Twentieth-Century
Literary Criticism

Guide to Gale Literary Criticism Series

For criticism on	Consult these Gale series
Authors now living or who died after December 31, 1959	*CONTEMPORARY LITERARY CRITICISM (CLC)*
Authors who died between 1900 and 1959	*TWENTIETH-CENTURY LITERARY CRITICISM (TCLC)*
Authors who died between 1800 and 1899	*NINETEENTH-CENTURY LITERATURE CRITICISM (NCLC)*
Authors who died between 1400 and 1799	*LITERATURE CRITICISM FROM 1400 TO 1800 (LC)* *SHAKESPEAREAN CRITICISM (SC)*
Authors who died before 1400	*CLASSICAL AND MEDIEVAL LITERATURE CRITICISM (CMLC)*
Authors of books for children and young adults	*CHILDREN'S LITERATURE REVIEW (CLR)*
Dramatists	*DRAMA CRITICISM (DC)*
Poets	*POETRY CRITICISM (PC)*
Short story writers	*SHORT STORY CRITICISM (SSC)*
Black writers of the past two hundred years	*BLACK LITERATURE CRITICISM (BLC)*
Hispanic writers of the late nineteenth and twentieth centuries	*HISPANIC LITERATURE CRITICISM (HLC)*
Native North American writers and orators of the eighteenth, nineteenth, and twentieth centuries	*NATIVE NORTH AMERICAN LITERATURE (NNAL)*
Major authors from the Renaissance to the present	*WORLD LITERATURE CRITICISM, 1500 TO THE PRESENT (WLC)*

ISSN 0276-8178

Volume 77

Twentieth-Century Literary Criticism

Excerpts from Criticism of the Works of Novelists, Poets, Playwrights, Short Story Writers, and Other Creative Writers Who Lived between 1900 and 1960, from the First Published Critical Appraisals to Current Evaluations

Jennifer Gariepy
Editor

Thomas Ligotti
Associate Editor

GALE

DETROIT · LONDON

STAFF

Jennifer Gariepy, *Editor*

Thomas Ligotti, *Associate Editor*

Susan Trosky, *Permissions Manager*
Kimberly F. Smilay, *Permissions Specialist*
Steve Cusack, Kelly A. Quin, *Permissions Associates*
Sandy Gore, *Permissions Assistant*

Victoria B. Cariappa, *Research Manager*
Michele P. LaMeau, Andrew Guy Malonis, Barbara McNeil, Gary J. Oudersluys, Maureen Richards, *Research Specialists*
Jeffrey Daniels, Tamara C. Nott, Tracie A. Richardson, Norma Sawaya, Cheryl L. Warnock, *Research Associates*
Corrine Stocker, *Research Assistant*

Mary Beth Trimper, *Production Director*
Carolyn Fischer, *Production Assistant*

Gary Leach, *Graphic Artist*
Randy Bassett, *Image Database Supervisor*
Robert Duncan, Michael Logusz, *Imaging Specialists*
Pamela Reed, *Imaging Coordinator*

Library of Congress Catalog Card Number 76-46132
ISBN 0-7876-2023-8
ISSN 0276-8178

Printed in the United States of America
10 9 8 7 6 5 4 3 2 1

Contents

Preface vii

Acknowledgments xi

Preface

Since its inception more than fifteen years ago, *Twentieth-Century Literary Criticism* has been purchased and used by nearly 10,000 school, public, and college or university libraries. *TCLC* has covered more than 500 authors, representing 58 nationalities, and over 25,000 titles. No other reference source has surveyed the critical response to twentieth-century authors and literature as thoroughly as *TCLC*. In the words of one reviewer, "there is nothing comparable available." *TCLC* "is a gold mine of information—dates, pseudonyms, biographical information, and criticism from books and periodicals—which many libraries would have difficulty assembling on their own."

Scope of the Series

TCLC is designed to serve as an introduction to authors who died between 1900 and 1960 and to the most significant interpretations of these author's works. The great poets, novelists, short story writers, playwrights, and philosophers of this period are frequently studied in high school and college literature courses. In organizing and excerpting the vast amount of critical material written on these authors, *TCLC* helps students develop valuable insight into literary history, promotes a better understanding of the texts, and sparks ideas for papers and assignments. Each entry in *TCLC* presents a comprehensive survey of an author's career or an individual work of literature and provides the user with a multiplicity of interpretations and assessments. Such variety allows students to pursue their own interests; furthermore, it fosters an awareness that literature is dynamic and responsive to many different opinions.

Every fourth volume of *TCLC* is devoted to literary topics. These topic entries widen the focus of the series from individual authors to such broader subjects as literary movements, prominent themes in twentieth-century literature, literary reaction to political and historical events, significant eras in literary history, prominent literary anniversaries, and the literatures of cultures that are often overlooked by English-speaking readers.

TCLC is designed as a companion series to Gale's *Contemporary Literary Criticism,* which reprints commentary on authors now living or who have died since 1960. Because of the different periods under consideration, there is no duplication of material between *CLC* and *TCLC*. For additional information about *CLC* and Gale's other criticism titles, users should consult the Guide to Gale Literary Criticism Series preceding the title page in this volume.

Coverage

Each volume of *TCLC* is carefully compiled to present:

- criticism of authors, or literary topics, representing a variety of genres and nationalities

- both major and lesser-known writers and literary works of the period

- 6-12 authors or 3-6 topics per volume

- individual entries that survey critical response to each author's work or each topic in literary history, including early criticism to reflect initial reactions; later criticism to represent any rise or decline in reputation; and current retrospective analyses.

Organization of This Book

An author entry consists of the following elements: author heading, biographical and critical introduction, list of principal works, excerpts of criticism (each preceded by an annotation and a bibliographic citation), and a bibliography of further reading.

- The **Author Heading** consists of the name under which the author most commonly wrote, followed by birth and death dates. If an author wrote consistently under a pseudonym, the pseudonym will be listed in the author heading and the real name given in parentheses on the first line of the biographical and critical introduction. Also located at the beginning of the introduction to the author entry are any name variations under which an author wrote, including transliterated forms for authors whose languages use nonroman alphabets.

- The **Biographical and Critical Introduction** outlines the author's life and career, as well as the critical issues surrounding his or her work. References to past volumes of *TCLC* are provided at the beginning of the introduction. Additional sources of information in other biographical and critical reference series published by Gale, including *Short Story Criticism, Children's Literature Review, Contemporary Authors, Dictionary of Literary Biography,* and *Something about the Author,* are listed in a box at the end of the entry.

- Some *TCLC* entries include **Portraits** of the author. Entries also may contain reproductions of materials pertinent to an author's career, including manuscript pages, title pages, dust jackets, letters, and drawings, as well as photographs of important people, places, and events in an author's life.

- The **List of Principal Works** is chronological by date of first book publication and identifies the genre of each work. In the case of foreign authors with both foreign-language publications and English translations, the title and date of the first English-language edition are given in brackets. Unless otherwise indicated, dramas are dated by first performance, not first publication.

- Critical excerpts are prefaced by **Annotations** providing the reader with information about both the critic and the criticism that follows. Included are the critic's reputation, individual approach to literary criticism, and particular expertise in an author's works. Also noted are the relative importance of a work of criticism, the scope of the excerpt, and the growth of critical controversy or changes in critical trends regarding an author. In some cases, these annotations cross-reference excerpts by critics who discuss each other's commentary.

- A complete **Bibliographic Citation** designed to facilitate location of the original essay or book precedes each piece of criticism.

- Criticism is arranged chronologically in each author entry to provide a perspective on changes in critical evaluation over the years. All titles of works by the author featured in the entry are printed in boldface type to enable the user to easily locate discussion of particular works. Also for purposes of easier identification, the critic's name and the publication date of the essay are given at the beginning of each piece of criticism. Unsigned criticism is preceded by the title of the journal in which it appeared. Some of the excerpts in *TCLC* also contain translated material. Unless otherwise noted, translations in brackets are by the editors; translations in parentheses or continuous with the text are by the critic. Publication information (such as footnotes or page and line references to specific editions of works) have been deleted at the editor's discretion to provide smoother reading of the text.

- An annotated list of **Further Reading** appearing at the end of each author entry suggests secondary sources on the author. In some cases it includes essays for which the editors could not obtain reprint rights.

Cumulative Indexes

- Each volume of *TCLC* contains a cumulative **Author Index** listing all authors who have appeared in Gale's Literary Criticism Series, along with cross references to such biographical series as *Contemporary Authors* and *Dictionary of Literary Biography.* For readers' convenience, a complete list of Gale titles included appears on the first page of the author index. Useful for locating authors within the various series, this index is particularly valuable for those authors who are identified by a certain period but who, because of their death dates, are placed in another, or for those authors whose careers span two periods. For example, F. Scott Fitzgerald is found in *TCLC,* yet a writer often associated with him, Ernest Hemingway, is found in *CLC.*

- Each *TCLC* volume includes a cumulative **Nationality Index** which lists all authors who have appeared in *TCLC* volumes, arranged alphabetically under their respective nationalities, as well as Topics volume entries devoted to particular national literatures.

- Each new volume in Gale's Literary Criticism Series includes a cumulative **Topic Index,** which lists all literary topics treated in *NCLC, TCLC, LC 1400-1800,* and the *CLC* yearbook.

- Each new volume of *TCLC,* with the exception of the Topics volumes, includes a **Title Index** listing the titles of all literary works discussed in the volume. In response to numerous suggestions from librarians, Gale has also produced a **Special Paperbound Edition** of the *TCLC* title index. This annual cumulation lists all titles discussed in the series since its inception and is issued with the first volume of *TCLC* published each year. Additional copies of the index are available on request. Librarians and patrons will welcome this separate index; it saves shelf space, is easy to use, and is recyclable upon receipt of the following year's cumulation. Titles discussed in the Topics volume entries are not included *TCLC* cumulative index.

Citing Twentieth-Century Literary Criticism

When writing papers, students who quote directly from any volume in Gale's literary Criticism Series may use the following general forms to footnote reprinted criticism. The first example pertains to materials drawn from periodicals, the second to material reprinted from books.

[1]William H. Slavick, "Going to School to DuBose Heyward," *The Harlem Renaissance Reexamined,* (AMS Press, 1987); excerpted and reprinted in *Twentieth-Century Literary Criticism,* Vol. 59, ed. Jennifer Gariepy (Detroit: Gale Research, 1995), pp. 94-105.

[2]George Orwell, "Reflections on Gandhi," *Partisan Review,* 6 (Winter 1949), pp. 85-92; excerpted and reprinted in *Twentieth-Century Literary Criticism,* Vol. 59, ed. Jennifer Gariepy (Detroit: Gale Research, 1995), pp. 40-3.

Suggestions Are Welcome

In response to suggestions, several features have been added to *TCLC* since the series began, including annotations to excerpted criticism, a cumulative index to authors in all Gale literary criticism series, entries devoted to criticism on a single work by a major author, more extensive illustrations, and a title index listing all literary works discussed in the series since its inception.

Readers who wish to suggest authors or topics to appear in future volumes, or who have other suggestions, are cordially invited to write the editors.

Acknowledgments

The editors wish to thank the copyright holders of the excerpted criticism included in this volume and the permissions managers of many book and magazine publishing companies for assisting us in securing reproduction rights. We are also grateful to the staffs of the Detroit Public Library, the Library of Congress, the University of Detroit Mercy Library, Wayne State University Purdy/Kresge Library Complex, and the University of Michigan Libraries for making their resources available to us. Following is a list of the copyright holders who have granted us permission to reproduce material in this volume of *TCLC*. Every effort has been made to trace copyright, but if omissions have been made, please let us know.

COPYRIGHTED EXCERPTS IN *TCLC*, VOLUME 77, WERE REPRODUCED FROM THE FOLLOWING PERIODICALS:

American Literary Realism, 1870-1910, v. XIV, Spring, 1981. Copyright © 1981 by the Department of English, The University of Texas at Arlington. Reproduced by permission of the publisher.—*The Antioch Review*, v. XXVII, Spring, 1967. Copyright © 1967 by the Antioch Review Inc. Reproduced by permission of the Editors.—*Canadian Historical Review*, v. LX, December, 1979. © University of Toronto Press 1979. Reproduced by permission of the University of Toronto Press Incorporated.—*Canadian Journal of Economics and Political Science,* v. XIX, August, 1953. Reproduced by permission.—*Harvard Law Review,* v. 64, February, 1951. Copyright 1951, renewed 1979 by Harvard Law Review Association. Reproduced by permission.—*Journal of Canadian Studies/Revue d'études canadiennes,* v. 12, Winter, 1977; v. 17, Winter, 1982-83; v. 20, Winter, 1985-86; v. 22, Winter, 1987-88. All reproduced by permission.—*The Journal of Economic History,* v. XXVI, December, 1966 for "The Content and Context of the Work of H. A. Innis" by Robert F. Neill. Reproduced by permission of the Cambridge University Press and the author.—*Kenyon Review,* v. 17, Summer-Fall, 1995 for "Mary Butts: Lost and Found" by Jascha Kessler. Copyright © 1995 by Kenyon College. All rights reserved. Reproduced by permission of the author.—*Melus,* v. 5, Fall, 1978. Copyright, MELUS, The Society for the Study of Multi-Ethnic Literature of the United States, 1978. Reproduced by permission.—*The New Hungarian Quarterly,* v. XXI, Winter, 1980 for "Literary Myth and Ethnic Assimilation" by Wilson J. Moses. © *The New Hungarian Quarterly,* 1980. Reproduced by permission of the author.—*The New York Times Book Review,* May 13, 1928, March 10, 1941. Copyright 1928, renewed 1956; Copyright 1941, renewed 1968 by The New York Times Company. Both reproduced by permission.—*PHYLON: The Atlanta University Review of Race and Culture,* v. XXXIV, March, 1973, v. XL, Fall, 1979; v. XLVII, June, 1986. Copyright, 1973, 1979, 1986 by Atlanta University. All reproduced by permission of *PHYLON./* v. IV, Winter, 1943. Copyright, 1943, renewed 1971 by Atlanta University. Reproduced by permission of *PHYLON.*—*Saturday Review of Literature,* v. XXIII, March 22, 1941. Copyright 1941, renewed 1968 Saturday Review magazine. © 1979, General Media Communications, Inc. Reproduced by permission of Saturday Review Publications, Ltd.—*The Southern Quarterly,* v. XXIV, Spring, 1986. Copyright © 1986 by the University of Southern Mississippi. Reproduced by permission.—*Studies in Black Literature,* v. 5, Spring, 1974. Copyright 1974 by the editor. Reproduced by permission.—*The University of Chicago Law Review,* v. 39, Fall, 1971. © 1972 by The University of Chicago. Reproduced by permission.

COPYRIGHTED EXCERPTS IN *TCLC*, VOLUME 77, WERE REPRODUCED FROM THE FOLLOWING BOOKS:

Auchincloss, Louis. From *Life, Law and Letters: Essays and Sketches.* Houghton Mifflin Company, 1979. Copyright © 1979 by Louis Auchincloss. All rights reserved. Reproduced by permission of Houghton Mifflin Company. In the United Kingdom by the author.—Basler, Robin. From "Here Lies the Woodpecker Who Was Zeus" in *A Sacred Quest: The Life and Writings of Mary Butts.* Edited by Christopher Wagstaff. McPherson & Company, 1995. Copyright 1995 by McPherson & Company. All rights reserved. Reproduced by permission.—Bone, Robert. From *The Negro Novel in America.* Revised Edition. Yale University Press, 1965. © 1958 by Yale University Press, Inc. Revised edition © 1965 by Yale University. All rights reserved. Reproduced by permission of the author.—Burton, David H. From *Oliver Wendell Holmes, Jr.* Twayne Publishers, 1980. Copyright © 1980 by G. K. Hall & Co. All rights reserved. Reproduced by permission of Twayne Publishers, a division of Simon & Schuster, Inc.—Burton, David H. From "Understanding 'The Common Law'" in *Oliver Wendell Holmes, Jr.—What Manner of Liberal.* Edited by David H. Burton. Robert E. Krieger Publishing Company, 1979. Copyright © 1979 by Robert E. Krieger Publishing Company. All rights reserved. —Campbell, Jane. From *Mythic Black Fiction: The Transformation of History.* The University of Tennessee Press, 1986. Copyright © 1986 by The University of Tennessee Press. All rights reserved. Reproduced by permission of The University of Tennessee Press.—Chatteron, Wayne. From *Irvin S. Cobb.* Twayne Publishers, 1986. Copyright © 1986 by G. K. Hall & Co. All rights reserved. Reproduced by permission of Twayne Publishers, a division of Simon & Schuster, Inc.—Creighton, Donald. From "Harold Adams Innis–An Appraisal" in *Culture, Communication, and Depen-*

PHOTOGRAPHS AND ILLUSTRATIONS APPEARING IN *TCLC*, VOLUME 77, WERE RECEIVED FROM THE FOLLOWING SOURCES:

Samuel Alexander

1859-1938

Australian-born English philosopher and critic.

INTRODUCTION

Alexander was among the foremost English realist philosophers of the early twentieth century. He is chiefly remembered for his *Space, Time and Deity* (1920), a systematic metaphysical inquiry into the nature of reality, consciousness, and God. Employing concepts of biology and psychology in addition to the methods of philosophical investigation, Alexander propounded his theory of "emergent evolution," the development of existence from primal space-time to successively higher levels, and posited the existence of God as an extension of the development of mind.

Biographical Information

Alexander was born in Sydney, Australia, in 1859. His father was a saddler who died before Alexander's birth. His mother later moved the family to St. Kilda, a suburb of Melbourne, where in 1871 Alexander entered Wesley College. He attended the University of Melbourne for two years, and while he left Melbourne without completing a degree, he had enjoyed a distinguished academic career. Moving to England in 1877, Alexander was awarded a scholarship to Balliol College, Oxford. In 1882 he became the first Jewish fellow of either Oxford or Cambridge, when he received a fellowship from Lincoln College, Oxford. Alexander maintained his position in Oxford until 1893, when he became professor of philosophy at the University of Manchester. He remained in Manchester for more than thirty years, becoming highly admired by his students and well-known within the wider cultural life of the city. From 1908 until 1911 he was president of the Aristotelian Society, a position to which he returned in 1936-37. He was elected to the British Academy in 1913. During 1917 and 1918, at the invitation of the University of Glasgow, Alexander developed a series of lectures summarizing his philosophical system. Known as the Gifford Lectures, these works provided the basis of his masterwork, *Space, Time and Deity*, 1920, an extensive consideration of such metaphysical questions as the nature of the space-time continuum and the existence of God. Alexander retired from academic teaching in 1924 but continued to give public lectures and in his later years devoted his attentions to matters of literary criticism and aesthetics. In 1930 he was awarded the Order of Merit. He died in 1938.

Major Works

Alexander's philosophical system is chiefly elaborated in his magnum opus, *Space, Time and Deity*, which repre-

sents the culmination of more than thirty years of academic research and teaching. In Alexander's view, metaphysical inquiry into the nature of reality and of such concepts as space, time, and value must utilize and reflect developments in the empirical sciences, including biology and psychology. In *Space, Time and Deity* Alexander maintained that neither space nor time can be comprehended without reference to the other and that all properties and values of nature arise out of the space-time continuum; in other words, out of motion.

Central to Alexander's philosophical system as outlined in *Space, Time and Deity* is the theory of "emergent evolution," a concept that dates from the works of the English philosopher and critic George Henry Lewes in the mid-1870s and which had been developed by Alexander's contemporary, the English zoologist and psychologist Conwy Lloyd Morgan. Rather than focusing on the sources of evolutionary development, emergent evolutionists concentrated on the process of evolution, in which the resulting advancement is greater than and is not reducible to the physical or chemical process through which it has emerged. For Alexander, as space-time reaches successively higher levels of complexity new qualities emerge. The first to emerge are the primary qualities of matter, including size and shape. Such secondary qualities as color then follow. Applying the reasoning of emergent evolution, Alexander posited the existence of God as a "level of existence" that would be realized in the development from body to mind to deity—from physical to mental to supramental. However, because the way in which God would be distinguished from mind cannot be predicted, Alexander maintained that the nature of God is unknowable.

In *Space, Time and Deity* Alexander also sought to elucidate questions of human perception, and his concept of "compresence" embodies his explanation of the cognitive relation of mind to objects and actions and of minds to other minds. Alexander held that an object may be *before* a consciousness but is not *in* it; consciousness *of* an object is not the same as consciousness of one's consciousness of the object. For example, an object such as a chair may be apprehended by a consciousness, but the chair is not located within that consciousness; and, the contemplation of the chair is distinct from thinking about the act of contemplating the chair. Further, since the contemplation of an object is itself an action, in Alexander's view it cannot be "contemplated" but only subjectively experienced, or "enjoyed."

While *Space, Time and Deity* represents the highest achievement of Alexander's career, he had earlier published works of philosophy and criticism analyzing the writings of G. W. Hegel and John Locke, as well as essays on evolutionary theory, ethics, and political philosophy. During the 1920s and 1930s he turned to such subjects as the philosophy of Baruch Spinoza and the realm of aesthetics. A posthumous collection, *Philosophical and Literary Pieces,* was published in 1939.

Critical Reception

Contemporary criticism of Alexander generally viewed his writings within the realist resurgence that flourished in American and English philosophy during the early twentieth century. Reviewers of *Space, Time and Deity* sought to explicate the extensive and systematic inquiry he presented and often praised particularly the comprehensiveness of his metaphysical system. However, within the decade such notable metaphysical works as M'Taggart's *The Nature of Existence* (1921) and Alfred North Whitehead's *Process and Reality* (1929) largely eclipsed Alexander's work, and his reputation subsided in the decades following his death. Some critics have suggested that his diminished status stems in part from the fact that he was connected with no movement or school and thus left no disciples engaged in the work of extending and refining his ideas. Yet Alexander has remained an attractive subject for numerous late-twentieth-century scholars, including Michael A. Weinstein, who summarized Alexander's appeal in 1984, writing, "The spirit of Alexander's philosophy is elegant passion,

something that is of vital importance for the sustenance of civilization. The elegance should not be taken to indicate indifference to public affairs . . . or retreatism . . . , but an understanding of philosophy's special role in describing experience comprehensively and reflectively, identifying its pervasive characters, relating them to one another, and judging them according to their importance."

PRINCIPAL WORKS

Moral Order and Progress: An Analysis of Ethical Consideration (philosophy) 1889
Locke (philosophy) 1908
The Basis of Realism (philosophy) 1914
Space, Time and Deity. 2 vols. (philosophy) 1920
Spinoza and Time (philosophy) 1921
Lessons from Spinoza (philosophy) 1927
Spinoza: An Address (philosophy) 1927
Beauty and Other Forms of Value (philosophy) 1933
Philosophical and Literary Pieces (philosophy and criticism) 1939

CRITICISM

Haldane (essay date 1920)

SOURCE: "Prof. Alexander's Gifford Lectures," in *Nature,* August 26, 1920, pp. 798-801.

[*In the following essay, Haldane considers Alexander's* Space, Time and Diety *in the context of Albert Einstein's general theory of relativity.*]

Prof. Alexander has written a book which requires more than cursory reading. It deserves careful study. For it embodies a thoroughly modern exposition of New Realism in full detail. Moreover, these two volumes are not merely the outcome of a sustained effort at accurate investigation. They are distinguished by their admirable tone and temper. The author is throughout anxious to understand and to represent faithfully the views of those with whom he is in controversy. His reading of what has been written by the great thinkers of other schools has been closer and more intelligent than that of most New Realists, and he displays no traces of arrogance. He has done all he could to appreciate the materials furnished, not merely by mathematical and physical science, but by biology and psychology; highly important fields for his inquiry.

These very merits of Prof. Alexander's method have, however, produced their drawbacks. They have driven him beyond the current conceptions of the New Realist type into others which are not always easy to reconcile with them. In the second volume, particularly, where the author is chiefly concerned with such problems as those of the nature of the tertiary qualities of reality, of value, and of deity, the treatment leaves the impression that the subject-matter passes beyond the limits which alone are for the method legitimate. None the less, the effort made to be consistent is a notable one. But under this head I must refer the reader to the book, for the only aspect of the doctrine in it with which space allows me to concern myself is its cardinal principle as applied to physical knowledge.

To begin with, it is necessary to be clear as to what is peculiar to himself and his school in Prof. Alexander's teaching. It is not sufficiently realised that to-day the New Realists comprise a variety of groups divided by differences that are of far-reaching importance. These differences relate to the nature attributed to mind. For some of the most prominent of the American New Realists mind has no characteristic at all that distinguishes it from its objective content. Seeing means colours occurring; hearing means sounds occurring; thinking means thoughts occurring. Mind is itself just a casual selection out of the field of consciousness, and has no nature distinct from that field. When we speak of a mind, the grouping arises out of relations possessed by the objective elements themselves, relations which exist quite independently of our own action in perceiving. Minds are thus subordinate groups in a larger universe of being which includes them, and which would be unaltered if minds disappeared from it. Consciousness is thus merely a demonstrative appellation.

Now for Prof. Alexander, and, I think, for most of the English New Realists, mind has a reality independent of its object. With the latter, whatever it is, it is "compresent." The act of perceiving is one reality, the object perceived is another. Left to itself, the activity which we call mind reveals the object, with its relations (which may be universals) just as they exist independently of it. But the activity is a separate reality, which does not belong to the ordinary object world, but reveals itself in consciousness, in which it is said by Prof. Alexander to be "enjoyed." Here we have dualism, a dualism which he gets over by referring the origin of the activity of mind and the object with which it is compresent, alike, to a final reality which is the foundation of both, an ultimate space-time continuum. This, inasmuch as the flow of time enters into its very essence, is not static, but dynamic. The activity which we are conscious of (in the form, not of perception, which is of objects, but of self-enjoyment) is therefore in its turn dynamic, and its character is that of a conation.

I am not sure that the Americans, notwithstanding their boldness, are not here on safer ground. They project everything, thought, feeling, and tertiary qualities, such as goodness and beauty, into what they call a non-mental world. Prof. Alexander is more cautious. With him the native hue of resolution is, at times at least, as he progresses in his enterprise, sicklied o'er with the pale

cast of thought. He seems to feel that he must retain something for a mental world. Starting with space and time as having no reality apart from one another, but as mere abstractions from aspects or attributes of the foundational reality, which is space-time or motion, the "stuff of which all existents are composed," he has to account for our actual experience. His foundationally existent activity breaks itself up into the complexes of which we are aware, and which possess, as belonging to their nature, certain fundamental and all-pervasive features which we recognise as categories. There result also qualities which appear in our experience. These form

> a hierarchy, the quality of each level of existence being identical with a certain complexity or collocation of elements on the next lower level. The quality performs to its equivalent lower existence the office which mind performs to its neural basis. Mind and body do but exemplify, therefore, a relation which holds universally. Accordingly, time is the mind of space, and any quality the mind of its body; or, to speak more accurately, mind and any other quality are the different distinctive complexities of time which exist as qualities. As existents within space-time, minds enter into relations of a perfectly general character with other things and with one another. These account for the familiar features of mental life; knowing freedom, values, and the like. In the hierarchy of qualities the next higher quality to the highest attained is deity. God is the whole universe engaged in process towards the emergence of this new quality, and religion is the sentiment in us that we are drawn towards him, and caught in the movement of the world towards a higher level of existence.

I have given the general result of his inquiry as summed up in the author's own words, those used by him in concluding his final chapter. But it would be unfair to suggest that the nature of this result can be appreciated from any isolated quotation. The whole book must be read. It is admirable alike in thoroughness of method and in command of material. Still, it is obvious that the entire edifice depends for its stability on its foundation, and that the author's conception of the ultimately real as being space-time, a continuum of point-instants or pure events entirely independent of mind, is the crucial point in his reasoning. If he is right, it must be in terms of this existent that all else must be capable of expression, and it cannot itself be expressed in terms of anything beyond itself. Of course, Prof. Alexander does not dispute that when we speak of space and time as of this character we are going beyond what we learn through sense, or intuitively, and are employing constructions of reflection. He is quite entitled to do this if a non-mental world can include universals, as he insists, in common with all New Realists. Our simplest experience is, as he says, "full of our ideas." The question is whether they belong to mind or to what is not mind. We shall see presently to what path this conclusion conducts.

At this stage we have to put before us the author's analysis of the relation of space to time, an analysis that seems to me altogether admirable. Space taken in abstraction from time has no distinction of parts. Time in so far as it is purely temporal is a mere now. To find a continuum we must find distinguishable elements. Without space there would be no connection in time. Without time there would be no points to connect. There is therefore no instant of time apart from a position in space, and no point of space except in an instant of time. The point occurs at an instant, and the instant occupies a point. The ultimate stuff of the universe is thus of the character of point-instants or pure events, and it is so that we get our continuum. The correspondence is, however, not a one-to-one, but a many-one, correspondence. For one point may occur at more than one instant, and one instant may, analogously, occupy several points.

Prof. Alexander thinks that he is here in full accord with Minkowski's well-known conception of an absolute world of four dimensions, of which ordinary geometry omits the fourth, the time element. When he wrote his book Einstein's doctrine of relativity was only fully known in its first form, the "special" theory, and Prof. Alexander believes that his view of the character of the space-time continuum has left him free to accept the so-called principle of relativity in this form. For it suggests really no more than the unification of the observations of two sets of observers who may be observing an absolute world in space-time, by means of formulas of transformation in which the observations of observers with one system of co-ordinates can be rendered in terms of the co-ordinates of observers with a different system. It may be, he says, that the formulas are not really independent, inasmuch as they are ultimately numerical, and numbers may be wholly dependent on an absolute space and time system. Thus it would be an absolutely identical set of relations which was observed from the two systems of reference, moving rectilinearly with a relative velocity which remained uniform.

But can this be accepted in the fresh light cast by the general theory of relativity, of which the special theory is now shown by Einstein to be a mere special case? Here metaphysicians have to look over a fence into ground at present mainly occupied by the mathematician. But not exclusively so occupied. The ground is in truth a borderland where mathematics and epistemology trench on each other, and the fence is not of barbed wire. We are, indeed, compelled to try to do the best we can with unfamiliar topics if we would get at the truth about the nature of reality. The relativity doctrine now extends to accelerating motion. It has also, apparently, been demonstrated that a principle of equivalence obtains according to which any changes which an observer takes to be due to what he supposes to be attraction within a gravitational field would be perceived by him in precisely the same way if the observer's system of reference were moving with the acceleration which was characteristic of the gravitation at the observer's point of observation. The combination of these principles gives us relativity of measurement in actual experience without restriction. The gravitational principle is, in addition, here based, not

on a supposed elementary law of gravitational *force,* whatever that means, which would leave us in metaphysical perplexities about action at a distance, but on elementary laws of the *motion* of bodies relatively to each other in a so-called gravitational field. There is no decision either for or against Euclidean geometry as a possible special case. But there is a decision that space, as a physical thing with unvarying geometrical properties, is to be banished, just for the same sort of reasons as the æther was banished before it. Only observable things are to be recognised as real in the new system of modern physicists.

It is therefore asserted by Einstein that, all motions and accelerations being relative to the system of reference of the observer, neither space nor time has physically independent objectivity. They are not measurable in themselves. They mean only the framework in which the minds of the observers arrange physical events, according to the conditions under which observation takes place. We may choose such frameworks as we please, but in point of fact we naturally choose so that the application of our method is the one that appears best adapted to the character of what we observe. The standard used will give their physical significances to our "geodetic lines." The apparent order in space and time has no independent existence. It manifests itself only in the events that present themselves as so ordered.

But the revolution in conception does not stop here. As so-called "gravitational fields" are everywhere present, the old special theory of relativity is nowhere an accurate account of phenomena. The velocity of light, for instance, cannot really be constant under all conditions. It is the things we observe in space and time that give to these their definite structure, and the relations in them of the things depend on the system of observation. To get at the fundamental law of the change which takes place in the space-time continuum we must look for the principle which governs the motion of a point in it as of the form of a differential law for the motion of such a point, not merely in a straight line in the Euclidean sense, but in a geodetic line which will be relative to any possible form of motion and acceleration in a gravitational field. If we can reach such a differential law under the aspect of an equation sufficiently elastic in its variables, we shall be able to fit into it mathematical expressions based on actual observation which give the "gravitational potentials" required for the application of the law. The form of the differential equation which expresses the law must therefore be such as to be applicable whatever may be the four co-ordinates of reference of the observer of motion in any conceivable gravitational field. The principle of equivalence necessitates this, and we get as the result a science of motion depending on the relativity of every kind of motion. All that is required is that the co-ordinates which are the variables in the equation of motion of a point-mass moving uniformly and rectilinearly should be so expressed as to be capable of transformation into the co-ordinates, whatever their shape, of any system of reference which moves in any path and has any accelerated motion whatsoever. This appears to have been done completely. The *result* is intelligible to the epistemologist who can even do no more than look across the boundary fence. The mathematical details and scaffolding he may be wholly unable to appreciate. But not the less does he feel compelled to take off his hat reverently before the shades of Gauss and Riemann, and before those who have been able to wield the mighty sword with which these great thinkers cut the knots that held physicists back from the unrestricted calculus of to-day, purified as it now is from the old assumptions.

Now the importance of this thorough-going application of the principle of the relativity of the character of the point-event continuum to the observer is obvious. It means relativity in significance for intelligence. As Prof. Eddington has recently remarked in a notable article in *Mind,* the intervention of mind in the laws of Nature is more far-reaching than is usually supposed by physicists. He develops this conclusion in a fashion which is impressive. Freundlich and Schick in their recent books insist on the same thesis.

But what does the word "mind" mean when used thus? Not a substance in space-time, as Prof. Alexander would have it. To start with, such an assumption would involve either the rejection of the modern doctrine of relativity as the school of Einstein has put it forward as dependent on interpretation, or something tending towards solipsism. Nor can mind mean substance in another aspect, that in which Berkeley and the Mentalists have sought to display it. Few competent students of the history of thought look on philosophy as shut up to such a view, the view which New Realism seeks to bind into the "egocentric predicament."

There is another interpretation of the meaning of mind in which it signifies neither any of these things nor yet an Absolute Mind apart from that of man, but just our own experience interpreted as being in every stage relative in its presentation, and not so merely in the relation of measurement. For Einstein's doctrine seems to be only a fragment of a yet larger and even more striking view of reality. Relativity is surely not to be confined to judgments based on the co-ordinates we employ in measurement. It may equally arise in other instances from the uncritical applications of conceptions concerned with quality as much as with quantity. From such a point of view reality, including human experience, is what it is only because we are ever unconsciously, under the influence of practical ends to be attained, limiting our systems of reference, interpreted in even a wider sense than that of Einstein. These may be limiting ends imposed on us by the mere fact that we are human beings with a particular position in Nature. The relativity of knowledge will thus assume the form of relativity of the real to general points of view, and will result in a principle of degrees extending through all knowledge and reality alike, which fall short of ideal completion. It is an old principle, as old as Greek thought. If it is true, it solves many problems and gets rid of the distinction between mental and non-men-

tal, between idealism and realism, between mind and its object. For it accepts the "that," and confines the legitimate problem to the "what." It also gets rid of the perplexing idea of an Absolute Mind as something to be conceived as apart from us while working in us.

The idea and the method, recurring as they do in ancient and modern philosophy, are worth study by those who feel the stimulus of the new atmosphere which Einstein has provided. They may find a convenient analogue to the special principle of relativity in Kant's "Critique of Pure Reason," with its investigation of the general conditions which are required in order to render any individual experience possible. If they seek for an analogue to Einstein's general principle, they may look either in the "Metaphysics" of Aristotle or in the "Logic" of Hegel. The greatest thinkers have presented resembling conclusions in varying language.

This path is one that is not easy to tread. It is as hard to enter on as is that of the metaphysician who has to try to understand the meaning for philosophy of the absolute differential equations which Einstein employs. Prof. Alexander, however, knows the direction, if he does not now look that way. And it may be that the difficulties with which the new principle of general physical relativity seems to threaten New Realism, with its non-mental and static reality, may lead him, with his openness of mind, to consider once again whether he should not wend his steps afresh towards the wicket-gate for a further pilgrimage. But whatever the direction in which he is looking, his new book is full of stimulating material, even as it stands.

Charles Hartshorne (essay date 1937)

SOURCE: "Mead and Alexander on Time," in *Beyond Humanism,* Willett, Clark & Company, 1937, pp. 242-52.

[*In the following essay, Hartshorne explicates and identifies weaknesses in Alexander's arguments in* Space, Time and Diety.]

George Herbert Mead was a great philosopher and certainly a humanist. Until his *Philosophy of the Act* has been published it will be too soon to pass judgment on his philosophy. But there are some aspects of his system which seem fairly well defined by his extant writings, and these aspects suggest the following criticisms. In his *Philosophy of the Present* Mead declares that each age creates its own past—not its own image of the past, for Mead seems to deny the validity of this distinction. The past *is* the best image we can construct on the basis of present experience in its past-pointing characteristics. The question then arises of how the past which we infer in this manner differs from the future which we may also infer. What is the direction of pastness? To this question Mead's writings seem to give only a cloudy answer. And in any case, it seems contradictory to assert that our efforts to know the past create the past we wish to know.

In Mead's own discussion we can feel the unwished-for but really inescapable naïve meaning of past as the "irrevocable," the settled and done for, contrasted with the future, the unsettled, which can be more and more settled in this way or in that as it comes closer and closer to the present. Mead admits that an absolutely fixed past is possible only theistically, but he considers only the old type of theism according to which the future is fixed also, and he rightly objects that in that case past and future lose their distinctness and time is explained away, not explained. But then is this not also the result if we make both past and future unsettled? The point is to distinguish them, and both old theism and Mead's humanism seem, though in opposite ways, to confuse them together. Is it not striking that Mead's paradoxical view was expressly adopted under the conviction that the only alternative was the medieval or Roycean absolute (which Mead mistakenly supposed was also Whitehead's doctrine)?

In theory of value Mead was a great thinker. But his view of the social nature of mind is dangerously unprotected against the conclusion that society is the only real locus of value. His sympathetic critic, Professor T. V. Smith, has warned against this danger.[1]

In any case, Mead's social psychology is compatible with organic sympathy, since the "mind" which, according to him, is generated by relations to other human organisms is mind as reflective consciousness, as understanding of "significant symbols," not mind as merely feeling and striving, and the embracing of these factors in a unity of awareness with its element of meaning as awareness "of" an environment. Or did Mead really think that *all* sense of meaning, including that involved in simple memory and desire and emotional attitudes, is due to "taking the role of the other" in the fashion which is achieved only by man? (That all life whatsoever is "social" in a broad sense Mead fully grants.)

Again, in *Movements of Thought in the Nineteenth Century,* Mead says that a physical object really is, in the perspective of the beholding organism, what it looks to be—colored, etc.[2] But the question between psychism and its critics concerns what the object is when *not* in the perspective of human perception, e.g., before animals existed on earth, or today when we are all asleep. Mead says the world is the totality of perspectives.[3] Then we must ask, What is the perspective that belongs individually to a molecule as a man's perceptions belong to the man? Does the molecule's perspective possess quality, and if so how can it lack feeling or sensation? Does it possess the past as real in the present, and then how can it lack memory? Is it subject to order, and then how can it lack some germ of purpose, i.e., of present pattern binding upon the future? Only if the *Philosophy of the Act* illuminates these questions will Mead's philosophy present a significant alternative to psychic naturalism.

Perhaps the most important of all recent efforts to interpret the world without resort to the cosmic psychic variables is that of S. Alexander in *Space, Time, and Deity.*

Alexander's view is that the only cosmic principle is space-time or, as he expresses it, pure motion. If one asks, Motion of what? Alexander replies, in effect at least, that there need be nothing to move except bits of motion themselves. In other words change of position can take place even though there is nothing at any position except change of position. This frank assertion of a paradox seems to me more honest intellectually than Santayana's pretense to possess in the term "matter" a key to what it is that has locus and that changes.

Out of pure motion "emerge" certain special properties ("local variables" in our terminology) such as quality, life, mind. But there are no cosmic variables, except bare space-time or motion, by which these local variables may be described.

In cosmic terms this system differs from older materialisms in three ways. First, space is held to be essentially temporal. Second, "matter" is given up as a cosmic principle except in so far as it means simply what is spatio-temporal. (This of course is the only positive meaning it ever did have.) Third, really new, unpredictable qualities perpetually appear in the universe. (The quality now emerging is deity, nascent divinity.) Because of these differences Alexander greatly objects to being called a materialist. When this charge is brought, he points out with great earnestness that he has described time as "the mind of space." But if asked what this means, and whether or not, by virtue of time, space thinks or feels, he replies that his metaphor must not be taken too seriously. The psychist cannot but suspect that Alexander has an intuition of the cosmic range of memory and expectation as essential to time, but has not clarified this intuition.

So far as I know, Alexander's is the only carefully elaborated, honest attempt (unless we should except Nicolai Hartmann's) to work out a non-psychic metaphysics which the twentieth century has so far witnessed. By virtue of his thoroughness and honesty the following difficulties appear plainly enough. First, pure structure is made independent of qualities. For space-time is nothing definite except a changing pattern of relations. "Relations of what?" remains unanswered. Second, the fact that space-time does in fact produce qualities is not explained. Third, there is in the system no ground of order in change.

It is also interesting that Alexander, writing a third of a century after Boutroux and Peirce had exploded the pretensions of determinism, tried to combine the absoluteness of law in physics with the absolute unpredictability of emergent properties.[4] Both absolutes are groundless obstacles to any understanding of time. It is also interesting that Alexander's quasi-materialism was not deliberately chosen as an alternative to a temporalistic panpsychism, but as an alternative to absolute idealism and ordinary materialism.

Alexander's point that space is inconceivable apart from time is an improvement over older materialisms, yet a weakness. For it is easier to overlook the emptiness of the concept of non-psychic reality in a static than in a dynamic context. That psychic reality is essentially dynamic is obvious, since thinking, feeling, striving, loving, hating, are all acts and since novelty and surprise are aesthetically valuable, and the very thought of their total absence is unbearable if we really strive to imagine it. But the blank notion of lifeless, insentient existence suggests no activity, for it suggests nothing definite, except, as Alexander says, the bare stuff of motion itself, and then it throws no light on what it is that moves. Becoming is a richer notion than being, and hence it reveals even more clearly the poverty of "matter" or of "non-psychic reality." If there is becoming, *something* must become which is not just a bit of becoming. Alexander's error is the universal one of all dualisms and materialisms, that of trying to explain the concrete by the abstract, "the fallacy of misplaced concreteness."

Alexander gives a very interesting argument for his rejection of quality as a cosmic variable.[5] He says that there is no "plan," or principle of variability, in quality similar to the plan of "humanity" as varied in Caucasian, Mongolian, and other races. He even doubts that there is any plan to color, and is confident that there is none uniting red and hard and sweet—all the sense qualities. Strangely, he says nothing about the continuity of colors, and of course nothing about the possibility that discontinuities among the different senses are due to the fact that human sense-feelings are not all possible feelings, but a restricted realization of these possibilities, even by comparison with other existent animals. Hence Alexander's conclusion that "quality" is only a collective name for red, sour, hard, etc., is hastily arrived at. Nor can it be justified, since no observation can prove the impossibility of qualities intermediate between red and sweet, or sweet and warm, or in general any discontinuity of this type. And the only plan of variability any universal can have is dimensionality, a continuous spread of values (admitting various discontinuous spreads as special cases).

Starting, as Alexander does, from motion as an ultimate, one cannot interpret quality and qualitative change. But if we start from the notion of qualitative changes as socially interlocked, sympathetically interacting with one another, motion becomes readily explicable.[6] For motion is change of relative position and position is determined by the principle: "My neighbor is he with whom I intimately interact" (Peirce). Hence motion is simply the changes in the degrees of interaction among qualitative changes. Furthermore, it is explicable why there should be such changes in interaction. For, given a certain feeling-quality in *A*, then the degree to which this quality is compatible with intimate relationship to a given quality in *B* is determined. To take an example on the human plane: If I am melancholy in such a settled way that it conflicts with my mood to be vividly aware of a cheerful neighbor, I shall tend to keep at a certain distance from cheerful persons and to seek out intimate relations with persons in a melancholy mood. But if I pass from this state to one

of feeling cheerless in a restless, painful way that makes me wish to be "cheered up," I shall seek out the society of happy people. The aesthetic unity of contrasting feelings which is necessary if feeling is not to be indefinitely destroyed by boredom or intolerable discord thus implies that changes in feeling-quality should be accompanied by changes in degree of relationship to other feeling-qualities, that is, by motion. And it matters not how simple the feelings may be, how subhuman or superhuman, for this law of unity in contrast is perfectly general and implies no higher degree of complexity than an electron may enjoy. Thus there is no riddle in the fact that our human feelings may produce motions in the human brain and muscles, for the parts of these organs sympathize with our changing feelings to such a degree as to involve sharp changes in their internal qualities, and from this their motion follows necessarily. The reverse process is equally explicable. Motion in the brain particles necessarily involves changes in their qualities, hence, by sympathy, qualitative changes in us. It also involves shifts in our relative intimacy with different parts of the brain (shifts of attention), so that one can truly say that consciousness moves.

It is easy to see why it is that science deals with motion as the causative factor rather than with qualitative change. All motion involves qualitative changes, but these are usually inaccessible to us by ordinary practical or scientific means. Only with animals a great deal like ourselves can we rather easily infer something about the feelings involved in their "behavior." With inorganic bodies, which do not as wholes feel, since the feelings of their parts are not pooled into a single aesthetic pattern, we find it much easier to infer analogy to ourselves in terms of mere behavior than in terms of feeling-quality. And the behavioristic analogy serves our purposes. Why does it do so? How can we know the shapes of things whose feelings we do not know? How can we separate what in our sensations is due to motion in the environment from what is due to qualitative change? It seems almost a sufficient explanation to say that the aesthetic unity of the world is such that when we take the motions by themselves, we find them characterized by a very definite quantitative pattern. Doubtless the complete aesthetic pattern involves qualities also. But these qualities evidently change in such a way as to involve motions (changes in the relations between qualitative changes) which, considered in abstraction from the qualitative side, yield fairly definite patterns of their own, somewhat as the pattern of a poem is relatively independent of the meanings of its words. Thus the final proof of the atomic theory of matter was the proof that if there is a definite law of heat, heat must be a mode of motion, whatever else it may be. In other words, our sensations can be predicted if we suppose changes in them to be correlated with motional changes in the environment and in ourselves and if we suppose these changes to follow certain patterns. Not that it does not matter what qualities there may be in the environment, but that it does not matter to us whether or not we *know* these qualities. For we do know this about them, that they are such as to be compatible with the patterns of motion which explain our sensations, and this is all we need to know. We get the results of the qualities in terms of motions and of the qualities of our sensations, and that satisfies us.

But the fact is that we do not in reality know the precise motions in nature, nor even anything much like them. We know statistical patterns and certain *limits* of motions, but the course of behavior of an individual electron inside these limits escapes us. We have positive grounds for denying that this behavior follows an absolute law by which it could be precisely predicted; but if we really knew the individual behavior of an electron up to a given moment, it might well be that we should be able to make a fairly close estimate of what it would do next. But also we should have some sympathy for it as an individual. We should know how long it has endured a given energy-state, how likely it is, by the general tolerance of electrons for given types of monotony, that it is "tired" of this state and ready to "react" away from it to something affording the relief of novelty. But the wonderful fact is that this knowledge would not for practical purposes tell us anything we need to know unless we could simultaneously observe millions of electrons in this individual fashion; and we should then have to have superhuman intelligence to put the facts together into a significant story. For we live on the macroscopic plane, where individual particles are insignificant.

It seems to come to this, that motion is decisive because, in abstraction from qualities, it yields the statistical patterns needed for our type of prediction and control of ourselves through control of the environment. The pattern of motions which is abstractable from the real but elusive changes of quality in the environment is continued into the body (not without some modifications no doubt, but to a significant extent), so that physiology is in a measure a mere complication of physics. But here motions and qualities begin to seem inseparable even for our knowledge. There is in a bright color a sense of exhilaration and in the sensation of black a "dead" quality which correspond to the fact that in one case the given part of the retina is stimulated, and in the other is merely left to its own internal energy or lack of it. And the cells or molecules concerned may be supposed to share (with appropriate qualifications) in such feelings of excitement or calm. Many other examples could be given (see the author's *The Philosophy and Psychology of Sensation*).

The facts on the whole seem entirely in agreement with the assumption that the ultimate or complete pattern of nature is a pattern in which qualities and motions are inseparable, but that the motion-patterns can be abstracted and, in statistical aspects, yield all the law we human beings can for most practical or scientific purposes desire; while, on the other hand, there is evidence that behind the statistical behavioristic laws there are patterns of individual behavior which could not be fully grasped apart from qualitative sympathy with the individuals. The study in which this double point of view enters even into scientific contexts is psychophysics. But

here we must note the difficulty that quality, in the strict sense of the non-structural properties of things, seems inevitably to elude reason, for reason deals with patterns, structures. In the book mentioned above I have tried to deal with this question, essentially by pointing out that qualities are similar to one another, and that similarity is a relationship subject to exact—in fact, geometrical—patterns. Starting with one's own sense qualities as origin, such relationships might conceivably lead to an insight even into the qualities of microscopic entities. But the problem will hardly be adequately formulated in our generation, one reason being that the advanced psychophysical knowledge which would make such a formulation useful is not yet at hand.

It is quite different with internal properties of a structural character, such as memory or purpose or complexity of feeling. It should be possible to make rapid progress in ascertaining how long on the average an electron vividly remembers or how far ahead it effectively anticipates. Physics can in this regard pass easily into a branch of comparative psychology, hindered indeed only by the fact that we do not deal directly with individuals. This psychology of structural properties is the only kind that is generally admitted to be possible even for animals, nay even for human beings, if we believe the behaviorists.

Alexander is right in choosing continuous dimensions for his cosmic variables; but variables of feeling-quality and of thought and volition may be continuous as well as those of space and time, and for philosophy may be even more important. Of course we have to abstract from any one set of particular thoughts or feelings or strivings, just as we do from any one set of space-time patterns. But to abstract from a whole infinite dimension such as the variables of thought or feeling are, is precisely the indefensible process of explaining concreteness by the merely abstract, that which is not even potentially concrete. Space-time is potentially all that particular patterns of motion are concretely, but it is not even potentially concrete particularizations of quality or thinking. It requires these latter particularizations for the particularization of its own dimensions, but the dimensions of qualitative particularization, for instance, are additional to the physical dimensions. The opponents of psychism have yet to explain what they take to be the relation of abstractions to the concrete. Peirce and Whitehead and Bergson have explained this most carefully. For them, to generalize the results of experience is to generalize experience itself. The variability of experience is itself experienced, by virtue of the sociability and the flexibility or freedom of the latter. Variability of a "reality" held to be distinguishable from all experience is, on the other hand, experientially meaningless. "Pure motion" is unimaginable not relatively but absolutely; it is a *contradiction* of the empirical variability—which is irreducibly more than four-dimensional—upon which the idea of motion and every idea must be based. The totality of irreducible dimensions of the experienceable variability of experience is the totality of irreducible dimensions of existence. The narrowness or provincial character of human experience, both with respect to what is "below" and what is "above" it, lies not in its dimensions, but in the limits of the "slice" of values humanly realized along these dimensions. If this statement is true, philosophical understanding is possible; otherwise it is not possible.

NOTES

[1] Cf. T. V. Smith, *Beyond Conscience* (McGraw-Hill Book Co., 1934).

[2] Mead, *Movements of Thought in the Nineteenth Century* (University of Chicago Press, 1935), p. 414.

[3] *Ibid.,* p. 315.

[4] Alexander, *Space, Time, and Deity* (The Macmillan Co., 1920), I, 326 ff.

[5] *Ibid.,* II, 328.

[6] On space as a pattern of sympathetic interconnection see Whitehead, *Adventures of Ideas,* pp. 226, 258-60; and *Process and Reality* (The Macmillan Co., 1929), Part IV.

G. F. Stout (essay date 1940)

SOURCE: "The Philosophy of Samuel Alexander (I.)," in *Mind: A Quarterly Review,* Vol. XLIX, No. 193, January, 1940, pp. 1-18.

[*In the following essay, Stout presents the first part of an extended analysis of Alexander's philosophical system, focusing on his concepts of mind, mental processes, and sensory perception.*]

According to Mr. Laird "no English writer has produced so grand a system of speculative metaphysics in so grand a manner since Hobbes in 1696 completed his metaphysical journey with the publication of *De Corpore*". I entirely agree. But this was not the kind of praise which pleased Alexander himself. When the plan of his philosophy first dawned upon him in all its brilliance, he hoped and was strongly tempted to believe that it was destined to be the "philosophy of the future". What he really longed for was confirmation of this estimate of the objective value of his work. Mere praise of its greatness or grandeur left him cold and finally bored him by its incessant repetition. Now I cannot myself admit that Alexander's system will be, or, at any rate, ought to be the philosophy of the future. There seem to me to be flaws in it fatal to any such claim. None the less, I feel strongly that the most promising path to this philosophy of the future is to be found in a critical reconstruction of Alexander's work, with the aim of correcting its defects while retaining its systematic character. He has asked the right questions and answered them in such a way that even where he is wrong his errors are most instructive. In discovering how he has gone astray we are guided to a more satisfactory

positive solution of the problems with which he deals. What is perhaps even more important, he has everywhere shown the essential connexion and interdependence of these problems and has thus bequeathed to his successors a most helpful and inspiring model of systematic thinking—of Architectonic.

It follows from the systematic character of his philosophy that if he goes astray in dealing with one fundamental question he is bound to go correspondingly astray in dealing with others. On the other hand, so far as we succeed in correcting one such error, we may hope to correct others on the same principle, and thus reconstruct the whole system in a more satisfactory form. It is in this way that each important philosopher learns from the work of his predecessors and progresses beyond it. The progress is of a peculiar kind determined by the peculiar nature of the philosophical problem. None the less it is quite real.

I cannot here attempt to reconstruct Alexander's philosophy. I must be content to recommend this reconstruction as a promising venture for younger men. I can here only indicate briefly some special points on which he seems to me to be mistaken.

Mind and the Cognitive Relation.

I begin with his treatment of the nature of mind as distinguished from and related to its objects. I do so because, as he tells us himself, it was in dealing with theory of knowledge that he was led on to ontological questions; also because this way of approach is most congenial to myself.

"Any experience whatever", according to Alexander, "may be analysed into two distinct elements and their relation to one another. The two elements which are the terms of the relation are, on the one hand the act of mind or the awareness and on the other the object of which it is aware; the relation between them is that they are together or compresent in the world which is thus far experienced."[1] Every part of this statement calls for close scrutiny. Let us begin with the cognitive relation and then consider the nature of the mental act or process.[2] It is to be noted at the outset, that the relation, as Alexander conceives it, is existential. In other words, the terms which enter into it have each an existence separate from that of the other. Further, the relation does not merely relate the nature of one term to that of the other, as is the case with mere resemblance or contrast. It is a real connexion relating the separate existence of each to the separate existence of the other.[3] We may now pass to the most startling point of Alexander's doctrine. He insists that the cognitive relation is in no way unique. Provided that one of the terms is a mental process or "act", any existential relation may be a cognitive relation. What is unique is not the nature of the relation but the nature of one of its terms—the mental process. He expresses this view in the most drastic way by asserting that all that is needed to constitute the cognitive relation is togetherness or compresence. Everything, according to him, is compresent with everything else inasmuch as they are all parts of one spatial-temporal universe. Why then are we not omniscient, seeing that a mental process is compresent with everything else? I can find no satisfactory answer to this question in Alexander. He holds that, in fact, however limited our knowledge of details may be, we are always cognisant, however dimly, of a whole embracing these details and extending indefinitely beyond them. "No experience . . . is isolated or has boundaries which shut it off rigidly from the rest of the world. . . . Every experience has its fringes, shoots out its corona into some larger whole which encircles it. . . . Every object we know is a fragment of an infinite whole."[4] I agree essentially with this statement. But it does not solve the difficulty I have raised. If it is sufficient to constitute the cognitive relation, that a mental process should be part of the same world with what it knows, it ought to know everything in detail. Finite minds ought to be omniscient and they certainly are not so. We may state the objection in another way. On Alexander's view, which I accept myself, compresence within one universe is not a special kind of relation; it is the most general condition of all relations, however diverse they may be in their specific nature. It covers indifferently such diverse relations as spatial contiguity, temporal succession, resemblance, greater and less, reason and consequence, etc. We give no account of the distinctive character of any of these by merely saying that they are cases of compresence. Now Alexander holds that in this respect the cognitive relation is exceptional. According to him it is not a specific kind of relation distinct in its own nature from all others. What is distinctive of it is only the nature of one of its terms. One of its terms must be a mental process. This condition being fulfilled, any existential relation is, at least potentially, a cognitive relation. So far as detailed knowledge is concerned, the potentiality becomes actual only under certain special conditions, *e.g.* the action of an external object on the organs of sense.

Why is it necessary to the relation that one of its terms shall be a mental process? I can find no possible answer to this question except that the reason lies in the peculiar nature of the relation. It is owing to the unique nature of the relation of cognition and cognitum that only minds can enter into it as cognitive. I believe Alexander would have recognised this if his mind had not been warped by his ontology. His ontology requires that all relations, at any rate all existential relations, shall be purely spatial-temporal. But cognition as here defined by him is an existential relation between particular processes in a finite mind and other things which are not mental. Hence, if he is to be consistent, he is bound to hold that the relation of knowing and being known is also spatial-temporal and nothing more. I submit that this is simply untrue. It is flatly inconsistent with the nature of the cognitive relation as we find it or, as Alexander would say, experience it.[5] Even if we admit that it always depends on spatial-temporal relations so as to be impossible without them, yet in its own nature it is neither spatial nor temporal. Even if we accept Alexander's very dubious contention that an individual mind is a spatial-temporal com-

plex, this does not remove the difficulty. What has to be shown is that it is nothing more. But the fact of cognition shows that it is something more.

Let us now consider the nature of the mental act or process. Alexander frequently speaks as if the mental process were itself cognition. It is an awareness of an object existentially distinct from itself. But such language is loose and inconsistent with his own fundamental position. What he really holds is that the mental act is cognitive only inasmuch as it enters into the cognitive relation. Within this relation it has a distinct nature and existence of its own. But its being in this relation is no more a mental act or process than being known is a physical act or process. Alexander does not make this clear until he is well advanced in the second volume of *Space, Time and Deity,* at ch. v, pp. 118-119. The relevant section is headed "Mind made up of Conations". Conation is to be taken as including such processes as "desire or endeavour or willing". But it is also used to cover mental excitements which are commonly regarded as passive, *e.g.* "passive acts of sense". In this wide application of the term every mental process is, according to Alexander, "a conation and is nothing else, except for the possible addition of feeling". "Cognition is not a separate kind of action from conation. It is not even a separate element in a mental act which can be distinguished from a conative element in the act. Cognition is nothing but the conation itself *in so far as it is compresent with and refers to an object.*"[6] "In so far as the conative act refers to its object, it is a cognition. The cognitive element therefore, of a mental act, is, to use a paradoxical expression, not anything distinctive of the act *as a process taking place in the mental substance itself. It signifies rather that the mental act refers to a cognitum.*"[7]

The mental act then is not in itself a cognitive process. It is so only in the sense that it enters directly into the cognitive relation on its cognitive side. But if it enters directly into the cognitive relation on its cognitive side, this only means, not that it is a knowing, but that it is that which knows. It is not cognition, but a cognitive subject. This is a startling paradox which Alexander simply ignores. It is true no doubt that we cannot desire anything or attend to it or be otherwise interested in it or occupied about it unless we are cognisant of it, however imperfectly. But for that very reason the conation itself cannot itself be the subject which is cognisant of the object. On the contrary, the conation, in order to exist as such, presupposes that the cognition is already present as part of the whole situation.

It seems obvious that Alexander's position here is quite untenable. But what alternative view can we substitute for it? Here if anywhere the conception of a transcendental self or pure ego seems called for. We seem to need a something definable only as "that which knows" or perhaps as "that which knows, feels and wills". But I agree with Alexander in rejecting this way out of the difficulty. We both substitute for the supposed "pure ego" the conception of the mind as a complex whole having a distinctive character and a distinctive form of unity marking it off from every other kind of complex whole, though in many ways its unity is analogous to that of a living organism. This complex whole is what the word 'I' stands for when I say that I know this or that, will or desire this or that, feel this or that. What is meant is that the knowing, willing and feeling enter into the constitution of the complex whole which is my individual mind or self and have no independent existence apart from it. This, be it noted, is not an exceptional use of language. When I say that my pen is in contact with the paper before me I mean that it has a point which is directly touching the paper. When I say that I digest food, I mean that my body, which I take to be part of myself, digests food. Further, it does so directly only through a part of itself—the digestive apparatus. The digestive apparatus is contained within its complex unity and functions only because it is so.

Now within an individual mind cognition is not found and, as I hold, cannot exist apart from some form of interest—of what Alexander calls conation. But if we are to examine the relation of cognition and cognitum for itself we must abstract from the conditions of its existence within the complex unity of the individual mind. Considering it in this abstract way, what do we find? I can find only the distinction and relation of what is cognised to the fact that it is cognised, of what is known to its knownness. From the purely abstract point of view I cannot find any distinction or relation between being known and knowing. I am not, in saying this, asserting a paradox. It is familiar common sense that there is no knowing apart from an 'I' which knows—a mind to which the knowing belongs. But I have deliberately left the knowing mind out of count, and it is for that reason that I can discover no knowing on the part of the mind, but only a being known on the side of the object. The proposition 'I know this or that' means that I *have* cognisance of this or that. In other words, it means that this is known within the complex unity of the individual mind. Its knownness belongs to the individual mind as *part* of its own being. From this a consequence follows which may be unpalatable to some modern realists. Inasmuch as knownness is only abstractly distinguishable from what is known and can have no separate being, it follows that objects, so far as they are known, must also in their own way enter into the constitution of the individual mind as a complex whole. Of course the condition "so far as they are known" is essentially important. I am not suggesting that objects are mental in any other respect. But so far as the mind has cognisance of them they are its own objects. So regarded, they are what are called ideas—what Ward calls presentations. As ideas or presentations they have characters and relations to each other of which they are otherwise incapable. Consider, for instance, association of ideas. Karlsbad is associated in my mind with my having had my hair cut there. This means that the thought of Karlsbad calls up in my mind the thought of the hair cutting. But the thought of Karlsbad and of the hair cutting and of the relation between them just is Karlsbad and the hair cutting and the

relation between them so far as I have cognisance of them. If they do not actually exist, yet, in so far as I have cognisance of them, they are at least objective possibilities dependent upon certain general conditions which cannot in the long run be merely possible.[8]

May we call knownness abstractly considered a *state* of the object known? Such language may seem appropriate inasmuch as the object may come to be known or cease to be known, at least to finite individuals, without ceasing to be the same object, as water may boil or freeze without ceasing to be water. But the suggested analogy breaks down in a most essential respect. When water boils or is frozen, its previous character is altered. But when what was previously unknown becomes known there is, in principle, no such alteration. The knownness is simply superinduced, leaving the other characteristics of the object, as it previously existed, unchanged. If this were not so, what is known could never be the same objectively as what was previously unknown. What we seek to know would never be the same as what we come to know. The questions we ask would never be answered.

Presupposing that we are cognisant of objects, it becomes possible to be interested in them—to be pleased or displeased with them, to seek to alter them or maintain them unaltered, to gain fuller knowledge of them. Such relations of the mind to its objects are essentially different from that which is involved in mere cognition abstractly considered. The terms which enter into it are existentially distinct. When the feeling of anger is part of the complex unity which I call myself I say that I feel angry. But the felt anger is existentially distinct from its object, from what I feel angry about. The same holds for all other ways of being interested. But the two terms of the relation being existentially distinct, there may be and there constantly is interaction between them. The object pleases or displeases me, and in being pleased or displeased with it I endeavour to act on it so as to maintain and enhance the pleasure or remove the pain. The mind as owning the feeling and conation is a subject interacting with its object. Though the objects are *its* objects only because it has cognisance of them, yet when we consider cognition in abstraction from feeling and conation, this antithesis of subject and object as existentially distinct and interacting with each other does not emerge. From this abstract point of view, we can say that the cognised objects, so far as cognised, are *in* the mind as a complex unity. But we cannot appropriately speak of them as for or before the mind, or as presented to the mind as if the mind confronted them and had dealings with them. It is quite otherwise when we consider the mind as owning feelings and conations. From this point of view the mind is a subject, and the mental life essentially consists in a transaction constantly going on between it and its objects. What we may call cognitive process essentially depends on this transaction. By cognitive process I mean, not a process in which cognition consists, for there is no such thing. I mean the passage from cognition to cognition, and especially from relatively vague and incomplete cognition to relatively distinct and complete cognition. This process could not go on without being sustained by conation and feeling.[9]

Sense-perception and the Status of Sensa.

Alexander draws a very sharp and sweeping distinction between the way in which each of us experiences his own mental processes—or, as I should prefer to say, his own subjective processes—and the way in which he experiences other things. The two kinds of experience are, according to him, mutually exclusive. As he holds, we only "enjoy" our own subjective processes and do not "contemplate" them; we contemplate other things and do not enjoy them. Now my main difficulty with his doctrine on this point is that I find something essentially akin to, if not identical with, what he calls enjoyment involved in what he calls contemplation and, on the other hand, something essentially akin to contemplation in what he calls enjoyment. My point is that he has confused a distinction between two elements involved in all knowledge through experience with a supposed distinction between two separate and mutually exclusive ways of experiencing. Postponing the treatment of "enjoyment", I shall first examine "contemplation", in order to show that his analysis of it is in this respect inadequate and incorrect. The question at issue is most sharply defined when we attempt to analyse the nature and conditions of perceptual illusion. To this topic Alexander devotes two chapters of *Space, Time and Deity* (Vol. II, chs. 7 and 8). Though I cannot accept his conclusions, I am full of admiration for the comprehensive and systematic way in which he states the relevant questions. His general doctrine, as I understand it, is that in all sense-perception what we perceive as existing actually does exist. Illusion is due to selection from, or distortion of, what actually exists as physical fact. In order to show that this is so Alexander distinguishes and examines in turn three kinds of appearances, which he calls *real* appearances, *mere* appearances, and *illusory* appearances.

The same thing appears differently to different persons or to the same person at different times according to their variable position relatively to it in space. Such differences, due only to the varying relative positions of the percipient, are said to be differences in the *real* appearance of things. What is distinctively characteristic of them is that they involve selection but not distortion. The difference between the object as it really is and as it is perceived is constituted by the partial nature of the perception. Only part of the object appears: but the part that does appear, appears as it really is. Alexander's attempt to justify this view in detail seems to me to break down completely. We need here examine only one typical example—the seeming increase or shrinkage in the size of things seen, according as they are nearer or more remote from the eye. A plate as measured by artificial instruments such as a tape or a yard measure, or by superposition of part of the percipient's body, *e.g.* the hand,[10] is, let us say, ten inches or three handbreadths in diameter. The size which is capable in principle of being measured in this way by physical units may be called physical or

objective size. What we call "the size of the plate" is physical size, and it has no other. When we contrast its objective or physical size with its apparent size the contrast is not between two kinds of size really belonging to the plate. What is meant is that the plate *seems* to be objectively either of the size it really is or larger or smaller than it really is. When I say that anything seems to some one, correctly or incorrectly, to be so and so, what is meant is either that the subject believes it to be so, or that conditions exist which tend to make him believe this and would lead him to believe it if he did not otherwise know better.

In this sense of "seems" the size of the plate seems to diminish as the distance between it and the percipient increases, though it really remains of the same size at all distances. As it recedes from him or he from it beyond a certain limit of distance,[11] it seems to be or seems as if it were smaller and smaller until it looks like a mere speck and finally vanishes. At one stage of the process it may seem not more than half an inch in diameter instead of ten inches. Apart from any such estimate in units of measurement, it seems as if it were very much smaller than it seemed to begin with, and very much smaller than another plate of equal size seen close at hand. Let us now consider Alexander's explanation of such facts. "The same plate," he tells us, "when near and far excites different extents of retinal tract and is seen in different sizes."[12] But how does the variable extent of the retinal excitement operate? It is in the answer to this question that the peculiarity of his view emerges. "The distance of the eye from the plate acts selectively. . . . The size which we see is a portion of the real geometrical size of the plate."[13] We must first make clear what Alexander means by *seeing* when we speak of "the size we see". The seeing is "immediate and sensory"; in other words, what is said to be seen is taken to be identical with the visual sensum as actually experienced, not merely thought or judged or believed or seeming to exist. It is the actual sensum which, according to Alexander, is identical with part of the size. The sensum is therefore a physical or objective size and in this respect does not differ at all from the "real geometrical size of the plate". The only difference is that it is part and not the whole of this real geometrical size. But what can be meant by the statement that it is part of the whole physical size of the plate which is thus actually experienced as a sensum? The meaning cannot be that as the plate seems to shrink with its increasing distance parts of it continue to be revealed in their real size while others vanish. All the parts together seem to shrink, so that what is true of the whole is true of each part. Further, if some were selected and others omitted, there would arise gaps between them of which there is no trace. We must suppose therefore that the gaps between them are in some way filled so as to constitute the single uninterrupted visual sensum as we actually experience it.[14] But if we reject the view that parts are thus selected and others rejected, what can be meant by saying that what is sensed is only part of the real size? So far as I can discover, in using such language we are only asserting in a clumsy way that the extent of the sensum is smaller than the real geometrical size of the thing seen. Let me add that I do not know how even this statement can be verified. For the size of the sensum as such is not capable of physical measurement.

Let us, however, grant that the size of the sensum is in some way a partial extract from the objective size of the thing. How far does this help him in accounting for the seeming diminution of the plate with increasing distance, and its seeming enlargement with decreasing distance? How in particular does he explain the fact that what seems to the percipient to grow smaller or larger is the whole size of the plate, not only a selection from it, and that if he knows from other sources that the plate as a whole continues to be the same size, he regards its seeming variations as unreal and for practical purposes disregards them? Indeed, for a certain near range of distance the plate does not even seem to vary in size, in spite of variations in the size of the visual sensum. Here the first question which emerges is how the percipient is cognisant at all of the whole size of the plate. For on Alexander's view only an extract from it is ever sensibly experienced.

But if it is not sensibly experienced and yet the percipient is cognisant of it, we must say that he only thinks of it. The thought together with the sensum enters into what Alexander, in agreement with ordinary language, would call the experience of seeing the plate. But *experience* in this sense should be distinguished from what I call actual or immediate experience, inasmuch as it includes besides this the thought of what is not actually experienced. We have next to inquire how the thought arises. Alexander, who recognises that it must be present, denies that it belongs to purely visual perception. "It is only in reference to space as touched and thought of in terms of touch that the plate itself seems to shrink as it moves further off. Considered in themselves as purely visual objects . . . the one patch of colour merely looks smaller than the other. If we know otherwise than by sight that they are appearances of the same thing, we say that the thing shrinks to sight as it recedes. But if we do not know this, there is no thought of shrinkage." Alexander does not, as I understand him, hold that touch perception reveals things in their size whereas sight fails so to reveal them. His position is more subtle. He holds that there are certain experiences of combined sight and touch which leave no doubt that the thing seen is the same as the thing touched, having the same place and the same extent, though the seeming size may vary for sight.[15] This size which is the same for what is seen and what is touched can only be the real or whole size of the object. "We have only to hold the plate in our hands and move it away . . . in order to assure ourselves that the touch and colour of the plate are in the same place. The touch remains of the same felt extent: the colour varies but the seen contour of the plate coincides in place with the felt contour." Alexander's analysis is defective. The felt contour is confined to the parts of the plate which the hands touch, and those parts are not seen because the hands screen them from the eye. The other side of the hands is seen in seeing the plate but, as he supposes, they and it seem to

shrink together as the distance is increased. But this assumption is wrong. For ordinary vision the seen object does not seem to shrink within this range of distance. I hold indeed as a verifiable matter of fact that the visual sensum does actually shrink with the varying extent of the retinal image. But this creates another difficulty for Alexander. His explanation of the seeming shrinkage as due merely to the diminution of the sensum breaks down. The seeming shrinkage is not merely due to what he regards as the smaller selection from the whole size, which according to him constitutes the sensum. None the less I agree with Alexander that experiences of this kind do give assurance that what is seen and what is touched are of the same size. The hand is an instrument for measuring the part of the plate on which it is superposed. It would do equally well if it were insensitive. Tactual perception is important mainly as evidence of contact. But sight can supply equally good evidence. I see my hand on the plate as I see a match on the table before me. In like manner the distance between the two hands, as determined by the angle made by the two arms, measures the distance from one side of the plate to the other, much as it might be measured with a pair of compasses. Motor sensations supply evidence of what this angle is. But within this near range of vision equally good evidence is supplied by sight. It is by sight alone that another person understands us when, in the absence of the plate, we indicate its size by holding our hands a certain distance apart. What measurement of this sort effects is to determine, however roughly, the physical or, as Alexander would say, the whole, size in terms of physical units supposed to remain at least sufficiently constant to be of some practical use. But we cannot thus attempt to determine what is the physical size, unless we start with the thought of it and the belief in its existence. As for the relation of the thought to the belief, we may safely adopt the Spinozistic position that belief in anything is inseparable from the thought of it unless the conditions preclude the belief. We may then confine ourselves to the question how the thought of it first arises. Is it primarily due to visual or to tactual perception or to both? To these I would add as a fourth alternative that it may be due not to touch alone but to touch in union with effort against resistance.[16] No one is likely to maintain that the thought belongs originally to visual and only derivatively to tactual perception. But the persistence of what I may call the Berkeleyan prejudice may lead some to regard it as belonging in the first instance to touch and only derivatively to sight. I can find no justification for this view. When we have set aside measurement by superposition and also effort against resistance, the case for touch rests only on the supposed constancy of tactual sensa. But they are not constant. They differ, *e.g.*, for the tip of the forefinger and the centre of the palm. If we hold with Alexander that in vision only part of the size of the thing seen is sensibly experienced we are bound to hold that in tactual perception only part of the size of the thing touched is sensibly experienced. Mere touch differs from sight in no way which can warrant us in asserting that it does, and that sight does not, primarily include the thought of "real geometrical size" as distinguished from the size of the sensum or from the seeming size of the object.

A more plausible case can be made out for touch in union with voluntary motor effort against resistance.[17] To touch there belongs an extensive sensum and the consequent apprehension of the thing touched as extended. In the experience of motor effort the extended thing as such is apprehended as if it were making a counter effort as a whole and in all its discernible parts. This resistance or counter effort is not part either of the tactual or of the motor sensum. It is thought of, not actually experienced. Hence the extension of the thing as resisting need not coincide with its extension as perceived under variable conditions by touch or sight. The real extension is the extension which offers resistance. Now I am ready to accept this analysis of the experience of effort against resistance as yielding the thought of and the belief in objective as contrasted with seeming extension. I would only add that since effort and resistance are reciprocal we are aware in this experience of the objective extension of our own bodies as included in the embodied self as well as of the thing which resists our efforts. The principle is that what acts and is acted on is so far real. But is this principle applicable only to motor effort against resistance? I submit that this is only one case, though a specially important one, of the interaction between subject and object which pervades our experience. Everywhere we find the antithesis of what we actively initiate and what is objectively determined for us and not by us. We need here only consider vision apart from touch and motor effort. It depends normally on our initiative whether we shall approach or recede from the thing seen, or remain still, or turn our backs on it. But however we proceed, it never depends wholly on our initiative what the size, shape, etc., of the thing shall seem to be or whether we shall see it at all. Suppose that we recede from it, keeping it in view; it seems to decrease in size in a way which is regular and uniform, provided that other relevant conditions remain unchanged. On this assumption we can command at will the series of seeming sizes. But we cannot thus determine *what* size it shall seem to be either initially or at any given distance. Further, the seeming diminutions in size as we retire from the thing seen do not always take place in the same uniform way. As we are receding from it, it may be receding from us, and it may itself increase or diminish. Such conditions, which are independent of our initiative, make a difference to the seeming size. In general we proceed on the sound principle that seeming change and difference which depend merely on our initiative are not objective. On the other hand, seeming change and difference which occur independently of our initiative may not be objective; for there are other sources of illusion. But in the absence of reasons to the contrary it presumably is so. It has at any rate passed an essential preliminary test.

I conclude that Alexander has no good reason for supposing that objective reference in visual perception is borrowed either from touch or from the union of sight and touch, even if we take touch to include motor effort. It is

plain also that he is wrong in denying that "real appearances" as such are free from illusion. If a plate far off seems to be objectively smaller than one near at hand which is objectively of the same size, the seeming is contrary to fact and therefore illusory. If the illusion is not corrected by knowledge gained from other sources, it involves false belief. I myself remember that in my early childhood when looking down from a cliff on a group of men below, I took them to be tiny dwarfs. I was astonished but not incredulous. I accepted the fact with "natural piety".

It makes no difference to the question at issue whether or not we accept Alexander's hypothesis that the size sensibly experienced is a selection from the whole objective size. For what I call seeming, whether illusory or not, is an affair of at least potential belief, not merely of immediate sensible experience. The sensum which is actually experienced cannot, as such, be illusory. The most radical defect in Alexander's epistemology is his failure to recognise the ambiguity of the term "experience". He habitually uses it in the very common and convenient sense in which it is synonymous with *knowledge through* or *by* experience. Understanding the term in this way, I agree with Alexander that all knowing is experiencing. But experience in this sense must in principle be sharply distinguished from what I call actual or immediate experience, whether this takes the form of sensation or the "enjoyment" of subjective processes. The latter is only one ingredient in knowledge through experience. It is the ingredient which justifies us in saying that it is through experience we know. The other ingredient is thought, and apart from this there would be no cognition. Even what we are actually experiencing is not cognised except in so far as it is thought of, and it is always thought of in connexion with what is not being actually experienced.

I have previously urged that it is difficult to attach any clear meaning to Alexander's view of the size of the sensum as a partial selection from the objective size unless we regard it as merely stating the unverifiable proposition that the sensible size is always smaller than the objective. But in spite of such difficulties many might be tempted to cling to it if it really gets rid, as Alexander supposes, of all representative theories of sense-perception. But we have just seen that it does nothing of the kind. Representationism[18] could be entirely avoided only if it were shown that the seeming objective size is identical with the whole objective size: and this on Alexander's view is far from being true.

For "mere appearances", such as the face we seem to see in a mirror or the straight oar that seems to be bent in water, the principle of selection confessedly breaks down. Alexander substitutes another which I cannot reconcile with obvious facts. In such cases Alexander's theory is that "we do not sense the thing of which we apprehend the mere appearance taken by itself but in connexion with some other thing which *modifies* it. What we sense or otherwise apprehend is not the thing by itself, but a new thing of which the thing forms a part; and *there is no reason to suppose that . . . the compound thing does not really possess what we sense.*"[19] "It may be impossible to perceive a thing alone, and the foreign thing may *distort* the object and make it not a real appearance but a mere appearance."[20]

Here Alexander is asserting two distinct and, as I think, incompatible propositions. (1) The thing seen, or what the percipient takes to be the thing seen, is really distorted by the intervention of a "foreign object". (2) What seems to be a character of the thing seen is objectively a character of a "compound object" of which this is only a part. Let us take first the theory of distortion. Wherein is the distortion supposed to consist? Alexander cannot mean, or at least ought not to mean, merely that the thing *seems* different from what it objectively is. For this is precisely what has to be explained; it is not the explanation. Nor can he mean merely that the sensum is distorted: for such distortion is relevant only in so far as it makes a difference to the seeming nature or place of the thing seen. These alternatives being excluded, there remains only one other, that the thing seen is objectively altered by the foreign object. Many passages in Alexander *prima facie* seem to imply this view. In particular it would account for his denial that "mere appearances" are illusory. But the theory is in violent conflict with admitted facts. The partially immersed oar is not really bent by the water or by the refraction of the light. The optical explanation is based on the assumption that it continues to be as straight as it was before it was dipped in the water. The refraction accounts for the bent sensum. But though the sensum is really bent the oar is not. Alexander analyses only one example at length, that of reflexion in a mirror supposed to be flawless. According to him we see the real thing exactly as it is, only it is displaced. Here I can only make the rude and crude comment that the real thing, *e.g.* a reflected face, is not displaced. It remains in front of the mirror and does not pass behind it: if it did, we should not see it at all, as the mirror would hide it. Nor is the visual sensum thus displaced: the only place the sensum can have is within the actually experienced field of visual sensation; it cannot move out of the field so as to get behind the mirror. It may be suggested that we immediately experience the reflected light: but the reflected light is not behind the surface that reflects it. The only tenable meaning I can attach to the statement that the face reflected is itself displaced, is that there seems to be a face where there really is no face, and that this illusory seeming is due to a real face's being reflected in the mirror. What we see is the reflexion and not the real face directly or indirectly. There is an experience, strangely neglected by Alexander, which seems decisive of this question. The spectator may see simultaneously the real face and the reflexion of it. There then seem to be two separate faces, each in its own separate place. One of them really exists where it seems to exist. The other does not exist at all, but only a reflexion of the first. But there really are two separate sensa, each actually experienced, in separate places within the actually experienced field of visual sensation. To convince any one who may doubt this let us discard the arbitrary assumption that the mirror is flawless. We have then another case of "mere appearance". But if the mirror is not flawless the sensum due to reflexion may differ grotesquely in shape from the sensum experienced in seeing the real face. But if they are really unlike they cannot be identical. I can make nothing of Alexander's other view that the seeming character or place of the object seen really belongs to a compound object of which it is part. The seeming place of the reflexion behind the mirror is not really the place of the compound object constituted by the mirror, the reflected face and the light passing between them. This compound object is not behind the mirror. On the whole, Alexander has signally failed to show that his mere appearances are not illusory.

We turn now to what Alexander himself admits to be illusory appearances. To account for these he again has recourse to "selection". But the selection is not, as in real appearances, from the perceived object; on the contrary, anything may be selected which is compresent with the percipient in the universe of which he is part. What determines the selection of this rather than that is not any objective condition but an appropriate mental process; and this is identified by Alexander with the neural process which is ordinarily said to be correlated with it. Alexander gives as an example the grey piece of paper which is seen as green by contrast on a red ground. "The paper itself is not green. But there is green in the world. The appropriate response of the mind to green is the kind of sensory act which the mind is at the moment performing, and accordingly it sees green." What is thus seen is not a "universal green" but an "individual sensum".[21] This highly ingenious theory is open to criticism in many ways. The green sensum is actually experienced as placed within a surrounding field of red. On the evidence of immediate experience it is as certain that it is in this place as that it is green. But the red which surrounds it is not supposed to be illusory or even a mere appearance. It is taken to be a real appearance. This means, according to Alexander, that the red actually experienced really belongs to the paper. It follows that the green which is really included within the red must also really be the objective colour of the paper.[22] But it is admitted that the paper which seems objectively green is in fact objectively grey. The conclusion seems unavoidable that the whole sensum is existentially distinct from any physical object. It is, however, real, though not physically real. Whether and in what sense it can properly be called mental is another question. Another obvious difficulty for Alexander is that he must assume that what is sensibly experienced in illusory appearances really pre-exists somewhere or other in the world. But this cannot be true of all that is sensibly present in dreams, delirium, etc. The only reply that Alexander can make is that such sensa are complex and that the elements which comprise them really pre-exist. But what we sensibly experience is actual, not merely potential. How are the constituent elements brought together so as to actualise the potentiality? On Alexander's view this must be the work of mind or of neural process. It follows that the mind or neural process must actually produce and not merely select such complex sensa. Further, as they are supposed by Alexander to be objective, the mind or neural process must produce them as objective facts—which is absurd. The outcome of this whole discussion is that, sensa being existentially distinct from whatever is physically objective, Alexander's doctrine of selection is quite untenable.

Am I then committed to a representative theory of sense-perception? I admit that I am. So is Alexander. He is bound to regard what is selected from the object as representing the whole object. But though I accept a representative theory of sense-perception I reject any representative theory of knowledge in general. The representative function of sensa, like all knowledge by way of representation, must be founded on an apprehension of some relation between what represents and what is represented; and this must in the long run be apprehended directly and not by way of representation. I have indicated my own positive view on this question in my book on *Mind and Matter*.

[1] *Space, Time and Deity*, Vol. I, p. 11. (Hereafter referred to as *S. T. and D.*)

[2] Alexander usually treats act and process as synonymous. At any rate the act is for him always a process.

[3] I gather that Alexander would hold that all relations are existential in this sense. But if so, I think that he is wrong.

[4] *S. T. and D.*, Vol. I, p. 23.

[5] I shall have occasion later to notice an ambiguity of the term *experience* which leads to confusion in Alexander's use of it.

[6] Italics mine.

[7] Italics mine.

[8] I do not wish to repeat here what I have said elsewhere about the nature and conditions of error and fiction.

[9] There is another reason why we naturally regard the mind as confronting the objects which are said to be present to it. The mind is commonly considered as embodied and its objects are taken to be external to the body as known through organic and motor sensation. So far as this is the case the confrontation is literal and not merely metaphorical.

[10] The use of the body or part of it as an instrument of measurement is different in principle from the perception of size through touch *sensation*, which is very vague and very variable for different parts of the skin, as is clearly shown by experiments expressly devised to test tactual sensibility. Alexander is confused on this point. He says, for instance, that it is only when "thought of in terms of touch that the plate itself seems to shrink as it moves further off". I should say "thought of in terms of physical measurement"—or more accurately "thought of in terms of magnitude which is capable of physical measurement".

[11] I shall have occasion to refer to this reservation later.

[12] *S. T. and D.*, Vol. II, pp. 193-194.

[13] *Ibid.*, p. 193.

[14] Otherwise there would be only a broken sketch or indication of the real shape, not a different shape which is what we perceive.

[15] I may add for touch also according as this takes place through different parts of the cutaneous surface.

[16] Alexander seems to offer yet another alternative in his account of intuition as a "way of apprehending" distinct from sense-perception. I shall deal with this topic later on. Meanwhile I am assuming that size, shape, etc., are perceived by the senses in essentially the same way as colour or heat.

[17] Alexander nowhere discusses this experience.

[18] Note that I am speaking of representative theories of *sense-perception*, not of knowledge in general. I shall return to this distinction later.

[19] *S. T. and D.*, Vol. II, p. 191. Italics mine.

[20] *Ibid.*, p. 185. Italics mine.

[21] *S. T. and D.*, Vol. II, p. 214.

[22] Or a selection from it: this makes no difference to my argument.

G. F. Stout (essay date 1940)

SOURCE: "The Philosophy of Samuel Alexander (II.)," in *Mind: A Quarterly Review*, Vol. XLIX, No. 194, April, 1940, pp. 136-49.

[*In the following essay, which comprises the second installment of his analysis of Alexander's philosophy, Stout discusses Alexander's distinction between the ways objects and mental processes are experienced, his treatment of the knowledge of other minds, and his conceptions of space-time, intuitive knowledge, and the emergent quality of nature.*]

Enjoyment and Contemplation.

Alexander draws a hard and fast distinction between the way in which we experience objects and the way in which we experience our own mental (*i.e.,* subjective) processes. We are said to *enjoy* the mental processes and to *contemplate* objects. Let no one suppose that this is only a new way of naming a distinction which can be readily understood and easily verified. At first I myself made this mistake. I took it to be in principle identical with the distinction between actual experience and thought. Then my main difficulty was with the view that only subjective processes and not sensa could be enjoyed, and also with the view that enjoyment and contemplation are mutually exclusive. But I soon discovered my mistake. The peculiarity of Alexander's view emerges with startling clearness in his denial that pleasure and pain are enjoyed. It is nonsense to say that the pain of a toothache or the pleasure of a lover in the presence of his beloved are not actually experienced. It is also nonsense to say that the pleasure and pain are existentially distinct and separable from the actual experiencing of them. Pleasure and pain exist only in being felt. When they are unfelt they not only cease to be known but altogether cease to be. I agree with Alexander that being pleased or pained is not the same as being conscious of the pleasure or pain. There is always the difference between what is known and the knowing of it. But in this case not only the knowing or being conscious but what we know or are conscious of is actually experienced and only exists in being actually experienced.

Let us now quote Alexander's own account of what he means by enjoyment as distinct from contemplation:—

> Take the perception of a tree or a table. This situation consists of the act of the mind which is the perceiving; the object of which it is aware is so much of the thing called tree as is perceived . . . ; and the togetherness or compresence which connects these two distinct existences into the total situation is called the experience. But the two terms are differently experienced. The one is experienced, that is, is present in the experience, as the act of experiencing, the other as that which is experienced. . . . The word 'of' indicates the relation between these two relatively distinct existences. The difference between the two ways in which the terms are experienced is expressed in language by the difference between the cognate and the objective accusative. I am aware of my awareness as I strike a stroke or wave a farewell. *My awareness and my being aware of it are identical.* I experience the tree as I strike a man or wave a flag.[1]

How, I ask, can my awareness and my being aware of it be identical? Such propositions are formally barred by Logic. What is known cannot be identical with its being known. Yet Alexander, when he speaks of awareness, means cognition. Everywhere he regards enjoyment as involving knowledge of what is enjoyed. Here he explicitly states that there is no difference between the enjoyment and the knowledge of it, between experiencing and the experience of the experiencing. What he says about the cognate accusative does not help him. For knowing is related to what is known not as striking to the stroke, but rather as striking to the object struck.[2] It is true that in the case of enjoyment the knowing is not existentially separate from what is known. But, as I have previously urged, the same is true of contemplation. Alexander's cognitive acts supposed to be existentially separate from the object

cognised are impossible fictions. There are indeed what Alexander calls conations, *i.e.,* ways in which the mind is interested in or occupied about the objects of which it is cognisant; and it may be that without such processes there could be no cognition. But in this respect there is no essential difference between contemplation and enjoyment. The enjoyed process consists in being interested in and occupied about its own object. But we may also be interested in and occupied about the enjoyed process itself as well as its object. In desiring food my attention may be wholly or almost wholly concentrated on the food as seen or smelled or thought of. But if satisfaction is postponed I become immediately interested in the desire itself. There follow exclamations such as: "I am dreadfully hungry; I would give the world for something to eat". Sometimes the interest in the enjoyed process is opposed to the interest in its object. This happens when we endeavour to suppress or conceal a desire such, for instance, as the morbid sexual cravings with which the psycho-analyst deals.

I conclude that "enjoyment" is not a way in which subjective states and processes are known, but a way in which they exist. I cannot see a fundamental difference between this way of existing and what I call being actually experienced. But I hold that sensa also are actually experienced. The question arises whether I am using the term with the same meaning when I apply it to sensa. If not, what is the difference? I have just pointed out that "enjoyment" of subjective processes is distinct from being cognisant of them. Is this also true of sensa as actually experienced? It seems too often assumed that the actual sensing of sensa consists only in knowing them by "direct acquaintance" instead of merely thinking of them. I cannot accept this view. What I find is that the actual experiencing is a necessary precondition of knowledge by acquaintance and is therefore not identical with it. It is no more identical with it than the placing of an object within my range of vision is identical with my seeing it. This is especially evident when the sensum is intensely pleasant or unpleasant or in other ways is in a high degree disturbing. Consider for instance a noise of overpowering intensity together with the organic sensa which accompany it. It is not my cognition of such sensa, however direct, but the sensa themselves which are so disturbing and intrusive. Their intrusiveness belongs to them as actually experienced and not as known. I cannot treat this question here with any approach to adequacy. I shall content myself with adding one argument which seems to me to have great force. If actual experience of sensa is just the same as knowing them by acquaintance it follows that nothing whatever can be sensibly experienced without being thus known. Further, nothing can be true of actual experience which is not true of the knowledge by acquaintance which is supposed to be identical with it. Now whatever is actually experienced is actually experienced in its completely determinate particularity. We cannot actually experience shape in general but only an entirely specific and particular shape. We cannot be actually experiencing a whole without actually experiencing each and all of its parts in their particular detail, as I can think of the town of Sydney without thinking of each and all of its particular roads, streets, etc. But if the actual experiencing of sensa is simply identical with knowing them by acquaintance, the knowledge by acquaintance must be no less particular and determinate. There ought to be no subconscious sensa. Every detail which is sensibly experienced ought to be separately discerned. But I am fully convinced that this is not so. If I ask myself what I am sensibly experiencing at any moment I find that only a relatively small part is discerned in detail. I am cognisant of the rest only inasmuch as I am cognisant of the whole sensible experience to which they belong. If I try to analyse this whole into its component parts, I find that I can pick out detail after detail, yet can never make the analysis complete. Further, the transition is quite different from that to new sensa, as when after seeing black I see white which was previously unseen. As each detail emerges into distinctness I am aware of something that I sensibly experienced before I discerned it—became *conscious* of it. I cannot here repeat what I and others have said in support of this doctrine of subconscious sensa. Some persons reject it as inherently absurd. But I have always found that they are really begging the question. They begin by assuming that what I call actual experience must be identical with knowledge by acquaintance. On this assumption I, of course, agree with them that there can be no subconscious sensa. Fully convinced, as I am, that they really exist, I can only infer that the assumption is false.

Can we distinguish enjoyment from sensible experience by saying that what is enjoyed actually exists only when it is actually enjoyed, whereas sensa may actually exist when they are not actually experienced? Once we have dismissed the view that sensa are selections from or distortions of objective facts, I can discover no evidence that they do in fact so exist, and it is at least doubtful whether they could do so. I am myself strongly inclined to agree with Berkeley that they could not. But even if we suppose that sensa can and subjective processes cannot actually exist without being actually experienced it does not follow that this is due to any fundamental difference in the way they are experienced. It may equally well be due to the difference between the nature of a subjective process and of a sensum.

Alexander, like James Ward, draws a hard and fast line between sensa and subjective process. He denies (though with some hesitation) that being pleased or pained by, with or about something is subjective or, as he would say, "mental". His reason is that pleasure and pain are sensory. It is curious that in this case at least he seems to have no way of directly determining what is mental. He has to fall back on this indirect criterion. To me it seems so clear that being pleased and the reverse are subjective that, if they are also sensory, I can only conclude that what is sensory constitutes or at least enters into the constitution of subjective states and processes. When we have got rid of the present alleged physical existence of sensa, this view does not present any insuperable difficulty. What stands in the way of it is a failure to distinguish the question of origin from the question of func-

tion. To be subjective is to be a way of being interested in something. Provided that this condition is fulfilled, a process is subjective whether or not it is partly or wholly sensory in its origin. In fact there seems to be good reason for asserting that subjective states are at least partly sensory in their origin.[3] I agree with Alexander that being pleased and pained essentially involve organic sensa with their feeling-tone. It is still clearer that the same is true of emotions such as fear and anger. Conation too normally involves experience of motor tension.

Knowledge of Other Minds.

In contrast with his usual thoroughness, Alexander's treatment of the way in which we know other minds strikes me as somewhat perfunctory. Generally he speaks of contemplation and enjoyment as if they were the only primary and direct "ways of apprehension". But when he comes expressly to deal with the knowledge one mind has of others he refuses to regard this as inferential. He adds it to contemplation and enjoyment as a third primary and direct way of knowing which he calls "assurance". He fully admits that knowledge of other minds *develops* through inference, just as knowledge of the physical world does. But in both cases the starting-point and precondition of the inferential process must be found in knowledge which is not inferential. So far I can follow him and in general accept his arguments. In particular, I agree with him that "the idea of a foreign consciousness, unless directly supplied by some experience to that effect, is something to which we have no clue in ourselves".[4] But I cannot accept Alexander's account of the conditions under which this primary knowledge of other minds arises. According to him it arises in the contemplation of a special kind of object. If we ask what kind of object this is, he answers that it is the kind of object in which we are socially interested. Alexander gives as examples "parental or filial affection, or sexual love, competition in pursuit of prey, or jealousy".[5] Now the very meaning of the term social interest as Alexander understands it implies that it cannot exist apart from the idea or thought of the existence of other minds. But just for that reason it is putting the cart before the horse to say that social interest is an antecedent condition which first gives rise in the individual to the thought of minds other than his own. Unless this is already present, there can be only contemplation of physical objects. "There is," says Alexander, "all the difference between grasping a hand which returns the pressure and grasping an unresponsive piece of flesh in the shape of a hand."[6] This is true. But the difference would not be appreciated if in grasping the hand we did not apprehend it as belonging to someone who was, or at least might be, capable of responsive feelings and desires. If this condition were not fulfilled, the pressure of the hand grasped would not be apprehended as a social response. It would be perceived merely as a physical fact. The same difficulty which Alexander finds in the theory of inference by analogy applies also to his own view. Social interest presupposes the thought of mental life other than our own and cannot therefore account for its existence.

My own view[7] is that the thought of mind other than our own and connected with our own is primary and universal in the constitution of experience and in this respect is on a level with the thought of physical objects as involved in sense-perception. The function of actually experienced sensa in sense-perception is fulfilled by actually experienced subjective processes in the knowledge we have of mental life other than our own. This knowledge develops in detail through inference, in which the analogy of the bodily appearance and motions of others to our own, and also the experiences of social response, play a most important part. Of the two, social response is the more fundamental and important.[8] Where and as far as these special clues fail, our apprehension of mental life beyond our own becomes comparatively vague and indefinite. But there is no reason for regarding it as baseless or unimportant. The primitive tendency, however, is to assume an individual life more or less analogous to our own individual selves even where special evidence for it is lacking. This anthropomorphic tendency is gradually corrected with advancing experience in much the same way as are primitive illusions of sense-perception, and just as the correction of perceptual error presupposes that sense-perception is always concerned with the objective world, however mistaken we may be about it, I submit that the same holds for the apprehension of mind other than our own.

Space-time and Intuition.

Alexander holds that there is a way of apprehending which he calls "Intuition," coming under the general head of contemplation, but distinct from Sense-Perception. I have postponed consideration of this way of apprehending because I find it impossible to examine it without first taking account of what seems to me most untenable in Alexander's ontology. In treating of sense-perception this complication did not arise. For there Alexander's fundamental ontological position was one which I share myself. It simply consists in the assumption that there really is a spatial-temporal universe, existing independently of being perceived. I should also agree that our knowledge of this universe is primarily direct in the sense in which 'direct' is contrasted with 'inferential'.

But his doctrine of intuition as a distinct way of apprehending is founded on a peculiar ontological theory of the ultimate constitution of the spatial-temporal universe. The basis of this theory is the view of *pure* space-time as existing independently of and even prior to the things, processes and qualities which are ordinarily said to exist in space and occur in time. From this pure space-time everything else develops, or, as he also puts it, pure space-time is the "stuff" of which everything else is made. It is as if he had said that pure number comes first and all countable things are evolved from it. Neither time nor space are anything at all apart from things and events which are not merely spatial and temporal but have other characters. Space is a universal order in which extended things and their parts are correlated and connected. Time is a universal order in which changes are correlated and connected.[9] The spatial order and the temporal mutually involve each other, and this fact is marked by the term space-time; and this, so far as I can see, is all that modern science means by it.

According to Alexander, pure space and pure time, considered apart from each other, are mere abstractions incapable of existing. But in their union as space-time they constitute one actual concrete process of great and ever-increasing complexity. In working out this view in detail he displays his own brilliance and ingenuity in a most impressive way. But what he says corresponds to nothing in my experience. It is all in the air, or rather in an airless region in which I at any rate find myself suffocated. I shall not, therefore, make any attempt to follow him in this part of his work.

What I am here especially concerned with is the correlation of pure space-time, as Alexander conceives it, with that peculiar way of apprehending it which he calls "Intuition". Pure space-time is according to him not perceptible by the senses either as a whole or in its parts. The proper objects of sense-perception consist in *qualities,* including under this head not only colours, sounds, smells, etc., but mass and energy[10] (what Alexander calls "materiality"). Pure unqualified space-time must therefore be apprehended otherwise than by sense-perception: this other way of apprehending is "Intuition". But intuition, though radically distinct from sense-perception, is none the less dependent on it. Apart from sense-perception intuition would be a mere faculty. The actual exercise of this faculty is indispensably conditioned by the perception of qualities. But this condition is also a limitation. We have no determinate apprehension of the particular parts of space-time which is not found in or derived from experience in which sense-perception accompanies and makes possible intuition. Intuition is, so to speak, in the dark except in so far as sense-perception strikes a light for it to see by. If it could be set free from this limiting condition, it would be an apprehension of the whole of space-time, including all its parts severally. "Comprescence," in the wide sense attached to that word by Alexander, would be all that is required for cognition. We are ourselves, according to him, parts of space-time. All other parts are therefore comprescent with us and would be known in all their detail, if intuition were not limited by sense-perception. Even with this limitation we are, according to Alexander, cognisant, not indeed of the whole of space-time, but of space-time as a whole.

This theory of intuition as a separate and independent faculty is essentially dependent on the ontological theory of pure space-time as a separate and independent existence from which qualities, including mass and energy, somehow "emerge". Holding as I do that pure space-time, apart from all that Alexander calls qualities, is an impossible abstraction incapable of existing by itself, I am bound to reject his doctrine of intuition as radically distinct from sense-perception. The reason why we cannot perceive pure space-time without qualities is that it can have no being without qualities any more than the qualities have any being apart from it. On the same principle, what Alexander regards as the indefinite apprehension of pure space-time as a whole is really the indefinite apprehension of the concrete universe as a whole including qualities and including mind as well as matter.

The Emergence of Qualities.

Let me begin by quoting Alexander's own formal and general account of what he means by "emergence" and by emergent qualities. "The world actually or historically develops from its first or elementary condition of Space-Time which possesses no quality except what we agreed to call the spatio-temporal quality of motion.[11] But as in the course of Time new complexity of motions comes into existence, a new quality emerges, that is, a new complex possesses as a matter of observed empirical fact a new or emergent quality."[12] To this we have to add that qualities emerge in a certain serial order, so that the earlier precondition the occurrence of the later.

Now it is undeniable that a whole as such has characters different both from those of its own constituent parts and from those of the relatively separate factors which by their combination and interaction contribute to form it. But it is not *any* character which may thus belong to the parts and not to the whole. The character of the whole is limited and conditioned by the nature of the parts. This follows from the very meaning of the term *whole*. For a whole is nothing else than all its parts as such. It is simply identical with all its parts united and inter-related in the way appropriate to that kind of whole. The nature of the whole as such exists only in so far as the natures of the parts contribute to form it. It cannot therefore be disparate from that of the parts, as a colour is disparate from a smell. The integral character must be an integration of partial characters having the same generic nature: it must be a determinate of the same assignable determinable. Sounds united in a certain kind of complex whole form a melody; but they cannot form a smell or a colour. If a smell or a colour accompanies the process, it must be referred to other conditions than the mere union of the sounds. Now it seems to me that Alexander's conception of emergence as interpreted by his application of it involves this absurdity. It introduces as characters of a complex whole, due merely to its complexity, characters which are entirely disparate in their nature from the nature of the parts which in their union constitute the whole.

He starts from a purely spatial-temporal process[13] which increases in complexity as it advances. When it has reached a certain kind and degree of complexity, the complex as a whole acquires a new character. The character is new in the sense that it is no longer merely spatial-temporal.

If it is not new in this sense it has not the distinctive novelty of an "emergent quality", such as belongs to the so-called secondary qualities where they occur. On the other hand, if it does have this kind of novelty, it cannot be accounted for as a character of the complex. For in whatever way or degree a purely spatial-temporal process may become complicated, the complication is not itself a transition to anything which is not pure space-time. All the parts of the resulting complex still remain purely spatial-temporal whether considered severally or in the union with each other which constitutes the whole. If a new quality occurs which has not this generic nature it must be due to other conditions or to no conditions at all.

According to Alexander, the first qualities to "emerge" are those which constitute "materiality", *e.g.,* mass and energy. His position here may be interpreted in two alternative ways, and I am not sure which he means to adopt. He may mean that "materiality" is nothing but a complex development of pure space-time, so that it can be analysed without residue into purely spatial-temporal process. But if this is so, the purely spatial-temporal process has not the novelty of an emergent quality. On the other hand, if anything is supposed to occur which is not a purely spatial-temporal development, we are faced with the difficulty I have already stated. The novelty has no kind of relevance to the conditions from which it is said to emerge. It might as well be supposed to "emerge" from nothing at all.

The same difficulty presents itself in a more obvious and acute form when we consider the so-called "secondary" qualities of matter. The word "secondary" is misleading. The "secondary" qualities are the only qualities properly so called. Mass, energy, etc., are quantitative and relational characters. They are not qualities in the sense in which sweetness and redness are so, as we experience them in sense-perception. Now the difficulty of accounting for such qualities properly so called has been acute for all who have held in any form the mechanical view of nature which has been prevalent among men of science and philosophers from the time of Galileo and Descartes to the present. The essence of the mechanical view is the assumption that such non-qualitative factors as local motion, position, mass and energy are alone operative in determining the course of events in the physical world. It followed either that qualities have no physical existence or that they are somehow derived from or produced by such non-qualitative factors. The second alternative seemed to them, as it does to me, impossible. No *mere* combination, redistribution or transformation of non-qualitative factors can result in the existence of qualities. This was for them as it is for me an analytical proposition. Hence they were compelled to fall back on the first alternative. They accordingly deny that "secondary" qualities really belong to physical objects. They are perceived as qualifying the physical objects, but the perception is illusory. I have the idea of the paper before me as white; but it is really neither white nor any other colour. It has no quality at all in the proper sense of the word. All that really exists in the object is the power to produce such illusory ideas in us. Now this view is decidedly rejected both by Alexander and myself. But we differ in our reasons. Alexander relies simply on the testimony of the senses. But as Descartes pointed out the senses are very fallible, and apart from other reasons we cannot safely assume that they do not deceive us even as regards the objective existence of qualities in general. On the other hand, Alexander entirely ignores and tacitly rejects the Berkeleyan argument which seems to me perfectly cogent. The Berkeleyan argument is that a world having only "primary qualities" (*i.e.*, quantitative and relational characters) is an impossible abstraction. Alexander on the contrary assumes that originally there was a universe empty of qualities. Hence he is bound to deal with the question: How do qualities arise in a non-qualitative world? He attempts to answer it by his conception of emergence. But the question does not arise from experience, but from his own presuppositions. And these presuppositions are not only intrinsically absurd; they are without a shred of empirical evidence. On the contrary, the concrete data of sense-perception show qualities everywhere and never mere extension, configuration and motion, and certainly never pure space-time. I accept "with natural piety" what is both suggested by the empirical evidence and required by the nature of the case. I assume that the qualitative aspect of the universe is as primary and universal as space-time, or as motion and configuration. New qualities occur as results of qualitative process, never of purely non-qualitative process. They no more do so than new motions and configurations result from purely qualitative process. Further, new qualities, like new motions and configurations, arise through *changes,* in which the old cease to exist in the transition to the new. Just so far as there is novelty, what previously existed vanishes. Previous positions of a moving body cease to be its positions as it passes to new ones. When red and yellow unite to form orange, the red and yellow as such cease to exist. The contrary holds good of what is called emergence. The emergent quality simply supervenes on and adds itself to the process from which it is said to emerge. The process might just as well exist and continue its course without the quality. If we suppose that the original space-time process was all that originally existed there is no reason why anything else should ever exist. If anything else does occur, it is a most misleading use of language to say that it emerges. All that we can say is that once it was not and now it is. But there is no process of change or transition through which it comes to be. In other words there is no process of emergence. But what is emergence if it is not a process? It can only be absolute creation—a concept which we should leave to the theologians.

Considered as a kind of causation, it is quite incapable of fulfilling the essential epistemological function of causation as what Hume calls "a principle of inference in matter of fact". If something occurs under certain circumstances, without any reason known or unknown why it should occur, there is no reason why it should occur again under similar circumstances in unobserved instances. As Hume pointed out, repetition of the conjunction, however frequent or uniform, makes no difference. In saying this I do not deny or belittle the logical value of repetition. My point is that inference to unobserved instances presupposes as a condition of its validity an

inference which covers also the observed instances. Frequency and uniformity of repetition has logical value only inasmuch as it makes it probable or practically certain that A and B are causally connected and not merely conjoined—in other words, that there is a general *reason* why B should follow or accompany A, a reason common to observed and unobserved instances. But in what is called "emergence" there cannot be any such reason.

The view that qualities and qualitative process are as primary in the constitution of the physical universe as space and time and spatio-temporal process, is natural to commonsense, and if we except the atomists it was the prevailing view in Greek philosophy and science. What has stood in the way of its acceptance in modern times is a certain scientific prejudice. Galileo and his successors found that what alone lends itself to exact, systematic and comprehensive treatment by physical science is spatial and temporal process, with the quantitative and other relations which it involves. Tacitly assuming that nothing but what thus lends itself to the purposes of physical science can be physically real, they banished all qualities properly so called from the physical world. Alexander, less consistently, admits that they now exist in it, but denies that they belong to its original constitution. Hence his doctrine of "emergence". But the assumption on which both he and they proceed is baseless. There is no reason why the limitations of scientific method should coincide with the limits of real existence.

[1] *S. T. and D.,* vol. i, pp. 11-12. Italics mine.

[2] I may point out that even the cognate accusative does not stand for just the same thing as its cognate verb. The verb, *e.g., strikes,* refers to a process with successive stages; the noun, *e.g.,* the *stroke,* refers to the completion of the process, when the stroke has been struck.

[3] I do not think that they are ever *wholly* sensory. But I have not time to discuss the question.

[4] *S. T. and D.,* vol. ii, p. 32.

[5] *Ibid.,* p. 33. Of course, this direct experience cannot be what I call "actual" experience but must be primary and non-inferential knowledge *through* experience. I had to argue this point in dealing with sense-perception. But here no argument is required.

[6] *Ibid.,* p. 34.

[7] Expounded in *Mind and Matter.*

[8] I hold Alexander to be wrong in regarding social response as the sole primary source of the thought of mind other than our own. But in all other ways what he says about it seems to me to be sound and admirably worked out.

[9] The correlation involved in measurement is of essential importance. Two extents are regarded as spatially equal

which would coincide if they were superposed. Two changes are regarded as taking the same time which, if they began simultaneously, would end simultaneously. Relative changes of position, distance, simultaneity and succession, comparative speed and slowness, are perceived in perceiving things and events. We cannot perceive pure space or time or space-time.

[10] This usage seems to take away the distinctive meaning of the word. For mass and energy are quantitative and relational, not qualitative characters.

[11] Which is not motion in any ordinary sense, but something which is *purely* spatio-temporal.

[12] *S. T. and D.,* vol. ii, p. 45.

[13] I have contended that such a process is an impossible abstraction. But I am here waiving this objection.

J. V. Bateman (essay date 1940)

SOURCE: "Professor Alexander's Proofs of the Spatio-Temporal Nature of Mind," in *The Philosophical Review,* Vol. XLIX, No. 3, May, 1940, pp. 309-24.

[*In the following essay, Bateman examines Alexander's proofs of the spatial and temporal nature of mind: his argument from introspection and his argument from the spatio-temporal properties of the neural processes.*]

According to Alexander, Space-Time is the simplest form of reality, out of which all finite existents—including minds—are made. Growth and creative process flow from the intrinsic nature of this primordial stuff; and the ensuing spatio-temporal configurations, with their differences of complexity and pattern, give rise to new levels of existents having new qualities, such as materiality, life and consciousness. While an emergent quality is grounded in the 'lower' level of existence from which it emerges, it is a new order of existent, unpredictable from the nature of its components and possessing its own special laws of behavior. For example:

> Mind is a new quality distinct from life, with its own peculiar methods of behaviour, for the reason already made clear, that the complex collocation which has mind, though itself vital, is determined by the order of its vital complexity, and is therefore not *merely* vital but *also* mental.[1]

It is important to note that while the empirical qualities of lower levels are carried up into the 'body' of a higher level, they are not carried up into the new quality.

> *Contrariwise the categorial characters are carried up into the emergent existent.* For everything is a complex of space-time and possesses the fundamental properties of any space-time, which are the categories. Hence, though life is not colored it is extended and in time, and this we have seen to be true of mind as well.[2]

If, then, mind is to accord with the fundamentals of his metaphysical system, Alexander must show that it is both spatial and temporal; more specifically, since consciousness is the distinctive feature of mind,[3] he recognizes the necessity of showing that space and time are "carried up" into the emergent quality mind or consciousness, and consequently, that mental acts are spatial and temporal. Now mental acts cannot be contemplated, they are enjoyed; consequently, the data relevant for demonstrating that mind or consciousness is spatial and temporal can only be disclosed in enjoyment. Although this condition of proof is required by the novel, unique, and autonomous nature ascribed to emergent qualities, and is prescribed definitely in many passages,[4] it tends to drift into an argument based on the spatio-temporal properties of the neural processes, which, being dependent on contemplation, would appear to be an *ignoratio elenchi.*

In outlining and examining these two arguments for the spatial and temporal nature of mind, attention will be primarily centered on the more difficult demonstration that mind is spatial. Furthermore, I shall not discuss the contentions that mental space and time is a piece of the space and time in which physical events occur, and that the time of mental events is spatial and their space temporal precisely as with physical space and time. These issues are obviously subsidiary to the problem of the general nature of mental space and time.

I

Proof of the Spatio-temporal Nature of Mind from Introspection. If enjoyment is thus the *nervus probandi* of the introspective proof of the spatio-temporal character of mind, it seems advisable—even at the risk of laboring with what is now a commonplace in philosophical terminology—to recall its scope and nature.

The relation of mind and its objects is one of "compresence". Compresence is not peculiar to the conscious level, but on the contrary, "It is the simplest and most universal of all relations",[5] and pertains between all finites irrespective of their level of existence. If one of the partners in the compresent relation be a mind, the act of mind "contemplates" its object and "enjoys" itself. The act of mind qua experien*cing* is enjoyed, the object upon which the act is directed is experien*ced* and contemplated. Consequently, enjoyment and contemplation are strictly correlative. Alexander thus extends the customary connotation of enjoyment, which restricts it to pleasurable experiencing. "It includes suffering or any state or process insofar as the mind lives through it."[6]

It is of the first importance for the subsequent discussion to note that Alexander will not allow that mind or its acts can be contemplated.[7] The possibility of introspection might seem to falsify this statement, but that is because introspection is being confused with extrospection. Introspection proper is the enjoyment of the acts of perceiving, remembering, thinking, etc. Extrospection is the contemplation of sensa or images in perceiving, imagining, and remembering.

> But the landscape I imagine or Lorenzo's villa on the way down from Fiesole that I remember with the enchanting view of Florence from the loggia, are no more discovered to me by introspection than the rowan tree which I perceive in front of my window as I write. These objects are presented to me by imagination or memory or perception, not by introspection, and are the objects not of introspection, but of extrospection, if such a word may be used, all alike.[8]

Again,

> The mind can never be an object to itself in the same sense as physical things are objects to it. It experiences itself differently from them. It *is* itself and *refers* to them. . . . I do not in introspection turn my mind upon itself and convert a part of myself into an object, I do but report more distinctly my condition of enjoyment.[9]

These typical passages elucidating and prescribing the nature of enjoyment, appear to render it a very elusive source of evidence. No reflective act may detect its message, for it immediately attaches itself to the act of reflection. It is so parasitical to contemplation and *in se* so precluded from objective reference of any sort, that it will not be surprising to discover that enjoyment cannot disclose either its own form, relationships or spatio-temporal attributes, and that Alexander's proof of the spatio-temporal character of mind from enjoyment appears to march only through the kindly offices of contemplation.

The proof that mind or consciousness is spatial begins by an appeal to introspection.

> My mind is for me, that is for itself, spread out or voluminous in its enjoyment. Within this vague extension or volume the separate and salient mental acts or processes stand out as having position, and 'direction'. My mind is streaked with these more pungent processes, as when a shoot of painful consciousness is felt or a sudden thought produces a new distribution in this extended mass. These streaks and shoots of consciousness have the vaguest position, but they have it; and such position and direction are most clearly marked in the higher acts of mind, imagination or desire or thinking, and especially when there is a change in what we call the direction of our thinking.[10]

It is to be particularly noted that the extensity and protensity of sensa, images, or any alleged mental content are not relevant for proving the spatio-temporal nature of mind. "By mental space and time, I do not mean the space and time which belong to our images and thoughts: these, according to our assumption, are nothing but physical space and time as they are represented in images and thoughts."[11] It is the '-ing' aspect of the mental act, the movement of consciousness enjoyed as 'direction' which is the clue to a correct understanding and appraisal of mental or enjoyed space and time. Direction of mental process is exemplified by Humpty Dumpty's poem in *Through the Looking Glass:* "I'd go and wake them if . . ." "We cannot do it, Sir, because . . ." where the forward and defeated movement of the mind is made the centre of attention.

Another illustration of mental direction is afforded by the memory and expectation of ourselves. I may remember how I felt when I heard my friend was dead, and this enjoyment has a different direction from the enjoyed expectation of myself going to Europe next year. It is important to note that these differences of direction are directly apprehended.

> It might be thought that when I remember myself, my enjoyment is a present one and is somehow referred to the past. But this again is a misreading. My enjoyment of myself in the past is enjoyed as past; and my expectation of myself in the future is enjoyed as future. They have the character of past and future written in their faces.[12]

> Whether in the study of past and future objects or in that of past and future states of ourselves, we have thus seen that our consciousness of past and future is direct, and is not the alleged artificial process of first having an experience of the present and then referring it by some method to the past or future.[13]

Direct apprehension of past and future is thus asserted to be an essential condition of enjoying direction and mental time.

The notion of enjoyed or mental space is more liable to misunderstanding. No student of *Space Time and Deity* will of course suppose that mental space is subjective. A more excusable misunderstanding is to confuse mental space with the spatial imagery of our memories and expectations. But the spatial imagery of my memory of a great pageant or even the spatiality of a purely imaginative construction is not mental or enjoyed space, but contemplated space. Mental space is the space in which the mind experiences itself as living—its direction *qua* functioning.

Particular emphasis on enjoyed space occurs in its alleged exemplification in the appreciation of passages quoted from Tennyson, Keats and Wordsworth—although the primary purpose of the quotations is to show that mental space and physical space belong to the same space.

"Let anyone who at all possesses sensory imagination think of the lines:—

> The same that ofttimes hath
> Charmed magic casements, opening on the foam
> Of perilous seas, in fairy lands forlorn,

and ask himself whether he is not conscious of the object described as somewhere in Space along with himself, that is, does not enjoy himself in an enjoyed space, along with an object somewhere in contemplated Space."[14]

I understand the intent of such passages to be that our thoughts proceed outwards from a focal point, which initially is simply *felt* as an absolute 'here' or centre. Without deliberation or even attention upon ourselves, objects and their spatial relationships are regarded as 'outwards' from an immediately felt 'me locus of reference'. Other illustrations of enjoyed space enlarge its span—a shoot of painful consciousness, and the vague premonitory shoots of consciousness which anticipate at times the winding up of a watch at night as contrasted with some other habit like turning off the electric light before going to bed.[15] Although no precision or accuracy of spatial descrimination is claimed for such habits and attitudes, a direction is enjoyed in the momentum felt as accompanying their functioning and in the tension of their frustration.

Just as with mental time, so mental or enjoyed space is direct. Spatial discrimination by immediate relationships could not occur without contemplative operations; and we are warned that if we try to find a direction of mental process which can be contemplated, we will find none, and the problem is queered from the outset.[16]

It may be mentioned that Alexander suggests that his doctrine of mental or enjoyed space offers a solution of how we localise pains and aches in our bodies and correlate mental and neural processes.[17]

II

If this outline correctly presents Alexander's introspective argument for his doctrine of mental space and time, its verity requires discussion of two points of fundamental importance:—(1) Does enjoyment disclose 'direction' of mental process and establish the fact of mental space-time?

(2) How far does enjoyed space and time assume importance in establishing the ontological status of mind?

(1) Does enjoyment disclose 'direction' of mental process?—I think the issue here is fundamentally the same as that raised by Broad in his review of *Space Time and Deity:*

> "Is enjoyment by a mind a mode of knowledge or only a mode of being?"[18] Alexander replied, "it is undoubtedly a mode of being, but not *only* a mode of being, for it is a kind of being which is knowing, and is at once a knowing of objects (in virtue of which relation it is called contemplation) and of itself. . . . Directly you speak of knowing by enjoyment, you have to add the proviso that this is not knowing of the enjoyment. Otherwise you would have the mind looking on at itself, which if the notion of enjoyment is valid, it cannot do, or at any rate does not do".[19] Again, "There are no two separate mental acts, one of enjoyment and one of contemplation. The mind, in enjoying itself,

has before it, and therefore contemplates, the object. Contemplation is a name for the same act as enjoyment, only in reference to the object. The enjoyment is at once a state of being of the mind itself, and that to which the object is revealed, and so is an act of knowing, Reciprocally, in knowing the object I know myself, not in the sense that I contemplate myself, for I do not do so, but in the sense that I live through this experience of myself."[20]

These quotations confirm the contention that no mediate operations of relating one state of mind and another can enter into enjoyment. Enjoyment must be taken at a gulp; and at first sight, its claim to be a mode of knowledge might seem to be simply another futile exhibit of an *apprehensio simplex.* I believe, however, that Alexander would argue that while he is committed to view enjoyment as a form of direct apprehension, it is not purely immediate; and that his doctrine of mental perspectives allows him to combine mediacy with directness of enjoyment. Broad's excellent summary of this doctrine is sufficient for our purposes.

> 'My mind at 10 o'clock today' does not consist simply of enjoyments whose date is 10 o'clock today. It consists of a certain selected group of enjoyments of various dates . . . past enjoyments which are remembered by me at 10 o'clock today and those future enjoyments that are anticipated by me at 10 o'clock today are to be included in the selection which constitutes 'my mind at 10 o'clock today'. . . .

If you now ask Alexander how he reconciles the presentness of my memory of yesterday's thought with the pastness of the thought and with the denial that the one contemplates the other, his answer will be, I take it: "The remembered thought is past for its date is yesterday; but there is a present memory of it, because this past enjoyment is included in that set of enjoyments of various dates which constitutes 'your mind at 10 o'clock today'."[21]

This ingenious suggestion is undoubtedly attractive. In the first place, it may appear to escape the difficulties attending the usual versions of immediate apprehension; for it would allow that a memory *qua* enjoyed—while not mediated by being the object of any contemplated activity—has a telescoped mediacy through its spatio-temporal connections with other mental acts. As Alexander puts it, "On the side of the enjoyment, too, we never have the single act appropriate to the object, but an act linked up with other acts."[22] In the second place, by providing a direct apprehension of the past, it avoids the well-known difficulties attending accounts of memory which make it derivative.[23] And, lastly, in the implied spatio-temporal continuity between mental acts, it can claim to make the basis of a unitary consciousness and continuous self concrete and intelligible.

The theory is not, however, free from difficulties. I shall not discuss the perplexities connected with the notion of a "mass of enjoyments at a moment"[24] or even a 'remembered enjoyment', except to mention that if 'enjoyment' in these contexts connotes the '-ing' aspect of a mental act, it appears to imply the attending to an act which itself involves attention—a feat which I regard as impossible. The crucial issue is, if memory and expectation are directly enjoyed as alleged, would they evidence *direction?* The unequivocal repudiation of any reference to a present in memory and expectation[25] eliminates a co-ordinate from which direction can be apprehended. Direction is essentially relational and can only be apprehended in a situation which transcends the self-sufficient pulse of enjoyment. This contention would also seem to apply to the apprehension of present, past, and future.

> Wholly from within any enjoyed present, that present has no external temporal boundaries. It has no laws in time. It is dateless and tenseless. . . . To view the present as occupying a temporal position is already to have transcended the present. The view requires a perspective wider than any which is accessible within the boundaries of presented and present.[26]

What is said here of the present applies equally to the past and future. The very characteristics of continuity, successiveness, and irreversibility attributed to Time by Alexander, involve the awareness of a time order which transcends the inarticulate directness of enjoyment. In short, temporal direction is contemplated not enjoyed.

The notion of enjoyed direction in mental space appears to me equally fictitious. Alexander anticipates a natural rejoinder to his notion of mental or enjoyed space.

> All this will seem to some to be founded on an elementary blunder of confusion between the locality of consciousness and the sensation derived from the scalp or the movements of the eyes. All our mental life is accompanied by these experiences, and when we talk of enjoyed space we are thinking of and misinterpreting what we learn about our head.[27]

Nevertheless, the view repudiated is not without distinguished adherents. Professor Stout writes:

> The self is an embodied self. Both embodied self, as engaged in the process of seeing and thing seen as 'external object' enter our total experience in essential correlation and contrast with each other. The thing seen is an external object for me, just because it is apprehended as spatially external to my body, and because my body and especially my eyes as implicated in the process of perceiving enter essentially into the constitution of my percipient self.[28]

Alexander allows that my body is a co-ordinate of reference when I ask 'where I am in the whole of space'. "I feel myself somewhere in my body or more particularly in my head. I am now contemplating the whole of space and localizing my enjoyed space in the same place as a contemplated object my body. . . ."[29] Nevertheless, he would maintain that the identification of mental and neu-ral space consequent upon knowledge about my central nervous system, itself depends upon the primacy and integrity of an enjoyed space. Now, undoubtedly, external reference in ordinary everyday experience appears to dispense with deliberate contemplation of its focal origin; but this is surely because a biologically useful and firmly engrained habit has rendered the bodily reference implicit. A speck of dust in the eye or a sore palate renders explicit the focal role of the seeing eye and tasting palate. But the really fundamental objection to Alexander's notion of enjoyed space and direction is that urged in the case of enjoyed time. The very nature of space—with its characteristics of coexistence and continuity—and direction—which is essentially a relation between spaces—cannot be apprehended without contemplative operations. As Professor Kemp Smith argues, categories—in the Kantian sense—are involved in the apprehension of Time and Space.

> The objects of intuition, time and space, are indeed apprehended as continuous; but, as we find upon analysis, such continuity already involves the employment of the category as a condition of its apprehension. For only as we employ the concept of whole and part can we apprehend specific times and specific spaces as being continuous, *i.e.,* as always being wholes, relatively to their constituent parts and yet at the same time as always being themselves parts of a time and space which transcend them.[30] . . .

It may be said that these difficulties are superseded by the doctrine of intuition. Alexander maintains that the spatial and temporal characteristics of objects are not apprehended by the senses but by intuition. The sense organs acquaint us with the secondary qualities of objects: intuition reveals their spatio-temporal properties. Since, however, our experience of external things is 'provoked' in us through sensation, we cannot *intuit* their spatio-temporal characteristics without sensing some of their secondary qualities.

> When I see a blue patch I see its blue quality, but I have intuition of its extent. I do not see a blue which possesses an extent, but I intuit an extent of space which I see blue. I do not apprehend an extended colour but a coloured extent.[31] Hence, Every sensory act contains in itself and consequently conceals or masks a simpler act of intuition.[32]

We are warned that this statement must not be interpreted so as to give rise to phantom difficulties with respect to the coordination of the acts of intuiting and sensing.

> There are not two acts of mind, but only one act of mind which in its sensory character apprehends the colour and in its intuitive character apprehends the place of it. We are conscious of a place coloured or of colour in a place.[33]

Nonetheless, in evolutionary development, Alexander would seem to hold that intuition is temporally prior to other modes of apprehension. "Intuition pure and simple is more elementary than sensation".[34] "Intuition is different from reason, but reason and sense alike are outgrowths from it, empirical determination of it."[35] *Conscious* intuition, however, is inextricably dependent upon sensation. "Intuition" is not to be had as consciousness in the absence of sensation (or else of course ideation).[36]

This brief outline of the doctrine of intuition is sufficient to show its important bearing on the topic of mental space-time. In the first place, if spatio-temporal relations are neither properties of sensa nor apprehended by sensation, it would give the quietus to the objection that mental space is really being confused with the contemplated space of sensations derived from the scalp or sensory organs. Secondly, it allows that directness of spatial apprehension which necessarily attaches to enjoyed space. But while the doctrine of intuition—with certain modifications—appears to me suggestive for contemplative operations, I find its application to enjoyed space and time another matter. In this regard, it must be remembered that since enjoyment is conscious, intuition will be "inextricably dependent upon sensations". The question arises, what is the contemplative act to which intuitive enjoyment of mental space is correlative? The answer appears to be, the intuiting of the space of the object. "The mind enjoys its own space through intuition of its object's space."[37]

> . . . A space which enjoys itself *consciously* or *mentally* as space (*e.g.,* a neural tract AB) contemplates the space of the object (*e.g.,* a line of colour ab), or rather has for its object an external, non-mental, contemplated space, contemplated that is in its form and position in total space.[38]

I cannot see that these passages are a correct description of the enjoyed correlative. It is not at all evident that contemplation by a conscious neural tract of *the space of a line of color* justifies us in saying that the neural tract thereby enjoys *itself* spatially, or still less that it thereby enjoys *its own space*. The enjoyed correlative in such an experience would be the *enjoyment of contemplating the space of the line of color.*[39] The mind's enjoyment of its own space—if it occurred—would seem to require a different correlative contemplative act. Of course, the facile transition between the contemplated space of the object apprehended and the mental space of the act is supposed to be "a direct consequent of the continuity of space-time, in virtue of which any point-instant is connected sooner or later directly or indirectly with every other".[40] But even if this be so, it is irrelevant for the discussion of *conscious* enjoyment. The enjoyment of continuity by point-instants is but a mythical analogy, and so far as conscious apprehension is concerned the intuition of the conscious neural tract is directed upon the spatio-temporal properties of the object presented in sensation. Apprehension of its own space and direction requires additional acts, and as I have argued contemplative acts.

The doctrine of intuition raises precisely the same issues already discussed in connection with 'direction', and I agree with Kemp Smith's contention that even intuition "involves the apprehension of meanings, and as factors indispensable to the possibility of such meanings, categorial relations".[41]

My conclusion then is that enjoyment does not disclose 'direction' of mental process nor is it capable of apprehending space in any shape or form. In both cases judgmental activity and contemplative operations of comparison are involved which transcend the directness essentially attaching to enjoyment.

(2) Alexander assigns to his conclusions about mental space and time the weighty ontological significance of establishing the spatio-temporal nature of mind. The basis of this conclusion appears to be two-fold (i) that the mind is as it enjoys, and, hence, the enjoyment of space and time constitutes the mind spatio-temporal, (ii) that the enjoyment is as the object contemplated.

> The mind enjoys *itself* as substance through intuition of an external substance.[42]

> When the mind is aware of number, it also enjoys *itself* as number.[43]

> The mind enjoys itself categorially in contemplating the corresponding categorial feature of the object which it contemplates.[44]

It might be supposed that the principle becomes a *reductio ad absurdum* in view of Alexander's account of illusion. If the mind is as it enjoys, then the mind is itself sweet, blue, infinite, and illusory in its enjoyment of sweet, blue, infinity, and illusion. But if enjoying illusion constitutes our mind illusory, illusion would be impossible, for "illusory appearances have their source in the mind itself".[45] As an *ad hominem* argument the contention misses fire, for illusory appearances are not regarded by Alexander as nonentities, but as real things seen awry or squintingly.

While we may agree with Alexander that the mind *is* its acts, not an entity apart from its act, and that "each of our acts in the appearance of the whole self as contained within its proper spatio-temporal enjoyed contour"; nonetheless, Berkeley's admonition that "those qualities (*viz,* extension and figure) are in the mind not by way of *mode* or attribute but only by way of *idea*",[46] seems applicable to the contention that the mind in enjoyment is as the object contemplated. I can only reiterate my belief that enjoyment is in such cases misdescribed, and that in contemplating the qualities and properties of an object, we do not enjoy ourselves under the same denominations, and do not acquire the qualities and properties of the objects apprehended.

Thus the introspective proof of the spatio-temporal nature of mind seems inconclusive for two reasons. Firstly, because enjoyment—despite the theory of perspectives—is intrinsically incapable of apprehending 'direction' which discloses the spatio-temporal nature of mind. Secondly, because, though it might be plausibly maintained that the mind is as it enjoys, it cannot be allowed that the mind in enjoying itself is as the objects contemplated.

III

Proof of the spatial nature of mind from the spatio-temporal properties of the neural processes. This argument appears inconclusive for several reasons. In the first place, the spatio-temporal properties of the neural processes are physical and contemplated. They are, therefore, irrelevant as evidence for proving the existence of mental space and time, which is enjoyed. In the second place, the identification of the neural and mental processes, on which the proof depends, is a virtual repudiation of the theory of emergence so vital to Alexander's cosmology, and commits him to the behaviorism which he explicitly repudiates.

I propose to keep in line with the previous discussion by concentrating on 'direction'. "The direction of a mental process is that of its specific anatomical or physiological path."[47] "Direction of the mental process means the actual movement within the neural space which is enjoyed in the identical mental space."[48]

Now, if by mental space is meant "the space in which the mind experiences itself as living or which it enjoys", how can the space and direction of neural processes which *qua* neural processes are neither enjoyed nor contemplated by their owner, be relevant to the discussion? The neural processes are not themselves apprehended nor are they apprehended as constituent facts in the contemplation of objects. As Alexander himself points out: "It is a commonplace that in seeing a tree I know nothing of the occipital movement, and when I think of the occipital movement I am not seeing the tree."[49]

It might, however, be contended that this interpretation is mistaken, since it concentrates attention exclusively on the neural processes; and that a more accurate analysis would show the direction and position of the neural process to be a relational affair determined by its com-presence with the appropriate object—"the form or pattern of the process is determined by its relation to its object".[50] Such would seem to be the presupposition of such statements as

> Thus not only does mind enjoy its own space through intuition of its object's space, but the enjoyed and the contemplated spaces both belong to the same space.[51]

> . . . A space which enjoys itself *consciously or mentally* as space (*e.g.,* a neural tract AB) contemplates the space of the object (*e.g.,* a line of colour ab) or rather has for its object an external non-mental, contemplated space, contemplated that is, in its form and position in total Space.[52]

Now as it has already been pointed out, it is not at all evident that contemplation by a neural tract of the space of a line of color justifies us in saying that the neural tract thereby enjoys itself spatially, or still less that it thereby enjoys its own space. The enjoyment in such an experience would be the *enjoyment of contemplating the space of the line of color.*[53] I fail to see that a transition from contemplation to enjoyment is provided, which would render the proof from the neural processes relevant for demonstrating the spatio-temporal nature of mind.

This proof is vitiated in a similar way by Alexander's repudiation of behaviorism and by the status of mind implied in his theory of emergence. Holt's behavioristic view of consciousness is rejected, because it fails to account for self-consciousness or self-experience as exhibited in enjoyment.[54] Epiphenomenalism is rejected, because there is no evidence that a neural process possessing the mental character would possess its specific neural character if it were not also mental. "A neural process does not cease to be mental and remain in all respects the same neural process as before."[55] The perplexities of Alexander's insistence that an emergent is "at once new and expressible without residue in terms of the processes proper to the level from which they emerge",[56] recurs in his identification of neural and mental processes and his like insistence on the unique, autonomous nature of mind. True, there is a distinction hinted at between merely neural processes and neuro-mental processes; but, even if we restrict our attention to the latter, emergence taken seriously recognizes that a new quality arises "constituting its possessor a new order of existent with its special laws of behavior".[57] One cannot affirm strict continuity between the various levels of existents and also maintain their emergent quality. To say "Each new type of existence when it emerges is expressible completely or without residue in terms of the lower stage and therefore *indirectly in terms of all lower* stages",[58] is surely a departure from the theory of emergence, and I might add, a fallacy of genetic explanation.

If emergent qualities are genuinely new they cannot be regarded as simply spatio-temporal complexes in disguise.

The proof of the spatio-temporal nature of mind from the spatio-temporal properties of the neural processes fails both in cogency of demonstration and is incompatible with Alexander's view of mind implied in his rejection of behaviorism and his doctrine of emergence.

[1] II 45, 46. All references, unless otherwise stated, are to *Space-Time and Deity.* S. Alexander, 2 vols., Macmillan.

[2] II 71 (Italics mine). This distinctive character of Alexander's version of Emergent Evolution is necessary to make it conform to his ontological monism and theory of categories, but I regard the attempted synthesis riddled with questionable logic. His difficulties are rooted in the fact that his ontology and categorial theory requires continuity between the different levels of existence, whereas continuity saps all the vitality from emergence.

[3] I am not concerned with the validity of this assertion. That it represents correctly Alexander's view may be

seen from the definition of mind in II 4: 81, the oft recurring expression "mind or consciousness" and the index heading "Mentality—Consciousness".

[4] I 93; II 89, 90. Preface to *New Impression,* xv.

[5] II 81, 82, 102.

[6] I 12.

[7] I 19. I am not concerned to discuss the validity of this contention, but to indicate that it prescribes a necessary condition for the proof of the spatio-temporal character of mind.

[8] I 18.

[9] II 89.

[10] I 97-8.

[11] P. 9. Abstract of Gifford Lectures, prepared by the author for his audience.

[12] Abstract p. 10: I ch. IV.

[13] I 133.

[14] I 99.

[15] I 212.

[16] Preface to *New Impression* xv.

[17] I 102.

[18] *Mind* XXX, 118, p. 129.

[19] *Mind* XXX, 120, pp. 420-21.

[20] Preface of *New Impression* xiv.

[21] *Mind* XXX, 118, p. 134.

[22] II 100.

[23] *Cf.* the masterly discussion by C. D. Broad in *Mind and its Place in Nature,* Ch. V.

[24] I 134.

[25] I 116, 133.

[26] G. P. Adams in *University of California Publications in Philosophy,* vol. 18, p. 211.

[27] I 101.

[28] G. F. Stout, *Mind and Matter,* 155; *cf.* Bk iv. Chap. 1 2.

[29] I 101.

[30] N. Kemp Smith, *Prolegomena to an Idealist Theory of Knowledge,* 134-35.

[31] II 164.

[32] II 148.

[33] II 148.

[34] II 201.

[35] II 147. In passing I might mention that from Alexander's epitomized version of Dr. Head's neurological studies, I find no support for regarding intuition as phylogenetically prior to sense. *Cf., e.g.,* "Pain, heat, and cold impulses cross in the spinal cord first, touch impulses later" . . . II 179, and the evidence that spatial apprehension is intimately connected with the cortex.

[36] II 147, 201.

[37] II 155.

[38] II 145.

[39] *Cf.* II 153. "In contemplating the action of the wind blowing down a chimney, *we enjoy first the act of contemplating the blowing wind,* and the standing chimney . . ." (Italics mine).

[40] II 144.

[41] N. Kemp Smith, *op. cit.* 132.

[42] II 155 (Italics mine).

[43] I 319. *Cf.* II 151 where the assertion is softened to "our enjoyment has number".

[44] II 144.

[45] II 211.

[46] Berkeley, *Principles* 49.

[47] I 110.

[48] II 128.

[49] I 109.

[50] II 117.

[51] II 155.

[52] II 145.

[53] It was gratifying to find this assertion supported by Mr. Hallet's comments on Alexander's use of enjoyment. "Thus the deliverance of immediate experience is that we enjoy the contemplation of the objects. It is only an out-

side observer (or the mind itself in thought) who says that what we enjoy is the neural process." *Aeternitas* 261. Again, "I understand Mr. Alexandcr to assert: when two things A and B are cognitively compresent, one of them (say A) is of the order of complexity to which the quality of consciousness or mind belongs. A then has (or is) a neural system which is innervated in response to stimulus from B which is mediated by ordinary physical or organic processes. This innervation is enjoyed by A, but not as a neural innervation; *it is enjoyed as the contemplation of B*" (*Ibid.* 262).

[54] II 111.

[55] II 8-46, 62-69.

[56] II 45.

[57] II 46.

[58] II 67 (Italics mine).

John Laird (essay date 1942)

SOURCE: "Samuel Alexander's Theism," in *The Hibbert Journal*, Vol. XL, No. 2, January, 1942, pp. 146-55.

[*In the following essay, Laird examines Alexander's views on the nature and existence of God.*]

Alexander was, quite certainly, a theist in his own Alexandrian way, a way that was never insincere. Indeed his "*nisus* theory of deity," to judge for instance from Mr Brightman's *Philosophy of Religion* (1940), seems by now to have taken its place as one of the accepted types of text-book theism. It has almost achieved respectability, like an eccentric old friend whose ways have become too familiar to startle.

A letter of Alexander's which came to me recently in rather an odd way, since it was sent me by the purchaser of a pamphlet into which it had been gummed, gives a more personal statement than was usual with its author.

> "I never was negative in respect of that subject [this letter runs] and never was even agnostic. I date from the agnostic time, but never subscribed to the prevailing belief (or want of belief). I daresay I may have expressed myself coldly (or, being younger, even scornfully) towards what I now call the elements of 'nonsense' in positive religions (I say nowadays [in private] that in spite of its manifest insufficiency I stick to Judaism because it contains less nonsense than the other religions known to me). But I think I have always been firm on thc central point."

I mean to make this letter (dated 31.8.31) in some sort the text of the present essay, for I want to include in its scope some account of the continuity of Alexander's views, and of the kind of thing that he accounted "nonsense."

Among Alexander's private papers there is one, professionally typed, on which he wrote in pencil "Read at Oxford about 1885?? to a society, James Bryce in the chair. First paper I wrote, I think." Its title was **"Fingerposts to Religion,"** and the substance of it was roughly as follows: The highroad to religion is "what for want of a better name may be called the religious consciousness." It is the sense of absolute dependence, Max Müller's sense of infinity, or the like. But there are also "fingerposts on the paths of science and conduct which point the way to religion," and it was these little things with a big message that Alexander attempted to discuss. What he said was not perhaps very thrilling. "A great intelligible world" was, as one might say, paulo-post-scientific; and he admitted that he did not have enough metaphysics to pass confidently from a single *intelligible* to a single *intelligent* universe. Similarly there were finger-posts from ethical science. From progress in conduct, and from the expanding moral world that progress creates

> "we go on to think of the whole world as completely used up for practical ends, no out of the way corner left which is not intelligible and turned into conduct, and which we think of such an ideal of conduct, to which we strive to approximate and which, because it is the fulfilment of what we ought to be, draws us towards itself by a natural affection."

On the other hand, he admitted (and, I think, without much regret) that the ethical finger-posts to theism were a good deal more ambiguous than the intellectual. God's goodness, if that word could be used at all, would have to be different in kind from human goodness.

About this time Alexander kept a sort of Commonplace Book. One passage in it, the only one which recorded his thoughts on theism, seems to me to be so significant that I ought to quote it almost in full, although it is rather prolix. Here it is:

> "To whom is the responsibility due? (1) Plainly to myself as representing the good character; as such it is conscience. (2) To the ideal as realised objectivity in God. This is the notion represented by the Last Judgement. *Conscience* seems to me (1 Nov. 1885) always to include this reference to myself as a tribunal of morality and so to be different from the moral sense. . . .

> "What is the connection between *conscience* as responsibility to my own self and *Duty to God?*

> "I might say conscience implies the existence in me of the Moral Law which is divine. But this is only a half-solution. For God is not exhausted by what happens at any moment to be the Moral Law. In what sense can God be called moral? Not as you or I because he chooses the better, because he has the affections of sense and uses the material thus afforded his will. (This seems to me the false half-suppressed postulate of a continuous future life beginning where the earthly leaves off.) Nor again as being a law of pure Reason: for this blinks the plain fact that morality as we know it is

conditioned by nature (this against Kant). In what sense, then? We have to remark:

"(1) In every moral act we do right absolutely— 'are pleasing in the sight of God'—are so far recognised by Him as one with Himself.

"(2) The *system* of moral duty is changing; man enters into a new order of moral relations as the 'moral law' alters, *i.e.* God's self-recognition in us grows; only its growth is not the same as the growth of our self-consciousness which is dependent (in a way to be considered) on sensuous affections, but goes on wholly in self-consciousness regarded as occupied wholly with itself. This, I think, is why we never can predict a new morality; when it comes it is a new fact; it is so much more of God revealed to us; and to God it is also so much more of Himself revealed. Only we must not use the word 'more' as if it meant that God went through a process in time; for, as we have seen, God is never imperfect, and even in imperfect morality is still absolutely God. It is only when *God is regarded as the actual recovery of Himself from the Nature in which he was lost* that we can speak of Him as gradually self-revealed. In every such recognition of God the whole of Him is present. The logical understanding may detect in the Idea of Him moral ideas which mean to pass one into the next by a logical necessity; but each superior idea containing the power in the process by which sense is rightly used is absorbed with the act in which self-consciousness recognises its own nature in the individual man. It is thus that God is all-present in each of his acts; in the very simplest the most complex can behold its own reflection. Everything, then, is transparent to God; God then is supremely moral because all moral law is in self-recognition of spirit. That is less for man than for God; for man it seems as far as he can go, but in God this moral law is seen in connection with all other things and their activities. It is the latent process of the human mind and the undiscovered invitations which Nature is yet to offer to him which determines a change of the Moral Law; but in God this moral law is already absorbed in the completed whole of processless activity which, as conditioned by bodily and mental powers, is to reappear as the never-ending struggle after higher and higher law. Therefore it is that God is wholly moral and yet we invest him in successive ages with different moral attributes."

There are certain faint echoes of this passage in Alexander's *Moral Order and Progress,* published in 1889, especially in the section on conscience; but the book, being a manifesto in support of evolutionary ethics, could have nothing to do with "a completed whole of processless activity." Ethics might be "near" metaphysics (p. 78), but all its standards were standards of adjustment and were moving standards. The moral life was a pursuit of the better, and of the bettering of the better, but never of the completed best. (Hence Green's "eternal self consciousness reproducing itself"— plainly the concern of the passage I have quoted—was not an ethical conception. Indeed Alexander ended his book by suggesting that religion was beyond morality, and that an all-too-moral religion was a religion misunderstood.)

He said the same thing to the end of his life about "values," holding that all values were human at their best and never divine. In most other ways, however, his philosophy, including his theism, made an immense stride between 1889 and 1920 when *Space, Time and Deity,* his next substantial book, appeared. What he believed himself to have accomplished is perfectly plain. As he thought, he had reached the point where he could establish a cosmic or metaphysical evolutionism instead of a merely scientific or ethical evolutionism. In other words, "processless activity," perfection in that sense, even if it was divine, could be seen to be a metaphysical impossibility, and the boundaries between science and metaphysics, or between moral science and theology, had to be drawn in a different place and on a different plan. God, if there were a God, would have to be an evolving God. For he would have to be genuine and not a myth, and all that is not evolving must be mythical.

I shall now attempt a brief discussion of the theism in *Space, Time and Deity,* with occasional references to subsequent essays and addresses of Alexander's. There was no substantial change in his later accounts of theism, but sometimes his later statements are neater or sharper or at any rate more conveniently quotable than those in *Space, Time and Deity.* [Hereafter cited as *S.T.D.*]

Abstractly put, the argument is as follows: We have (*a*) a general religious sentiment or emotion, a need of our being which demands its proper food as hunger does. As philosophers, however, our more pressing and our more professional business is (*b*) with the question whether common experience and/or the sciences have room for anything that could satisfy (or partially satisfy) this religious hunger, and, if they have room for such a thing, whether they actually house it. As a matter of method the second question should be tackled first. Answered, it should enable us to say whether the first is "verified" of the second.

In Alexander's exposition, "deity," "the quality of deity" "actual deity" (or "God"), "the *nisus* towards deity" and other such phrases are used in a way that often strains the attention if it is not downright misleading. Sentences like "Even God himself does not as actual God possess deity attained but only the *nisus* towards it" (*S.T.D.,* ii. 418) or "God is, if we may use such language, the power which makes for deity" (ii. 428) are instances. I shall therefore allow myself, quite frequently, to use other words.

The cardinal conception is what Alexander in a late essay called "the historicity of things." In other words, whatever is, is *in process* and is also *in progress.* That for him is essential, indeed quintessential, in all metaphysics. It elaborates the invincibility of the hyphen in "Space-Time" on which hyphen all Alexander's philosophy hung. "The restlessness of Time" is one of Alexander's descriptive phrases, but he was careful, indeed sedulous, to repeat that "restlessness" was not enough for historicity, *i.e.* for cosmic metaphysical evolution. The restlessness assumed a determinate direction. It was and became a progressive *nisus,* and the form that this *nisus* had taken was open to observation in common life and in the sciences. Space-Time had configured itself into materiality, certain material constellations had plunged into life, certain vital constellations had blossomed into neural patterns that "carry" what human beings call their "minds." This cosmic and metaphysical evolution is of the "emergent" type. In other words each stage is novel *in kind,* and is never deducible from the earlier stage, although it grows out of it. We may call this "the emergent ladder of the *nisus*" to indicate that there are distinct and decisive steps in the evolution, each such step being different in kind from its predecessor (being "emergent") and intelligible *après coup* but never in advance.

Obviously the ladder is an ambitious doctrine. If we accept the premiss (which I personally am unable to reject) that *process* belongs to the marrow of all existence, including God's, we might boggle at the further premiss that the *process* must be *progress,* and again at the gloss that such progress is quite clearly and specifically along the emergent ladder of the *nisus.* If Space-Time in its early career was a fluid sub-material magma the emergence of materiality would seem to be a universal cosmic step. But what of "life"? According to many (*e.g.* according to Sir Charles Sherrington in his recent *Man on His Nature*) "life" does not differ in kind from non-living chemical configurations. There is no such distinct rung on the ladder, and "mind" so far from being a new level in a biological constellation is something known, not by sense-observation, but in another way. (Alexander would have accepted a part of this in another side of his theory, but that other side as good as drops out of his theism.) Again a critic might be disposed to say that even if the ladder had been exemplified in the existence of this planet, it was only a planetary and not a cosmic ladder, and, for that matter, probably episodic even in a planetary way. The emergent ladder of the *nisus* might be quite a little ladder, and something of a cosmic curiosity instead of being that with which the entire universe was and had always been in travail.

Alexander would say (as I understand him) that the ladder is a faithful description of historicity as such, no more and no less. I find it difficult to believe that any metaphysical doctrine of invincible *progress* is not much more hazardous than a doctrine of invincible metaphysical *process,* not to speak of a progress as specific as Alexander's emergent ladder. Still, the conception, whether hazardous or not, is certainly possible, and, if it held, it would hold of everything that there was including whatever gods there were or were to be.

A second part of the theory should have an easier journey, for plainly we have to distinguish between the progressive *nisus* and the progress actually accomplished at any given time. The point in human experience is quite familiar. It is Hobbes's point in his criticism of the *summum bonum* of the ancients. According to Hobbes "there is no satisfaction but in proceeding" and "to have no desires is to be dead." In other words, a complete

good would be a good that had stopped. And that, in a living being, could not occur. If one appetition is stilled, another takes its place. Similarly, in the metaphysical way, we should have to say that the progressiveness of things, if invincible, could never be completed. If it were completed, time would be dead and existence would collapse into complete non-entity.

Here, however, I am moving a little too fast, for I have not explained the specific place of deity in this historicity. According to Alexander (*S.T.D.,* ii. 417) the sense of deity was "the sense of a new quality *above man* to which the whole world tends," that is, it was the *next* emergent rung in the ladder immediately above "mind." A certain progress in morals, æsthetics or science, say, would have nothing divine in it, and neither would an advance from man to superman if the superman did not differ *in kind* from man. Deity was the name for the rung in the ladder immediately above mind, and could not be less distinct from mind than mind was distinct from vegetative insentient existence.

Such a conception, in very many ways, may seem to be a most generous type of theism. It might extort a certain reluctant approval from M. Maritain and even from Herr Barth, for these authors, in very different ways, agree in insisting that the divine is altogether above the human, in kind as well as in degree, and is falsified if it is philosophised into an objective ideal of "perfect" knowledge like unto (although magnifying) all human knowledge (and similarly of the other human "values"). True, according to Alexander, what is asserted is necessarily an unknown God, an unknown "quality of deity." That, however, is scarcely a theological objection, and if it were an objection, an Alexandrian (although not, I think, Alexander himself) might say that the hiddenness of the emergent "God" was a consequence of *another* metaphysical principle which might be less certain than the ladder of emergent historicity. The principle in question is that any being "enjoys" (or experiences) itself, and knows itself in that way, and that any being except the lowest "contemplates" (or observes) what is lower than itself, but that no being can either enjoy or contemplate what is higher than itself, at any rate in the respects in which it is higher. This principle which seems largely to be a generalisation from the circumstance that we observe the bodies but not the minds of our fellows might appear to be rather shaky.

On the other hand, Alexander's doctrine seems to be crammed, if not even to be choked, with several serious difficulties. I shall now examine some of them.

(1) Most theologians would say that God, whatever else he may be, must as any rate be ultimate if he exists at all. According to Alexander the progressive historicity of things *would* be ultimate, the last word in any metaphysics, but God or deity, that is, the achievement of the next stage above "mind" in the ladder of emergence would not be ultimate at all. On the contrary, as soon as this level arose, there would be a straining after the next level, the level above mere deity. For every Jove there would be a

Prometheus. On the whole the conclusion here would seem to be that the *nisus* was more worshipful in the long run than the particular emergent stage that we call deity, but, no doubt, there may be a certain ingratitude in complaining of a "deity" that *ex hypothesi* is incommensurably higher than the best that is human.

(2) We may raise the question (although Alexander in *S.T.D.*, ii. 365, called it "trivial and scholastic") whether there *has* been the actual emergence of deity, *i.e.* whether the rung in the emergent ladder immediately above mind has ever been reached anywhere. Alexander says quite simply, that we don't know. But discussion is possible.

If it be assumed that minds have emerged rather late in the cosmic process, and not merely rather late in the history of this planet; if it be further assumed that the stage next above mind, that is, the stage of "deity," can only be reached through the stage of mind, then Alexander's "Ignoramus" might be an answer as good as it was simple. In other words if there were angels (and Alexander, half playfully, sometimes speaks of "angels" instead of "deity" when he is describing the next stage) and if we encountered them, we should necessarily encounter them unawares. That would be a consequence of Alexander's restriction of human awareness to "enjoyment" and "contemplation (*of the lower*)." By the same principle *we* couldn't be angels unawares. But there is nothing to forbid the belief that there may be plenty of angels *now,* and plenty of Jovian gods above angels, and plenty of Promethean gods above Jovian gods.

Such speculation is indeed "trivial and scholastic," but there is a more serious point. Alexander's metaphysics of the historicity of things is constructed on the principle that we *do* know that Space-Time came first in a non-material condition, that materiality supervened upon it universally, that sporadic, vitality, and, later, a still more circumscribed mentality supervened in the same way, and that the cosmos could have no room for "angels" or for "gods" until it had evolved through all these stages. I would suggest that we don't know anything of the kind, and have quite insufficient reasons for inferring it from the highly conjectural evidence that we may have concerning the origin of human minds on this planet. Let there be a hierarchy of levels of existence with the angelic or divine incommensurably above the human and mental. Let it also be granted that in a small corner of the universe, viz. in this planet, minds turned up rather late. What right have we to infer that superhuman levels may not have been established æons before life appeared on this planet? Since Alexander's conception of the historicity of things implies progress as well as process, we should have to say, I suppose, that deity could not be co-eternal with the world, or at any rate that some high level of existence (perhaps a level much higher than mere deity) could not come *first*. But if process and not progress is all that Alexander has proved (and I do not think he proved more), then divine process, or a process still higher, might very well be co-eternal with the universe. That is what many people believe who believe in God's

"eternity" and also in the "redemption" of the human race. Credible or not the conception implies no inconsistency.

(3) Alexander's repeated statements that *actual* "deity" would have to be finite may be rather too confident. In a way it was a consequence of his system, for he held that "deity" was an "empirical" (*i.e.* a scattered) quality and not a "categorical" (*i.e.* an all-pervasive) quality. Here, however, one may wonder whether, as so often, the system may not have manufactured difficulties which, without it, would not exist.

Certainly the most obvious interpretation of Alexandrian historicity would suggest the finitude of "deity." Only a smallish part of the living human body, namely the roof-brain, is fitted to "carry" mind. We should therefore naturally suppose that only a smallish portion of our minds would become able to "carry" deity. Alexander, however, recoiled from this particular way of looking at the story. The inference, he said, would be no better than if seaweed thinking (*per impossibile*) of the emergence of mind should conclude that it must be seaweed that would become mental. We should therefore, he said, be immensely more cautious in our inferences of this order.

Let us grant that the seaweed would have been naïvely sea-weedly. Nevertheless the inference that only a living body can become mental would be about as plain as any of Alexander's own plain stories. If all such suggestions were dropped, and if we thought of deity as "carried" not by a part of a mind that is "carried" by a brain (let us say, in some rapport between minds) what sort of life-line or what sort of mind-line would be left to cling to? Such a *rapport* might be between our minds (or the minds of the elect among us) and the minds of Martians and Saturnians. It might be a *rapport* between our minds and their stars, or more generally, a cosmic *rapport* that had nothing to do with the finite boundaries of living bodies and of living body-minds. So far as I can see the proof of the finitude of (actual) "deity" rests upon the finitude of the theatre (*i.e.* of the human body) in which the mental rung of the ladder of historicity invariably emerges from the merely vital rung. If bodily contours be held to be irrelevant, anything in the world may be supposed.

(4) Alexander invariably described the progressive *nisus* as a *nisus* of the universe and as in the passage I have already quoted, spoke of deity (*S.T.D.*, ii. 417) as "a new quality above man to which *the whole world* tends." For him the universe, all the spatiality of Space-Time, was "the body" of God. God's body was not finite although its emergent deity was.

Plainly, however, there can be no difference between the sense in which "the whole world" is straining towards deity, and the sense in which there has been straining towards mentality, that is to say, towards the emergence of my mind or of yours. Accordingly we have to say that even if there is a legitimate sense in which "the whole world" is "the body" of the minds that exist, it is not the usual sense. In the usual sense of language *the* body of my mind is a watery colloid substance of small dimensions and of very moderate powers. In terms of Alexandrian canons "the whole world" with its universal *nisus* is only the *Urleib* and not the *Leib* of any mind, its remote and not its proximate body. Similarly "the whole world" could only be the remote and not the proximate body of emergent deity, unless, as we saw under (2), deity, while presupposing minds as the rung in the ladder from which it ascends, is regarded as a pervasive and not as a limited actuality.

With these remarks I shall end my exposition of the science and natural theology of Alexander's theism. What remains for consideration is the question with which the theism of **Space Time and Deity** began, the question, namely, whether the science and the philosophy of deity "verified" and was able to satisfy the natural hunger of the religious sentiment. In general Alexander claimed that it did. Thus he said (**S.T.D.**, ii. 394) that his "speculative conception of God or deity . . . has appeared to be verified by religious experience." [It wouldn't much matter which "verified" which. The essential question is whether they agree.] In at least one passage, however, he said (**S.T.D.**, ii. 381), rather differently, that "speculatively we can arrive at the postulate of a world tending to deity *though we could not discover it to be worshipful.*" (Italics mine.)

One of the clearest accounts Alexander ever gave of this matter was in his admirably simple National Broadcast in the series "Science and Religion" (1930). In brief, what he said on that occasion was that there were two conspiring ways in which "belief in God is removed from being mere guesswork." One of these is our reverence for the mysterious greatness of things, our natural awe in the presence of what Otto called the "numinous." Punning, Alexander avowed himself "an Otto-man." He held, however, that the numinous would be a slender although never a negligible life-line for theism if it were not confirmed by the sciences themselves, and proceeded to argue that the deity to which the sciences pointed was truly something to be worshipped. Such deity was far more worshipful than the "god" of most philosophers. The philosophers worked with conceptions like truth, beauty and goodness, and tried to erect a God or Ideal of Perfection in whom there was no spot or blemish in respect of any of these "values." Of them Alexander said:

> "I can be enthusiastic for beauty or truth but I have no worship for them. They excite in me no religious feeling, though in many persons they may supply the place of religion, where no religion is felt. The mystics are right; we worship or love in God, not his goodness, but his godship or deity."

Yet he could not go all the way with the mystics, or with the creeds. The religion of natural devotion tended to be choked with mythology and to become its prey.

That was a gentler way of saying that he repudiated what in the letter I quoted at the beginning of this essay he privately called the "nonsense" of so many religions. But he was also saying that he repudiated the nonsense of

traditional philosophical theology, the nonsense of looking for deity in the wrong place and of attempting to adore the mere perfection of human attributes like moral goodness or intellectual insight when these, however much they might be "perfected," remained and had to remain wholly and definitely sub-divine.

It may seem difficult to dispute the force and the sanity of these comments, but whatever the mythologists may have to say about them, it seems to me that the decried philosophers should not be too readily acquiescent. Some of them would reply, I suppose, that they *did* worship the "values" (or some of the values) for which Alexander felt enthusiasm only, and never reverence. According to Kant (*Practical Reason,* Analytic, ch. iii.):

> "Fontenelle says 'I bow before a great man, but my mind does not bow.' I would add, before an humble plain man in whom I perceive uprightness of character in a higher degree than I am conscious of in myself, *my mind bows* whether I choose it or not. . . . Nay, I may even be conscious of a like degree of uprightness, and yet the respect remains."

It is not everyone, I concede, who has Kant's reverence for the moral law; and Alexander may have been wiser than Kant in this matter. But is it plain that he must have been wiser about it? If all you can say about the "higher" that is "divine" is that it is higher *in kind,* incommensurably higher than the highest that any man can find or can even conceive in himself, are you really showing force and sanity? Are you so very certain that the numinous which you worship has been enlightened at all by the night-lamps attached to the finger-posts of science and common experience? In short, can you be sure that you are attaching *any* intelligible meaning to the comparative "higher"?

It seems to me that this question is immensely difficult to answer with any approach to satisfactoriness on Alexandrian principles. Alexander's entire metaphysics of inevitable historicity or progressiveness professes to be based upon what I have called the ladder of emergent evolution. The nature of the ladder is that each emergent rung is a step higher than its immediate predecessor. Consequently an essential, perhaps *the* essential question is what precisely is meant by "higher." I have found no satisfactory answer in Alexander's pages. In so far as we are left to collect the answer from our experience, we should have to say that "higher" means whatever is common to the superiority of life over matter and of mind over life. But what is it that is common to these? The answer, so far as I can see, would have to be given in terms very similar to Herbert Spencer's "definite coherent heterogeneity." It would be an affair of efficient complexity, somewhat darkened by the reflection that each rung in the ladder differed *in kind* from its predecessor. Alexander's Spinozistic penchant for the view that virtue is just strength or availing, that goodness is just efficient or harmonious adjustment, that evil is either weakness or excrement is a corroboration so far as it goes.

If so, one can surely ask whether mind is higher than mere vegetative life solely or principally because of its more efficient complexity, and more generally *why* we should worship efficient complexity if it excels mind and mental values *in kind?* As it seems to me one might decline to worship efficient complexity with at least as good reason as Alexander had for declining to worship truth or beauty or righteousness, either in man, or in the "omniscience" and other traditional attributes of divinity, portrayed and elaborated by purblind and vain philosophers.

The most explicit statement of Alexander's that I have seen about the ultimate meaning of "higher in kind," occurs in a letter he wrote to Miss Hilda Oakeley in April 1921. I have her permission to publish it here. It runs:

> "'Higher' and 'lower' do not mean for me what can be judged beforehand to be higher and lower. My position rather is that the scale of levels is not intrinsically one of value, but of empirical differences which I call 'greater or less perfection' but without having an ideal of perfection (which is, I think, what you suppose). Perfection is an awkward name: I might have said 'difference of kind,' but I mean it in the sense in which one says that one man is a bigger man than another but not better. Now what I am trying to say is that value cannot be judged *a priori,* but is discovered experimentally, and that within each level the types which have value are those which can establish themselves. For the same reason deity is not a value, but a quality in the order of 'perfection,' but it is in the line of value because from the nature of the case it is the valuable types which by their persistence engender the next higher quality, I mean the quality which succeeds in the scale of qualities. All through, I am proceeding empirically and urging that you must first find out what value means and not use the conception *a priori.*"

I cannot see how anything could be less defensibly *a priori* than this statement that the "higher" *means* "the quality which succeeds in the scale of qualities."

A word in conclusion. I had meant this essay to be expository and even semi-biographical rather than critical, but sometimes I have lapsed into criticism if not even into polemics. I am sorry about that. The criticism was wrung from me, not willingly sought. Let me say, then, that for me at least there is a refreshment and an excitement in Alexander's pages that I could not easily put into words. He is rich, and deep and splendid and delicate in almost all that he says about theism. If it were not so I would not have written this essay.

The Earl of Listowel (essay date 1942)

SOURCE: "Samuel Alexander's Aesthetics," in *The Menorah Journal,* Vol. XXX, No. 2, July-September, 1942, pp. 145-60.

[*In the following essay, Listowel discusses Alexander's views on beauty in art and nature, noting Alexander's emphasis of the role of the spectator in artistic creation.*]

Those, like the present writer, for whom the late Samuel Alexander unlocked doors to new realms of wisdom and delight, or who basked in the sunshine of encouragement and kindly advice he gave so readily to younger men, will understand with what alacrity this opportunity was seized of paying a small tribute to the memory of so unusual and attractive a personality. To resurrect the mind that has built of its own fabric a mansion so vast that its chambers have room for every fact of experience and every theory of science will always provide a happy and appropriate memorial to one whose main business in life was the disinterested speculation idolized by the Greeks as the worthiest employment to which the human spirit can devote its powers. My own share in this labor of love is small and limited in scope; I want to fill in one corner of the picture of Alexander's philosophical system, by describing in some detail what he thought about Art and Beauty in their most important aspects and relations.

If one were to venture a conclusion from the sheer bulk and volume of Alexander's philosophical writings, one would say with little hesitation that aesthetics was his youngest and, after metaphysics, his favorite child. Putting ontology on one side as naturally the most serious topic for a born system-builder, nourished from intellectual infancy on the Bradleyan tradition, there was no branch of philosophy to which he devoted more time and study, or about which he wrote more voluminously and talked more incessantly, than the theory of the Beautiful. Prior to the production in 1920 of *Space, Time, and Deity* (two volumes), his *magnum opus,* he managed to find leisure in the interstices of teaching for one book on ethics and another on epistemology; but from that date until his death in September 1938, a span of eighteen consecutive years, he was constantly reading papers and publishing pithy manifestos on aesthetics alone of the many subjects that might have absorbed the unfettered attention of his final period.

It has happened on numberless occasions that a poet's creative impulse burned brightest in the years of his youth, growing steadily dimmer and more pedestrian with the passage of time; but crabbed age, with its passionless serenity and detachment from personal preoccupations, is more usually the blooming season for philosophy. It was certainly no disadvantage to Samuel Alexander that he took the plunge into aesthetics from the topmost pinnacle of fame, at a moment when he was already recognized on all sides as the leading spirit of his generation in British philosophy, and long after the laurels of academic prowess and professional success had lost whatever glamor they may once have had. In the cool evening of his life there was nothing left to distract him from the single-minded quest of truth.

But why, of the many unsailed seas he must have been tempted to chart, did his insatiable curiosity launch him on a last voyage into the rough waters of aesthetic theory? There is no certain answer to this question. What we do know is that the third person of the hallowed trinity whose members are Truth, Goodness, and Beauty had hitherto been sadly neglected as compared with the first two, and that a treatise on esthetics was urgently required as the coping stone of a neatly finished philosophical system. Yet it would be a grievous error to suppose that his fondness for the subject was due solely or even mainly to systematic grounds. Art, in its manifold shapes, attracted him irresistibly, and poetry in the wide sense most of all; Professor Muirhead has described his habit of reciting great chunks of Shelley to his friends.

His temperament was not that of the cold-blooded intellectuals whose main interest in a work of art is that of a surgeon in the corpse he has successfully dissected. The wealth of illustration in his writings affords us a glimpse—rare enough in a philosopher—of one who wrote and talked about Art because he really loved the pictures, statues, mansions, poems, novels, and plays that are its concrete manifestations. Communion with the fictitious characters of the dramatist and the inanimate figures of the sculptor or the painter was much easier for him than communication with real people, and one likes to think that much of the happiness denied him by his infirmity in personal relations was given back by a closer intimacy with the more distinguished inhabitants of an imaginary universe.

However that may be, the meticulous care he himself paid to the manner in which his ideas were expressed showed a keen appreciation of and a high esteem for verbal artistry. No writer practised more faithfully than he the precept he laid down about words being used by the literary artist for their own sake, and not as mere handcarts in which meanings are trundled about from one mind to another. Not that he ever allowed the philosopher in him to play second fiddle to the artist; his prose, for all the richness and harmony of its texture, is forged in the first instance to yield perfect clarity of definition, to sustain rigorous argument, and to convey to his readers the logical structure corresponding in the mind of man to the material structure of the world about us. A Pater or a Flaubert would probably have despised him as a mere craftsman.

He had in full measure those blessed gifts of good taste and minor executive ability that aesthetic theory can no more educe from the ungifted than racial theory can bestow blue eyes and flaxen hair upon the most naïve believers in Aryan superiority. Besides, the range of his appreciation was not limited by exclusive attachment to any single branch of fine art, or by an engrossing enthusiasm for any one school or style, classical or romantic, ancient or modern, to the detriment of the many other offshoots of the artistic faculty in the last five thousand years of history. His appetite for Beauty was insatiable, and his sensibility responded like a well-tuned instrument to every note that was struck upon it. One important and unhappy limitation does, however, deserve mention. The deafness that plagued him throughout his life, and grew painfully worse in his later years—one could only speak to him latterly through the black sound-box of an electrical instrument—shut him off from what many of us still

believe with Schopenhauer to be the queen of all the arts. For he listened to music at second hand, with the ears of competent but often one-sided critics, and that explains why his comments on the purest of the arts are scanty and strangely unsatisfactory as compared with what he writes about things seen or read with his own eyes.

Such was the psychological background of the most interesting contribution to a clear intellectual grasp of Art and Beauty made by any English writer on these topics since the time of Bosanquet. And now let me sketch, quite briefly and in broadest outline, Alexander's attitude to the principal problems, philosophical and psychological, of aesthetics.

II

Nowhere in Alexander's writings do we find any definition or even discussion of the nature and scope of the most recent outgrowth from the main stem of philosophy. We can only infer from the field over which he roams in the course of his inquiries that the object he is studying covers the whole range of our experience of the Beautiful in art and nature, and the relation in which it stands to our experience of the other values and to the total, all-inclusive reality of which our reflective consciousness is aware. The method of his research into this miscellaneous bunch of problems is the method he used throughout his philosophical work, the empirical method that leads from observed facts to broad generalizations and back again to the stubborn particulars by which they must be verified. It would be platitudinous nowadays to mention the *a posteriori* method in aesthetics were it not for certain Italian thinkers who still sin against the light. It is perhaps remarkable that Alexander never succumbed to the temptation that besets a system-builder to squeeze facts willy-nilly into the logical strait-jacket of his preconceptions. His happy blending of Herbert Spencer's patient epiricism with the bolder systematic sweep of Bradley and the giant figures of German idealism was nowhere more fruitful than in his treatment of aesthetics.

The more technically philosophical aspect of his intellectual task was to compare and contrast Beauty with the other members of the value trinity, to locate the rightful place of their common parent in the scheme of things, and to decide whether the Beautiful is a simple quality of outside objects or born of their relation to an artist's mind; for axiology, ontology, and epistemology are inalienable perquisites of the professional philosopher.

Let us take as our starting-point his definition of value, and follow out the path described by one of its consequences. "Value," he says in the second volume of *Space, Time, and Deity,* "in its greatest dilution and least intention is the relation between things in virtue of which one satisfies a want of another." Now as "wants" and their "satisfaction" permeate and pervade everything everywhere, and as possible sources of "satisfaction" are as varied and numerous as the "wants" they cater for, a value is not a prerogative of man or a faint gleam of what is changeless and abiding amid the flux of nature. Beauty, whatever the Platonic philosophers and theologians may say, is no better equipped than Goodness or Truth to furnish a short cut to a transcendent reality, for like all our values it is relative to the mentality of human beings and its future is inextricably bound up with their history upon earth. A little more humility, a little stricter impartiality, would convince us that the universe is not moulded to accommodate the needs and desires of our puny selves, but rather that our noblest cravings and boldest aspirations are simply a special instance of ordinary happenings observable at every level of organic and inorganic being.

Thus it is that we have below the philosophical values those "psychological" values which spring from the satisfaction of our biological urges—hunger, thirst, sexual need; the "economic" values arising from the relation between material wants and a limited number of material goods; and the "instinctive" values pervading animal and plant life from the complex organism of the anthropoid apes down to the pullulating unicellular families of ultramicroscopic bacteria. Descending yet lower in the scale of being, we find the drama of worth being vigorously enacted by the atoms and molecules of inorganic matter; for lo and behold, the lordly and bivalent oxygen atom refuses stoutly to be satisfied by anything less than the constant attendance of two hydrogen atoms. And what about the irresistible fascination, termed "natural election" by Professor Laird, of a magnet for the iron filings that fly like a flock of lovers to its embrace? It would seem, indeed, that wherever two things are related in time and space, they have a value for one another.

In the evolutionary cosmogony of Alexander, values in the narrower and human sense are the highest and most recent emergent from a changing but progressive universe. The infinite and everlasting space-time continuum—surely a modern version of Spinoza's substance—which encompasses all that is and carries in its womb all that is to be, has blossomed forth at immense intervals, by a process of spontaneous emergence, into the whirlwind dance of electrons, into the delicate tissues of living organisms, into the sudden light of consciousness, and into the rapturous awareness of values or ideals; and is still in travail with an unborn God who will be as superior to the most god-like man as he now is to the sanguinary carnivores of the jungle. Such, very briefly, is the relative but elevated function of Beauty in the life of man, and its proper status in the boundless empire of nature.

If we probe deeper into the separate values that lend dignity to personality and provide a fixed purpose among a welter of conflicting aims, we shall find that their worth derives from the satisfaction they give to certain deep-seated impulses we all share. Thus Beauty, we are told, "is that which satisfies the constructive impulse used contemplatively," while Goodness gratifies the social or herd impulse of the virtuous man, and Truth slakes the disinterested curiosity of the scientist and philosopher.

As seen from the viewpoint of the relative importance of mind and its environment in the manufacturer of value, fine art, in which the artist mixes in some sort his personality with his materials, stands mid-way between Goodness and Truth. For in science the brute facts of nature control and direct the mind, whereas virtue appertains to motives and draws all its nourishment from volitional sources. But these superficial differences only serve to mask an underlying identity; for Truth is the intellectual awareness of reality, the reflective self-consciousness of the whole unconscious universe, and therefore includes within its boundaries the Good and the Beautiful as well as much that is actively opposed or stonily indifferent to these highest values.

It might not unnaturally be supposed that so intransigent a realist as Alexander would have joined the school of thought that has singled out some common characteristic of external objects, such as the form with which they have been invested by natural forces or in which they have been moulded by man, as the hall-mark of the Beautiful in art and nature. Not so, however, for a mind sufficiently elastic to respond to the rich variety of experience. The "tertiary" qualities of things cannot be regarded like their "primary" and "secondary" qualities as real properties of the objects to which we attribute them, for Beauty does not belong to the full-blown rose in the same sense as its contour, its size, its color, its texture, or its fragrance. These so-called qualities are in fact the product of a unique combination of mind and matter, of subject and object, being a superior mongrel bred of the undeclared marriage between man and nature. "In every value," we are told in the second volume of *Space, Time, and Deity,* "there are two sides, the subject of valuation and the object of value, and the value resides in the relation between the two and does not exist apart from them." This happy compromise between realism and idealism enabled Alexander to avoid the pitfall of an undiluted subjectism as successfully as the snare of a naïve objectivism in aesthetics; for there can be no glimmer of Beauty in the universe without the work of art as well as the artist, without the sunset or the starlit sky as well as their human witness, without an assortment of material objects in an outside world as well as minds that people it with the animated figments of their happiest dreams.

An obvious but paradoxical conclusion is that when we wax enthusiastic about the beauty of natural scenery, we are really praising our own artistic perception of what would be a matter of utter indifference to the philistine onlooker or the domestic cat. The so-called "beauty" of nature is an illusion that not even Ruskin could shatter, for it is we who clothe its naked limbs with fine raiment spun from the thread of our own imaginations. In a pamphlet on *Art and Nature,* Alexander states as follows the problem as he saw it and its solution: "Does nature of herself possess beauty as what the philosophers call a tertiary quality? That is the question of my discourse, and the answer I am about to give is that she does not and that nature and works of nature possess beauty only so far as they are converted into works of art." It follows from this that we are all artists to a greater or a lesser degree when we discover beauty in the countryside, in the sea, or in the sky, and, like a painter or a poet, that we read into the impassive countenance of nature the storm and sunshine of the human soul. The relation of art to nature cannot be that of a copy to its original, and even the landscape painter never "imitates" literally a pleasing scene, for the artist's creative imagination is the common source of Beauty both in the fine arts and among the phenomena of nature.

So much for the narrowly philosophical side of Alexander's aesthetics; let us now pass on to his proposed solution of the remaining problems that confronted him.

III

Writers on aesthetics do not seem as yet to have been able to agree as to where they should look in order to lay a finger on the essence of our experience of the Beautiful. Philosophers have often found in the keenest appreciation of art or nature a direct revelation of some transcendent reality, psychologists have concentrated the bulk of their attention upon the frame of mind of the spectator, while those rare critics and art historians who have speculated about the nature of the fine arts have usually confined their inquiries to an analysis of its products. The most original feature of Alexander's theory of aesthetics is that he goes for its backbone neither to the keen enjoyment of the spectator nor to the material work of fine or applied art, but to the process of artistic production, exemplified in the labors of the creative artist. In this connection, there is a revealing *obiter dictum* on the views of Lipps at the end of a letter dated April 30, 1933; there he writes: "I have a suspicion, which may not be well-grounded, that he [Lipps] takes too much the point of view of appreciation and I like to approach the subject from the point of view of creation."

Now though the production of works of art depends to some extent on the technical procedure and the raw materials employed, it is an event in which the imagination and the emotions of the artist play the leading role. And being a psychological manifestation, it can only be studied scientifically with the assistance of psychological science. Alexander was never afraid to make use of psychology when it could help him to throw light on the problems of aesthetics. And, indeed, when he is not engaged in discussing purely philosophical questions, he is usually applying psychology to a sphere of mind which the professional psychologist has rarely ventured to explore.

Following in the footsteps of Herbert Spencer, Alexander tries to disentangle from among the manifold tendencies and impulsions that direct human actions the conative source peculiar to the activity of the artist. But he does not attempt to resuscitate the long-discredited impulse to play; instead he traces the origins of art to a sublimated and unpractical urge to material construction. According to the psychology of McDougall, it is an irresistible con-

structive instinct that sets the beaver to build, the bird to nest, and the nightingale to sing. In man this primordial instinct ceases to be blind and becomes purposive, though still subordinate to biological need; and we have the products of his handicrafts which are soon followed by the mechanical marvels of his technological inventiveness. Finally, emancipating himself from the dull task of providing for his daily needs, he begins to make things for the sheer joy of making them and without a thought for their usefulness or profitableness; the humble breadwinner at last becomes an artist. To use the writer's own words in his pamphlet on *Art and Instinct:* "The thesis which I submit to you is that the aesthetic impulse and the aesthetic emotion which goes with that impulse and is part and parcel of it are an outgrowth from the instinct of constructiveness, and are that impulse or instinct when it has become first human, and next, contemplative."

In his early comparison between "artistic" and "cosmic" creation, Alexander explains why the former event is not a prototype of the latter, and has no metaphysical significance. The brilliance and clarity of this psychological theory of artistic creation should not blind us to the fact that it is based on a more than doubtful analogy between animal instinct and human design, and that it ignores much of the little psychological material that has been collected by students of what is probably the toughest problem in aesthetics. It is difficult not to be persuaded that Alexander's most original contribution to the subject is also his most fragile, and that no aspect of his aesthetic doctrine is less likely to survive the legitimate criticism of his successors.

In his treatment of the arts he is at pains to dissociate himself from the popular fallacy of Croce, according to whom a work of art is made of mental stuff, being an "intuition" or "expression," and its material embodiment is merely a practical convenience whereby the artist shares his imaginative conception with like-minded people. Alexander maintains, in contradistinction to this view, that the artist's material actively influences his conception of the object he is fashioning or composing, and that the growth of a poem or a portrait goes on *pari passu* with the recitation of the verses and the brush work of the painter. There is a familiar ring about Alexander's emphasis upon the synthesis of form and content in the finished work of art when one calls to mind the unity of "characteristic" and "abstract" expressiveness in which Bosanquet summarizes the thesis of his *History of Aesthetics.*

The skill of the artist lies in his capacity for "imputing" a "meaning" to materials in themselves emotionally neutral by moulding them so that they become suggestive and eloquent to all beholders of the tenderness and defiance and despair, of the striving and the conflict, that stir in the depths of the struggling and sensitive soul. But a human significance can only be acquired by dumb, inexpressive objects when they have been invested with a form they lacked in the raw state, and there is as it were an organic relationship between the form or pattern of a work of art and its significance for the spectator. In the representative arts it is easy enough to distinguish between the subject and its formal treatment, but in abstract arts like architecture or textiles the two are fused and the subject is no more than the form itself. In his last publication on the subject of aesthetics, originally a broadcast lecture, Alexander writes as follows of the unity of form and content: "The artist's imputation of himself to his materials is represented by the form which he gives them." It would be a simple matter to show that this act of "imputation" is extremely similar in character to what earlier writers have called "aesthetic *Einfühlung*" or "Empathy," and that Alexander is here re-stating in his own terminology one of the cardinal tenets of modern aesthetics.

Branching out from the parent stem you get the separate members of the two related families of fine and applied art, and each of these derives an individual flavor from the material—words, tones, pigments, clay, glass, *et cetera*—used by the artist to embody and express his imaginative vision. Raw material in the crude state is thus a convenient principle for dividing art into its component elements. A distinction of some importance that Alexander liked to draw was between "beauty" and "greatness" in the arts. The latter quality is conferred by the subject-matter alone, so that a drama can be both beautiful and great, whereas a Chinese vase or a Persian carpet must content themselves to be just beautiful. Thus it is that supreme poets like Dante, Sophocles, or Shakespeare bring right home to us the mystery of life and death, reveal the tragic conflict between the forces of good and evil in the world, and show us by the enchantment of their impassioned language how courage and generosity can overcome the sluggish egoism that fetters the majority of human beings. Poets of this order are also, as Shelley claimed in his celebrated *Defence of Poetry,* prophets and preachers who turn the eyes of the multitude away from the trivialities of the daily round towards the shining heights of moral and intellectual achievement.

It is not often that aestheticians have laid so much emphasis on the intellectual content of an artistic object; but the stress is natural enough in a philosopher, and especially in one for whom poetry was an adored favorite among the arts. In this respect Alexander shares Volkelt's partiality for a *"menschlichbedeutungsvoller Gehalt"* wherever anything of profound human significance can suitably be enshrined and imparted by a work of art.

It follows from the conception of art as a mixing of the artist with his materials, and from an interpretation of natural beauty according to which the spectator is an artist travelling incognito even to himself, that there is an element of "illusion" in the appreciation of both art and nature. The "illusion" lies in our spontaneous attribution to physical objects of mental qualities they do not really possess. A vibrating string is neither glad nor sorrowful, a solid mass of marble or bronze is neither heroic nor defiant, a large volume of salt water neither laughs nor

rages nor laments. Yet the aesthetic "illusion" is not a mere perceptual error or a mistaken judgment, because we do not attribute the illusory quality to a real object as one of its genuine and lasting properties, but rather indulge in a passing fancy that we know full well to be fictitious for the duration and for the sake of the aesthetic experience. The pleasure inspired in us by things of beauty is the purely subjective side of the reaction, for it cannot be shared with or communicated to others. It is a private reverberation set up in our minds by communion with the beautiful in art or nature, and should not be regarded as an intrinsic element of the essential experience.

The obverse of this private side to our reactions in face of art and nature, a factor that fluctuates according to the sensibility of individual art lovers, is the public side that seems universally communicable and enables us to speak of standards of taste having general validity. The standard judgments of approbation and disapprobation, with all the fine shades that lie between the two, are laid down once and for all by the critical verdicts of the practised art critics, the connoisseurs, and the artists themselves; and in so far as our personal judgment approximates to or agrees with this standard aesthetic judgment we have good taste or the reverse. The objectivity and universal validity of the standard judgment is guaranteed in the last instance by the identity between the perfect critic's mind in the moment of contemplative delight and the imaginative vision of the artist himself. Actual diversity of taste in art can be accounted for as an aberration from the common norm due to the interference of personal idiosyncrasies or to the lack of sensibility among the cohorts of the indifferent. This bears out the common-sense view that what we actually like is not by any means always what we should like, and that taste can be improved by cultivation or allowed to deteriorate through neglect.

A word or two to wind up this exposition of Alexander's views about his attitude to the minor but interesting problem of the aesthetic categories. He starts by explicitly repudiating the Crocean denial of the very existence of these different types of experience, and sets out to describe a number of them in considerable detail. Curiously enough, he has nothing to tell us about the most fascinating variety of all from the standpoint of the philosopher—I mean tragedy and the tragic. That he had spent on this problem much time and thought is evident from a passage in a letter dated May 5, 1935: "I am now reading Volkelt's *Aesthetik des Tragischen,* and it's a very good book, but it could have been said in half the span." What conclusions he reached, or why he was unable to reach any at all, we shall never know. Caution forbids him to generalize broadly about "comedy or the comic spirit." But he relished the comic talent of Molière and offers us a theory of his type of comedy, according to which its essence is the humorous contrast between the average, commonsensical person who faithfully observes the social conventions, and the foibles and follies of those eccentrics who resent them and find the courage to rebel against them.

The beautiful in the narrow sense is that which lends itself to effortless aesthetic enjoyment apart from its handling by an artist, while the ugly is what in nature is repulsive or repellent but is transmuted into something aesthetically attractive by the skilful touch of the painter or the poet. This distinction is based on the subject-matter of the work of art, and follows Bosanquet's contrast between "easy" and "difficult" beauty. It is strange that in this connection he has nothing to say about the graceful. In his treatment of the sublime he sticks closely to A. C. Bradley's superb essay. Sublimity is a more than ordinary greatness in man or nature whereof the magnitude does not exceed our powers of imaginative sympathy. It is a "difficult" variety to appreciate because we must overcome the initial disharmony of terror or dismay by a strong effort of self-control before we can sympathize imaginatively with the awe-inspiring grandeur of the sublime object. He concludes these observations by an interesting and original discussion of the sharp contrast between the "classical" and "romantic" styles in art. He attributes their difference to the relative emphasis laid by the artist on the subjective and objective elements in the work of art; thus romantic art is more personal and has greater warmth of emotion, while classical art is colder and more impersonal in conception.

IV

In this essay I have contented myself with displaying Alexander's wares as prominently as possible in my shop window, with just here and there a sentence of praise or blame for what I estimate to be their quality; to have succumbed to the temptation of writing a critical study would have transformed my small effort from a brief article into a stoutish book. Yet I would not care to bid farewell to the friend and philosopher whose opinions I have endeavored to describe in these pages without one last word about his rightful place, so far as I am able with my scanty qualifications to judge, as an aesthetician among his fellow-aestheticians and in the British tradition of speculation on this sorely neglected philosophical topic.

I scarcely think he would himself have claimed to be in the same class as certain Continental authorities who have covered the whole field in systematic fashion; he lacked the time and, with advancing years, the energy to emulate the detailed and exhaustive inquiries of the greatest experts. Acknowledging an article I had sent him on British aesthetics, published in a German periodical, he wrote at the end of November 1934: "I accept humbly your reproaches of my want of vigour to do something really thorough and systematic. What I may yet contrive to do I don't know—but I think I can be most useful in taking up special topics." And so we had to content ourselves with the published lectures and papers on a number of these special topics, as a substitute for the slender volume we dared not hope to see.

Yet among English writers on aesthetics it would be hard to find a compeer in the ranks of his contemporaries, and even harder would it be to fill the gap he has left from among the rare aestheticians of the present day. The mantle of Bosanquet had fallen on his shoulders, and he wore it worthily though with a difference; for there is not one of the main problems of aesthetics, whether philosophical, psychological, or objective, that he did not illuminate by a treatment that was always fair and quite often original. No English philosopher who has grappled with this thorny subject in recent years better repays the student for his midnight oil, as well for his clear formulation of the essential problems and the spirit in which he advanced to meet them as for the theories he evolved for their solution.

In academic circles Croce was hailed at this time as the thinker who had said all but the last word on aesthetics, and the two stout volumes of his *Aesthetic* had become the *vade-mecum* of the average university lecturer and professor interested in the subject; but Alexander was not afraid to challenge orthodoxy when it became an excuse for loose thinking or a source of erroneous conclusions. He mentions Croce often in his writings, but it is almost always to refute a misleading fallacy to which the Neapolitan idealist had given currency. Alexander was a scholar in the true sense of the word, being familiar with all the leading authorities on his subject in the English, French, Italian, and German tongues. Judging from occasional conversations and some intermittent correspondence, I should say that his favorite authors were some voluminous and erudite Germans, whose work was so sound and thorough that he even forgave them the weariness of spirit caused by their native prolixity. He had a special liking for Dessoir, whose *Aesthetik und allgemeine Kunstwissenschaft* he was anxious I should translate. "Dessoir," he wrote in the spring of 1933, "seems to me so sane as well as complete."

I cannot myself conceive how a man with so many intellectual interests and attainments was able to read the prodigious number of books on one subject alone to which his scholarship testified. How well I remember my crestfallen astonishment when, soon after the publication of a history of modern aesthetics in which I cited with scholarly pride upwards of two hundred volumes in various languages, I received a letter from Alexander reminding me in the kindest way of two or three authors of some distinction who had escaped my attention. This was a shining example of those rare qualities of heart and mind that made Samuel Alexander one of the most encyclopedic scholars as well as one of the most inspiring and original thinkers in the long history of English philosophy.

John K. McCreary (essay date 1947)

SOURCE: "The Religious Philosophy of Samuel Alexander," in *The Journal of Religion*, Vol. XXVII, No. 2, April, 1947, pp. 102-13.

[*In the following essay, McCreary explicates Alexander's theological views, which posit the existence of God through the principle of emergence, or, the development of nature to successively higher levels.*]

Alexander is a representative of that movement of thought which may be termed Anglo-American realism; in his *Space, Time, and Deity,* he has offered the most complete metaphysical and religious system so far given by that group.[1] Much, if not most, of his work is occupied with mind—mind as in the order of realities which begins with mere events in space and time and ends with God. These data are for Alexander at once the most simple and the most complex in the universe. The present study is limited to his view of deity, treating space and time only with such sufficiency as will supply context for his religious thought. Alexander seeks to show what can be known on this subject and known consistently with the whole scheme of things we know and, also, with that sentiment of worship which is directed to God.

I. ALEXANDER'S CONCEPTION OF DEITY

I. DEITY AND GOD

Primarily, God may be defined as the object of the religious emotion or of worship. On the other hand, from the metaphysical approach, God may be defined as the being, if any, which possesses deity or the divine quality. The two approaches are complementary; but, whatever approach be adopted, in either case God is defined indirectly. There are no proofs of God's existence and nature. All pretended proofs introduce conceptions which are a priori in the bad sense of that phrase, in which it means not something experienced which is pervasive of all things but something supplied by the mind; in other words, such proofs desert the scientific interpretation of things along the lines indicated by experience itself, and they do this by a limited use of analogy. (Thus, in the famous ontological argument, nothing more is proved than that the totality of things is real, which is a bare tautology.)

Alexander thinks of deity as being the next higher empirical quality than mind. Out of the all-embracing stuff of space-time, the universe exhibits an emergence in time of successive levels of finite existence, each with its characteristic empirical quality. The highest of these empirical qualities known to us is mind or consciousness; deity is the next higher empirical quality to the highest we know—at any level of existence there is a next higher empirical quality which stands towards the lower quality as deity stands toward mind.

Time is, for Alexander, an element in the stuff of which the universe and all its parts are made and has no special relation to mind, which is but the last complexity of time that is known to us in finite existence. Bare time, in Alexander's hypothesis, whose verification he has been following in the previous stages of his thought, is now to find completion by the conception of God—bare time, as the soul of its space, performs toward it the office of soul as to its equivalent body or brain. And this elementary mind which is time becomes in the course of existence so complicated and refined in its internal groupings that there arise finite beings whose soul is materiality, or color, or life, or, in the end, what is familiar as mind.

There is a nisus in space-time, which, as it has borne its creatures forward through matter and life to mind, will bear them forward to some higher level of existence. Time itself, however, compels us to think of a later birth of time. We must ask how finite deities are related to the infinite God, for they themselves are finite gods.

Deity is thus the next empirical quality to mind which the universe is engaged in bringing forth. But our human altars are still raised to the unknown God. If we could know what deity is, how it feels to be divine, we should first have to become as gods.

But an attempt must be made; hence we ask: What is the being which possesses deity? Alexander finds that deity is not spirit or mind, for that, in principle, would commit us to making of God a being not higher in kind than minds. God's distinctive character is rather something new, or deity. God is the universe possessing deity. In the religious emotion we have the direct experience of something higher than ourselves which we call God, which is not presented through the ways of sense, as such, but through this emotion. The emotion is our going out, or endeavor, or striving toward this object. According to Alexander, speculation enables us to say wherein the divine quality consists and that it is an empirical quality, the next in the series which the very nature of time compels us to postulate, though we cannot tell what it is like.

What conception of God is required if we think of the universe as space-time engendering within itself in the course of time the empirical qualities of which deity is the one next ahead of mind? The answer is: God is the whole world as possessing the quality of deity. As such, the being of the whole world is the "body" and deity is the "mind." But, thus, the possessor of deity is not actual but ideal. As an actual existent, God is the infinite world with its nisus toward deity, or, as Alexander employs the phrase of Leibniz, as big, or in travail, with deity.

But Alexander does not identify God with space-time. On the one hand, he finds the totality of the world, which in the end is spatiotemporal; on the other, he finds the quality of deity engendered, or rather being engendered, within that whole. These two features are united in the conception of the world as a whole expressing itself in the character of deity, and it is this and not bare space-time which for speculation is the ideal conception of God.

Our philosopher admits, however, that the description of God as the whole universe, as possessing deity, or as in travail with deity is full of figurative language. Belief in God is an act of experience; but it is not an act of sight, for neither deity nor even the world as tending to deity is revealed to sense. Belief in God is an act of speculative and religious faith. So we find Alexander saying that the body of God is the whole universe and there is no body outside his and that God's deity is lodged in a portion of his body and represents that body. Since his body is infinite, his deity is infinite. God includes the whole universe, but his deity, though infinite, belongs to, or is lodged in, only a portion of that universe. (This is a physiological representation, like the representation on the brain of the different portions of the body which send nerve messages to the brain.) Not only is God infinite in extent and duration, but his deity is also infinite in both respects. God's body, being the whole of space-time, is omnipresent and eternal; but his deity, though not everywhere, is yet infinite in its extension and, though his time is only a portion of infinite time, his deity is—in virtue of what corresponds in deity to memory and expectation in ourselves—infinite in both directions.

Comparing us with God, Alexander remarks that we are finitely infinite. Our minds are infinite in the same way as God's deity. Our minds represent our bodies; deity represents God's body. Hence deity, unlike mind, is infinitely infinite.

But, while Alexander has been presenting an ideal conception of God for philosophy, he now makes a qualification of the greatest importance: God is actual. And only in the sense of travail, in the sense of straining toward deity, can there be an infinite actual God. Yet there is no actual infinite being with the quality of deity; there is, however, an actual infinite—the whole universe—with a nisus to deity, and this is the God of the religious consciousness (though that consciousness habitually forecasts the divinity of its object as actually realized in an individual form). God as an actual existent is always becoming deity but never attains it; he is the ideal God in embryo. The ideal, when fulfilled, ceases to be God, and yet it gives shape and character to our conception of the actual God and always tends to usurp its place in our fancy.

In the relation of God's deity to the matrix which is space-time, we are not to think of the latter as something which grows bigger in extent with the lapse of time; its space is always full and it grows older through internal rearrangements in which new orders of empirical finites are engendered. No matter, therefore, what quality the deity of God may be, his body is always simply the whole space-time.[2]

In contrast to the absolute spirit of idealism, which holds that finites, though real, are not real in their own right but are real appearances of the one absolute—a doctrine from which, for Alexander, the God of religion does not escape, he being in turn a real appearance but not ultimately real—our author brings what he considers a self-consistent truth; space-time itself, in his view, is the only absolute. He does not feel, as idealism asserts,[3] that there is contradiction in finitude or in the categories that describe and are constitutive of it. The measure of what is self-consistent is the nature of space-time itself.

We have already seen how the realization of such a quality (or spirit) means the appearance in the world of finite deities, so that infinite deity is but an ideal. But while, on the one hand, deity, i.e., God's mind, does not belong to the absolute; in God's body, on the other hand—which body is the whole of space-time and is absolute—the finites are not submerged and not transformed; they are constitutive portions of the absolute. Neither is God spirit, nor, far less, is the whole—or absolute, which includes spirit—itself spirit; nor is it deity; but it includes deity.

The well-attested fact that the lower life subserves, in the course of time, the higher is perverted in absolute idealism (according to Alexander) into the erroneous doctrine that there is a something higher (an absolute) in which all lower life is submerged and transformed, and this absolute is spirit, which is not even the highest empirical quality. Dowered with this empirical quality, the absolute claims to be above the empirical but would be itself empirical. This result is, to Alexander's mind, the inevitable outcome of taking the measure of consistency and contradiction from our thoughts (as in Bradley and Bosanquet) instead of from things themselves, and of pronouncing space and time to be contradictory; whereas it is only obedience to the nature of the one "mother" and "nurse" of all becoming which determines consistency and freedom from contradiction.

2. DEITY AND THE RELIGIOUS SENTIMENT

When we ask how we come by the cognition of God, we must answer that (as with love and hate, and appetite and aversion) it is because the world itself provokes in us a specific response which makes us aware of God, and this specific reaction is what has been described by Alexander as the outgoing to something in the world with which we are in communion. (We must note carefully the phrase "something *in* the world"; for Alexander holds that the world, space-time, does not itself arouse the religious sentiment.) W. James in his *The Varieties of Religious Experience* drew from his data the doctrine that in religion "the conscious person is continuous with a wider self through which saving experiences come."[4] Adopting this general idea, Alexander regards us as parts of space-time which throw out, as it were, feelers toward the rest of it so that we are thus accessible to its influences. The body of the universe affects our body, and the ultimate response in consciousness is this emotion. Like hungry appetite it is a conation whose object, God, is to it as food is to hunger. The religious conation which sets us in search of God is our groping-out to the reality which is God. It is the world in its nisus forward that grips the finite conative complex which is fitted to it. It excites religion in us, and we, in turn, feel the need of it.

The religious emotion or appetite has no specific organ through which it works. It depends upon the whole makeup or constitution of the mind and body and is the response of it to the whole of reality in its nisus toward a new quality. In that forward movement, due to the onward sweep of time, our minds are caught, and our religious response is at once the mark that we are involved in that nisus and that our minds contribute in their part toward it. This may be concealed from the cognitive mind; it is higher than mind. It makes itself felt in the religious sense, which discovers the world it sees to be clothed with divinity. The world is not merely what it is for the intellect alone; its nisus toward what is higher enters into its constitution, and, as impregnated with this tendency, it affects the mind by ways other than cognition, though interpretable in the ways of cognition. The whole world with its real tendency to deity stirs in us from the depths of our nature a vague endeavor or desire which shadows forth its object. Then intellect comes into play and discovers in detail the characters of this object and finds at last what it truly is, the tendency of the world forward toward a new quality.

James had called this of which Alexander now speaks an "unseen" or "mystical" world; but Alexander demurs from calling it the former or even the latter. For him it is partly seen and partly the object of thought; but it is its new quality, which is something higher than we know, that cannot be seen or understood, though its presence in reality is forced upon us both in philosophical conception and in the feeling which it evokes in us of itself.

This religious feeling itself suggests the notion of God which, when elaborated by reflection, is discovered to be that of the world big with deity. The world which works upon our religious sensibility and suggestibility is the actual world, but that actual world contains the seed of its future, though what future forms it will assume is hidden from us, except in so far as we can forecast it in spatiotemporal terms. As to the assurance of God, it may be said that we are assured of other minds through social emotion and of deity through a different response, the religious emotion. Each of them is specific to the object it discovers. But faith in other minds may be called practical assurance; faith in God we may be content to describe simply as faith. We are sure of one another's minds because we are social beings; but the social instinct or tendency is satisfied only by reciprocal actions on the part of others. There is no such reciprocal action from God, in Alexander's opinion. If we speak, as we must, in terms of God's response to us, there is no direct experience of that response except through our own feeling that devotion to God or worship carries with it its own satisfaction. The universe does not answer our prayers by overt external actions, as our fellows respond to our social approaches to them, except in the strength and sustainment which in its tendency to deity it gives to our minds. (Here Alexander comes as close as he ever does to mystical theology.) In both cases it is intercourse with the object which discovers it to us, but religious intercourse is different from social intercourse and is only called such by metaphor. In this respect our faith in God is nearer to simple sensation than our assurance of other minds. The assurance of God we cannot call surer than our assurance of other minds; both are equally sure but the former is simpler. Moreover, being infinite, God has higher and deeper attachments in the nature of things—as Berkeley recognized.

Even without the practical revelation of God, we can arrive, according to Alexander, at the postulate of a world tending to deity, though we could not discover it to be worshipful. The religious criteria of the conception of God are that he should be greater than man, a "universal" or all-inclusive being, different in quality from man, and, finally, responsive to man, so that he offers us, in W. James's language, "a solution of our uneasiness," whether that uneasiness is derived from our feebleness and finitude or from the more intimate sense of our shortcomings or even sin. This God would be worthy of man's trust.

Thus, the religious consciousness attests the philosophical conception that God's deity is the issue in time of a tendency or nisus in the world of which our minds and everything else of the nature of mind are the proximate highest outcome—an issue which is dependent on the nature of things lower than itself.

Further, as being the whole universe, God is creative, but the distinctive character of deity is not creative but created. As representing the whole of space-time, he is creative, because time is the moving principle that brings out the constant redistribution in the matrix which is equivalent to the birth of finite forms. Even then, it is, properly speaking, space-time itself which is the creator and not God. The body of God includes all the finites which have hitherto been evolved in the lapse of time, and what God is creative of is not these finites but the next empirical quality of deity. It is only when we look back and identify God's body with its previous stages and ultimately with space-time itself that we can speak of him as creator. God himself, i.e., the universe as tending to deity, is creative only of deity. On the other hand, deity owes its being to the pre-existing finites with their empirical qualities and is their outcome. God then, like all things in the universe—for space-time itself is not in the universe, whereas God, since his deity is a part of the universe, *is* in it—is in the strictest sense not a creator but a creature. Needless to say, he is not a creature of imagination or of thought but an infinite creature of the universe of space-time. When we think of God as that to which all things owe their existence, we are reversing the order of fact and are regarding the universe of space-time, which itself created all things, in the light of its highest empirical quality, which is not first but last in the order of generation. The notion of a creator-God is, for Alexander, a hybrid blending of the creative space-time with the created deity.

Hence God's body is space-time itself; his deity is located in an infinite portion of space-time, and it is, in fact, essentially in process and caught in the general movement of time

The contrast of Alexander's system with that of Spinoza is clarifying. For Spinoza, infinite space is an attribute of God and extension is part of God's constitution; but the other attribute which our minds can know of God is not time but thought. Hence since time is not an essential part of God's constitution, no satisfactory account can be given of how finite things come into existence. We understand why they are resolved into God but not how they issue from him. God is the reason or ground of finite things; but causality, in the proper sense, which requires time, subsists only in the concatenation of finite things with one another, not in their relation to God. Now, if in this scheme we substitute time for mind, the world of finites arises out of the mere restlessness of space-time. Mind then becomes nothing but a finite of a particular empirical rank. It is true also that the God, or substance, which is space-time, ceases to be the object of worship—that is, ceases as such, with mere attributes of space and time, to be God. He needs the empirical quality of deity. The extent of such modifications shows how a great speculative system like Spinoza's is disturbed by the alteration of a single item. (Alexander suggests, too, that we consider two illustrations. In the doctrine of the Platonic *Timaeus* let us introduce time into the space of which things are made by the creator; or, taking Kant's conception of the pure manifold of intuition, let us consider what changes are made in it if space and time cease to be contributions of the mind and forms of sense and are viewed as a priori constituents of things.)

3. THE RELATION OF DEITY AND VALUE

Religion as a sentiment is thus the outgoing of the whole universe in its process toward the quality of deity; and, just as space is apprehended by intuition, sensible qualities by sensation, universals by thought, and values by appreciation, so God is apprehended cognitively through the religious emotion by the assurance we call religious faith.[5]

The approach to God may be made in various ways: through the phenomena of nature, through the pursuit of truth, through art, or through morality. All our experiences may in their various degrees be schoolmasters to teach us the reality of God. In its primitive form it is the religious sense of awe which is felt in the presence of natural powers.[6] The universe in its nisus toward deity acts on the mind in a manner more closely allied to the affections produced by purely physical conditions than to the feeling of goodness or beauty.

Originally, religion and morality are not distinguished from one another but are differentiated later.[7] However, the relation of religion and morality is always of the closest. (The late J. Royce maintained that the explicit recognition of a religious community was Paul's distinctive contribution to the religious thought known as Christianity.)[8] But, though religion and morality begin with union, and religion always involves conduct, the sentiment of religion and the sense of moral value are, in Alexander's view, distinct; they are distinct in far greater degree than philosophy is distinct from physics which was separated out of philosophy. The religious emotion, Alexander holds, is as unique and self-sufficient as hungry appetite or love. For him it constitutes a sentiment which arises from a brute or crude conation of human nature. Were it not for this sentiment for deity, we should never arrive at religion from thinking of the problems that arise in our moral life.[9] But a passion for deity being present, it seizes

on moral and other values, treating them as conditions of the enjoyment of itself and offering a solution of the problems which they present. This brute instinct or tendency impels us toward the being in front of us, the quality of deity.

This deity is not a value but a quality. Deity belongs to the order of perfection rather than of value. God is for us the highest being in the universe. When God is considered in terms of value, the old problems of good and evil, etc., are forcefully felt; but, if the whole universe is, as in Alexander's conception, the body of God, this difficulty does not arise, for good and evil are present there together. Yet he hastens to say that deity is on the side of goodness. Deity is a type of perfection transcending human goodness or truth or beauty, and any lower form of valuable life; and it is different in its quality. To call God himself good is, if we think of his deity, a wholly inadequate designation, only legitimate because we use human terms and because we mean by it that God is the highest perfection. But if we are thinking of God as the whole world with a soul of deity, he is neither good nor evil, for in his body he includes both. Yet, though as deity God is beyond good and evil, his deity is on the side of goodness.

Space-time itself, by virtue of its own nisus, elaborates without forethought a "hierarchy of ministration" which, if it were produced by mind, would imply a past and all-wise forethought or providence. Deity is the distinctive quality of the higher type of perfection in this hierarchical line of forms. (Alexander practically repeats the position of Aristotle in his *scala universi*. The "how" of the hierarchy—not to speak of its "why"—Alexander finds insoluble.)

If it can be said in disagreement to Alexander's view concerning the good and evil problem that, after all, evil exists and, since the world is the body of God, evil cannot be dismissed from the nature of God, Alexander is prepared to assert that he is not declaring that evil does not exist in God—on the contrary, it is maintained to exist there—but he is only declaring that God's deity is on the side of good and not on the side of evil. The reason for this difficult conception is necessarily seen in that God is infinite, whereas the beings in the struggle out of which the distinction between good and bad and all other values is born are finite. As a healthy body, to go further, puts away from itself its disused or dead parts, so there is a space "outside" into which the excrements (of evil) can be discharged and maintain an independent existence. But, since God is infinite, there is no extrusion possible beyond his limits; there is no space outside him.

Deity in the universe as a whole is like life in a healthy body. All values are conserved in God's deity. Hence, religion is not primarily faith in the conservation of values but faith in deity—or in God with the quality of deity—and deity is seen to be in the line of value. But, since the religious sense is something more primitive and crude, it needs to be described as it actually is experienced, not as it is reflected about. In its essence religious sentiment is not a matter of value or appreciation. It is a crude recognition by, and on the part of, a mind that there is something with a distinctive quality above its own distinctive quality of mind. It is like the apprehension of color or life, except that we cannot say what the new quality is really like, for it is not revealed to sense or thought. Alexander, despite the condemnation this statement would bring from both empiricist and idealist philosophies of religion, asserts that we are only sure that the new quality is there—at least potentially.

Thus, as to the relation of deity and value: deity is the outcome of the onward sweep of all that is persistent and counts in the economy of the world. Human values are but the apex of all movement. (For deity is, even for reflection, not merely the conservation of what is precious to us but of what is precious to itself everywhere.) Value means, in its simplest terms, that the individual or type, any function of which is valuable, is not self-dependent but in its independence belongs to the whole space-time of which it is a complex. Every being has value or unvalue as part of the whole space-time; it has the nisus to a higher form in so far as it contributes to the general nisus of the world. Here, again, in Alexander the Aristotelian point of view emerges, which is seen in more detailed analysis in recent times in the work of A. N. Whitehead.[10] Men of transcendent gifts of perfection are thus in their degree examples of this nisus. (The ordinary theism, therefore, with its postulates concerning human intermediaries between us and God, conceives God as endowed with deity actually attained, and it acts consistently in believing the intermediator to be more than man, i.e., human and divine at once; it purchases consistency, however, at the cost of interposing the conception of a miraculous person in the world.)[11]

Value is, in the sense above indicated, conserved in deity; but we must recognize withal that not in deity but in God unvalues also are contained, not merely badness and ugliness and error, but, in the end, all impermanent forms of finite existence. The evil is a reality and has its finite existence, but by being resolved into the infinite whole out of which it sprang it undergoes alteration into value. Here the Hegelian trend in Alexander merges with the view exemplified in Royce and in more elaborate form in Whitehead. Perishing in the form of evil, ugliness, and wickedness, these finite realities are used up in a changed form for the purposes of deity. There is here, according to Alexander, a kind of purgation whereby God "unmakes to remake."[12] Deity is then neither good nor evil nor a value but a new perfection in which, so long as it is infinite and ideal, there is no distinction of values. But God, considered as his body, contains both evil and good, though as a whole he is neither, since terms of value belong only to finites.

In this problem of value we commit a theoretical fault, in Alexander's view, by emancipating God from time. Instead of asking why evil exists, we should know that God's deity sustains our goodness and discards our evil; thus the question is reversed. We should really see that God is helpless to prevent evil, for his deity is the outgrowth of good, and God does not foresee the evil or the good, but, in so far as he is equivalent to the whole world, he is himself the theater of the contest between value and unvalue. No theoretic consideration sustains the belief in a God who precedes his universe. Thus, for example, design is the effect of time, successive forms making use of their predecessors and perishing if they cannot. (This is an adumbration of Whitehead's concrescent process.) Evil is, again, like discord; discord and the passage in which it occurs are alike music. There is no resolution of discord (which is evil) on the level on which both good and evil exist. Resolution is effected on the higher level. The evil remains done, but by perishing in its evil form it may subserve deity. The discord remains a discord, but it does not enter into the higher quality, as such, as an ingredient. In this view Alexander (and Whitehead, cf. his Preface to *Process and Reality*) exemplifies certain phases of absolute idealism.[13]

The attempt at the betterment of things which we make is of course at once implicated. This attempt is implanted in us by the space-time out of which we are precipitated and secures the deity to which the world is tending. The conservation of value is attained in fact but not through the persistence of one valuable individual; rather this is done through the conservation of his ideal. The persistence of our human effort as a whole, however, is doing the work of preparing deity "in God's good time"—and place.

As to the question of pain suffered by God, pain exists in God's body as moral evil itself, but in God's deity there is no pain, nor anything corresponding to it; there is, according to Alexander, no pleasure there either. For pain and pleasure belong to the organic order, especially in the case of ourselves. Yet, following Aristotle, Alexander would say that God, not his deity, enjoys continuous pleasure.

In sum, deity is a quality different from spirit, while it owes its existence to the travail of the world which has reached the level of spirit. Deity is subject, so long as it is the infinite deity of God, to no distinction of evil or good or of any other values. It depends on values and is in the line of what is good but is itself a perfection not contrasted with imperfection. Values are conserved by the beings which think in their language. Alexander disagrees with Matthew Arnold's statement that there is a power not ourselves which makes for righteousness; he says that, if the power which makes for righteousness is not ourselves, there is no other power which makes for righteousness. God is the power, however, that makes for deity. It is because we ourselves make for righteousness that we have faith in this further nisus of the universe and are sustained by that sentiment so as to derive help from it in doing righteousness. Our minds and the values they create do not end the series of empirical values. Our virtue is only part of the presupposition on which depends the emergence of the next higher quality to mind which we call deity.

II. SUMMARY, EVALUATION, AND CRITIQUE OF ALEXANDER'S POSITION

Alexander's work constitutes a courageous, a generally definite, and quite original theology or philosophy of religion. His view of deity is unique. It is defined in terms of the principle of emergence, according to which nature rises to successively higher and superimposed levels.[14] Although the human mind is thus far pre-eminent, the principle of emergence implies higher levels beyond, which will be related to the human mind as this, in turn, is related to body. Deity is this prospective superiority viewed from below, and God is the supreme eminence or infinite being, viewed with reverent expectancy by man.

Surveying his work, we note that space and time have no reality apart from each other but are aspects or attributes of one reality, space-time or motion.[15] This is the stuff of all existents, that of which they are composed; and it breaks up of itself into these complexes within the one all-embracing stuff. Any portion of it—any space-time—possesses certain fundamental features which therefore belong to every existent generated within the universe of space-time. These fundamental pervasive features of things are the categories. Besides these features things possess quality (not a category) which is an empirical feature of things. Qualities form a hierarchy, the quality of each level of existence being identical with a certain complexity[16] or collocation of elements on the next lower level. The quality performs to its equivalent lower existence the office which mind performs to its neural basis. Mind and body do but exemplify, therefore, the relation which holds universally. Accordingly, time is the mind of space, and any quality is the mind of its object; or, speaking more accurately, mind and any other quality are the different distinctive complexities of time which exist as qualities. As existents within space-time, minds enter into various relations of a perfectly general character with other things and with one another. (This is the mark at once attesting Alexander's realistic and generally anti-idealistic position.) This accounts for the familiar features of mental life: knowing, freedom, values, etc. In the hierarchy of qualities the next higher quality to the highest is deity. God is the whole universe engaged in the process toward the emergence of this new quality, and religion is the sentiment in which we are drawn toward God and are caught in the movement of the world to this higher level. This last conception is in accord with the closing sentences of H. Bergson's *The Two Sources of Morality and Religion*,[17] in which he views the universe as a machine for the creating of finite gods.

The naturalistic theology Alexander offers is not without fascination for religious speculation. He has given it seriously yet not dogmatically, but rather in the casual spirit in which Whitehead has presented his similar cosmology in *Process and Reality*. It savors of something of that "overbelief" in which W. James so often and so deliberately indulged. Specifically, his comprehensive and systematic work has provided religious thought with an intellectual foundation for a naturalistic theism such as is embraced by F. R. Tennant in England and H. N. Wieman in the United States. On this view God is known in human life and in nature at large as that complex of interactions on which we depend and to whose essential structure men must conform if the maximum possible value is to be realized in human experience. Obviously, the details of this essential structure cannot be demonstrated in advance. God, as a principle of progressive integration making for the greatest human good, is, in Whitehead's phrase, "the lure for feeling in each emergent occasion, the eternal guide of desire."[18] God for us, then, is the whole universe as pregnant with and straining toward the quality of deity. What this quality is we cannot know, because it lies beyond our present experience; but we can know its relation to the quality of mind out of which it will emerge, since that is the same as the relation with which we are already familiar in the emergence of life out of matter and mind out of life.

Now, since the universe with its nisus toward deity is also the God of religious consciousness and worship, on Alexander's view, we can and should participate in the effort of God to bring deity into existence. Like James, Alexander believes that we should be fellow-workers with God. Thus, the religious sentiment which is directed to God is active as well as worshipful; it unites with the object of its adoration in the creation of value. This statement requires the comment further that, although in some respects Alexander's view of God is pantheistic—since it regards God as in a sense comprising the whole existing universe—yet Alexander is right in his insistence that his view is theistic, at least to the extent that it recognizes us to be finite individuals who have our independent consciousness and that we are distinct from God even when in communion with him in religious experience. Thus, God is immanent in the sense that he is present everywhere and he is transcendent in his forward reach to the attainment of deity. We cannot hold deity responsible for the evil now in the world because deity does not yet exist. We are to some extent responsible for what deity will be, i.e., for what good there will be in the world in the future. God and we, in unison, can make the world better and effect the emergence of deity.

[1] The Anglo-American realists include (admitting, of course, their individual divergencies) Russell, Moore, Santayana, Whitehead; mention may be made too of the exponents of "the New Realism"—particularly Perry and Holt.

[2] Alexander discovers no true world-soul but only a soul of space-time and a nisus in the world to deity.

[3] Cf. F. H. Bradley, *Appearance and Reality* (New York: Macmillan Co., 1902), *passim*.

[4] W. James, *The Varieties of Religious Experience* (New York: Longmans, Green & Co., 1902), p. 515.

[5] It is the problem of the philosophy of religion to state in significative terms the cognitive meaning of religious

emotion or faith. The difficulty of so doing is not sufficiently recognized by Alexander, who would be criticized, especially by logical empiricists, for so simple a statement of the problem.

[6] Cf. J. Oman, *The Natural and the Supernatural* (New York: Macmillan Co., 1931). It appears that Alexander at times is wont to grant that the world of space-time arouses the religious sentiment; his real view is that it does not. Precisely it is the world as tending toward deity that arouses this sentiment.

[7] As the special sciences were singled out of early Greek science, which was synonymous with philosophy.

[8] *The Problem of Christianity* (New York: Macmillan Co., 1913).

[9] For the view which Alexander denies, cf. W. G. de Burgh, *From Morality to Religion* (London: MacDonald & Evans, 1938).

[10] *Process and Reality* (New York: Macmillan Co., 1929).

[11] For the Christian view cf. E. Brunner, *The Mediator* (London: Lutterworth Press, 1934).

[12] One might ask how, since on Alexander's view space-time acts without forethought; and why not indeed the reverse—of good altered into evil? Whitehead's principle of concretion, or God, indicates the presence in the universe of an actual entity capable of selection; in this way he makes Alexander's contention more defensible.

[13] For the most aggressive alternative view cf. W. James, *A Pluralistic Universe* (New York: Longmans, Green & Co., 1909).

[14] A view which is elaborated by Lloyd Morgan (see his *Emergent Evolution* [London: Williams & Norgate, 1923] and other works) and which led him to acknowledge Alexander as one of his masters.

[15] Motion is a synonym for space-time in Alexander's cosmology.

[16] Morgan (*op. cit.,* pp. 18-19) speaks of it as a new mode of relatedness.

[17] New York: H. Holt & Co., 1935.

[18] Whitehead, *op. cit.,* pp. 521 ff.; see also the same author's *Religion in the Making* (New York: Macmillan Co., 1926), pp. 88-99.

John Passmore (essay date 1957)

SOURCE: "The New Realists," in *A Hundred Years of Philosophy,* Basic Books, Inc., 1966, pp. 259-80.

[*In the following essay, which was originally published in 1957, Passmore focuses on Alexander in a discussion of realist philosophers of the early twentieth century.*]

In the early years of the present century, it could no longer be presumed that Realism was intellectually disreputable, a mere vulgar prejudice. What a mind knows, Brentano and Meinong had argued, exists independently of the act by which it is known; Mach, and James after him—if they were still, from a Realist point of view, tainted with subjectivism—had at least denied that what is immediately perceived is a state of mind; and then Moore, seconded by Russell, had rejected that thesis which Idealists like Bradley and phenomenalists like Mill had united in regarding as indisputable: that the existence of objects of perception consists in the fact that they are perceived. The 'New Realism' brought together these converging tendencies; it owed much to Meinong, more to Mach and James, and it acknowledged the help of Moore and Russell in the battle against Idealism.

The first, in England, to formulate the characteristic doctrines of the New Realism was T. P. Nunn.[1] Best known as an educationalist, Nunn wrote little on philosophy, but that little had an influence out of all proportion to its modest dimensions. In particular, his contribution to a symposium on 'Are Secondary Qualities Independent of Perception?'[2] was widely studied both in England where, as we have already noted, it struck Bertrand Russell's roving fancy, and in the United States. Nunn there sustained two theses: (1) that both the primary and the secondary qualities of bodies are really in them, whether they are perceived or not; (2) that qualities exist as they are perceived.

Much of his argument is polemical in form, with Stout's earlier articles[3] as its chief target. Stout had thought he could begin by presuming that there are at least *some* elements in our experience which exist only in being perceived—he instanced pain. But Nunn objects that pain, precisely in the manner of a material object, presents difficulties to us, raises obstacles in our path, is, in short, something we must reckon with. 'Pain,' he therefore concludes, 'is something outside my mind, with which my mind may come into various relations.' A refusal to admit that *anything* we experience depends for its existence upon the fact that it is experienced was to be the most characteristic feature of the New Realism.

The secondary qualities, Stout had also said, exist only as objects of experience. If we look at a buttercup in a variety of lights we see different shades of colour, without having any reason to believe that the buttercup itself has altered; if a number of observers plunge their hands into a bowl of water, they will report very different degrees of warmth, even although nothing has happened which could affect the water's temperature. Such facts demonstrate, Stout thought, that secondary qualities exist only as 'sensa'—objects of our preception; they are not actual properties of physical objects.

Nunn's reply is uncompromising. The contrast between 'sensa' and 'actual properties' is, he argues, an untenable one. All the shades of colour which the buttercup presents to an observer are actual properties of the buttercup; and all the hotnesses of the water are properties of the water. The plain man and the scientist ascribe a standard temperature and a standard colour to a thing and limit it to a certain region of space, because its complexity would otherwise defeat them. The fact remains, Nunn argues, that a thing has not one hotness, for example, but many, and that these hotnesses are not in a limited region of space but in various places around about the standard object. A thing is hotter an inch away than a foot away and hotter on a cold hand than on a warm one, just as it is a paler yellow in one light than it is in another light. To imagine otherwise is to confuse between the arbitrary 'thing' of everyday life and the 'thing' as experience shows it to be.

In Nunn's theory of perception, then, the ordinary conception of a material thing is revolutionised; that is the price he has to pay for his Realism. A 'thing', now, is a collection of appearances, even if every appearance is independent of the mind before which it appears. Nunn's realism, at this point, is very like Mach's phenomenalism. The same is true of American New Realism.

Scottish 'common-sense philosophy', as we have already observed, dominated the American Universities during the greater part of the nineteenth century; nor was it entirely swept out of existence either by James's pragmatism or by Royce's idealism. Peirce, to take the most notable case, continued to admire that 'subtle and well-balanced intellect, Thomas Reid'; his 'critical commonsensism'[4] owed much to Reid and his school. When Peirce criticised Reid, furthermore, it was from a Realist point of view; Reid, he complained, had not wholly shaken himself free from the Cartesian doctrine of representative perception. 'We have *direct experience of things in themselves,*' Peirce wrote in 1896. 'Nothing can be more completely false than that we can experience only our own ideas. That is indeed without exaggeration the very epitome of *all* falsity.'

The American tendency towards Realism, however, had been vigorously opposed by Royce in *The World and the Individual* (1900). Realism was there defined as, above all, a defence of independence, and Royce criticised it as such. 'The world of fact,' Royce describes the Realist as maintaining, 'is independent of our knowledge of that world . . . the vanishing of our minds from that world would make no difference in the being of the independent facts we know.' Royce's counter-argument, lengthy, robust and ingenious, is designed to show that if independence is ultimate—not mere 'appearance'—then all relations, including the relation of knowledge, are impossible in principle. In trying to preserve the independence of the objects of knowledge the Realist ends, according to Royce, by destroying the very possibility of knowledge.

Royce's attack provoked an immediate reply from two of his former pupils, R. B. Perry and W. P. Montague.[5] Relatedness and independence, they argued, are perfectly compatible. The task of explaining in what 'independence' consists is not, however, an easy one; in England, Schiller had attacked Nunn on this very point. To give a satisfactory account of independence was one of the two main problems which confronted the New Realists; the other was to explain, without abandoning Realism, how reality is to be distinguished from illusion—that rock on which so many hopefully-launched Realisms have foundered.

American philosophical journals, in the first decade of the present century, contain a multitude of attempts to sketch a Realist philosophy which would deal satisfactorily with these problems. But New Realism did not come of age until the publication in 1912 of *The New Realism,* a co-operative volume with contributions by E. B. Holt, W. T. Marvin, W. P. Montague, R. B. Perry, W. B. Pitkin, and E. G. Spaulding.

The *New Realism* is the Realist equivalent of Idealism's *Essays in Philosophical Criticism.* A number of philosophers, by no means unanimous on every point, felt that they had in common a method of approach to philosophy, with the help of which they could satisfy their diverse aims. A manifesto,[6] it begins with a long explanatory preface and ends with a series of brief policy-speeches. The world of philosophy could no longer pretend ignorance of the fact that a new and revolutionary spirit of Realism was abroad.

In many respects, however, *The New Realism* had little to add except liveliness of statement to Moore's *Refutation of Idealism.* In other ways, again—in maintaining, for example, that philosophy is 'peculiarly dependent upon logic' and in defending the validity of analysis against the Idealist doctrine that 'the truth is the whole'—the New Realism is mainly important as a medium through which Russell's conception of philosophy was naturalised in America. Yet one must not overestimate the New Realism's indebtedness to English philosophy. Russell, after all, had learnt many of his most characteristic doctrines from William James, whom he describes as 'the most important of all critics of Monism'. The point most vital in the logic of *The New Realism*—that relations are external—James had particularly urged. Marvin summed up that doctrine with rare succinctness. 'In the proposition "the term *a* is in the relation *R* to the term *b*", *aR* in no degree constitutes *b,* nor does *Rb* constitute *a,* nor does *R* constitute either *a* or *b*.' From this it follows, presuming that knowledge is a relation, that the known is not constituted by its relation to the knower, or the knower by its relation to the known, or either knower or known by the fact that it is a constituent in the knowledge relation.

On so much, the New Realists agreed. There was not the same agreement about the nature of the knower or the nature of the known. When Russell referred favourably to the 'new Realism' he meant the 'neutral monism' which Perry and Holt had worked out under the influence of Mach, James and Nunn.[7] Other New Realists, Montague especially, were highly critical of neutral monism.

The Holt-Perry variety of realism is an out-radicalising of James's radical empiricism. James had denied that there is such an entity as 'consciousness'; its adherents, he wrote, 'are clinging to a mere echo, the faint rumour left behind by the disappearing "soul" upon the air of philosophy'. There are only 'experiences'; knowing is a relation between portions of pure experience. F. J. E. Woodbridge,[8] however, had objected that 'experience' can only be defined as that of which a conscious being is aware; to talk of 'experience', therefore, is already to presume the reality of consciousness. Perry and Holt recognised the force of Woodbridge's criticism, which they tried to meet by defining experience without making any reference, explicit or implicit, to consciousness.

For this purpose, they adapted to their ends another facet of James's many-sided philosophy. James had emphasised—this had been the theme of one of his earliest essays, 'Spencer's Definition of Mind' (1878)—that a human being is an organism, which has to maintain itself in an environment which sometimes favours, and sometimes threatens, its survival. Perry took over from James this emphasis on the human organism, and united with it a theory of perception which Bergson had sketched in his *Matter and Memory:* a mind's 'content', Bergson had argued, consists of that part of its environment to which its attention is momentarily directed. Mind, Perry concluded, is 'an interested response by an organism'. Our 'consciousness of a table', for example, consists simply in the fact that our nervous system is interested in the table. No entity, 'consciousness', is here involved, not even in the form of a 'mental act'.

Thus the familiar distinction between the 'private' contents of a particular consciousness and the 'public' world of science is, on the Holt-Perry view, quite unwarranted. James, in his 'How Two Minds Can Know One Thing' (*JP,* 1905), had suggested that an experience is 'mine' only as it is *felt* as mine, and 'yours' as it is *felt* as yours—which does not prevent it from being in fact both mine and yours. Following up this hint, Perry condemns as 'the fallacy of exclusive particularity' the argument that because something is in your mind it cannot be in my mind; if it were not for the fact that the contents of minds intersect, he maintains, any sort of inter-human communication would be impossible. No doubt, Perry admits, other people sometimes find it difficult to decide what I am thinking about—that is why it is plausible to suggest that the contents of my mind are private to me—but this difficulty, he says, never amounts to an impossibility. Even in the hardest of all cases, the case where I am remembering something, a careful observer, according to Perry, *could* apprehend what I have before my mind. 'My remembering London', he says, 'consists of such elements as my central attentive process, certain persisting modifications of my cerebrum, my original dealings, practical and neural, with London—and London itself.' All of these are open to public observation, in principle at least.

The central teachings of neutral monism ought by now to be clear. 'Consciousness' is abandoned; and so also are the 'act of awareness' and the 'sense-datum', in the form they take in Moore's theory of perception. Nothing exists except objective 'elements'. Knowing is a relation between such elements, a relation peculiar only in that at least one of its terms must be an organic process.

The usual objection springs to our lips. 'But what of error and hallucination? Are pink rats and bent sticks objective elements?' Holt is perfectly willing to accept this consequence. 'Every content,' he writes, 'subsists in the all-inclusive universe of being.' But surely, we protest, some contents are real, others unreal. 'As to what reality is,' Holt aloofly replies, in a passage which gave rise to more than a little shocked comment, 'I take no great interest.'

This is a natural enough answer, for on Holt's view the difference between the real and the unreal is an arbitrary convention. We set up a system of connected perceptions which, as Hume expressed the matter, we 'dignify with the name of reality'; we call a perception 'real', according to Holt, if it has a place in such a system, and 'unreal' if we wish to deny it the right of entrance to this exclusive society. As Russell mischievously put the same point, some perceptions form part of the 'official biography' of a thing—its staid, respectable behaviour under normal circumstances—whereas others are wild, abnormal, best forgotten, unless the epistemologist insists upon acting as a muckraker. The philosopher, Holt is saying, cannot be expected to bother his enlightened head with so merely respectable a distinction.

On the ordinary account of the matter, there is a sharp distinction between, say, those properties of a tree which 'really belong to it' and those, such as its perspective foreshortenings, which are 'unreal' or 'subjective'. But Holt follows Nunn in arguing that the innumerable geometrical projections of the tree—to any of which the nervous system may react—have each of them an equal right to be regarded as belonging to it even if it is convenient for practical purposes to describe a certain shape as its 'real shape'. The projections, it is clear, are all actual relations of the tree, and there is no precise way, Holt argues, of distinguishing between 'the tree' and 'its relations'. As in Nunn's case, then, the Holt-Perry defence of the commonsense view that the objects of perception exist independently of the perceiver culminates in what is anything but a commonsense view about the nature of the objects themselves.

American New Realism was, indeed, severely criticised on just this point. There was something suspect in the very ingenuity which Perry and Holt brought to bear upon their epistemology. The original group disintegrated; Holt became a distinguished psychologist, Perry a moral theorist and a scholar, Pitkin made his reputation by advising a multitude of readers how to be happy though forty; Montague continued to philosophise, but in a manner certainly not New Realist; neither Marvin nor Spaulding made substantial contributions to philosophy.[9] Yet the movement had made its impact. As Perry suggests in his *Realism in Retrospect* (*CAP*, 2), it was an important wing of the contemporary battle against Cartesianism; the New Realism attacked dualism in the interests of a theory more sympathetic to the empirical spirit of the age than Absolute Idealism could ever be. And whatever the difficulties in which the New Realists found themselves, the force of their polemics against Cartesianism and Absolutism was unaffected. Few philosophers, nowadays, would *wholly* reject the name of 'Realist'.

Marvin's contribution to *The New Realism* had borne the title 'The Emancipation of Philosophy from Epistemology'. An odd-sounding title; for Realism had ordinarily been, above all else, an epistemology. But in Marvin's eyes a Realist epistemology is important mainly because it leaves the philosopher free to undertake the study of 'metaphysics'—understood as an attempt to discover 'the highest generalisations warranted by our present knowledge'. If, as philosophers since Descartes had been accustomed to maintain, all knowledge is based upon knowledge of the contents of our own mind, then it seemed plausible to conclude that an inquiry into the human mind ought to precede any inquiry into reality itself; and the final effect of this circuitous approach to metaphysics had been the actual absorption of metaphysics, at least in empirical philosophies, into epistemology. If, on the other hand, knowing is merely one of the many external relations which link our experience, there is no reason to believe that a detailed epistemology is an essential propaedeutic to metaphysics. The metaphysician is thus emancipated, Marvin thought, from his servile dependence upon the epistemologist.

It was left to a British philosopher, Samuel Alexander, to work out a recognisably Realist metaphysics. His *Space, Time and Deity* was published in 1920, at the beginning of a decade remarkably productive of metaphysical systems; the first volume of McTaggart's *The Nature of Existence* appeared in 1921 and Whitehead's *Process and Reality* in 1929. *The Nature of Existence,* however, belongs in its essentials to the British 'neo-Hegelian' movement; *Space, Time and Deity,* like *Process and Reality,* has the New Realism behind it, even although it is by no means unaffected by Bradley and Bosanquet. And there is another vital difference between *Space, Time and Deity* and *The Nature of Existence;* McTaggart is trying to construct a strictly deductive metaphysics, Alexander to 'give a plain description' of the world in which we live and move and do our thinking. In his **'Some Explanations'** (*Mind,* 1921), Alexander goes so far as to assert that he *dislikes* arguments, a strange pronouncement from a philosopher. 'Philosophy,' he says, 'proceeds by description: it only uses argument in order to help you to see the facts, just as a botanist uses a microscope.' In an earlier article on **'Sensations and Images'** (*PAS,* 1910) his affiliations with Husserl are even more obvious; his method, he says, is 'an attempt to exclude philosophical presuppositions, and to state what is actually present in a given experience'. Nothing could be more remote from *The Nature of Existence,* which is argument through and through.

Alexander's method makes *Space, Time and Deity* a peculiarly difficult book to read and to discuss; in many respects, it is more like a work of literature than a philosophy. We expect from a philosopher a running thread of argument, interspersed with polemics. But there is very little of this in Alexander; he simply puts a hypothesis before us and then tells us to look and see how reasonable it all is, how admirably it squares with our experience. He does not exhort us, he does not argue with us, he merely bids us cast off our sophistication and look at the world through the naïve eyes of absolute innocence; yet the world he thus presents to us is complex and sophisticated in the extreme. Most philosophers have refused to follow his guidance; for all the acclaim which greeted its appearance, *Space, Time and Deity* is not now widely read. But it has its staunch admirers, some of them prepared to maintain that it is the most important contribution to philosophy our century has known.

When Alexander reached Oxford from Australia in 1877[10] his first contacts were with men of note in the Idealist movement—Green, Nettleship and A. C. Bradley were all tutors at Balliol in Alexander's time. He was naturally influenced by their teachings; and even when he broke with the Idealists, they continued to speak of him with a respect they rarely showed to New Realists—although this charity did not survive the bleakness of Cambridge, where McTaggart, forgetting his own blackened pots, complained of *Space, Time and Deity* that 'in every chapter we come across some view which no philosopher, except Professor Alexander, has ever maintained'. It would be inhuman to expect the arch-enemy of Time to praise its arch-prophet.

Influences of a distinctly different sort were also at work on Alexander; the new biology and the new experimental psychology won his admiration. Stout and Alexander, indeed, collaborated in the defence of psychology against its Oxford critics. Alexander's friends did not know whether to be amused or alarmed by his psychological experiments. This was not merely the enthusiasm of youth; *Space, Time and Deity* appeals more often to experimental psychology than to any other form of empirical inquiry. Similarly, the influence of biology, so apparent in Alexander's first book *Moral Order and Progress* (1889)—which belongs to the school of Leslie Stephen—was never wholly to be dissipated; conceptions derived from biology play an important part in *Space, Time and Deity*.

First, however, Alexander was to make his name as an epistemologist, in a long series of articles culminating in **'The Basis of Realism'** (*PBA,* 1914). The immediate stimulus which provoked Alexander's paper was the appearance of Bosanquet's *The Distinction between Mind and its Objects* (1913). In that book Bosanquet welcomed Realism as an ally in the Idealists' battle against the theory of representative perception and, what is ordinarily associated with it, the 'brickbat theory of matter'. But his final verdict on Realism was nevertheless adverse: it sinned gravely, he argued, by speaking of mind as if it were simply one particular entity in a world of particular entities. 'I should compare my consciousness to an atmosphere,' Bosanquet wrote, 'not to a thing at all. Its nature is to include. The nature of objects is to be included. . . . I never seem to think in the form "my mind is here and the tree is there".'

In sharp opposition, Alexander maintains that consciousness is a property of certain organic structures; the tree, for him, is not *in* my consciousness but *before* it, as an object 'compresent' with a conscious being. Alexander, indeed, was permanently influenced by Moore's 'Refutation of Idealism'; although he was attracted by the neutral monist reduction of the 'mental act' to an organic response he could never persuade himself wholly to reject the act-object analysis. For Alexander, however—and this brings him closer to Holt and Perry than to Moore— an act of mind is a *conation,* a response to an object. It is such a conation, not a cognitive act, which cognises an object.[11] And the 'content' of a mental act, for Alexander, is not a pale copy of its object; it consists in those psychological features peculiar to the mental act as a process—its intensity and its direction.

If this is the real situation, if knowledge is nothing more than the 'compresence' of a mental act and an object, how account, we might ask, for the very existence of views like Bosanquet's? What confuses Bosanquet, Alexander argues, is his acceptance of the common assumption that in contemplating an object we are at the same time contemplating the act which knows it. Then the consequence follows that in perceiving X my real object is not X but 'my consciousness of X', within which X is somehow an ingredient. Since, however, X is obviously not 'in my consciousness' in that sense of 'consciousness' in which it is identical with an individual mind, 'consciousness' has to be converted into a general 'medium' or 'atmosphere' within which things exist.

Alexander, however, is determined to retain the common-sense distinction between individual minds and their objects; he cuts the ground from under the Idealist argument by denying that we ever contemplate a mental act. Acts cannot be contemplated, but only 'enjoyed'—'lived through', as it is sometimes put. Thus 'our consciousness of an object' is never, for us, an object of contemplation; what we contemplate is the object, simply—although we at the same time enjoy the act which is conscious of it.[12] The mental act and its object are sharply sundered. Objects cannot be enjoyed, mental acts cannot be contemplated. From 'an angel's point of view'—the point of view of a being higher than ourselves—our conscious act would be an object; an angel would contemplate our conscious act as something compresent with its object. But we are not angels; for us the mental act exists only as an enjoyment.

To know an object, for Alexander, is to be a mental act compresent with it. The familiar question inevitably occurs to us: if its objects are compresent with the mind, how can it fail to apprehend them as they are? In reply,

Alexander, following Nunn, first of all admonishes us not to confuse between selective apprehension and error. A mind is conscious only of what stirs an impulse in it; its 'object' is not the complete thing with which it is compresent, but only a selection from that complete thing. This incompleteness is not, by itself, error. If two people see a table, one as a flat edge, the other as a corner, neither is in error, Alexander argues, unless he wrongly believes that what is true of his 'object' is true of the table as a whole. In general—a point Royce had also stressed—there is no error involved merely in *having* an object before our mind. If we look at a distant mountain, for example, we have blue before our minds; so far all is well: we make a mistake only if we go on to ascribe the blue to the distant mountain. Then we are confusing, according to Alexander, between one thing and another; we are imagining that an object lies within a certain spatio-temporal contour when it actually lies outside it. The error does not consist in our having a non-existent object before us but in our *misplacing* a real object.

The same analysis applies in principle, he tries to show, to more difficult cases. Suppose we wrongly believe that a patch of grey paper against a red background is green. In this case, there is no green anywhere in the neighbourhood of the paper, as there was blue in the neighbourhood of the mountain. But the important point, to Alexander, is that green at least exists *somewhere,* and it is there spread out over an expanse just as we now suppose it to be spread over the paper. Both the object apprehended and its mode of combination with other objects already exist in the world; our error lies in misplacing or mistiming them: we do not create a wholly novel object. This theory of error, which is essential to Alexander's Realism, is worked out in **Space, Time and Deity** with a wealth of detail which can here only be mentioned, not conveyed.

'The temper of Realism,' Alexander wrote in **"The Basis of Realism,"** 'is to de-anthropomorphize; to order man and mind to their proper place among the world of finite things; on the one hand, to divest physical things of the colouring which they have received from the vanity or arrogance of mind; on the other, to assign them along with minds their due measure of self-existence.' Thus Realism, as he conceives it, is naturalistic; for it, the human being is one finite thing amongst others, not the ruler and lord of the finite universe. Such a naturalism is usually condemned on the ground that, as Alexander expresses the accusation, it 'degrades mind and robs it of its richness and its value'. Alexander's aim in **Space, Time and Deity** is to put mind in its place without degrading it. For this purpose, a useful instrument lay near at hand: the theory of 'emergent evolution'. The conception of 'emergence' goes back at least as far as G. H. Lewes' *Problems of Life and Mind* (1875); but it had more recently been worked up into a theory of evolution by the philosopher-biologist C. Lloyd Morgan.[13] Lloyd Morgan hoped to tread a midway path between 'mechanism' and 'vitalism'. The mechanists had set out to show that organisms are 'nothing but' physico-chemical structures, which have assumed their present shape as a result of the operations of natural selection. For the vitalist, on the contrary, an organism possesses a 'vital force'; it is, indeed a medium through which life struggles towards perfection.[14]

Lloyd Morgan had no patience with vitalism as a biological theory. 'With all due respect,' he wrote in *Instinct and Experience,* 'for M. Bergson's poetic genius—for his doctrine of Life is more akin to poetry than to science—his facile criticisms of Darwin's magnificent and truly scientific generalisations only serve to show to how large a degree the intermingling of problems involving the metaphysics of Source with those of scientific interpretation, may darken counsel and serve seriously to hinder the progress of biology.' Vitalism, he argues, is not a scientific hypothesis, it is a metaphysics—a theory about the 'Source' of evolution, not a description of evolutionary processes. The theory of emergent evolution, on the other hand, purports to be a careful description of what actually happens in evolution, a description which at the same time brings to light the inadequacy of the 'mechanical' view that living processes are merely physico-chemical. In a genuine evolution, Morgan maintains—as distinct from the routine repetition of an established habit of action—there is always 'more in the conclusion than is contained in the premises'; in other words, the resultant process is never 'nothing but' the processes out of which it has evolved. Thus it is that modes of behaviour—consciousness, for example—can evolve out of physico-chemical processes without themselves being reducible to, although they are continuous with, such processes.

This doctrine of emergent evolution supplies the framework for Alexander's *Space, Time and Deity.* It might seem strange that a theory developed by a biologist for biology should be thus employed in a metaphysics; metaphysics is most often envisaged as a supra-scientific inquiry, in which science is, if not superseded, at least transcended. But for Alexander, metaphysics is itself a science, distinguishable from, say, physics only by its greater degree of comprehensiveness. Although its *method* differs from that of a natural science yet its conclusions must accord with the conclusions of scientists, and it can well take a hint from their discoveries. For its subject-matter is simply those pervasive features of things which are variously exemplified in the different fields of science: Space, Time, and the Categories.

Space and Time come first: 'it is not too much to say,' Alexander writes, 'that all the vital problems of philosophy depend for their solution on the solution of the problem what Space and Time are and, more particularly, how they are related to each other.' Philosophers have usually depreciated time; this is obviously true of Bradley and McTaggart, amongst recent philosophers, and the same can be said, to a large degree, of Russell. 'There is some sense,' he had written in *Our Knowledge of the External World,* 'in which time is an unimportant and superficial characteristic of reality. Past and future must be acknowl-

edged to be as real as the present, and a certain emancipation from slavery to time is essential to philosophical thought.' Any philosopher who approaches philosophy through logic is likely to argue in this way: on the face of it, implication is not a temporal relation and 'truth', as logic understands it, is eternal. One may note, in contrast, that for Alexander 'truth' is relative. 'Truth,' he says, 'varies and grows obsolete or even turns to falsehood'; to be 'true' is to be accepted by the 'social mind' and what that mind accepts varies from time to time.[15] And of inference, which like the Idealists he takes to be the subject matter of logic, he writes that it 'betrays most plainly that truth is not merely reality but its unity with mind, for inference weaves propositions into a system, and system and coherence belongs not to reality as such but only in its relation to a mind.' Not even truths, then, and not even logical relations are eternal; Alexander is 'taking time seriously' with a vengeance.

Bergson had already sought to rehabilitate time. But Bergson elevated time, Alexander thought, at the expense of Space, and in the process left it completely mysterious. In this respect, the opposition between Bergson and Alexander is complete: Bergson's philosophy is a protest against the interpretation of time in spatial terms, whereas Alexander maintains that this is how it *must* be interpreted, although equally, he grants, space must be interpreted in temporal terms. Neither space nor time, indeed, is intelligible in itself; each can be understood only by reference to the other, as an aspect of Space-Time.[16]

Alexander did not think it necessary to show in detail that time and space by themselves are unintelligible. In their negative arguments, he was prepared to follow Bradley and McTaggart: pure time would have to be at once pure succession and pure duration. But he does not conclude, as they did, that time is 'unreal'; we meet it in our experience, Alexander argues, and must describe it as we find it there. In that experience, however, it is never *pure* time; our experience is of the spatio-temporal. The succession we encounter in our concrete experience is the successive occupation of a place; the space with which we have dealings is not an undifferentiated inert mass but is at different instants diversely occupied. Once we recognise these facts, the 'contradictions' in Space and Time, Alexander thinks, lose their terrors.

On the naïve view of Space and Time, they are twin boxes within which things move about; in reaction against the 'box' theory, philosophers have attempted to identify Time with the relation of temporal succession and Space with the relation of spatial coexistence. But the relational theory of Space and Time, Alexander argues, ignores the fact that the terms in such relations are *themselves* spatial and temporal, and that it would involve a vicious infinite regress to try to reduce such spatio-temporality to a further set of relations. Furthermore—an objection which carries him to the heart of his metaphysics—'relation', like any other category, is intelligible only if it is interpreted as a mode of spatio-temporality. To use it to give an account of Space-Time is to reverse the true order of dependence.

Alexander proposes a third view of Space-Time: it is, he says, the 'stuff' out of which things are made (although in a Pickwickian sense of 'stuff', since matter is subsequent to Space-Time). This is not an easy theory to comprehend, nor do Alexander's elucidations and elaborations always relieve his readers' bemusement. Perhaps what he wants to say will be a little clearer in another form: Space-Time, he argues, is identical with Pure Motion; to say that Space-Time is the stuff of which things are made is to affirm that a thing is a complex of motions. 'Motion' is 'the occupation of points which successively become present'; and this occupation of a point by a succession of instants is precisely what Alexander means by 'Space-Time'. He would, he says, happily speak of the ultimate Stuff as Motion instead of Space-Time, were it not that we find it harder to represent to ourselves the idea of an all-encompassing Motion than that of an all-encompassing Space-Time. Alexander's metaphysics, indeed, is in many ways akin to that of Heraclitus; 'the universe', he says, 'is through-and-through historical, the scene of motion'.[17] A spatio-temporal universe, for him, is by its nature a universe in growth: this is the point at which Alexander's theory of Space-Time unites with the doctrine of emergent evolution.

The part of *Space, Time and Deity* on which Alexander particularly prided himself is Book II, *Of the Categories*. As we have seen, he regards the categories as the pervasive characters of things; this pervasiveness, he thinks, needs some explanation; it arises from the fact that the categories are properties or determinations of the primordial stuff, Space-Time. They belong to everything, just because everything is a complex generated in Space-Time.

We can illustrate the manner of his procedure by reference to two categories which have already occupied our attention in other contexts—universality and relation. There are, he argues, no 'particulars' and no 'universals'; everything is an 'individual', i.e. is both particular and universal. It is 'particular' in so far as it is distinguishable from other things of the same 'general plan of construction'; its 'universality' consists in the fact that the same plan of construction is repeated elsewhere, whether as the construction of that same finite being (as a marble keeps the same form as it rolls along the ground) or of different finite beings (as the marbles in a bag all have the same general construction). This possibility of repetition, Alexander argues, depends upon the uniformity of Space-Time, which enables a thing to change its place while retaining the same plan of construction. In that respect, to talk of 'universality', according to Alexander, is simply a way of drawing attention to Space-Time's uniformity. Furthermore, a 'plan' is simply a regular mode of behaviour; the universal, as Alexander describes it, is not a Platonic form, changeless, immutable and eternal, but a pattern of motions, 'instinct with Time'.

Relations, similarly, are essentially spatio-temporal. Alexander defines a relation as 'the whole situation into which its terms enter, in virtue of that relation'. Thus the maternal relation, for example, is a set of actions on the part of the mother and a set of actions on the part of the child, considered in so far as they 'establish a connexion' between mother and child or 'initiate a transaction' between them. A relation, therefore, is a concrete whole, not a vaguely-conceived 'link' between terms. Often, Alexander maintains, it is more important than the terms; as when, in time of war, although we are aware that the conflicts taking place involve men, we envisage the conflict-situation clearly, the individual men scarcely at all. But these are, comparatively speaking, matters of detail: the important point, for Alexander, is that a 'relation' is a spatio-temporal transaction between spatio-temporal constituents, the transactions having a 'sense' or a 'direction'. To put the same point differently, a relation is motions passing between systems of motions.[18]

From the Categories, Alexander passes in Book III to 'The Order and Problems of Empirical Existence' which many of his critics have considered to be the most profitable section of *Space, Time and Deity*. So far it has simply been said that the empirical qualities a thing possesses are 'correlative with' their underlying motions. But 'correlation' is an intolerably vague conception; the problem now is to make it more precise. The clue, he thinks, comes from the mind-body relation.

This is an unexpected suggestion; most philosophers have seen in the mind-body relation one of the most intractable of all philosophical problems. Alexander does not agree. Observation and reflection make it perfectly apparent, he thinks, that certain processes with the distinctive property of being conscious occur in the same places and at the same times as 'highly differentiated and complex processes of our living body'. The 'correlation' of mind and body consists, then, in the fact that *the very same process* which is experienced from within, or 'enjoyed', as a mental process can be 'contemplated' as a neural one.

Physiological processes of a certain type and complexity, according to Alexander, are conscious processes. Consciousness, to express the matter in terms of evolution, 'emerges' at a certain point in the development of living processes. No knowledge of physiology, he considers, could enable us *prior to experience* to predict that this quality would emerge, even although, after the event, we can determine the degree of complexity exhibited by those physiological processes which are conscious. 'Consciousness' is a novel, unpredictable quality, for all that it has its roots in, and is determined by, physiological processes.

Working with this 'clue to quality', Alexander describes the general pattern of emergence. When Space-Time or motion reaches a certain degree of complexity qualities emerge: first, the so-called 'primary qualities' such as size, shape and number, which are 'empirical modes of the categories', then secondary qualities like colour, which stand to the primary qualities as mind stands to body, then living processes, then mind—and deity. In each case, we must accept with 'natural piety' the fact that new qualities emerge; there is no 'explanation' of this fact, it just is the case.[19] The determination of the sequence and number of stages is, he says, a problem for natural science: the metaphysician must be content to sketch the general conception of a 'level of existence', and to illustrate the relationship holding between such levels.

We can now summarise Alexander's theory of finite existences. Every finite existence, in the first place, is compresent with (spatio-temporally connected with) other finite existences. A finite existence is a substance, i.e. a volume of Space-Time with a determinate contour; it is the scene of movements, which have each of them a history. They appear in time, exist through time, and end in time. There are three distinguishable aspects of a thing: its spatio-temporality, the processes which occur in it, and its plan of construction, or configuration. The first, from our point of view, is the thing's place, date, duration and extent; the second its qualities, perceived as sensibilia; the third is its 'nature', which we take as the object of our thought.

Alexander's theory of knowledge now finds its home within this metaphysical framework, as a special exemplification of it. A mind, like anything else, is a particular finite existence, and is 'compresent' with a variety of other finite existences. 'Compresence,' it is important to observe, does not connote simultaneity. Many of the events with which a mind is 'compresent'—or which, as Alexander also expresses the matter, form part of its 'perspective'—occurred a very long time ago, the events it perceives in the distant stars being a striking example. This, however, is not peculiar to mind; everything reacts to events which have already passed away. We can think of anything whatsoever as the point of departure for a 'perspective', which will include all those events in various places and of various dates to which it is related, with which, that is, it 'has transactions'. Space-Time, indeed, is built up of such perspectives, not of simultaneous cross-sections.[20]

How does Deity fit into this metaphysics? That is the question Alexander sets out to answer in Book IV of **Space, Time and Deity**. Deity, Alexander argues, is the next stage in evolution; it bears the same relation to mind as mind does to living processes and living processes to the physico-chemical. For us to predict its nature is impossible. To call Deity 'mind', for example, would be comparable to asserting that living processes are nothing but physico-chemical processes: Deity must no doubt *be* mind, but its distinctive properties will not lie in that fact.

Considered thus, Alexander admits, God is ideal rather than actual, in the making but not yet made. If we demand an actual God, that can only be 'the infinite world with its nisus towards deity'. Why, we may object, should we not describe Space-Time—which is both infinite and

creative—as God? One reason, according to Alexander, is that no one could worship, or feel a religious emotion towards, Space-Time; and it is the object of a metaphysics of deity to discover an entity towards which such an emotion is appropriate. He admits the abstract possibility that metaphysics might lead the philosopher to the conclusion that there is no such entity; but his own metaphysics, he considers, leads towards deity, not away from it. And this, he argues, is a point in its favour, for 'a philosophy which leaves one portion of human experience suspended without attachment to the world of truth is gravely open to suspicion'; the presumption must always be, he thinks, that to every appetite there corresponds an object which could satisfy it, and the religious emotion, on his account of it, is such an appetite, to be satisfied with no object less than Deity. That this Deity was very different from the God of ordinary religion, not least in the fact that there is no reason for regarding Deity as the last stage in evolution, did not seriously perturb Alexander.

A number of other philosophers were prepared to describe themselves as Realists, and felt the impact of Alexander's philosophy, without making the transition from epistemology to metaphysics. John Laird,[21] in such works as *A Study in Realism* (1920) expounded a 'down-to-earth' Realism—he liked to remember that his birthplace was near Reid's—in which the emphasis was critical and analytic rather than metaphysical. He admired Alexander greatly, and thought that Alexander's work overshadowed his own, but the atmosphere of his philosophy is that of Moore's Cambridge, where he had been a student; he did not move easily amid Alexander's abstractions. From his own Gifford Lectures *Theism and Cosmology* (1940) and *Mind and Deity* (1941) very little emerges in the way of a definite conclusion: no more than that a transcendental theism is 'not proven' although an immanent theism has some measure of attractiveness for a reasonable man.

Another Scottish Professor, the scholar N. Kemp Smith, author of classical commentaries on Descartes, Hume and Kant, stood much closer to Alexander, for all that he described himself as an 'Idealist'. His *Prolegomena to an Idealist Theory of Knowledge* (1924) is an attempt, as he expresses the matter, to formulate 'an idealist theory of knowledge along realist lines.'[22] There is, he argues, no necessary connexion between Idealism and subjectivism; subjectivism is metaphysically neutral, lending itself as much to the purposes of a Mach as to the purposes of a Berkeley. The Idealist can also be a realist; what he has to show, according to Kemp Smith, is not that reality is mind-dependent but that it incorporates 'spiritual values', that these, indeed, operate 'on a cosmic scale'. Thus much of Kemp Smith's argument is an attempt to demonstrate the many-sidedness of Nature, its richness and resourcefulness, quite in opposition to the tendency of many idealists to deaden Nature in order to make of mind the one enlivener.

Kemp Smith is able to absorb into his Idealism both Alexander's critique of subjectivism and his theory of natural processes. But he does not go all the way with Alexander, particularly in regard to the independence of secondary qualities. He agrees that sensa are not in the mind; he still thinks that they exist only in dependence upon an organism. They are on his view a biological device, enabling the organism to deal with an environment so complex that to see it accurately would be to find it overwhelming. When we look at water, for example, we see something continuous and stable, not a dervish-dance of molecules; and if we were not thus deluded, it would wholly bewilder us. We are deceived only because Nature is taking care of our interests.

Another philosopher who saw virtue in the resurgence of realism was C. E. M. Joad, who moved with it from 'The Refutation of Idealism' to *The Analysis of Matter*. But *The New Realism* was too pale and emaciated to claim a permanent lien over Joad's wide-ranging affections. Within a seam-bursting eclecticism, Russell, Bergson and Plato had somehow all to make room for themselves, as the representatives, respectively, of matter, life and value.[23] The result was a conglomeration of considerable popular appeal but little philosophical consequence. The fact remains that Joad—an invigoratingly polemical broadcaster, essayist and lecturer at a time when the ideal of 'good taste' was threatening to destroy personality—represented 'philosophy' to a large segment of the British public. What this proves, either about philosophy or about the British public, I should not care to say.

[1] On Realism generally, see *RIP* (1938); R. B. Perry: *Present Philosophical Tendencies* (1912); R. P. Kremer: *La theorie de la connaissance chez les néo-réalistes anglais* (1928) and *Le néo-réalisme américaine* (1920); R. W. Sellars; 'Current Realism in Great Britain and the United States' (*Monist*, 1927); A. K. Rogers: *English and American Philosophy Since* 1800 (1922); L. Boman: *Criticism and Construction in the Philosophy of the American New Realism* (1955); R. M. Chisholm: *Realism and the Background of Phenomenology* (1960, with bibliography).

[2] *PAS*, 1909; Schiller is his fellow-symposiast. See also Nunn's book *The Aims and Achievements of Scientific Method* (1907).

[3] 'Primary and Secondary Qualities' (1903) and 'Are Presentations Mental or Physical?' (1908), both in *PAS*.

[4] Commonsense, to Peirce, must be our starting-point; so far Peirce and Moore would be of the one mind. But any *particular* commonsense doctrine, Peirce also says, may turn out to be false, even although commonsense as a whole can never be abandoned. See R. M. Chisholm on 'Fallibilism and Belief' in *Studies in the Philosophy of C. S. Peirce* (ed. P. P. Wiener and F. H. Young, 1952); J. Buchler: *Charles Peirce's Empiricism* (1939); W. B. Gallie: *Peirce and Pragmatism* (1952).

[5] Montague in 'Professor Royce's Refutation of Realism' (*PR*, 1902) and Perry in 'Professor Royce's Refutation of Realism and Pluralism' (*Monist*, 1902). Compare James's attack on 'vicious intellectualism' (p. 110 above). See also Montague's 'Story of American Realism' (*Phil.*, 1937, reprinted in *Twentieth-Century Philosophy*, ed. D. D. Runes, 1943); R. B. Perry: 'W. P. Montague and the New Realists' (*JP*, 1954); obituaries of Perry by C. I. Lewis (*PPR*, 1957) and G. Deledalle (*Études Philosophiques*, 1957).

[6] This was an age of manifestos, in philosophy, in literature, and in politics. There are interesting points of comparison between *The New Realism* and the *Imagist Anthology* (ed. Ezra Pound, 1914). Contrast G. Ryle: 'On Taking Sides' (*Phil.*, 1937).

[7] Perry is the most devoted and scholarly of commentators on James; and he described Mach's *Analysis of Sensations* as 'among the classics of modern realism'. See Holt's *The Concept of Consciousness* (1914) and Perry's *Present Philosophical Tendencies*.

[8] Woodbridge was invited, but refused, to join the New Realist group. They saw in his articles, particularly in 'The Concept of Consciousness' (*JP*, 1905), a post-Jamesian realism akin to their own. See his 'Confessions' in *Contemporary American Philosophy* (Vol. II). His influence was mainly exerted through his teaching and his occasional articles; his major book is *The Realm of Mind* (1926). For a brief account of his philosophy, see H. T. Costello: 'The Naturalism of Frederick Woodbridge' (*Naturalism and the Human Spirit*, ed. Y. H. Krikorian, 1944).

[9] Montague attempted to construct a synthesis of realism, subjectivism, and 'critical realism'. This is an ambition characteristic of much American philosophy, with its fondness for odd combinations of '-isms'. The contributions to *Contemporary American Philosophy* bear such titles as 'problematic realism', 'personal realism', 'empirical idealism', 'temperamental realism'. On the whole, the American philosopher has expected to find himself with a system on his hands, which he is quite happy to label as an '-ism', in sharp, contrast with his contemporary British colleagues who prefer to think of themselves as remote from the clamour of schools and are more than a little offended when their critics refuse to take this disclaimer at its face-value. The sociologist may find ground for reflection in this contrast. Montague's epistemology is summed up in *The Ways of Knowing* (1925). The dialogue at the end of that book, participated in by a new realist, a critical realist and an Idealist—with Montague as Hylonous the *true* realist, reconciling their differences—is a useful presentation of the principal points at issue in the epistemological controversies of the present century, even if Hylonous is insufferably superior. For Spaulding, see his *The New Rationalism* (1918), and for Marvin, *A First Book in Metaphysics* (1912).

[10] One of a notable group of expatriates, of whom Gilbert Murray and Grafton Elliot Smith are perhaps the best known. Alexander likes to insist that his metaphysics is

'democratic' in spirit; it is not absurd to suggest that his Australian origins had a certain effect upon his revolt against Absolutism in metaphysics. It so happens that Alexander's work has been important in the development of Australian philosophy; the school centred around John Anderson in the University of Sydney owes much to the naturalistic and realistic tendencies in his argument. Many of those who have been in close contact with Anderson's work—not only his pupils and disciples— regard it as the most systematic presentation of a Realist philosophy. But he published only a few highly compressed articles brought together (with an introduction by J. A. Passmore) as *Studies in Empirical Philosophy* (1962). See in *AJP* G. Ryle: 'Logic and Professor Anderson' (1950) and J. L. Mackie's reply (1951), together with J. L. Mackie: 'The Philosophy of John Anderson' (1962). For Australian philosophy generally see J. A. Passmore: 'Philosophy' in *The Pattern of Australian Culture* (ed. A. L. McLeod, 1963). The writings of J. L. Mackie, P. H. Partridge, T. A. Rose, A. R. Walker, A. J. Baker, J. B. Thornton, G. F. McIntosh, D. M. Armstrong, J. A. Passmore, reveal in varying degrees Anderson's influence, which extends also into political philosophy, aesthetics and jurisprudence. For Alexander generally, see P. Devaux: *Le Systeme d'Alexander* (1929); J. M. McCarthy: *The Naturalism of Samuel Alexander* (1948); obituary notices by J. Laird (*PBA*, 1938), J. H. Muirhead (*Phil.*, 1939), G. F. Stout (*Mind*, 1940), A. Boyce Gibson (*AJP*, 1938); articles by G. F. Stout on 'The Philosophy of S. Alexander' (*Mind*, 1940); H. B. Loughnan on 'The Empiricism of Dr. Alexander' (*AJP*, 1931) and 'Emergence and the Self' (*Monist*, 1936); John Laird's preface to Alexander's *Philosophical and Literary Pieces* (1939); A. P. Stiernotte: *God and Space-Time in the Philosophy of Alexander* (1954); B. T. Brettschneider: *The Philosophy of Samuel Alexander* (1964).

[11] See his 'Foundations and Sketch-Plan of a Conational Psychology' (*Br. Jnl. Psych.*, 1911). Alexander thought he had learnt his conational psychology from Stout. But Stout thought otherwise. See his 'A Criticism of Alexander's Theory of Mind and Knowledge' (*AJP*, 1944) and 'Professor Alexander's Theory of Sense-Perception' (*Mind*, 1922).

[12] See John Anderson: 'The Non-Existence of Consciousness' (*AJP*, 1929); C. J. Ducasse: 'Introspection, Mental Acts, and Sensa' (*Mind*, 1936).

[13] In, for example, his *Instinct and Experience* (1912). Although Lloyd Morgan and Alexander stood shoulder to shoulder on many issues, Lloyd Morgan was not a Realist. For a brief statement of his philosophical position see 'A Philosophy of Evolution' (*CBP*, I); his philosophical ideas are worked out at greater length in his Gifford Lectures, *Emergent Evolution* (1923) and *Life, Mind and Spirit* (1926).

[14] A doctrine of this sort, which has its roots in Aristotle, had been maintained by that unorthodox novelist and publicist, Samuel Butler, in such works as *Life and Habit* (1877), composed at a time when the new orthodoxy was Darwinism. It was adapted for his own special purposes by Bernard Shaw in *Man and Superman* (1903) and *Back to Methuselah* (1921). The best known philosophical version of vitalism is Bergson's *Creative Evolution* (1907) in which the 'life force' appears as 'élan vital'. The theory of 'entelechies', as presented by the philosopher-biologist Hans Driesch in his *Science and Philosophy of the Organism* (1908), is another variety of the same mode of thought. See also the statesman J. C. Smuts: *Holism and Evolution* (1936).

[15] At this point, Alexander stands very close to Dewey and to Marx—in the long run, that is, to Hegel. See P. H. Partridge: 'The Social Theory of Truth' (*AJP*, 1936).

[16] A doctrine similar in certain respects had been maintained by physicists like Minkowski and Einstein. But Alexander's theory of Space-Time was arrived at, he says, by independent metaphysical speculation; he is glad to have the support of physics but makes no direct use of physical theory. Nor does he wholly accept the new physical conceptions. Indeed, one can easily detect two different approaches to Space-Time in Alexander, one relativist, the other not. See especially A. E. Murphy: 'Alexander's Metaphysics of Space-Time' (*Monist*, 1927); articles on *Space, Time and Deity* by C. D. Broad (*Mind*, 1921) with Alexander's reply 'Some Explanations'; G. Dawes Hicks (*Hibbert Jnl.*, 1921); R. B. Haldane (*Nature*, 1920); D. Emmet: 'Time is the Mind of Space' (*Phil.*, 1950).

[17] See particularly Alexander's essay on 'The Historicity of Things' (in *Philosophy and History* ed. R. Klibansky and H. J. Paton, 1936). This is in many ways a very useful account of Alexander's metaphysics, less encumbered with complications than *Space, Time and Deity*.

[18] There are, however, different threads in Alexander's theory of relations, which this brief account conceals. For something more satisfactory, see Murphy's *Monist* articles.

[19] See Alexander's 'Natural Piety' (*Hibbert Jnl.*, 1922, reprinted in *Philosophical and Literary Pieces*, 1939).

[20] For a presentation of this view, see particularly 'Some Explanations', and for criticism see Broad and Murphy (*op. cit.*). If we cut a cube into slices, Alexander argues, the slices do not 'add themselves together' to a cube; they are not, as separate slices, obviously slices of a cube. In contrast, if we move around a cube and take perspectives of it these perspectives overlap—'one cries out for the next to complete it'. In the same way, spatiotemporal perspectives 'demand' Space-Time for their completion, as slices of simultaneous events would not.

[21] See W. S. Urquhart's obituary in *PBA*, 1946.

[22] Kemp Smith's first important contribution to scholarship, his *Studies in the Cartesian Philosophy* (1902), had

already played a considerable part in the development of realism by drawing attention to weak points in the Cartesian dualism. See A. C. Ewing: 'N. K. Smith' (*PBA*, 1959).

[23] See 'A Realist Philosophy of Life' in *CBP* II and, for a longer version, *Matter, Life, and Value* (1929).

Michael A. Weinstein (essay date 1984)

SOURCE: "Spirit and Nature: Alexander's Early Writings," in *Unity and Variety in the Philosophy of Samuel Alexander,* Purdue University Press, 1984, pp. 12-32.

[*In the following essay, Weinstein discusses the development of Alexander's philosophical system from Hegelian idealism in the 1880s to Darwinism and Naturalism in the 1890s.*]

> May it not be that the inability of philosophy to understand the great body of facts familiar to us as variety, modification, multiplicity, accident, is not due to the weakness of nature, but suggests a problem for philosophy itself. (1886)
>
> The real answer to Hume is given by Darwinism. (1892)

Samuel Alexander's first approach to the problem of unity and variety was from the perspective of absolute or objective idealism. In his middle twenties, as Atkinson Lee reports, when late Victorian culture was reaching its florescence, Alexander "became immersed in the Neo-Hegelian philosophy."[1] Lee observes that it was to Alexander that "Mark Pattison gave the famous advice to go and steep himself in Hegel's philosophy, and then to forget all about it." Though Alexander claimed to have taken Pattison's advice and though he became an avowed naturalist in his early thirties, objective idealism exercised a deep, lasting, and, indeed, decisive influence on his thought.

From Hegel to Darwin

Alexander's encounter with idealism in the 1880s was neither superficial nor was it guided by a merely technical interest. John Laird, Alexander's literary executor and fellow realist, notes that Alexander's first paper, **"Fingerposts to Religion,"** which was delivered at Oxford in 1885, was securely within the idealist paradigm.[2] In **"Fingerposts"** Alexander enunciated the ideal of a fully meaningful cosmos. In no other writing than this initial one was he so confident an idealist, so willing to make unity the melody and variety the counterpoint. Considering the way in which moral experience suggests religious belief, Alexander expressed a vision of perfection recalling Josiah Royce's voluntaristic idealism. According to Alexander, from reflections on moral experience "we go on to think of the whole world as completely used up for practical ends, no out of the way corner left which is not intelligible and turned into conduct, and we

think of such an ideal of conduct, to which we strive to approximate and which, because it is the fulfilment of what we ought to be, draws us towards itself by a natural affection."[3]

All of the central themes of the last phase of nineteenth-century idealism are present in Alexander's description of the perfected world. Most importantly, the ideal is defined practically, in terms of conation and conduct. The world is conceived by him to be a perfect act in which no detail is indifferent to the fulfillment of the total purpose. Even after Alexander broke with idealism and became a leader of the British realists, he consistently accorded a primacy to conation over affection and cognition, preserving his adherence, though in successively altered forms, to the notion of a cosmos used up by conduct. Alexander's description of perfection also includes the theme of intelligibility. In the perfect act there is no confusion, no gratuitous variety, no separation of form from content. Each thing holds its essential place as a necessary contributor to the self-existence of the whole: each thing has an inalienable meaning as an integral participant in the totality. Following from the ideal of intelligible conduct is its spontaneous attraction for the finite will, which, when directed morally, makes explicit the implicit truth of unity with the cosmos within it.

Alexander's description of perfection shows the majesty of late Victorian idealism, a grandeur that has been lost altogether to twentieth-century thought. The idealism imbibed by Alexander held out the vision, originating in classical Greek philosophy, of a moralized cosmos. Georg Wilhelm Friedrich Hegel's approach to making the world a home for the human spirit, which was picked up by Alexander's more immediate influence T. H. Green, was more thoroughgoing than that of Plato and Aristotle. Hegelianism did not allow any separation of matter and form: there could be no obscurity in the world; nature had to yield effortlessly to the claims of spirit. Though finite spirit might suffer frustration and doubt, reason assured that the whole was meaningful. The great difficulty of Hegelianism, which was exposed in its many forms by the critics of idealism, was just the fault line that it opened up between the finite and the absolute spirits. Even if it might be shown in general that the real is rational, nature appeared accidental and history a slaughter bench to the finite mind. The grandeur of the absolute dazzled, but when the finite spirit blinked it might discover itself to be unhappy consciousness.

At some time in 1885, Alexander blinked and began having doubts about idealism, or, perhaps, he had never been so thoroughly dazzled. In that year he wrote two reviews for *Mind* that encapsulate his difficulties with idealism. Alexander's struggle with Hegelianism resembles those of Soren Kierkegaard, Karl Marx, and John Dewey, all of whom were so deeply challenged by absolute idealism that they thought it through to profound and original commitments. For Alexander the doubts about idealism were connected to the problem of transiting from the unity of the Hegelian idea to the variety of apparent nature. In a review of O. Pfleiderer's *Religionsphilosophie,* Alexander raised the question of unity and variety in terms of internal and external relations. Pfleiderer held that God's will is immediate and internal, and that it is "transformed into the mutual interactions of the bodies we know in the world" in a manner analogous to the way in which a general's will is translated into the movements of his army. Alexander did not find Pfleiderer's analogy to be enlightening and remarked that he could not understand how the idea of the transformation of God's will into actual events could be "anything more than a mere re-statement of the fundamental difficulty."[4] Yet Alexander was decidedly not ready to break with idealism over its "fundamental difficulty," because he added immediately that Pfleiderer's view was "fruitful" because it postulated "the rationality of the world in God, without which indeed faith and grace would be unmeaning terms." Alexander, then, was caught in 1885 between awareness of the "fundamental difficulty" of absolute idealism and what he would call in his next review its "central truth:" he could not make intelligible for himself the diversity of nature, but he was unwilling to deny the rationality of the world.

Alexander eventually resolved the tension evident in his review of Pfleiderer by rejecting absolutism, but until at least 1889 his work evinced that special form of unhappy consciousness which is engendered by the disillusionment with idealism. Hegel's work was in great part an effort to overcome the unhappy consciousness which results from the resistance of experienced nature to the spirit's demand for a meaningful world. It is one of the ironies of the history of philosophy and of the spirit itself that Hegel's thought was the major gateway to the unhappy consciousness for such figures as Kierkegaard, Miguel de Unamuno, and Jean-Paul Sartre. By making the unhappy consciousness the obstacle that he had to surmount on his ascent to theodicy, Hegel also made it the climax of the journey for those who could not or would not follow him. What was meant to be a way station became very easily a terminal, unless one could find a new direction in which to proceed. Alexander found such a new direction in the 1890s, but in the 1880s he approached positions later to be identified with existentialism.

Alexander's doubts further blossomed and his unhappy consciousness became more manifest in his review of Royce's *The Religious Aspect of Philosophy.* It has been noted already that Alexander was attracted most strongly by the voluntaristic strand of idealism, of which Royce was one of the most prominent expositors. Central to voluntaristic idealism was the notion of the cosmos as a moral entity, the fulfillment of a rational will. Yet in his engagement with Royce, Alexander found his greatest difficulty to be in squaring the vision of the moralized cosmos with the experience of nature for finite minds. Royce had argued that moral progress occurred through the gradual spiritualization of physical fact. Alexander responded that Royce's account of progress brought him "face to face" with the unresolved problem: "What then

is this nature, these physical facts; and how can God appear in the form of nature?"[5]

The heart of Alexander's review of Royce's first major work is an effort to formulate the fundamental difficulty of idealism satisfactorily. Alexander insists that the problem of how God can appear in the form of nature is not that of accounting for why God should have made the world. Remaining within the idealistic paradigm, Alexander could not make the world itself or even its rationality a problem, but could only query how that rationality is demonstrated in nature. Thus, he seeks to discover the implications of there being "a world of nature as opposed to spirit" and to find out how spirit can "so divest itself of its spirituality as to appear as nature." Yet Alexander does not follow his own guidelines and ends up asking what he had called the "unphilosophical" question: "What need is there for the Infinite thought so to reproduce itself in our finite thoughts as to appear in part unspiritual?"[6]

The difference between the questions of how spirit can divest itself of its spirituality so to appear as nature and why the idea should be reproduced in finite thoughts so to appear as in part unspiritual illuminates the line dividing a doubting within idealism and a doubting of it. To ask how spirit can appear as a partly unspiritual nature (a nature that does not appear to be completely used up for practical ends) is to require a more intelligible explanation than has been given of a process that has been presupposed: it is to raise the question of theodicy along Hegelian lines. To ask why the idea is reproduced in finite mind so as to appear in part unspiritual is to go along the path toward, though not to reach, what Albert Camus called "the absurd:" it is to counterpose finite spirit's demand for unity with nature to nature's apparent lack of response, and to demand, as Job did, satisfaction from God. Alexander approaches Camus's formulation of the problem of meaning, though he formally keeps within the idealist frame of reference, when he asks: "How can reality being present as it surely is, in the Infinite mind, yet be unlike our consciousness?"[7] The disparity, difference, or diversity of finite spirit and experienced nature was Alexander's entry way into unhappy consciousness, his way of raising the problem of evil. For the finite spirit, nature shows many aspects, such as pain, accidentality, superfluity, confusion, and conflict, which make nature appear to be unfriendly and alien to spirit. Once reject the belief in an "Infinite mind" and the opposition between nature and finite spirit becomes the starting point for thought rather than an incident in thought's development. Alexander did not make the move to the absurd in his review of Royce's work, but praised Royce because "the central truth of idealism is so easy to forget that we cannot be too grateful to anybody who reminds us of it in a way that puts it in fresh lights and connections."[8] Yet he also concluded that the problem of nature's apparent unspirituality for finite spirit was "the question which it will be the immediate business of philosophy to answer."

The Engagement with Hegel

Alexander's earliest philosophical writings were but preliminaries to his first major and sustained endeavor, **"Hegel's Conception of Nature,"** a commentary and criticism published in *Mind* in 1886. The Hegel essay is a remarkable work, not only because it brings to mature reflection the results of Alexander's encounter with idealism, but because it exposes the Hegelian roots of some of Alexander's most important later metaphysical ideas, particularly that of space-time as the "stuff" of being. In his characteristic self-effacing manner, Alexander declared that his purposes in the essay were "to give only a sketch of Hegel's general position as a philosopher of nature," to "represent Hegel's view of nature as simply as I can," and to "point out some of his merits and defects." The modesty of Alexander's declaration of intentions is in sharp contrast to the significance of his essay as a criticism of idealism and as a groundwork for his future thinking. The Hegel essay also shows that far from steeping himself in Hegel's philosophy and then forgetting all about it, Alexander was haunted by Hegel's thought and made a most strenuous effort to make it his own.

Alexander begins his discussion by noting that the *Philosophy of Nature* is "the most perplexing of Hegel's works" and that it is "nearly always mentioned with an apology," because it is "so fantastic and so poetical that it may often be thought not to be serious."[9] Most generally, the *Philosophy of Nature* is Hegel's attempt to reconceive the findings of the natural sciences so that the reflective experience of nature will be intelligible as a mediation between the science of logic and the science of the spirit. Nature, then, is connected with the logical idea and with the idea of spirit. With respect to the idea, "Nature is the self-liberation or the self-alienation, or the otherness, of the Idea;" whereas with regard to spirit, "Nature is that which is transcended so as to become Spirit."[10] From the preceding discussion of Alexander's 1885 writings, it is clear that he would have the greatest trouble with the transition from the idea to nature, and this, indeed, is at first the case. He states early in the commentary that the transition from idea to nature "is very obscure, and perhaps impossible," but, consistent with his approach of constructive criticism, he tries to make as much sense of it as he can.

The central difficulty of connecting nature with the idea is determining what it means for nature to be the "otherness" of the idea. As Alexander points out, "nature in the form of otherness" may mean "simply nature as other than the Idea," or it may mean "the Idea itself displaying otherness."[11] Alexander observes that the latter interpretation surely expresses "Hegel's real intention," but that the former accounts for "something of the satisfaction we experience in reading Hegel,—that though nature is transparent to the Idea it is different from it." But it is just this "ambiguity of nature in the form of otherness" which makes the transition from idea to nature "obscure" and "perhaps impossible." If nature is but the idea displaying otherness, as it must be for Hegel if reality is

unified, then that otherness can be nothing but the idea of otherness. Yet if nature is other than the idea, then its connection to the idea cannot be made intelligible; there can be no continuity between it and the idea. That the ambiguity of nature is built into Hegel's natural philosophy is shown by Alexander in his account of the logical character of nature. As the otherness of the idea, "of that which is always one and single and self-contained," nature is "the other as such, or it contains in itself the principle of otherness." It is just at this point that the problem of unity and variety becomes most acute in Hegel's philosophy. In order for nature to contain in itself "the principle of otherness," it "falls apart into a multitude of isolated parts or characters, all external to each other."[12] Alexander finds, then, that despite the requirements of his system Hegel must interpret nature as being different from the idea and not merely as the idea itself displaying otherness.

The fragmentation of nature into isolated parts, which will reappear in Alexander's metaphysics thirty years later as the breakup of space-time into finite complexes, introduces an ominous mystery into Hegel's thought. Nature, for Hegel, is, in "its first or immediate form," space, "the very abstract idea of self-externality, in which every part is indifferent to every other." The indifference of space when considered abstractly, its reduction to a mere blank, plays an important part in Alexander's later thinking, but in 1886 it is a springboard to the reflection that nature is constituted by the opposites of accidentality and necessity: "It is accidental because of the indifference of its parts; it is subject to necessity because in their indifference they are yet constrained within the unity of nature as a whole."[13] The constitution of nature through the opposition of accidentality and necessity means that nature is not altogether intelligible on its own terms. The natural sciences may group events under abstract laws, but the concreteness of the events is not exhausted by the statement or application of the laws.

The accidentality or indifference of nature, then, is "of its essence," and is exhibited to finite mind in "the wild confusion" of forms. Here Alexander comes close to describing the experience that Sartre named "nausea." For Alexander's Hegel, though nature is "transparent to Spirit," it is to finite mind "like a magic beryl, full of wild, fantastic shapes: it is a 'Bacchantic god:' it cannot preserve the outlines and limits of ideas and types, but in its profusion of forms, and in the monstrosities of organic life, it varies from them indefinitely."[14] The ominous mystery of nature is its inability to keep within its types. Alexander remarks that the unity "which we so much admire in nature" is regarded by Hegel not as its strength, but "as its weakness (*Ohnmacht*), its inadequacy." In one of the last essays he wrote, the 1936 **"Historicity of Things,"** Alexander returned to the theme of the weakness of nature, defending nature against Hegel's depreciation of it. Much of Alexander's work can be understood as a transvaluation of Hegel's judgment on the relative dignity of nature and spirit. It was, perhaps, the project of defending nature which saved Alexander from sinking into Sartre's viscous morass. In 1886, however, Alexander claims that Hegel's reluctance to admire "mere variety or multiplicity" evinces "the true instinct of the philosopher."

Hegel, according to Alexander, "sought relief from the broken lights of the Idea in the self-sufficiency of the Idea itself; the starry heavens bored him."[15] Otherness, though it was "Nature's law," was also nature's "primal vice or defect, out of which arose its effort to become what it implicitly is, Spirit." The revulsion against the "wild confusion" of nature, against the indifference of things to one another, and against the unintelligibility of things to the mind by virtue of their indefinite variation from form was brought within bounds for Hegel because he could turn his attention from the vitreous beryl to the diaphanous perfection of the idea. The essence of the Hegelian project, for Alexander, was the recovery from nature of the idea made manifest as spirit. Nature would have to show the imprint of the idea and the indefinite variation from type be revealed as the appearance of an intelligible reality. But the success of Hegel's project depended on a smooth transition from the idea to nature. One who could not make sense of such a transition might at last conclude that the idea was otiose and thus be left with no refuge from the "broken lights," which would no longer be diffracted from a single ray, but would just be themselves. Were the idea to be declared otiose, the problem would not be to find a reason why the idea transited to nature, but to determine why certain parts of nature (idealist philosophers) should have conceived of the idea and accorded it such importance.

Nausea, the specific revulsion against the weakness of nature, is the state of the finite spirit encountering the gratuitous excess of content over form. It evinces the frustration of spirit's aspiration to a meaningful unity of itself and what initially appears to be other to it. Whether or not Alexander experienced Sartrian nausea in its depths during his middle twenties, he described precisely the formal conditions for its emergence. His Hegel essay shows a suspension of judgment on the Hegelian system combined with a tendency to acknowledge the priority of variety over unity or at least their parity. Only in the 1890s would Alexander turn the tables on idealism and attempt to give a naturalistic account of finite spirit and its pretensions. In 1886 he is tentative, unwilling to bar the way to the refuge of objective idealism, but increasingly dualistic. The dualistic moment of thought, which brackets off the finite mind's experience of nature from any connection with the logical idea and the idea of spirit, is the starting point for a phenomenology of the finite spirit. The "wild confusion" of nature's forms and the difference of spirit aspiring to meaning from the failure of things to hold a place in any design are the first deliverances of such a phenomenology. In his Hegel essay Alexander provides the critical basis for a phenomenology of finite spirit, but does not develop one. In the second great period of his intellectual career, during the first decade of the twentieth century, he takes up the project of providing a dualistic account of mind and material, and follows it through, as one of his major endeavors, until the end of his life.

The degree to which Alexander in 1886 had advanced beyond a mere internal criticism of Hegel to a reformation of the fundamental problem of natural philosophy is shown by his specific criticisms of idealism. Recurring to the questions raised in his earlier reviews, Alexander asks: "What is implied in the notion of nature, and what is its connection with the divine idea?"[16] He notes that Hegel's solution of "the ultimate problem" is "plainly insufficient": "the transition is unclear from the Idea to nature." But now Alexander moves beyond the doubts of his reviews towards a new question. Having noted "the ambiguity of nature in the form of otherness," he cites as Hegel's "chief defect" the "failure to explain the variety of nature."[17] He argues that the self-externality of nature is a ground for inferring nature's "falling asunder" into apparently independent individuals, but not for the variation of these individuals from the "common type." Alexander speculates that Hegel would reply that "the confusion is of the essence of nature, and that philosophy has done its work when it has explained the existence of variety in general, and it is not called upon to deduce any individual thing, like the 'pen of Herr Krug'." Hegel's hypothesized response, however, does not satisfy Alexander because he does not believe that confusion (variation from type) can be inferred from mere self-externality. Hegel, comments Alexander, admits that "nature in her wildest freaks surprises us with a glimpse of the Notion," but he does not explain the "fact" of "this intermingling of notional and accidental."

Alexander concludes his criticism with the question which will guide all of his future thinking: "May it not be that the inability of philosophy to understand the great body of facts familiar to us as variety, modification, multiplicity, accident, is not due to the weakness of nature, but suggests a problem for philosophy itself?"[18] Alexander's encounter with Hegel, then, results in the shift from unity of meaning to variety of appearance as the starting point for philosophy. Henceforth, for Alexander, variety must not be ignored or wished away in the name of unity: the integrity of the parts must be honored. Yet he does not reject the Hegelian way of thinking altogether and emphasizes that the "distinguishing feature and merit" of Hegel's system "lies in Hegel's sense of concreteness and totality, his habit of regarding things as a whole, according to the place they occupy in the system of nature."[19] The aspiration for totality of vision also stays with Alexander throughout his career. The aims of preserving the integrity of the part and of interpreting the part as the member of a whole provide the deep tension that impels Alexander to philosophize. The dialectic of the resistance of nature to spirit and the will of spirit to subdue nature is the leitmotiv of Alexander's thinking. The acknowledgment of variety will push him towards a dualistic interpretation of mind and nature, but the will to system will pull him towards a comprehensive naturalism.

The Hegel essay is not only important because it is the decisive document exposing the grounds for Alexander's break with idealism, but because it shows how heavily Alexander relied on Hegelian concepts in his future thinking. A good case can be made that Alexander's *magnum opus, Space, Time, and Deity,* reproduces, with several strategic alterations, the substance of Hegel's natural philosophy. The middle portions of the Hegel essay are devoted to a straight-forward exposition of the "divisions" of Hegel's philosophy of nature. Hegel interprets the divisions of nature in accordance with the "order of thinking," which sorts nature out into a series of stages from least to greatest spirituality. The "order of thinking" is not, as Alexander points out, coincident with the "order of experience," that of temporal development or evolution. Hegel attempts "to arrange natural facts according to their logical function in the economy of nature," to exhibit the recovery of spirit from nature. The three stages into which Hegel divides nature—mechanics, physics, and organics—parallel Alexander's later order of emergence from space-time through matter to life. Only Alexander collapses Hegel's order of thinking into an evolutionary order of temporal development and adds "mind" onto the series as a natural quality.

Most significant for Alexander's later work is his discussion of Hegel's treatment of mechanics. Alexander's boldest conception is generally acknowledged to be the idea that "space-time" is the primal "stuff" of reality, out of which emerge qualitied substances.[20] Yet in the Hegel essay Alexander notes that, for Hegel, "matter is not that which comes first in the logical order of mechanical nature," but that space and time, which "together are abstract self-externality," "involve each other and combine to produce Motion, the soul of the world, which precipitates matter in its process."[21] Motion, further, depends on the idea of "place," "a point of space fixed in time," or what Alexander later calls a "point-instant," the building block of finite substance. The most difficult of Alexander's later claims—that space and time are mutually dependent, that space-time precipitates matter, and that qualities are objective—are all aired, without criticism or affirmation, in the Hegel essay. The idea of space-time is neatly expressed when Alexander argues that "such phrases as 'a point of time,' or 'an hour's distance from here to there,' are testimony that space and time are inseparable."[22]

Alexander's fundamental metaphysical principles, then, are present in his reading of Hegel's natural philosophy, thirty years before they are expressed in *Space, Time, and Deity.* Perhaps Alexander did not remember Hegel's philosophy of nature when he wrote his own metaphysics, but he obviously absorbed Hegel's thought into the deepest recesses of his mind. His strategic alterations of Hegelianism were to transform space-time, which for Hegel was the most abstract form in which "the Idea appears as Nature," into the "stuff" of reality; to bracket nature off from the idea and the spirit, and to naturalize mind; and to collapse the order of thinking into the order of experience. What for Hegel was a "logical rearrangement of experience," made intelligible by the project of recovering spirit from nature, became for Alexander a description of the genesis of things including the mind. Alexander's later metaphysics is a liberation of Hegel's

nature from the idea and the spirit—what for Hegel is self-external and, therefore, unintelligible except when referred to the self-centered idea, is for Alexander the self-sufficient foundation of being. When Alexander later says that his aim is to "take time seriously," he means by time primarily self-externality: Alexandrian naturalism is Hegelian in form and content, which is, perhaps, why it relies little if at all on the findings of the special sciences, including Albert Einstein's relativity theory. In his 1886 essay Alexander admires Hegel for "his concreteness or totality of view, the philosophical counterpart of common sense," and for refusing to regard "experience from many different points of view, or in abstraction, like the special sciences."[23] Alexander, too, strove to perfect the philosophical counterpart of common sense and was aided definitively in this endeavor by Hegel's thought.

Hegel's influence percolated in Alexander's mind for thirty years, and during that period there was little direct evidence of it. In 1892 Alexander contributed to a symposium on the perception of time and argued that the validity of the Kantian forms of space and time can be grounded in "that process of natural selection which extirpates all minds incapable of thinking in these forms": "The real answer to Hume is given by Darwinism."[24] The initial response of Alexander to the unhappy consciousness released by his criticism of absolute idealism was Darwinian naturalism. The transition from Hegel to Charles Darwin is marked in Alexander's 1889 review of volume III of Green's collected works. In his encounter with Green, Alexander notes that absolute idealism is based on "the belief in a divine mind of which the human mind is a reproduction under finite conditions," but he no longer holds that the great question of philosophy is to account for the transition from divine to finite mind.[25] His attention is fixed, instead, on Green's thesis that there is a spiritual unity in the mind which "makes mind disparate with all other things" and, therefore, does not allow mind's emergence to be explained by the "theory of evolution."

Alexander does not refute Green's thesis, but casts doubt on it by suggesting alternatives. Admitting that "nobody would deny that the mind is a different thing from a stone or a plant," Alexander queries whether it may not be possible to show "the gradations between all these different kinds of things." The denial of the possibility of showing continuity, he claims, is "derived from the fact that the mind not only feels but knows that it feels; not only knows but knows that it knows—is conscious of its own modes of behaviour."[26] Alexander, then, acknowledges the difference of mentality from other modes of being, and even calls self-consciousness "a most remarkable fact." But he adds quickly that the occupation of mind with itself has "analogies" in "lower stages." For example, when we feel one of our hands with the other "the feeler is also the felt," or when we bite our lips "the organ of eating feeds upon a part of itself." These examples are flawed because they presuppose a self-referential organism for whom the hands feel one another or the teeth and lips function for digestion. Yet they satisfy

Alexander who concludes that these "facts" suggest that "the mystery, if it be a mystery, of self-consciousness, has already begun lower down." In the second great stage of Alexander's career, the problem of self-consciousness becomes one of his major concerns, and he maintains the positions set out in the Green review, arguing that consciousness is different from other things but analogous and sometimes—in apparent contradiction—identical to them. But in 1889 his hopes were pinned on Darwinism as a paradigm which would unify diversity and make such "remarkable" facts as mind and value a bit more commonplace by relating them to "lower stages" of nature.

Nature and Value

The bulk of Alexander's written production in the late 1880s and early 1890s was not in the field of natural philosophy, but in ethics and political philosophy. While he was encountering Hegel on the deepest issues of metaphysics, Alexander was also writing a systematic treatise, **Moral Order and Progress** (1889), which firmly established his reputation as a first-rank philosopher in the late 1880s. J. H. Muirhead comments that **Moral Order and Progress** "stands along with Green's *Prolegomena* and Bradley's *Ethical Studies* as the high-water mark of nineteenth-century Oxford thought" in the field of ethics.[27] John Laird notes that the work "developed what may be called the Anglo-Aristotelian-Hegelian movement in British ethics in the direction of a sophisticated ethical theory."[28] Laird adds that by 1912 "Alexander had altered his views so considerably that he wanted the book to die." An examination of the major positions defended in Alexander's early treatise shows that Laird's description is only partly correct. Alexander states at the outset of his discussion that the work unites "ideas borrowed from biology and the theory of Evolution, which are prevalent in modern ethics, with a training derived from Aristotle and Hegel, and I have found not antagonism, but, on the whole, fulfilment."[29] The treatise, then, is a transitional work, an effort by Alexander to reconcile the idealism of his teachers, particularly that of Green, to whom he acknowledges "great" obligations, and the naturalism towards which he was turning. **Moral Order and Progress** in an instructive work for understanding Alexander's intellectual development because its transitional character exposes clearly some of the continuities and permanent conflicts in his thought.

Alexander evidences throughout his career dominant interests in metaphysics and in axiology, which in his later work are mediated by epistemological realism. In **Moral Order and Progress** he defines the relations between metaphysics and axiology in a way which will guide his future thinking. Following Hegel's lead, he allots to metaphysics investigation of "the questions which are left over for it by the other sciences," particularly the relation of the different divisions of reality to one another. Metaphysics works on ground that has been "prepared" for it by the special sciences and its ideas "though first in the order of importance, are not first in the order of discovery."[30] What human beings initially discover are their relations to one another and their desires for objects, both of which provide the material for ethics, which reflects upon the organization of conduct. Here Alexander foreshadows his later idea that metaphysics studies the most pervasive characters of things and places the characters which are more conspicuous to humans, because they appeal to desire, into a wider context. One of Alexander's overriding projects is to criticize the kind of thinking that confuses the order of discovery with the order of importance, and to show that the values which emerge in human society are continuous with natural processes. His general aim, then, in axiological inquiry is to interpret what comes first in the "order of discovery" as the final stage of the development described in the "order of importance."

Alexander's early treatise is from beginning to end marked by an ambiguity reflecting the difficult project of conciliating Hegel and Darwin. At the outset of the work, he places ethics among the "normative sciences," which "apply a standard," in contrast to the natural sciences, which "deal with assertions."[31] He begins, then, on the idealistic side of the polarity. But almost immediately he states that his project is to show "to what facts" ethical conceptions correspond. Throughout the work Alexander vacillates between defining a criterion for moral judgment and setting up a sociology of morals which is identical in significant respects to Emile Durkheim's account of solidarity in *The Division of Labor in Society*.[32] Following Aristotle, "the most nearly allied of all ancient thinkers to that mode of thought which is characteristic of the present day," Alexander's criterion of goodness is harmonious "adjustment of parts in an orderly whole," or an "equilibrium of powers" within each individual and over society as a whole.[33] The ideal of coherent individuals composing a coherent society, which seems to be transcendent over any specific social situation and but a formal definition of moral perfection, is later interpreted by Alexander to mean the prescriptions involved in any specific "equilibrium" achieved by a society. The "distinction of good and bad," then, corresponds to the "domination" of a particular human type which has come to "prevail" because its representatives have defined the "social equilibrium" through successful adaptation.[34]

Alexander attempts to mediate between the absolutist and historicist conceptions of morality by arguing that "morality is identical or eternal in virtue of its form." Though the form of the moral law is "a matter of dispute," when it is regarded as "the equilibrium of social forces in an order of conduct, it is *ipso facto* eternal and identical, being true wherever its conditions are found."[35] But Alexander's proposed "solution" is not convincing because it does not resolve the ambiguity contained in the notion of an "equilibrium of social forces." The equilibrium may be the universal ideal of a society in which each member has a harmonious will, which in turn is spontaneously harmonized with the wills of all other members, or it may be the prescriptions for conduct which have become dominant in any specific society during any period as the result of the struggle among competing ideas of goodness. If it is the former, then Alexander provides a possible standard to ground ethics as a "normative science," whereas if it is the latter, then Alexander offers a broad hypothesis for a sociology of morals based on a reading of what the "facts" are to which ethical conceptions, such as goodness, correspond. He cannot have it both ways unless he holds, as he decidedly does not, that all social orders propagate the ideal of goodness as he initially defined it.

In his ethical writings of the 1890s, the idealistic component of Alexander's thought recedes from explicit expression and Darwinian themes become clearly dominant. Behind the Darwinian figure a dualistic ground is sketched in to take the place of the discarded idealism, but it is not overtly acknowledged. Darwinism is so important for Alexander in the wake of his criticism of idealism because it provides him with an explanation of why, despite wide variation among individuals, types become stabilized: through the struggle for survival those individuals best construed to adapt to their environment and to adapt their environment to their needs form stable and lasting types. A process of mutual adaptation of each part to the others becomes for Alexander in *Space, Time, and Deity* the basis for declaring the cosmos itself to be progressive. But in his 1889 treatise Alexander still felt the pull of idealism strongly and concluded his work by enunciating a personal ideal, which is the counterpart of his initial social ideal and which anticipates the concepts of such twentieth-century existentialists as Gabriel Marcel ("fidelity") and Antonio Caso ("charity").[36] The highest ethical conception, according to Alexander, is not duty, but "free service to an order of life," which "gives vent" to the individual's energies. Alexander goes so far as to claim that "morality only implies that, however wide or narrow the society, the service should be rendered freely."[37] But he adds, evincing the tension of his transitional period, that "free service to a whole which is in continual progress is nothing but the analogy of animal life pushed forward one stage further." Alexander believed for a moment that he had found "fulfilment" and not "antagonism" in the encounter between Hegel and Darwin, but soon he would try to subordinate the "one stage further" to the "nothing but."

Naturalistic Doctrine

Alexander's transition to Darwinism and naturalism was completed in the early 1890s when he wrote a series of articles and reviews, contributed to symposia, and presented public lectures, all with the purpose of defending and propagating the view that human value is most adequately interpreted as a natural phenomenon. Never again in his philosophical career would Alexander be so polemical, so willing to engage opponents directly in debate, and so apparently confident about his own positions. The change in Alexander's thinking can be marked by his altered judgment of Aristotle, to whom he had recurred in *Moral Order and Progress.* By 1893 Aristotle was no longer an "ally" whose thought was genuinely akin to evolutionism. Aristotle's ideas now

resembled "the evolutionist doctrine so much," because Aristotle was "philosophizing a merely customary system of morals, in which moral observances fit into their places like the parts of an organism."[38] The leading work of Alexander's period of adherence to a clear-cut evolutionary naturalism is **"The Idea of Value,"** published in *Mind* in 1892, in which he gave his first systematic statement of the axiological theory which would, though in successively less positivistic forms, dominate his succeeding work. Alexander remained, at least formally, a naturalist throughout the rest of his philosophical career, though increasingly the dualistic component of his thought asserted itself until, at the end of his life, the naturalism retreated to the ground and the dualism became the figure.

Axiology was not, for Alexander, at any time in his career, an inquiry to be separated off from the rest of philosophical investigation. Alexander pursued his general problem of adjusting unity and variety in the special field of value theory. Value itself, for Alexander, refers to the relations through which social equilibria are maintained in the realms of conduct (ethics), appreciation (aesthetics), and cognition (theory of truth). Varying individual ideas of what is good, what is beautiful, and what is true are compromised and conciliated in a social process of adjustment, the resultants of which are norms enforced by sanctions, particularly that of approbation. Variety, then, precedes unity in the sphere of values, at least analytically. Society is a process of unifying diverse elements, or what Leonard Hobhouse, who was Alexander's friend and fellow liberal, called "conational unity."[39]

The social definitions of the values may be understood as analogous to the "types" which so interested and perplexed Alexander in his 1886 discussion of Hegel. At least with regard to human values, Alexander turned the tables on Hegel, and instead of wondering why particular things do not hold to their types, he attempted to account for the genesis of types from initial variety and for the maintenance and evolution of types against the variation and dispersion of individual components. Here Alexander falls squarely within the line of European vitalist thought for which unity is an achievement, an overcoming of diversity, chaos, entropy, or death. The dialectic of order and chaos in Alfred North Whitehead's thought, that of Eros and Thanatos in Sigmund Freud's reflections, and that of "ascending" and "declining" directions of life in Friedrich Nietzsche's philosophy all find an echo in Alexander's theory that value is the achievement of solidarity against the continual appearance of difference.[40]

Not only, however, did Alexander define value through a process of social unification, but he also sought to reduce the diversity of value from other natural phenomena, to make social or human process continuous with natural and in particular with biological process. **"The Idea of Value"** shows clearly that even at his most polemical Alexander was unwilling to adopt behavioristic or mechanistic interpretations of human activity, though he often veered in the direction of collapsing mind into nature. Most generally his positive accounts of human phenomena keep up a tension between mind and nature, and his criticisms of idealism emphasize a monistic naturalism. There is, then, a descriptive or phenomenological and dialectical side to Alexander's thought, and a dogmatic or naturalistic side. The phenomenological side is receptive to variety and is satisfied with the most tenuous of unities, whereas the naturalistic side demands an overriding principle of unification to contain the breakout of diversity.

The fine balance required by Alexander to sustain productive thought and to give just expression to its different sides is defined in **"The Idea of Value."** Alexander notes "two great dangers to which the mind is liable in scientific and especially in philosophic inquiry." The first danger comes from "the spirit which overlooks the patent distinctions of things, and merges their individuality in one sweeping and vague generalisation," whereas the second danger arises from "the spirit which loves discontinuity, which imagines that the cousinship of the more highly and less highly developed forms reduces both to the same low level of development."[41] Alexander's capacity and power of mind are founded in the presence of both of these "spirits" in his thinking, but in 1892 he was far more disturbed by the pluralistic spirit than by the monistic one. Having warned of the two dangers, he adds that since the "gift for perceiving resemblances is the mainspring of all comprehensive thinking" the unifiers "may well be forgiven because they loved much." The pluralist spirit, in contrast, "often arises from an imperfect success in comprehending the whole of a subject at once, and hence it is often found combined with vague and unfruitful generalisation."[42] Alexander's opposition to pluralism on the grounds that it often is based on weakness of mind shows how far by the 1890s he had retreated from insight into the "wild confusion" of nature's forms which had impelled his break with Hegel in 1886. Alexander had become distant from immediate experience and would only return to it again in the next decade.

The emphasis of **"The Idea of Value"** is on moral ideals, and the other values, truth and beauty, to which Alexander in later stages of his career would give much greater attention, are mentioned only in passing. Alexander's naturalism is forthrightly stated in the claim that "ideals are nothing but the formulations of desires."[43] In *Moral Order and Progress* he had argued that the idea of the end to be attained by a voluntary action "is present not merely *in* consciousness, but *to* consciousness," though he also insisted that the difference of will from desire is merely one of complexity.[44] In the 1892 essay no such distinction is made and the ideal is but "an object which floats before the mind in idea before it is affected in reality."[45] Alexander's target in his naturalistic period is the doctrine that moral ideas "stand alone," in some way cut off from biological and social life. Like Dewey, who criticized idealism on many of the same grounds as Alexander did, and who reduced the doctrine of timeless ideals to a projection of the "quest for certainty,"[46]

Alexander argues that separating idea from nature deprives value "of its material character." Those who make such a separation, who "maintain that the distinction of fact and value is *ultimate,*" fall victim to the "confusion of the practically invaluable with the theoretically unique."

On the dogmatic side of his thinking, Alexander's great proposal for reform throughout his career is the separation of the order of fact from the order of value. In a contribution to an 1891 symposium on whether the distinction between "is" and "ought" is ultimate and irreducible, Alexander argues, in response to Muirhead, that to hold "the 'is' to be dependent on the 'ought' because this 'ought' represents the real nature of human action" is to commit "the error of confusing the order of fact, of nature which always proceeds by efficient causation, with the order of significance."[47] An ideal, according to Alexander, may be more "significant" than a fact, but "in so far as the ideal works, it works only as a fact—as an idea in the mind of the person who possesses the ideal." Those who interpret the practically invaluable as the theoretically unique succumb to what another naturalist whose thought parallels Alexander's, George Santayana, called a "pathetic fallacy"[48]: they project their wish for the permanence and primacy of goodness into the cosmos, engage in wishful thinking. In Alexander's naturalism a moral and prophetic program cannot be separated from a theory of the nature of things: the criticism of wishful thinking grounds an attitude of "natural piety" embracing the realms of both theory and practice.

The direction of Alexander's thought during his first period of philosophical production can be understood by examining his interpretation of the major orders into which human experience is organized. Immanuel Kant had introduced into philosophy at the turn of the nineteenth century a sharp distinction between the perspectives of empirical science and moral freedom, the first ruled by causal law and the second by universalized conscience. Much of nineteenth-century philosophy, particularly idealism and the varieties of naturalism, like Alexander's, which derived from critical responses to idealism, were guided by the aim of unifying the dualism bequeathed by Kant. The form of the dualism with which Alexander first worked was the Hegelian distinction between the orders of experience and of thinking. In his Hegel essay Alexander observes that Hegel's philosophy of nature "is so difficult just because it demands the effort of following the order of thinking instead of the order of experience."[49] Hegel, says Alexander in 1886, uses the order of thinking, which is that of intelligible and purposive order, "to understand the forms of nature as they really are apart from the ordinary prejudices with which we approach the study of them." Nature as it is described by the empirical sciences is, for objective idealism, unintelligible because it does not display finality or meaning. Under the principle that reality is rational, the order of experience, which is organized by the empirical sciences, is subordinated to the order of thinking, which arranges the "types" displayed in nature according to their nearness to and distance from spirit. Hegel, then, attempted to resolve the Kantian dualism by holding the empirical order relative to the moral order, the latter of which was interpreted as the self-recovery of the idea from nature in the form of spirit.

The 1889 transition work, *Moral Order and Progress,* shows Alexander's break with idealism. The order of thinking is now renamed the "order of discovery" and refers to the interests which are closest to the spontaneous practical life of human beings. In contrast to the order of human interest is that of importance, which refers to the hierarchy of natural dependence described by the empirical sciences and especially by evolutionary biology. Here Alexander's transvaluation or inversion of idealism appears: for Hegel human practical interests are indicative of the way things are, whereas for Alexander in 1889 such interests tend to distort the proper apprehension of reality. By 1893 the order of importance has been renamed the order of fact and the order of discovery that of significance. The inversion of idealism is complete: what is significant depends upon an organization of fact which itself is lacking in value, at least from the immediately human standpoint. Reduced to a formula Alexander's position is that values are dependent upon facts and are themselves particular sorts of facts, whereas facts are not dependent upon values.

Alexander's naturalism as much as Hegel's idealism is an effort to bridge the dualism between "fact" and "value." It is, indeed, an Hegelian naturalism which does not ignore or attempt to suppress value and significance, but endeavors to find a place for them within experience as the natural sciences describe it. Yet the Alexandrian inversion of Hegel's thought contains within itself a new unsought and, unfortunately, unexamined, dualism between what Henri Bergson called the "practical viewpoint"[50] and a contemplative or theoretical viewpoint of scientific or more generally of systematic thinking. In his naturalistic version of the articulation of orders, Alexander implies that not only are human beings initially mistaken about the meaning or relevance of certain details of their experience, but that the very structure in which they spontaneously organize the components of their experience is delusive, leading them to believe that what is more valuable or most significant to them is also what is most real, most efficacious, and most permanent in the cosmos. Human beings would seem to be victims of what may be called a practical illusion which keeps them from taking the scientific or naturalistic standpoint towards themselves and the world. A thorough-going naturalism would interpret, as Nietzsche's did, the practical illusion as instrumental to the survival of the species, thereby setting up a self-conscious dualism between the requirements of theory and those of practice. Alexander, who was a partisan of progress and enlightenment in the line of Marx and Dewey, did not think through the duality or inverse relation between significance and fact, but sought instead for analogues of human value in what he called the "lower" rungs of nature, thus tempering the sharp split between distinctive orders

of value and fact implied and sometimes made explicit in his naturalistic critique of idealism.

The differences between and similarities of Alexander's new naturalism and the transitional thought of *Moral Order and Progress* are most evident in his treatment of value. The 1889 treatise was marked by an equivocation between the interpretations of ethics as a normative science and as a social science, which was expressed substantively as a tension between the social ideal of a harmony among integrated individuals and the social process of competition and conciliation resulting in shifting equilibria. In the 1892 essay on **"The Idea of Value,"** Alexander makes a strenuous attempt to absorb the ideal dimension into the social process, but succeeds only in duplicating the earlier equivocation, though in an attenuated and more obscure form. Alexander's basic problem is that if ethics is in any sense a normative science which applies a standard, that standard is either historically relative or it is independent in some way of specific historical situations. If ethics merely applies whatever standard is regnant at a certain place and time, then ethics may indeed be made a branch of practical sociology, but it will function merely to elucidate the preferences of those groups which have become dominant. If, in contrast, ethics applies a standard that can criticize existing normative systems, that standard cannot be supplied by naturalistic sociology. In his works of the 1890s, Alexander seems often to assume that existing social equilibria accord as best as they possibly can with ideal requirements. His assumption of maximum harmony between ideal and actual cannot be falsified empirically and has the consequence of justifying any social arrangement that appears.

Alexander's effort to devise a thoroughgoing naturalism is shown by his abandonment in the 1892 essay of the social ideal of integral harmony and the personal ideal of free service, and by his resort to a technical and sociological principle that value is "the efficiency of an act towards furthering or producing the social equilibrium."[51] Initiating the same sort of thinking as did his French contemporary Durkheim, Alexander argues that his functional definition of value implies that "value depends on the distribution of work, the division of labor" required for the social equilibrium. A human being, then, is "valuable" by virtue of being "efficient" in promoting "the work of society," whereas society, "being itself the standard of value, has the title to be such because it promotes the efficiency of each individual—these two results, the equilibrium of the whole society and the efficiency of each person in it, being effected at the same moment."[52]

Alexander's sociological theory of value, though it differs in content from his earlier and more idealistic account and though it purports to "remove" ethics from "the domain of metaphysics" and to class it, as Auguste Comte did, "as the last or psychical class of the natural sciences," contains nonetheless an equivocation between the ideal and the actual. According to Alexander, society has the "title" to be the standard of value. It gains this "title" by promoting the efficiency of each individual. Alexander, then, seems to rest his case on the claim that all societies are justified and have the title to be the standard of value by virtue of promoting the efficiency of each individual. However, since he has no independent measure of efficiency, all Alexander's claim amounts to is that every social situation is justified by the mere fact that it exists. It might be argued persuasively that "the equilibrium of the whole society and the efficiency of each person in it"—Alexander's naturalized version of the Hegelian identity of individual vocation and social function—is at least a necessary condition for the survival of a society, providing that membership in the society may be defined through a process of conflict in which those who do not fit in are excluded, perhaps by coercion. Any system of norms would be judged to further the survival of the society if it contributed to efficient equilibrium, but only so long as efficient equilibrium could be defined independently of the mere existence of social situations. But it is not obvious that in any but a technical and sociological sense that value is "the efficiency of an act towards furthering or producing the social equilibrium." Only a technocrat, perhaps, would make efficient equilibrium the object of activity, make it a self-conscious standard guiding practice. The criterion of efficient equilibrium, even if it could be defined independently of social fact, would constitute, then, a rather narrow definition of value, appropriate, perhaps, only for a specialized judgment of how effectively social systems function.

Alexander acknowledges that "equilibrium" is "not the object of practice" in his contribution to the 1891 symposium on the relation of judgments of "is" and "ought." The "idea of equilibrium," he says, "is a theory." Human beings do not, "as a general rule, act for the sake of the equilibrium which is characteristic" of a moral standard, but act because "they desire certain objects."[53] Objects which are "imposed" by the existing moral standard are "approved," whereas "acts which modify the existing standard" can "only be approved by reference to the new standard of which the reformer has a forecast." The "imposition of good conduct," then, "is the most flagrant instance extant of the tyranny of the majority," which works by means of disapproval by "that exclusive society for mutual admiration called good men, against whom the miserable wicked have no defense."[54] Alexander, thus, attempts to avoid the difficulties of using social equilibrium as a moral standard by substituting for it the consensus of those who "have arrogated to themselves the title of right." Value now is what is approved by those who call themselves "good men" and who can make their claim stick by applying social pressure against those who do not agree with them.

Alexander's new sociological interpretation, however, is no more satisfactory than the first one. If ethics is a normative science applying a critical standard, then the claim that an act or an object is good does not necessarily mean that it is approved by a social consensus, but at best that it should be so approved, whether or not it actually is. Alexander's "reformers" would seem to be in the odd position of having to wait until their reforms were approved by the social consensus before they could commend those reforms as "good." Alexander's consensus theory of value is similar to Justice Holmes's principle that "the law is what the courts say it is." Holmes's principle does not provide a judge with any guidance in deciding a case, nor does Alexander's theory provide any criteria for moral decision. That Alexander glimpsed the weakness of his consensus theory of value is shown by his return to the standard of social equilibrium, now as a guide for practice, because it is useful in directing "our action wisely to those objects which have the characteristics which experience and reflection have convinced us are proper to any end ever proposed as moral."[55] Alexander, however, does not give an account of the characteristics which are "proper to any end ever proposed as moral." Such an account would be the basis for an ethics, for a theory of what goodness is, rather than for a theory of the social conditions and consequence of ethical judgment.

Alexander's naturalistic theory of value can be illuminated by showing its structural similarities to the Hegelian theory of history. For Hegel, history displays rationality from the observer's viewpoint, whereas for participants, historical reality is filled with conflict and discontinuity. Similarly, the standpoint of the sociological observer in Alexander's theory of value reveals that social action functions to secure efficiency, whereas for participants in a society, action may appear to be a struggle among groups favoring competing standards, each attempting to achieve a dominant consensus. Alexander does not make such a clear distinction between perspectives in his reflections on value, nor does he have Hegel's advantage of appeal to the ideal of rational freedom as a criterion uniting the participant's and the observer's standpoints. Alexander's theory stands a technical and sociological criterion alongside a social fact (assuming that societies display consensus), and connects the two by the implied proposition that consensus on moral norms is instrumental to efficient equilibrium which in turn is instrumental to the survival of societies. Survival, then, is the final indicator of what characteristics are valuable, though Alexander insists that the significant question is what factors secure survival, not the survival itself. If Alexander's early naturalistic theory is defective from a moral viewpoint, it is because he confuses some of the qualities requisite for the survival of societies with the requirements for the good life. Persistence of a society is, indeed, a necessary condition for its goodness and even an element in its goodness, but it is not the only condition and the only element, nor is it a reliable indicator of the other conditions and elements. The high point of Alexander's ethical thinking was reached in his description of the idea of free service in *Moral Order and Progress*. Once he adopted the naturalistic standpoint he lost contact with the end-in-itself, the *raison d'être* of ethical theory.

The two perspectives implied in Alexander's early value theory are made explicit in the spiritual vision which culminates his naturalistic period. In a public lecture delivered to the Ethical Societies of Cambridge and London in 1892 and published that year as **"Natural Selection in Morals,"** Alexander attempts to refute the idea that the evolutionary theory is "hostile to the idea of any comprehensive system or structure in the world's history."[56] Enunciating the cosmic vision that will sustain his future thought, Alexander visualizes "how from the lowest forms of organic life, and probably from inorganic life below that, up to the highest forms of organic life, and again in the minds of men, piece by piece is added to the fabric and the meaning of the universe, the highest forms being linked on to those below them, and thence to the very lowest, representing *in petto* the laborious acquisitions of centuries."[57] Those, according to Alexander, whose minds "dwell upon the process by which the world is built, dwell upon the strife by which the unappropriate variations of creatures are extirpated." But while the "work" of history is secured by struggle, "each stage in it is attached to the preceding by the closest of ties, and when the eye turns away from the struggle it dwells on the bond which binds the sons of time together."[58] Here Alexander expresses for the first time his fundamental attitude toward existence, recommending the cultivation of a "natural piety which links together the successive types." Perhaps reflecting on the resolution of his own crisis of disillusionment with idealism, Alexander declares that "the history of humanity is like a life which a man should spend in a continual prayer of thanksgiving, the outpouring of ecstasy purchased at the price of inward conflict."[59]

Alexander's vision places him within the tradition which he would later define as that of the great Jewish mystics, including Baruch Spinoza and Bergson. It also approaches Martin Heidegger's idea of a "thinking which should be a thanking."[60] When Alexander's eye turns away from the struggles, variety, and discontinuities of immediate existence, it returns to gaze on the Hegelian series of types, ranged impeccably in the order of thinking. That vision of types transfigures naturalism and positivism, and provides, perhaps, the explanation for why Alexander was so untroubled by the moral implications of Darwinism. His naturalism, after all, was Hegelian, his thought fixed by his 1886 encounter with Hegel, and his vision a counterpart of the experience of a nature which cannot hold in place its types. . . .

NOTES

[1] Atkinson Lee, "Samuel Alexander," *The London Quarterly and Holborn Review*, 166 (October, 1941), p. 414.

[2] John Laird, "Samuel Alexander's Theism," *The Hibbert Journal*, XL (1941-42), p. 147.

[3] Ibid.

[4] Samuel Alexander, "Review of O. Pfleiderer, *Religionsphilosophie*," *Mind*, X (O.S.) (April, 1885), p. 286.

[5] Samuel Alexander, "Review of J. Royce, *The Religious Aspect of Philosophy*," *Mind*, X (O.S.) (October, 1885), p. 604.

[6] Ibid.

[7] Ibid.

[8] Ibid., p. 605.

[9] Samuel Alexander, "Hegel's Conception of Nature," *Mind*, XI (O.S.) (October, 1886), p. 495.

[10] Ibid., p. 498.

[11] Ibid., p. 516.

[12] Ibid., p. 500.

[13] Ibid.

[14] Ibid., p. 501.

[15] Ibid.

[16] Ibid., p. 516.

[17] Ibid.

[18] Ibid., p. 517.

[19] Ibid., p. 510.

[20] See for example, Michele Federico Sciacca, *Philosophical Trends in the Contemporary World* (South Bend, Ind.: University of Notre Dame Press, 1964), pp. 410-15.

[21] Alexander, *Mind*, XI (O.S.), p. 503.

[22] Ibid., p. 507.

[23] Ibid., p. 510.

[24] Samuel Alexander, "Has the Perception of Time an Origin in Thought?" *Proceedings of the Aristotelian Society*, II (O.S.) (1892-93), p. 53.

[25] Samuel Alexander, "Review of R. L. Nettleship (ed.), *Works of T. H. Green; Vol. III*," *The Academy*, 887 (N.S.) (May 4, 1889), p. 298.

[26] Ibid.

[27] J. H. Muirhead, "Samuel Alexander," *Philosophy*, XIV (January, 1939), p. 6.

[28] John Laird, "Memoir," in Samuel Alexander, *Philosophical and Literary Pieces* (John Laird, ed.) (London: Macmillan, 1939), p. 20.

[29] Samuel Alexander, *Moral Order and Progress: An Analysis of Ethical Conceptions* (London: Kegan Paul, Trench, Trubner, 1899), p. viii.

[30] Ibid., p. 78.

[31] Ibid., p. 1.

[32] Emile Durkheim, *The Division of Labor in Society* (Glencoe, Ill.: Free Press, 1947).

[33] Alexander, *Moral Order*, p. 18.

[34] Ibid., p. 306.

[35] Ibid., p. 295.

[36] For a discussion of Marcel on fidelity and freedom, see Thomas J. M. Van Ewijk, *Gabriel Marcel: An Introduction* (Glen Rock, N. J.: Deus Books, 1965). For a discussion of Caso on charity and freedom, see Michael Weinstein and Deena Weinstein, "The Ethics of Charity: Antonio Caso's Defense of Civilization," *Canadian Journal of Political and Social Theory*, IV, 3 (1980), pp. 69-82.

[37] Alexander, *Moral Order*, p. 410.

[38] Samuel Alexander, "Review of J. E. C. Welldon (tr.), *The Nicomachean Ethics of Aristotle*–and J. A. Stewart, *Notes on the Nicomachean Ethics of Aristotle*," *International Journal of Ethics*, IV (October, 1893), p. 125.

[39] Hobhouse's theory of the nature of society is most fully expressed in his *Social Development: Its Nature and Conditions* (New York: Henry Holt, 1924).

[40] See Sigmund Freud, *Civilization and its Discontents* (New York: W. W. Norton, 1962); Friederich Nietzsche, *Thus Spake Zarathustra* (Baltimore: Penguin, 1961); Alfred North Whitehead, *Process and Reality* (New York: Free Press, 1969).

[41] Samuel Alexander, "The Idea of Value," *Mind*, I (N.S.) (January, 1892), p. 36.

[42] Ibid.

[43] Ibid., p. 37.

[44] Alexander, *Moral Order*, p. 20.

[45] Alexander, *Mind*, I (N.S.), p. 38.

[46] John Dewey, *The Quest for Certainty* (New York: G. P. Putnam's Sons, 1929).

[47] Samuel Alexander, "Is the Distinction between 'Is' and 'Ought' Ultimate or Irreducible?" *Proceedings of the Aristotelian Society*, II (O.S.) (1891-92), p. 107.

[48] Santayana's similarities to Alexander are shown best in his *Reason in Common Sense* (New York: Collier Books, 1962), p. 21.

[49] Alexander, *Mind*, XI (O.S.), p. 510.

[50] Bergson discusses "the practical viewpoint" in his "The Perception of Change," in Henri Bergson, *The Creative Mind* (New York: Philosophical Library, 1946), p. 138.

[51] Alexander, *Mind*, I (N.S.), p. 55.

[52] Ibid.

[53] Alexander, *Proceedings of the Aristotelian Society*, II (O.S.), p. 104.

[54] Ibid., pp. 102-3.

[55] Ibid., p. 104.

[56] Samuel Alexander, "Natural Selection in Morals," *International Journal of Ethics*, II (July, 1892), p. 437.

[57] Ibid., pp. 437-38.

[58] Ibid., p. 438.

[59] Ibid., p. 439.

[60] See Martin Heidegger, "What is Metaphysics?" in Heidegger, *Existence and Being* (Chicago: Henry Regnery, 1949), p. 353.

FURTHER READING

Criticism

Brettschneider, Bertram D. *The Philosophy of Samuel Alexander: Idealism in "Space, Time and Deity."* New York: Humanities Press, 1964, 177 p.
    Extended examination of Alexander's philosophical system. Brettschneider devotes chapters to such topics as Alexander's concept and categories of Space-Time, his doctrine of emergent evolution, his theory of mind, and the systematic implications of his concepts of value, God, and deity.

Burtt, Edwin, A. "Some Individual Philosophies and Current Trends." In his *Types of Religious Philosophy*, pp. 409-48. New York: Harper & Brothers, 1939.
    Concise explication of Alexander's religious views and their relation to his thought as a whole.

Konvitz, Milton R. *On the Nature of Value: The Philosophy of Samuel Alexander.* Morningside Heights,

N.Y.: King's Crown Press, 1946, 119 p.
  Analyzes Alexander's writings on the nature of value within the context of the history of philosophy.

Lee, Atkinson. "Samuel Alexander." *London Quarterly and Holborn Review* CLXVI, sixth series, Vol. X (1941): 412-18.
  Appreciative memoir written by a former student. Lee sketches the main tenets of Alexander's philosophy and concludes that together with Conwy Lloyd Morgan and James Ward, Alexander "did most in this country to clear the way for the discussion, which is now proceeding, between science and philosophy, as to the meaning of evolution."

Maurer, Armand A. "Philosophy of Evolution." In *Recent Philosophy: Hegel to the Present,* edited by Etienne Gilson, Thomas Langan, and Armand A. Maurer, pp. 433-50. New York: Random House, 1962.
  Includes Alexander and Conwy Lloyd Morgan in a discussion of emergent evolutionary theorists in English philosophy. According to Maurer: "There is a certain romantic and poetic force in Alexander's conception of the universe and God, but its bold and fanciful speculation is far from convincing."

McCarthy, John W. *The Naturalism of Samuel Alexander.* New York: King's Crown Press, 1948, 111 p.
  Attempts "to show that the naturalistic basis of Alexander's thought is patent in his metaphysics, in his discussion of truth, of goodness, of art, and of religion."

Stiernotte, Alfred P. *God and Space-Time: Deity in the Philosophy of Samuel Alexander.* New York: Philosophical Library, 1954, 455 p.
  Focuses on Alexander's religious views in an attempt to analyze the "intellectual problem which underlies all religion."

"From Space-Time to Godhead: The Philosophy of Samuel Alexander, Jewish Genius in Metaphysics." *Times Literary Supplement* (23 March 1940): 146, 152.
  Appreciative reflection on Alexander's thought and academic career.

Tully, R. E. "Emergence Revisited." In *Pragmatism and Purpose: Essays Presented to Thomas A. Goudge,* edited by L. W. Sumner, John G. Slater, and Fred Wilson, pp. 261-77. Toronto: University of Toronto Press, 1981.
  Demonstrates how Alexander and C. D. Broad "deployed evolutionary theory in order to argue some basic issues in the theory of knowledge."

Wickham, Harvey. "The Colossus: I. Professor Alexander." In his *The Unrealists: James, Bergson, Santayana, Einstein, Bertrand Russell, John Dewey, Alexander and Whitehead,* pp. 219-25. New York: Lincoln Mac Veagh and The Dial Press, 1930.
  Excerpts concise passages of *Space, Time and Deity.*

Mary Butts

1890-1937

(Full name Mary Francis Butts) English novelist and short-story writer.

INTRODUCTION

Forgotten for nearly half a century, Mary Butts enjoyed a literary resurrection during the 1990s. A very modern figure, Butts lived in a glamorous, often sordid milieu that encompassed black magic, drugs, and sexual experimentation. Her reputation rests on a relatively small output that includes five novels and three short story collections. The most notable of her works are her 1937 memoirs, *The Crystal Cabinet,* and the two Taverner novels, *Armed with Madness* (1928) and *Death of Felicity Taverner* (1932).

Biographical Information

Butts was raised on a large country estate in rural Dorset and enjoyed close contact with nature during her early years. The death of her father and the remarriage of her mother, however, permanently altered the fabric of her world. Sent to boarding school, she became an unhappy young woman, as she would later recount in *The Crystal Cabinet.* After graduating from St. Leonard's School in St. Andrews, Scotland, in 1906, Butts enrolled in Westfield College of London University. But her time there was not long: in a characteristic act of defiance, she went to a horse race with a young instructor—a breach of decorum in Edwardian England—and the resulting disgrace left her little choice but to depart the college. After a period when she worked for the London County Council and made the acquaintance of such literary figures as Ezra Pound, H. D., and Rebecca West, Butts drifted to Paris in the years after the First World War. She married and had a child with the poet John Rodker, but soon left her husband for the painter Cecil Maitland. The two became involved in the clique surrounding the Satanist Aleister Crowley, and Butts experimented with drugs and a variety of heterosexual and homosexual relationships. She published her first novel, *Ashe of Rings,* in 1926, but in 1930 suffered a nervous breakdown and returned to England. There she wrote several more books, including *The Crystal Cabinet,* during the 1930s. She married a painter and cartoonist, Gilbert Aitken, but this relationship did not last either, and they separated in 1934. Butts died of a burst appendix in 1937, when she was forty-seven years old.

Major Works

At the age of thirty-four Butts published her first novel, *Ashe of Rings*, which was influenced by the bizarre world

of witchcraft and drugs which she inhabited at the time. Beginning two years later and falling on either side of her nervous breakdown in 1930 came the two Taverner novels, *Armed with Madness* in 1928 and *Death of Felicity Taverner* in 1932. They are the story of Scylla Taverner, who spends her life in the company of homosexual men, and the volumes are packed with sexual intrigue and deception. In the year of her death, Butts published *The Crystal Cabinet*, a memoir of her life to the age of twenty-two. In the 1990s, with the resurgence of interest in her work, the Taverner novels were reissued along with several collections of short stories.

PRINCIPAL WORKS

Ashe of Rings (novel) 1925
Armed with Madness (novel) 1928
Imaginary Letters (novella) 1928

CRITICISM

Edwin Muir (essay date 1925)

SOURCE: A review of *Ashe of Rings*, in *The Calendar of Modern Letters*, March 1925-July 1927, Frank Cass & Co. Ltd., 1966, pp. 476-78.

[*In the following review, Muir finds* Ashe of Rings *inconsistent and overly conventional, although he concedes that Butts has the potential to be a talented writer.*]

Miss Butts is a short-story writer of ability; in *Ashe of Rings,* she essays the novel with much the same technique as she used for the short story. This raises the question of technique. A short digression is, therefore, necessary.

By technique is generally meant the various means which a writer uses to express his vision. As such it is in every period a collective as well as an individual thing; the expression on the one hand, of what people call the spirit of the age, and, on the other, of the personality of the writer. And as in the political realm, as indeed in human life generally, there is here, too, a conflict between the individual and the mass, between the *Zeit Geist* which, if it could, would make us impersonal and undistinguishable vehicles of its expression, and ourselves as individuals desiring absolute utterance for our personal visions. No absolute freedom of this kind exists, in literature or in life, as we know; and so the writer who tries to escape the spirit of the age (an attempt which must always be hopeless in any case) is likely to attain less freedom than the one who, recognising it, wrestles with it for the prize of his personality. For the spirit of the age is not only a thing which limits the writer's expression (though that it does so we can recognise when we look back even upon such a recent era as the 'nineties); it is also the thing which gives most immediately what life may reside in what he says. But that life, it almost appears, can only be tapped at its living source, as Mr. Joyce tapped it in *Ulysses,* when one has struggled against the spirit of the age; for in the struggle, the deceptions, superficialities and fashions of the age are stripped away until, if the

writer is fortunate or honest, the point is reached where the age and he come into immediate contact, not by a conscious act merely, but through a kind of final necessity. The writer who does not resist his age, defending himself against all its claims crowding in upon him and overwhelming him, will belong to the literature of fashion. The writer who refuses to realise his age is not likely to belong to literature at all. The apparent exceptions to this rule, such as Blake, are not exceptions at all; for no one was more painfully concerned with his age than Blake. This brief generalisation, which could only be supported in a much longer argument, I must leave for the moment as it is.

Ashe of Rings is a striking example of the literature of fashion. Its technique is not essentially personal, as is the technique of writers so various as Mr. Joyce, Mr. Strachey, and Mr. Eliot; it is a technique which might at different moments belong to almost anyone who writes in the idiom of the time. It is a generalised technique and, therefore, never quite fits the situation or the emotion it is enlisted to convey; and so the general effect is always a little false. For it is only a technique which a writer has gradually perfected, not as an exercise, but always for specific and concrete ends, which will render at last his specific vision. Miss Butts' vision, one feels, is sometimes individual; but it is as if she translated it continuously into something which has scarcely anything to do with her or with it. The fault is a common one, though seldom illustrated with such brilliance as in *Ashe of Rings*; its prevalence is what makes it interesting. It is the fault of a large class of writing in which the inspiration is seen by the writer as one thing and the literary effect as something totally different; the first being susceptible of transposition in quite an arbitrary way into the second. When this transposition takes place, the inspiration, which is personal, becomes mere raw material to be manufactured into effects resembling other effects of the time: the unconscious error here, a very elementary one, being that if this process does not happen, the result will belong neither to the age nor to literature. This perennial error is betrayed in bad writing of all kinds; in melodrama, the West-end comedies of our time, the novelette, journalism; but it infects sometimes work which in happier circumstances might have been good. When this occurs it can only be a sign that in a particular writer the spirit of the age is manifesting itself with hesitation, for no writer would take the trouble to secure the outward signs of the age in his work if the influence of the age were felt overpoweringly by him. Miss Butts has made the mistake of trying to express the age instead of herself, which means that the *Zeit Geist* is not immanent in her, and has to be treated as subject-matter rather than expressed as content.

All this being so, it is not surprising that the story itself should turn out to be as old-fashioned as the style is modern. Miss Butts' characters are not merely good and evil; they are conventionally good and melodramatically evil. She is consistently on the side of virtue, a policy good in itself, but artistically a bad policy, for it inevitably makes the good characters appear prigs; and she does not even try to comprehend evil, again a bad policy, for the more comprehensible evil is made the more interesting aesthetically it becomes, as we may learn from Shakespeare, as well as from Dostoevsky. All this is elementary, yet Miss Butts' imagination ignores it, even if her style does not. That she has talent both her technique and her imagination, sentimental as it often is, tell us. If that talent were integrated, it might produce something above the ordinary. But at present it is not integrated, and from that fact flow all the main faults of the book.

Clifton P. Fadiman (essay date 1926)

SOURCE: "Old and New," in *The Nation*, New York, Vol. 122, No. 3181, June 23, 1926, p. 701.

[*In the following review, Fadiman admits Butts's talent, but dismisses* Ashe of Rings *as a contrived and outdated romance.*]

One of the many discoveries we owe to English romanticism is the sentiment of place. Somehow it was revealed in the early 1800's that localities, like persons, have active and sensible souls. It is such an adumbration of locale that should have formed the backbone of this very arresting novel [*Ashe of Rings*] by a writer of indubitable talent. As a matter of fact, there are two backbones—and the result is that we are faced with a museum curiosity, not an integrated work of art.

The earlier and more powerful section of the book is devoted to an evocation of the estate of Rings in England. From the arrogant lips of Anthony Ashe, master of Rings, we learn the fragmentary tale of the magic memories, the medieval horrors, the incantations that lie coiled and potent in the stony Druid circles which give the place its name. Ancestral witches, crucified sorcerers, hieroglyphic volumes, subtle caretakers who feed like vampires on the family tradition—the whole paraphernalia is effective in its way, the more so because old Anthony is shadowy and gnomic and his little daughter Van is another Ariel. There is little solidity of flesh and bone to intrude and dispel the atmosphere of place. Here Miss Butts's touch is firm and sensitive. She achieves a sort of spiritualized Gothic romance which substitutes the cumulative force of eerie legend for Anne Radcliffe's trapdoors and sanguinary nuns. If you are at all susceptible to the *frisson* here is *un nouveau*. But Van grows up, is exiled from the holy and enchanted Rings of her spirit, starves in London, lives in a garret, engages in artistic conversation, loves an artist-nihilist, and acts for the movies. She takes on reality, lives a separate organic life which is but feebly linked to the magic on which her childhood was nurtured. The realistic novelist steps upon the stage. The latter part of the novel, in which Van returns to the home of her fathers, struggles with its enemies, finds a brother, and loses a lover, is sheer mechanism. One perceives the synthesis. The joints show. The book as a whole collapses.

It is not to be denied that some very high art accompanies this fatal clash of material. Miss Butts understands the pattern of words, she has fine insights, and there is a certain rigorousness in her style which makes one regret that it has been expended on what is, after all, to the contemporary habit of thought, a decadent literary convention. For when all is said and done, places cannot live for us today as they did for the excited imaginations of Scott and Poe. A platitude, but a valuable one: this is a psychological age. Mary Butts would do well to ponder on the convincing exposition of this thesis contained in Virginia Woolf's essay, "Mr. Bennett and Mrs. Brown." Character is fate, it has been said. Certainly it seems to be the fate of the modern novel.

To an American particularly there is one other important element in the book which seems anachronistic. We can no longer be moved by the mystic tradition of family. The fungoidal mania that forces the Ashes to live as much and as deeply in the memory of their ancestors as in the consciousness of themselves hardly convinces us. The whole carefully built-up system seems rickety and unsubstantial. One remembers the devastating absurdity of that sentence in Donald Ogden Stewart's *The Crazy Fool*: "'We were Southerners—and proud . . . ,' he added simply."

The New York Times Book Review (essay date 1928)

SOURCE: "Sophisticated Fantasy," in *The New York Times Book Review*, May 13, 1928, pp. 9-17.

[*In the following review, the anonymous critic calls* Armed with Madness "*a sophisticated and most exquisitely written fantasy.*"]

When two or three years ago Mary Butts published a first novel called *Ashe of Rings* the few who read it were at once excited by its talents and puzzled by its contents; for here was a truly strange, a memorably strange feat of imagination which failed somehow to make sense. There was much beauty in the writing; there was much eeriness about the atmosphere; there was individuality to the characters. But what was the theme of the book (if, indeed, it had one) or on what milk these people had been suckled or of what past crimes the estate of Rings was guilty, no one could tell.

Now Miss Butts has published her second novel and called it *Armed with Madness*—a more explanatory title than *Ashe of Rings*. For it is very much the same kind of book, and one feels relieved to find Miss Butts herself admitting the madness of her characters. It permits one to stop seeking for esoteric meanings and motives, and enjoy the book as a sophisticated and most exquisitely written fantasy. It permits one to take her practical-joking sadists, her malevolent old men, her brain-ravaged introvert, her volatile Scylla with just a grain of humor or imagination of one's own; and to feel that one is not one's self altogether limited in experience simply because the events of *Armed With Madness* seem unusual.

Armed With Madness is the story of five Englishmen and one girl during a week's life. Scylla and Felix are brother and sister, high-born and poverty-stricken, and Picus and Clarence are two friends and distant relatives who live in a house near by. These four, with an aloof, fairly normal man named Ross, constitute a kind of highly and diabolically sophisticated group, with their own code, their own geatures, their own recondite ways of making themselves understood. A sixth person, an American named Carston, comes down to visit them, and finds himself the intended victim of a strange practical joke thought out by Picus, an unscrupulous kind of sadist with a perverted sense of humor. Picus buries a cup in a well, brings it up with a sword, supposes it to be a relic, and invokes the symbolism of the Holy Grail. The appearance of this cup proves strangely upsetting and leads to all sort of emotions and happenings just this side (and sometimes just the other side) of madness. A kind of diabolic malice and subtlety begins its interplay among these people, with their queer attachments, their quick jealousies and their unconventional attitudes. Before the end is reached Scylla has been tied to a statue and pierced with arrows. Clarence has tried to commit suicide. Felix has gone to Paris and brought back a hungry young Russian noble, and Carston has had his eyes opened to things undreamed of in his philosophy.

There is really no key which fits all the events of this book, some of which have as stripped and sharp a reality as one remembers, some of which seem the product of oversubtilizing, and others of which are turbid and inexplicable. Throughout the whole book runs a note of cruel and decadent sophistication oddly in contrast to the freshness and brightness and beauty of the writing, with its amazing imagery, its clean, natural sensuousness, its occasional pregnancy of significance. There is no question that Miss Butts is a poet, and hardly more that she is a writer of often distinguished prose. And once you enter her world, if you can accept and appreciate it as a world unto itself, what goes on becomes exciting and unpredictable, Aldous Huxley and William Blake walking hand in hand, with what results one can perhaps imagine.

Marianne Moore (essay date 1928)

SOURCE: "A House-Party," in *The Dial,* Vol. LXXXV, September, 1928, pp. 258-60.

[*In the following review of* Armed with Madness, *Moore praises Butts's lyrical writing style.*]

"The sea lay three parts round the house, invisible because of the wood. . . . The people who had the house were interested in the wood and its silence." "Poverty and pride, cant and candor, raw flesh and velvet" seem collectively to ask, "Are we never to have any peace, only adventure and pain?" to say "there is no good will left anywhere in the world."

They were Drusilla Taverner—"Scylla"; Carston, an American; Picus "unnaturally supple"; Carston "had seen him pick up something behind him with his hands as if it had been in front"; Clarence "with a feeling for decoration best served in cities." "One rougher and shorter, fairer, better bred, called Ross. Then a boy, Scylla's brother Felix Taverner."

"Ross arranged their chairs in the veranda while the storm banged about." "For an hour it rained, through sheet lightning, and thunder like a departing train, the hills calling one to another."

The Sanc-Grail is supposed to have been fished from the well, but "Picus had taken his father's cup . . . had run to small mystifications . . . had whistled up mystery with what was now undoubtedly a victorian finger-bowl."

"'We don't seem to have cleared up anything,' said Clarence.

'Cleared up,' said Picus chattering at them. . . . In this there was something that was not comic, in the dis-ease he imparted."

When consulted about disposing of the cup the vicar suggests replacing it where they got it. "'It seems to like wells,'" he said. "'And truth, if she prefers not to talk, can return to one.'"

"'Good,' said Picus, 'learn it to be a toad.'"

One sees the artist in Miss Butts, in her liking to watch "how violently, strangely, and in character people will behave," though an attitude of being surprising in matters of personal freedom seems needless. The iron hand of unconvention can be heavier than the iron hand of convention; and heresy in respect to this or that orthodoxy is perhaps a greater compliment to it than one sets out to pay, amounting really in the vehemence of protest, to subjection; to marriage and various other kinds of conformity Miss Butts pays compliments of this grudged, paining variety.

There are gruesome things here, as there were continually in the minds of the maddened conversers—"while high over them the gulls squalled like sorrow driven up." But there are many graces. And it is a triumph for the author that it is a mistake to recount anything she writes without recounting it in her own words. Sensitiveness sponsors defiance; it also sponsors homage to beauty. Strictness of touch and accurate drawing give "the endless turf-miles which ran up a great down into the sky"; "above the thunder a gull repeating itself . . . a little noise laid delicately upon the universal roar of air"; Carston "beautifying himself scrupulously and elaborately as a cat"; Picus' father, a collector with "a theory of the rights of owners to their property"—"prupperty: prupperty: prupperty";

Lydia (in London) "in a too short frock and a too tight hair-wave and a too pink make-up, reading the *Romaunt de la Rose*"; and Lydia's husband. "His method was to cut conversation, to interrupt whatever was said, and when he spoke, interrupt himself, so there should never be any continuity. Perfectly sound. . . . Could show them that not being a gentleman was worth something."

Little thicknesses are chipped away. Emphasis of writing and of attitude are equal, and as a change from the periodic sentence a syncopated rhetoric is pleasant; though emphasis without interruption amounts to no emphasis and one has the feeling that a mixture of code and declarative sentence may be best. There is much to notice, as one proceeds—rejecting, accepting, renovated and attentive. Would a Bostonian say, "I reckon" in the way in which Carston says it? Is flavour contributed or sacrificed by the elegiac curfew chime of current literacy— that is to say, by the interpolated aphorism: "When we were very young"; "meaning of meaning"; "portraits of the artist"; things from the Bible? But to doubt is merely a part of liking, and of feeling. One need not read Mary Butts if one has not a feeling for feeling. Her presentation of what one feels is here as accurate as of what one sees. Scylla "wished the earth would not suddenly look fragile, as if it was going to start shifting about. . . . There was something wrong with all of them, or with their world. A moment missed, a moment to come. Or not coming. Or either or both. Shove it off on the War; but that did not help." The "trick on Carston was ill-mannered, a little cruel. Also irrelevant." "What he could not have done, [to others] others could do [to him]." It is a compassionate view Miss Butts takes of this informed, formless party; of its "insolent insincerity" and seeming insufficiency—of Clarence smiling back at Picus "as if he had to smile under pain, his own, any one's," listening "till the time came when he could listen no longer, and hid his face, the awful pain rising in him drowning Picus' presence." "There was something in their lives spoiled and inconclusive like the Grail," she says. Some would say nothing in them was like the Grail. But Miss Butts is not palming anything off on us. We may make what we may of it. It is sympathy she offers us in Carston's reply when the vicar wonders "Whether a true picture of the real is shown by our senses alone." "All I can say is that I've never never been so bothered, never behaved so like a skunk, never so nearly fell dead in my tracks till I got down here and began to think about such things. It's unfashionable now, you know—"

Jascha Kessler (essay date 1995)

SOURCE: "Mary Butts: Lost . . . and Found," in *Kenyon Review,* Vol. 17, Nos. 3-4, Summer Fall, 1995, pp. 206-18.

[*In the following essay, Kessler surveys Butts's writings, arguing that her place in literary history be restored.*]

Literary history sometimes reads like archaeology, which, although another kind of historiography, presents some structural analogies to it. There are, for example, eras and epochs preserved from the past in earth and rock formations that reach back to beginnings; and those strata are often enough demarcated by disjunctions of the temporal continuity, which is seamless *per se.* Whether those "breaks" in the record are effected by mutations in climate, by volcanic eruptions and earthquakes, or else by catastrophes arriving from space is part of the puzzle that scientists sift and decipher in order to write the history of the planet. By now, of course, one can assert it was a nineteenth-century error to associate the backward-glancing achievement by which history is written, and therefore history itself, with the notion of progress, and more dubiously with that of evolution as progress. This is the error Henry Adams questioned in the biography of himself written in old age, the very title of which, *The Education of Henry Adams,* suggests that it needed a lifelong effort to educate his subject, himself, and to free his mind from illusion and prejudice . . . the better to comprehend the new century, which he foresaw would be radically different from his own, beginning with the harnessing of electricity.[1] What Adams opposed to the idea of progress was a skeptical, perhaps pessimistic, acceptance of an idea of evolution as change, but not necessarily advance, certainly if the doctrine was proposing hope as the necessary light toward the end, a greater glory, refulgent, illuminating what our human society might come to amount to. One lesson he seems to have tried to teach was that of the value of historical consciousness, coupled with self-consciousness, as a means of arriving—through retrospection, to be sure—at an understanding of history as a succession of periods abruptly, often discontinuously changed. In that, he read the meanings, as he knew them, of the geological strata. The difference between paleontology, archaeology, and history lies in this: that the changes occur to a species which can choose to learn because it records itself in language, tradition, and writing; hence, it remembers. The result is a complex consciousness that tells us: what changes also remains paradoxically the same. Paleontology and archaeology will show that Homo sapiens mastered fire and walked on the moon. That is the essential property the individual and the species exhibits. The hallmark of our proper existence is our creation of the historical perspective that shows us it is we who remain what changes. Little new in that: Heraclitus makes this observation in his apothegm about human nature: the man who crosses the stream the second time is not the same, nor is the stream itself the same.[2]

What I should like to have suggested, however, in my paralleling archaeology's mute history to the comment of the scholiast is simply that the latter is engaged in reading, not the periods in which their objects lived, but in studying and restoring documents to a dual existence, thereby apprehending them simultaneously as both past and present; which is to say, writings are things never quite dead, never as utterly and remotely extinct as the trilobite and the pterodactyl. An example of the liveliness of the lost and/or missing written work that illumines the remote past in a significant way might be the discovery and our subsequent efforts to "place" the Dead Sea Scrolls, a project still very much in controversial development for nearly half a century now. Here also violent events seem to have been the cause of their original disappearance from the historical continuum; the scrolls were hidden away for two millennia and found by accident, more or less well-preserved; moreover, the significance of the Qumran records remains in their bearing on the origins of the Christian religion itself, in terms of its remotest foundation and its present stability. The lability of religious establishments is well illustrated for us too by the fatal consequences to a writer like Salman Rushdie, who raised a question in a novel about the so-called "Satanic verses," which bear on the historical context of the issuing of the Koran itself. Nothing so arcane or immense is the subject of this discussion, however, which involves a relatively recent literary disappearance.

Mary Butts was born in 1890 and died rather too young of a ruptured appendix in 1937. Perhaps it was the catastrophe of World War II that took her work from view, just as the Depression had pretty much removed from the attention of the world of letters D. H. Lawrence, who had died in 1930 at forty-five. When she succumbed in the remote west of Cornwall, Mary Butts was not an unknown nor even obscure minor writer; quite the contrary, she was well and regularly reviewed all over England, and praised even over here by the poet Marianne Moore, who had observed in her review of *Armed with Madness,* "It is a triumph for the author that it is a mistake to recount anything she writes without recounting it in her own words. . . ." And, "One need not read Mary Butts who has not a feeling for feeling. Her presentation of what one feels is . . . as accurate as of what one sees."[3]

I cite an American critic because her judgment of the first of the two Taverner novels (recently reprinted more than sixty years after their first appearance) aptly conveys the subtle features of the historical situation. On the one hand, there was Moore's lively response to an outstanding feature of Butts's fiction: the power of her accurate prose to portray landscape, mood, and the "life of things." On the other, we have *our* present-day insight—made rather more inclusive and reflective by the passage of most of this catastrophic century—into *what* is conveyed by Butts's "feeling." One can say today that "feeling" is too understated a word to describe her passionate temperament and, more important, too vague to suggest the complexity of the cultural *issues* she took up in that novel. Much of the quality of her insistent vision and dark prophecy is necessarily absent from the ephemeral reviews that greeted her when she was alive, accurate and cogent as most of those were; certainly it was neither grasped nor appreciated for what it was, even though on the whole literary journalists then seem to have written better stuff than what passes for the casual notices offered in our newspapers. Perhaps we may be able to respond to her passion because we have begun to acknowledge the shadow of the apocalypse looming over the planet: we sense ourselves standing miserably advanced into a future she dreaded, on the far side of the chasm

broken open by World War II, the aftermath of which has been our irrevocable step into the atomic age. As its eclipsing shadow (and the political hysteria embodied in the symbol of Armageddon) advances—in all its various forms, nuclear catastrophes, famines, wars, disintegration of the very biosphere itself—we can see all too well what moved Mary Butts. Our sympathy, in short, derives from hindsight.

What should be remarked first, however, is that our interest in her is not just excited by the prospect of reviving interest in a writer as good as forgotten in her own country (although that would suffice, as it did when we were briefly reminded of Barbara Pym about ten years ago); nor is it a matter of enlarging the canon of remarkable writers, as occurred with Virginia Woolf more than a generation after her death (which would be reason enough). Rather, certain issues she dealt with remain part of our present cultural concerns. There is, for instance, the perennial question of autonomy for women, the problem of surmounting the many stubborn obstacles to self-realization and fulfillment as mature persons in a culture that makes *anyone's* accomplishment of maturity exceedingly iffy. Moreover, the struggle of women for "empowerment" is a terrible and confused one: it casts its penumbra over the complexity of sexual identity, of the dialectic of female and male relations, and the evolution of the individual's social roles in an emerging world society that reduces all persons to economic ciphers merely, and agents of consumerism. Beyond all that, though, in the case of Mary Butts it is precisely our potential reciprocation of her passion that should lead to her being unearthed and exhibited, as one would say of a buried hoard in archaeology. Toward that end credit is due to McPherson & Company, which is republishing Mary Butts in its new series of *Recovered Classics.* And, their recent publication of the two Taverner novels, bound in one volume, as well as a selection from three collections of her short stories, both in handsomely mounted and inexpensive editions, is admirable since it enables us to recognize her as someone who speaks to us today.

. . . . .

When I was nineteen and reading my way through what was then available of Virginia Woolf, that was in 1948-49—to the surprise of my favorite professor of English, who suggested Wells and Beerbohm but had almost nothing to say about Conrad or Joyce—my interest and admiration were elicited partly because there were affinities between the turbulence of our post-war years and the suffering of unstable sensibilities described in a novel like *Mrs. Dalloway,* or between the idea of coping with the ruined social and lost intellectual and artistic order of 1918-22, as in *To the Lighthouse.* Also, I was fascinated by the suppleness of her syntax, by her idiosyncratic use of the semicolon, and her verbal music, which flowed like a complex stream, ply upon ply, looking and sounding quite different from what one saw in James Joyce. Whereas Joyce's books constituted for me a veritable handbook and guide to the university of our Western culture, Woolf, his disparager and (not so) secret imitator, suggested quite another order of being: in short, they were not complementaries but, aesthetically, contraries. Still, read concomitantly both were handy to help fill out the range of possibility required to get a sense of what had been the modern, up to 1930. Fitzgerald's prose seemed in comparison uninventive to me, just a good, standard, polished style. Hemingway was obviously *sui generis,* an unusable genius: one could see already in 1948 that after *The Sun Also Rises* his influence had resulted in mannered imitation, his first American heirs, like Hammett and Cain and Chandler, working mainly in the genre novel, and his dialogue trick (as he termed it) absorbed by screenwriters. As for Faulkner, only *Sanctuary* was in print when he won the Nobel Prize for Literature in 1948, and that was written in the depths of the Depression as a gangster potboiler, or so he said.[4]

Apropos our reacquaintance with Mary Butts, D. H. Lawrence, who was just five years older, comes immediately to mind.[5] The two are scarcely from the same social stratum, nor did they have much if anything to do with one another personally, though they were both acquainted with some of the same Bloomsbury cast of characters. From his early discovery by Ford Madox Ford and acquaintance with the editor Edward Garnett, Lawrence was into and out of London bohemia until 1918, and several of its major players figure in, for example, *Women in Love* and *Aaron's Rod.* Both before and after the war, Lawrence had already begun to explore Germany and Italy, whereas Butts was to enter the fast society of London and Paris that Lawrence detested. Nevertheless, both writers have much in common temperamentally and in terms of their vision of the post-World War I world. While Lawrence after 1920 was to wander the world with Frieda, fulminating and agonizing over the collapse and disintegration of European civilization, Butts was fated to confront the wreckage as a woman: what she saw were the men who returned maimed, or walking wraiths; what she knew was the social frenzy and spiritual hysteria of the twenties in London and Paris. Still, Lawrence and Butts came to similar conclusions about what had happened to the world, and they are congruent in imagining what they believed might, indeed must, be done to remedy the present, if there was to be any hope for the future. They are of the same (quasimystical, shall we say) party, although they are not at all the same sort of prose writers. Roughly, one can say that Lawrence is fluent, full and clear in argument and thought, as well as poetic in his psychology and its projection of the subjective dynamic. Mary Butts's prose tends toward the laconic, the succinct, the terse; she is often syntactically eccentric, so that a page sometimes demands one's careful rereading, not only in order to parse the prose but to absorb her music, from which her meaning tends to emerge in disjunctive utterances: often she is most odd precisely when she is at her most sibylline (in which mode, she also can sound rather precious, and that can be off-putting, as writing is when the reader is obliged to make allowances). She has, nevertheless, a way of speaking that exerts its peculiar authority over the page. Lacking that authority, she could not convince the reader long enough to weave her net; indeed, her extraordinary tales would certainly dissipate their power to hold the reader even under the light of critical reflection.[6]

It will be helpful to open to Butts at first in *From Altar to Chimney-Piece,* sixteen stories selected from the thirty published in three gatherings (1923, 1932, 1938). This book offers a sampling of her themes and the range of her voice, which, incidentally, is so individual that one can almost hear her speaking: it is literally such a spellbinding voice that it seems a pity she was not recorded when she lived. Her characters are usually her contemporaries, starting about 1920: men who lived through the war and are spiritually paralyzed, or worse; younger men adrift after the war, heterosexual and homosexual, who can find little to do with themselves, with their lovers and wives, or for that matter with anyone; young women who are at a loss *vis-à-vis* the males they have to deal with, their lovers, bisexual or gay, their husbands or would-be husbands who are simply unable either to attain manhood or to preserve it. (Butts makes it abundantly plain that she believes manhood for a woman means much more than simple sexual potency.) About homosexuality, Butts is open and direct: her homosexuals and lesbians are people from her own set in London and France; she doesn't write self-consciously about her family, friends, or ambiguous "lovers." Rather she is blunt, decent; she is to be perceived as a woman involved yet also detached and tolerant. Her homosexuals are not (stereo)typed by their object choice; indeed, she is sympathetic and generous in her rendering of men who have no women in their lives. In **"The House Party"** (which she dedicated to Jean Cocteau), Butts describes a conventicle of sophisticated artists and aesthetes, the international gays of her *haute monde*—French, English, American—telling a wistful story of hope thwarted by a piece of rough trade; it is an unusually candid story, over which she casts the scumbled light of pagan paedeutic pederasty and Calvinistic damnation. Throughout the range of her stories she offers a gallery of sketches of English men and women, limited by her social acquaintance to the middle and upper classes; and her characters are eminently believable. In fact, most of them will strike the reader as faithful to what were surely their originals.

. . . . .

A recurrent theme in Butts's writing shows her as having been susceptible, even partially committed, to magic with a capital *M.* She seems to have been strongly attracted to the remnants of erstwhile druidical ritualism, fascinated by the uncanny. For us it may seem like a soft place in the hard, tough intellect she otherwise reveals, even in those stories explicitly devoted to the realm of the supernatural. Sometimes it has to do with historical nostalgia: her various Paris stories hint at the hugger-mugger and wickedness underlying and pervading the ancient districts of the Left Bank she loved, an archaic Paris opposed materially and spiritually to the cosmopolitan world of the Right Bank with its modern lights, traffic, and commerce. Perhaps she wants to cause a little disconcerting frisson in conjuring up the processes by which a questing, typically naive, soul may be swallowed up, right in walking distance of the Eiffel Tower. It should be recalled that there was an upsurge of obsessive, dark longings accompanying the Romantic Age, as expressed for instance in De Quincey and Beddoes; those impulses degenerated toward the close of the nineteenth century into spiritualism, into a fascination with evil and opium, reaching an intensity of sometimes cynical, sometimes desperate grotesqueness during the decadent Yellow Period of the 1890s. There was also to come in the Edwardian era a foolish or idle pursuit of psychologically dangerous practices, Rosicrucianism, Blavatskyism, Gurdjieffism, and so on. From today's prospect, the Satanism of most of those French and English occultists will appear somewhat futile, amounting to no more than the hapless flapping of Lucifer's once immense and now shrunken dark vans.[7] What subsist today are "rites" such as our plastic-masked, machine-produced Halloween costumes, assisted by lurid comic-strip movies, a last, popular, and thoroughly commercialized figuration for the kids of what were once great powers, now dwindled to exiguous hints of mystery even in Butts's altogether serious handling, as in her story **"With or Without Buttons."**[8]

What can be found in her Jamesian story about evil, **"From Altar to Chimney-Piece,"** is her latest treatment of such matters. There she shows us what she came to understand in her maturity: that evil was to be found only in forbidden ritual and trafficking with spooks; it was also very much a pathology, indeed, commingled as it is with sado-masochism, with the unrestrained egoism that uses some of the consequences of the modernist revolution as a blind for psycho-sexual cruelty, which she depicts as justifying itself through the surrealist manifesto yoked to Bolshevik radicalism.[9] In this powerful story, Butts cannily ties Cherry, the now-familiar twentieth-century figure of the questing girl, to Gertrude Stein's salon and to a form of purely psychological degradation; it's a nasty story that seems in retrospect to have been the cathartic by which she purged herself of her former fascination with the labyrinth of the magus.[10]

There is nevertheless a meaning to Butts's interest in the magical, which took another turn, much for the better, when she abandoned the degenerate sophisticates she had frequented in London and Paris and decided instead to seek the sacred. For her its realm now is to be found in natural mystery, the wilder and more primitive the better, which she located in the primeval and chthonic simplicity of the "black West" from which "the last lights . . . went." This can be understood as what Gerard Manley Hopkins meant in saying, "And for all this, nature is never spent; / There lives the dearest freshness deep down in things."[11] Her religious search is for that which was to be secularized during the atheistic existentialist heyday after 1945 as the "authentic." Mary Butts depicts it in her world of the Dorset country, where the Taverner novels take place.

Armed with Madness and *The Death of Felicity Taverner* are extraordinary books, what one likes to contemplate when thinking about permanent additions to the canon of the first rate. Read them with this clue in mind: that their stories of dysfunctional family and friends are imagined against a grand, quasi-allegorical backdrop, that of mental warfare, as Blake envisioned it.[12] Butts attempts the "visionary," what others from her world would indeed have called madness. The title itself, *Armed with Madness,* is a defiant irony meant to answer the doubter and skeptic she wants as her reader, because she has much to say about what "values" can still be found in the contemporary wasteland. She has this in common with D. H. Lawrence, especially the late Lawrence.[13] An important feature of Butts's machinery is mythomania, one of the hallmarks of poetry and fiction of the first half of this century, one of the features of what I call modern primitivism. She attempts to evoke, or to resurrect, and even to believe in ancient, non-Christian archetypes, powers or essences that once were projected in the forms of the various gods of the pagan world, especially those she derived from the Greek pantheon. She longs to believe in their reality, above and beyond the reality of human psychology,[14] and wishes to pin down evil and falsehood. In these novels, for all their strange poetry and vigorous, if sometimes brusque prose, Butts is nevertheless quite the worldly realist: her writer's voice is objective, detached, her viewpoint that of a dramatic artist. She is never coy, or fatuously the woman writer aiming for her books to sell as successfully as the trash of commercial *schwärmerei.* Butts is, in short, as serious as the Lawrence who found a sacred clearing in the virgin part of Nottingham forest for his Connie Chatterley to lie down in with Mellors, as serious as the Lawrence whose last novella depicts a sacred copulation between a Jesus awakened in his own flesh with a virgin dedicated to Isis.

What must encourage the reader to enter her world in the Taverner novels is the magisterial authority Butts displays in the first chapter of *Armed with Madness.* The narrator, felt immediately as a woman strong in her views, opens up with a challenge to her characters, saying to them in effect, All right, our civilization has been destroyed, millions of the best young men, our whole generation of lovers, husbands, leaders, scientists and artists, workers and all, have been killed off in the most murderous fashion in the Great War; millions of women are left stranded in the emptiness; society shall never again even hope to be what it was during the past hundred years; the world has changed course abruptly and is moving in ways unknown before; all has been lost—here we are, we few left alive, and what are we going to do with ourselves? Let us therefore stop our hand-wringing and our self-pitying whining, our effete nastiness and rottenness, our miserable existence in this Wasteland, and look for Life. (Her "few" are some half-men, either undecidedly sexually, or shell-shocked, manic-depressive, or amoral pretty fellows; she herself is situated amidst them like an earth goddess, as well as menaced by her more or less wicked relatives. There is as well an interesting foil: an American traveler who shows up, a thoroughly masculine and highly intelligent fellow, wholly, (luckily), innocent of European exhaustion. From the opening chapter of **Armed with Madness,** Butts's narrative vigor so braces, that one gladly joins her in what is to develop in both novels as the struggle of her small, *un*armed band of those who cling to a possibly redemptive Goodness against the active, determinedly Wicked.

It remains only to be suggested that the novels are quasi-Quest tales, quasi-detection fictions, although when I say "detection," I am thinking of the use to which Faulkner later put the genre in *Absalom! Absalom!* (written some years after Butts had published these novels). After opening her story upon a scene of devastation, cultural and personal, its characters' situation must be traced back to causes, which requires a tracing back to origins, a correction, *post hoc,* of the map of missteps and catastrophes; the source of some implanted evil, like the Fisher King's Wound, must be undone, before healing in some unknown future may occur. In the course of such a quest we will come to know ourselves and understand how we became what we are. In Butts's novels the enemies are the evil, worldly mother and her associates and dependents. The villain in **The Death of Felicity Taverner** is Felicity's husband, a widower when the book opens. But he is a *very* wicked fellow, not simply a man bereaved of a girl who was a paragon of all that is beautiful in womankind. Like Butts's own first husband, he is a Jew; he is also a Bolshevik, a Nihilist; moreover, he is not only the capitalist promoter and cynic, but a blackmailing extortionist who aims to publish the diaries of Felicity as upscale pornography for the collectors of limited editions.[15] Imagine! all these perversions of the Good resident in one energetic and ambitious man. In this reapparition of Shylock, presented here of course as a young man, Butts develops a stereotype familiar to her social class, and a cliché at the time, that of the pushy, vulgar, and insufferable intruder clambering into the ranks of aristocracy. Chaucer noted just that prejudice in the *Canterbury Tales,* implicit in the gentle nun who tells a ferocious tale depicting bloodthirsty Jews, and tells it long after the expulsion of the Jews from England. For Butts that once-upon-a-long-ago time accursed wanderer, that avaricious holder of the mortgage of a bankrupt, feudal nobility, is the embodiment of crass commercialism: indeed, he is now the avatar of the twentieth century: " . . . the jew [who] squats on the window sill, the owner / Spawned in some estaminet of Antwerp, / Blistered in Brussels, patched and peeled in London,"[16] as the often sanctimonious, sometimes pious Eliot put it in a vile sentence he preserved as part of his principal poetic oeuvre even after the Hitler decades and the Holocaust. His type is the essence of what is most hateful to her and has become familiar to everyone, whether Jew or Gentile, that of the modern entrepreneur: the developer who has no regard for beauty, whether of persons or of the natural world, let alone the arts of civilization, the one who proposes to transmogrify Butts's wild, sacred landscape into monotonous tracts for vacation villas, featuring such amenities as tennis, riding, and golf—in short, a forerunner of the impersonal conglomerators of today's consumerist society.[17]

Such wickedness can be off-putting indeed, given the horrors of those decades from 1930-1950; the more especially if her fiction is read narrowly, or as seeming to belong to the realistic mode, rather than what it is, allegorical and quasi-Expressionist. After all, Felicity herself is, from the opening pages of the novel, a memory, an ineffable wraith of a beauty that was supernal. Butts's point presumably is that her pagan eroticism, all ingenuous as it was, "Zeldaish" if you care to find a too-easy comparison from life, or "Caddyish," to use Faulkner's figure (and his later version, Temple Drake), is easily misunderstood and simply crushed in the hamfist of the butterfly's admirer: Beauty is the Good that Evil lusts after and yet cannot abide. One might ask, to think of Butts's absorption in classical mythology, why Aphrodite is married to Hephaestus, the sooty, crippled master of the forge? Or one might ask why the soul itself is trapped and darkened in its tenement of clay? Or why Young Goodman Brown believes his wife to be a witch? None of these typologies and parallels can mitigate, to be sure, the miserable, rank whiff of that fashionable, merely snobbish sort of anti-Semitism in Butts's narrative. And yet, she is nothing if not sophisticated. A perusal of her stories will reveal that she was a chronicler of her class and time, and fully conversant with its vices and its prejudices; that she attempted from the outset to surmount them by satirizing her society, and, in the Taverner novels, retreated in loathing from its excesses, in search of a life in what she hoped was the world in which the pristine might yet be found. That she had a complex attitude toward her peers and contemporaries is clear from the personae of the Taverner novels: shell-shocked veterans, confused mystifiers, exotic homosexuals, all men, in fact, and powerful, witchy women—a refuse of refugees from the blasted cultures of Europe, continental and English both. Butts's world is small and narrow and special. Her characters have had it with the City, in short. They are a rather motley bunch, yet fully developed fictional characters whose prototypes are the actors so briefly glimpsed in the various dramas of failed love constituting the narrative line of "The Waste Land." A blasé, even cynical eye might regard her passionate heroine as a Queen Bee (the young Frieda von Richthofen Weekley Lawrence Ravagli, for example); a better view would be gained by aligning one's perspective with that of the author: a woman in a world of half-men, each of them deficient or crippled in a different way. In **Armed with Madness,** the only "real" man is a handsome, intelligent, and vigorous American, who by definition is not party to the insanity of the Dorset cenacle that so attracts him at first; he is a prince who nearly makes his way to the couch of the Sleeping Beauty through the thick hedge of thorns that is Europe at the end of its civilization—only to understand (just in time? for him? for them?) that his safety, indeed his life, depends on a prompt escape from them all. It is a bittersweet Romance that is, ultimately, a profound anti-Romance. Butts in both works is using traditional devices; but she is also thinking her way toward some novel revelation of another way out of the abyss of her lifetime. She is "making it new," as Pound desired of the modern writer. To that end, as with so many of her generation of writers, she looks back toward the ancient world and reconsiders ancient stories. *Reculer pour mieux sauter.*

What did Butts arrive at in *Armed with Madness*? The True and the Good having been buried in the rubble of Western civilization after the cataclysm of World War I, she seems to have found her ultimate hope in what remains of the ultimate triad, whose light shines over Plato's world, what perhaps may always remain: Beauty. Having suggested that, one is stunned by this circumstance, which poses the theory of the following Taverner novel. Before it even opens, Felicity Taverner, a delicate, happy creature, a harmless, gentle, loving beauty who was as close as one can imagine to being a daughter of Aphrodite herself, as I have suggested, is found dead on a main road in the south of France. The ghost of her beauty is present from the first page; it hovers, as one reviewer remarked, like a perfume. Who killed Felicity, rather, *what* killed her, and why? Moreover, how did she come to be found lying smashed on the Mediterranean coast?

For the reader of Mary Butts, the unraveling of this mystery will provide her answer to questions we still ask today. It is not a complete answer; she was cut off from arriving at that by her sudden death. One cannot imagine what could have sustained her hope for beauty had. she lived through World War II. (Virginia Woolf, who had parallel preoccupations with the power of beauty to save, as we know, could not begin to face that time, but stuffed her pockets with stones and let herself drown.) She is a writer who may from her own magic casement open up a fresh view upon a world and a time she knew and that we look back upon as having been utterly forlorn: the pre-World War II epoch. Her importance lies in reminding us of what it was possible for a brave imagination to attempt, and one like hers seems to have been special and rare. Her gift is estimable, and she deserves to be recovered to her proper place in literature. Furthermore, to begin to read her now is to honor her courage,[18] which is not to say, given our novel circumstances and the condition of our degraded, disordered, and depraved culture, we are competent to come to terms with the answer she had begun to adumbrate when she died.

NOTES

[1] In a succinct, but most powerful formulation, it was for Adams the sign he called the Dynamo that would oppose, and inevitably replace, the icon of the Virgin that had for two thousand years dominated the civilization of Europe.

[2] The man, however, knows that he is not the same. On the morning of June 16, 1904, Joyce's Stephen Dedalus muses in *Ulysses* to that effect, observing that the man who leaves his house in the morning is not the man who returns to it that night, a proposition elaborated chapter by chapter throughout the novel. That contemplative musing shows us that we are no longer in the confident nineteenth-century world of change as progress; *Finnegans Wake* was to show us that Joyce had entered another universe altogether: that of the constancy of identity in the vast cycles of mutability, diurnal change, and historical change interfused in a state of sleep that is not a sleep at all, and a language that is no longer the language hitherto recognized as English, but is comprehensible only because it is, of course, recognizably English.

[3] Marianne Moore, "A Haute-Party," *The Dial* September 1928: 258-60. And I would add, *"and as accurate of what it is she thinks."*

[4] Perhaps it is Fitzgerald who provided Butts with the trick of quoting fragments of jazz lyrics in some of her stories; although she had *Ulysses* to hand, and mentions the name of James Joyce, she seems to have regarded him as someone not to be recommended as an example to aspiring young artists. (*Vide* her posthumously published story, "From Altar to Chimney-Piece.") She seems to have disregarded Hemingway, who was also working in Paris, even though his first novel certainly takes in the sort of crowd she ran with.

[5] Incidentally, in 1948 there were only easily available *Sons and Lovers* and *Women in Love*—the latter originally published in the United States, England during World War I being inhospitable to the Lawrences, and certainly not to his extraordinary masterpiece—and also a bowdlerized paperback of the third version of *Lady Chatterley's Lover.* Very little remained, in short, of this great writer until the revival of the late 1950s, sparked by the censorship trials of 1962-1963 both here and in England.

[6] That her fictional style is not merely a mannerism of her own is to be seen in her discursive prose, her last book and her autobiography, *The Crystal Cabinet: My Childhood at Salterns,* first published in 1937 and republished in 1988 (Beacon Press, Boston). In its extraordinarily interesting pages, Butts writes with the same voice one hears in the two Taverner novels. This is a book that should be read in conjunction with the fiction, and one hopes it may be returned to print so that certain useful insights into her themes will be made available to her reader. Her evocation of her infancy and childhood, her allusions to the sources and events of her early life, the beauties and hurts that obsessed her as a writer, her family situation primarily, are clearly laid out though not always consciously understood. It takes a bit of adroit reflection to link her characters, and much of what occurs, too, with certain vivid memories. Two examples may suffice: Butts mentions that a wryneck somehow got itself entangled in her mother's hair in the mysterious woods that backed the house at Salterns. In *Armed with Madness,* the principal character is married to a sexually ambiguous, half-mad man she calls Picus, or woodpecker. The wryneck is scansorial picoid bird, or wood-

pecker. In *The Death of Felicity Taverner,* the novel opens with the revelation of the death (by murder?) of that beauty, and one finds in *The Crystal Cabinet* a discussion of the traumatic event of the holocaust of her father's personal library (the books sequestered from the child, considered immoral by her mother—de Maupassant, Boccaccio, Burton's *1001 Nights,* et cetera). The child was forced to watch as her mother lit the pyre and declared that she was washing her father's hands clean! The grown woman cries out in her autobiography that she now understands that her mother has murdered beauty! Her passion is equivalent to that heard in Shakespeare's phrase: that Macbeth murdered sleep!

[7] Eliot recognized this in his last poems, remarking that when there was distress and turmoil among the nations, there was also an interest in fortune-telling. Recently the immense novel by Umberto Eco, *Foucault's Pendulum,* a wild, post-modern romp through the same Parisian purlieus Butts haunted, offered a compendious survey of hoary and dangerous satanical idiocies; it satirizes our vestigial obsession with what passes for the demonic, and consigns to the trashbin our rational and irrational pretensions to psychic powers that penetrate the veil of our limited understanding of the universe.

[8] Let's remember that before Yeats found his Blue Shirts, he was a devotee of mediumism and Rosicrucianism, and took quite seriously the same automatisms that the Surrealists treated as secular absurdities and irrational sources of new inspiration. For that matter, that very bad man, the black sorcerer Aleister Crowley, makes his appearance in Butts's short fiction, and echoes of Montague Summers flit through her shadows.

[9] Her term: in Butts, Surrealist and Bolshevist were a part of the same inhuman vanguard. And they were allied—until Stalin disjoined them in 1930 at the International Congress in Moscow, when he banished the Surrealists from the revolution. That was his perversion of Leninist Marxism, itself an enemy of democratic socialism.

[10] The story does offer echoes from James's *The Portrait of a Lady* and *The Ambassadors,* albeit its characters' fates are a condition of another leap into a more squalid netherworld than James had dealt with. A study of Butts might well find Butts making implicit references to the themes of old world/new world, innocence/corruption to be found in the American's latest novels.

[11] Gerard Manley Hopkins, "God's Grandeur." This sonnet might be taken as an apt credo for Butts's outlook, except that she is not a believer in the possibility that "the Holy Ghost over the bent / World broods with warm breast and with ah! bright wings." Rather, that yes, the world is "bent," but there is a mysterious power emanating from Gaea's breast, particularly as she herself, Butts, brooded over her Cornish landscape and listened to the wind and the waters.

[12] Butts is, after all, a descendant of the poet's patron, Thomas Butts. And it seems that Mary Butts's mother, a woman to be reckoned with in many ways, few of them admirable, to say the least, did sell off most of the artist's now priceless works in the family's possession. But another rendition of what can be understood as spiritual warfare is to be found, as English in type and origin as that of Butts, in J. R. R. Tolkien's epic, *The Fellowship of the Rings,* started in the late 1930s and completed in the 1950s.

[13] Cf. Lawrence's affinity to Blake was noticed by T. S. Eliot very early on, who attacked them both as false, heterodox prophets in the one collection he did not care to reissue, *After Strange Gods.*

[14] Though I don't think Butts would have bought into the Jungian flimflam we have seen sold in a big way since the 1950s, just as she was not for most of her life a believing Christian.

[15] Shades of Anaïs Nin, whose diaries, written industriously from the time she could hold a pen, became best-sellers in the 1980s, some edited, and rewritten, by the author and after her death by her widower, and her agent, for a liberated age's mass audience. Nin herself was not that much younger than Butts, though her time in Paris was in the 1930s, rather more than a decade later.

[16] T. S. Eliot, "Gerontion," *The Complete Poems and Plays, 1909-1950* (New York: Harcourt, 1952) 21.

[17] That the stereotype is scarcely to be defined as characterizing only Jews is readily suggested by Faulkner's satire of the same sort of type in his creation of the Snopes clan, as well as by Naipaul's and Narayan's Hindus. Volpone was no Jew, for that matter, but a figure who goes back to Plautus in Rome, Greek comedy, and further still into the Middle East.

[18] Not all her work is to be found, even in major libraries. Now, however, we do have available in one volume (also from McPherson & Company), *The Macedonian* and *Scenes from the Life of Cleopatra,* titled as *The Classical Novels* (with three short stories on classical themes included). In addition, the same publisher is scheduling a collection of essays by various writers; edited by Christopher Wagstaff, the work will contain an extensive bibliography for Mary Butts ("A Preliminary Checklist"), edited by Kenneth Irby and Christopher Wagstaff. (As of this writing, the publication remains untitled.)

Robin Blaser (essay date 1995)

SOURCE: "Here Lies the Woodpecker Who Was Zeus," in *A Sacred Quest: The Life and Writings of Mary Butts,* edited by Christopher Wagstaff, McPherson & Company, 1995, pp. 159-220.

[*In the following essay, Blaser provides an extensive analysis of* Armed with Madness, *as well as a survey of major themes in Butts's writings.*]

This essay on Mary Butts's *Armed with Madness* (1928) will, I fear, appear to be more an anthology than a commentary. My reasons are that her work is little known, few libraries have her twelve published volumes, and even the little that is written about her is hard to come by and confusing. I have chosen, therefore, to quote extensively and carefully. Her work belongs to the youth of twentieth-century writing, and the creative energy of it helps in the imagination of ourselves. An essay-story, then.

Mary Butts's reputation began with the publication of a volume of stories, *Speed the Plough,* in 1923. Her curious sense of the magic of personal meaning—the game of the possibility of a meaningful life—was there at the centre of those first stories. Ford Madox Ford's "Purposes," announcing the *Transatlantic Review* in 1923, included Mary Butts along with H. G. Wells, Conrad, Joyce, cummings, Pound, Eliot, Mina Loy, and Robert McAlmon. Among these, she is striking and remains so. In the history of the magazine *Pagany* (Boston, 1929-1933), put together by its original editor, Richard Johns, and Stephen Halpert in 1969, I find this statement with its strange lack of any sense of the passage of time:

> Johns' original intention was to limit his contributors to those who, whatever their ethnic background, were essentially Americans. One dictionary definition of native, "belonging to, or natural to, by reason of the circumstances of one's birth," would certainly include such writers as Ezra Pound, Gertrude Stein, Mary Butts, and Emanuel Carnevali, who despite their present expatriate status were born and bred in this country.[1]

Doubtless, this is simply confused writing—the point being the original intention. (Mary Butts died in 1937, and Gertrude Stein in 1946.) Here, the editor of *Pagany: A Native Quarterly,* taking its start and title from William Carlos Williams' *A Voyage to Pagany* (1928, but also a reminiscence of 1924)—joined by his collaborator—manages thirty-six years after the demise of his famous journal still to consider the quintessentially English Mary Butts of London, Dorset and Cornwall an American. This seems to have been part of her fate, for, as far as I can tell, it is in America that her reputation continued, avant-garde—now, I suppose the word is underground—and firm. Nevertheless, that original view, reflected upon by Johns and Halpert in *A Return to Pagany,* gives us a measure of her reputation in the 'twenties. Kenneth Rexroth wrote in his introduction to that volume:

> Many of them are now unjustly forgotten. They believed and hoped that the arts would be the instrument of a fundamental revolution of the human sensibility as such. They believed that the word or the pictorial image could be used to subvert the dead syntax by which human self-alienation had been grafted into the very structure of the brain and nervous system. They believed that The Revolution of the Word would liberate a new life meaning for man and sweep away dead shells from which meaning had been exhausted or had turned malignant.[2]

In preparation for that introduction, dated April 21, 1969, Rexroth read through a complete file of *Pagany*: "As I looked through it, it was just like Proust's madeleine." This youth of the twentieth-century literary effort included Mary Butts.

Williams' narrative of his year in Pagany—a tricky name for all of Europe—spent there at the behest of Pound, brings him back to America to search, as the New Directions book-blurb puts it, for "what is genuinely poetic at home."[3] What followed was, of course, *In the American Grain* (1925). It is useful to remember the final scene in *A Voyage to Pagany*:

> America, he began again haltingly, is hard to know.
>
> Yes, she answered, because she had made him serious so that he must speak his mind or say nothing.
>
> I think it is useful to us, he continued, because it is near savagery. In Europe, you are so far from it that maybe you will have to die first before you will live again.—But Dev was not such a fool.— Europe, I do not know, he corrected himself, I am seeing a few superficial moments only.
>
> But he had a quick pupil.—That is enough, replied Fräulein von J. I see now what I saw at the beginning. You are a savage, not quite civilized—you have America and we have not. You have that, yes, it is something.
>
> It is very difficult, said Dev. I am not a typical American. We have few natives left but they would not know me—
>
> You are holding on to something, she said.
>
> It is very difficult, Dev went on—something very likely to be lost, this is what—So he took out the flint arrowhead he had in his pocket and showed it to her.
>
> She was impressed. She held it hard in her hand as if to keep its impression there, felt the point, the edge, tried it, turned it over.
>
> Yes, she said, I have seen the same thing from our own fields, more finished work—but it is very far, very far. No one believes it is real. But this you carry in your coat? It is very strange. Where did you find it?
>
> In a corn-field in Virginia, there are many of them there.
>
> . . . . .
>
> Moving to rejoin Frau M. they saw that it was getting on into the afternoon and that they must be stepping along if they would be back in Rome by nightfall.
>
> You believe in America like a church, mused Fräulein von J. almost to herself.

Dev did not think so.

Do you believe then that the church is an enemy
to your belief?

Yes.

She looked away.

Oh come on, said Dev, let's get out of this.[4]

I have quoted so much in order to set Williams' "nativ-ist" position which *Pagany* adopted, never, rightly, ex-cluding the expatriates. Williams' quarrel with the "Europeanism" of Pound and Eliot became fundamental to his imagination. His insistence upon the return of lan-guage to a sense of place and to the rhythm and imagery of that place—which is a ground rather than a sky for being—defines the major effort of the modern writer and is a triumph of twentieth-century writing. And this gives us a clue to Mary Butts's place among these writers: the rhythm, imagery, and magic of her Dorset and Cornwall are dazzling—another grounding of imagination.

A "Manifesto" by William Carlos Williams appears in the first issue of *Pagany*:

> "The ghosts so confidently laid by Francis Bacon
> and his followers are again walking in the laboratory
> as well as beside the man in the street" [Scott
> Buchanan, *Poetry and Mathematics*, p. 18], the
> scientific age is drawing to a close. Bizarre derivations
> multiply about us, mystifying and untrue as—an
> automatic revolver. To what shall the mind turn
> for that with which to rehabilitate our thought
> and our lives? To the word, a meaning hardly
> distinguishable from that of place, in whose great,
> virtuous and at present little realized potency we
> hereby manifest our belief.[5]

The statement reflects Williams' profound interest in modern science, particularly in relativity theory and its implications for a relational imagination. His intention here is not anti-scientific, but rather he means to pick up the changed relation to an objective reality, which is implied, and Williams early recognized the fact. A rela-tional imagination then, rightly, turns to language "to rehabilitate our thought and our lives." As Robert Duncan puts it in another context, "Most importantly it is the word that carries with it the life-consciousness to be, the adventuring biological reality."[6] Immediately following Williams' manifesto in the original issue of *Pagany,* is Mary Butts's story, **"The House-party,"** dedicated to Jean Cocteau. This is a finely subtle, "politely sensual"—in the manner of the time—story about homosexual young men, accurate with a Jamesian kind of suggestiveness. But in Halpert-Johns's history of Pagany, this story is said to "Epitomize the amoral living of some of the wealthy English and American expatriates on the Continent." "In contrast," they continue, "Margery Latimer . . . searched the souls of simple-living Midwest American characters."[7] The problem of Mary Butts's reputation may well begin with this kind of careless, fearful comparison:

Throughout the first two years of *Pagany* Johns had given Mary Butts' decadent sparkle a full display. By the time the fourth issue was ready to be printed, Johns knew he would no longer accept further contributions from her so that space might be available for newer and lesser-known writers, who, in his opinion, had something more vital to say. Somehow in her shorter than usual story, **"Green,"** there seemed to blow a tempering wind through one of the untypically English country houses which generally housed an amorous imbroglio. Now Mary Butts was writing with tartness, almost as if she felt there might be a healthy future for a young couple in the heterosexuality of marriage, cleansed of the emotional friendships of other young men for the husband and the influence of a conniving, mantic mother. . . .

Mary Butts was always brilliant, and Johns was pleased to have had the opportunity to publish her works. . . . But this sign of good health on a generally fevered cheek was new and promising. One of her stories finally looked forward toward a balanced living, . . . an apt swan song for Mary Butts.[8]

One should not, perhaps, be too harsh in retrospect, but it is disappointing to find this stated in this way in 1969. The charge of decadence involves a moral imperative which defines life by exclusion, and I hasten to add, it has the effect of denying the search for a poetics of life that was the fundamental concern of many of *Pagany*'s writers.

This denial and the editorial changes consequent upon it are reflected in *Pagany* after the October-December, 1931 issue:

> The phasing out of Mary Butts and the introduction
> of John Cheever indicated that *Pagany*'s fourth
> issue for 1931 was one of transition, a final encore
> for a number of writers, yet far too subtle for the
> reader to notice.[9]

Faulkner's homosexual story, "Divorce in Naples," was rejected as "commonplace." "Twittering birds" such as Charles Henri Ford and Parker Tyler were out. Gertrude Stein's "nonsensical couplets had begun to pall." Johns himself had been troubled by the reception given his own tentative, defensive exploration (all fiction!) of a homo-sexual theme in his story "Solstice" (vol. 1, no. 4), which was clearly influenced by Mary Butts in its handling of unstated relations and in one instance, by her archetypal use of classical divinities to describe character—"a Cybele for young men to learn from." Pound himself was not making sense to Johns.[10] Pound's essay "The First Year of 'Pagany' and The Possibility of Criteria" (vol. 1, no. 1, 1931) with its instructions and its remarks on "Mr. Eliot's fatigue" and "M. Cocteau's adventures" had not apparently instructed Richard Johns. The remaining three issues of *Pagany* are memorable for, among other things, Cocteau's "The Laic Mystery" translated by Olga Rudge, Katherine Anne Porter's "Banquet for October," parts of Williams' *White Mule,* and Zukofsky's "'A'—First

Movement," but the adventure of the magazine was over. It began to follow another direction in modern American letters. Still, one notices that H. D. sent "Electra-Orestes" for the April-June, 1932, issue, accompanied by a letter in praise of the magazine, which closes: "You have been fortunate too, to have Mary Butts's exquisite stories."[11]

The turn in Mary Butts's reputation is nearly incomprehensible. In America, it is tied to a "decadence" already spotted in Richard Johns. Elsewhere, I've taken note of the false note in her British reputation as that is reflected in the spite and meanness of spirit of Douglas Goldring in his autobiographical *South Lodge* (1943), published six years after her death.[12] The tale of that relationship is the business of a biographer—one can only hope for a competent one with a mind as subtle and charmed as Mary Butts's. Her finest collection of short stories, *Several Occasions* (1932), is dedicated to Goldring. Suspicion begins there. The dedication tells us that he had once recognized something, and he tells us as much in an earlier autobiography, *Odd Man Out* (1935). But his own art could not openly praise the beauty of men as hers did, nor could he approach the adventure of the sacred which is her greatest concern. Biographical interest in Mary Butts will be trapped by the merely reductive if the sacred is not traced—tracked—in her work. That vitality I call the sacred begins with her childhood memories of Blake's paintings on the wall and his illuminated books on the shelves of a wondrous library that had come to the family through Blake's friend Thomas Butts. I suggest that Mary Butts's reputation, like that of H. D., suffered because of the complexity of the sacred in her twentieth-century mind, heart, and work.

· · · · ·

The adventure of the sacred is then the large issue in Mary Butts's work to which I wish to call attention. The realism of many of her stories is a record of the way lives flow into and out of this adventure. But it was the adventure itself which drew Mary Butts's attention in her most important works. And that adventure is entirely marked by the condition of the sacred in the modern world. It is this, I think, that drew, in turn, the attention of Pound and H. D.—her careful probing of the problem of it. This does not contradict her stand alongside Williams' "Manifesto." Nor is she contradictory, if we read her carefully, to Williams' interest in Einstein—"St. Francis Einstein of the Daffodils, *On the first visit of Professor Einstein to the United States in the spring of 1921*"—or to his fascination with Alfred North Whitehead's *Science and the Modern World* after first reading it in 1927. Both are concerned with the elemental, the ultimate, and the cosmos, which have to do with ground and place—so we are taught first by Hesiod, Oedipus at Colonus, and Lucretius. Theirs are two different ways of writing to a similar condition. Where Williams looked to science— post-Baconian and Newtonian—where he found the ghosts and so settled on the word and a newly posed language, a writer like Mary Butts sets up the contemporary with all its dazzle, free sexuality, sense and non-

sense, and finding the ghosts also, she turns to the archaic. And so it is, I assume, with one writer after another that the loosened, embattled relation to meaning, as that condition informs any meaningful life, turns up the ghosts—.

I want now to turn to Mary Butts's *Armed with Madness*:

> In the house, in which they could not afford to live, it was unpleasantly quiet. Marvelously noisy, but the noises let through silence. The noises were jays, bustling and screeching in the wood, a hay-cutter, clattering and sending up waves of scent, substantial as sea-waves, filling the long rooms as the tide fills a blow-hole, but without roar or release. The third noise was the light wind, rising off the diamond-blue sea. The sea lay three parts round the house, invisible because of the wood. The wood rose from its cliff-point in a single tree, and spread out inland, in a fan to enclose the house. Outside the verandah, a small lawn had been hollowed, from which the wood could be seen as it swept up, hurrying with squirrels, into a group of immense ilex, beech and oak. The lawn was stuck with yuccas and tree-fuchsias, dripping season in, season out, with bells the colour of blood.
>
> Once the house was passed, the wood gave it up, enclosed it decently, fenced a paddock, and the slip of dark life melted into the endless turf-miles which ran up a great down into the sky.
>
> The silence let through by the jays, the hay-cutter, and the breeze, was a complicated production of stone rooms, the natural silence of empty grass, and the equivocal, personal silence of the wood. Not many nerves could stand it. People who had come for a week had been known to leave next day. The people who had the house were interested in the wood and its silence. When it got worse, after dark or at mid-day, they said it was tuning-up. When a gale came up-Channel shrieking like a mad harp, they said they were watching a visible fight with the silence in the wood.
>
> A large gramophone stood with its mouth open on the verandah flags. They had been playing to the wood after lunch, to appease it and to keep their dancing in hand.[13]

Most striking in this passage which opens *Armed with Madness* is the silence, mysterious and unexplained. Its "tuning-up" proposes a primordial relation of sound and silence, even as the wit and magic of the gramophone stops us, first with laughter, then with a sense of the lives of those who play out the story to come. It is characteristic of Mary Butts's fiction that she adapts an older principle of narrative—somewhat akin to Greek drama in which the character is there for the sake of the action and not *vice versa,* or so Aristotle insisted that we understand the fact of the event in tragedy, which even in his time, following upon Plato's insistence that meaning was transcendent and abstract, needed to be straightened out.[14] Mary Butts's sense that a tale is told of human characters inside an action both older and other than themselves challenges that other sense of the novel in which character is interesting in and for itself. As a result of this different narrative technique, each character in a Butts novel remains a sketch poised within a realism of the elemental and mysterious. (That there is such a realism—that we are capable of it—Keats taught us long ago.) The expected psychological centre is displaced in such a way that, as in *Armed with Madness,* one is not always sure who is in charge of the narration which slips from one to another—the author included—allowing motivation and insight to wander.

The wood surrounding the house is old and sacred—that is to say, nurturing life-sanctities—very like the sacred wood of Butts's poem **"Corfe"** (addressed to Corfe Castle in Dorset), which Louis Zukofsky published in *An "Objectivist" Anthology* in 1932:

> But when I remember you Corfe, I remember
> Delphi
> Because your history also is a mystery of God.
>
> . . . . .
>
> Very sweet is the Sacred Wood
> In the gold clearing, in the mustard patch;
> But at night comes a change
> Like a gold ball thrown out
> And a black ball thrown in
> (Not sunset behind Tyneham Cap
> On a night without a moon.)
> But a shift of potencies
> Like a black ball thrown in
> And a gold ball thrown out
> And the players are princes
> Of the turf and the weed
> And the wind-moulded trees
> And the hazel thicket
> And the red blackberry thorn.
>
> Never trust a hemlock
> An inch above your mouth.
> An ice-green hemlock
> Is a lover
> In the wood.
> Now every way the wind blows this sweetie goes
> In the south
> Where goes the leaf of the rose
> And the evergreen tree.

The poem gives us a concentrated image of the magic of the wood that is a recurring interest in Mary Butts's work—here the night brings a "shift of potencies" represented by the reversed imagery of the gold and black balls, as though one could catch the potencies in a game, all leading to the storied and threatening hemlock become a lover.

Then, in the house, we meet the main characters: first Scylla and her brother Felix, and a strong, down-to-earth fellow, Ross, "a rare plant," who shares the house with them. An American, Dudley Carston, comes for a visit, the outsider to be tested. These four are joined by

Clarence and Picus, two men who share a cottage some distance away and who have come to stay in the house because, we are told, their well is low and polluted. One woman, five men, and Scylla's and Felix' old nurse who acts as house-keeper and general comforter. Nothing is ever told in the novel about the sexual relationship between Clarence and Picus, but we come to see the anguish and care of it as it falls apart, incapable of withstanding the test of the game that is played out in their lives. Scylla in the end wins the love of Picus. Clarence ends in madness and defeat, carving a punch bowl for Scylla. Felix escapes to Paris where he discovers Boris, a young, penniless, White-Russian prince whom he brings back to the house in the woods. Again, nothing is said about their relationship, though we understand enough. (Incidentally, it is Boris who prepares the plot for Butts's novel to follow *Armed with Madness, Death of Felicity Taverner,* 1932.)

Stated thus baldly, everything is lost except the tension, the possibilities, and a suggestiveness. These are not decadent, but serious and complex young lives. In Mary Butts's world, for whatever reason, male homosexuality is not a matter of decadence, but, rather, of the way lives turn. Boris, who appears near the end of *Armed with Madness* and whose first appearance in her work is in *Imaginary Letters* (dated 1924, published in 1928) is a case in point. *Imaginary Letters* begins Mary Butts's major work in fiction, though it appears very close to her life, and may be autobiographical. Here we meet Boris who will not stay still. Goldring tells us that Mary Butts had a special sympathy for these Russians, princes who had lost a world and were down and out in Paris. Boris is beautiful, underhanded, unstable, lost, homosexual, and unavailable. It is Boris, more fully imagined, who commits murder—mind you, as a gift—to save the land from a real estate development, parking lots and tourists in *Felicity Taverner.* In *Imaginary Letters,* we find the first care that brought him into her art, and there also we find anger that is womanly, direct and puzzled. He somehow starts the imaginary process. Boris, she writes, leads us "a pretty dance." "Capricious, selfish, insensitive." "Lecherous, drunken, bold, and chaste." The qualities build in the first pages—someone shapeless and changing. "He arouses equally unconquerable affection and despair." "A monster of vanity and pride." "He is cruel, devoted, jealous . . . ," this "black and green boy." The words create this figure, whom, in kind, most of us meet sometime in our lives. Protean love. He or she may be only ourselves, a desire, or perhaps that figure is out there, as Mary Butts says, "the cause of art in others."[15]

But, to return to *Armed with Madness,* the plot is not as simple as an outline of its interpersonal relations suggests. Picus and Clarence bring with them to the house in the wood a cup which they have discovered in their well—Felix, trying to help them, fished it out with a spear. The Grail, we guess immediately—"that mirage, symbol, archetype of unity and integrity that appeared to seers of the Middle Ages"—"around 1180, when the Latin Kingdom of Jerusalem was seen to totter," first with alarm and then spiritual defeat "in 1187, when Jerusalem fell."[16] In Mary Butts, the Grail is stunningly there and not there simultaneously, symbolic of a possible meaning and of a meaninglessness, neither of which conditions is privileged in the characters' lives. This profound symbol of spiritual fulfillment has returned again and again to modern letters, most brilliantly, I think, in Jack Spicer's *The Holy Grail,* but, then, Spicer was himself indebted to Mary Butts. Later in the novel, we find out that Picus has stolen the cup from his father, an antiquarian of some reputation, and that he planted it in the well and arranged for Felix to use a spear when trying to clear the well. The characters are, all of them, then caught up in an enactment of an old pattern. The interplay—the magic that meaning is, when it is love and a task of lives—among one woman and five men is a tale of a possible Grail. We never know whether the cup is simply a jade cup, an old altar vessel, an ashtray as it is once used in the novel, a spitting-cup, so used by Picus' father's mistress before her death, as the old man cruelly tells us, a poison-cup out of the East—jade is said to detect poison—or the Sanc-Grail. It is, of course, all of these in one way or another. In this way, Mary Butts tests the symbol and pursues her imaginative investigation of the condition of the sacred in our century.

The lives of Scylla and the five men around her shape a spiritual condition that is both frightening and, in the words of the novel, an "enormous lark"—like our own lives. "There was," she wrote, "something in their lives spoiled and inconclusive like the Grail story" (91). And this remark by the youngest of the characters, Felix, which he addresses to Ross, seems especially harsh:

> You're looking for something. I'm not. And I hope when you get it, you'll like it. Looking for the Sanc-Grail. It's always the same story. The Golden Fleece or the philosopher's stone, or perpetual motion, or Atlantis or the lost tribes or God. All ways of walking into the same trap (121).

Certainly, this is a very modern attitude toward the old unicity, but the trap is also sexuality, and Felix speaks his own young fear, confusion, and innocence. What he is looking for he does not yet know. The "trap" in Mary Butts is inchoate and personal, and it always leads to the puzzle of larger meaning.

Early in the novel, when Scylla and Ross are discussing the arrival of their American visitor, the narrator comments:

> "Give him a good time and see what happens." That was her part of their hospitality, whose rewards were varied and irregular. None of them, with perhaps the exception of Felix, could understand a good time that was not based on flashes of illumination, exercises of the senses. . . .
>
> Something long and white came up behind them out of the sea. An extra wave washed Felix a ledge higher. "Thank you," he said and skipped across.

A "pleasant memory" unites them, and

they became a triple figure, like Hecate the witch, amused, imaginative. They put on their things: Felix' pretty clothes, Ross' rough ones, the girl, her delicate strong dress. With their arms round her shoulders, they crossed the rocks and went up the cliff-path, and through the wood to the house (5, 6).

The deft touches, the careful realism—all coloured by the sudden simile of the witch, Hecate—begins a strange suggestiveness that will take us into the magic and witchery of their lives.

Strange suggestions accumulate throughout the novel. Early on, the reader stops over the name Scylla:

> They called her Scylla from her name Drusilla, altering it because they said she was sometimes a witch and sometimes a bitch (4).

Exactly, but the name also returns us to Greek lore— initially, to *The Odyssey* (12. 235) where we find this mighty daughter of Crataeïs, who lived in a cavern along the straits of Sicily, the rending, mangling, troubling face of the sea. Drusilla, on the other hand, returns us to the *Acts of the Apostles* (24) wherein St. Paul defends himself and his belief in Christ so strongly that he frightens the procurator Felix and his wife Drusilla, the daughter of Herod Agrippa I and sister of Herod Agrippa II. This curious method sets up layers in Butts's story of some very ordinary characters who are to become extraordinary through the serious game of their lives. The novelist appears to work by association and she expects us to. Here, the point is a lightly brushed blend of ancient and Christian heritage carried by contemporary people, if only in their names. Later in the novel, she will call this "the Freud game"—what do you remember of this or that. We need only let our minds play over the elements which the story brings together by association—ancient, Christian, and modern, noting especially the easily and almost sportively associated Scylla and Hecate, leading finally to a further association of love with violence and madness. Only at the end of the novel will we realize that we have been warned from the outset of a possible violence in this pursuit of the love-game which in Mary Butts is always an aspect of the sacred.

This is, perhaps, because the sacred, however we define it, is a power over one, such as love is. One may fail in entering upon the sacred or one may come through into an intelligence. At the beginning of the novel we have seen Poseidon momentarily, or perhaps we missed him: "Something long and white came up behind them out of the sea." A good source book, such as Morford's and Lenardon's *Classical Mythology,* will help me to summarize the depth of association that, I believe, Mary Butts wishes us to have. We should remember that Poseidon, god of the sea, is "violent in his loves." The god

> made advances to Scylla, the daughter of Phorcys and Hecate. Amphitrite was jealous and threw magic herbs into Scylla's bathing place. Thus

Scylla was transformed into a terrifying monster, encircled with a ring of dogs' heads. . . .

They remind us that

> Ovid (*Met.* 13. 917-68; 14. 1-71) tells us this same story about Glaucus, a mortal who was transformed into a seagod. It was he who fell in love with Scylla; when he was rejected, he turned to the sorceress Circe for help. But Circe fell in love with him and in her jealousy poisoned the waters of Scylla's bathing place.

And Hecate, the triple-figured—here amused and imaginative—descended from the Titans, who has her house in the depths of things

> is a goddess of roads in general and crossroads in particular, the latter being considered the center of ghostly activities, particularly in the dead of night. Thus the goddess developed a terrifying aspect; triple-faced statues depicted the three manifestations of her multiple character as a deity of the moon— Selene in heaven, Artemis on earth, and Hecate in the realm of Hades. . . . How different is the usual depiction of Artemis, young, vigorous, wholesome, and beautiful!

We also remember that Circe, a daughter of the Sun, is the aunt of Medea. So, the associations play around Mary Butts's novel. Violence, sexual frustration, and sexual transformation all lie in wait in this book. Irradiative associations inform the realism of the characters' young lives.

Throughout the novel there are introspective moments in which the narrator of the moment mulls his or her personal stake in this. Here, for example, Scylla goes to meet their American visitor in Starn, while Ross and Felix go picking mushrooms.

> It was all very well. She had told Felix to collect mushrooms and not allow Ross to experiment. He could get them in Ogham meads—What was she worried about? Money, of course, and love affairs; the important, unimportant things. Hitherto God had fed his sparrows, and as good fish had come out of the sea. But everywhere there was a sense of broken continuity, a dis-ease. The end of an age, the beginning of another. Revaluation of values. Phrases that meant something if you could mean them. The meaning of meaning? Discovery of a new value, a different way of apprehending everything. She wished the earth would not suddenly look fragile, as if it was going to start shifting about. . . . There was something wrong with all of them, or with their world. A moment missed, a moment to come. Or not coming. Or either or both. Shove it off on the war; but that did not help.
>
> Only Ross was all right—He never wanted anything that he did not get. Life had given it up and paid over Ross' stakes, because once his strong appetites were satisfied, he did not want anything in human

life at all. It was something to eat and drink, to embrace and paint. Apart from that, he knew something that she was only growing conscious of. And wouldn't tell. Not he—laughed at her for not knowing, and for wanting to know.

> Felix was quite different. Felix was scared. Fear made him brittle and angry and unjust. Without faith.
>
> Faith was necessary for the knowledge of God. Only, there were fifty good reasons for supporting the non-existence of God. Besides, no one wanted to believe that any more. That was the point. And it was a shame for those two men to make her go all that way through a valley, while they were grubbing about in the wind (10-11).

This haunted passage, ending in the strictly personal, is exact in its description of the modern predicament—the missed meaning of tradition, the loss and the change.

Scylla meets the American, Carston, rents a car and brings him back to the house in the woods. Meanwhile, Ross and Felix have interrupted their mushroom hunting to visit Clarence and Picus, which, as we have already noted, brings all four back to the house in the wood. The following passage allows us to watch the visitor size up the main characters.

> That was the situation for him, as he listened, translating, to the story Felix had to tell. Felix said that Ross and he had been to a place called Gault, and he'd sung to it. Presumably a dangerous place. They had then decided to call on distant friends, who might or might not be inhabiting a cottage on a place called Tollerdown. Anyhow, supposing they were not there, a rare species of hawk known as a honey-buzzard might be observed in the vicinity. On arriving they had found their friends (Scylla seemed to be the only woman in the group, a point for reflection) in difficulties owing to their well, shrunk by the drought, yielding nothing but dead hedgehogs. A digression on the use of soda-water to make tea. An excursion down the well to clean out the hedgehogs had led to a discovery. An odd cup of some greenish stone had been found, rather like pea-soup carnelian. The state of the well had necessitated the transfer of Picus and Clarence for an indefinite stay. "You're done in this country if your well gives out. Wait till ours does." Carston was not interested. This might interfere with his making love to Scylla, which he had decided was to be his expression of a successful visit. Unless he found out how to use it.
>
> Then Ross produced the cup suddenly, out of his pocket, and handed it round. Carston said:
>
> "That means nothing to me."
>
> "Been cut by hand," said Felix. "Is there a kind of opaque flint glass? Keltic twiddles, I think, very worn round the rim."
>
> A good deal was told Carston, casually, about Kelts

and Saxons and Romans and early Christianity; things completely over so far as he knew—Not that they talked about what he hadn't heard. Only they talked as if there was no time, no progress, no morality. He knew, of course, that there was no progress, and no morality.

Then Ross said, roughly and softly, as though he was loving something:

"The thing was that we fished it out with a spear."

Scylla said: "Ross, that's odd."

Clarence fidgeted attentively. Felix stared, and Carston saw the boy's tricky brilliant eyes light up. Picus was grave, a man so tall and thin he seemed to go on for ever. Unnaturally supple, he had seen him pick up something behind him as if it had been in front. He tried to think what a spear had to do with it.

Felix said, sharply:

"Good old Freud."

"Idiot!" said Ross, and turned away furious and contemptuous.

"It seems to me," said Scylla, "that people had to start some way of thinking of things. What they saw once they'd learned to think might be quite different from the things they'd learned on."

Then, to Carston, she said that odd things were always happening, and old patterns repeated themselves. That it was sometimes alarming when they did, and Freud very useful in the case of irrational fear. Very true, too, when there had been a row, and no one could feel what was just or what was not. Always look out for the suppressed wish that's taken the wrong turning. But that what had happened to-day was objective and odd.

Carston said:

"I think I'll have to ask you to explain a little more than that."

But Ross had turned round again. "I'm awfully sorry," he said. The insolent insincerity was not meant to be lost on Carston, but it was. "Put it down to the solstice or the heat."

"Tell us the news," said Felix. "We couldn't get back without our tea. Ross believes in perspiration. I don't."

Carston had come with elaborations of the best gossip. They listened to him—rather too attentively, he thought. At the same time there was something that spoiled his effects. It was the place, the faintly lit room mixing with the starlight outside. A shallow little green dish was lying among the glasses. Might have been made out of star-material. The woman had called it a diversion, but they weren't going to let him play. He began to dislike them, wish to humiliate them. Far too troubled to think how to do it.

Even Ross saw there was something wrong when he left them and went up to bed.

But this Carston had seen. Four ways of saying the woman good-night. Ross nodded to her. Felix embraced her. Clarence kissed her gallantly, with a flourish indicating affectionate indifference to their difference of sex. Picus, busy with a syphon, crooked his fore-finger at her across the room (19-22).

The next day, following up on this astonishing and annoying event of the cup and the confusing responses to it, Carston turns to Felix for information:

"Tell me more about your friends."

"Picus is Clarence' 'old man of the sea' only he's young. Clarence doesn't know it. Scylla says I'm hers. He only does one or two small things like whistling, but he does them perfectly. Riding and blowing birds' eggs. You saw how powerful his body is, but he's like a bird. Off in a flash. Hence the name. Picus was the Woodpecker.

"Clarence fights for him and with him. What he fights for, I don't know. Clarence is quite all right. A bit insincere, because he's afraid. And what he's afraid of, I don't know" (24-25).

The passage tells the reader a great deal in spite of its being limited by Felix' innocence. We need to remember the "old man of the sea" in the *Arabian Nights* and that he climbed on Sinbad's back and, then, refused to get off after having been carried across a stream. Finally, Sinbad made him drunk and shook him off. In ***Armed with Madness,*** Scylla breaks the pattern of dependence which holds the two men together.

Carston could only say: "Tell me more."

"Scylla's a different egg. If there is anything wrong about my sister, it's everything. I've said the word 'fear' at least ten times lately. This time it's my own." He horrified Carston—he was like a desperate butterfly, angry, petulant and white.—"It's she at one end, and Picus at the other, who get me going. It's because she wants everything to happen to its last possibility. That's how she gets kick out of life. Once a thing's got going, she'll understand it and manage it. And enjoy it. She'll never tone it down. Sort of woman who'd have mothered the house of Atreus, and though I owe her everything, it's wasted on me. She'll enjoy—"

"What will she enjoy?"

"What will happen out of what happened yesterday. Don't you see? That infernal Picus is a psychic if there ever was one. Or if there is such a thing."

"Does she believe in that?"

"Believing doesn't trouble her. Only what is going

to happen. She doesn't create situations. She broods them and they hatch. And the birds come home to roost. Some mighty queer birds. Truth isn't everyone's breakfast egg. She isn't happy till it's hatched. Calls it knowing where you are. I wish I knew where I was—" (25-26).

I have stopped over the associative nature of Mary Butts's use of names, and it is necessary to do so again: "Picus was the Woodpecker," as Felix has told us. This is the first mention in the novel of the peculiar provenance of this character's name. He is "like a bird"—"Off in a flash"—"Hence the name." Carston lets the matter pass. We know picus is one of the birds used in augury (Plautus)—a woodpecker, and we may remember Picus, son of Saturn, king of the aborigines of pre-Latin Italy and prophet who for spurning Circe was turned into a woodpecker (Ovid and Virgil). Such archaic elements require attention because they colour the characterization and inform the imagery.

Carston then continues to ask about Scylla whom he considers his primary interest until the Grail involves him also.

> Carston revised his ideas again about Scylla as a lover. He could only say: "But what can she and your friend Picus make out of what happened yesterday, anyhow?"
>
> "Don't you see? It was fishing it out of the well with that old spear—they always went together."
>
> "What went with what?"
>
> "The cup of the Sanc-Grail, of course. It and the spear, they always hunted in couples. You've heard of it. All sexual symbolism. I wish I hadn't."
>
> "Does sexual symbolism get you?" It would be news if it did.
>
> "I should worry. But the Sanc-Grail was a very funny thing. People used to think it was a shallow greenish dish. Those well-shafts on the downs might be any age. So might it. Tollerdown had a bad reputation, and I never heard of the Sanc-Grail doing anyone any good. With that moron Picus behind it, and that demon, my sister, in front of it."

Carston took stock of several things: what he remembered of the Grail story, the possibility of anyone behaving as if it had happened, and what that implied in human character. Felix's youth.

He said at last:

> "Don't tell me your sister is superstitious."
>
> "Not she. Better if she was. She'd read it up and do processions and things. It might be like that. But with her it won't get its home comforts. It will get vision."

On the last four words he changed, and Carston

saw the sister in the brother, in the elegant, frightened boy now explaining that what he wanted was not vision, but fashionable routine (26-27).

Such conversations not only delineate the quick changes of personality that fascinate Mary Butts—here, Felix's resistance to sexuality, his own and that of others, and Carston's slowly increasing awareness—they also forward the contemporary tension of the sacred as it belongs to imaginative life.

This tension increases as it is enacted by the characters—some of them named for ancient and archaic sanctities—and as they respond to their memories of medieval English Grail stories. Two scenes seem especially important. Ross goes up a hill to paint:

> Then he whistled as he drew, out of tune, but as though he was loving something. No nonsense about being the thing he loved, but like a lover, aware of the presence of what he loved everywhere.

Just so much is given us to suggest the special knowledge that had earlier eluded Scylla. Suddenly,

> There was a hard, explosive sound. Several mixed noises. A bird tore out of a thicket and crossed an open space, indirectly, frantically, and disappeared. He imitated its call and burst out laughing. "Woodpecker up to his tricks again." Then he went back to his work, straining his eyes (32).

We do not know that Picus of the novel is responsible, nor do we ever find out, but we do know that the Latin *picus* was a trickster. In addition, this is a kind of warning—mysteriously understood by Ross—well before we find out that Picus has tricked them all, for it is Picus who arranges to bring the spear and the cup together when Felix goes down into the well.

In the second scene, a doctor has come to check on Picus' health.

> The doctor said:
>
> "Shew me the cup you got out of the well."
>
> And when he had looked at it: "The luck of the country's with you. I'm glad to find a few roman pots. It isn't glass at all, too heavy. I think it's jade. It may have been set once. I tell you, it might have been the cup of a chalice." Intelligent interest. Carston felt quite friendly now towards the thing. The others were giving polite attention. Five people at once thinking about a spear. No, six. He was.
>
> "One has time to remember things, shooting about this country in a Ford. Do you know it makes me think of what I remember of the cup of the Sanc-Grail?"
>
> Picus said, meekly: "What was that?"
>
> Carston thought: 'How was that camp, or wasn't it? Would one of them pick up the challenge? Of

course, it was a challenge.' Ross said: "That's a long story," but Scylla leaned forward, excited, and said: "The best way to get that story out is for everyone to say what he thinks or feels or remembers. The Freud game really. Start, Felix!"

"Tennyson," said Felix.

"Oh, my dear," said Clarence, "those awful pre-Raphaelite pictures put me off it long ago."

Ross said: "A mass said at Corbenic."

"Wagner," said the doctor.

"A girl carrying it," said Carston, staring at Scylla and trying to play.

Scylla said: *"Quod inferius, sicut superius est."*

Picus said: "You haven't told me much."

"Second round," said Scylla,—"people enlarge on what they said before."

"I said Tennyson," said Felix, "because I hate the Keltic twilight. And nearly all its works. I hate it because it's a false way of telling about something that exists. No, a messy way. Responsible for the world's worst art. Now and then it nearly comes off. Milton left it alone, and I don't blame him. Tennyson made it idiotic with his temperance knights. Fixed it, too, enough for parody. Killed the unstated thing which I don't mind telling you scares me."

Clarence said: "I agree with Felix. I can't stand bad drawing."

Ross said: "At Corbenic, wherever that was, there was a different mass. It may have been the real thing."

The doctor said: "Parsival is like a great religious service to me."

Carston, embarrassed at his turn coming, saw their pained faces. He said: "I supposed the girl who carried it was the female spirit of life."

Scylla said: "I quote again: *'Here lies the Woodpecker who was Zeus.'*"

"Thank you," said Picus (37-39).

All the elements of the narrative are brought together almost violently in this exchange, whether or not the reader thinks that Scylla has taken the part of trickster. A certain amount of confusion is the result for both the characters and the reader, but I want to point out that this is part of the operational magic of the book—a concurrence and competition of layers of meaning. The history of the modern Grail is reflected from Tennyson to Wagner. Each character, except for Picus who is slyly noncommittal, expresses some tentative relation to the original spirituality that the Grail represented. The doctor's

taste is for the dramatic and ritualistic in religious matters, but we know so little about him that we can only trust his curiosity about the cup and try to measure his love of Wagner's *Parsifal.* The words "a great religious service" seem carefully chosen, though the service is hardly to be considered conventional. In contrast, Ross's suggestion that there was once a "real" mass—presumably with reference to transubstantiation—expresses contemporary loss. The doctor effectively brings the most important modern imagination of the Grail story—"like a belated inheritance," in Pierre Boulez' words—into the novel.[17] (*Parsifal* was first performed in 1882.) Again, I believe we need to stop—this time over Wagner's overwhelming presence in modern thought about the Grail. The doctor may represent the ordinary Wagnerite since he appears to hold the mistaken view that *Parsifal* is Christian. The knights of the Grail have been greatly modified when compared to those of Wagner's principal source, Wolfram von Eschenbach's thirteenth-century *Parzival,* and, as Martin Gregor-Dellin has noted, "the Grail itself has been divested of its Eucharistic function."[18] The doctor's remarks may simply reflect a modern sentiment for religion or a religious aestheticism. Still, I cannot help but think of Nietzsche's surprising recognition of the *Parsifal* Prelude: "Supreme psychological assurance with regard to what is intended to be said, expressed, *communicated.* . . . Such things exist in Dante, but nowhere else. Did ever a painter portray so melancholy a loving gaze as Wagner does with the final accents of his prelude?"[19]

Carston's view is perhaps the most twentieth-century and anthropological. Clarence, who will be driven mad in his helplessness, unlike Felix with whom he says he agrees, is attached to the merely stylish and mannered, a voice out of the 'twenties that could dismiss in the name of a newer, more geometric art, pre-Raphaelite, *art nouveau* and symbolist alike. Felix, with characteristic emotional energy, points to a profound aspect of all the Grail legends that whatever they were about was unstated— "Killed the unstated thing"—which leads to the modern arguments about Keltic sources and vegetation myths.

Scylla's responses are more gamesome and complex, in part because she has a clear motive—the winning of Picus. Her point is to push the edge, as Felix has warned us. Her first rather imperious and priestly sounding remark is a quotation from the most important of alchemical texts, the *Tabula Smaragdina,* the Emerald Table of Hermes Trismegistus. The complete quotation reads in translation:

> What is below is like that which is above, and
> what is above is like that which is below, to
> accomplish the miracles of one thing.[20]

It is striking that Scylla quotes from the Latin in which the text comes down to us—(the original text was probably Greek and may date back to the first or second centuries of the Christian era).[21] And it is remarkable that Scylla quotes only one half of this famous formula:

"What is below (inferius) is like that which is above (superius)." In so doing, she does not complete the alchemical formulation of the unity of all things; instead, she leaves the other characters and the reader with a fundamental statement of correspondence, understood, so to speak, from below whatever spiritual or transcendent is above. Scylla's phrase brings into the novel the ambiance of the Hermetic tradition—"a magical attitude to life." Titus Burckhardt, an engaged scholar of this tradition, remarks:

> The perspective of Hermetism proceeds from the view that the universe (or macrocosm) and man (or the microcosm) correspond to one another as reflections; whatever there is in the one, must also in some manner be present in the other. This correspondence may best be understood by reducing it to the mutual relationship of subject and object, of knower and known. The world, as object, appears in the mirror of the human subject.[22]

In Frances Yates's words, "the famous *Emerald Table*, the bible of the alchemists . . . gives in mysteriously compact form the philosophy of the All and the One."[23] But the tradition was not originally philosophical, however we abstract it; rather, it was a perceptual practice by way of image, metaphor and symbol. With this magical attitude in mind, one begins to reread some of the characters: Ross's love, which we have already noted, for example, probably represents an aspect of this view, and we return to Felix's remark that his sister would "read up on it and do processions and things," leading to "vision"—whatever that may turn out to be. Vision in Mary Butts's work repeatedly leads to a *dynameis* of experience, conflictual, creative, and harsh, rather than comfortable.

The novelist would have been fully cognizant of the controversy surrounding the lore of the *Hermetica* and of the occult tradition that derives from it, not only alchemy, but Cabbala, Tarot, Rosicrucianism, astrology, magic, theosophy, and the various texts of the mystery religious, Egyptian, Eleusinian and gnostic. What is often considered the "muck" of "religious back-waters." This disreputation sets aside the true imaginative value of such sources. She, born in 1890, like her peers, inherited the turmoil of belief and disbelief of the nineteenth century along with its literature and scholars. One thinks immediately of A. E. Waite's *Lives of the Alchemical Philosophers* (1888) and *The Hermetic and Alchemical Writings of Aureolus Philippus Theophrastus Bombast, of Hohenheim, called Paracelsus the Great* (1894), of J. Ferguson's *Bibliotheca Chemica* (1906), and of G. R. S. Mead's *Thrice-Greatest Hermes* (1906)—perhaps also E. A. Wallis Budge's *The Gods of the Egyptians* (1904)—to name only the most obvious whose influence remains current among those whose concern is with the lore of the human mind and imagination.[24] Such studies come into the play of imagination because they represent an anthropology faced with the direct imagination of a cosmos which is not a doctrine, an objectification, or abstraction. Such thought is always by way of protest against defini-

tion and determination, whether social or religious—Robert Duncan's "unregenerate archaic subscriptions." Duncan, discussing Allen Upward, writes of a time when "religion and childhood phantasy—the Christ and the Wizard King—are seen anew in the light of comparative folklore and the new anthropology. . . ."

> Anthropology, even as it presented itself in late nineteenth-century thought as having the grownup authority of a science, was also a development of the early nineteenth-century Romantic Vision of Man with its poetic and spiritualizing revaluations both of the Christian enthusiasms of the Seventeenth Century and of the Classical rationalism of the Eighteenth Century Enlightenment. Man—it was to be the persuasion of the new Sciences of Man—in his religions, even as in his dreams and in his romances and phantastic fictions, was everywhere at work to create at once a Self-Reality and a World-Reality.[25]

After Isaac Casaubon in 1614 dated the *Hermetica*—"though there may have been a man called Hermes Trismegistus of hoary antiquity, the *Hermetica* cannot have been written by any such person"—academic reason made the subject increasingly disreputable.[26] The battle for "reality"—first seen to be crucial in the poetry of William Blake—was given over to objectivity. Though the Hermetic tradition continued to be voiced, out of the Renaissance, well into our own century, the ability to understand this ancient and modern imagination of reality came increasingly to be more "occult"—"embarrassing," Auden said of this side of Yeats's work—until even the reputations of the scholars of it, such as Mead and Waite, were deprecated.[27] Mary Butts joins her peers in the use of this material—Yeats, Pound, and H.D. are the most obvious. (We should also, I think, recall such figures as A. R. Orage and especially Allen Upward whose work she is likely to have known.) She also had a strong interest in most things French and had lived in Paris, which suggests that she may have known the work of Sâr Péladan (1858-1918), such as his odd and cranky *Le Secret du Troubadour* which Pound had reviewed in 1906.[28] I also note that Péladan had himself established an Ordre de la Rose Croix du Temple et du Sanct Graal. Thus the combination of the Hermetic tradition with the Holy Grail was not unprecedented, but there is another precursor closer to home and to the new anthropology that we will consider shortly.

The lore of this multifarious tradition should be better known and acknowledged for what it is: a continuous activity of direct participation in the divine—the old sacred of the world that did not objectify reality or leave personal experience to a lonely, singular subjectivity. Its central concern is the activity of subject and object in the largest terms—cosmological and epistemological, which are not pretensions of art but fundamental to art. Mary Butts chooses the magical aspect of this old tradition—in personal lives to disturb and transform any singular dullness, and in a sense of the world to know that it is alive—so the gramophone plays to the wood. This "disreputable" side of Mary Butts's work is not simply nonsense. Her sense of magic is skillful at the same time that it is modernly tentative. In an essay of 1932, she writes:

> Magic has not yet been properly defined. In its *practise* it is, of course, very largely primitive science, misunderstandings by false analogy of the way things work, of natural law. But behind that there seems to remain a very peculiar kind of awareness, an awareness modified and sometimes lost by people whose life has been passed in towns. It is most difficult to describe. It has something to do with a sense of the invisible, the non-existent in a scientific sense, relations between things of a different order: the moon and a stone, the sea and a piece of wood, women and fish.[29]

In other words, the imagination and character of difference—what I have called a relational imagination which will have profound consequences in twentieth-century art.

This "awareness" is fundamental to a cultural conflict that continues into the present, involving the use and abuse of the human imagination. Blake is the first and greatest warrior of this conflict. His "mental fight" first clearly draws attention to the issue—that subject and object must meet, and it is in art that such a meeting is possible. Blake himself chose Newton to represent the contraction of reality—"Single vision and Newton's sleep." But the contraction goes back to the quarrel with the Hermetic tradition, as Frances Yates's distinguished studies inform us.

> In his eagerness to establish a purely objective view of nature as a mechanism, in his enthusiasm for pure mathematics as the only safe tool for objective enquiry, Descartes was left with the problem of mind somewhat embarrassingly on his hands. He provisionally solved the problem in a very crude way, by his so-called dualism, "one world consisting of a huge mathematical machine, extended in space; and another world consisting of unextended thinking spirits. And whatever is not mathematical or depends at all on the activity of thinking substance . . . belongs to the latter." Descartes even assigns an actual place in the body, the conarium or part of the brain, to this "thinking substance" which has to deal with everything which is not part of the vast external machine. This strangely inadequate way of dealing with mind did not long remain unquestioned and since Descartes' day many philosophers and thinkers have struggled with the problem of knowledge, of epistemology, of the relation between mind and matter. Nevertheless, this bad start of the problem of knowledge has never been quite made up. About the external world, man has discovered ever more and more. About his own mind, why he can reflect nature in it and deal with nature in it in this amazing way, he has made much less progress.

> Why was Descartes so contemptuous, even one might think, so afraid of the *mens* that he wanted to park it by itself, out of the way of the mechanical

universe and mathematics? Might not this be because of the struggle of his world to emerge from "Hermes Trismegistus" . . . and all that he stood for? The basic difference between the attitude of the magician to the world and the attitude of the scientist to the world is that the former wants to draw the world into himself, whilst the scientist does just the opposite, he externalises and impersonalises the world by a movement of will in an entirely opposite direction to that described in the Hermetic writings, the whole emphasis of which is precisely on the reflection of the world in the *mens*. Whether as religious experience or as magic, the Hermetic attitude to the world has this internal quality.

> Hence, may it not be supposed, when mechanics and mathematics took over from animism and magic, it was this internalisation, this intimate connection of the *mens* with the world, which had to be avoided at all costs. And hence, it may be suggested, through the necessity for this strong reaction, the mistake arose of showing the problem of mind to fall so completely out of step and so far behind the problem of matter in the external world and how it works. Thus, from the point of view of the history of the problem of mind and of why it has become such a problem through the neglect of it at the beginning of the modern period, "Hermes Trismegistus" and his history is important. . . . In any case we ought to know the history of what they discarded, if only to understand the motives which lay behind the triumph of mechanism. And that history uncovers the roots of the change which came over man when his mind was no longer integrated into the divine life of the universe. In the company of "Hermes Trismegistus" one treads the borderlands between magic and religion, magic and science, magic and art or poetry or music. It was in those elusive realms that the man of the Renaissance dwelt, and the seventeenth century lost some clue to the personality of that *magnum miraculum*.[30]

I have quoted at length this summary view both because it helps to clarify my own argument and because I believe the disreputation of this material may have tended to put Yates's work aside also.

In the four years between *Armed with Madness* and her essay *Traps for Unbelievers* (1932), it is clear that Mary Butts continued to study the magical and religious aspects of her concern, but with the new anthropology in hand. This essay is a major statement of her modern view: "The word Religion, with its vast connotations, is working its way into the category of shame-making or obscene":

> But with all this discarding, man, whether he likes it or not, whether he thinks about it or not, has been forced back (and that was the last thing he bargained for) onto the final, inescapable, and implacable question: "Is there anything there or not?" Anything at all? Or has the whole vast various structure been built out of nothing but my misunderstandings of phenomena and my suppressed wishes?[31]

One notices the characteristic, modernist concern with the loss of the old definition of being, the old metaphysical or God, but with that I wish to return to the magic of her imagination.

The "Freud game" passage in which Scylla insistently affirms the alchemical-magical tradition when faced with a possible Grail is rich in implication. In so doing, she proposes an interpretation of the Grail, that it is—in the words of the later essay, adapting a vocabulary from the new anthropology—the "Mana" or "virtus" of things:

> What a man or a woman will, if put to it, have no nonsense about, is the question of the "virtus" common and proper to both, their virility, courage, the source of each of their separate virtues. The best name for it is "Mana," the word which science has taken from the Polynesians; that which gives a man or a woman potency in every act or situation.[32]

The Grail, then, of the novel—"the unstated thing"—has to do with energy, act, and intelligence:

> Where a modern might ask: "What is it?" the medieval mind asked: "What must it have been?" No sacred object was conceivable outside of Christianity; therefore the search was for a known Christian relic with which it could be identified. By no later than 1200 two conflicting explanations had been advanced. One claimed that it was the cup with which Joseph of Arimethea caught the blood of Christ as it flowed down from His crucified body; in which case, the lance of the story was the lance of the soldier Longinus who pierced the side of the crucified Christ. The second claimed that it was the cup with which Jesus instituted the Eucharist at the Last Supper, and it was this second explanation which was to prevail among writers after 1225 or so. Meanwhile there was the confusing word "graal." Around 1200, the monk Helinandus of Beauvais sought in vain for a Christian tradition of the Grail, but his statements affirm the existence in Old French of a common noun "graal." It signified, he said, "a broad, deep dish," a kind of platter, and was derived from Latin "gradails" or "gradale" because such dishes were "pleasing" (grata) to guests![33]

And so the unstated—even unstateable—is the issue for the modern mind. In ***Armed with Madness***, Carston questions Scylla directly, rather than Felix:

> "And the new name for all this is our subconscious minds. And between Freud and Aquinas, I've managed to tell you about it completely wrong. For another of its names is intellectual beauty, and another, the peace of God."
>
> "D'you believe in God?"
>
> "I don't know. All we do know is what happens to faith based on catch-as-catch-can visions."
>
> "Weren't all religions based on that?"

> "They were, and look at them! But now you see why we felt we were being laughed at, dangerously, when we lifted that cup out of a well on the point of a spear?"
>
> Carston pulled himself together. "What did you mean by the other thing: *'Here lies the Woodpecker who was Zeus'?*"
>
> "A little poetry, a little witchery, a little joke. It's the same thing as I said before. Now I'll tell you something worse than what I said before.
>
> "Along with faith fit for people like us, and good taste which are where morals end, there is no goodwill left anywhere in the world. Which started to go first, or if they all went together, or which pushed the other out, I don't know. I've an idea that something else, a principle we haven't named yet, got rid of the lot."

Beginnings for an erotic conversation (41-42).

This last sentence is, of course, Carston's wry sense of the canny conversation with Scylla. Carston, as a character, always presents a near stereotype of the American who has lost all memory of the past: he belongs to the new, the direct, the simply sexual, until late in the novel; it is he who resolves as much of the Grail trick as is possible, a true modern Grail knight in that he asks the right questions.

Though Carston asks those questions, Scylla's answers on one level merely tease—"a joke," perhaps. (I think of a quotation Butts uses elsewhere: "Mais comme tu taquines éternité.") On another level, her remarks turn about the darkness of modern meaning—God become the unstated thing. She is sharp, bitter, and troubled, much as she was in her ruminations on the way to meet Carston.

Scylla has subtly shown her understanding of the whole business in her emphasis on "below" in the quotation from the *Emerald Table*. She has, if we could only follow—and she wants that possibility to be difficult and mysterious—indicated that the high mystery of the Grail is here at work among them, dangerously and laughingly; with the erudite reference to Picus the Woodpecker, she has, while mystifying everybody except Picus, tipped him off to the fact that she knows he is the trickster. Carston continues to question her:

> "Stay a minute. Maybe it's because I have no memories, but I don't see where the fun comes in."
>
> "Don't you call it fun to watch how violently, strangely and in character people will behave? Watch Ross, watch Clarence. Watch me." He was watching her (43).

Seriousness and laughter interplay in Mary Butts, even cruelly. But Carston's necessary question leads back to "Here lies the Woodpecker who was Zeus." With those words, bird-magic enters the layered meaning of the novel, and such magic leads directly to a chapter in Jane Harrison's *Themis* (1912, 2nd ed. 1927), a brilliant example of the new anthropology and of the new reading of the ancient world. There the mysterious phrase, as cited in Suidas, is given and translated:

εάδε κεῖταλ θανὼ . . . Πῖκος ὁ καὶ Ζεύς

—*"Here lies dead the Woodpecker who also is Zeus."*[34]

Scylla's version is carefully edited, removing the word "dead" and changing the tense to the past. The original suggests an ancient mythic event in which Zeus displaces or assimilates an indigenous Picus. The quotation has obviously been adapted to the magic of the narrative. Picus "lies" both because he is present and, in the tradition of Picus, the magician and trickster, he is lying in the matter of the cup. Picus who "was" Zeus is now the Picus of their own lives, setting off the recurring pattern of the search for the Grail.

Jane Harrison's discussion of Picus occurs in the chapter on magic, and she begins with a consideration of the word itself: "The word Μαδεία from which our word magic is derived was, among the Greeks of the classical days, never really at home." Yet, she notes that "the first dialogue that bears the name of Alcibiades" contains a surprising definition of the term. Of the four Persian "Royal paedagogues" chosen for their virtues—the wisest, the most just, the most prudent, the bravest—it is the wisest who teaches the magic (Μαδείαν) of Zoroaster. And it is Socrates who surprises when he explains: "The art of the magician is the service (θεραπεία) of the gods." Harrison remarks that " . . . in primitive Greece, as in Persia, magic had to do, if not with divinities (θεοί), yet at least with things divine, with sanctities (Τᾳ θεῖα). . . ." She reminds us of Picus in Aristophanes (*The Birds,* 480), in Vergil (*Aeneid,* VII. 170 ff), and in Ovid (*Metamorphoses,* XIV. 6 and *Fasti,* III). "Picus and Faunus are not regular *dei* like Jove, they are *numina,* spirits, genii, a bird spirit and a wood-spirit; like the Tree-King who watched over the Golden Bough, they haunt the dark groves."[35] Her argument that there existed sanctities before the anthropomorphic gods of sacrifice, suits Mary Butts's sense that we have returned to sanctities, personal and natural, unnamed things. Harrison concludes her remarks on indigenous Picus:

Finally Picus enshrines a beautiful lost faith, the faith that birds and beasts had *mana* other and sometimes stronger than the *mana* of man. The notion that by watching a bird you can divine the weather is preceded by the far more primitive notion that the bird by his *mana* actually makes the weather, makes and brings the rain, the thunder, the sunshine and the spring. Beasts and birds in their silent, aloof, goings, in the perfection of their limited doings are mysterious still and wonderful. We speak of zoomorphic or theriomorphic or ornithomorphic *gods,* but again we misuse language. Birds are not, never were, gods: there is no definite bird-cult, but there are an infinite number of bird-sanctities.[36]

Picus, she argues, can be seen in Ovid to have been preempted by the thunderer Zeus, but the name becomes a title of Zeus. The history of the curious Greek phrase which Scylla adapts to her purposes is complex:

Picus himself, according to the Byzantine syncretizers, knew that he was really Zeus. 'When he handed over the western part of his kingdom he died at the age of 120, and when he was dying he gave orders that his body should be deposited in the island of Crete, and that there should be an inscription:

'*Here lies dead the Woodpecker who also is Zeus.'*[37]

Crete is, of course, Zeus's ancient birthplace, indicating that the Greeks had never lost their sense that their gods were born of the earth. One can hear Mary Butts's laughter and feel her delight in the wildness of this history of the divine. She then prepares it again, through Scylla, in ***Armed with Madness.***

Jane Harrison's work leads us, in turn, to another great example of the new anthropology, A. B. Cook's *Zeus: A Study of Ancient Religion* (1914). Cook comments at length on the strange history of the phrase Πῖκος ὁ καὶ Ζεύς which cannot be traced beyond the second century—a "wild farrago" of world history put together by Byzantine chroniclers. But Cook notes:

In weighing . . . various hypotheses we must not lose sight of the fact that Πῖκος ὁ καὶ Ζεύς is consistently said to have been buried in Crete. Now the Idaean Cave has yielded a *tympanon* of the ninth or eighth century B.C., which represents the youthful Zeus or Zagreus in definitely Assyrian guise. . . . Moreover, we have seen reason to surmise that at *Hagia Triada* the soul of the prince embodying this deity took the form of a jay (*pica*)— a bird whose bright plumage suggested comparison with the woodpecker (picus). . . . It is, then, conceivable that the phrase Πῖκος ὁ καὶ Ζεύς finds its ultimate explanation in an actual Cretan cult, and that this cult was known, at least by tradition, to the chronographer who first tacked the history of Rome on to that of Assyria. When Euelpides in Aristoph. *av.* 480 spoke of Zeus as 'soon destined to restore the sceptre to the Woodpecker,' it was no mere flight of fancy but a genuine piece of folk-belief. . . .[38]

Indeed, it is Cook who begins the investigation of the phrase by calling attention to it in 1903, to be followed by Jane Harrison in 1912, W. R. Halliday's *Greek Divination* (1913), and J. Rendel Harris' *Picus Who Is Also Zeus* (1916). It is fascinating to trace the fun of what Mary Butts is likely to have read and then to note the serious side of her interest in archaic awareness.

The key to the violent combination of *Emerald Table,* Grail and ancient bird-magic, with which all these associations began, is, I believe, to be found in the work of still another scholar. Jessie Weston's studies of the

Arthurian cycle may all have been important to Mary Butts's imagination, but it is *From Ritual to Romance* (1920) that seems particularly suggestive. This book draws upon a large range of the new scholarship, so important to twentieth-century writers, including direct reference to Sir James Frazer, Franz Cumont, Anrich, Jane Harrison, G. R. S. Mead, and Sir Gilbert Murray. Especially important is Harrison's commentary on a Cretan Hymn of the Kouretes, which is addressed to Zeus as a "full-grown youth," not to the "most unreasonable and ungovernable of the Olympians." This is, of course, "Zeus-of-the-birth-cave" whose nature seems so strange to those who know only the later strata of myth in which Kronian Zeus is an overpowering sky-deity. In Harrison, this example becomes striking evidence for an older, archaic sanctity that is part of an original relation to nature.[39] Ms. Weston's use of this to approach the "secret of the Grail" is complex in that her ultimate endeavour is to trace all mystery religions back to such archaic vitalities. In so doing, she searches out the earliest Christian material available to her, what she called the "Naassene Document"—and here she draws upon G. R. S. Mead who analyzed and translated the document in *Thrice-Greatest Hermes.* His chapter on "The Myth of Man in the Mysteries" takes up this document, which Hippolytus (c. 222 A.D.) incorporates into his *Refutation,* and argues that it is a palimpsest: "an original pagan source," a "working over by a Jewish mystic of the time of Philo" (1st century B.C.), and a "Subsequent working over by a Christian Gnostic (Naassene) in the middle of the second century A.D."—all this edited by the arch-enemy of the Gnostics, Hippolytus. Ms. Weston is especially impressed by Mead's summary remarks: "The claim of these Gnostics was practically that Christianity, or rather the Good News of the Christ, was precisely the consummation of the inner doctrine of the mystery institutions of all nations: the end of them all was the revelation of the mystery of Man."[40] Drawing from this and from Frazer and Harrison, among others who sought archaic human nature, Weston concludes her famous argument: "The Grail story is not *du fond en comble* the product of imagination, literary or popular. At its root lies the record, more or less distorted, of an ancient Ritual, having for its ultimate object the initiation into the secret of the sources of Life, physical and spiritual."[41] However much we are disinclined to turn to Weston nowadays for an "explanation" of the Grail story—she seems so unaware of the place of narrative and imagination in thought and of the sheer energy of language—her book was startling in its day for good reason. Mary Butts had only to follow her own bent in the imaginative use of this scholarship to set about a novel in which "the unstated thing" would become active in contemporary terms. "Old patterns repeat themselves," one character tells us, and we may note that they are sometimes dangerously new.

Mary Butts was twenty when Roger Fry's first post-impressionist show opened in London—that is, when modernism first came to England, of which Virginia Woolf, looking back in 1924, would say in a lecture at Cambridge: ". . . in or about December, 1910, human character changed." "Think how little we know about character—think how little we know about art."[42] Cézanne, Van Gogh, Gauguin, Matisse, Picasso, Redon, Signac, Seurat were a storm for the English mind. For Mary Butts, behind this was the commotion of Victorian and Edwardian change, held together by what Samuel Hynes calls "established orders" until 1914-1918:

> As it was, the trauma of 1914-1918 ended the garden party as swiftly and rudely as a shower of hail or a four-letter word. It did so most dramatically within the fighting forces, though only after a good deal of bloody fumbling; but it also ended the more gracious aspects of the age. After the war there was never again so much money in the hands of the wellborn.[43]

With the established orders weakened what was left to responsible minds was the inheritance of change that the Victorians had left them:

> Victoria's reign had been a triumphant Age of Science; advances in geology, biology, and physics had not only affected the way men thought about their physical environment but had altered men's ideas of their relation to that environment—had brought, that is, a new cosmology and a new conception of the nature of change. It had been a scientific revolution, and, as is often true of revolutions, the revolutionaries in their moment of victory saw only their successes and not the new problems that success had created.[44]

This revolution with its resultant new cosmology also required a new anthropology, bits and pieces of which I have been considering. Most of this anthropology goes unnoticed now by a later non-classical, more "scientific" and structuralist anthropology. And, it should be noted, cosmology, new or old—not simply a detached logic of epistemology—is a fundamental activity of art, even if it is understood as self-expression. A new cosmology was the issue and remains so for the twentieth century.

One gets a charming view of this matter from Virginia Woolf's essay "The Cosmos," a review of *The Journals of Thomas Cobden-Sanderson, 1879-1922,* which she wrote in 1926:

> "'And what is Cosmos, Mr. Sanderson?' asks Sister Edith. 'What is the meaning of the word?' And then I go off like a rocket and explode in the stars in the empyrean." These two volumes are full of the sparks that fell from that constantly recurring explosion. For Mr. Cobden-Sanderson was always trying to explain to somebody—it might be Professor Tyndall ("I gave him my own view of human destiny, namely, the ultimate coalescence of the human intellect in knowledge with its other self, the Universe"), it might be Mr. Churchill, it might be a strange lady whose motor-car had broken down on the road near Malvern—what the word Cosmos meant. . . . we are left asking, with Sister Edith: "But, Mr. Sanderson, how does one 'fly to the great Rhythm'? What is the extraordinary ring of harmony within harmony that encircles us;

what reason is there to suppose that a mountain wishes us well or that a lake has a profound moral meaning to impart? What, in short, does the word Cosmos mean?" Whereupon the rocket explodes, and the red and gold showers descend, and we look on with sympathy, but feel a little chill about the feet and not very clear as to the direction of the road. . . . "My idea was magnificent; the act was ridiculous," he said. "Besides," he reflected, "nothing was explicable." And perhaps he was right.[45]

As Hynes observes, "Victorian science may have made metaphysics obsolete [still the work of our contemporary deconstructionists] but it had not destroyed men's metaphysical itch, and much of what one might generally call Edwardian science is concerned with the problem of restoring metaphysics to the human world."[46]

One effect of the new sciences, including the new anthropology, was that it implied and required a new psychology. We have seen Mary Butts, through Scylla and Felix, fooling around with Freud, which is not to say that she was not also serious. But the recognition of Freud came late to England, in fact, not until the War put his work to the proof.[47] Mary Butts was, thus, in the thick of the matter as she was writing. Nevertheless, she had available to her in her youth, the extraordinary work of Edward Carpenter and Havelock Ellis, which has a history of its own. As Samuel Hynes notes: "One field of scientific investigation in particular seemed to offer an escape from Darwinism—the field of mental events. Psychology . . . became in late-Victorian and Edwardian times the liberating movement in science, as the suffrage movement was in social relations, and socialism was in politics; and as such it attracted many of the same people."[48] We need to remember, in this context, that the Society for Psychical Research was founded in 1882, later to count both Freud and Jung as honorary members, and that the first English psychological journal, *The British Journal of Psychology,* begins in 1904, which, Hynes observes, withdrew from speculation "about the nature of sex"—"Edwardian England's principal contribution to modern psychology."[49] The acceptance of Freud in America came even later, and what Butts's editor Johns did not know and could not understand was the fact that something else was at work in her milieu. She may have known Carpenter's pamphlets of the 'nineties: for example, *Woman and her place in a free society* and *Homogenic Love and its place in a free society* (1896), but the influence of his *Love's Coming of Age* (1906) she can hardly have missed. The something else at work is likely, in part, to have been derived from Carpenter: "he sought human freedom, and when he wrote about sex it was about the sexual implications of the whole liberation of men."[50] His is the first voice of this in the English speaking world—except, once again, Blake. Carpenter's is also the first defense of homosexuality. There was also Havelock Ellis's great work in seven volumes, *Studies in the Psychology of Sex* (1897-1928). Ellis, with whom H. D. would work, sums up his own sense of his achievement:

I had done mankind a service which mankind needed, and which, it seemed, I alone was fitted to do. I had helped to make the world, and to make the world in the only way that it can be made, the interior way, by liberating the human spirit.[51]

However their contribution to later psychology is judged, they were pioneers and prophets who had spoken to one part of Mary Butts's life and art.

. . . . .

In order to clarify the interplay of all these intellectual and spiritual concerns in Mary Butts's work and before I turn to the final scene of *Armed with Madness,* I want to draw attention to a few passages in the essay of 1932, *Traps for Unbelievers*:

Jung has something to say about the value, the possibly unexhausted value, of classic religious symbolism and myth. It used to be fashionable to think that they had survived because of the motifs they supplied to the arts; we know now that it is more true to say that it was the quality of the belief which produced the works, and that each religion gets the art it deserves.

What sort of religion was it? . . . Then came the rise of anthropology and the science of comparative religions, and we have learned how to take fresh stock, compare Zeus with Jehovah, Aphrodite with Ashtaroth, and the pair of them with the Virgin; re-state Athene as a "functional daimon," as a vegetation spirit, as a totem, as a Luck; as an owl, as a feminist, as a wish-fulfillment; compare Orpheus and Osiris as Saviours, and both with Christ. It was a re-examination of extraordinary possibilities and value. Its exaggeration came from a desire to be primitive at all costs, to scour the cults and ceremonies for traces of totem-worship and fetish, for cannibalism and human sacrifice, for orgies and black magic, for exogamy and endogamy, and all the "gay science" of the anthropologist.[52]

Her critical mind goes over and over these new disciplines, never sentimental and never at rest.

So far as christian [*sic*] theology is concerned, it is all a question of date. We are still only emerging from its forms, the bones of them sticking up all about us, still dripping wet from that sea; and determined, or presumably determined, to get dry as soon as possible. Like all lately rejected things, about which we feel self-conscious, Christianity is going through a period of tabu, of being one of the things which are not done.[53]

And she continues:

So it would seem that the Gods, who for two thousand years have survived the organised forces of Christianity, are about to descend into a final twilight with their conqueror. As we have seen, they have not, like Christianity, become tabu, merely more and more symbolic, and what is more at the moment, artistically suspect. . . .[54]

We need only note, in this regard, her sensitivity, accurately outlined, to the growing positivism of scholarly thought and intellectual tradition.

Much of her concern seems involved in an analysis of the twentieth-century's translation of Renaissance humanism into a modern humanism of closure and its escape-hatch, power. Immediately following upon the remarks above comes one of Mary Butts's most prophetic and incisive admonitions:

> But the God to look out for is the God who does not put up a fight. His successes may not be spectacular, he has no hell up his sleeve, nor even much of a heaven. He is himself, for what he is worth. Take him or leave him, he makes no protest. Takes himself off, manifests himself in other ways, is called by another name. Until one is suddenly aware of him again, that his departure has been a feint, a trick that has been played on one by oneself.[55]

This is, I repeat, 1932, and this magical mind seems capable of reading European ideologies, including what was to happen to Communist practice, in a glass darkly. (Yeats's "Second Coming" which appears to go on coming is dated 1920.)

And who or what is this trickster that turns out to be ourselves?

> These Gods, "to whom a doubtful philosopher can pray, . . . as to so many radiant and heart-searching hypotheses," are no more and no less than so many descriptions man has made of himself. Descriptions that cover the ground pretty fully, the "subtle knot" retied, thread by thread. Man as an animal, as a prince, as a saviour, as a lover, as a phallos, as a warrior, as an artist, as a "magic," a flash of the hidden forces in nature. The subdivisions are often exceedingly delicate. Put together it is difficult to find one aspect of human nature or occupation or desire which is not personated. And always, as Professor Murray points out, the trivial or base, the obscene or irrational, the mysterious or the merely obscure and tiresome elements, are subordinated and kept within bounds. Which is, after all, what man likes to think about himself and do with himself.[56]

This is not exactly the euhemerism that the Sicilian came up with around 300 B.C. because it is Man who is deified in this argument, not an historical person or event, and it is the Man who burst out of the nineteenth century to find only Himself. Some few pages later, she returns to her point of departure and to the magic of the meaning she wove into her work:

> We have seen the universal discredit of christian monotheism. In an age of violent transition and discovery its old weakness has appeared again, its insufficient insistence on the wild, enchanting, incalculable force in nature, the mana of things, the non-moral, beautiful, subtle energy in man and in everything else, on which the virtue of everything depends.[57]

"We are," she concludes,

> back in the historical situation which Nietzsche described of a people "for whom God is dead, and for whom no baby-god is yet lying in his cradle." Back where we were at Alexander's death, with an instinct that is more than an instinct, a habit of life and a necessity for us, unsatisfied. Back in the blind and primitive assertion of that instinct; running after Luck and awaiting Destiny, or indulging ourselves in an orgy of mana, stripped of the morals and even of the tabus which once made it serviceable. Or, if we must specialise, back with certain people of the Hellenistic Age, in "chic" cults of the least of other men's divinities. . . . In common with the christian, the classic mind at its best insisted that, though it was possible for the divine and the human to mix, "man is not God and it is no use pretending that he is". . . . Something not very far off the deification of man is on us now, not, or not yet, of the kings and millionaires, but, and again, and this is primitive, of the conspicuous young men and women, our sexually desirable ones, whose nature it is to wax and wane and be replaced. Our Year-in-Year-out spirits, *eniautoi daimones,* "whose beauty is no stronger than a flower."

> Human nature was not meant for that strain. The stardust at Hollywood is full of dead stars. For the potency of the human god wanes, and his end is horror; rebirth, but for their human nature, terror. That is a story told in the Gospels as well as in *The Golden Bough.*[58]

One catches the translation of Frazer and Harrison into contemporary terms without Harrison's "beautiful lost faith" and a direction of vision very different from D. H. Lawrence's discovery of "blood-knowledge" in Frazer's *Totemism and Exogamy (Letters to Russell).* Nor does she here express herself as a companion of Bloomsbury, "the formulators," as Hynes puts it, "of that religion of art, intelligence, and human relationships that was born in Edwardian London and died in the Second World War."[59] She had, however, some respect from Virginia Woolf, for, having submitted an unnamed manuscript, she was invited to tea with Mrs. Woolf on Sunday, 29 October, 1922. It is also interesting to note that Virginia Woolf apparently intended to publish what must have been **Armed with Madness,** but rejected it for financial reasons: "Novels are the great bloodsuckers." In her *Diary* from which this information comes, Woolf seems interested in Mary Butts, but her judgment is clearly coloured by William Plomer's friend and Mary's brother, Anthony Butts. The entry for March 18, 1932, quotes him: "I cannot say anything of my sister—She is a bad woman—pretentious—I can see no merit in her books—pretentious. She corrupts young men. They are always committing suicide. She now has married Gabriel Atkins—without any character. They were given 25 decanters for their wedding." And Mrs. Woolf comments: "Tony is ashamed of Mary, who thus defiles the Butts blood." Many of these details are simply repeated by Goldring in *South Lodge.*

It is also notable in these passages from *Traps for Unbelievers* that they are preparation for her last two novels, *The Macedonian* (1933) and *Scenes from the Life of Cleopatra* (1935), which begin to track that "historical situation" by way of a life of Alexander, well founded on historical sources, and a feminist defense of the personality of Cleopatra who, of course, came to her position in Egypt as one result of the Macedonian's imperialism. Without biographical information, one can't be sure which came first, the essay or *The Macedonian,* since the preface to the latter is dated August, 1931. Still, I wish to say that her work is all of a piece, a deeply probing interrogation of an historical situation, which never ignores the "fun" that is part of the answer. *The Macedonian* closes with the death of Alexander, having delicately interwoven the characteristics of the public and private man:

> And Demosthenes was soon to say: "Alexander is not dead, for if he were, the whole earth would smell his body."
>
> But in the Serapeum, a priest sang:
>
> *"I praise him for his wars and quickness:*
>
> *"I praise him for his patience and far-seeing:*
>
> *"I praise him for his solitude and beauty:*
>
> *"I praise him for Clitus and Hephaestion:*
>
> *"I praise him for the fleet and the phalanx:*
>
> *"I praise him for Tyre and Alexandria:*
>
> *"I praise him for Arbela and Gedrosia:*
>
> *"I praise him for the East and the West.*
>
> *"I praise him that he is Alexander: and more than Alexander: and less.*
>
> *"I praise the Earth that she has restored to herself Alexander the Macedonian, son of Philip the Macedonian—being so nobly named—*
>
> *"That on her breast lies there*
> *he of the fairest-rare-*
> *hyacinth-curled hair,*
> *of the world famed."*[60]

This finely imagined hymn is no simple praise of the heroic; instead it is addressed to Earth who receives him and ends with the deft, personal touch of the "hyacinth-curled hair" reminding us of the boy from whose blood sprang the iris of that name, marked á á , "alas, alas!" (Mary Butts carefully credits not only Murray on Greek religion, but also Harrison's *Prolegomena to the Study of Greek Religion* and *Themis* for helping to tell this tale.) We are also to remember the long tradition that in 324, Alexander "officially" requested the Greek cities to recognize him as a god and another tradition that Alexander believed in his own divinity. The novel is a study of the man Alexander and that edge of power which we have called "gods" and which so tempted him in Persia and Egypt—a range of energy very like what Mary Butts calls the virtue of things.

Near the end of *Traps for Unbelievers,* we come upon another aspect of the intelligence of her work, which she drew from Nietzsche. This may already have been noted in *Armed with Madness* where, in Scylla's meditation as she goes to meet Carston at Starn, we come upon the phrases "Revaluation of values" and "Discovery of new value, a different way of apprehending everything." A Nietzschean concern, for Mary Butts, is not pretentious—though it might seem so to society writers such as her brother, Plomer, and Goldring—nor does it set her apart; rather, it firmly places her in the context of the most important English effort to come to terms with the change that marks the end of the nineteenth century and the beginning of the twentieth. The modern philosopher, *par excellence,* had long been a part of English literary thought during her lifetime, for, in the words of one writer at the turn of the century, Nietzsche made possible "a new habitation for the imagination of man."[61] The first English translations of Nietzsche were of aphorisms and began in New York in 1889 and in London in 1891.[62] After overcoming obstacles, machinations and delays, the editor, Oscar Levy, published *The Complete Works of Friedrich Nietzsche,* the final eighteenth volume in 1913. This important event meant that the young writers of the day had the texts at hand and would no longer be dependent upon such popular, poisonous introductions as Max Nordau's *Degeneration,* first published in English in 1895, "coincident" with Oscar Wilde's trials, and reprinted in a "Popular Ed." in 1913 and 1920—a thoroughly reactionary view which appears to have had profound consequences for both popular and literary understanding. David Thatcher's indispensible study, *Nietzsche in England, 1890-1914,* discusses this in detail for the first time. He notes that Wilde, in Nordau's book, "finds himself in the distinguished company of the pre-Raphaelites, Whitman, Gautier, Baudelaire, Maeterlinck, Tolstoy, Ibsen, Wagner, Nietzsche, and almost everybody of artistic account in the late nineteenth century, the writers, in fact, whom Havelock Ellis had praised in *The New Spirit* (1890)."[63] Behind this reaction, then, we have, as already noted, the recognitions of Havelock Ellis and Edward Carpenter—both strongly literary—who present the beginnings of a renewed, revalued literary psychology. And central to this psychology is Nietzsche whose "transvaluation of values" both implies and argues a changed psychological ground. Thatcher draws attention to the way in which this problem is slipped over in such studies as John A. Lester's *Journey Through Despair, 1880-1914: Transformations in British Literary Culture* (1968):

> This was, Lester maintains, a time of confusion and bewilderment, of disillusion and malaise; the transition from materialistic determinism to a world of chance and change involved "the urgent and pained necessity of a 'transvaluation of values,' to keep man's imaginative life alive under conditions which seemed unlivable."

But, for all the weight here upon that famous phrase, Nietzsche, in Lester's discussion, becomes one of the symptoms rather than harbinger and guide. That literary minds took up the imagination of an indeterminate human nature, founded in change and chance—among them Mary Butts—both before and after the meeting with Nietzsche is a major aspect of the profound meditation of twentieth-century thought. Thatcher cites two important passages from Nietzsche on this transvaluation, both of them available to the enquiring Mary Butts:

> These weeks I have employed in 'transvaluing values.'—You understand this trope?—After all, the alchemist is the most deserving kind of man there is! I mean the man who makes of what is base and despised something valuable, even gold. He alone confers wealth, the others merely give change. My problem this time is rather a curious one: I have asked myself what hitherto has been best hated, feared, despised by mankind—and of that and nothing else I have made my 'gold,' (Letter to Brandes, May 23, 1888, London, 1914),

and Nietzsche's definition of the "transvaluation of values,"

> an emancipation from all moral values, in a saying of yea, and in an attitude of trust, to all that which hitherto has been forbidden, despised, and damned (*Ecce Homo* in *Collected Works*, XVII, 92).

This issue of values, which involves a psychology, a practice and an imaginative structure, has been painful to think about for decades. Mary Butts, like many of her peers, seems to have simplified the problematic of "crossing over" inferred in the prefix "trans." The term "revaluation" is common in discussions of Nietzsche then and now. In *Traps for Unbelievers,* she, like Yeats in "The Second Coming," seems to have stopped over the moment of terror—a necessary moment, I think, in all such thought and one in which one notices the constant interweaving of cultural condition and imagination in twentieth-century art.

Having been reminded, in Thatcher's words, of "Havelock Ellis's judgment that Nietzsche was one of the greatest spiritual forces to appear since Goethe," I turn back, briefly, to brushstroke the strength of Nietzsche's presence in English literary thought. Phyllis Grosskurth's recent biography of Ellis (1980) notices that his judgement of Nietzsche is largely based on early work, which is true, but it is hardly likely, setting aside *The Will to Power* and *Ecce Homo,* that *Thus Spoke Zarathustra* "had nothing to say to him," given, as she also notices, that his "reality" is "based on a biological structure."[64] This opening, more likely through Freud than Ellis, will have an extraordinary history in modern letters by way of Charles Olson, Robert Duncan, and Michael McClure. Nietzsche has, indeed, been difficult to come to terms with, in large part because of the fascist preemption of his work, which translated what is first a psychological condition and then a problem of meaning on every level of the human structure—Mary Butts's "historical situa-tion"—into a monstrosity—her "terror." Only recently has a new effort been made to understand his influence on the modern imagination in such studies as Otto Bohlmann's *Yeats and Nietzsche* (1982), Ofelia Schutte's *Beyond Nihilism* (1984), and fundamentally, whether one is de-constructionist or not, Gilles Deleuze's *Nietzsche and Philosophy* (French, 1962; English, 1983). Deleuze:

> The sense of Nietzsche's philosophy is that multiplicity, becoming and chance are objects of pure affirmation. The affirmation of multiplicity is the speculative proposition, just as the joy of diversity is the practical proposition.[65]

The speculative character of modern art, especially writing, is often underestimated and undervalued. For Mary Butts and many another young writer, Nietzsche, in Thatcher's words, "was the philosopher *á la mode* in England between 1909 and 1913."[66] This influence grew dramatically with the appointment of A. R. Orage as co-editor of *New Age* in 1907—a socialist journal, one notes, and a factor in the hopes of the time. He was the author then of three books which have seldom been gauged, except by Thatcher, for their place in the modern imagination: *Friedrich Nietzsche: The Dionysian Spirit of the Age* (1906); *Nietzsche in Outline and Aphorism* (1907); and *Consciousness: Animal, Human, and Super-man* (1907)—this last one, for us startlingly published by the Theosophical Publishing Co. of London. With his appointment to the *New Age,* he carried these concerns into the currency of periodical publication. Thatcher adds this up: "From May, 1907, until the end of 1913—a period of five and a half years—Nietzsche's name is hardly absent from the pages of the *New Age.*"[67]

I think of the extraordinary range of public and private concern represented by the *New Age* and of its authors, particularly Ezra Pound. There, one finds, to name only one instance, Pound's "I Gather the Limbs of Osiris," a series of essays on his "New Method of Scholarship," a method of "luminous detail," 1911-1912. Pound's "Obituary: A. R. Orage" (1934) and "In the Wounds (Memoriam A. R. Orage)" (1935) remember the importance of *New Age* to his welfare, but his praise of Orage himself is mainly subsumed under their companionship in Douglasite economic reform. In the latter, Pound writes: "I had no interest in Orage's mysticism and am unqualified to define it. I was thankful he had it simply because it kept him in action."[68] There can be no doubt that Pound's sense of process is the contrary of Orage's "mysticism," but, though I have no time to bear it out here, a bridge can be made by way of Allen Upward's *The Divine Mystery* which Pound read as "a history of the development of human intelligence."[69] It is important, I think, to our understanding of Mary Butts's compounded elements in *Armed with Madness* to notice—Orage as our example—the connection between hermetical beliefs and Nietzsche, especially in the proposition of "Übermensch," best translated by Thatcher's "Beyond-Man."[70] That is to say, beyond the manhood so confused, determined and despairing that the arts had undertaken, along with Nietzsche, to answer with an undetermined imagination of human nature. Thatcher tells us that Orage's interest in Nietzsche began in 1900, following a chance meeting with Holbrook Jackson, "already an avid reader of *The Eagle and the Serpent*" (1898-1903), an early English, Nietzschean journal, and he cites Jackson's memory of what followed:

> We all developed supermania. He wanted a Nietzsche circle in which Plato and Blavatsky, Fabianism and Hinduism, Shaw and Wells and Edward Carpenter should be blended, with Nietzsche as the catalytic. An exciting brew.[71]

Such syncretism can be easily criticized, but it does demonstrate both the desperation and the effort of a new meaning. It is also an unprofessional and undisciplined response to the dialectics of Kant and Hegel.

More relevant to our literary interest here is, perhaps, a passage from Orage's *Friedrich Nietzsche: The Dionysian Spirit of the Age*:

> Friedrich Nietzsche is the greatest European event since Goethe. From one end of Europe to the other, wherever his books are read, the discussion in the most intellectual and aristocratically-minded circles turns on the problems raised by him. In Germany and in France his name is the war cry of opposing factions, and before very long his name will be familiar in England. Already half a dozen well-known English writers might be named who owe, if not half their ideas, at least half the courage of their ideas to Nietzsche. Ibsen seems almost mild by the side of him. Emerson, with whom he had much in common, seems strangely cool: William Blake alone among English writers seems to have closely resembled Nietzsche, and he who has read the *Marriage of Heaven and Hell,* and grasped its significance, will have little to learn from the apostle of *Zarathustra.*[72]

This led in turn to the affirmation of such affinity in *New Age* by its co-editor, Holbrook Jackson.[73] It is fair to say that the ability of twentieth-century readers to read Blake begins here. Without the necessary biographical underpinnings, I can only guess and speculate, but based on Mary Butts's autobiography, *The Crystal Cabinet* (1937), covering only her childhood, I can say with some assurance that her attentive sense of the Nietzschean problematic begins with Blake in whose work the issues of becoming, consciousness, and will are given a necessary vision. From Orage and the Nietzscheans, she seems also to have caught hold of a sense of our "historical situation" that Thatcher describes as "a relativist view of history in which all phenomena were interpreted in terms of the conflict of polarities, a philosophy of man which stressed his role as the noble protagonist in the drama of tragic existence. . . ."[74] A very ancient view which is reflected in Pound's Ulysses and Malatesta and in Mary Butts's Alexander as well as in the curious trickster quest of *Armed with Madness,* packed as it is with more ordinary-extraordinary personal affairs. On the one hand, as

one writer says of Hölderlin, in whose work, like Blake's, so much that we call modernism begins, "a precarious dialogue with the Other—whether this take the form of madness, revolution, or those gods of ancient Greece . . . vanished immediacies," and on the other, the "reinvention of antiquity out of the evidence of wreckage."[75] Blake and Nietzsche share a "consolidation of errors," psychological, social and religious, which "coincides with the revelation" of what they called the truth—that is to say, cultural belonging.[76] We have tended to give up this incredible compounding of theosophy, anthropology, psychology, reinvented antiquity, and Nietzsche consolidation—to leave it unstudied and unimagined—for the Freudian approach to mind, imagination and culture, also hailed by later issues of *New Age*. There are, it seems to me, good reasons to consider both Freud and Nietzsche as consolidators and "physicians of culture." For Mary Butts and many another who lived much longer facing into their work, the truth is a kind of indeterminacy of what we are. It is well to remember that Freud entered the English imagination late, and when he did, it was through this wide-spread interest in "mental events." Samuel Hynes takes note:

> Psychoanalytic ideas had spread more slowly in England than anywhere else in Europe or America. When Freud was made an honorary member of the Society for Psychical Research in 1911, he wrote to Jung that it was "the first sign of interest from dear old England"; the London Psycho-Analytical Society was not founded until two years later, in 1913, and then with only nine members, of whom only four ever practiced. Freud's methods became acceptable to the British medical world only after they had been proved in war-time treatment of shell-shock cases. . . .[77]

What is apparent and of enduring interest is, as Ellis, Carpenter, and Orage had discovered and argued publically with the considerable assistance of Nietzsche, art cannot be considered apart from the cultural condition in which it works. In this instance, a loss of cultural meaning. Mary Butts startlingly plays a game of hide-and-seek with such meaning.

. . . . .

Now, out of this labyrinth—necessarily speculative—of her heart and mind (I like her proposal of a speculative imagination), let us turn to the final scenes of *Armed with Madness*. Carston has managed to track down the source of the cup, and Picus produces a document to the effect that it was found in a church in 1881. The Rev. John Norris who could verify this is dead:

> Carston said:
>
> "Then we get nowhere."
>
> "Nowhere. Only in ghost-stories, and those not the best, do you get anywhere that way."
>
> "But what are we going to do with the damned

thing? It can't lie about the house like a green eye that doesn't wink. . . . This has been a fool's errand—"

"I have an idea," said the vicar. "Take it back to Tollerdown and replace it where you found it. If the next drought sends it up in a suspicious manner, well and good. It seems to like wells. And truth, if she prefers to talk, can return to one."

Carston said: "I like that."

"Good," said Picus, "learn it to be a toad" (196).

Meanwhile, Clarence has been spitefully informed by a letter from London that Scylla and Picus intend to marry, and Scylla, having found this out, goes to Tollerdown to talk with Clarence:

Clarence had not seen her. Unshaved, half-dressed, he was trying to torture the body of Picus, the statue he had done of him in clay. He had dragged it out against the quarry wall and pierced it with arrows of sharpened wood, feathered from a gull he had shot overnight.

Scylla found the door open and went softly in.

"Clarence, I've come all this way. Can I have tea?"

He heard the low voice, thought of the gull crying. She saw the bird's half-plucked body, bloody on the floor, and that there were papers torn in strips and little darts. She turned over a fold and saw her own body, and her cry was more like the gull. Bird-alone in the lonely room. Except for a ghost called Clarence, everything was empty. She thought:

'Run away: Can't: Where to? It's all empty, and my knees shake. And I'm curious. Curious and furious and only my body is afraid.'

Clarence wanted to be sure about the bird. He came in slowly, dazed with violence and grief. Bad conscience and fear of making a fool of himself nagged his blazing obsession. He saw Scylla at the door in silhouette, her scarf fluttering off the back of her neck, sweat-darkened curls appliquéd on her forehead, her hat thrown familiarly on a chair, her mouth open.

"Come and look," he said, and with the fingers of one hand dug into her collar-bone, led her through the kitchen into the half-circle of quarry behind.

She saw Picus in greenish clay, pricked with white feathers. Clarence had made him exactly as he was, a body she had known, for which hers ached.

"You see," he said, "I only had what I'd made of him to do it to."

There was an arrow through his throat, and his head had not fallen forward.

"You're going down the well, where the cup came—"

"Why, Clarence?"

"Best place for you, my fancy girl. If there's enough water, you'll drown. If there isn't, and I don't think there is, you'll break every bone in your body."

She could run like a lapwing, but he could run faster. She was strong as a tree-cat, but he could tear her in two.

"I came to bring you to Picus. He does not want you to be alone on Tollerdown. He is at Tambourne. Lydia sent you a silly letter because" (get his vanity if you can) "she is so in love with you that she's mad."

"And so are you, it seems. Gods! I'm a lucky chap. Unfortunately, Picus doesn't join the harem. He doesn't like me any more."

"Going to marry me, are you? You shall in a way. I mean to follow you down the well."

"Picus is at Tambourne, waiting for you."

"In time he will be here again. My body will fetch him."

"You are the most beautiful man in the world, but you won't be when they get you up out of the well."

He took her other shoulder in his fingers, thrusting them into the muscle-hollow under her neck, hurting her. She forgot him exacting, petulant; remembered him long before, beautiful, merry, inventive, good. And cruel now. Cruelty frightened her. She lied:

"Clarence, I am going to marry Carston—I teased Lydia—" He turned her towards the well.

"There will be one less of you bitches to come into our lives."

"We bear you, and I am no stronger in your hands than that bird. Why did you shoot a gull? It isn't done." Time seemed very precious. Only a thimbleful left. The well very near. The sun turning a little away from them.

"Woodpecker," she shrieked, and flung Clarence off, and ran to the statue. She had been careful not to say that name, and now saw Clarence hurrying to her, the mournful crazy mask splitting, the mouth turning up, the eyes shooting death at her. And Picus, pierced with arrows, smiled down his sweet equivocation. She heard: "That'll do better." He had a cord round his waist. He had cattleranched once: that was his lariat. She ran once round the statue. A second later he had thrown her, picked her up half stunned, and tied her against Picus. A black flint had cut her head, a patch of blood began to soak through the moon-fair hair.

Clarence walked back and stood by the kitchen door, fitting an arrow to the string. It ripped the skin on her shoulder and entered the clay. She saw another fly towards her and notch her forearm. Another, and there was a tearing pain below her left breast.

Three instants of pain, set in one of fear. Like a great jewel. Clarence stood by the kitchen door, sharpening an indifferent arrow. She made a supreme effort: not to scream much; not to betray herself. Then a moment of absolute contempt of Clarence. Then of pain. Then, as if she were looking out a window, into a state, a *clarté* the other side of forgiveness. Not by that route. She fainted (198-202).

Carston makes his way to Tollerdown to return the cup to the well and so interrupts this violent scene, just as Clarence is preparing another arrow. It is Clarence who is made to drop the cup in the well—"Plop went a noise a very long way below them" (205). This is no novel to bring in the police or social judgments. The next day Clarence cannot remember his actions; he only wishes to carve a punch-bowl for Scylla, but he is led, step following step by Picus, through exactly what he has done, the madness seeming to be a part of himself:

> Of Picus. Of the band he had grown up with. Of war, whose issues he had found too simple. Of their spiritual adventure he had not been equal to. Of the fool he had made of himself. The revenge his death would be. Not stay to be called Judas. *And bring our souls to His high city.*
>
> He took a step to the edge. Scylla jumped off the divan, and with her hand at her side, ran out to him.
>
> "Clarence, come in."
>
> She had hold of him as he had held her.
>
> . . . . .
>
> "Look," she said, and pulled off the handkerchief that tied her shoulder—"and my head is cut and my side. It was partly my fault that Lydia wrote to you. Go on carving while we talk."
>
> He did as she told him. Carston watched them. Like an idyll: a young lover making a present for his sweetheart, sitting on her bed. A harrow of wild geese with their necks out at flight. A border of fish (218-19).

In the end, Carston takes Clarence away to rest we are not sure where or for how long. Carston himself is asked to return to the house in the wood:

> "Our house is your house," said Scylla.
>
> "Besides," said Picus, "did you ever enjoy a summer more?"
>
> "Hasn't it been better than a movie? Leave Clarence at Tambourne and come over and look at Felix's find."

In his heart he knew he would not. Though there was continuity in this adventure, a circle like the design on Clarence's mazer, a ring near to a magic ring, he knew that nothing would induce him to go back to that poverty and pride, cant and candour, raw flesh and velvet; into that dateless, shiftless, shifting, stable and unstable Heartbreak House. Not for a bit. Off to Paris on his own folk adventure. In his last moments with them, looking at Clarence's bowl, he saw the changes in things.

> There had been an apple once. There had been an apple tree. When it gave no more apples, it had made fire, and a slice of its trunk had become a bowl cut out into birds. The bowl unless it was turned into fire again, would stop growing and last for ever. Things that came out of time, and were stopped; could be made over into another sort of time (220-21).

And, of course, the novel ends with Felix's "find," Boris, the cause of art and magic in others.

This return to the magic circle in the wood, to bird-sanctities and metaphors of them that colour the characters of Scylla and Picus is youthful and indeterminate of meaning, constantly endangered by violence. In the novel to follow *Armed with Madness, Death of Felicity Taverner,* as I have already noted, Boris takes murder to be a gift, and so implicates all the characters in his lack of understanding. The only figure in *Armed with Madness* who is truly armed is mad in loss and otherwise forgetful. A curious weight in the novel falls on Carston's meditation that "Things that came out of time, and were stopped; could be made over into another sort of time": art, perhaps, but, then, there is the commotion of lives, valued because it is not determined, or, for that matter, material.

I have laboured long over what is my own fascination with Mary Butts, and I have insisted that we remember the context and stake of her art because when memory goes, it leaves so many fine things behind. In closing this essay-story, I note that the transformation from determinism to chance and change—a matter of companionship between art and science, which companionship too often goes unnoticed because our sense of what we mean by science changes—brings us into twentieth-century art. It is one of the curiosities of this century that "reality" continues to be pre-empted by objectivity, which leaves us with a loose, even more preemptive subjectivity. Needless to say, this is destructive of imagination and our understanding of it. Closer to the necessary imagination are these remarks of Octavio Paz:

> in extirpating the notion of divinity, rationalism diminished man. It frees us from God but encloses us in an even more rigorous system. The humbled imagination avenges itself, and atrocious fetishes sprout from God's corpse: in Russia and other countries, the divinization of the leader, the cult of the letter of writings, the deification of the party; among us, the idolatry of the self. To be *one's self* is to condemn oneself to mutilation because man is perpetual longing to be another.

And so it is with Clarence's defeated desire for Picus and with Scylla's successful game to be with him—true also of Carston's departure for Paris and of Felix's finding Boris. We need, somehow, to arrive at such a perspective to understand our art and in this context, to read Mary Butts. Paz continues:

> The revolt of the romantic poets and their heirs was not so much a protest against the exile from God as a search for the lost half, a descent into the region that puts us in communication with the *other*. Therefore they did not find a place in any orthodoxy, and their conversion to this or that faith was never total. Behind Christ or Orpheus, Lucifer or Mary they were seeking that reality of realities we call the divine or the *other*. The situation of the contemporary poets is radically different. Heidegger has expressed it admirably: *We were too late for the gods and too early for being;* and he adds: *whose poem, already begun, is being.* Man is that which is incomplete, although he may be complete in his very incompletion; and therefore he makes poems, images in which he realizes and completes himself without ever completing himself completely. He himself is a poem; he is being always in a perpetual possibility of being completely and thus fulfilling himself in his non-completion. But our historical situation is characterized by the *too late* and the *too early*. Too late: in the tremulous light, the gods, already disappeared, their radiant bodies submerged below the horizon that devours all the mythologies of the past; too early: being, the central experience coming out of our selves to the encounter of its true presence. We are lost among things, our thoughts are circular and we perceive but dimly something, as yet unnamed, that is emerging.[78]

Mary Butts's grail, Felix's "unstated thing," and so on—[Mary Butts became unknown because men didn't like women that intelligent—because "closeted" writers like Plomer, Goldring, and Anthony Butts had more style than intellect—because the editor of *Pagany* was out of touch with her real effort—because Bloomsbury was "ignorant" of Nietzsche: he was "practically ignored by almost everyone known by me in the last seventy years, and I cannot remember even a discussion about him" (letter of Leonard Woolf to Thatcher, Oct. 17, 1968, cited by him, *Nietzsche in England,* p. 267)—because literary history gave too much credit to T. E. Hulme, which made the dropping of Nietzsche the easier, and the readership could become the new criticism which often had only the shadow of our art to talk about—because English Departments go on and on in an unintelligence of our cultural situation and the task of it in art—]

NOTES

[1] Halpert, Stephen, ed., *A Return to Pagany: The History, Correspondence, and Selections from a Little Magazine, 1929-1932* (Boston: Beacon Press, 1969), p. 17. Later, p. 41, it is said that "the exquisite *Armed with Madness*" has "introduced her to this country."

[2] Ibid., p. xiv.

[3] Williams, William Carlos, *A Voyage to Pagany* (New York: New Directions, 1970), back cover.

[4] Ibid., pp. 265-66.

[5] Halpert, reprint, p. 50.

[6] Duncan, Robert, "Introduction" to Allen Upward, *The Divine Mystery* (Santa Barbara, Calif: Ross-Erikson, 1976), p. xxviii.

[7] Halpert, p. 43.

[8] Ibid., pp. 335-36.

[9] Ibid., p. 337.

[10] Ibid., and p. 162.

[11] Letter printed in ibid., p. 444.

[12] My "Afterword" to Mary Butts, *Imaginary Letters* (Vancouver, B.C.: Talonbooks, 1979), pp. 64-5.

[13] Butts, Mary, *Armed with Madness* (London: Wishart, 1928), pp. 1-2. Page numbers for this novel will hereafter be given in the text.

[14] Brilliantly discussed in John Jones, *On Aristotle and Greek Tragedy* (London, Chatto & Windus, 1962), pp. 15 ff.

[15] My "Afterword," op. cit., pp. 75-6.

[16] Adolf, Helen, *Visio Pacis: Holy City and Grail* (The Pennsylvania State University Press, 1960), pp. 1 & 11.

[17] Cited in Martin Gregor-Dellin, *Richard Wagner* (New York: Harcourt, Brace, Jovanovich, 1983), p. 447.

[18] Ibid., p. 448.

[19] Cited in ibid., p. 457.

[20] This translation printed in John Read, *Prelude to Chemistry* (M.I.T. Press, 1966), p. 54. The translation is reprinted from G. F. Rodwell, *The Birth of Chemistry* (London, 1874). Mary Butts is likely to have known A. E. Waite's *The Hermetic Museum, Restored and Englarged* (London, 1893, two vols.).

[21] See John Read, ibid., pp. 51-5, for a summary discussion of the *Emerald Table,* its importance and the arguments about its age.

[22] Burckhardt, Titus, *Alchemy: Science of the Cosmos, Science of the Soul* (London: Stuart and Watkins, 1967), p. 34. See also James Webb's *The Flight from Reason: The Age of the Irrational* (London, Macdonald, 1971), p. 125, perhaps useful, but spoiled throughout by an unexamined privileging of Reason and no apparent understanding of the psychology of this undertaking.

[23] Yates, Frances A., *Giordano Bruno and the Hermetic Tradition* (London: Routledge and Kegan Paul, 1964), p. 150.

[24] See Kenneth Rexroth's measured introductions to G. R. S. Mead's *Fragments of a Faith Forgotten* and to A. E. Waite's *The Holy Kabbala*, both reissued by University Books, 1960.

[25] Duncan, op. cit., p. xv.

[26] Quoted and commented on in Yates, op. cit., p. 170.

[27] For the important opposition of such thought to Victorian values, see Samuel B. Hynes, *The Edwardian Turn of Mind* (Princeton University Press, 1968), especially his chapter "Science, Seers, and Sex." I am greatly indebted to this study, as will appear later in the essay.

[28] See Leon Surette, *A Light from Eleusis* (Oxford University Press, 1979), pp. 34 ff, for an interesting discussion of this in relation to Pound.

[29] Butts, Mary, *Traps for Unbelievers* (London: Desmond Harmsworth, 1932), p. 25.

[30] Yates, op. cit., pp. 454-55.

[31] Butts, *Traps*, pp. 12-13.

[32] Ibid., p. 40.

[33] From Helen M. Mustard's and Charles E. Passage's "Introduction" to Wolfram von Eschenbach, *Parzival* (New York: Vintage Books, 1961), pp. xl-xli.

[34] Harrison, Jane Ellen, *Epilogomena to the Study of Greek Religion and Themis* (New York: University Books, 1962), p. 109.

[35] Ibid., pp. 75 & 106-07.

[36] Ibid., p. 110.

[37] Ibid., p. 109.

[38] Cook, A. B., *Zeus: A Study of Ancient Religion* (New York: Biblo and Tannen, 1965), vol. 2, p. 697 n.

[39] Harrison, op. cit., p. 6 ff.

[40] Cited in Jessie L. Weston, From *Ritual to Romance* (New York: Peter Smith, 1941), pp. 144-45.

[41] Ibid., p. 191. For lack of space, I can here only refer the reader to Henry and Renee Kahane, *The Krater and the Grail: Hermetic Sources of the Parzival* (Univ. of Illinois, 1965).

[42] Cited and the exhibition discussed in Hynes, p. 325, taken from Virginia Woolf's "Mr. Bennett and Mrs. Brown"—"a paper read to the Heretics, Cambridge, on May 18, 1924"—published in *The Captain's Death Bed and Other Essays* (London: Hogarth Press, 1950), p. 91.

[43] Hynes, p. 13.

[44] Ibid., pp. 132-33.

[45] Woolf, "The Cosmos," in *The Captain's Death Bed*, pp. 79, 81, & 83.

[46] Hynes, p. 134.

[47] I wish to emphasize the usefulness of Hynes's discussion of this in the chapter already noted, "Science, Seers, and Sex," pp. 32-171.

[48] Ibid., p. 138.

[49] Ibid.

[50] Ibid., p. 151.

[51] Cited in Hynes, p. 159.

[52] Butts, *Traps*, pp. 35-6.

[53] Ibid., p. 33.

[54] Ibid., p. 37.

[55] Ibid., pp. 37-8.

[56] Ibid., p. 39.

[57] Ibid., p. 47.

[58] Ibid., pp. 49-50 & 51.

[59] Hynes, p. 154.

[60] Butts, Mary, *The Macedonian* (London: William Heinemann, 1933), pp. 209-10.

[61] John Davidson, cited in David S. Thatcher, *Nietzsche in England, 1890-1914* (University of Toronto Press, 1970), a valuable discussion, pp. 51-93.

[62] Helen Watterson in *Century Magazine* (New York, May, 1889) and John Davidson in *Speaker* (London, 1891), noted and discussed by Thatcher, ibid., p. 22.

[63] Thatcher, pp. 27 ff.

[64] Grosskurth, Phyllis, *Havelock Ellis* (Toronto: McClelland and Stewart, 1980), pp. 200-09.

[65] Deleuze, Gilles, *Nietzsche and Philosophy*, trans. by Hugh Tomlinson (Columbia University Press, 1983), p. 197.

[66] Thatcher, p. 42.

[67] Ibid., p. 235.

[68] Both are reprinted in Pound's *Selected Prose, 1909-1965,* ed. by William Cookson (New York: New Directions, 1973)—this quotation, p. 446.

[69] Pound, "The Divine Mystery" in *Selected Prose,* p. 403.

[70] See Thatcher, pp. 219 ff.

[71] Ibid., pp. 221-22.

[72] Cited in Thatcher, pp. 230-31.

[73] Noted in Thatcher, p. 234.

[74] Ibid., p. 233.

[75] Richard Siebuth's introduction to *Friedrich Hölderlin, Hymns and Fragments* (Princeton University Press, 1984), pp. 11 & 33, slightly adapted for my purposes.

[76] The notion of the "consolidation of error," adapted here, is from Brian Wilke and M. J. Johnson, *Blake's Four Zoas* (Harvard University Press, 1978), p. 141.

[77] Hynes, p. 164.

[78] Paz, Octavio, *The Bow and the Lyre,* trans. by Ruth L. C. Simms (University of Texas Press, 1973), pp. 247-48.

Barbara O'Brien Wagstaff (essay date 1995)

SOURCE: "The Effectual Angel in *Death of Felicity Taverner,*" in *A Sacred Quest: The Life and Writings of Mary Butts,* edited by Christopher Wagstaff, McPherson & Company, 1995, pp. 224-42.

[*In the following essay, Wagstaff contends that in* Death of Felicity Taverner *Butts confronted her personal demons and attempted to create the possibility for reconciliation and liberation of one's "ideal self."*]

With the publication of *Death of Felicity Taverner* in 1932, Mary Butts's trilogy of novels was complete. This book brings together Boris Polteratsky and the unnamed letter writer of *Imaginary Letters* (dated 1924, first published in 1928) and Scylla, Felix and Picus of *Armed with Madness* (1928). Before this third volume opens, Felicity Taverner, the cousin of Scylla, Felix and Picus, has died mysteriously in an automobile accident; and whether it was an accident, suicide, or murder, her death, her cousins are convinced, was caused by the hatred of her mother, brother and husband. The cousins soon realize that, not content with her death, Felicity's husband, Nicholas Kralin, seeks to defame her by putting out an edition of her letters with his interpretation of them and of her and also by developing the land she loved into a resort. Felicity's mother, Julia Taverner, who cares little

for her daughter though a great deal about the family name and the land, and Felicity's brother, Adrian, who cares only about himself, cannot prevent Kralin because they are too busy quarreling. Scylla, Picus and Felix do not know what to do, and, at last, it is Boris who acts, avenging Felicity by leading Kralin into a trap and drowning him.

The most traditional in style and form of her novels—almost a "romance"—and full of references to great English poets, this book is darker in outlook than her earlier novels and faces squarely the question of how to offset evil, a problem which remains unresolved. Hence, perhaps, a shift in focus, after this book, toward the divine and human interaction in history, and the emphasis on the God-man in the lives of such individuals as Alexander and Julian. It is as though Mary Butts had finally broken free from, exorcised, the demon of her personal past, and so found that historic imagination she had so long wished for. *Death of Felicity Taverner* plays a pivotal part in this liberation and discovery because it confronts the loss of the ideal self, Felicity, and the possibility of its partial recovery. What Felicity and her friends contend with largely through their devotion to each other and their land and through the alchemy of poetry will soon be grappled with in a bigger drama on a larger stage and with reinforcements.

In *Ashe of Rings,* Mary Butts's first novel, a character says, "I want to stop wickedness, and I don't know how."[1] Judy's malevolent hatred of Vanna in that book, like Kralin's of Felicity, is fierce. Judy would murder Van, but the Rings, an ancient precinct like Eleusis, protects Van who depends on the "signatures of potencies who are watching man" (174); however, she does not know how to include her friend Serge in this safety. She tells him, "When I was drawn up that night onto the Rings, and lay outstretched on the stone, I thought that I had done it for us both." "How could you save another?" he replies. "I see that now," she answers (284). In *Armed with Madness,* Scylla can not, as could Van, avert her own crucifixion, though she brings about a stronger community by feeling past her fear and Clarence's hatred to "a clarté the other side of forgiveness."[2] Then, in *Death of Felicity Taverner,* where there is no saving Felicity and where the "anti-life" menacing the characters and the land is extreme, the wickedness is stopped. Van's refuge, her reverence for Rings Hill and her "words of power" (*AR,* 280), so like Joyce's "words of silent power," is also Scylla's and Felicity's; staying in this sanctuary, they help make true, if only in part, Dante's assertion in his *Paradiso,* "There will be seen that which we hold by faith."

Like many individuals of her time, Mary Butts saw "sinister forces . . . a black cloud gathering to overwhelm us all,"[3] appearing partly in the form of "envy, hatred, malice and all uncharitableness'"[4] threatening community on a global as well as on a personal level. This dark cloud descends on the Taverners' home, as it was descending on the world, with the presence of the comfortless, and

Mary Butts, like her Scylla, felt that "we must combat it with the good, the pure, the sweet, the true."[5] The thunder at the end of T. S. Eliot's *The Waste Land,* pointing a way, says "Datta. Dayadhvam. Damyata." Van, Scylla and Felicity give and sympathize; but Shelley's awe-ful Prometheus, in whom Mary Butts finds "the meaning of human life,"[6] suggests that power, control, only comes with the spirit of charity.

Felicity never appears in the trilogy. She is not a character in *Armed with Madness,* and if she is the letter writer in *Imaginary Letters* she does not sign her name; and, by the time of *Death of Felicity Taverner,* she is a ghost, influencing and focusing the battle. What others say about her tends to reveal themselves, while what they do because of her helps reveal her. Like the grail in *Armed with Madness,* which disappears at the end of the novel, she is many things. Mrs. Taverner considers her a wanton; she cannot see her actions in any but a sexual light. Felicity climbs fences, she avers, to show off her legs. Adrian's view of his sister is colored by his mother's. Kralin, recognizing only personal gratification, calls Felicity "an erotic expert,"[7] and his relentless efforts to wipe out all trace of his wife suggests how much she disturbs him. Boris, who at first pretends not to have known Felicity, comes to see she is like the sister and mother and his own goodness destroyed in the Russian Revolution. Scylla, Felix and Picus see Felicity as Shelley did Keats. They would like to enhance her reputation and they try to incorporate what they understand of her in their lives. Called naive, repressed, loose and abnormal, Felicity suffers the artist's fate, and especially the true saint's, whose efforts to make earth a heaven are considered either immoral or unrealistic. As Scylla says of Felicity, she was "made for a particular kind of love . . . that the world at present has particularly no use for. . . . It was as good as any art to her. *'In whom alone love lives again'* and all that" (36).

"Who killed Cock Robin?" the nursery rhyme asks, and no one knows why the sparrow shot him with his bow and arrow, but all the creatures mourn. "Who kill'd John Keats?" writes Byron, continuing, "I says the Quarterly, / So savage and Tartarly; / 'Twas one of my feats." Scolded and berated by Mrs. Taverner, bullied by Adrian who denies the possibility of disinterested action, and hounded by Kralin who denies her very soul, Felicity, without pretension, without sufficient confidence in herself, lacks the instinct for self-preservation. Kralin speaks of her "Electra complex," and while she has no ability to get along with her mother, she cannot or will not retaliate with her knowledge of Adrian's patrimony, nor does she plead with Adrian nor try to justify herself to him; and, she will not use Felix's love for her. Instead, her hold on life weakened by the harsh judgments and misunderstanding of her family and the hatred of her husband, she dies. As Scylla sees it, "Her humility destroyed her. . . . She did not know her own power—her own discovery" (37). Without someone to help her, and without the disillusion to see what people are like, Felicity is helpless against the negation of Kralin whose talent is to undo what others do or would do.

Nicholas Kralin is Mary Butts's portrait of the devil in the modern world and probably also of her first husband, John Rodker, poet, translator and publisher. A Russian Jew, whom Boris, a Russian aristocrat, dubs a Red agent, a purveyor of obscene ikons (Rodker's publishing included erotica), Kralin is to Scylla and Felix the snake slithering through their Sacred Wood, a worm or slug leaving its trail of slime on their lives. He is the ultimate foreigner, alien to the honor, truth, beauty and love they value, and Boris cannot understand why Felicity's family allowed her to marry him. This picture of Kralin reflects the anti-Semitism of the period and the class-consciousness of England, but finally his evil, like that of Mary Butts's other monstrous characters, Jewish and non-Jewish alike, is his thorough denial of life, a rejection she knew from her reading of the Romantics and of myth and folklore, and also from her own experiences.

In *The Crystal Cabinet,* she describes her discovery as a young girl that "The world isn't like what people tell you. There are ugly things about like wolves running, and the Psalms are quite right" (*CC,* 114). Part of the ugliness is the contrast between the way people live and the way poetry, particularly Shelley's, describes living:

> [T]he crude world in which I found myself solitary was only a fire-bearer's apprenticeship. Perhaps only Shelley knows how I escaped the destruction of self-pity and unteachable priggishness.
>
> As to many generous children, it was the contradiction between the two worlds that bewildered as it hurt. Since goodness, loveliness, wisdom, adventure and high thoughts were so obviously preferable, why did people prefer ignorance, convention, commonness? All expressed in the unlovingness I felt around me on every side. Why didn't they listen to the men called philosophers who were there to show them? And to the painters and poets and great architects and men of learning? (*CC,* 125).

Throughout her stories, age constricts and prevents youth, ugliness attacks beauty, malice love, and spite generosity, an eternal conflict *Prometheus Unbound* depicts also, where Jupiter, the very spirit of constriction, hate, and the will-to-power endeavors to suppress the beauty, love and liberty of Prometheus. Besides the horror of Jupiter, there were the Norse myths, Odin hanging on the tree and Baldur's death, ballads and stories of bogies, and the child's awareness, in the woods especially, of "a much smaller, meaner form of supernatural life":

> Of every sort of kind and quality, in and out of doors; in patches, and often, as in the case of the great pine-tree, especially attached to things. God and your Angel took care of you through it—the Angel who was later to stand beside you, as his daimon by Socrates.
>
> "It" was infinitely less than God. The thought of God could send "it" scattering in an instant—if you remembered in time. Only there were bits of

it, come upon suddenly round corners, so terrifying that they caught you before you could remember Him. It was awfully interesting too. Things to explore when you were grown-up. And some of the gods even were "like" it—Hecate, of course, and Loki; and because of "it," in another grander way, people died when they saw Pan.

All this I found out for myself in the ancient garden at Salterns, and in the woods, in the salt-marshes and by the sea (***CC***, 139-40).

Mary Butts finds this "smaller, meaner form of supernatural life" depicted in Montague Rhodes James's ghost stories. In a review of his art of storytelling, the first published during his lifetime, she writes:

The evidence for their [good and evil potencies'] existence is, from many angles, as strong as the evidence for their non-existence. But—it is harder to follow; common-sense or even learned incredulity is essentially easier and simpler. Also more à la mode. . . . Perhaps the doubt felt about Doctor James' subject is not only shallow scepticism, but sound, self-protective sense. Better not—certainly for the majority—better not enquire too closely; ask too many questions as to the existence of such things. Everyone who has lived much out of doors feels something of what he tells. Not by association with tradition, but by a direct kind of awareness, an impact on the senses—and something more than the senses. It can be a recurrent, almost an overwhelming, experience. Much ancient bogey-lore was a rationalisation of it. Today we talk of suggestion, exorcise with the magic word "unscientific." But I doubt if our ignorant scepticism is any nearer truth than our ancestors' ignorant credulity.[8]

Unlike Algernon Blackwood "who relies on suggestion, a strengthening atmosphere in which very little ever happens; or rather one is not sure whether it has happened or not," M. R. James renders the supernatural and the horrible "unspeakably real, solid, present,"[9] through careful detailed descriptions of events or facts of history, setting, places, weather, and of what the characters observe as they run up against this malignity in the course of their daily lives and work. Blackwood's deep feeling for nature, his evocations of mountains, forests, lakes and rivers, particularly of landscapes remote from men's influence, enthrall by their sheer beauty, a sublimity human nature of itself cannot withstand, whereas many of the places and settings in Arthur Machen's tales and in M. R. James's stories threaten more. In their writings, the encounters with this other dimension are experienced as incursions which few survive intact, whereas in Blackwood the crossing-over can be a blessing. *John Silence* is Blackwood's series of stories about a doctor who helps others through a process of spiritual alchemy, an unusual Sympathy involving an active psychic negation and neutralization of evil forces and an identification with the good. It is intriguing that a work of occult fiction by Dion Fortune (Violet Mary Firth), founder of The Society of the Inner Light, entitled *The Secrets of Dr. Taverner* and widely read in its day, appeared in 1926.

"Taverner" the O.E.D. says is one who keeps a tavern and also one who drinks or takes intoxicating substances. "Felicity Taverner" encompasses an earthly and a heavenly nature and suggests intoxication whether by material or spiritual means. Robert McAlmon wrote that "Mary breathed in an exalted ecstasy of being,"[10] which other descriptions of her corroborate. Intoxication, whether by drink, drugs or the "words of power" in poetry and magic—all of which she knew by experience—may lead to transformation, and in her writings such transformation has often to do with love. In the works of Éliphas Lévi on magic, with which she was familiar, love is strongly identified with woman. Lévi discusses the relation between Christianity and the ancient mysteries and magic, bringing out the importance of knowing, daring, singleness of will, and silence, all of which the Taverners practise. Scylla's silence at her crucifixion in *Armed with Madness,* her dim realization that her business is "to bring order, proportion, light into what is happening. That where there has been falsehood and muddle, there shall be knowing and clearness, conception for misconception" (***DFT***, 122), saves her; and, in *Ashe of Rings,* Van is protected because of her knowledge of Rings and her relation to it.

The experience of the supernatural, central to Mary Butts's works, involves familiarity with woods, seashore, moor, cliff, birds, turf. As in myths and legends, these are sentient; they participate in the lives of humans. Her rendition of them includes the realism, the sense of danger, the evocation of place, as well as the terrible beauty of surroundings she admires in both James and Blackwood. What might be termed "Christian" and "pagan" elements coexist in her world. Her characters know the horror of nature and the supernatural, and also the supremacy of a love and a glory born not of themselves, as it is felt in the poetry of Spenser, Milton, Wordsworth and Shelley, authors crucial to her awakening as an artist.

Like the beasts in Arthur Machen's "The Terror" who reflect the hatred raging in the world from war, Kralin looms larger than human to Felicity and her cousins and Boris. It is an old belief that at those times when humans are less than human, the powers of evil rejoice and are more active; the little people are about more, and Boris's "fairy-tale mind" sees Kralin "with cheeks drawn in" carrying a bag containing "a small iced wind" he lets out in puffs (***DFT***, 205-06). This something about him they can only refer to as "the grey thing" or "le Kralinism" is the terror Boris imagines as pockets of poisoned air and Mary Butts experienced sometimes in the woods and encountered once on the Fifeshire sands, "inimical and deadly," "a focus, a column of energy, cold and vile and hateful, spinning there" (***CC***, 204).

Worshipping Nodens, God of the Abyss, "Not-Being, Un-Meaning, Un-doing" (***DFT***, 106), which Mary Butts gained an increased knowledge of from her visit to Aleister Crowley's Abbey of Thelema at Cefalù, Kralin causes Felicity to despair. Felix tells of her "panic-fear" of anything grey, of sea-mist and grey skies, which suggests to anyone interested in magic that Felicity was a victim of what some writers call a psychic attack, and which, they contend, is far commoner than is generally realized. The fear and oppression Felicity suffers from, her nervous exhaustion, the notion of evil odors and even the association of these with slime and the color grey are characteristics of such attacks, the imposition or intrusion of one will on another. Of course, literature and history and life are full of such instances of imposition though we still tend not to explore this aspect of events, but Mary Butts's works include it. As Picus says, "You can get a first in Greats or fly round inside the crater of Vesuvius, but what you depend on for your private life is your degree in witch-doctoring. How much you can smell-out the propitious from the unpropitious" (*DFT*, 24).

Married very young and having little experience of the world, Felicity has no nose for "the unpropitious" she meets in Kralin. Though her instincts to love are in the right direction, there is no John Silence to encourage her, and her cousins are too concerned with their own affairs to heed her danger. How could any of them believe in such a dark thing as Kralin? It takes them most of six weeks as the story unfolds to realize what he is like, and even Kralin is ignorant of the horror of himself, disgusted and impatient as he is with one of M. R. James's stories. The grey thing, like Felicity herself, is larger than the particular person or thing that manifests it.

In accompanying Felicity and a lover around Paris, Boris notices what they fail to see—not just "people hating what they should love" but "people practising how to kill what they do not like. Their ill-will *works*. And among certain people I know of in Paris, they know how to *make* it work. This they do for fun, or under some compulsion; or an order. How can I convince you? It was as if it had been decided on that she was to be crucified" (*DFT*, 84). He continues, "I knew that 'le Kralinism' had bitten into [her lover], and I did nothing. I, who knew enough to know that they were the condemned and that the grey web had been thrown over them. I let myself be its instrument" (*DFT*, 86).

Felicity's "crucifixion" recalls Scylla's as well as Van's and her ancestor's. None of these individuals is saintly in the usual sense, and the attacks on them are not wholly undeserved; but, each one is searching for a deeper community than those around her comprehend, and the vilification each suffers suggests how much such community threatens the security of identity which excludes the sacred. The story **"From Altar to Chimney-piece"** describes a group which practises a cult of cruelty, a "subjectivity run mad." A young girl with whom the narrator of the story is in love has been singled out as a victim, and as an old woman takes her dirty handkerchief and rubs out the name of Christ on the ancient ciborium now used as a candelabra, the narrator sees that her "contempt for . . . all that . . . makes life worth living, had something enormous about it."[11]

This denial of ties not only to other people but to things supernatural and natural for the most part undetected—to gods, places, trees, stars, animals—leads to the horror of Kralin. Modern individuals as Mary Butts depicts them in her works and discusses them in two essays, *Traps for Unbelievers* and *Warning to Hikers,* is cut off from both Nature and the divine, from what lies below and what is above; and, lacking these ties, their bonds with their fellows break also. To Kralin, who only appreciates the land for the revenge it affords and the money it will yield as a tourist attraction, everything, including sacred ikons, becomes an object.

The desecration of individuals, land and things which follows this unchecked subjectivity, which she also calls a "plague, a Black Death of the spirit" (*CC*, 138), can only be offset, Mary Butts's works suggest, by recontacting what John Shorthouse called "Eternal Truth manifested in Phenomena,"[12] in nature, myth, and art. In *Traps for Unbelievers* she speaks of the "very peculiar kind of awareness . . . [which has] to do with a sense of the invisible, the non-existent in a scientific sense, relations between things of a different order: the moon and a stone, the sea and a piece of wood, women and fish," an awareness which "has no more died in man than has his sight or any other of his senses; only he does not now try it out. . . ."[13] Van, Scylla, Felicity—mostly, it seems, it is women—have cultivated such a perception; they have grown up close to the sacred resident in poetry, music, and nature, and these come to their aid. A woman in the story **"Friendship's Garland"** is released from fear and regenerated by a tree, and in **"Green"**[14] a couple is protected from a Kralin-like character by their consciousness of the Hermes and Aphrodite power surrounding them. The denial of love, imagination, beauty, freedom, is real in Mary Butts's books, and just as a bad smell tends to overpower a sweet one, there is small hope for those who of themselves try to stand up to a Kralin; but, keeping tabu and preserving carefully their mana objects may get them through, unless, like Felicity, companionless, they find themselves pitted against Nodens himself. However, Felicity triumphs when the land, her cousins and Boris become a working community to help her.

Boris, who lives off his looks and wit and who drinks and takes drugs and avoids deep friendships all because of bad memories, is slowly transformed by his contact with the Taverners. He dates the hour of his ruin from his wish to be rid of his mother and sister when the family was fleeing Russia, a ruin he feels is symbolized by his losing an ikon his mother gave him. The letter writer of *Imaginary Letters* tries to dissuade him from accepting his ruin and following the usual remedy "not to think, to scurry through life to artificial oblivion"; but, it is not until the confrontation between his friends and Kralin that Boris sees his place in this "sad little war [they're] fighting" (*DFT*, 198, 234).

Scylla, Felix and Picus are ignorant at first of the operation of Kralin's destructiveness, unsure how it has killed their cousin until they encounter it firsthand. Only Scylla senses how to face Kralin. As she begins to feel sick and cold during a visit she pays him, she instinctively starts to play his game, "mean and sharp and of the ways of the world," telling him lies to put him off her track, and to think of such lines as *'Love your enemies'* and the one about the man *'who gave his enemy his plank and plunged aside to die'* (*DFT,* 176). She begins to control her awe and fear of him and summons up the power to tell him off and bring herself away from the interview intact though shaken. Later, the thought comes to her for them to call on the Elemental Spirits, but she wonders about their ability to solicit their aid; drawing closer together, she and Picus and Felix await the movement of events.

What they do not know and only gradually become aware of is that the ghost of Felicity is about. At first only a figure of speech, "the ghost" slowly materializes from a lover's dream to a felt presence a blackbird shouts at. She is so much in the hearts and minds of her family and friends that she cannot help coming to them. "This place is somehow full of Felicity," Adrian says, adding, after the ghost leaves, driven away by her mother and brother in death as in life, "Just now I felt a kind even of physical emptiness about us—There had been a sort of presence before" (*DFT,* 217, 222). Then, as Scylla and Boris stand on a crest overlooking the land and observe its beauties and discuss Kralin's plans, Boris's past and present experience merges with that of the Taverners, and "the ghost of Felicity Taverner," so identified and named for the first time, comes and sits down by her cousin "who moved a little, as though disturbed by an unaccountable breeze" (*DFT,* 242). Finally, she whom Scylla and Picus have seen as "a shape of bright darkness, blowing out flowers" and have felt as a third often with them, because, so at one with the land she loves "that the hills were her body laid-down, and 'Felicity' was said, over and over again, in each bud and leaf," she comes to accompany Boris as a third, a "confused transparency . . . as of a shadow threaded with brightness" when he leads Kralin to his death (*DFT,* 40, 256). "Ghost of Felicity, is not this what had to be? You know that, for we've felt you about us and you have not prevented us," observes Boris (*DFT,* 260).

This portrait of Felicity recalls Mary Butts's reading of M. R. James's story, "Lost Hearts," which seized her, she writes, with "terror and felicity."[15] Slowly, powerfully, this quiet land-cup with its sacred wood has been weaving its net of destiny. Its beauty has worked its magic on Scylla, Picus, Felix, and Boris, and though Kralin is insensitive to it, he is lured by his desire to use and destroy it. In James's story the ghosts of two children take revenge on their murderer and protect another child from the same fate. Mysterious figures, they present a terrifying spectacle, menacing and dreadful in a still, moonlit night. Thomas Nashe's line, "Brightness falls from the air," haunting Mary Butts's writing, not only suggests the terrible fall and loss of youth and beauty, like that of Keats and Cock Robin, but also the avenging spirit of such loss. Like the Erinyes who are also called Eumenides, Felicity is a bright darkness, which has less to do with orthodoxly Christian notions of good and evil than with the presences of places, objects, individuals and things unknown which can benefit or injure according to one's relation to them. Adrian, who is throwing away his "mana object" (*DFT,* 97), is making a wilderness of his life; and Kralin, who has no understanding of the powers of creatures and sacred objects and places and who enjoys turning gardens into deserts, becomes fish food. The land-cup with its wood, birds and cliffs towering above the sea, sacrosanct to Felicity and her cousins, is a magic ring changing Boris and drawing him in, thrusting out Kralin, protecting Scylla, Picus, Felix and itself. Like the providence Hamlet senses just before his duel with Laertes, which perhaps indicates how he is able at last to say "Let be," so the circumstance of Kralin's death has something large and inevitable about it, of which Boris's deliberation is only part. As an effectual angel, Felicity's ghost suggests such providence, the operation of divine powers coming into play when what Van calls "the art of life . . . to let things come" is practised (*AR,* 212).

Mary Butts writes that the link for her between the God of her fathers and her belief in the ancient gods "was my belief in the Guardian Angel" (*CC,* 137), and in Felicity are joined the Christian idea of love and the pagan reverence for nature which derive, at least in part, from Mary Butts's reading of Celtic literature, the Bible, Spenser, Milton and the Romantics—rhythms, lines, images and ideas of which appear throughout her writing. Angels, the host of heaven, come as messengers, holy ones, watchers, spirits in Genesis, Ezekiel, Daniel, Revelation and the gospels; and attendant spirits, spirits of nature, harbingers, heralds, angels and other bright ministers abound in Milton and Shelley. In the Book of Revelation angels and the earth help the woman fleeing the red dragon, and Shelley's Prometheus, buoyed by spirits of the hour and of earth and by unseen spirits, prevails through wishing no living thing to suffer pain. As in H. D.'s poetry, these luminous beings are real, not symbolic representations. Referring to Felicity, Adrian cites the lines from "Comus" about the "thousand liveried angels" who protect "saintly chastity," while Scylla's feeling of Felicity as a presence accompanying Picus and her at sea and through the woods evokes the divine creatures peopling Shelley's poems. The animated interchange between nature and humankind found in Romantic poetry helped Mary Butts to much of her vocabulary and experience. "The first thing that I remember is a puddle of yellow mud," *The Crystal Cabinet* begins, and then she describes tasting it. The venerative, receptive, alert passivity enabling Wordsworth to hear the "things forever speaking," and to feel "A presence . . . [which] rolls through all things,"[16] and to admit the blessings of all he beholds despite the dreary roar and commerce of daily life, informs Mary Butts's response to her surroundings.

> . . . there were times when the trees and stones and turf were not dumb, and [Scylla] had their speech, and the ruins rose again and the sunk foundations, and copse and clearing and forest changed places, and went in and out and set to

partners in their century-in, century-out dance. There were times, out on the high turf at sun-rise and set, when in the slanted light she saw their land as an exfoliation, not happening in our kind of time, a becoming of the perfected (*DFT,* 183).

This devotion to living in accord with this other is a transfiguring formula which has its counterpart in human relationships, however more difficult its terms be to apply. Though the war undermined this faith, as did most human relationships, in Mary Butts's books is felt the urgency of the need to bring the unimagined into play in the world. In a fever over Kralin's projected development of their land, Scylla invokes this Spirit, murmuring "'It will be all right only if we love each other enough'" (*DFT,* 263), almost the very words Boris's mother spoke to her family as they tried to escape and which "had dissolved the grain of his evil thought" (*DFT,* 195). Struggling to objectify Felicity's love, Scylla instinctively, increasingly cherishes what is sacred as Kralin's destruction looms ever more imminent; and, while Felicity found no Prometheus, Scylla has Boris, who rejoins community by stepping outside it.

In murdering Kralin, Boris performs an act of violence to equal his denial of others since that fatal day before a small tree outside a train station in eastern Russia when "for the first time . . . there came upon him hatred of his sister and his mother. . . . Into that pit of the spirit he had sunk with his father" (*DFT,* 194). One day out on the moor near the Taverners' home, as he muses over their situation, he sees the same tree and that Kralin is like it. Just as there is bad human nature, so is there bad nature, like the stone at Stone's End which causes evil thoughts or stops thought altogether and which Boris dubs "Kralin's Stone." Mary Butts speaks of the humming going on in everything which can be heard in stillness, a thought similar to Blackwood's that ideas come to people from trees and flowers. Of course, such thoughts are not always healthy for human beings, as many of Machen's and Blackwood's stories show; and Boris, familiar with the effects, if not with the process of such thoughts coming both from nature and from human beings because of his experience outside the train and his life in Paris, recognizes their characteristics in the Taverners' predicament.

From a lazy, petulant dependent, Boris changes to a determined, ruthless soldier, who having seen an enemy of his community, destroys it. In the context of Mary Butts's work, his act poses a question—Is not love, of itself, sufficient to offset Kralin? Scylla, Felix and Picus have retreated to their house, and though Scylla feels helpless, she clings to their love for each other. Again and again Mary Butts comes back to this redemptive capacity of love. Is Boris the *geburah* accompanying the *hesed* of his friends? His act is a reentry into a sympathy with others and with a locale which he has lost since leaving Russia, while it also puts him altogether outside the Taverners' world. Scylla sees that she and Picus and Felix must "be for honour what they [Kralin, Mrs. Taverner, Adrian] are for dishonour; for truth what they are for lies; for charity what they are for spite; for loveliness

what they are for filth"; and perhaps, at that instant of insight, the "release that felt like a glory [which] came about them, as though separate and converging paths of light lay to be walked on at their feet," suggests the bright darkness coming into action: "It was, at that moment, as though all that Kralin had done was to open a door onto a stadium set for the players of the sacred game. On which field he had his place also" (*DFT,* 160).

Begun for these characters in *Imaginary Letters,* played in *Armed with Madness,* and continued in *Death of Felicity Taverner,* the game of letting life alone, so that the divine rather than a mental machination can reach into and transform the human, is becoming more difficult. It has never been easy, and as the awareness of mental causation became more common around the turn of the century, as witness the proliferation of occult societies and literature, claims and accusations of mental manipulation and even of mental murder were not unusual. Anna Bonus Kingsford, for example, a doctor, and author with Edward Maitland of *The Perfect Way,* felt she succeeded in mentally assassinating some vivisectionists; in turn, she was herself thought to be a victim of mental murder. Mary Butts's associations, particularly in the early 'twenties, with occult groups and with practitioners of magic, such as Aleister Crowley and Cecil Maitland, surely increased her awareness of the perils of the mind unleashed, and certainly her writings indicate that to her the idea of mental malpractice was neither ridiculous nor farfetched. Though Boris's solution to Kralin hardly seems his author's, the question of what to do about such psychic malfeasance as Kralin is guilty of, of how to do as the thundering angel in *The Waste Land* advises and Shelley's *Prometheus* does, is unresolved. Kralin must be resisted, as Boris and Scylla resist quarreling because quarreling is what Kralin wants. Nature and the supernatural come to the aid of those who resist, but what would happen without Boris's intervention and what will happen because of it, is uncertain, though it hardly could be a fulfillment of Felix's wish that "someone be born . . . who will make *'On Heaven'* true" (*DFT,* 47). In *The Crystal Cabinet* Mary Butts recalls a teacher's comment, "Jacob was sent an angel. . . . There are blessings that are fought for—and others that cannot be earned or snatched, which are given only 'without money and without price'" (227-28).

Less terse and staccato in style and manner than *Armed with Madness, Death of Felicity Taverner* presents a greater madness. The 'twenties are over. The dancing, jazz and snatches of song integral to the spirit of *Armed with Madness* are mostly gone, and in their stead are long vigils in restless rooms and lines from "Lycidas." Scylla, Felix and Picus feel they will go mad if they cannot account for Felicity's death, and they only account for it by themselves encountering another madness, Kralin, and Boris's act of war. For years Boris has "been trying to find a happy-go-lucky way to kill himself" (*DFT,* 198), but rather than such disintegration, he is compelled into thought and action by his friends and their surroundings, tree, stone, moor and sea, a community which, he discovers, includes the felicity he has lost, and which demands each member's response.

In 1932 Mary Butts retired to a fishing village in Cornwall, it may be to draw close to those potencies which alone, perhaps, could help her to meet the coming world upheaval. Her childlike communion with beloved places and objects, and her awareness of poetry as a power, were her sustenance; and "blessed," she writes in **The Crystal Cabinet,** "are the grown-up people who have not lost [such communion]—a reminder of the conditions under which we enter the Kingdom of Heaven" (84). Later in the same book (118-19) she recounts an experience born of this lifelong conversation:

> It was in London, in the last lap of the war, when the air-raids were screaming out of the high winter sky. I was alone in a Hampstead studio, my first home by myself. The high fragile roof was made of glass, and the gun on the Heath shook the earth and the engines droned overhead, and suddenly panic came over me. I dared not go out through the dropping shrapnel, and the infernal things were zooming nearer and nearer overhead; and instantly the danger of it all and the horror were made clear to me, and I ran to try and hide myself in a little out-building, a dark hole full of wood, where the roof was low, and no airy brittle roof rose above me into shadows.
>
> I can only try and tell what happened as I tried not to crouch there. Which was an infinitely clear, infinitely quiet voice repeating: *'Love and man's unconquerable mind. Love and man's unconquerable mind';* and I was suddenly charged with knowledge that, somehow, it was important that I should command myself, that, in some unrealizable way, I had it in me to preserve or to destroy the meaning of those words.
>
> Repeating them, I went back; and inside the studio and the racket overhead there was a quiet into which I entered where both fear and death were swallowed up.

NOTES

1 Butts, Mary, *Ashe of Rings* (New York: Albert and Charles Boni, 1926), p. 294; hereafter cited parenthetically as *AR.*

2 Butts, Mary, *Armed with Madness* (New York: Albert and Charles Boni, 1928), p. 214.

3 McAlmon, Robert and Boyle, Kay, *Being Geniuses Together* (New York: Doubleday & Co., Inc., 1968), p. 124.

4 Butts, Mary, "Questionnaire," *The Little Review,* May 1929, p. 21.

5 *Being Geniuses Together,* p. 124.

6 Butts, Mary, *The Crystal Cabinet: My Childhood at Salterns* (London: Methuen & Co. Ltd., 1937), p. 116; hereafter cited parenthetically as *CC.*

7 Butts, Mary, *Death of Felicity Taverner* (London: Wishart & Co., 1932), p. 131; hereafter cited parenthetically as *DFT.*

8 Butts, Mary, "The Art of Montagu [*sic*] James," *The London Mercury,* Feb. 1934, vol. xxix, no. 172, pp. 315-17.

9 Butts, Mary, "The Art of Montagu James," p. 307.

10 *Being Geniuses Together,* p. 124.

11 Butts, Mary, *Last Stories* (London: Brendin Publishing Co., 1938), p. 166, p. 174.

12 Shorthouse, J. H., *John Inglesant* (London: MacMillan and Co., Ltd., 1881), p. x.

13 Butts, Mary, *Traps for Unbelievers* (London: Harmsworth, 1932), p. 25.

14 Butts, Mary, *Several Occasions* (London: Wishart, 1932).

15 Butts, Mary, "The Art of Montagu James," p. 306.

16 William Wordsworth, *Poems,* introd. Edwin Markham (New York and London: The Co-operative Publication Society, n.d.), pp. 236-37.

FURTHER READING

Biography

Blondel, Nathalie. *Mary Butts: Scenes from the Life.* Kingston, New York: McPherson, 1998, 554 p.
    Comprehensive biography of Butts that draws heavily on the unpublished diaries she kept from 1916 until her death.

> **Additional coverage of Butts's life and career is contained in the following source published by Gale Research:** *Contemporary Authors,* **Vol. 148.**

Irvin S. Cobb
1876-1944

(Full name Irvin Shrewsbury Cobb) American novelist, short story writer, journalist, essayist, and screenwriter.

INTRODUCTION

Although largely forgotten by the end of the twentieth century, during the years that followed the end of the nineteenth century and up to the time of the Great Depression, Cobb was known and loved not only as a writer, but as a national personality. His humorous stories, especially those surrounding his characters Judge Priest and Jeff Poindexter, earned him comparisons with his friend Will Rogers, and even with Mark Twain. But Cobb also wrote suspenseful tales which likewise inspired praise of his work as part of a grand American tradition, in this case the macabre stories of Edgar Allan Poe. Also a journalist, popular speaker, screenwriter, and actor, Cobb was a well-known public figure and a favorite of caricaturists, who depicted his prominent paunch and cigar. His work was a significant part of American literature in that his transition from the character of Judge Priest to that of the hapless "fat man" of numerous sketches marked a movement from nineteenth- to twentieth-century forms of humor.

Biographical Information

Cobb was born in Kentucky a decade after the Civil War, and he grew up surrounded by the images of the South that he would later preserve in his Judge Priest stories. In fact his father was one of several men who helped to form the model of the Judge, but the elder Cobb's story was not so lighthearted: he drifted into alcoholism, and his son had to quit school at age sixteen to support the family. Cobb entertained a number of ambitions, but ended up in newspaper work with the local *Paducah Daily News,* for which he became managing editor at age nineteen and in which capacity he served as local correspondent for the Chicago *Tribune.* In 1904, after a series of newspaper jobs in various states, Cobb—already a married man—set off to New York City alone to break into the newspaper business there. Partly through the clever use of a humorous form letter to editors, he gained a job with the *Evening Sun,* where he proved himself with a series of human-interest sketches on the Russo-Japanese peace conference in Portsmouth, New Hampshire, in 1905. Joseph Pulitzer hired him on the *New York Evening and Sunday World,* and Cobb's reputation as a humorist grew. He continued to cover straight news stories such as the infamous Harry K. Thaw murder trial, always doing so from a human-interest perspective. One of his most impressive talents was his ability to churn out copy of extremely high quality and quantity. Soon Cobb

began to produce short stories, first in the suspense genre; by the time he published his second book in 1912, he had introduced Judge Priest and friends to the world. Cobb followed this with a series of successful books, not just the Priest stories but a number of travel narratives, as well as his first-hand portrayal of events during World War I. During this time, Cobb also wrote for the *Saturday Evening Post* and later for the Hearst empire. His gentlemanly style of humor contrasted sharply with the acid wit of his contemporary H. L. Mencken. Cobb suffered large losses in the Wall Street Crash of 1929, and though he would recover financially through his involvement with Hollywood and as a popular and well-paid speaker, his role as an influential commentator rapidly ebbed. By the time he published his memoirs, *Exit Laughing,* in 1941, he had already become a figure of historical rather than current interest.

Major Works

Cobb published more than fifty books, hundreds of stories, and hundreds more sketches and essays, most of them humorous. Many of the latter he compiled in collections, of which *Cobb's Anatomy* (1912) and *Cobb's Bill-of-Fare* (1913) are representative. Later he applied his humorous style to travel narratives such as *Europe Revised* (1914); *Roughing It De Luxe*, a 1914 account of a trip out West; and *Some United States* (1926). He offered more serious journalistic accounts of current events, particularly World War I, in works such as *Paths of Glory* (1915). As for his fiction, he started out publishing suspenseful tales such as those found in *The Escape of Mr. Trimm* (1913), but his forte in the realm of fiction—as with nonfiction—lay in the area of humor. Most famous among his creations was Judge Priest, whose first stories were collected in 1912 as *Back Home*. The Judge was a quirky, somewhat absurd figure of a peculiarly Southern type, who, along with his friends, reminisced about the Civil War—the stories were set in the 1890s—while keeping an eye out for Yankees and other varmints. Almost as popular were the Judge's associates, particularly his black valet Jeff Poindexter, celebrated in *J. Poindexter, Colored* (1922). In spite of Cobb's stated desire to debunk myths about Southerners, he helps to perpetuate them with the stereotypical character of Jeff, who was fittingly portrayed by Stepin Fetchit in the 1934 John Ford film *Judge Priest*, in which Will Rogers played the title role. If Jeff and the Judge belonged to the nineteenth century, however, Cobb's "fat man" character is very much a creature of the twentieth. This figure—not so much a single character as a type that recurs in Cobb's work—made his most notable appearance in the writer's most popular book, *Speaking of Operations—* (1915), which sold some 100,000 copies in its first year of publication, described what Cobb viewed as his inhumane treatment at the hands of hospital personnel when he checked in for an appendectomy. Though the style was humorous, there was a somewhat frightening sense of the individual being swallowed in the machinery of modern life. The fat man was usually Cobb himself, as in *The Abandoned Farmers* (1920). Such work helped gain Cobb a reputation as an inheritor of Mark Twain's mantle; but, unlike Twain, he was apt to succumb to sentimentality and to avoid portraying genuine evil. Most of his later work continued along one of the threads he established in the 1910s and 1920s, and at the end of his career, Cobb summed up his life with his 1941 memoir, *Exit Laughing*.

PRINCIPAL WORKS

Back Home: Being the Narrative of Judge Priest and His People (short stories) 1912
Cobb's Anatomy (essays) 1912
Cobb's Bill-of-Fare (essays) 1913
The Escape of Mr. Trimm: His Plight and Other Plights (short stories) 1913
Europe Revised (travel essays) 1914

Roughing It De Luxe (travel essay) 1914
Paths of Glory; Impressions of War Written At and Near the Front (journalism) 1915
Speaking of Operations— (satire) 1915
The Abandoned Farmers (notebook) 1920
J. Poindexter, Colored (short stories) 1922
Some United States; A Series of Stops in Various Parts of the Nation with One Excursion Across the Line (travel essays) 1926
Exit Laughing (memoirs) 1941

CRITICISM

Pendennis (essay date 1917)

SOURCE: "My Types—Irvin S. Cobb," in *The Forum*, Vol. 58, October, 1917, pp. 471-86.

[*In the following essay, Pendennis interviews Cobb, discussing with him the inspiration for his characters.*]

Looking like Cyrano de Bergerac, in white flannels; hovering like a lazy bumble-bee over the honey-pots of literature, on a dreamy morning in August, Cobb prolonged his reputation for being the best newspaper man in the country.

Cyrano de Bergerac, as you remember, was a poet with a gift for wit in seeing life and a gallantry for believing well of his fellow-men. He should have been a Southerner. There was in him that slumbering soul of the rebel, slow to be roused, outwardly calm as the smooth face of the Mississippi, but deep and wide and threatening.

Irvin S. Cobb was born in Paducah, Ky., and although Illinois was just across the river, that did not inspire Paducah. When Cobb was a small boy, Judge "Billie" Bishop was the legal oracle of that community. In hundreds of southern towns there were judges to whom the people went for wisdom and good liquor. "Billie" Bishop was typical of most of them. A tall, portly, slow-moving human being, who always carried a huge cotton umbrella, wore a well educated goatee, and white duck suits in summer. Bald-headed, florid, poor, with the independence and the courage of a lion, he appeared sometimes childish, sometimes masterful, always kind.

He died fifteen years ago, in Paducah, before he became really distinguished in the world as the much loved Judge Priest, as Cobb re-christened him, calling him Priest because, as his name was Bishop, it seemed appropriate. He was a real man whose individuality sank deep into the heart and mind of little eight-year-old Cobb. At eight one does not expect one to be studying types for fiction. Obviously it behooves us to be cautious in the presence of our children; they may be spying into our hearts deeper than we can suspect.

Judge Priest comes to mind as the most definitely clear type of character that Cobb has given us. He abounds in the grandeur of simplicity, in the romance of Kentucky sentiment. In the years that have intervened since that young reporter first saw a story in him, the Judge has lain in all the glory of his remembrance, undisturbed in the heart of the writer who found him. So he has become an unconscious contribution to literature, where he belongs so perfectly.

To-day, in a diminutive Swiss chalet, gracefully set down on the edge of a miniature pond, Cobb communes with his typewriter. Faithful friend of intellectual stress and struggle, it has collaborated valiantly. It has come into its own. It rests now in that sylvan surrounding which many typewriters hope for, but rarely attain. It is safe among the hills that guard the Hudson, on its own estate of sixty acres. It has no doubt written the name for its retreat, since it is called Rebel Ridge, wherever in active duty of reconstruction its sphynx-like keyboard silently obeys the master's touch. It now has emerged from the atmosphere of haste and the noise of a newspaper where it worked so much more for so much less. Where it once upon a time turned out a thousand words for a paltry sum, now it hammers out words that are worth their weight in gold. Hence the lordly retreat, the surrounding peace, the music of the rustling leaves and the song of the birds to soften the click-clack of its own voice.

Cobb is a huge man. He towers upward and spreads out like a mature oak tree. He has been shedding acorns forty years, perhaps less than that. He began reeling off words in Paducah as a cub reporter. Then he came to New York and got a little more for them than in Paducah. Finally he became a "star" reporter and accumulated so much star dust that he turned into a comet, and the editors can't stay his soaring prices. His esteem for the reporter is his literary creed. He includes such creditable reporters as Balzac, Thackeray, Dickens, Wells, DeFoe, in that system. To be sure Arnold Bennett, Robert Hichens, and Henry James were not to be forgotten among the distinguished staff of literary posterity, but they were the editorial writers, not quite in tune with the words and music of those fellows who knew how to see a good story in the daily events about them. There was nothing said about genius, and that favorite word, technique, so gracefully used by the literary idler, was contemptuously ignored.

It is just as easy for him to write a story of twenty thousand words as it is for your stenographer to write a letter which you thought you dictated. It is not the length of a novel that has prevented him from writing it; it is the stretching of types. And then, like most thoroughbred characters, he has a weakness that upsets the classic mood, he bristles at the sound of a fire alarm. He might be in the third stanza of an ode to the Confederacy, but if a fire alarm sounded he would rush out into the thick of the smoke. If there were no smoke, no fire, he would

feel that he had done his duty as a reporter, that he had "covered it." I gather this from the source of all fact about a family man, his wife. He did not deny it; he did not condone it; he confirmed it in his analysis of types, his types.

It is barely six years since Cobb wrote his first short-story. It was written after he had reported the trial of a celebrated financier, and had seen him sentenced to the penitentiary at Atlanta. He recalled its nativity, briefly:

> Nothing could stop that man's mental poise, his grip of men. He was unscrupulous, cold, self-controlled, gigantic in management of men to do his own purpose. He could have revolutionized the finest jail system in the world. He did not stay in Atlanta long. I began wondering what could beat him. That was the theme of my first story. I made him escape from the detective on the train and get away in the woods. The train from which he escapes is wrecked. He finds a newspaper in which he reads that his body has been identified. He has only to communicate with his lawyer, hide for a while, and freedom is his, except for the handcuffs. At last they beat him. He wanders into a village and gives himself up. The handcuffs have beaten him.

Here was a type from which the source of many stories might flow; the one Cobb wrote about it was only a single phase of the character. His stories are usually studies of types, not editorial arguments about them, but incidents that reveal them. He explains it this way:

> There are two kinds of short-story writers—those who editorialize, who lead you into the mental state of the characters under pressure, and those who tell you the happenings to them in dramatic form. I think the reader likes to do his own thinking; therefore I favor the latter, the descriptive story of character in action.
>
> To see well, that is the chief thing, I think. Putting it down on paper can be acquired, but the vision is inherent. Not the editorial vision that argues with you, but the reporter's vision that tells you so that you can see as well as he.

"The literary photograph, which after all is the good reporter's impressions, is the best kind of a story," he added by way of explaining how he wrote his own.

> Thackeray had style, but he was a finely tempered reporter, a high-class newspaper man, with taste and discretion, a keen student of human nature. I pride myself upon being a good newspaper man, above all things. If I once focus on a man, I can remember every button on or off his coat, its size, its color. The man's accent, his voice, his words, his quality, his presence are all ineffaceable. In short I have his type. A sketch of him, however, is not sufficient; that alone does not conform to the needs of a story. I must know him years before, measure him with the yardstick of time, to place him in the proper atmosphere of dramatic value,

or shall we say fiction value. There is always the mysterious moulding process in the mind from which a type in fiction springs into being in after life. He blooms from the seed planted unconsciously in the past, the never-to-be-forgotten past. I suppose our boyhood belongs to that period. The first theatrical form of dramatic appeal I remember, was at St. Claire Hall, the Opr'y House of Paducah. There I thrilled to the terrors of "The Black Flag," "The Old Homestead," and other successes of that day. There was a curtain in the hall which represented a scene in Venice. I did not know it was Venice at the time, but I didn't care so much about where it was. There were some Venetian ladies and gentlemen very lightly clad coming down marble steps to get into a gondola or two. I recall that I was astonished at the light sort of clothing they were wearing, because in Paducah we sometimes had floods, and the river front was no place to go unless you were dressed for it. Years later I returned to my home town and drew a sketch of that curtain, which was accounted as being correct, even to the marble steps. This convinces one that the memory of a newspaper man is the best asset for a fiction writer. But the trouble is that most young writers never seem to consider their own actual experiences in life as sufficiently important to talk about. They will take sail in fancy to South Africa or to Hong Kong for local color, where they have never been. The reader is the first to resent this, because he will feel that the story is not written by a reporter who has been there. You can't read Balzac and fail to know that he is talking about something he has seen or absorbed from the vivid warmth of the human heart. He was a fine reporter, and his color is true to the spirit and passions of men and women. DeFoe was a good reporter, too, because he told of a new type, Robinson Crusoe, and he missed no incident of human interest in his story of him. If DeFoe had covered the Thaw trial he would have been writing about it yet. Stevenson was a fair reporter, although he had a literary taste that superimposed his narrative. He stopped to draw fine conclusions in the mood of the essayist. Stevenson would probably have written a good fire story that would have been rejected by a city editor, but would have been a masterpiece, none the less. Hichens writes too long to get the point, beautifully as he always does get to it. Of course, we all know what a complex reporter Henry James would have made, and what a difficult task the editors would have had with a story by Arnold Bennett—brilliant writers but lacking the brevity of the newspaper man's training.

I often receive requests from young writers to define the skill of technique. The word is in the dictionary, and that's all I know about it. The style of a man's work is chiefly a matter of good taste, I should think. His sentiment is a governing factor, but his judgment of what to say and what not to say is materially guided by his experience in writing for newspapers. The best technique I know of is to be had in that kind of work. To begin with, it simplifies a man's style, teaches him the difference between a fact and a dream, which is quite important when you begin to tell a story.

The personal element which enters into every good bit of literature I have ever read is found as constantly in the newspaper story as it is in fiction. How many readers do you suppose after reading a particularly well-written story in a newspaper think of the writer? A very large majority, I believe.

While all this may sound incompatible with our preconceived ideas of literary quality, Cobb has demonstrated only his own methods, his own way of writing a story, and he has gained a very large audience. His devotion to the newspaper as the foundation of literary success is a distinctly new note in literary expectation. There is much more to the making of a good short-story writer than merely the experience of reporting, which he claims as his chief instruction. There is the selection of types, and the assurance with which he places them in the lights and shadows of their own world. And there is the gift of humor that always underlies the life-like quality of Cobb's characters. Of this he said:

> Humor for the sake of the laugh, like the cartoon born for the test of the popular mood, has no lasting value. We will speak of Mark Twain as our greatest humorist, but we have received some of the greatest human messages in philosophy from him, some of the gems of literary thought. It was his deep and definite judgment of character that has given him posterity. Other men of lesser fame have written, perhaps, better humor, but it had no substance, no fine valor of feeling, no uplifting purpose. There must always be a serious, deep sincerity behind the best literature that distinguishes it from mere literary craftsmanship. There are a great many stories written to-day for a certain class of readers. Not that I think there should be such readers, because they too enjoy other stories when they are universally true, but they seem to require a certain sort of story, which is written particularly for them. The action is forced, the characters are dragged from the stock room of older romances when the world was groping in oil-lighted streets at night, and when every man carried a sword. The situations are improbable, the movement is jerky and forced.

> Such types are familiar, shopworn. The adventuress with a wicked French accent will have to go. The innocuous heroine who improved so rapidly on buttermilk and love will also have to fade into the oblivion from whence she came. But all these dummies of fiction still have their following, and they still appear in new clothes, up to their old tricks. These are no literary figures because they are old pretenders frankly dragged from the middle ages or the cavalier days, and sent to a department store for a ready-made outfit of language, style, and clothes. After all, it is what is unseen of the writer's nature that gives a story its value. We should find our types in our hearts, not in melancholy mood but smilingly, happily and faithfully.

> One's faith in human nature is an important factor in writing. Dickens had an endless source of kindliness. His humor was exactly the form that is found among the poor, who have that splendid bravery of turning their misfortunes into harmless

fun. Dickens gave us practical Christianity. Thackeray looked at his types with the blinking shrewdness of sly humor. I do not think that his satire was ever biting; it was too faithful to the balance of life for that. And, too, his characters were drawn with sympathy.

It is noticeable that one never could imitate literary masters. Their style, their feeling, their quality belonged to them exclusively. Every great writer has made his mark by writing not what he thought about life, but what he saw. His eyes were in his heart; his pen stirred as he felt. Above all things the literary masters bestowed upon us the blessing of seeing life hopefully. Even if, as in Edgar Allan Poe's case, we were thrilled by some horror, we still retained the flavor of superb poetry, of splendid imagination to which we all are heirs.

There is a limit to the scope of imagination that most trained writers discover in time. When we enter the secret chamber of our imaginations we are on hallowed ground. We should never enter alone; we should lead our type into it with us. Since we chose him or her from the selected ones of our memory, we clothe that type appropriately in the imaginative faculty of fanciful incident. The incidents, however, must be life-like, not a riot of action, but a sequence of natural events. We should, I think, be very intimate with our types, and very friendly. Even if we are compelled to betray the weaknesses of our types, we need not do so viciously. Ill feeling has no place in literary effort, any more than it should have a place in daily life.

There is no kind of work known, so hard, so exacting, requiring such gifts of artistic and accurate knowledge. Besides, successful writers are not born; they occur. There is probably a large undiscovered census of men and women who ought to be writers instead of what they are. Writing has always been regarded as a haphazard sort of business, preferably adopted by unknown genius. I have known of cases where young people have been forbidden to write under threat of being cut off in the parental will. No work exposes one to such suspicion as writing. Men have been shot for it, and many have not. Women have neglected their knitting to become magazine contributors, and the editors have helped them. It is often a business beset with disgrace and misunderstanding. Still, in spite of these drawbacks it is an occupation that is even coveted. Those who covet it most, however, need claim no special birthright for it. Painful as it may seem to those who cling to the long-haired tradition that it requires genius to write, I am convinced there are more short-haired men in pursuit of fireside comfort, who write well, than is suspected.

The shapeliness of an author has nothing to do with the shape of his work. He has to learn it, after he has discovered that he can write. The best moment of discovery is when a friend, an unselfish friend, asks him why he hasn't written that story about his own experience in a Harlem flat, or in a lawyer's office, or when he worked in a factory, instead of stories of wild adventures in a wilder world than ours.

A very successful writer had that experience. He began to write to increase his income, which was small, thanks to the liberality of a lawyer, whose sense of justice was always on the side of his own case. He wrote stories about dreadful things that were supposed to happen, that never happened, and sold them for modest sums. One day a friend suggested to him that he write about the people who came into the office during the day. He did, and so well that he became author of those internationally famous tales about "Potash and Perlmutter." Of course you may insist that a man who does that must have genius. I insist that he had industry and a photographic mind.

It is a peculiar fact among newspaper men that when they develop into the magazine story field they lose all interest in names. I remember when I was commissioned to go to the war zones in Europe, I discovered this. Just what use a war correspondent could be who was totally incompetent to advise the Admirals and Generals what to do in a strategic difficulty of the war, I did not know. Having no military knowledge, no army training, no chance of occupying a safe hill from which to see the armies at work, I had little hope of success at the front in the capacity of a war correspondent.

I pinned my faith for usefulness, however, upon one thing I knew I could do, to see well and find types that crystallize great facts in great moments. Their names did not matter. When we were being conveyed through Germany as prisoners, I said to one of our party: "You remember the names of the stations through which we pass, and when you name them to me I will remember all the types, the incidents, the dramas we saw in that region." Taking notes was forbidden, but the habit of memory, which is the key to good newspaper work, stood by me. Long after that journey ended, the mention of the name of a station brought back the memory of the spy we saw shot, or the despair of the woman who had her geese taken away from her by the soldiers, or many other facts.

That is how Cobb gets the types we all know.

The artist's vision, as Irvin Cobb has found it, is not the traditional dream of emotions, but an accurate, interesting, human story about men and women he has seen and known. His types are Americans, faithfully and sympathetically drawn. He has literally grafted the souls of men to the Americanism of his own feeling and good taste. His newspaper work was good because he met the world as he found it, not as he wished it could be. His types in fiction are among real people he has met. They are chiefly New Yorkers because he has lived in New York for twelve years, and known them best. It would seem, however, as though the reminiscent memories of his boyhood in Paducah had mellowed into literary fruition of greater depth and finer instinct than his types of more recent influence, and this in spite of the fact that he knows Washington in all its intricate subtleties and official life, and New York is the most vital experience of his life.

H. L. Mencken (essay date 1919)

SOURCE: "The Heir of Mark Twain," in *Prejudices: First Series*, Alfred A. Knopf, 1919, pp. 97-104.

[*In the following essay, Mencken finds Cobb's work "superficial and inconsequential."*]

Nothing could be stranger than the current celebrity of Irvin S. Cobb, an author of whom almost as much is heard as if he were a new Thackeray or Molière. One is solemnly told by various extravagant partisans, some of them not otherwise insane, that he is at once the successor to Mark Twain and the heir of Edgar Allan Poe. One hears of public dinners given in devotion to his genius, of public presentations, of learned degrees conferred upon him by universities, of other extraordinary adulations, few of them shared by such relatively puny fellows as Howells and Dreiser. His talents and sagacity pass into popular anecdotes; he has sedulous Boswells; he begins to take on the august importance of an actor-manager. Behind the scenes, of course, a highly dexterous publisher pulls the strings, but much of it is undoubtedly more or less sincere; men pledge their sacred honor to the doctrine that his existence honors the national literature. Moreover, he seems to take the thing somewhat seriously himself. He gives his *imprimatur* to various other authors, including Joseph Conrad; he engages himself to lift the literary tone of moving-pictures; he lends his name to movements; he exposes himself in the chautauquas; he takes on the responsibilities of a patriot and a public man. . . . Altogether, a curious, and, in some of its aspects, a caressingly ironical spectacle. One wonders what the graduate sophomores of to-morrow, composing their dull tomes upon American letters, will make of it. . . .

In the actual books of the man I can find nothing that seems to justify so much enthusiasm, nor even the hundredth part of it. His serious fiction shows a certain undoubted facility, but there are at least forty other Americans who do the thing quite as well. His public bulls and ukases are no more than clever journalism—superficial and inconsequential, first saying one thing and then quite another thing. And in his humor, which his admirers apparently put first among his products, I can discover, at best, nothing save a somewhat familiar aptitude for grotesque anecdote, and, at worst, only the laborious laugh-squeezing of Bill Nye. In the volume called *Those Times and These* there is an excellent comic story, to wit, **"Hark, From the Tomb!"** But it would surely be an imbecility to call it a masterpiece; too many other authors have done things quite as good; more than a few (I need cite only George Ade, Owen Johnson and Ring W. Lardner) have done things very much better. Worse, it lies in the book like a slice of Smithfield ham between two slabs of stale store-bread. On both sides of it are very stupid artificialities—stories without point, stories in which rustic characters try to talk like Wilson Mizner, stories altogether machine-made and depressing. Turn, now, to another book, vastly praised in its year—by name, *Cobb's Anatomy.* One laughs occasionally—but precisely as one laughs over a comic supplement or the jokes in *Ayer's Almanac.* For example:

> There never was a hansom cab made that would hold a fat man comfortably unless he left the doors open, and that makes him feel undressed.

Again:

> Your hair gives you bother so long as you have it and more bother when it starts to go. You are always doing something for it and it is always showing deep-dyed ingratitude in return; or else the dye isn't deep enough, which is even worse.

Exactly; it is even worse. And then this:

> Once there was a manicure lady who wouldn't take a tip, but she is now no more. Her indignant sisters stabbed her to death with hatpins and nail-files.

I do not think I quote unfairly; I have tried to select honest specimens of the author's fancy. . . . Perhaps it may be well to glance at another book. I choose, at random, *Speaking of Operations—,* a work described by the publisher as "the funniest yet written by Cobb" and "the funniest book we know of." In this judgment many other persons seem to have concurred. The thing was an undoubted success when it appeared as an article in the *Saturday Evening Post* and it sold thousands of copies between covers. Well, what is in it? In it, after a diligent reading, I find half a dozen mildly clever observations—and sixty odd pages of ancient and infantile wheezes, as flat to the taste as so many crystals of hyposulphite of soda. For example, the wheeze to the effect that in the days of the author's nonage "germs had not been invented yet." For example, the wheeze to the effect that doctors bury their mistakes. For example, the wheeze to the effect that the old-time doctor always prescribed medicines of abominably evil flavor. . . . But let us go into the volume more in detail, and so unearth all its gems.

On page 1, in the very first paragraph, there is the doddering old joke about the steepness of doctors' bills. In the second paragraph there is the somewhat newer but still fully adult joke about the extreme willingness of persons who have been butchered by surgeons to talk about it afterward. These two witticisms are all that I can find on page 1. For the rest, it consists almost entirely of a reference to MM. Bryan and Roosevelt—a reference well known by all newspaper paragraphists and vaudeville monologists to be as provocative of laughter as a mention of bunions, mothers-in-law or Pottstown, Pa. On page 2 Bryan and Roosevelt are succeeded by certain heavy stuff in the Petroleum V. Nasby manner upon the condition of obstetrics, pediatrics and the allied sciences among whales. Page 3 starts off with the old jocosity to the effect that people talk too much about the weather. It progresses or resolves, as the musicians say, into the wheeze to the effect that people like to dispute over what is the best thing to eat for breakfast. On page 4 we come to what musicians would call the formal statement of the main theme—that is, of the how-I-like-to-talk-of-my-operation motif. We have thus covered four pages.

Page 5 starts out with an enharmonic change: to wit, from the idea that ex-patients like to talk of their operations to the idea that patients in being like to swap symptoms. Following this there is a repetition of the gold theme— that is, the theme of the doctor's bill. On page 6 there are two chuckles. One springs out of a reference to "light housekeeping," a phrase which invariably strikes an American vaudeville audience as salaciously whimsical. The other is grounded upon the well-known desire of baseball fans to cut the umpire's throat. On page 6 there enters for the first time what may be called the second theme of the book. This is the whiskers motif. The whole of this page, with the exception of a sentence embodying the old wheeze about the happy times before germs were invented, is given over to variations of the whiskers joke. Page 8 continues this development section. Whiskers of various fantastic varieties are mentioned—trellis whiskers, bosky whiskers, ambush whiskers, loose, luxuriant whiskers, landscaped whiskers, whiskers that are winter quarters for pathogenic organisms. Some hard, hard squeezing, and the humor in whiskers is temporarily exhausted. Page 8 closes with the old joke about the cruel thumping which doctors perform upon their patients' clavicles.

Now for page 9. It opens with a third statement of the gold motif—"He then took my temperature and $15." Following comes the dentist's office motif—that is, the motif of reluctance, of oozing courage, of flight. At the bottom of the page the gold motif is repeated in the key of E minor. Pages 10 and 11 are devoted to simple description, with very little effort at humor. On page 12 there is a second statement, for the full brass choir, of the dentist's office motif. On page 13 there are more echoes from Petroleum V. Nasby, the subject this time being a man "who got his spleen back from the doctor's and now keeps it in a bottle of alcohol." On page 14 one finds the innocent bystander joke; on page 15 the joke about the terrifying effects of reading a patent medicine almanac. Also, at the bottom of the page, there is a third statement of the dentist's office joke. On page 16 it gives way to a restatement of the whiskers theme, in augmentation, which in turn yields to the third or fifth restatement of the gold theme.

Let us now jump a few pages. On page 19 we come to the old joke about the talkative barber; on page 22 to the joke about the book agent; on the same page to the joke about the fashionableness of appendicitis; on page 23 to the joke about the clumsy carver who projects the turkey's gizzard into the visiting pastor's eye; on page 28

to a restatement of the barber joke; on page 31 to another statement—is it the fifth or sixth?—of the dentist's office joke; on page 37 to the katzenjammer joke; on page 39 to the old joke about doctors burying their mistakes . . . And so on. And so on and so on. And so on and so on and so on. On pages 48 and 49 there is a perfect riot of old jokes, including the nth variation of the whiskers joke and a fearful and wonderful pun about Belgian hares and heirs. . . .

On second thoughts I go no further. . . . This, remember, is the book that Cobb's publishers, apparently with his own *Nihil Obstat,* choose as his best. This is the official masterpiece of the "new Mark Twain." Nevertheless, even so laboriously flabby a farceur has his moments. I turn to Frank J. Wilstach's *Dictionary of Similes* and find this credited to him: "No more privacy than a goldfish." Here, at last, is something genuinely humorous. Here, moreover, is something apparently new.

Grant Overton (essay date 1922)

SOURCE: "Cobb's Fourth Dimension," in *When Winter Comes to Main Street,* George H. Doran Company, 1922, pp. 166-86.

[*In the following essay, Overton provides an overview of Cobb's work.*]

i

A three-dimensional writer, Irvin S. Cobb has long been among the American literary heavy-weights. Now that he has acquired a fourth dimension, the time has come for a new measurement of his excellences as an author.

Among those excellences I know a man (responsible for the manufacture of Doran books) who holds that Cobb is the greatest living American author. The reason for this is severely logical, to wit: Irvin Cobb always sends in his copy in a perfect condition. His copy goes to the manufacturer of books with a correctly written title page, a correctly written copyright page, the exact wording of the dedication, an accurate table of contents, and so on, all the way through the manuscript. Moreover, when proofs are sent to Mr. Cobb, he makes very few changes. He reduces to a minimum the difficulties of a printer and his changes are always perceptibly changes for the better.

But I don't suppose that any of this would redound to Cobb's credit in the eyes of a literary critic.

And to return to the subject of the fourth dimension: My difficulty is to know in just what direction that fourth dimension lies. Is the fourth dimension of Cobb as a novelist or as an autobiographer? It puzzles me to tell inasmuch as I have before me the manuscripts of Mr. Cobb's first novel, *J. Poindexter, Colored,* and his very first autobiography, a volume called *Stickfuls.*

The title of *Stickfuls* will probably not be charged with meaning to people unfamiliar with newspaper work. Perhaps it is worth while to explain that in the old days, when type was set by hand, the printer had a little metal holder called a "stick." When he had set a dozen lines—more or less—he had a "stickful." Although very little type is now set by hand, the stick as a measure of space is still in good standing. The reporter presents himself at the city desk, tells what he has got, and is told by the city editor, "Write a stickful." Or, "Write two sticks." And so on.

Stickfuls is not so much the story of Cobb's life as the story of people he has met and places he has been, told in a series of extremely interesting chapters—told in a leisurely and delightful fashion of reminiscence by a natural association of one incident with another and one person with someone else. For example, Cobb as a newspaper man, covered a great many trials in court; and one of the chapters of *Stickfuls* tells of famous trials he has attended.

ii

Now about this novel of Cobb's: Jeff Poindexter will be remembered by all the readers of Mr. Cobb's short stories as the negro body servant of old Judge Priest. In *J. Poindexter, Colored,* we have Jeff coming to New York. Of course, New York seen through the eyes of a genuine Southern darkey is a New York most of us have never seen. There's nothing like sampling, so I will let you begin the book:

> My name is J. Poindexter. But the full name is Jefferson Exodus Poindexter, Colored. But most always in general I has been known as Jeff for short. The Jefferson part is for a white family which my folks worked for them one time before I was born, and the Exodus is because my mammy craved I should be named after somebody out of the Bible. How I comes to write this is this way:
>
> It seems like my experiences here in New York is liable to be such that one of my white gentleman friends he says to me I should take pen in hand and write them out just the way they happen and at the time they is happening, or right soon afterwards, whilst the memory of them is clear in my brain; and then he's see if he can't get them printed somewhere, which on the top of the other things which I now is, will make me an author with money coming in steady. He says to me he will fix up the spelling wherever needed and attend to the punctuating; but all the rest of it will be my own just like I puts it down. I reads and writes very well but someway I never learned to puncture. So the places where it is necessary to be punctual in order to make good sense and keep everything regulation and make the talk sound natural is his doings and also some of the spelling. But everything else is mine and I asks credit.
>
> My coming to New York, in the first place, is sort of a sudden thing which starts here about a month

before the present time. I has been working for Judge Priest for going on sixteen years and is expecting to go on working for him as long as we can get along together all right, which it seems like from appearances that ought to be always. But after he gives up being circuit judge on account of him getting along so in age he gets sort of fretful by reasons of him not having much to do any more and most of his own friends having died off on him. When the State begins going Republican about once in so often, he says to me, kind of half joking, he's a great mind to pull up stakes and move off and go live somewheres else. But pretty soon after that the whole country goes dry and then he says to me there just naturally ain't no fitten place left for him to go without he leaves the United States.

It seems that Judge Priest finally succumbed to an invitation to visit Bermuda, a place where a gentleman can still raise a thirst and satisfy it. Jeff could not stand the house without the Judge in it; and when an opportunity came to go to New York, Jeff went.

iii

The biographer of Cobb is Robert H. Davis, editor of *Munsey's Magazine,* whose authoritative account I take pleasure in reprinting here—the more so because it appeared some time ago in a booklet which is now out of print. Mr. Davis's article was first printed in *The Sun,* New York:

> Let me deal with this individual in a categorical way. Most biographers prefer to mutilate their canvas with a small daub which purports to be a sketch of the most significant event in the life of the accused. Around this it is their custom to paint smaller and less impressive scenes, blending the whole by placing it in a large gilded frame, which, for obvious reasons, costs more than the picture—and it is worth more. Pardon me, therefore, if I creep upon Mr. Cobb from the lower left-hand corner of the canvas and chase him across the open space as rapidly as possible. It is not for me to indicate when the big events in his life will occur or to lay the milestones of the route along which he will travel. I know only that they are in the future, and that, regardless of any of his achievements in the past, Irvin Cobb has not yet come into his own.
>
> The first glimpse I had of him was in a half-tone portrait in the *New York Evening World* five years ago. This picture hung pendant-like from a title which read "Through Funny Glasses, by Irvin S. Cobb." It was the face of a man scarred with uncertainty; an even money proposition that he had either just emerged from the Commune or was about to enter it. Grief was written on the brow; more than written, it was emblazoned. The eyes were heavy with inexpressible sadness. The corners of the mouth were drooped, heightening the whole effect of incomprehensible depression. Quickly I turned to the next page among the stock quotations, where I got my depression in a blanket form. The concentrated Cobb kind was too much for me.

A few days later I came suddenly upon the face again. The very incongruity of its alliance with laughter overwhelmed me, and wonderingly I read what he had written, not once, but every day, always with the handicap of that half-tone. If Cobb were an older man, I would go on the witness stand and swear that the photograph was made when he was witnessing the Custer Massacre or the passing of Geronimo through the winter quarters of his enemies. Notwithstanding, he supplied my week's laughter.

Digression this:

After Bret Harte died, many stories were written by San Franciscans who knew him when he first put in an appearance on the Pacific Coast. One contemporary described minutely how Bret would come silently up the stairs of the old Alta office, glide down the dingy hallway through the exchange room, and seat himself at the now historic desk. It took Bret fifteen minutes to sharpen a lead pencil, one hour for sober reflection, and three hours to write a one-stick paragraph, after which he would carefully tear it up, gaze out of the window down the Golden Gate, and go home.

He repeated this formula the following day, and at the end of the week succeeded in turning out three or four sticks which he considered fit to print. In later years, after fame had sought him out and presented him with a fur-lined overcoat, which I am bound to say Bret knew how to wear, the files of the Alta were ransacked for the pearls he had dropped in his youth. A few gems were identified, a very few. Beside this entire printed collection the New England Primer would have looked like a set of encyclopedias. Bret worked slowly, methodically, brilliantly, and is an imperishable figure in American letters.

Returning to Cobb: He has already written twenty times more than Bret Harte turned out during his entire career. He has made more people laugh and written better short stories. He has all of Harte's subtle and delicate feeling, and will, if he is spared, write better novels about the people of today than Bret Harte, with all his genius and imagination, wrote around the Pioneers. I know of no single instance where one man has shown such fecundity and quality as Irvin Cobb has so far evinced, and it is my opinion that his complete works at fifty will contain more good humour, more good short stories, and at least one bigger novel than the works of any other single contemporaneous figure.

He was born in Paducah, Kentucky, in June, '76. I have taken occasion to look into the matter and find that his existence was peculiarly varied. He belonged to one of those old Southern families—there being no new Southern families—and passed through the public schools sans incident. At the age of sixteen he went into the office of *The Paducah Daily News* as a reportorial cub.

He was first drawn to daily journalism because he yearned to be an illustrator. Indeed, he went so far as to write local humorous stories, illustrating them himself. The pictures must have been pretty bad, although they served to keep people from saying that his literature was the worst thing in the paper.

Resisting all efforts of the editor, the stockholders and the subscribers of *The Paducah Daily News,* he remained barricaded behind his desk until his nineteenth year, when he was crowned with a two-dollar raise and a secondary caption under his picture which read "The Youngest Managing Editor of a Daily Paper in the United States."

If Cobb was consulted in the matter of this review, he would like to have these preliminaries expunged from his biography. But the public is entitled to the details.

It is also true that he stacked up more libel suits than a newspaper of limited capital with a staff of local attorneys could handle before he moved to Louisville, where, for three years, he was staff correspondent of *The Evening Post.* It was here that Cobb discovered how far a humorist could go without being invited to step out at 6 a.m. and rehearse "The Rivals" with real horse-pistols.

The first sobering episode in his life occurred when the Goebel murder echoed out of Louisville. He reported this historic assassination and covered the subsequent trials in the Georgetown court house. Doubtless the seeds of tragedy, which mark some of his present work, were sown here. Those who are familiar with his writings know that occasionally he sets his cap and bells aside and dips his pen into the very darkness of life. We find it particularly in three of his short stories entitled **"An Occurrence Up a Side Street," "The Belled Buzzard,"** and **"Fishhead."** Nothing better can be found in Edgar Allan Poe's collected works. One is impressed not only with the beauty and simplicity of his prose, but with the tremendous power of his tragic conceptions and his art in dealing with terror. There appears to be no phase of human emotion beyond his pen. Without an effort he rises from the level of actualities to the high plane of boundless imagination, invoking laughter or tears at will.

After his Louisville experience Cobb married and returned to Paducah to be managing editor of *The Democrat.* Either Paducah or *The Democrat* got on his nerves and, after a comparison of the Paducah school of journalism with the metropolitan brand, he turned his face (see *Evening World* half-tone) in the direction of New York, buoyed up by the illusion that he was needed there along with other reforms.

He arrived at the gates of Manhattan full of hope, and visited every newspaper office in New York without receiving encouragement to call again. Being resourceful he retired to his suite of hall bedrooms on 57th Street West and wrote a personal note to every city editor in New York, setting forth in each instance the magnificent intellectual proportions of the epistolographer. The next morning, by mail, Cobb had offers for a job from five of them. He selected *The Evening Sun.*

At about that time the Portsmouth Peace Conference convened, and *The Sun* sent the Paducah party to help cover the proceedings. Upon arriving at Portsmouth, Cobb cast his experienced eye over the situation, discovered that the story was already well covered by a large coterie of competent, serious-minded young men, and went into action to write a few columns daily on subjects having no bearing whatsoever on the conference. These stories were written in the ebullition of youth, inspired by the ecstasy which rises from the possession of a steady job; a perfect deluge from the well springs of spontaneity. There wasn't a single fact in the entire series, and yet *The Sun* syndicated these stories throughout the United States. All they possessed was I-N-D-I-V-I-D-U-A-L-I-T-Y.

At the end of three weeks, Cobb returned to New York, to find that he could have a job on any newspaper in it. This brings him to *The Evening World,* the half-tone engraving, which was the first glimpse I had of him, and the dawn of his subsequent triumphs. For four years he supplied the evening edition and *The Sunday World* with a comic feature, to say nothing of a comic opera, written to order in five days. The absence of a guillotine in New York State accounts for his escape for this latter offence. Nevertheless, in all else his standard of excellence ascended. He reported the Thaw trial in long-hand, writing nearly 600,000 words of testimony and observation, establishing a new style for reporting trials, and gave further evidence of his power. That performance will stand out in the annals of American journalism as one of the really big reportorial achievements.

At about this juncture in his career Cobb opened a door to the past, reached in and took out some of the recollections of his youth. These he converted into **"The Escape of Mr. Trimm,"** his first short fiction story. It appeared in *The Saturday Evening Post.* The court scene was so absolutely true to life, so minutely perfect in its atmosphere, that a Supreme Court judge signed an unsolicited and voluntary note for publication, in which he said that Mr. Cobb had reported with marvelous accuracy and fulness a murder trial at which His Honour had presided.

Gelett Burgess, in a lecture at Columbia College, said that Cobb was one of the ten great American humourists. Cobb ought to demand a recount. There are not ten humourists in the world, although Cobb is one of them. The extraordinary thing about Cobb is that he can turn a burst of laughter into a funeral oration, a snicker into a shudder and a smile into a crime. He writes in octaves, striking instinctively all the chords of humour, tragedy, pathos and romance with either hand. Observe this man in his thirty-ninth year, possessing gifts the limitations of which even he himself has not yet recognised.

In appraising a genius, we must consider the man's highest achievement, and in comparing him with others the verdict must be reached only upon consideration of his best work. For scintillant wit and unflagging good humour, read his essays on the Teeth, the Hair and the Stomach. If you desire a perfect blending of all that is essential to a short story, read **"The Escape of Mr. Trimm"** or **"Words and Music."** If you are in search of pure, unadulterated, boundless terror, the gruesome quality, the blackness of despair and the fear of death in the human conscience, **"Fishhead," "The Belled Buzzard"** or **"An Occurrence Up a Side Street"** will enthrall you.

Thus in Irvin Cobb we find Mark Twain, Bret Harte and Edgar Allan Poe at their best. Reckon with these potentialities in the future. Speculate, if you will, upon the sort of a novel that is bound, some day, to come from his pen. There seem to be no pinnacles along the horizon of the literary future that are beyond him. If he uses his pen for an Alpine stock, the Matterhorn is his.

There are critics and reviewers who do not entirely agree with me concerning Cobb. But they will.

As I write these lines I recall a conversation I had with Irvin Cobb on the hurricane deck of a Fifth Avenue 'bus one bleak November afternoon, 1911. We had met at the funeral of Joseph Pulitzer, in whose employ we had served in the past.

Cobb was in a reflective mood, chilled to the marrow, and not particularly communicative.

At the junction of Fifth Avenue and Forty-second Street we were held up by congested traffic. After a little manœuvring on the part of a mounted policeman, the Fifth Avenue tide flowed through and onward again.

"It reminds me of a river," said Cobb, "into which all humanity is drawn. Some of these people think because they are walking up-stream they are getting out of it. But they never escape. The current is at work on them. Some day they will get tired and go down again, and finally pass out to sea. It is the same with real rivers. They do not flow up-hill."

He lapsed into silence.

"What's on your mind?" I inquired.

"Nothing in particular," he said, scanning the banks of the great municipal stream, "except that I intend to write a novel some day about a boy born at the headwaters. Gradually he floats down through the tributaries, across the valleys, swings into the main stream, and docks finally at one of the cities on its banks. This particular youth was a great success—in the beginning. Every door was open to him. He had position, brains, and popularity to boot. He married brilliantly. And then The Past, a trivial, unimportant Detail, lifted its head and barked at him. He was too sensitive to bark back. Thereupon it bit him and he collapsed."

Again Cobb ceased talking. For some reason—

indefinable—I respected his silence. Two blocks further down he took up the thread of his story again:

"—and one evening, just about sundown, a river hand, sitting on a stringpiece of a dock, saw a derby hat bobbing in the muddy Mississippi, floating unsteadily but surely into the Gulf of Mexico."

As is his habit, Cobb tugged at his lower lip.

"What are you going to call this novel?"

"I don't know. What do you think?"

"Why not 'The River'?"

"Very well, I'll call it 'The River.'"

He scrambled from his seat. "I'm docking at Twenty-seventh Street. Good-bye. Keep your hat out of the water."

Laboriously he made his way down the winding staircase from the upper deck, dropped flat-footed on the asphalt pavement, turned his collar up, leaned into the gust of wind from the South, and swung into the cross-current of another stream.

I doubt if he has any intention of calling his story "The River." But I am sure the last chapter will contain something about an unhappy wretch who wore a derby hat at the moment he walked hand in hand with his miserable Past into the Father of Waters.

For those who wish to know something of his personal side, I can do no better than to record his remarks to a stranger, who, in my presence, asked Irvin Cobb, without knowing to whom he was speaking, what kind of a person Cobb was.

"Well, to be perfectly frank with you," replied the Paducah prodigy, "Cobb is related to my wife by marriage, and if you don't object to a brief sketch, with all the technicalities eliminated, I should say in appearance he is rather bulky, standing six feet high, not especially beautiful, a light roan in colour, with a black mane. His figure is undecided, but might be called bunchy in places. He belongs to several clubs, including The Yonkers Pressing Club and The Park Hill Democratic Marching Club, and has always, like his father, who was a Confederate soldier, voted the Democratic ticket. He has had one wife and one child and still has them. In religion he is an Innocent Bystander."

Could anything be fuller than this?

iv

It was Mr. Davis, also, who in the *New York Herald* of April 23, 1922, made public the evidence for the following box score

	1st	2nd
Best Writer of Humour	Cobb	. . . . .
Best All-Round Reporter	Cobb	. . . . .
Best Local Colourist	Cobb	. . . . .
Best in Tales of Horror	Cobb	. . . . .
Best Writer of Negro Stories	. . . . .	Cobb
Best Writer of Light Humourous Fiction	Tarkington	Cobb and Harry Leon Wilson
Best Teller of Anecdotes	Cobb	Cobb

Not long ago a group of ten literary men—editors, critics, readers and writers—were dining together. Discussion arose as to the respective and comparative merits of contemporaneous popular writers. It was decided that each man present should set down upon a slip of paper his first, second and third choices in various specified but widely diversified fields of literary endeavour, and that then the results should be compared. Admirers of Cobb's work will derive a peculiar satisfaction from the outcome. It was found that as a writer of humour he had won first place; that as an all round reporter he had first place; that as a handler of local colour in the qualified sense of a power of apt, swiftly-done, journalistic description, he had first place. He also had first place as a writer of horror yarns. He won second place as a writer of darkey stories. He tied with Harry Leon Wilson for second place as a writer of light humorous fiction, Tarkington being given first place in this category. As a teller of anecdotes he won by acclamation over all contenders. Altogether his name appeared on eight of the ten lists.

Cobb lives at Ossining, New York. He describes himself as lazy, but convinces no one. He likes to go fishing. But he has never written any fish stories.

Thomas L. Masson (essay date 1931)

SOURCE: "Irvin Cobb," in *Our American Humorists,* Books for Libraries Press, Inc., 1931, pp. 91-103.

[*In the following essay, Masson praises Cobb's work and solicits from Cobb an overview of his career.*]

Irvin Cobb has written things about himself, I was about to add, "in a quite impersonal way," when I remembered that he had written about his being fat and had referred to the fact that he was homely, whereas he is nothing of the sort. Also, other people have written about him, but neither he, nor anyone else, has ever done him justice, not even Bob Davis, or Grant Overton.

Cobb is wrong about himself and others are wrong about him. I am the only one who really understands him, and yet to save me I cannot explain him in just the way that I should like.

I have said that Cobb is impersonal when writing about himself; what follows this brief introduction to him will emphasize what I mean. He does not take himself seriously but he does take his work seriously. This difference is very important, because it lies at the heart of most of our human relationships. Cobb has what I call literary integrity, but it is purely impersonal. The honesty of some people is so offensive that we wish the world were inhabited by more interesting criminals; not that the world isn't, but merely that even they try to be too honest about it.

Perhaps I can put it in another way by saying that Cobb is a natural man. And he is a natural workman. I have no doubt that he thinks he is homely. On the contrary, he is handsome. Handsome does not express just how Cobb looks, but if it did express it, that is the way Cobb would look. That is to say, he is very satisfactory to look at. I don't know of any man that I would rather look at than Irvin Cobb, and I am not joking about this. He has all the human qualities. And when he talks I could listen to him all the time. I might want to stop for meals, but if I did, I should want him sitting next to me.

The conversations of so many men have been so overrated. All through literature you read about what wonderful talkers some men were. There was Swinburne; there was Macaulay; there was Tennyson; there was Oscar Wilde. I have always believed that these men were overrated. I read once of how Swinburne (I remember now, it was in a book called *The Education of Henry Adams*) kept a whole company of people up until very late talking wonderful talk and reciting poetry. I don't believe it. He must have been a deadly bore. Indeed, Max Beerbohm indicates this. Few of us are honest when it comes to our literary opinions. The memory of some evening in which we drank too much hangs over us like a beautiful rainbow; stripped of its colors it is only Scotch and soda. When I say that I would rather listen to Cobb talk than to anybody else I know, I mean it in the right sense. Cobb is human. He is not thinking about himself except in the right way. He is sympathetic. He is broad-souled. His book **Speaking of Operations** is funny because, in reality—although it may seem quite the opposite—it is impersonal. I remember when it first came out in the *Saturday Evening Post*. A number of people spoke to me about it. "Have you seen that thing of Irvin Cobb's? It's immense." And so on. You see, they were all taking it to themselves. They thought it had happened to them. And that, I take it, is one of the tests of real humor.

Another test of humor is its popularity. If a lot of people read it, that shows that it has something to it. I heard this story, which may or not be true, but it is such a satisfactory story that I must tell it. It is about Mr. Cobb and Mr. Lorimer, the editor of the *Saturday Evening Post*. One day Mr. Lorimer went out to a newsdealer nearby to see how his paper was selling. And the newsdealer said:

"They ask me if there is anything in it by Cobb. If there is, they buy it. If there isn't, they don't."

Thereupon Mr. Lorimer said, "I must cut out Cobb."

I don't believe this story. But it is a good one. That is the main difficulty about the best stories. They are probably not true.

I was highly amused one day to pick up a book by Mr. H. L. Mencken, and read what he had to say about Cobb. He didn't like him. He said so. Mencken, so far as I have been able to discover in his writings, doesn't like anybody. Maybe he is right. Not to like anybody at all may be a creditable object for any man's ambition. It is a large undertaking. I have tried to dislike certain people at intervals, but in most cases have had to give it up. After pursuing the objects of my wrath persistently, I got tired out and ended by liking them, finding them in the long run much like myself. Even Mr. Mencken is under this handicap. After several pages in which he explains at some length why Cobb is not a humorist, or at least not a good humorist—in which he refers to the Cobb whisker motif, the Cobb wheeze, and the Cobb publisher, he winds up with:

> Nevertheless, even so laboriously flabby a *farceur* has his moments. I turn to Frank J. Wilstach's *Dictionary of Similes* and find this credited to him "No more privacy than a goldfish." Here, at last, is something genuinely humorous. Here, moreover, is something apparently new.

To have Mr. Mencken admit that Cobb has been guilty of something genuinely humorous and apparently new is certainly going some. But that shows what can happen even to a man like Mencken if he reads Irvin Cobb.

Cobb, in common with Abraham Lincoln, was born in Kentucky (in 1876). This—I regret to say I remember it—was the year of the great Centennial. The Centennial, as doubtless nobody but myself remembers, took place chiefly in Philadelphia. Cobb little knew in that year that he was destined in time to keep Philadelphia before the people by his later contributions in the *Saturday Evening Post*.

There is, however, one stain on his career—a dark spot that I hope he will have removed as soon as possible. He has permitted the publishers of *Who's Who in America* to state that he was a "staff humorist." We have all of us, at one time or another, been staff humorists. If you are any sort of a man when your first baby is born (and also subsequently), you become a staff humorist to that child by imitating the ribald antics of the common or garden horse. But to have this put down in cold print is quite another thing. That Cobb has permitted this to be done to him is another evidence of his humility, of the impersonal manner in which he regards himself. That man would let anything be said about him. After being born, he attended private schools, from which he recovered sufficiently to get into Dartmouth College, which honored him with a degree in 1918. Let me now, with the permission of the polite publishers of *Who's Who,* quote from that indispensable household adjunct:

> Shorthand reporter, contbr. to comic weeklies, reporter on local paper up to 17; editor *Paducah Daily News* at 19; staff corr. and writer "Sour Mash" column *Louisville* (Ky.) *Evening Post* 1898-1901 . . . represented *Saturday Evening Post* as war corr. in Europe; lectured throughout U. S. on "What I saw at the Front." Apptd. col. on staff gov. of Ky. 1918; Chevalier Legion of Honor (France) 1918.

As for Cobb's books, they are quite numerous, and many of them highly amusing. Personally, if I may be allowed, I like **"The Escape of Mr. Trimm"** best. His story of **"The Belled Buzzard"** is a masterpiece. There are highly distinguished critics in England who think he is the best short-story writer in America. As for his work as a humorist, he has written to me by request, as follows:

> Almost as far back as I distinctly can remember I tried to write funny stuff. At the grammar school I wrote alleged verses to accompany the pictures I drew. At that time my main ambition was to be a caricaturist. I had a small gift that way. My mother says I tried to draw pictures before I could walk, and, among her possessions, she treasures some drawings in color, terribly crude things, that I did before I was four years old.

> The first three things of mine that were ever published in a magazine were alleged comics—pen-and-ink drawings—which I sent to *Texas Siftings* when I was about fourteen years old. *Texas Siftings* printed them but forgot to pay me for them. However, I didn't crave any pay. Merely to see them printed was reward enough for me. In a scrap-book which I compiled when I was about fifteen—the only scrap-book, by the way, I ever made, and which I still have—two of the pictures from *Texas Siftings* are pasted. The third clipping got lost and I have forgotten its subject.

> I suppose, except for a bad turn in the family fortunes, I should to-day be a cartoonist, or a caricaturist, or an illustrator—probably a very bad one. I had grown through boyhood with the expectation of studying art and afterward taking it up as a profession. But, when I was sixteen years old, my father's very modest source of obtaining a livelihood failed him and it became necessary for me, a few months later, to leave school—which was no grief to me—and to go to work in order to help out with my earnings the family exchequer. I had grown up with the smell of printer's ink in my snoot. My favorite uncle, for whom I was named, was a country editor and one of the best paragraphers, I think, of the old school of Southern paragraphers founded by George D. Prentiss. My favorite play-place had been the cluttered editorial room of a little daily where this uncle of mine encouraged me to draw and try to write. A little further along I had carried papers over a route and on Saturdays I would hang about the newspaper shop and get pleasure out of the pretense that I was actually helping to get out the paper.

> So it was natural, I suppose, when it became incumbent upon me to get a job, that I should seek one in a newspaper office. I became a "prentice reporter," so-called, at a salary of $1.75 a week. I expect I was about the rawest cub that ever lived, but I had my share of energy if I had no other equipment. When I wasn't hustling after local items I was working over an old-fashioned chalk-plate trying to draw illustrations for news stories, and cartoons on local topics. Presently, though, my reportorial duties so broadened that I no longer found time for the picture-making end of the game, and with a few inconspicuous exceptions I have never tried to draw for publication since. Long ago I ceased to draw for my own amusement, and, with disuse, I have almost altogether lost the knack of it and the inclination for it.

> The editor of the paper on which I worked flattered my vanity and stirred my ambitions in a new direction by telling me he thought I had a turn for writing "funny stuff." Encouraged by him, I turned out bales of bum jingles and supposedly humorous comment on local subjects. And he was good enough to print the stuff; and a few subscribers were good enough to compliment it. I date the beginning of my downward career from that time.

> When I was nineteen a change in ownership of the paper threw him out of a job, and for a short while I filled his place with the title of "managing editor." I had the double distinction of being the youngest managing editor of a daily paper in the United States—and the worst one. When, a few months later, the publishers of the paper found out what ailed the paper they induced the editor to come back again to his former berth and I lost my peacock feathers and became once more a plain reporter. A photograph taken of me about this time proves what a plain reporter I was.

> However, I was not sorry, really, at being reduced to the ranks, because once again I had time and opportunity to write alleged funny stuff. A few of the state papers began copying my junk, and I derived considerable satisfaction thereby but no added glory, to speak of, since my copy was not signed. The paper got the credit instead.

> Two or three years later I moved to Louisville and became a political reporter on the *Evening Post.* On this paper I wrote an occasional column under the title "Kentucky Sour Mash." The column was made up of paragraphs, short articles mainly containing supposedly whimsical digs at politicians and public characters, and verses. My poetry was so wooden that it fairly creaked at the joints, but I could turn it out by the yard. Here's a curious thing: For twenty years now I have done no versifying, and I find it almost impossible to frame lines that will scan and rhyme, whereas this used to be the easiest thing I did. My wits have rusted here just as my hand has lost the trick of making pictures.

From the time I was twenty-five until I was twenty-nine, past, I wrote scarcely a line that was designed to be humorous. During that time I was the managing editor, back in Paducah, of the same paper, the *News,* upon which I had made my start; only now it was the *News-Democrat,* with linotype machines and a brief telegraph service. I worked day and night on routine editorial duties, with no opportunity for the lighter side of journalistic writing. Here, for the first time in my life, I discovered I had things called nerves.

I threw up my job, sent my wife and my year-old baby down to Georgia to stay for a while as non-paying guests at my father-in-law's house, and, with a hundred dollars of borrowed money in my pocket, landed in New York in the middle of the hottest summer of the Christian Era. I spent three weeks trying unsuccessfully to get a job—any kind of a job. When my money was almost gone I had an idea; born of desperation I suppose it was. I wrote out a form letter full of josh, telling how good I was and explaining that New York journalism needed me to make it brighter and better. I sent a copy of this letter to every managing editor in town. This, I suppose, might be called my first attempt at being humorous for a metropolitan audience. Inside of two days I had replies from six managing editors, including Arthur Brisbane, either offering me work right away or promising me the first available opening on their staffs. I went to work for the *Evening Sun.* At the outset I did reportorial work. In a few months I was writing a good half of the *Evening Sun's* Saturday back page of humor and, in addition, editing the page. Howsomever, what got me a job, at better pay on the *Evening World,* was not my humorous stuff but some straight news stories which I wrote for the *Sun.*

I stayed with the *Evening World* six years. I was a reasonably busy person. I was a reporter, a rewrite man, and at intervals a staff-correspondent on out-of-town assignments. I covered the two Thaw trials and probably a dozen other big criminal cases. Between times I wrote an average of three satirical or supposedly humorous signed articles a week for the magazine page of the *Evening World* and contributed special articles to the *Sunday World.* During the last four years of the six I spent under the *World* dome I wrote a page of humor under the titles: "The Hotel Clerk Says" and "Live Talks With Dead Ones" for the magazine section of the Sunday edition. In four years and twelve weeks I did not, on a single Sunday, miss filling my page. These articles were syndicated over the country, but I then regarded my humorous work, as I still do to a greater or less extent, as a sort of side-line, for my energies were largely devoted to handling news stories, and I did the lighter stuff at odd intervals between murders and fires. There used to be a saying in the *Evening World* shop that when, in a lull in city work, I sat down at my typewriter and stuck a clean sheet of paper into the machine and looked as though I were going to burst into tears, it was a sign that I was preparing to try to write something funny. I may add that, in this

regard, I have not greatly changed. I still regard humorous writing as about the most serious work a writing-man can do. I've never yet got a laugh out of anything I wrote in the line of humor. I trust that others have, occasionally, but I haven't.

My first attempt at out-and-out fiction-writing was made nine years ago at the end of a two weeks' vacation, when I was still on the *World.* It was a sort of horror story without a line in it that could be called humorous. I wrote it on a bet with my ally that I could write a straight serious fiction story and sell it to a reputable magazine. I won the bet. The *Saturday Evening Post* bought it and printed it. It was called **"The Escape of Mr. Trimm."** When my contract with the *World* expired I was emboldened to try magazine-writing for a means of livelihood, and I have been at it ever since. Perhaps a third of my output is what my friends are kind enough to call humor; the other two-thirds is made up of serious stuff—character yarns and descriptive articles, as when I went twice to the war for the *Post,* and straight fiction. I find that when I have written something of the humorous order it gives me an appetite, so to speak, to turn out a nice, gruesome, gory, Edgar-Allan-Poeish kind of tale, and vice versa. Personally, I would rather do the straight fiction; at the same time, I must confess that from the standpoint of popularity and financial returns in the form of book royalties, my most successful single piece of work is ***Speaking of Operations,*** which in book form has sold upwards of 300,000 copies in five years, which still is selling at the rate of 25,000 copies a year, and which by a majority of those who read it is regarded as being humorous, although my friend Mr. H. L. Mencken does not agree with them. He thinks it's sad, not to say dreary, and perhaps he is right.

One curious thing I have discovered: A man may write serious fiction for ten years or do straight reportorial work for ten years, but let him turn out one piece of foolery that tickles the public in its short-ribs and, from that hour, he is branded as a humorist.

I have no set rule or pet formulas for writing humor. First, I get an idea. I let it churn up and down a while inside my head until the butter-fats begin to form; then I sit down and write it. Usually, but not always, I rewrite it once, touching it up and smoothing off the corners, and then I let it go. I have found that about fifty per cent, roughly, of my lines and points come to me in conversation with persons congenially inclined. The other fifty per cent, about, hop on the paper during the throes of childbirth, when I am making the first draft of the copy. I have also found out that I am decidedly a poor judge of the humor-values of my own writings. What I think is going to be funny when I set it down frequently falls flat. What I do not regard as especially funny more often goes over well with the reader.

I said just now that I had no rules in writing humor.

I take that back. I have two rules which I endeavor to follow as closely as may be. In what I write with intent to be humorous I try to avoid giving offense to any individual. To my way of thinking, a joke that hurts the feelings of some one, or that leaves a sore spot on another's pelt, or that deals with the physical infirmities of men and women, is not such a very good joke after all. My other rule is this: When I write humor I seek, between the lines, to say to the reader: "Listen, old man, I'm about to poke fun at some of the foolish things you have done and said, but understand, please, that no matter how foolish you may have been in your time I'm a bigger ass than you ever can hope to be. We're both in the same boat, so bear with me while I make confession for the two of us." I am sure that if a humorous writer assumes this attitude and adheres to it the reader subconsciously falls into a state of mental sympathy with him and is more apt to like what is written.

If I may be permitted to lecture a few of my fellowlaborers, I would like to say that, in my opinion, the mistake some really humorous writers make is in assuming, wittingly or unwittingly, an air of superiority—in other words, it is as though they sat on a high pinnacle in a rarefied atmosphere of aloofness, looking down pityingly from that great height upon the foolish, futile, scrambling little human ants far beneath them, and stirring up those ants with barbed satire and clever ridicule. I am sure the reader resents this, even though he may not exactly know what it is that irritates him, and I am sure also another result is that these writers, real humorists though they may be, rarely are publicly recognized and acknowledged as humorists. The man who aspires to be known as a humorist must constantly be saying, not, "What fools *those* mortals be," but "What fools *all* mortals be—myself prominently included." To cite a few conspicuous and justly popular examples, Mark Twain and Bill Nye had this gift, and, among the living, George Ade and Don Marquis and Ring Lardner and Ellis Parker Butler and Ed Howe and Walt Mason—may their tribe increase—likewise have it.

Fred G. Neuman (essay date 1938)

SOURCE: "Style and Manner," in *Irvin S. Cobb: His Life and Letters,* Rodale Press, 1938, pp. 183-99.

[*In the following essay, Neuman outlines Cobb's methods of writing.*]

Those who look upon the writing profession as an easy thing meet with little encouragement from Irvin S. Cobb. The famous scribe once said that he could write "a million words about a pin," but he did not indicate it would be an easy undertaking. Some persons gather from the remark that the only requirements for literary work are pencil and paper. He says it is a toilsome business and must be learned like any other profession.

"You would not expect to become a lawyer, a doctor or a painter without a good many years of study, both in broad fundamentals and in technique," he said in advising beginners to go at it seriously. "Professional writing is not one whit less difficult to master than law, or medicine, or painting. The preparation is different, but no less arduous."

His stories, constituting a distant addition to the world's imaginative literature, have for years been an unfailing reservoir upon which earnest writers have drawn for plot, incident, and method. There is that indescribable touch about his artistry that instantly stamps him as a genius. Like a magic wand, his pen turns everyday things into romance and adventure. More of his short stories have been reproduced in anthologies and symposiums than can be said of any other living American. In one year eleven different published compilations carried as many stories by Mr. Cobb, attesting the wide favor of his creations.

Writing in the *American Magazine* for August, 1925, on the theme **"How to Begin at the Top and Work Down,"** Mr. Cobb gave his theory of short story writing. "It sometimes seems to me," he commented, "that every man, woman and child in the United States wants to write and is certain he or she can write. 'You know,' a young fellow remarks offhandedly, 'I think I'll become a writer. Why I wrote an essay the other day, and everybody told me it was wonderful. I think I'll send it to one of the big magazines.'"

Mr. Cobb is amused at the way aspiring writers contemplate the forum of letters. He has frequently remarked that "easy writing makes hard reading" and marvels at the loose methods employed by juvenile writers who consider speed the prime asset. Although the author of more than three hundred short stories, he avers none of them was dashed off at white heat.

"You should see me some morning when I'm in the mood for dashing off the stuff," said the wordsmith. "There I sit, dashing it off at the rate of about an inch and a half an hour, and using sweat for punctuation. I'm the sort of impetuous dasher that the Muir Glacier is. And so is every other writer who is getting away with it. They say Thackeray worked three weeks over a single paragraph, and then threw it away and started in all over again. Every smooth, easy, graceful line means another furrow in the head of its maker. Nearly every recorded statement which deals with verities means study, research, and patient inquiry."

Continuing, the author elucidated his remarks. "That expression, 'dash off a story,' gives me the pip!" he said, with less regard for elegance than force. "I never dashed off a story in my life, and in my opinion any story that is dashed off is bound therefore to be worthless. A story is like a loaf of bread; if the ingredients are slapped together and the dough is kneaded hastily, the bread is full of raw and indigestible and unsavory lumps; but if it is kneaded and kneaded and kneaded with painstaking care, the bread comes out sweet and smooth and vitalized."

The writer probably disparages himself a bit here, for his friend, Robert H. Davis, once wrote that Mr. Cobb was the only person he knew who could write a short story and carry on a conversation at the same time. The ability to do such a thing is unusual. Julius Caesar is said to have added two columns of figures at a time and Napoleon directed three officers in the same breath. In the case of Mr. Cobb, the feat may be ascribed to the many years he spent in newspaper offices, where both lobes of the brain are frequently called upon for a joint session. Ordinary noises do not distract from his train of thought, for he is accustomed to the roar and hubbub of the big city. Even the thunder of cannon at the battle front did not disturb his equanimity. But on the other hand, the cry of a child, or any distressing or unusual sound is annoying and commands his attention.

Like the late Arthur Brisbane, the prolific Kentuckian often utilizes his time while traveling to revise and make corrections in his work, but he does most of his actual composition at home. It may be in the drawing room of a fast-moving train en route to a speaking engagement that he pulls a manuscript from his pocket for final consideration, or in the quiet of a hotel room following the address where he can glance over what has been written.

Unlike many writers, Mr. Cobb does not prosecute his literary tasks during the late hours of night nor in the early morning. He goes to his workroom about eight-thirty o'clock in the morning and generally works till twelve-thirty. The practice of morning work was inbred during his newspaper days on evening papers, where following a hurried breakfast he rushed to the office and turned out his major copy before noon. Fannie Hurst follows a similar practice, turning out her important work before midday, as did also Rousseau.

He likes to write on Sundays and holidays. Gloomy days have no effect on his output. On the contrary, he turns out some of his liveliest yarns when clouds hang low. He is not a stickler for dismal weather, as was O. O. McIntyre; but given a pen and a clean sheet of paper, his mind is quickly relieved of the elements.

Like the old masters, Mr. Cobb writes all his copy in longhand. "When I turned to authorship I came to the conclusion that speed at which one writes with pen or pencil is the speed at which a mind under proper control can function best," the writer told Lee Shippey, columnist for the Los Angeles Times, in a chat in 1935. "I have tried dictation, but then the words stumbled all over one another." He does his literary work with a fountain pen, writing from three hundred to two thousand words a morning. His average is close to fifteen hundreds words.

The penman wears a French smock while at work and is usually puffing a typically masculine cigar, just as James Fenimore Cooper habitually chewed gum drops while in the throes of creative effort. The afternoons at home are often given to reading and correspondence, or making changes in manuscript.

He often maps out literary plans in some far-off retreat. Speaking of Mr. Cobb's mental activities on a camping trip in the north, Robert H. Davis says in *Canada Cavalcade* (1937):

> I remember the first season of the two that Irvin Cobb bivouacked at Ojuk and laid out a series of short stories, several of them Judge Priest tales and others equally well known. Parked in a hammock, a long cigar in his teeth and the prospect of good night fishing with a plug, the Paducah boy could do more thinking of a profitable sort at Ojuk Island than any man who ever set foot upon its golden strand.

Mr. Cobb says that writing a story is like reporting something. He maps out a fiction story just as he would a long newspaper article, holding that there is not a great deal of difference between news writing and fiction writing. He takes a plot from anything and tries to imagine the story as he would like to have it happen in real life if he were writing for a newspaper. Defoe's *Journal of the Plague Year*, Thackeray's *Vanity Fair*, and Mark Twain's *Huckleberry Finn* are examples of good reporting, he avers.

The writer says newspaper work offers a fine basis for story writing but often tends to hurtful speed. "Newspaper training is good in one way—it brings experience to a fiction writer better and quicker than any other occupation," says Mr. Cobb, seventeen years of whose drama-packed life were spent in newspaper offices. "It's bad in another way, for it tends to too much speed in writing and too much carelessness of the finer points."

Mr. Cobb alternates humor with his serious writing, according to the mood. "I do not disapprove of gloom," he says, claiming it is one of his standbys and often saves the day when he is trying to write something funny. "After I have spent several days trying to write something that will pass as humor, I know of no better way of chirking up than to sit down and write something full of shadows and skulls, smelling of the tomb and dripping the dark blood of sudden and mysterious death. If a character won't crack a Main Street quip for me, I drag him away to a Southern swamp and write up his tragic demise and subsequent decay. And this system works just as well with the reverse English on it. If I find that what I am writing fails to be as gloomy as it should, I bound back to the comic."

His workshop, or study, on the Pacific coast is a large upstairs room at the front from which one might view the ocean but for tall eucalyptus and bamboo trees. Yet from this coign he does not see the things about him but reaches far away for the background of stories destined to fill magazines and eventuate in outstanding books. This is his forte, his sanctuary, his kingdom.

Hundreds of books beckon from shelves of the large library. While the bulk of his literary treasures are in the study, stray volumes lie with delightful abandon in all parts of the house. The drawing room vies with the mental workshop above for its share of big books and little books, old books and new books. There are more than four thousand of them.

His favorite authors, "outside of Will Rogers and myself," are Robert Louis Stevenson, Kipling, Mark Twain, Anatole France, Abe Lincoln, Voltaire, Keats, Shakespeare, Lewis Carroll and Hans Christian Anderson.

The study, or his office, as he prefers to call it, is packed with things made by Indians, from a Navajo rug which practically covers the floor to the last Flathead buffalo spear crowded against the ceiling. At his feet also lies the pelt of a black bear, which, like the moose-head over the mantelpiece in the drawing room is a trophy of his chase for wild game. When he quits his workroom he is as likely to lay his smock on top of a Pawnee papoose-carrier as to hang it over a Sioux tomahawk decorated with a scalplock.

His former workshop at "Rebel Ridge" near New York City was an abandoned ice house one hundred and fifty feet from the home. The morning sun came in at the east windows and was reflected in a small pool beside which the brick structure sat. In its remodeled state the workshop resembled a hunting cabin or lodge. Notable among literary productions in these quarters were such books as *Life Among the Abandoned Farmers* and *J. Poindexter, Colored.* In all, he wrote about fifty stories at "Rebel Ridge."

Chief among the stories written while the Cobbs lived at the Algonquin Hotel in New York City may be mentioned **"Red Handed."** The humorous volume *One Third Off* was also written there. When a limner drew caricatures of New York's literary and playwriting grandees for the hotel's celebrity corner, Mr. Cobb was asked to autograph the burlesque of himself. At the jutting crevice of his mouth, he wrote: "What a place to throw old razor blades!"

From 1907 to 1913 the writer and his family lived at Park Hill, Yonkers, where he produced the early Judge Priest yarns and, in the field of humor, *Cobb's Bill of Fare* and *Cobb's Anatomy.* He had just turned out these humorous classics when he returned to New York City to make his home and was greeted at the station by reporters who questioned him as to why he made the change. "I have nothing to say against Yonkers," he replied, "but I believe New York has a future." Later, and until moving to California, the Cobbs maintained an apartment on Park Avenue for winter.

Philosophizing again on hasty story writing, the phrase-maker cited his own observations. "I have seen a good many manuscripts of would-be authors," he mused, "and what impresses me about them is the extraordinary slovenliness and lack of care they show. There are stupid inconsistencies; facts do not check up; a character is called Marion in one place, and Miriam in another, and Mary Ann in a third; punctuation is careless, and type-writing is often abominable. I can safely say I have never seen an amateur story that shows one-tenth the care and thought that I, or any other professional writer, think it essential to put on a story before I show it to an editor. And if that care and thought are necessary for an accepted writer with a waiting market, how much more necessary are they for the beginner entering the field and expecting to fight the enormous competition waiting there!"

During an interview at his suburban home, the writer disclosed the origin of most of his short stories. He said the things he visions in his working hours are the scenes of his past living and the people he has known. For many years he had no definite idea as to the source of fiction material, but agrees now that his younger days are the dormant caches that supply most of his short story data.

His first short story was **"The Escape of Mr. Trimm,"** which was suggested by the trial of a high-flying financier. He covered it as a reporter for the *New York Evening World.*

"That was more than twenty-five years ago," Mr. Cobb recently recalled. "The next winter I met Arnold Bennett, who told me that a successful writer must get his background, his basic material, from things that he thought, or felt, or did before he was thirty-five years old. I was approaching that age, and despite the sources of my first story, I didn't believe entirely in his statement. But I've thought about it since, and I've arrived at the conviction that Bennett was correct. All of my characters and most of the incidents are the result of my looking backward, sometimes unconsciously, over the memories of my experiences with life."

"Of course," he explained, "no single character is the counterpart of an individual, but everyone is made up of characteristics that I've observed in people that I've known. The trick is in selecting those characteristics which blend so harmoniously as to give the reader a vivid impression of actuality.

"So I'm sure that writing fiction is not really one of the creative arts. It's darn hard work; but it's merely the piecing together, the building up, of things a fellow's seen and heard, and the emotions he felt, into a unified form. That is the way all of my best work was done. Now I realize that Arnold Bennett knew what he was talking about, and that his remark set me to looking for material in the right direction—back over the life I have lived and the memories of the people I have known."

The happy marriage of sound and sense known as style of writing is simply a matter of good taste, in the opinion of Mr. Cobb. Jonathan Swift defined style the same way when he said it consists of "proper words in proper places," for the construction and application of words with due regard to clearness and variety determine the mode of expression. The English historian Green said Addison's style was "but a reflection of himself," which connotes Mr. Cobb's statement as regards taste.

"If you are ever going to be a writer, style is a thing which you laboriously must learn," the writer told a group of friends; "and then having acquired added wisdom you will forget part of it and chuck the rest of it out of the window and acquire a style of your own, which merely is another way of saying that if you have good taste to start with you will have what is called style in writing, and if you haven't got that sense of good taste you won't have style and nothing can give it to you.

"I think one of the banes of our young lives is being told what we should read to form our style. I'll begin my treason by saying that while Addison had a singularly clear style he didn't have anything else. If I had my childhood to live over I would tie a can to the essays of Charles Lamb and I would throw Bulwer-Lytton and his eighty-four pound works into the mill hole. The best I can say for George Eliot is that her works have all the glamour of antiquity. We are suffering from overreading of standard stuff. The world is full of people who have a magnificent style but nothing to wrap it around."

Mr. Cobb's style of writing is smooth and flowing, a pleasing combination of clear expression and force, euphony and beauty. Its unaffected movement gives truth to the assertion of William Wirt that "a simple style forms the best vehicle of expression." The sure rhythm and diction meet the precepts of Herbert Spencer in his essay on "The Philosophy of Style," by presenting ideas so they may be apprehended with the least possible mental effort. His rich vocabulary responds immediately to every demand, and he never has any difficulty in making himself clearly understood. Long and graceful sentences convey the writer's meaning with striking accuracy. Not only does he express his ideas perfectly, but he seems to achieve this result with apparent artlessness.

His metaphors and images are always fresh and new, and he never attempts a figure that is not complete. When he said a certain hazy individual had "as much sense of direction as an egg beater," the simile was absolute. The Cobb larder is heavily stocked with clever and pointed phrases—picturesque similes of a diverting and trenchant nature. The following are typical:

> Sizz like skyrockets.
> Noiseless as a mink.
> Shine like a wet seal.
> Pop like a bull-whip.
> Pampered like invalids.
> Skipped like ram goats.
> As nutty as a fruit cake.
> Stiff as a dried herring.
> Sore as a mashed thumb.
> Comfortable as an anvil.

> Quivered like proud flesh.
> Tumbling like shot rabbits.
> Sags like a fisherman's hat.
> Fleshless as a joint of cane.
> As limber as a string of fish.
> Cutting up like a trick mule.
> Fluctuate like a demented hen.
> Mixed together like jackstraws.
> No more privacy than a goldfish.
> Cuts loose like an avenging angel.
> Had a breath like a brandy sauce.
> He opened up like a family album.
> As neutral as a stop and go signal.
> Laced with red like a bloodshot eye.
> As misshapen as a dropsical woman.
> He has more kinfolk than a microbe.
> He had a disposition like a hangnail.
> Flew open like an engine-house door.
> Folded up like a condensed time-card.
> Snappy, like the click of a cash register.
> As vocal as a tree full of mocking birds.
> Trudging as steadily as a milkman's horse.
> Complexion like a stalk of bleached celery.
> He stiffened like a pointer on a warm scent.
> Gurgling like the last pint of suds in a sink.
> Crackled like the lightnings on Mount Sinai.
> Brief as the Z column in a pocket dictionary.
> Stands forth like carnival tags on a marquee.
> As crooked as a churnful of coon chitterlings.
> I had a tang in my mouth like an antique jug.
> Dovetailed and mortised like good cabinetwork.
> Sounds like a chapter out of a penny-dreadful.
> Left a taste in his mouth like a tintype factory.
> Imbibing his soup like a man bailing out a boat.
> Intermittently, like the click of a blind man's cane.
> As Southern as chicken gravy on a presiding elder's vest.
> Braced and steady, like a game man facing a firing squad.
> Riding on her speedboat was like being a jockey to a comet.
> As much out of place as a bald-headed eagle in a pet store.
> Tasted like rubber heels suffering from a brandy hang-over.
> Boring in and out, like a stubby needle going through a tick.
> Vandyked to a sharp point like evergreens in a cemetery.
> A pleasant swishing sound like a soft-shoe dancer starting on a jig.
> Groomed and polished, like a landed proprietor's blooded stock.
> Tastes like a place where an indisposed carrot spent the night.
> Dressed in white—all white, like a bride or a bandaged thumb.
> Overflowing like a crock of salt-rising dough in a warm kitchen.
> Make noises like a drunken Zulu trying to sing a Swedish folk song.
> It was like a gumboil that wouldn't heal; not serious but annoying.
> Busier than a boss canvasman when the show-train has been delayed by a washout.
> All gashed with wrinkles and seamed with folds, like the jowls of an ancient squaw.

Joined in, like the wind, the wood and the brass of
   an orchestra obeying the baton of the leader.
Love is like a butterfly: it may hover over a flower
   garden, and then again it may light on the city
   dump.
Tasting a good deal like a blotting-pad that has
   seen hard usage in the timekeeper's office of a
   crude-oil refinery.
My butler is the kind you see on the stage, with
   little side whiskers on each side of his face,
   like brackets inclosing a blankspace; so ( ).

Piercy's *Modern Writers at Work* (1930), which reproduces **"The Great Auk"** as a model short story, quotes
Mr. Cobb in the matter of keen discrimination in the use
and arrangement of words. "I do not feel qualified to give
others advice on how to write good English," Mr. Cobb
said. "That is a job I constantly am striving to learn.
Practice, hard work, reading the writings of real master-
writers—that's my system. In the face of my own constant failures to turn out copy which satisfies me, it still
is the best system I know anything about—the sole one,
in fact."

In the wide choice of Mr. Cobb's creations there is ready
evidence of the facility with which his pen is adapted to
every subject. The plots of stories are fascinating, often
uncanny, and abound in clever twists. Each story is fresh
and vital, not remote or shadowy as seen through several
thicknesses of theatrical gauze tending to blur details. His
deep pathos is tear-compelling. He is an eager student of
mankind and with his photographic pen paints an accurate picture of life. Delving deep into the hearts of men
and women, he brings to the surface their joys and sor-
rows, triumphs and failings, and moods and inward
thoughts. What he sees with his eye he reflects through
the mirror of sympathetic understanding, and this mirror
he keeps polished by constant rubbing of elbows with the
world. Fred Lewis Patton in *The New American Literature* (1930) notes that "in allusion, in vocabulary, in fictional fashions, in point of view, Mr. Cobb is always as
up-to-date as a college orchestra."

Whether the story at hand is one of sentiment, tragedy or
uproarious farce, it is characterized by an adequacy of
expression and subtle analysis. Robert H. Davis says Mr.
Cobb "writes in octaves, striking instinctively all the
chords of humor, tragedy, pathos and romance with either
hand."

As a descriptive writer, he has no peer among his contemporaries. Speaking of the Kentuckian's uncanny art of
observing things and method of describing them, Ellis
Parker Butler says: "Irvin S. Cobb writes of a person,
describing the front of him, and you know instinctively
that the man has one suspender button off in the back and
that both loops of his suspenders are hooked on the remaining button."

His poetic utterances are as redolent as roses and offer a
perpetual delight. There are whole chapters in **Chivalry
Peak** and **Red Likker,** for instance, where the author

woos like an angel. The flowing melody of his classic
prose suggests "the music of bells falling in cadence
sweet"; it is fluid and rippling, without a trace of effort.
An effulgence of language gives perfection to the sentimental moods and finer moments. **Some United States** is
strewn with tinseled phrases and jeweled periods. Page
after page of **All Aboard** is filled with wild beauty and
Both Sides of the Street, which records the author's visit
to South America, is rich with rhetorical decoration. One
is inclined to believe he was kissed by all the muses, as
any subject he touches is adorned.

The periodical known as *Word Beauty* questioned Mr.
Cobb among other well known Americans on what word
in the English language seemed to be the most beautiful
in sound. He selected "Chattanooga," a word of Indian
origin.

When asked which book in the vast storehouse of literature he would rather have authored than any other, the
Paducah sage chose Job, forty-two anonymous chapters
written long before Christ was born. "I would rather have
written it because in it, I think, there is more of majesty,
of poetry, of imagery and drama than in any book of
similar length known to me," Mr. Cobb said.

The judgment is well sustained, for the Book of Job is
recognized as the greatest poem in the world's great literature. Victor Hugo called it "perhaps the greatest masterpiece of the human mind."

Awards for literary achievement do not always balance,
the philosopher observed in his daily column upon reading that a man who wrote lovely verse died penniless.
"I'd rather do a ballad or a tale which, for one fleeting
hour, brought laughter or a thrill to a multitude, than turn
out a so-called classic which through generations would
moulder on the back rows of some library, hard by the
Bulwer-Lytton shelf and handily adjacent to the late
Charlotte Bronte," he declared.

Robert van Gelder (essay date 1941)

SOURCE: "The Last Autobiography," in *The New York
Times Book Review,* March 10, 1941, p. 4.

[*In the following essay, van Gelder reviews* Exit Laughing, *finding it entertaining, but ultimately unsatisfying.*]

Irvin S. Cobb learned his trade in a rugged school where
facility in writing was the reward for energy and vanity,
and where politeness was the price of safety. He has, of
course, been writing autobiography for years. A strong
instinct for self-preservation early taught him to believe
that the humor that picks on what is ridiculous in other
white men is a spurious brand. The proper study for the
genuine droll, he considers, is that droll himself, and as
Mr. Cobb has lived much of his life on the profits of
humor, he has inevitably written a great deal about himself. His early experiences in Paducah, Ky., where there

were plenty of guns left over from the Civil War and where a man had time to nurse an eccentricity into a definitely bad temper, have been a rich mine of material. His reportorial adventures in New York, and in Europe during the first World War, are almost as familiar as his operation.

That this should be so is proof of his good judgment. This old material, cast in new phrases and garnished with fresh anecdotes, makes the best part of this not-necessarily final autobiography. On the home grounds of his youth Cobb can show Cobb as eager, likable, a bear for work, an easily entertained young man who becomes adept at entertaining. But it is as though he had ballooned in some fashion when, after developing as one of the most skilled and efficient reporters of his time, he moved out into the big money fields of popular magazine writing and lecturing, and from then on never quite had touch with the sources of his own strength. There is a very clear line of demarcation. When he writes of the people he knew when he was young he presents characters who stand and move with the life that he puts into his descriptions of them. Later the people mentioned are all too often "important" heroes or despicable boors and cads. The once clear, friendly look has become, it seems, impossible.

The men and women of the Judge Priest stories came from Paducah, where Cobb was born and where, at 16, he obtained his first newspaper job. There had been Cobbs in Paducah since the early days, and his mother's people, members of the Saunders family, also had arrived not very long after the Revolutionary War. Cobb grew up in a nest of kinfolk, with uncles and aunts to spare. Judge Priest was physically a reincarnation of the late Judge William S. Bishop—"the high bald forehead, the pudgy shape, the little white paintbrush of a chin whisker, the strident high-pitched voice which, issuing from that globular tenement, made a grotesque contrast, as though a South American tapir had swallowed a tomtit alive and was letting the tomtit do the talking for him." Some of Judge Priest's mental attitudes were borrowed from Hal Corbett, a lawyer who spent most of his time running for office, and Mr. Cobb's father. For the bit players in the tales he drew from the Negro community. Connie Lee, who survives as the town's leading chiropodist—and is, by the way, the only survivor—was "Jeff Poindexter," Judge Priest's private retainer.

Irvin Cobb went to work at 16 because his father, hurt in the Civil War, determined, according to his son, to drink himself to death. He had lost his job with a steamboat line and had nothing left but an insurance policy which carried an anti-suicide clause. So very deliberately he set about to collect that insurance for his family. "He had health though, and was strong, and to accomplish this took four hard years." In the first year of his effort Irvin Cobb started writing news.

His apprenticeship was rigorous but it later paid full dividends. With a beginning salary of $1.75 a week, it was

his privilege to write just about all that he wanted to write, and he could always be sure that the people he knew would read him if he could keep his copy even moderately lively. He does not mention restrictions as to style—probably there were none. But there were the empty forms that must be filled, there were thousands of words to be put down every day.

At 19 Cobb was managing editor of the paper, but that didn't last long, as "the owners soon found out what was wrong with the paper." However at the age of 20, when his father died, he was earning twelve dollars a week, and his string as a correspondent was lengthening. Covering the best stories that Kentucky could provide and working so fast and hard that it was necessary to discover and make use of every natural gift in order to get through each day, he learned to write by free, popular writing. When, near the beginning of this century, he came to New York, he had tested himself to capacity and thus had a clear idea of what kind of performance he could turn in under stress. Success in New York came fairly rapidly and within a few years he was known as the highest paid reporter in the country, and George Horace Lorimer of *The Saturday Evening Post* had made a bid for his services—a bid that was promptly accepted. After that magazine correspondence, the lecture platform after-dinner speaking, Hollywood and much later, a few turns as an actor.

But now the emphasis changes and tales of Mr. Cobb's prowess as a big eater replace the earlier stories of work. William Randolph Hearst and Ray Long are not shown objectively as were the Monkey Wrench Corner idlers in Paducah or the bosses on *The Evening World*. There are "important people" introduced simply as "important people," with a few glib patches of praise pasted on them. And there are some curious now-it-can-be-told yarns that leave, it must be admitted a rather peculiar taste. We were not at war with Germany in 1914 but Mr. Cobb's story of the letter he brought from Germany for delivery to Franz von Papen in Washington is unavoidably unsavory. The same might be said of his barging in on President Wilson soon after we entered the war, intent on winning "me a pair of shoulder straps." Wilson refused his request that special influence be used to get him into the Army as an officer and told him that "the next time you want something at my hands let it be something worth your having and worth my giving." But he put his arm around Cobb's shoulders to take the sting out of the words, with the result that Cobb "came away with an enhanced chest expansion" that, to tell the truth, is still a bit noticeable.

William Allen White (essay date 1941)

SOURCE: "The Humor of the Self-Kidder," in *Saturday Review of Literature,* Vol. XXIII, No. 22, March 22, 1941, p. 5.

[*In the following essay, White praises* Exit Laughing *as a peculiarly American autobiography.*]

This book [*Exit Laughing*] is only incidentally the "life story" of Irvin S. Cobb. It is an adventure in humorous American humor. Taking it by and large, the humor in Irvin Cobb's autobiography, which bubbles like eternal Pierian springs on every page, is the humor of the self-kidder. He has a lot of stories about others, but if he laughs at a poor devil, it is only to reveal the fact that Cobb is not superior to the poor devil, but is his brother under the skin.

Mark Twain, at least in his earlier days, was a self-kidder. The travel stories of Mark Twain—*Roughing It, A Tramp Abroad, Innocence Abroad, Life on the Mississippi,* and his boys' stories, *Tom Sawyer* and *Huck Finn,* were pure self-kidding, and throughout this entire book, Irvin Cobb walks under a fool's cap, with chalked face and broad pantaloons, the everlasting clown who, despite his ribaldry and laughter, is pictured here scrupulously if unconsciously a gentleman and a scholar and a judge of good whiskey. Indeed a judge of good whiskey, who is, for the purpose of this narrative, slightly squizzed, so that he paints himself in perspective and, as Kipling put it, "Stands beside and sees himself behaving like a blooming fool." Indeed, again to quote Kipling, this book was obviously written by the gentleman and scholar and judge of good whiskey, as the story of one who "sits in clink without his boots, beholdin' how the world was made."

The skeleton of the autobiography puts down the facts of the life of Irvin Cobb; born in the little town of Paducah, Kentucky, in the third quarter of the nineteenth century, just after the close of what, at that time, was known in the north as the Rebellion, later was called the Civil War, and now, in polite society, is referred to as the War between the States. The War between the States was a national episode now rapidly glimmering across twilight's purple rim of our history. It is becoming a national myth. But the setting of that period of reconstruction during which Irvin Cobb came into consciousness as a boy and acquired his prejudices of youth, formed everywhere west of the Alleghenys a back-stage setting. War overshadowed life in the American South and West in the '60's, '70's, '80's, and until the turn of the century. In this overshadowing of American life, the Confederate viewpoint, a nice blending of hiccupping nostalgia and conscious, deliberate, and downright self-deception, furnished the spiritual landscape of Paducah and points south of Kentucky to New Orleans, east to Charleston, and back to Louisville. As a Southerner—and he proves his right to be one by bragging on his ancestors for two chapters—Irvin Cobb comes in this book, and all of his books bringing something precious and lovable into American life and letters. Cobb came from a region in the United States, where wealth had been wiped out by the war, where poverty was a badge of honor. Indeed, the South developed a bumptious scorn of the acquisitive life, which the Yankee North was patterning for the whole country in the third quarter of the old century and in the first third of the new century. That bumptious Southern scorn of the acquisitive pattern of life is after all, the secret key to the understanding and enjoyment of

Irvin Cobb's philosophy. That Southern attitude toward those predatory faculties of the Yankees in its very self makes for humor. A man who can look at a dollar without a spastic clutch for it it is, by all of the rules and tokens of the American game, slightly bughouse and conspicuously off his nut. So that Irvin Cobb, with the psychology of the busted South, coming into the American scene, north of the Mason and Dixon line, was laughable per se, ipse dixit, prima facie, and with all the giggleferious hereditaments thereunto appertaining!

Probably this attitude of absurdity which followed Irvin Cobb like a shadow molded his features. For his face provokes laughter in the mouths of the unthinking, who do not see that it is a serious, essentially sad, profoundly wise countenance. But some way Cobb can twist it, with scarcely a muscle's twitch, into a clowning grimace, without the slightest distortion. Mr. Cobb is known in his country as a humorist. But this story of his life as a newspaperman, from Paducah to Chicago to New York, from newspapers to magazines to books, and from books to the lecture platform to a place as a philosophic interpreter of our American scenes, is the story of a real man, a hard-working man, a conscientious man, tremendously impressed by the dignity and nobility of his profession.

This man's story of *Exit Laughing* is well worth reading, even if it were without embroidery, even if it lacked the gay, galluptious felicitation which sparkles from every page. Obviously the man whose unconscious portrait of dignity and sense of righteousness is delineated in this book, just had to be the friend of great figures of his generation. And so, as they pass in review here in these happy pages, we see Cobb and his friends walking in beauty, side by side, from the 1890s to the last tick of the clock of the 1940's. Probably no other biography that has been published in many years contains such vivid portraits of so many important Americans as this story of Irvin Cobb's. They are vivid because he has seen them, not as remote figures, but as faces across a table—maybe a dinner table, maybe a poker table, possibly a council table. He has seen them as friends, and he is certainly a friendly cuss. There is a strain of Newfoundland (and never poodle) in Irvin Cobb. Naturally, he never snaps, never barks, and never kicks dirt up behind him like a feist. He has aplomb and poise and carries his St. Bernard's rescuing whiskey flask to those in spiritual distress, with something like the sweet suavity of a duly registered practising angel. One can see that he brings out the best in his friends, and if he seems to be tromping through life on shell pink clouds of glory, with the rippling risibles of a happy humanity around him, it is because he makes his own environment.

I know of no book published in recent years which is so American as *Exit Laughing.* Its humor is Falstaffian. Shakespeare, on the whole, laughed with people, and not at them, and the Shakespearian quality of these pages, even if sometimes the rhetoric is a bit stagey, somewhat consciously mirthful, still, at the same time, is honest. It is always kind and wise.

Certainly this book could not have been written in Continental Europe, much less printed there. For it represents laughter, in life and in democracy. Here speaks the American spirit whose "sense of humor saves him whole!"

Judith D. Hoover (essay date 1986)

SOURCE: "Between Times: 19th Century Values in the 20th Century," in *The Southern Quarterly*, Vol. XXIV, No. 3, Spring, 1986, pp. 49-57.

[*In the following essay, Hoover discusses Cobb's shaping values, which she views as being rooted in the American South of the nineteenth century.*]

Irvin S. Cobb (1876-1944) had access to more of the media of mass culture in America than perhaps any other man of his day. He wrote two novels and more than 300 popular short stories, as well as speeches, jokes, quips, essays and opinion pieces for magazines; for more than ten years he reported daily human interest "news" for New York newspapers; he wrote screenplays and acted in films; he spoke to a national audience in his own radio program; he saw three of his plays produced on Broadway; he entertained "after dinner" to groups ranging from the elite of the business and professional world to Hollywood celebrities, small town Kentucky audiences and local fund-raising groups.

Cobb embodied the mind of the post-Civil War South as it struggled with questions of racial segregation, "Old South" cultural values, and economic and political upheaval. Judge Priest, his major fictional middle-class hero, and Jeff Poindexter, his most enlightened black voice, typified the old and the new South, while both struggled to live "by the rules" in a period when the rules were changing. Cobb's themes and sentiments upheld the traditional values of nineteenth-century life and literature. He maintained old style values of the intrinsic worth of the common man, of a sense of community, of good defeating evil, of care for the downtrodden.

Cobb's estimate of the worth of these values can be seen in a letter he wrote to James Whitcomb Riley in 1914 in response to "kind words" Riley had spoken about Cobb's work to a friend from Paducah, Kentucky, Cobb's home town. Cobb wrote, "I hope you'll believe me when I tell you that I would rather have your good opinion than the good opinion of any writing man in this country. . . . I found in your poems the kind of poems I have loved best . . . the poems that deal with every day people and every day homely things." Cobb once called Riley the "greatest poet of the people that America ever had" (Letter to Landon).

Cobb's narrative style, chronological order, formal structure, correct syntax and emphasis on reality all place him squarely in the nineteenth-century mold. How were the modernists of the early twentieth century different from this mold? How may we characterize the modernist change that occurred in the early twentieth century and locate Cobb in his proper place on either side of that line or straddling it?

Modernist writers, unlike Cobb, exchanged narration for ambiguity, imagery and symbolism (Lodge 3-4). They probed the unconscious, they challenged taboos and in some cases they saw their works repressed. T. S. Eliot argued against the writer's use of his own experiences. Poetry, he said, is made of poetry, and is not necessarily comprehensible, is not a reflection of the poet's life and times, feelings or perceptions. The poet's personality must be rendered extinct and he must become an intermediary or catalyst that aids in the creation of poetry but remains separate from it" (Eliot 7-11). Lionel Trilling, in his essay "On the Modern Element in Modern Literature," finds "the disenchantment of our culture to be a dominant theme in modern literature" (60).

Modernism seemed, to Cobb, to be a flight into chaos, necessitated by the questioning and rejection of old values and styles, with nothing concrete having been devised to replace them. The revolutionary modernists tore away at the structural forms and the underlying moral values at the same time. They claimed that life imitated art, but it seems clear that they and their art were reflecting the crisis of values that afflicted Americans during this period. While writers like Sinclair Lewis exposed the smallness, shallowness and meanness of village life, Cobb clung to his small town as a symbol of continuity.

Cobb expressed vehement opposition to modernist literature in letters, speeches and articles. He described the "young intellectuals" as the "literary bad boys of the East," whose "average age is approximately seventy years." These "self-appointed superior minds," who called business clubs like the Rotary "bourgeois" and "provincial" were his favorite target (**"Intellectuals are Target"**). In an attack on the "purveyors of superrealism and the deliberately chaotic style," Cobb accused them of being "so busy discovering sex and garbage they have forgotten beauty exists in the world." Cobb found their efforts to be up-to-date pitiful and impossible since "you have to wait until today has crystallized into yesterday before you can describe it accurately." He ridiculed another group of writers, observing that "Chicago woke up one morning and discovered that there were a lot of writers there. Bang! The Chicago School came into being." It was not that they were poor writers, some of them were good at their work, but they were lost in "a maze of words"; they were suffering from "nervous culture." They wrote "propaganda," and, Cobb said, "propaganda is never art" (**"Gompers and Cobb"**).

Cobb deplored the trend of equating smut with sex that he saw developing. He reminded his readers that sex had been around since the beginning of time and that some literary newcomer's "discovery" of it did not really make it new. It was not sex to which he objected because, as he said, "life is full of sex and literature must deal with life"

("**Slushy**"). It was the presentation of it in its sensation-alized and blatantly rebellious form that he found objectionable. Language still considered "improper" had become accepted on the stage and screen where it was considered merely "realism." If a truck driver said the same words in public, he would be arrested for using obscenity since he was not "artistic, but just a poor overworked slob of a vulgarian" (*Ladies and Gentlemen* 166).

Cobb feared censorship would result from this "superrealism." He acknowledged that perhaps it took such a group as the Legion of Decency to curb the trend toward "excesses" that developed early in the motion picture industry. He saw "no art" in a little boy writing "short and dirty words" on an alley fence, and he saw "no art in smut and filth acted out before a camera and flung upon a screen." The real problem, however, lay in "overzealous or bigoted prurient-minded censors" (*Exit*). He blamed censorship on "sensualship." "I believe in free speech," he insisted, "but I don't believe in it being free and easy. As for this notion of censorship, it merely is another expression of the desire to destroy individual liberty by sumptuary legislation which, made fat and greedy by the adoption of the Eighteenth Amendment, now would assault our rights again" ("**Censorship**").

Cobb's opposition to the prohibition amendment brings us to a sense of Irvin Cobb as liberal social critic, the point at which he begins to differ from the conservatism of the nineteenth century. His campaigns against prohibition, against religious bigotry, against oppression of the poor, all set him apart from nineteenth-century moral and social certainty and align him with the spirit of the twentieth century.

If Cobb's views seem to straddle both sides of the intellectual fence, however, his literary style does not, with the single exception of his use of poetic descriptive devices. He remained an adamant "purveyor of the deliberate *non*-chaotic style," to turn his epithet into a description of himself. He continued to use the narrative form to compose his stories, articles, essays and speeches. He preferred clarity to obscurity and "correct" form to experimentation. Cobb's subject matter reflected his feelings about the life he observed around him; his stories have heroes and villains, good guys and bad guys. His fiction is not made of fiction, but of experience. There is no glossing over of human frailties that typified many nineteenth-century novels, but his characters are not all bad or depressed or disillusioned, either. His villages are populated with those who are satisfied to be there, but we are not asked to believe, therefore, that they are unintelligent, unmotivated, stifled provincials in contrast to those who had the good sense to move.

Cobb's attitudes about social reform may throw him in with the progressives, but he did not write typical "progressive novels" with their naive heroes rising up through the corporate or political structure and finally acquiring enough power to overcome the evils of privilege. Nor were his heroes the beneficiaries of the "lucky accidents" of life, always in the right place at the right time, as in a typical Horatio Alger story.

If Irvin Cobb's criticism of his fellows has any weight, it must relate to his own literary status. What were his credentials as a writer? Contemporary criticism is mixed, but generally favorable. His first book of stories, *Back Home,* published in 1912, was praised both by H. I. B., a reviewer in the *New York Times,* and by the London *Bookman.* The first supported Cobb's notion of showing life in the South "without gilding that romance or adorning it with plumes borrowed from the helmet of Ivanhoe." His success was in "showing southerners as they really are with their weaknesses intact, but with pride and affection." Cobb gave a "true picture of a sadly misrepresented plain folk." From a European perspective, *Bookman* describes Cobb as a "South American who has gone to live in the North," who has written "unforced and curiously effective" stories, the "freshest things of the kind that have come out of America since Bret Harte wrote his first book." The stories were "clever," and "delightfully, humorously and poignantly human." Blanche Colton Williams in *Our Short Story Writers* called Judge Priest the best representative southerner ever found in literature, and compared Cobb with O. Henry, in that they both broke away from traditional types and created "real types." Cobb's greatest contribution was in his "interpretation of South to North and of generation to generation" (83). Robert H. Davis, writing in the January 1913 *Current Opinion,* felt that if Cobb were not an American, his "genius" would be recognized, but that Americans fail to take literature seriously. To Davis, Cobb's attributes were "style, restraint, narration, dialog, wit, subtlety, naturalness, and convincingness of plot" (57). The March 1913 *Bookman* called Cobb "someone who must be regarded rather seriously." Referring to Davis's lavish praise, *The Bookman* said that Davis had "probably read, or at least accepted or rejected more fiction," as editor of *Munsey's Magazine,* "than any other editor on earth," and so his opinion should count for something ("Concerning"). In a review of the volume *The Escape of Mr. Trimm* in 1914, the London *Bookman* called Cobb "proficient in humour and tragedy." It found the "**Mr. Trimm**" story "haunting in its grimness," and "**Occurrence Up a Side Street**" to be "worthy of Poe" and "suggestive of Maupassant."

By the 1920s a growing sophistication and a change in literary tastes, at least among critics, began to manifest itself in unfavorable reviews of Cobb's books. The characters Cobb and others had seen as "real" were beginning to seem superficial, and the humorous stories hardly worth a smile. Rather than growing and changing as a writer, Cobb simply sat still and turned out more of the same. H. L. Mencken's criticisms of Cobb's work began innocuously, but grew more sarcastic as time passed. Of *Back Home,* he said that "one feels that the author knows these people perfectly and what is more, that he loves them well." To Mencken, the result was "an excellent row of portraits, a bit old-fashioned, but altogether attractive" (qtd. in Neuman 98-9). By 1919, however, when

Mencken reviewed *Those Times and These,* he found only one "excellent comic story, **'Hark From the Tomb',**" lying in the book "like a Smithfield ham between two slabs of stale store-bread" (*Prejudices* 98). He saw nothing else even remotely good about Cobb in general, except a smile credited to Cobb—"no more privacy than a goldfish." Mencken said, "Here, at last, is something genuinely humorous. Here, moreover, is something apparently new" (103-4). Mencken claimed that this was his only detailed description of Cobb and that Doran, Cobb's publisher, had not sent him any of Cobb's books to review since then (Letter).

Some critics found fault in Cobb's readers, expressing disappointment that regardless of the quality of his work he still had a "large and devoted following," ("More of Cobb"). Others criticized Cobb for appealing to this mass audience by writing for magazines and characterized his readers as a "large, more or less heedless, public more anxious to be temporarily diverted than really entertained" ("Prose and Cons"). Occasionally, a particular piece of Cobb fiction met with the approval of the critics and the "heedless mass." *Red Likker* sold well and received praise as a firstrate book, full of "wisdom" and "intelligence" and "intimacy," a book that might "someday become an American classic" (**"Red Likker"**).

Reviews by individual newspapers may have little or no meaning when viewed alongside judgments made by a publisher's own professional staff. The archives of Bobbs-Merrill, Cobb's last publisher, contains readers' reports, inter-office memos, and publicity campaigns which, when combined with favorable reviews, throw a rather perplexing light on the reviewing process. A Bobbs-Merrill critic called Cobb's **"Choice of Jello or Rice Pudding"** about "as vapid as a title might be" (Memorandum). He or she rejected Cobb's next suggested title of "To Make a Long Story Short," but soothed Cobb's ruffled feathers by saying that they were looking for the right "commercial angle" in the title (Letter). Bobbs-Merrill wanted to cut Cobb's advance of $1000 on the book, eventually titled, *Faith, Hope, and Charity,* until reminded that "Cobb short stories sell better than ordinary short stories" (Note).

In promoting *Judge Priest Turns Detective* in 1936, Bobbs-Merrill turned the negative criticisms of their readers reports into positive aspects in their advertising. One reader noted that "if this book didn't bear the name of Cobb, it wouldn't get to first base with a publisher." Another complained that it was not a novel, as it claimed to be, but two long short stories or novelettes—and "just plain not very good." Cobb's well-known local Kentucky color seemed "all too familiar," and the "female impersonator device" and the "guilty friend of the family" were "such outworn gags that the modern detective story reader is apt to turn his nose up very high at them." The critic saw "no profit in publishing this book." Bobbs-Merrill publicity translated all this into: "Cobb paints with marvelous artistry the Kentucky scene he loves," scenes "delightfully familiar" to all Cobb's readers. The

book was a "double-barreled thriller"; the plot a "complicated yarn of who was murdered and why," and a "tasty and different dish for the jaded detective story fan" (Publicity layout). Unbelievably, highly favorable reviews came in to the publisher from daily papers in Columbus and Cincinnati, Ohio, St. Louis, Miami, Boston and New York (Collected reviews).

If reviews are a questionable measure of success, are sales any better? Cobb's autobiography made the bestseller list in 1941, the first of his books to do so, although alongside this listing, he is referred to as a "longtime favorite author and humorist" (Hackett 132). The little book *Speaking of Operations,* his humorous treatment of the care and non-feeding of the typical surgical patient and the original home of the goldfish simile, sold 300,000 copies in the first five years and had annual sales of 25,000 per year for the next five ("American Humorists"). All of his collected stories had previously been published in popular magazines, and, according to the Bobbs-Merrill memo, still sold well. George H. Lorimer claimed to have asked a newsdealer how his magazine was selling and the reply was, "They ask me if there is anything in it by Cobb. If there is, they buy it. If there isn't, they don't" ("Cobb, Literary Heavyweight").

Perhaps Lorimer's comment explains why in 1925 Cobb was renowned as the world's highest paid short story writer, receiving $3500 to $4000 per story rather than the standard $500 to $1000 ("Cobb, Highest Paid"). A pure dollars and cents measure of success gave Cobb a lifestyle he desired, even down to a liveried, white Cadillac with his initials in gold on the door. It also gave him a sometimes begrudged, sometimes enthusiastic recognition from fellow writers. In Thomas Wolfe's *Look Homeward, Angel,* a young boy, hawking his wares, extolled the virtues of the *Saturday Evening Post,* saying, " . . . on page 29 you have a story by Irvin S. Cobb, the g-g-g-greatest living humorist" (99).

Early in his writing career Cobb faced the changes inherent in the modernization of literature. His use of forms and structures did not reflect the change, as that of other writers did. Cobb disapproved, as well, of the use of the "sensuous" aspects of life as topics of rhetorical invention. He refused to see the Babbits and the Elmer Gantrys as important; his Main Street represented hearth and home, not pettiness and ennui. Yet, he was no Pollyanna, he saw and wrote about injustice, the problems of the poor and the powerless. He looked at America, at small towns, at the South, at New York and New Orleans. He made fun of people and institutions and himself. He was a local colorist in its least flattering sense, but he was also more than that. In its diversity of settings, points of view, purposes, choices of language style, genre and impact, his work was multicolored.

Although Cobb has been neglected for most of the forty years since his death, the Popular Press has recently published a new biography by Anita Lawson, a professor at Murray State University near Cobb's hometown of

Paducah. If this book succeeds in renewing an interest in Cobb's work, what will a new generation of readers find? At a glance Cobb seems to reflect only the bigoted opinions of his time. Those who use specific racial terms and write or speak in dialect are labeled racists, and rightly so, because changes in American attitudes have resulted in revision of what is considered appropriate language. His harshness toward immigrants, a common American affliction after World War I, conflicts with his reverence for the poor and downtrodden. His anti-intellectualism, so simplistic and so unyielding, makes Cobb a perfect target for intellectual critics today.

Cobb's lengthy sentences, his word pictures that describe scenes and people down to the last detail, his slowly evolving plots and his digressions from "the point" combine to render his stories too time-consuming for modern readers who want the details cut to a minimum, leaving "just the facts." The change to the visual medium of television has reduced the need for lengthy descriptions and encouraged a preference for being "shown" rather than "told." It has also lessened an appreciation for a well-turned phrase, or a cleverly and laboriously thought out metaphor. Even Cobb's horror stories hold no terror for those accustomed to the *Jaws* or *Friday the Thirteenth* variety. However, Judge Priest, minus Jeff Poindexter, could have been Marcus Welby or Grandpa Walton, or any of the other paternalistic television heroes. Indeed, the "heedless mass" with the need to be "diverted" rather than "entertained" perfectly describes the intellectual view of today's television audience, with the half-hour situation comedy the equivalent of the humorous short story.

Like all those who struggle with change, Cobb had choices to make. He chose to adapt in ways that proved to be beneficial. He fully embraced the new media perhaps because they were geared toward satisfaction of a mass audience. Cobb was highly motivated to speak directly to the people. He chose to oppose cynicism about the common man and about life's potentialities that typified the modernist era. He rejected changes in form and literary style as he rejected irreverence for older values. He was a true conservative in his plodding, methodical effort to preserve the status quo, but a progressive in his campaigns for social justice. The laws of nature mandate that a species must change or die. In the areas of his work in which he refused to change, Cobb is dead today, but if one scrapes away the remnants of nineteenth-century thinking, the man stuck between times still lives.

WORKS CITED

"American Humorists: Irvin S. Cobb." *The Journal of the National Education Association* 14 (Mar. 1925): 102.

B., H. I. "Irvin S. Cobb, Who Strikes the True Note of Southern Life." *New York Times* 8 Dec. 1912.

Bobbs-Merrill Archive. Collected reviews. Lilly Library, Indiana University, Bloomington.

———. Letter from D. L. Chambers to Irvin Cobb. 13 March 1934.

———. Memorandum from Andy to Mr. Chambers. 13 March 1934.

———. Note from D. C. to Lawrence. 9 April 1934.

———. Publicity layout.

———. Unsigned readers reports.

"Censorship or Not." *The Literary Digest* 23 June 1923: 29.

Cobb, Irvin S. *Back Home.* 1911.

———. *Exit Laughing.* Indianapolis: Bobbs-Merrill, 1941.

———. "Peace on Earth." *Ladies and Gentlemen.* New York: Cosmopolitan, 1924.

———. Unpublished letter to Hugh McKenna Landon. 21 Sept. 1915. James Whitcomb Riley MSS. Lilly Library, Indiana University, Bloomington.

———. Unpublished letter to James Whitcomb Riley. Not dated, but sent from North Hatley, Canada, where Cobb visited in 1914. Riley MSS.

"Concerning Irvin Cobb." *The Bookman* 37 (Mar. 1913): 14-15.

Davis, Robert H. "An Attempt to Place Irvin S. Cobb Among the Immortals." *Current Opinion* 54 (Jan. 1913): 57.

Eliot, T. S. *Selected Essays.* London: Faber and Faber, 1972.

"Gompers and Cobb Jabbing the Literati." *The Literary Digest* 22 Dec. 1923: 26-27.

Hackett, Alice Payne, and James Henry Burke. *Eighty Years of Best Sellers.* New York: Bowker, 1977.

"Intellectuals are Target for Cobb." *Louisville Herald* 1 Jan. 1925.

"Irvin Cobb, Highest Paid Short Story Writer." *Louisville Herald* 1 July 1925.

"Irvin Cobb, Our Leading Literary Heavyweight." *Current Opinion* 74 (Feb. 1923): 231-32.

Lawson, Anita. *Irvin S. Cobb.* Bowling Green University: Popular, 1984.

Lodge, David. *Modernism, Anti-Modernism, and Post-Modernism.* Birmingham: U. of Birmingham, 1976.

Mencken, H. L. *Prejudices, First Series.* New York: Knopf, 1919.

————. Unpublished letter to John Wilson Townsend. Not dated. Townsend MSS. Eastern Kentucky University Library, Richmond.

"More of Irvin Cobb." *Boston Transcript* 11 Nov. 1916.

Neuman, Fred G. *Irvin S. Cobb, His Life and Achievements.* Paducah, Ky.: Young, 1934.

"Prose and Cons of Irving Cobb." *Boston Transcript* 11 Aug. 1926.

"Red Likker." *Boston Transcript* 21 July 1929.

"Review of *Back Home.*" *The Bookman* 43 (Jan. 1913): 237.

"Review of *The Escape of Mr. Trimm.*" *The Bookman* 46 (July 1914): 187.

"Slushy Sex Books." *Louisville Times* 19 Apr. 1924.

Trilling, Lionel. "On the Modern Element in Modern Literature." *The Idea of the Modern.* Ed. Irving Howe. New York: Horizon, 1967.

Williams, Blanche Colton. *Our Short Story Writers.* New York: Moffat, 1922.

Wolfe, Thomas. *Look Homeward, Angel.* New York: Scribner's, 1929.

Wayne Chatterton (essay date 1986)

SOURCE: "Tales of the Eerie, the Bizarre, and the Grotesque," in *Irvin S. Cobb,* Twayne Publishers, 1986, pp. 108-23.

[*In the following essay, Chatterton examines Cobb's horror stories.*]

In a letter to editor Thomas Costain (12 May 1941), Irvin Cobb suggested that the firm of Doubleday, Doran, consider publishing in one volume "twelve or fifteen of the so-called 'horror yarns' I've done, including such as **'Darkness,' 'The Escape of Mr. Trimm,' 'An Occurrence up a Side Street,' 'The Exit of Anse Dugmore,' 'The Belled Buzzard,' 'One Block from Fifth Avenue,' 'Fishhead,' 'Snake Doctor,' 'The Gallowsmith,' 'Three Wise Men of the East Side,'** etc."[1] Later in the same letter, Cobb said of the suggested collection, "Some of these stories had quite a vogue. Some are now forgotten, probably. And some people apparently have forgotten or never knew that I wrote plenty of grim-like blood-and-guts tales in former years."

This collection was never published,[2] but four years later another company published a broader anthology containing eight of these grim stories.[3] The gratuitous interest apparently caused Cobb to reassess his previous assumption, and he expressed pleasure with this evidence that his humorous works had not entirely eclipsed his serious ones.[4]

Cobb felt that he had reason to wonder whether he had been too long pigeonholed as a humorist before he wrote his first piece of outright fiction. That piece was also his first "horror story." That story, **"The Escape of Mr. Trimm,"** appeared in the *Saturday Evening Post* on 27 November 1909 when Cobb was thirty-three and still working on the *Evening World.* By his own admission, this was his favorite among the nearly three hundred short stories he wrote in his lifetime.[5]

Cobb himself has provided the simplest explanation of how and why he began to shift from the comic to the horrifying. In his answer to an epistolary interviewer he once wrote, "I find that when I have written something of a humorous order it gives me an appetite, so to speak, to turn out a nice, gruesome, gory, Edgar-Allan-Poeish kind of tale, and vice-versa."[6] But others have sought more objective reasons for this conjunction of humor and horror. "A strong sense of the grotesque and the whimsical finds material quite as readily in the dark as in the bright sphere of life. It is this feeling of the whimsical that is Irvin Cobb's most precious possession."[7]

The origins of Cobb's penchant for writing "grim-like" tales may have lain farther back in his literary development than he realized at the time when he deliberately set himself the task of writing **"The Escape of Mr. Trimm."** His most fruitful sources for this kind of story were newspaper accounts and court records, especially when he had some personal involvement with the events. For his first involvement of this kind on a grand scale, one can go all the way back to his "Sourmash" days on the *Louisville Evening Post,* when he had followed the career and eventually the trial of the political demagogue William Goebel and was on the scene of his assassination.

Because Cobb had helped carry the bleeding body from the murder scene, he was able to write his news story as an observer. His closeness to this gory affair made a strong impression upon him, and as one writer observes, "Critics claim the effect of this tragic episode is shown in the occasional stories of horror that Cobb has penned."[8] Though any assumption of this kind must remain speculation, it is difficult to believe that an experience so violent, so bloody, and so early in his career would not have quickened the part of Cobb's creative consciousness that eventually led him to write his "horror" stories.

The speculation gains credibility when it is coupled with the knowledge that Cobb made his first attempt to evoke the grotesque and macabre in a short piece he wrote for the Louisville paper during the time when he also reported the Goebel murder for the same paper. This was a twelve-hundred-word descriptive essay that he later exhumed from a trunk and elaborated into one of his most chilling short stories, **"Fishhead."**[9]

Cobb's fondness for **"The Escape of Mr. Trimm"** is understandable. He has explained the origins of this story and the circumstances of its writing more frequently than for any other story he wrote. With passage of time the versions of his account vary in some details, but the main outlines remain constant.[10] The constant factors are these. At some time during 1908-9, while doing one of his regular tasks for the *Evening World,* Cobb found himself among other reporters who were covering the court trial of Charles W. Morse, a flamboyant and high-speculating financier who had run afoul of the law after the "baby panic" of 1907-8. A fearless plunger and superb confidence man, Morse took over his own defense and by endless ploys, ingenious argument, and studied brashness he came near to beating "open-and-shut" charges with which his high-priced lawyers could not seem to cope. He was, however, justifiably sentenced to twelve years in the Atlanta prison. His ability to mold circumstances to his advantage led Cobb to remark to a colleague that such a man could never be kept long in any prison or anywhere under constraint, that nothing would "break him."

With this story in his mind, he one day made a bet with his wife that he could write a piece of fiction without "an intentionally funny line in it," and could sell it to a top fiction market. Though Mrs. Cobb was skeptical, he had great confidence in his idea. He was convinced that the conception of the story was a sure thing even if he proved inadequate in the technical aspects of fiction.

In Cobb's story, the instrument that defeats this clever and powerful man is one of the simplest devices imaginable—a pair of three-dollar disposable handcuffs. Clamped upon his wrists by a slow-witted but practical-minded marshall at the beginning of the train ride to prison, these cheap circlets defy every effort Mr. Trimm makes to foil them. They stay tight through a train wreck from which Mr. Trimm is thrown, otherwise free and entirely unhurt, while the mangled body of another man is identified as his. The cuffs remain through a time of hope when Mr. Trimm speculates that now, in secret, he might be able to get one of his retained lawyers to send him some of his own money for a change of identity and a life of luxury in some foreign country. They stay through the inexorable wearing away of hope as one by one each more desperate effort fails. They stay and even tighten on his bloody, mangled wrists through a slow but steady moral and physical disintegration. They are there when, disheveled and starved and sick and utterly abject, he almost eagerly gives himself up to a country constable.

Cobb was right. The elements of the story are those of one of the most reliable of all short story lines. Moreover, Cobb's painstaking development of concrete details and his careful management of the mounting action gave every evidence that he had a high aptitude for fiction

writing. There is an account to the effect that, under the title **"The Grip of the Law,"** he first offered the story to *Everybody's Magazine.* There, editor Theodore Dreiser rejected it, not because he did not like it, but because he did not want to offend his publisher, who had once been a business partner with Morse.[11] At any rate, the *Saturday Evening Post* took it immediately, and as Cobb remarks, "I won my bet, and gave up earning an honest living as a newspaper reporter and turned fiction writer."[12]

TALES OF TERROR AND PATHOS

When Cobb turned the true story of Charles W. Morse into fiction, the most unsavory aspects of Morse became submerged in the character of the wealthy Mr. Trimm, in whom prevailed the traits of monumental cleverness and supreme self-confidence. As a result of the transfiguration, Mr. Trimm becomes a person who is capable of evoking a degree of sympathy that his real-life model could not. As terror mounts in him, and after almost superhuman endurance he gives way to despair, he becomes increasingly pathetic. In varying combinations and degrees, Cobb uses these elements in half a dozen other stories, some of which, like **"The Escape of Mr. Trimm,"** are among his best.

Cobb had an extraordinary talent for creating fictional settings that are so eerie and bizarre as to cause pathos to arise from something that borders upon or becomes part of terror itself. None of his stories accomplishes this ascendance more effectively than does **"The Great Auk."**[13] Cobb got the idea for the story from sportswriter Bozeman Bulger, who told him about an old actor who went around declaring that he had spent the day at the seashore. The truth was that this old trouper lived in a deserted theater and had begun to live according to illusions that were impressed upon his mind by exotic scenes painted on the old backdrops.[14]

Bulger thought the idea comic, but to Cobb, with his abiding interest in the theater, the plight of the old actor seemed most sorrowful. Having worked with theater people, Cobb knew that the golden age of versatile repertory acting had yielded to the specialists, to actors who were trained for only one kind of part. This "cracked" anachronism of a bygone time suggested to Cobb's imagination a great repertory actor who had become in his own sphere of life an extinct species like the Great Auk.

For the sake of his story, Cobb conceives the characters of a young playwright and a somewhat older director who have been looking vainly for an actor to play a grandfather role. Remembering one of the best of the actors who a quarter-century ago had been able to perform all kinds of parts, the director takes the playwright to an abandoned, forgotten theater far downtown. Inside, they find themselves among eerie and unwholesome surroundings. "The place looked dead and smelled dead and was dead. . . . heavy-laden with boneyard scents—rot and corrosion and rust and dust . . . taints of moulded leather and gangrened metal, of wormgnawed woodwork and moth-eaten fabrics" (227).

In this mausoleum of the dramatic art the old actor appears on a derelict stage where, with consummate brilliance, he performs one classic scene after another, taking all parts. Though he plays as if to a full house, the only visible spectator is a little gutter-gamin who claps and whistles wildly at the performance. For so doing, he has the privilege of sleeping in the theater on cold nights. The two hidden spectators agree that no other actor could do their grandfather part remotely as well as this "Great Auk" of the stage world. But they understand also that the old actor is hopelessly insane. "Every haunted house is entitled to its ghost," says the director (243). So they leave an old actor to his haunts.

In **"Darkness,"**[15] also, pathos is the outgrowth of an interaction between a sympathetic character, Dudley Stackpole, and surroundings that are so eerie and bizarre as to inspire horror. At the Stackpole mill, Dudley had once been forced into an unequal and unsought gunfight. In the confrontation, one of the Tatum brothers had been shot and killed, and Dudley had been acquitted as having acted in unavoidable self-defense. Thereafter, Stackpole has lived in obsessive fear of darkness, convinced that in the dark his imagination will conjure up Tatum's agonized face. In his house, the lights always burn in all the rooms. He sleeps fitfully and only in the brightest possible light. He leaves the house only in broad daylight. He wears only sad-toned clothing. The skin of his face has become the color and texture of an abandoned hornet's nest. He rarely speaks to anybody: "He would make you think of a man molded out of a fog; almost he was a man made of smoke" (15).

One day a dying man in a faraway town confesses that he, not Stackpole, had killed Tatum. An old enemy of the Tatums, this man took advantage of the confusion at the mill to hide and kill Tatum. Now Stackpole can sleep again in comforting darkness. He can become the normal, happy, social being he once was. But the people of the town do not react accordingly.

They have become accustomed to Stackpole as he has been all these years. They resent what seems to them unwarranted familiarity when he speaks to them. They behave as though he is depriving them of something when he is no longer the Dudley Stackpole who has become the town character. Worst of all, the safe, comforting, concealing darkness he has yearned for is now an enemy in itself. As soon as he turns out the lights at night, he is stricken with a nameless horror of the darkness merely as darkness. It smothers. Unable to bear the darkness or to live longer in ceaseless bright light, he turns on the gas to find peace only in death.

Cobb's awareness of the dark as a common property of terror is borne out by another story, **"Blacker Than Sin,"**[16] in which he uses blackness to instill in his readers an almost overweening sense of horror. In this story,

however, the setting is not the source of the horror, as in **"The Great Auk."** It arises here from the contrast between the normalcy of everyday life in a small Southern town and the sinister blackness of a woman's daily costume.

The main line of the story is this. One Major Foxmaster has appeared in a rather sleepy little town, and after a considerable time he has succeeded in becoming accepted by the residents. But one day a small, erect, slender woman appears there also. Dressed from top of head to the ground in a black dress and veil, she begins to follow the major everywhere he goes. She moves soundlessly and seemingly without movement, as though she floats rather than walks. She never speaks to the major or to anyone. She never interferes with him in any way. But she is always there. Though her identity is a mystery in the town, rumor says that the major had wronged her and abandoned her as a young girl, that everywhere he has fled she finds him, to get her vengeance in this way.

The imagination of the town is fired by her presence, and the people speculate endlessly about her. But the major never acknowledges her presence. He goes his way as if she does not exist. He does so, that is, until he has grown old and stooped and his step has become an old man's step. Then he realizes that the woman in black seems unchanged by the years. Still she floats behind him, straight and strong as on the day he wronged her. Now he begins thinking her a supernatural avenger. At length he loses his composure. He whirls upon her in the public street. He tears away her veil, staggers backward, clutches at his chest. Behind the veil he has seen a face as black as the Pit—**"Blacker Than Sin."** And he has fallen dead of sudden heart stoppage.

Only then does the town have its answer. The real avenger had come there, but she had died some time ago. Upon her death she had altered her will to the effect that her young black housemaid would perpetuate the major's torment until he expired, whereupon the maid would legally inherit her mistress' considerable estate.

This story is better crafted than are the previous ones. In it there is less padding, less authorial philosophizing, and the climactic disclosure is managed cleanly and convincingly. It is an austere story, for which it is the more effective.

"The Exit of Anse Dugmore" is essentially a revenge story in which the act of revenge takes a strange, unexpected, and sentimental turn. When Anse Dugmore, the central character, shoots and kills one of the Tranthams in a feud, he is sentenced to life at hard labor. Within four years, he is so far gone with consumption that the governor sets him free to die at home. There he finds that his wife has taken his two little boys and has "gone over" to Wyatt Trantham, who is now head of the enemy clan.

To most of the other people in the story it seems that Anse Dugmore "never had any more feelings than a moccasin snake" (191), but the truth is that his "dumb, unuttered love" (195) for his two boys is the only thing that has kept him alive at all. Slowly coughing up his life's blood, he drags himself to a hillside above the main trail and lies in ambush for Wyatt Trantham to ride his mule home from Christmas shopping in the town. When the time comes, knowing that he has only life enough to pull the trigger, Anse brings his rifle sight to rest on his enemy's chest and begins to squeeze the trigger. At the same instant, Wyatt takes a toy drum from his saddle bags, and Anse can also see sacks of Christmas candy and other gifts of the kind loved by little boys. As Trantham looks at the Christmas presents, he hears a long, gurgling sigh from the hillside, and then goes on his way. When searchers find the body of Anse Dugmore, his finger is still tight against the trigger.

Though Cobb's sentimentality is as obvious as his fondness for contrivances, he does succeed in making Anse Dugmore believable, pathetic, and even admirable—evidence of considerable competence in the storytelling craft.

In **"The Gallowsmith,"** however, Cobb manages a transformation as unlikely as that of Anse Dugmore, and he does it more convincingly. It is a story based upon the potentially devastating effects of a suddenly awakened imagination in a man who never knew he had one, and in whose profession no man can allow himself to have one. His calling is that of public hangman.

At sixty-five or so, Jacob Dramm appears to have all the best qualities for a man in so melancholy a profession. His only physical restriction is a long-standing heart condition, but in compensation he is by nature unexcitable, methodical, meticulous with detail, and beyond everything else literal and practical of mind. He averages twelve executions a year and is well satisfied that he has accomplished each with maximum efficiency and minimum discomfort to the condemned. When one execution is over, it is a job well done and entirely out of mind. He considers himself a respectable officer of the state.

But the time comes when a hard and arrogant desperado refuses to accept his doom as others have done. While the gallowsmith makes his routine preparations, the condemned man lays a curse upon him. He, the criminal, will come back to haunt his hangman, and he will take his soul to hell along with his own. For Jacob Dramm, this is a new and disturbing experience. He is unaware that he is hurrying his procedure. As a consequence, the man does not die instantly with a broken neck. He dangles at the end of the rope, slowly strangling. The whole body writhes and jerks in what seems demonic gyrations. The crimson glow of the just-risen sun projects this Devil's dance upon the prison wall, and the image burns itself into the mind of the hangman.

The event has awakened in Jacob Dramm an unknown faculty—that of the imagination. Never having had one, he finds it uncontrollable. All day he wanders the streets in torment. Back home, late at night, he steps on and only half kills a deformed mouse that has crawled in from outside. Still disturbed, he partially raises the blind and absent-mindedly tosses the mouse through the open window. Then, lying alone in the sinister darkness, his imagination playing and replaying the awful scene of the morning, he is transfixed by something he sees through the window. The frame is filled with a brilliant, flickering crimson light. In that square is a dangling figure, kicking and writhing in eternal torment.

Next morning the sheriff finds Dramm's corpse lying in the bed. The hangman's heart has stopped and there is terror on his face. Outside the window, in a neighbor's yard, a pile of autumn leaves is still smoldering. In the window frame dangles the body of a deformed mouse, its tail tangled in the sashcord.

Aside from its almost too-heavy reliance upon coincidence at the conclusion, this tale is a startling excursion into the fictional use of the psychology of terror. From the opening paragraph it builds upon the sinister occupation of the hero and upon his believable if almost subhuman detachment from its implications. As a result, the unexpected and rampant emergence of an uncontrollable imagination is a fearful thing. This story is probably the best in a group of Cobb's tales that have in common some degree of horror, and with whose central characters one is likely to be sympathetic.

TALES OF TERROR AND THE GROTESQUE

In another group of Cobb's "horror" tales, the central characters tend to be malefactors or utter grotesques. Some are a bit of both. By and large, they are not persons for whom most people are likely to feel sympathy.

Among these stories **"The Belled Buzzard"** (*E*, 54-76) is the least satisfactory from a technical point of view. But it is also the most widely celebrated. In this story Squire Gathers, an old man with a young wife, has shot and killed a young itinerant whom the squire suspects of philandering with his wife. Leaving the murder gun and the body where they may not be found for years, the old man is satisfied with his work and goes his way ostensibly without fear or qualm of conscience. However, as in Poe's "Telltale Heart," the murderer's conscience will not be still. The deus ex machina is a buzzard, supposedly carrying a never silent cowbell. It circles incessantly over the squire's house, sounding the bell and driving the murderer almost insane. At the end of the story, someone stumbles upon the body of the murdered man and the authorities arrange a coroner's inquest. As a justice of the peace, the squire is called upon to conduct the proceedings. There, with the body of his victim upon display, he manages to keep a cool demeanor. But now he hears again the sound of the bell. It comes closer and closer, until it seems to be outside the door of the inquest room. At this point the squire breaks. In an instant he is utterly insane. He throws himself upon the floor, confessing his guilt over and over. The door opens, and into the room walks a little boy. He is ringing a cowbell he has found somewhere and has appropriated as a toy.

A far better use of the psychological power of local superstition appears in **"Snake Doctor."**[17] In this story, the superstition holds that the dragonfly—known in the North as the devil's darning needle—is a malign insect that ministers to ailing moccasin snakes. It is known therefore as the snake doctor. By a similar association, the titular character in the story is known in his locality as Snake Doctor. Rives by name, this man is a grotesque whose appearance and movements are peculiarly snake-like. Moreover, he lives alone in the middle of a dense and tangled area where snakes abound. He makes his living by catching them in order to sell their skins and the oils he renders from them. He is regarded as a friend and even kin to the snakes. In return, they protect him from harm. He is thought, also, to have a fortune hidden in his cabin, with a pet snake to guard it.

The action of the story is rapid and complicated, but the basic sequence of events is this. An avaricious neighbor erroneously suspects his wife of cohabiting with Snake Doctor, though she is really a kind-hearted soul who goes to Snake Doctor's cabin once a day to tend him in a sickness. So the husband contrives an intricate and seemingly foolproof plan to kill Snake Doctor and steal his money without implicating himself. But he shoots his wife by mistake and finds himself in the dark cabin, searching for the cache of money.

He thrusts his hand into a hole in the cabin wall. At the same instant he dimly sees there the head of a snake. In horror he withdraws his hand but feels a stab of pain on a fingertip. Fang marks! Blindly he runs from the cabin. But in the tangled weeds outside the cabin he dies slowly and in great pain, feeling every symptom of snake bite. An attending physician, however, says that he has never known a human being to actually die from the bite of a moccasin snake. In the cabin, Snake Doctor's "fortune" of ninety-seven dollars remains untouched inside a hole in the wall, a hole that is lined with coils of barbed wire and guarded by a stuffed snake, posed as if to strike. The story won the O. Henry Memorial Award as the best short story published in 1922.[18]

"January Thaw"[19] is basically a simpler story. But the tissue of the scheme contrived by the murderer is extraordinarily fragile, and the horror that arises from the failure of his plan creates in him a much slower and more tortuous form of disintegration. Before murdering his partner in crime, a man named Champney works out a "foolproof" plan for disposing of the corpse. The two men have hidden out during the winter in one of the northeastern villages where people come to ski. According to local custom, most visitors have built across an open slope all kinds of grotesque sculptures made of snow. Feeling clever and superior, Champney has propped up his partner's corpse and built a snow sculpture around it. Now it appears to be merely another of the countless snow statues that decorate the slope.

Returning to his rooming house at the edge of the slope after he has concealed the corpse, the murderer breaks his leg on some ice and must stay in the house until it mends. He is in no hurry, since old-timers have said that the snow stays late into the spring. But Champney has not been told of a very short interval called the "January thaw." This quick thawing frequently melts all the snow before the regular winter season resumes. So Champney sits looking helplessly through his window for a whole day while the snow turns to slush. In mounting terror he stares while the snow covering drips from the body of his victim. By nightfall he knows what every person in the village will see the next morning. In the dark, he drags his broken leg across the slope. But his solicitous landlord finds him gone, follows his trail onto the slope, and finds him crouched at the base of a melting statue. Possessed by an insane compulsion, Champney is scooping up armfuls of slush and trying to plaster it back upon the stark white legs of a propped-up corpse.

The "purest" of all Cobb's horror stories, however, is **"An Occurrence up a Side Street"** (*E,* 79-95). Though Cobb has spoken of his penchant for turning from humor to a "Poe-ish" kind of tale, and though many critics and reviewers have compared his "horror" stories to those of Poe, this is Cobb's only story to have something of the structure as well as the flavor of Poe. The main reason the story justifies this comparison is that when Cobb selected the essential ingredients for the story he pared away everything else in order to focus upon the moment of horror. This moment is the brief span of time that begins after the sense of horror has become intolerable to the characters. It ends only with the catastrophe to which the horror has been building.

"An Occurrence up a Side Street" is one of Cobb's earliest attempts to write fiction. He found inspiration for the story in newspaper accounts of a bizarre contemporary murder case. According to these accounts, the two culprits, a man and a woman, committed murder—a most gory and messy one—in the bathroom of a downtown flat. Then they find that there is no safe hiding place except the last place anybody might think to look, in the apartment itself. The police have completed their investigation and have removed the body. But they have sealed the door and placed a guard in the street outside, so that none of the evidence can be disturbed. The murderers have gained entry through a rear cellar window that is known only to them. Here they are, then, prisoners at the scene of their own worst nightmare, with the corpse gone but all the gore remaining.

To Cobb's credit, he appears to have realized—better than with any other story he wrote—that the tale he wanted to tell was confined entirely within the walls of that apartment. Accordingly, **"An Occurrence up a Side Street"** begins and ends there, with only a "flashback" or two for explanation of necessary background.

The city is in the grip of a heat wave. Because the prisoners cannot open windows without disclosing their presence to the guard on the street below, the apartment is stifling. The man sits at a table peeling an overripe peach. The woman moves constantly back and forth to the window to see whether the policeman is still on guard. In the heat of the night, the odor of the peach seems heavy and oversweet and sticky. Upon the closed white bathroom door are thousands of fat, buzzing, green-bodied flies. In a heavy clump they have clustered upon the white porcelain door-knob and around the key-hole, where they are "forever cleaning their shiny wings and rubbing the ends of their forelegs together with the loathsome suggestion of little gravediggers anointing their palms" (*E*, 88).

Having conspired to commit an unspeakable crime so that they can be together, the two lovers are now "stuck" with each other. They are alone against the world, with nothing in common save the thing they most loath. Now they loath each other and want nothing more than to be rid of each other. So the man has a motive in peeling an overripe peach, just as the woman has one in her prowling across the room behind his chair. She wants to keep him in front of her, and in view at all times. But in a rare moment when she is watching something outside, he pours two glasses of cheap, warm champagne. Into her glass, he drops a liquid that has a strong peach odor. At the same time, he breaks open the pit of the peach. Unaware of what he has done, but seeing her chance, the woman steps behind him and plunges into his eye a ten-inch hatpin. He dies instantly, and with hardly any blood. She notices a glass of champagne on the table, and in a surge of relief she tosses it down, sensing the strong smell of peach but thinking it the broken peach pit. She falls dead beside him.

Despite the wrenching contrivance, **"An Occurrence up a Side Street"** is Cobb's best story. His focus upon the crucial situation eliminates his usual philosophical excursions and his tendency to overelaborate contributing circumstances. Since the horror has been building for a considerable time before the opening paragraphs, Cobb is able to plunge directly into the stream and to develop the sense of horror with a fullness and impact that his other stories do not achieve. All in all, Cobb has brought to this story a discipline and a focus unusual in his fiction.

One other tale belongs in this group, though it is unlike the rest of Cobb's "horror" stories. The story is **"Fishhead"** (*E*, 242-57). Its substance is not folklore in the ordinary sense, though some form of folklore is an important element in the story. The world of **"Fishhead"** lies in some borderland where folklore and natural history meet the supernatural. There is something in it, too, of the kind of mythology that builds tales around creatures that are part man and part animal, but belonging to neither species.

The freak of nature known as "Fishhead" seems more fish than man. Though his natural element is air, though he walks erect, though he lives as a man lives—in a shack at the edge of a stagnant bayou of Reelfoot Lake—he seems otherwise a nearer kin to the monstrous and obscene catfish indigenous to those waters: "His skull sloped backward so abruptly that he could hardly be said to have a forehead at all; his chin slanted off right into nothing. His eyes were small and round with shallow, glazed, pale-yellow pupils, and they were set wide apart in his head and they were unwinking and staring, like a fish's eyes. His nose was no more than a pair of tiny slits in the middle of the yellow mask. His mouth was the worst of all. It was the awful mouth of a catfish, lipless and almost inconceivably wide, stretching from side to side" (*E*, 247). According to the lore of the lake, his mother had been frightened by one of the big fish before he was born.

It is said that these big fish are Fishhead's only friends, for people fear him, especially at night, when he swims and cavorts with the fish and even feeds with them, eating whatever they eat. At sunset he always walks barefoot to the end of a huge fallen tree that extends far out into the deep water, and there he squats in the dark. According to local superstition, a strange booming sound that carries across the lake is the cry that Fishhead makes to call the big fish to his log at sundown.

The two Baxter boys have pledged themselves to murder Fishhead in revenge for a beating that Fishhead had once given them. One day at sundown they come secretly, paddling a pirogue, to shoot him when he comes to the end of his log. They stand in their boat and fire from behind another fallen tree. But the recoil of the gun knocks them into the water. Mortally hit by a load of heavy buckshot, Fishhead is able to make his great, booming cry before he slips quietly into the water. Neither of the Baxter boys is ever seen again. The big fish have come to Fishhead's call, and they have pulled the murderers to the bottom of the lake.

"Fishhead" is more an expanded incident than a short story. Yet it has the fullness of substance and characterization that are necessary to a short story, and it has all the impact of a short story. Its hybrid form is probably the result of its being expanded from a short descriptive essay for a newspaper column. At any rate, it is in a unique fashion the eeriest, the most grotesque, and the most horrifying of all Cobb's fictional narratives.

STORIES OF COMPLICATION AND SUSPENSE

Among the "horror" stories that Cobb mentions in his letter to Costain is **"Three Wise Men of the East Side."**[20] In several important ways, however, it does not appear to belong with the genuine horror tales. Like some other stories by Cobb, the main element in them is not so much horror as complication of plot and the building of suspense.

A category of marginal "horror" tales might include such stories as **"The Luck Piece"**[21] and **"Faith, Hope and Charity"**[22] along with **"Three Wise Men of the East Side."** All of them are eerie. Each contains a moment of real terror, but the moment is for the most part unsustained, so that the terror develops mostly as a by-product of involved action. In some instances, terror is at best incidental to most other elements of the story.

"The Luck Piece," for instance, opens with fast action that leads to an eerie struggle during which the hero-figure accidentally shoots and kills a man who wants to kill him. This action occurs in a dark alley, late at night, just before the crowds begin to leave the theaters a block or so away on Broadway. Beyond this episode, the protagonist's urgent flight from the police could become terrifying. But terror is dissipated in a contest of wits between the murderer and a wily old detective who knows the culprit's mind and habits, and whom the culprit fears therefore above all.

"Three Wise Men of the East Side" is a complicated death-row story of mutual double- and triple-cross. There is always horror in a man's waiting for his own execution, but in this story, the horror has been resolved almost before the story opens. It has been preempted by the one-upmanship of the condemned man's plot to choose his own time and method of death. Further, even the horror of suicide is mitigated by the sense of victory that comes with his foiling the authorities.

He bribes his lawyer to smuggle in a cyanide pill that he can swallow just before he goes to the death chamber. He also bribes a guard to slip it to him at the chosen moment. But the guard gives him a fake pill, a harmless one. The condemned man has a few moments of intense horror as he realizes that the pill has not worked and that he must die in the electric chair. But afterward the lawyer finds that the "reward" in the bank vault is only burglar tools, and the guard finds that his $1,000 bribe is counterfeit.

Similarly, in **"Faith, Hope and Charity"** each of three prisoners has a morbid fear of dying in the way his country has condemned him to die. A Frenchman has a horror of dying by the guillotine; a Spaniard by the garotte; an Italian by live burial. Together they escape from a train in the Sonoran Desert of Mexico, and each goes his own way. But in their flight, the Frenchman is accidentally beheaded by a malfunctioning elevator, the Spaniard is accidentally garotted by the shrinking of rawhide around his neck, and the Italian is accidentally buried alive in a box canyon.

The three stories are grounded in horror, and horror remains in them as a kind of threat. But the horror is metamorphic. Instead of materializing in its own form, it becomes urgency of survival, complicated scheming, hurried action. Horror ceases to be the main ingredient and becomes the means by which emerges one of Cobb's favorite effects—a combination of irony and grim humor.

A PECULIAR HORROR

Cobb had good reason to suggest that his "so-called" horror stories be collected and published together. They constitute an extraordinary anthology of a kind that seems always to have found readers. It would be unfortunate, however, if these stories were to be advanced as Irvin Cobb's answer to Edgar Allan Poe. There is little in them of "the misty mid region of Weir," of the broody supernatural madness that pervades "The Fall of the House of Usher," or of the glooming cavern-world of "The Cask of Amontillado." Save for the grotesque biologic mutation called **"Fishhead,"** Cobb's people are caught up in the affairs of everyday living. They are in this world and of this world, and their horrors are recognizable as the depths into which worldly affairs can plunge those who are susceptible to bizarre and outré circumstance. The result is a peculiar horror that belongs only to Cobb.

The typical summary of Cobb's horror tales is that "Nothing better can be found in Poe's collected works. One is impressed not only with the beauty and simplicity of his prose, but with the tremendous power of his tragic conceptions and his art in dealing with terror."[23] Such generalized references as this have diverted later commentators from searching out the real qualities of his horror tales and from attempts to discover more defensible reasons for their effectiveness.

For reasons yet more obscure and disturbing, the impact of Cobb's "horror" stories upon readers of his day has come from the tales that are least good from a technical standpoint. It is difficult to understand why **"The Belled Buzzard"** was an overwhelming success with the general reading public during the decades when the other "horror" tales were appearing in the magazines. But this story appears to have been a favorite, and this kind of critical thinking has hindered development of more defensible attitudes toward all of Cobb's fiction.

A few cooler heads have appeared, but they have not prevailed. Sloane Gordon, for instance, perceived the dichotomies of public taste in this regard, and he wrote, "The critical public has voted his **'The Belled Buzzard'** as Cobb's best effort. There are lots of people who don't think so. But Cobb himself likes it immensely. It has been compared to some of Poe's most shuddery productions. It doesn't compare with them. But it's a corking story."[24] In this kind of assessment lies something nearer the truth about the remarkable "horror" stories of Irvin Cobb. They are probably better stories than most students of the genre have realized.

NOTES

[1] This unpublished letter is in the Cobb collection at the University of Kentucky. It is one of four original handwritten letters sent to the university from the offices of Doubleday & Co., Inc., New York, at the request of Mr. Lawrence S. Thompson, who was then director of libraries at the university. Mr. Costain was then an editor at Doubleday.

[2] In the cover letter (7 February 1951) that accompanied the four Cobb letters mentioned in note 1, Ethel M. Hulse

of Doubleday, Doran, wrote, "The project was never carried out."

[3] *Cobb's Cavalcade* (Cleveland, 1945), 125-260.

[4] B. D. Zevin, in ibid., 12.

[5] Here was the "funny fat man," no longer with new excursions into humor, but with a gripping short story about a man enduring almost superhuman adversities.

[6] In Masson, *Our American Humorists,* 101.

[7] Stuart, "Irvin S. Cobb," 270.

[8] Henderson, "Irvin S. Cobb," 11.

[9] See Arthur Bartlett Maurice, "The History of Their Books," *Bookman* 69 (July 1929): 104.

[10] Besides the previously cited "My Story That I Like Best," see also, among other accounts, Cobb's *Exit Laughing,* 332 ff.; his contribution to *My Maiden Effort,* published for the Author's League of America (Garden City, N.Y., 1921), 40-42; Pendennis, "'My Types'—Irvin S. Cobb," 473; and Maurice, "The History of Their Books," 511.

[11] Maurice, "The History of Their Books," 511.

[12] "My Maiden Effort," 42.

[13] *Local Color* (New York, 1916), 204-43.

[14] Maurice, "The History of Their Books," 513-14.

[15] *Sundry Accounts,* 11-56.

[16] *Local Color,* 129-59.

[17] *Snake Doctor,* 11-48.

[18] See *First Prize Stories, 1919-1960* (Garden City, N.Y., 1960), 51-68.

[19] *Faith, Hope and Charity* (Cleveland, 1942), 129-52.

[20] *Ladies and Gentlemen,* 202-25.

[21] *From Place to Place,* 156-205.

[22] *Faith, Hope and Charity,* 11-38.

[23] Overton, *When Winter Comes to Main Street,* 176.

[24] Gordon, "The Story of Irvin S. Cobb," 278. Even among Cobb's close friends and acquaintances were some discriminating readers who could see little in "The Belled Buzzard." Tom Waller, for instance, whom Cobb personally selected to read the eulogy at his funeral, was outspoken about this matter. "I could never see much in 'The Belled Buzzard,'" he said, "but I am impressed by some of the others." See my interview with Waller.

FURTHER READING

Biography

Lawson, Anita. *Irvin S. Cobb.* Bowling Green: Bowling Green State University Popular Press, 1984, 254 p.
    Most comprehensive study of Cobb's life and career.

Criticism

Maurice, Arthur Bartlett. "The History of Their Books: Part VII, Irvin S. Cobb." *Bookman* Vol. 69 (July 1929): 511-14.
    An engaging overview of Cobb's stories and of his method of writing.

Walker, Stanley. "Mellow and Friendly As His Native Bourbon." *New York Herald Tribune* Vol. 17, No. 29 (March 16, 1941): 1-2.
    A review of *Exit Laughing* with a hint of nostalgia for the heyday of Cobb's career, when his name was well-known and his writing in fashion.

Additional coverage of Cobb's life and career is contained in the following sources published by Gale Research: *Dictionary of Literary Biography*, Vols. 11, 25, and 86.

Sutton Griggs

1872-1930

(full name Sutton Elbert Griggs) American novelist and nonfiction writer.

INTRODUCTION

On the strength of his five novels, Griggs became an influential figure in African-American fiction during the period between Reconstruction and the Depression. His influence rests not on his ability as a craftsman—critics have tended to judge Griggs's work harshly for its limits in characterization and plot—but on his political foresight. Written in an age characterized by "Jim Crow" laws and militant white supremacy, works such as *Imperium in Imperio* (1899) called for blacks to take action against whites in order to establish a separate nation in the Southeast. Few were prepared to take the steps demanded by Griggs; only in a later era would African-American critics pay homage to an author who, in spite of his shortcomings as a stylist, offered sometimes uncannily accurate political prophecies.

Biographical Information

Born the son of a Baptist minister, Griggs grew up in Texas, and graduated from Bishop College in the town of Marshall in 1890. He attended Richmond Theological Seminary, finishing in 1893. Following his ordination, he assumed his first pastorate in Berklcy, Virginia. In 1895 he moved to Tennessee, first to East Nashville and then Memphis, and in 1897 married Emma Williams. The couple had no children, and for the next three decades Griggs would devote himself to his church and his writing. Griggs wrote five novels and published them—at his own expense—over a period of nine years. As a self-published author with a high personal stake in his books' success, he sold them door-to-door, which one critic has cited as a reason for the greater impact of his work over that of contemporary Charles Chesnutt. But Griggs turned to nonfiction following the publication of his last novel in 1908, producing a number of full-length books and tracts on issues of concern to African Americans. His philosophy had mellowed over the years, and whereas he had begun by implicitly advocating armed struggle against the white government of the United States, he ultimately became more accommodationist in his views. His financial losses from his books ended a plan to rebuild his Memphis church, and in the latter years of his life Griggs returned to Texas. There he became pastor of his father's old church in Denison, then moved to a position as leader of a Baptist organization in Houston just before his death.

Major Works

Griggs's primary impact came through his novels, and secondarily by means of nonfiction works such as

Wisdom's Call (1911). Among the themes of his fiction are racial violence; the need for a separate black nation; questions of racial purity arising from the mixing of bloodlines because of white men raping black women; and the endurance of suffering by patient black characters, usually women. By far the most significant of his novels is his first, *Imperium in Imperio*, whose two central figures are the dark-skinned and poor Belton Piedmont and his friend Bernard Belgrave. Bernard is light-skinned, and he lives well because his mother is "kept" by a white man—presumably his father—yet he proves the more politically radical of the two friends. He becomes leader of the "Imperium in Imperio" (Empire within the Empire), a black nationalist movement, whereas Bernard dies of execution by the Imperium for his failure to support its radical plan to wage war on the United States. The novel is filled with improbable events, including Belton's miraculous survival of hanging, shooting, and an attempted dissection; or the suicide of Bernard's fiancee Viola, who kills herself rather than contribute to further miscegenation by marrying a mulatto. Belton, Bernard, and Viola—respectively the cautious conservative, the hot-headed revolutionary, and the longsuffering woman who accepts death before dishonor—reappear in other Griggs novels. In *Unfettered* (1902), for instance, there is the passive Harry Dalton, the "ebony-like Apollo" Dorlan Worthell, and the woman they both love, Morlene. White characters are often vicious race-baiters like Horace Christian in *Overshadowed* (1901), who keeps a black mistress; but in *The Hindered Hand* (1905) a white prosecutor risks his reputation in an unsuccessful bid to bring a lynch mob to justice. *Pointing the Way* (1908), Griggs's last and least critically acclaimed novel, was also his most accommodationist in tone. It involves a wide array of characers and a confusing plot, but at the center of it are familiar Griggs characters such as the heroic Baug Peppers, who ultimately brings a case before the Supreme Court, and his mixed-race bride, Eina. After *Pointing the Way*, Griggs turned to nonfiction, producing works such as *Wisdom's Call*, in which he developed themes of black self-reliance that had appeared in his novels. *The Story of My Struggles* (1914) presented those ideas in an autobiogrphical light; and in works such as *Life's Demands* (1916) and *Guide to Racial Greatness* (1923), Griggs applied his considerable learning in the natural and social sciences to questions that concerned African-Americans of his day.

PRINCIPAL WORKS

Imperium in Imperio (novel) 1899
Overshadowed (novel) 1901
Unfettered (novel) 1902
The Hindered Hand; or, The Reign of the Repressionist (novel) 1905
Pointing the Way (novel) 1908
The Race Question in a New Light (nonfiction) 1909; enlarged as *Wisdom's Call*, 1911
The Story of My Struggles (autobiography) 1914
Life's Demands; or, According to the Law (nonfiction) 1916
Guide to Racial Greatness; or, The Science of Collective Efficiency (nonfiction) 1923

CRITICISM

Hugh M. Gloster (essay date 1943)

SOURCE: "The Negro in American Fiction," in *PHYLON: The Atlanta University Review of Race and Culture*, Vol. IV, No. 4, Winter, 1943, pp. 335-45.

[*In the following essay, Gloster profiles Griggs as a leader among those African-American novelists whose work challenged racial stereotypes portrayed in the writings of white Southerners such as Thomas Dixon.*]

During the period of disfranchisement Thomas Nelson Page and Thomas Dixon, Jr., were outstanding among those Southern writers who abetted anti-Negro legislative action by showing the black man to disadvantage before the American reading public. Page was preeminently the perpetuator of the plantation motif which had received emphasis before the Civil War in the works of such writers as John Pendleton Kennedy, W. A. Carruthers, John Eston Cooke, and James W. Hungerford. In the opinion of Page, the ante-bellum South enshrined the "sweetest, purest, and most beautiful civilization" the nation has ever known; and in such works as *In Ole Virginia, or Marse Chan and Other Stories* (1887), *The Old South* (1892), and *Social Life in Old Virginia* (1897) he paints a gorgeous plantation scene peopled by chivalric, benevolent aristocrats and contented, doting slaves. But Page was more than the retrospective romancer of a vanished feudal society: he was also the ardent sponsor of a reconstructed South in which the Negro would be kept in a subordinate position. In this latter capacity he helped to expedite disfranchisement and other legalized handicaps applied to freedmen. His novel *Red Rock* (1898), for example, is chiefly an apotheosis of Southern bluebloods and a disparagement of scalawags, carpetbaggers, Negro politicians and Northern missionaries. A more forthright statement of his racial attitude, however, is given in "The Negro Question," an essay in which he, after marshaling arguments to prove the backwardness and inferiority of the black man, states

> These examples cited, if they establish anything, establish the fact that the Negro race does not possess, in any development which he has yet attained, the elements of character, the essential qualifications to conduct a government, even for himself; and that if the reins of government be intrusted to his unaided hands, he will fling reason to the winds and drive to ruin.[1]

Though demanding Anglo-Saxon supremacy, Page at least approved educated Negroes who "knew their place," and never attempted to exculpate the Ku Klux Klan of all guilt for lawlessness. On the other hand, Dixon voiced the very epitome of Negrophobia in two novels which he describes as follows

> . . . . *The Leopard's Spots* was the statement in historical outline of the conditions from the enfranchisement of the Negro to his disfranchisement.

> *The Clansman* develops the true story of the "Ku Klux Klan Conspiracy," which overturned the Reconstruction régime.[2]

As a matter of fact, neither of the two works is a realistic rendering of history. Betraying its incendiary sensationalism by such chapter titles as "A Thousand-Legged Beast" and "The Black Peril," *The Leopard's Spots: A Romance of the White Man's Burden, 1865-1900* (1902) is mainly concerned with complimenting the slaveholding landlords; attacking the carpetbaggers, scalawags, Freedmen's Bureau, Northern missionaries, and Negro politicians and intellectuals; ridiculing Yankees whose liberal racial theories do not obtain in actual social situations; establishing the Negro as a degenerate, inferior, irresponsible, bestial creature, "transformed by the exigency of war from a chattel to be bought and sold into a possible beast to be feared and guarded";[3] decrying intermarriage because it would destroy through Africanization the racial integrity of the Anglo-Saxon; and extolling the Invisible Empire as the defender of the weak, the expeller of thieves and parasites, the preserver of Aryan culture, and "the old answer of organized manhood to organized crime."[4] The eulogy of the Invisible Empire is continued in *The Clansman; An Historical Romance of the Ku Klux Klan* (1905), dedicated to the author's uncle, a former Grand Titan of the hooded order, and converted in 1916 by D. W. Griffith into *The Birth of a Nation,* one of the most popular and inflammatory box-office attractions in the history of the American motion picture industry.

Aroused by the literary libels of the schools of Page and Dixon as well as by political, social, and economic discrimination and persecution, Negro authors undertook to offset the misrepresentations of Southern propagandists by defending and glorifying the black man. Among the Negro fictionists of the *fin de siécle* and of the first decade of the present century, who participated in this campaign of racial apology and extollment were Frances Ellen Watkins Harper, Charles W. Chesnutt, J. McHenry Jones, Pauline E. Hopkins, Charles Henry Fowler, G. Langhorne Pryor, George Marion McClellan, J. W. Grant, and Sutton E. Griggs. In this group Griggs was outstanding because of his productivity and influence.

The author of five race-motivated novels—*Imperium in Imperio* (1899), *Overshadowed* (1901), *Unfettered* (1902), *The Hindered Hand* (1905), and *Pointing the Way* (1908)—Griggs not only operated his own publishing company but also, during his travels as a prominent minister and orator, promoted an extensive sale of his works among the black masses of the country. Though virtually unknown to white American readers, his novels were probably more popular among the rank and file of Negroes than the fiction of Chesnutt and Dunbar. Militant and assertive, Griggs chronicled the passing of the servile black man and hailed the advent of the intellectually emancipated Negro

> The cringing, fawning, sniffling, cowardly Negro which slavery left, had disappeared, and a new Negro, self-respecting, fearless and determined in the assertion of his rights, was at hand.[5]

In view of Griggs' active literary career and forthright demands for racial justice, it is somewhat surprising that but one historian of twentieth century Negro literature[6] has mentioned his work as a novelist and that no scholar in this field has treated at length the significance of his contribution.

Griggs' first novel, *Imperium in Imperio,* is a fantastic account of a national Negro political organization. The main characters are dark-skinned Belton Piedmont and mulatto Bernard Belgrave, graduates of Stowe (Roger Williams?) and Harvard universities respectively. Invited by Piedmont, Fairfax joins the Imperium in Imperio, an agency secretly formed "to unite all Negroes in a body to do that which the whimpering government childishly but truthfully" said it could not do. Elected president of the Imperium, Fairfax urges the open revolt of the Negro and proposes a demand for the surrender of Texas and Louisiana, the former to be retained and the latter to be ceded to foreign allies in return for aid. Opposing Fairfax, Piedmont advocates that Negroes voluntarily segregate themselves in Texas to work out their destiny. The Imperium adopts Fairfax's plan and offers Piedmont a choice between cooperation and death. At the expiration of his time limit Piedmont offers himself to be shot, and Griggs asks

> When will all races and classes of men learn that men made in the image of God will not be the slaves of another image?[7]

Though weakened by melodramatic situations, idealized characters, and stilted conversation, *Imperium in Imperio* is the first American Negro novel with a strictly political emphasis. Besides exposing miscegenation, oppression, and Jim-Crowism, it attacks the exploitation of the black man in American politics and stresses the need for an agency to protect Negro interests not safeguarded by the government. While extravagant in conception, *Imperium in Imperio* exhibits the racial outlook that produced the National Association for the Advancement of Colored People and other organizations striving for the full participation of the Negro in American democracy.

In *Overshadowed,* his second novel, Griggs surveys the national scene with a feeling of futility. In the preface he foresees a hard road ahead for the Negro, "whose grandfather was a savage and whose father was a slave," in a social order evolved and dominated by the Anglo-Saxon. With Richmond, Virginia, as its main background, *Overshadowed* traces the love of Erma Wysong and Astral Herndon. While Herndon is in college, John Benson Lawson, an ex-governor's son, engages Dolly Smith to procure Erma as a mistress. Unknown to young Lawson is the fact that Dolly is the sister of Erma's mother, the unfortunate victim of an earlier liaison with his father. To obtain revenge, Dolly eventually brings young Lawson to court, where she makes public the illicit affairs of the father and son. As a result of the trial, the ex-governor loses his mind, Dolly is tarred and feathered, and young Lawson receives a jail sentence. Later Herndon and Erma, having married and become the parents of a boy, are surprised one winter night by the coming of Erma's brother John, who had been placed in the chaingang for the murder of a master workman who insisted that labor unions bar Negroes. Soon after his arrival John dies of exposure, and Erma quickly succumbs to shock and grief. A white friend subsequently advises the grieved husband that the adoption of a Booker T. Washington racial philosophy would ease his burden

> Your status here is but due to conditions inherent in the situation. Why not bow to the inevitable,

accept conditions as you find them, extract from life as much good as can come from well-directed efforts, and beyond this point have no yearnings? Develop character, earn money, contribute to the industrial development of the country, exercise your wonderful capacity for humility, move continuously in the line of least resistance and, somehow, all will be well.[8]

Rejecting this counsel and later discarding the idea of emigration to Africa because "it, too, is overshadowed," Herndon buries his wife in mid-ocean, where "there abides no social group in which conditions operate toward the overshadowing of such elements as are not deemed assimilable."[9]

The thesis of *Overshadowed* is that the Negro must face a racial handicap in all parts of the world and particularly in the United States and Africa. Attention is focused, however, upon the American scene, where miscegenation causes the death of Erma and her mother, the suicide of Dolly, the insanity of ex-Governor Lawson, the imprisonment of his son John, and the loss of Herndon's wife and mother. The novel also exposes the instability of Negro employment, the exclusion of the Negro by labor unions, and the maladministration of justice in Southern courts. Especially interesting is the subtle attack upon the racial platform of Booker T. Washington. It is after an optimistic speech by Washington, for example, that Erma persuades her brother to make a confession which eventually results in his miserable death. A further veiled thrust at the Tuskegee educator's program is made when Herndon rejects Washingtonian arguments for remaining in America and severs relations with all lands in which the Negro is oppressed. Generally speaking, *Overshadowed* paints a gloomy picture of Southern racial difficulties and offers slight prospect for adjustment in the immediate future.

"It is the aim of *Unfettered,*" states Griggs in an introductory note to his third novel, "to lead the reader into the inner life of the Negro race and lay bare the aspirations that are fructifying there."[10] The action opens with the death of a Tennessee plantation owner who leaves the bulk of his wealth to a nephew, Lemuel Dalton, but at the same time provides liberally for an old Negro nurse and a beautiful mulatto girl named Morlene. After dispossessing the colored beneficiaries of his uncle's will, Lemuel almost provokes a riot by wounding Harry Dalton, a young Negro who had overcome him some years earlier. Concluding that formal training had caused Harry and his sister Beulah to assume social equality and "that the only safe education for the Negro was the education that taught him better to work," angered whites drive the pair out of the community and thereby cause a mass exodus of black folk. Later Beulah, believed to be the inciter of the migration, is killed during an attack by a group of young white men. In order to avoid further bloodshed, the whites draft as a mediator a Negro school teacher, a typical representative of the professional man whom Griggs calls perhaps "the greatest conservator of peace in the South, laboring *for* the Negroes by the *appointment* of

the whites, being thus placed in a position where it was to his interest to keep on good terms with both races."[11] After reluctantly marrying Harry, Morlene goes with him to a nearby city, where she meets Dorlan Warthell, a successful Negro politician who is at once attracted by her unusual beauty. Warthell, who is at odds with the Republican Party, aims to use the Negro vote to force the United States to grant ultimate liberty to the Philippine Islands. Angered by Warthell's intention, a treacherous congressman engaged Harry to take the Negro politician's life; but Morlene overhears the plot, warns the intended victim, and deserts her husband. Left by his wife and repudiated by right-thinking Republicans, Harry sacrifices himself to save the lives of a woman and her children. Thereupon Warthell proposes to Morlene, who promises to consent if he will outline a plan which will unfetter the mind of the Negro and enable the two races to live together in peace and amity. When Warthell submits his project, entitled "Dorlan's Plan," Morlene immediately agrees to become his wife. Meanwhile Lemuel's young Northern bride, who has been taught by her husband to hate and fear the Negro, becomes so hysterically frightened upon seeing a colored boy that she suffers a fatal fall from horseback. Painfully aware of the dire effects of misinstructing his wife, Lemuel realizes that interracial good-will is necessary for the happiness and welfare of both groups in the South.

Like *Overshadowed, Unfettered* provides a dismal picture of race relations. The opposition of prejudiced Southern whites to the education of the Negro is set forth, and an analysis is made of the motives underlying intimidation and segregation. Especially interesting are the political views of Warthell, who, though distrustful of the Democrats because their "chief tenets are the white man's supremacy and exclusiveness in government," nevertheless recognizes no unseverable party ties. In his advocacy of the liberation of the Philippines, moreover, Warthell manifests a world-wide as well as a national concern for the advancement of darker races.

As a statement of racial policy, however, the most important section of *Unfettered* is the appended essay called "Dorlan's Plan: Sequel to *Unfettered: A Dissertation on the Race Problem.*"[12] This essay, which is a serious approach to the problem of racial adjustment in the United States, points out that the major task is to institute merit and not color as the standard of preferment. Since the oppression of the Negro stems from unfortunate circumstances of the past, the race is urged to "meet and combat the timorous conservatism that has hitherto impeded our progress." The Negro is advised not to rely wholly upon the Republican Party. Listed as necessary in the task of preparing the race for a better future are character development, worthy home life, public school education for the masses, technological institutions for the training of industrial workers, and universities for the development of "men capable of interpreting and influencing world movements, men able to adjust the race to any new conditions that may arise." Land ownership and a back-to-the-farm movement are recommended. Good government and simple justice, not race supremacy and partisan patronage, are defined as the desirable goals of Negro political action. The cultivation of the friendship of the white South as well as of the moral support of other sections of the country and of other civilized nations is also emphasized as a *sine qua non* of enlightened racial policy. In the promotion of this program the support of the orator, journalist, literary artist, painter, sculptor, and composer is solicited. As a statement of desirable procedure for the colored people of the United States, "Dorlan's Plan" is a forerunner of James Weldon Johnson's *Negro Americans, What Now?* (1934) and numerous other guides to interracial harmony in the United States.

In his next novel, *The Hindered Hand,* Griggs explores the tragic results of miscegenation in the South and attacks the biased portrayal of the Negro in Dixon's *The Leopard's Spots*. The tragedy sometimes caused by interbreeding is shown in the lives of a mulatto couple's three children—Tiara Merlow, who, because of her dark complexion, is early separated from her family in order to make "passing" easier for her parents and the other two children; the Reverend Percy G. Marshall, who is killed by a Negro when seen holding his sister Tiara in his arms; and Eunice Seabright, who, after being forced into an unhappy marriage with a white man, becomes demented when her racial identity is revealed. Concerning Eunice's insanity a Northern specialist says

> The one specific cause of her breakdown is the Southern situation which has borne tremendously upon her. That whole region of the country is affected by a sort of sociological hysteria, and we physicians are expecting more and more pathological manifestations as a result of the strain upon the people.[13]

The effect of American caste upon the Negro is considered in Tiara's defense of her mother:

> My mother is dead and paid dearly for her unnatural course. But do not judge her too harshly. You people who are white do not know what an awful burden it is to be black in these days of the world. If some break down beneath the awful load of caste which you thrust upon them, mingle pity with your blame.[14]

The maladministration of justice in the South is mirrored in the unwarranted lynching of Foresta Crump and Bud Harper in Mississippi. An investigator, upon asking a white native whether mob action against the Negro couple was caused by "the one crime," receives the following explanation

> That's all rot about one crime. We lynch niggers down here for anything. We lynch them for being sassy and sometimes lynch them on general principles. The truth of the matter is the real "one crime" that paves the way for a lynching whenever we have the notion, is the crime of being black.[15]

At a subsequent trial of the lynchers a young prosecuting attorney becomes a political outcast for demanding justice, and the jury sets the mobbers free.

In the first and second editions of *The Hindered Hand,* a review of Dixon's *The Leopard's Spots* appears in the form of a conversation between two of the characters of the novel, but in the third edition this discussion in amplified in a review at the end of the book. Even in the third edition, however, *The Leopard's Spots* is mentioned in the body of the novel when A. Hostility, in a fruitless effort to enlist Negro aid in a Slav movement against the Anglo-Saxon, calls the attention of Tiara's lover, Ensal Ellwood, "to the book written for the express purpose of thoroughly discrediting the Negro race in America."[16] Ellwood is disturbed by the literary campaign against the Negro

> Ensal thought of the odds against the Negro in this literary battle: how that Southern white people, being more extensive purchasers of books than Negroes, would have the natural bias of the great publishing agencies on their side; how that Northern white people, resident in the South, for social and business reasons, might hesitate to father books not in keeping with the prevailing sentiment of Southern white people; how that residents of the North, who essayed to write in defense of the Negro, were laughed out of school as mere theorists ignorant of actual conditions; and, finally, how that a lack of leisure and the absence of general culture handicapped the Negro in fighting his own battle in this species of warfare.[17]

In "A Hindering Hand, Supplementary to *The Hindered Hand:* A Review of the Anti-Negro Crusade of Mr. Thomas Dixon, Jr.,"[18] Griggs states that Dixon's malice derives from the traditional dislike of the Southern poor white for the Negro and that his purpose is to effect the expulsion of those having African blood from the United States. To accomplish this aim, according to Griggs, Dixon attempts "to thoroughly discredit the Negroes, to stir up the baser passions of men against them, and to send them forth with a load of obloquy and the withering scorn of their fellows the world over, sufficient to appall a nation of angels." Among the propagandistic techniques allegedly used by Dixon are the depiction of the Negro as the lustful despoiler of white womankind, the portrayal of degenerates as representative types of black men, and the attribution of natural inferiority to those of African extraction. In consideration of Dixon's methods and materials, Griggs submits the following epitaph for the author of *The Leopard's Spots*

> This misguided soul ignored all of the good in the aspiring Negro; made every vicious offshoot that he pictured typical of the entire race; presented all mistakes independent of their environments and provocations; ignored or minimized all the evil in the more vicious elements of whites; said and did all things which he deemed necessary to leave behind him the greatest heritage of hatred the world has ever known. Humanity claims him not as one of her children.[19]

Though weak according to artistic standards, *The Hindered Hand* is the most elaborate attack upon Thomas Dixon in American Negro fiction. In addition, the book presents the well-worn themes of miscegenation and racial injustice, and shows the Negro mind weighing open revolt and emigration to Africa[20] against bearing the burdens of an ethnic minority in the United States. The denial of political rights is designated as the chief factor which "causes the Ethiopian in America to feel that his is indeed 'The Hindered Hand.'"[21]

Like *The Hindered Hand, Pointing the Way* treats interbreeding and politics in the South, but ends upon a more hopeful note. Letitia Gilbreath, spinster daughter of a white man and his ex-slave mistress, considers it "a shocking crime for two dark persons to marry each other" and therefore undertakes to compel her niece Clotille to become the wife of Baug Peppers, a mulatto lawyer. Clotille, however, loves Conroe Driscoll, her dark-skinned college sweetheart, and, while studying in Boston, invites Eina, a beautiful English-Spanish-Indian girl, to her Southern home in Belrose with the hope that the visitor would marry Peppers and thus leave her free to wed the young man of her choice. After reaching Belrose, Eina becomes seriously interested in Peppers; but Seth Molair, a white attorney who admires the attractive newcomer, warns her that "to work, to eat, to sleep, to die is the utmost programme that organized society in the South offers" the Negro, and informs her that she may not mingle socially with both races

> . . . . In the South social freedom is not permitted, for reasons that I need not discuss here. Whoever affiliates socially with the one race in the South is denied the social life of the other.[22]

After Eina asks whether there is any hope for interracial harmony, Molair replies

> The one thing needed in the South is political cooperation between the better elements of whites and the Negroes, but the manner of the coming of emancipation, enfranchisement, and elevation to high public station seems to have riveted the Negro into one party, while the terror of being ruled by an alien and backward race has chained the real strength of the white race into an opposing party. . . . As long as there is a bitter political war between the Negroes and the whites of the South, how can conditions change?[23]

Resolving to bring about better race relations in Belrose and definitely aligning herself with the Negro group, Eina persuades Peppers to ask Molair to run for mayor on a platform pledging justice to all citizens. Moved by the ruthless murder of a colored youth by a white chaingang guard, Molair enters the race and wins the election. His impartial and progressive administration, during which Driscoll becomes a captain in the municipal fire department, not only draws national attention and presidential commendation, but also elicits the enthusiastic interest and financial support of a millionaire ex-Southerner who opposes the steady northward migration of Negroes and resolves to improve the status of the blacks and poor whites of the South. Successful in her campaign for better race relations in Belrose, Eina induces Peppers to test

Southern disfranchising legislation before the Supreme Court. Assisted by a bequest from Letitia, who earlier died in a fire in which Driscoll made a fatal effort to save her life, Peppers carries a test case to the highest tribunal in the land and makes an eloquent plea for the enfranchisement of his people. The novel closes with praise of the Belrose experiment and with the marriage of Peppers and Eina.

Pointing the Way emphasizes the tragic consequences of intra-racial prejudice by showing how the happiness of lovers is thwarted through the efforts of a color-conscious old maid to force her niece to marry a mulatto. The novel also seeks to show that the political cooperation of the races in the South not only contributes to the solution of the problems of that section but also to the general improvement of conditions throughout the country. While deficient according to standards of art, *Pointing the Way* adds to Griggs' reputation as a political propagandist in fiction.

At this place it might be well to draw a few comparisons between Griggs and his well-known contemporary, Charles W. Chesnutt. To begin, both employ the conventional subject-matter of miscegenation, color prejudice, and racial oppression. Unlike Chesnutt, however, Griggs recommends a way to a better life for his people. Rejecting open revolt, exodus to Africa, and the program of Booker T. Washington, he offers the solution of political cooperation with the white South and alignment with whatever party offers the Negro the fullest participation in government. Unlike Chesnutt again, Griggs tends to glorify black pigmentation, as the following description of Warthell, the hero of *Unfettered,* indicates: "As to color he was black, but even those prejudiced to color forgot that prejudice when they gazed upon this ebony-like Apollo."[24] While ridiculing the color line within the race in several of his works, Chesnutt nevertheless shows a predilection for mulattoes and occasionally uses certain black stereotypes which most of his Negro contemporaries disdained. As an artist, however, Chesnutt is the superior in every way, for weaknesses in plot, characterization, and diction loom obtrusively in the novels of Griggs.

But regardless of his failings as an artist, Griggs is a significant pioneer in the history of American Negro fiction. Like Oscar Michaux and J. A. Rogers today, he personally distributed his books among the masses of his people. In his novels he shows the advantages of racial organization as a technique for gaining the full benefits of American democracy, answers the writers who belittled and vilified the Negro before the national reading public, points unerringly to the distorting influence of prejudice and discrimination upon members of both races, and manifests a deep humanitarian interest in the welfare of oppressed peoples in other parts of the world. Most important of all, he is one of the earliest symbols in American Negro fiction of the spiritual emancipation of his people and the first important author of the political novel among his race in this country.

NOTES

[1] *The Old South*, p. 324.

[2] *The Clansman*, p. v.

[3] *The Leopard's Spots*, p. 5.

[4] *Ibid.*, pp. 150-151.

[5] *Imperium in Imperio*, p. 62.

[6] Sterling Brown in *The Negro in American Fiction* (1937), pp. 100-101. Professor Brown briefly discusses *Unfettered* and *The Hindered Hand*, two of Griggs' five novels.

[7] *Imperium in Imperio*, p. 252.

[8] *Overshadowed*, p. 215.

[9] *Ibid.*, p. 217.

[10] *Unfettered*, p. 5.

[11] *Ibid.*, p. 56.

[12] *Ibid.*, pp. 217-276.

[13] *The Hindered Hand, or The Reign of the Repressionist*, p. 249.

[14] *Ibid.*, p. 238.

[15] *Ibid.*, p. 136.

[16] *Ibid.*, p. 206.

[17] *Ibid.*, p. 207.

[18] [In the essay], Griggs states that he does not intend "to deal with Mr. Dixon's second book [*The Clansman*] bearing on the race problem, it being the hope of the writer to give that matter serious and independent attention." *Ibid.*, p. 298. This investigator has found no record of such a study of *The Clansman* by Griggs.

[19] *Ibid.*, p. 332.

[20] In appended "Notes to the Serious," Griggs, somewhat anticipating Marcus Garvey, declares that the idea of a Negro exodus to Africa is his own dream and not the wish of most American Negroes:

> The overwhelmingly predominant sentiment of the American Negroes is to fight out their battle on these shores. The assigning of the thoughts of the race to the uplift of Africa, as affecting the situation in America, must be taken more as a dream of the author than as representing any considerable responsible sentiment within the race, which, as has been stated, seems at present thoroughly and unqualifiedly American, a fact that must never be overlooked by those seeking to deal with this grave question in a practical manner. *Ibid.*, p. 297.

[21] *Ibid.*, p. 292.

[22] *Pointing the Way*, p. 26.

[23] *Ibid.*, p. 41.

[24] *Unfettered, op. cit.*, p. 71.

Robert Bone (essay date 1958)

SOURCE: "Novels of the Talented Tenth," in *The Negro Novel in America*, Revised Edition, Yale University Press, 1965, pp. 29-50.

[*In the following excerpt, Bone looks at Griggs's novels within the framework of African-American political conditions at the time of their writing.*]

Griggs was a prominent Baptist minister and a popular lecturer on the race problem. Having written five novels in the space of ten years (1899 to 1908), he organized his own publishing company in Nashville, Tenn., to promote their sale and distribution. The novels are badly written and tractarian in the extreme, but Griggs' very militancy represents something of a culmination. This militancy deserves closer examination, however, if only because of current misconceptions regarding it. Hugh Gloster has written extensively of Griggs, both in an article in *Phylon*[1] and in *Negro Voices in American Fiction*. He has treated Griggs as a political thinker of some stature whose views on the race question compare well with those of James Weldon Johnson.[2] He has found in Griggs not a forerunner of the New Negro but "the novelist of the New Negro" incarnate.

The term "New Negro" was coined by Alain Locke during the 1920's, to express the new spirit of dignity and manhood which animated the postwar generation of Negro youth. The New Negro was distinguished by his refusal to accept subordinate status; he had decisively rejected the slavemindedness which taught the Old Negro to know his place. But freedom in the psychological sense is a process of becoming. At what point in this process is Sutton Griggs? On occasion he is militant and challenging, as Dr. Gloster avers. At other times he is conciliatory to the point of servility. His militancy has its source in a fanatical Negro nationalism; his servility, in a political outlook which is essentially feudal. The former mood is well illustrated by *Imperium in Imperio* (1899); the latter, by *Pointing the Way* (1908).

In his first novel, Griggs displays the classic attitudes of Negro nationalism. He is almost pathologically antiwhite and scarcely less antimulatto.[3] He toys with a solution to the race problem which is both revolutionary and separatist. His hero, described throughout as a "race patriot," leads a secret student society in revolt under a black flag; later he joins a revolutionary underground government which plans to seize Texas as a base for a separate Negro nation. To be sure, the hero of the novel repudiates these excesses in the end. But the symbolic drama which is being enacted is clear enough. Griggs' blind impulse toward retaliation and revenge is striving for mastery with a more moderate, and more realistic approach.

The author's next three novels,[4] while not as blatantly black-nationalist as *Imperium in Imperio,* are essentially cut from the same cloth. *Pointing the Way* (1908), however, far from being "militant and challenging," is conciliatory and accommodationist. In the words of a minor character: "Good white people kin lead de cullud folks ef dey will jes' 'gree ter do so."[5] The heroine of the novel, in attempting "to bring the better elements of white and colored people together," seeks the assistance of Seth Molair, a young white man whose family is described in the following terms: "The Molairs had never ceased under freedom to exercise a paternal care over all those who had belonged to the family in the days of slavery" (p. 111). Illustrative of the kind of "equality" which Griggs espouses is Molair's campaign for mayor of a small Southern town, undertaken with the support of the colored community. After winning the election, he courageously makes a Negro college graduate captain of the municipal fire department! (A place for everyone, and everyone in his place.)

At one point in the novel Griggs gives the game away: "just as the Negroes had great faith in *their* white folks, the whites, as a rule, had great faith in *their* Negroes" (italics in original). Here, in an unguarded moment, Griggs reveals the paternalistic relationship which lies at the heart of his feudal psychology. In spite of his rhetoric about Negro rights, in the last analysis Sutton Griggs is an old-fashioned Southerner who relies on the "Quality white folks" to provide a solution to the race problem. He must therefore be willing to make certain compromises and opportunistic arguments. This approach to Southern politics can of course be argued on its merits, but it is certainly not the approach of the New Negro.

Sutton Griggs' vacillation between one pole which is militant and fantastic and another pole which is realistic and accommodationist faithfully reflects the political dilemma of the Negro intellectual prior to World War I. The ideological contradictions which plagued Griggs were not personal but historical. He and others of his generation were caught in an iron vise which precluded political action that was at once militant and realistic. DuBois' Niagara Movement and the subsequent founding of the NAACP marked a decisive change in the strategy of the Negro leadership, from a perspective of manipulating Southern paternalism to one of independent struggle. But before this strategy could be implemented, a vast population shift from South to North and from farm to city was necessary. The urban migration, which only made itself felt after World War I, gave the Negro leadership a mass base capable of supporting an independent struggle.

Militancy is one thing; translating it into effective political action is another. Too often Negro nationalism, for all its militancy, is politically Utopian. The most militant of the early novelists, insofar as they were realistic, were obliged to be more or less accommodationist. Conversely, insofar as they remained militant and uncompromising, their political strategy was bound to have a certain Utopian ring. *Pointing the Way* by Sutton Griggs and *The Colonel's Dream* (1905) by Charles Chesnutt represent one horn of this dilemma; *The Quest of the Silver Fleece* (1911) by DuBois and *The Immediate Jewel of His Soul* (1919) by Herman Dreer, with their Utopian agrarian communities, represent the other. All of these novelists were forerunners of the New Negro, but scholars should resist a tendency to date the New Negro movement too early in order to gloss over the long period of accommodationist politics which preceded it.

NOTES

[1] "Sutton Griggs, Novelist of the New Negro," *Phylon* (fourth quarter 1943), pp. 335-45.

[2] *Negro Voices in American Fiction,* p. 62.

[3] See the crude mutilation fantasies involving whites in *Imperium in Imperio,* pp. 13, 35, and 152. Note also the characterization of Bernard throughout the novel, and Viola's refusal to marry a mulatto, pp. 173 ff.

[4] *Overshadowed* (1901), *Unfettered* (1902), *The Hindered Hand* (1905).

[5] *Pointing the Way,* p. 99.

Robert E. Fleming (essay date 1973)

SOURCE: "Sutton E. Griggs: Militant Black Novelist," in *PHYLON: The Atlanta University Review of Race and Culture,* Vol. XXXIV, No. 1, March, 1973, pp. 73-7.

[*In the following essay, Fleming explores aspects of violence—real and imagined—in Griggs's novels.*]

Sutton E. Griggs has customarily been held up as an early example of the militant black novelist, especially in his first novel, *Imperium in Imperio* (1899). The most vigorous promoter of this point of view has been Hugh M. Gloster; Robert A. Bone, while differing with Gloster on the degree of militance which Griggs displays, is in basic agreement with his view of *Imperium in Imperio.* However, the recent republication of Grigg's best-known novel makes it available to a greater number of readers, who must question the degree to which Griggs subscribes to his characters' beliefs and attitudes. An examination of the novel as a whole and of the techniques used suggests that Griggs is neither as militant nor as inconsistent as he has seemed to some critics.

Hugh M. Gloster presents Griggs as a forerunner of modern black militants in his introduction to the 1969

Arno Press edition of *Imperium in Imperio.*[1] Earlier, in *Negro Voices in American Fiction,* Gloster emphasized the novelist's militancy, contrasting Griggs with less politically motivated contemporaries such as Paul Laurence Dunbar and Charles W. Chesnutt.[2] More significantly, Gloster's summary of the plot of *Imperium in Imperio* deals almost exclusively with the last third of the novel, the section concerning the secret political organization of black people from which the novel takes its name.[3] The climactic event of the book is the debate and passage of a resolution to embark on a military venture which includes a complex plan to sabotage the U.S. Navy. By means of civil war with the United States and alliance with her foreign enemies, the Imperium plans to gain control of Texas and Louisiana. To focus, as Gloster does, on this admittedly militaristic part of the plot is doubly misleading, not only because the first two thirds of the novel is ignored, but also because the protagonist of the novel, Belton Piedmont, opposes the military role of the Imperium and makes an impassioned plea against the course of action favored by the majority.

In *The Negro Novel in America,* Robert A. Bone questions Gloster's interpretation of Griggs' militancy and suggests that such an interpretation has led to "current misconceptions" of the novelist's stance.[4] According to Bone, Griggs is ideologically confused about the stance he wishes to assume: "On occasion he is militant and challenging, as Dr. Gloster avers. At other times he is conciliatory to the point of servility. His militancy has its source in a fanatical Negro nationalism; his servility, in a political outlook which is essentially feudal. The former mood is well illustrated by *Imperium in Imperio.*"[5] Bone goes on to analyze Griggs' later works, which seem to retreat from violent militance, as expressions of the author's conciliatory attitudes. He views Griggs' dilemma both in psychological terms—"Griggs' blind impulse toward retaliation and revenge is striving for mastery with a more moderate, and more realistic approach"—and in historical terms—"Sutton Griggs' vacillation between one pole which is militant and fantastic and another pole which is realistic and accommodationist faithfully reflects the political dilemma of the Negro intellectual prior to World War I. The ideological contradictions which plagued Griggs were not personal but historical."[6] While correctly pointing out certain inconsistencies in Griggs' total literary output, Bone fails to acknowledge that even in the first and most militant of his works Griggs expresses an aversion to violence, though he realizes that some black people regard it as inevitable.

Griggs speaks out against racial injustice more openly and forcefully than most of his contemporaries, and he does so by employing a variety of techniques, which range from open denunciation to ridicule.[7] His propagandistic purpose is quite obvious in his direct and often heavy-handed dramatization of instances of bigotry and injustice. When Belton Piedmont first goes off to school, it is to a ramshackle building which once housed a white Baptist congregation, but which "had been condemned as unsafe by the town authorities."[8] The white teacher enrolls Belton while muttering audibly, "Another black nigger brat for me to teach."[9] Later, when he attends a black college founded by Northern liberals, Piedmont finds that even there the only black teacher on the staff is barred from eating with the white professors. Piedmont is dismissed from his first job because of his political activity, suffers from jim crow treatment in a railroad coach in Louisiana, and is refused service in a white restaurant. Then, in a melodramatic series of events, he is hanged, shot, and nearly dissected by a curious white surgeon.

Not content with presenting discrimination and brutality dramatically, Griggs frequently intrudes in his own voice to make explicit comments on the results of racial prejudice. Such is the case in the following passage, which treats Piedmont's problem after losing his second job because he has followed his principles:

> Belton began to cast around for another occupation, but, in whatever direction he looked, he saw no hope. He possessed a first class college education, but that was all. He knew no trade nor was he equipped to enter any of the professions. It is true that there were positions around by the thousands which he could fill, but his color debarred him. He would have made an excellent drummer, salesman, cashier, government official (county, city, state, or national) telegraph operator, conductor, or anything of such nature. But the color of his skin shut the doors so tight that he could not even peep in.[10]

Neither Bone nor Gloster mentions another noteworthy propaganda technique employed by Griggs—his use of broad comic scenes which ridicule the exaggerated dignity of the white master race. An extended example occurs at the beginning of the novel and has as its target Mr. Tiberius Bracchus Leonard, the pompous white schoolteacher who is to become Belton's first white enemy. Leonard is standing on the top step at the entrance to the schoolhouse when Belton's mother brings him to school to enroll him.

> To emphasize his disgust, he drew back so that Mrs. Piedmont would pass him with no danger of brushing him. He drew back rather too far and began falling off the end of the step. He clutched at the door and made such a scrambling noise that the children turned in their seats just in time to see his body rapidly disappearing in a manner to leave his feet where his head ought to be.
>
> Such a yell of laughter as went up from the throats of the children![11]

When Leonard leaves the school to have his head dressed, one of the children mimics him by conducting a mock class, while another leaves a bent pin on the teacher's chair; Leonard returns, having regained his dignity, and promptly loses it again by sitting on the pin. In a later chapter, Belton makes a laughing stock of his teacher by causing him to fall through a hole in the floor as the finale of graduation ceremonies. Griggs is obviously far from subtle as a writer of comedy, but his creation of a white Steppin Fetchit type relieves the more serious and straightforward social criticism which forms so large a part of the novel.

Thus, Griggs' techniques perform different but complementary functions. His dramatic and authorial expositions of racial injustice are both informative and effective; they are designed to appeal to the white reader's sense of fair play as well as to win sympathy for black people. His comic scenes not only relieve the generally somber tone of the novel but also further the author's cause: Griggs attempts to change undesirable attitudes of whites by showing readers how ridiculous it is for people to feel superior merely because of their race. Still another approach, similar in some ways to the methods of the Black Panther Party of our day, is the appeal to fear. It is the use of this approach that has created misunderstanding about Griggs. Like Sam Greenlee in his recent novel *The Spook Who Sat by the Door* (1969), Griggs uses realistic and concrete details to give substance to an essentially fantastic vision. In order to achieve a frightening prophetic effect, both Greenlee and Griggs use hyperbole; by exaggerating possible reactions of blacks to injustice, they attempt to convince the reader that immediate reforms are imperative if the nightmare of black revolution is to be averted.

In his appeal to the reader's fear, Griggs foreshadows the introduction of the Imperium by pointing out causes for growing discontent. For example, he notes that black college graduates like Belton Piedmont find themselves educated but unemployable: "They grew to hate a flag that would float in an undisturbed manner over such a condition of affairs. They began to abuse and execrate a national government that would not protect them against color prejudice, but on the contrary actually practiced it itself."[12] Such conditions lead men to join the Imperium, a secret government which made "use of all [the] secret orders already formed by negroes"[13] and which was founded "to secure protection for their lives and the full enjoyment of all rights and privileges due American citizens."[14] To make the Imperium seem real and believable, Griggs presents in detail the society's history, organization, financing, and procedures. However, under the leadership of Bernard Belgrave, Piedmont's boyhood rival, the society becomes more militant. In his first speech as president of the Imperium, Belgrave stirs the anger of the members by reminding them of the suffering they have undergone as a race—slavery, exclusion from good jobs, deprivation of civil rights, inferior education, unfair treatment in the courts, and the horrors of mob rule. He asks how blacks are to obtain freedom. Amalgamation with the white race and emigration to Africa are both rejected. Finally, a speaker rises "to stick a match to the powder magazine which Belgrave had left uncovered in all their bosoms."[15] He favors war, and his suggestion is enthusiastically accepted.

At this point Belton Piedmont, second only to Belgrave in the Imperium hierarchy, rises to dissent. In a twenty-page speech he argues that conditions are not as bad as Belgrave has suggested and that since emancipation conditions have been better. He urges a course of action he feels will achieve their goals without bloodshed: revelation of the Imperium's existence; warning that its members intend to gain their rights; and, if these means fail, the peaceful move of all black people to the state of Texas, where their numbers will enable them to control the state government. The forces that favor war win, and Piedmont, who refuses to condone premeditated mass murder, is executed.

Thus, Griggs uses the Imperium plot as the most powerful weapon in his attack on racial injustice; he resorts to fear in order to motivate those readers who have not been moved by reason, sympathy, or laughter. Although the Imperium plot is fantastic, Griggs bases it on facts: the large number of black people in the United States; their growing discontent; and the Anglo-Saxons' chronic underestimation of the Negro character. However, the novel is neither a blueprint for nor a call to violence; indeed, Griggs' use of Belton Piedmont as his hero, rather than the more militant Bernard Belgrave, indicates where his true sympathy lies. The note on which the novel ends provides further evidence of Griggs' viewpoint. One of the members, Bert Trout, has been influenced by Piedmont's plea for peace and exposes the plot with the warning that crushing the Imperium will only postpone the inevitable racial holocaust unless its root causes are eradicated: "I only ask as a return [for this disclosure] that all mankind will join hands and help my poor downtrodden people to secure those rights for which they organized the Imperium. . . . I urge this because love of liberty is such an inventive genius, that if you destroy one device it at once constructs another more powerful."[16] Surely Bert Trout speaks for the author in these closing lines of the novel.

The fact that Griggs presents the Imperium plot as a narrowly averted tragedy does not lessen his importance as an early militant writer. At a time when Booker T. Washington's soothing tones were filling the ears of white people everywhere, it took boldness and daring for Griggs to suggest, even in fantastic terms, that the black population could be capable of organized revolt. However, it is important to read his novels as he wrote them, and not to ascribe to him a tendency toward violence which he never displayed. If we read *Imperium in Imperio* as a warning of possible violence to come, but not as an endorsement of that violence, Griggs' later "accommodationist" novels proceed more logically from his first.

NOTES

[1] Preface to Sutton E. Griggs, *Imperium in Imperio* (New York, 1969), pp. iii-viii.

[2] Revised edition, New York, 1965, pp. 56-67.

[3] *Ibid.,* pp. 57-58. See also Gloster's "Sutton E. Griggs: Novelist of the New Negro," *Phylon,* IV (Fourth Quarter, 1943), 337-38.

[4] Revised edition, New Haven and London, 1965, pp. 32-33.

[5] *Ibid.,* p. 33.

[6] *Ibid.,* pp. 33-34.

[7] Griggs does not confine himself to attacks on white people, but also attempts to awaken and foster black pride by showing black people in favorable lights. Piedmont becomes the best student in his class and is later an admirable leader in spite of difficulties created by race prejudice. Two other characters, a black college professor and the intended fiancee of Bernard Belgrave, are also presented as admirable and principled individuals, unlike most of the white characters in the novel.

[8] Griggs, *op. cit.,* p. 8

[9] *Ibid.,* p. 9.

[10] *Ibid.,* p. 129.

[11] *Ibid.,* p. 9.

[12] *Ibid.,* p. 131.

[13] *Ibid.,* p. 194.

[14] *Ibid.,* p. 183.

[15] *Ibid.,* p. 225.

[16] *Ibid.,* p. 265.

Campbell Tatham   (essay date 1974)

SOURCE: "Sutton Griggs' Imperium in Imperio," in *Studies in Black Literature,* Vol. 5, No. 1, Spring, 1974, pp. 7-15.

[*In the following essay, Tatham examines Griggs's* Imperium in Imperio *as a guide to radical political action.*]

> Be convinced . . . that the past is no forbidden vista upon which we dare not look, out of phantom fear of being, as the wife of Lot, turned into pillars of salt. Rather the past is an omniscient mirror: we gaze and see reflected there ourselves and each other—what we used to be, what we are today, how we got this way, and what we are becoming. To decline to look into the mirror of Then . . . is to refuse to view the face of Now.
>
> —Eldridge Cleaver, *Soul on Ice*

> To ask questions . . . is equivalent to a new and itensified declaration of war . . . look at us and know us and you will know yourselves, for *we* are *you,* looking back at you from the dark mirror of our lives!
>
> —Richard Wright, *12 Million Black Voices*

I propose to examine a mirror—at first, seemingly quaint and antiquated, irrelevant to a search after not what should have been, but what was and may still be; I propose to ask questions, to risk a declaration of war.

A 'mirror'; a novel: *Imperium in Imperio.* Is no one willing to dust off the frame of this work? Is it so obviously irrelevant to the face of now, having been published more than seventy years ago? Granted, the frame seems chipped with age, the surface streaked, perhaps cracked. Yet distortions, chips, streaks, cracks—might these not most appropriately reflect the dislocated images of our time? Perhaps, but at best we are embarking on an ambiguous adventure.

There are, to be sure, Guides—the Critics, voices reflecting their limited experience in this curious antique shoppe:

Addison Gayle, Jr.: " . . . the novel of this virtually unknown nineteenth-century writer."[1]

Robert A. Bone: "[Griggs'] militancy has its source in a fanatical Negro nationalism; his servility, in a political outlook which is essentially feudal . . . In his first novel, Griggs displays the classic attitudes of Negro nationalism. He is almost pathologically anti-white."[2]

A Black critic, a White critic—for them, the past of Sutton Griggs' novel is no forbidden vista; it is merely an aberration, of minimal historical interest, ultimately tedious, hardly worth mentioning. In fact, their fellow critics find it unworthy of any mention whatever: search (vainly) through the works of David Littlejohn, Edward Margolies, and C. W. E. Bigsby—all three professing to deal with the Negro Novel, none having anything to say about *Imperium in Imperio.* Hoyt Fuller, always eager to scold white professors and whitewashed black critics, marks the beginnings of the black novel with "the advent of Paul Laurence Dunbar and Charles W. Chesnutt, toward the end of the nineteenth century"; only then did we have "works that qualified as literature according to those whose prerogative it is to make such judgments."[3] Sutton who?

There is, of course, Hugh Gloster, who would appear to have a virtual monopoly on Griggsiana. The competition is not keen. Even Gloster is not greatly interested. His insights are not startling, scarcely provocative: "Though weakened by melodramatic situations, idealized characters, and stilted conversation, *Imperium in Imperio* is the first American Negro novel with a strictly political emphasis . . . While extravagant in conception, *Imperium in Imperio* exhibits the racial outlook that produced the National Association for the Advancement of Colored People and other organizations striving for the full participation of the Negro in American democracy."[4] The novel advocates striving for full participation in American democracy? Surely Gloster must be thinking of another book, perhaps one by Chesnutt . . . Fortunately, the original novel is again available, and we are afforded further insights by Gloster in the form of an introduction. His vision has not improved: "[Griggs] offers a program of political cooperation with the white majority and the withdrawal of the black population into a separate state as the surest road to freedom, justice, and equality for the Negroes of this country."[5] Can the surest road to freedom entail both cooperation with and separation from the white power structure? Gloster's logic keeps pace with his critical sensitivity. It is worth noting, however, that he has changed in at least one respect. In 1943, when he first glanced over Sutton Griggs, the novel was "extravagant in conception"; in 1969, "American Negroes who espouse black beauty, black pride, black militancy, and black separatism are the ideological successors of Dr. Sutton E. Griggs."[6] It may be that American Negroes have in fact changed more than Dr. Gloster himself. He declines to elaborate.

In 1899, the year of *Imperium*'s publication, the notion of a vast, underground network dedicated to the creation of a separate black state may indeed have seemed extravagant in conception. Memories of Nat Turner must have faded, Marcus Garvey was yet to appear, nation-building-time was unheard of. Was Griggs the progenitor of the Spook who sits by the door?

Consider the ingenious plot articulated by Bernard Belgrave, the novel's protagonist; the organization is to purchase secretly land in Texas, stockpile weapons, infiltrate the navy, negotiate with potentially sympathetic foreign powers; at an appropriate time, the state capitol is to be seized, the navy sabotaged, and the United States government ordered to cede Texas and Louisiana to the Imperium; Louisiana is to be offered in payment to the foreign allies, while Texas will permit "The Negro [to] have an empire of his own, fertile in soil, capable of sustaining a population of fifty million people" (252). A truly extravagant conception?

Consider the ingenious plot articulated by Imari Abubakari Obadele, the protagonist of a rather real structure, the Republic of New Africa: the organization is to purchase secretly land in Mississippi, stockpile weapons, infiltrate government agencies at all levels, negotiate with potentially sympathetic foreign powers; at an appropriate time, a plebescite is to be held, the independence of five southern states declared, a petition put before the United Nations, industry sabatoged (only if necessary, of course), freedom attained. Extravagant? Perhaps. Obadele is apparently taken seriously; he writes, as of now, from a prison cell in Jackson, Mississippi, where he was arrested after a confrontation with the police of that state.

Imperium in Imperio, a nation within a nation, nation-building time.

Obadele calls for the training of guerilla units, equipped with "radios, medical kits, field packs, tent, and arms: 30-06 rifles (preferably M-1 Garand), the 12-guage shotgun, and/or the M-1 carbine, and plenty of ammunition"; Obadele calls for a contribution from every black family

of $105 per week, "the maintenance cost of one military unit in the field"; Obadele issues his call in one of the most prominent black periodicals.[7] Does anyone listen? Is the RNA simply cashing in on the fashionable rhetoric-of-revolution? It can't happen here, not really? On August 18, 1971, in the 'confrontation' that led to Obadele's arrest, a white policeman was killed and two others wounded.

Which may 'prove' nothing. Still, the Mirror of Then may sharpen our perception of the face of Now.

> As an artist, however, Chesnutt is the superior in every way, for deficiencies in plot, characterization, and diction loom obtrusively in the novels of Griggs.
>
> —Hugh Gloster

Griggs encases *Imperium in Imperio* within a masterfully ironic framework, the distorted vision of its processed narrator, Berl Trout. As his name might suggest, Trout is confused—snarled and gullible—and confusing. To avoid becoming unnecessarily snarled and confused himself, the reader should at least keep in mind that the events are reflected through the consciousness of this conspicuously unreliable narrator. 'Reflection' or 'refraction'? In the field of our encounter with the novel, it is especially difficult to locate and maintain our bearings. Griggs has decentered our experience: there is no central 'point-of-view' to which we can unambiguously assent, certainly no position we can confidently attribute to the author.

The 'author,' one "Sutton E. Griggs" (not be be confused with the actual-author, Sutton E. Griggs), pretends to have been "well acquainted with Berl, as we fondly call him" and promises to "vouch for his truthfulness anywhere" (xi). Standard strategy: the more the 'author' insists on the truthfulness of his narrator, the more we are forced to sensitize ourselves to the artifice of the fiction. "Griggs" claims possession of certain documents which could supply "indisputable proofs of every important statement" (xii). Are we to smile indulgently, recalling Hawthorne in the attic of the customs house and countless other spurious gestures toward 'realism'? No, for we, too, may yet have "perfect faith in the truthfulness of his narrative" (xii)—if not in the events and characters as such, then in the truly ambiguous psychological foundations underlying them. We need not vouch for the veracity of *what* Berl Trout says, obviously; we may nonetheless vouch for the veracity of the *saying*. The ironies turn back on themselves and compel us to say 'yes' and 'no' simultaneously. And continuously, throughout the novel.

"I am a traitor"—the first words of the narrator. This speaker, whom the 'author' insists we trust, announces that he has "violated an oath that was as solemn and binding as any ever taken by man on earth" (1). Thus, before we engage the narrative content, we must confront the involuted ironies of "Berl Trout's Dying Declaration." Questions arise. A traitor to whom? He refers to "the sacred trust of a loving people"—does Trout "betray" the Imperium? or does he act against black people everywhere? or against Blackness-as-such? Trout himself appears uncertain, tangled in conflicting levels of abstraction. He stumbles through his unconvincing justification/declaration, moving from "myself," to "the race," to "the whole family of man" and "all races," to "the earth," finally to "God" (2). A familiar pattern, no doubt, not unrelated to the archetypal "double-consciousness" described by DuBois: unwilling to assume the responsibility for his concrete individuality, Trout swims through progressively broader abstractions, hoping to lose himself in the whole human family, the earth, God. Committed to all races, he need commit himself to none in particular and can 'betray' the trust of his people: professing involvement in the whole human family, he can effectively disengage himself from himself. Double consciousness, then, as articulated by DuBois, can lead to Bad Faith, as articulated by Sartre. And Trout must indeed be a traitor—to himself, to his people, to existence.

Yet to judge Trout is such terms is to implicate ourselves in the same Bad Faith we profess to discover in his 'confession.' Clearly, he is seeking to shirk the responsibility for his act of betraying the Imperium; but as soon as we imply that he should in fact "be-responsible" to an organization or to a people, we are guilty of invoking the self-delusion of an abstraction. *People* exist, The People do not, How can we scoff at Trout's hypocrisy—and then support those who call for All-Power-to-the-People? Gabriel Marcel claims to stand for "an obstinate and untiring battle against the "spirit of abstraction"; reflecting upon his experience (especially that of the Nazi Occupation of France), he finds that "as soon as we accord to any category, isolated from all other categories, an arbitrary primacy, we are victims of the spirit of abstraction"—with the seemingly inevitable result that, ourselves victims of delusions, we systematically victimize others by denying them individuality reality: *The Jews* could be exterminated, by individuals who would shudder at the sight of a dog run over in the street.[8] Yet Marcel also admits that "abstraction, as such, is a mental operation to which we must have recourse if we are seeking to achieve a determinate purpose of any sort."[9] And 'the spirit of abstraction" is itself an abstraction . . . The abstractions would seem to mirror each other, inversions of reciprocal degrees of Bad Faith. But are the meditations of a French philosopher relevant to the pressing realities of the struggle of racial freedom?

Consider two statements by Frantz Fanon, seen by many as a Revolutionary Prophet:

> (1) I do not come with timeless truths . . . These things I am going to say, not shout. For it is a long time since shouting has gone out of my life . . . Fervor is the weapon of choice of the impotent . . . I find myself—I, a man—in a world where words wrap themselves in silence; in a world where the other endlessly hardens himself . . . My life should not be devoted to drawing up the balance sheet of Negro values . . . In the world through which I travel, I am endlessly creating myself . . . I am my

own foundations. My final prayer: O my body, make of me always a man who questions!"[10]

> (2) Individualism is the first to disappear. The native intellectual had learnt from his masters that the individual ought to express himself fully. The colonialist bourgeoisie had hammered into the native's mind the idea of a society of individuals where each person shuts himself up in his own subjectivity, whose only wealth is individual thought. Now the native who has the opportunity to return to the people during the struggle for freedom will discover the falseness of this theory."[11]

To be sure, much happened in the eleven years separating Fanon's polarized positions. Can we say, simplistically, that he transcended his early reactionary individualism, that he attained the "intellectual decolonization" advocated by Sekou Toure? But Toure, even as he attacks "the individualistic and racist heresies of which the black world will have been the last and most tragic victim," also recommends that one "re-adapt oneself to one's deep-seated values, to one's own activity, to one's peculiar mentality."[12] What is one's peculiar mentality if not individualistic? The rehtoric is confusing, snarled. To be an individual is reactionary, to be committed to 'mankind' is a racist ploy to mask the oppression of concrete communities, to return to The People is to achieve salvation; to espouse the fervor of Negro values is to reveal inner impotence, to avoid individual thought is to betray one's own concrete deep-seated values, activity, and peculiar mentality. To be committed to a cause—any cause, be it The Whole Human Family or The People—is to attempt to escape from the self; to be committed to the Self is to close off avenues of community action, and thus to insure continued oppression.

Consider the reflections of Richard Sennett:

> We are beginning to see in certain social upheavals a familiar and depressing character type, a new leader consumed by a desire for a more human order yet who also reveals a terrible kind of inhumanity, a rigid, insatiable search for a life he can never achieve. The flowering of a pain-transcending, timeless ideal seems to push such leaders to act in ways that contradict the humanity and openness of the specific reforms they espouse.[13]

The ideals of Berl Trout, or Imari Obadele, or Frantz Fanon—they all involve the killing of people, in the name of The People. "There's no such thing as a nonviolent revolution," said Malcolm X; "revolution is bloody, revolution is hostile, revolution knows no compromise, revolution overturns and destroys everything that gets in its way."[14] Must not, then, revolution or counter-revolution destroy the very values it professes to stand for—be they values oriented to a community or to the preservation of individual freedom?

Consider again the view of Richard Sennett:

> The feeling of common identity . . . is a counterfeit of experience. People *talk* about their understanding

of each other and of the common ties that bind them, but the images are not true to their actual relations. But the lie they have formed as their common image is a usable falsehood—a myth—for the group . . . But in the purification of a coherent community image, fear rather than love of men's 'otherness' prevails. Out of this fear is bred the counterfeit of experience. The 'we' feeling, which expresses a desire to be similar, is a way for men to avoid the necessity of looking deeper into each other.[15]

At what point does the 'myth' of The People cease to be viable and become an instrument of oppression—practiced either by the individual upon himself, through deliberate self-deception, or by the community he pretends to support? To protect the myth, the community must purge all elements of discord, all evidence of essential differences, including factors within its own structure (reflective intellectuals). Conversely, the act of Berl Trout, justified in the name of all mankind, entails the suppression of his own people. But are we, is anyone, in a privileged position and thus able to make such judgments? Are we not all implicated? Yet, given the stakes (literally, survival), can we afford not to judge?

Yes, many would insist. For to ask such questions is to exhibit precisely the reactionary intellectualism encouraged by the forces of oppression. The conquered must be kept divided; ideally, the divisiveness will arise and be maintained within themselves.

But consider the recent assessment made by Carolyn Rodgers:

> Fantasy can be good (imagination is a better word), but also destructive, as it can totally remove us from harsh realities. It can obscure and create erratic unrealistic self-destructive behavior . . . We have screamed our hurt enough . . . We have ridiculed the hunkie but we still have not dealt with who we are, how we feel, *really,* how we live, *truly.*[16]

Berl Trout surely swims through a destructive fantasy. Which of us does not? Yet we do judge him—and ourselves—because we must, if we are to engage what Carolyn Rodgers calls the "WHOLE TRUTH." For Berl Trout, as he himself realizes, is "doomed to die" (2), to be replaced by . . . whom? Perhaps by someone with a more destructive fantasy? Someone like Bernard Belgrave and his 'myth' of the Imperium? Someone like Imari Obadele and his 'myth' of the RNA? Beset with ambiguity, still we must judge, for we are implicated in both. Griggs offers reflective perspectives, but no resolution.

The problematic of the narrative position, then, mirrors the central issue of the novel as a whole. Take, for example, a definitive episode, one that leads to Bernard's radical commitment to the Imperium. His dream of marrying Viola is doomed, for she has determined to fight "the evil" of miscegenation, which she views as a white plot to sap the integrity and vitality of pure Blackness.

Because of this stance, her "first step was to solemnly pledge God to never marry a mulatto man" and thereby further pollute the Race. Unfortunately, Bernard is a mulatto man. Their marriage, accordingly, is "not to be"; for, decides Viola, "I had to choose between you and my race" (175). She chooses the Race—and commits suicide, instructing Bernard to "lead our people forth from this accursed land," assuring him that in so doing she "shall not have died in vain." At first, the issue seems clear enough: Viola is heroic in her willingness to sacrifice herself for the People. Moreover, the narrator is predictably uneasy by this racial commitment and attempts to blur the scene with a flood of mawkish, sentimental rhetoric: "Dropping a tear of regret on the little darling who failed to remember that we have one atonement for all mankind and that further sacrifice was therefore needless, we pass out and leave the loving ones along with their dead" (175). Indeed, Viola's involvement with the destiny of the Race is preferable to Trout's pious reminder of some "Atonement of all mankind," not to mention the grotesque hypocrisy of his vision of this proud woman who represents all that threatens his own untenable position, this vision of her as "the little darling." Is it such an episode that leads Robert Bone to refer to Griggs' "fanatical Negro nationalism"?

A slight pause, however, reveals flaws in such a hasty interpretation. Viola is an extremely ambiguous spokeswoman for black nationalism: she is, we are informed, "exceedingly tender of heart" (162), given to melodramatic fits of screaming (173), very much the self-conscious Heroine of a romantic novel. Her views on miscegenation—scientifically, politically, emotionally ludicrous as they are—are based entirely on a book she happened to read. Her fervor is suspect. "I do not trust fervor," wrote Fanon; "every time it has burst out somewhere, it has brought fire, famine, misery . . . And contempt for man."[17] Passionate fervor seems generated by the spirit of abstraction and breeds, in turn, unrealistic self-destructive behavior, In the case of Viola's fantasy, it is literally suicidal. Is Griggs suggesting that commitment to any such 'myth' (the myth of Black purity — what Fanon once called, abstractly, "The *Fraud* of a black world"[18]) is, by definition, self-destructive? Or does he 'intend' us to distinguish between Viola's misplaced idealism and Bernard's firm determination to free the Race? Viola signs her conspicuously contrived suicide-note as "Viola Belgrave"—yet she has not married Bernard; indeed, her refusal to become his wife motivated her own death. Does Griggs suggest that Bernard is, in a sense, 'married' to Viola anyway, and thereby contaminated by her suicidal dedication to abstractions? To be sure, Bernard turns to the broader social contest and decides that "these abominable horrors shall cease" and that the Race "must separate," for "Viola demands it and Bernard obeys" (176). Yet this only gives rise to further questions: we must ask whether Bernard's involvement with the Imperium is due to his commitment to the People or to his commitment to the memory of the dead Viola. Are the "horrors" he would end those inflicted on his people—or are they those reflecting only his frustration at not possessing the object of his personal desire? Of course, Viola's motive (choosing the Race) may be admirable, and her act foolish; similarly, Bernard's motive may be foolish, and his act (leading the Imperium) admirable. Trout clearly feels that both figures are misguided, but we cannot trust Trout in any case. And Griggs neutrally exposes the complexity of the situation, leaving us to judge. If we can. For which of us can be sure of his own motivation, permeated with ambiguity as every active choice must be?

Such ambivalence dominates this novel. Opposed (seemingly) to Bernard's vision is his mirrored *Doppelganger*, Belton Peidmont. At first, his position seems clear, reflecting a point of view suspiciously like that of the narrator. Thus, Belton appears to fit the classic definition of the House Nigger, as formulated (abstractly?) by Malcolm X: "If the master's house caught on fire, the house Negro would fight harder to put the blaze out than the master would . . . He identified himself with his master, more than the master identified with himself. And if you came to the house Negro and said, 'Let's run away, let's escape, let's separate,' the house Negro would look at you and say, 'Man, you crazy. What you mean, separate? Where is there a better house than this?'"[19] Archetypically, Belton's early graduation speech lauds "The Contribution of the Anglo-Saxon to the Cause of Human Liberty" (32); his final plea for moderation, an attempt to blunt the revolutionary fervor of Bernard's leadership of the Imperium, reaffirms his love of the master's house:

> While all of the other races of men were behind the ball of progress rolling it up the steep hill of time, the negro was asleep in the jungles of Africa. (231)

> Allow me to note this great fact: that by enslavement in America the negro has come into possession of the great English language. He is thus made heir to all the richest thoughts of earth. (232)

> Nor must we ever forget that it was the Anglo-Saxon who snatched from our idolatrous grasp the deaf images to which we prayed, and the Anglo-Saxon who pointed us to the lamb of God that takes away the sins of the world. (232)

> We must change the conception which the Anglo-Saxon has formed of our character. (244)

> Our beloved President, in his message to this Congress, made a serious mistake when he stated that there were only two weapons to be used in accomplishing revolutions. He named the sword (and spear) and ballot. There is a weapon mightier than either of these. I speak of the pen. If denied the use of the ballot let us devote our attention to that mightier, weapon, the pen. (246)

And so on. Seemingly a grim parody of the sort of "accomodation' recommended by Booker T. Washington, who infamously announced: "it is at the bottom of life we must begin, and not at the top. Nor should we permit our grievances to overshadow our opportunities . . . The wisest among my race understand that the agitation of questions of social equality is the extremest folly, and that progress in the enjoyment of all the privileges that will come to us must be the result of severe and constant struggle rather than of artificial forcing."[20] So: the slaves should be grateful; after all, they have been well paid—in the coin of the English language, western religion, and 'progress'—and, anyway, artificial forcing (that is, standing for human dignity) is the extremest folly. The anti-logic is patently grotesque, and tragic in its implications. Nor can we overlook the oddly prophetic foreshadowing of Malcolm's insistence on choosing between "the bullet and the ballot." If anything, Griggs is too obvious: Belton = The House Nigger.

Moreover, Griggs hints at some of the elements that might lead to such a colonized spirit. Belton's mother is a parody of the equally archetypal 'Black Mammy,' inculcating the values of ('white') respectability and ('white') education. "There was a conflict in her bosom between her love and her ambition" (15), we are told; the warped ambition triumphs and seemingly justified E. Franklin Frazier's reflections on the sickness of the Black Bourgeoisie. Belton's education is accordingly processed. He accepts the self-serving advice of Mr. King, the familiar White Liberal: "Always seek for and appeal to that [good] side of their [white] nature" (47). At college, he learns to beseech God "to enable him and his people, as a mark of appreciation of what had been done for the race, to rise to the full measure of just expectation and prove worthy of all the care bestowed" (51); "the deepest passion of his soul," obviously, becomes "Equality of the races" (55). He subsequently permits himself to be infatuated with a light-skinned woman, courts her in a manner sure to delight anyone steeped in sickly sentimentality. He is outraged when their child turns out to be light-skinned—assuming that she has consorted with a white man—but is equally disconcerted when (magically, it seems) the child becomes progressively darker, "until he was a shade darker than his father" (256). Symbolizing, no doubt, the hint of future rejection of bourgeois values by coming generations. When he earns, in spite of himself, the anger of some white townspeople and is threatened with lynching, "he made no resistance, having unshaken faith in God" (155). And so on. "Since the world of make-believe cannot insulate the black bourgeoisie completely from the world of reality," Frazier pointed out, "the members of this class exhibit considerable confusion and conflict in their personalities."[21]

Apparently, he joins the Imperium, even helps to organize it, only to subvert it, to instill in it the spirit of abstract accomodation, to ensure against its leading to the fiery destruction of the Master's house: "I love the Union and I love the South" (252), Belton unabashedly admits. How can we avoid concurring in Bernard's harshly apt judgment of the spineless Belton: "If I live I shall surely proclaim your infamy to our people and slay you besides. The curse of our doomed race is just such white folks' niggers as you are" (184)? "Know the real enemy," advises Don Lee[22]; and the real enemy, instructs Malcolm, is "Negroes who are nothing but modern Uncle Toms, twentieth-century Uncle Toms, to keep you and me in check, to keep us under control, keep us passive and peaceful and non-violent."[23] When it gets down, Toms must be offed, even before the man is taken on, everyone knows that, right?

So simple, so straightforward, surely we can have no difficulty in judging the misguided Belton? At first, the mere fact that Berl Trout so blatantly idolizes him is enough to earn our contempt. But then: it seems too simple, too straightforward. We must reflect further.

At the start, we note a strange inversion of the archetype: most often, the modern Tom is portrayed as a Black Intellectual—recall Chesnutt's Dr. Miller, Wright's Cross Damon, or Baldwin's Leo Proudhammer; often, also, this figure is conspicuously light-skinned (symbolizing his orientation to 'whiteness'). But Belton is emphatically Black (the more radical Bernard, in an ironic inversion of the myth, is light-skinned); and Belton is far closer to the 'soil,' to the People, than the remote and aristocratic Bernard could ever be. Moreover, Belton's mother, for all her bourgeois aspirations, has the strength and vitality, the determination (if perhaps misdirected) of the Black Peasant; Bernard's mother, on the other hand, was the mistress of a white senator and radiates pride in her cultural attainments (a most prominent characteristic of the Black Bourgeoisie). It is Belton who first joins the Imperium, for whatever motive; it is Belton who alone strikes down a white oppressor, although his instinctive attempt to seek protection from the white governor of the state makes it difficult to interpret this episode (157-158). It is Belton who continually considers the most effective political tactics, who believes that open warfare must be suicidal, that a carefully modulated policy of developing a growing political base of power is necessary, and who warns against acting out of rage or the lust for revenge—motives which can only blind the organization and lead it into a suicidal holocaust. We cannot help but recall that Malcolm X, although he warned of the coming choice of the bullet over the ballot, often warned (ironically?) against "forming rifle clubs and going out looking for people" and finally opted for a larger perspective: "My mind is wide open to anybody [including whites] who will help get the ape off our backs."[24] Belton's motives are obviously suspect. But can the content of his advice be so easily dismissed?

We note, also, that when Belton is ultimately executed for betraying the Imperium, Bernard appears to succumb to a literally insane and self-destructive lust for revenge: he determines to destroy white America for the personal injuries inflicted on him, for putting him in the role of a bastard unacknowledged by his white father, for looking on his mother as a harlot, for making Viola's suicide (a charge for which no evidence is supplied in the novel), for forcing him to kill his friend. No pious dedication to the freedom of his People; Anglo-Saxons must become "richer food for the buzzards" because Bernard Belgrave

has been insulted and ill-used (263). An ominous ego-trip? Or was this central to his motivation all along?

If we are willing to reflect honestly, how many messiahs set out to reform the world—'reforms' seen essentially as a means of redressing the personal affront to their self-image? Can we dismiss the warning of Dr. Lovejoy, the dangerously vapid president of Belton's processed university? That warning against the possible consequences of accepting "the designation of a hero": "I exhort you to not play with fire, merely for the sake of the glare that it may cast upon you. Use no crisis of self-aggrandizement . . . If you heed my voice, you shall become true patriots. If you disregard, it, you will become time-serving demagogues, playing upon the passions of the people for the sake of short-lived notoriety" (66-67)? Indeed. But how are we to distinguish between the True Patriots and the demagogues? "We must not voodoo the people, nor dissolve them in emotion and confusion," warned Fanon; and he was particularly fearful of a leader whose "contact with the masses is so unreal that he comes to believe that his authority is hated and that the services that he has rendered are being called in question. The leader judges the ingratitude of the masses harshly, and every day that passes ranges himself a little more resolutely on the side of the exploiters."[25] Is not Bernard dangerously close to embodying Fanon's fears?

The line between the individual who sacrifices himself unselfishly for the People and the individual who responds primarily to an inner need for glorified recognition—that line is narrow, difficult to trace, perhaps impossibly ambiguous. We are necessarily situated in the present, feeling the burden of that present together with the weighty echoes of the past, struggling to respond unselfishly and to anchor our own freedom in the freedom of all; yet it is, ultimately, *our* situation, and our perceptions are inescapably bound to that centrality of our sense of Self. Who, after reflecting on the inner complexities and contradictions of his feelings, thoughts and deeds, would presume to accept the designation of Hero? Or are the truest heroes those who systematically refrain from self-reflection and who passionately commit themselves to concrete action? But they might also be the truest demagogues. And how are we to judge? And yet we must, somehow; for the real enemy may not be the oppressor, or the collaborator—but rather the incipient dictator who begins in sincerity but who becomes increasingly motivated by the need to purify and protect his self-image.

Because we live in a nation seemingly hovering on the brink of racial war, we are implicated by the very fact of our existence in these times. Berl Trout's judgment appears intolerable. He mourns "the spirit of conservatism" that died with Belton, although there may be a mixture of ironic uncertainty when he adds, "He was the last of that peculiar type of Negro heroes that could so fondly kiss the smiting hand" (262). In spite of the terrible difficulties in assessing the inner motives of Bernard, must not his vision become at least preferable? Yet can we, authentically, ignore Trout's sense that the "well-organized, thoroughly equipped Imperium was a serious menace to the peace of the world," that it might result in "a conflagration, which, unchecked, would spread destruction and death all around" (263)? Of course: in the Cause of Freedom, destruction and death must be justifiable, perhaps inevitable, certainly necessary . . . But Trout's anguished sense of the approaching apocalypse must haunt us, today, aware as we cannot help but be of its immanent possibility:

> I felt that beneath the South a mine had been dug and filled with dynamite, and that lighted fuses were lying around in careless profusion, where any irresponsible hand might reach them and ignite the dynamite. I fancied that I saw a man do this very thing in a sudden fit of uncontrollable rage. There was a dull roar as of distant rumbling thunder. Suddenly there was a terrific explosion and houses, fences, trees, pavement stones, and all things on earth were hurled high into the air to come back a mass of ruins such as man never before had seen. The only sound to be heard was a universal groan; those who had not been killed were too badly wounded to cry out. (264).

We, who have heard that thunder already in dimensions that Griggs could scarcely envision—we, who have seen the ruins of post-war Europe, the blank despair in the faces of bombed-out Japan, the seemingly endless destruction of southeast Asia—we, who have heard the groans of a generation of refugees throughout the world—how are we to judge which hands are responsible and admirable, and which are tainted with self-destructive rage?

In 1945, Maurice Merleau-Ponty struggled to understand the enduring significance of the Nazi Occupation of his nation. With determined courage and in spite of his own commitment to the Resistance, he discovered that "when we looked closely at things, we find culprits nowhere but accomplices everywhere."[26] He was himself inclined to accept the many-faceted importance of the individual, the unique and necessarily concrete situatedness of the isolated man; yet he found himself in a world in which people were tortured *because* they were "Frenchmen," in which people were exterminated *because* they were "Jews"—a world, that is, which turned a myth into a frightening reality. "An anti-Semite," he observed, "could not stand to see Jews tortured if he really saw them, if he perceived that suffering and agony in an individual life—but this is just the point: he does not see Jews suffering; he is blinded by the myth of *the* Jew. He tortures and murders the Jew through these concrete beings; he struggles with dream figures, and his blows strike living faces."[27] And did not the individuals in the Resistance, themselves, struggle also with dream figures, with "Collaborators." whom they could not afford to see as individuals? And do we not have our own living faces to haunt us, the terror in the eyes of the Vietnamese woman moments before the torturous events at My Lai? Who is not an accomplice? No one's hands are clean.

More recently, James Baldwin expressed the anguish of similar ambiguity in *Tell Me How Long the Train's Been Gone*. Leo Proudhammer participates in a civil rights rally and feels a powerful sense of 'community': "Yes, we on the platform were united in our social indignation, united in our affliction, united in our responsibility"; yet he simultaneously experiences his own personal estrangement, the realization that no one else could "imagine such a journey as my own."[28] Is Leo merely the victim of a colonized spirit? He listens to a young black girl sing about "deliverance," an optimistic gesture of hope—and he marvels at her innocence when she later seems to enjoy the food provided at the rally: "Then I wondered if I was right to give her a fried chicken dinner which she could enjoy. Maybe I should have given her a dinner which would cause her to overthrow the table and burn down the house. But I did not want her to vomit or to burn: I wanted her to live."[29] Wherever he turns, Leo discovers undecipherable ambiguity, the duality that Griggs projected into the separate characters of Belton and Bernard:

> I was beginning to apprehend the unutterable dimensions of the universal trap. I was human, too. And my race was revealed as my pain—my pain—and my rage could have no reason, nor submit to my domination until my pain was assessed; until my pain became invested with a coherence and an authority which only I, alone, could provide.[30]

The universal trap: I am human in a world which disavows, systematically, my humanity; I am situated within a community of others, yet would maintain the integrity of my own being—which seems to isolate me from that same community; my acts must be founded on some sort of coherence and authority—yet they are only *my* acts, and the authority I, alone, can provide, even as I cannot seem to trust the authority which I ultimately *am*. I am haunted by the possibility that it is already too late, that the train's been gone, long gone, and that, like Leo, I shall find myself, "Presently, standing in the wings again, waiting for my cue."[31] If I follow Belton's way, I may gain some sense of inner coherence, but will always bear the burden of doubt as to my relationship and responsibility to my immediate community; if I follow Bernard's way, I may gain a sense of active purpose and togetherness with others, but will always bear the burden of doubt as to my own motives and right to proclaim my authority. The price of thoughtful reflection may well be paralysis, yet the price of willed blindness must be oppression; to obey with one's eyes closed is the beginning of panic, yet to perceive and to question is to risk sinking beneath staggering ambiguity.

Such are some of the reflections provoked by Griggs' novel. Who is not, in a sense, a nation within a nation, a mixture of tangled motives and conflicting feelings? Might that not be the WHOLE TRUTH? But who would dare to tell it? Who would risk such an ambiguous adventure?

> I find myself suddenly in the world and I recognize that I have one right alone: That of demanding human behavior from the other.

One duty alone: That of not renouncing my freedom through my choices.

—Frantz Fanon, *Black Skin, White Masks*

"Appearance and its reflections sparkle and crackle. Shall you not regret appearance and its reflections?" . . .

"No. I am tired of this closed circle. My thought always returns upon myself, reflected by appearance, when, seized by disquiet, I have thrown it out like a tentacle."

"But it returns to you. Toward whatever side you turn, it is your own countenance that you see, nothing but that. You alone fill the closed circle."

—Cheikh Hamidou Kane, *Ambiguous Adventure*

NOTES

[1] "The Harlem Renaissance: Towards a Black Aesthetic," *Midcontinent American Studies Journal*, XI (Fall 1970) 82.

[2] *The Negro Novel in America*, Revised Edition (New Haven, 1958), p. 33.

[3] "The New Black Literature: Protest of Affirmation," *The Black Aesthetic*, edited by Addison Gayle, Jr. (Garden City, 1971), p. 352.

[4] "Sutton Griggs, Novelist of the New Negro," *Phylon*, IV (1943), 337-338.

[5] Sutton Griggs, *Imperium in Imperio*, with a preface by Hugh M. Gloster (New York, 1969), pp. vi-vii. All further references to *Imperium in Imperio* will be to this edition.

[6] *Ibid.*, p. iii.

[7] "The Struggle Is for Land," *The Black Scholar*, III (February 1972), 24-36.

[8] *Man Against Mass Society*, translated by G. S. Fraser (Chicago, 1962), pp. 1, 155-156.

[9] *Man Against Mass Society*, p. 155.

[10] *Black Skin, White Masks*, translated by Charles Markmann (New York, 1967), pp. 7, 9, 229, 230, 231.

[11] *The Wretched of the Earth*, translated by Constance Farrington (New York, 1963), p. 47.

[12] "The African Elite in the Anti-Colonial Struggle," *The Black Scholar*, III (January 1972), 2-11.

[13] *The Uses of Disorder*, (New York, 1970), p. 21.

[14] "Message to the Grass Roots," *Malcolm X Speaks* (New York, 1966), p. 9.

[15] *The Uses of Disorder*, pp. 36-39.

[16] "Uh Nat'chal Thang—The WHOLE TRUTH—US," *Black World* (September 1971), pp. 7, 9.

[17] *Black Skin, White Masks*, p. 9.

[18] *Ibid.*, p. 229.

[19] "Message to the Grass Roots," pp. 10-11.

[20] *Up From Slavery*, in *Three Negro Classics* (New York, 1965), pp. 147, 149.

[21] *Black Bourgeoisie* (New York, 1957), p. 25.

[22] "A Poem to Complement Other Poems," *Don't Cry, Scream* (Detroit, 1969), p. 37.

[23] "Message to the Grass Roots," p. 12.

[24] *Malcolm X Speaks*, pp. 43, 213.

[25] *The Wretched of the Earth*, pp. 200, 166.

[26] *Sense and Non-Sense*, translated by Hubert L. and Patricia A. Dreyfus, (Evanston, 1964), p. 141.

[27] *Ibid.*, p. 143.

[28] (New York, 1969), p. 84.

[29] *Ibid.*, p. 87.

[30] *Ibid.*, p. 76.

[31] *Ibid.*, p. 370.

Roger Whitlow (essay date 1978)

SOURCE: "The Revolutionary Black Novels of Martin R. Delany and Sutton Griggs," in *Melus*, Vol. 5, No. 3, Fall, 1978, pp. 26-36.

[*In the following essay, Whitlow compares and contrasts* Imperium in Imperio *with Martin Delany's novel of slave revolt,* Blake.]

From the outset of the Black experience in America there has existed a plethora of interpretations of what role blacks do have in the operation and values of the country, as well as of how blacks should respond to the country and its laws and institutions—and ambivalence has always prevailed. The early arguments (white initiated, but, in part, black endorsed) ran: slavery is not the best of conditions, and it is, indeed, trying to be considered a cipher in the eyes of both social convention and the law, but there is an opportunity to have a religious experience [read: *Christian* experience] which otherwise would be lacking in black lives. It never was a good argument, of course, and it broke down for most people, black and white, who could think at all by the turn of the nineteenth century.

But later a more perplexing ambivalence emerged—made more perplexing by the fact that, following Emancipation, blacks did seem to have some options—oppression (social, political, economic, and legal) on one hand, as against the *promise* (and occasional actuality) of opportunity in all of those areas, on the other. Was open revolt still called for? If so, to what *specific* end? Or should America and her various corruptions simply be abandoned? If so, in favor of what new geographical location? Or was perpetual "in-house" agitation against injustice the most practical course of action? Obviously, given the relatively few revolts and the relatively few blacks who have abandoned America—historically, most black Americans have chosen this last option.

It is probably equally accurate to say, however, that many of the best black minds have argued, with conviction and logic, the wisdom of the other positions. Two such thinkers and writers were Martin R. Delany, a physician and social theorist, and Sutton Griggs, a Baptist minister and race lecturer. What these men have in common is that they wrote the only two revolutionary novels written by black Americans in the nineteenth century, Delany's *Blake; or, The Huts of America* (published serially, intermittently, between 1859 and 1862), and Griggs's *Imperium in Imperio* (1899). The theories of black revolution in the novels, however, take substantially different directions. Delany, writing before the Emancipation Proclamation, used as a revolutionary model a by then familiar slave-insurrection scheme like the ones planned by Gabriel Prosser in 1800, Denmark Vesey in 1822, Nat Turner in 1831, and John Brown in 1859.

Griggs, on the other hand, broke new ground with a plan calling for confiscating a specific region of the United States (in this case, Texas), for evicting the white residents, and for turning that region into a black nation. Griggs's idea is only partly like the historical plan of Edwin McCabe, who in 1889-90 attempted to attract large numbers of blacks to the Oklahoma Territory so that when Oklahoma became a state, blacks would have numerical superiority, hence statewide political control; unfortunately for McCabe, who, unlike one of Griggs's heroes, viewed himself as a politician rather than as a black nationalist, white migration into the Territory proved so considerable as to preserve white numerical superiority, though McCabe did help found a number of all-black towns, like Langston. Griggs' idea was, in fact, a prototype, a prophetic version of what would emerge in the 1930s (and again, more loudly, in the 1960s) with Muhammed Fard, Elijah Muhammed, and their Black Muslim doctrine of black separatism.

Martin Delany took a very personal interest in insurrectionary ideas and movements. Jean Fagan Yellin records Delany's historic "Chatham meeting" with John Brown in 1858:

Although what happened at Chatham [Canada] is disputed, historians agree that at Brown's request Martin R. Delany arranged for a number of black men to meet with Brown and a dozen of his Kansas followers in a small schoolhouse on May 8, 1858. There he introduced Brown, who according to minutes kept by one of his men, explained "the general features of the plan of action in the execution of the project. Mr. Delany and others spoke in favor of the project and the plan, and both were agreed to by general consent." After Delany moved that they swear an oath of secrecy, in the name of "citizens of the United States, and the oppressed people," they considered a "Provisional Constitution" which outlined a government appropriate to a group waging guerrilla warfare. Delany and the other members of the Convention adopted and signed the document, elected officers of the provisional government, and made John Brown commander-in-chief.[1]

Eight months later, Delany wrote his only novel, *Blake; or The Huts of America*[2] which Yellin describes as "a revolutionary handbook outlining the organization of a guerrilla army of black liberationists."[3] The most authoritative writer on the life of Martin Delany, Victor Ullman, says that *Blake*'s "real contributions [are] not to literature, but to a knowledge of the slaves."[4] Indeed, the novel, though absorbing, does have literary weaknesses, the chief being the stilted language of the protagonist Henry Blake, who is Cuban-born and well-educated, but who was sold illegally into American slavery by the captain of a ship on which he was working. Typical of Blake's language in his own explanation of his plans: "I now impart to you the secret, it is this: I have laid a scheme, and matured a plan for a general insurrection of the slaves in every state, and the successful overthrow of slavery" (p. 39)—rather pedantic, actually.

The novel is weak—or perhaps naive—too, in its assumption that an individual like Blake could move throughout the South, as well as throughout Cuba, and single-handedly set in motion something as hugely complicated as two simultaneous national race revolutions. For all of that, *Blake* is a fascinating novel, and though it is not, as Floyd Miller describes it, "clearly the most important black novel of this period and, for the social historian, one of the most significant and revealing novels ever written by an Afro-American,"[5] it remains a useful compendium of ante-bellum slave conditions, as well as a well articulated model of that slave-insurrection plan which many, black and white, considered during the nineteenth century—and which a few did try.

Delany understood well the entangling legal-economic-social-political network which many have called the "slavocracy." *Blake* opens near Natchez, Mississippi, on the plantation of Colonel Stephen Franks. His house guests are Northerners with property interests in Cuba. Mrs. Ballard tells him, "You, I'm sure, Colonel, know very well that in our country commercial interests have taken precedence of all others, which is a sufficient guarantee of our fidelity to the South" (p. 4). And, sometime later, her husband, Judge Ballard, explains his opinion of the position of blacks before the law:

> My opinion, sir, is a matter of record, being the first judge before whom a case was tested, which resulted in favor of the South. And I go further than this; I hold as a just construction of the law, that not only has the slaveholder a right to reclaim his slave when and wherever found, but by its provision every free black in the country, North and South, are [sic] liable to enslavement by any white person. They are freemen by sufferance or slaves-at-large, whom any white person may claim at discretion. It was a just decision of the Supreme Court—though I was in advance of it by action—that persons of African descent have no rights that white men are bound to respect! (p. 61)

Both Martin Delany and his protagonist Henry Blake recognize that this system is collapsible only through violent force. Maggie, Blake's wife, is sold to the Ballards and is later taken to Havana—hence the later Cuban connection. Henry Blake, in reality a free man, has suffered slavery in order to be with her and their child. When he returns from a trip he had been sent on by Colonel Franks and finds his wife gone, Blake becomes furious, and begins immediately to set his plan in motion. Taking a "note of passage" from Colonel Franks, Blake leaves the plantation, saying to other slaves as he goes: "You may see me in six months, and might not in eighteen. I am determined, now that I am driven to it, to complete an organization in every slave state before I return, and have fixed two years as my utmost limit" (p. 42). With that Blake—in a plan incredibly more comprehensive than anything Denmark Vesey or George Boxley ever dreamed of—moves secretly by night from the "huts" (slave cabins) of one plantation to those of another, explaining his rather vague plan for general uprising and seeking support. As Blake travels, Delany has an opportunity to enumerate instances of brutality directed toward blacks, thus pointing out that his way (and Blake's) is the only one. On a Mississippi plantation the reader is shown what was to become a stock feature of nineteenth-century black fiction, an astonishing example of white cruelty—in this case an overseer forcing a bizarre performance from a small slave boy for the amusement of his employer's guests:

> Shortly there came forward, a small black boy about eleven years of age, thin visage, projecting upper teeth, rather ghastly consumptive look, and emaciated condition. The child trembled with fear as he approached the group.
>
> "Now gentlemen," said Grason, "I'm going to show you a sight!" having in his hand a long whip, the cracking of which he commenced, as a ringmaster in the circus. . . .
>
> "Wat maus gwine do wid me now? I know wat maus gwine do," said this miserable child, "he gwine make me see sights!" when going down on his hands and feet, he commenced trotting around like an animal.

> "Now, gentlemen, look!" said Grason. "He'll whistle, sing songs, hymns, pray, swear like a trooper, laugh, and cry, all under the same state of feelings."
>
> With a peculiar swing of the whip, bringing the lash down upon a certain spot on the exposed skin, the whole person being prepared for the purpose, the boy commenced to whistle almost like a thrush; another cut changed it to a song, another to a hymn, then a pitiful prayer, when he gave utterance to oaths which would make a Christian shudder, after which he laughed outright; then from a fullness of his soul he cried:
>
> "O maussa, I's sick! Please stop little!" casting up gobs of hemorrhage. (p. 67)

Blake is forced to kill a threatening overseer in Mississippi, then he moves on to Texas, then to Arkansas, about which Blake [Delany] makes one of his many regional judgments: "Neither the robes of state nor gown of authority is sufficient to check the vengeance of awakened wrath in Arkansas. Law is but a fable, its administration a farce" (p. 88). About Virginia, Blake says, "The restrictions here concerning Negroes and mulattos are less rigid" (p. 115). And about the "good treatment" accorded slaves in Kentucky, Blake says: "That's the very mischief of it. . . . 'Tis this confounded 'good treatment' and expectation of getting freed by their oppressors, that has been the curse of the slave. All shrewd masters, to keep their slaves in check, promise them their freedom at their, the master's death, as though they were certain to die first" (p. 127).

In Part II, set in Cuba, where he has traveled in search of his wife, Blake encounters numerous examples of Cuban mistreatment of slaves: one of whom is a man named George, once spirited, but now after consistent beatings, subjugated: "He's completely broken, sir, and humble as a dog. The last chastisement that Goodman gave completely reduced him, taking out the last remnant of his manhood, so that he's as spiritless as a kitten" (p. 175). The social climate in Cuba is very tense. The revolutionary poet, Placido, Blake's cousin, is stirring the same discontentment among the slaves that Blake stirred in the American South—and Blake joins him in his efforts.

At this point the black nationalist organization takes on a normal structure with the creation of a provisional government:

> The provisional organization consisted of Placido, Director of Civil Government; Minister of State, Camina; Minister of Justice, Carolus Blacus; Minister of Foreign Affairs, Castina; Postmaster General, Antonio Blacus; Minister of War and Navy, Montego.
>
> The Army regulations were: Henry Blake, Commander in Chief of the Army of Emancipation; Juan Montego, General of First Division; Pedro Castina, General of Second Division; Ferdinand Recaud, General Third Division; Stephen Rivera,

General of Fourth Division; Gofer Gondolier, Quartermaster General. Thus organized, the oppressed became a dangerous element in the political ingredients of Cuba.

Already the atmosphere of sentiments began to change, the weather of prospects to alter, the sunlight of promise grow dim, the day of anticipation darker, and clouds of the downtrodden were seen in specks, to gather throughout the island. The signs of the public zodiac were warningly significant of an approaching storm, though a great way off, yet the calculation of the political calendar paid no attention to it.

Moved by a solemn sense of the import of the momentous subject before them, and the great responsibility of the undertaking, Blake in a few words thus impressingly addressed them:

"Brethren, sisters, men and women of Cuba!—The like of tonight's gathering, save in a neighboring island years before any of us had an existence, in this region is without a parallel; and as the Lord lives, and my soul bears witness that he does, I will do all that in my power lies to carry out the decrees of this Council!" (pp. 256-57)

Here the novel, in its present form, ends (the final installment has remained lost); and so, the reader never learns whether the American and Cuban revolutions which are ready for triggering, actually take place or what the outcome might be—though the fate of the numerous insurrections tried in nineteenth-century America would suggest dim possibilities of success indeed, at least in the United States.

It is really an unendable plot anyway. The necessity of plausibility suggests the certain failure of one or the other of the two-step revolutionary scheme (as nearly all of the well-known slave insurrections were): 1) set the revolutionary catapult for release, and 2) release it. Even if Gabriel's thousand or more armed slaves had not been turned back by the torrential rains and thoughts of bad omens and had actually killed all of the whites that they encountered in Richmond; even if Nat's troops had not fallen into disorder and had killed 6,000 white plantation dwellers instead of 60; even if John Brown had not been trapped in the arsenal at Harper's Ferry, and, further, if nearby slaves actually had shown up at the schoolhouse to receive arms, and further yet, if they all had started their "wave of freedom" across the countryside—what then? All of these plans—and Delany's—had in common the notion that slavery could be broken if enough emancipated slaves traveled enough miles and killed enough whites. But it remains an untested plan—and both logic and American social-political-economic-military reality dictate against its ever having been successful.

For a period after Emancipation there was hope for black people to forge ahead in American society, but as the decades passed, Jim Crowism and violence threw up obstacles and a despairing people looked for solutions other than that given by Booker T. Washington at Atlanta

in 1895. In many ways as biting as *Blake* is Sutton Elbert Griggs's *Imperium in Imperio* (1899),[6] based upon the idea of a secret black government in the United States, the leaders of which eventually decide to form a separate black nation in the state of Texas. The novel opens with an announcement from the author, one of those fictional statements of authenticity, which begins:

The papers which are herewith submitted to you for your perusal and consideration, were delivered into my hands by Mr. Berl Trout.

The papers will speak for themselves, but Mr. Trout now being dead I feel called upon to say a word concerning him.

Mr. Berl Trout was Secretary of State in the Imperium in Imperio, from the day of its organization until the hour of his sad death. He was, therefore, thoroughly conversant with all of the details of that great organization. (p. i)

Next comes Berl Trout's own "Dying Declaration," which, in part, reads:

I am a traitor. I have violated an oath that was as solemn and binding as any ever taken by man on earth.

I have trampled under my feet the sacred trust of a loving people, and have betrayed secrets which were dearer to them than life itself.

For this offence, regarded the world over as the most detestable of horrors, I shall be slain.

Those who shall be detailed to escort my foul body to its grave are required to walk backwards with heads averted.

On to-morrow night, the time of my burial, the clouds should gather thick about the queenly moon to hide my funeral procession from her view, for fear that she might refuse to longer reign over a land capable of producing such a wretch as I. . . .

While I acknowledge that I am a traitor, I also pronounce myself a patriot.

It is true that I have betrayed the immediate plans of the race to which I belong; but I have done this in the interest of the whole human family—of which my race is but a part. (pp. 1-2)

Following this excellent dramatic opening, Griggs sets out to explain how the secret black government, the Imperium in Imperio ("the empire within an empire"), originated and how two men, the "pure" black Belton Piedmont and the mulatto Bernard Belgrave, come to be its leaders and how they split, finally, on the direction which the Imperium should take. The action begins in 1867 when Belton, then eight, and Bernard, then nine, enter a Southern "colored school." In keeping with Griggs's plan for making his most noble characters "pure" black (Robert Bone says of Griggs, "He is almost pathologically antiwhite and scarcely less antimulatto"[7]—something of an overstatement), in connection with an oratorical contest in which Belton and Bernard compete, the reader is told that "Bernard did not have the incentive that Belton did" (p. 30). Belton outmatches Bernard in the contest, but the white judges are reluctant to give the award to a black over a mulatto: "That black nigger has beat the yellow one all to pieces this time, but we don't like to see nigger blood triumph over any Anglo-Saxon blood. Ain't there any loop-hole where we can give it to Bernard anyhow?" (p. 35). Even at this early stage of the novel, two ideas are beginning to emerge which will come to maturity in the course of the work: 1) Blacks must work against far longer social odds than mulattos, and 2) Despite this handicap, blacks are more resourceful and honorable than mulattos—and substantially more so than whites.

After graduation from the public schools, the two young men go to college, Bernard to Harvard to study law and the classics, Belton to Stowe University in Nashville to prepare for a career as a teacher. After Belton leads a successful student strike to force an end to segregated dining facilities, the narrator says: "The cringing, fawning, sniffling, cowardly Negro which slavery left, had disappeared, and a new Negro, self-respecting, fearless, and determined in the assertion of his rights was at hand" (p. 62). Bernard, on the other hand, during his experience at Harvard, learns that he is the son of a wealthy United States Senator and that, at his father's death, he will inherit ten million dollars—an astronomical sum at that time, and another effort by Griggs to "load" the case against Bernard for his later purpose.

A few years later, Bernard, who has been elected a Virginia Congressman, receives a brief letter from Belton: "Come to Waco at once" (p. 177). Belton meets Bernard in Waco, Texas, then drives him five miles out of town, where Bernard sees "a high stone wall enclosure. In the middle of the enclosed place, upon a slight elevation, stood a building four stories high and about two hundred feet long and one hundred and eighty feet wide" (p. 178). This, it turns out, though called Thomas Jefferson College, is the seat of government of the Imperium in Imperio; and, after he is "tested" for his race loyalty, Bernard is informed that he has been elected President of the Imperium and that he has several months to decide if he will accept the office.

Bernard is told that the Imperium has existed for years and was originally founded by a wealthy "Negro scientist who won an international reputation by his skill and erudition" (p. 191). He is told, further, that the Imperium has a "well organized judiciary" (p. 195) and a single-branch Congress which "passes laws relating to the general welfare of our people, and whenever a bill is introduced in the Congress of the United States affecting our race it is also introduced and debated here" (p. 195). After examining the government, Bernard "found it well nigh perfect in every part and presented a form of government unexcelled by that of any other nation" (p. 199).

Bernard accepts the Presidency, but, in his opening message to the Imperium, discord between himself and Belton begins to emerge—all the more unbelievably because Bernard, who until now, has been a loyal part of (and has prospered from) the existing American economic and political systems, now becomes almost rabidly militant. As he summarizes the position of blacks in industry, education, the courts, and politics (a very informed summary, incidentally), he concludes that armed revolution is called for, and shortly afterward, a resolution of war is passed by the Imperium, with Belton casting the only negative vote.

Here the novel takes a strange turn, one which may, in part, be explained by Robert Bone's statement that "Griggs's blind impulse toward retaliation and revenge is striving for mastery with a more moderate, and more realistic approach."[8] It has already been noted that Bernard, the "establishment" figure, at this point turns warlike. So there is a reversal in the character of Belton, consistently the rebel throughout the novel, who now, in saying "a few words on behalf of the South," makes such racism-endorsing observations as: "Our grotesque dress, our broken language, our ignorant curiosity, and, on the part of many, our boorish manners, would have been nauseating in the extreme to [white] men and women accustomed to refined association" (p. 235); and "Our race has furnished some brutes lower than the beasts of the field, who have stirred the passions of the Anglo-Saxon as nothing in all of human history has before stirred them" (p. 237).

With this, Belton enters a "moderate" counter-resolution (the age-old moderate-militant social conflict is well articulated here) calling for making public the existence of the Imperium to show whites "that the love of liberty in our bosoms is strong enough to draw us together into this compact government" (p. 244); for spending "four years in endeavors to impress the Anglo-Saxon that he has a New Negro on his hands and must surrender what belongs to him" (p. 245); and, finally, for migrating to "the state of Texas, working out our destiny as a separate and distinct race in the United States of America" (p. 245). Given the hard doses of reality that Belton has experienced throughout the novel, his trust in white America seems naive. He is still Griggs's hero, for Bernard has become an almost hysterical fanatic, presumably showing the mulatto as an unstable personality type.

Now apparently intent upon the actual destruction of the United States, Bernard submits one last resolution—certainly black nationalism with a vengeance—one which is adopted by the Imperium:

> 1. Reconsider our determination to make known the existence of our Imperium, and avoid all mention of an emigration to Texas.

2. Quietly purchase all Texas land contiguous to states and territories of the Union. Build small common-place huts on these lands and place rapid fire disappearing guns in fortifications dug beneath them. All of this is to be done secretly, the money to be raised by the issuance of bonds by the Imperium.

3. Encourage all Negroes who can possibly do so to enter the United States Navy.

4. Enter into secret negotiations with all of the foreign enemies of the United States, acquainting them of our military strength and men aboard the United States war ships.

5. Secure an appropriation from Congress to hold a fair at Galveston, inviting the Governor of Texas to be present. It will afford an excuse for all Negro families to pour into Texas. It will also be an excuse for having the war ships of nations friendly to us, in the harbor for a rendezvous.

6. While the Governor is away, let the troops proceed quietly to Austin, seize the capitol and hoist the flag of the Imperium.

7. We can then, if need be, wreck the entire navy of the United States in a night; the United States will then be prostrate before us and our allies.

8. We will demand the surrender of Texas and Louisiana to the Imperium. Texas, we will retain. Louisiana, we will cede to our foreign allies in return for their aid. Thus will the Negro have an empire of his own, fertile in soil, capable of sustaining a population of fifty million people. (pp. 251-52)

Little is left. Belton resigns from the Imperium, knowing that, according to the constitution, such an act means execution. "Bernard gave the word of command to fire, and Belton fell, a corpse. On the knoll where he fell he was buried, shrouded in an American flag" (p. 261). The Imperium never carries out Bernard's wild plan for revolution, however, for Berl Trout, himself a member, betrays the plan to the American government, and the Imperium is crushed. *Imperium in Imperio* is a fascinating novel, though, like *Blake,* it certainly is, as Hugh Gloster suggests, "fantasy."[9] The idea that seven million two hundred fifty thousand individuals (the black population) could keep such an organization secret is, put mildly, ridiculous—especially when one recalls that nearly all of the groups planning slave uprisings in the nineteenth century, often numbering no more than ten or twenty persons, were betrayed. It is, in fact, as ridiculous as it is pointless for a secret Congress to debate at length bills over which it can never have any influence whatever.

Nonetheless, despite these weaknesses and despite the fact that the reader is never quite sure how far Griggs wants the idea of black nationalism to go, there are valuable insights in the work. For, while back-to-Africa versions of black nationalism had begun as early as 1815 (with the venture of Paul Cuffee, a black American ship-builder and trader, to transport thirty-eight blacks from America to Africa) and had emerged on notable occa-

sions with James Whitfield (with a Central-American variation) and Martin Delany himself in the 1850s, with Henry McNeal Turner at the turn of the century, and with Marcus Garvey in the 1920s, the actual taking of an American region and converting it into a black nation was a concept not seriously popularized until Muhammed Fard in the 1930s. Griggs then, unlike Delany who looks back to the slave-insurrection model, is breaking new ground (Delany does so only insofar as he was the first to introduce the issue of Cuban slavery and, particularly, of simultaneous uprisings) on the matter of race revolution by presenting a scheme which looks forward to a form of black nationalism which would not be seriously considered by many until well into the new century.

NOTES

[1] Jean Fagan Yellin, *The Intricate Knot: Black Figures in American Literature, 1776-1863* (New York: New York University Press, 1972), p. 193.

[2] *Blake* has had a rather unusual printing history. The first twenty-six chapters were published serially in *The Anglo-African Magazine* between January and July, 1859, but no further installments were published. Then the entire novel was published serially by *The Weekly Anglo-African* newspaper between November, 1861, and May, 1862. The novel was not published in book form until 1970. All page references are made to the 1970 Beacon Press edition published in Boston and edited by Floyd J. Miller.

[3] Yellin, p. 199.

[4] Victor Ullman, *Martin R. Delany: The Beginnings of Black Nationalism* (Boston: Beacon, 1971), p. 200.

[5] See Floyd Miller's introduction to the Beacon Press edition of *Blake.*

[6] Originally published in Cincinnati by the Editor Publishing Company. All page references are to the Mnemosyne reprint published in Miami in 1969.

[7] Robert A. Bone, *The Negro Novel in America,* rev. ed. (New Haven: Yale Univ. Press, 1965), p. 33.

[8] Bone, p. 33.

[9] Hugh Gloster, *Negro Voices in American Fiction* (Chapel Hill, North Carolina: University of North Carolina Press, 1948), p. 57.

Wilson J. Moses (essay date 1979)

SOURCE: "Literary Garveyism: The Novels of Reverend Sutton E. Griggs," in *PHYLON: The Atlanta University Review of Race and Culture,* Vol. XL, No. 3, Fall, 1979, pp. 203-16.

[*In the following essay, Moses evaluates Griggs's place within the tradition of the nationalist novel adn discusses his use of African-American literary conventions.*]

The distinguished black American scholar arna bontemps was once heard to express his objections to white critics making more of the novels of Sutton Griggs than Bontemps felt they deserved. Perhaps Bontemps suspected the motives of his white colleagues and intended to halt, at the outset, a subterfuge that would ultimately lead to the ridiculing of black literature by displaying unrepresentative and pathetically weak figures. Or perhaps Bontempts simply felt that he, along with all other black literary figures, was being patronized, and resented it.[1] Sutton Elbert Griggs, like all artists, had weaknesses as well as strengths, and his writing, like even the greatest art, was sometimes flawed. The older generation of black critics have certainly not been guilty of overstating the strengths of Sutton Griggs. And if there has been any sinister conspiracy on the part of the white literary establishment to elevate his work, with all of its supposed inferiority, to public view, I am completely unaware of it. Griggs has been a prophet singularly without honor, either among his own people or in the larger society. With the exception of the noted Afro-American critic, Hugh M. Gloster, there have been few readers to treat Griggs with any serious appreciation. There is a bitter irony here, because Griggs was perhaps the first black writer consciously to attempt to create a distinctly Afro-American philosophy of literature and a body of writing to go with it.

From the 1930s to the 1950s, when black historical and literary scholarship were understandably preoccupied with the fight against segregation, there was little concern for emphasizing the black American separatist tradition. Literary black nationalism, as exemplified in the novels of Sutton Griggs, was usually disparaged. Rayford Logan, the distinguished historian and pioneering Pan-Africanist, estimates that Griggs "probably had more Negro readers than did Chesnutt and Dunbar." He nonetheless offers the stringent criticism that Griggs's novels had "little literary merit and presaged the black chauvinism of Marcus Garvey." Logan is correct in attributing to Griggs a proto-Garveyist nationalism, although he does not support his view that this amounted to a stylistic shortcoming.[2]

Logan's appraisal was not atypically harsh. Sterling Brown in *The Negro in American Fiction,* speaks of Griggs's novels as "counterpropaganda." *Unfettered* (1902) is characterized as "a hodgepodge," and its prose is described as "trite and pompous." Brown sees *The Hindered Hand* (1905) as "also a bad novel. . . . All of the darker phases of the South appear in the book, but melodramatically, unrealistically."[3] Hugh Gloster, who views Griggs as "a significant pioneer in the history of American Negro fiction," admits nonetheless "his failings as an artist."[4] Robert Bone, a white scholar, belittles Gloster's insight that Griggs was a political thinker of stature, and finds his social philosophy confused and contradictory, vacillating between blatantly fanatical "Negro nationalism" and conciliatory servility.[5] Bone's attack on Gloster is supported by David M. Tucker, another white scholar.[6] Arthur P. Davis and Saunders Redding see Griggs as sharing a weakness "common to many other black authors of his era: he was too much concerned with the Race Problem and too little with the art of fiction."[7] S. P. Fullinwider, a white scholar, is fascinated by Griggs's complexity and finds his "rugged intellectual honesty . . . astonishing."[8]

Griggs was not only concerned with writing about the "race problem"; he was concerned also with writing for black audiences. Rayford Logan has speculated that Griggs was able to appeal to a significant number of black readers. W. E. B. DuBois also spoke to this issue and noted that Griggs was unlike his contemporary, Charles Chesnutt, who, as is well known, sought acceptance from the white reading public, and even went so far as to conceal his racial identity in his search for publishers. In DuBois's estimation, Griggs's strident racialism "spoke primarily to the Negro race."[9]

One would think that in the past decade's flurry of activity in the setting up of black studies departments, and in the search for methods and discipline to determine the distinctively "Black" elements of Afro-American art, Sutton Griggs might have been "discovered" and reexamined. Nothing of the sort has happened. Black Studies specialists have continued to focus upon those writers who meet orthodox criteria of literary excellence, rather than turning their attention to neglected writers like Griggs. Authors like Jean Toomer, Ralph Ellison, Amiri Baraka, and Ishmael Reed have had widespread appeal to the literary establishments, white and black. Their stylistic accomplishments are of the sort that scholars are taught to recognize. One does not wish to ignore the accomplishments of the foregoing authors, nor to demean the critical insights of those who have appreciated them. Still, it would seem that if Afro-American literature specialists are to justify themselves and their professional existence as specialists—with singular insights and privy knowledge, that are not shared by non-specialists—then they will have to attempt to adopt methods that will aid them in the analysis of novelists like Griggs, who have so far been avoided by perplexed conventional critics.

Since Griggs has commonly been assumed by such knowledgeable black contemporaries as DuBois, Logan, and Charles Alexander[10] to have been reasonably influential among the literate black working class, he seems to have appealed to the same audience as Marcus Garvey, and like Garvey, Griggs was a successful orator before black audiences. His literary theory may indeed be seen as literary Garveyism, for it was strongly nationalistic. The purpose of literature was, he felt, to serve the masses of black people. It was to provide a basis for racial unity and at the same time to create channels of legitimate leadership. He recognized that the political potential of black Americans was severely limited by illiteracy, and he issued a call that was understandable enough for a novelist who did not wish to restrict his appeal to white readers, but hoped to find an audience among Afro-Americans.

> To succeed as a race we must move up out of the age of the voice, the age of the direct personal appeal, and live in an age where an idea can influence to action by whatever route it drifts one's way.
>
> When the time arrives that the Negroes are capable of being moved to action on a large scale by what they read, a marked change in the condition of the race will begin instantly and will be marvelous in its proportions.[11]

Griggs saw the need for the creation of a "Negro Literature," not only for the creation of particular works whose authors happened incidentally to be black, but for an integral body of literary tradition that would be readily identifiable as belonging to Afro-Americans. "Not a single race that has no literature is classified as great in the eyes of the world," he said. A nation's leaders could not "foster the patriotic spirit" without preserving their insights for future generations, "and those races that have no literature are devoid of a method of embalming."[12]

That Griggs's writing on the purposes of literature seems to neglect artistic concerns in favor of considerations chiefly political should not mislead us into thinking that his novels are without their aesthetic delights. His writing style is splendidly primitive, clear, forceful, and colorful. Primitive writing has never achieved the same degree of respectability as "primitive" music or sculpture, for example. We have no concept such as *folk novel* in the critical vocabulary, and such a term might be useful to describe certain aspects of Griggs's work, because in order to appreciate Griggs, one must either overlook or else learn to enjoy his stylistic "imperfections," just as one willingly overlooks the often flawed plots and characterizations in Shakespeare's plays, or the flat characterizations of Bunyan. To say that great art is flawed is not to say that it lacks beauty; one can learn to appreciate the beauty of Griggs's style, if one can learn to appreciate such untrained painters as Edward Hicks and Henri Rousseau. Good art does not have to be "life-like," and indeed Griggs's often is not. But if his characters have a pasteboard quality, perhaps there is a reason.

Edward Bland, a black critic, once observed that black literature of the late nineteenth century falls into a "pre-individualistic" mode.

> In the pre-individualistic thinking of the Negro, the stress is on the group. Instead of seeing in terms of the individual, the Negro sees in terms of "races," masses of peoples separated from other masses according to color. Hence, an act rarely bears intent against him as a Negro individual. He is singled out not as a person but as a specimen of an ostracized group. He knows that he never exists in his own right but only to the extent that others hope to make the race suffer vicariously through him.[13]

Clearly this holds certain implications for the way in which characters are drawn, for indeed in many black novels of the nineteenth century, including those of Martin Delany, Sutton Griggs, and William Wells Brown, one feels that the characters are not individuals, but personifications of ideas common in Afro-American nonfiction such as racial ambivalence, or the "two-souls" motif, and black nationalistic themes.

The two souls motif is prominent in all five of Griggs's novels, which give fictional form to an idea stated in DuBois' *The Souls of Black Folk*, that the black American individual experiences a sense of "two-ness":

> An American, a Negro; two souls, two thoughts, two unreconciled strivings; two warring ideals in one dark body, whose dogged strength alone keeps it from being torn asunder.[14]

Several of Griggs's major characters display this "two-ness." Dorlan Warthell in *Unfettered* (1902) is a Negro American, committed to the advancement of the black cause in the United States. At the same time he has a commitment to the elevation of the entire black race throughout the world. His goal of advancement for black Americans is inextricably bound up with the cause of Universal Negro Improvement. Ensal Ellwood in *The Hindered Hand* (1905) struggles manfully to realize his American nationality throughout the novel, but finally decides that he cannot continue to live as an American and still discharge his duties to his race. Bernard Belgrave in *Imperium in Imperio* (1899) is probably the most striking example of the two souls theme illustrated in an individual character. Bernard, a mulatto, combines the supposed emotionalism of the African personality with all the cruel intellectual cunning and insatiable spirit of the European. Also noteworthy, however, is Belton Piedmont in the same novel, who is torn between his desire to be a loyal and patriotic American and his need to fight for racial survival by the use of Un-American tactics.[15]

At the climax of *Imperium in Imperio* Bernard and Belton address a congress of black leaders in America, assembled in a huge subterranean chamber. Bernard calls for war against the United States, arguing that only by acts of violence can blacks prove themselves equal to or worthy of association with whites.

> To the martyr, who perishes in freedom's cause, death comes with a beateous smile and with most tender touch. . . . if we die on the mountain side, we shall be shrouded in sheets of whitest snow, and all generations of men yet to come upon the earth will have to gaze upward in order to see our whitened forms.[16]

The symbolism of the foregoing cannot be ignored. Bernard desires to have his fallen form "whitened" if only in death. The frustration of Bernard in his half-caste status symbolizes the frustration of all black Americans in their ambiguous status—both Negro and American.

Belton's response to Bernard's bloodthirsty cry is that black people cannot force whites to accept them, and that there is no point in suicide. Blacks must make one final attempt to pursuade whites to grant them justice. If that should fail, then, and only then, Afro-Americans must seek a separate destiny and whites must face the consequences of having created an *Imperium in Imperio*. In such a spirit, Belton introduces the following resolution to the black congress:

> Resolved: That we spend four years in endeavors to impress the Anglo-Saxon that he has a New Negro on his hands and must surrender what belongs to him. In case we fail by these means to secure our rights and privileges we shall all, at once, abandon our several homes in the various other states and emigrate in a body to the State of Texas, broad in domain, rich in soil and salubrious in climate. Having an unquestioned majority of votes we shall secure possession of the State Government.[17]

But Belton's proposed alternatives are not radical enough for Bernard. He insists upon either the total intermixture or the total separation of the black and the white nations in America. Thus he rebels against the ambiguous role of blacks in America which is symbolized in his own schizophrenic personality and half-caste station. Bernard proposes full-scale revolutionary black nationalism.

> . . . Encourage all Negroes who can possibly do so to enter the United States Navy. . . .
>
> Enter into secret negotiations with all of the foreign enemies of the United States, acquainting them of our military strength and men aboard the United States war ships. . . .
>
> We can then, if need be, wreck the entire Navy of the United States in a night; the United States will then be prostrate before us and our allies. . . .
>
> We will demand the surrender of Texas and Louisiana to the Imperium. Texas, we will retain. Louisiana, we will cede to our foreign allies in return for their aid. Thus will the Negro have an empire of his own, fertile in soil, capable of sustaining a population of fifty million people.[18]

The novel ends with the execution of Belton, unable to reconcile his black nationalism with his love for America, and with the madness of Bernard, unable to live with the cruel ambivalence of white America.

Aside from the "two-ness" experienced by the characters in *Imperium in Imperio,* another duality is present. This is manifested in Griggs's use of dual protagonists to represent a conflict of ideals within the race. Belton and Bernard represent two antagonistic sets of traits commonly associated with the personalities of Afro-Americans. Belton represents the heroic Uncle Tom personality in the best sense. He is quietly courageous, loyal, enduring, and he possesses the Christian virtue of transcending hatred and revenge and desiring the salvation of his op-

pressor. The wrathful, vindictive Bernard is a no less common stereotype, and a no less valid characterization of black American attitudes. The mounting tension between the two characters represents the warring opposites within the soul of each individual black American and the conflicting goals of leadership within the race.

The Hindered Hand is also concerned with this variation on the "two souls" theme. Its principal characters are Earl Bluefield, "so light of complexion that he could easily have passed for white," and Ensal Ellwood, "a fine looking fellow" of dark complexion. As in *Imperium in Imperio* the black protagonist is used to symbolize the virtues of classical Negro conservatism. He has a frank and dignified manner, a calm fortitude, and an instinctive sense of Christian virtue. The mulatto is bitter and vengeful. He gathers about himself a "Spartan band . . . five hundred men who are not afraid to die" and with these he plans to seize the state capitol and "When the city awakes tomorrow morning it will find itself at our mercy." (p. 144) Ensal attempts to dissuade Earl from his mad plan but when he fails to do so, the novel is forced to a crisis. Ensal and Earl meet to wrestle at midnight on a bridge above a river that divides their city.

Black nationalist themes are given greater prominence in *Imperium in Imperio* than in any of Griggs's other novels, but this is not the only one in which they are present. Black nationalism and two of its variant forms known as Pan-Africanism and "Ethiopianism" are present in several of Griggs's works. Pan-Africanism is a philosophy that emphasizes the spiritual unity of all black people. It is based on the idea that all blacks are victimized to some extent by the doctrine of white supremacy and that none of us are free till all are free. The liberation of the African continent from all manifestations of colonialism is its chief goal. Pan-Africanists believe that the uplift of Africa is an essential step in the uplifting of blacks in the United States. Griggs was among the group of Pan-Africanists that included DuBois, who believed that a concern for the uplift of Africa did not mean any lessening of concern for problems in the United States. For this group, Pan-Africanism meant what the Zionist movement meant to American Jews, "the centralization of race effort and the recognition of a racial front."[19] Such a variety of Pan-Africanism makes its appearance in *Unfettered* (1902), Griggs's third novel.

Unfettered is the story of Dorlan Warthell who is in love with Morlene Dalton, a beautiful mulatto, widowed during the course of the novel. Morlene refuses to marry Dorlan until he can create a plan for organizing the political efforts of Afro-Americans and improving their position in the United States. Dorlan is able to come up with such a plan, partly due to his own intellectual ability and hard work and partly due to help from an unexpected source. One morning while standing in his own front yard, Dorlan observes a motley procession of lower-class blacks following a parade of Negro musicians down the street. They present a rather untidy and boisterous appearance and Dorlan muses,

Now those Negroes are moulding sentiment against the entire race. . . . Be the requirement just or unjust the polished Negro is told to return and bring his people with him, before coming into possession of that to which his attainments would seem to entitle him. It is my opinion that there must be developed within the race a stronger altruistic tie before it can push forward at a proper gait. The classes must love the masses. . . . [20]

It is in the midst of this altruistic reverie that Dorlan's vision encounters a fantastic sight.

Dorlan's eye now wandered from the people to the band. In the midst of the musicians he saw a cart pulled by five dogs hitched abreast. In the cart stood a man holding aloft a banner which bore a peculiar inscription.

Dorlan read the inscription on the banner and looked puzzled. Coming out of his gate he kept pace with the procession, never withdrawing his eye from the banner. He read it the second, third, and fourth and fifth times. At length he called out, "Hold! here am I." The occupant of the cart leapt up and gazed wildly over the throng, endeavoring to see the person that had spoken.[21]

As it turns out, the cart's occupant is an emissary from Africa, the inscription on the banner is the motto of a princely African family and comprehensible to Dorlan because he is the descendant of an African king, sold into slavery as the result of an ancient feud. Furthermore, as Kumi, the African emissary reveals, there is a long-hidden treasure and Dorlan's family lore is the only key to its whereabouts. Dorlan is not expected to return to Africa in order to reclaim the treasure, for as Kumi tells him,

"In the event that the government of the tropics is to be conducted from the temperate zones, we tropical people will desire Negroes to remain in the temperate zones, to advocate such policies and from such alliances as shall be for our highest good.

So, it may turn out to be the best for you, our king, to remain here, for our welfare, owing to our peculiar environments, depends, just now, as much upon what others think of us as upon what we ourselves may do."[22]

The speech of Kumi is not so improbable as it may seem. We must remember that Pan-Africanists from Africa, Alfred C. Sam, Orishatukeh Fadumah and Edward Wilmot Blyden, proselytized among the less educated classes of black Americans during the period of Griggs's career as a novelist, a fact noted with ridicule by Joel Chandler Harris.[23] Griggs, however, seems to have found the activities of such sojourners worthy of serious regard. It would therefore seem impossible to achieve a full appreciation of him without some understanding of Pan-Americanism in its literary and political manifestations, especially as these are expressed in the writing of other

black men and women of letters. One such literary manifestation of Pan-Africanism is the Ethiopian theme.

Ethiopianism, an important tradition in black literary and intellectual history, has been described by numerous students of the black religious experience.[24] It derives its name from a biblical verse often referred to by black preachers and writers, "Princes shall come out of Egypt; Ethiopia shall soon stretch forth her hands unto God." (Psalms 68:31). Like most biblical quotations, the verse is subject to a number of interpretations limited only by the exegetical powers of the interpreter. Since the late eighteenth century, however, it has usually been interpreted to mean that Africa and her scattered peoples have a divine mission to fulfill in the course of history. Ethiopianism is essentially a view of history, then, and it consists of more than the mere reference to Ethiopia as a literary allusion. One of the best descriptions of Ethiopianism comes to us from the racist author Daniel Thwaite in his paranoid book, *The Seething African Pot* (1936). He attributes the rise of Ethiopianism to the sojourn of the African Methodist Episcopal Bishop Henry McNeal Turner in South Africa during 1898. Thwaite saw Turner as inaugurating Ethiopianism on the basis of his speeches throughout the land and cited him in a typical passage:

"Africa," roared the bishop, "is a new land, a new world; she needs new men, and we are the men she needs. Arise, Africa! for Ethiopia is holding out her arms, not as a suppliant, as the white men call her, but to incite us to throw out our arms like boxers, seize the enemy, chuck him out and conquer the first place among peoples."[25]

Ethiopianism, as defined by Thwaite and other observers, is clearly more than vague allusions to Ethiopia, but rather a cry for world revolution and universal elevation of the status of African peoples.

The title of *The Hindered Hand* signals the Ethiopian theme of Griggs's fourth novel, the struggle of races and nations for world dominance. It is concerned with the black perception of this world-struggle and characterizes Anglo-Saxon dominance as a cosmic disorder that "circles the globe in an iron grasp."[26] This iron grip of Anglo-Saxon dominance which denies to Negroes their political rights "more than all other factors, causes the Ethiopian in America to feel that his is indeed 'The Hindered Hand.'"[27]

The Hindered Hand is, like *Imperium in Imperio,* a novel of conspiracy. In its pages Griggs is concerned with racial politics in America, but no less concerned with the struggle of racial forces on an intercontinental scale. One of the novel's most interesting and prophetic characters is Mr. A. Hostility, who is "the incarnation of hostility to that [Anglo-Saxon] race, or to that branch of the human family claiming the dominance of that strain of blood."[28] Mr. Hostility is a Pan-Slavist who hopes to enlist the aid of Afro-Americans in his struggle against Anglo-Saxon power. Griggs's work is prophetic, for he anticipates the theory of Oswald Spengler that Russia would fuel the revolutionary struggles of colored races in the twentieth century.[29] But *The Hindered Hand* was written in 1905, when the Russian revolution was still only a gleam in Lenin's eye.

The Hindered Hand is not a cheerful book. It ends with most of its main characters either dead or driven insane; and two of them sail for Africa.

> to provide a home for the American Negro . . . should the good people of America, North and South grow busy, confused or irresolute and fail, to the subversion of their ideals, to firmly entrench the Negro in his political rights, the denial of which and the blight incident thereto, more than all other factors, cause the Ethiopian in America to feel that his is indeed "The Hindered Hand."[30]

Griggs was, as we have seen, interested in Pan-Africanism. He had ties to such proponents of the movement as W. E. B. DuBois and Charles Alexander. In an addendum to *The Hindered Hand* Griggs admitted to an interest in the "Back to Africa" movement, an interest not necessarily shared by all Afro-Americans.

> The overwhelmingly predominant sentiment of the American Negroes is to fight out their battles on these shores. The assigning of the thoughts of the race to the uplift of Africa, as affecting the situation in America, must be taken more as the dream of the author rather than as representing any considerable responsible sentiment within the race, which, as has been stated, seems at present thoroughly and unqualifiedly American, a fact that must never be overlooked by those seeking to deal with the grave question in a practical manner.[31]

The presentation of such sentiments as these gives credence to the statement of Rayford Logan that Griggs was a literary black nationalist and that his philosophy presaged that of Marcus Garvey.

Sutton Griggs's interest in folklore should not go ignored in this discussion of nationalism in art. A concern with folkloristic themes is characteristic of much nationalistic art in the nineteenth century. Earlier black writers like Frederick Douglass, Martin R. Delany and William Wells Brown had shown occasional interest in folklore or had used folk songs and folk tales in their writings. Griggs seems, however, to have been the first black writer to have laced his novels thoroughly with the flavoring of Afro-American "jokelore" and folksy humor. In this respect, at least, he was a novelist of the "New Negro" and he even rivalled the writers of the Harlem Renaissance in his concern for capturing the thought and feeling of the black masses—both urban and rural. Griggs's concern for black folklore did not focus upon animal stories of the sort that Joel Chandler Harris popularized, however. He was more interested in the folk mythologizing of sociological and historical experiences that had actually occurred in the patterns of black life in the South.[32]

The fact that Griggs was a preacher gave him an intimate knowledge of the lives of the masses of the black working poor. He came to know them, not only through the practice of his ministerial duties, but also because of his efforts to disseminate his writings, which he sold from door to door, distributed on the campuses of the black schools, and peddled to workers at their places of employment during lunch hours.[33] Griggs had a keen sense of irony and bitter humor, and seems to have taken seriously—but not too seriously—his role as a moral leader and man of letters. He was able, therefore, to laugh at stereotypes of the black preacher, which he included in two of his novels. In *Imperium in Imperio,* he relates a well-known story of a preacher who is invited to dine at the home of a poor woman and her several children. Two of the children, having been promised biscuits and chicken after the minister is done, watch from the loft as he makes his progress through the meal. As he reaches for the last biscuit they are so overcome with dismay that they lose their balance and topple out, dropping to the floor.[34] In *Overshadowed,* a more sinister type is described. Reverend Josiah Nerve, ridiculous and pompous, burns down his church in order to collect the insurance.[35]

Griggs's novels are also concerned with political folk mythologies. For example, *The Hindered Hand* is often discussed as a counter-myth or as a response to Thomas Dixon's racist novel, *The Leopard's Spots.*[36] Griggs's last novel, *Pointing the Way,* introduces the memorable character Uncle Jack, who is a sophisticated counter-myth to Uncle Remus. Joel Chandler Harris, creator of Uncle Remus, clearly felt that both his own work and that of Harriet Beecher Stowe had defended slavery as a civilizing agency and as a favorable portrayal of the childlike and "feminine" virtues of the black race, as well as the nobility of the master class.

> I trust I have been successful in presenting what must be, at least to a large portion of American readers, a new and by no means unattractive phase of negro character—a phase which may be considered a curiously sympathetic supplement to Mrs. Stowe's wonderful defense of slavery as it existed in the South.[37]

Both Uncle Remus and Uncle Jack represent what DuBois once referred to as "the faithful, courteous slave of older days, with his incorruptible honesty and dignified humility."[38] Like Uncle Remus, Uncle Jack tells his story of the Civil War years and of how he stayed on the plantation and "looked atter de wimmins wid er eagle eye."[39] Griggs, however, has endowed his faithful old Negro with complexity that Uncle Remus lacks. Uncle Jack, like Uncle Remus, remains loyal to his white folks after the Civil War, but unlike Uncle Remus, he develops a sense of political responsibility. Uncle Jack is sympathetic to the newer generation of black leaders who, "wants things ter move 'cordin' ter some principull,"[40] while Uncle Remus considers them to be audacious upstarts. "I kin take a bar'l stave an' fling mo' sense inter a nigger in one minnit dan all de school-houses betwixt dis en de State er Midgigin."[41]

Of course it would be wrong to assert that any and all uses of folkish elements constitute literary nationalism. At the same time, folk themes are an important component of nationalistic art. The folksy and socially perceptive humor of Uncle Jack is perhaps the strongest element of Griggs's last novel. Indeed he is hardly the minor character that Bone would have us believe he is.[42] Uncle Jack is the missing link between the "Old" and the "New" Negro. He dies forgiving his white oppressors, and expressing his enduring love for them, but he dies defending his right and the right of even the most illiterate class of black people to vote. Griggs's Uncle Jack, then, like Harris's Uncle Remus and Stowe's Uncle Tom, has his political functions. While Uncle Jack is not portrayed as a black nationalist, he does represent ideals of grass roots political consciousness and black political unity that often characterize nationalistic rhetoric. Finally, Griggs's decision to transform the traditional stereotype of the contented plantation darky into a vehicle for progressive political thought is consistent with his nationalistic belief that the strength of black Americans must rise up out of the hearts of the people rather than descending from a superior Washingtonian technocracy or a DuBoisean talented tenth.[43]

With respect to the literary merit of Sutton Griggs, I feel that he deserves a more patient hearing than he has received. He is a forceful, colorful, and entertaining writer. He is capable of moving his readers—especially his black readers—very deeply. Griggs has a particular relevance for today, for he wrote in a time of white backlash, a time when white America was forcibly retracting those rights and privileges that had been ceded to black people during Reconstruction.

The pleasure to be derived from the novels of Sutton Griggs can be enhanced for those who have some understanding of the intellectual tradition in which he wrote and of some of the other figures who wrote in that tradition. This naturally implies understanding those writers who have already gained a modicum of respectability, like Charles W. Chestnutt and Paul Laurence Dunbar, but an understanding of the black nationalistic ministers who were writers, like Henry McNeal Turner and Orishatukeh Fadumah, is also very helpful. These writers, like Griggs, were educated black clergymen, fueling the fires of the black nationalism of the working classes. I have identified several characteristically black American motifs in the novels of Sutton Griggs, and have tried to demonstrate the usefulness of analyzing Griggs in connection with Pan-Africanism, Ethiopianism, and the Two Souls theme. There is no denying that Griggs was profoundly influenced by traditions outside the black world, as well. After all, he was a well-educated cosmopolitan man. His writing is full of allusions (and direct references) to Thomas Huxley, Benjamin Kidd, Prince Kropotkin, Herbert Spencer, and other social theroists of the day.[44] In better times, Griggs might have taught social anthropology in a university—but no such opportunities were present at the turn of the century, so Griggs wrote sociology in the form of the sentimental novel. He also wrote books on social

theory and race relations that were not fictional.[45] Griggs was a serious thinker and an entertaining writer. If he has not been fully appreciated, it is not because his writing lacks depth.

Rayford Logan's assessment of Sutton Griggs as a literary black nationalist and precursor of Marcus Garvey seems insightful. The hostility of earlier generations of black scholars towards black nationalism and Garveyism probably accounts in part for their failure to perceive his literary merits. If I may speak for the younger generation of black scholars, I will assert that many of us are inclined to look at Garveyism and at black nationalism as phenomena to be studied objectively—neither to be ignored nor responded to in purely emotional terms.[46] When we turn to the question of evaluating his contribution to literature, we must compare Griggs to other Christian polemical writers. British critics have long defended the crude yet vivid beauty of works like *Pilgrim's Progress* and *Everyman* with the argument that these works enshrine the essential values of the societies that produced them as well as the eternal verities that have dominated life on this planet.[47] One might argue in the same vein that Griggs with his understanding of laughter in the face of suffering, gentility amidst squalor, and toughness behind a mask of subservience has managed to filter universal truth through the prism of Afro-American nationalism. Griggs gave us five novels, each of which is worth more than one reading. Taken together, they provide us with a more insightful picture of life in the black South at the dawn of this century than social science alone is capable of providing.

NOTES

[1] Bontemps' objections were expressed during an institute on Afro-American culture at the University of Iowa during the summer of 1970. Griggs is conspicuous by his absence from standard anthologies of black literature published since the late 1960s. An exception is the excellent text by Arthur P. Davis and Saunders Redding, *Calvalcade: Negro American Writing from 1760 to the Present* (Boston, 1971). Robert Bone has done a lazy job on Griggs in *The Negro Novel in America* (New Haven, 1958). He mistakenly refers to Uncle Jack in *Pointing the Way* (Nashville: The Orion Publishing Company, 1908) as a minor character, and falsely states that "the term 'New Negro' was coined by Alain Locke during the 1920s. . . ." Griggs, of course, had already used the term in *Imperium in Imperio* (Cincinnati: The Editor Publishing Company, 1899). The earliest occurrence of the term that I have thus far been able to locate is in the title of an address. "The New Negro," delivered on January 21, 1896, by John M. Henderson at the Bethel Literary Association mentioned in John W. Cromwell, *History of the Bethel Literary and Historical Association* (Washington, D.C., Published by the Association, 1896), p. 30. Also see William Pickens, *The New Negro* (New York: Neal, 1916), and Booker T. Washington, *A New Negro for a New Century* (Chicago: American Publishing House, 1900). Hugh Gloster is correct in dating the New Negro

Movement from the late nineteenth century, and it is Bone who is incorrect when he attempts to fault Gloster for so doing. See Gloster, "Sutton Griggs, Novelist of the New Negro," *Phylon* IV, No. 4 (Fourth Quarter, 1943), 335-45 and Gloster, *Negro Voices in American Fiction* (Chapel Hill, 1948). August Meier in *Negro Thought in America* (Ann Arbor, 1963), p. 258, traces the term *New Negro* to circa 1895.

2 Logan comments on Griggs's popularity and proto-Garveyism in *The Betrayal of the Negro* (New York, 1965), pp. 357-58.

3 Sterling Brown, *The Negro in American Fiction* (Washington, D.C.: The Associates in Negro Folk Education, 1937), pp. 100-01.

4 Gloster, "The Novelist of the New Negro," p. 345.

5 Bone, *op. cit.,* p. 33.

6 David M. Tucker, *Black Pastors and Leaders* (Memphis, 1975), pp. 71-2. Tucker's book involves some serious misreadings of some of Griggs's critics, and his interpretation of Griggs as a disgruntled intellectual who became an Uncle Tom is based upon hearsay.

7 Davis and Redding, *op. cit.,* p. 163.

8 S. P. Fullinwider, *The Mind and Mood of Black America* (Homewood, Illinois, 1969), p. 74.

9 DuBois mentions Griggs's appeal to black readers in "The Negro in Literature and Art," *Annals of the American Academy of Political and Social Science,* XLIX (September, 1913), 236.

10 Charles Alexander was the publisher of *Alexander's Magazine,* funded by Booker T. Washington and published in Boston as a counter agent to William Monroe Trotter's *Guardian, Alexander's Magazine* was ironically notable for its sympathy for Back-to-Africanism, which Washington tended to disparage. Alexander published two reviews of Griggs's *The Hindered Hand,* one on October 15, 1905, the other on August 15, 1906. A photograph of Griggs was published with each article.

11 Griggs, *Life's Demands, or According to Law* (Memphis: National Public Welfare League, 1916). pp. 51-2.

12 *Ibid.,* p. 98.

13 Quoted in Ralph Ellison, *Shadow and Act* (New York, 1966), p. 95.

14 W. E. B. DuBois, *The Souls of Black Folk* (Chicago: McClurg, 1903), p. 3.

15 In addition to *Imperium in Imperio,* already mentioned, Griggs wrote four other novels: *Overshadowed* (Nashville: Orion, 1901); *Unfettered* (Nashville: Orion, 1902);

The Hindered Hand (Nashville: Orion, 1905); *Pointing the Way* (Nashville: Orion, 1908). Reprints are available from Books for Libraries and AMS Press.

16 *Imperium in Imperio,* pp. 220-21.

17 *Ibid.,* p. 245.

18 *Ibid.,* pp. 251-52.

19 DuBois, "Reconstruction and Africa," *Crisis,* XVII, No. 4 (February, 1919), 166.

20 *Unfettered,* pp. 160-61.

21 *Ibid.,* p. 161.

22 *Ibid.,* pp. 167-68.

23 Joel Chandler Harris describes Uncle Remus's total lack of interest in "dat Liberious country" in *Uncle Remus Returns* (New York, 1918), pp. 158-65. Alfred C. Sam is discussed in William E. Bittle and Gilbert Geis, *The Longest Way Home* (Detroit, 1964). Mention is also made of Fadumah. Blyden's American tours are mentioned in Edwin S. Redkey, *Black Exodus* (New Haven, 1969).

24 See George Shepperson, "Ethiopianism and African Nationalism," *Phylon,* XIV, No. 1 (First Quarter, 1953), 9-18; St. Clair Drake, *The Redemption of Africa and Black Religion* (Chicago, 1970); Jomo Kenyatta, *Facing Mt. Kenya* (London, 1938); Daniel Thawaite, *The Seething African Pot* (London, 1936); F. Nnabuenzi Ugonna, Introduction to the London, 1969 reprint edition of J. E. Casely Hayford's *Ethiopia Unbound* (London, 1911); Wilson J. Moses, "The Poetics of Ethiopianism; W. E. B. DuBois and Literary Black Nationalism," *American Literature,* XLVII, No. 3 (November, 1975), 411-26.

25 Thwaite, *op. cit.,* p. 38.

26 *The Hindered Hand.* p. 243.

27 *Ibid.,* p. 298.

28 *Ibid.,* p. 202.

29 Oswald Spengler, *The Hour of Decision,* translated from the German by Charles Francis Atkinson (New York, 1934). See especially pp. 208-09. "Russia has removed its 'white mask' . . . has again become Asiatic with all its soul, and is filled with a burning hatred of Europe."

30 *The Hindered Hand,* p. 298.

31 *Ibid.,* p. 303.

32 Although it should be remembered that Harris dealt with two varieties of folklore in his tales of Uncle

Remus. The animal lore was no more important than the lore of the contented darky, unconcerned about his political and economic welfare.

[33] Griggs tells of his attempts to market his works privately in *The Story of My Struggles* (Memphis: The Author, 1914), p. 14.

[34] *Imperium in Imperio,* pp. 20-22. As a child, I heard my father tell this same story. After I became acquainted with Griggs's version of it I showed the passage to my father, who could remember hearing it from his mother.

[35] *Overshadowed,* pp. 73-81.

[36] See, for example, Sterling Brown's discussion of *The Hindered Hand* as "counter-propaganda," *op. cit.,* pp. 100-01. Also see John Daniels, "A Negro's Answer to 'The Leopard's Spots,'" *Alexander's Magazine* I, No. 6 (October 15, 1905), 31-33.

[37] Joel Chandler Harris, *Uncle Remus: His Songs and His Sayings* (New York, 1908), p. viii.

[38] W. E. B. DuBois, *The Souls of Black Folk,* p. 80.

[39] *Pointing the Way,* p. 59; cf., *Uncle Remus,* pp. 201-14.

[40] *Pointing the Way,* p. 150; cf., *Uncle Remus,* pp. 231-33.

[41] *Uncle Remus,* pp. 255-56.

[42] Bone's misinterpretation of Uncle Jack, one of the dominant figures of *Pointing the Way,* and one of Griggs's most memorable creations, can only be attributed to Bone's not having read the book; see *The Negro Novel,* p. 33.

[43] Martin Delany in his novel *Blake* (Boston, 1970) endows the plantation slaves with subtlety, wit and the ability to deceive their masters while wearing a mask of subservience; see pp. 12 and 44-48. Also see William Wells Brown, *Clotel, or, The President's Daughter* (London, 1853), pp. 99-100.

[44] To chart all of the influences of the social sciences upon Sutton Griggs would be a mammoth task, far outside the scope of this paper, which is concerned with his contributions as a novelist. Within the novels, however, he does allude to Benjamin Kidd, *Unfettered,* pp. 244, 167; *The Hindered Hand,* p. 147, utilizes some of Kidd's theories concerning climatological influences under racial temperament, but no direct reference to Kidd is made. The evolutionists, Charles Darwin and Prince Kropotkin, are mentioned in *Unfettered,* p. 235. Darwin is also discussed in *Overshadowed,* p. 168. Most of Griggs's references to social Darwinists and other social theorists are to be found in his social studies, however.

[45] The following works by Griggs are concerned with social theories: *The One Great Question: A Study of Southern Conditions at Close Range* (Nashville: Orion, 1907); *Wisdom's Call* (Nashville: Orion, 1911), which alludes to the work of Thomas Henry Huxley, p. 117; Ray Stannard Baker, p. 122, and demonstrates a fair knowledge of the opinions of contemporary political leaders. *Life's Demands, or, According to Law* (Memphis: National Public Welfare League, 1916) attempts to work out an exact scientific approach to race relations. In this work, Griggs works out an exact ideology based on the writings of Kropotkin and Darwin, pp. 34-35, and elsewhere. *Guide to Racial Greatness, or, The Science of Collective Efficiency* (Memphis: National Public Welfare League) makes copious references to theories in the social sciences and the biological sciences.

[46] My own article, "Marcus Garvey: A Reapprasial," *The Black Scholar* IV, No. 3 (November/December, 1972), is a poor example of this spirit of objectivity. It was indeed a step along the way to my becoming appreciative of Garvey's importance, but an extreme rejection of the uncritical adulation of him. An example of the more sophisticated treatment of Garvey and black nationalism that is becoming widespread is Tony Martin, *Race First* (Westport, Connecticut, 1976). Also of high quality is Robert Hill's essay in John Henrik Clarke, *Marcus Garvey and the Vision of Africa* (New York, 1974).

[47] The grand old work on John Bunyan and a classic in its own right is John Brown, *John Bunyan: His Life Times and Work* (Boston and New York, 1886). See especially pages 282-300. British literary historians have long justified works within their own tradition on moral, political, or historical grounds. An application of such methodology might well be justified for proponents of black studies who wish to secure a fair hearing for Griggs.

Wilson J. Moses (essay date 1980)

SOURCE: "Literary Myth and Ethnic Assimilation," in *The New Hungarian Quarterly,* Vol. XXI, No. 80, Winter, 1980, pp. 131-36.

[*In the following essay, which was originally presented as a lecture at an American Studies conference, Moses contrasts Griggs's views on ethnic assimilation in America with those of the Jewish writer Israel Zangwill.*]

Israel Zangwill (1864-1926) was a man of two souls. As one biographer contends, "He was passionately devoted to the values of the Jewish past as enshrined in the ghetto, but at the same time, he sought to escape from what he felt to be the ghetto's restrictiveness." He was born in London of a poor Russian immigrant family, educated at the Jews' Free School in the East End of London, where he later became a teacher. He published prolifically, essays, stories, and plays, becoming known for his "Dickensian" portrayals of types of London

Jewry. But the best known contribution that Israel Zangwill made to the thought of the modern world was a phrase that he donated to American culture. It is a phrase taken from the title of his now almost forgotten play, *The Melting Pot.* It is with the theme of this play that I am concerned here. Stated succinctly, and in its author's words the central idea is that "America is God's crucible, the great "melting pot," where all the races of Europe are "melting and reforming." The plot is as follows:

It is 1908, and young David Quixano, a Russian Jewish violinist, has recently arrived in America to live with his Uncle Mendel, a piano teacher, and Mendel's aged mother, who finds it hard to give up her old country ways and speaks no English. They have a good hearted, though sporadically ethnocentric, servant girl named Kathleen. She is Irish, of course, and provides much amusement with her attempts to speak Yiddish and to remember the family's orthodox rituals and customs. At one point, Kathleen exclaims in exasperation that the Pope himself could not remember so many religious rules and dietary laws. One evening the family is visited by Vera Revendal, an idealistic young woman, who has recently emigrated from Russia. Her English is perfect because her parents, Czarist aristocrats (though of modest means) were able to provide her with an English governess. Vera asks David to play his violin at her settlement house, although, as she explains apologetically, she will not be able to offer a fee. But David responds with passion,

> A fee! I'd pay a fee to see all those happy immigrants you gather together—Dutchmen and Greeks, Poles and Norwegians, Welsh and Armenians. If you only had Jews, it would be as good as going to Ellis Island.

Ellis Island in New York is, of course, the symbolic gateway through which so many turn-of-the-century immigrants were herded before being officially admitted as residents. It was on Ellis Island that they often had their first contact with industrial bureaucracy, as they were issued their papers, and sometimes even, due to the carelessness or callousness of petty officialdom, new names. Once ashore, they usually found homes in immigrant neighbourhoods. There they came into contact with the settlement house movement. This was an urban reform idea, originating among the educated classes to alleviate the cultural and spiritual poverty of the communities in which the immigrants often resided. Settlement houses existed for the purposes of assisting the immigrants in finding health, education, and social welfare services. They also provided artistic, political, and intellectual activities for the neighbourhoods they served. As an idealistic, upperclass young woman, Vera Revendal would have been a typical settlement house type. As an immigrant from a Russian aristocratic family, she would have been extraordinary.

David, as we soon realize, is quite certain that she is the very "Spirit of the Settlement." He shares with her—because he is certain that she will understand—a rhapsody on the meaning of America as he sees it.

"Here you stand, good folk," think I when I see them at Ellis Island, here you stand in your fifty groups with your fifty languages and histories, and your fifty blood hatreds and rivalries. But you won't be long like that, brothers, for these are the fires of God you've come to—these are the fires of God. A fig for your feuds and vendettas! Germans and Frenchmen, Irishmen and Englishmen, Jews and Russians—into the Crucible with you all! God is making the American. . . . the real American has not yet arrived. He is only in the Crucible, I tell you—he will be the fusion of all races, perhaps the coming superman.

David and Vera begin to fall in love, despite the fact that he knows she is from his native town of Kishineff, and a member of that class who murdered his mother, his father, and his sister in a program. Needless to say, his Uncle Mendel does not approve of the romance, but, says David, "The ideals of the fathers shall not be foisted on the children. Each generation must live and die for its own dream." Just as the young lovers have vowed "to throw off the coils of the centuries" and harken to the voice of "the living present," Vera's father enters. He is Baron Revendal, a stubborn and narrow man, who carries a pistol to defend himself from the anarchists, whom he believes to lurk behind every lamp post. David recognizes the Baron as the commander of the soldiers who stood coldly looking on while a mob hacked his mother and sister to bits. David staggers out the door; Vera collapses in tears, but the drama is to have a happy ending.

Herr Pappelmeister, an intelligent and sympathetic German conductor, peruses the score of the symphony that David has been composing. He recognizes, naturally, that David's composition is a work of genius and performs it before an admiring audience, who respond with half an hour of frenzied applause. David is overcome by the ideals represented in his "New World Symphony," and his heart is softened towards Vera. The curtain falls as the lovers turn their backs on the European past and pledge themselves to the future symbolized by an America that is not so much a nation as a negation of all traditional nationalisms.

There were others who found it more difficult to harbour such optimistic hopes for the future of America. Sutton Elbert Griggs was a black American Baptist minister, who between 1899 and 1908 wrote and published five novels. In all of them he is concerned with the barriers between the races and pessimistic concerning any possibility of the black and white populations over successfully merging into a united and happy people. Thus in his first novel, ***Imperium in Imperio,*** Griggs describes the black population as a nation within a nation. He sees the only hope for survival among blacks as the creation of an invisible government with war-making powers and a sense of steadfast unity in the face of white America. At the end of the story, all the main characters, save one, have been lynched, murdered, or driven to suicide. The sole survivor, now quite mad, stands beside the grave of a fallen compatriot, plotting revenge upon the United

States with the aid of European allies, and delivers the following soliloquy:

> Float on, proud flag, while yet you may. Rejoice, oh ye Anglo-Saxons, yet a little while. Make my father ashamed to own me, his lawful son; call me a bastard child; look upon my pure mother as a harlot; laugh at Viola in the grave of a self-murderer; exhume Belton's body, if you like, and tear your flag from around him to keep him from polluting it! Yes, stuff your vile stomachs full of all these horrors. You shall be richer food for the buzzards to whom I have solemnly vowed to give your flesh.

In his second novel, *Overshadowed,* Griggs has his protagonist completely renounce all ties to the United States. As he boards a ship in New York harbour, his friends inquire of him where he is bound.

> "Are you returning to your fatherland?" anxious friends, gathered at the pier, inquired.
>
> Astral replied, "It, too, is overshadowed. Aliens possess it."

When the ship is in mid-ocean, Astral finally makes a declaration of his plans.

> "I, Astral Herndon, hereby and forever renounce all citizenship in all lands whatsoever, and constitute myself A CITIZEN OF THE OCEAN, and ordain that this title shall be entailed upon my progeny unto all generations, until such time as the shadows which now envelope the darker races in all lands shall have passed away, away, and away.

In Sutton Griggs' third novel, *Unfettered,* the hero is brought into an international plot, led by members of his long lost tribe in Africa. In his fourth novel, *The Hindered Hand,* Griggs' black hero is invited to join in a conspiracy of the Slavic world against the Anglo-Saxon. A cadaverous white man in a brown derby presents himself at his front door and announces that he is the incarnation of hostility to those who identify with the Anglo-Saxon race.

> "The world, you see, will soon contain but two colossal figures, the Anglo-Saxon and the Slav. The inevitable battle for world supremacy will be between these giants. Without going into the question as to why I am a Pro-Slav in this matter, I hereby declare unto you that it is the one dream of my life to so weaken the Anglo-Saxon that he will be easy prey for the Slav in the coming momentous world struggle."

The hero successfully resists the temptation to throw in with America's enemies, but nonetheless becomes increasingly alienated and spends the last several chapters of the book travelling to and from Africa. He finally decides to take his family to the Fatherland for good, in order "to provide a home for the American Negro."

In all of Sutton Griggs' novels the theme of permanent separation of the races finally wins out in the end. Only in death do the black and the white people ever meet, for, in several instances, Griggs mentions that a faithful Negro retainer is sometimes buried at the foot of his master's grave. This is indeed the final note of his last novel, *Pointing the Way.* The best that could be hoped for in Griggs' novelistic America was a spirit of mutual respectful avoidance between white and black.

The contrast between the two views, presented by Israel Zangwill and Sutton Griggs, will perhaps provide us with some insights into the theme of this conference, "Origins and Originality of American Culture"; for Israel Zangwill, American culture represented a break with the past, something completely new. It is clear that Zangwill identified deeply with the mass experience of the 1,500,000 Jews who left Eastern Europe between 1900 and 1914. Some 90 per cent of this group settled in the United States, where despite the many hardships they encountered, they nonetheless found conditions better than in Czarist Russia. But for the Afro-Americans of whom Sutton Griggs wrote, conditions in the United States were far different. For them, the American South was just as brutal as the tyranny of the Czars. The environment in which the vast majority of black American peasants lived closely resembled the environment known to Russia's Jews.

The biases of Zangwill's point of view did not allow him to see this. To be sure, he did have Baron Revendal defend the Jewbaiting of Russia by asking of an American, "Don't you lynch and roast your niggers?" And David Quixano, in one of his speeches throws both "black and Yellow" into the crucible along with his assortment of Europeans. Yet, if one examines the appendices to the 1913 edition of *The Melting Pot,* one finds that Zangwill gives his approval to such traditional Anglo-Saxon ideas as the following:

> . . . the prognathous face is an ugly and undesirable type of countenance . . . it connotes a lower average of intellect and ethics . . . white and black are as yet too far apart for profitable fusion. Melanophobia, or fear of the black, may be pragmatically as valuable a racial defence for the white as the counter-instinct of philoeucosis, or love of the white, is a force of racial uplifting of the black.

The comments appended to *The Melting Pot* are clearly intended to disassociate its author from the charge that he advocates contamination of the white race. It is possible for Zangwill to advocate the cultural and genetic assimilation of Jews into the rest of America, so long as the Jews, like David Quixano, are willing to give up their memories of the Old World and abandon the faith of their fathers. But Zangwill knew full well that a play advocating interracial marriage could never have been produced in Washington, D.C., of 1908, where *The Melting Pot* had its very successful premier, and was dedicated, by permission, to President Theodore Roosevelt. This same

President Roosevelt had once been severely criticized as an advocate of race mixing because he had eaten at the same table with Booker T. Washington.

From the perspective of the black American writer, America has never appeared so unique as Zangwill believed it to be. And even white American writers contemporary to Zangwill had some reservations concerning the myth of the Melting Pot. Upton Sinclair believed that assimilation into American life was a painful, even an unhealthy process. His novel, *The Jungle,* is said to have turned Theodore Roosevelt's stomach, with its description of the filthy conditions under which Eastern European immigrants worked in Chicago meat packing houses. Sinclair showed how the healthy, robust customs of Slavic peasants soon were obliterated in the dehumanizing industrial slums of Chicago. He showed how the family disintegrated under the stresses of poverty, hunger, and unfamiliarity with urban conditions. And the descriptions painted by Upton Sinclair and others of the type, who came to be known as "muckrakers," led to health, education, and welfare reforms that benefited all Americans.

Settlement house workers, far from encouraging the complete eradication of all European ethnic traits, realized the importance of encouraging the immigrants to retain the essence of their ethnic heritages. Jane Addams, the dean of settlement house organizers, told in her minor literary classic, *Twenty Years at Hull House,* of her efforts to assist the children of immigrants in learning to appreciate the skills, crafts, arts, and ways of life brought to America by their parents and grandparents. She also praised Jewish and German immigrants for their intellectual interests and felt that all Americans might learn from their habits of political and literary discussion. Rather than assuming that all European traits must be eradicated, the best of the settlement workers encouraged immigrants to preserve the nurturing elements of their European cultures.

In all fairness to the Melting Pot school, they too believed that America benefited from the cultural influx of various nations. Even the Negroes had contributed a "comic spirit" or a sort of "spiritual miscegenation" which had led to 'rag time' and the sex dances that go to it. But the essential importance of genetic mixing to the Melting Pot theory cannot be denied. Zangwill articulated a belief that many Americans found acceptable at the time, and that the majority of Americans still find acceptable. The American ideal is to forget the European past and become fully American. This implies intermarrying with other Americans. When an Irishman named John F. Kennedy marries a French woman named Jacqueline Bouvier, this is seen as the storybook wedding that logically fulfills the American dream. The Melting Pot ideal works as well for the Jews as for others, with the passing of years, as they become more and more removed from the ghettoes of New York's lower East Side. The increasing secularization of society aids the process. At present some thirty per cent of American Jews marry outside their faith. The proportion increases the farther we are from the East Coast. The minuscule occurrence of intermarriage between black Americans and other ethnic groups is not much affected by the passage of generations or internal migration. Intermixture between blacks and whites had diminished to almost nothing since the emancipation of the slaves. White men are no longer able to have their way with black women.

The statistics do not lie. Although it has become fashionable among some American sociologists and ethnologists to deny that the melting pot ideal still predominates in America, the fact is that among fourth generation Americans, religion and national origin seem to matter very little, if at all, in the selection of one's mate. But America, like every other culture, has its unassimilable ethnics. It is only when race is added to ethnicity that the melting process is considered undesirable. And even Israel Zangwill, during the heyday of his ideal, subscribed to the view that the black population would be better off founding its own separate state, or perhaps setting sail for Liberia, as did the hero of Sutton Griggs' novel, *The Hindered Hand.*

John Vassilowitch, Jr. (essay date 1981)

SOURCE: "The Example of 'Horace Christian': A Central Irony in *Overshadowed*," in *American Literary Realism, 1870-1910,* Vol. XIV, No. 1, Spring, 1981, pp. 60-9.

[*In the following essay, Vassilowitch examines the rise and fall of the white racist Horace Christian, a character in* Overshadowed.]

Overshadowed (1901) is the second novel written by turn-of-the-century black author Sutton Griggs. Historian S. P. Fullinwider calls the book, correctly, "In part . . . a sermon against assimilation; against the degrading effects of the white man's values."[1] While overstating his case somewhat, Hugh Gloster is also correct in emphasizing the destructive role that miscegenation plays in the story.[2] Griggs's essential aversion to both cultural and sexual assimilation with white America sets the tone throughout *Overshadowed* and gives some unity to its otherwise rather loosely-constructed plot. Nevertheless, scholars have completely overlooked a key pun, developed intricately and at length, that announces in ironically religious terms this dual aversion central to Griggs's story. The pun involves a white politician named Horace Christian, whose deadly sexual frame-up of an innocent, nameless "Negro" and whose own seduction of black Margaret Marston form crucial episodes in the book.[3] In the view of Griggs, himself a Baptist minister, Christian embodies the worst values of his race. Horace's account of the sexual frame-up and subsequent lynching shows him to be a briber, a racial murderer, and a racist hypocrite, while the Marston seduction episode shows him also to be a liar, an interracial fornicator, and a drunkard. Phonologically, his name is almost identical to "Whore-Race Christian," and this ironic pun implies that the white race often prostitutes, figuratively speaking, the religious and moral values it professes. Moreover, Griggs believes that blacks like Margaret Marston adopt such debased values at the risk of becoming "Whore-Race Christians" themselves—literally as well as figuratively.

When Horace Christian first appears in *Overshadowed,* Griggs's narrator implicitly makes the character a kind of white Everyman by describing him in deliberately vague terms. He notes: "Horace Christian was slightly below the medium in stature, had dark eyes and facial features of the most commonplace type. There was no marked peculiarity about him, nothing that would so impress you that you could point him out again if you saw him in a crowd" (p. 130). On a more literal level, Christian is a state legislator who has just been returned to the Virginia House of Delegates in Richmond. His reelection campaign was unusually difficult, however, and he discusses at some length with a fellow legislator named Stewart the problems he had to overcome. This review comprises a lynching narrative during which the nominal Christian reveals himself as emphatically un-Christian in his behavior—indeed, as a racist hypocrite who, while appearing honorable and courageous, will stoop to bribery and even murder to achieve his political ends.

According to Horace, his black constituents were the source of his reelection difficulties. In the past he had found them easy enough to handle: "'On previous occasions I had paid out a little money and bought up the Negro vote to such an extent as to secure my election'" (p. 130). But this time his Republican opponent—a repentant ex-Confederate general—was so formidable that something more than the usual bribes was needed to get Christian the black vote. The "'brilliant'" (p. 131) expedient that the latter finally hit upon involved a racial murder and a tortuous rationalization:

> "I reasoned . . . that my only salvation lay in doing something to get the gratitude of the Negro. Just now all the gratitude of the Negroes is lavished upon Southern whites who denounce lynching. I decided to get an anti-lynching record. But I could not get that record without a lynching. If I was to get to the Legislature and have a finger in the pie, I must have a lynching. The question had reduced itself to this simple proposition; no lynching, no seat in the Legislature, or a lynching and a seat in the Legislature. I argued with myself that it would not matter so much with the universe if one more innocent Negro were lynched. Just one more name to the long list of innocents slain would not be such a great addition. Besides, I argued, if the lynching spirit goes on, some innocent Negro will soon be lynched and nothing gained, but in my case there is something to gain—a seat in the Assembly at a most opportune time." (pp. 131-132)

Thus, by inventing an argument replete with Swiftian irony, the legislator was able to "justify" a conclusion at once religiously and morally grotesque—that his "'only salvation'" lay in murder. Since, however, the only sort of salvation that really interests this Christian is political rather than religious, his casuistic exercise had its desired effect: "'Having toned my conscience down, I began to concoct my scheme. Of course, that was the easiest part of the job'" (p. 132).

With his freshly "toned-down" conscience, Christian then attended to the unsavory details of his pseudo-ethical lynching scheme. To begin with, the plan required the sexual frame-up of a black man—a grimly ironic circumstance in view of Horace's own sexual appetite for black women. The legislator tells Stewart: "'You know that in the chivalrous South whenever a white woman throws out a hint against a Negro, he might as well make his will. I decided to take advantage of this chivalrous feeling and make it serve my purposes. A false charge was trumped up against a Negro, and he was soon in the hands of a mob'" (p. 132).

Once the anonymous "'nigger tramp'" (p. 165) had been successfully framed and was at the mercy of his would-be lynchers, the scenario called for racist Christian to provide the man with a phony defense. The politician played his role to the hilt. Indeed, so convincing was his hypocritical display that he made believers of both black constituents and black victim. Horace recalls:

> "According to prearranged plans, the Negro was being led forth to the place where he was to be hanged, when I came upon the scene and besought the mob to halt. This they did, and listened to remarks from me, denunciatory of their proposed actions. Only the leaders knew of my true relation to the whole affair.
>
> "The fury of the mob had been aroused to such a pitch that nothing could induce them to desist. That Negro did look at me so appealingly, evidently regarding me as his only possible hope. Finally the crowd became impatient at listening to my harangue. They started off with the Negro. I then drew my pistol as if about to kill and be killed for his sake. I was overpowered in short order; but that one deed, the drawing of that pistol, has made me solid forever." (pp. 132-133)

Thus, the sordid charade was a complete success. Only as an afterthought does Christian note its real, human cost: "'The poor Negro was taken near the scene of the alleged crime and was hanged and riddled with bullets'" (p. 133).[4]

Still, Christian remains essentially unrepentant for his sins. When Speaker of the House Lanier suddenly arrives on the scene, the ensuing dialogue underscores this point:

> "A nigger stood in the way of my coming to the Legislature, so I just killed him. I have been telling Stewart about it," said Christian.
>
> "In cold blood?" asked Lanier.

"Oh, it's a small matter about the sort of blood," laughed Christian. "Killing a nigger does not amount to anything. A man isn't popular these days unless he kills a nigger. I have got mine." Lanier looked at Christian contemptuously. The subject was so disgusting that he hastened to discard it at once. (p. 135)

In *Overshadowed* Lanier—"a large, tall man, of grave aspect, and of a commanding appearance" (p. 135; see also p. 213)—serves as a foil to Horace and a reflector of the author's own moral judgment. Griggs clearly shares the Speaker's feelings of contempt and disgust for the unremorseful briber, murderer, and hypocrite.

Lanier's visit marks the end of the Christian lynching narrative and the beginning of the Christian seduction episode. The Speaker tells Horace and Stewart that he has come "'on the queerest mission possible'" (p. 135) at the request of Mrs. Turner, widow of a former Richmond mayor. Having recently made black people her pet project, this eminent lady has now "'decided to use a number of Negro girls to kill off inimical legislation relative to the Negro race'" (p. 136). More specifically, Lanier explains, Mrs. Turner "'wishes to hold at her house a number of fetes at which no one shall be present but about twenty young Negro women of the very purest and highest type in their race, together with an equal number of the leaders in the Legislature'" (pp. 136-137). She hopes that, through such an arrangement, the "'inimical'" racial legislation pending in the Virginia House will succumb to "'the power of social influence'" (p. 136). In the seduction episode, Christian—who with Stewart accepts Lanier's invitation to participate in this improbable scheme—shows himself to be a liar, fornicator, and drunkard. He also continues to indulge in the sort of racist hypocrisy that has already proved so beneficial to his political career.

Horace lies to Lanier when the latter, on behalf of Mrs. Turner, outlines a code of conduct for her interracial parties. On one aspect of the code the Speaker is especially insistent: "' . . . as the honor of Mrs. Turner's house is at stake, you are implored by her to pledge me upon *your honor* to treat the girls as ladies. They come from the best homes, and a misfortune would be a most damaging and blighting affair. Do you promise?'" (p. 137). The response is as dishonest as it is quick: "'Oh, yes; we promise you faithfully,' said Christian, winking slyly at Stewart" (p. 138). Unlike Lanier, Horace does not hold honor "'sacred'" (p. 137) and has no intention whatever of keeping his promise.

Nevertheless, Mrs. Turner's parties take place with Horace Christian in attendance. At these gatherings the white politicians and black women spend much time discussing two racist measures then being considered in the state legislature: "'a separate coach bill'" and "'a law so dividing the school funds that Negro children shall get only that proportion of school money that comes from taxes paid on Negro property'" (p. 136). As legislative debate on these proposals reaches a climax, so does

Christian's dishonesty. Racist Horace rises in the Virginia House and delivers a hypocritical speech reminiscent of his performance at the lynching. Griggs's narrator relates: "At length the day for voting on the two measures came. . . . Excitement ran high as man after man arose and spoke in ringing tones in denunciation of the measures. When the measures in their turn were submitted to a vote they were defeated by safe majorities. . . . It was conceded by all that the speech of the day was delivered by the Hon. Horace Christian. He spoke with so much eloquence and power and so far excelled his every previous effort, that friend and foe united in giving him unstinted praise" (pp. 141-142).

Once more, "the Hon." Horace Christian is able to dupe his black constituents and achieve a political coup. His performance also enables him to achieve a sexual conquest. At a victory celebration given by Mrs. Turner, Christian is effusively congratulated for his eloquence by black Margaret Marston, a regular participant in the interracial parties. With appropriate Biblical allusion (and sexual symbolism), the narrator notes the seduction that soon occurs: " . . . the serpent had crept into the Garden of Eden. These fetes went on during the entire session, Mrs. Turner fearing that an attempt might be made to resurrect the bills and pass them. It was afterwards remembered that on two or three occasions all of the young women were present but Margaret and that on these same occasions Horace Christian was likewise away" (p. 143). Before very long, Marston becomes pregnant and leaves Richmond. After her departure Christian consoles himself by visiting a black "house of ill-fame" and drinking himself into a stupor—his last dissipation of the novel (pp. 156-157; see also p. 162).

Throughout the seduction episode, Christian—lying, hypocritical, lustful, drunk—contrasts sharply with Lanier, whose feelings and attitudes continue to mirror the moral outrage of Sutton Griggs. When the Speaker discovers Horace's affair with Margaret, he becomes "enraged": "Horace Christian's slighting reference to his [Christian's] having killed a Negro came back to him now. Christian's utter disregard of the solemn promise made to him relative to treating the Negro girls as ladies intensified Lanier's contempt for his moral nature" (p. 152). When Lanier finally confronts Christian with "'your little intrigue with Margaret Marston'" (p. 153), Horace remains thoroughly unrepentant. Indeed, he comports himself like a pulp-fiction villain: "'Ha, ha, ha! Have you heard of that? I did not know it was out. I suppose there will soon be a young African calling me daddy. Ha! Ha! Ha!'" (p. 153). The Speaker's already considerable contempt for Horace's "toned-down" conscience and "moral nature" now erupts into disgust so intense that Lanier "could hardly repress manifestations of his repugnance" (p. 153). Moreover, at one point Griggs's intrusive narrator himself alludes to "the baseness of Horace Christian" (p. 149).

Finally, Lanier (acting no doubt as the author's moral instrument) decides that the unrepentant Christian must die for his sins. Accordingly, the Speaker concocts a highly complicated scheme to substitute Horace for a black prisoner on death row. The unlikely plan not only succeeds, but also results in a consummate irony. It causes Christian, the agent of an innocent black man's hanging, to be hanged publicly himself—in "darky" disguise and, technically, for a crime he did not commit. As Horace is being led to the gallows, the ironic parallel between the two incidents is made most emphatic. Unaware that he is the victim of mistaken identity, Christian wrongly attributes his predicament to the discovery of his own crime: "The picture of the Negro tramp whose murder he had caused for political purposes, crowded before his gaze. He shook tremblingly and began to stagger" (p. 165). No moment of truth for Christian here, however. Fear for life, rather than any ethical awakening, explains his intense anguish.

Arriving at the foot of the gallows, Horace suddenly realizes the true nature of his predicament and tries to divulge his real identity. In doing so, he engages in an unwitting parody of the traditional Christian "deathbed confession." With ironic appropriateness, he is still "the very embodiment of abject terror"—but for selfish, not religious, reasons—and just before his death even invokes God's name—but to imprecate, not supplicate (pp. 165, 166). "[P]iteously," this makeshift "darky" now whines his pseudo-confession to the crowd: "'I am a white man, I killed a nigger; I am a white man, I killed a nigger'" (p. 166). Ironically, however, Horace's admission of guilt is in no way a sign of true Christian repentance or of reconciliation with God. It is not even, properly speaking, an admission of guilt. Rather, it is nothing more than a restatement of his belief that "'Killing a nigger does not amount to anything'"—a racist appeal directed to fellow bigots (not God) and designed to save his skin in this world (not his soul in the next). Far from repenting his sins, Christian reaffirms them.

Ultimately, the parodic confession proves completely ineffective in the here as well as the hereafter. The narrator describes Horace's final moments: "As his body shot down, his last words were 'O God, I killed a—.' The sentence was finished in the other world. A few convulsive jerks, and the murderer of an innocent fellow being and the despoiler of virtue had gone to his reward" (p. 166). Horace's ironic "reward," then, is that he must complete both his pseudo-confessional "sentence" and his murderer's "sentence" "in the other world." In other words, Christian quite clearly is consigned to hell.

Thus, by his repeated prostitution of Christian moral and religious values, Horace Christian—that nondescript white Everyman—certainly lives up to his ironic name. Furthermore, Griggs shows that those blacks who also adopt such debased values become "Whore-Race Christians" themselves—always figuratively, and often literally. Horace's black paramour, Margaret Marston, is a case in point.

Early in *Overshadowed* Griggs's narrator introduces Marston as an indolent "Negro society belle" (p. 31) who is entirely supported by her mother, an industrious washerwoman. Margaret herself refuses to help in any way and cites, as the basis for her refusal, the example provided by white people: "'White girls occupying the social station in their race that we do in our race would suffer themselves to be carried out of their homes dead before they would perform such menial tasks'" (p. 37). Marston serves as a foil to black protagonist Erma Wysong, a hard-working, pious domestic servant whom Griggs's narrator effusively describes as "a heroic figure, a beautiful, noble girl, who stands unabashed in the presence of every ill" (n. pag.). Indeed, *Overshadowed* ends with the narrator exclaiming "All hail to Erma!" (p. 219), and earlier she is even spoken of as "being in an especial sense the handmaid of God" (p. 198). Wysong is also the handmaid of Sutton Griggs and surely expresses his sentiments when she prophesies: "'This idea that work is disgraceful is destined to ruin thousands of Negro girls who are going to try to play "lady" and abstain from employment'" (p. 43; see also pp. 42-43, 67-68). More specifically, Erma tells Marston's mother: "'It would be so grand . . . if you could get Margaret out of that false notion of life, borrowed from the white people in the South'" (p. 44).

Thus, the "Negro society belle" (and budding "Whore-Race Christian") and the "handmaid of God" are set on a collision course. When Wysong advertises for work as a domestic servant, Marston extravagantly denounces her as disgraced, "'ruined . . . forever,'" and worse than dead (pp. 37, 36, 32; see also pp. 31, 33)—rather ironically, in view of Margaret's later adventures with Horace Christian. She decides that the godly Erma must somehow be humiliated and, with help from a friend, initiates a perverse "crusade" (p. 37) for that purpose. Before long, Marston "was stirring up the entire city against an orphan girl whose only offense was that she had decided to obey the Bible injunction to labor six days in the week" (p. 46; see also pp. 55-56).

It is ironically fitting that the climax of the "crusade" occurs in a religious context. One Sunday morning in the Leigh Street Church, Margaret—like Horace Christian, a master manipulator—has the dubious pleasure of witnessing and participating in a public humiliation that she herself has arranged. When Erma, deliberately shunned by Marston and the rest of the congregation, must take a seat alone in the amen corner, a "Negro doctor" (p. 57) becomes outraged at Wysong and demands her expulsion:

> "Do you think that the white folks would allow a white servant girl to sit on the front pew in their church? We shall never amount to anything as a race until we learn to do as white people," said the indignant doctor.

> "Well, what would you say do, doctor?" inquired the . . . obsequious usher.

> "What do! what do! Why, what would white people do? Put her out! Put her out!" exclaimed the doctor.

The ushers nearly tumbled over each other to get to Erma to do what they supposed white people would do to a white servant girl under similar circumstances. (p. 58)

Marston and her cronies see neither irony nor contradiction in expelling a servant girl from church one moment and worshiping "the God of the Nazarene carpenter lad" (p. 58) the next. Thus, long before Margaret Marston meets Horace Christian, her religious and ethical values are thoroughly debased. By mindlessly imitating corrupt white standards, the "Negro society belle" has herself become a full-blown "Whore-Race Christian."

Her introduction to Horace, however, gives Margaret an opportunity to become a "Whore-Race Christian" in a more literal sense. With her value system already distorted, she welcomes the chance to be Christian's mistress. In fact, it may be said that she seduces him as much as he seduces her. Just after Horace's much-praised speech to the House of Delegates, Marston and the legislator find themselves together at Mrs. Turner's victory celebration. Griggs's narrator describes the scene:

> In one corner of the room on a divan sat Margaret Marston and Horace Christian. . . . She half murmurs, "Yes, Mr. Christian I have been trying ever so hard to get near you all the evening. I must, Oh I must congratulate you on that speech. It was most masterly." Her manner and her tones . . . awakened sinister thoughts in Mr. Christian. . . . She continued, "Oh, it was just grand! I could have—could have—just—just kissed you. There, now, it is out." So saying she arose and casting a timid look in his direction went to another part of the room. . . . (pp. 142-143)

Marston, then, is a willing victim—if, indeed, she is a victim at all.

After Margaret becomes pregnant by Horace, there are hints that she may eventually find herself working in a black whorehouse like the one patronized by her white lover. She writes a letter to Erma and in it announces: "'Our family physician came to see me this morning, and he tells me that I am a ruined girl. I know only too well that all he says is true. So I am going to New York to do I know not what'" (p. 148). That Marston will continue on this "'downward journey'" (p. 149), however, is by no means certain, for her letter also contains evidence that she has begun to overhaul the disastrous value system responsible for her predicament. In an act of true Christian repentance that contrasts sharply with Horace's parody at the gallows, she confesses and apologizes for her role in the Leigh Street Church incident. She tells Wysong: "'I was the one who worked up that sentiment against you and caused your ejection. I, the one who was above work, trying to act like the white society girl, should have been thrown out instead of yourself. It was my idleness, my failure to earn money, my attempt to keep up with the fashions set by the wealthy that has wrought my ruin'" (p. 148). Moreover, Marston now sees Christian for what he is—one who wrecks homes and

"'prey[s] upon our morals'" (pp. 148, 149). Still, whether her belated shock of recognition will be enough to save Margaret is left an open question.[5]

Overshadowed has been called "a gloomy, pessimistic novel."[6] The despairing tone owes much to the sinful and unrepentant Horace Christian—briber, murderer, racist hypocrite, liar, fornicator, drunkard—and to all the white "Whore-Race Christians" whom he symbolizes. In the opinion of Sutton Griggs—and to his dismay—Margaret Marston and far too many other blacks find this collective example morally and even physically seductive. The Baptist author-minister, however, deems it both a religious travesty and moral obscenity. Thus, Griggs's black readers may take as an ominous warning the ironic fact that Horace Christian makes his final appearance in *Overshadowed* disguised as a "darky" and hanging from the end of a rope. While black people are perfectly free to imitate the destructive example of the "Whore-Race Christians," they do so at their own peril.

NOTES

[1] S. P. Fullinwider, *The Mind and Mood of Black America: 20th Century Thought,* Dorsey Series in American History (Homewood, Ill.: Dorsey Press, 1969), p. 76.

[2] According to Gloster, " . . . miscegenation causes the death of Erma and her mother, the suicide of Dolly, the insanity of ex-Governor Lawson, the imprisonment of his son John, and the loss of a wife and a mother by Herndon." Hugh M. Gloster, *Negro Voices in American Fiction* (1948; rpt. New York: Russell & Russell, 1965), p. 59. See also Gloster's earlier study "Sutton E. Griggs: Novelist of the New Negro," *Phylon,* 4 (Fourth Quarter 1943), 338-339.

[3] See Sutton E. Griggs, *Overshadowed* (Nashville, Tenn. Orion Publishing Co., 1901), Chs. 16-17, 19-22. Future references will be to this edition and be parenthetically included in the text.

[4] For all his faults, Christian is not entirely without moral sense. Occasionally, he shows some awareness that no amount of rationalization, Swiftian or otherwise, can absolve him from blame in the lynching, and thereby becomes more credible as a character. Horace's account of his actions and reactions the night after the lynching is a striking case in point. He tells Stewart:

> "That night I could not sleep. . . . Something drew me irresistibly to the scene of the lynching. The murdered Negro was yet hanging there, and by the light of the moon . . . I saw a horrible sight. The face was ploughed up with bullets, his eyes were bulging out, his stomach was ripped open and his entrails were visible. On his breast there was a placard, and an inward voice seemed to say to me, 'Read!' With my hair rising on my head and the strangest feeling I ever had in my life stealing over me, I crept up to the body. I could not see distinctly, so I struck a match and read

these words: 'Whatsoever a man soweth, that shall he also reap.' I looked up at the bulging eyes, and they seemed to be trying to speak to me and say, 'Thou art the man.' My strength failed me, and I fell forward, and, clutching at anything to keep from striking the ground, caught hold of the dead Negro. My weight, added to his, broke the rope, and we fell down together, my head getting caught under his mangled form." (pp. 133-134; see also pp. 129, 153)

Unnerved by his recollection of the mutilated corpse and Biblical warning, Christian at this point abruptly ends his account.

[5] Arlene Elder, who has recently provided the most thorough analysis of *Overshadowed* to date, thinks that the question is not left quite so open. She says of Margaret: "That someone as spoiled and indolent as she will succeed in salvaging her life seems unlikely." See Arlene A. Elder, The "'Hindered Hand': Cultural Implications of Early African-American Fiction," *Contributions in Afro-American and African Studies,* Number 39 (Westport, Conn.: Greenwood Press, 1978), p. 81.

[6] Judith R. Berzon, *Neither White Nor Black: The Mulatto Character in American Fiction* (New York: New York Univ. Press, 1978), p. 213.

Jane Campbell (essay date 1986)

SOURCE: "A Necessary Ambivalence: Sutton Griggs's *Imperium in Imperio* and Charles Chesnutt's *The Marrow of Tradition*," in *Mythic Black Fiction: The Transformation of History,* The University of Tennessee Press, 1986, pp. 42-63.

[*In the following excerpt, Campbell explores the ways in which Griggs's* Imperium in Imperio *and Charles Chesnutt's* The Marrow of Tradition *reflected the moral climate of their time.*]

The fiction of Sutton Griggs and Charles Chesnutt emerges from post-Reconstruction despair, both writers crafting romances that bespeak vast promise, that give voice to black heroism in the face of devastating odds. Both resort to the Genteel Tradition in order to supplant degrading stereotypes. At the same time, both launch indictments of education for the limited advantages it offered Afro-Americans. Finally both create two heroes, one militant and one accommodationist, heroes that reflect Griggs's and Chesnutt's ambivalence toward their mythmaking role.

Griggs especially strives to awaken his audience to blacks' innate power; his notion of black solidarity, autonomy, and separatism cemented by creative thinkers conjoins the myth of the messiah with his faith in Western rationality. His saviors must unite their intellectual and visionary capacities to deliver Afro-America from its sense of powerlessness, effect political change, and, ultimately, reorder the world. For Griggs, post-Reconstruction's overwhelming constraints on black America dictate identification with transcendent figures, for suffering and death constitute everyday realities. Although Griggs's ideal leadership rests on an educational foundation, he insists that black thinkers must not forget their folk roots or seek to assimilate. In keeping with such thinking, he jettisons Brown's reverence for light skin, encouraging pride in blackness. Given the dangers implicit in Griggs's endorsement of revolt, however, his dramatization of revolt divides in two, and one of his messiahs becomes an accommodationist.

Griggs employs a number of strategies in the mythmaking process. Romance, his primary device, serves him well for projecting his utopian vision of black political power embodied in a gigantic secret society designed to rectify social injustice. His heroes and heroines occupy the upper reaches of human possibility, hovering close to divinities in their abilities to survive attempts on their lives, and in their intellectual and artistic talents, qualities that occasion instant stardom. Just as the romance allows for characters of ideological rather than psychological magnitude, so too does romance plotting free the narrative from the burden of verisimilitude. His heroes' talents enable them to unify Afro-America, creating a national organization that exceeds the limits of plausibility in its size and power. To elucidate his allegiance to blackness, Griggs designs a subplot in which one of his heroines commits suicide rather than produce light-skinned children with her suitor. To dramatize the healing power of laughter, Griggs makes use of the oral narrative mode, reinforcing trickster figures' centrality in black life. Aside from his reliance on Sentimental Heroines, the Genteel Tradition and inflated diction, Griggs has trouble incorporating historical events into his narrative, and he repudiates African historical connections. Despite his limitations, however, Griggs remains the first black artist to dramatize an appreciation of dark skin and political separatism and as such anticipates later historical fiction.

Imperium in Imperio presents an account of the lives of Belton Piedmont and Bernard Belgrave, childhood companions who struggle to develop and receive recognition for their talents in a racist society. Whereas their white grade-school teacher victimizes Belton because of his poverty and dark skin, he appears to favor Bernard, a well-to-do mulatto. Despite their opposite treatment, the two protagonists achieve equal academic credentials in grammar school and enter college. Belton's political leanings become clear when he launches a successful student protest on campus, subsequently organizing a secret society to secure black rights. After Belton and Bernard graduate from college, both embark on careers, encountering all the stumbling blocks that typify post-Reconstruction. Eventually Belton builds his secret society, the Imperium in Imperio, to great proportions and recruits Bernard to serve as president. Ultimately, when Belton refuses to join a militant plan, he agrees to be executed by the Imperium, as policy dictates. Griggs's romance concludes with an epilogue written by the man who has betrayed that plan in order to subvert the race war that would result.

Griggs's protagonists are essentially one-dimensional, representing two heroic alternatives: pacifist and militant.[1] Both undergo numerous trials that demonstrate to the audience the value of "manly" behavior, offering a mythology of power and heroism. Repeatedly mistreated and thwarted by the grammar school teacher who considers him a "nigger brat," Belton still develops into a superior student who receives a full scholarship to a black college on the strength of his commencement address. When Bernard is being considered for president of the Imperium in *Imperio*, he undergoes initiation rites including a real firing squad and actual gallows. Both characters repeatedly receive accolades; Belton's graduation speech is "everywhere . . . hailed as a classic."[2] Bernard's achievements at Harvard are likewise "so remarkable that the Associated Press telegraphed the news over the country" (85). The demonstration Belton organizes at Stowe University is so successful that it triggers similar revolts in many schools throughout the United States. Both become involved in politics. Bernard, in fact, is elected to Congress but is denied the office because of typical post-Reconstruction fraud at the polls. Ultimately, when the two are involved in the Imperium, nearly every black in the country regards them as heroes.

Like other romances of its era, *Imperium in Imperio* reflects the Genteel Tradition, an unfortunate but inescapable influence. Not only Belton and Bernard but their lovers Antoinette and Viola reach the zenith of middle class respectability. It would never have occurred to Griggs to have created heroes and heroines who speak black English. Rather, he employs diction epitomized by the formula, "Take that, you knave" (185). Viola leaves a suicide note paralleling in style most of the sentimental romances of the time: "If in the shadowy beyond, whose mists I feel gathering about me, there is a place where kindred spirits meet, you and I shall surely meet again" (175). Another device with which Griggs underlines his characters' gentility is their attire. Belton, though making his initial appearance in a patched jacket and an elaborately described collection of hand-me-downs, later sports "a most beautiful and costly silk handkerchief" that he stows "in the tail pocket of his handsome Prince Albert suit of lovely black" (70). Inevitably, houses are furnished with "exquisite taste."

Female characters are both genteel and remarkable, befitting their suitors: "Miss Viola Martin was a universal favoirte. She was highly educated and an elocutionist of no mean ability. She sang sweetly and was the most accomplished pianist in town. . . . She was most remarkably well-informed on all leading questions of the day, and men of brain always enjoyed a chat with her. . . . In all religious movements among the women she was the leading spirit" (100). Antoinette is no less extraordinary. She is "famed throughout the city for her beauty, intelligence and virtue. . . . She neither sang nor played, but

her soul was intensely musical and she had the most refined and cultivated taste in the musical circle in which she moved" (113-14). According to the dicta of the popular sentimental romance, women must not only be described as virtuous, but they must prove their virtue through suffering. Just as Belton and Bernard undergo trials to prove their manhood, Viola and Antoinette demonstrate that they are appropriate models for their audience. Because Viola believes that a union between two mulattoes such as herself and Bernard will cause the race to grow pale and to deteriorate, she commits suicide, an act the reader is encouraged to view as a noble, if misguided, sacrifice. Antoinette, too, possesses heroic powers. When she gives birth to a white baby, Belton abandons her, assuming she has been unfaithful. Later, of course, her virtue is revealed, but her suffering continues when Belton is executed by the Imperium. Significantly, Griggs, unlike Brown, Harper, and Hopkins, refuses the tragic mulatto theme, maintaining that black skin is purer than white. And although Griggs's emphasis on gentility seems quaint, even amusing, to contemporary audiences, he wrote as do all writers from within a particular era, and his insistence on racial pride and heroism far outweighs his conventionality. Of primary significance is the characters' participation in the myth-making process that Griggs deems indispensable to fiction of historical nature.

For Griggs as for Brown the miraculous creates a sense that not only survival but transcendence of oppression are within reach. As do most romances, *Imperium in Imperio* abounds with coincidences, escapes from peril, and astounding, even improbable, events. Often such events intertwine with post-Reconstruction conditions to suggest that with sufficient agility and ingenuity blacks can combat their situation. One of the most spectacular of such incidents involves Belton's entrapment by the Klan (called "Nigger Rulers") who shoot and hang him as punishment for entering a white church and helping a white girl find the correct place in her hymnal. By chance the bullet merely penetrates the skin at the base of his skull, failing to enter the brain; luckier still is the whites' impatience to get on with the dissection of "such a robust, well-formed, handsome nigger," for they cut him down before he has time to die (156). Once on the operating table, Belton has his valor tested when the doctor cuts and pricks the victim's skin to assure himself that he is dead. Belton, of course, does not flinch. When the doctor conveniently places his dissecting tool next to Belton, the protagonist seizes the opportunity to stab the doctor, lay him out on the table, and leave a note to head off his pursuers. Even carrying a bullet in his head, Belton makes his way to Baton Rouge—not to escape, but to turn himself over to the governor. When it seems that Belton is doomed, Bernard is employed as a *deus ex machina*. With an eloquence comparable only to that of Daniel Webster, the narrator informs the audience, Bernard pleads the case before the Supreme Court and secures an acquittal.

Dramatizing these events without excessive narrative intrusion, Griggs leads the reader to identify with his protagonists and thus succeeds in indirectly commenting upon many aspects of contemporary history. That blacks were segregated from white churches and subject to lynching for infractions of the Jim Crow code is illustrated by the results of Belton's "impudence" in suggesting that a white girl was too stupid to locate the correct page in her hymnal. Since post-Reconstruction, blacks have been caught in a double-bind: self-assertion assures chastisement for impudence; aloofness from whites guarantees castigation for surliness. *Imperium in Imperio* as well as *The Marrow of Tradition* and *The Quest of the Silver Fleece* abound with scenes fictionalizing this historical truth. Also illustrative of the mood of the time is the suggestion of the white church's hypocrisy (a legacy from the slave narratives) and the utter corruption of supposedly moral members of white society. The postmaster, a government employee, heads the Nigger Rulers, and the doctor, who has dedicated himself to saving lives, finds joy in sacrificing this "fine specimen" to an experiment that is clearly counterfeit. Because the nineteenth century regarded science with both awe and suspicion, the scene becomes doubly significant. For murdering Belton, the postmaster receives from the doctor a keg of whiskey, symbolic of dissipation in much black literature. Ultimately, these incidents conclude so as to satisfy the tastes of a late-Victorian audience: the postmaster is punished, the hero resurrected.

Thus these events describe the mood and morals of the time; furthermore they illustrate the oral narrative, a tradition rooted in folklore and music, a tradition crucial to black literature. Because Griggs established his own publishing company, promoting his fiction among the entire black community, Gloster postulates that his novels were more widely read than those of Chesnutt and Dunbar.[3] Whatever the case, Griggs, like Harper and Hopkins, strove to approach his audience by way of the popular mode, one that would appeal to a wide readership. The popular mode deriving from the oral narrative utilizes formulaic style (epithets) and protagonists with whom the audience can easily identify, and it relies on formula episodes as well. Most familiar of these formulas are those employed in the western or the detective story. In "Prolegomena to a Study of the Popular Mode in Narrative," James Mellard asserts: "If we are going to understand 'pulp' fiction or the 'slicks,' the western, the detective or science fiction, the soap, the confession, or the adventure, we must come to understand their structural conventions and formulas as fully as the scholars of the oral tradition understand Homer's themes and plots."[4] By the same token, to read *Imperium in Imperio* properly, the reader must view it according to the conventions Griggs employed, rather than denigrating it because it fails to satisy demands outside its scope.

The episode described above, that of Belton's capture, escape, and acquittal, presents him with several obstacles he must overcome. By considering for a moment the fictional forms mentioned earlier—the western, for example—the reader may realize that the protagonist often confronts several obstacles within an episode, each of

which must be dispensed with in order for the protagonist to triumph. Viewed within this context, Belton's actions seem predictable to the extent that the reader assumes he will ultimately outsmart his antagonists. Yet in much the same way that the audience of a tragedy knows the outcome of events but is engaged by the working out of these events, the audience of the popular narrative stays with the story in order to discover the author's variation of the formula. Employing the conventions of the popular mode, Griggs suggests that, though seemingly entrapped by a kind of historical destiny, blacks can attain heroic or mythic stature and eventually change the course of that destiny by outwitting the opponents they confront.

Robert E. Fleming speaks of Griggs's use of comedy to "ridicule the exaggerated dignity of the white master race."[5] Particularly does he refer to those scenes involving the practical jokes played on Tiberius Leonard, Belton and Bernard's grammar school teacher. From placing a tack on Leonard's chair to contriving an elaborate device to drop him into a cistern at the culmination of graduation exercises, these scenes derive from a humorous tradition easily recognizable as oral. The gradual piling up of details which lead inevitably to a disastrous conclusion is a device which demands that the audience, consciously or unconsciously, predict that conclusion. As with the episode involving Belton's escape, the audience waits to see the way the teller will vary this formula. Griggs, of course, assumes that the audience has as little regard for Leonard as do he and the romance's characters. In transforming a figure who is historically real, who is indeed horrifyingly familiar, into a victim of clever jokes, Griggs reiterates much the same notion as with the use of formula episodes. Blacks may respond to oppression in various ways; by laughter they may revolt against and transcend it. Thus black oral tradition contributes to the mythology Griggs creates.

Many of the jokes achieve success because they are directed at a teacher. For an audience whose primary identification does not lie with the academic world, the teacher functions as a time-worn target for humor. Contemporary American films, televison programs, and comic strips continue to exploit the audience's ambivalence toward and alienation from education, as well as their anger toward authority figures. For Griggs's audience, Leonard is drearily emblematic of teachers available to blacks. Griggs takes pains to describe the stigma attached to teaching in a black grammar school and makes clear that Leonard's criminal past has made him unfit for any other career. But Griggs's mythologizing of history reaches far beyond a condemnation of the poor quality of teachers. *Imperium in Imperio* fictionalizes historical reality and at the same time debunks the educational theories of Booker T. Washington and William Wells Brown.

The romance opens with Belton's mother sending him off to school because she is determined to expose him to all available education. Tiberius Leonard favors Bernard over Belton because of his own shady associations with

Bernard's white father; however, because he pits the two boys against each other, they strive to outdo each other. Upon graduation Belton obtains a teaching position, yet when he starts a newspaper that decries fraud at the polls, he is fired. With this incident, Griggs exposes the relationship between education and politics, suggesting that the teacher must function as a puppet to survive, that the intention of education is not to encourage independent thinking or integrity but to reward students and teachers for docility. Thus Griggs implies that the educational philosophy of Booker T. Washington accommodates itself to political corruption. To undermine Brown's concept that black education will inevitably lead to joy and prosperity, the narrator informs us that though Belton's aid to the Republican party entitles him to a high position in the post office, his color consigns him to a post as stamping clerk. Shortly afterward, his refusal to support a racist candidate for Congress causes him to lose his job with the post office. Although educated, Belton is victimized by a corrupt environment because he lacks Bernard's influential white father and his light skin. Contrary to Brown's and Harper's doctrine of black "perfectability" leading to the creation of an ideal society, Griggs maintains that this "perfection" leaves Belton at the mercy of a society preferring expediency to integrity. Finally Belton takes a position as president of his alma mater. Significantly, the only hope for an educated black man during post-Reconstruction is to return to his own community; white culture refuses to acknowledge his talents. En route to his new life Belton encounters the ethic of Jim Crow: he is literally thrown off a train for refusing to leave a first-class coach; he is refused service in a restaurant; and he is harassed by the Klan. Promising prosperity and joy, education brings instead frustration, alienation, and a more acute sense of injustice.

But *Imperium in Imperio* does not totally indict education. Rather, Griggs rejects the myth that education necessarily serves as a tool by which blacks can achieve material success in white society and replaces this notion with an emphasis on education as a process that should develop critical and creative thinking so that blacks can alter oppressive conditions. Such thinking is essential for the members of the Imperium, the secret society Belton creates. An organization intended to operate in the political arena, the Imperium suggests Du Bois's Niagara Movement (of which Griggs was a member) that later evolved into the NAACP. The Imperium, however, limits its membership to blacks. The legendary quality of the Imperium is clear, for its members number 7,250,000 and its treasury $850 million. Further, the Imperium represents a separatist government that will settle legal differences without needing to resort to the bigoted white system. The Imperium boasts an army, a congress, and a constitution.

The political philosophy of the Imperium crystallizes when a black postmaster's house is burned, he and his family shot. This event, one that actually occurred in 1898 in Lake City, South Carolina, precipitates a meeting to decide black-white relations in this country. There follows Bernard's discourse on injustices of the period: the relegation of blacks to a physical rather than a mental plane, the Jim Crow laws, the emasculating intentions of education, the prejudice of the courts, and the practice of mob rule. Imperium members propose three solutions: amalgamation, African emigration, and war. At the third suggestion Belton recoils, his rebuttal taking an accommodationist position. Attributing to the Ango-Saxon a culture superior to that of "primitive" Africa, he urges the Imperium to adopt the tenets of Christianity taught them by this "superior" culture. Rather than engage in race war, he resolves that the Imperium devote four years to impressing whites of the New Negro's talents. Should that fail, Belton proposes that the members of the Imperium emigrate to Texas, "working out our destiny as a separate and distinct race . . ." (245). Belton's proposal is defeated the next day by that of Bernard, who resolves to enter into secret negotiations with foreign enemies and seize Texas by force. Because Belton will not accede to this plan, Belton agrees to be punished by execution.

Belton and Bernard, then, occupy the two horns of the dilemma faced by blacks in turn-of-the-century America. With the suggestion to "work out destiny," Belton echoes Booker T. Washington's Atlanta Address of 1895. Possibly, Griggs had in mind the Washington-Du Bois controversy, with Belton representing Washington, Bernard, a more militant Du Bois. But both positions created doubts for the black audience. Belton's non-violent stance and his insistence on Christian humility gained a sympathetic ear; in fact, such tactics later proved effective for Martin Luther King. But his notion of the inferiority of African culture mirrors the very indictments that whites were using to perpetuate oppression. Tragically, Belton has come to accept a stereotyped, erroneous view of Afro-American history, a view that remains dominant until well into the twentieth century. Bernard's insistence on militance, though laudable for its loyalty to the black community, raised fears of race suicide, heroic but futile. To ascertain Griggs's position, the reader might be tempted to take Belton's death as an endorsement of militance. But Berl Trout, who foils the Imperium's plans, urges in the epilogue that humanity must unite to secure black rights "because love of liberty is such an inventive genius that if you destroy one device it at once constructs another more powerful" (165). *Imperium in Imperio,* then, should be read both as an incentive to black solidarity and as a warning that unless the black's place in history changes for the better, violence will inevitably erupt.

Griggs shies away from returning to his racial past, and in *Imperium in Imperio* he concentrates most of his energies on analyzing the historical moment, on creating a mythical society to rectify the horrors of that moment. The work begins about the time of the Compromise of 1877; unlike Harper and Hopkins, Griggs chooses not to approach the subject of slavery at all. Instead, *Imperium in Imperio* focuses on events contemporaneous with the time of its publication and reveals that late nineteenth-century blacks were largely controlled by prejudice. Even so, his mythology insists, blacks can reshape their environment, primarily through education and adoption of white middle-class speech and cultural mores. Griggs believes that Afro-Americans' political understanding must be sophisticated; however, the action taken on the strength of that understanding remains unclear. Unable to endorse either total accommodation or total militance, Griggs merely depicts these two positions through Belton and Bernard. And much of *Imperium in Imperio*'s strength and complexity derives from Griggs's failure to take a position, for his romance documents the ambivalence characteristic of the period's black intellectual.

Charles Chesnutt's *The Marrow of Tradition* (1901) also fictionalizes the bewilderment of a man full of righteous anger but incapable of abandoning hypnotic security. Far angrier in tone than any of Chesnutt's earlier works, this romance, like *Imperium in Imperio,* employs two black characters, one conciliatory, one militant. Unable to embrace militance, yet consumed with rage, Chesnutt remains ambivalent toward blacks' proper position in history; each character depicts a possible mode of being. As Griggs responded to post-Reconstruction's socio-historic pressures, so too did Chesnutt. Just as an actual event— the murder of Postmaster Cook and his family—spurred Griggs on to interpret contemporary history, so did the race riot in Wilmington, North Carolina, provide part of Chesnutt's impetus. Occurring in the same year—1898— the two events furnished Griggs and Chesnutt with dramatic material to transform into fiction and myth at once. [As shown elsewhere in *Mythic Black Fiction*], such events are not isolated ones, the climate of the 1890s being so vicious that it allowed for numerous such occurrences. The year 1898 spawned mobs in Greenwood County, South Carolina, where many blacks were shot and hanged. In 1900, mobs robbed and assaulted blacks for three days in New Orleans. During this time, in fact, the proportion of lynching was increasing in the South.[6]

Like his fellow post-Reconstruction writers, Chesnutt responds to the dehumanization of blacks, and his primary emphasis is self-definition. In the manner of many black writers, he uses messianic figures to point to traditionally Christian virtues without making direct reference to Christianity. Thus he mythologizes endurance and dignity in the face of adversity, demonstrating the transcendence of suffering he wants his audience to acknowledge in the black community. Moreover, Chesnutt depicts black visionary qualities, particularly intuitive wisdom, to arrive at a notion of the various ways Afro-Americans are empowered to change history. Literacy, a central fixture of Chesnutt's mythmaking, has the potential to demonstrate black intellectual agility, if not to provide social mobility.

The romance, with its emphasis on heroic characters who triumph over corrupt forces, is an ideal strategy for depicting Chesnutt's myth. His three central characters form a kind of trinity engaged in battle with the unholy "Big Three," Chesnutt's fictionalization of typical post-Reconstruction politicos. Romance also allows him to uproot prevailing stereotypes, particularly those promulgated by the Plantation Tradition, and redesign them from a black perspective. Generally speaking, Chesnutt's mythmaking in *The Marrow of Tradition* centers on educated blacks, fleshed out by the Genteel Tradition, the Sentimental Heroine, and the tragic mulatto, devices to further his insistence on assimilation. At the same time, however, he offers an uneducated working-class hero, Josh Green, whose messianic capabilities emerge when he avenges slavery's injustices. Two other paradigmatic characters, William and Janet Miller, both of whom are educated, dramatize dignity and refusal to misuse power. Both can see beyond the mammoth injustices inflicted on them to envision an ideal world, and they behave according to the dictates of that world without sacrificing their integrity. Perhaps because Chesnutt views his racial past as humiliating, or perhaps because he assumes his audience views it thus, he cannot incorporate that past into his mythology. While such omission may or may not constitute a fictional flaw, one cannot ignore more obvious flaws: *The Marrow of Tradition* suffers from the stock devices of the sentimental romance, including overplotting, and its language is as stilted as that of most romances of its day. Nevertheless, if examined within the mode Chesnutt chooses, *The Marrow of Tradition* cannot justly be criticized for melodrama or implausibility or for flat characterization or plot contrivances, for Chesnutt deliberately employs such strategies to convey his fictional mythology.

Both Griggs and Chesnutt sought to counteract stereotypes and create heroes for their audiences, but these audiences differed from one another. Earlier it was noted that a larger number of blacks read Griggs' fiction than read either Chesnutt's or Dunbar's. Chesnutt failed to reach a large black audience, in part, because in some instances he chose not to reach that audience. In a letter to Houghton Mifflin, December 14, 1899, Chesnutt wrote that he did not favor advertising or reviews from the majority of black newspapers. His reason involved this theory: "Most of them are grossly illiterate, and their readers, generally speaking, buy comparatively few books."[7] Thus while he, like Griggs, tried to merge historical issues with popular fictional strategies to attract a large readership, his major audience was not the black working class but those whites and middle class blacks suffering the influence of the plantation tradition of Joel Chandler Harris, Thomas Nelson Page, and, later, Thomas Dixon.

Harris and Page's fictionalization of pre-war times, albeit ludicrously simplistic or historically inaccurate, did provide impetus for Chesnutt. In addition, Chesnutt reacted as vehemently as Hopkins to newspapers of the time that vilified blacks as brutes lurking in the shadows, intent on raping innocent white women. With *The Marrow of Tradition,* he wished to confront the lack of reality of black characters presented to American society. Moreover, Chesnutt envisioned himself as crusading against what he perceived as the "subtle, almost indefinable feeling of repulsion toward the Negro, which is common to most Americans."[8] As a result, *The Marrow of Tradition* strives to develop multi-faceted characters.

Chesnutt accomplishes this characterization in part because he realized that black characters, though functioning as counter-stereotypes, need not necessarily appear divine. White characters, he saw, needed to occupy roles other than villainous ones—or at least needed motivation for villainous acts. Proceeding from these assumptions, Chesnutt created Jerry, a black character whose class interests preclude moral action, and Old Mr. Delamere, a truly benign member of the gentry. During slavery Jerry would have experienced a certain degree of protection from his master, but as a freedman he is on his own, shrewdly ascertaining that his well-being depends on obsequiousness. Disloyal to whites and blacks alike, he contributes to the near-lynching of an innocent black man. Although a victim of racism, Jerry is at no time presented sympathetically. Rather, he reveals the dehumanization resulting from the New South's mores. Whereas the Plantation Tradition made much of the suffering freedman, Harris and Page chose not to depict the reality of his condition as did Chesnutt. Many of Chesnutt's characters resemble Plantation Tradition types; however, each transforms the original to explode and replace contemporary myths. Consequently, *The Marrow of Tradition* both parallels and parodies the romances of its literary adversaries, revising both history and historical fiction.

Primarily, Chesnutt addresses the Plantation Tradition through contrasting the old and the new. For Harris and Page, who wished to perpetuate the notion that the South had deteriorated since the Civil War, it was necessary to show the benevolent paternalism of the old masters. Old Mr. Delamere, whose faith in the innocence of his servant Sandy Campbell obliterates his faith in his own grandson, exemplifies this sort of ideal gentleman. In contrast, his grandson Tom, emblematic of the new order, is portrayed as a whiskey swilling, insensitive rake, who not only cheats at cards, defying the code of the Southern gentleman, but robs (and possibly murders) his own aunt to pay off his gambling debts. More hideous still, he frames the loyal servant who raised him, almost causing Sandy's lynching. Had Chesnutt depicted Old Delamere as a stereotypic Southern gentleman, the reader might feel bewildered by Chesnutt's apparent use of the Plantation Tradition. Actually, Chesnutt transmutes stereotypes into real historical figures, presenting Delamere's loyalty to Sandy in historically accurate fashion: Sandy is found innocent simply because Delamere's blacks had been carefully raised, in other words, socialized. White romancers would have lionized the beatific Southern gentlemen of the past; however, they would have avoided showing that men such as Delamere produced dissolute grandsons such as Tom. Chesnutt's mythmaking, then, recreates and undercuts the Plantation Tradition.

Servants, too, embody contrasts between antebellum and post-Civil War periods. Just as Chesnutt opposes Sandy,

the ultimate innocent, to Jerry, the sycophant, he juxtaposes the faithful old Mammy Jane with a combative new nurse. Significantly, however, Mammy Jane, while genuinely kind, is appallingly self-righteous, as shown by her response to her employer's claim that Mammy Jane has no peer: "Deed dere ain't, honey; you is talkin' de gospel truf now! None er dese yer young folks ain't got de trainin' my ole mist'ess gave me. Dese yer new-fangle schools don' l'arn 'em nothin' ter compare wid it."[9] Through this speech, Chesnutt underscores the nature of the servant's compliment to her mistress, her firm resolve to identify with the power of the ruling class. In contrast, the nameless nurse is described as passing through racial adolescence: "she was in what might be called the chip-on-the-shoulder stage, through which races as well as individuals must pass" (42). With the phrase "as well as individuals," Chesnutt slyly suggests that all readers, white as well as black, have at one time manifested the "pugnaciousness" which post-Civil War blacks stood accused of originating. Through these and other devices, Chesnutt seeks to dispel Plantation Tradition myths.

To further mythologize black history, Chesnutt resorts to the Genteel Tradition, that delimiting but inevitable set of values in the turn-of-the-century romance. Amusingly, when Chesnutt wishes to symbolize Tom Delamere's utter depravity, he reveals a bureau drawer's contents. To his horror, Old Mr. Delamere discovers "bottles of wine and whiskey; soiled packs of cards; a dice-box with dice; a box of poker chips, several revolvers, and a number of photographs and paper-covered books at which the old gentleman merely glanced to ascertain their nature" (223). Chesnutt's handling of black characters further reinforces genteel values. William Miller, the young doctor, is rarely called by his first name; that the reader knows him as "Dr. Miller" seems pretentious and formal. In addition it has led several critics to call him "Adam," his father's name. Miller and Janet, his wife, speak white English at all times and struggle to influence "the best people" (190). In one episode a train conductor forces Miller to ride in the Jim Crow car, and he briefly shares his quarters with some farm laborers whose noise and dirty clothes he finds "offensive" (61). That he must ride with them galls his class sensibilities. Chesnutt's willingness to exploit the tragic mulatto theme constitutes a more serious limitation. Miller and Janet are both mulatto; in fact the primary emotional impact of *The Marrow of Tradition* hinges on Janet's relationship with Olivia Carteret, her half-sister, and Olivia's refusal to acknowledge Janet's existence, much less her right to their father's estate. Bearing a strong family resemblance to Olivia, Janet is nevertheless denied social acceptance by the white community. Chesnutt's purpose in emphasizing Janet's color is much the same as his predecessors; by stressing the physical similarity between Olivia and Janet he hopes to elicit white sympathy and identification. Whereas Harris and Page emphasize the mulatto's "tainted nature," Chesnutt deplores the racial mixture because it leads to isolation. Janet and her husband, though financially stable, are as Chesnutt described himself, "neither 'nigger,' white, nor 'buckrah.' Too 'stuck up' for the colored folks, and, of course, not recognized by the whites."[10]

As with Brown, Harper, and Hopkins, the appeal to whiteness suggests an underlying sense of racial supremacy disturbing in a writer seeking to counter white supremist's romances. Chesnutt himself, however, would have found such criticism irrelevant because he unabashedly envisioned part of his "high, holy purpose" as promoting assimilation.[11] Through assimilation, he felt, racial prejudice would vanish. That such a notion is politically anathema to black nationalists is obvious. But even in Chesnutt's time the tragic mulatto theme was considered sentimental. According to the 1860 census, only 12 percent of the black population was mulatto.[12] By 1900 the census did not solicit such information, but there is little reason to believe the figures had altered significantly. For most blacks the mulatto was not tragic but fortunate, enjoying special privileges denied darker Afro-Americans. Thus for some black readers Chesnutt dwelled on sentiment for its own sake. Significantly, neither Griggs nor Du Bois exploits the tragic mulatto theme. Finally, the reader must regret Chesnutt's use of the theme as indicative of his imprisonment in a cliché.

A more appealing device of Chesnutt's romance to counter stereotypes is his emphasis on characters' extraordinary qualities. Josh Green, Dr. Miller, and Janet Miller possess heroic potential, each serving a distinct ideological function. Josh Green exhibits the most obvious heroism, and the modern reader can identify with him more easily than with the Millers. The reader first glimpses Josh, "a huge Negro, covered thickly with dust," through Miller's eyes. Poles apart from the well-mannered doctor, Josh immerses his head in a water trough and shakes himself "like a wet dog." In contrast to Miller, who has paid first-class train fare, Green has hopped on a car without paying. To Miller, Josh is "an ordinarily good-natured, somewhat reckless, pleasure-loving negro" (59). Therefore he is surprised to see Josh's expression change to one of intense hatred when he glimpses Mc Bane, a fellow passenger. During a Klan incident Mc Bane has shot Josh's father and traumatized his mother so that she has never regained her sanity; Josh is determined to avenge these deeds. Even while he regards Josh as a "dusty tramp," Miller admires his dedication to revenge (59). Most blacks, Miller admits to himself, want to forget their history, a "dark story." Josh, on the other hand, remembers his and "shapes his life to a definite purpose" (112). Josh remains unintrigued by middle-class manners and mores. His sympathy, language, and behavior lie entirely with the black working class, and his life purpose is to rectify the wrongs done to them, wrongs symbolized by his mother's disrupted sanity.

Chesnutt further stresses Josh's heroism through opposing his militant stance to Miller's accommodationist principles. Whereas Miller attempts, with no success, to convince the indifferent whites of Sandy Campbell's innocence, Josh proposes that blacks take up arms and surround the jail. Even when Miller refuses to join Josh's resistance group against Mc Bane and Carteret's raid on the black citizenry, the rebels proceed fearlessly without him, disregarding his warning that resistance is suicidal. The ensuing riot provides Josh with his long-awaited confrontation with Mc Bane. While more than one critic has lambasted this scene for its melodramatic qualities, the scene clearly ignores the demands of verisimilitude and moves into the realm of romance. Josh, a "black giant, famed on the wharves for his strength," amazes the crowd with his immunity to the endless rain of bullets. "Armed with a huge bowie-knife, a relic of the civil war," and a smile which "seemed to take him out of mortal ken," Josh plunges the weapon into Mc Bane's heart. Given the post-Reconstruction era, Chesnutt cannot endorse Josh's violence, finding it necessary to query, "One of the two died as the fool dieth. Which was it, or was it both?" (309). Nevertheless, Josh's larger-than-life status remains intact. He occupies a pivotal position in black historical fiction, a man who would "ruther be a dead nigger any day dan a live dog," thus contributing to the mythologizing process (284).

Dr. Miller's heroism is more elusive, but Chesnutt does mean him to serve as a paradigm, even though Miller laments his own advice to disband the resistance group as "not heroic but . . . wise" (283). Dr. Miller belongs to the segment of black culture Du Bois designated as the "talented tenth." Colleagues here and abroad regard him as the best in his field, and he has performed a remarkable operation that has gained him recognition in a medical journal. Moreover, his humanitarian instincts have led him to dedicate personal funds to establish and maintain a black hospital in the South rather than in the less oppressive North or in Europe because he regards his mission as remaining with his people, contributing "to their uplifting" (51). Despite repeated slights and insults, such as being denied entrance to Carteret's home, where a Northern doctor has invited him to assist at a delicate operation, he maintains impeccable dignity. The romance's final scene pushes Miller's self-command beyond the point any ordinary man could endure. His hospital reduced to rubble by a racial massacre perpetrated by Carteret, his own son shot during the holocaust, Miller is approached by Olivia Carteret to save her son's life by performing a tracheotomy. During several impassioned, irrefutable speeches, Miller outlines the moral situation: Major Carteret is a murderer, while he is a victim; Major Carteret represents injustice, while he represents justice. In short, Miller, as the only doctor who can save Carteret's son from death, occupies the messianic throne of power. Satisfying as his power appears to the audience, Miller, like Chesnutt, cannot reconcile himself to the militance his position suggests. Just as Chesnutt edges away from Josh's violent attack on Mc Bane, he takes the reins from Miller and hands them to Janet, allowing her to perform her mythic function.

Janet's heroic potential is almost as difficult to perceive as is Miller's, but when viewed within its historical context, her heroism emerges clearly. Serving, like her husband, to counter prevailing Plantation Tradition stereotypes, she is college-educated, well-read, and unlike the so-called "impudent new negroes," unfailingly gracious and polite. In fact Janet is the quintessential Sentimental Heroine: aside from her role as tragic mulatta, she is "an exhaustless fountain of sympathy" who all her life has "yearned for a kind word, a nod, a smile," from her sister Olivia Carteret (65-66). Despite Janet's self-abnegation, Chesnutt wants his audience to view her as an extraordinarily sensitive and introspective woman. In reflecting on her all-forgiving nature, Janet muses that she has often rebuked herself for her spineless behavior and poor self-concept. She attributes these flaws to the "taint of slavery" (66). Janet's meditations are not apt to arouse in the reader a sense of her heroism, in the traditional sense. Unlike Josh, her remembrance of her history does not lead her to "shape [her] life to a definite purpose" and avenge the wrongs done to her ancestors. In contrast to Josh, she feels more shame than anger in connection with the history that has "tainted" her; or, more to the point, she has internalized her anger rather than directing it toward an appropriate target. What is heroic is her willingness to confront her own docility and to examine its supposed origins. Chesnutt obviously views Janet as a woman concerned with the nature of truth, a woman who has access to profound realities. His confidence that "when the heart speaks, reason falls into the background" explains why Janet's decision to allow Miller to perform the tracheotomy is not simply a retreat from militance, for Chesnutt believes she possesses a penetrating intuitive understanding of truth (66).

The Marrow of Tradition's final moments permit Janet to turn around a potentially humiliating confrontation with her sister and achieve tragic greatness. Chesnutt stresses her mythic qualities: "she towered erect, with menacing aspect, like an avenging goddess" (326). When Olivia, fearing that Janet will not send Miller to her baby's aid, exercises her last effort at manipulation by offering Janet the portion of their father's estate to which his will already entitles her, Janet retorts scornfully, "I throw you back your father's name, your father's wealth, your sisterly recognition. I want none of them—they are bought too dear! . . . But that you may know that a woman may be foully wronged, and yet may have a heart to feel, even for one who has injured her, you may have your child's life, if my husband can save it!" (329). Compared to the narrow, petty selfishness of her sister, she emerges as heroic, almost saintly. *The Marrow of Tradition* concludes with Miller entering the Carteret house. Still, the reader remembers not this seeming defeat but Janet's superb victory over the groveling, ignominious Olivia. Indeed, Janet's nearly superhuman dignity during her last speech ensures her mythic stature. Each of the romance's heroic characters has suffered tremendous loss: Josh Green lies dead, Dr. Miller's hospital stands in ruins, Janet is deprived of her child and her inheritance. But the three characters remain ennobled—not by suffering but by their ability to transcend that suffering. Putting aside personal,

selfish motives, each acts with dignity even in the face of degrading circumstances. Each, larger-than-life, achieves legendary status, suggesting that blacks would be better equipped to lead than whites if given positions of power.

Did Chesnutt's characters not triumph in this fashion, his romance would be unbearably depressing, for he fictionalizes in meticulous detail post-Reconstruction politics. Carteret, Belmont, and McBane convey through their values and actions Chesnutt's concept of history. With the leaders of the white supremacy movement, Chesnutt explains the forces behind disenfranchisement. Major Carteret, editor of the *Morning Chronicle,* the organ of the political party defeated in the last election, seeks to reinstate the old South for his son's sake. Carteret, who believes in "the divine right of white men and gentlemen," represents those for whom the Southern code's external manners easily symbolize true morality (34). As William L. Andrews has demonstrated, Chesnutt has modelled Carteret on an actual person, Josephus Daniels, "who, as editor of the *Raleigh News and Observer* . . . conducted an anti-fusion, anti-Negro press campaign during the election year of 1898." General Belmont, Andrews establishes, is likewise based on a real historical figure in Wilmington politics, Alfred Moore Waddell.[13] Belmont, a lawyer aspiring to be governor, is entirely unscrupulous. In Chesnutt's moral hierarchy, Belmont retains his gentlemanly position primarily as a result of birth, education, and shrewdness. In short, unlike Carteret, he is the sort of man who before the war would have turned his head when his slaves were mistreated. "Captain" McBane, whose title is purely fictitious, epitomizes the old South's obliteration. Whereas before the war McBane would have served as an overseer, slavery's abolition, coupled with his ambition, has allowed him to move from manual laborer to political aspirant. Benefiting from illegally-acquired wealth, McBane seeks a political office to ensure the status formerly denied him. Thus he perches on the bottom rung of the ladder, below Carteret and Belmont.

Their campaign to repeal the Fifteenth Amendment through convincing North Carolina that blacks should never have received the vote is for each of these men only a tool to further his own ambitions. Finally, they possess a frightening amount of political power. What Carteret and Belmont lack in effrontery McBane makes up for; what McBane lacks in influence Carteret and Belmont counterbalance. As a result, "the Big Three" constitute an invincible force. With these characters and the massacre they bring about (for which Carteret disclaims responsibility when the wholesale murder repels his sensibilities) Chesnutt suggests that if history is cyclical, it is so because men like these desperately need the security previous eras afforded. To be sure, blacks are floundering in a post-Reconstruction morass, but the Big Three, as well, stumble through unknown territory, struggling to forge stable identities. Carteret and Belmont can best forge these identities by reinstating the old order. By identifying with this order, Mc Bane can blot out his past's humiliation. Through these characters, John Reilly writes, "Chesnutt exposes the fundamental similarity of white men who mistakenly believe themselves to be distinctly different because of social class and manners."[14] *The Marrow of Tradition* demonstrates that history is shaped by humanity's psychological needs, its insecurities and weaknesses. Analyzing the white supremacy campaign's success, the narrator reflects that selfishness, rather than patriotism, humanism, or spirituality, "is the most constant of human motives . . . burrowing unwearingly at the very roots of life" (239). Perhaps because Chesnutt spent much time with whites, he arrives at a vision of history that recognizes the degree to which blacks' and whites' fates intertwine. Selfishness motivates all of us, the only hope lying with those who can put aside selfishness and behave morally. Both black and white characters exhibit this ability: Old Delamere, who intervenes on Sandy Campbell's behalf, acts as morally as do Josh, Miller, and Janet. J. Noel Heermance makes a case for the optimism Chesnutt exhibited most of his life. Pointing to a statement to Walter Hines Page in 1899 that blacks were "moving steadily upward," Heermance argues that even in the period of Chesnutt's most profound despair, he never failed to believe in the future amelioration of blacks' condition.[15] For Chesnutt, as for Griggs, life is grim. Yet while *Imperium in Imperio* reveals bewilderment at the proper means to confront that life, *The Marrow of Tradition* conjectures that even when nothing can be gained except the assurance of dignity and heroism, by refusing to misuse power blacks can transcend oppression.

Griggs and Chesnutt both rely on their own era's historical events to furnish fictional material. Like Brown, they do little more than allude to a past whose "primitiveness" precludes the possibility of heroic figures for their audience. Both flirt with militance, yet neither can fully endorse that militance. Whereas each decries the paucity of reward gained through education, each takes pains to provide genteel, educated blacks to counteract stereotypes. Both romances embody the desire to provide legendary figures who dispel myths of inferiority and populate a realm of heroic possibility. For the post-Reconstruction romancer, the need to create a positive mythology was monumental. But the unabashed heroism of *Iola Leroy* and *Contending Forces* ultimately eludes Griggs and Chesnutt. To repudiate white cultural values as does Josh Green, or to embrace militance, as do both Josh and Bernard, suggests the very dehumanization these writers fight so hard to erase. Accordingly, to accept white mores while refusing to fight back, as do Belton and Dr. Miller, means betrayal of one's race, loss of integrity. Even Janet achieves her heroism at the expense of joy. Many blacks today believe their dilemma mirrors the one Griggs and Chesnutt depict. Yet *Imperium in Imperio* and *The Marrow of Tradition* disclose a far more constrictive culture, one that totally denies black humanity and achievement, forcing its writers to take refuge in a heroism tempered by bitterness and ambivalence.

NOTES

[1] S. P. Fullinwider points out in *The Mind and Mood of Black America: 20th Century Thought* (Homewood, Ill.: Dorsey Press, 1969), 75, that in four of Griggs's romances two such heroic figures mirror Griggs's own ambivalence.

[2] Sutton Griggs, *Imperium in Imperio* (1899; rpt. New York: Arno, 1969), 40. All further references to this work appear in the text.

[3] Hugh M. Gloster, *Negro Voices in American Fiction* (1948; rpt. New York: Russell and Russell, 1965), 57.

[4] James M. Mellard, "Prolegomena to a Study of the Popular Mode in Narrative," *Journal of Popular Culture* 6 (1972), 8.

[5] Robert E. Fleming, "Sutton E. Griggs: Militant Black Novelist," *Phylon* 34 (1973), 75.

[6] Woodward, *The Strange Career of Jim Crow*, 87.

[7] Chesnutt Papers, as quoted in William L. Andrews, "A Reconsideration of *Charles Waddell Chesnutt: Pioneer of the Color Line*," *College Language Association Journal* 19 (1975), 144.

[8] Journal, May 29, 1880, Charles Waddell Chesnutt Collection, Erastus Milo Cravath Memorial Library, Fisk Univ., Nashville, Tenn., as quoted in J. Noel Heermance, *Charles W. Chesnutt: America's First Great Novelist* (Hamden, Conn.: Archon, 1969), 19.

[9] Charles Waddell Chesnutt, *The Marrow of Tradition* (1901; rpt. Miami: Mnemosyne, 1969), 41. All further references to this work appear in the text.

[10] Chesnutt Papers, as quoted in Andrews, "A Reconsideration," 142.

[11] Helen Chesnutt, *Charles Waddell Chesnutt: Pioneer of the Color Line* (Chapel Hill: Univ. of North Carolina Press, 1952), 21.

[12] Woodward, *The Strange Career of Jim Crow*, 16.

[13] William L. Andrews, *The Literary Career of Charles W. Chesnutt* (Baton Rouge: Louisiana State Univ. Press, 1980), 180.

[14] John Reilly, "The Dilemma in Chesnutt's *The Marrow of Tradition*," *Phylon* 32 (1971), 34.

[15] Heermance, *Charles W. Chesnutt*, 137.

Stephen C. Tracy (essay date 1986)

SOURCE: "Saving the Day: The Recordings of the Reverend Sutton E. Griggs," in *PHYLON: The Atlanta Uni-*

versity Review of Race and Culture, Vol. XLVII, No. 2, June, 1986, pp. 159-66.

[*In the following essay, Tracy offers a look at Griggs's style as a preacher.*]

Although critics as early as Sterling Brown in 1937 recognized the artistic deficiencies of Sutton E. Griggs, they have also recognized that Griggs at times transcended these artistic limitations by striking an early, semi-militant stance in literature—as a political novelist, adversary of Thomas Dixon, and champion of fictional heroes with black pigmentation.[1] Hugh Gloster wrote that "American Negroes who espouse black beauty, black pride, black militancy, and black separatism are ideological successors of Dr. Sutton E. Griggs," at least the Griggs of the early novels.[2] Robert Bone agreed with this assessment, though he identified in Griggs a vacillation between militancy and accommodation, a vacillation that was not a personal but an historical phenomenon.[3] Robert Fleming correctly identifies accommodationist leanings in Griggs' first novel, *Imperium in Imperio* (1899), where Belton Piedmont is the hero rather than the more militant Bernard Belgrave.[4] Perhaps Arlene A. Elder best characterizes Griggs and his "middle-class revolutionary" stance:

> . . . his books cry out for Black independence and self-reliance on American soil, but also insist that progress will depend upon "conservative" leaders in both races. He strongly rejects violence, a possibility that he explores fully and often, as a means of righting wrongs, yet just as strongly urges full political participation by Blacks and peaceful, but militant social action.[5]

Progressively in the latter part of his life Griggs immersed himself in his work with the Baptist church, particularly around 1920. At that time Griggs moved to Memphis and, beset by financial problems, offered a conciliatory hand to whites, garnering him the reputation as the "Negro Apostle to the White Race."[6] This section of Griggs's career rightfully interests the literary critics much less than his earlier, more militant period; however, there is material from the 1920s, previously unnoticed, that should be of great interest.

The revised edition of R. M. W. Dixon and John Godrich's *Blues and Gospel Records 1902-1943* lists six sides under the name of Reverend Sutton E. Griggs, recorded in Memphis, Tennessee on September 18 and 29, 1928. It seems highly likely that these sides are by *the* Sutton Griggs: he was an ordained Baptist minister, corresponding Secretary of the Education Department of the National Baptist Convention in Nashville, pastor of the Tabernacle Baptist Church in Memphis (though he apparently left there for Texas in 1926), and author of nonfiction prose published in Tennessee as late as 1927). After I had made these various connections between the writer and recording artists, I received a review copy of Paul Oliver's *Songsters and Saints: Vocal Traditions on Race Records,* which devoted two paragraphs to one of the Griggs recordings. Oliver describes the sermon that

referred to racial tension as being told in "measured phrases," and describes it as having a "pointed, even platitudinous moral."[7] There is a suggestion in the book that this may be the novelist Griggs, but Oliver explores none of the biographical details (indeed, he suggests that the recording artist is Methodist because of his delivery), though he does suggest that the Reverend's delivery is "literary."[8]

Although this is the religious Griggs and not the novelist, the recordings themselves are fascinating and important in that they provide insight into Griggs' technique as a speaker and into the way he mixed the oral and written traditions in his sermons. The following transcriptions and discussions hopefully will present insight into Griggs' religious and political stance near the end of this life.

What follows are discographical details and transcriptions of Griggs' recordings.[9]

Rev. Sutton E. Griggs, vocal with two soprano vocals, two alto vocals, tenor vocal, and piano.

Tuesday, September 18, 1928. Memphis, Tenn.

47055-2 **"Saving the Day"**

Victor V38516

> "Saving the Day." My text is the seventeenth verse of the third chapter of Joshua, reading thus: "And the priests that bare the ark of the covenant of the Lord stood firm on dry ground in the midst of the Jordan, and all of the Israelites passed over on dry ground, until all the people passed clean over Jordan." I am now to tell you of the salvation wrought in modern times in a river by a group of Negroes. The Mississippi River was hammering away at a given point in her levee. Behind the trembling embankment of earth the people watched in an agony of fear. Their property and their lives were being menaced by a sea of angry waters that seemed to have chosen that spot for one last mad effort to break through and roll at liberty over the land teeming with life and pregnant with the coming harvest. Skilled engineers with the previous history of the river before them had spent the full force of their judgment in the construction of the levee but, as the situation proved, had failed to give perfect security. The state and federal governments had exercised their full power in trying to meet the situation created, but the waters lashed and roared and laughed their best efforts to scorn. The citizens from the surrounding regions gathered in mass at the chief point of danger and were rushing sand bags to the front with all the speed at their command. In spite of all this, a break came. And with a gurgle of joy the waters of the mighty Mississippi started through. In the twinkling of an eye, a band of Negroes offered their bodies as temporary sand bags. Wedging their forms into the break, they formed a human wall, and at the

imminent peril of their lives, held the furious waters in leash until sand bags could be rushed to the break. And thus the day was saved.

Singing: Refrain:

    Group: Roll Jordan, roll (x2)

        I want to go to heaven when I die

        Go ahead Jordan, roll.

    Griggs: O sister you ought to have been there.

    Group: Yes my Lord.

    Griggs: Or sitting in the corner

    Group: To hear Jordan roll.

    Group: Refrain

47056-1 "A Hero Closes a War"

Victor 21706

"A Hero Closes a War." In the fourth chapter of Micah and the third verse we have these words: "They shall beat their swords into plowshares, and their spears into pruninghooks: nation shall not lift up sword against nation, neither shall they learn war anymore." It was in Chesapeake Bay one dark night during the World War. An open boat was carrying a crew composed of white and Negro men. The boat capsized, throwing the entire crew into the water. There was now a scramble for the bottom of the upturned boat and some white men gained possession. They sought to keep it for the sole use of the whites, thinking that there would not be room enough for all. Feeling thus, they knocked back any Negro reaching the boat. Seeing the racial conflict, one Negro swam away, secured a white man struggling in the water, and took him to the boat, handing him to his white comrades. He did another white man the same way. Next he brought a Negro. Some of the men sought to deny asylum, but they were made to desist by other white men, and the Negro was taken aboard. From that time on, the swimmer could bring white or colored indiscriminately. The race war was over. That unknown Negro, in the dark of night in the water, menaced by death, was willing to bear the temporary implication of being a traitor to his race, a thought that must have flashed through the minds of his fellows because of the war that was raging. But he had their ultimate good in mind, and so persisted. With us, it is day, not night. We are safe ashore, not threatened with drowning. Under these circumstances, far superior to those of this Negro hero, come what will or may, let us have the vision and the courage to go forth helping the various races of mankind to tolerate one another on the bottom of the upturned boat in the troubled, tempestuous sea of life.

Singing: Soprano: Going to lay down my burden

    Group: Down by the riverside (x3)

    Soprano: Going to lay down my burden

    Group: Down by the riverside

        To study war no more.

    Group: Ain't gonna study war no more (x6)

Wednesday, September 19, 1928

47058-1 "Self Examination"

Victor 38516

"Self Examination." Paul says, in the eleventh chapter of First Corinthians and the twenty-eighth verse, "let a man examine himself." One of the greatest problems of religion is that of concentrating a man's attention upon himself. We are too apt to be found examining our neighbors rather than ourselves. Often we pass a point of a sermon to the other fellow when it should remain with us. I wish to illustrate my text by giving the interpretation of another text by a fellow minister. The minister said,

Old man prodigal son wasted his money his father gave him. When his money runned out, he pulled off his coat and sold it. When *dat* money was gone, he pulled off his vest and sold *dat*. When *dat* money was gone, he pulled off his top shirt and sold *dat*. When *dat* money was gone, he pulled off his undershirt and sold *dat*. When he done *dat*, he had come to himself. And my text says, "And when he come to himself, he said, 'I will arise and go to my father.'"

I exhort each one to practice constantly self examination. The world will be far better when each of us considers himself and not his neighbor.

Singing: Refrain

    Griggs: It's me

    Group: It's me, it's me, O Lord,
        Standing in the need of prayer.
        It's me, it's me, it's me, O Lord,
        Standing in the need of prayer.

    Soprano: It's not my brother but it's me, O Lord,

    Group: Standing in the need of prayer.
        It's not my brother but it's me, O Lord,
        Standing in the need of prayer.

    Group: Refrain

Soprano: It's not my sister but it's me, O Lord,

Group: Standing in the need of prayer.
          It's not my sister but it's me, O Lord,
          Standing in the need of prayer.

Group: Refrain.

47058-2 "Self Examination"

Unissued Test[10]

The text of this unissued test is substantially the same as the issued take. The line "When he done *dat,* he had come to himself" is changed in this text to "When he done *dat,* he had come to hisself." The "himself" of the following sentence is changed to "hisself" as well. The "himself" of the final sentence of the sermon is unchanged.

47060-1 "A Surprise Answer to Prayer"

Victor 21706

"A Surprise Answer to Prayer." My text is Luke, eleventh chapter, first verse: "teach us to pray." Sometimes when we are praying to move the people instead of God, we would be shocked to find some of our prayers answered. A wake was being held in a church one night over a man supposed to be dead. One of the brethren of the church, anxious to win a reputation as a pray-er, got on his knees, closed his eyes tightly, and began to pray in a loud voice. He besought God time and again to raise the corpse from the dead, calling (to the) attention to the fact that God had raised Lazarus from the dead. The praying of the brother and the shouting of the sisters awakened the man supposed to be dead, and he sat up. The people rushed wildly out of the house. The praying brother became disturbed over the silence that came after the people were gone. He kept one eye shut for God's sake and opened one for his own sake. The open eye revealed the man supposed to be dead sitting up and facing him. He reached for his knife, shouting to the revived man, "Doggone you, don't you move. Don't you move, I say. If you do, if you're not dead I'll kill you." He was threatening to murder to get rid of the answer to his prayer. Likewise, we would be surprised oft times if our prayers were really answered.

Group: There are four and twenty elders on their knees (on their knees) (x2)
    And we'll all rise together and face the rising sun.
    O Lord, (O Lord) have mercy if you please.

There are children in the fiery furnace on their knees (on their knees) (x2)
    And we'll all rise together and face the rising sun.
    O Lord, (O Lord) have mercy if you please.

47060-2 "A Surprise Answer to Prayer"

Unissued Test

In this take, "to win a reputation as a pray-er" is changed to "to win a reputation as a great pray-er." Griggs does not stumble over his words in the next sentence by putting "(to the)" in the wrong place. He changes "God had raised Lazarus" to "Jesus raised Lazarus." This take deletes the sentence "He kept one eye shut for God's sake and opened one eye for his own sake," changing the following sentence to "Opening his eyes, he saw the man supposed to be dead sitting up and facing him." He changes "Don't you move, I say" to "I say, don't you move." Lastly, his final sentence reads, "Likewise, we often would be surprised to have our prayers really answered."

The manner of performance on these recordings does indeed say much to us about Griggs' values. Godrich and Dixon state that "These titles are very 'Europeanized' and of very little gospel interest,"[11] and it is certainly true that these recordings have none of the vivacity, drama, or exhortative drive of recorded Baptist preachers like the Reverend J. M. Gates, the Reverend J. C. Burnett, or the Reverend A. W. Nix, or the spontaneity of sanctified or jack-leg preachers. He is not the type of oral folk preacher about whom James Weldon Johnson wrote in *God's Trombone* or Zora Neale Hurston depicted in *Jonah's Gourd Vine.* For one thing, the lack of significant textual variation in available alternate takes suggests that Griggs either has memorized or is reading a fixed text rather than improvising around basic ideas and phrases and establishing a rhythmic unit for his bursts of text as an oral folk preacher would do.[12] This may in fact be due to the artificiality of the recording studio and the time constraints of the length of a 78 RPM phonograph record. Griggs, of course, was not a folk preacher, and he does not evidence their concerns with formulas, rhythm, metrics, repetition, parallelism, and spontaneity. He would be classified, based on these recordings, as a "manuscript preacher" by the so-called spiritual preachers, whose sermons are oral, spontaneous and chanted. Griggs seems to lean toward the manner of the "spiritual preacher" in his imitation of another preacher in **"Self Examination."** It should be noted, however, that these recordings do not necessarily reflect his normal demeanor as a preacher because, as I have already said, they were recorded in an artificial environment. Griggs sounds very stiff and uncomfortable, putting accents on unimportant words and, often, enunciating as clearly as possible. He very rarely uses any changes in pitch or attack to emphasize any points, though a notable exception is in **"Self Examination,"** where he illustrates his text by referring to the textual interpretation of another minister. In this section Griggs attempts to imitate, just a little, a black preacher whose speech is not as sophisticated as his own, pronouncing his *th* sounds as *d,* twice changing the *himself* of the issued take to *hisself* in the test, and making slight use of parallelism and repetition to build up some drive. Still, both takes are very stiff, hardly emotionally rousing at all. Neither does he vocally dramatize the rather humorous story he tells in **"A Surprise Answer to Prayer,"** seeming content to allow the content to carry the message by making his manner of delivery calm and controlled and "reasonable."

Furthermore, the music that follows each of the short sermons lacks the fire and vocal effects characteristic of African-American religious singing despite the fact that the songs are African-American religious songs. There are no "worried" or drawn out notes, no dramatic pauses, no exhortations or cries or percussive effects. The singing is, rather, of the type that one might hear in a white Baptist or Methodist church, straightforward and unadorned, and Griggs and the singers enunciate as clearly in song as Griggs does when he preaches. The final effect of the manner of performance is not to excite emotionally, but to interest socially and to promote a temperate, middle-class approach.

Two of Griggs' sermons deal with racial disharmony, and the actions that define heroes in Griggs' stories reveal, once again, a middle-class approach to racial matters though, as Oliver points out, **"A Hero Closes a War"** was "almost alone among recorded sermons in making any specific reference to racial tension."[13] The heroes of **"Saving The Day"** accomplish what history, science, and governments cannot by selflessly offering themselves as "temporary sand bags" to stop the rush of water. By comparing this group of "Negroes" to the priests of the Israelites, Griggs seems to be seeking to prove the worthiness of "the Negro" through these people. Griggs avoids the fact that, very often, in flood times blacks were pressed into service on levees and forced to work until they dropped, as described in Richard Wright's "Down By the Riverside," which could have taken its setting from the 1927 flooding of the Mississippi River. That flood, the river's worst flood disaster in recorded history, happened the year before Griggs' recordings. Given this circumstance, their willingness to sacrifice their lives to save lives and crops seems an effort to prove their "nobility." Like his depiction of his hero in **"A Hero Closes A War,"** this heroic action involves the self-sacrifice of some blacks to save everyone else, and the language describing the storm is elevated and "literary," personifying the river.[14]

Racial conflict is more obvious in **"A Hero Closes A War"** in the actions of whites to prevent blacks from regaining their positions in a capsized boat. Although the story implies that whites and blacks were all "in the same boat" at one time, it still suggests that it is the "Negro's" responsibility to sacrifice, to prove his worthiness so that he may be accepted by the offending whites. Griggs has no problem with this circumstance, or with the implication that two whites must be saved before one "Negro." He anticipates that there may be some criticism of this attitude, recognizing that some "Negroes" might call his hero a traitor to his race and some whites might still not be appeased, but he insists that the self-sacrifice is for the common good. He never mentions any necessity for

whites to act decently in the first place. However, it is very interesting that Griggs acknowledges a racial war that coincided with World War I, that was amplified as white and black soldiers fought, in this case, side by side. In fact, Griggs gets a bit ambiguous when he discusses this. After "the race war was over," he discusses the feeling of the "fellows" toward the swimmer, who they might have considered a traitor to his race "because of the war that was raging." To which war was Griggs referring: the World War, the race war, or the private war between the two groups of soldiers? It is likely that Griggs was referring to the last of these, but the ambiguity might suggest unrest because of the World War as well. Finally, it should be noted that these two "racial" sermons were not released on the same 78 RPM record. Rather, each sermon was coupled with a "non-racial" one despite the fact that the racial sermons were recorded on the same day. Perhaps this indicates a hesitancy to release a record that deals too extensively with racial subjects; perhaps it indicates a desire to capitalize on the subjects of the sermons on two records instead of one. The reason behind the pairings will probably never be definitely known.

Finally, these recordings reflect Griggs' growing preoccupation with racial cooperation that involved the potential loss of African-American lives, pride, and style. The burden of proof, of being worthy of the respect of whites, resided with blacks who could treat themselves as inanimate objects (sand bags), aid those who denied them safety and equality, and imitate the manners of speech and performance that would help "legitimize" them in the eyes of whites. If Griggs was praying for racial cooperation, the surprise answer he most likely would have got from many whites would not have been the idealized one he presented in **"A Hero Closes A War,"** but a resounding "no." He seems to have been willing to endure that patiently until it changed.[15]

NOTES

[1] Sterling Brown, *Negro Poetry and Drama and The Negro in American Fiction* (1937; rpt. New York, 1972), pp. 100-01.

[2] Hugh M. Gloster, Preface, *Imperium in Imperio* by Sutton Griggs (New York, 1969), p. iii.

[3] Robert Bone, *The Negro Novel in America* (New Haven, 1962), pp. 33-4.

[4] Robert E. Fleming, "Sutton E. Griggs: Militant Black Novelist," *Phylon,* 34 (March 1973): 77.

[5] Arlene A. Elder, *The Hindered Hand: Cultural Implications of Early African-American Fiction* (Westport, Conn., 1978), p. 70.

[6] Thomas Oscar Fuller, *History of the Negro Baptists of Tennessee* (Memphis, 1936), pp. 76-7.

[7] Paul Oliver, *Songsters and Saints: Vocal Traditions on Race Records* (Cambridge, England, 1984), p. 146.

[8] Ibid., pp. 146-47. In a textual note on p. 298, Oliver does refer the reader to discussions of Griggs by Janheinz Jahn and Leroi Jones.

[9] The discographical details are taken from Robert M. W. Dixon and John Godrich, *Blues and Gospel Records 1902-1943* (Essex: Storyville Publ., 1982), p. 287.

[10] The two unissued tests discussed in this article are not listed in the discography. However, it does include two sermons recorded for Victor but not issued: "Speaking the Truth" and "Keeping the Peace," copies of which I have not been able to locate.

[11] Dixon and Godrich, op. cit., p. 287.

[12] For a good discussion of the folk preacher see Bruce Rosenberg, *The Art of the American Folk Preacher* (New York, 1970).

[13] Oliver, op. cit., p. 146. Oliver's assertion applies to sermons recorded during the 1920s and possibly the early 1930s.

[14] In what I have transcribed as "laughed their best efforts to scorn," Griggs pronounces *laughed* as *loft,* throwing into doubt whether this transcription is correct. If it is, it is perhaps a rather affected pronunciation. This is the only word in any if the transcriptions about which there is any doubt.

[15] Thanks go to music historian and discographer, Roger Misiewicz, who loaned me copies of the recordings by Sutton Griggs.

FURTHER READING

Bibliography

Inge, M. Thomas; Maurice Duke; and Jackson R. Bryer, eds. "Bibliographies." In *Black American Writers: Bibliographic Essays*, Volume I: *The Beginnings Through the Harlem Renaissance and Langston Hughes*, pp. 133-60. New York: St. Martin's Press, 1978.
    Writings by and about Griggs and his contemporaries such as Charles Chesnutt, with listings of reference books and other works on the African-American literature of the era.

Page, James A., and Jae Min Roh. "Griggs, Sutton E." In *Selected Black American, African, and Caribbean Authors: A Bio-Bibliography*, pp. 111-12. Littleton, Col.: Libraries Unlimited, 1985.
    Listing of Griggs's novels, with both their original publication dates and their re-publication dates in the 1960s and 1970s.

Criticism

Bell, Bernard W. "The Early Afro-American Novel: Historical Romance, Social Realism, and Beyond." In *The Afro-American Novel and Its Tradition*, pp. 37-75. Amherst: University of Massachusetts Press, 1987.
    Comparative essay on Griggs's *Imperium in Imperio* and the works of other writers before and after the Civil War.

Byrd, James W. "Five Early Afro-American Novels." *Southwest Review* LVII, No. 3 (Summer 1972): 262-64.
    Brief review of Griggs's five novels, with an emphasis on their prophecies regarding black nationalism, the Cold War, and other aspects of the mid-twentieth century.

Davis, Arthur P., and Saunders Redding, eds. "Sutton Elbert Griggs (1872-1930)." In *Cavalcade: Negro American Writing from 1760 to the Present*, pp. 163-67. Boston: Houghton Mifflin, 1971.
    A brief overview of Griggs's career, followed by a selection from *The Hindered Hand*.

Gayle, Addison, Jr. "Paradigms of the Early Past." In *The Way of the New World: The Black Novel in America*, pp. 60-70. Garden City, NY: Anchor Press/Doubleday, 1975.
    A review of Griggs's novels, with a defense against attacks on him by Robert Bone and other critics.

Gloster, Hugh M. "Sutton E. Griggs." In *Negro Voices in American Fiction*, pp. 56-67. New York: Russell & Russell, 1948.
    Overview of Griggs's novels, which Gloster briefly contrasts with those of Charles Chesnutt.

Hedin, Raymond. "Probable Readers, Possible Stories: The Limits of Nineteenth-Century Black Narrative." In *Readers in History: Nineteenth-Century American Literature and the Contexts of Response*, edited by James L. Machor, pp. 180-205. Baltimore: Johns Hopkins University Press, 1993.
    Examines a tradition of writings on black revolt, starting with Nat Turner's *Confessions* (1831) and ending with *Imperium in Imprerio*.

Additional coverage of Griggs's life and career is contained in the following sources published by Gale Research: *Contemporary Authors,* Vol. 123, and *Dictionary of Literary Biography*, Vol. 50.

Oliver Wendell Holmes, Jr.

1841-1935

American jurist.

INTRODUCTION

Holmes was one of the most renowned and controversial justices to serve on the United States Supreme Court. Appointed by Theodore Roosevelt in 1902, Holmes took his seat on the bench at a crucial transition point in American judicial history, when questions of the efficacy and applicability of the Constitution arose with the rapidly changing social conditions of the time. Despite his great popularity and influence, Holmes was known as the "Great Dissenter" for his consistent refusal to support the decisions of his fellow justices.

Biographical Information

Holmes was born in 1841 to one of Boston's most prominent families. On both sides of his family, he counted as ancestors such American luminaries as the Puritan poet Anne Bradstreet and the Quincys and Jacksons of early American politics. His grandfather, Abiel Holmes, was an admired Calvinist preacher and writer, and his father, Oliver Wendell Holmes, Sr., was a leading physician as well as an eminent author. Family connections allowed the young Holmes contact with the New England intellectual circle that included the essayist Ralph Waldo Emerson. In 1857 Holmes entered Harvard College, graduating in 1861. When the Civil War broke out, Holmes postponed his planned entrance to Harvard Law School to join the 20th Massachusetts Volunteers, in which he served until 1864. Evidence supports the claim of many biographers that Holmes placed far greater importance on his service in the war than on his academic studies in the shaping of his character; he was wounded three times, and the diary he kept during the war was later published with the title *Touched with Fire*. Holmes earned his law degree in 1866 and the following year cofounded the firm Shattuck, Holmes and Munroe, where he remained until 1882. During this time, Holmes also edited the *United States Law Review* and the *American Law Review*. In 1872 he married Fanny Dixwell, who later figured strongly as "the Mrs." in Holmes's popular public persona. From 1870 to 1882 Holmes was a lecturer and professor at Harvard Law School and the Lowell Institute in Massachusetts. A series of lectures he delivered at the Lowell Institute was published in 1881 as *The Common Law*, which brought him international renown as a great legal scholar. In 1883 Holmes became an associate justice of the Supreme Judicial Court of Massachusetts; in 1899 he was promoted to chief justice. Two years later President Theodore Roosevelt appointed Holmes to the United States Supreme Court. A vigorous

supporter of majority rule and free speech, Holmes used his command of language to pen his famously persuasive dissensions. Influenced personally and professionally by his friends William James and Charles Sanders Peirce, both American philosophers associated with the Pragmatist school, Holmes developed as a judge a keen ability to infuse complicated legalese with common sense and accessibility. He served on the Supreme Court until his retirement at the age of 91; he died in Washington, D.C., three years later.

Major Works

Although he was voted class poet for his graduating class at Harvard, Holmes's writing did not engage public notice until the publication of his lecture series *The Common Law* in 1881. Therein he delineated the judicial theory that would propel his career for the next fifty years. Holmes posits in *The Common Law* that it is not logical abstractions upon which judicial practice is based, but varying responses to constantly evolving social issues and problems. Applied throughout his career, this theory was particularly compelling during and after the First World War, when questions of free speech and the place of democratic ideals in the United States and abroad arose with the advent of fascism and communism. Holmes expressed his beliefs regarding free speech most markedly in *Schenck vs. U.S.* (1919), in which he argued that only speech that represents a "clear and present danger" should meet with legal recourse; otherwise, Holmes wrote in *Abrams vs. U.S.*, a "free trade in ideas" was integral to the flourishing of truth and justice. Legal historians have since noted the later distortion of Holmes's intent in *Schenck vs. U.S.* by subsequent United States justices. Most notably, the phrase "clear and present danger" was liberally and widely perverted in the Cold War of the 1950s to suit conservative political leanings. Nevertheless, Holmes was known during his lifetime for his support of civil liberties, as voiced in his strong dissent in cases approving the use of wiretapping and the conviction of a conscientious objector. In addition to his legal writings, Holmes wrote essays, letters, "wit and wisdom" works, and speeches, most of which were published after his death. The diary he kept as a young soldier in the Civil War and the letters he wrote during that period were published in 1946 as *Touched with Fire: Civil War Letters and Diary of Oliver Wendell Holmes, Jr., 1861-64.*

Critical Reception

Reception of Holmes's body of work has varied widely. Hailed by many as a liberal renegade, relying on American pragmatism and upholding civil liberties with a healthy skepticism, Holmes was nonetheless at times sharply criticized by others as a proto-fascist. H. L. Mencken, in his review of *The Dissenting Opinions of Mr. Justice Holmes*, found Holmes's dissension amusing, but maintained that the Justice was anything but liberal in his social and political beliefs. Others accused Holmes of undiscriminating and dangerous utilitarianism. Regardless of such censure, Holmes, along with his fellow Justices Louis Brandeis and Roscoe Pound, is remembered for his fairness and integrity as well as for his progressive ideas regarding the application of the principles of the American Constitution to social issues in a turbulent era.

Justice Holmes to Doctor Wu: An Intimate Correspondence (letters) 1935
Some Table Talk of Mr. Justice Holmes and "the Mrs." (nonfiction) 1935
The Black Book of Oliver Wendell Holmes (nonfiction) 1936
Justice Oliver Wendell Holmes: His Book Notices and Uncollected Letters and Papers [edited by Harry C. Shriver] (nonfiction, letters, and essays) 1936
The Judicial Opinions of Oliver Wendell Holmes: Constitutional Opinions, Selected Excerpts, and Epigrams (nonfiction) 1940
Holmes-Pollock Letters: The Correspondence of Mr. Justice Holmes and Sir Frederick Pollock, 1874-1932. 2 vols. (letters) 1941; published as *The Pollock-Holmes Letters: Correspondence of Sir Frederick Pollock and Mr. Justice Holmes, 1874-1932*, 1942
The Mind and Faith of Justice Holmes: His Speeches, Essays, Letters and Judicial Opinions (speeches, essays, letters, and nonfiction) 1943
Touched with Fire: Civil War Letters and Diary of Oliver Wendell Holmes, Jr., 1861-64 (letters and diary) 1946
Holmes-Laski Letters: The Correspondence of Mr. Justice Holmes and Harold J. Laski, 1916-1935. 2 vols. (letters) 1953
The Wit and Wisdom of Oliver Wendell Holmes, Father and Son (nonfiction) 1953
The Holmes Reader: The Life, Writings, Speeches, Constitutional Decisions, etc., of the Late Oliver Wendell Holmes (nonfiction and speeches) 1955
Occasional Speeches (speeches) 1962
The Holmes-Einstein Letters: Correspondence of Mr. Justice Holmes and Lewis Einstein, 1903-1935 (letters) 1964
Holmes-Sheehan Letters: The Letters of Justice Oliver Wendell Holmes and Canon Patrick Augustus Sheehan (letters) 1976
Progressive Masks: Letters of Oliver Wendell Holmes, Jr., and Franklin Ford (letters) 1982
The Formative Essays of Justice Holmes: The Making of an American Legal Philosophy (essays) 1984

PRINCIPAL WORKS

The Common Law (nonfiction) 1881
Speeches by Oliver Wendell Holmes, Junior (speeches) 1891; enlarged edition, 1896-1934
The Soldier's Faith: An Address by Oliver Wendell Holmes (lecture) 1895
Collected Legal Papers (nonfiction) 1920
The Dissenting Opinions of Mr. Justice Holmes (nonfiction) 1929
Representative Opinions of Mr. Justice Holmes (nonfiction) 1931

CRITICISM

Oliver Wendell Holmes, Jr. (essay date 1896)

SOURCE: "The Path of the Law," in *Oliver Wendell Holmes, Jr.,—What Manner of Liberal?*, edited by David H. Burton, Robert E. Kreiger Publishing Company, 1979, pp. 21-37.

[*In the following essay, originally published in 1896 in the* Harvard Law Review, *Holmes details his belief that legal considerations should rely on empiricism and reason rather than traditional absolutes.*]

When we study law we are not studying a mystery but a well known profession. We are studying what we shall want in order to appear before judges, or to advise people in such a way as to keep them out of court. The reason why it is a profession, why people will pay lawyers to argue for them or to advise them, is that in societies like ours the command of the public force is intrusted to the judges in certain cases, and the whole power of the state will be put forth, if necessary, to carry out their judgments and decrees. People want to know under what circumstances and how far they will run the risk of coming against what is so much stronger than themselves, and hence it becomes a business to find out when this danger is to be feared. The object of our study, then, is prediction, the prediction of the incidence of the public force through the instrumentality of the courts.

The means of the study are a body of reports, of treatises, and of statutes, in this country and in England, extending back for six hundred years, and now increasing annually by hundreds. In these sibylline leaves are gathered the scattered prophecies of the past upon the cases in which the axe will fall. These are what properly have been called oracles of the law. For the most important and pretty nearly the whole meaning of every new effort of legal thought is to make these prophecies more precise, and to generalize them into a thoroughly connected system. The process is one, from a lawyer's statement of a case, eliminating as it does all the dramatic elements with which his client's story has clothed it, and retaining only the facts of legal import, up to the final analyses and abstract universals of theoretic jurisprudence. The reason why a lawyer does not mention that his client wore a white hat when he made a contract, while Mrs. Quickly would be sure to dwell upon it along with the parcel gilt goblet and the sea-coal fire, is that he foresees that the public force will act in the same way whatever his client had upon his head. It is to make the prophesies easier to be remembered and to be understood that the teachings of the decisions of the past are put into general propositions and gathered into text-books, or that statutes are passed in a general form. The primary rights and duties with which jurisprudence busies itself again are nothing but prophecies. One of the many evil effects of the confusion between legal and moral ideas, about which I shall have something to say in a moment, is that theory is apt to get the cart before the horse, and to consider the right or the duty as something existing apart from and independent of the consequences of its breach, to which certain sanctions are added afterward. But, as I shall try to show, a legal duty so called is nothing but a prediction that if a man does or omits certain things he will be made to suffer in this or that way by judgment of the court;—and so of a legal right.

The number of our predictions when generalized and reduced to a system is not unmanageably large. They present themselves as a finite body of dogma which may be mastered within a reasonable time. It is a great mistake to be frightened by the ever increasing number of reports. The reports of a given jurisdiction in the course of a generation take up pretty much the whole body of the law, and restate it from the present point of view. We could reconstruct the corpus from them if all that went before were burned. The use of the earlier reports is mainly historical, a use about which I shall have something to say before I have finished.

I wish, if I can, to lay down some first principles for the study of this body of dogma or systematized prediction which we call the law, for men who want to use it as the instrument of their business to enable them to prophesy in their turn, and, as bearing upon the study, I wish to point out an ideal which as yet our law has not attained.

The first thing for a business-like understanding of the matter is to understand its limits, and therefore I think it desirable at once to point out and dispel a confusion between morality and law, which sometimes rises to the height of conscious theory, and more often and indeed constantly is making trouble in detail without reaching the point of consciousness. You can see very plainly that a bad man has as much reason as a good one for wishing to avoid an encounter with the public force, and therefore you can see the practical importance of the distinction between morality and law. A man who cares nothing for an ethical rule which is believed and practised by his neighbors is likely nevertheless to care a good deal to avoid being made to pay money, and will want to keep out of jail if he can.

I take it for granted that no hearer of mine will misrepresent what I have to say as the language of cynicism. The law is the witness and external deposit of our moral life. Its history is the history of the moral development of the race. The practice of it, in spite of popular jests, tends to make good citizens and good men. When I emphasize the difference between law and morals I do so with reference to a single end, that of learning and understanding the law. For that purpose you must definitely master its specific marks, and it is for that that I ask you for the moment to imagine yourselves indifferent to other and greater things.

I do not say that there is not a wider point of view from which the distinction between law and morals becomes of secondary or no importance, as all mathematical distinctions vanish in presence of the infinite. But I do say that that distinction is of first importance for the object which we are here to consider, a right study and mastery of the law as a business with well understood limits, a body of dogma enclosed within definite lines. I have just shown the practical reason for saying so. If you want to know the law and nothing else, you must look at it as a bad man, who cares only for the material consequences which such knowledge enables him to predict, not as a good one, who finds his reasons for conduct, whether inside the law or outside of it, in the vaguer sanctions of conscience. The theoretical importance of the distinction is no less, if you would reason on your subject aright. The law is full of phraseology drawn from morals, and by the mere force of language continually invites us to pass from one domain to the other without perceiving it, as we arc sure to do unless we have the boundary constantly before our minds. The law talks about rights, and duties, and malice, and intent, and negligence, and so forth, and nothing is easier, or, I may say, more common in legal reasoning, than to take these words in their moral sense, at some stage of the argument, and so to drop into fallacy. For instance, when we speak of the rights of man in a moral sense, we mean to mark the limits of interference with individual freedom which we think are prescribed by conscience, or by our ideal, however reached. Yet it is certain that many laws have been enforced in the past, and it is likely that some are enforced now, which are condemned by the most enlightened opinion of the time, or which at all events pass the limit of interference as many consciences would draw it. Manifestly, therefore, nothing but confusion of thought can result from assuming that the rights of man in a moral sense are equally rights in the sense of the Constitution and the law. No doubt simple and extreme cases can be put of imaginable laws which the statute-making power would not dare to enact, even in the absence of written constitutional prohibitions, because the community would rise in rebellion and fight; and this gives some plausibility to the proposition that the law, if not a part of morality, is limited by it. But this limit of power is not coextensive with any system of morals. For the most part it falls far within the lines of any such system, and in some cases may extend beyond them, for reasons drawn from the habits of a particular people at a particular time. I once heard the late Professor Agassiz say that a German population would rise if you added two cents to the price of a glass of beer. A statute in such a case would be empty words, not because it was wrong, but because it could not be enforced. No one will deny that wrong statutes can be and are enforced, and we should not all agree as to which were the wrong ones.

The confusion with which I am dealing besets confessedly legal conceptions. Take the fundamental question, What constitutes the law? You will find some text writers telling you that it is something different from what is decided by the courts of Massachusetts or England, that it is a system of reason, that it is a deduction from principles of ethics or admitted axioms or what not, which may or may not coincide with the decisions. But if we take the view of our friend the bad man we shall find that he does not care two straws for the axioms or deductions, but that he does want to know what the Massachusetts or English courts are likely to do in fact. I am much of this kind. The prophecies of what the courts will do in fact, and nothing more pretentious, are what I mean by the law.

Take again a notion which as popularly understood is the widest conception which the law contains;—the notion of legal duty, to which already I have referred. We fill the word with all the content which we draw from morals. But what does it mean to a bad man? Mainly, and in the first place, a prophecy that if he does certain things he will be subjected to disagreeable consequences by way of imprisonment or compulsory payment of money. But from his point of view, what is the difference between being fined and being taxed a certain sum for doing a certain thing? That his point of view is the test of legal principles is shown by the many discussions which have arisen in the courts on the very question whether a given statutory liability is a penalty or a tax. On the answer to this question depends the decision whether conduct is legally wrong or right, and also whether a man is under compulsion or free. Leaving the criminal law on one side, what is the difference between the liability under the mill acts or statutes authorizing a taking by eminent domain and the liability for what we call a wrongful conversion of property where restoration is out of the question? In both cases the party taking another man's property has to pay its fair value as assessed by a jury, and no more. What significance is there in calling one taking right and another wrong from the point of view of the law? It does not matter, so far as the given consequence, the compulsory payment, is concerned, whether the act to which it is attached is described in terms of praise or in terms of blame, or whether the law purports to prohibit it or to allow it. If it matters at all, still speaking from the bad man's point of view, it must be because in one case and not in the other some further disadvantages, or at least some further consequences, are attached to the act by the law. The only other disadvantages thus attached to it which I ever have been able to think of are to be found in two somewhat insignificant legal doctrines, both of which might be abolished without much disturbance. One is, that a contract to do a prohibited act is unlawful, and the other, that, if one of two or more joint wrongdoers has to pay all the damages, he cannot recover contribution from his fellows. And that I believe is all. You see how the vague circumference of the notion of duty shrinks and at the same time grows more precise when we wash it with cynical acid and expel everything except the object of our study, the operations of the law.

Nowhere is the confusion between legal and moral ideas more manifest than in the law of contract. Among other things, here again the so-called primary rights and duties are invested with a mystic significance beyond what can be assigned and explained. The duty to keep a contract at common law means a prediction that you must pay damages if you do not keep it,—and nothing else. If you commit a tort, you are liable to pay a compensatory sum. If you commit a contract, you are liable to pay a compensatory sum unless the promised event comes to pass, and that is all the difference. But such a mode of looking at the matter stinks in the nostrils of those who think it advantageous to get as much ethics into the law as they can. It was good enough for Lord Coke, however, and here, as in many other cases, I am content to abide with him. In Bromage *v.* Genning, a prohibition was sought in the King's Bench against a suit in the marches of Wales for the specific performance of a covenant to grant a lease, and Coke said that it would subvert the intention of the covenantor, since he intends it to be at his election either to lose the damages or to make the lease. Sergant Harris for the plaintiff confessed that he moved the matter against his conscience, and a prohibition was granted. This goes further than we should go now, but it shows what I venture to say has been the common law point of view from the beginning, although Mr. Harriman, in his very able little book upon Contracts has been misled, as I humbly think, to a different conclusion.

I have spoken only of the common law, because there are some cases in which a logical justification can be found for speaking of civil liabilities as imposing duties in an intelligible sense. These are the relatively few in which equity will grant an injunction, and will enforce it by putting the defendant in prison or otherwise punishing him unless he complies with the order of the court. But I hardly think it advisable to shape general theory from the exception, and I think it would be better to cease troubling ourselves about primary rights and sanctions altogether, than to describe our prophecies concerning the liabilities commonly imposed by the law as those inappropriate terms.

I mentioned, as other examples of the use of the law of words drawn from morals, malice, intent, and negligence. It is enough to take malice as it is used in the law of civil liability for wrongs,—what we lawyers call the law of torts,—to show you that it means something different in law from what it means in morals, and also to show how the difference has been obscured by giving to principles which have little or nothing to do with each other the same name. Three hundred years ago a parson preached a sermon and told a story out of Fox's Book of Martyrs of a man who had assisted at the torture of one of the saints, and afterward died, suffering compensatory inward torment. It happened that Fox was wrong. The man was alive and chanced to hear the sermons, and thereupon he sued the parson. Chief Justice Wray instructed the jury that the defendant was not liable, because the story was told innocently, without malice. He took malice in the moral sense, as importing a malevolent motive. But nowadays no one doubts that a man may be liable without any malevolent motive at all, for false statements manifestly calculated to inflict temporal damage. In stating the case in pleading, we still should call the defendant's conduct malicious; but, in my opinion, at least, the word means nothing about motives, or even about the defendant's attitude toward the future, but only signifies that the tendency of his conduct under the known circumstances was very plainly to cause the plaintiff temporal harm.

In the law of contract the use of moral phraseology has led to equal confusion, as I have shown in part already, but only in part. Morals deal with the actual internal state of the individual's mind, what he actually intends. From the time of the Romans down to now, this mode of dealing has affected the language of the law as to contract, and the language used has reacted upon the thought. We talk about a contract as a meeting of the minds of the parties, and thence it is inferred in various cases that there is no contract because their minds have not met; that is, because they have intended different things or because one party has not known of the assent of the

other. Yet nothing is more certain than that parties may be bound by a contract to things which neither of them intended, and when one does not know of the other's assent. Suppose a contract is executed in due form and in writing to deliver a lecture, mentioning no time. One of the parties thinks that the promise will be construed to them at once, within a week. The other thinks that it means when he is ready. The court says that it means within a reasonable time. The parties are bound by the contract as it is interpreted by the court, yet neither of them meant what the court declares that they have said. In my opinion no one will understand the true theory of contract or be able even to discuss some fundamental questions intelligently until he has understood that all contracts are formal, that the making of a contract depends not on the agreement of two minds in one intention, but on the agreement of two sets of external signs,—not on the parties' having *meant* the same thing but on their having *said* the same thing. Furthermore, as the signs may be addressed to one sense or another,—to sight or to hearing—on the nature of the sign will depend the moment when the contract is made. If the sign is tangible, for instance, a letter, the contract is made when the letter of acceptance is delivered. If it is necessary that the minds of the parties meet, there will be no contract until the acceptance can be read,—none, for example, if the acceptance be snatched from the hand of the offerer by a third person.

This is not the time to work out a theory in detail, or to answer many obvious doubts and questions which are suggested by these general views. I know of none which are not easy to answer, but what I am trying to do now is only by a series of hints to throw some light on the narrow path of legal doctrine, and upon two pitfalls which, as it seems to me, lie perilously near to it. Of the first of these I have said enough. I hope that my illustrations have shown the danger, both to speculation and to practice, of confounding morality with law, and the trap which legal language lays for us on that side of our way. For my own part, I often doubt whether it would not be a gain if every word of moral significance could be banished from the law altogether, and other words adopted which should convey legal ideas uncolored by anything outside the law. We should lose the fossil records of a good deal of history and the majesty got from ethical associations, but by ridding ourselves of an unnecessary confusion we should gain very much in the clearness of our thought.

So much for the limits of the law. The next thing which I wish to consider is what are the forces which determine its content and its growth. You may assume with Hobbes and Bentham and Austin, that all law emanates from the sovereign, even when the first human beings to enunciate it are the judges, or you may think that law is the voice of the Zeitgeist, or what you like. It is all one to my present purpose. Even if every decision required the sanction of an emperor with despotic power and a whimsical turn of mind, we should be interested none the less, still with a view to prediction, in discovering some order, some rational explanation, and some principle of growth for the rules which he laid down. In every system there are such explanations and principles to be found. It is with regard to them that a second fallacy comes in, which I think it important to expose.

The fallacy to which I refer is the notion that the only force at work in the development of the law is logic. In the broadest sense, indeed, that notion would be true. The postulate on which we think about the universe is that there is a fixed quantitative relation between every phenomenon and its antecedents and consequents. If there is such a thing as a phenomenon with these fixed quantitative relations, it is a miracle. It is outside the law of cause and effect, and as such transcends our power of thought, or at least is something to or from which we cannot reason. The condition of our thinking about the universe is that it is capable of being thought about rationally, or, in other words, that every part of it is effect and cause in the same sense in which those parts are with which we are most familiar. So in the broadest sense it is true that the law is a logical development, like everything else. The danger of which I speak is not the admission that the principles governing other phenomena also govern the law, but the notion that a given system, ours, for instance, can be worked out like mathematics from some general axioms of conduct. This is the natural error of the schools, but it is not confined to them. I once heard a very eminent judge say that he never let a decision go until he was absolutely sure that it was right. So judicial dissent often is blamed, as if it meant simply that one side or the other were not doing their sums right, and, if they would take more trouble, agreement inevitably would come.

This mode of thinking is entirely natural. The training of lawyers is a training in logic. The processes of analogy, discrimination, and deduction are those in which they are most at home. The language of judicial decision is mainly the language of logic. And the logical method and form flatter that longing for certainty and for repose which is in every human mind. But certainty generally is illusion, and repose is not the destiny of man. Behind the logical form lies a judgment as to the relative worth and importance of competing legislative grounds, often an inarticulate and unconscious judgment, it is true, and yet the very root and nerve of the whole proceeding. You can give any conclusion a logical form. You always can imply a condition in a contract. But why do you imply? It is because of some belief as to the practice of the community or of a class, or because of some opinion as to policy, or, in short, because of some attitude of yours upon a matter not capable of founding exact logical conclusions. Such matters really are battle grounds where the means do not exist for determinations that shall be good for all time, and where the decision can do no more than embody the preference of a given body in a given time and place. We do not realize how large a part of our law is open to reconsideration upon a slight change in the habit of the public mind. No concrete proposition is self-evident, no matter how ready we may be to accept it, not even Mr. Herbert Spencer's. Every man has a right to do what he wills, provided he interferes not with a like right on the part of his neighbors.

Why is a false and injurious statement privileged, if it is made honestly in giving information about a servant? It is because it has been thought more important that information should be given freely, than that a man should be protected from what under other circumstances would be an actionable wrong. Why is a man at liberty to set up a business which he knows will ruin his neighbor? It is because the public good is supposed to be best subserved by free competition. Obviously such judgments of relative importance may vary in different times and places. Why does a judge instruct a jury that an employer is not liable to an employee for an injury received in the course of his employment unless he is negligent, and why do the jury generally find for the plaintiff if the case is allowed to go to them? It is because the traditional policy of our law is to confine liability to cases where a prudent man might have foreseen the injury, or at least the danger, while the inclination of a very large part of the community is to make certain classes of persons insure the safety of those with whom they deal. Since the last words were written, I have seen the requirement of such insurance put forth as part of the programme of one of the best known labor organizations. There is a concealed, half conscious battle on the question of legislative policy, and if any one thinks that it can be settled deductively, or once for all, I only can say that I think he is theoretically wrong, and that I am certain that his conclusion will not be accepted in practice *semper ubique et ab omnibus.*

Indeed, I think that even now our theory upon this matter is open to reconsideration, although I am not prepared to say how I should decide if a reconsideration were proposed. Our law of torts comes from the old days of isolated, ungeneralized wrongs, assaults, slanders, and the like, where the damages might be taken to lie where they fell by legal judgment. But the torts with which our courts are kept busy today are mainly the incidents of certain well known businesses. They are injuries to person or property by railroads, factories, and the like. The liability for them is estimated, and sooner or later goes into the price paid by the public. The public really pays the damages, and the question of liability, if pressed far enough, is really the question how far it is desirable that the public should insure the safety of those whose work it uses. It might be said that in such cases the chance of a jury finding for the defendant is merely a chance, once in a while rather arbitarily interrupting the regular course of recovery, most likely in the case of an unusually conspicuous plaintiff, and therefore better done away with. On the other hand, the economic value even of a life to the community can be estimated, and no recovery, it may be said, ought to go beyond that amount. It is conceivable that some day in certain cases we may find ourselves imitating, on a higher plane, the tariff for life and limb which we see in the Leges Barbarorum.

I think that the judges themselves have failed adequately to recognize their duty of weighing considerations of social advantage. The duty is inevitable, and the result of the often proclaimed judicial aversion to deal with such considerations is simply to leave the very ground and foundation of judgments inarticulate, and often unconscious, as I have said. When socialism first began to be talked about, the comfortable classes of the community were a good deal frightened. I suspect that this fear has influenced judicial action both here and in England, yet it is certain that it is not a conscious factor in the decisions to which I refer. I think that something similar has led people who no longer hope to control the legislatures to look to the courts as expounders of the Constitutions, and that in some courts now principles have been discovered outside the bodies of those instruments, which may be generalized into acceptance of the economic doctrines which prevailed about fifty years ago, and a wholesale prohibition of what a tribunal of lawyers does not think about right. I cannot but believe that if the training of lawyers led them habitually to consider more definitely and explicitly the social advantage on which the rule they lay down must be justified, they sometimes would hesitate where now they are confident, and see that really they were taking sides upon debatable and often burning questions.

So much for the fallacy of logical form. Now let us consider the present condition of the law as a subject for study, and the ideal toward which it tends. We still are far from the point of view which I desire to see reached. No one has reached it or can reach it as yet. We are only at the beginning of a philosophical reaction, and of a reconsideration of the worth of doctrines which for the most part still are taken for granted without any deliberate, conscious, and systematic questioning of their grounds. The development of our law has gone on for nearly a thousand years, like the development of a plant, each generation taking the inevitable next step, mind, like matter, simply obeying a law of spontaneous growth. It is perfectly natural and right that it should have been so. Imitation is a necessity of human nature, as has been illustrated by a remarkable French writer, M. Tarde, in an admirable book, "Les Lois de l'Imitation." Most of the things we do, we do for no better reason than that our fathers have done them or that our neighbors do them, and the same is true of a larger part than we suspect of what we think. The reason is a good one, because our short life gives us no time for a better, but it is not the best. It does not follow, because we all are compelled to take on faith at second hand most of the rules on which we base our action and our thought, that each of us may not try to set some corner of his world in the order of reason, or that all of us collectively should not aspire to carry reason as far as it will go throughout the whole domain. In regard to the law, it is true, no doubt, that an evolutionist will hesitate to affirm universal validity for his social ideals, or for the principles which he thinks should be embodied in legislation. He is content if he can prove them best for here and now. He may be ready to admit that he knows nothing about an absolute best in the cosmos, and even that he knows next to nothing about a permanent best for men. Still it is true that a body of law

is more rational and more civilized when every rule it contains is referred articulately and definitely to an end which it subserves, and when the grounds for desiring that end are stated or are ready to be stated in words.

At present, in very many cities, if we want to know why a rule of law has taken its particular shape, and more or less if we want to know why it exists at all, we go to tradition. We follow it into the Year Books, and perhaps beyond them to the customs of the Salian Franks, and somewhere in the past, in the German forests, in the needs of Norman kings, in the assumptions of a dominant class, in the absence of generalized ideas, we find out the practical motive for what now best is justified by the mere fact of its acceptance and that men are accustomed to it. The rational study of law is still to a large extent the study of history. History must be a part of the study, because without it we cannot know the precise scope of rules which it is our business to know. It is a part of the rational study, because it is the first step toward a deliberate reconsideration of the worth of those rules. When you get the dragon out of his cave on to the plain and in the daylight, you can count his teeth and claws, and see just what is his strength. But to get him out is only the first step. The next is either to kill him, or to tame him and make him a useful animal. For the rational study of the law the backletter man may be the man of the present, but the man of the future is the man of statistics and the master of economics. It is revolting to have no better reason for a rule of law than that so it was laid down in the time of Henry IV. It is still more revolting if the grounds upon which it was laid down have vanished long since, and the rule simply persists from blind imitation of the past.

Let me take an illustration, which can be stated in a few words, to show how the social end which is aimed at by a rule of law is obscured and only partially attained in consequence of the fact that the rule owes its form to a gradual historical development, instead of being reshaped as a whole, with conscious articulate reference to the end in view. We think it desirable to prevent one man's property being misappropriated by another, and so we make larceny a crime. The evil is the same whether the misappropriation is made by a man into whose hands the owner has put the property, or by one who wrongfully takes it away. But primitive law in its weakness did not get much beyond an effort to prevent violence, and very naturally made a wrongful taking, a trespass, part of its definition of the crime. In modern times the judges enlarged the definition a little by holding that, if the wrong-doer gets possession by a trick or device, the crime is committed. This really was giving up the requirement of a trespass, and it would have been more logical, as well as truer to the present object of the law, to abandon the requirement altogether. That, however, would have seemed too bold, and was left to statute. Statutes were passed making embezzlement a crime. But the force of tradition caused the crime of embezzlement to be regarded as so far distinct from larceny that to this day, in some jurisdictions at least, a slip corner is kept open for thieves to contend, if indicted for larceny, that they should have been indicted for embezzlement, and if indicted for embezzlement, that they should have been indicted for larceny, and to escape on that ground.

Far more fundamental questions still await a better answer than that we do as our fathers have done. What have we better than a blind guess to show that the criminal law in its present form does more good than harm? I do not stop to refer to the effect which it has had in degrading prisoners and in plunging them further into crime, or to the question whether fine and imprisonment do not fall more heavily on a criminal's wife and children than on himself. I have in mind more far-reaching questions. Does punishment deter? Do we deal with criminals on proper principles? A modern school of Continental criminalists plumes itself on the formula, first suggested, it is said, by Gall, that we must consider the criminal rather than the crime. The formula does not carry us very far, but the inquiries which have been started look toward an answer of my questions based on science for the first time. If the typical criminal is a degenerate, bound to swindle or to murder by as deep seated an organic necessity as that which makes the rattlesnake bite, it is idle to talk of deterring him by the classical method of imprisonment. He must be got rid of; he cannot be improved, or frightened out of his structural reaction. If, on the other hand, crime, like normal human conduct, is mainly a matter of imitation, punishment fairly may be expected to help to keep it out of fashion. The study of criminals has been thought by some well known men of science to sustain the former hypothesis. The statistics of the relative increase of crime in crowded places like large cities, where example has the greatest chance to work, and in less populated parts, where the contagion spreads more slowly, have been used with great force in favor of the latter view. But there is weighty authority for the belief that, however this may be, "not the nature of the crime, but the dangerousness of the criminal, constitutes the only reasonable legal criterion to guide the inevitable social reaction against the criminal."

The impediments to rational generalization, which I illustrated from the law of mercy, are shown in the other branches of the law, as well as in that of crime. Take the law of tort or civil liability for damages apart from contract and the like. Is there any general theory of such liability, or are the cases in which it exists simply to be enumerated, and to be explained each on its special ground, as is easy to believe from the fact that the right of action for certain well known classes of wrongs like trespass or slander has its special history for each class? I think that there is a general theory to be discovered, although resting in tendency rather than established and accepted. I think that the law regards the infliction of temporal damage by a responsible person as actionable, if under the circumstances known to him the danger of his act is manifest according to common experience, or according to his own experience if it is more than common, except in cases where upon special grounds of policy the law refuses to protect the plaintiff or grants a privilege to the defendant. I think that commonly malice, intent, and negligence mean only that the danger was manifest to a greater or less degree, under the circumstances known to the actor, although in some cases of privilege malice may mean an actual malevolent motive, and such a motive may take away a permission knowingly to inflict harm, which otherwise would be granted on this or that ground of dominant public good. But when I stated my view to a very eminent English judge the other day, he said: "You are discussing what the law ought to be; as the law is, you must show a right. A man is not liable for negligence unless he is subject to a duty." If our difference was more than a difference in words, or with regard to the proportion between the exceptions and the rule, then, in his opinion, liability for an act cannot be referred to the manifest tendency of the act to cause temporal damage in general as a sufficient explanation, but must be referred to the special nature of the damage, or must be derived from some special circumstances outside of the tendency of the act, for which no generalized explanation exists. I think that such a view is wrong, but it is familiar, and I dare say generally is accepted in England.

Everywhere the basis of principle is tradition, to such an extent that we even are in danger of making the role of history more important than it is. The other day Professor Ames wrote a learned article to show, among other things, that the common law did not recognize the defense of fraud in actions upon specialties, and the moral might seem to be that the personal character of the defence is due to its equitable origin. But if, as I have said, all contracts are formal, the difference is not merely historical, but theoretic, between defects of form which prevent a contract from being made, and mistaken motives which manifestly could not be considered in any system that we should call rational except against one who has privy to those motives. It is not confined to specialties, but is of universal application. I ought to add that I do not suppose that Mr. Ames would disagree with what I suggest.

However, if we consider the law of contract, we find it full of history. The distinctions between debt, covenant, and assumpsit are merely historical. The classification of certain obligations to pay money, imposed by the law irrespective of any bargain as quasi contracts, is merely historical. The doctrine of consideration is merely historical. The effect given to a seal is to be explained by history alone.—Consideration is a mere form. Is it a useful form? If so, why should it not be required in all contracts? A seal is a mere form, and is vanishing in the scroll and in enactments that a consideration must be given, seal or no seal.—Why should any merely historical distinction be allowed to affect the rights and obligations of business men?

Since I wrote this discourse I have come on a very good example of the way in which tradition not only overrides rational policy, but overrides it after first having been misunderstood and having been given a new and broader scope than it had when it had a meaning. It is the settled law of England that a material alteration of a written contract by a party avoids it as against him. The doctrine is contrary to the general tendency of the law. We do not tell a jury that if a man ever has lied in one particular he is to be presumed to lie in all. Even if a man has tried to defraud, it seems no sufficient reason from preventing him from proving the truth. Objections of like nature in general go to the weight, not to the admissibility, of evidence. Moreover, this rule is irrespective of fraud, and is not confined to evidence. It is not merely that you cannot use the writing, but that the contract is at an end. What does this mean? The existence of a written contract depends on the fact that the offerer and offeree have interchanged their written expressions, not on the continued existence of those expressions. But in the case of a bond the primitive notion was different. The contract was inseparable from the parchment. If a stranger destroyed it, or tore off the seal, or altered it, the obligee could not recover, however free from fault, because the defendant's contract, that is, the actual tangible bond which he had sealed, could not be produced in the form in which it bound him. About a hundred years ago Lord Kenyon undertook to use his reason on this tradition, as he sometimes did to the detriment of the law, and, not understanding it, said he could see no reason why what was true of a bond should not be true of other contracts. His decision happened to be right, as it concerned a promissory note, where again the common law regarded the contract as inseparable from the paper on which it was written, but the reasoning was general, and soon was extended to other written contracts, and various absurd and unreal grounds of policy were invented to account for the enlarged rule.

I trust that no one will understand me to be speaking with disrespect of the law, because I criticize it so freely. I venerate the law, and especially our system of law, as one of the vastest products of the human mind. No one knows better than I do the countless number of great intellects that have spent themselves in making some addition or improvement, the greatest of which is trifling when compared with the mighty whole. It has the final title to respect that it exists, that it is not a Hegelian dream, but a part of the lives of men. But one may criticise even what one reveres. Law is the business to which my life is devoted, and I should show less than devotion if I did not do what in me lies to improve it, and, when I perceive what seems to me the ideal of its future, if I hesitated to point it out and to press toward it with all my heart.

We must beware of the pitfall of antiquarianism, and must remember that for our purposes our only interest in the past is for the light it throws upon the present. I look forward to a time when the part played by history in the explanation of dogma shall be very small, and instead of ingenious research we shall spend our energy on a study of the ends sought to be attained and the reasons for desiring them. As a step toward that ideal it seems to me that every lawyer ought to seek an understanding of economics. The present divorce between the schools of political economy and law seems to me an evidence of how much progress in philosophical study still remains to be made. In the present state of political economy, indeed, we come again upon history on a larger scale, but there we are called on to consider and weigh the ends of legislation, the means of attaining them, and the cost. We learn that for everything we have to give up something else, and we are taught to set the advantage we gain against the other advantage we lose, and to know what we are doing when we elect.

There is another study which sometimes is undervalued by the practical minded, for which I wish to say a good word, although I think a good deal of pretty poor stuff goes under that name. I mean the study of what is called jurisprudence. Jurisprudence, as I look at it, is simply law in its most generalized part. Every effort to reduce a case to a rule is an effort of jurisprudence, although the name as used in English is confined to the broadest rules and most fundamental conceptions. One mark of a great lawyer is that he sees the application of the broadest rules. There is a story of a Vermont justice of the peace before whom a suit was brought by one farmer against another for breaking a churn. The justice took time to consider, and then said that he had looked through the statutes and could find nothing about churns, and gave judgment for the defendant. The same state of mind is shown in all our common digests and textbooks. Applications of rudimentary rules of contract or tort are tucked away under the head of Railroads or Telegraphs or go to swell treatises on historical subdivisions, such as Shipping or Equity, or are gathered under an arbitrary title which is thought likely to appeal to the practical mind, such as Mercantile Law. If a man goes into law it pays to be a master of it, and to be a master of it means to look straight through all the dramatic incidents and to discern the true basis of prophecy. Therefore, it is well to have an accurate notion of what you mean by law, by a right, by a duty, by malice, intent, and negligence, by ownership, by possession, and so forth. I have in my mind cases in which the highest courts seem to me to have floundered because they had no clear ideas on some of these themes. I have illustrated their importance already. If a further illustration is wished, it may be found by reading the Appendix to Sir James Stephen's Criminal Law on the subject of possession, and then turning to Pollock and Wright's enlightened book. Sir James Stephen is not the only writer whose attempts to analyze legal ideas have been confused by striving for a useless quintessence of all systems, instead of an accurate anatomy of one. The trouble with Austin was that he did not know enough English law. But still it is a practical advantage to master Austin, and his predecessors, Hobbes and Bentham, and his worthy successors, Holland and Pollock. Sir Frederick Pollock's recent little book is touched with the felicity which marks all his works, and is wholly free from the perverting influence of Roman models.

The advice of the olders to young men is very apt to be as unreal as a list of the hundred best books. At least in my day I had my share of such counsels, and high among the unrealities I place the recommendation to study the

Roman law. I assume that such advice means more than collecting a few Latin maxims with which to ornament the discourse,—the purpose for which Lord Coke recommended Bracton. If that is all that is wanted, the title "De Regulis Juris Antiqui" can be read in an hour. I assume that, if it is well to study the Roman law, it is well to study it as a working system. That means mastering a set of technicalities more difficult and less understood than our own, and studying another course of history by which even more than our own the Roman law must be explained. If any one doubts me, let him read Keller's "Der Romische Civil Process und die Actionen," a treatise on the praetor's edict, Muirhead's most interesting "Historical Introduction to the Private Law of Rome," and, to give him the best chance possible, Sohm's admirable Institutes. No. The way to gain a liberal view of your subject is not to read something else, but to get to the bottom of the subject itself. The means of doing that are, in the first place, to follow the existing body of dogma into its highest generalizations by the help of jurisprudence; next, to discover from history how it has come to be what it is; and, finally, so far as you can, to consider the ends which the several rules seek to accomplish, the reasons why those ends are desired, what is given up to gain them, and whether they are worth the price.

We have too little theory in the law rather than too much, especially on this final branch of study. When I was speaking of history, I mentioned larceny as an example to show how the law suffered from not having embodied in a clear form a rule which will accomplish its manifest purpose. In that case the trouble was due to the survival of forms coming from a time when a more limited purpose was entertained. Let me now give an example to show the practical importance, for the decision of actual cases, of understanding the reasons of the law, by taking an example from rules which, so far as I know, never have been explained or theorized about in any adequate way. I refer to statutes of limitation and the law of prescription. The end of such rules is obvious, but what is the justification for depriving a man of his rights, a pure evil as far as it goes, in consequence of the lapse of time? Sometimes the loss of evidence is referred to, but that is a secondary matter. Sometimes the desirability of peace, but why is peace more desirable after twenty years than before? It is increasingly likely to come without the aid of legislation. Sometimes it is said that, if a man neglects to enforce his rights, he cannot complain if, after a while, the law follows his example. Now if this is all that can be said about it, you probably will decide a case I am going to put, for the plaintiff; if you take the view which I shall suggest, you possibly will decide it for the defendant. A man is sued for trespass upon land, and justifies under a right of way. He proves that he has used the way openly and adversely for twenty years, but it turns out that the plaintiff had granted a license to a person whom he reasonably supposed to be the defendant's agent, although not so in fact, and therefore had assumed that the use of the way was permissive, in which case no right would be gained. Has the defendant gained a right or not? If his gaining it stands on the fault and neglect of the land-owner in the ordinary sense, as seems commonly, to be supposed, there has been no such neglect, and the right of way has not been acquired. But if I were the defendant's counsel, I should suggest that the foundation of the acquisition of rights by lapse of time is to be looked for in the position of the person who gains them, not in that of the loser. Sir Henry Maine has made it fashionable to connect the archaic notion of property with prescription. But the connection is further back than the first recorded history. It is in the nature of man's mind. A thing which you have enjoyed and used as your own for a long time, whether property or an opinion, takes root in your being and cannot be torn away without your resenting the act and trying to defend yourself, however you came by it. The law can ask no better justification than the deepest instincts of man. It is only by way of reply to the suggestion that you are disappointing the former owner, that you refer to his neglect, having allowed the gradual disassociation between himself and what he claims, and the gradual association of it with another. If he knows that another is doing acts which on their face show that he is on the way toward establishing such an association, I should argue that in justice to that other he was bound at his peril to find out whether the other was acting under his permission, to see that he was warned, and, if necessary, stopped.

I have been speaking about the study of the law, and I have said next to nothing of what commonly is talked about in that connection,—text-books and the case system, and all the machinery with which a student comes most immediately in contact. Nor shall I say anything about them. Theory is my subject, not practical details. The modes of teaching have been improved since my time, no doubt, but ability and industry will master the raw material with any mode. Theory is the most important part of the dogma of the law, as the architect is the most important man who takes part in the building of a house. The most important improvements of the last twenty-five years are improvements in theory. It is not to be feared as unpractical, for, to the competent, it simply means going to the bottom of the subject. For the incompetent, it sometimes is true, as has been said, that an interest in general ideas means an absence of particular knowledge. I remember in army days reading of a youth who, being examined for the lowest grade and being asked a question about squadron drill, answered that he never had considered the evolutions of less than ten thousand men. But the weak and foolish must be left to their folly. The danger is that the able and practical minded should look with indifference or distrust upon ideas the connection of which with their business is remote. I heard a story, the other day, of a man who had a valet to whom he paid high wages, subject to deduction for faults. One of his deductions was, "For lack of imagination, five dollars." The lack is not confined to valets. The object of ambition, power, generally presents itself nowadays in the form of money alone. Money is the most immediate form, and is a proper object of desire. "The fortune," said Rachel, "is the measure of the intelligence." That is a good text to waken people out of a fool's paradise. But, as Hegel says, "It is in the end not the appetite, but the opinion, which has to be satisfied." To an imagination of any scope the most far-reaching form of power is not money, it is the command of ideas. If you want great examples read Mr. Leslie Stephen's "History of English Thought in the Eighteenth Century," and see how a hundred years after his death the abstract speculations of Descartes had become a practical force controlling the conduct of men. Read the works of the great German jurists, and see how much more the world is governed today by Kant than by Bonaparte. We cannot all be Descartes or Kant, but we all want happiness. And happiness, I am sure from having known many successful men, cannot be won simply by being counsel for great corporations and having an income of fifty thousand dollars. An intellect great enough to win the prize needs other food beside success. The remoter and more general aspect of the law are those which give it universal interest. It is through them that you not only become a great master in your calling, but connect your subject with the universe and catch an echo of the infinite, a glimpse of its unfathomable process, a hint of the universal law.

H. L. Mencken (essay date 1930)

SOURCE: "Mr. Justice Holmes," in *A Mencken Chrestomathy,* edited by H. L. Mencken, Alfred A. Knopf, 1942, pp. 258-65.

[*In the following review of* The Dissenting Opinions of Mr. Justice Holmes, *originally published in the* American Mercury *in May 1930, Mencken pronounces Holmes's decisions "interesting as literature" because of his "easy-going cynicism," but argues against the widely-held notion that Holmes was a political liberal defending freedom.*]

Mr. Justice Holmes's dissenting opinions [presented in ***The Dissenting Opinions of Mr. Justice Holmes***] have got so much fawning praise from Liberals that it is somewhat surprising to discover that Mr. Lief is able to muster but fifty-five of them, and even more surprising to hear from Dr. Kirchwey that in only one case did the learned justice stand quite alone, and that the cases "in which he has given expression to the judgment of the court, or in which he has concurred in its judgment, far out-number, in the ratio of eight or ten to one, those in which he felt it necessary to record his dissent."

There is even more surprising stuff in the opinions themselves. In three Espionage Act cases, including the Debs case, one finds a clear statement of the doctrine that, in war time, the rights guaranteed by the First Amendment cease to have any substance, and may be set aside summarily by any jury that has been sufficiently inflamed by a district attorney itching for higher office. In *Fox vs. the State of Washington* we learn that any conduct "which shall tend to encourage or advocate disrespect for the law" may be made a crime, and that the protest of a man who believes that he has been jailed unjustly, and threat-

ens to boycott his persecutors, may be treated as such a crime. In *Moyer vs. Peabody* it appears that the Governor of a State, "without sufficient reason but in good faith," may call out the militia, declare martial law, and jail anyone he happens to suspect or dislike, without laying himself open "to an action after he is out of office on the ground that he had no reasonable ground for his belief." And in *Weaver vs. Palmer Bros. Co.* there is the plain inference that in order to punish a theoretical man, A, who is suspected of wrong-doing, a State Legislature may lay heavy and intolerable burdens upon a real man, B, who has admittedly done no wrong at all.

I find it hard to reconcile such notions with any plausible concept of Liberalism. They may be good law, but it is impossible to see how they can conceivably promote liberty. My suspicion is that the hopeful Liberals of the 20s, frantically eager to find at least one judge who was not violently and implacably against them, seized upon certain of Mr. Justice Holmes's opinions without examining the rest, and read into them an attitude that was actually as foreign to his ways of thinking as it was to those of Mr. Chief Justice Hughes. Finding him, now and then, defending eloquently a new and uplifting law which his colleagues proposed to strike off the books, they concluded that he was a sworn advocate of the rights of man. But all the while, if I do not misread his plain words, he was actually no more than an advocate of the rights of law-makers. There, indeed, is the clue to his whole jurisprudence. He believed that the law-making bodies should be free to experiment almost *ad libitum,* that the courts should not call a halt upon them until they clearly passed the uttermost bounds of reason, that everything should be sacrificed to their autonomy, including, apparently, even the Bill of Rights. If this is Liberalism, then all I can say is that Liberalism is not what it was when I was young.

In those remote days, sucking wisdom from the primeval springs, I was taught that the very aim of the Constitution was to keep law-makers from running amok, and that it was the highest duty of the Supreme Court, following *Marbury vs. Madison,* to safeguard it against their forays. It was not sufficient, so my instructors maintained, for Congress or a State Legislature to give assurance that its intentions were noble; noble or not, it had to keep squarely within the limits of the Bill of Rights, and the moment it went beyond them its most virtuous acts were null and void. But Mr. Justice Holmes apparently thought otherwise. He held, it would seem, that violating the Bill of Rights is a rare and difficult business, possible only by summoning up deliberate malice, and that it is the chief business of the Supreme Court to keep the Constitution loose and elastic, so that blasting holes through it may not be too onerous. Bear this doctrine in mind, and you will have an adequate explanation, on the one hand, of those forward-looking opinions which console the Liberals—for example, in *Lochner vs. New York* (the bakery case), in the child labor case, and in the Virginia case involving the compulsory sterilization of imbeciles—and on the other hand, of the reactionary opinions which they so politely overlook—for example, in the Debs case, in

Bartels vs. Iowa (a war-time case, involving the prohibition of foreign-language teaching), in the Mann Act case (in which Dr. Holmes concurred with the majority of the court, and thereby helped pave the way for the wholesale blackmail which Mr. Justice McKenna, who dissented, warned against), and finally in the long line of Volstead Act cases.

Like any other man, of course, a judge sometimes permits himself the luxury of inconsistency. Mr. Justice Holmes, it seems to me, did so in the wiretapping case and again in the Abrams case, in which his dissenting opinion was clearly at variance with the prevailing opinion in the Debs case, written by him. But I think it is quite fair to say that his fundamental attitude was precisely as I have stated it. Over and over again, in these opinions, he advocated giving the legislature full head-room, and over and over again he protested against using the Fourteenth Amendment to upset novel and oppressive laws, aimed frankly at helpless minorities. If what he said in some of those opinions were accepted literally there would be scarcely any brake at all upon lawmaking, and the Bill of Rights would have no more significance than the Code of Manu.

The weak spot in his reasoning, if I may presume to suggest such a thing, was his tacit assumption that the voice of the legislature was the voice of the people. There is, in fact, no reason for confusing the people and the legislature: the two, in these later years, are quite distinct. The legislature, like the executive, has ceased, save indirectly, to be even the creature of the people: it is the creature, in the main, of pressure groups, and most of them, it must be manifest, are of dubious wisdom and even more dubious honesty. Laws are no longer made by a rational process of public discussion; they are made by a process of blackmail and intimidation, and they are executed in the same manner. The typical lawmaker of today is a man wholly devoid of principle—a mere counter in a grotesque and knavish game. If the right pressure could be applied to him he would be cheerfully in favor of polygamy, astrology or cannibalism.

It is the aim of the Bill of Rights, if it has any remaining aim at all, to curb such prehensile gentry. Its function is to set a limitation upon their power to harry and oppress us to their own private profit. The Fathers, in framing it, did not have powerful minorities in mind; what they sought to hobble was simply the majority. But that is a detail. The important thing is that the Bill of Rights sets forth, in the plainest of plain language, the limits beyond which even legislatures may not go. The Supreme Court, in *Marbury vs. Madison,* decided that it was bound to execute that intent, and for a hundred years that doctrine remained the corner-stone of American constitutional law. But in late years the court has taken the opposite line, and public opinion seems to support it. Certainly Dr. Holmes did not go as far in that direction as some of his brother judges, but equally certainly he went far enough. To call him a Liberal is to make the word meaningless.

Let us, for a moment, stop thinking of him as one, and let us also stop thinking of him as a *littérateur*, a reformer,

a sociologist, a prophet, an evangelist, a metaphysician; instead, let us think of him as something that he undoubtedy was in his Pleistocene youth and probably remained ever after, to wit, a soldier. Let us think of him, further, as a soldier extraordinarily ruminative and articulate—in fact, so ruminative and articulate as to be, in the military caste, almost miraculous. And let us think of him still further as a soldier whose natural distaste and contempt for civilians, and corollary yearning to heave them all into Hell, was cooled and eased by a stream of blood that once flowed through the Autocrat of the Breakfast Table—in brief, as a soldier beset by occasional doubts, hesitations, flashes of humor, bursts of affability, moments of sneaking pity. Observe that I insert the wary word, "occasional"; it surely belongs there. On at least three days out of four, during his long years on the bench, the learned justice remained the soldier—precise, pedantic, unimaginative, even harsh. But on the fourth day a strange amiability overcame him, and a strange impulse to play with heresy, and it was on that fourth day that he acquired his singular repute as a sage.

There is no evidence in Dr. Holmes's decisions that he ever gave any really profound thought to the great battle of ideas which raged in his time. He was interested in those ideas more or less, and now and then his high office forced him to take a hand in the battle, but he never did so with anything properly describable as passionate conviction. The whole uproar, one gathers, seemed fundamentally foolish to him. Did he have any genuine belief in democracy? Apparently the answer must be no. It amused him as a spectacle, and there were times when he was in the mood to let that spectacle run on, and even to help it on, but there were other times when he was moved to haul it up with a sharp command. That, no doubt, is why his decisions show so wide a spread and so beautiful an inconsistency, baffling to those who would get him into a bottle. He could, on occasion, state the case for the widest freedom, whether of the individual citizen or of the representative lawmaker, with a magnificent clarity, but he could also on occasion give his vote to the most brutal sort of repression. It seems to me that the latter occasions were rather more numerous than the former. And it seems to me again, after a very attentive reading of his decisions, that what moved him when he was disposed to be complacent was far less a positive love of liberty than an amiable and half contemptuous feeling that those who longed for it ought to get a horse-doctor's dose of it, and thereby suffer a really first-rate belly-ache.

This easy-going cynicism of his is what gave his decisions their peculiar salacity, and made them interesting as literature. It separated them sharply from the writings of his fellow judges, most of whom were frankly dull dogs. He had a considerable talent for epigram, and like any other man who possesses it was not shy about exercising it. I do not go so far as to allege that it colored and conditioned his judgment, that the apt phrase actually seduced him, but certainly it must be plain that once his mood had brought him to this or that judgment the announcement of it was sometimes more than a little affected by purely literary impulses. Now and then, alas, the result was far more literature than law. I point, for example, to one of his most celebrated epigrams: "Three generations of morons are enough." It is a memorable saying, and its essential soundness need not be questioned, but is it really judicial, or even legal, in form and content; does it offer that plain guidance which the higher courts are supposed to provide? What of the *two* generations: are they too little? I should not want to be a *nisi prius* judge if all the pronunciamentoes of the Supreme Court were so charmingly succinct and memorable—and so vague.

The average American judge, as everyone knows, is a mere rabbinical automaton, with no more give and take in his mind than you will find in the mind of a terrier watching a rathole. He converts the law into a series of rubber-stamps, and brings them down upon the scalped skulls of the just and unjust alike. The alternative to him, as commonly conceived, is quite as bad—an uplifter in a black robe, eagerly gulping every new brand of Peruna that comes out, and converting his pulpit into a sort of soapbox. Mr. Justice Holmes was neither, and he was better than either. He was under no illusions about the law. He knew very well that its aim was not to bring in the millennium, but simply to keep the peace. But he believed that keeping the peace was an art that could be practised in various ways, and that if one of them was by using a club then another was by employing a feather. Thus the Liberals, who long for tickling with a great and tragic longing, were occasionally lifted to the heights of ecstasy by the learned judge's operations, and in fact soared so high that they were out of earshot of next day's thwack of the club. I suspect that Dr. Holmes himself, when he heard of their enthusiasm, was quite as much amused as flattered. Such misunderstandings are naturally grateful to a skeptic, and they are doubly grateful to a skeptic of the military order, with his professional doubt of all persons who think that they think. I can imagine this skepticism—or, if you chose, cynicism—giving great aid and comfort to him on January 1, 1932, when he entered the chamber of the Supreme Court for the last time, and read his last opinion.

The case was that of one James Dunne, an humble bootician of Eureka, Calif., and the retiring justice delivered the majority opinion. Dunne had been tried in California on an indictment embracing three counts. The first charged him with keeping liquor for sale, the second with possessing it unlawfully, and the third with selling it. The jury acquitted him on the second and third counts, but found him guilty on the first. His counsel thereupon appealed. The evidence as to all three offenses, it was shown, was precisely the same. If the prisoner was innocent of two of them, then how could he be guilty of the third? Mr. Justice Holmes, speaking for himself and all his fellow justices save one, swept away this question in the following words:

> Consistency in the verdict is not necessary. Each count in an indictment is regarded as if it was a

separate offense. If separate indictments had been presented against the defendant for possession and for maintenance of a nuisance, and had been separately tried, the same evidence being offered in support of each, an acquittal on one could not be pleaded as *res judicata* of the other. Where the offenses are separately charged in the counts of a single indictment the same rule must hold.

I am not learned in the law, but the special gifts of a lawyer are surely not necessary to see that this judgment disposed completely of the prohibition of double jeopardy in Article I of the Bill of Rights. What it said, in plain English, is that a man may be tried over and over again for what is essentially the same offense, and that if one, two, three or *n* juries acquit him he may yet be kept in the dock, and so on *ad infinitum* until a jury is found that will convict him. And what such a series of juries may do may be done by one single jury—by the simple device of splitting his one offense into two, three, four or *n* offenses, and then trying him for all of them. In order to go free he must win verdicts of not guilty on every count. But in order to jail him all the prosecuting attorney needs is a verdict of guilty on one.

I commend this decision to Liberals who still cherish the delusion that Dr. Holmes belonged to their lodge. Let them paste it in their Sunday go-to-meeting hats. And I commend to them also the astounding but charming fact that the one judge who dissented was Mr. Justice Pierce Butler, for many years the chief demon in their menagerie. This is what he said:

> Excluding the possession negatived by the finding under the second count, there is nothing of substance left in the first count, for its specifications were limited to the keeping for sale of the identical drinks alleged in the second count to have been unlawfully possessed. . . . The evidence having been found insufficient to establish such possession, it cannot be held adequate to warrant conviction under the first count. The finding of not guilty is a final determination that possession, the gravamen of both counts, was not proved.

Felix Frankfurter (essay date 1938)

SOURCE: "Property and Society," in *Mr. Justice Holmes and the Supreme Court*, Cambridge, Mass.: Harvard University Press, 1938, pp. 13-45.

[In the following essay, Frankfurter discusses Holmes's views on constitutional property rights issues.]

The United States got under way nearly one hundred and fifty years ago, and only seventy-seven men have shaped its destiny, in so far as law has shaped it. To understand what manner of men they were who have sat on the Supreme Bench is vital for an understanding of the Court and its work. Yet how meager is our insight into all but a very few. A lawyer's life before he becomes a judge, like that of an actor, is largely writ in water unless he has had a rich political career. And legal opinions are not conducive to biographical revelation. On the whole, we have a pitifully inadequate basis for understanding the psychological and cultural influences which may be the roots of judicial opinions. The obvious map to the minds of the justices—the opinions of the Court—is deceptive precisely because they are the opinions of the Court. They are symphonies, not solos. Inferences from opinions to the distinctive characteristics of individual justices are treacherous, except in so far as a man's genius breaks through a collective judgment, or his vivid life before he went on the bench serves as commentary, or as he expresses individual views in dissent or through personal writings. Not to speak of the present Court, Mr. Justice Holmes possessed these qualities of personal genius perhaps in richer measure than any member in the Court's history.

The Chief Justice of Massachusetts became Mr. Justice Holmes of the Supreme Court on December 4, 1902, and resigned on January 12, 1932. He was thus a member of the Court for more than a fifth of its entire active history, and participated in more than a third of its adjudications. More important than these items of duration or volume is the historic significance of the period. Long-maturing social forces which the Civil War released or intensified found powerful political expression just about the time that Mr. Justice Holmes went to Washington. Time did not abate these conflicts. And so it came about that the Court, during his whole thirty years, was sucked into political controversies more continuous and of more immediate popular concern than at any time in its history.

To the discerning, the burst of capitalistic activity following the victory of the North early revealed that reconciliation of unfettered individual enterprise with social well-being would be the chief issue of politics. A letter by Mr. Justice Miller, written in 1878, which has recently come to light, is a straw showing the way the wind was blowing. Miller, an appointee of Lincoln and probably the most powerful member of his Court, kept a close watch on events in Washington as well as from the vantage point of the agricultural Middle West, where he travelled much on circuit:

> I have met with but few things of a character affecting the public good of the whole country that has shaken my faith in human nature as much as the united vigorous, and selfish effort of the capitalists,—the class of men who as a distinct class are but recently known in this country—I mean those who live solely by interest and dividends. Prior to the late war they were not numerous. They had no interest separate from the balance of the community, because they could lend their money safely and at high rates of interest. But one of the effects of the war was greatly to reduce the rate of interest by reason of the great increase in the quantity of the circulating medium. Another was by the creation of a national funded debt, exempt from taxation, to provide a means for the investment of surplus capital. This resource for investment was quadrupled by the bonds issued by the States,

by municipal corporations, and by Rail Road companies. The result has been the gradual formation of [a] new kind of wealth in this country, the income of which is the coupons of interest and stock dividends, and of a class whose only interest or stake in the country is the ownership of these bonds and stocks. They engage in no commerce, no trade, no manufacture, no agriculture. *They produce nothing.*[1]

Mr. Justice Miller was here describing early manifestations of the impact of technological science upon society. Finance capital was in its early stages. Its evolution since Mr. Justice Miller wrote has been analyzed in Veblen's writings and in Brandeis' *Other People's Money;* the pungent details are recorded in the massive volumes of the Pujo and the Pecora investigating committees. In brief, technological advances led to large-scale industry, large-scale industries flowered into mergers and monopolies, thereby producing in considerable measure a subordination of industry to finance. On the social side came the shift from a dominantly agricultural to an urbanized society. Big business stimulated modern trade unionism. Since modern politics is largely economics, these conflicting forces soon found political expression. After several abortive attempts, the various agrarian and progressive movements, in combination with organized labor and other less defined groups, three times won the presidency. For the "square deal" of Theodore Roosevelt, the "new freedom" of Woodrow Wilson, and the "new deal" of Franklin D. Roosevelt have a common genealogy. Disregarding for the moment detailed or minor differences, the three eras which these slogans summarize derived from efforts to reconcile modern economic forces with the demands of a popular democracy.

The result of the process of economic concentration in the half century since the Miller letter is luminously conveyed by some Treasury figures. I quote from Solicitor General Robert H. Jackson in his recent report on the Sherman Law:

> In 1932, according to the statistics of the Bureau of Internal Revenue, 53 percent of all corporate owned assets in this country was held by 618 corporations, which constitutes only 0.2 of 1 percent of the number of corporations reporting. Five percent of the corporations owned 85 percent of all corporate owned wealth in 1932. More than 50 percent of all the net income enjoyed by corporations in 1932 went to 232 corporations, while of the country's manufacturing corporations 1.2 percent of the total number accounted for 63 percent of the aggregate net profits. In 1934 the only group of corporations to earn an aggregate net profit was the group whose assets exceeded $50,000,000. Thus, the process of concentration was continuing.

> There was likewise a high degree of concentration in the ownership of these corporations. 1929 was a banner year for stock ownership and in that year the 3.28 percent of the population who filed individual income tax returns accounted for the

receipt of more than 83 percent of all dividends paid to individuals. And 78 percent of those dividends reported were received by 0.3 of 1 percent of our population.

The effect of this centralization is reflected in the distribution of national income. In 1933 the Bureau of Internal Revenue statistics show that there were only 1,747,740 taxable individual incomes in the United States and nearly one-third of all the property reported as passing by death was found in less than 4 percent of the estates. Brookings Institution's studies of 1929 show that about 6,000,000 families, or 21 percent of all families, had family incomes of less than $1,000 annually, and that 36,000 families in the high income brackets received as much of our national income in that year as 11,000,000 families with the lowest income.[2]

Instead of using dry figures Mr. Bernard Baruch, who is uniquely equipped to describe it, has portrayed the present economic scene by a few swift strokes:

"In the industrial east, at least, individual initiative had begun to merge into corporate collectivism" around the end of the 19th century, attaining its fullest effect in the decade following the world war. It has long since replaced "the older capitalism" as the dominant force in our economic life.

Naturally, there is only one means of controlling this collectivist growth in corporate enterprise. Government regulation must be extended to a direct proportionate degree. This is a sine qua non which business must accept.[3]

Short of the immediate issues of today, Mr. Justice Holmes' period of service on the Court covered the years of most intense interaction between government and business. Barring the tariff and the National Bank Act there were only two important measures of economic legislation on the federal statute books when Mr. Justice Holmes came to the Court, and these two, the Interstate Commerce Act of 1887 and the Sherman Law of 1890, had only somnolent vitality. Nor had state legislation, after the flurry of the Granger days, proved itself an effective device for social control over economic circumstance. Theodore Roosevelt's presidency marked the change. Under him the federal government for the first time embarked upon a positive program of social welfare. Through use of the taxing power and by regulatory legislation, not only were abuses to be remedied but benefits to be achieved for the common man. A vast field of hitherto free enterprise was brought under governmental supervision. Regardless of the political complexion of successive administrations, the area of national oversight of business was extended. From 1903 to 1932, an invigorated Interstate Commerce Commission, the Federal Trade Commission, the Federal Reserve Board, the Farm Loan Board, the Tariff Commission, the Federal Power Commission, the Railroad Labor Board followed each other in quick succession.

This vigorous legislative movement was partly a reflex of energetic state action and partly stimulated states to ac-

tion. Wisconsin, under the elder La Follette, and New York, under Charles E. Hughes, took the lead in effective state regulation of utilities. In the decade between 1910 and 1920 all but half a dozen states enacted workmen's compensation laws. Local anti-trust laws, shorter hours acts, minimum wage laws, blue-sky laws, banking laws, conservation enactments, illustrate only some of the topics on which laws came from the forty-eight states for eventual judgment by Mr. Justice Holmes' Court.

In this response of legislation to the new world created by modern industry, the United States was merely repeating British experience. The American story of agitation, investigation, and legislation is registered in the well-known British blue books, containing reports of royal commissions on modern economic and industrial problems, as they have manifested themselves in Great Britain and throughout the British Dominions. This struggle between the individualistic habits of the early nineteenth century and legislation as a means of effectuating the common interest is familiar to every reader of Dicey's brilliant *Law and Opinion in England.*

Such were the problems, however embedded in legal forms and phrased in legal jargon, that came to Mr. Justice Holmes for adjudication.

What equipment did he bring to the Court for dealing with these problems? What qualities did President Theodore Roosevelt look for, in appointing a Supreme Court justice at this time? Most things are kept from us that touch the intimate history of the Court, and so we are seldom allowed to share the private thoughts of a president on the considerations which moved him in making a Supreme Court appointment. Thanks to Senator Lodge, the elder, to whom President Roosevelt unburdened his mind, we do know both the hopes and the doubts that he felt about Mr. Justice Holmes' qualifications for the Supreme Bench, at that particular time:

First of all, I wish to go over the reasons why I am in his favor. . . . The labor decisions which have been criticized by some of the big railroad men and other members of large corporations, constitute to my mind a strong point in Judge Holmes' favor. The ablest lawyers and the greatest judges are men whose past has naturally brought them into close relationship with the wealthiest and most powerful clients, and I am glad when I can find a judge who has been able to preserve his aloofness of mind so as to keep his broad humanity of feeling and his sympathy for the class from which he has not drawn his clients. I think it eminently desirable that our Supreme Court should show in unmistakable fashion their entire sympathy with all proper effort to secure the most favorable possible consideration for the men who most need that consideration.

Now a word as to the other side. . . . In the ordinary and low sense which we attach to the words "partisan" and "politician," a judge of the Supreme Court should be neither. But in the higher sense, in the proper sense, he is not in my judgment fitted for the position unless he is a party man, a constructive statesman, constantly keeping in mind his adherence to the principles and policies under which this nation has been built up and in accordance with which it must go on; and keeping in mind also his relations with his fellow statesmen who in other branches of the government are striving in cooperation with him to advance the ends of government. . . .

. . . The majority of the present Court who have, although without satisfactory unanimity, upheld the policies of President McKinley and the Republican party in Congress, have rendered a great service to mankind and to this nation. The minority—a minority so large as to lack but one vote of being a majority—have stood for such reactionary folly as would have hampered well-nigh hopelessly this people in doing efficient and honorable work for the national welfare. . . .

Now I should like to know that Judge Holmes was in entire sympathy with our views, that is with your views and mine . . . before I would feel justified in appointing him. Judge Gray has been one of the most valuable members of the Court. I should hold myself as guilty of an irreparable wrong to the nation if I should put in his place any man who was not absolutely sane and sound on the great national policies for which we stand in public life.[4]

In taking account of the general philosophy of a prospective member of the Supreme Court towards major public issues likely to come before it, Theodore Roosevelt was merely following the example of other presidents, notably Lincoln in appointing Chase as Chief Justice. The psychological assumptions made by Theodore Roosevelt and Lincoln that the past in which a man is inured may have a powerful effect upon his future decisions are supported by weighty judicial experience. In the intimacy of family correspondence, Mr. Justice Miller has given us a glimpse of the personal influences which shape impersonal legal opinions:

It is vain to contend with judges who have been at the bar the advocates for forty years of rail road companies, and all the forms of associated capital, when they are called upon to decide cases where such interests are in contest. All their training, all their feelings are from the start in favor of those who need no such influence.[5]

We have been educated to an awareness of the enormous rôle which the unconscious plays in ordinary life, and the best of judges are beginning to realize, as Mr. Justice Holmes did long ago, how profoundly important it is that a judge be on his guard lest he read "his conscious or unconscious sympathy with one side or the other prematurely into the law." When judges decide issues that touch the nerve center of economic and social conflict, the danger, in de Tocqueville's phrase, of confounding the familiar with the necessary is especially hazardous. The matter was put with candor by Lord Justice Scrutton, a great English judge:

The habits you are trained in, the people with whom you mix, lead to your having a certain class of ideas of such a nature that, when you have to deal with other ideas, you do not give as sound and accurate a judgment as you would wish. This is one of the great difficulties at present with Labour. Labour says: "Where are your impartial Judges? They all move in the same circle as the employers, and they are all educated and nursed in the same ideas as the employers. How can a labour man or a trade unionist get impartial justice?" It is very difficult sometimes to be sure that you have put yourself into a thoroughly impartial position between two disputants, one of your own class and one not of your class.[6]

Unlike the great men on the Court before him, Mr. Justice Holmes had been singularly outside the current of public affairs or of interest in them. He was essentially the philosopher who turned to law. Ultimate issues of the destiny of man, not the evanescent events of the day, preoccupied his mind. That he did not read newspapers revealed neither affectation nor a sense of superiority; it mirrored his worldly innocence. When Senator Lodge tried to induce him to run for governor, with the bait that it would inevitably lead to a seat in the United States Senate, Mr. Justice Holmes blandly replied: "But I don't give a damn about being Senator." And yet, though he did not bring to the Court the experience of great affairs, not even Marshall exceeded him in judicial statesmanship. Other great judges have been guided by the wisdom distilled from an active life; Mr. Justice Holmes was led by the divination of the philosopher and the imagination of the poet.

Because he had an organic philosophy, he was not distracted by the infinite diversity of detail in the appearance of the same central issues. No one realized better than he that, while principles gain significance through application, concrete instances are inert except when galvanized into life by a general principle. And so it is perhaps more true of him than of any other judge in the history of the Court that the host of public controversies in which he participated was subdued to reason by relatively few guiding considerations. This was true whether he was called upon to strike a balance between the claims of property and its obligations, or between the rights of individuals and their duties, or between the limits of state action and the authority of the federal government.

Indeed, underlying all the myriad forms of these great problems is an antecedent issue. What is the rôle of a judge in making these adjustments between society and the individual, between the states and the nation? The conception which a judge has of his own function, and the fastidiousness with which he follows it, will in large measure determine the most delicate controversies before him. Justices of the Court are not architects of policy. They can nullify the policy of others; they are incapable of fashioning their own solutions for social problems. The use which a judge makes of this power of negation is largely determined by two psychological considerations. It depends first on the judge's philosophy, conscious or implicit, regarding the nature of society; that is, on his theory of the clash of interests. This, in turn, will influence his conception of the place of the judge in the American constitutional system.

Mr. Justice Holmes' view of the play of forces in society hardly differed from that of Madison in his classic statement in the *Federalist:*

> Those who hold and those who are without property have ever formed distinct interests in society. Those who are creditors, and those who are debtors, fall under a like discrimination. A landed interest, a manufacturing interest, a mercantile interest, a moneyed interest, with many lesser interests, grow up of necessity in civilized nations, and divide them into different classes, actuated by different sentiments and views. The regulation of these various and interfering interests forms the principal task of modern legislation, and involves the spirit of party and faction in the necessary and ordinary operations of the government.[7]

Thirty years before he went on the Supreme Court, Mr. Justice Holmes expressed this view in his own way:

> This tacit assumption of the solidarity of the interests of society is very common, but seems to us to be false . . . in the last resort a man rightly prefers his own interest to that of his neighbors. And this is as true in legislation as in any other form of corporate action. All that can be expected from modern improvements is that legislation should easily and quickly, yet not too quickly, modify itself in accordance with the will of the *de facto* supreme power in the community, and that the spread of an educated sympathy should reduce the sacrifice of minorities to a minimum. . . . The objection to class legislation is not that it favors a class, but either that it fails to benefit the legislators, or that it is dangerous to them because a competing class has gained in power, or that it transcends the limits of self-preference which are imposed by sympathy. . . . But it is no sufficient condemnation of legislation that it favors one class at the expense of another; for much or all legislation does that; and none the less when the *bona fide* object is the greatest good of the greatest number . . . if the welfare of all future ages is to be considered, legislation may as well be abandoned for the present. . . . The fact is that legislation in this country, as well as elsewhere, is empirical. It is necessarily made a means by which a body, having the power, put burdens which are disagreeable to them on the shoulders of somebody else.[8]

Mr. Justice Holmes never forgot that the activities of government are continual attempts by peaceful means to adjust these clashes of interest, and he was equally mindful of the fact that the body to whom this task of adjustment is primarily delegated is the legislature. And so he gave complete loyalty in his work as a judge to the major premise of Marshall "that it is a *Constitution* we are expounding."[9] He scrupulously treated the Constitution as a broad charter of powers for the internal clashes of society, and did not construe it as though it were a code which prescribed in detail answers for the social problems of all time.

Thus, the enduring contribution of Mr. Justice Holmes to American history is his constitutional philosophy. He gave it momentum by the magic with which he expressed it. Great judges are apt to be identified with what lawyers call great cases. The achievements of his great predecessors have, on the whole, to be recounted through an analysis of specific decisions, their meaning and their consequences. Mr. Justice Holmes' specialty was great utterance. He dealt with intrinsic significance, not with meretricious, because evanescent, importance. "Great cases," he himself has said, "are called great, not by reason of their real importance in shaping the law of the future, but because of some accident of immediate, overwhelming interest which appeals to the feelings and distorts the judgment." He saw the vital in the undramatic; to him, inconspicuous controversies revealed the clash of great social forces. And so the significance of his genius would evaporate in any analysis of specific decisions. In his case, form and substance were beautifully fused. His conception of the Constitution must become part of the political habits of the country, if our constitutional system is to endure; and if we care for our literary treasures, the expression of his views must become part of our national culture.

The Constitution is, of course, a legal document, but a legal document of a fundamentally different order than an insurance policy or a lease of timberland. For the Justice, the Constitution was not primarily a text for dialectic but a means of ordering the life of a progressive people. While its roots were in the past, it was projected for the unknown future:

> . . . the provisions of the Constitution are not mathematical formulas having their essence in their form; they are organic living institutions transplanted from English soil. Their significance is vital not formal; it is to be gathered not simply by taking the words and a dictionary, but by considering their origin and the line of their growth.[10]

> . . . when we are dealing with words that also are a constituent act, like the Constitution of the United States, we must realize that they have called into life a being the development of which could not have been foreseen completely by the most gifted of its begetters. It was enough for them to realize or to hope that they had created an organism; it has taken a century and has cost their successors much sweat and blood to prove that they created a nation. The case before us must be considered in the light of our whole experience and not merely in that of what was said a hundred years ago.[11]

While the Supreme Court is thus in the exacting realm of government, it is itself freed from the terrible burdens of governing. The Court is the brake on other men's actions, the judge of other men's decisions. Responsibility for action rests with legislators. The range of the Court's authority is thus very limited, but its exercise may vitally affect the nation. No wonder John Marshall spoke of this power of the Court as "delicate."[12]

No man who ever sat on the Court has been more keenly or more consistently sensitive than Mr. Justice Holmes to the dangers and difficulties inherent in the power of judges to review legislation. For it is subtle business to decide, not whether legislation is wise, but whether legislators were reasonable in believing it to be wise. In view of the complexities of modern society and the restricted scope of any man's experience, tolerance and humility in passing judgment on the worth of the experience and beliefs of others become crucial faculties in the disposition of cases. The successful exercise of such judicial power calls for rare intellectual disinterestedness and penetration, lest limitation in personal experience and imagination operate as limitations of the Constitution. These insights Mr. Justice Holmes applied in hundreds of cases and expressed in memorable language:

> It is a misfortune if a judge reads his conscious or unconscious sympathy with one side or the other prematurely into the law, and forgets that what seem to him to be first principles are believed by half his fellow men to be wrong. . . . When twenty years ago a vague terror went over the earth and the word socialism began to be heard, I thought and still think that fear was translated into doctrines that had no proper place in the Constitution or the common law.[13]

> While the courts must exercise a judgment of their own, it by no means is true that every law is void which may seem to the judges who pass upon it excessive, unsuited to its ostensible end, or based upon conceptions of morality with which they disagree. Considerable latitude must be allowed for differences of view as well as for possible peculiar conditions which this court can know but imperfectly, if at all. Otherwise a constitution, instead of embodying only relatively fundamental rules of right, as generally understood by all English-speaking communities, would become the partisan of a particular set of ethical or economical opinions, which by no means are held *semper ubique et ab omnibus.*[14]

If these had been merely the views of a closet philosopher they would not have aroused dissent, nor would they have been seriously noticed. But when they were made the effective instruments of adjudication they became fighting issues. By cutting beneath the surface of decisions Mr. Justice Holmes exposed their psychological and sociological roots. While in the eighties and nineties our economy was in process of drastic transformation, members of the Supreme Court continued to reflect the economic order in which they grew up. Between the presidencies of Grant and the first Roosevelt, *laissez faire* was the dominant economic social philosophy, and it was imported into the Constitution. Temporary facts were translated into legal absolutes; abstract conceptions concerning "liberty of contract" were erected into constitutional dogmas. Malleable and undefined provisions of the Constitution were applied as barriers against piecemeal efforts of adjustment through legislation to a society permeated by the influence of technology, large-scale industry, progressive urbanization, and the general dependence of the individual on economic forces beyond his control. The due process clauses were especially the destructive rocks on which this legislation foundered. Judge Learned Hand, one of the most eminent of our judges, has said that the requirement of due process is merely an embodiment of the English sporting idea of fair play. In England, particularly from the time of the Campbell-Bannerman government, the same causes that induced American legislative attempts led to a continual Parliamentary modification of the system of private enterprise. The scope of this trend in England is revealed by a few tell-tale figures. The social services established by this legislation have entailed an increase in expenditure from 19*s*. 2*d*. per capita in 1900 to £8 16*s*. 6*d*. in 1934; and about a third of the national income of Great Britain is now spent through public channels.[15]

Yet as late as 1905 the Supreme Court held it unconstitutional to limit the working hours of bakers to ten,[16] and as recently as 1936 the Court adhered to its ruling that it was beyond the power both of the states and of the nation to assure minimum wage rates for women workers obviously incapable of economic self-protection.[17] Every variety of legislative manifestation to subject economic power to social responsibility encountered the judicial veto.

The doctrinal process by which the majority reached such results was thus explained by Mr. Justice Holmes in dissenting from his brethren in the Minimum Wage case:

> . . . The only objection that can be urged [against a minimum wage law for women for the District of Columbia] is found within the vague contours of the Fifth Amendment, prohibiting the depriving any person of liberty or property without due process of law. To that I turn.

> The earlier decisions upon the same words in the Fourteenth Amendment began within our memory and went no farther than an unpretentious assertion of the liberty to follow the ordinary callings. Later that innocuous generality was expanded into the dogma, Liberty of Contract. Contract is not specially mentioned in the text that we have to construe. It is merely an example of doing what you want to do, embodied in the world liberty. But pretty much all law consists in forbidding men to do some things that they want to do, and contract is no more exempt from law than other acts.[18]

The practical meaning of this operation of judicial review was put by the late Judge Hough with characteristic pungency: "No man has seen more plainly that the court was measuring the legislature's reasons by its own intellectual yardstick than has Justice Holmes; none more keenly perceived that the notations thereupon marked those results of environment and education which many men seem to regard as the will of God or the decrees of fate."[19] Against this subtle danger of the unconscious identification of personal views with constitutional sanction Mr. Justice Holmes battled during all his years on the Court. For a short time after the bake-shop case his views were in the ascendant. Chief Justice White was heard to attribute to the influence exerted by President Theodore Roosevelt no inconsiderable share in the shift of the Court's emphasis. The fact is that for less than a decade, between 1908 and the World War, the Court did allow legislation to prevail which, in various aspects, regulated enterprise with reference to its social consequences and withdrew phases of industrial relations from the area of illusory individual bargaining.[20]

But those who had assumed a permanent change in the Court's outlook were soon disappointed. Changes in the Court's personnel and in the general economic and social climate of the Harding-Coolidge era soon reflected themselves in decisions. Until after the 1936 election, the Court was back to the high tide of judicial negation reached in the Lochner case, in 1905. Mr. Justice Holmes' classic dissent in that case will never lose its relevance:

> This case is decided upon an economic theory which a large part of the country does not entertain. If it were a question whether I agreed with that theory, I should desire to study it further and long before making up my mind. But I do not conceive that to be my duty, because I strongly believe that my agreement or disagreement has nothing to do with the right of a majority to embody their opinions in law. It is settled by various decisions of this court that state constitutions and state laws may regulate life in many ways which we as legislators might think as injudicious or if you like as tyrannical as this, and which equally with this interfere with the liberty to contract. Sunday laws and usury laws are ancient examples. A more modern one is the prohibition of lotteries. The liberty of the citizen to do as he likes so long as he does not interfere with the liberty of others to do the same, which has been a shibboleth for some well-known writers, is interfered with by school laws, by the Post Office, by every state or municipal institution which takes his money for purposes thought desirable, whether he likes it or not. The Fourteenth Amendment does not enact Mr. Herbert Spencer's Social Statics. . . . Some of these laws embody convictions or prejudices which judges are likely to share. Some may not. But a constitution is not intended to embody a particular economic theory, whether of paternalism and the organic relation of the citizen to the State or of *laissez faire*. It is made for people of fundamentally differing views, and the accident of our finding certain opinions natural and familiar or novel and even shocking ought not to conclude our judgment upon the question whether statutes embodying them conflict with the Constitution of the United States.[21]

This was the great theme of his judicial life—the amplitude of the Constitution as against the narrowness of some of its interpreters. And so, having analyzed with brave clarity the governing elements in the modern economic struggle, he did not shrink from giving his analysis judicial recognition. "One of the eternal conflicts out of which life is made up," he wrote, more than forty years ago, "is that between the effort of every man to get the most he can for his services, and that of society, disguised under the name of capital, to get his services for the least possible return. Combination on the one side is patent and powerful. Combination on the other is the necessary and desirable counterpart, if the battle is to be carried on in a fair and equal way."[22] Mr. Justice Holmes therefore found nothing in the Constitution to prevent legislation which sought to remove some of the more obvious inequalities in the distribution of economic power.

Economists and historians are now largely agreed that the resistance to a natural and responsible trade unionism has been one of the most disturbing factors in our economy. Had the views of Mr. Justice Holmes prevailed, the Constitution would not have been used as an obstruction to the healthy development of trade unionism. More than thirty years ago he protested when a majority of the Court invalidated an act of Congress against the "yellow dog" contract which, as a matter of history, was drawn by Richard Olney and sponsored by President Cleveland. The need for legislation to remove disabilities against the effective right of association by workers became more manifest with time. State after state, therefore, passed laws to assure trade unions the opportunity which they already had in the rest of the English-speaking world. But a majority of the Court remained obdurate and imposed a doctrinaire view of the Constitution against such legislation.[23] One can only surmise what would have been the gain to social peace and economic security had the dissenting views expressed more than twenty years ago by Mr. Justice Holmes been the Court's views:

> In present conditions a workman not unnaturally may believe that only by belonging to a union can he secure a contract that shall be fair to him. . . . If that belief, whether right or wrong, may be held by a reasonable man, it seems to me that it may be enforced by law in order to establish the equality of position between the parties in which liberty of contract begins. Whether in the long run it is wise for the workingmen to enact legislation of this sort is not my concern, but I am strongly of opinion that there is nothing in the Constitution of the United States to prevent it. . . . [24]

Law, he was well aware, not merely confirms property interests; it helps to create them. The availability of legal remedies may itself be a potent instrument of economic power. Correspondingly, the withholding of such remedies may affect the balance of conflicting interest in the economic struggle. Mr. Justice Holmes denied that the Constitution stereotyped any particular distribution of economic power for all time. With the clean precision of a surgeon he uncovered the process by which, under the guise of deductive reasoning, partial claims were given the shelter of the Constitution as comprehensive interests of property:

> Delusive exactness is a source of fallacy throughout the law. By calling a business "property" you make it seem like land, and lead up to the conclusion that a statute cannot substantially cut down the advantages of ownership existing before the statute was passed. An established business no doubt may have pecuniary value and commonly is protected by law against various unjustified injuries. But you cannot give it definiteness of contour by calling it a thing. It is a course of conduct and like other conduct is subject to substantial modification according to time and circumstances both in itself and in regard to what shall justify doing it a harm.[25]

By a steady extension of doctrines which, to Mr. Justice Holmes, had no justification in the Constitution, a majority of the Court persistently denied exertions of the legislature toward reconciling individual enterprise and social welfare. Abstract conceptions regarding property and "liberty of contract" were the swords with which these measures were struck down. Mr. Justice Holmes was finally roused to an unusual judicial protest. His dissent from the decision of the majority in declaring unconstitutional a New York statute regulating theatre-ticket scalping fully reveals his mind. It also gives a glimpse of the importance he attached to art throughout life:

> We fear to grant power and are unwilling to recognize it when it exists . . . when legislatures are held to be authorized to do anything considerably affecting public welfare it is covered by apologetic phrases like the police power, or the statement that the business concerned has been dedicated to a public use. The former expression is convenient, to be sure, to conciliate the mind to something that needs explanation: the fact that the constitutional requirement of compensation when property is taken cannot be pressed to its grammatical extreme; that property rights may be taken for public purposes without pay if you do not take too much; that some play must be allowed to the joints if the machine is to work. But police power often is used in a wide sense to cover and, as I said, to apologize for the general power of the legislature to make a part of the community uncomfortable by a change.
>
> I do not believe in such apologies. I think the proper course is to recognize that a state legislature can do whatever it sees fit to do unless it is restrained by some express prohibition in the Constitution of the United States or of the State, and that Courts should be careful not to extend such prohibitions beyond their obvious meaning by reading into them conceptions of public policy that the particular Court may happen to entertain. Coming down to the case before us I think, as I intimated in *Adkins v. Children's Hospital,* 261 U. S. 525, 569, that the notion that a business is clothed with a public interest and has been devoted to a public use is little more than a fiction intended to beautify what is disagreeable to the sufferers. The truth seems to me to be that, subject to compensation when compensation is due, the legislature may forbid or restrict any business when it has a sufficient force of public opinion behind it. Lotteries were thought useful adjuncts of the State a century or so ago; now they are believed to be immoral and they have been stopped. Wine has been thought good for man from the time of the Apostles until recent years. But when public opinion changed it did not need the Eighteenth Amendment, notwithstanding the Fourteenth, to enable a State to say that the business should end. *Mugler v. Kansas,* 123 U. S. 623. What has happened to lotteries and wine might happen to theatres in some moral storm of the future, not because theatres were devoted to a public use, but because people had come to think that way.
>
> But if we are to yield to fashionable conventions, it seems to me that theatres are as much devoted to public use as anything well can be. We have not that respect for art that is one of the glories of France. But to many people the superfluous is the necessary, and it seems to me that Government does not go beyond its sphere in attempting to make life livable for them. I am far from saying that I think that this particular law a wise and rational provision. That is not my affair. But if the people of the State of New York speaking by their authorized voice say that they want it, I see nothing in the Constitution of the United States to prevent their having their will.[26]

Taxation is perhaps the severest testing ground for the objectivity and wisdom of a social thinker. The enormous increase in the cost of society and the extent to which wealth is now represented by intangibles, the profound change in the relation of the individual to government and the resulting widespread insistence on security, are subjecting public finance to the most exacting demands. To balance budgets, to pay for the costs of progressively civilized social standards, to safeguard the future and to divide these burdens fairly among different interests in the community, put the utmost strain on the ingenuity of statesmen. They must constantly explore new sources of revenue and find means of preventing the circumvention of their discoveries. Subject as they are, in English-speaking countries, to popular control, they should not be denied adequate latitude of power for their extraordinarily difficult tasks.

Mr. Justice Holmes never yielded to finicky limitations or doctrinaire formulas, drawn from the general language of the Constitution, as a means of circumscribing the discretion of legislatures in the necessarily empirical process of tapping new revenue or stopping new devices for its evasion. He did not have a curmudgeon's feelings about his own taxes. A secretary who exclaimed, "Don't you hate to pay taxes!" was rebuked with the hot response, "No, young feller. I like to pay taxes. With them I buy civilization." And as a judge he consistently refused to accentuate fiscal difficulties of government by injecting into the Constitution his own notions of fiscal policy. Nor did he believe that there was anything in the Constitution to bar even a conscious use of the taxing power for readjusting the social equilibrium. One of his last utterances gives the general flavor of his many opinions in tax cases:

> I have not yet adequately expressed the more than anxiety that I feel at the ever increasing scope given to the Fourteenth Amendment in cutting down what I believe to be the constitutional rights of the States. As the decisions now stand, I see hardly any limit but the sky to the invalidating of those rights if they happen to strike a majority of this Court as for any reason undesirable. I cannot believe that the Amendment was intended to give us *carte blanche* to embody our economic or moral beliefs in its prohibitions. Yet I can think of no narrower reason that seems to me to justify the present and the earlier decisions to which I have referred. . . . It seems to me to be exceeding our powers to declare such a tax a denial of due process of law.

> And what are the grounds? Simply, so far as I can see, that it is disagreeable to a bondholder to be taxed in two places. Very probably it might be good policy to restrict taxation to a single place, and perhaps the technical conceptions of domicil may be the best determinant. But it seems to me that if that result is to be reached it should be reached through understanding among the States, by uniform legislation or otherwise, not by evoking a constitutional prohibition from the void of "due process of law," when logic, tradition and authority have united to declare the right of the State to lay the now prohibited tax.[27]

I have indicated the general direction of Mr. Justice Holmes' judicial mind on the great issues of the constitutional position of property in our society. During most of his thirty years on the Supreme Bench, and especially during the second half of his tenure, his were not the views of a majority of the Court. But the good that men do lives after them. About a year ago the old views of Mr. Justice Holmes began to be the new constitutional direction of the Court.[28] His own constitutional outlook was, throughout a long life, free from fluctuations. This was so because it was born of a deeply rooted and coherent philosophy concerning the dynamic character of the American Constitution and of a judge's function in construing it. If he threw the weight of his authority on the side of social readjustments through legislation it was not because of any faith in panaceas in general or in measures of social amelioration in particular. He personally "disbelieved all the popular conceptions of socialism," and came dangerously close to believing in the simplicities of the wage-fund theory.[29] But his scepticism and even hostility, as a matter of private judgment, toward legislation which he was ready to sustain as a judge only serve to add cubits to his judicial stature. For he thereby transcended personal predilections and private notions of social policy, and became truly the impersonal voice of the Constitution.

NOTES

[1] Charles Fairman, "Justice Samuel F. Miller—A Study of a Judicial Statesman," *Political Science Quarterly,* L (March 1935), 15, 21.

[2] *Report of the Attorney General for the Fiscal Year 1937,* p. 36.

[3] Letter in *Springfield Republican,* Saturday, March 26, 1938, p. 6.

[4] *Selections from the Correspondence of Theodore Roosevelt and Henry Cabot Lodge,* I (New York, 1925), 517-19.

[5] Fairman, in *Political Science Quarterly,* L, 43, n. 4.

[6] Scrutton, "The Work of the Commercial Courts," *Cambridge Law Journal,* I (1921), 6, 8.

[7] *The Federalist,* No. 10 (sesquicentennial ed., Washington, 1937), p. 56.

[8] Holmes, "The Gas-Stokers' Strike," *American Law Review,* VII (1873), 583, reprinted in *Harvard Law Review,* XLIV (March 1931), 795.

[9] McCulloch v. Maryland, 4 Wheat. 316, 407 (U. S. 1819).

[10] Gompers v. United States, 233 U. S. 604, 610 (1914).

[11] Missouri v. Holland, 252 U.S. 416, 433 (1920).

[12] Fletcher v. Peck, 6 Cranch 87, 128 (U. S. 1810).

[13] Holmes, *Collected Legal Papers* (New York, 1920), p. 295.

[14] Otis v. Parker, 187 U. S. 606, 608-09 (1903).

[15] Frankfurter, "Foreword," *Yale Law Journal,* XLVII (1938), 515, 516.

[16] Lochner v. New York, 198 U. S. 45 (1905).

[17] Morehead v. New York *ex rel.* Tipaldo, 298 U. S. 587 (1936).

[18] Adkins v. Children's Hospital, 261 U. S. 525, 568 (1923).

[19] Hough, in *Harvard Law Review,* XXXII, 232, n. 2.

[20] *E.g.,* Muller v. Oregon, 208 U. S. 412 (1908); Bunting v. Oregon, 243 U. S. 426 (1917).

[21] 198 U. S. 45, 75-76 (1905).

[22] Vegelahn v. Guntner, 167 Mass. 92, 108 (1896).

[23] Adair v. United States, 208 U. S. 161 (1908).

[24] Coppage v. Kansas, 236 U. S. 1, 26-27 (1915).

[25] Truax v. Corrigan, 257 U. S. 312, 342-43 (1921).

[26] Tyson & Bro. v. Banton, 273 U. S. 418, 445-47 (1927).

[27] Baldwin v. Missouri, 281 U. S. 586, 595-96 (1930).

[28] West Coast Hotel Co. v. Parrish, 300 U. S. 379 (1937).

[29] See Plant v. Woods, 176 Mass. 492, 505 (1900).

Daniel J. Boorstin (essay date 1941)

SOURCE: "The Elusiveness of Mr. Justice Holmes," in *The New England Quarterly,* Vol. XIV, No. 3, September, 1941, pp. 478-87.

[*In the following essay, Boorstin examines Holmes's social philosophy outside of the constitutional issues he decided professionally.*]

The thought and personality of Mr. Justice Holmes have suffered from affectionate neglect. In proportion to his stature he has received less adequate interpretation than any other American of his generation. He has become the victim of his acolytes, who, in heaping sacrifices at his altar, have obscured the image of their idol. A survey of the literature about the great Justice shows numerous collections of dedicatory essays, giving him deserved adulation and the homage which men can understandably feel compelled to give to such a rare spirit among lawyers. The principal biography is written in a similar vein. But these works have not greatly helped to reveal in the character of Mr. Justice Holmes the great significance which his life holds for the student of American thought. The best statement of his elusive philosophy is still made in his own words. And for this reason several recently published volumes are of especial interest. Mr. Harry C. Shriver has edited a selection of the judicial opinions of the Justice during the nineteen years while he sat on the bench of the Supreme Judicial Court of Massachusetts.[1] He has done a service in making more generally available documents on a portion of Mr. Holmes's career little known to laymen. Although the lawyer may regret that his decisions on other than constitutional questions are not adequately represented,[2] and may feel that the wisdom in the epigrams culled by Mr. Shriver is often obscured by the omission of the facts of cases in which the epigrams were stated,[3] the volume is one which should interest the layman and help him form a fuller picture of the Justice's social views.

The crucial materials for formulating Justice Holmes's social philosophy, if they have not all been accessible to the layman, have for some time been in print in the law reports. But until now his personal philosophy has had to be drawn almost entirely from his speeches. Therefore the publication of the **Holmes-Pollock Letters,** comprising a correspondence of nearly sixty years with the eminent English legal scholar, Sir Frederick Pollock, is particularly welcome.[4] The two volumes of this correspondence provide rich additional material for an attempt to define more precisely this aspect of Holmes's thinking,

and the careful and restrained editing of Professor Mark DeWolfe Howe deserves the highest praise. Although the letters throughout maintain a characteristic dignified reserve, and although the readers of Holmes's judicial opinions, his **Speeches,** his **Collected Legal Papers,** and his previously published letters to William James[5] are already familiar with many of his phrases and ideas, the continuity of the correspondence and the variety of the subjects here covered, as well as the occasional interplay with Sir Frederick Pollock, paint in many lines and shadows that have heretofore been lacking. The self-assurance and clarity of the speeches are often absent, but the reader is rewarded by the feeling that he is being allowed to share the process of the great Judge's thought as he is organizing and stating his doubts. Throughout the correspondence, Justice Holmes appears as a subtle, sensitive mind of catholic and cultivated interests. And if the letters occasionally seem bookish or self-conscious, if they sometimes seem to lack personal warmth, they are always intense and concerned with the kind of questions—indeed the whole gamut of questions—that must concern civilized men.

Dr. Johnson once said of Sir Isaac Newton that if he had lived among the Greeks he would have been worshipped as a god. Mr. Justice Holmes came as near apotheosis in his own day as perhaps any other American. And yet it is singularly difficult to imagine his thought and character transferred to another age. For the great Judge was no system-builder. His social philosophy—if one is to be articulated for him—must be pieced together as a mosaic of decisions on particular issues which he met during his years as Judge and Chief Justice of the Supreme Judicial Court of Massachusetts, and later as Associate Justice of the Supreme Court of the United States. The work of exegesis has not been wholly successful; it is not certain that he would have accepted any of the systems made for him by his disciples. The newly-published correspondence with Sir Frederick Pollock reveals more of the tantalizing elusiveness of Holmes's personal philosophy, and helps account for the fact that many of his disciples have simply given themselves up to a reverent homage. The inadequacy of labels like "liberal" and "conservative" quickly appears, and it becomes increasingly evident that here was a man so sensitive to contemporary thoughts and feelings, so eager to wreak himself upon life, and so responsive to the variety, color, and sound of life that he embodied many of the conflicting currents and attitudes of his day. In his earnestness to encompass all philosophies and yet to commit himself to none, his personal world of ideas was a world of doubt and conflict.

Mr. Justice Holmes, the product of a New England conservative tradition, clearly felt the tug of opposing forces. His family background drew him in the direction of respectability, elegance, and the genteel tradition. But the individuality of the Justice was intensely liberal; he was a man of extra-ordinary intelligence who was eager and happy to see a world of change. He was finally unable to reconcile these two aspects of his personality, although an apparent resolution took the form of a faith in conflict, in the process and struggle of life. Indeed, "conflict," physical and intellectual, is a *leitmotif* of the correspondence. On October 21, 1895, he opened his letter to Sir Frederick, "Thirty-four years ago today was my first battle. I was shot through the breast at Ball's Bluff & it always seems something of an anniversary to me."[6] That was written in the Judge's fifty-fifth year. Nearly a third of a century later, when he was over eighty, he still celebrated the anniversary, and headed a letter to Sir Frederick, "Beverly Farms, September 18, 1927 Antietam was 65 years ago yesterday."[7] In his serious utterances he used most frequently the metaphors of battle. He liked to call himself "an old soldier." In his speech on his predecessor as Chief Justice of Massachusetts, Holmes concluded by saying, "With a kind of desperate joy we go back to the fight."[8] The figure of battle which characterized the active life to him, also represented to him the world of ideas and of moral values. As early as 1895, he wrote to Pollock of the qualities necessary to make a lawyer a "fighting success."[9] In a significant letter in the summer of 1925, again employing the metaphor of battle, he wrote:

> I think the proper attitude is that we know nothing of cosmic values and bow our heads—seeing reason enough for doing all we can and not demanding the plan of campaign of the General—or even asking whether there is any general or any plan. It's enough for me that this universe can produce intelligence, ideals, etc.—*et superest ager.*[10]

By a paradox, this most reflective of recent American jurists seemed to admire the study of law not so much because it was philosophical as because it dealt with the world of conflicting interests—where the discords of the market place were given all the drama and dignity which men's everyday disagreements can be given in human society. In 1870, only a half-dozen years after he had taken up legal study, he wrote, "It is the merit of the common law that it decides the case first and determines the principle afterwards."[11] The personal philosophy that led him to find this charm in the common law was expressed many years later, in 1897, in a public tribute to a fellow judge:

> But I know of no true measure of men except the total of human energy which they embody—counting everything, with due allowance for quality, from Nansen's power to digest blubber or to resist cold, up to his courage, or to Wordsworth's power to express the unutterable, or to Kant's speculative reach. The final test of this energy is battle in some form—actual war—the crush of Arctic ice—the fight for mastery in the market or the court. . . . It is one thing to utter a happy phrase from a protected cloister; another to think under fire—to think for action upon which great interests depend.[12]

Like the true soldier, Holmes sometimes seemed more interested in the process and strategy of the fight than in the cause for which the fighting was being done. The conflicts of interests in society were essential to the drama of life. The judge was a sort of *deus ex machina,* interested not so much in removing conflict as in resolving it. He found Brooks Adams's philosophy of history exciting and was much concerned with his theory of the place of conflict in history,[13] although he naturally did not find the pessimism of the man congenial.[14] Despite this interest in the fight and his desire to preserve the equal opportunities of the fight for all men in society, Holmes distrusted "fighting faiths,"[15] and particularly the faiths of reformers—men with whose social philosophy his has been often identified. They represented the "upward and onward,"[16] men who must have seemed to the Justice more concerned with the cause than with the struggle.

Holmes's curiosity about the new philosophies entering on the battlefield of ideas and his interest in the drama of intellectual history only confirmed him in his distrust of systems of thought. Since "time has upset many fighting faiths," and "the best test of truth is the power of the thought to get itself accepted in the competition of the market, and that . . . is the only ground upon which [men's] wishes safely can be carried out,"[17] the validity of systems would naturally be affected by the conditions of the market. He wrote from Washington in 1905, "am just turning to Santayana's last two volumes of *The Life of Reason* which I like better than any philosophy I have read—or nearly so. . . . But more and more I am inclined to belittle the doings of the philosophers while I think philosophy the end of life."[18] The philosophy which Justice Holmes asserted again and again was one which he thought freed him from the bonds of any particular system, and which may have seemed to him actually to evade some of the central problems of philosophy. This was his philosophy of "can't helps." As he wrote in the summer of 1906:

> I always start my cosmic salad by saying that all I mean by truth is what I *can't help* thinking and that I have no means of deciding whether my can't helps have any cosmic worth. They clearly don't in many cases. I think the philosophers usually are too arrogant in their attitude. I accept the existence of a universe, in some unpredicable sense, just as I accept yours—by an act of faith—or by another can't help, perhaps.[19]

Over twenty years later, in 1929, he was writing in the same vein, insisting that "the *I* can't help is the ultimate. If we are sensible men and not crazy on-*ists* of any sort, we recognize that if we are in a minority of one we are likely to get locked up and then find a test or qualifications by reference to some kind of majority vote actual or imagined."[20] Close as this attitude may seem to the doctrines of pragmatism, Mr. Justice Holmes would not call himself a pragmatist, perhaps partly because of the temperamental incompatibility which he came to feel with William James, and partly because he preferred the individualism of his personal philosophy.[21]

More and more it appears that Mr. Justice Holmes's belief in conflict and in free competition among ideas was connected somehow with the conflicts in his own life and with his difficulty in deciding what he really believed. In May of 1919 he wrote:

> Brandeis the other day drove a harpoon into my midriff with reference to my summer occupations. He said you talk about improving your mind, you only exercise it on the subjects with which you are familiar. Why don't you try something new, study some domain of fact. Take up the textile industries in Massachusetts and after reading the reports sufficiently you can go to Lawrence and get a notion of how it really is. I hate facts. I always say the chief end of man is to form general propositions—adding that no general proposition is worth a damn. Of course a general proposition is simply a string for the facts and I have little doubt that it would be good for my immortal soul to plunge into them, good also for the performance of my duties, but I shrink from the bore—or rather I hate to give up the chance to read this and that, that a gentleman should have read before he dies. I don't remember that I ever read Machiavelli's *Prince*—and I think of the Day of Judgment. There are a good many worse ignorances than that that ought to be closed up. I don't know how it will come out. The spring here is enchanting.[22]

Although he had written as early as 1886, "All that life offers any man from which to start his thinking or his striving is a fact,"[23] although his legal philosophy continually lends itself to characterization as Legal Pragmatism, Mr. Justice Holmes in his personal philosophy was often inclined to take refuge in a kind of mysticism. The theme of the "unknowable" runs through his letters as it runs through his speeches. However important the pragmatic attitude in his way of thinking, there was also a large transcendental element. Commenting on James's *Pragmatism,* he significantly remarked, "And I now see, as I have seen in his other books that I have read, that the aim and end of the whole business is religious. . . . taking that as the significance of the whole business I make it my bow."[24] He himself made the link between mysticism and his own "can't help" philosophy when he wrote in 1918, "It is true that beliefs and wishes have a transcendental basis in the sense that their foundation is arbitrary. You can not help entertaining and feeling them, and there is an end of it."[25] In the same year he was writing to Pollock, "I am a mystic in the sense of believing myself to be an intelligible moment of the unintelligible, but not at all in that of supposing that by purging myself of all activities that the Cosmos has implanted I can get nearer to the central power and have a private conversation with God."[26]

The more one reads in this lively correspondence, the more Mr. Justice Holmes appears as the inquiring, restless, liberal mind, full of conflict and doubt—more interested in the multifariousness than in the moral of life. There is at once a note of optimism and of detachment. The reader cannot help perceiving the tension and inner conflict of a man who saw and understood much of the world, who was philosophical by nature and conservative by environment, but who dared not formulate a philosophy, and could not accept one ready-made. It is singularly difficult to trace development in Mr. Justice Holmes's thought; the uncertainty, the doubt, and the enquiry continued for the whole of the fifty-eight years of the correspondence. Without elaborating the connection with his social philosophy, it is obvious that between Holmes's own uncertainties and faith in the conflict in life and his eagerness to preserve for other people in society the opportunity of a fair fight, whether on the economic or on the intellectual level, there must have been some relation. The figure of Mr. Justice Holmes emerges as the prototype, on the highest intellectual level, of intelligent, self-conscious individualism in the expanding America of the late nineteenth and the early twentieth centuries. Individualism, in the dynamic form in which Mr. Justice Holmes prescribed it for the state, made him friends among socialists and radicals. But individualism as a personal philosophy, although when combined with the tradition of the culture of gentlemen it could make the warm intellectual relations of his friendship with Sir Frederick Pollock, still left him alone and in doubt, torn between pragmatism and mysticism, and finally reposing his faith in the struggle of life. "For high and dangerous action teaches us to believe as right beyond dispute things for which our doubting minds are slow to find words of proof. Out of heroism grows faith in the worth of heroism. The proof comes later, and even may never come."[27]

NOTES

[1] *The Judicial Opinions of Oliver Wendell Holmes: Constitutional Opinions, Selected Excerpts and Epigrams, as Given in the Supreme Judicial Court of Massachusetts (1883-1902),* Harry C. Shriver, editor (Buffalo, New York, 1940).

[2] Cases of interest which might have been included are those on instructions to juries (Loftus *v.* Inhabitants of North Adams, 160 Mass. 161) and on admissibility of evidence (Commonwealth *v.* Hannah Welch, 163 Mass. 372), interesting for its analogy to later wire-tapping cases.

[3] *E.g.,* the epigrams from Hamilton *v.* West End Street Railway Company (309) and from Stack *v.* New York, New Haven, and Hartford Railroad (316 f.).

[4] *Holmes-Pollock Letters: The Correspondence of Mr. Justice Holmes and Sir Frederick Pollock, 1874-1932,* 2 volumes, edited by Mark DeWolfe Howe (Cambridge, 1941).

[5] R. B. Perry, *Thought and Character of William James* (Boston, 1935), I, 504 ff., and II, 458 ff.

[6] *Holmes-Pollock Letters* (hereinafter referred to by volume and page numbers only), I, 64.

[7] II, 205.

[8] Silas Bent, *Justice Oliver Wendell Holmes* (New York, 1932), 224. Some other uses of the figure of battle in speeches occur on pages 137 f., 218, and 353. Of Bertrand Russell, Mr. Justice Holmes wrote to his correspondent on May 2, 1925, "But I think he is something of a sentimentalist, and does not talk well of war." II, 158.

[9] I, 65.

[10] II, 163.

[11] Bent, 346, quoting from an unsigned editorial in the *American Law Review*, I, 5. *Cf.*, for example, the dicta against "general reasoning" and "too broadly generalized conceptions." Shriver, 285 and 289.

[12] Bent, 137 f.

[13] I, 64 f., 76 f., 124, and 187.

[14] I, 73.

[15] *Cf. The Dissenting Opinions of Mr. Justice Holmes,* Alfred Lief, editor, (New York, 1929), 50.

[16] I, 201. *Cf.* the remark of Mr. Holmes to his secretary, about 1916: "I'm afraid Brandeis has the crusading spirit. He talks like one of those upward-and-onward fellows." Bent, 281.

[17] *The Dissenting Opinions of Mr. Justice Holmes,* 50, quoted from Abrams *et al v.* United States, 250 U.S., 616, at 630.

[18] I, 122.

[19] I, 126. *Cf.* the strikingly similar statements at I, 139, and II, 251 f.

[20] II, 255 f. *Cf.* Santayana's remark that James believed philosophy to have a Polish Constitution, *Character and Opinion in the United States* (New York, 1920), 82.

[21] "*I* think pragmatism an amusing humbug—like most of William James's speculations, as distinguished from his admirable and well written Irish perceptions of life." I, 138 f. *Cf.* I, 140, and R. B. Perry, *Thought and Character of William James* (Boston, 1935), II, 458 ff.

[22] II, 13 f. In 1897, Mr. Holmes had written, "For the rational study of law the black-letter man may be the man of the present, but the man of the future is the man of statistics and the master of economics." *Collected Legal Papers,* collected by Harold J. Laski (New York, 1920), 187.

[23] *Collected Legal Papers,* 30. Examples of his pragmatic attitude to the law may be found in the *Holmes-Pollock Letters, e. g.,* definition of "a right," II, 212; and "The Path of the Law," in *Collected Legal Papers,* 167 ff.

[24] I, 140.

[25] *Collected Legal Papers,* 312.

[26] I, 274. *Cf.* II, 207 f.

[27] Quoted in Bent, 123.

John A. Garraty (essay date 1949)

SOURCE: "Holmes's Appointment to the U. S. Supreme Court," in *The New England Quarterly,* Vol. XXII, No. 3, September, 1949, pp. 291-303.

[*In the following essay, Garraty traces the personal and political considerations of Holmes's appointment to the Supreme Court.*]

Early in July, 1902, Associate Justice Horace Gray, troubled by failing health, responded to the urgings of his family and his physician and wrote a letter to President Theodore Roosevelt. Further service might seriously endanger his health, he told the President, and therefore he must resign immediately or upon the appointment of his successor, whichever the President wished.[1]

His replacement, of course, was a matter for the determination of the Chief Executive subject to the approval of the Senate, but custom imposed certain limitations on the field of choice. In the first place, Judge Gray was a Massachusetts man. His successor, therefore, almost certainly would come from New England, probably from the Bay State itself. In 1902 the Supreme Court was one hundred and thirteen years old; for eighty-two of these years its Bench had been graced by a Massachusetts citizen. The rest of New England might not think so highly of this record. "There are judges in these outlying districts," the *Hartford Courant* pointed out, "quite as eminent for learning and well-dowered with all the judicial virtues as the Massachusetts judges." Yet the facts had to be faced. The new judge *might* come from anywhere in the United States, but it was extremely unlikely that he would be found more than fifty miles from Boston.[2]

A second factor also limited the selection. The Massachusetts senators would have to be consulted and their approval obtained, for "senatorial courtesy" would prevent the confirmation of any man not supported by them. Horace Gray's replacement must be satisfactory to two key figures—George Frisbie Hoar and Henry Cabot Lodge. The venerable Senator Hoar's career in the Upper House ran back uninterrupted to 1877, and if he no longer ranked as a leader in the Republican party, he was still a man of great prestige who could not be ignored. Lodge, though a relative newcomer in the Senate, held a position there second to none by virtue of his relation to Roosevelt, whose best friend and close political adviser he was. So, while the President would make the final choice, it would not be an unrestricted one.

In the early months of 1902, as it became clear that Gray would probably quit his post, interested parties began to speculate. Late in February, textile manufacturer Eben S. Draper suggested in a letter to Senator Lodge that a good candidate for the vacancy, if and when it occurred, would be United States Circuit Court Judge Francis Cabot Lowell. Lowell was a member of an old and eminent family, and had much to recommend him. Trained in the law, he had also served in the lower house of the Massachusetts legislature and on the Boston Common Council, and had achieved some recognition as historian and man of letters.[3] But Lodge had another candidate, equally distinguished. "There are others as you know with very strong claims," he wrote Draper on March third, and went on to indicate that his own favorite was the Chief Justice of the Massachusetts Supreme Court—Oliver Wendell Holmes, Jr.[4]

By any superficial standard Holmes would seem a choice that a man like Draper could have accepted with pleasure. In background and training he was very similar to the manufacturer's own Boston-born and Harvard-trained candidate. Yet Draper's reaction was almost violent. Holmes's appointment would be a grave mistake, he informed Lodge, and hastened to assure him that his own lay opinion could be amply buttressed by consultation with the Massachusetts legal fraternity. "While it would naturally be difficult to get lawyers to express this opinion under all the circumstances," Draper wrote, "they think that [Holmes] is erratic, and that he is not a safe man for such an important position."[5] Draper did not explain this attitude, but no explanation was necessary. Holmes was "erratic" and not "safe" because of certain opinions he had offered from the bench of the Massachusetts Court—opinions highly disturbing to a conservative cotton manufacturer and to many equally conservative lawyers. For instance, he had taken the "erratic" position that peaceful picketing by striking workers should not be terminated by an injunction in the case of Vegelahn v. Guntner, in 1896. In Plant v. Woods, Holmes had even ventured to opine that within certain limits a secondary boycott by a labor union was legal. A judge who had said, "I think that unity of organization is necessary to make the contest of labor effectual," was not, to men like Draper, a person properly to be entrusted with the interpretation of the Constitution of the United States.[6] Lowell held no such heretical views, but if he would not do there were others. When, in mid-May, a report from "well-informed professional circles" appeared in the papers that the ailing Gray might be replaced by Senator Hoar's nephew, corporation counsel Samuel Hoar, Draper was quick to switch his allegiance. "I feel perfectly certain that the appointment of Mr. Hoar would give a great deal better satisfaction to all the business interests of the state than would the appointment of Judge Holmes," he wrote Lodge.[7]

But Lodge himself was not upset by Holmes's radical views on the rights of organized labor; he and his friend in the White House rated another matter as far more important. The Supreme Court was badly split over what he called the "Porto Rican cases"—the Insular cases dealing with the constitutional relations of the United States and its newly-acquired overseas possessions. In Downes v. Bidwell, for example, the Court had divided five to four in upholding what one of the dissenting Justices called the right of Congress to keep a territory "like a disembodied shade, in an intermediate state of ambiguous existence for an indefinite period."[8] To imperialists like Roosevelt and Lodge, this state of things was desirable, and they were very much afraid of any change of opinion in the precariously balanced Court. In the Downes v. Bidwell decision there had been two different majority opinions and two dissenting ones—clearly there was no certainty that future cases would not alter the balance. Justice Gray had been one of those who had made up the all too uncertain majority. Therefore his successor must have similar views on such matters. Holmes, Lodge thought, filled the bill, and this to a great extent accounts for his support of the Chief Justice of his state. "I am absolutely for Holmes unless he should be adverse on Porto Rican cases, which I am informed he is not," the Senator wrote Roosevelt.[9]

When Lodge reached his home at Nahant after the adjournment of Congress in June, he called on Justice Gray and talked with him at length about his successor. Gray, Lodge later informed Roosevelt, agreed that Holmes was a suitable man for the job. Roosevelt had in previous conversations indicated approval, but he had not definitely committed himself, so Lodge (knowing that Gray's resignation would be forthcoming very soon) now put Holmes's case before the President forcefully. Besides his brilliance and profound learning, as the Chief Justice of Massachusetts, he was the logical choice, the Senator urged. "It would be hard to pass him by—hard on him." While it was true that men like Samuel Hoar and certain other lawyers disliked him because of "his one or two labor decisions," many others felt differently. "I have been talking quietly with lawyers here," Lodge went on, "& there is no doubt that the great body of the bar would strongly approve. Our ex-Att'y Gen'l Knowlton a very strong man is an example of these." Just how widely Lodge had carried his investigations of legal opinion in Massachusetts is not apparent, but the example he chose was not a fair one. Knowlton had a special interest in Holmes's promotion, for Governor Crane had promised him the Chief Justiceship if Holmes were moved up before his own term expired. "Knowlton . . . was most anxious for my appointment and showed it with a *naïveté* that made me smile," Holmes himself wrote years later. "He knew that the outgoing governor would appoint him to my place and wanted to fasten it before the new governor came in." But, of course, Lodge was doing his best to make a case for his friend. Holmes's stand on labor matters he thought "of no importance really." "It would I confess be a sore disappointment to me if you should decide . . . to pass Wendell over. . . . I am very fond of him & he is in line for the promotion."[10]

Roosevelt's answer to this letter has been published and widely quoted by students of both Holmes and the Supreme Court. It need only be summarized here. The President agreed with Lodge both as to the Judge's qualifications and the unimportance of his labor views. He even said, "The labor decisions . . . constitute to my mind a strong point in Judge Holmes' favor." But he too stressed the territorial cases and added another *caveat*. In February, 1901, on the one-hundredth anniversary of John Marshall's elevation to the Supreme Court, Holmes had delivered an address on Marshall in which he had not expressed what Roosevelt considered proper enthusiasm for the great Chief Justice. That speech had been "unworthy," Roosevelt declared, and had demonstrated "a total incapacity to grasp what Marshall did." It was important that Holmes be a party man in the Marshall sense as well as a good judge. Roosevelt demanded assurance on this point and authorized Lodge to put the question frankly to the candidate. If he seemed sound, Lodge was to have him go to Oyster Bay for a final talk before the announcement of the appointment.[11]

This letter reached Lodge at Tuckernuck (a small island off Nantucket owned by his friend and Harvard classmate, William Sturgis Bigelow) where he was vacationing. "I agree most profoundly with everything you say," he replied. "I can put it to Holmes with absolute frankness & shall, for I would not appoint my best beloved on that bench unless he held the position you describe." The Senator immediately dispatched a note to Holmes making an appointment to see him, and then returned to the mainland. Their conference was a success.

"I told the President you had always been a Republican and never a Mugwump," said Lodge.

"A Mugwump!" Holmes replied stoutly. "I should think not. Why they are mere elements of dissolution."[12]

Having passed this test, Holmes went to Oyster Bay for the final interview with "TR." He arrived on July 24, but the President was away, and his return was delayed by a heavy fog; so their talk did not take place until the following morning. When it did it was eminently successful. Roosevelt was "entirely satisfied," and Holmes left with the knowledge that he would be nominated. "The way he put his wishes to me . . . was a reward for much hard work," the Judge later explained to Lady Pollock. But Roosevelt was not ready to make his decision public. "He said his mind was made up, but asked me not to mention [it] except to you," Holmes wrote Lodge, and went on to thank the Senator for his "kind feeling" and help. Lodge was naturally pleased, for Holmes was a life-long friend. "I felt sure that you would [be satisfied] for he is our kind right through," he told Roosevelt when he heard the results of the Oyster Bay meeting.[13]

Though Roosevelt had approved Lodge's choice the picture was not yet complete, for Senator Hoar was very unhappy about the appointment. This accounts for Roosevelt's warning to Holmes that the subject must not yet be discussed publicly. The old Senator was vacationing at the Isles of Shoals, and Lodge wrote to him there

telling him the news. Hoar's reply bristled with disapproval. "I do not agree with you about Chief Justice Holmes," he wrote. "His accomplishments are literary and social . . . not judicial. . . . In his opinions he runs to subtleties and refinements, and no decision of his makes a great landmark in jurisprudence." Hoar went on to say, as Draper had earlier, that the great weight of Massachusetts legal opinion would be hostile to the choice of such a man. He did not mention the labor opinions but hinted at them darkly. "It will be a pity if the Democratic judges . . . while a minority in numbers, shall be believed by the people to comprise the solid strength of the Bench," he wrote. Not content with this, Hoar wrote to Roosevelt, but in a strangely different vein. He said nothing against Holmes, but complained of the way the appointment was being made. "There is no doubt of the absolute right of the President to make such appointments on such advice as he chooses, or without advice, if he prefer," he admitted. But he made it quite plain that he did not like the way Roosevelt was handling the question. "The old method . . . in making these great and irrevocable appointments, has been to let the public know of the vacancy, to allow a reasonable time for all persons interested, especially the members of the legal profession, and the representatives of the States immediately concerned, to make known their opinions and desires. . . ."[14]

The President was eager to placate Hoar and offered in his answer to this letter to hear and consider any evidence against Holmes which could be presented. He had not consulted Hoar sooner, he said, because he had assumed that the Chief Justice of Massachusetts would be a perfectly satisfactory choice in the eyes of any Massachusetts man. Also, he had not known until very recently that Justice Gray was going to quit. But he was firm in his determination to make the announcement quickly unless Hoar could advance some clear proof that Holmes was unfit. "It seems to me desirable," his letter concluded, "to announce how [the] place is to be filled forthwith."

Lodge also wrote Hoar once again, trying hard to soothe his colleague's ruffled feelings. "I cannot feel that you do justice to judge Holmes in his legal capacity," he said, but added with the proper humility of one who had never practised law, "although I should never for a moment think of setting my opinion against yours on such a question." He mentioned influential lawyers who had expressed satisfaction with Holmes—Judge Gray himself, Knowlton, of course, and former Attorney General Richard Olney. This seemed to have no effect at all, for Hoar's next letter took up the story where he had left it: "I always talk with lawyers, when I meet them about the State, about the Court. It is as common a subject of conversation as the quality of the President of the United States is among men interested in politics. . . . I never heard anybody speak of Judge Holmes as an able judge. He is universally regarded as a man of pleasant personal address . . . but without strength, and without grasp of general principles."[15]

As their correspondence progressed so fruitlessly, Lodge came to realize that while Hoar was not pleased with the choice of Holmes, what he most seriously resented was the fact that rightful deference had not been made to the Senior Senator from Massachusetts himself. "I feel about it," he had written candidly to Lodge on August seventh, "somewhat as the late Peter C. Bacon, the Dominie Sampson of the Worcester Bar, did when he heard that a neighbor was going to shoot his dog. He said with great indignation, 'If he gives me notice and then shoots my dog, I don't care, but if he shoots my dog without giving me notice, I shall be mad.'"

Hoar was in a delicate position in opposing Holmes. As Roosevelt had indicated, the fact that the candidate was already the Chief Justice of the Massachusetts Supreme Court would prevent any Massachusetts man from *publicly* questioning his qualifications, and Hoar was no exception. Also, since Hoar's nephew, Samuel, had been mentioned for the coveted vacancy, any serious objection by the Senator to Holmes might be interpreted as a desire to promote a member of his own family. Lodge and Roosevelt both understood Hoar's dilemma but did not wish to injure his sensibilities. Hoar undoubtedly understood it too and in time came to accept it. "The proposed appointment will be considered by the general public as entirely respectable," he admitted to Lodge finally, "and those members of the profession whose opinion is of any value will have to make the best of it." Needless to say, he was speaking for himself, for Lodge finally was able to inform the President, "Mr. Hoar still growls mildly about Holmes not being a great lawyer but he is quieting and is good-natured already and all is well."[16]

With Senator Hoar reconciled if not satisfied there was no longer need for delay; on August 11 Roosevelt announced the appointment. There was no inordinate stir in the press when the story broke. The news was, the *Literary Digest* summarized, "generally considered . . . more interesting than momentous." Much stress was placed upon Holmes's labor dissents, and there was a good deal of speculation on the territorial issue which had loomed so important to Roosevelt and Lodge. "If Justice Holmes disagreed with the recent findings of the court in the insular cases, his vote would overturn the majority," admitted the *Digest,* "but he is said to agree with the court's findings and no disturbance is looked for in that quarter." On the other hand, the *New York Herald* pictured the fate of America's overseas possessions as trembling in the balance. The conservative *Boston Transcript* was on the surface satisfied, but could not hide the fears inspired by *Vegelahn v. Guntner,* though it did not refer to the case directly. "His striking originality of mind will help him when it does not hinder," its editorial remarked primly, and went on at some length in praise of the retiring Justice Gray, characterizing him as "the greatest judge in the language[!]" But the *Boston Globe,* catering to more plebeian temperaments, called Holmes both an "ornament" and a "strong addition" to the court who would bring to the bench the fruits of his "liberal and well stored mind," and the Democratic *Boston Post* seemed thoroughly satisfied with what it referred to as the "wise and admirable choice" of the President.[17]

The amazing thing about the entire episode of Holmes's appointment to the Supreme Court was that neither the press nor the figures who played any important part in it appreciated the significance of what was happening. The new Justice's conception of the dynamic nature of law, so clearly expressed as early as 1881 in his great book, *The Common Law,* and his belief that the courts should not interfere with legislative action aimed at social improvement even when property rights were in the process restricted, were practically ignored. The newspaper reaction was bitterly depressing to Holmes himself, who almost alone seems to have appreciated what important effects his particular approach was to have on American judicial thinking. "They don't know much more than that I took the labor side in Vegelahn *v.* Guntner," he complained to his friend Sir Frederick Pollock. He also resented the "incompetence and inadequacy of the ordinary talk" of the people. This was particularly true of those who might have been expected to know better—Senator Hoar, for instance, whose opinions quoted above of Holmes as a judge certainly add nothing to his own legal reputation. And if Hoar is to be believed, most of the lawyers in Massachusetts seem to have been equally weak in appraising their great colleague. Neither Roosevelt nor Lodge was a lawyer (Lodge had a degree, but never practiced) and may perhaps be excused for not appreciating Holmes's legal philosophy. Yet they were both made very unhappy in later years by certain decisions which even a cursory reading of Holmes's Massachusetts opinions should have led them to expect. Roosevelt particularly was put out by Holmes's dissents in some of the anti-trust cases, of which the Northern Securities Case was the most important. Writing to Lodge in 1906, the President declared:

> Nothing has been so strongly borne in on me concerning lawyers on the bench as that the *nominal* politics of the man has nothing to do with his actions on the bench. His *real* politics are all important. From his antecedents, Holmes should have been an ideal man on the bench. As a matter of fact he has been a bitter disappointment. . . .

In the Northern Securities Case Holmes held, in effect, that combinations as such did not constitute restraint of trade. Was this surprising—coming from the man who had said in his Vegelahn *v.* Guntner dissenting opinion, "It is plain from the slightest consideration of practical affairs, or the most superficial reading of industrial history, that free competition means combination. It seems to me futile to set our faces against this tendency."[18]

Both Lodge and Roosevelt had questioned Holmes about his "politics" before his nomination to the Court. If either had understood the man and his point of view, it would have been easy to uncover his stand on industrial combinations. Yet neither appreciated the simple fact that Holmes applied the same standard to a combination of capitalists as he applied to a combination of laborers. Holmes took a position in the Vegelahn Case which was favorable to labor, and from this Roosevelt assumed that he was opposed to trusts. Nine times out of ten this might have been a safe assumption, but if the President had understood Holmes he would have realized that this was the tenth time. Holmes decided cases on legal principles, not on what *he* thought was right or wrong. Lodge and Roosevelt asked him if he was a Republican. He said, "yes," so they made him an Associate Justice of the Supreme Court. But this did not make him a Republican Supreme Court Justice in the sense that Roosevelt and Lodge wanted him to be.

Probably, in their prenomination quizzes, neither the President nor the Senator went into the trust question at all. Lodge was interested mainly in the territorial issue, and here the candidate's views were similar to his own both personally *and* judicially. Neither Lodge nor any other imperialist had ever any reason to quarrel with Holmes's opinions in the insular cases with which he dealt. Roosevelt was worried about party regularity as well as imperialism, but was manifestly satisfied when Holmes said that he was not a Mugwump—that he disapproved of "independents" in politics. Being a politician he could not appreciate that Holmes the judge was not Holmes the Republican private citizen. So he was unhappy later not because he had been deceived but because he had not understood. He had only himself to blame.

As Holmes said years later, it was all "rather comic."[19] Roosevelt "looked on my dissent to the *Northern Securities Case* as a political departure," he wrote Sir Frederick Pollock in 1921, and offered an estimate of Roosevelt which demonstrated clearly that he understood "TR" far better than "TR" understood him. "He was very likeable, a big figure, a rather ordinary intellect, with extraordinary gifts, a shrewd and I think pretty unscrupulous politician. He played all his cards—if not more. *R. i. p.*"[20]

NOTES

[1] Gray to Roosevelt, July 9, 1902, in Roosevelt Papers, Library of Congress. Gray had suffered a stroke in February, and was failing rapidly. He died on September 15, 1902. In accepting the resignation, Roosevelt told Gray that if the opening had occurred he would have been raised to the Chief Justiceship. Roosevelt to Gray, July 11, 1902, in Roosevelt Papers.

[2] Catherine Drinker Bowen, *Yankee from Olympus* (Boston, 1944), 343; *Literary Digest,* xxv, 214-215 (August 23, 1902).

[3] Draper to Lodge, February 28, 1902, in Lodge Papers, Massachusetts Historical Society; Ferris Greenslet, *The Lowells and Their Seven Worlds* (Boston, 1946), 329-330.

[4] Lodge's first choice would have been William Henry Moody, but he knew that Moody's age (he was a mere stripling by judicial standards—only forty-nine) was against him. Moody was elevated to the Supreme Bench in 1906.

[5] Draper to Lodge, March 7, 1902, in Lodge Papers.

[6] Plant *v.* Woods (176 Mass. 492), quoted in Dorsey Richardson, *Constitutional Doctrines of Justice Oliver Wendell Holmes* (Baltimore, 1924), 32.

[7] *Boston Globe,* May 18, 1902; Draper to Lodge, June 13, 1902, in Lodge Papers.

[8] Downes *v.* Bidwell (182 U. S. 244), 1901; Chief Justice Fuller dissenting.

[9] Lodge to Roosevelt, June 5, 1902, in Lodge Papers.

[10] Lodge to Roosevelt, July 7, 1902, in Lodge Papers; Holmes to Sir Frederick Pollock, May 17, 1925, in Mark DeWolfe Howe, editor, *Holmes-Pollock Letters* (Cambridge, 1941), II, 161. Knowlton was appointed Chief Justice by Crane when Holmes resigned. After Holmes's appointment had been announced, Knowlton even went so far as to urge Holmes to resign from the Massachusetts Court immediately, arguing that failure to do so would prejudice the Senate against his confirmation. See Lodge to Roosevelt, August 20, 1902, in Henry Cabot Lodge, editor, *Selections from the Correspondence of Theodore Roosevelt and Henry Cabot Lodge: 1884-1918* (New York, 1925), I, 527.

[11] Roosevelt to Lodge, July 10, 1902, in *Selections from the Correspondence of Theodore Roosevelt and Henry Cabot Lodge: 1884-1918,* I, 517-519.

[12] Lodge to Roosevelt, July 19 and 26, 1902, in Lodge Papers. Lodge could have had no doubts about Holmes's regularity. In 1884, when most of Boston was scornful of Lodge, and his best friends were cutting him on the street because of his support of Blaine, Holmes was one of the few who stood up for him and supported him cordially, William Lawrence, *Henry Cabot Lodge: A Biographical Sketch* (Boston; 1925), 40.

[13] Roosevelt to Lodge, July 25, 1902, in Roosevelt Papers; Holmes to Lady Pollock, September 6, 1902, in *Holmes-Pollock Letters,* I, 105; Holmes to Lodge, July 25, 1902, and Lodge to Roosevelt, July 26, 1902, in Lodge Papers.

[14] Hoar to Lodge, July 29, 1902, in Lodge Papers; Hoar to Roosevelt, July 28, 1902, in Roosevelt Papers.

[15] Roosevelt to Hoar, July 30, 1902, in Roosevelt Papers; Lodge to Hoar, August 8, 1902, and Hoar to Lodge, August 11, 1902, in Lodge Papers.

[16] Hoar to Lodge, August 7 and 11, 1902; Lodge to Roosevelt, August 17, 1902, Lodge Papers.

[17] *Literary Digest,* XXV, 214 (August 23, 1902); *Public Opinion,* XXXIII, 229 (August 21, 1902); *Boston Globe,* August 13, 1902.

[18] Holmes to Pollock, September [?], 1923, in *Holmes-Pollock Letters,* 1, 106; Roosevelt to Lodge, September 4, 1906, in Lodge Papers; Vegelahn *v.* Guntner (167

Mass. 92), quoted in *Constitutional Doctrines of Justice Oliver Wendell Holmes,* 30.

[19] Holmes to Lewis Einstein, April 1, 1928, quoted in Felix Frankfurter, "Oliver Wendell Holmes, Jr.," *Dictionary of American Biography,* Supplement I, 422.

[20] Holmes to Pollock, February 9, 1921, in *Holmes-Pollock Letters,* II, 63-64.

Irving Bernstein (essay date 1950)

SOURCE: "The Conservative Mr. Justice Holmes," in *The New England Quarterly,* Vol. XXIII, No. 4, December, 1950, pp. 435-52.

[*In the following essay, Bernstein argues that Holmes's social and political philosophy were not ideologically liberal, but that Holmes was actually a classical conservative.*]

A cherished American myth is that Oliver Wendell Holmes, Jr., was a liberal. This notion, as baseless as the tale of Washington and the cherry tree, was born during the great jurist's life and persists in the national folklore since his death. Walton Hamilton wrote in 1941, "It has taken a decade to elevate . . . Holmes from deity to mortality."[1] The time has come to lay the ghost of "Holmes and Brandeis dissenting."

Holmes, in fact, was as profound, as civilized, and as articulate a conservative as the United States has produced. Although he eludes the neatly wrapped and labelled package, his views speak for themselves.

As a young officer during the Civil War, Holmes wrote his sister, "I loathe the thick-fingered clowns we call the people— . . . vulgar, selfish and base. . . . " Age produced no sea-change. When Carl Becker visited Holmes late in life, he was asked,

"Becker, do you love the human race?"

"I've never discovered anything within myself which you, Mr. Justice, would define as a heart overflowing with human kindness, but I wish them well."

"I don't, Becker. God damn them all, I say."[2]

Holmes, in fact, was a firm believer in capitalism who looked with distrust upon governmental intervention in economic life. Monopolies won his respect, while he regarded unions and strikes suspiciously. The search for security, Holmes felt, was humbug. He was a confirmed nationalist who disparaged international machinery to promote peace. By the same token, he regarded war as the highest expression of man's destiny. "What moved him," H. L. Mencken has observed, "was far less a positive love of liberty than an amiable and half contemptuous feeling that those who longed for it ought to get a horse-doctor's dose of it, and so suffer a really first-rate belly-ache."[3]

I

Holmes's views were shaped primarily by three forces: his personal history and social status, his experience in the Civil War, and the doctrine of Evolution. For Holmes the accident of birth in 1841 was a stroke of fortune. He entered life with unsurpassed background and endowments, a member of the intellectual aristocracy of New England in the age of her flowering.

Few Americans, excepting perhaps an Adams or a Lee, could claim a more distinguished lineage. His ancestors, arriving in the seventeenth century, embedded themselves like native rock in the New England soil. Holmes wrote in the Harvard Class Album for 1861: "All my three names designate families from which I am descended. A long pedigree of Olivers and Wendells may be found in the book called *Memorials of the Dead in Boston.* . . . Of my grandfather Abiel Holmes, an account may be found in the biographical dictionaries."[4] Abiel, who married the daughter of the president of Yale, occupied the pulpit at Christ Church, Cambridge, and wrote *The Annals of America.* He was a Calvinist and a Federalist. Abiel's son Oliver studied medicine and became Professor of Anatomy in the Harvard Medical School. He was, as well, the genial, albeit acutely class-conscious, Autocrat of the Breakfast Table. He wrote: "You can't keep a dead level long. . . . If all the cities of the world were reduced to ashes, you'd have a new set of millionaires in a couple of years or so, out of the trade in potash."[5] He was a Republican.

The maternal side of Holmes's ancestry produced fewer books but possessed greater wealth and social standing. Colonel Jacob Wendell lost forty buildings in the great Boston fire of 1760. His son Oliver sat in the Senate and Council of the Commonwealth and was a judge and a passionate Federalist. The Wendells were related to the Jacksons, Cabots, Eliots, Quincys, and Bradstreets, and had their portraits done by Copley and Stuart. Judge Oliver Wendell's daughter Sally married Abiel Holmes. Their son Oliver Wendell took Amelia Jackson as his bride. Her father owned one of the most impressive homes in Boston and was a distinguished judge of the Superior Court of Massachusetts.

Oliver Wendell Holmes, Jr., went to Harvard. Indeed, he could not go elsewhere, for, as he wrote, "We love every limb of Harvard College."[6] Sally Wendell's father and both her grandfathers had gone there. Dr. Holmes's great-uncle had been treasurer, Judge Wendell a fellow, and Judge Jackson an overseer of Harvard College. Dr. Holmes had attended the institution, becoming a member of Hasty Pudding and Porcellian, and had returned later to take his chair in medicine. Oliver, Jr., made the same clubs, as well as Phi Beta Kappa. When war came he enlisted in the Twentieth Massachusetts Infantry, "the

Harvard Regiment." After military service he returned to study law.

Holmes's career advanced in a straight line from one success to the next: law practice in Boston, editor of the *American Law Review,* author of **The Common Law,** professor at the Harvard Law School, judge and then Chief Justice of the Supreme Judicial Court of Massachusetts, and Justice of the Supreme Court of the United States. The greater part of his life was spent in the cloistered calm of the bench. Holmes did not know financial insecurity and, in fact, left a substantial fortune when he died. He married Fanny Dixwell, daughter of the principal of his Latin School, who was his constant companion through a long life. Their home, however, was never warmed by the presence of children.

Holmes received all the personal endowments the gods could offer. He possessed a powerful, disciplined intellect, sparkling wit, and a masterful command of language. In him a handsome face and strong body joined with the excellent health that carried him through ninety-three years. He was well over six feet tall, with strong shoulders, a high brow, a distinguished nose, and searching eyes. Holmes's manner was noble, gracious, and often dazzling. Chief Justice Hughes found beneath his "judicial robe the chivalry of a knight."[7]

The process of reaching maturity in New England's golden age brought a quality of wholeness to Holmes's personality and mind. His father, who was in the literary mainstream himself, wrote: "We all carry the Common in our heads as the unit of space, the State House as the standard of architecture, and we measure off men in Edward Everetts."[8] Celebrated figures were at his house for tea—Emerson, Lowell, and Dr. James Freeman Clarke. Emerson, in fact, read young Holmes's college essay on Plato; he did not care for it. As a boy Holmes witnessed the *Flying Cloud* glide down the ways in East Boston. His family summered at the "old Wendell farm" near Pittsfield, where Melville and Hawthorne lived nearby. His father took him to meetings of the Saturday Club at the Parker House where he rubbed minds with Emerson, Dana, Agassiz, Longfellow, and Whittier.

The combination of these elements gave Holmes unusual personal security. As Hamilton has remarked, "Holmes never had to be introduced. . . . He was somebody. . . . Status opened doors, set presumptions in his favor, saved embarrassment and bother."[9] As a consequence, professional and social climbing were absent from his life. His attention was never diverted; security gave him release and freedom from inhibition. He was gifted, in the words of Justice Cardozo, with "serenity . . . , and gentleness, and most of all, benignancy—the benignancy of a soul that has fashioned its own scale of values, and in those deeply graven markings has found the quietude of peace."[10]

"What we most love and revere generally," Holmes wrote, "is determined by early associations." His youth-ful associations gave him a passionate devotion to the past and particularly to the old in New England. "The reverence for venerable traditions remains. I feel it in my fingertips. . . . I love every brick and shingle of the old Massachusetts towns." He preferred books in his library that "were on shelves before America was discovered," prints on his walls "that go back two or three hundred years." Old associations became part of his being and when they were wrenched from him "roots are torn and broken that bleed like veins." He was delighted to have outlasted Taney, to be "the oldest judge who ever . . . remained sitting on our bench."[11]

Of his great-grandmother Temperance Holmes it was said, "To the affairs of her household she was assiduously and unweariedly attentive, and never ate the bread of idleness." Holmes shared her passion for hard work. John Ropes declared that he never knew anyone to study law so ferociously. "He was as busy as a witch in a gale." On the Supreme Court he alone inflicted "cruel and unusual punishment" upon himself by taking extensive notes on argument and by refusing secretarial help. "The mode in which the inevitable comes to pass is through effort."[12] Expenditure of energy, however, was pointless without the quest for the superlative. Holmes declared,

> No man has earned the right to intellectual ambition until he has learned to lay his course by a star which he has never seen. . . . Only when you have worked alone,—when you have felt around you a black gulf of solitude more isolating than that which surrounds the dying man . . . will you have achieved.[13]

Although Holmes titillated his friends with naughty words, his taste, like his moral conduct, was impeccably respectable. He nodded approvingly when Chief Justice Taft forbade a western judge to enter court without a waistcoat. Of Ernest Hemingway he wrote, "I wonder at the illusion that one is more real if one evokes sordid situations and bad smells, than if one invites one's readers to fresh air and agreeable and even noble people. . . . Let him leave his garbage."[14]

II

The Civil War was the searing and maturing experience of Holmes's life. "The generation that carried on the war," he declared, "has been set apart. . . . Through our great good fortune, in our youth our hearts were touched with fire. It was given to us to learn at the outset that life is a profound and passionate thing."[15] Half a century after Appomattox he caught himself "deeply and unexpectedly" moved by the Unknown Soldier ceremony.

The Twentieth Massachusetts saw action in many of the major battles of the war, losing five-eighths of its men, killed and wounded. At Ball's Bluff on October 21, 1861, a ball entered Holmes's left breast and came out behind the right, missing the heart and lungs. That night, blood dripping from his mouth; he considered taking poison in anticipation of death. He recovered to fight in the Peninsula Campaign in 1862, where he suffered nothing worse than body lice, scurvy, and diarrhea. In September he was hit in the neck at Antietam. Holmes confided to his diary, "The South have achieved their independence."[16] In the second Battle of Fredericksburg he was wounded a third time, shrapnel splintering the bone and tearing the ligaments of his heel. The following summer he wrote his mother, "I honestly think the duty of fighting has ceased for me—ceased because I have laboriously and with much suffering of mind and body *earned* the right . . . to decide for myself how I can best do my duty."[17] Holmes was mustered out on July 17, 1864, having risen from lieutenant to lieutenant-colonel.

The war taught Holmes that life is a struggle, that peace is an idle dream. He wrote of the League of Nations,

> Man at present is a predatory animal. I think that the sacredness of human life is a purely municipal ideal of no validity outside the jurisdiction. I believe that force, mitigated so far as it may be by good manners, is the *ultima ratio,* and between two groups that want to make inconsistent kinds of worlds I see no remedy except force. . . . Every society rests on the death of men.[18]

For Holmes, then, danger became an end in itself. Heidelberg students "with their sword-slashed faces inspire me with sincere respect." A broken neck is not a waste, but "a price well paid for the breeding of a race fit for . . . command."[19] Similarly, the will to fight became a vital object.

> That . . . faith is true and adorable which leads a soldier to throw away his life in obedience to a blindly accepted duty, in a cause which he little understands, in a plan of campaign of which he has no notion, under tactics of which he does not see the use.[20]

The war, in addition, made Holmes a confirmed nationalist. During the conflict with Spain, for example, he confessed pleasure in "hearing some rattling jingo talk." War also caused him to take a knightly view of honor— "that for which . . . , if need be, we are willing to die."[21]

The measure of a man can be taken in his heroes, and Holmes's combined the warlike virtues. Nansen captivated him by an ability to be "gay in the face of death, . . . capable, though a complex and civilized man, to lark like a boy and rejoice over a bellyful of blubber."[22] Corporate empire builders like Jim Hill won his admiration by their mastery and ruthlessness.

The war, finally, penetrated his idiom. Holmes would break into Civil War slang in conversation, and his speeches and letters are replete with war imagery. He would "fire off" an opinion; "when you have taken one trench there is always a new firing line beyond."

III

Darwin retaught Holmes at the level of generalization what he had already learned in experience on the battlefield. The doctrine of Evolution was the central concept

of the age in which he came to maturity, the subject of eager debate at Harvard and the Saturday Club. Holmes, like his contemporaries William James, John Fiske, and Henry Adams, devoured *The Origin of Species*. He later explained to Morris Cohen that the difference between his father's and his own generations lay in "the influence of the scientific way of looking at the world."[23]

Darwin, who had himself drawn heavily upon Malthus, foresaw that when scholars in other fields no longer looked at life as a "savage looks at a ship" a grand untrodden field of inquiry would open.[24] The historical school of jurisprudence transplanted the evolutionary hypothesis to the study of law. Maitland, Maine, Dicey, Pollock, Vinogradoff, and, not least among them, Holmes, substituted a biological for a mechanical view of society.

For Holmes the study of law became the study of history. He opened his great work **The Common Law** with this classic statement:

> The life of the law has not been logic; it has been experience. The felt necessities of the time, the prevalent moral and political theories, intuitions of public policy, avowed or unconscious, even the prejudices which judges share with their fellowmen, have had a good deal more to do than the syllogism in determining the rules by which men should be governed.[25]

If ideas, like the bone structure of the horse, evolve in response to environment, "truth is the majority vote of that nation that could lick all others."[26] In this epistemology the law and the Constitution become working instruments rather than God-given commandments. Legislation then reflects that interest in society which has competed successfully against others. The free market place, like the proving ground of Nature, must be preserved in law, in politics, in economics, and in speech. There is no room for sentimentality; the imbecile, the maimed, and the sick should be killed off.

Evolution freed the mind of the post–Civil War generation to move to the Right. The rampant capitalism of the age was justified because it had prevailed. Holmes's admired Jim Hill pointed out that "the fortunes of the railroad companies are determined by the law of the survival of the fittest."[27] Holmes, similarly, did not look unfavorably on the rise of great business combinations.

IV

The ideas Holmes evolved in his formative years supply the keys to his economic and legal philosophies. Francis Biddle has observed that his economic education stopped at the age of twenty-five.[28] Holmes worshipped at the shrine of orthodoxy; Adam Smith, Ricardo, and Malthus would have been pleased with his views. Malthus, moreover, deeply influenced Holmes as he had Darwin earlier. "This fellow," Holmes declared, "has stuck a sword into the very bowels of the principle of population."[29]

The heart of his economics was the individual. Holmes would give the entrepreneur virtually unfettered freedom with the assurance that a progressive economic society and a reasonable distribution of wealth would result. Ownership was a gateway, not a terminus, for "large ownership means investment, and investment means the direction of labor towards the production of the greatest returns."[30] These returns were consumed by the many rather than by the few. His hobby was to abjure talk of money and to examine the flow of products. The wheat, the cloth, and the railway travel were consumed by the masses rather than by the rich. If great fortunes were redistributed equally the level of national income would rise hardly at all. Needless to say, he opposed "tinkering with the institution of property."[31]

In this light, movements seeking the reform or reconstitution of economic society won his distrust. Holmes regarded the stirrings of the Progressive era as "unrest" and reserved searching skepticism for the domestic policies of the first Roosevelt. Socialism was an unscientific system for transferring burdens from the weak, who deserved them to the strong, who did not. It rested, he felt, on dramatic contrasts: "Look at the big house and the little one." He took a dim view of the notion that selfishness would disappear in any social order. "I cannot but reflect that my neighbor is better nourished by eating his own bread than by my eating it for him."[32]

The collectivist tendency, Holmes believed, was not only "an empty humbug" but constituted a danger to the safeguards in bills of rights. The drive for security, whether in the form of preventing cruelty to animals or socialism, left him cold. He had no sympathy for a society in which people "may be comfortable or may shine without much trouble or any danger." A famous phrase summarized his views: "I have no belief in panaceas and almost none in sudden ruin."[33]

To labor Holmes held out the iron law and the wage fund. The notion that unions could win a larger share of national income for workers as a whole was "pure phantasy." Organizations might gain more for their own members "at the expense of the less organized and less powerful portion of the laboring mass. They do not create something out of nothing."[34] Of strikes "I cherish no illusions," while the English General Strike of 1926 "fills me with sadness and apprehension." He worried lest "that noble people is facing ruin." Holmes's advice to labor carries a familiar ring: "Eternal hard work is the price of a living." He distrusted social legislation, refusing to become sentimental about child labor and doubting the value of a statutory minimum wage.[35]

Holmes was undisturbed about monopoly, nor did he regard bigness as a curse. "Prosecution for being, and not for doing, [is] . . . justified under no proper principle of the law."[36] Trustbusting, Holmes felt, undermined natural selection in the market place. The Sherman Act was "a humbug based on economic ignorance," while the Interstate Commerce Commission was unfit to be entrusted with rate-making. The wastes in competition, such as advertising and duplication of establishments, were "the very things the trusts get rid of." When the Dr. Miles Medical Company fixed retail prices by resale price maintenance contracts, Holmes considered the company better able to determine a reasonable price than the courts.[37]

In summary, Holmes was contented with the status quo. Upon his appointment to the Supreme Court, he wrote, "Some . . . of the money powers think me dangerous, wherein they are wrong."[38]

v

Holmes's legal philosophy rested upon an analysis of sovereignty, the source of power in government. Diverse groups within a society are in constant conflict and government is the arena for the clash of interest. "Wise or not, the proximate test of a good government is that the dominant power has its way."[39] In a democracy power is expressed in majorities. "If the will of the majority is unmistakable, and the majority is strong enough to have a clear power to enforce its will, . . . the courts must yield, as must everybody else."[40]

Legislation, accordingly, is an extension of the will of the dominant interest. It is "a means by which a body, having the power, put burdens which are disagreeable to them on the shoulders of somebody else."[41] A law cannot be condemned for favoring one class as against another since all laws do that. As a consequence, there are few, if any, scientific criteria for measuring legislation. "I am so sceptical," Holmes observed, "as to our knowledge about the goodness or badness of laws that I have no practical criticism except what the crowd wants." He felt certain that the crowd would not want what it does if it knew more, "but that is immaterial."[42]

In Holmes's legal universe the law was in a constant state of flux. Each generation and community refashioned it in accordance with "the felt necessities of the time." Hence custom and usage were decisive shaping elements. In Hamilton's words, "The genius of the common law broods over Holmes's world."[43]

With these premises Holmes became the classic exponent of the doctrine of judicial restraint. In his view the common law was the great area of court action, while the people through their legislatures were primarily responsible for constitutional law. The American federal system, however, permitted no such neat division of labor. The solution for judges, therefore, was to refrain from asserting their own views except under compelling circumstances. The Constitution in this light was a broad charter of powers rather than a code prescribing in detail and for all time the answers to social problems. Holmes said,

> Long ago I decided that I was not God. When a state came in here and wanted to build a slaughterhouse,

I looked at the Constitution and if I couldn't find anything in there that said a state couldn't build a slaughterhouse I said to myself, if they want to build a slaughterhouse, God-dammit, let them build it.[44]

Judicial restraint is a two-edged blade that cuts impartially. It may serve liberals seeking to regulate industry as well as conservatives wishing to restrict labor. In the historical context of Holmes's term on the bench, however, its greatest value was to those who pressed for restrictions on business and assistance to labor. This, at bottom, is the source of the Holmes liberal myth.

Illustrations of his "liberal" opinions abound, usually with reservations on the merits. Oklahoma, for example, enacted a statute guaranteeing bank deposits which was challenged as a violation of the due process clause of the Fourteenth Amendment. The Court sustained the law, Holmes holding, "We fully understand . . . the very powerful argument that can be made against the wisdom of the legislation, but on that point we have nothing to say, as it is not our concern."[45] Holmes, in his dissent in *Truax v. Corrigan,* deprecated use of the Fourteenth Amendment beyond "the absolute compulsion of its words" to prohibit social experimentation by the states, "even though the experiments may seem futile or even noxious to me."[46] In *Coppage v. Kansas* the Court nullified a state law prohibiting yellow-dog contracts. "Whether in the long run," Holmes's dissent argued, "it is wise for the workingmen to enact legislation of this sort is not my concern, but I am strongly of the opinion that there is nothing in the Constitution of the United States to prevent it."[47]

By the same token, judicial laissez faire sometimes produced "conservative" results. During a labor dispute, Governor Peabody of Colorado had Charles Moyer, president of the Western Federation of Miners, arrested and imprisoned ten weeks with no charge. Since, as events proved, there was no basis for the detention, Moyer sued for deprivation of liberty without due process. Holmes, speaking for the Court, refused to assert judicial authority. "So long as such arrests are made in good faith . . . the Governor is the final judge. . . . The ordinary rights of individuals must yield. . . . Public danger warrants the substitution of executive process for judicial process."[48] Holmes's dissent in the *Dr. Miles Case* is another illustration. He held the company's judgment superior to the Court's in pricing its products even at the cost of a resale price maintenance system.

The foundation of Holmes's legal structure was free speech. Some, at least, of his utterances, in Zechariah Chafee's view, are fit to stand beside Milton's *Areopagitica* and Mill's *On Liberty*. In *Schenck v. U.S.* Holmes set forth the fundamental "clear and present danger" doctrine.[49] In *Abrams v. U.S.* he lodged his faith in "free trade in ideas—that the best truth is the power of the thought to get itself accepted in the competition of the market."[50] Free speech for Holmes was a Darwinian arena in which ideas would struggle for survival. It was

at the same time a prop of a conservative society. As he wrote the Harvard Liberal Club, "With effervescent opinions the quickest way to let them get flat, as with the not yet forgotten champagnes, is to let them get exposed to the air."[51]

Holmes, however, was not an extremist on free speech, "in which," he wrote, "I have no very enthusiastic belief." On the Massachusetts bench, for example, he sustained a conviction for speaking on the Boston Common without a permit. "For the Legislature absolutely or conditionally to forbid public speaking in a highway or public park is no more an infringement of the rights of a member of the public than for the owner of a private house to forbid it in his house."[52] This decision was invoked by Mayor Hague when he banned free speech in Jersey City. Holmes in *McAuliffe v. New Bedford* upheld the town's right to discharge an officer for political activity. "The petitioner may have a constitutional right to talk politics, but he has no constitutional right to be a policeman."[53]

Holmes compromised himself on free speech most notably in the *Debs Case*. The leader of the Socialist Party was convicted and imprisoned under the Espionage Act for an address criticizing the war policy of the Wilson Administration. Holmes for the Court accepted the jury's verdict without looking behind it, failed to examine the constitutionality of the statute, and refrained from applying his own "clear and present danger" test.[54]

Holmes's conservatism on the bench was clearly apparent in cases involving contracts. For a man beset with doubts about the cosmos, contract had the virtue of specificity. His dissent in *Bailey v. Alabama* illustrates this preoccupation in disregard of the status of the Negro in the South. In 1907, Bailey, a colored farmhand, entered into a contract with an employer to work for a year at twelve dollars per month. He received a fifteen dollar advance and was to get $10.75 each month, the remainder to be charged against the advance. After one month Bailey quit without refunding the money, clearly an illegal act under an Alabama statute. The Supreme Court ruled that the contract constituted peonage and was invalid under the Thirteenth Amendment. Holmes, however, dissented. "If the contract is one that ought not to be made, prohibit it. But if it is a perfectly fair and proper contract, I can see no reason why the State should not throw its weight on the side of performance."[55]

Pennsylvania Coal Co. v. Mahon is in the same vein. The company, by deed executed in 1878, conveyed surface property to a householder but expressly reserved the right to remove underneath coal with the grantee assuming all risks and waiving any claims for losses that might result. A Pennsylvania statute of 1921, however, forbade mining in such a way as to cause subsidence of habitations. It admittedly destroyed the contract rights of the company and the question was whether the police power could be stretched to cover the law's constitutionality. The Court through Holmes held the statute invalid. "What makes the right to mine coal valuable is that it can be exercised with profit. To make it commercially impracticable to mine certain coal has very nearly the same effect for constitutional purposes as appropriating or destroying it." Brandeis dissented.[56]

VI

"In the structure of the beetle . . . ;" Darwin wrote, "in the plumed seed which is wafted by the gentlest breeze; . . . we see beautiful adaptations everywhere and in every part of the organic world."[57] Holmes was just such an adaptation, perhaps the most complete and certainly one of the most appealing figures to grace American history. He has, in fact, entered the pantheon of our heroes, and the myth-makers show no sign of tiring in their busy labors.

A prime function of the hero is to campaign in the politics of the generations that follow. The struggle for Jefferson's legacy and the long shadow that Franklin Roosevelt casts in death are illustrations. In the contest for protagonists the Democrats have the advantage. They point to Jefferson, Jackson, Woodrow Wilson, and the second Roosevelt. The Republicans claim only Lincoln and Theodore Roosevelt, and in both cases there are reservations. Although conservatives have failed to seize the opportunity, in Holmes they could embrace another champion. Their failure to perceive his political value is typical of the anti-intellectual strain in the American Right.

Holmes's value to conservatism is enhanced precisely because he exposed himself to liberal ideas. The free range of his intellect and his extraordinary tolerance offered him the opportunity to examine all views. In 1893, for example, he paid a call at the "humble shrine" of a Boston labor leader. "Sir," he said, "I am Judge Holmes of the Supreme Judicial Court. . . . As a good citizen I like to understand all phases of economic opinion. What would you like if you could have it?" They "discoursed several times with some little profit."[58] Holmes's conservatism, therefore, was of a most impressive and rare variety. His convictions stemmed from knowledge and cerebral mechanics rather than prejudice. He was, in fact, rarely capable of thinking in stereotypes.

There is little likelihood, however, that progressives will give up Holmes without a struggle and they are not without weapons. He was certainly more liberated, if not more liberal, than his reactionary colleagues on the Court. The doctrine of judicial restraint, moreover, led him to affix his signature to many opinions that encouraged social experimentation. Finally, there was in Holmes an elusive, sometimes an impish, quality that confounds any group that seeks to claim him entirely. He was, at bottom, himself.

NOTES

[1] Walton Hamilton, "On Dating Mr. Justice Holmes," *University of Chicago Law Review,* IX (1941), 1.

[2] Hamilton, "On Dating Mr. Justice Holmes," 9 n.

[3] "The Great Holmes Mystery," *American Mercury,* XXVI (1932), 124.

[4] Quoted in Frederick C. Fiechter, Jr., "The Preparation of an American Aristocrat," New England Quarterly, VI (1933), 4.

[5] Quoted in Silas Bent, *Oliver Wendell Holmes* (New York, 1932), 29.

[6] Oliver Wendell Holmes, *Speeches* (Boston, 1918), 29.

[7] "Mr. Justice Holmes," *Harvard Law Review,* XLIV (1931), 679.

[8] Quoted in Bent, *Holmes,* 34.

[9] "On Dating Mr. Justice Holmes," 5.

[10] "Mr. Justice Holmes," *Harvard Law Review,* XLIV (1931), 691.

[11] Boyd H. Bode, "Justice Holmes on Natural Law and the Moral Ideal," *International Journal of Ethics,* XXIX (1919), 399; Holmes, *Speeches,* 75, 92; Holmes to Sir Frederick Pollock, November 5, 1923, M. De W. Howe, editor, *Holmes-Pollock Letters* (Cambridge, 1941), II, 123; Holmes to Doctor Wu, November 2, 1928, *Justice Holmes to Doctor Wu, an Intimate Correspondence, 1921-1932* (New York, n.d.), 51.

[12] Francis Biddle, *Mr. Justice Holmes* (New York, 1942), 49, 75, 80; Holmes to Dr. Wu, November 2, 1928, *Holmes-Wu Correspondence,* 52.

[13] Holmes, *Speeches,* 24.

[14] Richard Walden Hale, *Some Table Talk of Mr. Justice Holmes and "The Mrs."* (Boston, 1935), II; Holmes to Sir Frederick Pollock, August 20, 1928, *Holmes-Pollock Letters,* II, 227; Holmes to Owen Wister, n.d., quoted in Bent, *Holmes,* 17.

[15] Holmes, *Speeches,* 11-12.

[16] M. De W. Howe, editor, *Touched With Fire, Civil War Letters and Diary of Oliver Wendell Holmes, Jr.* (Cambridge, 1946), 72.

[17] *Touched With Fire,* 143.

[18] Holmes to Sir Frederick Pollock, February 1, 1920, *Holmes-Pollock Letters,* II, 36.

[19] Holmes, *Speeches,* 63.

[20] Holmes, *Speeches,* 59.

[21] Holmes to Lady Pollock, June 9, 1898, *Holmes-Pollock Letters,* I, 87: Holmes, *Speeches,* 26.

[22] Holmes to Lady Pollock, April 11, 1897, *Holmes-Pollock Letters,* I, 73.

[23] Holmes to Morris R. Cohen, February 5, 1919, Felix S. Cohen, editor, "The Holmes-Cohen Correspondence," *Journal of the History of Ideas,* IX (1948), 14.

[24] *The Origin of Species* (New York, 1861), 422.

[25] Quoted in Max Lerner, editor, *The Mind and Faith of Justice Holmes* (Boston, 1943), 51-52.

[26] Quoted in Felix Frankfurter, editor, *Mr. Justice Holmes* (New York, 1931), 150-151.

[27] Quoted in Richard Hofstadter, *Social Darwinism in American Thought, 1860-1915* (Philadelphia, 1945), 31.

[28] *Holmes,* 86-87.

[29] Quoted in Bent, *Holmes,* 17.

[30] Quoted in Lerner, *Mind and Faith,* 389.

[31] Quoted in Lerner, *Mind and Faith,* 393.

[32] Holmes to Sir Frederick Pollock, February 26, 1911, *Holmes-Pollock Letters,* I, 175-176; H. C. Shriver, editor, *Justice Oliver Wendell Holmes, His Book Notices and Uncollected Letters and Papers* (New York, 1936), 140.

[33] Quoted in Lerner, *Mind and Faith,* 390.

[34] *Plant v. Woods,* 176 Mass. 492, 504 (1900).

[35] Holmes to Dr. Wu, May 5, 1926, *Holmes-Wu Correspondence,* 36; Holmes to Sir Frederick Pollock, September 19, 1919, *Holmes-Pollock Letters,* II, 25; *Hammer v. Dagenhart,* 247 U. S. 251, 277 (1918).

[36] Quoted in Dorsey Richardson, *Constitutional Doctrines of Justice Oliver Wendell Holmes* (Baltimore, 1924), 49.

[37] Holmes to Sir Frederick Pollock, May 25, 1906, April 23, 1910, *Holmes-Pollock Letters,* I, 123-124, 163; *Dr. Miles Medical Co. v. Park and Sons Co.,* 220 U. S. 373, 409 (1911).

[38] Holmes to Sir Frederick Pollock, August 13, 1902, *Holmes-Pollock Letters,* I, 103.

[39] Quoted in Lerner, *Mind and Faith,* 378.

[40] *Book Notices and Uncollected Papers,* 98.

[41] *Book Notices and Uncollected Papers,* 108.

[42] Holmes to Sir Frederick Pollock, April 23, 1910, *Holmes-Pollock Letters,* I, 163.

[43] "On Dating Mr. Justice Holmes," 20.

[44] Quoted in Alpheus Thomas Mason, *Brandeis, A Free Man's Life* (New York, 1946), 572-573.

[45] *Noble State Bank v. Haskell,* 219 U. S. 104 and 575 (1911).

[46] 257 U. S. 312, 343 (1921).

[47] 236 U. S. 1, 28 (1915).

[48] *Mover v. Peabody,* 212 U. S. 78 (1909).

[49] 249 U. S. 47 (1919).

[50] 250 U. S. 616, 624 (1919).

[51] Quoted in Bent, *Holmes,* 6.

[52] *Commonwealth v. Davis,* 162 Mass. 510 (1895).

[53] 155 Mass. 216 (1892).

[54] *Debs v. U. S.,* 249 U. S. 211 (1919). See Max Lerner's comments, *Mind and Faith,* 297-300.

[55] 219 U. S. 219, 245 (1911).

[56] 260 U. S. 393 (1922).

[57] *Origin of Species,* 60-61.

[58] Holmes to Sir Frederick Pollock, January 20, 1893, *Holmes-Pollock Letters,* 1, 44.

Mark DeWolfe Howe (essay date 1951)

SOURCE: "The Positivism of Mr. Justice Holmes," in *Harvard Law Review,* Vol. 64, No. 4, February, 1951, pp. 530-46.

[*In the following essay, Howe examines Holmes's posthumous reputation.*]

On the occasion of the ninetieth birthday of Mr. Justice Holmes, his successor on the Supreme Court of the United States said that Holmes was "for all students of the law and for all students of human society the philosopher and the seer, the greatest of our age in the domain of jurisprudence, and one of the greatest of the ages."[1] At the conclusion of his essay, Mr. Justice Cardozo quoted from a letter which he had received from Holmes saying that he had always believed that neither place, nor power, nor popularity "makes the success that one desires, but the trembling hope that one has come near to an ideal."[2] Mr. Justice Cardozo was reminded by these words of the wistful confidence of Keats: "I think I shall be among the English poets after my death." And Cardozo went on to say that "there was no 'fool's paradise' for Keats" and to predict that there would be none for Holmes.[3]

Nearly twenty years have passed since Cardozo predicted that Holmes' trembling hope would be realized, and it is time to inquire whether the prediction has been fulfilled. Though many would think it obvious that time has done nothing to diminish the stature of Holmes, in recent years there have been such frequent efforts to belittle his reputation, to discredit his philosophy of law, and to disparage his achievements as a judge that Cardozo's prediction cannot be considered wholly fulfilled. When Holmes died in 1935 would any columnist, even the most irresponsible, have had the temerity to describe him as "the cynical and senile brutalitarian"? It seems clear that he would not. Yet it is with these delicate words that Westbrook Pegler has characterized Mr. Justice Holmes.[4]

It would be pleasant for those who believe that Cardozo's estimate of Holmes was justified, to write off the fulmination of Pegler as the outburst of an isolated, malignant temper. Unfortunately, however, Pegler's slur upon the memory of Holmes represents something more significant than a small boy's blasphemous efforts to attract attention. The theme which he so stridently plays had earlier been played to smaller audiences by far more responsible persons. Pegler's rendition is coarser than theirs, but the melody is unmistakably the same.

The first elaborate formulation of the thesis that Holmes' philosophy of law is anti-democratic, un-American and totalitarian in tendency was in an essay by Father John C. Ford[5] and a year later it was restated by Father Francis E. Lucey.[6] The next article in which the criticism was repeated was by Ben W. Palmer of the Minneapolis bar. His first paper, under the somewhat flashy title, "Hobbes, Holmes, and Hitler," appeared in 1945,[7] and having brought forth a number of enthusiastic letters to the editor of the *Journal* was followed by another, "Defense Against Leviathan,"[8] along the same lines. It is not my purpose to deal with these particular efforts to persuade the American people that the philosophy of Holmes was repugnant to the principles of American civilization. The criticism of Fathers Ford and Lucey, popularized by Mr. Palmer and perverted by Mr. Pegler is so firmly grounded in the Catholic philosophy of law that were I to attempt to meet it directly I should find myself quickly engaged in a theological controversy beyond my competence to discuss. All I need say of the essays of Father Ford and Father Lucey is that they take a position which it was almost inevitable that members of the Jesuit Order would take: Holmes not only proclaimed himself a skeptic in matters of religion and denounced man's relentless effort to give human values a more than human significance, but he denied the existence of that law of nature upon which the Catholic philosophy of law is based. It would have required no special insight to predict, twenty years ago, that Jesuit teachers of law would find Holmes' skepticism philosophically unacceptable.

The criticism of Holmes with which I shall deal has been most effectively stated by Professor Lon Fuller of the Harvard Law School. To date Professor Fuller has not directed his attention to the achievements of Holmes as judge and has discussed only the shortcomings of his philosophy of law as expressed in writings other than judicial opinions. This makes it suitable that I should accept those same limits.

I am strongly persuaded that Professor Fuller has expressed in his writing on Holmes a point of view which many lawyers have come, perhaps unconsciously, to share—a feeling not only that Holmes' philosophy of law was inconsistent with the highest traditions and aspirations of Western thought, but that his scale of moral and political values was badly suited to measure the needs of a progressive and civilized society. As I understand the thesis, it is that Holmes, child of Hobbes, is the American father of legal positivism. By positivism in law Professor Fuller tells us that he means "that direction of legal thought which insists on drawing a sharp distinction between the law *that is* and the law *that ought to be*."[9] The justification for classifying Holmes as a positivist, within this definition, is found by Professor Fuller in many of Holmes' utterances, perhaps nowhere more clearly than in passages from his well-known address on **"The Path of the Law."**[10] There he told his audience, first, that the student of law must come to recognize as fundamental the distinction between law and morality, and, second, that law was not usefully to be defined in terms of right and wrong and the principles of ethics, but should be considered to be nothing more esoteric than an informed and prophetic judgment as to what the courts will do in fact. With that positivist tendency in Holmes' thought, Professor Fuller contrasts the philosophy of natural law—"the view which denies the possibility of a rigid separation of the *is* and the *ought,* and which tolerates a confusion of them in legal discussion."[11] He asks the present generation of lawyers to abandon the positivism of Holmes and to return to the earlier and healthier conviction that there is nothing shameful in the association of law and morality.

My first concern will not be with the merits of the philosophical issue which Professor Fuller has so persuasively presented. It will rather be with a problem upon which he touched in passing—that is, the considerations which led Holmes to accept the positivist theory of law. When Hobbes first formulated the principles of positivism he gave an explicit reason for his effort to separate the domain of morals from the province of jurisprudence; he wanted men to obey even those rules of law which they believed to be unjust. Holmes, says Professor Fuller, never made it clear what prompted him to accept the dichotomy and has thus made our task of comprehension peculiarly difficult. He suggests, however, that Holmes' Civil War experience bred in the young soldier a sentimental enthusiasm for the heroism of obedience, which in the mature philosopher became blind respect for authority as such.[12] Though Professor Fuller does not quote Holmes' most famous pronouncement on the virtue of the soldier's faith, he undoubtedly had in mind the Memorial Day speech of 1895 in which Holmes had spoken these words:

> I do not know what is true. I do not know the meaning of the universe. But in the midst of doubt,

in the collapse of creeds, there is one thing I do not doubt, that no man who lives in the same world with most of us can doubt, and that is that the faith is true and adorable which leads a soldier to throw away his life in obedience to a blindly accepted duty, in a cause which he little understands, in a plan of campaign of which he has no notion, under tactics of which he does not see the use.[13]

I should not hesitate for a moment to agree that this passage reflects most significantly the mixing of skepticism and romanticism in Holmes' faith. My disagreement with Professor Fuller is with his suggestion that when Holmes spoke thus romantically of the soldier's sustaining faith he was indirectly committing himself to a positivist theory of law which, according to Professor Fuller, puts fiat above reason in the legal process.

Before discussing Holmes' theory of law one should consider his theory of morality, and, in order to comprehend his principles of ethics, one should look at the circumstances in which his mind and character came to their maturity. Catherine Drinker Bowen in *Yankee from Olympus,* has popularized the notion that Dr. Holmes, the Justice's bouncing father, was an insignificant figure of such consuming personal vanity and petty conceit that his son gained no significant profit from growing up in his household. This is a most misleading picture of the Doctor and a completely inadequate interpretation of the relation between father and son. It disregards entirely the fact that Dr. Holmes, throughout his whole life, was struggling vigorously to break away from the oppressive traditions by which American thought and American morality had, in his father's generation, been so effectively suffocated. Perhaps the Doctor was never able to shake himself entirely free from those traditions—he refused to read novels on Sunday—but with respect to the basic intellectual and moral issues of his day, he stood invariably with those men of vision who insisted that the questions which the advance of science had put to man should not be answered by the outworn formulas of Calvinism and the threadbare precepts of Protestant morality. The seeds of skepticism which had been planted in the mind of the medical student in Paris blossomed in the maturity of the novelist and essayist who asked of the old order whether its settled pieties had any other justification than familiarity. When he suggested that the sin of Elsie Venner might find a truer explanation and a more Christian understanding if its sources were approached through science rather than through Calvinism, he was asking that skepticism be given rights. He saw as persistent and inescapable the American's obligation to re-examine every article of national faith, whether political or religious. "To think," he said, "of trying to waterproof the American mind against the questions that Heaven rains down upon it shows a misapprehension of our new conditions. If to question everything be unlawful and dangerous, we had better undeclare our independence at once; for what the Declaration means is the right to question everything, even the truth of its own fundamental proposition."[14] An alert young man, brought up in a household presided over by a father so wholeheartedly

dedicated to the cause of free inquiry, could scarcely fail to start his life with the conviction that the first consequence of the scientific revolution must be the development of a skeptical mind.

Nurtured in that belief, Holmes must have found many, if not all, of the aspects of the Harvard College which he entered in the fall of 1858 hopelessly benighted. The sponge of complacency with which Professor Francis Bowen, Professor of Natural Religion, Moral Philosophy, and Civil Polity, erased the writing on the wall was the product of Harvard's stubborn assurance that reason and morality, religion and piety had discovered the final answers to the mysteries of the universe, and that the teacher's responsibility to his students was to explain those answers and develop an appropriate humility before the altar of unalterable truth. Is it any surprise that the young Holmes, encouraged by his father to ask on all occasions the unanswerable question, in his senior year had to be publicly admonished by President Felton for "repeated and gross indecorum in the recitation room of Professor Bowen"?[15] In his junior year Holmes had written an undergraduate essay in which he had offended the pieties of his teachers by suggesting that "duty is not less binding had the Bible never been written, or if we were to perish utterly tomorrow."[16] This rather pallid expression of skepticism aroused the anger of a more orthodox classmate, who published a protest against the Emersonian tendencies of Holmes' thought, and suggested that his ideas were "barbarous in the province of reason and practical piety."[17] It is not unlikely that the satisfaction which Holmes found in disturbing the intellectual tranquilities of his teachers and his fellow students added fresh impetus to the skeptical instinct. It is certain, in any case, that his reading as an undergraduate followed those frontiers of inquiry to which the scientific impulse was carrying philosophical and ethical speculation.

As Holmes' college course came to its end, he found himself, under the influence of his father and his times, far from the moorings of religious faith which his New England ancestors had laid and to which most of his contemporaries were still fixed. Having lost all confidence that moral convictions may find sufficient justification in the dogma of religion, Holmes' search was for a system of philosophy, or, perhaps, for a way of life, which would give some assurance that a sense of duty had validity in a universe which must be explained in scientific terms. Where the normal processes of intellectual growth would have led him had tranquility not been shattered by the outbreak of the Civil War no one can say. It is possible that his early admiration for Emerson might have led him to attempt to systematize the Emersonian insights, and that out of that effort might have come a philosophy quite different from that which the circumstances of war in fact produced. That, however, is the idlest speculation, for the War did come, and with it the need for again examining the foundations of morality.

Although in later life Holmes indicated that he had small sympathy for men of strong belief and distrusted the crusading spirit of the reformer, when the Civil War broke out it is clear that he was moved to join the Union forces by an abolitionist fervor. He acknowledged later that he shared the emotional state of the abolitionists—a state which he came to dislike because "it catches postulates like the influenza."[18] I am not concerned at the moment, however, with the later development of Holmes' thought but with the significant fact that the young man, who during his college course had come to the conviction that morality could no longer find its justification in a theology which science had shown to be unacceptable, went to war convinced that the cause for which he fought was noble and right. It may even be said that he went in a spirit of some defiance, anxious to prove to a complacent older generation that a skeptic in religion was not necessarily a skeptic in other things, and that though science had turned the creed of Harvard and of his ancestors to dust and ashes, the Puritan's standard of morality and duty still survived. In the very thick of war he wrote to Charles Eliot Norton that it was only by preserving his conviction that the War was the holy crusade of the nineteenth century that he was able to keep his hand to the sword.[19] Certainly there is no indication that at the opening of the War, Holmes had become a skeptic in matters of morality. His father's influence had carried him far on the way to emancipation from tradition; it had led him to repudiate the religious and the intellectual assumptions upon which Harvard's decencies and Boston's proprieties were built, but it had not led him seriously to doubt that the accepted standards of behavior had an external or preordained validity. Those to whom postulates are as catching as the influenza are unlikely to look skeptically upon the disease and are susceptible to its infection simply because of the conviction that each postulate reflects at least a facet of the cosmic truth.

If Holmes went to the War a convinced abolitionist, what was it that led him thirty-four years later in his Memorial Day speech to say categorically: "I do not know what is true. I do not know the meaning of the universe"? The answer to this question is not to be found in the maturing process of the intervening years, setting the young man's crusade in historical perspective. It is rather to be found in the drama of the Civil War itself—a drama so vast in its political and physical aspects that one easily overlooks its no less exciting and confusing moral aspects. The Twentieth Regiment of Massachusetts Volunteers, which Holmes joined immediately after his graduation, reflected the national confusion and the whole uncertainty of purpose by which the Union effort from first to last was frustrated. Among the officers with whom Holmes was most intimately associated was his classmate, Penrose Hallowell, Quaker and abolitionist, whose religious convictions condemned war and whose reforming faith made participation in war seem necessary. Another friend was William Francis Bartlett who gravely doubted the justice of the Northern cause, yet fought gallantly with its armies, losing a leg with the Twentieth Regiment, returning to command another regiment of volunteers, and ultimately rising to the rank of Major General at the age of twenty-six. Of other friends the

most intimate was Henry Abbott. From the very first Abbott proclaimed himself a Copperhead, throughout the War cursed the purposes and abilities of Lincoln, condemned the strategy of the northern armies, and denounced the emancipation of the slaves as unconstitutional. Yet he fought with supreme courage in every battle in which the Twentieth was engaged, refused promotion which would have taken him to safer posts, and, when he finally fell in the Wilderness, was mourned by generals and privates as their heroic brother.

Read in this context of association and experience Holmes' Memorial Day speech takes on a very different meaning from that which his latter-day critics have given it. The young man who had joined the army in the conviction that the cause of abolition made the Civil War the moral crusade of the nineteenth century, found that those who saw it as the blundering effort of politicians to achieve through force ends which were beyond the constitutional limits of their power, were capable of a selfless heroism equalling if not exceeding his own. What wonder is there, then, that such a young man, already skeptical in matters of religious faith, should find himself at the War's end doubtful that "the right" as he conceived it had a better claim to universal validity than "the right" so differently conceived by his neighbor. Perhaps a man of relentless rationalism, having discovered that he neither knows what is true nor has solved the riddle of the universe, would have been satisfied to settle down, cushioned by his skepticism, to observe the silly antics of mankind—affirming nothing, denying nothing. Perhaps a man of firmer complacency would have returned from the War convinced that the greater sacrifices which wounded and dead comrades had made for the cause as they saw it were less significant than the sacrifices which he had made for the cause as he had seen it. But it is not surprising that a sensitive spirit and a skeptical mind, remembering such friends as Henry Abbott, gave neither the cynical nor the complacent answer to the problem of intense experience and came out of the War, despite all doubt, convinced of one truth "that the faith is true and adorable which leads a soldier to throw away his life in obedience to a blindly accepted duty, in a cause which he little understands, in a plan of campaign of which he has no notion, under tactics of which he does not see the use."

To read Holmes' Memorial Day Address as the creed of an authoritarian is totally to disregard its context; to suggest that he there was saying that might makes right, that the *is* is more important than the *ought*, distorts his thesis beyond recognition. It is to read his eloquent address to veterans as if it were a law review article on jurisprudence. This is not to say that Holmes never permitted oratory to get the better of judgment, or to deny that he let himself too frequently use the language of arms to dispose of questions of morality; it is only to ask that we take appropriate account of the influence which the experience of the Civil War had in moulding the contour of his skepticism.

If this interpretation of Holmes' intellectual development is accepted, it means that when he began the study of law in the fall of 1864 he had passed through two decisive phases of his growth. First, he had shaken off the religious faith on which so many of the assumptions of the world around him were based, and, second, he had learned from the War that personal taste in morals does not establish universal or objective truth in ethics. Skeptic in faith and skeptic in morals, he quickly found, however, that the world around him, particularly the world of legal theory in which he moved at the Harvard Law School, was heavy with the stagnant complacency of the pre-War years. The law in books was a conglomerate of Coke's artificial reason and Kent's equally artificial morality. Outside of books, the law, to be sure, was less burdened with pretension and piety, for such judges as Shaw in Massachusetts and Gibson in Pennsylvania had shown that good sense and the adjustment of English principle to American reality could make the law an effective instrument of government. Yet the words of Rufus Choate, spoken to the pre-War generation, still struck chords of sympathy in the minds of the post-War generation of lawyers. Choate had insisted that our national need was for "reformation of our individual selves," not for reform of our legal institutions. Describing the body of the law which he considered so deserving of preservation, Choate had said:

> The judge does not make it. Like the structure of the State itself, we found it around us at the earliest dawn of reason, it guarded the helplessness of our infancy, it restrained the passions of our youth, it protects the acquisitions of our manhood, it shields the sanctity of the grave, it executes the will of the departed. Invisible, omnipresent, a real yet impalpable existence, it seems more a spirit, an abstraction,— the whispered yet authoritative voice of all the past and all the good,—than like the transient contrivance of altogether such as ourselves.[20]

It is difficult for the present generation of lawyers to realize that when Choate spoke in these terms he was not simply indulging his passionate weakness for oratory, but was defining the prevailing concept of law. The concept was not appreciably shaken for most American lawyers until the 1880's. That it was shaken then was due primarily, perhaps, to the effort of Sir Henry Maine and others of the historical school to examine the institutions of the law with the same scientific detachment which Darwin had shown in examining the physical world around him. It was, of course, inevitable that Holmes, if he could be persuaded that law offered the same opportunity for generalization which the new philosophy and the new science offered, would join those scattered forces which were seeking to rid the law of its analytical and moral dogmatism. His first struggle was to persuade himself that the law did offer large opportunities for creative speculation. Shortly after the end of his law school course, if not earlier, he became convinced that the satisfaction which his philosophical instinct was seeking could be found in the law. During the fifteen years which passed between his graduation and his first appointment to judicial office, his energies were dedicated to the task of showing that a critically accurate understanding of the

law would only be possible after two steps had been taken. First, its analytical traditions must be subjected to the same rigorous and skeptical inspection to which science had subjected theology. Second, its moral postulates, imbedded in the old complacency, must be reexamined without fear and without deference to settled pieties.

I need not discuss the first efforts which he made in essays and in book reviews to achieve those tasks. The fruits of all those efforts were brought together in *The Common Law*. The most significant achievements of that book were two. He made it impossible for later generations of lawyers to accept as valid Coke's maxim that "reason is the life of the law," and compelled them instead to accept as true the conflicting maxim that "the life of the law has not been logic; it has been experience."[21] He thus led American legal scholarship to follow the historical rather than the purely logical—even theological—methods which had threatened to dominate legal thought. The other achievement, less apparent though it may have been, was no less significant. It was to call attention to the fact that though moral conceptions had been of predominant importance in the initial formulation of rules of law, time and experience had given to the language of morality as it survives in law, a meaning substantially different from that which it originally possessed. In the first cases in which such moral concepts as those of "fraud," "malice," and "negligence" had been fruitfully utilized, the concepts had relatively clear dimensions. As time passed, however, the words had lingered in the law, still laden with deceptive implications of morality, but infused with a new meaning and serving new purposes. Generalizing the tendency of growth, Holmes found that the terms of subjective morality had acquired in the law an objective meaning quite different from that which they had at first possessed.

So far as I know, the latter-day critics of Holmes do not cite *The Common Law* to show that his creed was that of the positivist who asserts that law must concern itself exclusively with the *is* and never bother itself with the *ought*. Yet his address on **"The Path of the Law"** to which they have so frequently taken exception says little if anything more than what he had already said in *The Common Law*. The differences in emphasis are largely the result of the fact that *The Common Law* was a volume written for sophisticated and mature lawyers, whereas **"The Path of the Law"** was an address to students. Each effort, however, was the expression of the same philosophical concern of which I have already spoken. In talking to students, Holmes asked them at the outset to look behind the surface of traditional definitions to the stuff of the law. For generations, students had been told that law is "a system of reason" and had been charged by their elders to remember that it is "a deduction from principles of ethics." We may have forgotten the words of Rufus Choate, but, to the audience which Holmes addressed, the suggestion that the invisible and omnipresent law was "the whispered yet authoritative voice of all the past and all the good" still had persuasive eloquence. Read with appreciation of the circumstances in which the address was delivered, **"The Path of the Law"** is anything but the formulation of a totalitarian creed. It is a philosopher's plea that theory should be founded in fact; an historian's argument that experience tells more of truth than does eloquence.

The passages in the **"The Path of the Law"** to which Holmes' critics have taken most frequent objection opened with the suggestion that it was desirable to dispel a prevailing confusion between morality and law. In order to dramatize the suggestion, he urged that the student should look at the law from the standpoint of the bad man—a hypothetical figure who was concerned neither with moral right nor with moral wrong, and whose only interest was in knowing what sanctions society might bring to bear upon him if he followed a course of lawless conduct. Such a man, Holmes indicated, might have a more accurate understanding of the meaning in law of such words as "fraud," "malice" and "intent" than a student nurtured in the pieties of Rufus Choate. If Holmes' historical analysis in *The Common Law* was accurate and perceptive, it is hard to see how his dramatic reiteration of the same analysis in **"The Path of the Law"** became totalitarian. Professor Fuller and Holmes' other critics have not, so far as I know, argued that he was mistaken in saying that the language of morality when used in the law loses much of its ethical content. When Holmes' critics show that he was wrong in that matter, it will be time for them to show the error of his philosophical way. While that thesis remains unrefuted, however, the friends of Holmes are likely to believe that the current criticism of his views is founded either in misunderstanding of his argument or in an unimaginative, literal-minded reading of **"The Path of the Law."**

The misinterpretation seems almost willful when one remembers that Holmes prefaced his argument with the following paragraph:

> I take it for granted that no hearer of mine will misinterpret what I have to say as the language of cynicism. The law is the witness and external deposit of our moral life. Its history is the history of the moral development of the race. . . . When I emphasize the difference between law and morals I do so with reference to a single end, that of learning and understanding the law. For that purpose you must definitely master its specific marks, and it is for that I ask you for the moment to imagine yourselves indifferent to other and greater things.[22]

Is this the language of one who sought to make law a matter not of reason but of fiat and who was not concerned with questions of the *ought* and only interested in the *is?* Does it indicate a repudiation of the conviction so firmly stated in *The Common Law* that "rules of law are or should be based upon a morality which is generally accepted"?[23] Professor Fuller says nothing of this prefatory caution nor does he refer to that other passage in **"The Path of the Law"** in which his positivist villain spoke of the direction which he thought the path should

follow. "I look forward," said Holmes, "to a time when the part played by history in the explanation of dogma shall be very small, and instead of ingenious research we shall spend our energy on a study of the ends sought to be attained and the reasons for desiring them."[24]

Professor Fuller has not, of course, overlooked such passages as those which I quote. He dismisses them with the casual statement that Holmes "did not always himself remain faithful to the program for a rigid separation of law and morals laid down in his early essays."[25] It is my thesis that Holmes never laid down the program which Professor Fuller ascribes to him, that from first to last he insisted that the ultimate source of law is the moral judgment of the community. He felt, however, that understanding of the law would be more perceptive than it had been if one saw morality as its source rather than its content. If Holmes' critics would limit their efforts to the task of showing that this conviction was mistaken they might succeed, but that success would not establish their present thesis that his philosophical concern was solely with the *is* and never with the *ought.*

Professor Fuller, with others, treats Holmes' definition of law—the prediction of what the courts will do in fact—as another aspect of the positivist's refusal to let conceptions of morality play their appropriate part in the legal process.[26] Once more this seems to involve an almost willful refusal to understand his thesis and his definition. Believing as Holmes did that "the law is the witness and external deposit of our moral life," it is inconceivable that he should ask lawyers to leave out of their predictions of what courts might be expected to do in fact—in other words, out of their consideration of law—all attention to the influence of morality on the minds of judges and jurors. What he was asking was that lawyers and judges should think things and not words, and become conscious of their responsibility to bring decisions into conformity with current standards of morality. Holmes once said that the strength of Mr. Chief Justice Shaw lay in his "accurate appreciation of the requirements of the community whose officer he was," and that few judges "have lived who were his equals in their understanding of the grounds of public policy to which all laws must ultimately be referred."[27] In **"The Path of the Law,"** the alleged source of all imperfection, Holmes spoke of the utility of history, and described its use by lawyers as "the first step toward an enlightened skepticism, that is towards a deliberate reconsideration of the worth"[28] of rules of law. "It is revolting," he went on to say, "to have no better reason for a rule of law than that so it was laid down in the time of Henry IV. It is still more revolting if the grounds upon which it was laid down have vanished long since, and the rule simply persists from the blind imitation of the past."[29] Remembering such utterances as these, how is it possible to accept Professor Fuller's statement that Holmes' "avowed purpose" was "to cut the law loose from the ethical considerations that have shaped it"?[30]

The critics of Holmes might, perhaps, admit that they have exaggerated the positivist elements in his theory of law. Should they make that admission, I believe that they would return to the assault on other lines of battle. They would tell us, first, that the effort which he made to look at law from the bad man's point of view added nothing to our understanding of its character. I should be willing to admit that if his effort is read as an attempt to reach the heart of a philosophical problem, it was not entirely successful. It usually takes something more than a shift in emphasis to achieve profound insight. What Holmes was seeking to do was to put the familiar and valid thesis of *The Common Law* in dramatic terms, to suggest to his audience that their understanding of law would be more penetrating if they washed its precepts in cynical acid, and in doing so, discovered that its language of subjective morality was deceptive. Perhaps his effort was an artistic failure, possibly the dramatic image of the bad man was bound to distract the attention both of the speaker and the audience from the philosophic point in issue. If Holmes' failure was merely artistic, however, criticism of his effort should be concerned with that failure and not with the thesis which he sought to establish.

The other line of attack which I believe that Holmes' critics might be expected to follow would be the assertion that whatever his own philosophy may have been, he put it in such terms as to encourage his disciples to the commission of philosophic sin. By asking lawyers to think of themselves as bad men, by urging them to separate law and morality, by telling them that law is simply a prediction of what courts will do in fact, he started the train of positivism on its journey to cynicism. This visiting of the sins of the children upon their father seems a somewhat harsh sentence, particularly when it is imposed by the philosophers who ask that morality should play a part in law. If the misinterpretations of Holmes' beliefs by some of his disciples have been similar to those of his critics, the primary blame is on disciples and critics alike and not on Holmes. Again, however, I think it only proper to acknowledge that Holmes may deserve some blame for crediting his audience with an imagination greater than they possessed. Though I have spoken of his distrust of the rhetorical excesses of Rufus Choate, he himself was an effective orator and allowed himself, perhaps too frequently, to express philosophic doctrines of great subtlety in the dramatic language of oratory. To say this, however, is only to repeat my earlier point that legitimate artistic criticism is not necessarily valid philosophic criticism.

If my efforts thus far have met with any success, I trust that I have demonstrated that Holmes did not deny that a primary source of law is the realm of moral standards in which society has its being, and that he considered the first responsibility of the lawyer and judge to be that of bringing the law into conformity with those moral standards. It may be asked, however, whether this deference to morality had any substantial significance if Holmes denied, as he did, that our moral standards have objective—or, as he liked to say, cosmic—significance. Those persons whose articles of religious faith include the conviction that the Law of Nature has real existence and that virtue as we conceive it lies at the heart of reality, are

compelled, of course, to believe that when Holmes repudiated the absolute in morals, he destroyed the ethical foundations of the law. For those of us, however, who doubt the cosmic significance of human values, I wonder whether the rejection of the absolute necessarily entails such destructive consequences. May not the value which is merely human have an influence on law as decisive as that which is gloriously absolute? Only if one is persuaded that it may, will it be possible to accept the interpretation of Holmes' philosophy of law which I have suggested. For if it is believed that standards of behavior, which are sustained by human sanctions only, may not lay claim to the honors of morality, then Holmes, by giving no other support to those standards than the taste and preference of men, denied that morality is a source of law. Such critics as Professor Fuller, however, do not purport to defend the absolute. The character of their misinterpretation follows a direction which suggests that his real offense, in their eyes, may be his moral skepticism, not his legal positivism.

This suggestion, that the true ground of their hostility to Holmes is something different from what it appears to be, is not, I believe, an insolent effort on my part to charge his critics with intellectual dishonesty, or a sly attempt to suggest that I know them better than they know themselves. For it seems to me that it is at this point of inquiry that we reach an issue of transcendent importance. That issue concerns problems of metaphysics and ethics more directly than it does questions of law, yet it is inescapably presented in the philosophy of Holmes. The question to which I refer is this: are we intellectually willing and emotionally able to accept that total skepticism which led Holmes to question whether man has a cosmic significance "different in kind from that which belongs to a baboon or a grain of sand"? There are many indications that our stomachs are not strong enough to accept the bitter pill which Holmes tendered us. Professor Fuller is not the only legal philosopher who is asking us to return, if not to the whole of the tradition of natural law, then at least to a significant portion. Although Professor Fuller has given to the concept of natural law a meaning substantially different from that which history has given it, his use of the familiar words is significant of a desire, shared by many thinkers of our generation, a desire to reinstate the monarchy of absolutes—no longer perhaps as an absolute monarchy but one subject to the constitutional restraints of scientific reason. This new doubt of our generation whether the skepticism of Holmes did not carry us too far is partly the result of the glimpse which Hitler gave us of cynicism triumphant. We have begun to ask ourselves whether, despite Holmes, there are not some standards of decency so fundamental and so permanent that they may properly be described as absolute. The legitimacy of such inquiry is beyond question; the one serious danger is that the glib journalism of such mountebanks as Westbrook Pegler will persuade us that there is no difference between the skepticism of Holmes and the cynicism of Hitler.

Those who are encouraging the revival of natural law, though they do not ask us to receive it with all its implications of divine authority, seem to me to be seeking shelter from skepticism beneath the deceptive security of a phrase. The security is sure to be deceptive so long as the phrase embraces no concepts more serviceable than those of social convenience, utility and the public need. If that is all that is included in this new law of nature which is being offered us as an alternative to the positivism of Holmes, it seems to me clear that we are only being asked to swap phrases in the middle of the philosophic stream. The problem of getting across will still be with us. The problem of defining law, the problem of deciding cases, and the never-ending problem of determining through what processes and by what standards the influence of morality on law is to be made effective, remain as they were when Holmes considered them. The danger to be feared in this effort to revive the concept of natural law is that it will lead us unconsciously back to the shop-worn absolutes of an earlier day. If criticism of Holmes proceeds without protest along the lines which it has recently followed, we shall soon find ourselves persuaded that skepticism inevitably breeds cynicism. To avoid that danger we are likely to become fearful of skepticism and seek solace in the delusive concept of natural law.

None of Holmes' serious critics has charged him with cynicism. As Professor Fuller has pointed out, Holmes found it possible to escape the despair which might seem the natural consequence of total skepticism by a romantic faith in the fruitfulness of struggle and of action. By putting his faith in the language of arms he used a tongue which to our generation is distasteful. I see no reason, however, for holding the language which experience made natural to him too much against him. His temperament, like ours, demanded some form of assurance that things are, or at least may be, better than they seem to the eye of reason. The experience of the Civil War, the memory of friends who had died for causes which they did not understand, provided him with the materials for faith. We might find that faith more lovable if its context had been less military. But we, who are also seeking for a faith which will give us protection from our own skepticism, should not be hypercritical of one whose search was inspired by impulses like our own. I wonder, in the end, whether a revived though pallid faith in the law of nature is not less healthy than his. If we should accept it, are we not likely soon to find ourselves not only allied with those who repudiate the achievements of skepticism but eager to rediscover the comforts of the absolute? If that eagerness becomes predominant in our philosophy, we shall be obliged once more to free ourselves from the old shackles. We would do better to stand by Holmes' faith and his skepticism than to repudiate both.

[1] Cardozo, *Mr. Justice Holmes,* 44 *Harv. L. Rev.* 683, 684 (1931).

[2] *Id.* at 691.

[3] *Id.* at 692.

[4] See *Boston American,* Dec. 18, 1950, p. 34.

[5] Ford, "The Fundamentals of Holmes' Juristic Philosophy" in *Phases of American Culture* 51 (1942).

[6] Lucey, *Natural Law and American Legal Realism,* 30 GEO. L.J. 493 (1942).

[7] Palmer, *Hobbes, Holmes, and Hitler,* 31 *A.B.A.J.* 569 (1945).

[8] Palmer, *Defense Against Leviathan,* 32 *A.B.A.J.* 328 (1946).

[9] Fuller, *The Law In Quest of Itself* 5 (1940).

[10] Holmes, "The Path of the Law" in *Collected Legal Papers* 167 (1920).

[11] Fuller, *op. cit. supra* note 9, at 5.

[12] *Id.* at 106-07.

[13] Holmes, *Speeches* 59 (1913).

[14] *The Professor at the Breakfast Table, 2 Works of Dr. Oliver Wendell Holmes* 295 (1892).

[15] Tilton, *Amiable Autocrat,* 264 (1947).

[16] Holmes, *"Notes on Albert Durer,"* 7 *Harvard Magazine* 41 (1860).

[17] 7 *id.* at 144.

[18] Unpublished letter, Holmes to Harold Laski (Sept. 18, 1918).

[19] *Touched with Fire* 122 n.I (Howe ed. 1946).

[20] I *Works of Rufus Choate* 436 (1862).

[21] Holmes, *The Common Law* I (1881).

[22] Holmes, *Collected Legal Papers* 170 (1920).

[23] Holmes, *The Common Law* 44 (1881).

[24] *Id.* at 195.

[25] Fuller, *op. cit. supra* note 9, at 117.

[26] Fuller, *Reason and Fiat in Case Law,* 59 Harv. L. Rev. 376, 383-84 (1946).

[27] Holmes, *The Common Law* 106.

[28] Holmes, *Collected Legal Papers* 186 (1920).

[29] *Id.* at 187.

[30] Fuller, *supra* note 26 at 384.

Saul K. Padover (essay date 1960)

SOURCE: "The American as Skeptic: Oliver Wendell Holmes (1841-1935)," in *The Genius of America: Men Whose Ideas Shaped Our Civilization,* McGraw-Hill Book Company, Inc., 1960, pp. 249-70.

[*In the following essay, Padover discusses Holmes's role on the Supreme Court as a pragmatic dissenter.*]

When twentieth-century Americans speak of judges, they are likely to think first of Oliver Wendell Holmes. He had the superb qualities that symbolize greatness in a jurist—striving for truth, tolerance of ideas, skepticism in the face of dogma, urbanity of manner, grace of expression, philosophic balance and, in the words of Judge Learned Hand, "above all, humility before the vast unknown." There has never been another American judge quite like Holmes, the Boston Brahmin who graced the United States Supreme Court for nearly a third of this century. His impact on America, particularly in the crucial area of judicial thought and posture, has been pervasive and lingering.

Holmes was not merely *a* justice of the Supreme Court; he was a special kind of justice. His uncommonness derived not from any originality of particular juridical theories or precedent-shattering judicial decisions—he was often a dissenter from the majority on the Court—but from his personality. The Holmes character and style had a distinct flavor, as unique as a work of art. Peculiarly American in one sense—in his pragmatism plus humaneness—he was also exceptional in the American political-democratic tradition. A salty Yankee seasoned in intellectual brine, Holmes was a dedicated skeptic, cheerfully doubting the noblest tenets of his countrymen, and gleefully questioning the most devoutly held certainties of his philosophical friends.

Henry Stimson gives one example, that of Holmes' disagreement with the noted Harvard philosopher Royce (1855-1916): "He talked of his old arguments with Josiah Royce. He laughed and laughed over them. He said that the trouble with Royce was that whenever he, Holmes, got him cornered, he would take refuge in saying, 'Well, I am in the bosom of God'; while Holmes would reply, 'Nonsense, you are just in a rathole that I have cornered you in.'"

As free of cant as his predecessor John Marshall, whom he admired considerably, Holmes was blessed with that rare form of intellectual grace known as wit. In addition, his mind was fortified by a buoyancy positively Voltairean in its irreverence and cultivated by a philosophic curiosity that matched Jefferson's. According to Justice Felix Frankfurter, Holmes reminded judges that "in order to be weighty they need not be heavy." For all his erudition, Holmes was never heavy.

Oliver Wendell Holmes, Jr., was born in Boston on March 8, 1841, the son of a father whose reputation has been eclipsed by the subsequent renown of his son. Like the Adams family, the Holmeses belonged to the New England aristocracy. "All my three names," young Holmes wrote in the Harvard College album of the Class of 1861, "designate families from which I am descended. A longer pedigree of Olivers and Wendells may be found in the book called *Memorials of the Dead in Boston.*" From this line of ancestors, the future justice inherited much of his sturdy independence; from his father came his good humor and the sharpness of his wit. "Two and two," the father wrote in *The Poet at the Breakfast-Table,* "do not always make four, in the matter of hereditary descent of qualities. Sometimes they make three and sometimes five." It was five in the case of his son.

Oliver Wendell Holmes, Sr. (1809-94) was a celebrated figure whose rationalism and humor are reminiscent of another native Bostonian, Benjamin Franklin. The senior Holmes was a physician by profession and a writer by avocation. Professor in (and dean of) the Harvard Medical School, Dr. Holmes was the author of popular verse, psychological novels, and amusing books, the best known of which were the *Breakfast-Table* series (*The Autocrat of the Breakfast-Table,* 1858; *The Professor at the Breakfast-Table,* 1860). The witty professor did not spare even the profession of medicine, to which he contributed learned articles. "I firmly believe," he said in an address to the Massachusetts Medical Society, "that if the whole *materia medica* as now used could be sunk to the bottom of the sea, it would be all the better for mankind—and all the worse for the fishes."

The cheerful irreverence and raillery of the father seeped into the thought of the son. The wry humor and skepticism of Holmes the physician is echoed in the judge. "Of course everybody likes and respects self-made men," the senior Holmes wrote in *The Autocrat at the Breakfast-Table.* "It is a great deal better to be made in that way than not to be made at all." There is an echo of this in Justice Holmes' dissenting opinion in the Northern Securities Company case. In Holmes, Sr.'s *Pages from an Old Volume of Life* we have in a nutshell the son's basic aproach to the philosophy of the law: "Of relative justice law may know something; of expediency it knows much; with absolute justice it does not concern itself."

Next to heredity and the immediate environment—"We are all tattooed in our cradles with the beliefs of our tribe; the record may seem superficial, but it is indelible," his father wrote—the most enduring influence on the younger Holmes' life was the Civil War. At its outbreak, when President Lincoln called for 75,000 volunteers, the twenty-year-old Harvard senior enlisted in the infantry. Characteristically, "he was walking down Beacon Hill with Hobbes' *Leviathan* in his hand," according to a contemporary, when he was informed that he had been commissioned a first lieutenant.

As an officer in the Twentieth Massachusetts Volunteers, young Holmes saw some of the bloodiest fighting of the war. He was wounded three times, twice severely and once almost mortally. At the Battle of Ball's Bluff (October 1861), Lieutenant Holmes was shot in the chest. He reports in his crisp diary: "I was hit at 4 1/2 PM. . . . I felt as if a horse had kicked me and went over—1st Sergt Smith grabbed me and lugged me to the rear a little way & opened my shirt and . . . the two holes in my breast & the bullet. . . ." Years later he told a friend ironically, "When I was dying after Ball's Bluff, I remembered my father's saying that death-bed repentances generally meant only that the man was scared." After recovery, he returned to the front as a captain. During the Battle of Antietam (September 1862), he was shot in the neck. He wrote home the next day:

> My Dear Parents . . . Usual luck—ball entered at the rear passing straight through the Central seam of Coat & waistcoat collar coming out towa [rd] the front on the left hand side—yet it don't seem to have smashed my spine or I suppose I should be dead, or paralyzed or something—It's more than 24 h'rs & I have remained pretty cocky, only of course feverish at times. . . . [His father diagnosed the wound: "*Through* the neck,—no bullet left in wound. Windpipe, food-pipe, carotid, jugular, half a dozen smaller, but still formidable vessels, a great braid of nerves, each as big as a lamp-wick, spinal cord—ought to kill at once, if at all. *Thought not* mortal, or *not thought* mortal—which was it?"]

In "My Hunt After the Captain," published in the *Atlantic Monthly* in December 1862, Dr. Holmes told movingly how he had sought his "first-born" through many towns in Maryland and on the road to Philadelphia. He finally found him being fussed over by adoring ladies in the home of Mrs. Howard Kennedy in Hagerstown, twelve miles from Antietam. After a long convalescence, Holmes returned to duty, fought again in Maryland and at the Battle of Fredericksburg (May 1863), was once again wounded, this time by a piece of shrapnel that shattered his heel. He was finally mustered out of service on July 17, 1864, with the rank of lieutenant colonel.

Holmes never forgot the Civil War; it left an indelible imprint on his soul. Many decades later he wrote in a letter to Sir Frederick Pollock in 1920, "I loathe war—which I described when at home with a wound in our Civil War as an organized bore—to the scandal of the young women of the day, who thought that Captain Holmes was wanting in patriotism."

The Civil War battles, some of the most sanguinary in history up to that time, matured him as a man, steeled his character, and deepened his insight into the fragility of human existence: "As long as man dwells upon the globe, his destiny is battle, and he has to take the chances of war." He lost forever the easy optimism of his countrymen. To have proved himself in battle—in a war that tried the souls of men and tested the nation's existence—was to have undergone an experience which, Holmes said, was "incommunicable." Only battle-tested veterans, men who knew what it was to fear for life, what it meant to see their own bodies bleeding and their comrades torn

to pieces could understand the searing experience of war. Matchless, enduring, and elevating, the experience set him and his generation apart from their fellows. This is how Holmes put it, in a Memorial Day address to the veterans of the Grand Army of the Republic at Keene, New Hampshire, in 1884, in almost mystic tones:

> Through our great good fortune, in our youth our hearts were touched with fire. It was given to us to learn at the outset that life is a profound and passionate thing. While we are permitted to scorn nothing but indifference, and do not pretend to undervalue the worldly rewards of ambition, we have seen with our own eyes beyond and above the gold fields the snowy heights of honor, and it is for us to bear the report to those who come after us. . . . Our dead brothers still live for us, and bid us think of life, not death—of life to which in their youth they lent the passion and glory of the spring. As I listen, the great chorus of life and joy begins again, and . . . our trumpets sound once more a note of daring, hope, and will.

In the autumn of 1864, Lieutenant Colonel Holmes entered Harvard Law School, after considering and rejecting other possible careers, among them art and writing. There he formed a close friendship with William James, and they engaged in continuing philosophical arguments. But Holmes did not let philosophical speculation, in which he was to have a lifelong interest, interfere with his chosen profession. Even after graduation in January 1866 and admission to the bar the following year, he devoted himself to the technical study of the law with an absorption that baffled his friends. "For two or three months," Holmes wrote to "Dear Bill" James in December 1867, "I debauched o' nights in philosophy. But now it is law—law—law. My *magnum opus* was reading the *Critique of Pure Reason*." The next April he again wrote to James:

> Since I wrote in December I have worked at nothing but the law. Philosophy has hibernated in torpid slumber, and I have lain "sluttishly soaking and gurgling in the devil's pickle," as Carlyle says. It has been necessary—if a man chooses a profession he cannot forever content himself in picking out the plums with fastidious dilettantism and give the rest of the loaf to the poor, but must eat his way manfully through crust and crumb—soft, unpleasant, inner parts which, within one, swell, causing discomfort in the bowels.

Such concentration unavoidably assured Holmes' career. He had the qualities needed for success. Handsome, elegant, brilliant, hard-working, ambitious, he was bound to rise to eminence. The speculative William James, observing his friend's single-minded pursuit of his legal career, remarked perceptively that "my Wendly boy" was "composed of at least two and a half different people. . . ." One was a philosopher, and the other a somewhat cynical and hard-minded lawyer bent on success. On the Supreme Court, Holmes was to show these distinct parts of his character on more than one occasion.

Success came with fair rapidity. At thirty he became lecturer on constitutional law at Harvard and editor of the

American Law Journal. Three years later he edited and annotated the twelfth edition of Chancellor Kent's *Commentaries on American Law,* a four-volume work that was then the bible of American lawyers. In 1881, Holmes published *The Common Law,* consisting of the Lowell Lectures he had delivered the previous year and which became a landmark in the realistic study of American jurisprudence. It made his reputation as a jurist. His fame was now such that in 1882, at the age of forty-one, he was offered a professorship at Harvard and an appointment to the Judicial Supreme Court of Massachusetts. Holmes accepted the judgeship. "To think of it," his sprightly seventy-three-year-old father said with delight, "—my little boy a Judge and able to send me to jail if I don't behave myself."

In 1902, after Holmes had served on the Massachusetts bench for nearly twenty years (the last three as chief justice), Theodore Roosevelt appointed him to the United States Supreme Court. President Roosevelt knew Holmes' reputation as a legal scholar and admired him as a Civil War hero, but he first wanted to make sure that the Boston Brahmin judge was a liberal like himself, a man in "entire sympathy with our views." After the two Massachusetts senators, Henry Cabot Lodge and George F. Hoar, presumably reassured the President of the acceptability of Holmes' views, the appointment was confirmed by the Senate, in December 1902. Roosevelt, expecting in Holmes a pliable judge, was soon to be angrily disappointed.

For the white-haired Holmes, lean, erect, and sparkling at sixty-one, the appointment to the Supreme Court was the beginning of a great new career. He was to remain on the supreme bench, its ornament and its legend, through half a dozen presidential administrations until he resigned, still hale and racy, at ninety. By an historic coincidence, the humor of which would have delighted Holmes, the last case he heard on the Supreme Court was the first for a lawyer who was destined to become its chief justice within a quarter of a century. As Earl Warren relates the incident, he argued his first case before the Supreme Court on a Friday in June 1930; the next Monday Justice Holmes announced simply: "I won't be there tomorrow," and never returned to the Court. Chief Justice Warren, telling the incident, remarked that his friends have accused him of driving Holmes from the Supreme Court: "One look at you and he said 'I quit.'" Holmes died in 1935, ninety-four years old.

What Holmes had brought to the Supreme Court was not only a finely tempered and keenly cultivated mind but, more important, a special point of view, a philosophy of life and society that was not swayed by the winds of temporary doctrine or transient opinion. In a deeper sense, Holmes the Supreme Court justice, although called upon to deal with crucial questions of practical life, was above the battle in that he refused to become emotionally involved in the political currents or commitments of the moment, whether liberal, reformist, pacifist, or Socialist. Actually, he was not particularly interested in such cur-

rents. "As you know," he wrote to Harold Laski, "I am not much on politics." Not subject to what he called the "hydraulic pressure" of public opinion, Holmes occasionally surprised or shocked his liberal friends with judicial decisions that ran counter to prevailing emotions. Thus, taking a common-law position in defense of property, he dissented from the majority in the trustbusting Northern Securities Company case in 1904. And he again offended liberal opinion when he concurred, on the implied ground of national defense, with the majority in the sentencing of a Socialist leader in the free-speech case of Eugene V. Debs.

This case involved Eugene Victor Debs (1855-1926), founder of the American Socialist Party and its five-time presidential candidate. Under his leadership, the Socialist Party, which increased its presidential vote from about 97,000 in 1900 to nearly one million in 1920, dropped its Marxist phraseology but retained its Marxist ideology. Its 1912 platform, for example, blamed the capitalist system for nearly all the ills that afflict mankind, including armaments, crime, slums, child labor, insanity, and prostitution. Tried in Federal Court for advocating pacifism in World War I, Debs addressed the judge in September 1918, with brave eloquence before receiving sentence.

The case reached the Supreme Court on appeal, and Holmes, in *Debs v. U.S.* (1919), wrote the unanimous opinion of the Court upholding the sentence. He was not, of course, against free speech or against Debs as a socialist, although he despised both Debs and socialism. "I wonder," he wrote to Laski in April, "if Debs really has any ideas. What I have read of his discourse has seemed to me rather silly—and what he said about the judgment against him showed great ignorance." But, in a technical sense, Debs *did* violate the law, as Holmes wrote to Sir Frederick Pollock: "There was no doubt that the Jury was warranted in finding him [Debs] guilty or that the act [Espionage Act of 1917] was Constitutional. Now I hope the President will pardon him and some other poor devils with whom I have more sympathy." Holmes was unhappy about the whole thing. "I hated to have to write the *Debs* case," he admitted in a private letter to Herbert Croly in May, "and still more those of the other poor devils before us the same day and the week before. I could not see the wisdom of pressing the cases, especially when the fighting was over and I think it quite possible that if I had been on the jury I should have been for acquittal but I cannot doubt that there was evidence warranting a conviction on the disputed issues of fact." President Wilson refused to pardon Debs, but President Warren G. Harding did so in 1921.

To American liberals, those who most warmly admired Holmes, he was a baffling phenomenon. They expected him to pursue a consistently liberal line on the bench, but he eluded their pattern. His conception of the function of a judge was not theirs. John Dewey suggested that, if liberalism meant faith in human intelligence and respect for ideas as the supreme force in the solution of social problems, then Holmes was a liberal. If it meant an acceptance of prevailing doctrines of political reform just because they were regarded desirable or noble at any given moment in history, then he was hardly one. In truth, Holmes was a conservative much of the time and a pragmatist all the time. As Dewey said: "He has no social panacea to dole out, no fixed social program, no code of fixed ends to be realized." What Holmes was guided by was not tailored doctrine but skeptical philosophy and the experience of life.

There was a duality in Holmes as a judge. On the one hand he was a disciplined jurist bound by a profound respect for the law as it existed; on the other, he was a philosopher who viewed the human condition from the vantage point of universality. On one level, the law was a hard taskmaster, holding society together in an orderly framework of daily exigencies. On another level, the law, being pragmatic, local, and subject to amendment and alteration, had no cosmic significance. To a philosopher, no man-made statute really mattered much in the long view of history. This cosmic awareness tinctured Holmes' thinking and provided him with a pervasive skepticism—and humility—in areas that many men, including judges, considered certainties. Speaking before the Harvard Law School Association in New York in 1913, Holmes enunciated his judicial philosophy with almost Olympian detachment:

> I have no belief in panaceas and almost none in sudden ruin. I believe with Montesquieu that if the chance of a battle—I might add, the passage of a law—has ruined a state, there was a general cause at work that made the state ready to perish by a . . . battle or a law. Hence I am not much interested one way or the other in the nostrums now so strenuously urged. I do not think the United States would come to an end if we lost our power to declare an Act of Congress void. . . . I do not pin my dreams for the future to my country or even to my race. I think it probable that civilization somehow will last as long as I care to look ahead— . . . perhaps also bred to greatness and splendor by science. I think it not improbable that man . . . may have cosmic destinies that he does not understand.

In Holmes' philosophy there was a kind of suspension of philosophy, at least of the traditional variety. Systematic philosophers, who seemed to know the answers to the most thorny problems of man and the universe, left him unconvinced. He was equally skeptical of moralists—"I naturally shrink from the moral tone," he wrote to Laski—and critical of dogmatists. He felt that none of the claimants to certainty really knew enough to substantiate their sweeping assertions about truth and the human condition. Large generalizations, including judicial decisions, were merely expressions of the "longing for certainty" to be found "in every human mind." But, he said, "certainty generally is illusion, and repose is not the destiny of man." Objecting to what he called "delusive exactness," Holmes insisted on intellectual humility and suspension of judgment in the presence of the unknown. "I think none of the philosophers sufficiently humble," he

told William James in a letter in which he made some critical remarks on James' *Pragmatism*. And he wrote to Laski, "Why should we not be humble—why not willing to admit that the primordial wiggle of the first churning of chaos came before our time?"

The only thing that was meaningful, Holmes reiterated in his writings and speeches, was life itself—the plain, unvarnished reality of daily existence, with its joys and conflicts. The dynamism of human life was its own justification; it could not fit into preconceived theories. "From the point of view of the world," he said to the Boston Bar Association in March 1900, "the end of life is life. Life is action, the use of one's powers. . . . Life is an end in itself, and the only question as to whether it is worth living is whether you have enough of it." Holmes used a similar expression some eighteen years later in a letter to Sir Frederick Pollock: " . . . Realize life as an end in itself. Functioning is all there is—only our keenest pleasure is in what we call the higher sort. I wonder if cosmically an idea is any more important than the bowels."

In a private letter to a friend, William James complained that Holmes' philosophy was "immature" and "unworthy" of a judge: "It is curiously childish to me." But to Holmes it was mature. Faith in life as a continuing struggle and experimentation was at the base of his approach to law. Nothing in human affairs, he held, was either sacrosanct or permanently fixed. Everything, including the federal Constitution, which Holmes had sworn to uphold, was flexible and subject to change. "The Constitution," he said in a famous statement, which echoed that of Jefferson a century earlier, "is an experiment, as all life is an experiment."

Holmes was one of the pioneers in the pragmatic study of jurisprudence. Even before Charles Sanders Peirce, William James and John Dewey developed the theories of pragmatism and revolutionized social thought in America, Holmes analyzed the law, not as an immutable system, but as an experimental process. In *The Common Law* he challenged the prevailing theories of natural law—which assumed absolute doctrines of eternal (unchanging) truths—with his assertion that the "life of the law has not been logic: it has been experience." Law, he went on to explain, was the product of time and experience, rather than handed-down dogma:

> The felt necessities of the time, the prevalent moral and political theories, intuitions of public policy, avowed or unconscious, even the prejudices which judges share with their fellow-men, have had a good deal more to do than the syllogism in determining the rules by which men should be governed.

Law, to Holmes, was not an *ought* but an *is*. Personal preferences or pet legal theories had little to do with the hard reality of law as it existed at any given time. Law was subject to alteration by orderly processes as a result of "felt necessities," but while on the statute books and backed by the sovereignty of government, it remained a brute fact of life. "When I talk of law," Holmes wrote to Laski in 1917, "I talk as a cynic. I don't care a damn if twenty professors tell me a decision is not law if I know that the courts will enforce it." The old veteran of the Civil War had no illusions about the sacredness of human life vis-à-vis the needs of government. Holmes frankly and cheerfully accepted the idea of the use of force as a social and political necessity—whenever the occasion arose. Every society, he said, "rests on the death of men." Government does not hesitate to kill "when it sees fit and can."

"I think that the sacredness of human life," Holmes wrote to Pollock (in 1920), "is a purely municipal ideal of no validity outside the jurisdiction. I believe that force, mitigated so far as may be by good manners, is the *ultima ratio,* and between two groups that want to make inconsistent kinds of worlds I see no remedy except force."

Like Dewey, Holmes took a relativist position on moral values and judgments. Consistent with his rejection of natural law, he asserted the idea that truth in human relations was subject to changing conditions as seen and experienced by individuals. As such, its validity was personal instead of cosmic. To William James, of whose metaphysical theories he was dubious, he wrote in 1907: "I have been in the habit of saying that all I mean by truth is what I can't help thinking. The assumption of the validity of the thinking process seems to mean no more than that. . . . I have learned to surmise that my *can't helps* are not necessarily cosmic can't helps—that the universe may not be subject to my limitations; and philosophy generally seems to me to sin through arrogance. It is like the old knight-errants who proposed to knock your head off if you didn't admit that their girl was not only a nice girl but the most beautiful and best of all possible girls. I can't help preferring champagne to ditch water.—I doubt if the universe does."

Holmes developed his relativistic position concerning truth and values more fully in **"Natural Law,"** an article published in the November 1918 *Harvard Law Review.* It is interesting, as Professor Arnold Brecht has pointed out in his comprehensive work, *Political Theory* (1959), that Holmes' relativism was close to that of pre–World War I German jurists and sociologists, whose writings the Justice "did not seem to know." (The essence of the relativist argument was that truth and value judgments, matters of personal preference, were not subject to scientific proof.)

Holmes felt that one man's choice of values was as good as another's—an opinion, Professor Brecht reminds us, almost identical with that expressed by Max Weber in his epochal 1904 article, "'Objectivity' in Social Scientific and Social Political Knowledge." An individual may strongly assert his preferences and even fight for them, but he cannot prove them by reason or theorize them into universality. "I don't talk much of rights," Holmes said, "as I see no meaning in the rights of man except what the crowd will fight for."

Holmes' article in the *Harvard Law Review* is couched in terms more personal than is the wont of theoretical philosophers. It contains the quintessence of his relativistic and skeptical attitude toward both life and law:

> There is in all men a demand for the superlative, so much so that the poor devil who has no other way of reaching it attains it by getting drunk . . . this demand is at the bottom of the philosopher's effort to prove that truth is absolute and of the jurist's search for criteria of universal validity which he collects under the head of natural laws. . . . Certitude is not the test of certainty. . . . I love granite rocks and bayberry bushes, no doubt because with them were my earliest joys . . . others, poor souls, may be equally dogmatic about something else. . . . The jurists who believe in natural law seem to me to be in that naive state of mind that accepts what has been familiar . . . as something that must be accepted by all men everywhere . . . a right is only the hypostasis of a prophecy . . . behind these legal rights is the fighting will . . . to maintain them . . . ; but that does not seem to me the same thing as the supposed *a priori* discernment of a duty or the assertion of a pre-existing right. A dog will fight for his bone.

Skepticism in the face of dogmas and relativism in regard to values underlay Holmes' legal thinking and help explain his role as the "Great Dissenter" on the Supreme Court. His dissents—in which Justice Louis D. Brandeis usually joined after his appointment to the Court in 1916—became celebrated for the independent position they embodied and for the matchless style in which they were couched.

Although Louis Dembitz Brandeis (1856-1941) is coupled with Holmes as a Great Dissenter, the two men were not intimate and did not altogether share the same philosophic outlook. Both were men of large liberal spirit, particularly in the field of free speech, but of widely different temperaments. Holmes' predilection was for legal and philosophical reasoning; Brandeis' propensity was for economic data. Holmes built his cases like a worldly philosopher; Brandeis constructed his like an academic social scientist. Holmes was an amused and amusing skeptic; Brandeis was a dead-serious believer in reform. "I'm afraid Brandeis has the crusading spirit," Holmes once said with ironic affection. "He talks like one of those upward-and-onward fellows."

It was that crusading spirit that had caused such a storm of opposition when President Wilson appointed Brandeis to the Supreme Court in January 1916. The most powerful conservatives of the day, among them seven former presidents of the American Bar Association (including William Howard Taft, Joseph H. Choate, and Elihu Root), opposed the nomination and attacked Brandeis' public as well as private life. "The propaganda in this matter," President Wilson wrote, "has been very extraordinary and very distressing to those who love fairness and value the dignity of the great professions." The opposition to Brandeis, partly motivated by anti-Semitism, was mainly due to his reputation as a liberal who had for years fought stubbornly for social justice and economic equality. Brandeis considered big business monopolies the greatest single danger to American democracy. He advocated government regulation of unrestrained economic bigness, protection of small business, freedom of labor to organize, and other social reforms, such as pensions, sick benefits, and unemployment insurance. He may justly be regarded as the father of the New Deal (of which he did not always approve, primarily because its governmental powers were becoming "too big").

To the advocacy of his social-economic reform program, in writings, speeches, and testimony before Congress, Brandeis brought a mastery of economic detail and a knowledge of the total national economy that was unprecedented, especially in a lawyer and judge. He had the rare gift of marshalling his ideas with a precision of language and (in the words of Charles A. Beard) "a display of stubborn and irreducible facts knit closely together" that was overwhelming in its impact. Before his appointment to the Court he had given freely of his time in the service of causes which he considered just and democratic.

"Some men," Brandeis said in 1911, "buy diamonds and rare works of art; others delight in automobiles and yachts. My luxury is to invest my surplus effort, beyond that required for the proper support of my family, to the pleasure of taking up a problem and solving, or helping to solve, it for the people without receiving any compensation. Your yachtsman or automobilist would lose much of his enjoyment if he were obliged to do for pay what he is doing for the love of the thing itself. So I should lose much of my satisfaction if I were paid in connection with public services of this kind. I have only one life, and it is short enough. Why waste it on things I don't want most? I don't want money or property most. I want to be free."

Brandeis' idealism and his known mastery of the complex data of modern life were the reason the equally reform-minded Woodrow Wilson selected him for the Supreme Court.

On the Court, Justice Brandeis' liberal position remained unchanged. In the fields of civil liberties and economic justice his judicial opinions were so unswerving that one prominent educator likened him to Lincoln. "You two," Alvin Johnson wrote to Brandeis (November 1936), "seem to me the two most serenely implacable democrats in all history."

Brandeis upheld his social philosophy either in separate opinions or in concurrence with Holmes' dissents. The two justices continued to respect one another. "I don't see much of him," Holmes wrote to Laski in 1920, "except in Court but he is a great comfort to me." And again the next month: " . . . and that makes me think of Disraeli and the affection that he inspired, and that makes me ask whether loveableness is a characteristic of the better class

of Jews. When I think how many of the younger men that have warmed my heart have been Jews I cannot but suspect it. . . . Brandeis, whom many dislike, seems to me to have this quality and always gives me a glow, even though I am not sure that he wouldn't burn me at a slow fire if it were in the interest of some very possibly disinterested aim. I don't for a moment doubt that for daily purposes he feels to me as a friend—as certainly I do to him."

Holmes did not, of course, always dissent, nor did he always agree with the liberal Brandeis. Much of the time, in fact, Holmes agreed with his "brethren" on the bench, the majority of whom were conservative in their economic outlook. He shared his fellow justices' antipathy for economic radicalism, but on grounds more sophisticated than theirs. He considered radical theorists and socialists fools or worse; they were "shriekers," whose proclaimed passion for economic equality, he said, was "merely idealizing envy." They simply had no grasp of the facts and meaning of life. The advocacy of "wholesale social regeneration" through "socialized property," Holmes wrote in the *Illinois Law Review* in 1915, was an "empty humbug." It ignored human beings as individuals with their immense range of talents, efforts and aspirations. "I never read a socialist yet from Karl Marx down," Holmes told Harold Laski, "and I have read a number, that I didn't think talked drool."

Holmes felt equal disdain for such American radicals as Henry George, Thorstein Veblen, and Eugene Debs. He disliked theories and legislative acts based upon them that involved the dangerous business of what he said was "tinkering with the institution of property." It is not too surprising, therefore, that he concurred with the conservative majority in about three fourths of the cases in which the Supreme Court held state legislation contrary to the Fourteenth Amendment.

The key words in the Fourteenth Amendment (1868), under which much state legislation in the economic sphere after the Civil War was challenged in the courts, were:

> No State shall make or enforce any law which shall abridge the privileges or immunities of citizens of the United States; nor shall any State deprive any person of life, liberty, or property without due process of law.

The amendment was originally designed to provide protection for the civic rights of the newly enfranchised Negroes, but the *due process* clause was used increasingly by the federal courts to strike down social-economic legislation that was distasteful to conservative property interests—and that had nothing to do with the rights of Negroes.

In some cases, Holmes wrote the majority opinion for the Court. But his dissents, qualifying him for the exclusive title of the Great Dissenter, were Olympian in their disregard for precedent.

There were two general areas in which his dissents were conspicuous. One was his blunt rejection of dogmatic interpretations of the federal Constitution. The other was his approach to the problem of free speech.

Although he shared his colleagues' aversion for radicals and radical legislation, he did not accept the dogmatic economic and legal theories they used to justify their decisions. His rejection of dogmatism in Supreme Court rulings—in itself a major service in the cause of open-mindedness—is best seen in three important cases, those of *Lochner v. New York* (1905), *Truax v. Corrigan* (1921), and *Tyson Bros. v. Banton* (1927).

The Lochner case was of special significance because it was one of the first to deal with social legislation in the field of labor protection. It involved a New York state law limiting the hours of labor in bakeries to ten a day and a maximum of sixty a week. The act was passed under the general "police powers" of the state and was designed to protect the health of the bakers. Challenged as a violation of "liberty of contract" under the Fourteenth Amendment, the Supreme Court upheld the challenge by a vote of five to four, and declared the law invalid. The majority opinion, written by Justice Rufus W. Peckham, went beyond the immediate act and stated sweeping political-economic principles that all but destroyed the power of any states to legislate in the welfare field. "The act," Justice Peckham wrote, "is . . . an illegal interference with the rights of individuals, both employers and employees, to make contracts regarding labor upon such terms as they may think best."

In addition to that of Holmes, there was a dissenting opinion written by Justice John M. Harlan in which Justices Edward D. White and William Rufus Day concurred.

But Holmes' dissent became a landmark in sociological jurisprudence, in what Roscoe Pound has described as the pragmatic movement in the law that aimed at "putting the human factor in the central place." Holmes started out with a blunt rejection of Peckham's underlying assumptions. "This case," he wrote, "is decided upon an economic theory which a large part of the country does not entertain." Whether a judge personally liked a law or not, it was not his business to deny the "right of a majority to embody their opinions in law." The statute books were full of laws (many of them upheld in previous Supreme Court decisions) that were unwise or tyrannical—Sunday laws, lottery laws, school laws, tax laws—and yet within the right of the citizens to enact them. The New York state act regarding the bakers was in the same category. It was now being declared invalid, Holmes suggested, not because it violated the Fourteenth Amendment—it had nothing to do with that Amendment—but because it did not fit into the preconceived economic doctrines of the judges. "The Fourteenth Amendment," Holmes wrote in a passage that was to echo through the decades, "does not enact Mr. Herbert Spencer's Social Statics" (a teleological work, published in 1850, which contained the usual Spencerian generalizations unblemished by empirical

data). The smuggling of dogmatic doctrines into the Constitution to justify the judges' economic bias was, in Holmes' view, bad law and bad policy.

"But a constitution," he continued, "is not intended to embody a particular economic theory, whether of paternalism and the organic relation of the citizen to the State or of *laissez faire*. It is made for people of fundamentally differing views, and the accident of our finding certain opinions natural and familiar or novel and even shocking ought not to conclude our judgment upon the question whether statutes embodying them conflict with the Constitution of the United States."

He took a similar position in *Truax v. Corrigan,* which involved labor, and in *Tyson Bros. v. Banton,* which concerned theater tickets. In both instances, Holmes rejected *a priori* theories and upheld the right of the states to legislate without hindrance by the Supreme Court. In *Truax v. Corrigan,* the Court invalidated an Arizona statute which provided that no injunctions could be issued against peaceful picketing. Chief Justice William Howard Taft, in a five-to-four decision, held that the Arizona act was unlawful in that picketing, being inherently an attack on property, violated the *due process* clause of the Fourteenth Amendment.

In his majority decision, Justice Taft wrote that picketing was "a direct invasion of the ordinary business and property rights" and that such experimentation as was involved in the Arizona law was unlawful: "The Constitution was intended . . . to prevent experimentation with the fundamental rights of the individual." Professor Felix Frankfurter, a future justice of the Supreme Court, commented in *The New Republic* (1921) that the decision ignored American economic realities: "For all the regard that the Chief Justice of the United States pays to the facts of industrial life, he might as well have written this opinion as Chief Justice of the Fiji Islands."

Holmes dissented. He protested, with a touch of irony, against the dangers of "delusive exactness in the application of the Fourteenth Amendment" (by which the judges confused picketing, as a potential threat to business, with established property rights) and insisted that legislatures had a right to pass laws to remedy or redress evils. "Legislation may begin where an evil begins." He reiterated that it was not the Supreme Court's business to interfere with legislation on the ground that it did not coincide with the judges' economic theories:

> I must add one general consideration. There is nothing I more deprecate than the use of the Fourteenth Amendment beyond the absolute compulsion of its words to prevent the making of social experiments that an important part of the community desires, in the insulated chambers afforded by the several States, even though the experiments may seem futile or even noxious to me and to those whose judgment I most respect.

Similarly, in the Tyson case, in which the Supreme Court held that a New York state law setting a 50-cent limit on the mark-up of theater tickets was unconstitutional—taking away the rights of property without *due process*—Holmes dissented and repeated his belief that the powers of the legislature must not be curbed to fit the bias of the judges:

> I think the proper course is to recognize that a State legislature can do whatever it sees fit to do unless it is restrained by some express prohibition in the Constitution of the United States or of the State, and that Courts should be careful not to extend such prohibitions beyond their obvious meaning by reading into them conceptions of public policy that the particular Court may happen to entertain. . . . I am far from saying that I think that this particular law a wise and rational provision. That is not my affair. But if the people of the State of New York speaking by their authorized voice say that they want it, I see nothing in the Constitution of the United States to prevent their having their will.

In his dissents connected with the free-speech cases, Holmes was equally outspoken. Here he not only challenged the prevailing passions of intolerance—generated by World War I—but explored the difficult concepts and practices of free speech on a philosophical level reminiscent of Jefferson. Among the most important cases in which Holmes expressed his dissenting opinions were: *Abrams v. U.S.* (1919), *Gitlow v. N.Y.* (1925), *U.S. v. Schwimmer* (1928), and *Olmstead v. U.S.* (1928). These cases dealt with what he called the "free trade in ideas."

But here again his position was not an absolute one. Even in this crucial area of intellectual freedom, Holmes did not always dissent. As in other instances involving social legislation, so also in matters affecting freedom of speech he sometimes sided with the majority. This was particularly true in cases involving the national security, where the Civil War veteran took a high patriotic position. In such notable cases as *Schenck v. U.S.* (1919) and, as noted, *Debs v. U.S.,* both upholding limitations on freedom of speech in wartime, Holmes not only concurred with the majority but wrote the opinion for the Court.

The Schenck case concerned the general secretary of the Socialist Party, who was jailed under the Espionage Act of 1917 for sending through the mails, particularly to the armed forces, pacifist leaflets. The Supreme Court upheld the conviction. In handing down the opinion, Holmes formulated the famous "clear and present danger" doctrine as a test of free speech. He took the position that freedom of speech was not an absolute value, good at all times and at all places, but a relative one. His argument in *Schenck v. U.S.* was that speech was not being prohibited because the ideas involved were inherently undesirable, but because under certain circumstances—opposing recruitment and spreading demoralization among the troops in wartime, for example—words could endanger the war effort. What Holmes was saying in effect was that Schenck and other defendants similarly situated should remain in jail, not because they advocated

pacifism and socialism but because they did so at the wrong time. "When a nation is at war many things that might be said in time of peace are such a hindrance to its effort that their utterance will not be endured so long as men fight." In other words, the test of freedom of speech was not its *substance* but its *circumstance*. He wrote in the Schenck case:

> We admit that in many places and in ordinary times the defendants in saying all that was said in the circular would have been within their constitutional rights [under the First Amendment]. But the character of every act depends upon the circumstances in which it is done. . . . The most stringent protection of free speech would not protect a man in falsely shouting fire in a theater and causing a panic. . . . The question in every case is whether the words used are used in such circumstances and are of such a nature as to create a clear and present danger that they will bring about the substantive evils that Congress has a right to prevent.

To a philosopher like Holmes, it must have been evident that the "clear and present danger" doctrine that justified limitation on freedom of speech was neither clear nor adequate. It could serve a momentary purpose, under pressures of war, but it was not sufficient to stand by itself as a doctrine governing man's rights and responsibilities in a free society. Moreover, the "clear and present danger" argument came perilously close to agreeing with the ultraconservatives and antidemocrats who have always held that freedom of speech was all right in its way, but not in a crisis. This was a manifest absurdity, and it would be surprising if Holmes was not troubled by it. For if freedom of speech had any meaning at all, it meant freedom to speak when it was unpopular to do so, precisely because it was unpopular. Obviously there is no problem when everybody agrees with everybody. Holmes himself said in the Schwimmer case (1928) that the principle of free thought meant "not free thought for those who agree with us but freedom for the thought that we hate."

It was this principle that Holmes developed in *Abrams v. U.S.* (1919), which followed hard on that of Schenck, and subsequent free-speech cases. His dissent in the Abrams case sounded as if he regretted his decision in Schenck; it was a complete reversal of his position. Just as he agreed with the majority that Schenck was guilty of distributing leaflets, so he disagreed with his colleagues that Abrams was guilty for doing almost precisely the same thing at approximately the same time. Jacob Abrams had thrown down from a loft in New York City leaflets urging that workers refuse to produce arms that were to be used for intervention in the Russian Revolution. Under the Espionage Act this was considered an "intent" to curtail or cripple the prosecution of the war, and Abrams was sentenced to twenty years in prison. The Supreme Court, with Justices Holmes and Brandeis dissenting, upheld the conviction. Technically, Holmes' dissent revolved around the meaning of the word *intent*. He did not regard Abrams' intent incitement enough to cause a direct limitation of war production. "Nobody can suppose," Holmes wrote, "that the surreptitious publishing of a silly leaflet by an unknown man . . . would present an immediate danger that its opinions would hinder the success of the government arms."

But Holmes went beyond the technicalities. He took the opportunity to explore the inner meaning of free speech, especially in a crisis, something he had failed to do in the Schenck case. Apart from intent, what was the real question in the Abrams case? It was, Holmes asserted, the right under the Constitution to express ideas and beliefs, no matter how silly, provided they were honestly held. He considered Abrams' socialist faith a "creed of ignorance and immaturity," but this was no excuse whatever for the government to punish him for his opinions. Like Voltaire and Jefferson before him, Holmes now elucidated the principles of free opinion in timeless terms. He rooted them in the Constitution as being integral to its whole spirit. The words, in the Abrams case, stand as a monument to intellectual freedom:

> Persecution for the expression of opinions seems to me perfectly logical. If you have no doubt of your premises or your power and want a certain result with all your heart you naturally express your wishes in law and sweep away all opposition. . . . But when men have realized that time has upset many fighting faiths, they may come to believe . . . that the ultimate good desired is better reached by free trade in ideas,—that the best test of truth is the power of the thought to get itself accepted in the competition of the market. . . . That, at any rate, is the theory of our Constitution. It is an experiment as all life is an experiment. . . . While that experiment is part of our system I think that we should be eternally vigilant against attempts to check the expression of opinions that we loathe and believe to be fraught with death.

Note the similarity to Jefferson. In his *Notes on the State of Virginia* (1785) Jefferson had written: "Reason and free inquiry are the only effectual agents against error. . . . They are the natural enemies of error, and of error only. . . . It is error alone which needs the support of government. Truth can stand by itself."

Holmes concluded this dissenting opinion by saying that he regretted he could not "put into more impressive words" this belief that in their conviction . . . the defendants [in the Abrams case] were deprived of their rights under the Constitution of the United States."

In the Gitlow and Schwimmer cases, Holmes continued and elaborated his reasoned defense of free expression. Benjamin Gitlow was convicted for publishing a revolutionary pamphlet. The Supreme Court upheld the sentence mainly on the ground that the Marxist pamphlet was a "direct incitement" to revolution. Holmes pointed out that his Schenck case criterion of "clear and present danger" did not apply to Gitlow, that the defendant's "redundant discourse" had little chance of starting a radical conflagration, and that there was no current danger of an attempt to overthrow the government by a small mi-

nority like that. In the absence of any such peril to the nation, Holmes could see no justification for punishing Gitlow for his opinions. Under the Constitution and in the free market place of ideas, Gitlow had a right to offer his opinions, even though they were inflammatory:

> It is said that this manifesto was more than a theory, that it was an incitement. Every idea is an incitement. It offers itself for belief and if believed it is acted on unless some other belief outweighs it . . . the only meaning of free speech is that they [beliefs] should be given their chance and have their way.

In the Schwimmer and Olmstead cases, both in 1928, Holmes extended his championship of freedom to include the advocacy of pacifism and the rejection of government-approved wiretapping. Rosika Schwimmer had had her application for citizenship rejected on the ground that she had been a pacifist. In his dissent, Holmes [Chief Justice Charles Evans Hughes, and Justices Brandeis and Stone also dissented] attacked the Court's decision on two main grounds: that her belief in pacifism was neither dangerous nor silly, and that even if it were both, she still had a right under the Constitution to voice it. "She is an optimist," Holmes wrote, "and states . . . her belief that war will disappear. . . . I do not share that optimism." But it was absurd to assume that hatred of war would not make her a good citizen. In the Olmstead case, which involved the tapping of a bootlegger's wire by federal agents to prove his violation of the prohibition laws, Holmes disagreed with the majority that such a procedure was lawful or constitutional. Wiretapping, he held, was a violation of the Fourth and Fifth amendments, and as such, was a "dirty business." Evidence illegally obtained was a "criminal act." There was no justification for its use by the government, even for the apprehension of criminals. "We have to choose," Holmes wrote in his dissent, "and for my part I think it less evil that some criminals should escape than that the government should play an ignoble part."

Such was the over-all pattern of Holmes' thought. He was an unflinching realist, acutely aware of the relativity of values, moved by no dogmas, pursuing what he conceived to be the truth with an overpowering sense of philosophic humility. In human affairs, he took the long, detached view. But despite his Olympian aloofness, he could be stirred. When Alvin Johnson, in 1933, organized a committee to rescue European scholars driven out by Hitler, Felix Frankfurter asked Justice Holmes to be a sponsor. To Frankfurter's surprise, the Judge, then in his ninety-second year, eagerly accepted, saying: "I have never joined anything to promote a cause. This is different. Nothing less is involved than the history of civilization."

Holmes displayed a tolerant regard for the human mind, no matter what its direction. Without necessarily respecting the content of other people's ideas or convictions, he nevertheless championed their right to voice them. "With effervescing opinions as with the not yet forgotten champagnes," he wrote to the Harvard Liberal Club in 1920, "the quickest way to let them get flat is to let them get exposed to the air." He was in favor of what he called the "aeration" of ideas.

Holmes' greatness as a judge and jurist lies in this: Even in dissents, he spoke from the awe-inspiring platform of the Supreme Court in defense of the most crucial of all public values—freedom of the mind. The ideas embodied in his opinions and dissents became the intellectual property of his countrymen and ultimately even their laws. The skeptical Great Dissenter, in precisely that role, was the conscience of America, perhaps despite himself.

Francis Biddle (essay date 1961)

SOURCE: "The Attacks on Justice Holmes," in *Justice Holmes, Natural Law, and the Supreme Court,* The Macmillan Company, 1961, pp. 27-49.

[*In the following essay, Biddle discusses the reaction of many priests at Jesuit law schools against Holmes after Holmes's letters were published posthumously.*]

The attacks on Justice Holmes were stirred into life by the publication of his letters a few years after his death—there was hardly enough in the opinions and speeches to shock the well-bred ear of the average man; and the priests, who wrote most of the criticism, must have spent many hours combing the letters to sustain their view that here was a modern antichrist worthy of their mettle. The Justice's admirers came to his defense, but only here and there, and with dignity and caution, as if the charges were not worth answering, and it was simply a matter of misunderstanding their hero. It would be pointless, however, to get into this battle of words in the law journals, in itself hardly an engrossing subject, were it not for the fact that it represents not merely misunderstanding, but two points of view about the law and the proper approach to its application that are fundamentally opposed, and touch the roots of its life.

The first letters published (in 1936) were to John C. H. Wu, a young Chinese student with a solemn philosophic bent, who would later be a judge of the Shanghai Provisional Court. The letters to Sir Frederick Pollock—the English scholar descended from David Pollock, a saddler to George III, whom Holmes called "one of the very most learned men I ever saw in any age"—appeared in 1941, the correspondence covering a friendship that lasted for almost sixty years. Finally came the letters to Harold Laski (1916 to 1935), an obscure, frail young Englishman, instructor in government at Harvard, who was taken by Felix Frankfurter, then teaching at the Harvard Law School, to see Holmes at Beverly Farms in the summer of 1916.

Holmes's correspondence was enormous—many of his letters are still unpublished—he wrote everything in longhand, and he spent as much pains on his letters as he did on his opinions, and short occasional addresses to a group of veterans or a meeting of the bar. I would not deny that he had an eye cocked for posterity, particularly in the letters; but the chief reason for his concentrated and minute exertions was his lifelong habit of reaching for perfection, not unrelated to his deeply ingrained way of never laying down a book he had begun—if you start something you must finish it. It was therefore like him to exclaim, "How one hates a book while one is reading it!"

Holmes's letters to Pollock are more restrained, more sober than what he wrote Laski, and display more legal scholarship, as if to show his friend that since he became a judge he had not given up reading what was being said about the nature and sources of law. The letters to Laski carry the wit and insight and charm of his talk; Laski is indiscreet—and brilliant. Everything about Holmes is there; and one feels that the younger man's broad culture and omnivorous reading, even allowing for his boasts about it—"I can't believe that you read all the books you mention," Holmes bursts out, *he* couldn't swallow books like oysters—and the fact that Laski's point of view was teasingly alien to the Justice's challenged him to do his utmost in the long-drawn intellectual duel.

Holmes said what he liked in the letters—he must have sometimes felt penned in among his brethren in Washington—which range over a broad field of life and law, of literature and philosophy, of the beliefs and doubts of men. They are written with lucidity and concision, without consciousness of the need to exercise discretion which the opinions and public talks necessarily imposed. Of course he repeats himself; and the repetitions show how little the ideas he held most closely, the "can't helps," as he called them, changed over the years. I don't mean to say that these beliefs could not have been found in the opinions and his occasional addresses; but they lack the atmosphere of casual ease in which friends indulge when they do not fear being quoted, at least until the lapse of time takes from their talk the sting of the contemporary. Holmes must have felt a boyish pleasure of indulging in expressions, which, particularly to the canonical, were more shocking than the ideas which they were intended to convey.

. . . . .

Following the upheaval of a great war, or of profound economic and scientific changes, traditions break down and the truths of yesterday are no longer accepted; men look for spiritual guidance outside their own limited experience, and grasp at religion to reestablish their sense of direction. Today is such a time. Side by side with the present mood of violence and despair there is a reaction against cynicism, a demand for the comfort of the mystical, a desire to be reassured and to be instructed. "The insecurities of our age today," Reinhold Niebuhr has observed, "strongly tempt this generation, not to the utopianism of yesterday but to flight into any kind of storm cellar of religious security, whether this be Biblicism . . . or emphasis on the uniqueness of the church." It is not surprising, therefore, that natural law—

which in the past has promised so much—has had a revival in the Catholic law schools, somewhat doctrinaire, in an endeavor to clarify and to justify its tenets.

Among those who drew their moral sustenance from natural law, Holmes's reputation must have suffered under the assaults of certain Roman Catholic priests teaching in Jesuit law schools, whose charges I shall presently examine. I do not believe that their extreme views and lack of restraint in the manner of expressing them represent the thought of Jesuits as a body, many of them enlightened legal scholars. Though of course they accept the principles of natural law, these principles do not differ greatly from the ethical concepts of Protestants, or of members of other denominations, or of men of good will who happen to be freethinkers. One does not have to be a cleric to be an upright man, and most thoughtful lawyers talk the same language. Yet several of my friends, who are prominent Catholic lawyers and judges, and whose opinions and views I respect, have gathered the impression from reading the law-review articles that we shall consider, that Holmes was a cynic, who thought of law as nothing but the application of force; that he believed that morals, basically conceived, were but the expression of individual taste, and had nothing to do with law; and that he held that the proper function of a judge was to carry out what the majority had already decided, whether it was right or wrong.

I do not think that Holmes's ultimate place in history, or the tradition that has grown up around the nation's memory of him as an heroic and noble figure, will be affected by these onslaughts, sometimes highly personal and ungoverned. Yet it seems to me appropriate to meet them—they have not, I think, been adequately answered outside law-school journals. That I loved and admired Justice Holmes makes it difficult for me to resist this opportunity to talk about him and his detractors. But this is not merely a matter of coming to the defense of a great man whom little men are trying to pull down. Holmes's contribution to law—his insistence on examining objectively the facts which explain its life and its direction—involves keeping open the doors of the mind in a world which increasingly, I feel, is closing about us. The attacks are leveled against the emancipation of law from superstition—a task to which everything in Holmes was dedicated.

. . . . .

I do not propose to define natural law, or to discuss its often contradictory tenets. But it is essential to know in the most general way some of the claims of natural law which the critics of Justice Holmes had in mind in order to understand why he rejected them, and the reasons he was attacked for doing so. This rejection, as we have seen, was leveled at all moral absolutes, particularly if they were confused with law.

There have been many schools of natural law, which is speculative and dogmatic, and its range has been used to cover the whole field of morals. It is said, for instance, that the International Military Tribunal at Nuremberg applied natural law. It did not; but punished what the charter, under which it operated, designated as *crimes against humanity.* It may be replied that this reference was itself taken from natural law; but that is true only in the most general sense. The phrase was an expression of the reaction of the conscience of the community against evils which seemed so shocking that they must be considered "crimes." That is the way in which the common law of crime largely developed, and many early crimes were not spelled out in any statute, or in the decree of a sovereign. Like the doctrine of equity, natural law has had marked influence on English common law, although it is not the same as common law, and has never absorbed it.

Since the substance of natural law is a statement of what is thought to be moral, it is not surprising to find it invoked on both sides when controversy arises. In our Declaration of Independence the assertion that all men are endowed by their Creator with certain unalienable rights is drawn from natural law; yet such a ringing and noble expression of faith did not prevent Americans from writing slavery into their Constitution; or Southerners from claiming in the Civil War that slavery was sanctified by the laws of nature. Albert Dicey, the English scholar, said of natural law that it had often been a name for the dictates of expediency. It has noticeably influenced American thinking, and many of its pronouncements are indistinguishable from the democratic outlook of normal Americans. Generally speaking it is today not thought of as a church doctrine but as the assertion of certain general rights to be taken for granted: men have a *right* to liberty; they have a *right* to happiness; they have a *right* to fair trial. Some hold that men are born with these rights; others that God gives them to men. Few pause to ask who enforces the rights, and how, and whether rights that cannot be enforced are in fact inalienable.

Often, natural law is spoken of as that body of moral behavior practiced in the community by men of good will over a long period of years, so that it has come to be universally accepted as a broad canon of decencies on which most men agree. Again, where such generality is assumed, awkward questions are forgotten or overlooked. Does natural law exist in a civilization dominated by Communist dogma? If not, was it ended at a certain time and place, or does it still hover, as it were, "a brooding omnipresence in the sky"—to use Holmes's apt phrase—which will descend to earth when the time is ripe; or is there a natural law of Communism which has its own set of dogmatic absolutes? Such questions are by no means irrelevant, as the kind of natural law espoused by the Roman Catholic Church claims that its precepts are universal and eternal.

. . . . .

The concentrated criticism of Holmes began in 1941 when the Reverend Francis E. Lucey, S.J., a writer who theretofore had been, comparatively speaking, unknown, published an article in *Social Science* called "Jurisprudence and the Future Social Order." Other priests joined in the attack, chiefly in the legal periodicals of the Catholic law schools, but Father Lucey was in the front ranks, continually coming back to do battle, distinguished from his associates by his intemperate language, the increasing length of each article, and his admirable collection of Holmes's aphorisms, largely drawn from the letters, to prove his points. Father John C. Ford, S.J., in the same year addressed the annual convention of the Jesuit Philosophical Association on "The Fundamentals of Holmes' Juristic Philosophy." A month later the Reverend William J. Kenealy, S.J., Dean of the Boston College Law School, at the celebration of the Red Mass in that city, using for the title of his pronouncements "The Majesty of the Law," indicated his conviction that the alien philosophies of Kant, Hume, Herbert Spencer, John Stuart Mill, Hobbes, Marx, and now Holmes were "cutting away at the foundations of American jurisprudence," and might "topple the superstructure which we are proud and happy to call our American Way of Life." It is not inaccurate to suggest that Father Kenealy's exhortations were more rhetorical than lucid.

There were other, similar attacks, and a debate in the *American Bar Association Journal,* which stirred up a lively controversy among lawyers for a brief moment of time. Fred Rodell of the Yale Law School, and Mark Howe of Harvard, wrote law-review articles contrasting Holmes's views with those of the Jesuits, which drew blood from Father Lucey, for he rushed back to the attack—he did not think much of these two professors, though Rodell was "not quite as smooth and snide as Howe."

The charges against Holmes are about the same in all the articles and addresses: he was a skeptic and cynic who believed in no God and had no principles; he considered that law was nothing but the use of force, and that might makes right; he discarded all absolutes, including natural law, and defined truth as the vote of the majority; and he described morals as nothing but a curb on the normal human inclination to get your feet in the trough.

. . . . .

As I suggested, Holmes's skepticism was by no means complete, but was balanced and humanized by a sturdy belief in the things he cared about. He shared with other men of his time acceptance of the ordinary decencies—courage, abstinence, truth, a sane mind in a healthy body, honesty, and loyalty. These did not differ in any marked degree from those which these priests acknowledged. But Holmes would not call them eternal because he was a philosophic as well as a religious skeptic. His detractors could not concede that anyone who rejected God could be a good man.

Nor did Holmes hold that the essence of law was physical force, as Father Ford asserted, trying hard to understand

this terrifying unbeliever whom he could not help admiring; and Father Ford had no grounds for surmising that from this it followed that Holmes believed that might makes right. What Holmes did say—and repeated in various ways—was that law was a *statement of the circumstances in which the public force will be brought to bear upon men through the courts.* On reflection Father Ford might have accepted such a statement as a commonplace. When Holmes talked of law he always meant the same thing—the law that lawyers practice and judges declare, and from which human beings suffer; the law that permits a policeman to shoot an escaping felon, or a sheriff to manacle a kidnaper, or a judge to send a man to jail for refusing to testify. And in that sense law—what we call positive law—is based on force, and can hardly be said to exist unless it can be enforced. To Holmes law, like sovereignty, was a fact. The only external limit that he could see to the power of the lawmaker was the limit of power as a question of fact. This had nothing to do with the difficulty of finding out who the sovereign was, or the tacitly recognized *de facto* limits of the power of the most absolute sovereign (or state) that ever was. So when he talked of law he talked like a cynic. He didn't "care a damn if twenty professors" told him that a decision was not law if he knew that the courts would enforce it. When he spoke of the lawmaking power he meant concurrence of all the necessary organs of government in putting an enactment into execution.

Holmes was not talking about Father Ford's absolutes, floating somewhere as ideals in men's minds, essences of what law should be (but hardly ever is). So Holmes said—and Father Ford held up his hands—"Just so far as the aid of the public force is given a man, he has a legal right, and this right is the same whether his claim is founded in righteousness or iniquity." Is not this carefully exact? Holmes is not discussing the problem of what makes law, or inspires it, or influences its direction, or what it should be; he is telling us in hard, clear, definite language what it is: "Law being a practical thing, must found itself on actual forces."

Father Ford had been brought up, theologically speaking, on St. Thomas Aquinas and his doctrine that *all* law is based on natural law implanted by God in man. But he would not, I take it, have denied that force had its place in the enforcement of law, and that it must often be used to make law effective. Yet he would not admit that you could build law on the use of force to the exclusion of everything else, as he supposed Holmes did, an anti-Christian idea that seemed to dismiss morals from law, and narrow it to brute force. But Justice Holmes's observation about force was a description of what he saw happen. It was not an attempt to exhaust the definition of law or to reduce it to a single formula. No one who had read *The Common Law* with understanding, or studied Holmes's contribution to law over half a century, could possibly have made the foolish mistake of believing that Holmes meant to banish other conceptions of law by this particular criterion. To him law involved many other attributes—it was an expression of life, the formulation of community desires, the act of a legislature or the decree of a sovereign, the intuition or prejudice of a judge written into an opinion; but—and he thought it vitally important to keep repeating the idea in the striking form of an oversimplification—all law rested on the exercise of force for its fulfillment.

Father Ford, trembling a little as he tries to hold his spear in place, takes the next step: if law is based on force no law can be absolute, and what Holmes called rights are not fundamental or eternal, since they rest on the ephemeral and temporary quality of force.

By definition Holmes uses the word *right* in the narrow legal sense as something that can be enforced, not in the secondary and more ambiguous meaning of a desirable end, such as the pursuit of happiness, an activity to which men may believe they are entitled but which cannot be achieved through a court of law.

The children at Little Rock did not enjoy their right to go to a public school until United States troops saw to it that the right was enforced. When by statute the Nazi regime destroyed the right of the German-Jewish population to live where they pleased, to own their own property, to come and go freely, to marry Gentiles—in a word to enjoy the common decencies of tolerance and equality of living won for human beings over the long centuries— Jews no longer enjoyed *rights* in the Holmesian sense. That they existed undiminished in Father Ford's head (or heart), or in that distant Heaven where Jews take their place with Christians and Mohammedans, since natural law is universal; or in the mind of God, since natural law came from Him—assuming all these subjective absolutes of religion, which may be peculiarly important to those who have been deprived of the enforcement of their legal rights on earth, can it be doubted that Father Ford would have admitted that there is such a thing as an enforceable legal right? And the Justice would have answered that that was all he meant; and that those were the only kind of rights he was talking about. His own views were "simple and brutal" when he considered *legal* rights.

But Holmes knew that even though a sovereign does create legal rights, and makes you obey them, he is often hopelessly wrong morally. Holmes did not dismiss human aspirations, and remembered that they embodied principles that men had died for, and that it was well not to forget, the "right"—particularly for him—to think and talk freely. He believed in the articulation of these rights, but was not prepared to say that they were eternal. He lamented the tendency "toward underrating or forgetting the safeguards in bills of rights that had to be fought for in their day and that still are worth fighting for." What he understood by human rights was what a given crowd would fight for successfully. Old Louis Agassiz, he remembered, once said that in some part of Germany if you added a farthing to the price of a glass of beer there would be a revolution. If that was true, to have beer at the current price was one of the rights of man in that place.

Father Ford can have his absolute law, Holmes would say, if he keeps within his jurisdiction, the imagination of the faithful, and does not trespass on Caesar's sterner magistracy, where courts apply the rules that govern men. And that is what Holmes said in a dozen different ways, some of which Father Ford finds pretty hard to understand, as indeed they are.

Holmes's tight condensations—there is hardly ever an extra word to ease the understanding—do not tend to clarify his basic meaning. He liked to say that he wrote for the one man who did understand—but sometimes Holmes missed him.

. . . . .

Father Ford bravely tackles the Justice's famous statement in his article on *Natural Law,* which has proved the target for so many shafts: "But for legal purposes a right is only the hypostasis of a prophecy—the imagination of a substance supporting the fact that the public force will be brought to bear upon those who do things said to contravene it—just as we talk of the force of gravitation accounting for the conduct of bodies in space." Even Sir Frederick balked a bit at this—the word "hypostasis" was known to him only as a theological term—in what sense did Holmes use it? To start his definition of law, Holmes replied, he employed the word in the sense in which it is used by the modern lawyer, as a statement of the circumstances in which the public force would be brought to bear upon men through the courts: that is the prophecy in general terms. "So we prophesy that the earth and sun will act towards each other in a certain way. Then we pretend to account for that mode of action by the hypothetical cause, the force of gravitation, which is merely the hypostasis of the prophesied fact and an empty phrase. So we get up the empty substratum, a *right,* to pretend to account for the fact that the courts will act in a certain way." And this applied even to a right which Father Ford regards as absolute and God-given. Holmes added, almost as if he were trying to be doubly offensive: "I think our morally tinted words have caused a great deal of confused thinking." But Father Ford makes no comment, after quoting this passage, but merely adds that Pollock agreed with Holmes about *right,* an ambiguous word meaning an expectation that the court would assist you, in case of interference with certain of your *lawful* liberties, or that you could call on the court for redress of some form. Apparently Sir Frederick was highly respectable company!

What did *morally tinted* mean? Father Ford, pondering, and putting all these assertions together, concluded that Holmes divorced the ethical from the legal order. That is an accurate reflection; but the priest went on to add that Holmes denied *any* relation between law and morals. Apparently Father Ford had either not read Holmes or not understood what he was talking about. The Justice invariably assumed the relationship of morals and law, insisting, as I have noted, that the prevalent moral and political theories have had their part in determining the rules whereby men are governed. He did not wish his hearers to misinterpret what he had to say about force as the language of cynicism: "The law is the witness and the external deposit of our moral life. Its history is the history of the moral development of the race."

. . . . .

As a lawyer, Holmes used the word "theories"; Father Ford, a priest, spoke of "principles." Holmes, unlike Father Ford, never experienced an absolute. He called his preferences "prejudices" because as an historian he realized how the "prejudices which judges share with their fellow-men" had shaped the rules of law, and he had watched those of some of the other justices on the Court on which he sat prevent them from upholding laws which interfered with the dogma of laissez faire which they held sacred. Father Ford should have known what Holmes meant by *morally tinted,* for he quotes at length from Holmes's wonderful address, **"The Path of the Law,"** at the dedication of a new hall of the Boston University School of Law in 1897.

If you want to know the law, and nothing else, Holmes had said, you must look only for its material consequences, which you can predict, like a "bad man," who cares only for results, not like a good one, who finds his reasons for conduct "in the vaguer sanctions of his conscience." The law is full of phraseology drawn from morals, and talks about *rights* and *duties, malice, intent,* and *negligence*—and nothing is easier in legal reasoning than to take these words in their moral sense. So we speak of the rights of a man meaning to mark the limits of interference with individual freedom prescribed by conscience, or by our ideal. Yet many laws have been passed and enforced which go beyond the limit of interference, and are condemned by the most enlightened public opinion. Therefore nothing but confusion can result from assuming that the rights of man in a moral sense are equally rights in the sense of the Constitution and the law.

If the training of lawyers, Holmes believed, led them habitually to consider more definitely and explicitly the social advantages on which the rule they lay down must be justified, they sometimes would hesitate where now they are confident, and see that really they were taking sides upon debatable and often burning questions. And judges—"There is a tendency to think of judges," Holmes wrote Laski in 1926, "as if they were independent mouthpieces of the infinite, and not simply directors of a force that comes from the source that gives them their authority. I think our court has fallen into the error at times and it is that that I have aimed at when I have said that the Common Law is not a brooding omnipresence in the sky and that the U.S. is not subject to some mystic overlaw that it is bound to obey." To Holmes there was no such thing as *the* common law *in abstracto.*

And that is precisely how he thought of natural law—a mystic overlaw, not law in any true sense, theology or

morals if you like, but not law. The demand for the superlative that we find in all men was at the bottom of the philosopher's effort to prove that truth was absolute, and of the jurist's search for criteria of universal validity which he collects under the head of natural law. That is why the jurists who believed in natural law seemed to him to be "in that naive state of mind that accepts what has been familiar and accepted by them and their neighbors as something that must be accepted by all men everywhere." To a Jesuit priest, reared on natural law, Holmes's view that it was but a product of wishful thinking must have sounded blasphemous.

. . . . .

The underlying difference between the views of Justice Holmes and the Jesuits boils down to whether or not you believe in absolutes; or, more accurately put, whether you think they have an existence of their own, outside the mind of man. Apparently natural law, for instance, in addition to existing in the mind of the Creator, and in the mind of man when he exercised his reason in order to find it, was conceived as something with a separate being of its own, irrespective of divine or human recognition. Holmes had never experienced it, and, not believing in revelations which he had not shared, denied its external validity. The unwillingness to accept less than being on the ground floor with God did not impress him much except as a fact of psychology. The assumption of a knowledge of ultimate truth implied a kind of arrogance that he distrusted. Why should we not be humble? Why not admit that the first primordial wiggle came before our time?

By no means a humble man himself, Holmes experienced humility when he thought of the universe, of which he was so minute a part. His comments were most caustic when he was dealing with those who were sure that they had universal truth by the ears. "I think the proper attitude," he wrote to Pollock, "is that we know nothing of cosmic values and bow our heads—seeing reason enough for doing all we can and not demanding the plan of campaign of the General. . . . It's enough for me that this universe can produce intelligence and ideals." He could not go along, he said in another letter, with "some mystical works of men seeking to lift themselves by the slack of their own breeches, and demanding that the final compulsions under which we reason, love, etc., should be admitted as of cosmic validity. I stop short of that. All I mean by truth is the road I can't help travelling. What the worth of that *can't help* may be I have no means of knowing. Perhaps the universe, if there is one, has no truth outside the finiteness of man." This position is not an extreme one. It does not exclude another's experience of faith, but implies it is not his—Holmes knows his own, but would not force it on anyone else.

He thought clericism childish, and at times was a little disturbed at exhibitions of ecclesiastic power. But he had such a conviction that it was doomed that he did not care to hurry its fate; and, ad interim, it helped to keep order.

He also questioned the postulate of science that everything can be explained. He had a sense of the mystery of the universe, and thought it unlikely that we know anything about it or have faculties that fit us to do more than adjust ourselves to it and to live. He had faith in the prevalence of reason, but was aware how long reason may be kept under by what man wants to believe.

Such a point of view, it may be conceded, would not be popular among believers in the reality of eternal truth.

But all this is in the realm of speculation. The issue raised by the detractors of Holmes is sharper and more immediate than any found in the play of moral theorizing. Holmes never went out of his way to discuss natural law, except for the casual reference that I have described; or indeed, any other religion—systems, whether religious or philosophic, bored him. He had no particular objection to indulgence in their intricacies if they did not impinge on his own field of law. He did not agree with what Edmund Burke, whom he liked to quote, had said about law—that it sharpened the mind only to narrow it. To Holmes law was the reflection of man's life on earth; and, more particularly, the story of the experience of his own people, and was therefore worthy of the devotion of a lifetime. He had discovered that law was not the same as morals, which differed from creed to creed, and that it was highly dangerous to try to preserve it in the form of a moral absolute—for life kept changing and absolutes did not. He had seen men clothe their predilections in the generalities of ideals that had become standardized, and close their minds to an appropriate solution of the practical problem of decision that was before them.

. . . . .

That natural law is taught in Roman Catholic law schools as part of the education of a lawyer deflects him from the modern approach to law as a science, dragging theology back into law from which, as in the teaching of medicine and other professions, it had long since been banished, except in the Catholic schools. Only Catholic law schools teach that natural law has a higher and more august sanction than human law; that laws in contravention of natural law are invalid; and that any statute or decision conflicting with natural law is inherently vitiated. In other schools "law" is not taught as being eternal, and could not be, for the modern lawyer, pragmatic and scientific as far as possible in his approach, has learned to keep his law and religion apart. It is to this separation that the Catholic teachers object.

The Catholic doctrine—fundamentally inconsistent with separation of Church and State—goes much further than the concept that, in determining whether he should resist a particular law thought to be evil a man should bide by the dictates of his conscience, since it insists that he must obey the dictates of his Church, irrespective of the expressed will of his sovereign. To the Catholic, natural law is what the Church says it is.

This potential conflict is, however, more startling in theory than in practice, for a theorem of the Church holds that although the basic tenets of natural law never change, their application varies. Thus right to a fair trial is said to be basic, unchangeable, a law of God and of nature; but a particular application of this general right, such as the right to trial by a jury, is not a natural law right, and therefore not absolute, and may be given or withdrawn by the State. One is eternal, the other temporary. Since questions of law arise on specific issues, and not over the discussion of principles, there is in practice little conflict between natural law and the law of the sovereign.

But the effect of such a doctrine on the development of law is important. Even if now for practical purposes there is little conflict—although for hundreds of years the struggle for temporal power between Church and State was savage and continuous—the suggestion that there is a higher lawgiving power than the State postulates the theological approach. This way of looking at law is against everything that Holmes stood for.

. . . . .

Father Lucey, coming back to the attack, in an article which he called "Holmes—Liberal—Humanitarian—Believer in Democracy?" admitted that once upon a time he had been charmed by the Justice's style and the "end results of his opinions involving personal liberties," but later had an uneasy feeling that there was something wrong with his idol. For the next few years he read and reread everything that Holmes had written. And what did he find? "A philosophical skeleton of life and law, of man and morals that was horribly deformed."

This language, like Father Kenealy's, partakes of the rhetorical; but in spite of its ineptness we do get a sense that Father Lucey was upset. He insisted that skepticism, pragmatism, and evolution were the influences which inevitably led to Holmes's position. Holmes would not have liked to be called a pragmatist, for the word indicated a philosophy which he thought ridiculous, so that when Laski spoke of "the implicit pragmatism" of Holmes's attitude, the Justice answered that *the judging of law by its efforts and results* did not have to wait for William James or Roscoe Pound for its existence.

But skepticism and pragmatism were characteristic of the age in which the father had been reared, and against which his Church, knowing the disastrous fashion in which indulgence in such heresies endangered her own authority, had continually thundered. Therefore to find these influences displayed by still another great man could hardly account for the father's choler. I suspect that what really shocked the priest was Holmes's language rather than his views. As the old song goes, It wasn't so much as what he said as the orful way he said it! Father Lucey may have remembered, although he did not quote it, what Holmes said about the martyr—that he was *a pigheaded adherent of an inadequate idea.*

Holmes opened himself widely to criticism. In spite of the fact that he distrusted sweeping statements, and all his life resisted their pressure, he could, for the sake of a telling *bon mot* or neat aphorism, let out the most absurd generalities, worded as if they were self-evident truths, as when he said to Laski that "all law means I will kill you if necessary to make you conform to my requirements." Sometimes he goes on to explain what he means—law, he adds here, is what the sovereign orders: "If in fact Catholics or atheists are proscribed and the screws put on, it seems to me idle to say that it is not law because by a theory that you and I hold . . . it ought not to be." He keeps coming back to the idea that men either agreed or fought: "When men differ in taste as to the kind of world they want the only thing to do is to go to work killing."

It was all right if you did not take Holmes literally, did not go along with the inclusive sweep of his oversimplifications. His theory that law was nothing more than the prophecy of what the judge would hold, was useful for the counseling lawyer—for the solicitor—but not for the trial lawyer bent on persuading the court, the barrister: law is of course something more than prophecy.

In his article on natural law Holmes remarked that he used to say, when he was young, *that truth was the majority vote of that nation that could lick all others.* Father Lucey comments eloquently: "This of course was Hitler's test . . . the theme song of the Storm Troops as they made their pragmatic functional approach to Poland, Czechoslovakia, Norway, Holland, Belgium, and France." But the father did not mention that Holmes went on to explain the sense in which he had made the remark: "Certainly we may expect that the received opinion about the present war [the First World War] will depend a good deal upon which side wins (I hope with all my soul it will be mine), and I think that the statement was correct in so far as it implied that our test of truth is a reference to either a present or an imagined future majority in favor of our view." This was not unlike Mr. Dooley's line about the Supreme Court's following the elections—neither was the whole truth and nothing but the truth, but each had a core of meaning.

Holmes had written Pollock that when one thinks coldly he could see no reason for attributing to man a significance different *in kind* (he did not say in degree) from that which belongs to a baboon or to a grain of sand. Father Lucey seized on the phrase but lost its point: "Stripped of a soul and innate dignity," he lamented, "man is only as significant as a baboon or grain of sand." What Holmes meant was that since the universe was without guidance, there was no one to assert differences or draw comparisons. Holmes would not have admitted that there was no difference between himself and Father Lucey, or between Father Lucey and a baboon. He meant only that, cosmically speaking, the universe did not make the distinction. Father Lucey, one would have thought, would have hesitated to speak about what went on inside the complex and subtle mind which he called Holmes's world, and to say that for Holmes there were no values inside the law or outside it. Holmes's values were as precious to him as Father Lucey's; but no man as dog-matic as Father Lucey could ever admit that a freethinker could have a creed that was noble.

Twenty years later Holmes wrote along similar lines to Pollock that a platitude had come home to him with quasi-religious force. He had been repining at the thought of his slow progress—how few ideas he had or had picked up—when it occurred to him to think of the total of life, and how the greater part was wholly absorbed in living and continuing life—victuals, procreation, rest, and eternal terror. Why not accept the common lot? An adequate vitality would say: "God—what a good sleep I've had." "My eye, that was a dinner." "Now for a rattling walk." Functioning is all there is—only, our keenest pleasure is what we call the higher sort. "I wonder," he finished, "if cosmically an idea is any more important than the bowels." The bowels! No wonder Father Lucey called Holmes "an animal man"—a designation which would have mightily pleased our Judge—and added that Holmes's concept of democracy embodied "a strong jungle odor."

One accusation Father Lucey made that might have angered Holmes—a patently unfair charge—was that if "the law on the books clashed with Holmes's evolutionary theory Holmes could stretch the law and try to work off his theory." Holmes spent his life keeping his own preferences and theories out of his opinions. It was a small and mean observation, and Father Lucey made no attempt to support it by citing any decision. Now and then the father becomes personal, sneering that Holmes spent his spare time with youngsters "whom he felt were the smart minds of their generation and the elite of the future." The priest must have had some individuals in mind, although he does not name them—Owen Wister, Justice Frankfurter, Walter Lippmann, Lord Eustace Percy?—they came to be numbered among the elite. Finally Father Lucey whips himself into a mild canonical frenzy, pelting "the Yankee from Olympus" (to use the father's words) with soft absolutes—*skepticism, evolutionism, positivism, and pragmatism*—that reduce men to "a pestilence-driven multitude, the prey of a blind evolutionary climate!"

This is no inconsequential battle, he cries, not only for Americans, but for the entire world. If universal agnosticism prevail it will mean the end of Democracy, because there can be no Democracy without protection of absolute natural rights. . . . Holmesian philosophy was infiltrating the public schools. Had not J. Edgar Hoover testified before the Kefauver Committee that we are in a moral depression, and added, as one of the reasons, that the name of God could not be mentioned in many of our schools? The Holmesian philosophy had reached the very summit—we find "the Chief Justice of the United States [Fred M. Vinson] proclaiming in an official document [Father Lucey means an opinion]: *Nothing is more certain in modern society than the principle that there are no absolutes . . . all concepts are relative.*" But the father does not believe that the Chief Justice really realized the implications to which he was committing himself.

. . . . .

At times Father Lucey seems to be angry with what eludes him. But the difference between the two men is not principally a question of misunderstanding. It comes down to a determination of the *sources* of general principles. The Catholics say that they come from God, and have a validity entirely independent of their human acceptance. For Justice Holmes they are derived from the consensus of the community embodied in the long tradition of the law, of the dominant beliefs of the culture of which he felt himself a part, and of the Constitutional provisions expressing that culture.

Put simply, and without the paradoxes and teasing oversimplifications, Holmes's beliefs are neither radical—for our day and age—nor disturbing: the belief that men make their own laws; that these laws do not flow from some mysterious omnipresence in the sky, and that judges are not independent mouthpieces of the infinite; that since morality is human in its origin and its end, men should be permitted to discover what is for them desirable and how it should be achieved, and allowed to indulge in their own legislative experiments to better their lot—they are not fools for doing what they want to do; that the justification of any rule of law is that it helps to bring about a desired social end; that law must change to follow the needs of man; that all doctrine must be adjusted to these needs; that the law when ascertained should be obeyed, but will not be ascertained by reference to vague generalities, or by fumbling over the familiar; and finally that we cannot think beyond the reach in time of our own society, so that the claim of a special code to respect is not that it represents first principles but simply that it exists and is the one to which we have become accustomed.

. . . . .

There can never be reconciliation between the dogmatic mind and the free mind. In spite of efforts to bridge the gap between those who cherish some Being outside their own world because they cannot bear the terror of standing alone, and men like Holmes who find their strength and faith within themselves, the chasm remains, and it is idle to deny its depth. The fanatic believer, who cannot view those who do not agree with him except as evil men, must never be tolerant, for tolerance might open the gates of understanding.

Edmund Wilson (essay date 1962)

SOURCE: "Justice Oliver Wendell Holmes," in *Patriotic Gore: Studies in the Literature of the American Civil War*, 1962. Reprint by Northeastern University Press, 1984, pp. 743-96.

[*In the following essay, Wilson provides a biographical sketch of Holmes.*]

With the Oliver Wendell Holmeses, father and son, the theology of Calvinism has faded, but its habits of mind persist. The father of Dr. Holmes was Abiel Holmes, a Connecticut preacher, who came to occupy in Cambridge, Massachusetts, the pulpit of the First Congregational Church. He had been educated at the Yale Divinity School, which at that time stood somewhat to the left of the fundamentalist Princeton Theological Seminary but still kept closer to Calvinist orthodoxy than the Harvard Divinity School, already infected in the twenties with the fashionable Unitarianism. Abiel Holmes was himself not severe in the matter of doctrine: he appears in the novels of his son in the characters of the Congregational ministers who are surreptitiously humanizing their creed. But he found himself, in his Cambridge church, between a new liberalizing party and the still powerful old orthodox Calvinists. Under pressure of an orthodox newspaper and especially, among the clergy, of Lyman Beecher, the father of Harriet Beecher Stowe, he abandoned the now common practice of exchanging Sunday pulpits with other Congregationalist ministers, regardless of their theological views. But his parish was attainted with liberalism and did not care to have Dr. Beecher, with whom Holmes had been led to exchange, assailing them from the pulpit with the menace that if they should yield to the Unitarian heresy, a "moral desolation" would "sweep over the land." Dr. Holmes in his novels made his kindly old ministers escape from the pressures of orthodoxy, but the contrary had been true in the case of his father, who barred liberal preachers from his pulpit and was forced to resign by his congregation and to set up a Second Congregational Church.

The effect of this on Abiel's son, at that time a student at Harvard, was to stir in him a strong opposition to the traditional Puritan theology, which he came to feel was wholly monstrous and a hindrance to human progress. He said that his whole conception of the place of man in the universe had been upset at some point in his childhood by seeing the planet Venus through a telescope. Through the study and practice of medicine, he tried to substitute the discipline of science for the discipline of the old morality. I have spoken of his *One-Hoss Shay* as a parable of the break-up of Calvinism; and his novels are intended to show that destructive or peculiar tendencies on the part of an individual are due not to Original Sin but to "prenatal influence" (at that time taken seriously even by the medical profession), special heredity or early trauma. The first of these novels, *Elsie Venner,* published in 1861, so outraged the Protestant clergy that one religious paper as far away as Chicago made a point of denouncing each instalment as the story came out in the *Atlantic Monthly.* Yet Holmes himself, as he tells us, was never to succeed completely in freeing himself from the Calvinist inculcations: he could never, to the end of his life, allow himself to read novels till sundown on the Sabbath, and there always went on in his mind a dialogue between the inherited doctrine and the new scientific point of view.

The young Wendell, who could start from the point to which his father had succeeded in advancing, was not troubled by these hauntings from the past and put the old

New England God behind him—though, as we shall see, in his temperament and his type of mind, he was much closer to the Puritan breed than his father. He had read Herbert Spencer at Harvard and had incurred a rebuke from the President for answering back a professor who was teaching a course on the Evidences of Religion. But during his service in the Civil War, he was subjected to a desperate ordeal, which, instead of having the effect, as such ordeals sometimes do, of impelling him to turn to God, caused him definitely to dismiss this Deity. He had enlisted when he was only just twenty, in April, 1861, and he had been badly wounded in the chest at the Battle of Ball's Bluff in October. "I thought I was a gone coon," he wrote to Frederick Pollock long afterwards, and he was actually not expected to live. "I happened to have a bottle of laudanum in my pocket and resolved if the anguish became unbearable to do the needful. A doctor (I suppose) removed the bottle and in the morning I resolved to live." But in the meantime the crisis had occurred. Here is his own account of it, written down almost immediately afterwards, an effort at self-observation—very remarkable on the part of so young a man—which shows his courage and the strength of his intellect:

> Much more vivid [than his recollection of what was actually happening] is my memory of my thoughts and state of mind for though I may have been light-headed my reason was working—even if through a cloud. Of course when I thought I was dying the reflection that the majority vote of the civilized world declared that with my opinions I was *en route* for Hell came up with painful distinctness—Perhaps the first impulse was tremulous—but then I said—by Jove, I die like a soldier anyhow—I was shot in the breast doing my duty up to the hub—afraid? No, I am proud—then I thought I couldn't be guilty of a deathbed recantation—father and I had talked of that and were agreed that it generally meant nothing but a cowardly giving way to fear—Besides, thought I, can I recant if I want to, has the approach of death changed my beliefs much? & to this I answered—No—Then came in my Philosophy—I am to take a leap in the dark—but now as ever I believe that whatever shall happen is best—for it is in accordance with a general law—and *good & universal* (or *general law*) are synonymous terms in the universe—(I can now add that our phrase *good* only means certain general truths seen through the heart & will instead of being merely contemplated intellectually—I doubt if the intellect accepts or recognizes that classification of good and bad). Would the complex forces which made a still more complex unit in *Me* resolve themselves back into simpler forms or would my angel be still winging his way onward when eternities had passed? I could not tell—But all was doubtless well—and so with a 'God forgive me if I'm wrong' I slept—But while I was debating with myself Harry Sturgis bulged upon the scene—I don't remember what I said—I know what I wanted—it was the cool opinion of an outsider—a looker-on—as a *point d'appui* for resistance or a πoυ στω from which to spring aloft, as the case might be; at any rate a foreign substance round which

my thoughts could crystallize—Sturge I hear says I was very profane, to this effect—"Well Harry I'm dying but I'll be G. d'd if I know where I'm going"—But I doubt it although a little later I swore frightfully—to the great horror of John O'S. who tried to stop me thinking I was booking myself for Hell rapidly. Sturge thereat with about his usual tact, begun "Why—Homey—you believe in Christ, don't you" etc. with a brief exposition of doctrine argumentatively set forth—I gave him my love for Pen whom I'd not yet seen, & the same message home which I subsequently gave the Fire Zouave Surgeon and Sturge departed.

He had denied God and still survived, and that was the end of God in the cosmogony of Oliver Wendell Holmes, who was never again tempted to believe and who lived to be over ninety.

The young Holmes's experience of the Civil War, besides settling for him the problem of faith, also cured him, and cured him for life, of apocalyptic social illusions. Perhaps no one had enlisted at the beginning of the war with a more devoted ardor than Holmes. "It is almost impossible here," says Higginson in his *Cheerful Yesterdays,* "to reproduce the emotions of that period of early war enlistments. . . . To call it a sense of novelty was nothing; it was as if one had learned to swim in air, and were striking out for some new planet. All the methods, standards, habits, and aims of ordinary life were reversed, and the intrinsic and traditional charm of the soldier's life was mingled in my own case with the firm faith that the death-knell of slavery itself was being sounded." The memory of that early exaltation was to remain with Holmes all his life. He had been almost as much carried away by the novels of Walter Scott as any of his Southern contemporaries, and, as late as 1911 we find him writing to the Baroness Moncheur, wife of the Belgian ambassador: "Just now I am having one of my periodic wallows in Scott. He also is dear to most people, I suppose—but the old order in which the sword and the gentleman were beliefs, is near enough to me to make this their last voice enchanting in spite of the common sense of commerce. The same belief was what gave interest to the South, but they paid for it by their ignorance of all the ideas that make life worth living to us. But when you see it in costume, with people who could not have heard of evolution, belated but in its last and therefore articulate moment, Oh what a delight it is." This spirit of romantic chivalry he brought to the Abolitionist cause, by which he afterwards said he was "moved . . . so deeply that a Negro minstrel show shocked me and the morality of *Pickwick* seemed to me painfully blunt," and he had acted as a bodyguard to Wendell Phillips when there was a threat of his being mobbed at an anti-slavery meeting. He had left college in his senior year and forfeited graduation in order at once to enlist.

He thus accepted the war as a crusade, and, even in the April of 1864, when he had been through some of the worst of the fighting, he forced himself to continue to do so. "I have long wanted to know more of Joinville's

Chronicle than I did," he writes to Charles Eliot Norton apropos of an article of his, "but the story seems to come up most opportunely now when we need all the examples of chivalry to help us bind our rebellious desires to steadfastness in the Christian Crusade of the 19th century. If one didn't believe that this was such a crusade, in the cause of the whole civilized world, it would be hard indeed to keep the hand to the sword; and one who is rather compelled unwillingly to the work by abstract conviction than borne along on the flood of some passionate enthusiasm, must feel his ardor rekindled by stories like this."

For this cause and in this crusade, the young Oliver Wendell Holmes, as we have already seen, had faced death at the very beginning: "It is curious," he wrote in the account of his wounding from which I have already quoted, "how rapidly the mind adjusts itself under some circumstances to entirely new relations—I thought for a while that I was dying, and it seemed the most natural thing in the world—the moment the hope of life returned it seemed as abhorrent to nature as ever that I should die." He went home on leave to recover, but returned to his regiment the following March (in the second year of the war). He was wounded again at Antietam in September: the bullet went through his neck and just missed his windpipe and jugular vein. He was shipped home again for six weeks; then, in the middle of November, was ordered back. He had a moment of extreme discouragement. From Virginia, three days later, he writes: " . . . with the crack brained Dreher & obstinate ignoramus Shepherd as act'g Col & Lt. Col. the Regt is going to H——L as fast as ever it can or at least no thanks to them if it isn't—I wouldn't trust it under them for a brass tuppence in a fight—They'd send it to the devil quicker even than Gen. Sumner and I've pretty much made up my mind that the South have achieved their independence & I am almost ready to hope spring will see an end—I prefer intervention to save our credit but believe me, we never shall lick 'em.—The Army is tired with its hard [work?], and its terrible experience & still more with its mismanagement & I think before long the majority will say that we are vainly working to effect what never happens—the subjugation (for that is it) of a great civilized nation. We shan't do it—at least the Army can't—" In December he writes to his father: " . . . —I never I believe have shown, as you seemed to hint, any wavering in my belief in the right of our cause—it is my disbelief in our success by arms in wh. I differ from you . . . —I think in that matter I have better chances of judging than you—and I believe I represent the conviction of the army—& not the least of the most intelligent part of it—The successes of wh. you spoke were to be anticipated as necessary if we entered into the struggle—But I see no farther progress—I don't think either of you realize the unity or the determination of the South. I think you are hopeful because (excuse me) you are ignorant. But if it is true that we represent civilization wh. is in its nature, as well as slavery, diffusive & aggressive, and if civ. & progress are the better things why they will conquer in the long run, we may be sure, and will stand a better chance in their proper province—peace—than in war, the brother of slavery—brother—it is slavery's parent, child and sustainer at once—At any rate dear Father don't because I say these things imply or think that I am the meaner for saying them—I am, to be sure, heartily tired and half worn out body and mind by this life, but I believe I am as ready as ever to do my duty—" He had dysentery that winter and was wounded in the heel at Fredericksburg on May 1 of the following year.

The young soldier now spent ten months at home; but he returned to the army again in January, 1864. He had become a lieutenant-colonel and was made aide-de-camp to Major General Horatio Wright, who was stationed above the Rapidan. In Wright's corps there were only the remnants of Holmes's Massachusetts Twentieth Regiment. The friends with whom he had graduated from Harvard, the officers he had fought beside, were mostly dead. Some thought that he himself was not fit to serve; but he went through the terrible battles of the Wilderness: Spottsylvania, North Anna, Cold Harbor. In May, he performed an exploit of which he was rather proud. He describes it as follows in a letter to his parents:

> The afternoon of the 29th I had my narrowest escape—Dispatch to carry—important—don't spare y'r horse—gallop—1 mile—small boy (one well known as Col. Upton's scout) retreating at a run—reports fired at 2 reb. cav^y—looked round for forces—one straggler (infty) one (unarmed) man on mule, one sick officer—& boy—I spy 4 of our cav^y foraging dismiss former forces & order them with me—trot—when boy was shot at gallop—bend in road—woods cease—bang—bang—whiz—whiz—about 20 reb^s in line—"Halt. Surrender" I pulled up & sung out "friends" deceived by number and darkness of their clothes—They keep on shooting then I saw & put in licks for straight ahead—Anon a fellow comes riding down the road—I think I'll gobble him—he to me "Halt Surrender" I see others on R. of road—he is unslinging his carbine as I get to him, I put my pistol to his breast & pull—enclosed cap snaps—then I run the gauntlet—bang—whiz—Halt—Surrender lying along the neck of my horse—Got my dispatch through & return in triumph to find myself given over for lost—

But in spite of a certain exuberance here, we have come a long way from the boyish exhibitionism of the days just before Ball's Bluff. His diaries and letters, both, become more and more confused and disjointed. The action is moving so fast that we hardly know where we are: yells and firing, shells bursting, brains spattering. The dead are piled in trenches at the edge of the wood, and the trees have been shot to splinters.

> Before you get this, he writes to his parents on May 16, 1864, you will know how immense the butchers bill has been—And the labor has been incessant—I have not been & am not likely to be in the mood for writing details. I have kept brief notes in my diary wh. I hope you may see some day—Enough, that these nearly two weeks have contained all of fatigue & horror that war can

furnish—The advantage has been on our side but nothing decisive has occurred & the enemy is in front of us strongly intrenched—I doubt if the decisive battle is to be fought between here and Richmond—nearly every Regimental off—I knew or cared for is dead or wounded—

I have made up my mind to stay on the staff if possible till the end of the campaign & then if I am alive, I shall resign—I have felt for sometime that I didn't any longer believe in this being a duty & so I mean to leave at the end of the campaign as I said if I'm not killed before.

He was later annoyed with his father—the natural annoyance of the man in the field with the immoderate belligerence of the people at home—for misunderstanding this letter. He had long ago, however, grown used to the slaughter. "It's odd," he had written fifteen months before, "how indifferent one gets to the sight of death—perhaps, because one gets aristocratic and don't value much a common life. Then they are apt to be so dirty it seems natural—'Dust to Dust'—I would do anything that lay in my power but it doesn't much affect my feelings." But he has just been through much of the worst of the war. He has constantly expected to be killed, and we gather that he wrote notes to his parents before he went into battle, and no doubt, as many soldiers at Cold Harbor did, pinned them onto his clothes. He seems to have destroyed them later when he was going over these papers. But in the meantime, he writes as follows: "rec^d y'r letters of 21d 22d the latter fr. dad, stupid—I wish you'd take the trouble to read my letters before answering—I am sure I cannot have conveyed the idea, rightfully, that I intended resigning before the campaign was over (i.e. next winter just near the end of my term of service)—then I probably shall for reasons satisfactory to myself—I must say I dislike such a misunderstanding, so discreditable to my feeling of soldierly honor, when I don't believe there was a necessity for it—I shall stay on the staff and wish you'd notify the Governor to commission new field officers to the 20th I waive promotion—I am convinced from my late experience that if I can stand the wear and tear (body & mind) of regimental duty that it is a greater strain on both than I am called on to endure—If I am satisfied I don't really see that anyone else has a call to be otherwise—I talked with Hayward the mentor of the Regt & told him my views on the matter—I am not the same man (may not have quite the same ideas) & certainly am not so elastic as I was and I *will not acknowledge the same claims upon me under those circumstances* that existed formerly—a day & a half have passed since I wrote last word—it is quarter to 12 between May 31 & June 1 I have just been riding through black woods after some H^{d}Qrs—and we are going to have another of those killing night marches as soon as we can start out of a country worse than the wilderness if possible—I have hardly known what a good night's sleep was since the campaign opened—constantly having, as tonight, to be up all night—" "I started in this thing a boy," he later—in June—wrote his parents. "I am now a man and I have been coming to the conclusion for the last

six months that my duty has changed." In July he was mustered out: his three years' enlistment was over.

The conclusions to which Holmes had been brought under pressure of his service in the Civil War were to effect in fundamental ways the whole of his subsequent thinking. But his relation to the war was peculiar. He did not like to refight its battles; he did not care to read about it. Over and over to his correspondents, he reiterates this reluctance to revert to the years of the war, making exceptions only for Lord Charnwood's *Lincoln* and for John S. Mosby's memoirs, which had been sent him by "old Mosby," as he calls him, "the famous guerilla man on the Southern side." He even extends this disinclination to Thucydides, of which, when he gets around to it at the age of eighty-three, he writes to Sir Frederick Pollock: "It isn't the kind of thing I like to read—just as I hate to read of our Civil War." Nor is he concerned with the consequences of the war. By that summer of 1864, he had had quite enough of the army and was eager to embark on a learned career. He started in at Harvard Law School that autumn and graduated in 1866. By this time Lincoln was dead, and there had died with him any possibility of a clear and decent policy toward the South. The struggle had commenced in Congress which was to culminate in the attempt on the part of the Radical Republicans to drive President Andrew Johnson from office. During the years when Holmes was first practising law in Boston and editing the *American Law Review,* the exposures of the squalid scandals of the Grant administrations were being one after another exposed in the papers. But Holmes, who was later deliberately to make a practice of not reading the newspapers, seems already to have adopted the policy of dissociating himself from current events. An account of the impeachment of Andrew Johnson confines itself, says his biographer, Mr. Mark De Wolfe Howe, to the purely legal aspects of the trial without giving any intimation of approval or disapproval. Holmes was solely intent on his own success, a success for which he was quite prepared to pay any cost in effort it demanded.

The young Holmes had brought out of the war a tough character, purposive, disciplined and not a little hard, a clearly defined personality, of which his humor and affable manners, his air of being a man of the world and the ready susceptibility to feminine attraction which he sometimes a little paraded, ["Oh, to be eighty again!" he is said to have exclaimed at ninety when passing a pretty woman on the street.] could never quite embellish the bleakness. His concentration on his work, his grim industry, were astonishing to those who knew him at the time when his career was still to make. It was said of him by one friend that he knew more law than anybody else in Boston and by another that he, the friend, had "never known of anyone in the law who studied anything as hard as Wendell." He had been worried at first by a feeling that this profession was unrewarding and sterile. Like his father, he had always had a strong taste for literature and had even once thought of becoming a poet. A sonnet that he wrote in the army has a throb of the emotional power of which I have spoken above as redeeming in that period the verse of the amateur in contrast to the rhymed editorial. He was to speak of his early forebodings in regard to the career he had chosen in an address to a college audience in 1897: "There were few," he says, "of the charts and lights for which one longed when I began. One found oneself plunged in a thick fog of details—in a black and frozen night, in which were no flowers, no spring, no easy joys. Voices of authority warned that in the crush of that ice any craft might sink. One heard Burke saying that law sharpens the mind by narrowing it. One heard in Thackeray of a lawyer bending all the powers of a great mind to a mean profession. One saw that artists and poets shrank from it as from an alien world. One doubted oneself how it could be worthy of the interest of an intelligent mind. And yet one said to oneself, law is human—it is a part of man, and of one world with all the rest." And working hard and working uphill, stubborn tension of the will and the intellect, were natural, even necessary, for Holmes; they were a part of his Puritan heritage. He produced his great book *The Common Law*—in 1880, when he was thirty-nine—by dint of dogged application in the evenings. "I can assure you," he wrote his friend Pollock, "it takes courage and perseverance to keep at a task which has to be performed at night and after making one's living by day." He told a friend that he hoped by this book to supersede Blackstone and Kent and that he aimed to become, first, Chief Justice of the Supreme Court of Massachusetts, then Justice of the Supreme Court of the United States.

This ambition and his relentless pursuit of it were dismaying to some of his friends. A man who knew him well, James Bradley Thayer, a partner in the law firm for which Holmes first worked, said of him that, in spite of his "attractive qualities and solid merits," he was "wanting sadly in the noblest region of human character,—selfish, vain, thoughtless of others;" and one of his ex-secretaries, not himself a New Englander, once said to me that Holmes had a streak of "the mean Yankee."

His relations with William and Henry James are, in this connection, particularly significant. Holmes and William, as young men, were extremely close. Holmes's mind was fundamentally philosophical, rather than either legal or literary, and they had discussed the great problems together; but Holmes, in his later years, when, in spite of his professions of skepticism, his negative convictions had become quite rigid, felt that James had gone rather soft, that he was giving in to religion and leaving a loophole for the supernatural. Their sympathies became more and more imperfect, and William James, in his letters to Henry, makes his own feelings almost ferociously clear: "The more I live in the world," he wrote in 1869, "the more the cold-blooded, conscious egotism and conceit of people afflict me. . . . All the noble qualities of Wendell Holmes, for instance, are poisoned by them, and friendly as I want to be towards him, as yet the good he has done me is more in presenting me something to kick away from or react against than to follow and embrace." And years later (1876), when he has been to visit the Holmeses at Mattapoisett, he writes Henry that Wendell

"is a powerful battery, formed like a planing machine to gouge a deep self-beneficial groove through life; and his virtues and his faults," James adds, "were thrown into singular relief by the lone-someness of the shore, which as it makes every object, rock or shrub, stand out so vividly, seemed also to put him and his wife under a sort of lens for you. . . ."

In the case of Henry James, I have been told on good authority that when Holmes went to see him on his visits to England, he was in the habit rather brutally of baiting him on account of his expatriation, as if he were shrinking from the dust and heat of life in his native country; and it is evident from James's correspondence with Holmes that when the former revisited the United States in 1910-11, the latter was not quite sure that the former would want to see him. The intimation of this in a letter brought out all that was most feminine in Henry James, and one is reminded of James's story *Poor Richard,* published forty-four years before, and evidently inspired by the holiday that he and Holmes and another ex-soldier had spent in North Conway, New Hampshire, with James's cousin Minnie Temple. "I ask myself frankly today, dear Wendell,—or rather, still more frankly, ask *you*—why you should 'feel a doubt' as to whether I should care to see you again and what ground I ever for a moment gave you for the supposition that the 'difference in the sphere of our dominant interests' might have made 'a gulf that we cannot cross.' As I look back at any moment of our contact—which began so long ago—I find myself crossing and crossing with a devotedness that took no smallest account of gulfs, or, more truly, hovering and circling and sitting on your side of the chasm altogether (if chasm there were!)—with a complete suspension, as far as you were concerned, of the question of any other side. Such was my pleasure and my affection and my homage—and when and where in the world did you ever see any symptom of anything else?" But Henry James, too, had his reservations. When Holmes had sent him a Memorial Day address delivered at Harvard in 1895, he wrote William: "It must have been rarely beautiful as delivered. It is ever so fine to read, but with the always strange something unreal or meager his things have for me—unreal in connection with his own remainder, as it were, and not *wholly* artful in expression. But they are 'very unique'—and I shall write to him in a high key about this one."

This address—*The Soldier's Faith*—illustrates in a striking way the paradox of Holmes's attitude toward the Civil War. Though he did not want to hear about it, though he seems to have felt little interest in it as an episode in American history, he had it with him, nevertheless, all his life. That he has managed to survive his regiment has become for him a source of pride, and in writing to correspondents, even to those whom he does not know well and even as late as 1927, he rarely fails to signalize the dates of the Battles of Ball's Bluff and Antietam, at both of which he had been wounded, by some such note as "31 years and one day after Antietam," "Antietam was 65 years ago yesterday," "We are celebrating Antietam, where if a bullet had gone one eighth of an inch differently the chances are that I should not be writing to you." It is as if he were preening on paper his formidable military mustaches, for the trimming of which, he mentions to Pollock, he depends upon a favorite Washington barber. (John De Forest wore a similar pair, and Ambrose Bierce's, although not of the handlebar type, had also the military bristle. Neither of these, however, was at all on the scale of Holmes's.) "It may well be," says Mr. Howe, "that of the two wars, the war in fact and the war in retrospect, it was the latter which was dominantly formative of [Holmes's] philosophy." He seems now to have completely lost sight of the angry young man who had once rebelled against the butcheries of Cold Harbor and the Wilderness. He comes finally to insist on the dignity of war as an exercise in personal virtue. "I do not know what is true," he wrote in *The Soldier's Faith.* "I do not know the meaning of the universe. But in the midst of doubt, in the collapse of creeds, there is one thing I do not doubt, that no man who lives in the same world with most of us can doubt, and that is that the faith is true and adorable which leads a soldier to throw away his life in obedience to a blindly accepted duty, in a cause which he little understands, in a plan of campaign of which he has no notion, under tactics of which he does not see the use."

He seems now to approve of all wars—at least those in which the English-speaking peoples take part. At the time of our war with Spain, he writes Pollock that the sound of a military band recalls to him "old days": "It gives one a certain ache. It always seems to me that if one's body moved parallel to one's soul, one would mind campaigning less as an elderly man than as a young man"; and he "confesses to pleasure" in hearing, on the part of his friend Brooks Adams, "some rattling jingo talk after the self-righteous and preaching discourse, which has prevailed to some extent at Harvard College and elsewhere." Writing to Pollock when the Boer War is going on, he wishes the British "a speedy success"; and writing to Harold Laski in 1916, he assures him of the ancient Romans that, "It did those chaps a lot of good to live expecting some day to die by the sword." When Pollock, after World War I, visiting France in 1928, writes Holmes of his indignation at the idea of "preaching to the French" that they ought to forget what the Germans have done to them, he replies, "I agree with your condemnation of armchair pacifists on the general ground that until the world has got farther along war not only is not absurd but is inevitable and rational—although of course I would make great sacrifices to avoid one." A saying of Rufus Choate's about John Quincy Adams that the latter "had the instinct for the jugular"—Holmes's own having been barely missed when he was shot through the neck at Antietam—was to become one of his favorite phrases.

These evidences of abiding pugnacity, when piled up as I have done with them above, may give the impression that Holmes was a tiresome old professional veteran, always ready to rattle his saber; but actually he was much too well-bred and much too serious-minded ever to let

himself become boring or ridiculous. With his essentially philosophic mind, which was speculative but also very rigorous, he must account for the war and his part in it in terms of a general philosophy, and it is here that his honesty as a thinker is to be seen at its most impressive. There is no cant about the war in Holmes; for a Northerner of his generation, he permits himself a minimum indulgence in conventional special pleading and obscuration of actuality by myth. It is true that although at one point in the war he had come to believe that the Union was aiming at "the subjugation . . . of a great civilized nation," he was to become, when the war was over, distinctly contemptuous of the Southerners and to write to Senator Albert J. Beveridge: "I hope that time will explode the humbug of the Southern Gentleman in your mind—not that there weren't a few—and not that their comparatively primitive intellectual condition didn't sometimes give a sort of religious purity of type, rarer in the more civilized and therefore more sceptical northerner. But the southern gentlemen generally were an arrogant crew who knew nothing of the ideas that make the life of the few thousands that may be called civilized." Elsewhere he goes even further and declares that he has never known a Southerner whom he considered to be a gentleman. But he always accepts realistically and indeed makes the basis of his system—legal as well as historical, since law, in Holmes's conception, is always molded by history—the action of the Union and its consequences.

He has repudiated the gospel of the militant God; he thinks that God has had nothing to do with it. The New England theocracy is gone forever. "I can't help an occasional semi-shudder," he says in a letter to Laski of May 8, 1918, "as I remember that millions of intelligent men think that I am barred from the face of God unless I change. But how can one pretend to believe what seems to him childish and devoid alike of historical and rational foundations? I suppose such thoughts would be as likely to occur to you about Valhalla or the Mahometan hell as about this. Felix [Frankfurter] said so himself the other night—but I was brought up in Boston—and though I didn't get Hell talk from my parents it was in the air. Oh—the *ennui* of those Sunday morning church bells, and hymn tunes, and the sound of the citizen's feet on the pavement—not heard on other days. I hardly have recovered from it now. I am glad to remember that when I was dying after Ball's Bluff I remembered my father's saying that death-bed repentances generally meant only that the man was scared and reflected that if I wanted to I couldn't, because I still thought the same."

That Holmes had begun to think early about the problem of moral relativity and actually to formulate the conceptions which were to govern his thinking in later life we have seen from his reflections on his escape from death after his wounding at Ball's Bluff. He had decided already at twenty that "good" and "general law" were "synonymous terms in the universe," that "good only means certain general truths seen through the heart and will instead of being merely contemplated intellectually," and that he doubted "if the intellect accepts or recognizes that classification of good and bad."

What is left, without God's direction, is simply a conflict of forces, in which the party that wins rules the roost. Mr. Howe, in his searching biography, has shown how Holmes's point of view owed a good deal to Darwin's theory of the survival of the fittest and to the positivism of Auguste Comte, as well as to the pragmatism of Charles S. Peirce, who had been one of Holmes's circle in Boston. Such thinkers as Peirce had rejected the authority of both divine and "natural" law. Moral values could not be decided in any objective way, and if two sets of values conflicted, the question of which should prevail could only be decisively settled by one side's suppressing the other. "Pleasures are ultimates," Holmes writes to Laski on August 5, 1926, "and in cases of difference between ourself and another there is nothing to do except in unimportant matters to think ill of him and in important ones to kill him. Until you have remade the world I can class as important only those that have an international sanction in war." It is amusing but very characteristic that this dictum about fundamentals should have been prompted by a difference of opinion between Holmes and his British correspondent as to the merits of Jane Austen's novels, for which Holmes, like Mark Twain, did not care; but it was none the less a serious expression of the Justice's fundamental ideas. The question of the dulness of Jane Austen leads him to argue his pragmatic position, and this pragmatic position implies his attitude toward the Civil War. The Unionists and the Southern secessionists had had, from Holmes's point of view, a serious difference of opinion about matters sufficiently important to warrant their resorting to arms. The Northerners had had to kill the Southerners in order to keep the South in the Union. And thus, at least, Holmes is never misleading. He does not idealize Lincoln; he does not shed tears about slavery. He does not call the planters wicked; he merely says that they are not truly "civilized." In his opinions on cases in the South in which the court has been intimidated by a mob, he will censure its legal procedure, but he never, even off the bench, gives way to moral indignation.

The rights, then, in any society, are determined, after a struggle to the death, by the group that comes out on top. Holmes is always insisting on the right to kill, to establish authority by violent means, to suppress in a crisis, as Lincoln did, subversive or obstructive speech. In peacetime, the sovereign power has the right to impose its policies, and the function of the laws that it passes is to see that these are carried out.

Quotations from Holmes could be multiplied to demonstrate his philosophy of *force majeure*—as they could be on any other point of his thinking, for in his papers and correspondence he repeated his opinions again and again, often in the same words. One may quote from his letters to Laski and Pollock such passages as the following. To Laski, October 26, 1919: "I fear we have less freedom of speech here than they have in England. Little as I believe

in it as a theory, I hope I would die for it and I go as far as anyone whom I regard as competent to form an opinion in favor of it. Of course when I say I don't believe in it as a theory I don't mean that I do believe in the opposite as a theory. But on their premises it seems to me logical in the Catholic Church to kill heretics and [for] the Puritans to whip Quakers—and I see nothing more wrong in it from our ultimate standards than I do in killing Germans when we are at war. When you are thoroughly convinced that you are right—wholeheartedly desire an end—and have no doubt of your power to accomplish it—I see nothing but municipal regulations to interfere with your using your power to accomplish it. The sacredness of human life is a formula that is good only inside a system of law." There is of course on Holmes's part a certain inconsistency here, to which we shall return in a moment. To Laski, January 14, 1920: "I repeat my old aphorism that everything is founded on the death of men—society, which only changes the modes of killing—romance, to which centuries, that is generations, of dead, on the memorial tablets of a great war, are necessary." And on the following February 1, he expressed the same idea to Frederick Pollock: "I loathe war—which I described when at home with a wound in our Civil War as an organized bore—to the scandal of the young women of the day who thought that Captain Holmes was wanting in patriotism. But I do think that man at present is a predatory animal. I think that the sacredness of human life is a purely municipal ideal of no validity outside the jurisdiction. I believe that force, mitigated so far as may be by good manners, is the *ultima ratio,* and between two groups that want to make inconsistent kinds of world I see no remedy except force. I may add what I no doubt have said often enough, that it seems to me that every society rests on the death of men . . ." And to Laski on May 20 of the same year: "Perhaps you respect the self-assertion a little more than I do," he writes apropos of Randolph Bourne, who had opposed our intervention in the first World War. "If I may quote my favorite author (as Thackeray says) with regard to his objections to treating a man as a thing—a means—and not as an end in himself, 'If a man lives in society, he is liable to find himself so treated!' I have no scruples about a draft or the death penalty."

I do not mean at all to depreciate Holmes by pointing out the special emphasis that he put upon killing. This was the heritage of the Civil War. Ambrose Bierce, as we have seen, after a similar experience, was obsessed by the idea of death, and he succumbed to its morbidity as Holmes did not. Holmes's long and hard service as a soldier had, besides, given him something else which was to become excessively rare in the period after the war, when most Northerners wanted to forget or to disguise what had happened. For a young man who has always lived comfortably and accepted the security of convention, it may be an educational advantage for him to see his society with the bottom knocked out, its most honored institutions threatened and its members, irrespective of class, thrown together in conflict to the death or in obligatory coöperation. The law had broken down in

America; the Constitution had gone to pieces. It was impossible for an honest man of Holmes's probing intelligence to pretend that the law was a sacred code, which had simply to be read correctly. He always saw it as a complex accretion, a varied assortment of rules that had been drawn up through more than a thousand years and which represented the needs and demands of people existing in particular places at particular periods of history. He was not the first writer to examine the law from an historical point of view, and he must have been influenced by *Ancient Law,* the pioneering book by Sir Henry Maine, which was published in 1861. But in his treatise on *The Common Law* he, too, was a pioneer in examining our legal code in the light of its historical origins. The book begins with a statement of the attitude and method of the author which has now become a classical formulation: "The life of the law has not been logic: it has been experience. The felt necessities of the time, the prevalent moral and political theories, intuitions of public policy, avowed or unconscious, even the prejudices which judges share with their fellow-men, have had a good deal more to do than the syllogism in determining the rules by which men should be governed. The law embodies the story of a nation's development through many centuries, and it cannot be dealt with as if it contained only the axioms and corollaries of a book of mathematics." He unravels with subtlety and coolness many curious misunderstandings by which antiquated statutes have been carried along and have been made to mean something quite different from what they did in their remote beginnings. He shows, also, how ancient ideas of morality still color the language of modern law and how modern ideas of morality are read back into language where they do not belong. Holmes's interest in the law, as he often says, is anthropological and sociological as well as philosophical. He likes to treat tradition lightly, to insist that a law's long existence is no reason for not repealing it tomorrow; yet, skeptical though he is, he believes in the general validity of any corpus of law as the expression of the dominant will of any considerable social group.

How, then, in view of this philosophy, was it possible for Oliver Wendell Holmes to become, in the nineteen-twenties, a great hero of the American "liberals," who were intent upon social reforms and who leaned sometimes pretty far to the Left?

There was a certain element of comedy in this situation. Besides believing that might made "rights," Holmes could not, in his economic views, have been further from Harold Laski and the editors of the *New Republic,* and he was as contemptuous of what he called "the upward and onward" as H. L. Mencken was of what he called "the uplift." He was actually, in certain ways, intellectually closer to Mencken than to his favorite young friend Laski, to whom he writes (February 10, 1920): "I took malevolent pleasure in Mencken's *Prejudices,* which devotes a chapter to speaking ill of [Thorstein Veblen]. Do you know that writer [Mencken]? With various foibles, he has a sense of reality and most of his prejudices I

share." The economic views of Holmes did not admit of redistribution of wealth, and they had never, as has been said by Mr. Francis Biddle, changed at all since he was twenty-five. "On the economic side," he writes to Laski on January 8, 1917, "I am mighty skeptical of hours of labor and minimum wages regulation, but it may be that a somewhat monotonous standardized mode of life is coming. Of course it only means shifting the burden to a different point of incidence, if I be right, as I think I be, that every community rests on the death of men. If the people who can't get the minimum are to be supported, you take out of one pocket to put into the other. I think the courageous thing to say to the crowd, though perhaps the Brandeis school don't believe it, is, you now have all there is—and you'd better face it instead of trying to lift yourselves by the slack of your own breeches. But all our present teaching is hate and envy for those who have any luxury, as social wrong-doers." He had a conception of "the stream of products," as he called it, as something with which one should not try to tamper. "For instance, take taxation—," he writes Laski, May 17, 1917, "if you stop with preliminary machinery you think of breaking up great estates and old families by an inheritance tax or of cutting down great profits by an income tax—if you pass by means to ends you see that any form of considerable taxation means withdrawing so much of the stream to feed, clothe, and house those whom the Government elects to feed, clothe, and house—and that the rest of the crowd must have so much less." And he had been permanently influenced by Malthus. "To my mind," he says in a letter of May 24, 1919, "the notion that any rearrangement of property, while any part of the world propagates freely, will prevent civilization from killing its weaker members, is absurd. I think that the crowd now has substantially all there is—and that every mitigation of the lot of any body of men has to be paid for by some other or the same body of men—and I don't think that cutting off the luxuries of the few would make an appreciable difference in the situation."

The only possibility for human improvement that he seems to have been able to envisage is some process of breeding a "selected race." He mentions this in a letter to Pollock of February 1, 1920; and he seems to be referring to a theory which he has already rather remotely invoked without elaborating upon it in a paper of five years before, **"Ideals and Doubts"** (reprinted in *Collected Legal Papers*): "I believe that the wholesale social regeneration which so many now seem to expect, if it can be helped by conscious, coördinated human effort, cannot be affected appreciably by tinkering with the institution of property, but only by taking in hand life and trying to build a race." This last reference to building a race is illuminated by passages in unpublished letters. To Lady Leslie Scott he had written in 1912: "As to eugenics I don't exactly know what your government could undertake if they wanted to tackle it. But, as you probably know, I have thought from before the days of Galton that it was the true beginning, theoretically, of all improvement. The folly, to my mind, of socialism is that it begins with property instead of with life. I remember saying to Arthur

McLellan in the Army—the day will come when the boss will say we shall be wanting some statesmen (artists, manufacturers or whatnot) in thirty years—John A376 and M2—which I think embodied the principles in sufficiently concrete form." And to another correspondent, in 1917, he professes a profound contempt for any variety of socialism which does not try to remold life rather than rearrange property and to put to death all the people who do not come up to a certain standard. But he does not, so far as I have been able to find, enlarge on this proposed solution. One cannot be sure whether Holmes is thinking of eugenics or education.

There were, however, two important matters as to which the opinions of Holmes seemed to be often on the same side as those of the liberals: labor and free speech. In the course of his twenty years—1882-1902—as a judge of the Massachusetts Supreme Court (and Chief Justice from 1899), he had sometimes dissented in cases where the right to strike or to picket was being denied by his colleagues, and this had horrified conservative Boston and gained him the reputation of being rather a dangerous man, a reputation which provoked some strong protests when in 1902 he was appointed by Theodore Roosevelt to the Supreme Court of the United States. "They don't know much more," he wrote Pollock, "than that I took the labor side in *Vegelahn v. Gunther* and as that frightened some money interests, and as such interests count for a good deal as soon as one gets out of the cloister, it is easy to suggest that the judge has partial views, is brilliant but not very sound . . ." In the United States Supreme Court itself, he continued to pursue this policy of not hesitating to decide against the money interests." He dissented, for example, with Louis Brandeis, from a majority decision which declared unconstitutional an Act of Congress that prohibited the transportation from one state to another of the products of factories in which children were employed, contending that if Congress had the power to regulate interstate commerce in such matters as fraudulent drugs and the transportation of girls for purposes of prostitution, it had also the power to prohibit the transportation of "the product of ruined lives." In writing this dissenting opinion, he evidently feels some sympathy for the children; but he had no special feeling for labor. He seems instinctively to have turned away from the dingy industrial world with which these opinions dealt. He said once that his only firsthand contact with Massachusetts industrial life had been occasionally taking out, in his youth, the girls from the Lawrence factories. It is true that his long friendship with Louis D. Brandeis, whom he had known when the latter taught at Harvard Law School and with whom he was later associated when Brandeis, in 1916, was appointed to the Supreme Court by Wilson, did something to call his attention to the badness of working conditions and the odds against which labor was struggling. He writes at the same time to Pollock and to Laski, in May 1919, when he is already seventy-eight years old—using in both cases the same murderous metaphor—that "Brandeis the other day [I quote from the letter to Pollock] drove a harpoon into my midriff with reference to my summer occupations. He said you talk about improving your mind, you only exercise it on the subjects with which you are familiar. Why don't you try something new, study some domain of fact. Take up the textile industries in Massachusetts and after reading the reports sufficiently you can go to Lawrence and get a human notion of how it really is." But, Holmes goes on to say, "I hate facts. I always say the chief end of man is to form general propositions—adding that no general proposition is worth a damn. Of course a general proposition is simply a string of facts and I have little doubt that it would be good for my immortal soul to plunge into them, good also for the performance of my duties, but I shrink from the bore—or rather I hate to give up the chance to read this and that, that a gentleman should have read before he dies. I don't remember that I ever read Machiavelli's *Prince*—and I think of the day of Judgment." And to Laski, in June of the following year: "In consideration of my age and moral infirmities he [Brandeis] absolved me from facts for the vacation and allowed me my customary sport with ideas." In his attitude toward any dispute at law between working class and "money interests," Holmes felt himself so incomparably superior to the common run of either that it cost him no struggle of conscience to announce what he thought was just, and, in writing certain opinions, he even felt, I think, a certain lofty relish, *"le plaisir aristocratique de déplaire."*

In the matter of free speech, he was perhaps somewhat inconsistent, in philosophy, if not in practice. We have seen this in one of the quotations above. He does not like to hear people talk about the "class war" in the United States, and he is reluctant to extend to a dominant group *inside* an established society the same authority that he willingly assumes for a conquering over a conquered nation: "When I talk of law I talk as a cynic," he writes Laski (December 3, 1917). "I don't care a damn if twenty professors tell me that a decision is not law if I know that the courts will enforce it. . . . And I understand by human rights what a given crowd will fight for (successfully)." He had already expressed similar opinions in a letter of September 15, 1916, but had added: "All my life I have sneered at the natural rights of man—and at times I have thought that the bills of rights in Constitutions were overworked—but these chaps [Faguet and Hazlitt, whom he has just been reading] remind me, if I needed it . . . that they embody principles that men have died for, and that it is well not to forget in our haste to secure our notion of general welfare." (Note that what justifies these principles is that men have allowed themselves to be killed for them.)

It may be that the influence of his new friends the liberals counted for something with Holmes in his opinions after the first World War in cases in which the issue of free speech was involved. In the cases of Schenck and Debs, he had upheld, under the wartime Espionage Act, convictions for obstructing the draft. But he had reacted to the wartime intolerance against any sort of expression of radical opinion, as he invariably did, after the Civil War, to fanaticism of the Left or the Right. He writes Laski in connection with Debs on March 16, 1919: "The federal judges seem to me (again between ourselves) to have got hysterical about the war. I should think that the President when he gets through with his present amusements [Wilson's visit to Europe in the interests of the League of Nations] might do a little pardoning." And to Pollock on April 5: "I am beginning to get stupid letters of protest against a decision that Debs, a noted agitator, was rightly convicted of obstructing the recruiting service so far as the law was concerned. I wondered that the Government should press the case to a hearing before us, as the inevitable result was that fools, knaves, and ignorant persons were bound to say he was convicted because he was a dangerous agitator and that obstructing the draft was a pretence. How it was with the Jury of course I don't know, but of course the talk is silly as to us." In the Abrams case, which followed in the same year, dissenting with Brandeis from the majority opinion, Holmes took a strong line in favor of Civil Rights and tried to square the right to free speech with his philosophy of the rights of power. Russian immigrants had scattered some leaflets in which—though the authors made plain that they were not opposed to the war against Germany—the munition workers were urged to strike against the armed intervention by the United States in opposition to the Russian Revolution. Holmes held that even this exhortation did not constitute "resistance to the United States." "In this case," he goes on, "sentences of twenty years' imprisonment have been imposed for the publishing of two leaflets that I believe the defendants had as much right to publish as the Government has to publish the Constitution of the United States now vainly invoked by them. Even if I am technically wrong and enough can be squeezed from these poor and puny anonymities to turn the color of legal litmus paper—I will add, even if what I think the necessary intent were shown—the most nominal punishment seems to me all that possibly could be inflicted, unless the defendants are to be made to suffer not for what the indictment alleges but for the creed that they avow—a creed that I believe to be the creed of ignorance and immaturity when honestly held, as I see no reason to doubt that it was held here, but which, although made the subject of examination at the trial, no one has a right even to consider in dealing with the charges before the Court." He now, in his final paragraph, reverts to his theory that repression is the prerogative of established power: "Persecution for the expression of opinions seems to me perfectly logical. If you have no doubt of your premises or your power and want a certain result with all your heart you naturally express your wishes in law and sweep away all opposition. . . . But when men have realized that time has upset many fighting faiths, they may come to believe even more than they believe the very foundations of their own conduct that the ultimate good desired is better reached by free trade in ideas— that the best test of truth is the power of the thought to get itself accepted in the competition of the market, and that truth is the only ground upon which their wishes can safely be carried out. That, at any rate, is the theory of our Constitution. It is an experiment, as all life is an experiment. Every year if not every day we have to wager

our salvation upon some prophecy based upon imperfect knowledge. While that experiment is part of our system I think that we should be eternally vigilant against attempts to check the expression of opinions that we loathe and believe to be fraught with death, unless they so imminently threaten immediate interference with the lawful and pressing purposes of the law that an immediate check is required to save the country. I wholly disagree with the argument of the Government that the First Amendment left the common law as to seditious libel in force. History seems to me against the notion. I had conceived that the United States through many years had shown its repentance for the Sedition Act of 1798 by repaying fines that it imposed. Only the emergency that makes it immediately dangerous to leave the correction of evil counsels to time warrants making any exception to the sweeping command, 'Congress shall make no law . . . abridging the freedom of speech.' Of course I am speaking only of expressions of opinion and exhortations, which were all that were uttered here, but I regret that I cannot put into more impressive words my belief that in their conviction upon this indictment the defendants were deprived of their rights under the Constitution of the United States."

The important point here is that, in firm disregard of the panic created by the Russian Revolution, he is giving the foreign radicals the benefit of a doubt. This opinion provoked a fierce outburst on the part of John Henry Wigmore, the Dean of Northwestern Law School, which Holmes characterized as "bosh," but it brought from Harold Laski a paean of praise. It may be that in the climate of appreciation provided by the liberal group the spirit of Puritan protest was coming to life in Holmes after the paralyzing stroke to his idealism administered by the Civil War, in which the Abolitionist protest against slavery had been discredited by his practical experience, and his incipient sympathy with the protest of the South had been killed by the victory of the North and by a realistic recognition of the power of the latter to impose its will. But the liberals of the post–World War period were now slaking Holmes's thirst for intercourse with men of ideas. They stimulated and entertained him as well as gave him the admiration he craved. He had always been rather lonely, since the days of the Harvard philosophers, for the intellectual companionship of equals. His long correspondence with Sir Frederick Pollock, a sort of English opposite number, like Holmes a great legal scholar with wide-ranging historical and literary interests—which began in the middle seventies and continued to the end of Holmes's life—shows how eager he was for this. "I . . . must vent a line of unreasoning— rage I was going to say—dissatisfaction is nearer . . ." he writes to Pollock of the newspaper comments on his appointment to the United States Supreme Court. "They are so favorable that they make my nomination a popular success but they have the flabbiness of American ignorance. I had to get appreciation for my book in England before they dared say anything here except in one or two quarters. . . . It makes one sick when he has broken his heart in trying to make every word living and real to see a lot of duffers, generally I think not even lawyers, talking with the sanctity of print in a way that at once discloses to the knowing eye that literally they don't know anything about it. . . . If I haven't done my share in the way of putting in new and remodeling old thought for the last 20 years then I delude myself. Occasionally some one has a glimpse—but in the main damn the lot of them." Later on, in 1917, he writes enthusiastically about Laski, the brilliant young Jew from Manchester then lecturing on politics and history at Harvard: "He goes with some of the younger men like Frankfurter and the *New Republic* lot, who make much of your venerable uncle and not only so, but by bringing an atmosphere of intellectual freedom in which one can breathe, make life to him a good deal more pleasant."

But the further these liberals incline toward the Left, the less can Holmes accept their conclusions. "I have begun Karl Marx's book," he had written Pollock in 1893, "but although he strikes me as a great man I can't imagine a combination less to my taste than Hegel and political economy"; and he writes later, in 1912, that Proudhon was "a man of insights, who ends by boring you as all men with issues and panaceas in their head do, especially if you think you know the answer," and that "I liked to have him walk into Karl Marx as a plagiarist and a humbug, after K. M.'s bullying everybody else as a bourgeois intelligence." Of "the accursed Trotsky's" autobiography he writes to Laski (July 10, 1930): "I am interested enough not to throw the book aside but I shall be glad when I am done with it. I don't like him and the book seems to have a dominant purpose to blow his own horn at the expense of Stalin. I feel the tone that I became familiar with in my youth among the abolitionists. He to be sure takes his principles for granted. I should like to see them stated. If he still believes in Marx I thought that *Capital* showed chasms of unconscious error and sophistries that might be conscious." The certainty of one's moral rightness, the absolute confidence in one's system always set up in him the old antagonism. "He seems to me," he writes Harold Laski in September, 1918, of the pacifist activities of Bertrand Russell, "in the emotional state not unlike that of the abolitionists in former days, which then I shared and now much dislike—as it catches postulates like the influenza"; and in October, 1930, when he has been reading Maurice Hindus's *Humanity Uprooted*, "His account of the Communists shows in the most extreme form what I came to loathe in the abolitionists—the conviction that anyone who did not agree with them was a knave or a fool. You see the same in some Catholics and some of the 'Drys' apropos of the 18th amendment. I detest a man who knows that he knows." The agitation over the Sacco-Vanzetti case had the same effect on Holmes. He received an appeal by counsel for the defendants for a writ of habeas corpus on August 10, 1927, in the week when the two Italian anarchists were condemned to be executed for a supposed murder, and ten days later an appeal for an extension of time in order to apply to the Supreme Court for writs of *certiorari* and for a stay of execution while the application was pending. Both of these Holmes denied on the ground, in the first instance, that he "had no authority to take the prisoners

out of the custody of a State Court having jurisdiction over the persons and dealing with the crime under a State law," and in the second, because, as he says, he "thought no shadow of a ground could be shown on which the writ could be granted." These appeals had been made in the hope that the Justice would recognize an analogy between the Sacco-Vanzetti case and a Southern Negro case of a few years before in which he had formulated the majority decision in granting a writ of habeas corpus for five men convicted of murder in a court which, as Holmes says, was dominated by a mob, "ready to lynch the prisoner, jury, counsel and possibly the judges if they did not convict"; but he declined to accept this analogy: the prejudices alleged in the Massachusetts court were not really the same thing; in any trial some prejudice could be alleged. And why so much fuss over Sacco and Vanzetti when "a thousand-fold worse cases of Negroes come up from time to time, but the world does not worry about them." The demonstrations at home and abroad, a shower of denunciatory or pleading letters and the blowing-up of the house of one of the jurors had the effect of getting the old Justice's back up. "My prejudices," he writes Laski, after the executions, "are against the convictions, but they are still stronger against the run of the shriekers. . . . The *New Republic* had an article that seemed to me hysterical. . . . So far as one who has not read the evidence has a right to an opinion I think the row that has been made idiotical, if considered on its merits, but of course it is not on the merits that the row is made, but because it gives the extremists a chance to yell." In December of the following year: "[Felix Frankfurter] is convinced of their innocence—but I was not convinced that too much talk had not been made on the theme. The *New Republic* recurs to it from time to time. But the *New Republic* strikes me as having become partisan in tone of late judging from an occasional glance. It seemed to nag at Coolidge—and I rather think believes a number of things that I don't. I come nearer to reading it than I do reading any other newspaper—but I can't be said to read that."

The extent to which Holmes was a "liberal" has therefore been considerably exaggerated; but it is true that the "American Renascence," which began first to stir under Theodore Roosevelt, which was manifesting itself quite vividly when our armies got back from France and which reached in the course of the twenties at least almost the dignity of an Enlightenment, did make Holmes a conspicuous figure and cause him to be generally recognized in the intellectual world as the truly great man he was. His prestige at the Harvard Law School seems steadily to have increased with the years, and in the same year, 1914, that the *New Republic* was founded, Felix Frankfurter, a sort of disciple of Holmes, or at least in certain respects a continuator of the Holmes tradition, became a professor there. Holmes had always been fond of young people—he had no children of his own, and he was now much sought after and honored by younger men of congenial tastes. Every year he was supplied with a secretary who had graduated from Harvard Law School—a post for which the qualifications were not only special competence in legal studies but historical and cultural interests which would make him a companion for Holmes. The old Justice begins to appear—as he has never in his life done before—in the light of an established sage, a god of the national pantheon. His books are reprinted and read; his minor papers collected and published. In following his correspondence, one feels that he smiles more and growls less. He knows, and the public knows, that Justice Holmes has become a classic. In the reaction against the gentility, the timidity, the sentimentality of American cultural life, he is seen to have been a humanist, a realist, a bold and independent thinker, who has required of himself from the first to meet the highest intellectual standards and who has even, with little public encouragement, succeeded in training himself to become also a distinguished writer. *The Common Law,* though lucid in intention, is so compact and so closely reasoned that it is sometimes opaque to the layman, and one is relieved to hear even from lawyers that they sometimes find it difficult reading. But in general Holmes's legal studies are so elegantly and clearly presented, so free from the cumbersome formulas and the obsolete jargon of jurists, that, though only an expert can judge them, they may profitably be read by the layman.

As for the speeches and non-legal essays, they ought to be read by everyone. One guesses that it is only Holmes's atheism, his lack of conventional patriotism and his complete incapacity for the optimism which, in that period of national self-congratulation, had become almost obligatory for public figures—Holmes thought that even William James was too open-minded and exuberant—which have kept them out of school and college textbooks. The younger Holmes was not, like his father, a fluently felicitous writer; but his literary sense was developed in a remarkable, if limited, way. One feels sometimes that this sense is quite subtle, as when, in a letter to Owen Wister, he compares the effects of light on light in Dante's *Paradiso* with Andrew Marvell's "green thought in a green shade," or when he comments, in a letter to Laski, on Alfred de Musset's stories: "He is like the flowering of an apple tree and hardly lives beyond the moment of copulation, but I can't believe that knowing but essentially second-rate Remy de Gourmont that we now know that A. de M's phrase is empty. Charm is one of the few things that survive." But there is also a certain unwillingness to let himself go with the poets. He firmly maintains that Macbeth, on hearing of the death of his lady, would hardly have been likely to soar into the "Out, out, brief candle" speech; and, having put himself through the *Odyssey* in Greek, he doubts whether it has been really worth while. He is torn between a moral obligation to make himself acquainted with the classics and a feeling that they are out of date, that it is more profitable to read something modern. But he developed, for his occasional pieces, a literary style of his own which conforms to the same austere ideal as his professional legal papers. He worked very hard over writing, and he gave to these short pieces a crystalline form as hard and bright as Pater's flame. They are perfect, and they are undoubtedly enduring—since their value lies not merely in the style, by

means of which he "makes every word tell": it is almost impossible for Holmes even to touch upon any problem of legal interpretation or to compose a brief memorial for some old colleague of the Boston bench or bar without assigning it or him to a place in a larger scheme.

It is Holmes's special distinction—which perhaps makes him unique among judges—that he never dissociates himself from the great world of thought and art, and that all his decisions are written with awareness of both their wider implications and the importance of their literary form. He was not merely a cultivated judge who enjoyed dipping into belles lettres or amusing himself with speculation: he was a real concentrator of thought who had specialized in the law but who was trying to determine man's place, to define his satisfactions and duties, to try to understand what humanity is. It is this that makes Holmes's correspondence, as well as his more formal writings, so absorbing and so fortifying and a very important part of his *"œuvre."* In spite of his strong negative predispositions, he will not relinquish a fundamental skepticism as to human convictions and systems, and he is always alert and attentive, always inquiring and searching, to find out some further answers. "The book is pretty thick with suggestions, . . ." he writes Pollock when he is reading Spengler. "I don't value his conclusion, but do his *aperçus.* Isn't that so of all theorists and system makers. . . . Yet when one suspects that a man knows something about life that one hasn't heard before one is uneasy until one has found out what he has to say." Through his long lifetime—Holmes died at ninety-four—he seems never to falter or to become fatigued in the discharge of his professional duties or in the eager intellectual life which occupied him beyond his profession. Among the sequences of correspondence so far published, Holmes is to be seen at his best in his long exchange of letters with Pollock. With Laski, a much younger man, whom he did not know till 1916, there is never the same intimate relationship; and Laski sometimes falsifies his side, in his effort to keep the old man amused, by resorting to a certain amount of flim-flam. But in the correspondence with Pollock, in which both are as free as was possible for men of their generation from common nineteenth-century prejudices, as they discuss their professional interests and boundlessly range beyond them—Frederick Pollock was a great linguist and traveller—through a friendship that lasted six decades, we see Holmes on his highest level.

Of his generation that fought in the Civil War and among the really gifted men whose characters and subsequent careers were profoundly modified by it, Holmes the younger perhaps stands alone as one who was never corrupted, never discouraged or broken, by the alien conditions that the war had prepared. How was it that he managed to survive, to function as a first-rate intellect, to escape the democratic erosion?

He was indeed a very special case. It is plain that his unshakable self-confidence, his carapace of impenetrable indifference to current pressures and public opinion was due partly to the impregnable security of belonging to the Boston "Brahmin" caste. This term had been invented by Dr. Holmes, and the peculiar position of the caste, its conception of its own special function, is explained in the opening chapters of his novel *Elsie Venner*. The Boston Brahmins, says Dr. Holmes, are not only distinct from any other group in New England, they differ from any other aristocracy in the world. There are, to be sure, in New England, families who seem to rise by suddenly making money, but they lose it in the third generation, and they cannot become Brahmins. The distinguishing mark of the Brahmin is that, from generation to generation, he maintains a high tradition of scholarship: the Brahmins are all preachers, lawyers, doctors, professors and men of letters. Some rough ambitious young boy may come to college from the New England countryside and prove able to compete with a Brahmin, but this is rather an exceptional event, and if one finds a young man with an unknown name, not "coarse" and "uncouth" like the countryman, but slender, with a face smooth and pallid, features "regular and of a certain delicacy," whose eye is "bright and quick," whose lips "play over the thought he utters as a pianist's fingers dance over their music," whose "whole air, though it may be timid, and even awkward, has nothing clownish," you may be sure that his mother was a Brahmin. There must of course at some point have been money to supplement the aptitude for learning. The author of *Elsie Venner* does not say this in so many words, but he admits that it is sometimes possible for a Brahmin to become impoverished and that in that case he may marry property. Now, Oliver Wendell Holmes the elder had himself married the daughter of a Jackson, a justice of the Massachusetts Supreme Court, whose family, successful merchants, owned most of the large town of Pittsfield (where Oliver, Jr., spent his boyhood summers), and the son married Fanny Bowditch Dixwell, the granddaughter of the celebrated author of that Bible of the New England sea trade, the *Practical Navigator,* and the daughter of Epes Sargent Dixwell, who had read law in Judge Jackson's office and later, with a reputation as the best classical scholar in Boston, been headmaster of the Boston Latin School, at which Oliver, Jr., had studied.

It would be easy, by appropriate quotation, to create the impression that Holmes was an egregious social snob of a peculiarly provincial kind. His contempt for the common run of men had come out very strongly at the time of the war, when for the first time he had had to have some contact with it. "While I'm living *en aristocrate*," he had written his sister on his way back from furlough to rejoin his regiment, "I'm an out-and-outer of a democrat in theory, but for contact, except at the polls, I loathe the thick-fingered clowns we call the people—especially as the beasts are represented at political centres—vulgar, selfish and base." We have seen his opinion of Southerners and their pretentions to be considered gentlemen. Of even the Philadelphians he writes Pollock that, "While not infrequently having the manners of the great world," they have "somehow . . . always . . . struck me as hopelessly injected with the second rate, when I have seen

them in their law, on which they pride themselves—but I would not breathe this aloud." He hardly ever mentions the Jameses without referring to the fact that they are Irish, with, in Henry's case, an intimation of underbreeding in comparison to the Anglo-Saxon and, in William's, an implication that, though lively and full of eloquence, he is not quite to be taken seriously. (His attitude toward the Jews is quite different. Through his intelligence and his love of learning, his sharpness of mind and his humor, he has obviously more in common with certain of his Jewish colleagues than with most of his Gentile ones; and there is also no doubt the traditional prestige which the Jews have had in New England, due to the self-identification of the Puritans with the Old Testament Israelites. Holmes is said to have believed that the Wendells were Jewish—they were originally Vondals from Holland; and he seems to have regarded the intellectual Jew as a special variety of Brahmin.)

Holmes's attitude toward the ablest of the Presidents under whom, as a soldier or a judge, he had served was invariably patronizing. He was not at first impressed by Lincoln: "Few men in baggy pants and bad hats," he wrote to one correspondent, "are recognized as great by those who see them." And to Beveridge: "Until I was middle-aged I never doubted that I was witnessing the growth of a myth. Then the revelation of some facts and the greatness of some of his speeches—helped perhaps by the environing conviction of the later world—led me to accept the popular judgement—which I do, without a great deal of ardor or very great interest in the man." Of Theodore Roosevelt, by whom he had been appointed to the Supreme Court, he writes Pollock that he "was very likeable, a big figure, a rather ordinary intellect, with extraordinary gifts, a shrewd and I think pretty unscrupulous politician. He played all his cards—if not more." Roosevelt had apparently expected Holmes, in return for his appointment to the Court, to vote in support of the President's measures, and when Holmes had soon failed to do this in dissenting from a majority decision, in the Northern Securities case, which held that this company had violated the Sherman Anti-Trust Act, the President—by way of third parties—emphatically expressed his displeasure. The response of the Brahmin judge to such an explosion of pique on the part of a successful New York politician was a lofty New England contempt. In the same letter quoted above, he tells Pollock that "a Senator in his [Roosevelt's] day" had said that "What the boys like about Roosevelt is that he doesn't care a damn for the law." Holmes continues, "It broke up our incipient friendship . . . as he looked on my dissent to the *Northern Securities Case* as a political departure (or, I suspect, more truly, couldn't forgive anyone who stood in his way). We talked freely later but it never was the same after that, and if he had not been restrained by his friends, I am told that he would have made a fool of himself and would have excluded me from the White House—and as in his case about the law, so in mine about that, I never cared a damn whether I went there or not." It is amusing, in view of this, to remember the acute sensitivity—the Coolidges being an old Massachusetts family—of his suspicion that the *New Republic* is "nagging" at the pygmy Coolidge. It has been thought that his reluctance to intervene in the Sacco-Vanzetti case was due to a stubborn unwillingness to impugn the Massachusetts bench, on which he himself no longer sat—a reluctance which he had not felt, in the Negro and the Leo Frank cases, in regard to the Southern judiciary.

It will, however, be seen that there runs all through this the special ideal of the Brahmin, whose superiority is not merely social. The Philadelphians, though sometimes good-mannered, are decidedly second-rate at law; the Irish, though gifted, lack rigor; Lincoln, though he wore baggy trousers and though he could hardly be interesting to a Brahmin, did in his speeches have moments of greatness. And it is greatness, not a polished complacency—though, to be sure, a better turned-out greatness than that of which Lincoln was capable—at which Holmes himself always aims. When he says—it is a favorite phrase—that someone is "a great swell," he never means that he is socially brilliant but always that he is preëminent intellectually—a top expert in some department or a profound and original thinker. When he speaks of "touching the superlative"—another favorite phrase—he always means excelling in one's work. After the funeral of Mahlon Pitney, one of his Supreme Court colleagues, he writes Pollock, "He could not touch the superlative, and when he first came to the bench riled me by excessive discourse. But he took his work seriously, was untiring in industry, had had some experience of life, and as Brandeis always said and, I came to think, truly had intellectual honesty that sometimes brought him out against his prejudices and first judgment." And elsewhere in a letter to Pollock: "I am looking forward with curiosity to the new Chief Justice [William Howard Taft]. He marked a fundamental difference in our way of thinking by saying that this office always had been his ambition. I don't understand ambition for an office. The only one that I feel is to believe when the end comes, for till then it is always in doubt, that one has touched the superlative. No outsider can give you that, although the judgment of the competent, of course, helps to confidence—or at least to hope. Between ourselves I doubt if Mr. T. can do that."

It was not true, as we have seen, that Holmes had never been ambitious for office; but it *was* true that, having attained it, he wanted to feel that he stood in the highest rank of a non-official scale of values. How eager he was for assurance of this appears in a letter to Pollock just after his eighty-first birthday: "I have had some letters and one or two notices in the paper that have touched me deeply. They have said what I longed to hear said and would almost willingly have died to hear twenty years ago"—that is, in 1902, when Roosevelt had appointed him to the Supreme Court and when Holmes had complained to Pollock of the lack of recognition of his merits, as he was later sometimes to complain that he was not fully accepted as "a great judge." "The only thing an internal man cares for," he writes Dean Wigmore in 1910, "is to believe he is taking the right track for intellectual mastery. Only a few men in this world . . . can do

anything to assure one's ever-doubting soul about that." There is surely something of Calvinism in this: the anxiety, the undermining doubt as to whether one has really been Elected. Holmes is Calvinist in his concentration on making certain of his own élite status, as well as in his almost complete lack of interest in other people as individuals. There is no gossip in Holmes's letters, very little discussion of personalities; when he expresses an opinion of somebody, it is always in terms of his abilities, that is, of his eligibility to be counted among the Elect. He read a good many novels—he seems to have had a special liking for French ones—and in Washington he and his wife went to the theater every Thursday night; but he did not care much for biographies. His reading is dominated by a sense of duty and a Puritanical fear of idleness. He feels that he must grapple with certain works, quite apart from any pleasure they give him, and, once having begun a book, no matter how dull or verbose it is, he must read every word to the end. He is always imagining—this is humorous, of course, but it shows a habit of mind—that God, at the Judgment Day, will ask him to report on the books which he ought to have read but hasn't. Yet in all this he shows a humility which redeems a certain narcissism. He likes to believe of others, whatever their reputations, that they have not really touched the superlative, and his biographer says that he is grudging in acknowledging his debt to his predecessors; but of certain people—Pollock, for example—he seems somewhat to stand in awe, and he is always confessing his deficiencies. One feels that he is not very far from Calvin's conception of "the Communion of Saints." Calvin readily admitted that his clergy on the earth were not free from non-Elect elements; but this alloy did not impair the true church, which consisted of those who were saved, whether living or already in Heaven, and who constituted a kind of club from which everyone not saved was excluded. So Holmes finds his only solidarity with the classical "great swells" of the past and with the few possible "great swells" of the present and future.

Now, despite the fact that Holmes as a judge is dealing constantly with concrete cases of men in relation to men and in spite of his insistence that "the life of the law" has been not logic but historical experience, in spite of the common sense that he brings to the application of his principles—in spite of all this, it would seem that dedication to an ideal of excellence which is not to save others but to justify oneself must cut one off from the rest of society. He had no children to bring to his notice the problems of the contemporary world, and is said not to have wanted any, since he feared they would distract him from his great objective. In Holmes's effort to touch the superlative by practising his juristic profession with all its drudgery and its hard limitations, he evolves the conception of the "jobbist" and even forms a kind of jobbists' club, which, however, except by correspondence, may not involve personal contacts. The jobbist is one who works at his job without trying to improve the world or to make a public impression. He tries to accomplish this professional job as well as it can be accomplished, to give it everything of which he is capable. The jobbist is alone with his job and with the ideal of touching the superlative—which in his grandfather Abiel Holmes's time would have been called being chosen for salvation.

The extent to which the grandson succeeded, after his service in the Civil War, in remaining aloof and detached from the life of the United States was a phenomenon of a very uncommon kind. He is at first, when appointed to the Supreme Court, as he writes Pollock, "more absorbed, interested and impressed than ever I had dreamed I might be. The work of the past seems a finished book— locked up far away, and a new and solemn volume opens. The variety and novelty to me of the questions, the remote spaces from which they come, the amount of work they require, all help the effect. I have written on the constitutionality of part of the Constitution of California, on the powers of the Railroad Commissioners of Arkansas, on the question whether a law of Wisconsin impairs the obligation of the plaintiff's contract. I have to consider a question between a grant of the U.S. in aid of a military road and an Indian reservation on the Pacific coast. I have heard conflicting mining claims in Arizona and whether a granite quarry is 'Minerals' within an exception in a Railway land grant and fifty other things as remote from each other as these." But though the Holmeses had made one trip to the Coast in 1888 and spent two weeks at Niagara Falls, it would never have occurred to the Justice to pay a visit to any of these places or even to read them up. And not only does he resist the suggestion that he look into the conditions of American labor, he even makes it a rule not to see the papers, which he feels are a waste of time. "I don't read the papers," he writes Pollock, in 1905, "or otherwise feel the pulse of the machine." It was mainly through Mrs. Holmes that he acquired any knowledge of current events. Of American business he knew almost nothing, only as much as his cases compelled him to learn. "We are sitting and having cases that I dislike about rates and the Interstate Commission. I listen with respect but without envy to questions by Brandeis and Butler using the words of railroading that I imperfectly understand" (to Laski, 1929). But he tried to give the business man his due, and he cherished a strange idealization of James J. Hill, the Western railroad magnate, against whose monopolistic operations the government had intervened in the Northern Securities suit and whose case had been supported by Holmes in the dissent which had infuriated Roosevelt. "I regard a man like Hill," he tells Pollock in 1910, "as representing one of the greatest forms of human power, an immense mastery of economic details, an equal grasp of general principles, and ability and courage to put his conclusions into practice with brilliant success when all the knowing ones said he would fail. Yet the intense external activity that calls for such powers does not especially delight me." And to Laski in 1923: "I . . . don't sympathize with your artist friends in their loathing for business men. It seems to me merely an illustration of the inability of men to appreciate other forms of energy than that which is natural to them. I am not, and I fear could not be a business man—but the types that I have in

mind seem to me among the greatest. This is a disinterested appreciation of what generally is disagreeable to me." He had been in fact almost as little prepared as Lincoln or Grant or Lee to understand the social-economic developments that followed the Civil War, and he seems to have had as little to do personally with the tycoons whom he tries to praise as with the factory workers of Lawrence. If he *had* known them from personal contact, as had that other Boston Brahmin, the younger Charles Francis Adams, who became an expert on railroads and eventually President of the Union Pacific, Holmes would no doubt have agreed with him when he said, in his testy New England way: "A less interesting crowd I do not care to encounter. Not one that I have ever known would I care to meet again, either in this world or the next; nor is one of them associated in my mind with the idea of humor, thought or refinement." (This reference to the next world would seem to have something to do with the New England assimilation of the Communion of Saints to a kind of superior club.)

The real key to Holmes's attitude to business, as to many other aspects of life, is to be found in the distaste for facts and the preference for "general propositions" which he expresses, in the quotation above, in connection with Brandeis's efforts to interest him in factory conditions. This is one of his recurrent themes. He tells Laski, in a letter of January 16, 1918: "My difficulty in writing about business is that all my interest is in theory and that I care a damn sight more for ideas than for facts." And so he further confesses to the same correspondent (October 9, 1921) that his conception of Jim Hill as his "favorite" man of action has been derived "not from knowledge of Hill but from a theoretic construction of what he might have been." To Pollock he writes in 1904: "I never knew any facts about anything and always am gravelled when your countrymen ask some informal intelligent question about our institutions or the state of politics or anything else. My intellectual furniture consists of an assortment of general propositions which grow fewer and more general as I grow older. I always say that the chief end of man is to frame them and that no general proposition is worth a damn." He repeats this in a letter to Pollock seventeen years later, adding, "We are not sure of many things and those are not so."

Though he is still always inquiring into the destiny of man, he can no longer believe that the human race is necessarily of any importance. He writes to Pollock when he is seventy-eight: "I have just read Marvin, *The Century of Hope,* an interesting conspectus of the modern period inspired by a rather deeper belief in the spiritual significance of man than I am able to entertain and a consequently greater faith in the upward and onward destiny of the race." This readiness to conceive of the human race as an insignificant detail of the universe seems also to be traceable to Calvin, who believed that mankind was nothing in comparison with the omnipotence and infinity of God. In the letter just quoted and another that follows, Holmes even allows himself the concession of using the word God: "I only don't believe, i.e. have no affirmative belief, that man was necessary to God, in order to find out that he existed (if the cosmos wears a beard, as to which I have no opinion). It seems to me probable that the only cosmic significance of man is that he is part of the cosmos but that seems to me enough. . . . It strikes me that these philosophers [such as Ralph Barton Perry of Harvard] have gone round the globe to get to the spot close to which they stood before they began to philosophise—also that they still show their theological inheritance by assuming the special cosmic importance of man. I see no reason to believe that God needed him otherwise than as he may need all that is." But he usually speaks in terms of a beardless universe, and it is one of his recurring contentions that it is foolish to revolt against this universe—in the manner of the angry romantics—because man is a part of this universe and cannot differentiate himself from it in such a way as to create an issue as between himself and it.

As for transforming human society, the old Justice—having lost in the war the high hopes of the Northern crusade and fallen back on a Calvinist position which will not admit the realization of the Kingdom of God on earth—must simply, as a jurist and a jobbist, submit to the dominant will of the society he has sworn to serve. He sometimes detested the laws that this society made him enforce and would, as we have seen, sometimes seize upon the benefit of a doubt to declare himself in the opposite sense. He did not approve of the Sherman Anti-Trust Act and had no sympathy with the Volstead Act, which deprived him of the bottle of champagne which it had always been his ritual to drink with his wife on the occasion of their wedding anniversary. If the business men made the laws, he would have to accept their authority; if the people should decide to vote for socialism, he would have to accept that, too—and it was always from the point of view of assessing this latter possibility that he did his occasional reading in the literature of socialism.

So Holmes achieved isolation, remaining unperturbed and lucid, through the whole turbid blatant period that followed the Civil War—with its miseries of an industrial life that was reducing white factory workers to the slavery which George Fitzhugh had predicted, with its millionaires as arrogant and brutal as any Carolina planters, with the violent clashes between them as bloody as Nat Turner's rebellion or John Brown's raid upon Kansas, with its wars in Cuba and Europe that were our next uncontrollable moves after the war by which we had wrested California from the Mexicans and the war by which we had compelled the South to submit to the Washington government. These events touched him only at secondhand in the cases that came up before his tribunal and which elicited his crystalline opinions. His Brahminism, his high-minded egoism and his philosophic temper of mind had equipped him with an impenetrable integument.

Eventually the country at large came to join Holmes's colleagues in the law and his later-coming liberal admirers in assigning to him a consecrated authoritative role, though certainly the public in general knew as little about his work and ideas as they had when he was appointed to the Supreme Court. It was partly, no doubt, the prestige of longevity when the ancient has retained his faculties, partly the feeling of awe—of which I have spoken in connection with Lee—inspired by the rare survival of the type of the republican Roman, irrespective of what he now stands for: Justice Holmes was perhaps the last Roman. But there was also, I think, something more which was not inconsistent with these. The popular feeling about Holmes was illustrated in a striking and touching way in the reception by Eastern audiences, sixteen years after Holmes's death (in 1951), of a rubbishy film about him with the title *The Magnificent Yankee*. It was significant that what most moved these audiences were not the parts that were personal and sentimental but the scenes, all too few and inept, in which the hero's moral courage was shown. They seemed to be responding to these with a special enthusiasm of reassurance because they were made to feel—at a moment of the national life particularly uncertain and uncomfortable: the end of Truman's second administration—the Korean War, the Hiss trial, the rise of McCarthy—that here was a just man, a man of the old America who, having proved himself early in the Civil War, had persisted and continued to function through everything that had happened since, and had triumphed in remaining faithful to some kind of traditional ideal. But what *was* this ideal they applauded? I have tried to make out what Holmes meant to them. Independence and fair-dealing, no doubt; rectitude and courage as a public official; and a conviction that the United States had a special meaning and mission to devote one's whole life to which was a sufficient dedication for the highest gifts.

Was this Holmes's own understanding of the "job" to which he found himself committed? When he died in 1935 at the age of ninety-four, it appeared that he had left bequests of $25,000 each to Harvard and to the Boston Museum of Fine Arts, but all the rest of his very modest fortune—something over $270,000—to the government of the United States. There was much speculation over this. It was true that his wife was dead, that, childless, he had not even any relatives to whom such a sum might have been useful. But why had he not bequeathed it to Harvard Law School or some other institution to be used for some specific purpose? I have heard two quite different explanations, both suggested by younger men who had seen a good deal of Holmes. One felt that his failure to do this was due simply to a lack of imagination. Having rarely, so far as is known, given a penny to a cause or a charity, indifferent to the improvement of others while preoccupied with the improvement of himself, it never came into Holmes's head to contribute to the usefulness of an institution. The other of Holmes's friends believed that, on the contrary, there was a definite point in Holmes's disposal of his money. He had fought for the Union; he had mastered its laws; he had served in its highest court through a period of three decades. The American Constitution was, as he came to declare, an "experiment"—what was to come of our democratic society it was impossible for a philosopher to tell—but he had taken responsibility for its working, he had subsisted and achieved his fame through his tenure of the place it had given him; and he returned to the treasury of the Union the little that he had to leave.

G. Edward White (essay date 1971)

SOURCE: "The Rise and Fall of Justice Holmes," in *The University of Chicago Law Review,* Vol. 39, No. 1, Fall, 1971, pp. 51-77.

[In the following essay, White follows Holmes's image in America, from his extreme popularity to the later disillusionment about his ideals widely adopted after his death.]

Occasionally the American nation sees itself in the life of one of its citizens. Something about the experiences, background, attitudes, or accomplishments of an individual seems particularly evocative of American culture, or at least a vision thereof. Such a life was that of Justice Oliver Wendell Holmes. In addition to being a man of great popular appeal,[1] Holmes has held considerable interest for the intellectual community. From the publication of Holmes's *The Common Law* in 1881 until the present day, legal scholars, philosophers, political scientists, historians, literary critics, and journalists[2] have attempted to understand and articulate the qualities that have made Holmes, in their eyes, an especially noteworthy representative of American civilization. This article traces the changing image of one man in the eyes of American intellectuals through the years—the "rise and fall" of Justice Holmes.

I. INTRODUCTION

American intellectuals have focused on Holmes in three capacities: as Brahmin, as ideologue, and as stylist. The shifting image of Holmes in the American scholarly community reflects changes in the attitude of intellectuals toward Holmes in each capacity.

The term Brahmin suggests Holmes's close association with a Boston tradition of social privilege and intellectual enterprise. During the twenty years following Holmes's birth in 1841, Boston and its surrounding countryside produced the first major concentration of intellectual activity in American history. The individuals who made contributions, which ranged from discoveries in natural science to poetry, were from wealthy or socially respectable families. Many had traveled to Europe in their youth, some for educational purposes; many had attended Harvard College, some also reading law for a time; a distinct minority, such as the Adamses, had served in the government.[3]

Of those names associated with Brahminism—Parkman, Agassiz, James, Lowell, Emerson, Longfellow, Parker, to

list some—that of Holmes was among the most celebrated. At his son's birth Dr. Oliver Wendell Holmes, Sr. had already gained notice for an emotional appeal on behalf of the threatened *U.S. Constitution.*[4] During Holmes's youth his father had enhanced his professional status with an influential paper on puerperal fever[5] and ultimately emerged as the leading social historian of his time with the publication of *The Autocrat of the Breakfast Table.*[6] The success of the elder Holmes and the equal success of Holmes, Jr. in a different area of endeavor, coupled with an unmistakable tension between father and son,[7] has served as a starting point for scholarly explorations into the relationship between Holmes and his heritage. The explorations have revealed a relationship rich in ambiguities.

The Brahmins were "gentlemen" at a time when that style of life was still considered a profession. Gentlemanliness stood not only for educated refinement in intellect, taste, and culture, but also for snobbishness and class consciousness. There is abundant evidence that Holmes was as fastidious, clubbish, and condescending as any of his peers.[8] Moreover, he possessed high intellectual standards and was generally critical of even those works he considered worth reading.[9] He also held rather elitist political views, confessing late in his life that the only justification he found for a government's undertaking to rectify social ills was "an aristocratic assumption that you know what is good for them better than they (which no doubt you do)."[10]

Alongside these aristocratic characteristics, however, existed counter-tendencies. After a convivial youth as Harvard undergraduate and clubman, Holmes largely withdrew from social contacts with his peers for approximately ten years. He had virtually no intimate friends during his adult life, but his major correspondence friendships were with non-Brahmins. Although he fervently desired to make an intellectual name for himself before his fortieth birthday,[11] he was contemptuous of his father's role as all-purpose man of letters.[12] If Holmes favored government by elites, he believed in sharply curtailing the powers of the elitist judicial branch;[13] if he "loathe[d] the thick-fingered clowns we call the people . . . —vulgar, selfish, and base,"[14] he praised "that instinct that makes the American unable to meet his fellow man otherwise than simply as a man."[15]

Holmes's ideology was as ambiguous as his identification with his heritage. He emerged from adolescence an agnostic and an opponent both of time-honored moral pieties and of inexorable axioms governing scholarship. Later in his life, his agnosticism merged with a theory of government that stressed the importance of power relationships. Nevertheless, he retained an apparently passionate devotion to the act of believing in ideals—as distinguished from any particular ideals themselves—and a faith in the redeeming powers of social evolution. The combination of these potentially contradictory precepts has confounded those who have studied Holmes as ideologue. The "nutshell" words for Holmes abound: positivist,[16] Darwinist,[17] skeptic,[18] cynic,[19] idealist,[20] romanticist,[21] mystic,[22] progressive,[23] patriot.[24] Each suggests an aspect of his thought, but no one word can accurately describe the whole.

Holmes has been equally interesting to American intellectuals as a judicial stylist. In a profession in which the mode of expression characteristically has been technical, formal, depersonalized, and restrained, Holmes's opinions are remarkable for their absence of technicalities, their informality, their liveliness, and their poetic flights of language. Holmes's style is better described as a deviation from the judicial norm than as an improvement on it. If clarity, precision, and "reasoned elaboration"[25] can be said to be ideals of judicial opinion writing, Holmes appears to have eschewed these goals in the pursuit of terseness and ambiguity. His opinions have been called as difficult to understand as they are easy to read.[26]

In each of the above capacities, then, Holmes is not only interesting but controversial. As Brahmin, he provokes comment at two levels: his position evokes the tension of social privilege and intellectual superiority in an increasingly socially mobile and mass-educated society; his behavior contains the emotional conflict inherent in a man rejecting his social heritage. As ideologue, his stances raise a series of questions, among them whether power should be the controlling basis of social arrangements and whether social evolution is inevitable. As stylist, his method of judicial communication invites inquiries as to the value of a decision-making process that expresses its conclusions by unelaborated formulae.

The ambiguities and controversy surrounding Holmes have emerged as his image has changed in the eyes of the American intellectual community. Commentators have woven his thoughts and attitudes into their own social, political, or intellectual preoccupations. As those preoccupations have shifted, the image of Holmes has changed accordingly.

II. The Changing Image of Justice Holmes

Holmes's image may be evaluated in six time segments: (1) 1881 (publication of *The Common Law*) to 1902 (appointment to the Supreme Court), (2) 1903 to 1931 (retirement from the bench), (3) 1932 to 1940, (4) 1941 to 1949, (5) 1950 to 1959, and (6) 1960 to the present. Broadly speaking, each time segment is marked by a dominant intellectual attitude; these attitudes I have termed scientism, progressivism, hero worship, demythology, a sense of alienation, and libertarianism-egalitarianism. The time segments are, of course, only approximations for the sake of convenience, since changes in intellectual attitudes do not occur with chronological precision. The segments are intended to convey a general sense of the points in time at which one overriding perception of Holmes began to be replaced by another, rather than to demarcate any abrupt changes in intellectual attitude.

The term "image," as used in this article, is a construct representing the perceptions of a variety of articulate

individuals about a public figure. Like any construct employed to derive collective meaning from individual attitudes, it is imperfect. This imperfection flows from the diversity of intellectual viewpoints during any historical period. The primary purposes of this investigation of Holmes's reputation are to emphasize the complexity of the process by which the reputation of a judge is established and to demonstrate the way in which the image of a man is shaped by the attitudes of his critics.

A. *1881-1902: Holmes as Scientist*

The late nineteenth century intelligensia in America were obsessed with what would now be known as model building. Religious and spiritual principles appeared to them to have been made obsolete by more measurable rules of science. The universe, they had discovered, could be explained in terms of recurrent, predictable phenomena such as evolution and competition. Holmes's *The Common Law,* his contemporaries felt, was in the mainstream of the scientific movement in that it systematized jurisprudence on the basis of observable social phenomena rather than through intellectual abstractions. The theories advanced by Holmes, such as the external standard of liability in tort law, were said to rest on "a series of scientific observations" and were thought to indicate "the advance which the common law is now making toward a more scientific structure than it has ever before possessed."[27] By announcing that the felt necessities of the time governed the formulation of policy in the courts, Holmes was setting forth a tangible set of materials on which to erect a jurisprudential system, hence bringing "the . . . office of the courts . . . into unaccustomed clearness."[28] By 1899 a commentator announced that *The Common Law* was "everywhere regarded as a scientific work."[29]

Scientism, in the late nineteenth century, was intellectual radicalism, since it attempted to shift the source of scholarly axioms away from the intuitions and abstractions of an educated elite of religious believers. To believe in science was to challenge established faiths. Insofar as it questioned a set of traditional social values, scientism was associated with political radicalism, and there were those who thought that Holmes had tendencies in this direction. In 1899 two law reviews labeled Holmes a radical, pointing particularly to his dissent in *Vegelahn v. Guntner,*[30] in which Holmes had disassociated himself from a majority ruling upholding an injunction prohibiting peaceful picketing by strikers and had announced that "combination [on the part of labor] is a necessary and desirable counterpart [of combination on the part of capital] if the battle is to be carried on in a fair and equal way."[31] Reviewers found such "radical" language "strange . . . from a man of [Holmes's] environments."[32]

Late nineteenth century intellectuals were most interested in Holmes as ideologue. His privileged social position was not regarded as significant to commentators—the only negative remarks made about Holmes's heritage were issued by Wendell Phillips, himself a Brahmin, who complained in 1895 about the unfortunate tendency of Holmes and other of his contemporaries to equate war with heroism.[33] As a stylist, Holmes suffered from too facile an identification with his father. Those who attempted to analyze his opinions or writings invariably prefaced their remarks with a reference to the literary contributions of Dr. Holmes. At his sixtieth birthday, after twenty years on the Massachusetts bench, Holmes had not fully emerged as a unique and original figure. What reputation he had made for himself by 1902 flowed mainly from his efforts to make the study of the law more scientific.

B. *1903-1931: Holmes as Progressive*

The late nineteenth century intellectual community insisted that formal logical arguments rest on a more scientific foundation than intuitive personal insights, but it was by no means prepared to abandon the use of abstract, deductive reasoning as an academic and pedagogic tool. Syllogistic reasoning from assumed intellectual principles represented the primary mode of thought and expression of the time. After 1900, however, not only the content of particular academic axioms but the formalistic reasoning process itself came increasingly under attack.[34] Antiformalism in the early twentieth century intellectual community was a manifestation of the broader ideological movement known as progressivism. Progressivism emphasized the constantly changing nature of society and the need for testing social propositions and intellectual theories on the basis of contemporary experience. It resisted abstractions that could not be shown to be responsive to modern social conditions and was consequently hostile to intellectual discourse that appeared to rest on untested or untestable assumptions. In particular, progressivism denied the existence of permanent "laws" that governed intellectual disciplines. It preferred dominant academic or ideological trends to emerge through a process of experimentation whereby those ideas or policies that proved useful in achieving "progress" achieved dominant status until they were replaced by still more "progressive" concepts.[35]

In its political form, the progressive movement believed in the management of government by experts responsible to but not deferential toward the public. Progressives sought to expand the public sector of government in order to substitute decision making by an educated, efficient group of impartial administrators for decision making by partisan representatives of special interest groups. Progressive public policy envisaged the expansion of the executive branch of government, primarily in the form of administrative regulatory agencies, at the expense of Congress and the courts. Progressives urged federal or state legislation that attempted to create executive regulatory schemes and demanded a large measure of judicial tolerance for such legislation. They were particularly incensed at the attempts by judges to substitute nineteenth century economic axioms for empirical analyses of contemporary economic conditions.[36]

The reexamination of American social values stimulated by progressivism led ultimately to a reexamination of the

movement itself. In its early years, at the opening of the twentieth century, the movement simultaneously embraced empirical relativism and moral absolutism, advocating social change in accordance with time-honored standards of behavior, such as honesty, industry, and temperance. But as its adherents became more impressed with the impermanence of ideas and institutions, they came to question the inviolability of their once-cherished moral principles. The result was a sweeping attack on the dominant social mores of the late nineteenth century, which were dismissed as "Victorian" and "Puritan."

Holmes's career on the Supreme Court coincided with the dominance of progressivism as an intellectual force in American life. His relationship with the movement itself was complex. Insofar as progressivism meant social or political reform, Holmes had little sympathy for the movement. In 1915 he told John Wigmore that "the squashy sentimentalism of a big minority of our people about human life" made him "puke." Among that minority Holmes placed those "who believe in the upward and onward—who talk of uplift, who think that something particular has happened and that the universe is no longer predatory."[37] Holmes continued to believe in nineteenth century concepts of classical economics, which the progressives repudiated, and nineteenth century social theories, such as that proposed by Malthus, which assumed an inherent imperfectibility in the bulk of mankind. He failed to share in any degree the progressives' faith in man's innate goodness or their missionary zeal to inculcate others with their moral beliefs. He remained throughout his life supremely indifferent to social welfare schemes of any sort, with the possible exception of eugenics.[38]

Nevertheless, the progressives found Holmes an especially attractive and sympathetic judicial figure and contributed to the growth of his stature. By an accident of history, Holmes ascended the Supreme Court bench at a time when a series of constitutional issues were before the Court that progressives considered to be of great importance. The issues involved the constitutionality of state and federal legislative schemes, such as workmen's compensation and wages-and-hours regulation, in which governmental bodies asserted control over private economic relationships. This power the progressives regarded as essential to their campaign to reduce the influence of "special interests." In a series of opinions from 1903 to 1923, Holmes announced his willingness to tolerate legislative experiments and his contempt for judges who used constitutional provisions to further their own social or economic prejudices.[39] The paradigmatic situation Holmes addressed in these years was that posed by *Lochner v. New York*,[40] in which Justice Peckham, for the majority, had found a New York statute establishing maximum work hours for bakers inconsistent with the due process clause of the fourteenth amendment because it interfered with the right of laborers to work as many hours as they wished. Holmes found Peckham's position to be an artificial application of the so-called liberty-of-contract doctrine[41] in the face of conditions in the baking industry that rendered that doctrine meaningless. He stressed the reasonableness of beliefs on the part of New York legislators that the working environment of bakers was deleterious to their health and deferred to these beliefs, without endorsing the soundness of the maximum hours law itself.

Progressives considered Holmes's exposure of the deficiencies of abstract judicial reasoning and his tolerance for the programs of legislative majorities to be manifestations of judicial statesmanship of the highest order. In a series of articles, Felix Frankfurter celebrated Holmes for his ability to separate his personal views from his legal opinions, for his resistance to doctrinaire interpretation, for his understanding of social and economic forces, and for his willingness to allow legislative experimentation.[42] Frankfurter's opinions were echoed by others, including James Tufts,[43] Roscoe Pound,[44] and John Dewey.[45] Praising Holmes's grasp of "economic forces," Charles Carpenter declared in 1929 that "no judge who has sat upon the bench has ever been more progressive in his attitude."[46] Walter Wheeler Cook and Jerome Frank saw in Holmes's interpretation of his office the advent of a new school of jurisprudence. Cook asked rhetorically in 1921: "How many . . . among law teachers, not to mention judges and practicing lawyers, . . . 'consider the ends which [legal] rules seek to accomplish, the reasons why those ends are desired, what is given up to gain them, and whether they are worth the price?'" "[M]uch missionary work remains to be done," Cook maintained, "before the methods of legal thinking exemplified [by Holmes] become characteristic of . . . the leaders of the legal profession."[47] Frank, nine years later, hailed Holmes for "abandon[ing], once and for all, the phantasy of a perfect, consistent, legal uniformity. . . ." "As a consequence," Frank felt, "whatever clear [sense] of legal realities we have attained in this country in the past twenty-five years is in large measure due to him. . . . [Holmes] has developed that remarkable tolerance which is the mark of high maturity. . . . His legal skepticism is clear, sane, vital, progressive. . . ."[48]

One of the social issues to which progressives turned their attention was the place of social privilege in American society. On one level, progressivism was a movement to expand the classes of beneficiaries of governmental reforms and consequently to achieve a more egalitarian society. On another, it represented a reentry of social and intellectual elites into positions of public influence. In specific reforms such as the conservation movement, progressive rhetoric emphasized the importance of diffusing the power of monopolists and of improving the life style of small farmers, while progressive programs envisaged the management of conservation programs by an educated elite of technocrats.[49] In general terms, social privilege was not itself regarded as an evil by progressives, provided that individuals of high status demonstrated a sense of social responsibility and a concern for the less fortunate classes.

With some strain, early twentieth century commentators sought to demonstrate these qualities in Holmes. They attempted this through association of Holmes with two symbols: the socially conscious Puritan and the aristocrat as democrat. The first symbol was an artful redefinition of Puritanism. For early twentieth century American intellectuals, Puritanism symbolized a moral rigidity and parochialism that came increasingly to be considered old-fashioned. But it also suggested an adherence to the dictates of one's conscience. Certain supporters of Holmes tended to stress his *social* conscience, which they linked to his Puritan heritage. They insisted that Holmes was "a Puritan whom doubt had civilized" so that his "Puritan strength" appeared not as a religious dogma but as a "simple conviction" that the democratic ideals of American civilization should be upheld.[50] Life for Holmes was "a rich but a responsible adventure" in which the "natural Puritan aristocracy" functioned as caretakers of democracy.[51]

Thus Holmes, especially during his last years on the bench, came to be considered "an aristocrat with a genuine interest in the welfare of the common man."[52] Those attracted to the symbol of Holmes as an aristocratic democrat emphasized the social implications of his free speech opinions. In these cases the defendants whose rights Holmes championed were conspicuously disadvantaged persons, being impoverished immigrants.[53]

Holmes's style was not controversial among members of the early twentieth century intellectual community. Their overriding concern was that judicial opinions not exhibit the abstract reasoning characterized by Roscoe Pound as "mechanical jurisprudence";[54] on this point Holmes's opinions were eminently satisfying, since they eschewed that process altogether. Holmes's tendency toward formulaic expression was seen by commentators as fresh rather than cryptic. Judge Benjamin Cardozo, himself an aspiring stylist, remarked that "one almost writhes in despair at the futility . . . of imitation or approach" upon confronting Holmes's "pointed phrases."[55]

In his metamorphosis from scientist to progressive, Holmes stood on the threshold of deification. He stepped from his father's shadow by transcending his privileged background through tolerance and sympathy for thoughts and life styles foreign to his own. To observers of progressive persuasion his sense of the impermanency of ideas and intellectual axioms became "realism" or "sociological jurisprudence"; his willingness to defer to the wishes of those holding positions of political power became a belief in social experimentation; his tendency to believe that social upheavals were infrequent and that words alone rarely threatened the fabric of society became a faith in free speech; his general indifference to social problems and political issues became enlightened judicial self-restraint. He lacked only a historical vindication of his attitudes toward judicial decision making and political arrangements—which, after 1931, he received.

C. *1932-1940: Holmes as Myth*

Reviewing in 1941 the ten years that had passed since Holmes's retirement, Walton Hamilton found that

Holmes had emerged as a "deity . . . an Olympian who in judgment could do no wrong. His opinions were norms by which to measure the departures of his Court from the true path of the law." "The neat phrase, the quotable line," Hamilton observed, "were ultimates; and beauty of form was commuted into wisdom of utterance. For the Court, but especially in dissent, thus spake Holmes and the subject was closed."[56] The years from 1932 to 1940 witnessed the apotheosis of Holmes. His human qualities were enhanced in the eyes of the world: the moving radio address on his ninetieth birthday;[57] the gracious retirement, accompanied by a memorable letter to his fellow justices;[58] the tranquil declining years when, to one observer, his face fairly glowed with an inner radiance.[59] His death, three days short of his ninety-fourth birthday, was cause for inspired reflection—here was a life that could be said to have been fully lived, in terms of both longevity and accomplishment.

Other elements contributed to the deification of Holmes. At a time when economic privilege was in disrepute but gracious life styles retained a romantic attraction,[60] Holmes's role as transcendant Brahmin maintained its fascination. His brand of jurisprudence was labeled "realistic;" it served as an inspiration for legal scholars who desired to publicize the human and institutional factors operative in judicial decision making and to eradicate once and for all deductive logic from the judging process.[61] His tolerance for experiments in legislation and his relativist approach to ideas contrasted sharply with the stubborn absolutism of the Justices who struck down New Deal legislative programs. As the primary responsibility for reform shifted from the states to the federal government, those who believed that a vast expansion of federal power and activity was needed to save the nation imagined that Holmes would have supported their efforts. He thus became a liberal as well as a realist.

The transcendant Brahmin theme was popularized by the appearance in 1932 of the first full-length biography of Holmes, written by the journalist Silas Bent. Holmes, for Bent, expanded the Puritan view of human nature—that man is inherently selfish—to a "noble conception of a realistic and rationalized science of law." He "perceived that jealousy and envy . . . were in fact when sublimated the basis of human justice." As a consequence, he came to advocate a mode of lawmaking that gave each man fair scope to pursue his own self-interest. Bent saw this as evidence that Holmes had "freed himself from the group loyalties and prejudices and passions which are a heritage of those reared in the security of the genteel tradition." "Never," he maintained, "was aristocrat less class-conscious."[62] Others pursued this tack. "Of the many achievements of Justice Holmes," Adolf Berle wrote in 1935, "none is more glorious than that of transcending the bounds of his apparent emotional security."[63] Augustin Derby, a former clerk to Holmes, found him "the most democratic of men, . . . entirely without pose."[64]

If Bent polished Holmes's image as aristocratic democrat, Karl Llewellyn served a similar function in the emergence of Holmes as realist. Llewellyn had himself been one of the early and major spokesmen for realism—in 1930 and 1931 he had written law review articles that announced the emergence of a realistic jurisprudence which combined a sense of the sterility and artificiality of legal rules with a belief in the importance of manipulation and rationalization in governmental decision making.[65] This point of view was not original, Llewellyn maintained; "Holmes' mind had travelled most of the road two generations back."[66]

By the date of Holmes's death, realism had become a major intellectual force among American legal scholars. Llewellyn took the occasion to pay tribute to the contribution of Holmes to the movement. Because of Holmes's work, Llewellyn maintained, "it is no longer heresy to argue that judges have 'molecular' law-making power. . . . It is . . . no longer heresy to argue that there is no brooding omnipresence in the skies, but that the true measure of law . . . is: what, in particular, can or will anybody do about it, here and now? It is no longer heresy to see constitutional law as a field in which economic forces, prejudices and personalities play in an intricate, semi-concealed game, law, politics and statesmanship together. . . ."[67]

The most compelling image of Holmes in the nine years after 1931, however, was that of liberal. The major representation of him in that role was made by Felix Frankfurter in *Mr. Justice Holmes and the Supreme Court,* published in 1938. Frankfurter had himself made the transition from progressive to New Dealer without strain[68]—he saw the experiments of the Roosevelt administrations as enlightened recognition of the need to adjust social policies pragmatically in order to meet the demands of an increasingly complex civilization. In Frankfurter's view, Holmes "threw the weight of his authority on the side of social readjustments through legislation." Holmes analyzed "with . . . clarity the governing elements in the modern economic struggle," Frankfurter maintained, "[and] found nothing in the Constitution to prevent legislation which sought to remove some of the more obvious inequalities in the distribution of economic power." He "[did not] believe that there was anything in the Constitution to bar even a conscious use of the taxing power for readjusting the social equilibrium." He "was loath to find a governmental vacuum . . . where there was no intersection of federal and state authority."[69] In short, Holmes was an ancestral New Dealer, as he had been for Llewellyn an ancestral realist.

The intellectual community of the 1930s was quick to support Frankfurter's interpretation. Perhaps the most enthusiastic acclaim came from the *New York Times,* which described Holmes as the "liberal and lovable philosopher" whose "scores of opinions . . . testif[ied] to his liberalism"[70] and who was "known through the world for his liberal interpretations of the law in cases involving property rights and personal rights."[71] Upon Holmes's death the *Times* called him the "chief liberal of [the] supreme bench for 29 years."[72]

The 1930s thus saw Holmes elevated to demigod by the intellectual community.[73] If he had been "the idol of the progressives who believed that America must evolve and change,"[74] he was even more revered by the reformers of the 1930s, who had added to their criteria for statesmanship a commitment to majoritarian relativism and a "realistic" approach to social planning. Although he symbolized the grandeur of a more distant, and for some a more gentlemanly, era, he also appeared—particularly in light of the Court-packing crisis and the "switch in time"—distinctly a man of the times.

D. *1941-1949: Demythologizing*

Holmes's reputation had been too closely linked to an implicit set of social priorities not to be altered with the replacement of that set by another. His unequivocal deference to the whims of majorities was destined to become a subject of controversy as the intellectual community lost faith in the judgment of sheer numbers. As early as 1919 it had been suggested that Holmes believed "that there can be . . . no standard of evaluation except the principle that might makes right."[75] In 1940 Lon Fuller had pursued a similar line of analysis in observing that Holmes's influence as a judge "fell far short of being commensurate with his general intellectual stature." Fuller attributed this condition to Holmes's "notion that the law is something severable from one's notions of what it ought to be."[76] The absence of any overriding set of moral values in Holmes's jurisprudence caused increasing anxiety in the intellectual community after 1941, when ideals of civilization and justice seemed challenged in a variety of ways by the Axis powers.

The most sensational manifestation of this anxiety was a series of articles by Jesuit theologians and law professors which linked Holmes's ideology with that of totalitarian regimes. Between 1941 and 1943, four critiques of this nature appeared. Two of the articles, written by Francis Lucey, attempted to show that Holmes's philosophy was "akin to Hitler's" and that if adopted "would be the death knell of our democracy."[77] For Holmes, Lucey maintained, "there [were] no moral oughts, . . . just plain, unadulterated physical force of the majority imposing itself on all." "If . . . Holmes was correct," Lucey concluded, "Hitler is correct."[78] John Ford published a similar piece in 1942 which summarized Holmes's thought as follows: "The essence of law is physical force. Might makes legal right. The law is to be divorced from all morality. There is no such thing as a moral ought—it is a mere fiction. . . . There is no absolute truth. . . . There is too much fuss about the sanctity of human life. To the state man is a means to be sacrificed if necessary in the interest of the state. The ultimate arbiter of all life is physical force." These attitudes scandalized Ford, who saw them as the ultimate rationale for facist and communist dictatorships.[79] The fourth such critique of Holmes, written by Paul Gregg, equated Holmes's "pragmatism"—a philosophy which for Gregg assumed that "ideas, logic, reason, morals, and all else, are merely tools by which plans of action are forged and made to work"—with "the latest social experiment in Nazi Germany." "Who can say," Gregg asked, "that the United States, at some future time, will not be dominated by bureaucrats whose social philosophy is kindred to that of Hitler, Goering, Goebbels, and Himmler?" "[T]otalitarianism and dictatorship," Gregg felt, "can live and flourish under pragmatism. . . . If totalitarianism ever becomes the form of American government, its leaders, no doubt, will canonize as one of the patron saints Mr. Justice Holmes. For his popularization of the pragmatic philosophy of law has done much to pave the way."[80]

The ideas advanced in these four articles were popularized by Ben Palmer in an essay entitled "Hobbes, Holmes, and Hitler," which appeared in the *American Bar Association Journal* in 1945. In Palmer's view, "the fact that Holmes was a polished gentleman who did not go about like a storm-trooper knocking people down and proclaiming the supremacy of the blonde beast should not blind us to his legal philosophy that might makes right, that law is the command of the dominant social group." Holmes's jurisprudence, for Palmer, sanctioned "the iron fist of absolute power wielded without possibility of external restraint because of any protest of impotent individuals or minorities." "If totalitarianism comes to America," Palmer maintained, " . . . it will come through dominance in the judiciary of men who have accepted a philosophy of law that has . . . its fruition in implications from the philosophy of Holmes."[81]

The association of Holmes with totalitarianism sparked a debate that was, in its ramifications, to preoccupy legal scholars in America for a further decade. At the core of the debate was the question whether the American legal system embodied any absolute moral principles or whether it merely exemplified contemporary social norms. In the 1940s it seemed especially distressing for American intellectuals, particularly those of a religious persuasion, to deny that lawmaking in the United States flowed from unalterable humanitarian principles. In other parts of the world, denial of such standards seemed to have created patently inhumane governments. America had made a commitment to combat these nations, and philosophies that assumed that "whatever works is right" appeared intolerable to those who supported this struggle.

The Jesuit attack on Holmes, then, was an extreme manifestation of a general tendency of intellectuals in the 1940s to reassess Holmes's philosophy in relation to their own thinking. At a time when "pragmatism" and "realism" had evolved, in some circles, from words suggesting progressive social reform to words heralding the coming of totalitarianism, one group of Holmes's critics maintained that such labels were inadequate to describe the breadth and depth of his character. These critics defended Holmes by emphasizing the complexities and contradictions in his thought. Daniel Boorstin suggested in a 1941 article that "the inadequacy of labels like 'liberal' and 'conservative' quickly appears" in describing Holmes. "In his earnestness to encompass all philosophies and yet to commit himself to none," Boorstin maintained, Holmes made "his personal world of ideas" one "of doubt and conflict." He "clearly felt the tug of opposing forces": his "New England conservative tradition" and his "intensely liberal individuality."[82] Max Lerner noted in Holmes "a deep conflict between skepticism and belief, between mind and faith, between a recognition that men act in terms of a cold calculation of interests, and a recognition also that they are moved by symbols." Holmes tried, in Lerner's view, "to construct a philosophy of life for himself which would allow him to take account of both strains."[83] Francis Biddle referred to Holmes's "dualism of skeptic and moralist, of doubter and preacher." "He distrusted affirmations," Biddle felt, "yet . . . made them with an oversimplification that was only partially concealed by the form of witty aphorism which they usually took."[84]

To be sure, the 1940s were marked by some older images of Holmes. Felix Frankfurter persisted in emphasizing Holmes's ability to "transcend his emotional attachments." "New Englander of New Englanders in his feelings all his life," Frankfurter wrote of Holmes in 1944, "[he] disciplined himself against any kind of parochialism in his thinking. . . . He reached the democratic result by . . . his disbelief in ultimate answers to social questions. Thereby he exhibited the judicial function at its purest."[85] Morton White maintained that Holmes was "a serious comrade-in-arms of the liberal, progressive, and professional movement for reform" and felt that his "intellectual outlook was permeated with a good many of the ideas that were stirring the liberals of his time."[86] But the tone of the commentators had altered. If the Jesuit critics and their popularizers were regarded as aberrational, they nonetheless symbolized an unconscious decision by American intellectuals to, as Walton Hamilton put it, "elevate Mr. Justice Holmes from deity to mortality."[87] From that decision emerged a complex image of Holmes as a man whose thought and character contained contradictory forces and whose apparently facile self-assurance masked the considerable strain he must have felt in attempting to reconcile them. If the passions of the war-scarred 1940s stimulated some of the most savage evaluations of Holmes, they also generated some of the most mature.

E. *1950-1959: Sense of Alienation*

Whatever Holmes had been to American intellectuals from 1880 through the 1940s, he had been relevant. His relationship to his heritage, his approach to constitutional issues, his jurisprudential principles had touched on powerful themes for the intellectual community. But after 1950, critics of Holmes tended increasingly to reveal their sense of the widening gulf between his world and theirs. The man who had been dateless for Hamilton in 1941 suddenly became dated.

The decade commenced with a continuation of the impassioned debate that had begun in the 1940s. Harold McKinnon denounced Holmes's philosophy as "a symbol of our intellectual wretchedness, a conspicuous example of our abandonment of those spiritual, philosophical and moral truths that have been the life of the western tradition."[88] Father Lucey also returned to the attack, again comparing Holmes to Hitler.[89] Supporters of Holmes continued to defend him. Fred Rodell wrote that "Holmes took pains to make clear . . . that his skepticism had never bred in him the cynicism of defeat and despair, and that, in the realm of ought-to-be, he held strong moral and ethical views concerning decency and justice among mankind."[90] Mark DeWolfe Howe stated that Holmes "did not deny that a primary source of law is the realm of moral standards in which society has its being, and . . . considered the first responsibility of the lawyer and judge to be that of bringing the law into conformity with those moral standards." Howe's essay was colored by a sense that his generation was affected by concerns that had not affected Holmes. The adverse criticism of Holmes's skepticism, Howe felt, was "partly the result of the glimpse which Hitler gave us of cynicism triumphant. We have begun to ask ourselves whether, despite Holmes, there are not some standards of decency so fundamental and so permanent that they may properly be described as absolute." Having experienced a sense of the depths of man's inhumanity to man, Howe and his contemporaries of the 1950s were not, in his judgment, "intellectually willing and emotionally able to accept that total skepticism which led Holmes to question whether man has a cosmic significance 'different in kind from that which belongs to a baboon or a grain of sand.'"[91] They needed to believe that moral principles buttressed the universe; that civilization imposed limits on man's behavior. "Holmes' words are read now," Henry Hart wrote in 1951, "when the foundations of all things are being re-examined. The moral claims of settled law in a constitutional democracy must not today be overlooked."[92] Holmes himself had not experienced the horrors of a wholly amoral world. Charles Wyzanski emphasized Holmes's faith in the ultimate triumph of reason. Wyzanski attributed this faith to the fact that "Holmes wrote before the world had fully appreciated the wickedness of which civilized man is capable. He knew not the Nazi concentration camps . . . nor the Communist disciplined subordination of man's interest in truth to man's interest in material progress."[93]

Intellectuals of the 1950s thus felt that Holmes's conclusions were founded on assumptions about the nature of man that differed from their own. This view led critics to treat him as a figure from another age, an approach that occasionally led to debunking[94] or redefinition[95] of his political views. In the main, however, alienation from Holmes took the form of attempts to place him at a distant point in time. This was the major thrust of the three principal books written about Holmes in the 1950s; Henry Steel Commager's *The American Mind,* Samuel Konefsky's *The Legacy of Holmes and Brandeis,* and Mark DeWolfe Howe's *Mr. Justice Holmes: The Shaping Years.* Commager identified Holmes with "the progressive movement['s] . . . inability to fulfill itself without imposing far reaching readjustments upon the legal mechanics of economy."[96] Konefsky found Holmes "backward" and "singularly static" in "his conception of the economic universe" and maintained that his thought was "filled with a good many fallacies and superficial preconceptions which he assumed to be basic truths," including his "imperturbable confidence in the capacity of society to defy artificial meddling with its natural evolution."[97] Howe saw Holmes's aesthetic judgment as "responsive to older modes of expression and earlier moods of feeling." His biography of Holmes, Howe observed, was largely "an essay in intellectual history."[98]

The works of the 1950s presented a composite picture of Holmes as a man whose thought failed, despite its breadth, to encompass the problems of mid-twentieth century existence. A series of inevitabilities ruled Holmes's world: iron economic laws, natural selection of ideas and social policies, the continual progress of civilization. These inevitabilities marked the thought of an older age where, in light of a series of consoling faiths, men could afford to be skeptical. Life in the mature twentieth century, in the minds of American intellectuals, encouraged no such faiths.

F. *1960—: Holmes and Libertarianism-Egalitarianism*

In the 1960s, attention turned to the problems caused by the inequalities and diversities among Americans. Integration—racial, psychological, cultural—became a dominant concept as the decade opened. Intellectuals emphasized once more the responsibilities of elites to those less privileged and stressed the fundamental values—liberty, democracy, egalitarianism, impartial justice—that bound Americans together. Critics of Holmes asked again whether he had understood the social obligations of leadership or the consensual values embedded in the process of lawmaking in America. Their answer, by and large, was negative on both counts. Critics alleged that as both a man and a judge Holmes had been indifferent to the needs of the underprivileged. They pointed to the distance Holmes felt between himself and less socially and intellectually privileged Americans, and to his apparent lack of concern for civil-liberties interests in certain cases.

"It would be easy . . . to create the impression," Edmund Wilson wrote of Holmes in 1962, "that [he] was an egregious social snob of a peculiarly provincial kind."[99] Commentators on Holmes as Brahmin did occasionally attempt to foster that impression,[100] but they were far more concerned with what Wilson called the "carapace of impenetrable indifference to current pressures and public opinion" in Holmes, "due partly to the impregnable security of belonging to the Boston 'Brahmin' caste."[101] Distance, withdrawal, isolation, and detachment became the chief aspects of Holmes's Brahminism that interested critics. Mark DeWolfe Howe emphasized Holmes's prolonged withdrawal from society and his feeling that his destiny lay in areas, such as scholarship, that were isolated from the world at large.[102] Yosal Rogat accentuated Holmes's "preoccupation with the theme of the observer—the spectator." "[His] participation in public, and perhaps even in private, experience had an attentuated

quality," Rogat wrote, "and [he] withdrew, perhaps consciously, from important areas of shared human experience."[103] Saul Touster provided a charitable explanation for Holmes's Brahmin detachment. "Holmes," Touster maintained, "was . . . a profoundly injured spirit." "The deadening of sympathetic feelings, the Olympian aloofness, the spectator view, . . . the disbelief in causes" were devices "by which he somehow [could] gain distance from the world." Touster found that Holmes's "expressions of sympathy and doubt and feelings for the distress of the Negro were suppressed" in his later life; "suppression of feeling," he maintained, "may be the product not of the absence of feeling, but an excess of it."[104]

Others in the 1960s viewed aloofness in Holmes less sympathetically. Francis Biddle, in an otherwise laudatory assessment, described Holmes as "an aristocrat and a conservative" who "had little sympathy with the sufferings and failures of mankind, and no urgent desire to change their lot."[105] Rogat felt that "to a remarkable degree, Holmes simply did not care. . . . Precisely because he thought that 'the crowd' was unwise, he expected them to destroy the way of life that he preferred. But he would have thought it immature to be deeply concerned about that imminent destruction."[106] Robert Faulkner saw Holmes's skepticism and deference to majority views as manifestations of "a certain disdain toward minorities and the weak generally."[107]

For intellectuals of the 1960s, belief in certain fundamental guarantees of equal treatment for minorities and certain permanent individual rights was an important aspect of enlightened social thought. In the context of their own full-blown libertarianism-egalitarianism, representatives of the American intellectual community found Holmes's response to civil liberties shocking. Rogat, the leading critic, set out to disprove the widely held belief that Holmes was a champion of civil liberties. In cases involving "various claims to civil and political rights that arose out of the Civil War Amendments," for example, Rogat maintained that Holmes was "consistent" in "denying the claimed right" and "weighed the substantive claim to equality lightly." In alien cases Holmes "wrote as if anyone seeking entry was merely a suppliant." "Nowhere" did he "help in framing a remedy to secure a constitutional right. He did not develop further any inchoate right or liberty, or broaden the scope of those which were already established." In short, Rogat found that "the accepted image of Holmes as uniquely libertarian owes more to fantasies unloosed by the attractiveness of his personality than to the realities of his career." Holmes's striking insensitivity to civil rights and liberties stemmed, Rogat maintained, from a "fundamentally impoverished account of legal phenomena." He "did not sufficiently distinguish a crude system of social control, resting on naked power, from a distinctively legal method of control." He seemed "never . . . to have perceived, and certainly never acknowledged, the extent to which general commitments to fairness, generality and neutrality are built into the idea of legality and constitute part of its meaning. . . . Holmes spoke as if a legal sysem were simply a mechanism to enforce by whatever means, the desires of the dominant group," ignoring the extent to which law in America was premised on notions of equitable attention to the needs of minorities and guarantees of equal justice.[108]

Faulkner also found that an "orientation by moral and political ends [was] absent from Holmes' jurisprudence." Holmes, for Faulkner, "left vacant [the] essence [of judicial decision making]: a reasonable view of what constitutes justice in America." The "besetting and deepest flaw of Holmes' thought" was a tendency to prefer abstractions to "humane ends." Instead of giving attention to the pressing needs of interests at particular points in time, Faulkner argued, Holmes subscribed to a "fundamentally optimistic fatalism" which allowed history to usurp the role of the judge in doing justice. Holmes believed, according to Faulkner, that "man's interests are automatically ever better served. . . ." "[He] presupposed . . . the justice of history."[109]

Critics of the 1960s expanded the concept of civil liberty in finding Holmes wanting as a civil libertarian. Writers of the 1920s and 1930s who had hailed Holmes as a champion of civil liberties had made assumptions about the nature of rights in civilized society different from those made by their counterparts in the 1960s. They had assumed that liberties—such as that of contract and that of speech—were not absolutes, but were subsumed in the consensual values of contemporary America. Their view was that expressed by Justice Brandeis in two decisions in 1921: "Rights . . . must be remoulded, from time to time, to meet the changing needs of society."[110] "All rights derive from the purposes of the society in which they exist; above all rights rises duty to the community."[111] They considered Holmes a libertarian because in certain decisions he had protected freedom of speech where it did not immediately threaten national interests. For Holmes, the liberty flowed not from any inherent right of the individual but from the interest of society in a free flow of ideas. By the 1960s, however, the standard of libertarianism had altered; a social definition of civil rights seemed inequitable. Racial equality seemed to demand a philosophical definition that provided for the inherent equality of individuals and the absolute nature of human rights. No longer could society have one standard of rights for one set of persons and a second for another—that constituted a deprivation of inalienable guaranties. In this context Holmes's easy approval of majoritarian discriminations against minorities appeared unconscionably nonlibertarian.

The 1960s marked the nadir of Holmes's image. Critics seemed unwilling to undertake charitable interpretations of any of his characteristics: his Brahminism was considered snobbishness, diffidence, and insensitivity; his ideological presuppositions were thought to exhibit both a shocking indifference to humanitarian values and a complacent insularity about the inevitability of progress. The great repute in which Holmes had been held in earlier years seemed to critics of the 1960s to be a glaring example of the distasteful set of values that had dominated American civilization in their immediate past. The ideal they held of a society whose guardians perceived the democratic and egalitarian principles at its core clashed with qualities and beliefs they found in Holmes.

III. HOLMES AND THE CRITICS: A CONCLUDING ASSESSMENT

Despite its diversity, the critical literature on Holmes almost uniformly fails to assess him on his own historical terms. Holmes was, first and foremost, a late nineteenth century intellectual radical. He was concerned with smashing existing fixed systems of the universe and substituting a fluid one. *The Common Law* was his most telling work—it was critical of the quasi-religious formalistic logic of his time and supportive of two fluid organizing concepts, history and community values. At the close of the nineteenth century, Holmes attempted through science to make the concept of community values a tangible, measureable one. In this task he foreshadowed the efforts of social planners in the early twentieth century. But as that century dawned, Holmes gave up his effort and came to rest on the belief that the universe was unknowable, that ultimate values were in the end merely personal prejudices, and that change comes through the fluctuating superiority of such prejudices. Ultimately his ideology presumed an open and ever-changing system of intellectual intercourse—an unregulated market of ideas. This was his famous skepticism.

Because Holmes equated prevailing social values and ideals with prejudices, his ideology was profoundly apolitical. Late nineteenth century commentators made the mistake of identifying his intellectual radicalism with political radicalism. The progressives also erred in thinking that since Holmes believed in fluidity and change, he, like they, ascribed a positive value to change. But in giving up any belief in scientific measurement of social desires, Holmes had also given up a faith in the ability of social planners to achieve progress through an enlightened reordering of social priorities. If beliefs could not be measured, he felt, they could not be ranked. He thus rested on "what the crowd wants." The progressives, in contrast, wanted to educate the "crowd" to desire those things that the progressives believed right-thinking twentieth century Americans should desire.

The hero worshippers of the 1930s made a similar error in their evaluations of Holmes. They ascribed to him the positive as well as the negative components of attitudes, whereas Holmes held only the negative. Because Holmes believed that ideas should have free expression—a belief he often justified by saying that the process of airing those ideas would convince people of their absurdity—and because some of his free speech decisions had involved members of minority groups, Holmes became a protector of minorities and a transcendant Brahmin. His approach to free speech, in fact, assumed the ultimate impotence of all forms of unpopular expression. Because Holmes was critical of nineteenth century judicial formalism and had demonstrated a consciousness of the element of bias in judicial decision making, he was said to support the whole of realism. But Holmes did not believe that psychology was the major component of decision making, and he opposed the kind of empirical internal study of institutions that the realists advocated. Because Holmes had taken a passive stance toward state experimentive schemes in the 1910s and 1920s, critics of the 1930s assumed that he would be not only equally passive toward the federal programs of the New Deal, but sympathetic to what the New Deal represented. But Holmes had never been enthusiastic about paternalistic legislation. He took a fatalistic view of man's nature and muttered about who was going to "pay the bill."

The demythologizers of the 1940s, though more sensitive than their earlier predecessors to the complexities in Holmes, still regarded him as "dateless." His apolitical, laissez faire skepticism was read as the equivalent of those bogeys of the 1940s, pragmatism and totalitarianism. Only in the 1950s did intellectuals begin to see a gap between Holmes's universe and their own. This perception appeared largely in the form of strained efforts to make him "moral" in 1950s terms—to show that had he comprehended the horror of totalitarian regimes he would have demonstrated greater concern for political values.

The critics of the 1960s continued to view Holmes through the lens of contemporary events. Their annoyance at his apparent absence of concern for libertarian principles rested on an expanded definition of liberties. Like the progressives, writers of the 1960s matched all previous eras against their own; Holmes, whose thought was shaped in a world that had far different notions of "liberty" and "equality," was destined to fall short of their standards.

But if Holmes asks, on one level, to be judged by the standards of his age, he invites, on another level, judgment by a more timeless standard: the capacity for being human. Here one finds a disturbing dissonance between Holmes's very conspicuous social and professional success—it is hard to imagine a life less marred by physical, social, or economic deprivations or one marked by a greater length and breadth of achievement—and his gloomy musings that "the crowd has substantially all there is,"[112] that "we all are very near despair,"[113] that men are like "flies,"[114] and that man has no more cosmic significance than a baboon or a grain of sand.[115] The specter of the eminent Holmes uttering such misanthropy smacks of the "old cardinal" prose of Henry Adams that Holmes himself decried.[116]

Holmes's skepticism appears to have been less a striving for a positive goal than a facile means of avoiding commitment, whether to beliefs institutions, or mankind itself. One is struck by the comments of Holmes that he had remained childless because he could not bear bringing children into the world and because he preferred the less-involved paternalism he felt for his law clerks.[117] These statements suggest a desire to evade the responsibilities and emotional attachments of close involvement with other human beings, or perhaps the adoption of a misanthropic pose to prevent others from probing into areas of his life in which he felt vulnerable.

It is disappointing to find a man who was fortunate enough to be made aware in his lifetime of the full measure of his accomplishment (how many men are able to hear themselves called "the greatest of our age in the domain of jurisprudence, and one of the greatest of the ages"[118]?), yet who seemed to be so indifferent, at times savagely so, to the lives of his fellow mortals. To be sure, Holmes had his values—civilization, the martial virtues, and, in his own sense, democracy and even liberty. He also had high standards of intellectual performance. But the richness of his mind, the power of his intellect, and even the depth of his feelings tended to degenerate into a cranky negativism that, given his stature, seems peculiarly distasteful. It is Holmes's articulated refusal to take pride in being human that marks him as one of the least "heroic" of America's heroes.

NOTES

[1] Holmes has been the only Supreme Court Justice in American history whose life has been the subject of a Broadway play, *The Magnificent Yankee,* which appeared in 1951.

[2] The enumerated groups compose the "American intellectual community" for the purposes of this essay. Journalists include writers for the *New York Times,* the *New York Herald Tribune,* the *Christian Science Monitor,* and certain periodicals of popular scholarship, such as the *Nation* and the *New Republic.*

[3] *See generally* V. Brooks, *The Flowering of New England* (1936).

[4] O.W. Holmes, Sr., *Old Ironsides, Boston Daily Advertiser,* Sept. 16, 1830.

[5] O.W. Holmes, Sr., *The Contagiousness of Puerperal Fever, New England J. Medicine and Surgery*, Apr., 1843.

[6] O.W. Holmes, Sr., *The Autocrat of the Breakfast Table* (1858); *see* M. Howe, *Holmes of the Breakfast Table* (1939).

[7] *See* C. Bowen, *Yankee From Olympus* (1943); M. Howe, *Justice Oliver Wendell Holmes: The Shaping Years, 1841-1870* (1957).

[8] *See* Hamilton, *On Dating Justice Holmes*, 9 U. Chi. L. Rev. 1 (1941); Kurland, *Portrait of the Jurist as a Young Mind*, 25 U. Chi. L. Rev. 206 (1957); Llewellyn, *Holmes*, 35 Colum. L. Rev. 485 (1935); Sergeant, *Oliver Wendell Holmes*, 49 New Republic 59 (1926).

[9] Hamilton, *supra* note 8; Llewellyn, *supra* note 8.

[10] Letter from Oliver Wendell Holmes to Harold Laski, July 23, 1925, in 1 *Holmes-Laski Letters* 762 (M. Howe ed. 1953).

[11] M. Howe, *Justice Oliver Wendell Holmes: The Proving Years, 1870-1882* (1963).

[12] M. Howe, *supra* note 7, at 19-21.

[13] *E.g.*, Lochner v. New York, 198 U.S. 45, 74 (1905) (dissenting opinion).

[14] Quoted in *Touched with Fire: Civil War Letters and Diary of Oliver Wendell Holmes, Jr.* 71 (M. Howe ed. 1947).

[15] Quoted in *The Occasional Speeches of Justice Oliver Wendell Holmes* 25 (M. Howe ed. 1962).

[16] Howe, *The Positivism of Mr. Justice Holmes*, 64 *Harv. L. Rev.* 529 (1951).

[17] Rogat, *Mr. Justice Holmes: A Dissenting Opinion*, 15 *Stan. L. Rev.* 3, 254 (1963).

[18] M. Lerner *The Mind and Faith of Justice Holmes* (1943).

[19] Mencken, *The Great Holmes Mystery*, 26 *American Mercury* 123 (1932).

[20] M. Howe, *supra* note 7.

[21] *Id.*

[22] Boorstin, *The Elusiveness of Mr. Justice Holmes*, 14 *New England Q.* 478 (1941).

[23] R. Faulkner, *The Jurisprudence of John Marshall* 227-28 (1968).

[24] Villard, *Issues and Men: The Great Judge*, 140 *Nation* 323 (1935).

[25] *Cf.* H. Hart & A. Sacks, *The Legal Process* (tentative ed. 1958).

[26] Rogat, *supra* note 17, at 9-10.

[27] Book Review, 26 *Albany L. J.* 484, 486 (1882).

[28] Book Review, 15 *Am. L. Rev.* 331 (1881).

[29] Note, 33 *Am. L. Rev.* 753, 754 (1899).

[30] 167 Mass. 92, 104 (1896).

[31] Id. at 108.

[32] Note, *Judge Holmes' Opinions*, 60 *Albany L. J.* 118 (1899).

[33] Phillips, Sentimental Jingoism, 61 *Nation* 440 (1895).

[34] *Cf.* M. White *Social Thought in America* (1968).

[35] *Cf.* D. Noble, *The Paradox of Progressive Thought* (1958).

[36] *Cf.* White, *The Social Values of the Progressives: Some New Perspectives*, 70 S. *Atlantic Q.* 62 (1971).

[37] Quoted in M. Howe, *supra* note 7, at 25.

[38] *Cf.* Rogat, *supra* note 17, at 282-89.

[39] *E.g.*, Adkins v. Children's Hospital, 261 U.S. 525, 567 (1923) (dissenting opinion); Truax v. Corrigan, 257 U.S. 312, 342 (1921) (dissenting opinion); Hammer v. Dagenhart, 247 U.S. 251, 277 (1918) (dissenting opinion); Adair v. United States, 208 U.S. 161, 190 (1908) (dissenting opinion); Lochner v. New York, 198 U.S. 45, 74 (1905) (dissenting opinion); Otis v. Parker, 187 U.S. 606 (1903).

[40] 198 U.S. 45 (1905).

[41] *Cf.* Pound, *Liberty of Contract*, 18 *Yale L. J.* 454 (1909).

[42] Frankfurter, *The Constitutional Opinions of Mr. Justice Holmes*, 29 *Harv. L. Rev.* 683, 691, 693, 694 (1916); Frankfurter, *Twenty Years of Mr. Justice Holmes' Constitutional Opinions*, 36 *Harv. L. Rev.* 909, 927, 929 (1923); Frankfurter, *Mr. Justice Holmes and the Constitution*, 41 *Harv. L. Rev.* 121, 132, 134 (1927).

[43] "Holmes has . . . firmly set himself against a slack universe of legal conceptions and a rigidly fixed social order" and "has sought to give man room to express his advancing needs in an orderly progressing society." Tufts, *The Legal and Social Philosophy of Mr. Justice Holmes*, 7 A.B.A.J. 359 (1921).

[44] Pound discussed Holmes's "conscious facing of the problem of harmonizing or compromising conflicting or overlapping interests. . . . " Pound, *'Judge Holmes's' Contributions to the Science of Law*, 34 *Harv. L. Rev.* 449, 450 (1921).

[45] Dewey stressed Holmes's "impatience with the attempt to settle matters of social policy by dialectic reasoning from fixed concepts" and his "faith that . . . our social system is one of experimentation, subject to the ordeal of experienced consequences." Dewey, *Justice Holmes and the Liberal Mind*, 53 *New Republic* 210, 211 (1928).

[46] Carpenter, *Oliver Wendell Holmes, Jurist*, 8 ORE. L. REV. 269, 270 (1929).

[47] Cook, Book Review, 30 *Yale L. J.* 775, 776 (1921).

[48] J. Frank, *Law and the Modern Mind* 253, 257, 259 (1930).

[49] *Cf.* G. White, *The Eastern Establishment and the Western Experience* (1968).

[50] Littell, *Books and Things,* 3 *New Republic* 100 (1915).

[51] Sergeant, *Oliver Wendell Holmes,* 49 *New Republic* 59, 60 (1926).

[52] Pollard, *Justice Holmes, Champion of the Common Man,* N.Y. Times, Dec. 1, 1929, Sec. 4, at 4, col. 1.

[53] *E.g.,* United States v. Schwimmer, 279 U.S. 644, 653 (1929) (dissenting opinion); Schenck v. United States, 249 U.S. 47 (1919); Abrams v. United States, 250 U.S. 616, 624 (1919) (dissenting opinion). In the correspondence attendant upon the *Schwimmer* decision, in which WASP militarist Holmes made courteous replies to the tributes of Russian Jewish pacifist Rosika Schwimmer, readers saw another manifestation of the Brahmin's tolerance for ideologies and life styles alien to his own. *See* Sergeant, *supra* note 51, at 60.

[54] Pound, *Mechanical Jurisprudence,* 8 *Colum. L. Rev.* 605 (1908).

[55] Cardozo, *Mr. Justice Holmes,* 44 *Harv. L. Rev.* 682, 689 (1931).

[56] Hamilton, *supra* note 8.

[57] Reprinted in *Justice Oliver Wendell Holmes: His Book Notices and Uncollected Letters and Papers* 142 (H. Shriver ed. 1936).

[58] *Id.* at 143.

[59] C. Bowen, *Yankee From Olympus* 413 (1943).

[60] *Cf.* D. Wecter, *The Great Depression* (1948).

[61] *Cf.* W. Rumble, *American Legal Realism* (1965).

[62] S. Bent, *Justice Oliver Wendell Holmes* (1932).

[63] Berle, *Justice Holmes: Liberal,* 24 *Survey Graphic* 178 (1935).

[64] Derby, *Recollections of Mr. Justice Holmes,* 12 *N.Y.U.L.Q. Rev.* 345, 345-46 (1935). Max Lerner called Holmes "the very perfection and flowering of the New England aristocracy." Lerner, Book Review, 46 *Yale L. J.* 904, 908 (1937). Morris Cohen found him to have "intellectual power and the true liberal attitude that enabled him to rise above his hereditary class prejudices." Cohen, *Justice Holmes,* 82 *New Republic* 206, 207 (1935).

[65] *E.g.,* Llewellyn, *A Realistic Jurisprudence—The Next Step,* 30 *Colum. L. Rev.* 431 (1930); Llewellyn, *Some Realism About Realism,* 44 *Harv. L. Rev.* 1222 (1931).

[66] Llewellyn, *supra* note 65, at 454.

[67] Llewellyn, *Holmes,* 35 *Colum. L. Rev.* 485, 487-88 (1935).

[68] The transition was not so easy for others; many progressives parted company with the New Deal. *See* O. Graham, Jr., *An Encore for Reform* (1967).

[69] F. Frankfurter, *Mr. Justice Holmes and the Supreme Court* 44, 36-37, 43, 86 (1938).

[70] *N.Y. Times,* Jan. 13, 1932, 1, at 3, col. 4.

[71] *Id.* at col. 6.

[72] *N.Y. Times,* Mar. 6, 1935, 1, at 1, cols. 2-3.

[73] Amidst the shower of praise for Holmes in the 1930s came an occasionally querulous or critical note, foreshadowing a later shift in tone. H.L. Mencken felt that there was "no evidence in Holmes' decisions that he ever gave any really profound thought to the great battle of ideas that raged in his time." Holmes had "no . . . genuine belief in democracy," Mencken argued, and his decisions demonstrated "a widespread and beautiful inconsistency." Further, the "peculiar salacity" of Holmes's opinions, which made them "interesting as literature," derived in Mencken's opinion from an "easy-going cynicism." Holmes, Mencken felt, "had a considerable talent for epigrams," and when "once his mood had brought him to this or that judgment the announcement of it was sometimes more than a little affected by purely literary impulse. . . . [T]he result was . . . now and then . . . far more literature than law." Mencken, *The Great Holmes Mystery,* 26 *American Mercury* 123, 124 (1932). Kenneth Reiblich, in a 1939 analysis of Holmes's conflict-of-laws opinions, found that "certain concepts seemed to be accepted [by Holmes] as apriori truths and applied with little indication of the realism which one might have expected to find." Reiblich found puzzling the "conviction that Mr. Justice Holmes, the liberal and realist, becomes in conflict of laws the conservative and conceptualist." Reiblich, *The Conflict of Laws Philosophy of Mr. Justice Holmes,* 28 GEO. L.J. 1, 12, 20-21 (1939). Meanwhile, Walter Nelles and Samuel Mermin had concluded that "in his approach to labor questions Holmes was free from all such sentimentality as is expressed in talk of 'human rights' or 'brotherhood of man.' There was no humanitarian softness in his head." Nelles & Mermin, *Holmes and Labor Law,* 13 *N.Y.U.L.Q. Rev.* 517 (1936).

[74] Villard, *Issues and Men: The Great Judge,* 140 *Nation* 323 (1935).

[75] Bode, *Justice Holmes, Natural Law, and the Moral Ideal,* 29 *Internat'l J. Ethics* 397 (1919).

[76] L. Fuller, *The Law in Quest of Itself* 62-63 (1940).

[77] Lucey, *Jurisprudence and the Future Social Order,* 16 *Social Sci.* 211 (1941).

[78] Lucey, *Natural Law and American Legal Realism* 30 *Geo. L. J.* 493, 512, 531 (1942).

[79] Ford, *The Fundamentals of Holmes' Juristic Philosophy,* 11 *Fordham L. Rev.* 255. 275 (1942).

[80] Gregg, *The Pragmatism of Mr. Justice Holmes,* 31 *Geo. L. J.* 262, 284, 293, 294 (1943).

[81] Palmer, *Hobbes, Holmes, and Hitler,* 31 *A.B.A.J.* 569, 571-73 (1945).

[82] Boorstin, *The Elusiveness of Mr. Justice Holmes,* 14 *New England Q.* 478, 480-81 (1941).

[83] M. Lerner, *The Mind and Faith of Justice Holmes* 373 (1943).

[84] F. Biddle, *Mr. Justice Holmes* 95 (1942).

[85] Frankfurter, *Oliver Wendell Holmes,* 21 *Dictionary of American Biography* 417, 423 (1944).

[86] M. White, *supra* note 34, at 104, 74.

[87] Hamilton, *supra* note 8, at 1.

[88] McKinnon, *The Secret of Mr. Justice Holmes,* 36 *A.B.A.J.* 261, 345 (1950).

[89] Lucey, *Holmes—Liberal—Humanitarian—Believer in Democracy?,* 39 *Geo. L. J.* 523, 548, 553 (1951).

[90] Rodell, *Justice Holmes and His Hecklers,* 60 *Yale L. J.* 620, 623 (1951).

[91] Howe, *The Positivism of Mr. Justice Holmes,* 64 *Harv. L. Rev.* 529, 544-45 (1951).

[92] Hart, *Holmes' Positivism—An Addendum,* 64 *Harv. L. Rev.* 929, 937 (1951).

[93] Wyzanski, *The Democracy of Justice Oliver Wendell Holmes,* 7 *Vand. L. Rev.* 311, 319 (1954).

[94] Martin Hickman's "reappraisal" of Holmes revealed "a man arrogant beyond the ordinary, a man of narrow and oligarchical sympathies," whose "indulgence of the legislature . . . rested at least as much on contempt as on tolerance." The stereotype of Holmes that he "was a champion of free speech and civil rights, that he was compassionate and solicitous for the defenseless," Hickman argued, was not supported by "an examination of the cases." There "is a hollow ring to the finely turned phrases." Hickman, *Mr. Justice Holmes: A Reappraisal,* 5 *W. Pol. Q.* 66, 83, 73 (1952). Merle Pusey, in his biography of Charles Evans Hughes, wrote that the "Holmes whom the judges knew had little in common with the humanitarian crusader of the same name who has so often been extolled in print. Holmes' brethren knew that he didn't care a straw for the 'social' or 'progressive' legislation that he was said to be heroically defending. . . . [They] were well aware of his scorn for any deviation from the result he thought the law required because that result might be 'unjust' to the individuals concerned." I. M. Pusey, *Charles Evans Hughes* 287, 289 (1951).

[95] Irving Bernstein announced that the "cherished American myth . . . that Oliver Wendell Holmes was a liberal" was "as baseless as the tale of Washington and the cherry tree." Holmes, according to Bernstein, was "as profound, as civilized, and articulate a conservative as the United States has produced." He was "a firm believer in capitalism who looked with distrust upon governmental intervention in economic life. Monopolies won his respect, while he regarded unions and strikes suspiciously. . . . Movements seeking the reform or reconstruction of economic society won his distrust. . . . Free speech for Holmes was a Darwinian arena in which ideas would struggle for survival. It was at the same time a prop of a conservative society." Bernstein, *The Conservative Justice Holmes,* 23 *New England Q.* 435, 445, 449 (1950).

[96] H. S. Commager, *The American Mind* 874 (1950).

[97] S. Konefsky, *The Legacy of Holmes and Brandeis* 59, 24, 64, 303 (1956).

[98] M. Howe, *supra* note 7, at 10, vi.

[99] E. Wilson, *Patriotic Gore* 784 (1962).

[100] *E.g.,* Rogat, *The Judge as Spectator,* 31 *U. Chi. L. Rev.* 213, 230 (1964).

[101] E. Wilson, *supra* note 99, at 782-83.

[102] M. Howe, *supra* note 11, at 1-8, 256 (1963).

[103] Rogat, *supra* note 100, at 230.

[104] Touster, *In Search of Holmes From Within,* 18 *Vand. L. Rev.* 437, 470, 450-51 (1965).

[105] F. Biddle, *Justice Holmes, Natural Law and the Supreme Court* 7 (1961).

[106] Rogat, *supra* note 100, at 255.

[107] R. Faulkner, *The Jurisprudence of John Marshall* 253 (1968).

[108] Rogat, *supra* note 17, at 254-55, 24, 305, 308; Rogat, *supra* note 100, at 225.

[109] R. Faulkner, *supra* note 107, at 264-65, 263, 247-49.

[110] Truax v. Corrigan, 257 U.S. 312, 376 (1921).

[111] Duplex Co. v. Deering, 254 U.S. 443, 488 (1921).

[112] 1 *Holmes-Laski Lftters* 207 (M. Howe ed. 1953).

[113] O. W. Holmes, *Collected Legal Papers* 248 (1920).

[114] 2 *Holmes-Laski Letters* 946 (M. Howe ed. 1953).

[115] *Cf.* Howe, *supra* note 91.

[116] Rogat, *supra* note 100, at 230-31.

[117] Letter and Memorandum from Learned Hand to Mark DeWolfe Howe, Apr. 29, 1959, in M. Howe, *supra* note 102, at 8; Derby, *supra* note 64, at 352.

[118] Cardozo, *Mr. Justice Holmes,* 44 *Harv. L. Rev.* 682, 684 (1931).

G. Edward White (essay date 1976)

SOURCE: "The Integrity of Holmes' Jurisprudence," in *Intervention and Detachment: Essays in Legal History and Jurisprudence,* Oxford University Press, 1994, pp. 75-99.

[*In the following essay, White traces the concurrence of the tenures of Justices Holmes and Louis Brandeis with the rise of modern judicial liberalism.*]

A sharp distinction between "nineteenth-century" and "twentieth-century" phases of the American judicial tradition has some artificial features. Older jurisprudential attitudes and theories of judging persisted after 1900; their persistence, in fact, is one of the features of American judicial history in the twentieth century. The striking twentieth-century changes in the intellectual climate in which judicial decisions were made, discussed in this [essay], . . . should not create an inference that the nineteenth century, by contrast, was static in its jurisprudence; the difference is one of degree. Finally, the prominence given in this [essay] to modern liberalism as a force helping to redefine judicial attitudes cannot . . . be read as suggesting that an ideological dimension to judging in America is peculiar to the twentieth century.

Nonetheless, a major reorientation of the American judicial tradition did occur sometime shortly after 1900. The oracular theory of judging ceased to be regarded as a universal principle, eventually became a minority viewpoint, and subsequently lost academic respectability altogether. Although none of the basic challenges of appellate judging in America disappeared, the intellectual context in which they were faced was altered. That process of alteration was part of a more general re-examination of attitudes and values in America, out of which emerged the ideology of modern liberalism.

The standard referents for political thought during most of the twentieth century have been the terms "conservatism" and "liberalism." So ubiquitous has been their usage that they have ceased to function as sharp characterizations and have become symbolic instruments of rheto-ric. The incorporation of the term "liberalism" into our contemporary vocabulary in this fashion has some historical significance, since the term had, at its modern origins, a precise and revolutionary meaning. It had suggested then a radically new ideological perspective, based on a rejection of longstanding assumptions about the way in which society ought to be organized and on the creation of a novel relation between the individual citizen and his government. "Liberalism" has lost its original meaning largely because its premises have become so widely and loosely accepted. Before the 1920s the term, in its modern sense, was barely known; by the 1950s it was academically respectable to argue that liberalism had been the dominant ideology in the history of American civilization.[1]

The origins of modern liberalism in America coincided with the Supreme Court tenures of Justices Oliver Wendell Holmes and Louis Brandeis. The coincidence was accidental but of great import. The social thought of Holmes and Brandeis was not decisively affected by the emergence of twentieth-century liberalism, nor were their interpretations of their office markedly influenced by any desire to act as models of modern liberal judges. But the advent of liberalism provided critics of the judiciary with a new perspective from which to evaluate judicial performance. This perspective revealed innovative and contemporary elements in the jurisprudence of Holmes and of Brandeis and led to their apotheosis as heroic liberal judges.

I

Modern liberalism began in America with an insight, which dawned around the outbreak of World War I and revived in the 1920s, that the cultural unity of American civilization was disintegrating. There were numerous diverse manifestations of this perception, ranging from nervous reaffirmations of the purity of Anglo-Saxon America to attacks upon traditional symbols of virtue and respectability.[2] Linking these myriad forms of protest was a feeling that the core values of American culture had become meaningless slogans, capable of countless self-serving interpretations and hence no longer capable of functioning as a code of honorable behavior. As though for the first time, skeptics of the period saw that every unifying value engendered its own countervalue: morality begat hypocrisy; progress, exploitation; religiosity, bigotry; refinement, snobbishness; democracy, philistinism. As older consensual values became tarnished, former success models became figures of irony and pathos. The captain of industry, the self-made man, and the super-salesman were each regarded as having had a part in creating the stock market crash of 1929 and the ensuing depression.

Another perception followed from the original consciousness of value disintegration. Mature industrialism had created inequities and left a residue of victims. While rewarding a large segment of the nation's citizens, it had ignored or hurt other segments. It had not, for instance, eradicated poverty, or measurably improved the welfare of industrial laborers, or helped the increased percentage of elderly persons, or improved the quality of rural life. For these groups, progress had not necessarily been beneficial; for them industrialization had not brought success.

Over time, the sense of a wholesale loss of consensual American values merged with the perception of the costs of industrial progress to produce an affirmative ideology that supplanted the scattered "reform" movements of the late nineteenth and early twentieth centuries. The chief catalyst in the appearance of modern liberalism as a positive social philosophy in America was the crisis produced by the Depression of the 1930s. That crisis gave an immediacy to reform proposals that had been articulated in the 1920s by persons such as the advocates of a welfare state in Great Britain.[3] The principal innovation of modern liberalism was its utilization of the state as an agent to fill the void left by consensual value disintegration. The state, in this role, became a permanent force for social planning, order, and enlightened progress, substituting its administrative procedures for the discredited set of traditional values. It articulated common national goals by fiat and conceived and executed social policies consistent with those goals. The goals were not elaborately linked to consensual values; they were more often the tentative formulations of those who managed the state. The pursuit of social goals represented a form of coerced coherence necessitated by crisis and the dissolution of a previous value consensus.

Liberalism, at the time of its origin, represented a modification of some of the tenets of preceding reform movements in the light of a twentieth-century crisis in values. It retained a belief in an active, positive government; it also supported expansion of the class of government wards and beneficiaries. But it modified many of the substantive assumptions of advocates of one or another form of paternalism, embodying them, if at all, in standards of fair procedure. A comparison of liberalism with populism and the early-twentieth-century reform movement of progressivism illustrates the modifications. The populists and progressives both supported legislation intended to benefit industrial laborers; so did the liberals of the New Deal. The rhetorical emphasis of the first two groups was on removing the conditions—such as excessive size in industrial corporations and exploitation of workers by employers—that prevented workers from achieving freedom and independence in their jobs. The rhetorical emphasis of liberalism was on securing for industrial workers a forum, through unionization and collective bargaining, in which their interests could be fairly and equally represented. For populists or progressives, reform often had a moral content, evidenced in idealized roles for its beneficiaries, such as that of free and independent yeomen for industrial workers. Liberal reformers were not so much concerned with the life-style or moral character of those whose causes they supported as with insuring them a fair opportunity to air their grievances and promote their own self-interests.[4]

Although the idea of professionals in government was first articulated in the twentieth century by progressives, liberals gave it a new interpretation. The progressives, borrowing notions advanced by late-nineteenth-century elite reformers, argued that the presence in government of persons of high social and economic status would stimulate a revival of moral values because such persons would be above corruption and beyond the influence of special interests.[5] Liberals, though retaining a belief that government should be managed by elites, equated elite status more with technical and administrative expertise than with wealth or social position. This modification was in keeping with the assumption of modern liberals that professionalism's essential impact was to be felt in efficient and fair governmental procedures.

At its inception liberalism was an ideology based less on a commitment to shared values than on a response to their perceived disintegration. But as it evolved, its constant attention to the plight of casualties of progress became itself a value, often articulated as humanitarianism. As the victims of twentieth-century life came to include not only economic minorities but also ethnic, religious, or racial groups, a paradox developed. Humanitarianism compelled support for those whose minority status was made manifest by usurpations of their civil rights and liberties. Yet policies conceived and implemented by governmental officials inevitably produced such usurpations. What was the proper liberal response to government suppression of dissident speech in wartime, to wartime incarceration of naturalized American citizens who had retained or previously held citizenship in an enemy nation, to the invasion of welfare recipients' privacy by government agencies? Liberalism had as its major premise the validity of positive governmental intervention to further individual rights; what happened when the state acted to suppress them?

The paradoxes in modern liberalism were reflected in its ideals for judicial performance. On one hand, liberalism asked judges to reach results in keeping with the substantive values it cherished, such as those that sustained affirmative governmental action to alleviate economic and social inequalities or to help disadvantaged persons. On the other hand, liberalism asked judges to interpret their office in a professional manner—and by the 1920s judicial professionalism had taken on a new meaning. The model of judging embodied by Field had encountered strong criticism from legal scholars. The model permitted (so critics charged) an unwarranted imposition of the social and economic views of judges on the public at large. The apparent refusal of many members of the judiciary to respond to changed social conditions only exacerbated the situation.[6] Indeed some states, thwarted by the courts in their attempts to enact social welfare legislation, had responded by imposing elective checks, such as recall, on the performance of their judges. Two early-twentieth-century jurisprudential theories, Sociological Jurisprudence and a then nameless one that was eventually called Realism, had gained prominence on the strength of arguments that judging was a highly politicized and idiosyncratic process and that effective judicial performance could come only from constant attention to the social context of decisions, a full recognition by judges of the role that bias played in decision-making, and serious efforts on the part of the judiciary to confine the scope of its powers.[7]

The stunning effect of this criticism, in terms of the history of appellate judging, was its discrediting of the oracular theory of judicial decision-making. Deference by the judiciary to legislative activity was required (the critique maintained) for the reason that law could be shaped in the process of judicial interpretation to harmonize with the predilections of the judge. To claim that judicial theories of social organization or economics were outmoded was to imply that the law could be made synonymous with the social attitudes of judges. The vast majority of nineteenth-century jurists had not ignored the fact that judges had social attitudes, but they had insisted on a separation of those attitudes from the fabric of the law itself. Discovering the law remained a process independent of one's personal convictions, despite the social ramifications of discoveries. Sociological Jurisprudence and Realism found the separation between "law" and the interpretations of its officials to be artificial. Realism eventually took the step of equating law with the idiosyncratic judgments of judges and other lawmakers, but this step was not necessary to discredit the oracular theory of judging. All that was needed was the triumph of the belief that judges were, even in a limited sense, lawmakers rather than simply law finders.

All these factors combined to make what came to be called judicial self-restraint an important professional value. Competent professionalism, as defined by a set of academic critics in the early twentieth century, demanded that judges abandon the use of their office to bar "excessively democratic" legislation. Such a response was grounded simply on bias and was therefore intellectually unjustifiable. The appellate judiciary should not substitute its views on social issues for those of the legislature; the latter branch was far better suited to perceive and respond to social change. Judicial professionalism, if not humanitarianism, thus dictated deference on the part of judges to the affirmative governmental actions supported by liberals.

From the time of Holmes's appointment to the Court in 1902 through Brandeis's appointment in 1916 to Holmes's retirement in 1932, the general tenets of liberalism and its double-edged mandate for the judiciary gained increasing acceptance. At the same time a large number of appellate judges, including a shifting majority of the Justices on the Supreme Court, continued to scrutinize and invalidate social welfare legislation, often using language that suggested a continued belief in the oracular theory of judging. In most instances the scrutinized legislation constituted an intervention in behalf of disadvantaged groups or individuals. From a liberal perspective, judicial self-restraint in such cases facilitated desirable results. For reasons primarily related to their approach to judging, Holmes and Brandeis both protested against judicial involvement in the great majority of such cases and were subsequently hailed as modern liberals.[8] In a smaller set of cases, the limits of government power to suppress individual rights were tested. Here the Holmes-Brandeis hegemony broke down, and differences between their jurisprudential views were revealed. In this latter group of cases their images as liberals became somewhat clouded, and some of the inherent contradictions in judicial liberalism were first exposed.

II

The conspicious advantages of Holmes's youth—his family being socially prominent, economically comfortable, and at the center of Boston's intellectual community—only served to fire his ambition to divorce himself from his heritage and to distinguish himself in his own right. His father was not merely a competent physician and well-known poet but also a leading public figure of his time; he loved publicity, social companionship, and good conversation, and his public reputation was thereby so deeply entrenched that when the younger Holmes was appointed to the Supreme Court in 1902, at age sixty-one, he was chiefly described as Dr. Holmes's son.[9] Holmes reacted early and sharply against the stature and impact of his father. He was as solitary and self-preoccupied as his father was garrulous; as serious and introspective as his father was effervescent and glib. Dr. Holmes thought his son given to "looking at life as a solemn show where he is only a spectator";[10] William James, less charitable, found in him a "cold-blooded, conscious egotism and conceit."[11] For his part, Holmes thought his father "largely distracted into easy talk and occasional verse": had Dr. Holmes been "less popular," said his son, "he might have produced a great work."[12]

In Holmes's college years he seemed eager to arrive at some organizing ideological or philosophical principle that would isolate his way of thinking from that of his family circle. He rejected his father's religious views and at one point believed that "an all-comprehending science has embraced the universe . . . generalizing and systematizing . . . every vagary of the human mind."[13] In the 1850's, as the gap between North and South widened, Holmes became a rabid abolitionist and, when war came, enlisted in a regiment of Massachusetts volunteers in the Union army. Once at war, however, he found that life resisted a neat intellectual ordering and that the rightness or wrongness of beliefs was largely irrelevant. From these experiences came the celebrated paradoxes on which Holmes built his mature philosophic stance. Searching for general principles was the ultimate in intellectual satisfaction, but no generalization was worth a damn; fighting for ideals was heroic, but ideals were meaningless in themselves.

One can see the presence of these paradoxes in Holmes's scholarship, written largely in the nineteenth century; in his general attitude toward the relation of governmental institutions to social change; and in his interpretation of his judicial office. In his most extensive and impressive piece of scholarship, *The Common Law* (1880), he adopted an analytical technique that was to become characteristic: exposure of the fallacies of a prevailing system of thought, substitution of a counter-system, denial of the "truth" of that counter-system. In *The Common Law* the discarded system was nineteenth-century "logic," by which Holmes meant the formalistic, religion-based logic that reasoned downward syllogistically from assumed truths about the universe; the proposed counter-system was "experience," the changing "felt necessities" that reflected current social values and were altered by time and circumstances. Yet experience did not always produce wisdom, and change was not always for the better; so Holmes's system was not a model for lawmaking but merely a fatalistic acceptance that law was not so much the embodiment of reason as a manifestation of dominant beliefs at a given time.

Similar messages were conveyed in his two other major contributions to legal scholarship of the nineteenth century. In an essay, **"The Path of the Law,"** he denied that the law was "a system of reason" or a series of "deduction[s] from principles of ethics";[14] it was simply an embodiment of the ends and purposes of a society at a given point in its history. One could study current social purposes and, by referring legal rules to them, better understand the course of legal development. One could not, however, treat some purposes as invariably true or timeless and erect a logical jurisprudence on them. In another essay, **"Law in Science and Science in Law,"** he argued, in fact, that one could even measure, through the techniques of statistics and economics, the intensity of the "competing social desires" that clashed in a lawsuit and, having made that measurement, arrive at a decision that kept law "in accord with the wishes and feelings of the community." But science, though a helpful tool, could not be thought of as an ultimate organizing principle. There would probably never be, Holmes felt, a "commonwealth in which science [was] everywhere supreme." It was only "an ideal—but "without ideals what is life worth?"[15]

Holmes apparently never read a newspaper (at least in his later life), and kept informed on contemporary events mainly through correspondence and conversation. Although he once said that academic life was half-life, his life-style while a judge, particularly during his tenure on the Supreme Court, was cloistered, focused on intellectual pursuits, and entirely isolated from national government and politics. Yet Holmes had no difficulty forming opinions on current political issues and resolving, as a judge, delicate questions of government. So integrated and flexible was his philosophic stance that it could absorb new issues, ideals, and events without disturbing its essential balance.

Life, Holmes assumed, was in constant flux, ideals gaining and losing primacy; one could not alter this process, however devoted one was to a particular viewpoint. The temporary triumph or defeat of ideas was determined by the unregulated intellectual marketplace. Hence there was no harm in tolerating the expression of ideas but no guarantee that any idea could survive for all time. Since America was a republic, majority opinion determined the acceptability of views, and a majority had the right to impose its beliefs on minorities. The principal vehicle for majoritarian expression was the lawmaking branch of the government; legislative power, grounded on majoritarian sentiment, was therefore limitless. But a majoritarian power to suppress minority viewpoints could be exercised only when the activities or viewpoints of a minority could reasonably be said to subvert social goals espoused by the prevailing majority. Up to that point, dissenting actions or opinions were protected, since they had a right to enter the intellectual marketplace to become "popular" or to be confined to oblivion.

Accordingly, the legislative branch of government could suppress speech, but only if the speech in question were clearly subversive of majoritarian social goals.[16] It could sterilize imbeciles if the ultimate eradication of mental defectives from the population were an end receiving majority support and if sterilization could reasonably be said to further that end.[17] It could prevent aliens from owning guns if the belief of a majority that aliens were inclined more than citizens to violence could be deemed reasonable.[18] A citizen might nonetheless campaign all his life against a war, in behalf of imbeciles, for equal treatment for aliens, or for the broader ideal of freedom to act and speak in a dissenting vein. American society had long recognized the latter ideal, and Holmes believed that he would be as willing as others had been to die for it.[19] But at some point civilized living in America required the recognition that unpopular views were ultimately impotent because the sentiments of the majoritarians determined the path of the law; and short of revolution, the laws of a majority were to be obeyed.

If Holmes's polity worked smoothly, dissenting actions and viewpoints continually beat against the wall of majoritarianism, the majority acted against them, and clashes in "social desires" resulted. The resolution of these clashes was the task of the courts, which held the "sovereign prerogative of choice."[20] But their freedom of choice was severely limited. To some extent, courts were bound by the choices of their predecessors; it was not generally the province of judges to "undertake to renovate the law."[21] Even on those occasions when precedents gave no guidelines, a series of institutional constraints derived from Holmes's notion of majoritarian sovereignty limited judicial freedom. The judiciary, not being elected representatives of the majority, was [not] to substitute its views for those of legislatures. The judiciary did not necessarily protect even constitutional rights against legislative infringement. All individual rights, for Holmes, were ultimately held at majority sufferance. Vindication of a right that the majority chose to circumscribe required a revolution and the forcible installation of a new majority.

Over and over, in his years on the Supreme Court, Holmes sounded these themes. Paternalistic social-welfare legislation was challenged before the Court; Holmes, who liked to play the cranky Social Darwinist, muttered about the frivolity or foolishness of the legislation but upheld the legislature's power to enact it. This interpretation of the judicial function came to be called tolerant or self-restrained or even statesmanlike by Holmes's admirers. Holmes, professing disdain for the last appellation, privately coveted it.[22]

In the end Holmes's intellectual vantage point was compatible with the opposing impulses that lurked, unarticulated, within him. He felt pride in the democratic and egalitarian consciousness of Americans, yet he was an intellectual and social snob, contemptuous of the "crowd." His personal relations were marked by barriers and distance. The archetypal Holmes friendship was a correspondence friendship, with the other participant being inaccessible to Holmes except for occasional visits. Even the most persistent of his correspondents, such as Harold Laski, rarely got beyond a certain level of intimacy. When Laski proposed, after many years of letters, that he call Holmes by his first name, he was summarily rebuffed.

Although much of Holmes's communication with others was at the level of intellectual abstraction, he also had an earthy, bawdy side, which punctuated his talk and occasionally his writings and revealed itself in his covert private life. Much of the distinctiveness of Holmes's style came from his juxtaposition of earthy or homely language with abstract ideas; although he held the two impulses apart in his activities, in his thoughts they easily intermeshed. "I wonder," he once said, "if cosmically an idea is any more important than the bowels."[23]

The internal tensions in Holmes ultimately led him to a fatalistic dependence on paradox and impotence, and this formed the basis of his jurisprudence. Consciously or unconsciously, he perceived the opposing impulses in himself, and gave up attempting to reconcile them. Whether man was inherently evil or perfectible, whether change ever constituted progress, even whether he himself existed—a question he took seriously—were unanswerable riddles. The easy solution was to acknowledge "ultimate facts"—power, force, and change—and let the "goodness or badness of laws" turn on "what the crowd wants," even though the crowd, "if it knew," would not want what it did.[24]

III

Late in his career Holmes came increasingly to parallel Brandeis, who had joined Holmes on the Court in 1916, in his voting record on certain constitutional issues. Chief Justice William Howard Taft, who was never enthusiastic about Brandeis as a colleague, said that in his later years Holmes was "so completely under the control" of Brandeis that it gave Brandeis two votes instead of one.[25] A 1927 press comment claimed that Holmes and Brandeis had "achieved a spiritual kinship that mark[ed] them off as a separate liberal chamber" of the Court.[26]

The kinship of Holmes and Brandeis was one of the accidents of history. Neither their temperaments nor their philosophies were similar; the congruence of their views was largely a matter of time and circumstance.

As a young man Brandeis coveted the symbols of Holmes's inheritance: social prestige, affluence, and access to the Boston intelligentsia. The son of German immigrants who had settled in Kentucky, he entered Harvard Law School at eighteen in 1875 and rapidly became entranced by the intellectual atmosphere of Cambridge, determining for himself the "rising lights" among his professors[27] and "carefully not[ing] the names and addresses of eminent people."[28] He felt, as a Southerner, a Jew, and not a college graduate, that gaps existed between himself and his peers; he strove to narrow those gaps by adopting the life-styles of those about him. He was successful enough in this endeavor to lay the groundwork for a prospective law partnership in Boston with Samuel Warren, a wealthy socialite, and to secure for himself and his wife, a Jew from New York, a moderate degree of acceptance on the part of Boston society.[29]

Once economically and socially comfortable, however, Brandeis did not blend into Holmes's world. He was mindful, as he said to a close friend, that "whatever I have achieved, or may achieve is my own, pure and simple, unassisted by the fortuitous circumstances of family influence or social position,"[30] and he retained a distance from the life in the trappings of which he surrounded himself. He joined clubs in order to "captivate" potential clients,[31] insisted that his wife adopt conventional upper-class dress standards, and dabbled in gentlemanly politics, such as civil service reform; yet in 1891 he attributed "the little successes I may have had" to "pressure from within" that stemmed from "a deep sense of obligation" rather than from "the allurement of a possible distinction."[32] Obligation for Brandeis meant adherence to a code of rigid personal standards, which included the tenets of self-denial, distaste for excess in any form, and moral righteousness. It was as though he were compelled by his conscience to follow these standards, with success following naturally upon them.

The Brandeis code justified, among other things, low heat in his law office to save expense, a short working day (to keep one's mind fresh), disdain for drinking, dancing, and like pursuits, the zealous molding of the lives of the underprivileged so that paupers might achieve "moral growth,"[33] distaste for sloppy and inefficient business practices, and eventually, in his maturity, adoption of the public as his client in a series of lawsuits designed to dissolve the monopolistic positions held by gas utilities, life insurance companies, banks, and the New Haven Railroad. It was not important to Brandeis that in those suits he actually represented competitors of the various industries rather than their consumers. What was important was that his clients recognize the value of moderation, efficiency, and social responsibility in their business practices. The proper task of the legal profession was to aid them in that recognition. Lawyers at large should occupy the position Brandeis had carved out for himself: one of "independence between the wealthy and the people, prepared to curb the excesses of either."[34]

By the time of Brandeis's appointment to the Court, against the protests of an influential segment of the Boston legal and commercial community, who felt that the combination of an economic reformer and a Jew was too much to tolerate, the eligible beneficiaries of his wisdom were numerous. He had scrutinized business trusts and concluded that excessive size produced economic waste. The trust-busting aspects of Woodrow Wilson's New Freedom were largely his creation.[35] Scientific management, the efficiency-oriented program created by the engineer Frederick Taylor, had become one of his causes, even though it was opposed by labor unions whose members he wanted to liberate from their industrial slavery. The moral fervor of Zionism and its passion for social planning attracted him, and he began to deplore assimilation on the part of American Jews, calling it "national suicide."[36] He lobbied for reform of the banking industry and was one of the draftsmen of the Federal Reserve Act, which initiated national control over the distribution of currency and credit. Even institutions of government became objects of Brandeisian crusades. As counsel for *Collier's Weekly,* which had exposed mismanagement of Interior Department resources, Brandeis publicized the cause of a middle-level employee of Interior who had been muzzled for uncovering inefficiency and corruption in his superiors.

As with Holmes, a juxtaposition of competing impulses formed the core of Brandeis's philosophy. In his case the impulses were those of freedom and self-restraint. Excess size, inequities, or inefficiencies choked or stifled individual initiative, he believed, but success and accomplishment were ascribed to self-abnegation and a conservation of human resources. Brandeis found industrial laborers his "most congenial company,"[37] and regarded the industrious among them as heroes (but was infuriated to see them smoking cigarettes). For him they were to be a counterpoint to the "intense materialism and luxuriousness"[38] of economic royalists. Freedom came, as it had in his case, from self-denial. In countless attempts to ingratiate himself with the eminent in Boston, in endless chilly days with overcoats substituted for radiators, in the husbanding of his early savings bonds, the moderation of pleasures, and the renunciation of luxuries were found the bits and pieces of Brandeis's eventual independence. When he joined the Court he was financially secure and beholden to no class or interest group. He was also convinced of his own righteousness, and zealous to impose his life-style on others.

The cosmic reach of Brandeis's philosophy suggested that he might come to the Court with developed views on the proper function of the judiciary. In actuality he had given little thought to the specific task of appellate judging, tending to include judges within his general observations on the legal profession. Two themes were central to his interpretation of law practice: the importance of empirical observation, and the lawyer's duty to be an intermediary between his clients and the public. Confronted with a legal problem, Brandeis sought to gather "the facts," and his great powers of organization and synthesis made fact analysis one of his special arts.

The facts having been collected and sifted, a course of action emerged. Each problem, he felt, formed the evidentiary basis of its own solution, since a sufficient supply of empirical data clarified the costs and benefits of various legal approaches. With the solution at hand, the next task was to persuade a client of its virtue. Here again, a grasp of "facts," including an understanding of the client's temperament, was a lawyer's best weapon. Empirical analysis, then, led to an inductive reasoning process in which costs were weighed against benefits; the process yielded a strategy with independent validity; a lawyer proceeded to persuade his client to adopt that strategy; in so doing, he not only gave good advice but influenced social policy and preserved his independence as well.

Judging, for Brandeis, was simply another exercise in this method. It was not a process of "reasoning from abstract conception," but one of "reasoning from life," taking "notice of facts."[39] In his first years on the Court, Brandeis seemed to make almost no distinction between his opinions and the briefs he had written as an advocate. He set forth the factual basis of his inquiry, undertook an extensive empirical investigation (complete with technical references), made a cost-benefit analysis of the effects of various policy choices made by a lower court or a legislature, chose the most efficient solution, and lobbied for it. In a case in his first year on the Court, *Adams v. Tanner,*[40] which considered the constitutionality of a Washington statute prohibiting employment agencies from charging fees, Brandeis asked himself what was "the evil which the people of Washington sought to correct," why had they chosen "the particular remedy embodied in the statute," and what had been "the experience . . . of other states or countries in this connection."[41] Fifteen pages of labor statistics provided the answers. Private employment agencies had been corrupt and inefficient. It was reasonable for the people of Washington to want to eradicate corruption and inefficiency, and just for the Court to promote their cause.

For Holmes, this sort of partisan documentation was out of place in a judicial opinion[42]—and tedious as well. Holmes was not concerned with showing the positive value of paternalistic or regulatory legislation, but merely that its basis was reasonable. Therein lay a vital difference between him and Brandeis. Both men, as judges, believed that a legislative majority could infringe upon individual rights. "Above all rights," Brandeis said in one opinion, "rises duty to the community."[43] But whereas Holmes simply accepted the ultimate logic of that view, Brandeis needed to be personally convinced of the rightness of the majority's action. He was not receptive to, indeed was suspicious of, governmental power in the abstract, but when that power was being used for a moral purpose, he welcomed it. For example, Brandeis believed that economic independence and political democracy were interrelated. Excess size in enterprises was not only wasteful, he felt, but posed a threat to individual self-reliance, since the enterprise, as a unit, came to wield power over its own employees and other American citizens. Hence the use of governmental power to reduce the size of giant corporations amounted to a crusade for individual freedom. There was nothing inherently attractive in governmental power, however; "Big Government" was as much a potential threat to the individual as "Big Business."

Holmes, in contrast, recognized the "fact" of majority sovereignty and suggested to oppressed minorities that they consider revolution. In the historic struggles between the increasingly omnipotent governments of the twentieth century and various sets of individual rights, Holmes's reaction to government intervention—if he thought it anything but arbitrary—was generally passive; Brandeis's selectively enthusiastic or hostile. Consequently Holmes was almost uniformly indifferent to individual rights or liberties, whether economic or civil, whereas Brandeis, despite his view that all rights were ultimately subsumed in a broad obligation to society, occasionally approximated the stance of a civil libertarian.

IV

Of the thousands of opinions written by Holmes and Brandeis during their tenure on the Court, perhaps the most revealing, if not necessarily the most influential, were those in which they considered the effect of governmental regulation on two sets of liberties—first, the Fifth and Fourteenth Amendments' alleged guarantees of "liberty of contract"; second, the First and Fourteenth Amendments' guarantees of free speech.

The doctrine of liberty of contract, originally hinted at by Cooley in *Constitutional Limitations,* was developed in state courts in the 1880s,[44] was slowly and obliquely incorporated in Supreme Court decisions in the late 1880s and 1890s,[45] and was explicitly, though irregularly, accepted by a Court majority between 1905 and 1923.[46] Its advocates postulated an inalienable right in employers and employees to buy and sell their goods or services on terms they chose, deriving this right, originally, from the Fourteenth Amendment's protection against state interference with liberty and property. Later a similar gloss was made on the Fifth Amendment's protection of liberty and property rights from interference by the federal government, making liberty of contract a philosophical principle as well as a constitutional doctrine. In its most extreme form, liberty of contract declared that any governmental attempt to regulate private contractual relations was presumptively invalid. It was that presumption that jeopardized much of the welfare legislation of the early twentieth century.

Judicial use of the liberty-of-contract doctrine to invalidate paternalistic legislation became an object of controversy in the first decade of the twentieth century. Oppo-nents of the doctrine, among them Roscoe Pound and Theodore Roosevelt, suggested that it was unsound for two reasons: it ignored "new conceptions of the relation of property to human welfare,"[47] and it exemplified an artificial process of judicial reasoning in which predetermined beliefs were developed pseudologically "in the teeth of the actual facts."[48] If every man held his property subject to the general right of the community to regulate its use, property and contract rights were not inalienable. To exaggerate their importance in judicial formulas such as liberty of contract, which ignored the disadvantaged position of industrial workers in modern America, was to fail to adjust "[legal] principles and doctrines to human conditions."[49] This failure invited a characterization of judges as reactionaries or antiquarians.

Holmes identified himself with the opponents of liberty of contract in his first Supreme Court opinion, but his opposition stemmed from a different source. The case, *Otis v. Parker,*[50] tested the constitutionality of a California statute prohibiting sales of stock shares on margin. Holmes dismissed a claim that the statute limited unduly the freedom of adult persons to make contracts, by invoking his view on the proper allocation of institutional power in America. The fact that a statute could be said in a general way to violate the Constitution did not end the inquiry, he maintained, for "general propositions do not carry us far." The appropriate question for the Court in cases involving legislative infringement of "liberties" was not whether judges thought the statute "excessive, unsuited to its ostensible end, or based on [disagreeable] conceptions of morality," but whether it had a rational purpose and could be said to be a reasonable exercise of legislative power.[51]

At the outset of his career on the Court, then, Holmes indicated that his opposition to the liberty-of-contract doctrine could not be grounded on any enthusiasm for the paternalistic legislation that he sustained against its challenge. He thought that hours-and-wages laws merely "shift[ed] the burden to a different point of incidence";[52] he professed indifference toward "legislation to make other people better";[53] he did not believe that "wholesale regeneration" could be achieved "by tinkering with the institution of property."[54] He simply acquiesced in the apparent fact that "the liberty of a citizen to do as he likes" was "interfered with . . . by every state or municipal institution which takes his money for purposes thought desirable, whether he likes it or not."[55] When a legislative majority believed that an "important ground of public policy" called for restraint of individual liberties, Holmes felt that the Constitution permitted that restraint. "[T]he right to make contracts at will that has been derived from the word liberty in the [Fifth and Fourteenth] Amendments," he observed, had "been stretched to its extreme."[56]

From *Lochner v. New York* through *Adair v. U.S.* to *Adkins v. Children's Hospital,* the last a 1923 case invalidating the constitutionality of a minimum-wage law in the District of Columbia as an undue interference with the liberty to contract, Holmes protested against the use of the doctrine and all such "general propositions of law" to decide "concrete cases." But his protest stemmed from a general proposition of his own: "the scope of state sovereignty" was "a question of fact."[57] By this phrase Holmes meant that governmental interference with individual liberties was permissible in circumstances in which that interference could be shown to be grounded on some rational basis or tied to the achievement of some important public purpose. Whether it could be so shown or so tied was a matter of quasi-empirical proof, proof of the seriousness and rationality of the legislature's purpose. The importance and seriousness of a given purpose varied with time, but the test of its rationality was majority sentiment. A majority might behave irrationally, however, and not every interference with liberties was justifiable. The mere fact that legislation infringing individual rights furthered a public purpose did not prevent judicial inquiry into its reasonableness. Such inquiries, however, could only be made on an *ad hoc* basis.

Nowhere in Holmes's approach was there an attempt to demonstrate the particular worth of a piece of legislation. He would support a paternalistic statute only to the extent of conceding that an economic or social inequality existed and that the disadvantaged group could fairly convince a majority that the inequality ought to be alleviated. Thus, in his dissent in *Coppage v. Kansas,*[58] a 1915 case that struck down a Kansas statute prohibiting employers from preventing their employees from joining labor unions, Holmes stated that "in present conditions a workingman not unnaturally might believe that only by belonging to a union can he secure a contract that shall be fair to him,"[59] but stopped well short of endorsing the value of labor unions.

In contrast to this fatalism and indifference was the righteousness and zeal of Brandeis. Liberty of contract arguments stimulated Brandeis to demonstrate the value of the legislation being challenged. His interest was not so much in exposing the sterility of judicial decisions that reasoned downward from preconceived beliefs as in showing that the preconceptions themselves were unsound in light of the "facts" of twentieth-century life in America. The liberty-of-contract doctrine was inadequate, he felt, not so much because it represented the inappropriate judical promulgation of a particular economic theory, but because it assumed an equality of bargaining power between employees and employers when it did not actually exist, or because it failed to recognize that, in modern life, considerations of social welfare could transcend the exercise of individual rights.

For Brandeis there were good theories and bad theories, purposes that were noble and purposes that were illegitimate. A Washington statute forbidding employment agencies from receiving fees for their services had been passed in response to a number of "evils" incumbent upon that practice, including waste, inefficiency, and corruption.[60] An Arizona law forbidding the use of injunctions in labor disputes had been partially motivated by the inequitable and heavy-handed use of the practices and by the divided state of public opinion as to its efficacy.[61] A Nebraska statute fixing maximum weights for loaves of bread was attempting to eradicate unfair competition among bakers and frauds on the public.[62]

Brandeis's support for legislative infringements on individual rights, in short, varied with his enthusiasm for the goals envisaged by the legislation. In certain areas of life he believed firmly that persons should be protected against their own self-destructive tendencies, requiring not only moral guidance but a degree of coercion. Consumption of alcoholic beverages was one of these areas. For Brandeis "evil [was] sure to flow from the appetite of men for stimulating liquors."[63] He supported prohibition legislation and, as a judge, he granted to the federal government and the states a wide scope of power to implement it. A provision of the War-Time Prohibition Act of 1918 preventing the sale of liquors in bond was not an unconstitutional taking of property.[64] Congress and the states had power to enact legislation designed to suppress traffic in intoxicating liquors even if that legislation regulated alleged non-intoxicants such as beer and malt liquor.[65] The presence of intoxicating liquor in a car rendered it forfeitable to the government regardless of whether the car's owner knew of the liquor's presence.[66] The amount of liquor dispensed by physicians for medicinal purposes could be limited by Congress.[67]

Brandeis did not apply uniformly his belief that a paternalistic government should protect members of the public against themselves. In the area of free speech he seemed to move, in the course of his career in the Court, toward a stricter standard of judicial scrutiny for regulatory legislation than he advocated in cases involving property and contract rights. Holmes, as well, appeared in free speech cases to be giving greater deference to individual rights than his theory of majoritarian sovereignty would allow.

Free-speech cases in the early twentieth century underscored the anxieties that centered around the place of consensual norms and values in American civilization. Freedom to express dissident and unpopular sentiments had been a traditional American value, part of the nation's revolutionary heritage. But World War I, an increasingly diverse and heterogeneous population, and the international success of alternative ideologies to capitalism and democracy combined to·produce a perception that dissident attitudes and values could threaten national security. As the ethnic and cultural heritage of American citizens became more diffuse, pressures for national unity against outside threats increased. The result was a strident reaffirmation of the values and norms that allegedly unified Americans in the face of their disintegration. Dissident speech raised the troublesome problem of defining what beliefs early twentieth-century Americans still held in common.

Holmes came to free-speech cases with an attitude he once expressed by saying "I see no meaning in the rights of man except what the crowd will fight for."[68] There were no such things as natural rights for Holmes, only the right of majorities to impose their opinions on minorities and the correlative right of minorities to overthrow the majority. But exchange of ideas, in a democratic society, was an essential part of the continual replacement of majorities by other majorities. Little as Holmes believed in the inalienability of free speech, he said, he hoped he would die for it; although time had "upset many fighting faiths," the "ultimate good desired" was best achieved by "free trade in ideas."[69]

Holmes thus appears to have accepted, in addition to the "ultimate fact" of force on which governmental power rested, an intermediate basis of legitimacy. In democratic societies, at any rate, one way in which majorities held power was by convincing citizens of the rightness of their beliefs. They imposed their views on others and suppressed dissenting opinions, but they also attempted to justify their own actions. Quite often in America, Holmes believed, majorities "doubt[ed] [their] power or [their] premises."[70] There was something about American civilization that lent an uneasy status to the naked use of power. Holmes did not go on record as applauding this uneasiness. He took pains, in fact, to stress that power was the essential rationale for governmental acts. But he recognized it and built his analysis of free-speech questions upon it.

Holmes began his free-speech decisions by stressing the power in legislatures to suppress speech and, having established that premise, attempted to work out an accommodation between majoritarian sovereignty and the First Amendment. In *Patterson v. Colorado,*[71] a 1907 decision, he allowed the Colorado Supreme Court to hold in contempt a man who had published articles criticizing its motives, announcing in the process that the First Amendment's protection extended primarily to prior restraints on speech, not to speech that had been published. In the 1915 case of *Fox v. Washington,*[72] which sustained the constitutionality of a statute punishing any speech that had a tendency to encourage or incite the commission of a crime, he made no inquiry into the actual consequences of the speaker's words.

But in *Schenck v. United States*[73] and *Abrams v. United States,* two 1919 cases, he appeared to be moving toward a practical compromise between governmental power and free expression, embodied in the "clear and present danger" test articulated in *Schenck.* The proper judicial inquiry in speech cases, Holmes maintained, was "whether the words used are used in such circumstances and are of such a nature as to create a clear and present danger that they will bring about the substantive evils that Congress has a right to prevent."[74] Under this test, circulars urging persons subject to the draft to resist conscription could be suppressed and their authors punished, but circulars urging munitions workers to support the Russian Revolution of 1917 were constitutionally protected.[75] The first endangered the American military effort in World War I, since the authors attempted to prevent the government from amassing a fighting force. The second did not have a similar effect, since the United States was not at war with Russia.

The test for clear and present danger was grounded on a paradox that became increasingly apparent, especially as used by Brandeis in cases in the 1920s. The test began with the assumption that free speech was not an absolute right, despite the First Amendment. It endorsed governmental infringement on individual liberties in principle and tolerated specific infringements. But it also set limits on the power of a legislative majority to suppress speech and permitted the judiciary to determine those limits. A court, under the test, could take a free-speech case away from the jury if it decided that the words sought to be suppressed had not in fact created a clear and present danger to majority security. The test could thus be seen, as Brandeis said in *Schaefer v. United States,*[76] as a "rule of reason":[77] a means by which judges scrutinized the rationality of legislative acts. As a rule of reason, it could conceivably be used the way late-nineteenth-century judicial rules of reason had been used—namely, as a means of allowing the judiciary to make substantive judgments on the worth of legislation.

Here Brandeis's confidence in the inherent soundness of his own judgments prevailed over his tendency to interpret the range of judicial powers narrowly. He believed that a careful analysis of the facts of a case could lead one to truth. When the insights generated by an inquiry into facts harmonized with his own predilections, conclusions became irresistible. Once he had drawn conclusions, he was not particularly tolerant of opposing views, nor terribly anxious, as a judge, to allow them much weight. In *Schaefer* he decided that the publication of newspaper articles expressing skepticism about the professed intent of the United States to send troops to Europe was so far from being an immediate danger to the American war effort that "no jury in calmness" could find it such. Accordingly, the test for clear and present danger dictated withdrawal of the case from jury consideration.[78] Similarly, in *Pierce v. United States,*[79] after carefully studying a Socialist Party leaflet that depicted the horrors of war and asserted that the Morgan interests were behind the war effort, Brandeis concluded that it was a mere expression of opinion that had even recognized its own impotence in inducing resistance against the war.

In these cases Brandeis was making a gloss on Holmes's test that Holmes himself was not entirely prepared to accept. Brandeis was concerned not only with the close connection of the suppressed speech to the occurrence of a preventable evil, but also with the seriousness of the evil that might occur. Holmes, in the 1919 cases in which he had formulated the test, had been interested primarily in the chronological relation of the speech to the evil. Brandeis believed that mere chronological proximity was not enough. If the evil that the speech induced was relatively trivial, the speech should be protected. In *Gilbert v. Minnesota*[80] a lobbyist was convicted, under a Minnesota statute prohibiting public speeches against the war effort, for stating that conscription should be subject to popular vote and that "if they conscripted wealth like they have conscripted men, this war would not last over forty-eight hours."[81] Holmes voted to sustain the conviction and uphold the statute's constitutionality; Brandeis dissented. The statute created a blanket prohibition of public speech against enlistment or in behalf of pacificism, Brandeis maintained. No effort was made to inquire into the purpose of the speech or to ascertain whether the speaker's remarks could reasonably be expected to induce others to perpetrate truly serious evils.

As free-speech cases moved outside the context of World War I, this difference in focus between Holmes and Brandeis persisted, even though it did not again result in their casting opposing votes. In *Gitlow v. New York*,[82] a 1925 case, a Socialist was convicted under the New York Criminal Anarchy Act of 1902 for advocating mass strikes and hostile action against the bourgeoisie. Holmes, in dissenting from the Court's decision sustaining the conviction against a free-speech challenge, distinguished between the advocacy of ideas in the abstract, and concrete attempts to induce others to carry out those ideas immediately. The "redundant discourse" of Gitlow, he maintained was not "an attempt to induce an uprising against government at once," but "at some indefinite time in the future."[83]

Brandeis joined this dissent, but his subsequent concurrence two years later in *Whitney v. California*[84] indicated that he was concerned with the seriousness as well as the imminence of the resulting evil. He read the test for clear and present danger, he said, as meaning that whenever the "fundamental rights of free speech and assembly" were allegedly invaded, a defendant could raise three questions: whether "there actually did exist at the time a clear danger"; whether "the danger, if any, was imminent"; and "whether the evil apprehended was one so substantial as to justify the stringent restriction interposed by the legislature."[85] The first two questions were questions of fact, the third was a question of law. A court could determine that the evil perceived was not sufficiently serious to merit legislative interference with free speech, and so withdraw the case from the jury. The judicial deference to legislative wisdom championed by Brandeis in liberty-of-contract cases did not always apply in speech cases.

Holmes joined Brandeis in his *Whitney* concurrence, but the facts of the case qualified his support. The defendant in Whitney had been convicted under a California criminal statute for participating in the organization of a state Communist Labor Party. The statute prohibited persons from becoming members of organizations that advocated violence as a means of inducing social or political change, and thus attempted to punish those who merely associated with persons who advocated or practiced violence. A majority of the Court peremptorily sustained the statute. Brandeis, however, thought that the statute might be constitutionally defective as applied to Miss Whitney. Her association with Communists, he argued, did not by

itself constitute a sufficiently imminent danger to the security of the State of California. But there was other evidence that might have suggested that Miss Whitney and her associates posed an immediate threat to California's security; and thus Brandeis tolerated her conviction. His focus, ultimately, was thus on the imminence of the danger rather than the seriousness of the perceived evil. This focus was consistent with that of Holmes in *Gitlow*.

At the very end of his career, Holmes seemed to have accepted the notion of reversing the presumption of constitutional validity in speech cases. In *Near v. Minnesota*[86] a majority of the Court invalidated a statute allowing injunctions against newspapers that had printed allegedly defamatory material. In the process, the majority, through Chief Justice Charles Evans Hughes, asserted the importance of keeping the press immune from censorship of its publications and claimed the power to weigh the serious public evil caused by authority to prevent publication against the evils suppressed by the statute.[87] In this, the last speech case decided before Holmes's retirement, he and Brandeis were both members of the majority. Whether Holmes's acquiescence stemmed from his belief that protection from "prior restraints" formed the core of the First Amendment or whether he had actually endorsed Brandeis's gloss on his original clear-and-present-danger test is unclear.

Also in 1931 came one of the last liberty-of-contract cases of the twentieth century, *O'Gorman v. Hartford Ins. Co.*,[88] in which a New Jersey statute regulating the fees paid to local agents by insurance companies was challenged as a violation of the Fourteenth Amendment's due process clause. Brandeis, in a majority opinion sustaining the statute, made the familiar analysis of evils and remedies he had made in earlier liberty-of-contract cases and then invoked the presumption of the constitutionality of legislative acts to dispose of the case. Holmes voted with the majority. The entire five-man majority of *O'Gorman*, which included Justices Holmes, Brandeis, Hughes, Stone, and Owen Roberts, adopted a rule of presumptions for liberty-of-contract cases differing from that used for speech cases. Conversely, the four dissenters in *O'Gorman*—Justices Butler, McReynolds, Sutherland, and Van Devanter—proclaimed the inviolability of freedom to contract, but, as dissenters in *Near*, argued that legislative attempts to curb speech were presumptively valid. By 1931 liberty of speech had apparently come to occupy the exalted place once reserved for liberty of contract, while liberty of contract had been discredited.

Holmes and Brandeis had played an important part in a process that ultimately led to temporary placement of First Amendment liberties in a constitutionally "preferred position" over economic liberties. This development, when it was made manifest by the Court in 1945,[89] was hailed as a victory for liberalism and a tribute to the influence of the foremost judicial liberals of the early twentieth century, Holmes and Brandeis.[90] But rather than demonstrating the compatibility of liberalism with Holmes's and Brandeis's interpretations of their office, the liberty-of-contract and speech cases had unearthed the paradoxical nature of the modern liberal blueprint for judicial performance.

v

Holmes had taught that ideas and values, whether employed by judges or by others, were not absolutes but products of changing social conditions. Brandeis had taught that the empirical indices of change could be observed and analyzed and that, by this process, public policies could be made responsive to the dictates of contemporary life. Liberalism, as it coalesced into a definable ideology, drew upon both these insights. American society after World War I was marked by a simultaneous collapse of allegedly timeless values and norms and a pervasive need for governmental policies that responded to the newly perceived facts of modern industrial life. To an extent, Holmes helped make palatable a world without consensual norms, while Brandeis sought to show how governmental institutions could intervene to make that world more livable. Each contributed to the belief of modern liberalism that an activist state could provide both security and progress.

But if some strands of the thought of Holmes and Brandeis were harmonious with liberalism, others were not. The dissonance that thus resulted highlighted the uneasy role of the appellate judiciary in the liberal state. Holmes had been a leading late-nineteenth-century intellectual radical. His quarrel with that century's faith in universal axioms had made him an early-twentieth-century juristic reformer, exposing the essential subjectivity of the oracular approach to judging. With his distaste for intuitive judicial decision-making came an exaltation of self-restraint, and in the liberal world of fragmented values judicial self-restraint seemed eminently sensible. Holmes was hence a professional judge for liberals: the "completely adult jurist," to Jerome Frank.[91] But he was no humanitarian. He not only tolerated but actually believed in the principle of majoritarian repression of minority rights. He rejected the notion that free speech was an absolute right as surely as he rejected the inalienability of a liberty to contract. He was indifferent to the civil rights of blacks, Orientals, and aliens;[92] he was often satisfied with summary forms of procedural due process. His clear-and-present-danger test cut both ways: it carved out an area of constitutionally protected speech but also justified widespread suppression of "dangerous" expression. In short, Holmes abjured close scrutiny of repressive legislation as well as of welfare legislation. Hours and wages laws were sanctioned, but so were statutes requiring the compulsory sterilization of mental defectives.

Brandeis, as well, fell short of the paradigm of a liberal judge. Sometimes, as in the wartime prohibition cases, he assumed the presence of a consensus of values on moral issues that liberalism denied, thereby reaching what were perceived as illiberal results.[93] On other occasions his deviance from liberalism exhibited itself in his methods, as in those speech cases where through his gloss on the clear and present danger test he appeared to be endorsing a subjective form of judicial decision-making that the professional canons of liberalism repudiated. Brandeis was a liberal in his result-orientation only to the extent that liberalism endorsed Brandeisian social policies; he was a liberal in methodology only to the extent that judicial self-restraint fostered results that he thought sensible.

The careers of Holmes and Brandeis hence illustrated the tension in judicial liberalism between "right" results and "right" methods. That tension had been implanted in the movement at its origin. The early-twentieth-century critics of "mechanical" jurisprudence objected not only to methods but to results as well. They disliked conservatism in the appellate judiciary as much as they disliked subjective activism. Their critiques assumed that the liberty-of-contract doctrine represented unsound social policy as well as illogical reasoning, and that assumption rested on their own strong perception of the common goals of American civilization. But as the substantive content of consensual American values became increasingly difficult to perceive after World War I, judicial self-restraint took on an expanded meaning. It was not merely a check against wrong-headed subjectivity but also a means by which the judiciary assured that the decisions of the institution best suited to discern and reflect majoritarian sentiment—the legislature—were given their proper weight. Since the state had become a substitute for value consensus, its legislative fiats should be supported as buffers against anarchy.

The concept of an expansive regulatory state rested, however, on the premise that it would be responsive to the needs of disadvantaged minorities. Otherwise the egalitarian and democratic traditions of America would vanish, and liberalism would be synonymous with totalitarianism. The state was permitted to regulate private conduct only to the extent that its regulations were fairly implemented, and also conferred benefits on the disadvantaged that outweighed the costs to everyone else. Not every manifestation of majoritarian sentiment was to be tolerated; some legislative policies were illiberal. The only institution capable of scrutinizing the fairness of legislative activity was the judiciary; hence, judges in the liberal state should use their expertise in interpreting the Constitution to undertake that scrutiny. They should presume legislation to be constitutionally valid, but be prepared to override that presumption.

The harmony of methods and results envisaged by this conception of judicial performance was fated to dissolve in instances where pressure for national solidarity clashed with pressure to vindicate minority rights. The speech cases represented one such instance in which judicial self-restraint did not produce liberal results. Holmes and Brandeis, both of whom, in varying degrees, believed in tolerating legislative judgments and in vindicating free expression, struggled with the dilemma posed by these cases. Their eventual resolution, at least in the *Near* case, appeared to subordinate a liberal methodology to the achievement of liberal results. As a result of that case and other instances in which they seemed to champion the disadvantaged, they were apotheosized as liberals. That apotheosis, however, ignored the differences between them and minimized the inherent contradictions in modern liberalism's mandate for the judiciary. The considerable skills of Holmes and Brandeis—the keenness of their minds, their capacity for eloquence, the coherence of their thought—did not make any easier for them the task of squaring approved liberal results with approved liberal methods of judging. They, at least, were acute enough to see a potential tension between methods and results. Other early-twentieth-century members of the Supreme Court, who opposed modern liberalism in any form, failed to perceive a distinction between judging and vindicating one's social or political preferences. That failure generated another threat to the independence of the American appellate judiciary.

NOTES

[1] See generally L. Hartz, *The Liberal Tradition in America* (1955).

[2] The discussion to follow draws on insights in H. May, *The End of American Innocence* (1959); R. Wiebe, *The Search for Order* (1967), and P. Conkin, *The New Deal* (1967).

[3] E.g., H. Laski, *Authority in the Modern State* (1919).

[4] No effort is made here to deny the possibility of a divergence between the publicly expressed and the privately held views of supporters of either populism or progressivism. Both movements attracted persons from a variety of social and economic backgrounds, and various theories have been advanced as to their collective motivations for reform. Compare J. Chamberlain, *Farewell to Reform* (1932), with R. Hofstadter, *The Age of Reform* (1955), and G. Kolko, *The Triumph of Conservatism* (1963). In contrast to that of the New Dealers, the rhetoric of populists and progressives appears laden with moral appeals and visions of an idyllic society. For an expression of the contrasting tone taken by liberals, see T. Arnold, *The Symbols of Government* (1935). These different angles of vision may have reflected fundamentally different social perspectives. See H. Graham, *Encore for Reform: The Old Progressives and the New Deal* (1967).

[5] For the late-nineteenth-century version of this view, see J. Sproat, *The Best Men* (1971). See generally White, "The Social Values of the Progressives: Some New Perspectives," 70 *South Atlantic Quarterly* 62 (1971).

[6] See, e.g., Pound, "Mechanical Jurisprudence," 8 *Colum. L. Rev.* 605 (1908); Dodd, "Social Legislation and the Courts," 28 *Pol. Sci. Q.* 1 (1913).

[7] Examples of the two schools in the period discussed are Pound, "The Theory of Judicial Decision," 36 *Harv. L. Rev.* 641, 802, 940 (1923); Oliphant, "A Return to Stare Decisis," 14 *A.B.A.J.* 71, 159 (1928). See generally White, "From Sociological Jurisprudence to Realism," 58 *Va. L. Rev.* 999 (1972).

[8] E.g., R. Jackson, *The Struggle for Judicial Supremacy* 312 (1941): "Holmes and Brandeis have not only furnished the highest expression but they have been the very source and the intellectual leaders of recent liberalism in the United States."

[9] See White, "The Rise and Fall of Justice Holmes," 39 *U. Chi. L. Rev.* 51, 56 (1971).

[10] O. W. Holmes, Sr., 3 *The Complete Writings of Oliver Wendell Holmes* 59, 142 (13 vols., 1900).

[11] William James, Oct. 2, 1869, quoted in R. Perry, 1 *The Thought and Character of William James* 307 (2 vols., 1935).

[12] Holmes to Felix Frankfurter, June 26, 1928, in Holmes Collection, Harvard Law School.

[13] Holmes, "Notes on Albert Dürer," 7 *Harvard Magazine* 41, 43-44 (October 1860).

[14] Holmes, "The Path of the Law" (1896), reprinted in *Collected Legal Papers* 167, 172 (1920).

[15] Holmes, "Law in Science and Science in Law" (1899), reprinted in id. at 210, 242.

[16] See discussion of free-speech cases *infra*.

[17] *Buck v. Bell*, 274 U.S. 200 (1927).

[18] *Patsone v. Pennsylvania*, 232 U.S. 138 (1914).

[19] Holmes to Harold Laski, in M. Howe, ed., 1 *Holmes-Laski Letters* 217 (2 vols., 1953).

[20] Holmes, "Law in Science and Science in Law," *supra* n.15 at 239.

[21] Id.

[22] See Holmes to Harold Laski, January 13, 1923, in 1 Howe, ed., *supra* n.19, at 473-74.

[23] Holmes to Sir Frederick Pollock, in M. Howe, ed., 2 *Holmes-Pollock Letters* 22 (2 vols., 1961).

[24] Holmes to Pollock, in 1 Howe, ed., *supra* n.23 at 163.

[25] Quoted in H. Pringle, 2 *The Life and Times of William Howard Taft* 969 (2 vols., 1939).

[26] Charles G. Ross, *St. Louis Post-Dispatch,* quoted in I. Dillard, ed., *Mr. Justice Brandeis, Great American* 14 (1941).

[27] Brandeis to Otto Wehle, March 12, 1876, in *Public Papers of Louis D. Brandeis,* U. Louisville Law School.

[28] A. Mason, *Brandeis: A Free Man's Life* 42 (1946).

[29] See id. at 103.

[30] Brandeis to Charles Nagel, July 12, 1879, in *Public Papers, supra* n.27.

[31] Brandeis to Amy Brandeis Wehle, Jan. 2, 1881, in id.

[32] Brandeis to Alice Goldmark, quoted in Mason, *supra* n.28 at 75.

[33] Testimony before the Committee of the Board of Aldermen in the Case and Management of Public Institutions, 3 *Report* 3631-32 (1874).

[34] L. Brandeis, *Business—A Profession* 321 (1914).

[35] See generally A. Link, *Wilson: The New Freedom* (1956).

[36] Brandeis, "A Call to the Educated Jew," 1 *Menorah Journal* 15 (1915).

[37] Brandeis to Alfred Brandeis, June 18, 1907 in *Public Papers, supra* n.27.

[38] Brandeis, *Business—A Profession, supra* n.32, at liv-lvi.

[39] Brandeis, "The Living Law," 10 *Ill. L. Rev.* 461, 465 (1916).

[40] 244 U.S. 590 (1917).

[41] Id. at 597, 600 (dissent).

[42] Holmes wrote Laski that on one occasion he had told Brandeis that the latter was "letting partisanship disturb his judicial attitude." 1 M. Howe, ed., *supra* n.19 at 128.

[43] *Duplex Co. v. Deering,* 254 U.S. 443, 479, 488 (1921) (dissent).

[44] E.g., *In re* Jacobs, 98 N.Y. 98 (1885); *Millett v. People,* 117 Ill. 294 (1886); *Godcharles v. Wigeman,* 113 Pa. 431 (1886).

[45] *Powell v. Pennsylvania,* 127 U.S. 678, 687 (1888) (Field, J., dissenting); *Hooper v. California,* 155 U.S. 648, 659 (1895) (Harlan, Brewer, Jackson, JJ., dissenting); *Frisbie v. United States,* 157 U.S. 160 (1895); *Allgeyer v. Louisiana,* 165 U.S. 578 (1897); *Holden v. Hardy,* 169 U.S. 366 (1898).

[46] E.g., *Lochner v. New York,* 198 U.S. 45 (1905); *Adair v. United States,* 208 U.S. 161 (1968); *Adkins v. Children's Hospital,* 261 U.S. 525 (1923).

[47] Theodore Roosevelt, *Autobiography* (1919), reprinted as *The Autobiography of Theodore Roosevelt* 334 (1958).

[48] Pound, "Liberty of Contract," 18 *Yale L. J.* 454, 462 (1909).

[49] Id. at 464.

[50] 187 U.S. 606 (1903).

[51] Id. at 608-9.

[52] Holmes to Laski, in 1 Howe, ed., *supra* n.19 at 51.

[53] Id. at 42.

[54] Holmes, *Collected Legal Papers, supra* n.14 at 306.

[55] *Lochner v. New York, supra* n.46 at 75 (dissent).

[56] *Adair v. United States, supra* n.46 at 191 (dissent).

[57] Holmes to Laski, in 1 Howe, ed., *supra* n.19 at 21.

[58] 236 U.S. 1 (1915).

[59] Id. at 26, 27 (dissent).

[60] *Adams v. Tanner, supra* n.40.

[61] *Truax v. Corrigan,* 257 U.S. 312, 354 (1922) (dissent).

[62] *Burns Baking Co. v. Bryan,* 264 U.S. 504, 517 (1924) (dissent).

[63] Brandeis, "The Anti-Bar Law," address before the Joint Committee on Liquor Law of the Massachusetts Legislature, Feb. 27, 1891, in *Public Papers, supra* n.27.

[64] *Hamilton v. Kentucky Distilleries Co.,* 251 U.S. 146 (1919).

[65] *Jacob Ruppert v. Caffey,* 251 U.S. 264 (1920).

[66] *United States v. One Ford Coupe,* 272 U.S. 321 (1926).

[67] *Lambert v. Yellowley,* 272 U.S. 581 (1926).

[68] Holmes to Laski, in 1 Howe, ed., *supra* n.19 at 8.

[69] *Abrams v. United States,* 250 U.S. 616, 630 (1919) (dissent).

[70] Id.

[71] 205 U.S. 454 (1907).

[72] 236 U.S. 273 (1915).

[73] 249 U.S. 47 (1919).

[74] Id. at 52.

[75] *Abrams v. U.S., supra* n.69 at 624 (dissent).

[76] 251 U.S. 466 (1920).

[77] Id. at 482 (dissent).

[78] Id. at 482-83.

[79] 252 U.S. 239, 253 (1920) (dissent).

[80] 254 U.S. 325 (1920).

[81] Quoted in Z. Chafee, *Free Speech in the United States* 290 (1941).

[82] 268 U.S. 652 (1925).

[83] Id. at 673 (dissent).

[84] 274 U.S. 357 (1927).

[85] Id. at 372, 379 (concurrence).

[86] 283 U.S. 697 (1931).

[87] Id. at 708.

[88] 282 U.S. 251 (1931).

[89] *Thomas v. Collins,* 323 U.S. 516 (1945).

[90] See generally R. Cushman, "Clear and Present Danger in Free Speech Cases," in M. Konvitz and A. Murphy, *Essays in Political Theory* 311 (1948).

[91] J. Frank, *Law and the Modern Mind* 253 (1930).

[92] See generally Rogat, "Mr. Justice Holmes: A Dissenting Opinion," 15 *Stan. L. Rev.* 3, 254 (1963).

[93] E.g., Mason, *supra* n.28 at 567: Brandeis's "stand in [cases involving] 'moral' issues" was "strangely out of key with his customary liberalism."

Louis Auchincloss (essay date 1979)

SOURCE: "The Long Life and Broad Mind of Mr. Justice Holmes," in *Life, Law and Letters: Essays and Sketches,* Houghton Mifflin Company, 1979, pp. 1-19.

[*In the following essay, Auchincloss provides an overview of Holmes's life and career.*]

Few men have seen as much of our history, and from such advantageous viewpoints, as Oliver Wendell Holmes, Jr. As a boy in Massachusetts he met veterans of the Revolution. He went to school in a Boston shaken by abolition. He fought through the Civil War, and it is said

to have been his voice that shouted the rough warning to Lincoln when the President exposed his high hat above the ramparts at Fort Stevens. With peace Holmes became a lawyer and a great scholar. He served as a judge for half a century, first on the high bench of Massachusetts and then on the United States Supreme Court. And at the age of ninety-two, just retired, he received an early official visit from the newly elected Franklin D. Roosevelt. ("Why are you reading Plato, Mr. Justice?" was the President's genial opening.) That such a span of life should have been granted to a man so competent to use it is a rare event in the history of any nation.

Holmes was born in 1841 in Boston, into a world that regarded itself as the intellectual and commercial center of the nation. His father, Dr. Oliver Wendell Holmes, was not only one of America's favorite poets and novelists; he was also a distinguished medical practitioner who published a paper on the contagiousness of puerperal fever which saved the lives of thousands, perhaps millions, of women. On his mother's side the infant was a grandson of Justice Charles Jackson of the Supreme Judicial Court of Massachusetts, on which bench Holmes was later to sit not only as an associate, but as chief justice.

The Holmeses were not rich, but they were comfortably off. Dr. Holmes, a wit and a raconteur, was in high demand at intellectual gatherings. Charles Sumner, Emerson, and Longfellow were close friends and frequent callers at his house. Such a background has been regarded by many as a check to the creative impulse. Henry Adams, born three years before Oliver Wendell Holmes, Jr., under the very shadow of the State House, claimed that he had been less equipped for life in nineteenth-century America than if he had started as a polish Jew, "a furtive Yacoob and Ysaac still reeking of the Ghetto, snarling a weird Yiddish to the officers of the customs." Holmes, however, had little use for such self-dramatization. He selected from his background what tools he needed for the life that he wished to lead, and discarded the rest as best he could. He grew up into a tall, lean, strong young man, strikingly handsome yet of a cool disposition, tolerant, amused, incessantly curious, but with a certain disdain for the mob and an iron determination to lead his life by his own lights no matter what people or forces might stand in his way.

He was one of eighty in the Harvard class of 1861, graduating just as the Civil War began. Although he was repelled by what he saw as the excesses of the abolitionists and although he was always fond of many Southerners, there was no question in his mind but that the Union had to be preserved, and he enlisted at once in the Twentieth Massachusetts Regiment, known as the "Harvard Regiment," in which he was soon commissioned. Many of the intellectuals of his generation, including Henry and William James, did not take up arms in the war. Holmes did not seem particularly critical of such men. He believed that each man should make up his own mind. During his three years' service, he was three times badly wounded: in the chest at Ball's Bluff, in the neck at Antietam, and in the heel at Fredericksburg.

After Antietam the enthusiastic and emotional Dr. Holmes rushed to his son's side, taking care to record the dramatic events of his journey in an article for the *Atlantic Monthly,* "My Hunt After 'The Captain.'" The son noted this, as he also noted his father's undoubted affection. He was always just, but his father's florid style was not to be his. As he later said, the Harvard Regiment never wrote about itself in a newspaper.

Holmes always regarded his military service as the most intensely lived part of his existence. In later years when commercial greed seemed to engulf America, he was to feel that the long absence of the cruel test of warfare was making people soft. On the whole, although he admired men like the railroad tycoon James J. Hill, whom he regarded as representing "one of the greatest forms of human power," he preferred warriors to stockbrokers. And in a Memorial Day address at Harvard in 1895 he made a statement which today sounds remarkably bellicose: "War, when you are at it, is horrible and dull. It is only when time has passed that you see that its message was divine . . . For high and dangerous action teaches us to believe as right beyond dispute things for which our doubting minds are slow to find words of proof. Out of heroism grows faith in the worth of heroism. The proof comes later, and even may never come. Therefore I rejoice at every dangerous sport which I see pursued. The students at Heidelberg, with their sword-slashed faces, inspire me with sincere respect. I gaze with delight upon our polo players. If once in a while in our rough riding a neck is broken, I regard it, not as a waste, but as a price well paid for the breeding of a race fit for headship and command."

In light of the above, the way that his own military career ended may seem curious. The Twentieth Regiment had been enlisted for three years, and Holmes was entitled to be discharged in the summer of 1864. In July of that year, when the war had still eight of its bloodiest months to run, he resigned his commission and returned to Boston to study law. But Holmes never sought excuses, and he insisted in this as in all his other actions, on his individual prerogative. Here is what he wrote his parents:

> I started this thing as a boy. I am now a man and I have been coming to the conclusion for the last six months that my duty has changed. I can do a disagreeable thing or face a great danger coolly enough when I *know* it is a duty—but a doubt demoralizes me as it does any nervous man—and I honestly think the duty of fighting has ceased for me—ceased because I have laboriously and with much suffering of mind and body *earned* the right . . . to decide for myself how I can best do my duty to myself, to the country, and, if you choose, to God.

As an old man Holmes came to question the validity of this decision. But it was certainly consistent with his concept of independence. He never shrank before the enemy, nor did he shrink before the prospect of what his family and friends might think of his packing up and going home before Richmond had been taken. Certainly he never regarded this decision as qualifying his right to extol the military virtues to youth.

After Harvard Law School, Holmes was admitted to the Massachusetts bar in 1867. He practiced for a short time with his brother, Edward Jackson Holmes, and then joined the firm that became known as Shattuck, Holmes & Munroe, the Boston partnership with which his name has been predominantly associated. He had a general practice, with considerable litigation, but his great passion was exploring the origins of law to establish a theoretical basis for fundamental legal doctrine. In the course of the decade and a half before his appointment to the bench, Holmes dedicated most of his nights and weekends to this scholarship. Thus, even as a busy lawyer, he was able to edit the twelfth edition of Kent's *Commentaries on American Law* in 1873, and in 1881, just before his fortieth birthday, he brought out his own enduring classic, **The Common Law**.

These years of law practice and scholarship constitute a rather arid period in the history of Holmes's personality. The man who in 1897 could write to a friend of the divinity of vitality, the wonderful capability of complex and civilized man to "lark like a boy," is scarcely perceptible in the midnight toiler. Yet this was also the period of his marriage, at thirty-one, to Fanny Dixwell, a few months older than himself, daughter of the headmaster of the school he had attended in preparation for Harvard. Mrs. Holmes, who lived almost as long as her husband, had a character that is difficult to piece out. Her complete devotion to Holmes has always been recognized. But she was a shy woman of few or no intimates. She was an efficient housekeeper, a serious artist in needlepoint, and a woman of strong will, few words, and sharp wit. Her adoration of her husband was probably intensified by the childlessness of their marriage, and she never interfered either with his work or with his pleasures. For example, she rarely accompanied him on his summer trips to England, giving as her excuse her dislike of the Atlantic voyage. But I suspect that she knew how much he loved the intellectual companionship of his English friends and felt that she was a drag on such expeditions.

Holmes and his wife lived at first with his parents, which could not have been easy for Fanny. That he must have considerably neglected her, working so intently, there can be little doubt. In the opinion of William James, at that time one of his best friends, all of Holmes's noble qualities were poisoned by "cold blooded, conscious egotism and conceit," and William's mother, writing to her novelist son Henry in England, said of him: "His whole life, soul and body, is utterly absorbed in his last work [the Kent *Commentaries*]."

Henry James was more perceptive than his brother. He was always one to appreciate the necessary loneliness of hard work, and he recognized in early youth that Holmes was destined to a great success, although "in a speciality." In later years Holmes visited Henry James on trips to England, and the latter perceived that the former's personality never essentially changed. Henry speculated that this quality of being inalterable might spring from a failure to live. This may seem a strange comment to be made about a warrior and a busy judge by a fussy old literary bachelor who had avoided military service in the Civil War, but its significance will be appreciated by those critics who have found in Holmes's Olympian detachment a suggestion of occasional heartlessness, or at least indifference, to his fellow man. Henry put it more agreeably when he described Holmes as moving through life "like a full glass carried without spilling a drop."

James Bradley Thayer, who collaborated with Holmes in the editing of Kent's *Commentaries,* felt that Holmes had treated him badly in arrogating to himself most of the credit, and Charles W. Eliot, the president of Harvard, was indignant when Holmes in 1882 resigned a professorship, which he had just accepted at the Law School, to accept the governor's appointment to the Supreme Judicial Court of Massachusetts. But on Holmes's side it must be pointed out that he indeed had done the major work on the *Commentaries,* and that he had written a letter to President Eliot when he accepted the Harvard appointment, reserving the privilege to resign it if appointed to any judicial post.

It seems, on balance, that Holmes's friends were severe on him in this period. He had to support himself, and he would have had to give up his greatest goal in life had he not used every available minute for hard work. He was not a man of overweening ambition, but when it was a question of those things about which he cared, such as the credit for a book that he had largely written, or the acceptance of a judicial post that might never be offered again, he could act with a speed and determination that may have had an air of ruthlessness. Once Holmes was convinced that what he was doing was the right thing, judged entirely by his own standards, he did not give a damn what anyone else thought.

Holmes, in *The Common Law,* explored the origins of civil and criminal liability in Anglo-Saxon, German, and Roman law. His famous statement, on the very first page, that the life of the law has not been logic but experience, seems obvious enough today, but we must remember that he was a pioneer. He sought to articulate a theoretical basis for fundamental legal doctrine in a way that differed significantly from the attempt of many of his contemporaries to deduce legal rules from absolute principles. Such theorists had a tendency to idealize law, to see it as a constantly perfected process emanating from judicial inductions and deductions, possibly inspired, if not directed, from a higher sphere. Holmes would have none of this. Law was simply the product of history and legislation. Its substance at any given time pretty nearly corresponded with what was then "understood to be convenient."

Convenience, that was the key—convenience of the majority. Accidents were bound to happen, with damage to some, and the most convenient solution for society was to let the loss lie where it fell. Holmes points out that in early law the damaging thing could be surrendered to the plaintiff as a *total* compensation: the body of the debtor to his creditor, the biting dog to the bitten person. As civilization advanced, the debtor was allowed to buy back his body, and the owner of the dog his animal. The absolute liability of the thing became the absolute liability of its owner. Thus, initially, a moral responsibility was at the bottom of the defendant's liability to pay. He had owned the offending thing at his peril.

Holmes now embarks on the development of his great thesis: that the development of law is, in the last analysis, the transmutation of this moral standard into an external one. Society may start with moral responsibility, but that is soon found to be practically inadequate. Actual intent cannot be the test; it must be *imputed* to persons who behave in a certain way:

> A man who intentionally sets fire to his own house, which is so near to other houses that the fire will manifestly endanger them, is guilty of arson if one of the other houses is burned in consequence. In this case, an act which would not have been arson, taking only its immediate consequences into account, becomes arson by reason of more remote consequences which were manifestly likely to follow, whether they were actually intended or not.

This is true, as Holmes proceeds to establish, in civil as well as criminal liability. The law frequently penalizes, or forces to pay, "those who have been guilty of no moral wrong and who could not be condemned by any standard that did not avowedly disregard the personal peculiarities of the individuals concerned." Under the common law, a man acts at his peril. But it would have been going too far for courts to hold a man responsible for all the consequences of his acts. He was only responsible for the *foreseeable* consequences, not those that he had actually foreseen but those which a prudent man (as defined by a judge or jury) *would* have foreseen. Thus, conduct that is criminal or tortious is conduct that the average member of the community would regard as such. Such conduct we must all avoid, or pay the damages or be jailed or even hanged. But "the tests of liability are external, and independent of the degree of evil in the particular person's motives or intentions."

Holmes rode his horse of the external standard a bit hard through other fields of law. He seemed intent on obliterating the entire question of morality. In contracts he argued that there was no duty on the part of a promisor to perform, but simply an election to choose between performance and the payment of damages. And a "right," he claimed, was nothing but a prophecy: a prognostication that society would back one up if one took such and such a stand. In later years he liked to quote his old professor at Harvard, Louis Agassiz, who had said that in parts of Germany there would be a revolution if one added two cents to the cost of a glass of beer. Presumably, the privilege to buy beer at a certain rate had become a right in that place and time.

If one were to assess *The Common Law* today as a work of legal history, it might receive only indifferent marks. The texts available to Holmes in the 1870s were often corrupt. The Anglo-Saxon material, for example, began to reach definitive form only three decades later. Yet the book still remains important for its expression of legal theory. His conception of the external standard has had its logical consequence in our modern tendency to eliminate guilt from liability, as seen in workmen's compensation laws and in no-fault automobile insurance.

I have dwelt at some length on *The Common Law* because I believe that it represents the culmination of Holmes's immersion in matters intellectual. For the next fifty years he was too busy a judge to write books, but he never changed his fundamental views from those stated in 1881. Idealists have attacked his materialism. Is there not an implication in his legal philosophy that moral standards have no place even in the realm of the conscience? Has a man no obligation to his neighbor but what the average citizen conceives as such? Can morality be reduced to simple good manners? And is a good deed good even if directed by an evil motive? Or a bad deed bad even if directed by a good one? Did Holmes not reject all religion?

He was, it was true, an agnostic, perhaps an atheist. He never considered that man was central, or even necessarily important, to the cosmos. He did not believe in a life after death. When his wife died, it took the persuasion of his brothers on the court, apprehensive of the scandal of such godlessness in high places, to induce him to have any funeral service at all. But there was never any question of his own moral standards. He may have laughed at himself for being the heir to a puritan background, but he did not kick against its restraints. He had a deep sense of the importance of being a gentleman—in the best sense of that word—even in a cold and indifferent universe. How can rational men be Christians? he asked Sir Frederick Pollock, the eminent British legal authority, and here is how he answered his own question: "It is like the justification of conventions—I respect a tall hat or the cult of monogamy not from the internal self-satisfaction of the accidents of space and time but from the consideration that the inward necessity of man to idealize must express itself in inadequate and transitory symbols of no value in themselves but reverent for the eternal movement of which they are the momentary form."

Holmes's work on the Supreme Judicial Court of Massachusetts represented a highly creative period in the development of law, and he came to be a leading, if not the dominant, figure of that bench. From the beginning, in 1882, he was happy in his new work. He loved being able to apply his knowledge in the philosophy of law to actual cases, and he found the judicial experience an exciting one. There are few positions in the world of practical affairs where a man can be so much of a scholar and a philosopher as that of judge. Holmes's life was with ideas; he had no use for facts except insofar as they gave rise inductively to general propositions. Years later, in 1919, he was to describe to Sir Frederick Pollock the feelings aroused in him by Justice Louis Brandeis's criticism of his slighting of economic statistics:

> Brandeis the other day drove a harpoon into my midriff with reference to my summer occupations. He said you talk about improving your mind, you only exercise it on the subjects with which you are familiar. Why don't you try something new, study some domain of fact. Take up the textile industries in Massachusetts and after reading the reports sufficiently you can go to Lawrence and get a human notion of how it really is. I hate facts. I always say the chief end of man is to form general propositions—adding that no general proposition is worth a damn.

Holmes was an ambitious man, but his ambition lay along severely restricted lines. When his friend Henry Cabot Lodge suggested that he should run for governor of Massachusetts as a step toward becoming a senator, he replied simply, "But I don't give a damn about being senator." He said of Napoleon, "I am not interested by men whose view of life does not interest me." But he was intensely interested in judicial work and looked forward to an even larger opening than was offered by the highest bench of Massachusetts.

Washington was watching him. His reputation for liberalism stood him in good stead under the new administration of Theodore Roosevelt. Holmes's dissent in *Vegelahn v. Guntner* had alarmed the capitalist world, although the simple language with which he presented the conflict of capital and labor seems indisputable today:

> One of the eternal conflicts out of which life is made up is that between the effort of every man to get the most he can for his services, and that of society, disguised under the name of capital, to get his services for the least possible return. Combination on the one side is patent and powerful. Combination on the other is the necessary and desirable counterpart, if the battle is to be carried on in a fair and equal way.

However, when Theodore Roosevelt appointed Holmes an associate justice of the United States Supreme Court in 1902, it was only after careful consultation with Holmes's and Roosevelt's good friend Lodge, who was then a senator. The President was characteristically candid. He wanted to be sure that Holmes was a good party man, in entire sympathy with Roosevelt's views. Lodge was reassuring, and the appointment was made. Everything went well, from the President's point of view, until the case of *Northern Securities v. United States,* two years later, when Holmes dissented from the opinion of the majority, which held that the merger of the Northern Pacific and Great Northern railroads was in violation of the Sherman Antitrust Act. Holmes refused to be swept along in the wake of Roosevelt's trust busting. He pointed out that the supposed evil countered by the statute was a union between parties to exclude strangers, a combination to keep rivals out of the business and to ruin those already in it. The statute in no way prevented a combination of companies with the object of increasing the total amount of business performed. Size alone was not objectionable. If it were, he observed, either the Great Northern or the Northern Pacific might already be considered too large.

Theodore Roosevelt was irate. He made his opinion known that Holmes had truckled under to the power of big business, and exclaimed in disgust that he could carve a judge with more backbone out of a banana. It was said that he even contemplated excluding Holmes from further invitations to the White House. Holmes cared little. He always professed a liking for Theodore Roosevelt and an admiration for his way of getting things done, but he never had much respect for his intellect.

Holmes remained on the Supreme Court for thirty years, resigning when he was ninety, in 1932. Meanwhile, he and Justice Brandeis became famous for their dissents against majority opinions. It is a truism to point out that many of these dissents have since become the law. What are today regarded the fundamental rights of workers and unions were long denied because of the judicial doctrine of the sacredness of liberty of contract. Holmes had no particular predisposition toward legislative regulation of business or in favor of labor unions, but his old belief that law represented the convenience of the majority induced him to be very strongly of the opinion that legislatures must be given a wide latitude to experiment.

Dissenting from a majority opinion that denied the power to New York State to set a fifty-cent limit for the markup of theater ticket prices, Holmes said:

> Lotteries were thought useful adjuncts of the State a century or so ago; now they are believed to be immoral and they have been stopped. Wine has been thought good for man from the time of the Apostles until recent years. But when public opinion changed it did not need the Eighteenth Amendment, notwithstanding the Fourteenth, to enable a State to say that business should end . . . What has happened to lotteries and wine might happen to theaters in some moral storm of the future, not because theaters were devoted to a public use, but because people had come to think that way.

He was inclined to take a more narrow look at state or federal statutes which cut down on freedom of speech. Where this occurred in time of war, he had to be convinced that there was a clear and present danger to the state in the prohibited utterance. Here, in *Abrams v. United States,* is one of his most eloquent arguments in favor of the "experiment" of the Constitution:

> But when men have realized that time has upset many fighting faiths, they may come to believe even more than they believe the very foundations of their own conduct that the ultimate good desired is better reached by free trade in ideas—that the best test of truth is the power of the thought to get itself accepted in the competition of the market, and that truth is the only ground upon which their wishes safely can be carried out. That, at any rate, is the theory of our Constitution. It is an experiment, as all life is an experiment. Every year if not every day we have to wage our salvation upon some prophecy based upon imperfect knowledge. While that experiment is part of our system I think that we should be eternally vigilant against attempts to check the expression of opinions that we loathe and believe to be fraught with death, unless they so imminently threaten immediate interference with the lawful and pressing purposes of the law that an immediate check is required to save the country.

The rather fuzzy, sentimentalized picture of Holmes, developed by the great claque of his admirers in his old age, as a persistently fighting liberal, always on the side of the underdog, can be misleading. Holmes was first and foremost a judge. Because he did not think it proper for a court to weigh the wisdom of a statute and to superimpose upon a legislature the court's own economic or social predilections, he was inclined to sustain rather than throw out new laws. As a good percentage of such laws during his long tenure on the Supreme Court tended toward the restraint and regulation of big industry, he is sometimes thought to have been in favor of a regulated society. Yet in his correspondence he again and again denies any such predisposition.

He scoffed at socialism, claiming that "the crowd" already had pretty much of the national wealth and asserting that the palaces and yachts of the rich amounted only to a drop in the bucket. He repeatedly expressed his admiration for the giants of industry who seemed to strike him as bigger men than do-gooders and uplifters. And more than once, in defending free speech in his correspondence, he said that it was the right "of a fool to drool." Once even, in a moment of impatience, he exclaimed to the lady sitting next to him at dinner that he "loathed" most of the things that he decided in favor of.

There were times, indeed, when Holmes struck some of his contemporaries as the very reverse of liberal. He regretted the prosecution by the government of cases against antiwar propagandists, but he sustained its right to bring them, and after the *Debs* decision a package addressed to him with a bomb was intercepted in the post office. He defended the right of the state of Washington to prosecute the publishers of a pamphlet celebrating the glories of nudism because it encouraged "a disrespect for the law," and in *Baily v. Alabama* he dissented from the majority opinion and argued the constitutionality of an Alabama statute (the so-called Negro peonage law) that made a worker's refusal to perform labor as agreed presumptive evidence of an intent to defraud the employer. Holmes here refused to admit the climate of local prejudice:

> We all agree that this case is to be considered and

decided in the same way as if it arose in Idaho or New York. Neither public document nor evidence discloses a law which, by its administration, is made something different from what it appears on its face, and therefore the fact that in Alabama it mainly concerns the blacks does not matter . . .

But the opinions just cited are intended only to demonstrate the variety of his thinking. If he loathed some of the things he decided for, it must be remembered that he also loved deciding things that he loathed. He knew that the law could only develop healthily in the way that it had always developed—as a combination of history and legislation, and that for such development judicial restraint was essential. Justice Felix Frankfurter, who succeeded Benjamin Cardozo, who succeeded Holmes, was Holmes's closest disciple in this philosophy, and lived to see his principles discredited by liberals.

Holmes was always an omnivorous reader. Books seemed to provide him with a life that was as necessary as his work on the Court. Again and again in his letters we find him yearning for the summer vacation at Beverly Farms, when he would be able to read all day. His list of titles is so long and various that it is hard to make many generalizations about it, but one may note a primary interest in current books by philosophers of law, history, and science. Holmes wanted to know every possible theory of man's role in the cosmos. Yet he was always willing to try any other work that a trusted fellow reader suggested, and his efforts in this respect were nothing if not thorough. We see him, for example, plunging into the famous French critic Sainte-Beuve at the suggestion of British political scientist Harold Laski and not really much enjoying the experiment, yet refusing to give up until he had read fourteen volumes of the *Causeries du Lundi* and all of that mammoth work, *Port-Royal.* He read fiction with less enthusiasm but with considerable insights. He admired the young Ernest Hemingway with reservations, and Willa Cather without them. He read Alfred North Whitehead and Morris Cohen and Bertrand Russell and Oswald Spengler—and also Milt Gross and Anita Loos.

His wide reading brings one inevitably to his correspondence, which is closely bound up with it. Five volumes of this have now been published, including the Holmes-Pollock letters and the Holmes-Laski letters. Holmes and Sir Frederick Pollock were contemporaries and lifelong friends, and both were legal scholars, philosophers, and aristocrats. Both were reserved, independent, strong-minded men. In the correspondence, which covers nearly sixty years, their minds met on every kind of legal, political, social or literary problem. The letters make fascinating reading even for those not versed in law.

Holmes's letters to Harold Laski are a bit less interesting. Laski was a generation younger and treated his correspondent with marked deference. Holmes was very fond of him, but he was inclined to use him as a literary retriever. He wanted the names of all the books Laski was reading, and he was supplied with a feast. Yet he did not always, as with Pollock, follow up on topics that Laski

evidently wished to discuss. At rare moments, however, Holmes would let himself go in a bit of natural description. One can only wish that there were more of such passages as the following: "The event of the week has been the opening of the Freer Gallery in the Smithsonian grounds—a beautiful building—with a square in the middle a patch of green, a little fountain and two peacocks and a peahen. The lady it is said will have nothing to do with one of them and he flocked apart and took the sunlight. The other displayed his fan and shivered with amorous anticipations."

Fanny Holmes died in 1929 at the age of eighty-nine, and Holmes wrote to his friends that she had made life poetry for him. He said that he was glad that she had gone first, for he felt—and one is sure correctly—that she would have been worse off without him than he without her. It was only too evident that he had constituted her entire life, whereas she had hardly expected—or even wanted—to constitute all of his. In the following year Charles Evans Hughes was appointed chief justice, and Holmes wrote to Laski that he had lunched at the White House, and that Mrs. Hoover had told him that the President would have liked to appoint him but had thought that he should not be burdened. Indeed, he did not want the appointment; he no longer cared for anything that anyone could give him. On January 12, 1931, he retired from the Court. Harvard Law School continued to send him one of its brightest graduates each year, to be his law clerk and secretary, until his death in 1935, just before his ninety-fourth birthday.

In the final years Holmes became a national hero and was inundated, almost to the point of asphyxiation, with laudations. His fame extended far beyond the legal field, and he was elevated to a kind of old national darling to thousands who could not have understood a page of *The Common Law.* Holmes's attitude about this outburst of fame was amiable enough, but he was never one to value highly any praise that was not discriminating. A word of approval from Sir Frederick Pollock was worth a thousand hosannas. His life had been a happy one, because he had had his chance and had used it, the chance to break his heart "in trying to make every word living and real." The only tragedy would have been to have missed it, a thought which had haunted him in the long campaigns of the Civil War. He never forgot the friends of the Twentieth Regiment who had lost their chances at Ball's Bluff, or Antietam, or Fredericksburg.

David H. Burton (essay date 1979)

SOURCE: "Understanding The Common Law," in *Oliver Wendell Holmes, Jr.—What Manner of Liberal?,* edited by David H. Burton, Robert E. Krieger Publishing Company, 1979, pp. 13-20.

[*In the following essay, Burton outlines Holmes's major points in* The Common Law.]

In the opening sentence of the great book Holmes spoke his objective: "to present a general view of the Common

Law." He proposed a methodology: "We must alternately consult history and existing theories of legislation." And finally he stated his purpose: To understand the law, for while today "there are a great many rules which are quite sufficiently accounted for by their manifest good sense, . . . there are some which can only be understood by reference to the infancy of procedure among the German tribes, or to the social condition of Rome under the Decemvirs." In laying down these general propositions Holmes offered two caveats. "One, is that of supposing because an idea seems very familiar and natural to us, that it has always been so." The other is "the opposite of asking too much of history. We start with the man full grown. It may be assumed that the earliest barbarians whose practices are to be considered, had a good many of the feelings and passions as ourselves." Asking his listeners—and later on his readers—to bear in mind such principles Holmes proceeded to expound the common law with boldness and originality.

He first construed the early forms of liability, holding that "early English appeals for personal violence," for example, "seem to have been confined to intentional wrongs." "Intentional" character implied moral culpability, to be sure. But could an inanimate thing, a falling tree, a runaway wagon, in any way be considered morally responsible for injuries sustained in an accident? For that matter, could the ferocious dog be held responsible for biting his owner's neighbor? Moral culpability must be confined to moral agents. Yet early law took vengeance upon the offending object: the fallen tree whose chips were scattered to the wind. As civilization advanced, vengeance was replaced by compensation and liability was transferred from the agent to the responsible owner. As Holmes pointed out: "The customs, beliefs, or needs of a primitive time establish a rule or a formula. In the course of centuries the custom, belief, or necessity disappears, but the rules remain. The reason which gave rise to the rule has been forgotten, and ingenious minds set themselves to inquire how it is to be accounted for. Some ground of policy is thought of, which seems to explain it and reconcile it with the present state of things; and then the rule adapts itself to the new reasons which have been found for it, and enters on a new career." As an example Holmes suggested that in Roman legal procedures the desire for revenge applied initially to torts, a practice which sooner or later was applied to a breach of contract, because "the remedies for the two is not found ready made." Furthermore, Holmes argued for similarities between Roman law and German tribal custom, that is, vengeance developed imperceptibly toward a non-violent satisfaction for the injury committed while moral culpability replaced the animism ascribed to ships, wagons, and mad dogs.

Conclusions drawn from such considerations enabled Holmes to reject the conservative understanding of law as something fixed and final. Looked at logically, "each new decision follows syllogistically from existing precedent. . . . Precedents survive in the law long after the use they once served is at an end and the reason for them

forgotten. The result of following them must often be failure and confusion from the merely logical point of view." So much for form. But what about the substance—the law? Law is made by judges on "considerations of what is expedient for the community concerned. Every important principle which is developed by litigation is in fact and at bottom the result of more or less definitely understood views of public policy; most generally, to be sure, under our practice and traditions, the unconscious result of the instinctive preferences and inarticulate convictions, but none the less traceable to views of public policy in the last analysis." Law, in Holmes's own words, was administered by able and experienced men who know too much to sacrifice good sense to the syllogism. This explication of early forms of liability concluded on two notable observations: One, the law "is forever adopting new principles from life at one end, and it always retains old ones from history at the other, which have not yet been absorbed or sloughed off." In so saying, Holmes was stating a basically pragmatic principle as applied to the law. Two, "while the law does still and always, in a certain sense, measures legal liability by moral standards, it nevertheless, by the very necessity of its nature, is continually transmuting those moral standards into external or objective ones from which the actual guilt of the party concerned is wholly eliminated." This latter axiom he then set about to demonstrate by an examination of criminal law.

Holmes commenced his treatment of criminal law by contending that presentment was "the child of vengeance," and this desire "imparts an opinion that its object is actually and personally to blame." But the question is whether such a standard is still appropriate in contemporary society. While admitting that any form of punishment satisfied a thirst for vengeance in some way, and that criminal law had improved only gradually, still the modern view of criminal law, Holmes thought, must be punishment meted out to protect society from actions harmful to it and to its members. Punishment is not intended to reform the criminal but to deter crime. If the prisoner pays with his body, society benefits. This social reference is crucial, of course, to Holmes's understanding of all law. In criminal matters as well as in others, "the first requirement of a sound body of law is that it should correspond with the actual feelings and demands of the community, whether right or wrong." Holmes believed that the law should not encourage the passion of revenge, either in individuals or the state.

The social aspect of criminal law was brought out in still another way. Taking direct issue with the Kantian proposition that the individual can never be sacrificed, can never be treated as a means to an end, Holmes asserted: "probably most English-speaking lawyers would accept the preventive theory without much hesitation." No society has ever admitted that it could not sacrifice individual welfare to its own existence, as both military conscription and the right of eminent domain demonstrate." Such a contention led Holmes to utter one of his most famous dicta: "the *ultimata ratio*, not only *regnum*, but of private persons, is force, and that at the bottom of all private relations however tempered by sympathy and all the social feelings, is justified self-preference." What Holmes was speaking in favor of was that the general principles of criminal and civil liability were the same. If the criminal were judged morally, not socially, his abnormal instincts, his want of education, his lack of intelligence, and whatever other defects he might exhibit would have to be taken into account. Yet for the most part these matters were subordinate to what was thought best by society for society as specified in laws and judicial opinions. The individual, therefore, was a means, "a tool to increase the general welfare at his own expense." Such a position, Holmes was to admit, was not an all-encompassing rule. For example, the principle of killing in self-defense is sanctioned by society—and in the interest of society—even though the act of killing is indeed intentional. On the other hand, ignorance of the law can never be allowed to excuse its violation. Society would surely be the loser if it permitted violations of the law because the offender could plead ignorance. The social fabric would disintegrate, and society would be doomed. Without intending to deny the possible importance of "personal unworthiness," the purpose of criminal law was "to induce external conformity to rule." Even so, personal blameworthiness "was judged according to standards set by society." This was exemplified in Holmes's argument that according to current morality, a man is not so much to blame for an act done under the disturbance of great excitement, caused by a wrong done to himself, as when he is calm." The matter of house burning was another set piece employed by Holmes to illustrate his views. A man may intentionally destroy his own property. But if his house is in close proximity to others and these houses are fired in consequence, he is guilty of arson in as much as the effect of his action has had evil social results. Holmes neatly summarized his theory of criminal liability as follows: "All acts are indifferent *per se*. Acts are rendered criminal because they are done under circumstances in which they will probably cause some harm which the law seeks to prevent. The test of criminality in such cases is the degree of danger shown by such experience to attend that act under those circumstances." In this step by step way, the social character of criminal activity was elucidated and established.

Having delineated the social origins of law in matters relating to civil liability and crime, Holmes proceeded to apply the same yardstick to torts. The business of the law of torts, as he stated it in *The Common Law*, "is to fix the dividing line between those cases in which a man is liable for harm he has done, and those in which he is not." In such actions if the law requires satisfaction "the reason for doing so must be found in some general view of conduct which every one may fairly expect and demand from every other, whether that other has agreed to it or not." The law of torts admittedly abounds in moral phraseology—malice, fraud, intent, and negligence—all of which imply that a guilty person must have had some moral shortcoming. While certain authorities, like Austin, accepted such a conclusion, others insisted that man al-

ways acted at his own peril. Holmes proposed to advance an alternate theory, namely, that man acted at his own peril in so far as society would expect a prudent man to act and to foresee the consequences of his actions. And in as much as the expectations of society change, the law itself may change accordingly. Such modifications in the expectations of society were always "politic," that is according to public policy, or what the public would support. As Holmes wrote: "A man may have as bad a heart as he chooses, if his conduct is within the rules." The standards of the law were external standards. Law was wholly indifferent to the internal phenomenon of conscience. It was in his discussion of torts that Holmes offered one of his most insightful descriptions of the life of the law.

> The growth of the law is very apt to take place in this way. Two widely different cases suggest a general distinction, which is a clear one when stated broadly. But as new cases cluster around the opposite poles, and begin to approach each other, the distinction becomes more difficult to trace; the determinations are made one way or the other on a very slight preponderance of feeling, rather than of articulate reason; and at last a mathematical line is arrived at by the contact of contrary decisions, which is so far arbitrary that it might equally well have been drawn a little farther to the one side or the other, but which must have been drawn somewhere in the neighborhood of where it falls.

> In this way exact distinctions have been worked out upon questions in which the elements to be considered are few. For instance, what is a reasonable time for presenting negotiable paper, or what is a difference in kind and what a difference only in quality, or the rule against perpetuities.

Just as law grew in response to the needs of society so social requirements took precedence over those of the individual. The law "does not attempt to see men as God sees them." It only considers what is blameworthy in the average man, a determination made by society and not by moral theories.

The "actual wickedness of the kind described" in the use of such words as fraud or malice, "is not an element in the civil wrongs to which those words are applied," thought Holmes. The basis of liability in torts was the knowledge of what effect the actions performed would have. One example, fraud, may suffice to illustrate Holmes's viewpoint. Deceit was a necessary element in fraud and as such was a "notion drawn from the moral world, and in its popular sense distinctly imports wickedness." The "elements which make it immoral are the knowledge that the statement is false, and the intention that it shall be acted upon." But the defendant in an action involving fraud is not chargeable because he committed an immoral act but because of proof that the defendant knew the other party intended to act upon deceitful information. "The standard of what is called intention is thus really an external standard" of known circumstances. Looked at critically "we find the moral side shade away." Notwithstanding such bold assertions of the social cast of the law Holmes was prompted to state "the moral starting-point of liability in general should never be forgotten, and the law can not without disregarding it hold a man answerable for statements based on facts which would have convinced a wise and prudent man of their truth." Such a concession to morality was indeed a qualified one, for Holmes went on to observe that "starting from the moral ground [the common law] works out an external standard of what would be fraudulent in the average prudent member of the community, and requires every member at his peril to avoid that." In such a context Holmes was led to make one of his most succinct explanations about the growth of law.

> The theory of torts may be summed up very simply. At the two extremes of the law are rules determined by police without references of any kind to morality. Certain harms a man may inflict even wickedly; for certain others he must answer, although his conduct has been prudent and beneficial to the community.

> But in the main the law started from those intentional wrongs which are the simplest and most pronounced cases, as well as the nearest to the feeling of revenge which leads to self-redress. It thus naturally adopted the vocabulary, and in some degree the tests, of morals. But as the law has grown, even when its standards have continued to model themselves upon those of morality, they have necessarily become external, because they have considered, not the actual condition of the particular defendant, but whether his conduct would have been wrong in the fair average member of the community, whom he is expected to equal at his peril.

For Holmes the socially external standard must always be the determining standard.

This critical approach to the law Holmes illustrated in his treatment of bailment. Admitting that the only existing theories on the subject came from Germany and that "the German philosophers who have written upon the law have known no other system than Roman," some rules which he discovered in his research lay clearly against what the German legal theorists had come to regard as first principles. At least Holmes wanted to avoid the hasty assumption that such principles were universal. He had discovered procedures which were kindred to early German folk-laws in fact. While not claiming that the law of bailment was of pure German descent, it possessed enough German elements in Holmes's judgment to challenge the German philosophers who had insisted on Roman sources. Occasionally in *The Common Law* the author was satisfied to question existing assumptions without offering a new thesis fully limned.

A critical attitude was sustained in Holmes's discussion of "possession." He again came out openly and unequivocally against the "*a priori* doctrines of Kant and Hegel" as well as those of "the speculative jurists of Germany,

from Savigny to Ihering." Disagreement arose from the German claim to universal authority. To Holmes the "possessing of a right as such was intrinsically absurd." Tracing theories from Kant back to Rousseau and the Massachusetts version of the American Bill of Rights, which stressed the freedom and equality of men, he dismissed them one and all in as much as they made man an end unto himself. Thus, if an individual was in possession of a thing, the law protected him in that possession because it was an extension of the self. Absolutism of this sort was anathema to Holmes. He was "one who saw in the history of law the development of society" and who was "apt to think that the proximate ground of law must be empirical." "Law being a practical thing must found itself on actual forces." Possession was to Holmes a matter of instinct which he was prepared to argue forcefully.

> It is quite enough, therefore, for the law, that man, by an instinct which he shares with the domestic dog, and of which the seal gives a most striking example, will not allow himself to be dispossessed, either by force or fraud, of what he holds, without trying to get it back again. Philosophy may find a hundred reasons to justify the instinct, but it would be totally immaterial if it should condemn it and bid us surrender without a murmur. As long as the instinct remains, it will be more comfortable for the law to satisfy it in an orderly manner, than to leave people to themselves. It if should do otherwise, it would become a matter for pedagogues, wholly devoid of reality.

In short, instinct was "that mightier body of law than the Roman."

Because Holmes was writing about "possession" at a time when property rights had taken on a sacred patina in American society, he was moved to discuss the nature of "rights" at some length in his chapter on Possession. It may be particularly useful to quote him fully, for by inference he was evaluating all rights, not excluding the "inalienable rights" of life, liberty and the pursuit of happiness as expressed in the American tradition.

> A legal right is nothing but a permission to exercise certain natural powers, and upon certain conditions to obtain protection, restitution, or compensation by the aid of the public force. Just so far as the aid of the public force is given a man, he has a legal right, and this right is the same whether his claim is founded on righteousness or iniquity. Just so far as possession is protected, it is as much a source of legal rights as ownership is when it secures the same protection.

> Every right is a consequence attached by the law to one or more facts which the law defines, and wherever the law gives any one special rights not shared by the body of the people, it does so on the ground that certain special facts, not true of the rest of the world, are true of him. When a group of facts thus singled out by the law exists in the case of a given person, he is said to be entitled to

the corresponding rights; meaning thereby, that the law helps him to constrain his neighbors, or some of them, in a way in which it would not if all the facts in question were not true of him.

Such considerations were of course legal. "What may be their relation to moral rights if there are any, and whether moral rights are not in like manner logically the offspring of moral duties, are questions which do not concern." Such concern was for the speculative philosopher who approached the law from outside, while the jurist came to his subject from within.

What Holmes was doing in his analysis of the law was imparting to it objectivity by reference to the rules of society and public policy. This he carried over to his discussion of contracts, one of the most sensitive and historic of all legal considerations. The common element in all contracts was a promise. One promise may be distinguished from another—for example, I promise you one hundred bales of cotton—by the degree of power possessed by the promisor over the event involved. But according to Holmes, the law does not require the promisor to have any assurance that he either can or will deliver on the promise made. In the moral world it may be an obligation to promise only what one can fulfill, but not so at law. "I take it that a man may bind himself at law that any future event shall happen." By so arguing Holmes escaped the idea that a contract was a "qualified subjection of one will to another, a kind of limited slavery."

Equally practical for contemporary social requirements, damages levied in a breach of contract were not as great as those justified in tort. Furthermore, when contracts were voided the law displayed no concern with the actual state of the party's mind. "In contract, as elsewhere, [the law] must go by externals and judge parties by their conduct." If there are distinctions which might account for voided contracts, these distinctions were "founded in experience, not in logic," an observation which leads back unerringly to the prolegomena of *The Common Law.*

David H. Burton (essay date 1980)

SOURCE: "The Shaping of Wendell Holmes," in *Oliver Wendell Holmes, Jr.,* Twayne Publishers, 1980, pp. 13-35.

[*In the following essay, Burton recounts major influences on Holmes's thinking and surveys his early writings.*]

The law was part of Oliver Wendell Holmes, Jr.'s, natural inheritance. Lawyers had been in the family at least from the time of the sixteenth century—Thomas Holmes of Gray's Inn—and judges, too, a maternal grandfather, Charles Jackson, having been a justice of the Supreme Judicial Court of Massachusetts. For his part, immediately upon completion of Civil War service, Holmes

commenced his legal studies at Harvard and for the next seventy years, down to his death in 1935, his career never deviated from his commitment to understanding the meaning and usage of law. As a student, attorney, scholar, judge, Supreme Court justice, and elder legal statesman, Holmes came to value the law not as an abstruse exercise but as a living, vital aspect of American society. But Holmes, who was born in Boston on March 8, 1841, had a wider birthright than the law itself, however much in after years he was drawn to it. A world of thought, a native city of intellectual and moral preoccupation, a family diverse in learning and accomplishment, a father of wisdom widely proclaimed, all this and the total of its implications passed on to Wendell Holmes. By the time he had reached the age of twenty he had come to know who he was and what he was, though he was far less sure of what he wanted to become. If a number of elements associated with both "thinkers" and "doers" met in him, he was the richer for it. But the intersection of so many and varied strains, at the same time, made for a tension between father and son, between reality and the theory of law, between a conception of man and the cosmos—tensions which Holmes never completely exorcised and which in a unique way help to account for his distinctive place in the historical unfolding of law in America.

I *INHERITANCE*

Holmes's world of thought had roots in the Puritan mind. Just as John Cotton and his generation had sought to reconcile divine revelation with a thriving humanism, producing thereby an imposing if ephemeral Puritan synthesis, Holmes encountered a similar conflict between traditional attitudes and scientific imperatives in his study and uses of the law. No system builder, he nonetheless reflected his Puritan forebears in an earnest search for truth. Unable ultimately to capture that elusive commodity either in constitutional provision or in judicial opinion, Holmes was fated to remain an active philosopher-judge for all his years. He retained throughout an awe bordering on reverence for the "august Puritan figures" from the past. His own especial dedication to the law was the result of his Puritan temperament. For him "life was its own answer. He was a workman who found the stuff and patterns within himself, whose reward was their union."[1] Yet Holmes saw clearly that he had outgrown the Puritan faith, while valuing its legacy of earnest endeavor. "Even if our mode of expressing wonder, our awful fear, our abiding trust in the face of life and death, and the unfathomable world has changed, yet at this day, even now, we New Englanders are still leavened with the old Puritan ferment; our doctrines may have changed, but the cold Puritan passion is still here."[2] Such words as these, delivered on the occasion of an historic anniversary of the founding of the First Church in Cambridge, where his grandfather Abiel Holmes was once pastor, acknowledged his Puritan debt.

Because the Puritan beliefs had yielded to the frontier as well as to the new learning of the century of Enlightenment when Massachusetts grew from colony to province to state, Holmes came to respect eighteenth-century thought and to imbibe its revolutionary philosophy. American freedom was bred in his bones and one day he would answer a call to arms in defense of the Constitution and the Union, edifices built as much on ideas as on action. By the time Holmes was born, however, rationalism had been generously streaked with romanticism and reform was in the air. If America was to be true to its promise, it had to cleanse itself of slavery and a dozen other evils. Holmes as a young man surely was touched by such moral fervor which aimed at nothing less than a national rededication. He was a convinced abolitionist in the 1850s while at Harvard and viewed his Civil War enlistment in part as a commitment to the destruction of human slavery. But like his father, who refused to become either an abolitionist or a pacifist, he would remain aloof from causes and crusades once the passions unleashed by war had a chance to cool. Holmes was, in fact, a true Yankee, "torn between a passion for righteousness and a desire to get on in the world."[3] In the tension discoverable in his outlook, the distance between "is" and "ought" he kept manageable because of the eminently human faith and optimism of men like Ralph Waldo Emerson, whom he knew so well as a boy. Years later Holmes recounted to a friend how one day he met Emerson unexpectedly on the street and on impulse said to him, "If I ever do anything, I shall owe a great deal to you—which is true."[4] Whatever authority the new scientific postulates about the nature and the fate of man were to have on the developing mind of Holmes, the hopefulness of the reforming generation left a lasting mark on a nature which remained openly friendly to honor and sacrifice. "You and I," Holmes was to write to his close friend Sir Frederick Pollock years later, "believe that high-mindedness is not impossible to man."[5]

It requires no flight of imagination to visualize that meeting of Holmes, the boy, and Emerson, the mystic, on the streets of Boston. Boston was a city famous for its great men of philosophy and literature and every kind of learning. To happen on an Adams or a Longfellow or to glimpse Asa Gray or James Russell Lowell was typical of life in that holy place. It was the "hub of the universe," according to Holmes's phrase-making father, Dr. Holmes, "the Autocrat of the Breakfast Table," and the intellectual world revolved around it. Boston filtered the elements derived from the larger realms of thought beyond its boundaries. Not that the city gave its approval to certain beliefs only. The Boston mood could be open and expansive, albeit capable of parochialism and intellectual priggery of a high order if the occasion warranted it. Had not the Autocrat himself pronounced that Bostonians "all carry the Common in our heads as the unit of space, the State House as the standard of architecture, and we measure off men in Edward Everetts as with a yardstick." The Saturday Club, with its storied membership meeting monthly at the Parker House, was the field for Boston's intellectual jousts. Here ideas flowed as copiously as did the wine, and if the results did not strictly add up to *in vino veritas,* the pursuit and isolation of falsity in man, mind, and morals was a game superbly played. To be

detached and critical was a Boston hallmark with which Holmes readily identified, though in his years as a legal scholar and jurist he did not succumb as Boston did to the complacent belief that his judgments were necessarily correct because he had uttered them.[6]

In the longer view Holmes would not feel comfortable as Indian summer engulfed New England. His eye was fixed on a farther, wider horizon, where Boston certainties might appear as "a jingle of words with a jangle of contradictory meanings."[7] Apart from such considerations of the mind, Boston was home to Wendell Holmes. "I've always lived in Boston," was the terse statement in his college autobiography for the Harvard Alumni Album, a remark offered with the quiet pride of an Athenian of old.[8] It was a town to be enjoyed for its houses and gardens, its streets and architecture, its buildings reminders of a rich, persuasive history, and all these things replete with a thousand personal associations as well. It was a place to return to for refreshment after days of battle or months of numbing fatigue on the Supreme Court.

In that same sketch for the Harvard Album there is an apt description of Holmes's family and his sense of it. "All my three names," he wrote, "designate families from which I descended. A long pedigree of Olivers and Wendells may be found in the book called 'Memorials of the Dead—King's Chapel Burying Ground.' . . . Some of my ancestors have fought in the revolution; among the great grandmothers of the family were Dorothy Quincy and Anne Bradstreet ('the tenth muse'); and so on. . . ."[9] His earliest American forebear was one David Holmes, born in England about 1635, died in Milton, Massachusetts, 1666. Within a brief time the Holmes family became both plentiful and successful. John Holmes, David's son and a surveyor of some skill, built a sawmill and began accumulating land. John's son was "Deacon" Holmes, and after him came another David, who was a Revolutionary War officer, then the Rev. Abiel Holmes, a Yale man and a clergyman who was the father of Dr. Holmes and thus the grandsire of Wendell Holmes. The first Wendells were in America by 1640, coming out of Holland. On the Wendell side of the family Holmes was related to Wendell Phillips, Richard Henry Dana, and William Ellery Channing. Added to this, Wendell's father had married a second cousin, Amelia Jackson, giving the impression that the family was at once numerous, distinguished, and closely knit. Amelia Jackson's father, Judge Jackson, was a landowner who provided his daughter and son-in-law with their family house in Montgomery Place as a wedding gift, a successful businessman and a jurist. If the Holmes side of the family was noted for its learning with a dash of piety, the Jacksons introduced a preference for the practical which was to serve Wendell Holmes in good stead. Unlike his contemporary, young Henry Adams, Holmes grew up in Boston conscious of the place his ancestors had prepared for him in life and happy with the prospects. When in 1872 he married Fanny Bowditch Dixwell, the New England connection was complete. Fanny was the granddaughter of the well-known writer on navigation Nathaniel Bowditch; her father, E. S. Dixwell, a brilliant student two classes ahead of Dr. Holmes at Harvard, was a proper Boston schoolmaster. The wild streak in the Dixwell blood—it was said that John Dixwell had helped in the execution of Charles I—had been transmuted to a quiet *joie de vivre,* of which Fanny Bowditch Dixwell, luckily for Wendell Holmes, enjoyed a generous share.[10]

II *FATHER AND SON*

Unlike many sons of a famous parent, Wendell Holmes managed to escape from the long shadow cast by his father. Indeed, unlike most children so favored, he came to exceed his parent in age and in historical reputation, if not in wisdom. But growing up under the roof as well as the shadow of the Autocrat was not a condition easily borne, despite the obvious advantages it entailed. The more Wendell learned the more he was likely to argue with his father and dissent in the bargain. If it is remembered further that Holmes brought his bride to his father's house and did not establish his own home until three years had passed, the opportunities for distemper between an egoistic father and his intellectually aggressive offspring must have been numerous. Wendell, anxious to go his own way, saw in his father's household presence, as in his household erudition, too much of what was intimidating and inhibiting. But the clash of two such self-confident personalities—including the possibility at least that in later years the younger Holmes took a special pleasure in the prospect of outstripping his father in the world of men and affairs—cannot disguise the influence which Dr. Holmes exerted on his eldest boy.[11] For one thing, freedom of thought in religious matters passed clearly enough from father to son. For another, it appeared to "observers of hereditary talent," that Holmes Jr.'s "subtle and original following out of analogies and the presentation of familiar elements in fresh lights" could be seen as derived on a straight line from Dr. Holmes.[12] More basic was the son's scientific attitude of mind: antimetaphysical, skeptical of development of constants and universals beneath the flux of change—all this learned at home far more so than at school. As Dr. Holmes was prone to view free will as illusory, substituting heredity and environment for Calvinistic predestination, Judge Holmes, for example, came to doubt the deterrent value of criminal punishment, holding that most criminal actions were but responses to stimuli. Wendell agreed unequivocally with his father that man's free will was often severely limited by chance circumstances and surroundings. Like his father he was dubious about the prospect of self-direction. Human frailty caused them both to question conventional concepts of moral responsibility. Though young Holmes found it uncongenial to confide in Dr. Holmes as to the origins and direction of his philosophical ideas, his broader frame of reference owed much to his father's scientific convictions. Nor for all of the irritants present in their relationship, real as they were but undoubtedly exaggerated with the retelling, should the natural affection of father and son be ignored. What may have been lacking in sentiment was made up for by admiration and respect.

The birth of Dr. Holmes's first son was for him an occasion of pride and promise. He wrote his sister, Ann, within hours of the event, describing the baby as "a little individual who may hereafter be addressed as——— Holmes, Esq. or The Hon———Holmes, M. C. or His Excellency———Holmes, President."[13] Such hopes are perhaps no more common to men of distinction than to others, even though the air of confidence in Dr. Holmes's fancy was thoroughly consistent with his Brahmin mentality. By the age of six "o.w.h."—his father used this style of designating the little edition of O.W.H.—was attending a Dame's school and in the autumn of 1848 enrolled at a boys' academy run by a T. Russell Sullivan. The master was a former Unitarian minister who lost no occasion, whether the subject be the delivery of pure water to the city or the prospecting for gold in California, to invoke the name and the wonderful power of the Lord. After four years under Sullivan's tutelage, Holmes entered Dixwell's Private Latin School in Boylston Place, having impressed Master Sullivan with "habits of application," "proficiency in all the English branches," and a "love for study."[14]

III *SCHOOL AND BOOKS*

Epes Sargent Dixwell, whose son-in-law Holmes was to become, had some claim to recognition as a classical scholar. Though he had read law and had engaged in a little practice, his true calling was that of schoolmaster. With an eye trained on the Harvard College entrance examination which stressed Latin, Greek, ancient history, and mathematics, Dixwell provided his charges with a solid grounding in these fundamentals. No narrow pedant himself, as his interest in conchology and membership in the Boston Society of Natural History testified, Dixwell saw to it that his students also read French and German and studied English as well as modern history, though these lastnamed subjects were approached with a good deal less intensity. Such formalities aside, Dixwell seems to have discovered in the young Holmes an apt companion for walks and talks after school as the two made their way home; and their friendship remained steadfast in the years to come.

In conjunction with schooling Holmes had an outlet for his budding literary tastes in the novels of Walter Scott— *Ivanhoe, Old Morality,* and the *Fortune of Nigel*—as well as the writings of Dickens, Thackeray, Tennyson, and Macaulay. Lesser authors of the caliber of Mayne Reid, G. R. P. James, and Sylvanus Cobb, Jr., also offered Holmes stories of interest. Such boyhood enthusiasms as he displayed in reading Scott, for example, who was his favorite, provided a wholesome balance to the classical-language drills he daily faced at Dixwell's. Beyond school, and especially from his father and his mother, young Wendell learned the code of a humanized Christian ethic. Honor, courage, honesty, diligence, fidelity, while they all might be assumed, were nevertheless inculcated by precept not more than by example. But it was a practical morality Holmes tended to embrace as well as a highly personalized one, which even as a youngster he put to use. One of his recollections from childhood had to do with this practical brand of morality. Was it ever right to lie, he once asked his cousin and closest chum, John T. Morse, Jr., as the two boys were playing one day on Boston Common. When his companion answered "No," Holmes offered him a supposition. Suppose, he said, they were to see a man who, running toward them terrified of pursuers he knew to be close at his heels, bounded into a nearby thicket. Would it be wrong, queried Holmes, to deny to the pursuers any knowledge of the whereabouts of the man? Both boys concluded that it might be indeed the right and necessary thing to do in order to save the hare from the hounds.[15] In morality, as in the law, circumstances were known to alter cases.

Holmes was to survive three woundings during the Civil War, no little tribute to his good luck and to a certain physical toughness and resilience. As a youth he was not devoted to outdoor sports, and it was not until his army days that he learned to ride. Holmes is best thought of as a typical lad of his time. His greatest fun was sleighing on the hills of Boston. He also liked to row on the Charles, a pastime his father greatly encouraged. In 1849, when Wendell was about eight years old, Dr. Holmes built a summer house for the family near Pittsfield on land which had been in the family for generations. The site was on the Lenox Road and was called Canoe Meadows; it encompassed some 280 acres. Such a place was perfectly suited to children's holidaying, for by this time the Holmes family had expanded to include a sister, Amelia, and a brother, Edward. Here the children were free to fish and swim, pick berries, and explore the woodlands round about. This was the red-skin interlude for Wendell which schools introduce between the fast flowing tears of the child and the man: sitting at Xanthus-side amidst the camp fires or witnessing the battle in the West Country where Arthur fell. Holmes later spoke of these days as "my first recollections of the country—and what we love and revere is largely determined by our earliest memories."[16]

By his mid-teens Holmes had discovered a fresh and unusual outlet for his energies and his imagination. He had attained a feel for art and procured a set of etching tools and materials. Never minded to devote his life to drawing, this interlude proved great fun for him and at the same time diversified and enlarged his appreciation of the world about him. The knowledge he acquired of the techniques of woodcut, wood-engraving, and line-engraving was remarkable. Such drawings as he made were carefully done, proficient if not inspired; but he was shortly convinced that his efforts lacked "that final wiggle of genius.[17] Later, at Harvard, Holmes wrote a piece for the *Harvard Magazine,* **"Notes on Albert Dürer,"** in which he sought to fuse his instinctive yen for art and his developing philosophical outlook. In fact his appreciation of art and artists remained a consistent part of him, though in later years he might be more prone to utilize his fondness for art to point up a larger moral observation. Addressing the Fiftieth Anniversary Dinner

of his Harvard class in 1911, for example, he offered the thought: "Life is painting a picture, not doing a sum," one of those capsulized judgments with which he delighted his circle.[18]

Meanwhile Holmes also fed his spirit with more serious reading. Lamb's *Dramatic Poets* and *The Prometheus of Aeschylus* were books taken from library shelves to be read with evident satisfaction. Vaughan's *Hours with the Mystics* he pondered while still at Dixwell's, a book which he was later to tell Pollock constituted a "transit from boy to man."[19] And he had commenced a serious consideration of Plato which grew out of his course in Greek at school. Emerson—"Uncle Waldo," as Holmes affectionately knew him—had advice when Wendell confided to him that he was reading Plato: "You should read Plato at arm's length. Say to him: 'You have been pleasing the world for two thousand years; see whether you can please me.'"[20] Emerson's counsel appealed to him; his own critical awareness had begun to take shape and direction. He had clearly outgrown Dixwell's Private Latin School and was as ready as any of his age for entrance into Harvard College. His father might have said he was more ready than most of his fellow students. As it turned out, Harvard was to be a set of expectations, some fulfilled and some not, for O. W. Holmes, Jr., Class of '61.[21]

IV *HARVARD COLLEGE*

The disappointments attending Holmes's years at Harvard (1857-1861) were born of incongruity; yet, paradoxically, this same incongruity enabled Holmes to forge for himself an inquiring and critical mind. He was no more trained to ask big questions or to challenge the traditional assumptions which governed the educational enterprise of Harvard College in the 1850s than were Master Dixwell's other graduates. Nor was he at first minded to do so. He made the transition from school to freshman year in college easily enough because the difference between the two was a matter not of a kind but of degree. By the close of his course of studies, however, he had become disenchanted with the limiting effect of indoctrination, recitation, and institutional discipline which summarized the educational life-style at Cambridge in those years. By formally and semi-officially seeking to deny Holmes (and to his fellow students as well) the spectrum of universal knowledge, by dismissing as insignificant Darwin's scientific findings, for example, the intellectual authority over her students which Harvard wished to exercise produced the reverse effect on Holmes. Like certain of his college friends, William James among them, Holmes wanted to twist the tail of the cosmos, and was not content to be the receptacle into which traditional morality and philosophical orthodoxy might be poured in carefully measured quantities. If Harvard was "an emphatic and unbuilding force in the life of Holmes," she taught her students, in Holmes's own phrase, "in ways not to be discovered, by traditions not to be written down, help[ing] men of lofty nature to make good their faculties."[22] As Holmes's mind fleshed out, Harvard College proved less and less able to contain it. After a while he would no longer seek to conform, and for the last three years, with an increasing intensity, he agitated against the educational system.

The intellectual cross-purposes of institution and student notwithtanding, the total of Holmes's life at Harvard was not merely tolerable but pleasant to the point of enjoyable. As a freshman he took rooms at Mr. Danforth's on Linden Street, adjacent to but beyond the College Yard. He remained in residence there for his four years, thus avoiding the worst disciplinary features of dormitory life. All in all these arrangements provided more suitable an environment than living in college, giving Holmes a better chance to study, reflect, and write; he had come to Harvard seriously bent on learning. He was also active in the social clubs: the Institute, the Hasty Pudding, the Porcellian, and the Alpha Delta Phi. For a while at least he was a member of the Christian Union, an organization pointedly opposed to the highly orthodox and religiously rigorous Christian Brethren.[23] If little is known of the young collegian's social life beyond Harvard, in the drawing rooms of the best families of Boston and Cambridge, there is no reason to hold that the handsome and articulate son of Dr. Holmes lacked for female admirers. In his **"Notes to Account of My First Wound,"** composed just after his first Civil War encounter at Ball's Bluff, he wrote: "While I was lying on the island, one of the thoughts that made it seem particularly hard to die was the recollection of several fair damsels whom I wasn't quite ready to leave."[24] Certainly he made close friends with fellow students. Norwood Penrose Hallowell, a Philadelphia Quaker who was to be the Orator of the Class of '61—as Holmes was Class Poet—was the best among them. Hallowell later served in the Twentieth Massachusetts Volunteer Infantry, Holmes's regiment, was wounded at Antietam, and remained a life-long friend.

It would have been remarkable had young Holmes not strayed beyond the boundaries of College discipline and decorum as rigidly laid down and relentlessly enforced by the faculty, regulations which President Eliot in his 1869 inaugural address slightingly referred to as "petty." Sanctions were placed on an endless list of indulgences large and small: smoking in the Yard, missing chapel, breaking windows (something of an undergraduate obsession), blaspheming. The result was a state of near-constant warfare between faculty and students. By living off campus Holmes avoided conflict with a good many of these rules, not that he was inclined to break them all. Rather his resistance to the ways of Harvard was concerned more with what he was taught, not with how he was to behave. As one of the three senior editors of the *Harvard Magazine* he drew the ire of President Felton when disrespectful language characterizing a retiring professor found its way into the columns of the magazine. On another occasion the faculty voted a public admonition to Holmes for "repeated and gross indecorum in the recitation of Professor Bowen."[25] Bowen's insistence on religious orthodoxy as the one sound foundation for hu-

man behavior had simply become too much for Holmes in his senior year. Given the number of temptations a maturing, critical student must have encountered along the way, the infrequency of penalties levied against Holmes may be the more significant factor after all for estimating his self-restraint. Such considerations, furthermore, may be best seen as unavoidable obstacles which simply had to be overcome if students were "to make good their faculties." In the case of Holmes he made good the opportunity to pass out of Harvard not merely as one experienced in protesting against the system but as one equipped with a personal and noble philosophy which, having fashioned it himself, became part of him.

Wendell Holmes left a considerable record of his progress along the paths of the learning and the intellectual independence for which he is well remembered. His sophomore essay, **"Books,"** is a useful early reference point. In its passages Holmes insists that students must not be content with creeds which define all the possibilities and then say, "Thus far shall ye think, and no farther." He contends, instead, that "we *must,* will we or no, have every train of thought brought before us while we are young. . . ."[26] This call for an intellect open to the universe was not, at so early a phase of his Harvard career, a hostile reaction to the college's orthodoxies; the sentiments and convictions expressed in **"Books"** were matters of the Holmesian temperament. He was, as he would remain, concerned with "conclusions, or of such facts as enabled him to arrive at conclusions, on the great issues of right and wrong and on the relation of man to God." By calling for a life of the mind, as opposed to a life taken up merely with events, Holmes argued that books must be the starting point. Not alone the works of Shakespeare, Montaigne, and Goethe, but Plato and Confucius, and "the Buddhist and Zoroastrain sacred books" as well. As he remarks in his essay, "books are but little seeds after all, seeming insignificant before the merest weed of real life; but they lie soaking in our minds and when we least expect it, they will spring up, not weeds but supporters that will be our aid in the sorest struggles of our life."[27] Behind the sententious prose of the Harvard sophomore Holmes's mind was beginning to coil. It would draw together tighter and tighter over the course of his schooling before and after the Civil War, set to spring loose upon the law as upon all of life.

The case for books having been amply stated, what books in particular appear to have absorbed Holmes's energies in these years, apart from college texts like Bowen's *The Principles of Metaphysical and Ethical Science Applied to the Evidences of Religion* and Thomson's *Law of Thought* which were typical of the standard reading in most courses he took? Plato's *Dialogues* was a constant companion. He also studied Fichte's *Contribution to Mental Philosophy,* contemplated Butler's *Ancient Philosophy* and Cousin's *Modern Philosophy,* and returned again and again to Vaughan's *Hours with the Mystics.* The ongoing struggle to fashion his own peculiar intellectual outlook, and the drift of that outlook away from traditional, orthodox moorings was evident in his reading of

Lowes's volumes *Comte's Philosophy of the Sciences* and *Biographical History of Philosophy*. These latter books no doubt helped to polarize Holmes's thinking on the methods of truth-seeking and the possibilities of truth-finding without, in the end, convincing him of the logical positivist's confident dismissal of all that can not be seen and measured as irrelevant.

Holmes became one of those thinkers who quite frankly and firmly insisted on reading philosophy from the point where he stood in historical time backward to the ancient Greeks. " . . . I regard pretty much everything, and especially the greatest things, in the way of books, as dead in fifty, nowadays in twenty years," he told one friend in 1909. "The seeds of thought germinate and produce later seeds. The old structures are remodeled and have electric lights put in." He then went on to describe himself as one who "thinks that Philosophy and the philosophy of history really have advanced within recent times. . . . "[28] In light of these assertations, the formative potentiality of his Harvard years is registered unmistakably in an essay, **"Plato,"** which he published in the October 1860 issue of the *University Quarterly,* an intercollegiate journal of undergraduate opinion. Following the advice of Emerson not to accept Plato's philosophy unless, in fact, Plato pleased him, Holmes undertook to apply his growing skepticism to some of Plato's favorite generalizations. "Man is man, again Plato also says, just as far as he partakes of humanity. . . . But here, as it seems to me, there is a serious confusion introduced . . . owing to the admitting equally, without distinction, the simple ideas like those in which mathematical truth is dependent . . . and those like humanity, which is a purely general statement. In other words, as long as we have faith in reason we must believe in the truths of mathematics . . . while we see at least no such necessary existence for the ideas of humanity, etc." Holmes discovers an "unhappy fallacy" in Plato in that he confounded conclusions present in logic with conclusions drawn from new data. Admitting that Plato's philosophy is a "vast step" in introducing more accurate and well defined thought than had previously existed, "it still needed a complete remodeling before it would suffice as a consistent cosmology." "Our chemists do know more really than the best of the alchymists . . . and so with ancient metephysics." For Holmes "we start far beyond the place where Plato rested." Nevertheless, there is in this essay a lingering regard for the "intuitive faculty" in man which makes the position of its author a trifle ambiguous. His quarrel is not so much with Plato as a thinker but with those who continued to quote Plato, oblivious to the rise of science which rendered Plato, not useless, but anachronistic. Plato's value to the philosopher is still real; seeing "a really great and humane spirit fighting the same fight as we ourselves" was inspiring.[29] Yet Plato's answers were, in the main, out of date. No less a philosopher than Emerson had read this essay on Plato in draft form. "I have read your piece," he told the young Holmes. "When you strike at a king, you must *kill* him."[30] Yet for Holmes and his intellectual world the time was not yet ripe for dismissing Plato and his answers altogether. He could

still talk sincerely of coming to know the "necessary ideas" which are part of the "mind of the Creator," while trusting more in science than in intuition.[31]

"Notes on Albert Dürer," which Holmes wrote over the summer months of 1860, showed a similar propensity.[32] Dürer's treatment of religious subjects attracted him because his drawing technique appealed to the draughtsman in him and because contemplation of the artist's work yielded meaning for him. It was the mood which Dürer was able to evoke—the ultimately tragic fate of mankind—and not so much the religious message of the pictures which fascinated him. Indeed, in this essay, Holmes is prepared to say that Dürer, like Plato, had become outdated if one sees only and even primarily the message of salvation. "The growth of civilization increases our faith in the natural man and must accordingly detract from the intense and paramount importance attached in darker times to the form of the story embodying the popular religion." Yet Holmes's attraction to Dürer's drawings, with their unavoidable overtones of religious spirituality, remains unexplained, save by his temperamental need to fathom the fullest meaning of man which itself tends to suggest a residual belief, or faith in God. Unable to accept the faith of an age that was passed, he was not ready to take "the leap into the dark" on the reassurances of science. And so he focused in his **"Notes on Albert Dürer"** on man himself. His description of Dürer's *Meloncolia* spoke something of his youthful anguish. "That solitary picture is the true picture of his [man's] soul, in its strength and its weakness; powerful, but half overcome by the many objects of its universal study; crowned with the wreath of the elect and beautiful with an ideal genius, but grave with thought and marked with the care of the world; winged, yet resting sadly on earth."[33] That the art and thought of Dürer appealed to Holmes for more than half a century is clear from a 1923 letter in which he wrote of his collection of Dürer engravings and woodcuts, many of them having been in his possession since the Civil War. The consistent tension which is discoverable in the whole range of Holmes's life of the mind is traceable in some part to the impressions made by Dürer's work, which itself seemed to want to suspend judgment between God and man, Heaven and hell.

v *CALL TO ARMS*

Wendell Holmes's final term at Harvard was an unsettled one. The imposition by orthodox professors of principles of metaphysics and *laissez-faire* economics was but part of the discontent. The Civil War was bearing down on Harvard men no less than on other Americans, and Holmes was caught up in these great events which led on to strife. Wendell Phillips had once again stirred Boston in favor of the cause of abolition. Lincoln's call for volunteers to put down the Southern rebellion broke the spell of uncertainty and indecision which hung across the land. Holmes was, for the moment at least, an abolitionist. Within two weeks of the presidential proclamation of April 15, 1861, he had enlisted as a private soldier in the

Fourth Battalion of the state militia and had commenced training at Fort Independence in Boston Harbor. Harvard College was suddenly remote. Once it was clear that the Fourth Battalion was not slated for immediate action, both Holmes and his father had some sober second thoughts about the college career which was so near successful completion. It was possible for him to remain in military service and yet take the examinations for his degree. The willingness of the faculty to accept him back on these terms, the fact that he had already been elected Class Poet, and the time required for his application for a commission to be processed all conspired to enable Holmes to graduate Harvard with the Class of 1861. Then, on July 23, 1861, within a week of commencement exercises, Oliver Wendell Holmes, Jr., aged twenty, was commissioned a lieutenant and joined A Company, Twentieth Massachusetts Volunteer Infantry. The Civil War awaited him.

VI *LESSONS OF WAR*

The transition from peace to war was a swift and painful one for Wendell Holmes. Commissioned in July 1861 and ordered South with his regiment in September, he was wounded the next month in the battle of Ball's Bluff. "Hit in the beginning of the fight," he wrote his mother from a military hospital two days later, to which he added hopefully, "we'll lick 'em yet though."[34] Such were the ways during the first months of the Civil War: raw recruits led by unseasoned officers with heavy casualties the usual result—as Holmes's own experience testifies. Commission in hand and with little enough training, he was expected to lead troops, green and feckless youth for the most part drawn from New England farms and villages, into battle. As dangerous as such a situation was to the soldiers in the ranks, it was both hazardous and harrowing for the junior officers who had to assume responsibility for leadership while facing the same risk of death as the men under their command. Nothing that Wendell Holmes had known in life had prepared him for this ordeal. But perhaps Harvard had helped to ready his response. At college he had worked hard to refine a "noble philosophy" in which he could truly believe and by which, in consequence, he could guide his behavior. Battle would be the first, and possibly the supreme, test of that philosophy.

Like all citizen-soldiers Holmes was to learn by doing and, perchance, by dying—the lot of "the infantry of the line [which] stood the great slaughter."[35] The three separate wounds he received, at Antietam, September 1862, and at Fredericksburg, May 1863, in addition to Ball's Bluff, October 1861, are reminders of how constant was the danger to life itself, how often luck or fate played a part in survival. Nor was Holmes indifferent to such considerations. "My Dear Parents," he wrote just after being hit at Antietam, "Once more I back it as per hint of yesterday's letter—Usual luck—ball entered at the rear passing through the central seam of coat & waistcoat collar coming out to the front of the left side. . . ." Luck today; fate tomorrow: "now as ever I believe that what-

ever shall happen is best."[36] And so the war came to Wendell Holmes.

For every soldier who survives the ravages of battle there must always remain two wars: the war in fact and the war in memory. But more rare is the veteran who displays a peculiar need to recall battles, toast old wounds years afterwards, relive personal tragedies, and commemorate great events and great friends as did Holmes. In consequence he tended to impart a patina of unreality to the horrors he spoke and wrote of, once he was *hors de combat*. Perhaps it was only an effort to cast out the devils which are war's daily companions and which continue to haunt old soldiers despite the years. The evidence that he reflected on the war and its lessons is overwhelming. In writing to Frederick E. Pollock he noted: "I always think that when a man has once had his chance—has reached the table land over his difficulties—it does not matter much whether he has more or less time allowed him in that stage. The real anguish is never to have your opportunity. I used to think that a good deal during the war."[37] And he told Harold Laski, one of his confidants, more than half a century after Appomattox, "The army taught me some great lessons—to be prepared for catastrophe—to endure being bored—and to know that however fine a fellow I thought myself in my usual routine, there were other situations alongside and many more in which I was inferior to men that I might have looked down upon had not experience taught me to look up."[38]

Other equally serious and far-reaching lessons he learned as well. The three distinctive elements which stand out in Holmes's reaction to the Civil War are strikingly alike components discernible in his later intellectual growth. Soldiering did not thwart so much as it nurtured that development in altogether novel ways. Holmes came to treat the duties and the dangers of war pragmatically. He learned by doing and readily saw, at peril to his life, that old habits might have to be discarded and new skills acquired if military success was to be achieved. His ability to adapt was proven regularly in battle. Success was tantamount to survival. What contributed to survival in one situation might have to be avoided in another, as the demands of the engagements shifted. Beyond these everyday considerations, men like Holmes viewed the war as a matter of efficiency versus inefficiency. They thought of winning the war in practical, pragmatic terms, rather than according to the enthusiasms of the home front. Duty for them could depend "less in relation to great causes and more as a matter of doing the necessary tasks in an efficient way."[39] Individual survival and military success were linked to the least wasteful and quickest methods of victory.

Whatever the ingredient of luck, soldiers in action feel, as Holmes felt, that survival is bound up with the will to struggle, the will to survive, perhaps bound up even with the momentary illusion of immortality in this life. To the soldier who continues to function as a human being, and Holmes for all his exposure to brutality remained intensely human, war does not appear as it might seem to the generals—that is, an awesome use of lives to gain an objective. It is more intimately involved with an individual's desire to stay alive, however reckless or selfless his behavior under fire. Viewed from without war is an inexorable mechanism for destruction; but from within it is each individual's determination not to be destroyed. There is discoverable in any battle condition, and in the larger context of war, a curious blending of pragmatic and social Darwinist elements which for Holmes worked themselves out under circumstances certain to leave a lasting impression.

The cause which made Holmes's struggle against extinction and his pragmatic response to survival appeal to him as worthwhile comes through as a reminder that, at this stage in his growth, tradition and traditional values could have an almost decisive place. There was no pressing need on his part to enlist in the Union Army; no special social stigma attached to those young men of his generation who did not enlist. While a great many Harvard graduates did join the fight, not a few of his social class—and the young Henry Adams and William Everett come to mind—did not. Those who shunned military duty were not stirred by the same noble impulse which stirred Wendell Holmes. If his service was an expression of a youthful rebellion against parental and institutional authority, his avowed purpose, to help in the destruction of slavery, placed his decision in a context of values. Beyond that we may be sure that Holmes's response to the presidential call for volunteers was patriotic in a direct and ennobling way. Lacking the social compulsion to enter the army, there was a compelling Puritan sense of duty to be performed. The call to arms came not alone from Lincoln but from across the years, across the generations of Puritan forebears. Giving an account of his conduct at Ball's Bluff, Holmes saw himself as acting "very cool and did my duty I am sure."[40] On another occasion he described himself as 'heartily tired and half worn out body and mind by this life, but I believe I am as ready as ever to do my duty."[41] Evidence from Holmes's record of service bears out the primacy of duty in his set of working values.

The concept of duty figured throughout Holmes's wartime letters and diary and was registered in his postwar reflections. In his Memorial Day Address at Keene, New Hampshire, May 30, 1884, he praised the duty he judged his own to be in celebrating the sacrifice of his intimate friend Henry L. Abbott, killed at Cedar Montain, August 1862. Of Abbott Holmes said, "He was indeed a Puritan in all his virtues without a Puritan austerity; for when duty was at an end he who would have been master and leader became the chosen companion in every pleasure a man might honestly enjoy. In action he was sublime."[42] Even as Holmes was nearing the end of his enlistment and found himself thoroughly whipped by the war, duty remained paramount. "I honestly think that the duty of fighting has ceased for me," he wrote his mother in June of 1864, "ceased because I have laboriously and with much suffering of mind and body *earned* the right . . . to decide for myself how I can best do my duty to myself,

to the country, and, if you choose, to God."[43] In like vein he told Charles Eliot Norton about the same time: "If one did not believe this war was a crusade in the cause of the whole Christian world it would be hard to keep the hand to the sword."[44] Such thoughts as these coming at the end of Holmes's long trial as a soldier expose the deep roots of conviction regarding the war. Furthermore, the acknowledgment of absolute values in his scheme of living helps to delineate his traditionalism. Later intellectual adventuring would supply rationales for pragmatic adaptation and struggle for survival which battlefield experience had woven into his subconscious. No such philosophical justification for the absolute demands of duty and loyalty would be forthcoming, however, so that Holmes's reasons for making the sacrifices attendant to the war would remain the same reason which enabled him, some thirty years afterward, to praise as "true and adorable that which leads a soldier to throw away his life in obedience to a blindly accepted duty. . . ."[45] Uncertain of the meaning of the universe, the demands of duty remained absolute. If remembrance of battles past was the only consideration causing the mature Holmes to proclaim a belief in absolutes, that in itself is some measure of the impact of the Civil War on the young Boston aristocrat who was so eager to join the fight in 1861.

VII *WAR'S LASTING EFFECTS*

Years after the event, Holmes advised one friend that since "the Civil War the world never seemed quite right again."[46] His insistence upon such a judgment demands a careful assessment of the particular ways in which he had been changed by his wartime experiences, or at least what evolving characteristics of mind and faith found nourishment or possibly confirmation in the agonies of battle. Traits of the mature Holmes are easily related to the war, traits ambivalent in a revealing fashion. Aristocratic, yet democratic; detached, but involved; stoic while passionate; callous, though tender; convinced of life as a quaint adventure of the protoplasm without losing sight of man's innate dignity—these were the contradictions which distinguished the impact of the Civil War on Wendell Holmes.

Holmes had volunteered in 1861 out of an aristocratic sense of responsibility which was part of his New England birthright. Duty to him was inbred rather than deliberated. Yet the Civil War stripped away the artificialities of social rank by throwing individuals back on their own resources, as Holmes came quickly to appreciate. His first sergeant, when he commanded G Company, was Gustave Magnitzky, an immigrant newly arrived from Polish Prussia. Holmes's estimate of Magnitzky was the description of a natural aristocrat: "quiet and steady under fire, quiet and effective in camp, modest, distinguished in bearing and soul. . . ."[47] He was prepared to give him rank equal to that of an Abbott or a Hallowell in the company of soldiers and gentlemen. Wendell's democracy was the equal of his aristocratic sense.

It has been argued to good effect that the war promoted in Holmes his Olympian detachment in the face of a war, or a world, calling for answers to unanswerable questions.[48] Furthermore, he himself once conceded that "in the Civil War I formulated to myself the value of prejudice and being cocksure for achievement."[49] Some of the very passages from his wartime letters which underscore his sangfroid are interlaced, however, with Holmes's frustration at not being able to stop the loss of life which he was witness to. "It is odd how indifferent one gets to the sight of death—perhaps, because one gets aristocratic and don't [sic] value much a common life—Then they are apt to be so dirty it seems natural—'Dust to Dust'— I would do anything that lay in my power but it doesn't much offset my feelings."[50] Similar evidence shows how the stoic remained the passionate young man. Having announced his decision to leave the army: "so I mean to leave at the end of the campaign as I said, if I am not killed before," in the same letter he described "the intense yearning" for "home and parents" which he said immediately precedes a campaign.[51]

The toughness of the mature Holmes is axiomatic. "I believe that force is the ultimate ratio" and "three generations of imbeciles are enough" are vintage Holmes. Such views no doubt found a source in the horrors of the war so often recalled. He could speak with callous measure of heavy battle losses as "the butcher's bill" at a point when the war was "kill-kill all the time." Yet he did not descend to the brutish level. "A thousand loving thoughts this Sunday Morng [sic]." "Day beautiful and quiet," "Love to all" are phrases common in his letters and diary during those days when he was his most disdainful of life. His soul-searching over the decision to be mustered out of the army arose from the inner thoughts of a person who continued to weigh his behavior in a human scale of values.

Holmes's doubts about his meaning in the cosmos subsequent to his first wound—"Would the complex forces which made a still more complex unit in *ME* resolve themselves back into simpler forms or would my angel be still winging his way onward when eternities had passed?"[52]—soon gave way to his own peculiar agnosticism. This is not the same as saying that life was futile. The Civil War taught Holmes that life had a worth in itself, that there was an ineffable value to battles fought, and better still, to battles won, a quality which lent dignity and carried within it its own purpose. It will not do to draw from Holmes's oft-quoted remarks in speeches long after the events, including the famous **"Soldiers' Faith."** Better to listen to the man at arms who took sure if quiet pride in soldiering and especially in his regiment. "I really very much doubt whether there is any Regt, wh. can compare with ours in the Army of the Potomac. Everyone says this who belongs to a good Regt. but still I fancy I am right from the evidence of many things."[53] In his regiment Holmes had a mirror for his own sense of devotion to duty and accomplishment. The regiment became his "beloved 20th." It identified him positively with something outside himself, something he believed in and was intensely loyal to. By giving loyalty to an absolute, namely, the unyielding principle of duty, Holmes verified the truth of that principle. In his own later phrase, truth is what I "can't help" believe. Coming at a time when such lessons were indelibly written, Wendell Holmes left the war touched not alone by fire but by the spirit of man's strange and perplexing purpose.

NOTES

[1] Learned Hand, "Mr. Justice Holmes," *Mr. Justice Holmes,* Felix Frankfurter, ed. (New York, 1931), p. 131.

[2] Oliver Wendell Holmes, "The Puritans," *Speeches* (Boston, 1913), p. 21.

[3] The phrase of Samuel Eliot Morison in *The Maritime History of Massachusetts* (Boston and New York, 1921), p. 188.

[4] Holmes to Patrick Augustine Sheehan, Oct. 27, 1912, *Holmes-Sheehan Correspondence,* David H. Burton, ed. (Port Washington, N.Y., 1976), p. 51.

[5] Holmes to Sir Frederick E. Pollock, June 20, 1928, *Holmes-Pollock Letters,* Mark deW. Howe, ed., 2 vols. (Cambridge, Mass., 1941), II, 223.

[6] Van Wyck Brooks, *New England: Indian Summer 1865-1915* (New York, 1940), looks back from 1865 to "Dr. Holmes's Boston." See pp. 1-22.

[7] The phrase is that of Charles S. Peirce as applied to absolutes in philosophy. *Collected Papers of Charles S. Peirce,* Charles Hartshorne and Paul Weiss, eds., 6 vols. (Cambridge, Mass., 1933-1935), I, 357. Peirce was a close friend of Holmes during the days of the Metaphysical Club, 1868ff.

[8] Quoted in Frederick C. Fiechter, Jr., "The Preparation of an American Aristocrat," *The New England Quarterly* VI: 1 (March, 1933): 3-28.

[9] Ibid., p. 4.

[10] There are useful genealogical tables dealing with Holmes's descent and his mother's family in Catherine Drinker Bowen, *Yankee From Olympus* (Boston, 1944), pp. 6, 80. See also Silas Bent, *Justice Oliver Wendell Holmes* (New York, 1932), p. 26, and Mark deW. Howe, *Justice Oliver Wendell Holmes, Jr., The Shaping Years, 1841-1870* (Cambridge, Mass., 1957), pp. 31-32.

[11] Bowen, p. 100.

[12] Arnold L. Goldsmith, "Oliver Wendell Holmes Father and Son," *Journal of Criminal Law, Criminology and Political Science* 48:4 (Nov.-Dec. 1957): 394-98 passim.

[13] Bowen, p. 81.

[14] Quoted in Howe, p. 5.

[15] Fiechter, pp. 7-8.

[16] Holmes to Sheehan, Aug. 14, 1911, *Holmes-Sheehan Correspondence,* p. 44.

[17] Bent, p. 45.

[18] Holmes, "The Class of '61," *Speeches,* p. 96.

[19] Holmes to Pollock, Dec. 7, 1927, *Holmes-Pollock Letters,* II, 207.

[20] Bent, pp. 42-43.

[21] Ibid., p. 69.

[22] Holmes, "Harvard College at War," *Speeches,* p. 14.

[23] Howe's chapter, "Harvard College," is best relied on for an awareness of this aspect of Holmes's background; see Howe, *The Shaping Years,* pp. 35-79.

[24] Holmes, *Touched with Fire,* Mark deW. Howe, ed. (Cambridge, Mass., 1947), p. 32.

[25] Howe, *The Shaping Years,* p. 62.

[26] Ibid., p. 44.

[27] Ibid., p. 45.

[28] Holmes to Sheehan, July 17, 1909, *Holmes-Sheehan Correspondence,* pp. 27-28.

[29] Holmes, "Plato," *University Quarterly* II: 1 (Oct. 1860): 205-17 passim.

[30] Quoted in Howe, *The Shaping Years,* p. 54.

[31] Holmes, "Plato," p. 210.

[32] Holmes, "Notes on Albert Dürer," reprinted in Wolfgang Stechow, "Justice Holmes' Notes on Albert Dürer," *Journal of Aesthetics and Art Criticism* VII: 2 (Dec. 1949): 119-24.

[33] Ibid., p. 119.

[34] Holmes to Amelia Jackson Holmes, Oct. 23, 1861, *Touched with Fire,* p. 13. This volume includes the wartime letters of Holmes as well as portions of his diary for 1861-1864, and as such is the major source for understanding the effects of the Civil War on Holmes.

[35] Holmes to Harold J. Laski, May 4, 1924, *Holmes-Laski Letters,* Mark deW. Howe, ed. 2 vols. (Cambridge, Mass., 1953), I, 615.

[36] Holmes to parents, Sept. 18, 1862, *Touched with Fire,* p. 64.

[37] Holmes to Pollock, Dec. 21, 1886, *Holmes-Pollock Letters,* I, 29.

[38] Holmes to Laski, Dec. 16, 1926, *Holmes-Laski Letters,* II, 905.

[39] George M. Frederickson, *The Inner Civil War* (New York, 1968), p. 172.

[40] Holmes to his mother, Oct. 23, 1861, *Touched with Fire,* p. 13.

[41] Holmes to his father, Dec. 20, 1862, *Touched with Fire,* p. 80.

[42] Holmes, "Memorial Day," *Speeches,* p. 8.

[43] Holmes to his mother, June 7, 1864, *Touched with Fire,* p. 143 (italics in original).

[44] Holmes to Charles Eliot Norton, April 17, 1864, quoted in *Touched with Fire,* p. 122, n. 1.

[45] Holmes, "The Soldiers' Faith," *Speeches,* p. 58.

[46] Holmes to Lewis Einstein, *The Holmes-Einstein Letters,* James B. Peabody, ed. (New York, 1964), p. xvi.

[47] Howe, *The Shaping Years,* p. 86.

[48] See especially Touster, *In Search of Holmes from Within, Vand. Law Rev.,* 438 (1964-1965).

[49] Holmes to Lewis Einstein, April 12, 1925, *The Holmes-Einstein Letters,* p. 235.

[50] Holmes to his mother, Dec. 15, 1862, *Touched with Fire,* p. 78.

[51] Holmes to his parents, May 16, 1864, *Touched with Fire,* pp. 122-23.

[52] Holmes Diary, *Touched with Fire,* pp. 27-28.

[53] Holmes to his father, March 29, 1863, *Touched with Fire,* pp. 90-91.

G. Edward White (essay date 1994)

SOURCE: "The Integrity of Holmes' Jurisprudence," in *Intervention and Detachment: Essays in Legal History and Jurisprudence,* Oxford University Press, 1994, pp. 75-99.

[*In the following essay, White addresses apparent contradictions in Holmes's judicial actions and writings.*]

Writing about Oliver Wendell Holmes can be likened to playing Hamlet in the theatre: it is a kind of apprenticeship that legal scholars undertake as a way of measuring their fitness to endure the academic travails ahead. Holmes himself engaged in a similar rite of passage when he wrote an essay on Plato as a Harvard undergraduate.

Plato's thought, Holmes claimed, "needed a complete remodeling"; Holmes' generation "start[ed] far beyond the place where Plato rested."[1] Ralph Waldo Emerson, to whom Holmes showed a draft of his essay, suggested that "[w]hen you strike at a king, you must kill him."[2] The urge to strike at Holmes has been recurrent, and the man, as a jurist, is far from dead.

Ten years ago I suggested that Holmes' reputation was on the decline, and complained about his "articulated refusal to take pride in being human."[3] In an intellectual culture dominated by liberal humanism, I surmised, Holmes would not be likely to fare well: he was not much of a liberal and certainly not a humanist. Once again Holmes seems to have triumphed over his critics. His thought has had a capacity to contain insights sufficiently diverse and contradictory to appeal to someone regardless of prevailing intellectual fashions. And the gap between Holmes and prevailing opinion has narrowed rather than widened in the 1970s. The "disturbing dissonance" I found between Holmes' "very conspicuous social and professional success" and his "gloomy musings that . . . man has no more cosmic significance than a baboon or a grain of sand"[4] presupposed an obligation in those whom life has favored to believe in the optimistic possibilities of living. Optimism is harder to come by these days; what I called a "cranky negativism"[5] in Holmes now seems more like sensible resignation. At any rate, interest in Holmes has dramatically revived,[6] and I should not like to be thought of as having given up on him too soon.

My concern in this essay is with a feature of Holmes that, for all that has been written on him, scholars are just beginning to address. The feature involves an apparent discontinuity between Holmes' theory of judging in the private law and public law spheres. Holmes' famous book *The Common Law*[7] reads like a credo for activist judging in pursuit of broad general principles of law; judges are to help arrange legal subjects in what Holmes called a philosophically continuous series.[8] His constitutional opinions on the Supreme Court, by contrast, extol the virtues of judicial deference. How is Holmes simultaneously the reformer of private law and the passive public law judge? How could the same judge who wanted to take all grade crossing cases away from juries[9] feel comfortable allowing legislatures to make all sorts of discriminatory classifications, so long as they were arguably rational?[10] Are these tendencies another example of the internal contradictions in Holmes' thought, which have been so regularly pointed out? Or is there a basic, if latent, integrity to Holmes' jurisprudence?

The reason this inquiry may be put as a fresh proposition so late in the history of scholarship on Holmes is that scholars have thus far given only limited attention to his experience as a judge on the Supreme Judicial Court of Massachusetts. Although Holmes was sixty-one when appointed to the Supreme Court of the United States, he remained a Justice for over twenty-nine years and made his public reputation as a Justice. Early scholarship on

Holmes paid almost no attention to his years as a Massachusetts judge, and although a major biography, that of Mark DeWolfe Howe,[11] was begun in the 1950s, Howe died before he addressed the Massachusetts cases. Howe's last volume on Holmes appeared in 1963;[12] there was a gap of nearly fifteen years before any detailed treatment of Holmes' Massachusetts years appeared.[13]

The explanation for this neglect of Holmes' state court opinions is obvious. Scholarship in American legal history that emphasized private law subjects languished in the 1950s and 1960s; there was little interest in the opinions of any state court judges. Further, there was so much else in Holmes' career of interest—his early scholarship, his Supreme Court opinions, his engaging correspondence—that scholars could justify neglecting what seemed to be a collection of boring, insignificant Massachusetts cases.

Holmes himself, as we will see, found his state cases relatively trivial and dull exercises. His opinions are not particularly path-breaking, rarely detailed, and not even the rich source of aphorisms and epigrams that his Supreme Court opinions are.[14] But the experience of being a state court judge, when taken in connection with the other two major roles of Holmes' career—scholar and Supreme Court Justice—was a vital link in the forging of Holmes' jurisprudence. The experience of a Massachusetts judgeship transformed Holmes' thought from its expansive, conceptualistic, reformist early form to its cryptic, skeptical later variety. It was on the Massachusetts bench that Holmes came to adopt his familiar posture of resignation, a posture he had never expected to adopt as a judge.

This essay traces the evolution of Holmes' jurisprudence in the three major phases of his career. The first section discusses Holmes' early scholarship, which culminated in *The Common Law* in 1881, and the theory of judging that Holmes held at the time of *The Common Law*'s publication. Section II examines the process by which Holmes' ideas about judging private law cases became modified with his experiences as a Massachusetts judge, and contrasts the scholarship he produced between 1882 and 1902 with his earlier efforts. Section III discusses the relationship of Holmes' revised theory of judging, which had been developed in a private law setting, to his approach to public law cases as a Supreme Court justice. The fourth section assesses some of the implications of Holmes' jurisprudence for contemporary judging.

I THE EARLY SCHOLARSHIP: ORDER AND ACTIVISM

Holmes' early life, as a practitioner in a Boston firm, a lecturer and professor at Harvard, and an author and editor for the *American Law Review,* has been one of the most fully examined phases of his career.[15] We know that by the 1870s Holmes had become attracted to the idea of "analys[ing] what seem to me the fundamental notions and principles of our substantive law [and] putting them in an order."[16] Beginning in 1870 he published a series of unsigned articles and book reviews, primarily in the *American Law Review,* in which he argued that the purpose of legal scholarship should be "classification," by which he meant the organization of a subject "from the most general conception to the most specific proposition or exception in the order of logical subordination."[17]

We know, as well, that Holmes found the subject of Torts a particularly fruitful one to examine in this fashion. After an original judgment that Torts was "not a proper subject for a law book,"[18] Holmes, by 1873, had concluded that "there is no fault to be found with the contents of [Torts] text-books."[19] Torts appealed to Holmes because it seemed to be a subject ripe for classification. While earlier Torts treatises had attempted to associate concepts, like trespass, evidence, and defamation, that bore no "cohesion or legal relationship" to one another, Holmes became convinced that some fundamental notions and principles could be derived.[20] He claimed that "an enumeration of the [tort] actions which have been successful, and of those which have failed, define[d] the extent of the primary duties imposed by the law."[21] This was in keeping with his belief that "form[s] of action" could be made "to correspond to every substantial duty," and thereby "embod[y] in a practical shape a classification of the law."[22] Holmes discovered that the tort writs could be divided into three groups, one requiring culpability as a prerequisite for liability, another indifferent to culpability, and a third determining culpability from "motives of policy . . . kept purposely indefinite."[23]

The last category of wrongs introduced for Holmes the standard of modern negligence, which he seized upon as a clarifying principle for tort law. Eight years after his preliminary survey of tort writs he was prepared to argue, in *The Common Law,* that the negligence principle had increasingly dominated tort law.[24] That shift from analytic classification to philosophical synthesis was characteristic of his scholarship in the late 1870s. In five articles in the *American Law Review*[25] between 1876 and 1880 Holmes revealed a new style of scholarship. His subjects and his explorations were primarily historical; his purpose, however, was not merely to clarify the historical origins of doctrine, but to claim that doctrine could not be understood apart from its historical origins. A historical exploration of a legal subject, for Holmes, revealed its essentials: its standards of liability, its core elements, its character. History, he later said, was "the first step . . . towards a deliberate reconsideration of the worth of those rules."[26] "History sets us free and enables us to make up our minds dispassionately whether the survival which we are enforcing answers any new purpose when it has ceased to answer the old."[27]

The pattern of scholarship first introduced in Holmes' articles on tort law thus continued through other subjects to culminate in *The Common Law.* As Mark Howe has shown,[28] *The Common Law* was a reformist work in two senses of the word. In his efforts to show that all the common law fields—criminal law, property, torts, and contracts—had arguably been governed by shifting exter-

nal standards of liability throughout their history, Holmes was attempting to reform jurisprudence by emphasizing the derivation of general principles rather than the pleading of specific writs. Uncertainty would be reduced in the law if common law subjects were arranged according to general principles and lawyers recognized that those principles were simply manifestations of current community preferences. The study of law was thus to proceed from the individual case through history to the derivation of general principles. This would require, among other things, a basic change in the way law was taught and practiced.

Holmes was also advocating another kind of reform in the *The Common Law.* Since certainty and predictability were desirable goals for the legal profession, those institutions in the legal system that fostered certainty should be rewarded at the expense of those that appeared to hinder its pursuit. In his 1873 essay on torts Holmes expressed what he took to be the view of "many whose opinion is entitled to respect" that "negligence [was] always and in the nature of things a question for the jury."[29] This echoed a position he had taken two years earlier, when he said that "we suppose it is wholly for the jury to say whether the party has used such care as a reasonable and prudent man would have used under the circumstances of that particular case."[30] But by 1880 Holmes had changed his mind about the efficacy of allowing legal standards to be formulated by juries. In *The Common Law* he complained about "leav[ing] all our rights and duties throughout a great part of the law to the necessarily more or less accidental feelings of a jury," arguing that "the sphere in which [a judge] is able to rule without taking [jury] opinion at all should be continually growing."[31] This was in keeping with his belief that "the tendency of the law must always be to narrow the field of uncertainty."[32]

Holmes' early scholarship, in its final phases, thus envisaged a "creative epoch"[33] in late nineteenth-century American private law in which a philosophically oriented class of scholars would join with a class of judges who had acquired "a fund of experience"[34] to develop broad, predictable rules. The pursuit of order in American jurisprudence would be fostered by judicial activism. Given Holmes' confidence in the techniques of analysis he had used in *The Common Law* and in the principles he had derived as a result of their use, it was hard for him to imagine that others could not do likewise. But those others would have to be persons capable of understanding the law and its history, and dedicated to the goals of certainty, predictability, and coherence. Judges were such persons.

One of the curiosities of Holmes' early life is why, after finding his scholarly labors finally coming to fruition as he approached forty, he did not regard a life of future scholarship with more enthusiasm. After severely pressing himself to secure some scholarly achievement by his fortieth birthday—the result of which was some petty competitiveness with other scholars, a neglect of his home life, and a "fearful grip upon his work" that made him "a melancholy sight" to one observer[35]—Holmes, who had written *The Common Law* while in active law practice, was then given an opportunity to continue a life of scholarship. By November 1881, he had been offered a position on the Harvard Law School faculty, subject to the contingency of funds being raised to endow a new professorship, and had indicated his readiness to accept. In his letter of acceptance, however, Holmes reserved the right "not . . . to feel bound in honor not to consider" a judgeship should one subsequently be offered him.[36]

Less than a year later, after finally accepting Harvard's offer of a professorship in jurisprudence, Holmes resigned to go on the Supreme Judicial Court of Massachusetts. The circumstances of his resignation—he consulted no one on the Harvard faculty and accepted the judgeship three hours after it was offered—produced a good deal of bitterness at Harvard. James Bradley Thayer, who had helped raise funds for the professorship that brought Holmes to Harvard, poured out his resentment in a diary. "[W]ith all his attractive qualities and his solid merits," Thayer concluded, Holmes was "wanting sadly in the noblest region of human character,—selfish, vain, thoughtless of others."[37] Much later, when Felix Frankfurter was considering joining the Harvard faculty, Holmes wrote him that "academic life is but half life—it is withdrawal from the fight in order to utter smart things that cost you nothing except the thinking them from a cloister." He also said, in the same letter, "My wife thinks I unconsciously began to grow sober with an inarticulate sense of limitation in the few months of my stay in Cambridge."[38]

Apparently Holmes was unsure where a scholarly life would take him. He wrote James Bryce shortly after his decision to take the judgeship that he "had already realized at Cambridge that the field for generalization inside the body of the law was small and that the day would soon come when one felt that the only remaining problems were of detail"[39] The choice, he later wrote to Harold Laski, seemed to be "between applying one's theories to practice and details or going into another field."[40] Judging appeared to provide "an all round experience," and a "share in the practical struggle of life."[41] It "hardens the fibre," Holmes later said, and "is more likely to make more of a man of one who turns it to success."[42] Had he stayed at Harvard he would have felt that he "had chosen the less manly course."[43]

The striking feature of Holmes' conception of the academic and judicial worlds at this point in his career is not his sense that academic life was more cloistered or less "manly" than a judgeship. It is rather his feeling that "the field for generalization inside the body of the law was small" and that "as a philosopher" Holmes needed to "extend his range."[44] Holmes apparently believed that his labors on *The Common Law* had resulted in a comprehensive theory of jurisprudence, that he was not likely to modify that theory, and that the remainder of academic life, if he stayed in the law, would be filling in the details.[45] This was not as limited a conception of scholarship as it might first appear. Holmes was reluctant to abandon an insight once he had formulated it; nearly forty years after publishing *The Common Law* he defended its findings against critics.[46] Moreover, the seminal work of many scholars is done early in their careers, and there are temptations to rest on one's reputation and "fill in the details." Holmes may have understood that there was not much more he could do, at least in the private law subjects that held his greatest interest, after he had plumbed their depths in *The Common Law.*

But if Holmes was interested in "generalization" and the pursuit of "tempting [philosophical] themes,"[47] why did he choose to become a judge? He never made the reasons for his choice explicit, but he appears to have thought that if he were going to "apply one's theories to practice and details," performing that function in "the practical struggle for life," rather than in a "cloister," would be more satisfying. Academic detail was just nit-picking; judicial detail was "the gradual weaving of one's contribution into the practical system of the law."[48] Judging was to provide a means by which the theories of *The Common Law* were to have an impact on "business in the world."[49]

One cannot review Holmes' choice to forego academic life for a judgeship without sensing that he was proceeding under the assumption that judging would give him an opportunity to put his theories into practice. He had spent too much time deriving his views on contracts, the criminal law, property, and torts to regard them merely as "smart things"; his jurisprudence was the jurisprudence of reform. Here was an opportunity to put his reforms into action, to rewrite the corpus of Massachusetts jurisprudence. Here was an opportunity to be an activist judge creating an orderly, predictable system of laws.

II The Supreme Judicial Court: Deflated Expectations

In 1900, after nearly twenty years as a judge, Holmes asked himself "what is there to show for this half lifetime that has passed?"[50] He had considered "[a] thousand cases, many of them upon trifling or transitory matters." He "would have liked to study to the bottom and to say his say on every question which the law has ever presented." He would have liked to "invent new problems which should be the test of doctrine, and then to generalize it all and write it in continuous, logical, philosophic exposition, setting forth the whole corpus with its roots in history and its justifications of expedience." Instead he had decided a great many dull cases. That was "life," he felt; "we cannot live our dreams."[51]

The experience of judging had not conformed to Holmes' expectations. He had contemplated being able to study cases "to the bottom," to "say his say" fully on matters of common law doctrine, to use existing cases as a means of anticipating "new problems," and perhaps even to "generalize it all." For the most part he had not been able to do these things. There was not enough time to study cases in depth. Saying one's say fully ran the risk of offending one's colleagues: opinions were joint projects. Lawyers, litigants, and even judges were not interested in a case as an index of future doctrinal development; practical issues were at stake, results had to be reached and decisions made. And the common law, as it evolved in the Massachusetts Supreme Judicial Court, was hardly a "continuous, logical, philosophic" system. It was better described as a series of largely desultory cases that were decided without much attention to the "whole corpus."[52]

Decisionmaking on the Massachusetts court was best captured by the old metaphor that Holmes had first written in his 1873 essay, **"The Theory of Torts,"**[53] where he had speculated on the development of the law:

> Two widely different cases suggest a general distinction, which is a clear one when stated broadly. But as new cases cluster around the opposite poles, and begin to approach each other, the distinction becomes more difficult to trace; the determinations are made one way or the other on a very slight predominance of feeling, rather than articulate reason; and at last a mathematical line is arrived by the contact of contrary decisions, which is so far arbitrary that it might equally well have been drawn a little further to the one side or to the other.[54]

Rather than studying cases to their bottom, appellate courts made determinations on a "predominance of feeling." The "mathematical lines" drawn by courts were "arbitrary." Clear distinctions evolved into intuitive preferences.

A random survey[55] of Holmes' torts opinions on the Massachusetts court provides an entry to his work as a state judge. Torts had been the private law field in which Holmes had arguably made his greatest scholarly contributions. It is possible to claim that in essays such as **"The Theory of Torts"** and **"Trespass and Negligence,"**[56] and in *The Common Law,* Holmes had supplied a principle for late nineteenth-century tort law—the modern negligence principle—that allowed torts to develop its identity as a discrete branch of law. Holmes' achievement had been to see that it was possible to speak of the myriad tort writs as manifestations of a general civil duty owed by everyone not to carelessly injure others. The concept of this duty of very great generality and the limitation of the duty through the fault principle—reasonable conduct under the circumstances—were major catalysts to the growth of modern tort law. Almost all the leading torts theorists of the late nineteenth century—Thomas Cooley,[57] Melville Bigelow,[58] John Wigmore,[59] Jeremiah Smith[60]—owed their conception of the subject as dealing with universally imposed civil duties to Holmes.[61]

What were the tort cases that Holmes, with this rich scholarly background, considered on the Massachusetts court? Holmes wrote over 400 torts opinions, the most he wrote on any legal subject and nearly one-third of his

entire output. Of these only three were dissents.[62] One would have thought with this amount of cases, the very high percentage of majority opinions, and Holmes' understanding of the intellectual foundations of tort law, he would have had ample opportunity to put his scholarly theories into practice. Instead his torts opinions were exceptionally routine. Two opinions in the 1883 term merely disposed of evidentiary exceptions taken by the defendant at trial.[63] A third was a conventional assumption-of-risk case that was decided on its facts.[64]

Only in *Cowley v. Pulsifer,*[65] a case testing the limits of the record libel privilege, did Holmes attempt an elaborate discussion. The case involved publication in a newspaper of the contents of a petition to remove an attorney from the bar. Before the petition had been presented to the court or entered on the docket, it appeared in the paper. Holmes stated that "no binding authority has been called to our attention which precisely determines this case, and we must be governed in our conclusion mainly by a consideration of the reasons upon which admitted principles have been established."[66] He then grounded the decision on a distinction between proceedings in open court, which could be recorded without subjecting the recorder to a libel suit, and "preliminary written statement[s] of a claim or charge."[67] The record libel privilege did not extend to the latter.

Trivial torts cases again outnumbered significant ones in the 1884 term. Of the seven cases in which Holmes wrote opinions, two simply disposed of exceptions,[68] one held that the technical requirements for a libel had been made out,[69] one allowed an action for diverting water to be maintained by a citizen of another state,[70] one refused to find contributory negligence as a matter of law where an officer in an act of arresting a person stepped into a partly covered well in the darkness,[71] and one labeled the actions of a deputy sheriff misrepresentations of facts.[72] Only in *Dietrich v. Northampton*[73] did Holmes find a case on which he could ruminate. There a pregnant woman slipped on a defective highway constructed by the town of Northampton and suffered a miscarriage. She recovered for her physical injuries, and the deceased child's administrator sought to recover for the child's death. The case raised a number of issues, including whether infants could maintain actions for injuries suffered before birth, whether an injured fetus was a "person" entitled to legal redress, and whether the common law of negligence had a different standard of liability from that imposed on towns for failure to maintain highways in proper repair. For Holmes the case turned on the proposition that "no case, so far as we know, has ever decided that, if the infant survived, it could maintain an action for injuries received by it while in its mother's womb."[74] That dictum was to survive in tort law for seventy-five years.[75]

The 1890 Term contained more cases that approximated the typical late nineteenth-century tort action: the industrial accident leading to a suit in negligence. None of the negligence cases, however, involved more than a simple application of reasonable conduct standards to their facts. An employee assumed the risk when he passed close to a band saw, slipped, and put his hand on it.[76] A conductor of a streetcar was not contributorially negligent when knocked off the car by a protruding post from an excavation barrier.[77] A husband and wife injured at a grade crossing where the gates were up and no whistle or bell was sounded by the approaching train were entitled to have the question of their contributory negligence decided by a jury.[78] A commuter who, ignoring closed gates, walked behind one train and was hit by another on a neighboring track was grossly negligent as a matter of law.[79] A town had a responsibility to repair a mudhole in a road that caused the driver of a wagon to injure himself when he drove off the road to avoid it.[80] An unauthorized person using a water closet in a railroad station was owed no duty of care by the railroad, and no liability ensued when he was killed by a train that ran off its track.[81] The maintenance of a heavy steam hammer by a car wheel company was not a nuisance.[82]

Only one case in the Term, *Burt v. Advertiser Newspaper Co.*,[83] presented Holmes with an opportunity to clarify legal doctrine. Burt was a libel action against the *Boston Daily Advertiser* for a series of articles on fraud in the New York customs house. Two brothers, James and Silas Burt, were mentioned in the articles; James Burt, a broker, was accused of "outrageous sugar frauds"[84] and Silas Burt, a naval officer, of having a "long-time connection with some of the most disreputable elements in the New York custom-house."[85] In response to a letter of protest the *Advertiser,* while conceding that Silas Burt had not been accused of any wrongdoing, said that James Burt's practices "hold the New York custom-house up as a national disgrace."[86] The question raised by the Burt case was the scope of the *Advertiser's* privilege of "fair criticism upon matters of public interest."[87] That privilege, Holmes held, did not extend to the publication of false facts. It was the criticism—the opinions of the critics—that was privileged. Holmes distinguished between "private inquiries . . . about a private person,"[88] such as "answers to inquiries about the character of a servant"[89] and comment on public matters. The *Advertiser's* reasonable belief that its allegations about James Burt were true did not constitute a defense, Holmes noted: "A person publishes libelous matter at his peril."[90] The Burt case furnishes a good example of nineteenth-century common law attitudes toward freedom of the press in defamation cases. Not even a showing that a reasonable editor would have believed the false facts about James Burt to be true would have helped the *Advertiser.* Strict liability was the standard in defamation cases.

The 1891 Term produced no significant torts cases. The city of New Bedford was exonerated from liability for nuisance when a homeowner who connected his drain with a sewer, which concededly had a narrow outlet, had his basement filled during a heavy rainstorm with water and sewage.[91] A person who fell down unlighted cellar stairs in the course of delivering wood was held to assume the risk of an open cellar being near the house.[92] A case where a woman fell down a lighted flight of stairs was not sufficient for res ipsa loquitur, and could be taken from the jury since its elements were "permanent, few, and simple."[93] A workman who set on fire a shafting box soaked with oil, thereby damaging the owner's premises, was negligent as a matter of law.[94] And a traveler who picked up a loose telephone wire in a road, and was injured from electric current, was considered to be owed a duty by the city of Cambridge, which had negligently allowed the wire to fall into the road.[95] In none of the above cases did Holmes' opinions extend beyond a few paragraphs.

By the 1901 Term Holmes had become Chief Justice, and his workload had increased. He wrote Sir Frederick Pollock in 1899 that he "had more to do than ever," and that he had been taking on himself "perhaps rather a lion's share."[96] But the torts cases were no more significant than they had been in the 1880s or 1890s. Holmes found no contributory negligence in a parent whose child had been run over by a wagon in a quiet road,[97] but did find it where another child was run over by an electric car in a "teeming" city street.[98] He upheld a jury's verdict that a street railway car had negligently run into a baker's wagon that had been lawfully driving on the streetcar tracks,[99] construed a dram shop act to impose liability on the owner of a bar who illegally sold liquor to a person who while intoxicated stumbled into the path of a train,[100] and refused to impute to a passenger the alleged contributory negligence of a driver of a coal wagon.[101] He found a spout that spilled water on a sidewalk, causing ice to form, to be a nuisance, and its owner strictly liable for the injuries of a pedestrian who slipped on the ice.[102] He held that proof that a woman had committed adultery was not a defense against calling her a dirty old whore.[103] He allowed recovery from emotional distress when accompanied by a slight physical injury.[104] He found a gateman who inexplicably stood between the tracks of a railroad and was killed by a freight train in the process of coupling and uncoupling cars to be contributorially negligent.[105] And he denied recovery to a postal clerk who had sued the railroad owning the train on which he was unloading mail for injuries suffered when a car from another railroad negligently hit that train.[106]

In only one torts case that Term was there a glimpse of the kind of role Holmes might have expected himself to play as a judge. In *Patnoude v. New York, New Haven, and Hartford Railway*[107] a street railway company and the New York, New Haven and Hartford Railroad had agreed to unload a streetcar at a point on the railroad's tracks near the streetcar company's barn. The unloading process required the temporary dismantling of a fence that shielded the tracks from an adjoining highway. While the fence was dismantled and the streetcar, covered with a white canvas, was resting on a flat car of the railroad, a rider drove by on the adjacent highway and his horse, startled by the sight of the streetcar, reared and threw him. The question was whether the railroad was liable in nuisance or in negligence.

"As in many cases," Holmes said in his opinion finding for the railroad, "two principles or social desiderata present themselves, each of which it would be desirable to carry out but for the other, but which at this point come into conflict." It was "desirable that as far as possible people should be able to drive in the streets without their horses being frightened, [and it was also] desirable that the owners of land should be free to make profitable and otherwise innocent use of it." A "line has to be drawn to separate the domains of the irreconcilable desires, [but] such a line [could] not be drawn in general terms."[108] In the *Patnoude* case, however, the condition of the railroad's car and fence was transitory, and its potential for frightening horses did not necessarily mean that it was unlawful.[109] Torts cases involved drawing lines, balancing irreconcilable desires, and giving common-sense interpretations to facts. General propositions were not much help in deciding them.

With *Patnoude* one can see how far Holmes' conception of judging had evolved from the one he held when first appointed to the Massachusetts court.[110] While he had enjoyed getting to the bottom of things and formulating generalizations as a scholar, such activities were not easily related to appellate judging. The facts of individual cases were so diverse, and the competing principles so generally worthy, that arbitrary line-drawing was the inevitable result. Such line-drawing could not be generalized. Setting forth "the whole corpus" of law, or "writ[ing] it in continuous, logical, philosophic exposition"[111] were tasks beyond the reach of judges, who had to decide difficult, limited, and largely trivial cases.

Holmes had learned two lessons from his experience on the Supreme Judicial Court of Massachusetts. The first lesson was that cases inevitably presented conflicts between desirable social principles, and judges simply had to choose. That choice was an act of policymaking, not an inevitable unfolding of common law principles. The second lesson was that since such choices were arbitrary, and since the process of line-drawing could not be generalized, judging was a far more modest and less creative activity than Holmes expected. These lessons fostered two judicial habits in Holmes: the habit of deferring especially arbitrary policy choices to some other body, such as a legislature or a jury, that arguably reflected community sentiment; and the habit of not agonizing over the reasoning that justified an arbitrary choice. By the time Holmes left the Massachusetts court in 1902 his opinions were already notable for their brevity, their assertiveness, and their cryptic language. It was as if Holmes recognized that his decisionmaking process was largely arbitrary and decided to get on with it.

The Massachusetts years were also notable for a significant change in the attitudes expressed in Holmes' scholarship. *The Common Law,* I have argued,[112] had been a reformist tract, seeking to show by example that a thorough canvass of private law subjects could yield some clarifying and organizing principles. One message of *The Common Law* was that such principles were there to be extracted and applied to real-life situations by judges. The meaning of a private law subject, Holmes seemed to

be saying, could be found in this body of intelligible principles.

By 1897, when he delivered his address, **"The Path of the Law,"**[113] Holmes was offering a very different definition of the meaning of law. Notwithstanding the claims of "some text writers" that law was "a system of reason" or "a deduction from principles of ethics or admitted axioms," law could be most accurately described as "prophecies of what the courts will do in fact."[114] While the "language of judicial decision" was "mainly the language of logic," behind the "logical form" lay "a judgment as to the relative worth and importance of competing legislative grounds." Judicial decisions were "opinion[s] as to policy" that merely "embod[ied] the preference of a given body in a given time and place."[115] The "duty" of judges was to weigh "considerations of social advantage."[116]

"The Path of the Law" had stressed lesson one of Holmes' experience as a judge: while judges may attempt to cloak their decisions in logic, the decisions were instinctive policy preferences. **"Law in Science and Science in Law,"**[117] delivered two years later, stressed lesson two. Holmes had some faith in science as a vehicle for measuring the social desires that he saw competing in a case.[118] He conceded that an "absolutely final and quantitative determination" could only occasionally be reached "because the worth of the competing social ends which respectively solicit a judgment for the plaintiff or the defendant cannot be reduced to number and accurately fixed."[119] Since policy grounds lay behind the use of legal rules, a "quantitative comparison" of the competing social desiderata seemed desirable. Such a comparison led Holmes back to a variant on his original passage from **"The Theory of Torts."**[120]

> In our approach towards exactness we constantly tend to work out definite lines or equators to mark distinctions which we first notice as a difference of poles. . . . When [we] ha[ve] discovered that a difference is a difference of degree, that distinguished extremes have between them a penumbra in which one gradually shades into the other, . . . [we realize that we have] to draw the line, and an advocate of more experience will show the arbitrariness of the line proposed by putting cases very near to it on one side or the other. But the theory of the law is that such lines exist. . . . We like to disguise the arbitrariness, we like to save ourselves the trouble of nice and doubtful discriminations.[121]

Thus Holmes concluded that judging ended up being the arbitrary resolution of "a conflict between two social desires, each of which seeks to extend its dominion over the case, and which cannot both have their way." In making that resolution judges were "exercis[ing] the sovereign prerogative of choice."[122] They were "weigh[ing] the reasons for the particular right claimed and those for the competing right." Their solutions could not be in general terms, because "generalities [were] worse than useless."[123] Their solutions were bound to rest on "general grounds of policy blindly felt."[124]

Such were the lessons of twenty years on the Massachusetts bench. And there were two curious, and potentially contradictory, corollaries to those lessons. Since legal decisions were at bottom choices between competing social policies, it was essential that such choices reflect the wishes and feelings of the community, so that the law might keep pace with current thought.[125] Judge-made law had a tendency to prefer the logical form to the candid policy statement, and consequently sometimes became ridden with anachronistic rules and outmoded propositions. Especially in doubtful cases, then, Holmes thought that the practice of deferring policy choices to the jury was a good one: juries were apt to "introduce into their verdict a certain amount. . . . of popular prejudice."[126] In a case like *Patnoude,* where a right to ride without fear of injury conflicted with a right to use property in a profitable manner, one could label as a question of fact whether the use that invaded the right was negligent, and let a jury decide which social desideratum it preferred. A sense of the arbitrariness of judicial decisionmaking, then, led to a desire to defer, in close cases, to a more community-minded tribunal.

At the same time, however, that sense of arbitrariness led to a desire to exercise the sovereign prerogative of choice. Holmes had no particular confidence that juries "could see further into things or form a saner judgment than a sensible and well trained judge."[127] He thought that a well-trained judge could "follow the existing body of dogma into its highest generalizations," then "discover from history how it has come to be what it is," and finally "consider the ends which the several rules seek to accomplish"[128] and make a choice. Indeed, he thought that a judge need not do all those things; he might have liked to have done them, but he had not done them often in his opinions. What he had done was to see the internal conflict presented by a case, measure the competing social desires in his mind, and make an arbitrary choice. Having done that, he had made use of logic and his own command of language, and had produced an opinion. Judging in that manner was not difficult, so long as one recognized what one was doing.

In these two peculiarly divergent corollaries lay the seeds of Holmes' constitutional jurisprudence. Holmes' opinions on the Supreme Court were of two very different types. The first type, which brought him public acclaim,[129] emphasized the unsoundness of judges substituting their judgment on social issues for that of legislatures. Legislatures, like juries, were repositories of contemporary prejudices; there was something to be said for letting them decide difficult policy questions. In this deferential stance Holmes appeared as a judge aware of his own limitations, an appearance that was deceptive. The second type of opinion that Holmes produced on the Court resembled many of his private law opinions in Massachusetts: it was a brief, cursory, and cryptic determination of a difficult and complex issue. In the first type

of opinion Holmes seemed chastened by the recognition of his arbitrary power; in the second he seemed to revel in it.

III THE SUPREME COURT: A "JOB" MENTALITY

After being appointed to the Supreme Court in 1902 Holmes wrote Pollock of his delight with his new position. "I am . . . more absorbed, interested and impressed than ever I had dreamed I might be," he said. "The variety and novelty to me of the questions, the remote spaces from which they come, the amount of work they require, all help the effect."[130] But before long Holmes began to see recurrent themes. Most questions before the Court were questions of degree; beneath "the lion's hide" of a case was "the same old donkey of a question of law."[131] Holmes could write two opinions a week, finishing the first one assigned to him at a Saturday conference by Tuesday and the second by Saturday. In listening to counsel argue before the Court he could summarize an argument before the lawyer had finished making it. His law clerks, whom he hired from 1905 on at the suggestion of John Chipman Gray, Ezra Thayer, or Felix Frankfurter, had very little legal research to do: Holmes wrote his own opinions, asking only for an occasional citation. The clerks paid his bills, answered routine correspondence, read to him in his last years, and above all were sounding boards on contemporary issues. When another justice needed research help, Holmes lent them out.[132]

Despite the "burning themes" that appeared in constitutional cases and despite the great public attention that his opinions, especially his dissents, received, Holmes primarily thought of his work on the Supreme Court as a "job." In 1928 Holmes wrote Lewis Einstein that "when I am on my job I don't care a damn what you want or what [a President] wants."[133] Yosal Rogat once likened Holmes' attitude toward his work on the Supreme Court to that of a pony express rider who "had to undertake a dangerous and exhausting series of rides in order to insure the survival of the city." While Holmes may have ridden hard, he "was not motivated by the city's survival. . . . Rather, he executed the assignment simply because he had undertaken it and. . . . to bring back a map of the terrain."[134] Repeatedly in his Supreme Court opinions Holmes conveyed this sense of detachment. He once said in a dissent that "[t]here is nothing that I more deprecate than the use of the Fourteenth Amendment . . . to prevent the making of social experiments . . . in the insulated chambers afforded by the several States, even though the experiments may seem futile or even noxious to me."[135]

Detachment seems the most accurate term to characterize Holmes' stance on the Supreme Court. He was not merely skeptical; his emotions were for the most part not engaged. To put it more precisely, his emotions were stimulated by the professional features of his work but not by its substance. Few judges could pack more emotion into an opinion, but the emotion was not often generated from compassion for the litigants or concern for the seriousness of the issue at stake. It was the emotion of a literary talent, a person who liked the sound of memorable phrases. Holmes' aphorisms were original and incisive; they were also repeated often.

One can see Holmes' stance of detachment as a culmination of his intellectual history. By all accounts he was not only serious about philosophy and jurisprudence as a young man; he was in dead earnest. He clung to his manuscript on Kent, taking it with him to meals; he taught himself German so as to be able to read the contribution of German jurists in the original; he worked nights on the lectures that became *The Common Law;* he allegedly married Fanny Dixwell, whom he had known most of his life, only when someone else mentioned that she was pining away out of love for him.[136] From the 1870s, when he first began to think and write about jurisprudence, to the time he went on the Supreme Judicial Court of Massachusetts, he was a passionate and zealous legal reformer, eager "to say his say on every question which the law has ever presented." And then, as we have seen, the futility of his grand design revealed itself. Cases were not vehicles for propounding a grand theory, but merely clusterings around poles; judging was not writing law "in continuous, logical, philosophic exposition" but an exercise in the arbitrary drawing of lines. One could not live one's dreams: "We are lucky enough if we can give a sample of our best."[137]

Holmes' sense of his professional role thus radically contracted over time, and his reduced expectations combined with traits of personality to produce detachment. Acquaintances of Holmes had from his early years noted his apparent indifference to others. His father thought he "look[ed] at life as at a solemn show where he is only a spectator";[138] William James called him "a powerful battery, formed like a planing machine to gouge a deep self-beneficial groove through life";[139] James Bradley Thayer, embittered over Holmes' leaving Harvard for the Massachusetts court, had said that he was selfish, vain and thoughtless.[140] Holmes did not read a newspaper, paid little attention to contemporary affairs, had most of his intimate friendships with persons from whom he was physically separated, and once said that he was glad that he had no children.[141] The themes that engaged him, such as intellectual effort and war, were related to central personal experiences. Beyond that he seemed content to "do my job in the station in which we were born."[142]

Holmes' job at the Supreme Court consisted of, in many instances, reviewing the constitutionality of actions of a legislature. In such cases Holmes forged his famous attitude of deference, which was seen as humility and "self-restraint" by admirers and had the added advantage of sustaining "progressive" legislation about which a number of early twentieth-century intellectuals were enthusiastic.[143] Deference to legislative policymaking was consistent with the views Holmes had developed on the Massachusetts court. In twenty years on that court he had held unconstitutional only one Massachusetts statute.[144] His general attitude was expressed in an advisory opinion on the constitutionality of the legislature's authorizing

towns to buy coal and wood and sell them to their inhabitants as fuel.[145] "[W]hen money is taken to enable a public body to offer to the public . . . an article of general necessity," Holmes wrote, "the purpose is no less public when that article is wood or coal than when it is water or gas or electricity or education, to say nothing of cases like the support of paupers, or the taking of land for railroads."[146]

Deference, of course, was consistent with Holmes' belief that judging was an arbitrary exercise in policy choices, and, that being so, some policy choices were better made by more "representative" bodies of government. He may have been motivated to express his views more openly, however, by the clumsy policymaking of his contemporaries on the Supreme Court. In the first years of the twentieth century the constitutionality of a number of pieces of "welfare" legislation was tested by the Court. The legislation sought to regulate the working hours of certain occupations or persons, to insure minimum wage standards, to eliminate child labor, and other such "reforms." Holmes was not personally sympathetic to most of the legislation, but he was even less sympathetic to the treatment of it by majorities on his Court. Those majorities had invalidated the legislation by the use of the "liberty of contract" doctrine, which Holmes later called a "dogma."[147] Liberty of contract was objectionable to Holmes in that it attempted to decide "concrete cases" on the basis of a "general proposition" that was suspect as a matter of textual interpretation and debatable as a matter of economic theory.[148] The Court had sustained many legislative acts that interfered with freedom of contract, and the Constitution was "not intended to embody a particular economic theory."[149] To transform the Fourteenth Amendment into an ideological creed was to "pervert" it.[150]

It is instructive to dwell on what Holmes thought was wrong with the majority's decisions in such liberty of contract cases as *Lochner v. New York,*[151] *Adair v. United States,*[152] and *Adkins v. Children's Hospital.*[153] He did not object to the substance of the doctrine itself; he would have "to study it further and long" before endorsing it or rejecting it.[154] Nor did he necessarily object, at least as a general proposition, to the Court's substitution of its judgment for that of a legislature. What he objected to was the clumsy use of a "dogma" to decide questions that ought to have been decided by a consideration of the ends that rules seek to accomplish, the reasons those ends are desired, what is given up to gain them, and whether they are worth the price.[155] Such a consideration was presumptively suited to a legislative judgment, and if the Court were to distrust that judgment it ought to do so in a manner that did not so transparently expose the "convictions or prejudices" of its members.[156]

In deferring, Holmes thus neither espoused the worth of legislation nor expressed concern that judges ought to leave policy decisions to someone else. He merely felt that if judges were going to make arbitrary choices, they ought not to base those choices on vulnerable dogmas.

Thus the principal problem with decisions like *Lochner* was not that the Court based its judgments on an economic theory, although Holmes said that a constitution was not made to embody economic theories,[157] but that it based its judgments on a theory that "a large part of the country does not entertain."[158] While a constitution was "made for people of fundamentally differing views," the views that counted were those of the majority.[159] Policymaking in America was largely a majoritarian activity; where minorities, such as the courts, made policy, they had better keep their "theories" in line with popular sentiment.

Holmes' deference thus sustained repressive legislation as much as benevolent legislation. The Pennsylvania legislature could, under a wild game protection act, keep aliens from owning firearms because its members believed that aliens were more prone to violence in this area than native citizens.[160] The Virginia legislature could sterilize persons thought to be feebleminded because it assumed that imbecility bred imbecility and that imbeciles were a burden on the state.[161] The Iowa legislature could forbid the teaching of all languages except English in public schools because it believed that in this fashion German culture and influence within the state would be reduced.[162] Congress could restrict speech so long as the words created "a clear and present danger that they will bring about the substantive evils that Congress has a right to prevent,"[163] and those evils might be defined by mass prejudice. The most one could expect of legislation, Holmes had written very early in his career, was that it "modify itself in accordance with the will of the de facto supreme power in the community."[164] Keeping "the sacrifice of minorities to a minimum" was dependent on "the spread of an educated sympathy."[165]

Students of Holmes have found his posture of deference so fascinating that they have defined his entire career on the Court in terms of it.[166] But the bulk of Holmes' Supreme Court opinions were cases in which he did not defer to a legislative policy judgment, but rather made one himself, and made it, as he had on the Massachusetts, court, with relatively little attention to exposition. Three cases are representative: *Baltimore and Ohio Railroad v. Goodman,*[167] *United Zinc & Chemical Co. v. Britt,*[168] and *Pennsylvania Coal Co. v. Mahon.*[169]

In *The Common Law* Holmes, in the course of arguing that courts should increasingly take negligence cases away from juries, supported his argument with some observations about grade crossing accidents. "If the whole evidence," he wrote, "was that a party . . . stood on a railway track, looking at an approaching engine until it ran him down, no judge would leave it to a jury."[170] On the other hand: "If the whole evidence was that he attempted to cross a level track, which was visible for half a mile each way, and on which no engine was in sight, no court would allow a jury to find negligence."[171] These examples suggested to Holmes that "the limit of safety" in grade crossing cases "could be determined almost to a foot by mathematical calculation."[172] *Goodman* was a

grade crossing case in which Holmes attempted to prove that point. Nathan Goodman, the driver of a truck, was approaching a grade crossing at the speed of about five to six miles an hour. The crossing was over a level section of track, but Goodman's view on one side was obscured by a section house, so that he could not see anything until he was about twenty feet from the first train rail, and "then the engine was still obscured by the section house."[173] Goodman continued to cross the tracks, was hit by a train going at least sixty miles an hour, and was killed.

After stating the facts Holmes announced that "it appears to us plain that nothing is suggested by the evidence to relieve Goodman from responsibility for his own death."[174] He then overturned a jury verdict for the driver, holding that Goodman was contributorially negligent as a matter of law. He declared that "if a driver cannot be sure otherwise whether a train is dangerously near he must stop and get out of his vehicle, although obviously he will not often be required to do more than to stop and look."[175] This was a clear standard of conduct and was to be "laid down once for all by the Courts," although "the question of due care very generally is left to the jury."[176]

Goodman seems to have been a case in which Holmes had forgotten the lessons of his Massachusetts experience. He may have continued to believe in 1927 that "the limit of safety" in grade crossing cases "could be determined almost to a foot," and he may have been correct that under the circumstances Goodman was negligent. But "mathematical calculation" or Holmes' "stop, look and listen" exercise was not going to fix the limits of safety in grade crossing cases. Some drivers might follow Holmes' standard, get back in their cars, and then get hit by a train that was plainly obvious from a considerable distance. Were they to be exonerated? Others might decide not to get out of their cars because of the dangers of approaching traffic. Were they necessarily negligent? Holmes' formula ended up being a good argument for retaining jury discretion in grade crossing cases, and seven years later the Supreme Court, with Justice Cardozo treading carefully, abandoned the formula.[177]

Goodman shows Holmes anxious not only to make a judgment himself but to deprive juries of the opportunity to make that judgment in subsequent cases. The case was striking in that it lent itself to Holmes' "competing desiderata" analysis. A policy of allowing drivers to drive on the streets without being injured competed with a policy of allowing railroads to use their property in profitable ways. In *Patnoude* Holmes had said that the line that "had to be drawn to separate the domains of the irreconcilable desires" could not be "drawn in general terms."[178] In *Goodman* he had attempted to do so. One could hardly call his posture deferential.

Holmes' decision in *Britt* was somewhat less ambitious. He sought to ascertain the limits of the "child trespasser" doctrine, by which landowners were deemed to owe a duty of care to children trespassing on their premises if the children could be said to have been attracted onto the premises by something on the land. Examples were railroad turntables, ponds, and excavations. In the *Britt* case two boys were camping near land where the United Zinc & Chemical Company had formerly operated a sulphuric acid plant. The company had abandoned the plant but left its foundations, in which residue from sulphuric acid and zinc sulphate remained. Water had accumulated over the foundations, giving the area the appearance of a pond, but the water, although clear, had been poisoned by the residue. The two boys investigated the site, a little over 100 feet from a dirt road, were poisoned, and died.

Holmes distinguished previous child trespasser cases on the grounds that the United Zinc & Chemical Company did not know that children had been in the habit of visiting the site and had not maintained the site adjacent to the road. "[I]t is at least doubtful," he wrote, "whether the water could be seen from any place where the children lawfully were." There had been no inducements, Holmes felt; there was no evidence that the water had "led [the boys] to enter the land." There was no pattern of children trespassing on the land that might have informed the United Zinc & Chemical Company of potential dangers. Even the presence of roads close to the site were not invitations: "[A] road is not an invitation to leave it elsewhere than at its end."[179]

Britt seems to have been a case ideally suited to leave to a jury, and as such raises the question why Holmes did not adopt that course of action. Child trespasser cases inevitably turn on their facts: how much of an "inducement" the dangerous substance was, how much awareness the landowner had of trespassers, how easy the dangerous substance was to reach, etc. Given the fact that landowners had long been held to owe no duty to trespassers, the child trespasser doctrine seemed designed for those circumstances where a landowner knew that he was maintaining a dangerous substance on his land and knew or should have known that it would be attractive to children. If the railroad turntable was a paradigmatic attractive nuisance, since it was adjacent to a roadway and since it was the kind of substance that would appeal to children as a place to play, a pond near an abandoned building was not far from that paradigm. The only complicating factors in the *Britt* case were that the company apparently had no experience with trespassers on the site and that the site was not adjacent to the road. But those were surely not conclusive on the question of liability, given the very dangerous condition of the pond. The case seemed designed to be decided by the "common sense" of a jury.

It appears that some of the same tendencies that motivated Holmes to lay down the "stop, look and listen" standard in *Goodman* were at work in *Britt*. In his early career Holmes had been dismayed at the unpredictability and uncertainty of jury-made rules: If the child trespasser doctrine was to be invoked or not invoked depending on the sympathies of a jury, it was not a doctrine whose existence helped landowners (or potential trespassers)

plan their affairs. Holmes seems to have wanted to use the *Britt* case as a means of confining the doctrine to those cases where a landowner had notice of children trespassing near a dangerous substance on his property. So formulated, the doctrine's impact would be greatly reduced, since it could never be invoked against a landowner in a "first accident" case. Once two boys had died as a result of coming into contact with a zinc company's dangerous abandoned plant it is unlikely that the company would permit the plant to remain in that condition; at a minimum it would post conspicuous warnings. Only if the company did nothing and a second accident involving children occurred would the child trespasser doctrine come into play. That was a predictable state of affairs; it was also unlikely to happen.

Goodman and *Britt* may suggest that Holmes' "activist" decisions on the Supreme Court were confined to those instances where he had engaged himself as a scholar. But many of Holmes' most famous opinions came in areas, such as the First Amendment, that he had not addressed in his early career, and in some of these opinions he dropped his usual pose of deference to legislatures. The line of first amendment cases, stretching from *Abrams v. United States*[180] through *Gitlow v. New York*,[181] *Whitney v. California*,[182] and *United States v. Schwimmer*[183] to *Near v. Minnesota*,[184] was one set of examples: Holmes attempted to fix the outer limits of legislative regulation of speech. *Nixon v. Herndon*,[185] a case invalidating a Texas primary system that excluded blacks from participation, was another. Holmes said for the Court: "States may do a good deal of classifying that it is difficult to believe rational, but there are limits."[186] *Olmstead v. United States*[187] was yet another: there Holmes read the Fourth and Fifth Amendments to prohibit the use of illegally seized evidence in a criminal prosecution. The case invoked "two objects of desire, both of which we cannot have," Holmes said; "we must . . . make up our minds which to choose."[188] He was unwilling in that instance to let a legislature make the choice.

Nor was Holmes willing to defer to a legislative judgment in *Mahon*.[189] There the Pennsylvania legislature had passed a statute that forbade the mining of anthracite coal on land in such a way as to endanger structures erected on the surface of the land in question. A landowner sought to apply the statute to prevent the Pennsylvania Coal Company from mining on land he had bought from the company. The company had expressly reserved subsurface rights to the land and had also retained the right to remove coal from beneath the surface. Since the contract between the coal company and the landowner had been made prior to the passage of the statute, the question was whether the statute was an unconstitutional deprivation of existing property and contract rights.

Holmes, for a majority of the Court, held that it was. "The general rule," he announced, "is, that while property may be regulated to a certain extent, if regulation goes too far it will be recognized as a taking." Here the Pennsylvania legislature had provided no compensation for the mining companies, and thus had infringed their rights. "We are in danger of forgetting," Holmes noted, "that a strong public desire to improve the public condition is not enough to warrant achieving the desire by a shorter cut than the constitutional way of paying for the change." Even if the statute had been passed "upon the conviction that an exigency existed," the "question at bottom [was] upon whom the loss of the changes desired should fall."[190]

Compensation cases such as *Mahon* involved "question[s] of degree," Holmes said, and "therefore [could] not be disposed of by general propositions." That being said, he did not defer to legislative balancing. The Pennsylvania statute went "beyond any of the [compensation] cases decided by this Court." A strong public desire for property did not itself justify a taking without compensation; otherwise the legislature could invoke its police power "more and more until at last private property disappears."[191]

Mahon was not different for Holmes from the speech cases or from *Nixon v. Herndon:* there were limits to what states could do under their discretionary authority. Commentators have reacted differently to *Mahon* because Holmes protected property rights rather than personhood rights, but Holmes made no such jurisprudential distinctions. When he invoked the Constitution to invalidate a legislative restriction on rights, that was because the legislature had gone "too far." What was "too far" was a "question of degree," but sometimes the answer was obvious. When it was, Holmes saw no reason—"exigencies" notwithstanding—to defer to legislative judgments.[192]

Neither conventional political labels nor common terms from jurisprudence help clarify Holmes' stance on the Supreme Court. Several commentators have shown that his opinions are imperfectly described as "liberal" or "conservative."[193] This article suggests that they are no more satisfactorily described as "activist" or deferential. When Holmes' tenure on the Supreme Court is subjected to detailed analysis, two striking and hitherto largely unremarked features appear. First, Holmes was nowhere near as activist in private law cases as his early scholarship suggested he might have been, but he was more activist, if anything, than he had been on the Supreme Judicial Court of Massachusetts. The *Goodman* and *Britt* opinions were in some sense throwbacks to his earlier theory, formulated as a scholar, of how negligence cases ought to be decided. Holmes retained on the Supreme Court the idea that most cases presented policy choices between competing "social desiderata," and while this led him toward deference to legislatures in many cases, it did not prevent him from making choices in others. He believed the choices to be arbitrary, but he made them anyway. Calling Holmes an advocate of self-restraint on the Court does not fully capture him.

Second, while Holmes saw that at the bottom of nearly every Supreme Court case was a choice between competing public policies, he was not deterred by that realization from making a prompt decision. If he chose to defer to a legislature, he spent very little time justifying the legislature's actions: the simplest bow to minimal rationality generally sufficed. Sometimes, in cases like *Patsone v. Pennsylvania,*[194] Holmes did not even seem to be lingering over the question of legislative rationality. In that case he blithely accepted the legislature's premise that aliens were more dangerous to wildlife than citizens. Nor was Holmes any less peremptory when he chose to upset a legislative judgment. That the Texas legislature had gone too far in *Nixon v. Herndon* was "too clear for extended argument."[195] That the Pennsylvania statute in *Mahon* went "beyond any of the cases decided by this Court" needed only to be stated.[196]

The overwhelming impression of Holmes' performance on the Supreme Court, then, is the same impression one gets of his performance in Massachusetts. Here was a judge whose principal interest seems to have been in having cases decided, written up, and disposed of. The vivid sentence with which Holmes ended his opinion in *Britt,* "a road is not an invitation to leave it elsewhere than at its end."[197] captures the mood in which Holmes appears to have written most of his opinions. The sentence is striking, but it is not much help, either as a general statement or as an explanation of the case. Travelers leave roads at a variety of places—indeed almost no one who travels on a road leaves it at its end. A road, in fact, is not an "invitation" to leave it at all; if anything, it is an invitation to take it somewhere, as being an easier place on which to travel than a field or a stream. But the sentence is designed to dismiss the argument that the presence of the road in *Britt* may have been an enticement to travel near the poisoned site. The sentence does "dismiss" that argument, but only through a largely erroneous statement that captures our attention. It is as if having turned a phrase Holmes decided that he had said enough, and could get on to something else. Holmes makes cases seem like toys scattered in a child's room: The idea is to pick them up and put them in place, not to linger over the differences among them nor to give some more special meaning than others. When the job is over, the room is clean; the toys are "put away."

IV REMEMBERING HOLMES: WHAT DOES HE LEAVE US?

However much Holmes is written about or ignored, his reputation seems secure. I have suggested that his reputation may contain some erroneous components, such as the idea that he was consistently an apostle of judicial self-restraint, but that is not to suggest that it will not endure. Three of Holmes' contributions seem so significant as to resist even the most aggressive form of historical debunking. First, he identified judging as an exercise in intuitive policy choices at a time when few other judges or jurists were prepared to concede that judging was anything other than finding and applying preexistent legal principles. For Holmes to see that cases were repositories of clashing policies was a keen enough insight; for him to come upon that insight in the midst of a jurisprudential climate that denied any policymaking component to judging was remarkable.

Second, Holmes helped develop a significant corollary to his insight that judges were policymakers. The corollary was his theory of deference, and while he did not originate the theory nor practice it exclusively, several of his opinions were powerful arguments for its use. This was particularly true in the public law area, and most particularly true in Supreme Court cases, where Holmes' version of good sense was juxtaposed against tortured judicial efforts to preserve "dogma" at all costs. The accident of Holmes' being on the Supreme Court at a time when legislatures had become more active, and the Court had not developed a theory of responding to that activism, made him one of the original spokesmen on the Court for a theory of constitutional adjudication that was to have great influence in the twentieth century. While Holmes was never as zealous a proponent of self-restraint as some of his disciples, his opinion in *Lochner* gave deference intellectual respectability.

Third, as the last sentence from *Britt* illustrates, Holmes had a distinctively arresting style. No Supreme Court Justice matched Holmes in this regard; only Robert Jackson occasionally came close. The holdings of Holmes' opinions may be forgotten, but the epigrams remain. "A word is . . . the skin of a living thought";[198] "[g]reat cases like hard cases make bad law";[199] "[t]he Fourteenth Amendment does not enact Mr. Herbert Spencer's Social Statics";[200] "the best test of truth is the power of the thought to get itself accepted in the competition of the market";[201] "[t]hree generations of imbeciles is enough."[202] Not one of these sentences was necessary to the decision in the case in which it appeared; all contain overstatements or ambiguities. Each, however, helps to universalize the act of opinion writing, to make it a process of communicating at the deepest levels of human experience. When a judge can write in that fashion subsequent generations will be gripped by his style. No notes of dissatisfaction with his opinions as guidelines for future conduct will fully detract from his appeal. Holmes wrote lines that spanned time.

But can one remember Holmes as more than the author of arresting epigrams? Does his jurisprudence leave us a foundation for thinking about judging? Here it seems that on some issues Holmes seems so overwhelmingly right that one wonders how a contrary position was ever seriously maintained, and on other issues Holmes seems so disinclined to explore questions once he has raised them that one is tempted to conclude that an important function of his jurisprudence is to cut off thinking at preliminary stages.

Holmes may have thought, when he was at the fever pitch of his scholarly efforts in the 1870s, that, while absolute certainty might be unattainable, fields of private law could be made more certain, in the sense of being more regularized and predictable. The impulse toward certainty is a strong one in legal scholarship: recently we have seen the "laws" of welfare economics offered as yet another source of regularizing the common law. But we should have learned the lesson Holmes had learned after sixteen years as a judge: "[c]ertainty generally is illusion, and repose is not the destiny of man."[203] Too many variables exist for certainty in the law to be realizable: the discrete personalities and idiosyncracies of judges and other lawmakers; the changing intellectual climates in which research is conducted, which affect the normative dimensions of research and thereby insure that scholarly contributions will never be timeless; the fortuitous allocation of talent and incentives among counsel for one side or another; the strange ways in which the facts of a case compel a rule, which then evaporates when the facts fade into memory. Holmes may have been sensible, as a young scholar, to search for certainty; had he not thought it attainable he might not have tried to study private law subjects to their bottom. But he was even more sensible to abandon certainty as a judge. His metaphor of "growth" in the law, a series of decisions clustering around two poles and finally being separable only by an arbitrary line, rings truer than all the pronouncements that law can be made "scientific." I would not call Holmes' metaphorical description a process of growth, merely one of change, but I think as a description it is uncontroverted.

Does it follow, then, that since certainty in jurisprudence is elusive, humility and deference are the only appropriate lawmaking postures? Here I think Holmes' own indifference and the misguided labors of his disciples have contributed to lend prominence to a theory of judging that possesses serious limitations. During Holmes' tenure judicial deference resulted in legislation that helped alleviate some of the inequalities of rampant industrialism; in the 1950s and 1960s a similar version of deference would have perpetuated malapportioned legislatures, racially segregated facilities, the absence of legal representation for impoverished persons, and restrictions on the use and dispensation of birth control devices. The simple truth that law cases in America serve as a forum for testing conflicting ideas about public policy does not suggest that all such decisions should be made by "representative" or "community-minded" bodies, such as legislatures or juries. Sometimes the choices of the public are benighted or hasty or prejudiced; sometimes the majority oppresses those who differ with it. Holmes taught us that judges, if unchecked, will make justice synonymous with their own prejudices. The Warren Court taught us that legislatures will do the same.

Deference or activism is thus a function of time and place and of the seriousness of the issues at stake. Sometimes a court does well to defer: the issues are volatile, the public divided, the principles hard to grasp. At other times a court seemingly has an obligation not to defer: a more representative body has forgotten elementary principles of justice and needs to be admonished by an institution whose popularity is not so dependent on majoritarian whim. It stretches Holmes beyond recognition to make him a Warren Court Justice, but he had his own areas, ranging from speech to subsurface mining, where he found majoritarian solutions defective. Still, while one would like to blame Holmes' disciples for the agonized state in which self-restraint theory found itself after World War II, Holmes set it on that path.[204] He found legislative rationality in too many mere pretexts, he tolerated repression in the name of democracy too often. Before long judges who considered themselves intellectuals and "liberals" in the tradition of Holmes were allowing legislatures to compel school children to salute the flag and to require that college professors go on record as opposing Communism.[205] Holmes' theory of deference had led them there; his having scrapped the theory when it suited him did not excuse his putting it on the market for others to misuse.

Linked to Holmes' beliefs that certainty was an illusion and that deference was often a sensible judicial posture was his conviction that judicial decisions were at bottom arbitrary exercises. As we have seen, the discovery of arbitrariness led Holmes in two directions, toward deference and also toward a "job mentality" that emphasized deciding cases so that they could be decided. Arbitrariness raises two separate issues: are we resigned to its presence, and, if so, what can we do about it? As to the first, to sense that human decisionmaking is arbitrary seems to me the beginning of wisdom about the way persons conduct their affairs. All of us have our memories of a nakedly arbitrary decision, ranging from a situation when two devotees of one side of an issue forgot the date of a meeting and the other side won by a single vote, to a situation where a committee was deeply divided on the resolution of an academic matter and finally decided in accordance with the views of the sole member who prepared written comments. Beyond those examples, all of us sense that many decisions are made that would have been made differently had different personnel been involved, had the timing of events been different, or had the issue been presented in different form. Holmes was right to see arbitrariness built into every discretionary decision; he was also right not to be afraid of it.

But does arbitrariness provide a justification for the kind of limited explanations for decisions that Holmes so regularly produced? Here it seems to me that one can advance two interpretations of the purpose of a judicial decision, and the explanations that one produces for one's results will be affected by the interpretation one chooses. One can see the decisions of cases as single existential phenomena: They occur, they dispose of a controversy, they cease to have an existence. Or one can see such decisions as communications beyond the immediate controversy, directed, potentially, at future litigants, future judges, commentators, the general public. If one holds to the first view there is not much point in advancing extensive justifications for one's results. New cases will necessarily be different; a whole host of variables will serve to distinguish them from the past, and prior explanations will not prove much use. I think that in many instances Holmes adopted this view, or at least was sufficiently skeptical of the utility of extensive explana-

tions and sufficiently motivated to get on with the job that he acted as if he adopted it. On other occasions, of course, Holmes regarded a decision as a means of communicating more extensively; he did not dissent just to see how many memorable phrases he could turn.

The idea that judicial opinions communicate to audiences beyond the immediate parties in the dispute is one that once led me to characterize constitutional adjudications as a dialectical process.[206] The dialectical theory holds that judicial decisions, at least when they interpret the Constitution, are in a kind of provisional state of acceptance; they possess the authority of the court that delivers them but their eventual acceptance—their legitimacy—has not been achieved. The process of legitimation involves a testing, over time, of the justifications advanced for the given interpretation. Of course the interpretation yields a definite result, and the controversial nature of the result will play a part in how swiftly or how searchingly the interpretation is tested. But the process occurs to some extent in all decisions.

When a decision is being "tested," the pressure points of its explanatory apparatus may make a difference in how fully it becomes legitimated. To take a contemporary example, an opinion that seems not yet to have reached the status of being legitimated is *Roe v. Wade,*[207] which is eight years old at this writing. *Roe v. Wade*'s indeterminate status is partially a function of the controversial nature of the issue it purports to resolve: abortion is not an issue easily "settled" in one fashion or another. The decision's indeterminate status seems also linked, however, to its explanatory strategy, which chose to emphasize the state of medical knowledge about when a life is "in being" as a crucial determinant for when an abortion is permissible. Such an emphasis, of course, renders the decision vulnerable to changes in the state of medical knowledge. If the time a life is said to come into being were to recede, in the view of a dominant number of qualified medical practitioners, until a point so close to conception that any abortion would be a termination of "life," *Roe v. Wade*'s guidelines for abortion, which allow a mother unrestricted autonomy to terminate a pregnancy in the first trimester, might be threatened. In that instance *Roe v. Wade* could be taken as a communication into the future that was eventually found lacking in persuasive power due to the outmoded assumptions on which it rested.

Such seems to be the fate of many constitutional opinions. But one might argue that this form of communication, regardless of its vulnerability, is preferable to the cryptic, assertive form adopted by Holmes in many of his opinions. An explanation like that advanced in *Roe v. Wade* seems to be saying: "Here are my choices, between life and the autonomy of personhood; my decision to choose one over the other is necessarily arbitrary, but is influenced by some assumptions about the medical nature of 'life'; if those assumptions are subsequently called into question, another arbitrary choice may result." Holmes' explanations rarely sought to communicate in so extended a fashion. Indeed when Holmes retreats to the kind of language he used to explain his results in such cases as *Patsone*—a reasonable man might well think aliens are dangerous to wildlife[208]—one gets the impression that his tongue is in his cheek; that he is using the convention of deference to cut off communication rather than to open it up.

Here, finally, I come back to Holmes' job mentality. There are many cases, he seems to be saying, where the choices are between generally desirable policies that happen to conflict; we must prefer one or the other; we will surely not invariably prefer that one on every occasion; we have a case to decide; let's get on with it. But that method tells us precious little about why one policy should prevail over another even in this case. It seems to tell us, in fact, only that the judge made a choice; another judge might have decided differently. That message leads us to **"The Path of the Law"** and the "prophecies of what the courts will do in fact,"[209] to the idea that law is synonymous with the arbitrary fiats of officials, and to related cynical revelations. If we end up endorsing such cynicism, Holmes can take some of the credit.

But I think Holmes intended to convey something more in his cryptic explanations. I think he was attempting to show that in a truly "hard" case, if you force an extended explanation, that explanation will crumble to pieces on reflection. And as one explanation after another crumbles, one is left with the fact of judicial power, the force of judicial intuition, and the way the law has of correcting itself over time. After a while, Holmes seems to say, it is not the explanations that count—they all crumble, eventually—but the decisions. One's job as a judge becomes to decide—that is what people count on one to do; that is what judges have the power to do where ordinary people do not—and not to agonize about why. Cryptic explanations, then, are intended to cut off thinking about issues that are sufficiently complicated and difficult to benumb one's mind. At some point one has to stop thinking and choose. It may be that Holmes' view of judging makes sense—and if it does, the concept of a dialectic of constitutional adjudication seems so much academic gossamer—but even if it cuts off thought and explanation too soon, it may not be the easy way out. The easy way out may be to pretend that sooner or later some disinterested, reasoned justification will emerge mysteriously out of one's ruminations as one tries to decide a case. Holmes looked to the bottom of cases and saw only his own reflection. Should we probe so far, we might conclude that reasoning in epigrams was preferable to more extended ratiocinations. Length is not the equivalent of depth.

NOTES

[1] Holmes, *Plato*, 2 *U.Q.* 205, 206 (1860).

[2] Letter from Oliver Wendell Holmes to Elizabeth Shepley Sergeant (Dec. 7, 1926), *quoted* in 1 M. Howe *Justice Oliver Wendell Holmes* 54 (1957).

[3] White, *The Rise and Fall of Justice Holmes*, 39 *U. Chi. L. Rev.* 51, 77 (1971).

[4] *Id.* at 76.

[5] *Id.* at 77.

[6] In the past two academic years, Harvard Law School, Northwestern University School of Law, the University of Illinois School of Law, and the American Society for Legal History have devoted lectures or symposia to Holmes' work, and Professors Patrick Atiyah, Robert Cover, Grant Gilmore, Robert Gordon, Morton Horwitz, Saul Touster, and Jan Vedder, as well as Judge Benjamin Kaplan, have delivered papers on various features of Holmes' career.

[7] O.W. Holmes, *The Common Law* (1881).

[8] O.W. Holmes, *The Solider's Faith*, in *Occasional Speeches* 73, 78-79 (M. Howe ed. 1962).

[9] *See infra* text accompanying notes 171-78.

[10] *See infra* text accompanying notes 161-66.

[11] M. Howe, *Justice Oliver Wendell Holmes* (vol. 1, 1957; vol. 2, 1963).

[12] 2 *id.*

[13] *See* Tushnet, *The Logic of Experience: Oliver Wendell Holmes on the Supreme Judicial Court*, 63 *Va. L. Rev.* 975 (1977).

[14] There are a few exceptions. *See, e.g.,* Crocker v. Cotting, 170 Mass. 68, 71, 48 N.E. 1023, 1024 (1898) ("The jurisdiction is not affected by a defendant's recalcitrance"); Laplante v. Warren Cotton Mills, 165 Mass. 487, 489, 43 N.E. 294, 295 (1896) ("A boy who is dull at fifteen probably was dull at fourteen"); Lincoln v. Commonwealth, 164 Mass. 368, 378, 41 N.E. 489, 491 (1895) ("All values are anticipations of the future").

[15] *See, e.g.,* 1 M. Howe, *supra* note 11, at 245-86 (Boston law practice); 2 *id.* at 26-95, 253-83 (Harvard years); *id.* at 1-95 (*American Law Review* experience).

[16] Letter from Oliver Wendell Holmes to James Bryce (Aug. 17, 1879), *quoted in* 2 M. Howe, *supra* note 11, at 25.

[17] *The Arrangement of the Law—Privity*, 7 *Am. L. Rev.* 46, 47 n.2 (1872).

[18] Book Notices, 5 *Am. L. Rev.* 341 (1870).

[19] *The Theory of Torts*, 7 *Am. L. Rev.* 652, 659-60 (1873).

[20] Book Notices, *supra* note 18, at 341.

[21] *The Theory of Torts*, *supra* note 19, at 659-60.

[22] Book Notices, 5 *Am. L. Rev.* 359 (1871).

[23] *The Theory of Torts, supra* note 19, at 659.

[24] O.W. Holmes, supra note 7, at 89.

[25] *See* 2 M. Howe, *supra* note 11, at 136.

[26] O.W. Holmes, *The Path of the Law,* in *Collected Legal Papers* 167, 186-87 (1920).

[27] O.W. Holmes, *Law in Science and Science in Law,* in *Collected Legal Papers* 210, 225 (1920).

[28] 2 M. Howe, *supra* note 11, at 196-97.

[29] *The Theory of Torts, supra* note 19, at 658.

[30] Book Notices, 5 *Am. L. Rev.* 536 (1870).

[31] O.W. Holmes, *supra* note 7, at 124-26.

[32] *Id.* at 127.

[33] *Id.* at 89.

[34] *Id.* at 124.

[35] Letter from Mrs. Henry James to Henry James, Jr., *quoted in* 1 R. Perry, *The Thought and Character of William James* 519 (1935).

[36] Letter from Oliver Wendell Holmes to Charles W. Eliot (Nov. 1, 1881), *quoted in* 2 M. Howe, *supra* note 11, at 261.

[37] Thayer, Memorandum (Dec. 22, 1882), *quoted in* 2 M. Howe, *supra* note 11, at 268.

[38] Letter from Oliver Wendell Holmes to Felix Frankfurter (July 15, 1913), *quoted in* 2 M. Howe, *supra* note 11, 282.

[39] Letter from Oliver Wendell Holmes to James Bryce (Dec. 31, 1882), *quoted in* 2 M. Howe, *supra* note 11, at 280.

[40] Letter from Oliver Wendell Holmes to Harold Laski (Nov. 17, 1920), *quoted in* 2 M. Howe, *supra* note 11, at 281.

[41] Letter from Oliver Wendell Holmes to James Bryce (Dec. 31, 1882), *quoted in* 2 M. Howe, *supra* note 11, at 280-81.

[42] Letter from Oliver Wendell Holmes to Felix Frankfurter (July 15, 1913), *quoted in* 2 M. Howe, *supra* note 11, at 282.

[43] Letter from Oliver Wendell Holmes to James Bryce (Dec. 31, 1882), *quoted in* 2 M. Howe, *supra* note 11, at 281.

[44] *Id.* at 280.

[45] *Id.*

[46] Letter from Oliver Wendell Holmes to Harold Laski, (Feb. 1, 1919), *quoted in* 2 M. Howe, *supra* note 11, at 137.

[47] Letter from Oliver Wendell Holmes to Harold Laski (Nov. 17, 1920), *quoted in* 2 M. Howe, *supra* note 11, at 281.

[48] Letter from Oliver Wendell Holmes to Lady Clare Castletown (Mar. 5, 1897), *quoted in* 2 M. Howe, *supra* note 11, at 282.

[49] Letter from Oliver Wendell Holmes to Felix Frankfurter (July 15, 1913), *quoted in* 2 M. Howe, *supra* note 11, at 282.

[50] O. W. Holmes, *Speech at Bar Dinner,* in *Occasional Speeches* 122, 123 (M. Howe ed. 1962).

[51] *Id.*

[52] *Id.*

[53] *The Theory of Torts, supra* note 19.

[54] *Id.* at 654.

[55] Even the term "random survey" may impart too much rigor. I have examined Holmes' torts opinions in three time periods from 1881 to 1902. Adjustments were made if the number of opinions in a given year seemed too low to be revealing. I was interested in the significance or insignificance of the case, as suggested by Holmes' opinion and subsequent treatment of the opinion, and in comparisons between Holmes' jurisprudential perspective in one time frame and another.

[56] Holmes, *Trespass* and *Negligence,* 14 *Am. L. Rev.* 1 (1880).

[57] *See* T. COOLEY, *A Treatise on The Law of Torts* 628-58 (1880).

[58] *See* M. BIGELOW, *The Law of Torts* 106-16 (8th ed. 1907).

[59] *See* 1 J. WIGMORE *Select Cases on The Law of Torts* 7-8 (1912).

[60] *See* Smith, *Tort and Absolute Liability—Suggested Changes in Classification,* in *Selected Essays on The Law of Torts* 176, 189-90 (1924).

[61] *See* G. White, *Tort Law in America* 6-62 (1980).

[62] May v. Wood, 172 Mass. 11, 14, 51 N.E. 191, 192 (1898) (Holmes, J., dissenting); Nash v. Minnesota Title

Ins. & Trust Co., 163 Mass. 574, 586, 40 N.E. 1039, 1042 (1895) (Holmes, J., dissenting); Hanson v. Globe Newspaper Co., 159 Mass. 293, 299, 34 N.E. 462, 464 (1893) (Holmes, J., dissenting).

[63] McMahon v. O'Connor, 137 Mass. 216 (1884); McAvoy v. Wright, 137 Mass. 207 (1884).

[64] Williams v. Churchill, 137 Mass. 243 (1884).

[65] 137 Mass. 392 (1884).

[66] *Id.* at 393.

[67] *Id.* at 394.

[68] New Salem v. Eagle Mill Co., 138 Mass. 8 (1884); Purple v. Greenfield, 138 Mass. 1 (1884).

[69] Hurley v. Fall River Daily Herald Pub. Co., 138 Mass. 334 (1885).

[70] Mannville v. Worcester, 138 Mass. 89 (1884).

[71] Learoyd v. Godfrey, 138 Mass. 315 (1885).

[72] Burns v. Lane, 138 Mass. 350 (1885).

[73] 138 Mass. 14 (1885).

[74] *Id.* at 15.

[75] The first case to extend a right of action for prenatal injuries was Verkennes v. Cornifa, 229 Minn. 365, 38 N.W.2d 838 (1949). Dietrich v. Northampton, 138 Mass. 14 (1884), was not limited until Keyes v. Construction Serv., Inc., 340 Mass. 633, 165 N.E.2d 912 (1960).

[76] May v. Whittier Mach. Co., 154 Mass. 29, 27 N.E. 768 (1891).

[77] Powers v. Boston, 154 Mass. 60, 27 N.E. 995 (1891).

[78] Merrigan v. Boston & A. R.R., 154 Mass. 189, 28 N.E. 149 (1891).

[79] Debbons v. Old Colony R.R., 154 Mass. 402, 28 N.E. 274 (1891).

[80] Pomeroy v. Westfield, 154 Mass. 462, 28 N.E. 899 (1891).

[81] Dillon v. Connecticut River R.R., 154 Mass. 478, 28 N.E. 899 (1891).

[82] Wesson v. Washburn Car Wheel Co., 154 Mass. 514, 28 N.E. 679 (1891).

[83] 154 Mass. 238, 28 N.E. 1 (1891).

[84] *Id.* at 241, 28 N.E. at 3.

[85] *Id.* at 239, 28 N.E. at 2.

[86] *Id.* at 241, 28 N.E. at 3.

[87] *Id.* at 242, 28 N.E. at 4.

[88] *Id.* at 243, 28 N.E. at 4.

[89] *Id.* at 242, 28 N.E. at 4.

[90] *Id.* at 245, 28 N.E. at 5 (citations omitted).

[91] Buckley v. New Bedford, 155 Mass. 64, 29 N.E. 201 (1891).

[92] Walker v. Winstanley, 155 Mass. 301, 29 N.E. 518 (1892).

[93] Pinney v. Hall, 156 Mass. 225, 226, 30 N.E. 1016 (1892).

[94] Perry v. Smith, 156 Mass. 340, 31 N.E. 9 (1892).

[95] Bourget v. Cambridge, 156 Mass. 391, 31 N.E. 390 (1892).

[96] Letter from Oliver Wendell Holmes to Frederick Pollock (Dec. 1, 1899), in 1 *Holmes-Pollock Letters* 98 (M. Howe ed. 1941).

[97] Walsh v. Loorem, 180 Mass. 18, 61 N.E. 222 (1901).

[98] Cotter v. Lynn & B.R.R., 180 Mass. 145, 61 N.E. 818 (1901).

[99] Vincent v. Norton & Taunton St. Ry., 180 Mass. 104, 61 N.E. 822 (1901).

[100] McNary v. Blackburn, 180 Mass. 141, 61 N.E. 885 (1901).

[101] Murray v. Boston Ice Co., 180 Mass. 165, 61 N.E. 1001 (1901).

[102] Davis v. Rich, 180 Mass. 235, 62 N.E. 375 (1902).

[103] Rutherford v. Paddock, 180 Mass. 289, 62 N.E. 381 (1902).

[104] Homans v. Boston Elev. Ry., 180 Mass. 456, 62 N.E. 737 (1902).

[105] Tirrell v. New York, N.H. & H.R.R., 180 Mass. 490, 62 N.E. 745 (1902).

[106] Stoddard v. New York, N.H. & H.R.R., 181 Mass. 422, 63 N.E. 927 (1902).

[107] 180 Mass. 119, 61 N.E. 813 (1901).

[108] *Id.* at 120-21, 61 N.E. at 814.

[109] *Id.*

[110] *See supra* text accompanying notes, 50-61.

[111] O. W. Holmes, *supra* note 50, at 123.

[112] *See supra* text accompanying notes 28-32.

[113] O. W. Holmes, *supra* note 26, at 167.

[114] *Id.* at 172-73.

[115] *Id.* at 181.

[116] *Id.* at 84.

[117] O. W. Holmes, *supra* note 27, at 210.

[118] *Id.* at 226.

[119] *Id.* at 231.

[120] For the original passage from *The Theory of Torts,* see *supra* text accompanying note 54.

[121] O. W. Holmes, *supra* note 27, at 232-33.

[122] *Id.* at 239.

[123] *Id.* at 242.

[124] *Id.* at 232.

[125] *Id.* at 238.

[126] *Id.* at 237-38.

[127] *Id.* at 237.

[128] O. W. Holmes, *supra* note 26, at 198.

[129] *See, e.g., Dewey, Justice Holmes and the Liberal Mind,* 53 *New Republic* 210, 211 (1928); Frankfurter, *The Constitutional Opinions of Judice Holmes,* 29 *Harv. L. Rev.* 683, 691-94 (1916); Pound, *Judge Holmes' Contributions to the Science of Law,* 34 *Harv. L. Rev.* 449, 450 (1921).

[130] Letter from Oliver Wendell Holmes to Frederick Pollock (Dec. 28, 1902), in 1 *Holmes-Pollock Letters, supra* note 96, at 109.

[131] Letter from Oliver Wendell Holmes to Frederick Pollock (Dec. 11, 1909), in 1 *Holmes-Pollock Letters, supra* note 96, at 156.

[132] For the reminiscences of one of Holmes' law clerks on these matters, see Derby, *Recollections of Mr. Justice Holmes,* 12 N.Y.U.L. REV. 345, 349-50 (1935).

[133] Letter from Oliver Wendell Holmes to Lewis Einstein (Apr. 1, 1928), in *Holmes-Enstein Letters* 279 1964

[134] ROGAT *The Judge as Spectator,* 31 *U. Chi. L. Rev.* 213, 244 (1964).

[135] Truax v. Corrigan, 257 U.S. 312, 344 (1921) (Holmes, J., dissenting).

[136] *See* C. Bowen, *Yankee From Olympus* 259-61, 270-74 (1945). Bowen's account of Holmes's life is partially fictionalized and undocumented, so one cannot be sure the conversation ever took place.

[137] O. W. Holmes, *supra* note 50, at 123-24.

[138] O. W. Holmes, SR., 3 *The Complete Writings of Oliver Wendell Holmes* 142 (1900).

[139] Letter from William James to Henry James (July 5, 1876), *quoted in* 1 R. Perry, *supra* note 35, at 371.

[140] Thayer, *supra* note 37.

[141] *See* 1 M. Howe, *supra* note 11, at 8.

[142] *Holmes-Cohen Correspondence,* 9 *J. Hist. Ideas* 10 (1948).

[143] *See* White, *supra* note 3, at 56-61.

[144] Lorden v. Coffey, 178 Mass. 489, 60 N.E. 124 (1901).

[145] Opinion of the Justices, 155 Mass. 598, 607, 30 N.E. 1142, 1146 (1892) (opinion of Holmes, J.).

[146] *Id.*

[147] Adkins v. Children's Hosp., 261 U.S. 525, 568 (1923) (Holmes, J., dissenting) (overruled in West Coast Hotel Co. v. Parrish, 300 U.S. 379 (1937); *see* G. White, *The American Judicial Tradition* 164-67 (1976).

[148] Lochner v. New York, 198 U.S. 45, 76 (1905) (Holmes, J., dissenting).

[149] *Id.* at 75 (Holmes, J., dissenting).

[150] *Id.* at 76 (Holmes, J., dissenting).

[151] 198 U.S. 45 (1905).

[152] 208 U.S. 161 (1908).

[153] 261 U.S. 525 (1923) (overruled in *West Coast Hotel Co. v. Parrish,* 300 U.S. 379 (1937)).

[154] 198 U.S. at 75 (Holmes, J., dissenting).

[155] *See, e.g., Adkins,* 261 U.S. at 568 (Holmes, J., dissenting).

[156] *Lochner,* 198 U.S. at 75 (Holmes, J., dissenting).

[157] *Id.* (Holmes, J., dissenting).

[158] *Id.* (Holmes, J., dissenting).

[159] *Id.* at 76 (Holmes, J., dissenting).

[160] Patsone v. Pennsylvania, 232 U.S. 138 (1914).

[161] Buck v. Bell, 274 U.S. 200 (1927).

[162] Bartels v. Iowa, 262 U.S. 404, 412 (1923) (Holmes and Sutherland, JJ., dissenting).

[163] Schenck v. United States, 249 U.S. 47, 52 (1919).

[164] *Summary of Events, The Gas-Stokers' Strike*, 7 Am. L. Rev. 582, 583 (1873).

[165] *Id.*

[166] *See, e.g.,* F. Frankfurter, *Mr. Justice Holmes and The Supreme Court* 36-45 (1938).

[167] 275 U.S. 66 (1927).

[168] 258 U.S. 268 (1922).

[169] 260 U.S. 393 (1922).

[170] O. W. Holmes, *supra* note 7, at 128-29.

[171] *Id.* at 129.

[172] *Id.*

[173] *Id.*

[174] *Id.*

[175] *Id.* at 70.

[176] *Id.*

[177] Pokora v. Wabash Ry., 292 U.S. 98, 106 (1934).

[178] *See supra* text accompanying notes 108-109.

[179] 258 U.S. at 276.

[180] 250 U.S. 616, 628-31 (Holmes, J., dissenting) (stating that defendant had right to publish leaflets supporting Russian revolution and attacking United States policy).

[181] 268 U.S. 652, 672-73 (1925) (Holmes and Brandeis, J J., dissenting) (stating that Socialist Party member should not have been convicted of criminal anarchy merely because he advocated a proletarian dictatorship).

[182] 274 U.S. 357, 379 (1927) (Brandeis and Holmes, J J., concurring) (overruled in Brandenburg, v. Ohio, 395 U.S. 444 (1969) (per curiam)) (stating that mere advocacy of the desirability of proletarian revolution is protected speech but intent to commit serious present crimes is not protected).

[183] 279 U.S. 644, 653-55 (1929) (Holmes, J., dissenting) (stating that a Quaker should not be denied United States citizenship because of her pacifist views).

[184] 283 U.S. 697 (1931) (Minnesota statute authorizing "previous restraints" of periodicals that publish defamatory or malicious articles held unconstitutional infringement of freedom of press).

[185] 273 U.S. 536 (1927).

[186] *Id.* at 541.

[187] 277 U.S. 438, 469 (1928) (Holmes, J., dissenting) (overruled in Katz v. United States, 389 U.S. 347 (1967)).

[188] *Id.* at 470 (Holmes, J., dissenting).

[189] 260 U.S. 393 (1922).

[190] *Id.* at 412-16.

[191] *Id.* at 415-16.

[192] See, *e.g., id.*

[193] For a recent collection of such efforts, see D. Burton, *What Manner of Liberal?* 155-56 (1979).

[194] 232 U.S. 138 (1914).

[195] 273 U.S. at 541.

[196] 260 U.S. at 416.

[197] 258 U.S. at 276.

[198] Towne v. Eisner, 245 U.S. 418, 425 (1918).

[199] Northern Securities Co. v. United States, 193 U.S. 197, 400 (1904) (Holmes, J., dissenting).

[200] Lochner v. New York, 198 U.S. 45, 75 (1905) (Holmes, J., dissenting).

[201] Abrams v. United States, 250 U.S. 616, 630 (1919) (Holmes, J., dissenting).

[202] Buck v. Bell, 274 U.S. 200, 207 (1927).

[203] O. W. Holmes, *supra* note 26, at 181.

[204] *See* White, *supra* note 3, at 64-71.

[205] For an example of one justice's agonized attempts to adopt Holmes' theory of deference to mid-twentieth-century cases, see H. Hirsch, *The Enigma of Felix Frankfurter* (1981).

[206] White, *The Evolution of Reasoned Elaboration: Jurisprudential Criticism and Social Change*, 59 Va. L. Rev. 279, 296-98 (1973).

[207] 410 U.S. 113 (1973).

[208] *See supra* note 161 and accompanying text.

[209] *See supra* note 114.

FURTHER READING

Bibliography

Aichele, Gary J. "Bibliographic Essay." In *Oliver Wendell Holmes, Jr.: Soldier, Scholar, Judge*, pp. 197-205. Boston: Twayne Publishers, 1989.
  Lists primary and secondary sources on Holmes's work and life.

Biography

Bowen, Catherine Drinker. *Yankee from Olympus: Justice Holmes and His Family*. Boston: Little, Brown and Company, 1944, 473 p.
  Traces Holmes's family History from his grandparents' marriage in 1800 until his death in 1935.

Novick, Sheldon M. *Honorable Justice: The Life of Oliver Wendell Holmes*. Boston: Little, Brown and Company, 1989, 522 p.
  Biography that attempts to tell Holmes's life story "with sympathy, but without apology," including some of the less well-understood aspects of Holmes's opinions and character.

Criticism

Commager, Henry Steele. "Masters of the New Jurisprudence: Pound and Holmes." In *The American Mind: An Interpretation of American Thought and Character since the 1880s*, pp. 374-90. New Haven: Yale University Press, 1950.
  Examines the advent of the theory of natural law in the American judicial system with the appointment of Justices Holmes, Pound, and Brandeis.

Dewey, John. "Oliver Wendell Holmes." In *Characters and Events: Popular Essays in Social and Political Philosophy*, edited by Joseph Ratner, pp. 100-06. New York: Henry Holt and Company, 1920.
  Discusses Holmes's social philosophy.

Greene, Nathan. "Mr. Justice Holmes and the Age of Man." *Wayne Law Review* 6, No. 3 (Summer 1960): 394-412.
  Explains Holmes's place in the twentieth-century debate over civil liberties.

Hamilton, Walter H. "On Dating Mr. Justice Holmes." *The University of Chicago Law Review* 9, No. 1 (December 1941): 1-29.
  Reviews Holmes's body of work, attempting to place him in the historical context of American law.

Lippman, Walter. "To Justice Holmes on His Seventy-Fifth Birthday." In *Men of Destiny*, pp. 242-44. New York: The Macmillan Company, 1928.
  Laudatory comment on Holmes's remarkable impact on American law.

Plucknett, Theodore F. T. "Holmes: The Historian." *Harvard Law Review* XLIV, No. 5 (March 1931): 712-16.
  Discusses Holmes's contributions to the study of legal history, particularly in his book *The Common Law*.

Rogat, Yosal. "The Judge as Spectator." *The University of Chicago Law Review* 31, No. 2 (Winter 1964): 213-56.
  Uses the second volume of Mark DeWolfe Howe's biography of Holmes to examine Holmes's role on the bench as a "spectator," distancing himself from particular schools of thought but nonetheless leaving a unified body of work.

Whittemore, Robert Clifton. "Oliver Wendell Holmes." In *Makers of the American Mind*, pp. 421-37. New York: William Morrow and Company, 1964.
  Reviews Holmes's life and overall influence on American social and judicial trends.

Additional coverage of Holmes's life and career is contained in the following source published by Gale Research: Contemporary Authors, Vol. 114.

Harold Adams Innis

1894-1952

Canadian economist, historian, and essayist.

INTRODUCTION

In the years between the world wars, economist Harold Innis became the first Canadian intellectual to attract significant international recognition. His work was revolutionary in several regards. He showed that the railroads had replaced the trade routes of the earlier fur industry, and thus reinterpreted Canada's development as something which took place because of its geography rather than in spite of it, as had been previously supposed. His views of history made use of the "staple theory of economic development," which approached the story of a nation's evolution as a chronicle of various "staples"—fur, timber, fish—at the center of its economy. Such an interpretation was particularly applicable to Canada, which as Innis showed, had an economic environment quite unlike that of the United States or Britain. By treating Canada as an economic entity separate from its influential mother country and its powerful neighbor to the south, Innis inaugurated a new era in Canadian studies. In spite of his emphasis on individualism and a free market, his focus on economics as a determining factor in a nation's political history helped to draw a following, long after his death, among Marxists. His career and work fell into two phases, the first of which was marked by the publication of *The Fur Trade in Canada* (1930), and which focused on the study of economic factors in the development of Canadian history. After the Second World War, Innis directed his attention to the means by which civilizations propagate themselves through modes of communication. These ideas, which he developed in *Empire and Communications* (1950), would have an impact far beyond Canada, in part through their influence on his more famous countryman, Marshall McLuhan.

Biographical Information

Innis was born in southwestern Ontario, and raised by strict Baptist parents. Though in later life he did not belong to any organized religion, the influence of his upbringing would be felt in many particulars of his life and work, perhaps most notably in his emphasis on both personal freedom and personal responsibility. Educated at local high schools and later at Woodstock Collegiate Institute, to which he had to commute many miles by train every day, he enrolled at McMaster University in 1913. At McMaster, a Baptist college then located in Toronto, Innis was lonely and lacking sufficient funds, but he managed to graduate with honors in 1916 as a political economy and philosophy major. By then Canada had entered World War I, and Innis enlisted in the army

as a private. During fighting at Vimy Ridge in France he was wounded with shrapnel in his leg, and he spent the next year in the hospital. The war would have an enormous influence on Innis, who saw firsthand the manner in which governments manipulated their fighting men through control of information. He also came to believe that Canadians' sacrifices entitled them to a greater degree of political and cultural independence from Britain than they had previously enjoyed. After the war, he finished his M.A. at McMaster and entered the doctoral program at the University of Chicago. There he came under the influence of several notable academicians, particularly F.H. Knight, and met Mary Quayle. In 1921 he married Quayle, who would also become a writer on economic and historical subjects. Innis's doctoral thesis would become his first published work, *A History of the Canadian Pacific Railway* (1923). Having obtained his doctorate in 1920, he accepted a position in the political economy department of the University of Toronto. The department took an interdisciplinary approach, combining studies in a number of social sciences, and Innis applied a similarly wide range of disciplines to his first major work, *The Fur Trade in Canada.* During the 1930s, the university environment was torn by the increasing politicization of professors, a movement of which Innis disapproved strongly. But when the next world war began, and his left-wing colleague Frank H. Underhill came under fire for his anti-British opinions, Innis placed his by then considerable influence in Underhill's defense. With the war raging overseas, Innis remembered the lackluster reception he and his comrades had received following the First World War, when they descended on institutions unprepared for the onslaught of new students. Therefore he helped to ready his university for an influx of eager young soldier-students who would arrive after the end of the hostilities. During this time, he came under the influence of his colleague Charles Cochrane, a classical historian whose *Christianity and Classical Culture* (1940) examined the decline of Rome in terms of the Romans' inability to develop a sustaining intellectual framework that took account of Christianity's rise. Soon after the German surrender, he visited the Soviet Union as part of a small Canadian delegation, and recorded his observations in a diary that would not be published for another four decades. While in Russia, he began to consider the differing strains of Western civilization which had created a society similar to, but quite different from, that of Europe. These influences may have led in part to his shift away from strictly economic studies, and toward an examination of the influence of communications on civilization. Innis received a number of awards in his lifetime, and was celebrated by scholars throughout North America and Europe. He died of cancer in 1952.

Major Works

Innis's work fell into two phases: the period between the world wars, when he focused his attention chiefly on Canadian economic history, and the years following World War II, when the role of communications in the rise and fall of civilizations became his primary subject. Following his study of the Canadian Pacific Railway, the doctoral dissertation which he published in 1923, Innis wrote a highly specialized study called *The Fur-Trade of Canada* (1927), which he broadened and published three years later as *The Fur Trade in Canada.* He intended the book, as its subtitle indicated, to be an introduction to Canadian economic history, and in it he brought to bear a variety of disciplines in his examination of the fur trade's effect on the evolution of Canada as a political entity. In this volume, he sketched out the essentials of his staple theory as he applied it to the Canadian situation, portraying his land's economic history in terms of its shift from one staple to another, each a primary export to the United States and Europe. He further developed these ideas in *The Cod Fisheries* (1940), whose thesis in part was that "European civilization left its impress on North America through its demands for staples products." The second and much shorter—but potentially more significant—phase of his writing began with a series of books in the early 1950s, each comprising lectures or essays on the relationship of the modes of communication to the power structure of the civilization that pro-

duces them: *Empire and Communications, The Bias of Communication* (1951), and *Changing Concepts of Time* (1952). Innis was particularly interested in the effect of one type of "bias" or another. There was the bias of time, motivated by forms of communication made to last for centuries, but not particularly adapted to the easy spread of information across distances—e.g., stone tablets. And there was the bias of space, encouraged by modes such as printed material which are easily disseminated through a great area, but are not made to last. Another theme was the use of a dominant medium by a dominant group, whether priests, the military, nobles, or businesspeople: this control of the medium, he posited, would lead to stagnation, and the ultimate usurping of authority by a rival group possessing modes not susceptible to the dominant bias.

PRINCIPAL WORKS

A History of the Canadian Pacific Railway (history) 1923
The Fur-Trade of Canada (history) 1927
The Fur Trade in Canada: An Introduction to Canadian Economic History (history) 1930
Problems of Staple Production in Canada (nonfiction) 1933
Settlement and the Mining Frontier (history) 1936
The Cod Fisheries: The History of an International Economy (history) 1940
Political Economy and the Modern State (essays) 1946
Empire and Communications (lectures) 1950
The Bias of Communication (essays) 1951
Changing Concepts of Time (essays) 1952
Essays in Canadian Economic History [edited by Mary Quayle Innis] (essays) 1956
The Idea File of Harold Adams Innis [edited by William Christian] (essays) 1980
Innis on Russia: The Russian Diary and Other Writings [edited by William Christian] (journals) 1981

CRITICISM

W. T. Easterbrook (essay date 1953)

SOURCE: "Innis and Economics," in *Canadian Journal of Economics and Political Science,* Vol. XIX, No. 3, August, 1953, pp. 291-303.

[*In the following essay, Easterbrook delineates phases of Innis's career as a writer on economics.*]

Over the three decades of teaching and research allotted Harold Innis, no subject concerned him more than the state of economics. He looked to economic history to enrich and broaden economic thought, and he sought to explain fashions in economics and to make economists intelligible to themselves. Although Veblen's influence left its mark on his work, Innis remained throughout a disciple of Adam Smith and no name appears more frequently in his observations on economics past and present. His plea was, as he put it, for "a general emphasis on a universal approach" and in his unfinished paper he writes, "The economic historian must test the tools of economic analysis by applying them to a broad canvas and by suggesting their possibilities and limitations when applied to other language or cultural groups."[1]

Apart from this search for perspective in economic thought there were other elements of continuity in Innis's thinking which give his life's work a coherence and a unity whether his interest centred on Canadian economic history or the duration powers of empires. It is scarcely necessary here to refer to his dislike of concentrations of power in any form or to his uncompromising belief in the free and creative powers of the individual, attitudes which stamp his research from beginning to untimely end. In his writings on economic history, technological change, free or controlled, links past and present. In his more specific references to economics, the pricing system provides the key to his reflections on the state of the subject. Early in his work there is present the same price-technology dichotomy that is to be found throughout Veblen's writings; later Innis sought to resolve this dichotomy in his studies of communication in which he saw technology and pricing as elements interacting with politics, law, and religion in a larger network of human relationships.

If one word may be used to bring to a focus his research in economic history and his observations on the state of economics, it is *industrialism,* its antecedents, course, and consequences in economic and cultural change. It is used in the following pages to set out the principal phases in Innis's enquiries and to aid in outlining his reflections on economics in each of these phases. Examination of his writings in terms of their timing and content, of his readings over the whole period of his studies, and of available correspondence suggest a number of turning points in his explorations which mark off successive phases on the way to what was to be, I think, a philosophy of history.

The first, or Veblen phase, ends with the publication of *Problems of Staple Production in Canada.*[2] In this early phase he was concerned with the antecedents of industrialism in Canada and in his major work of this stage, *The Fur Trade in Canada,*[3] he set out the conditions for the rise of the old industrialism of coal and iron, canals and railways, wheat and tariffs. His studies at this time were marked by emphasis on the drive of technology and the efficiency of the pricing system.

The second phase begins with the article **"Economic Nationalism,"**[4] an article which serves as an introduction to his studies in the new industrialism of mining, pulp

and paper, and hydro-electric power and his growing interest in the limitations of the pricing system and the economics of disturbance. This phase comes to a close with his *Cod Fisheries* volume,[5] a work which carried him beyond his earlier interest in staples to reflections on the problems of empires, the impact of machine industry in exposed regions, and the broader implications of technological change and marketing influences. As such it marks the end of his basic research in Canadian economic history.

In the third phase his reflections on industrialism take a new turn. Although there are suggestions of the change in his writings of the late 1930's, a glance at his reading indicates that in the summer of 1940 he turned abruptly to an intensive study of technological and pricing factors in the area of mechanized communications beginning with printing and the press. In his published work, the article **"The Newspaper in Economic Development"**[6] may be regarded as the first fruit of his new inquiries, and his work for the next five years or so consists mainly of explorations along lines suggested in this key article. The researches of this phase represent a strenuous attempt to apply more broadly the methods of analysis which had yielded such rich returns in his studies of Canadian problems.

The fourth and final phase was ushered in with the publication of the article **"Minerva's Owl."**[7] This along with his *Empire and Communications*[8] comes closest to a complete survey of his unpublished volume on the history of communications. We find him working back from the industrialization of communications to its antecedents in early empires as he had worked back in Canadian economic history to the antecedents of industrialism in Canada.

Although it is possible to mark out some such phases as these in Innis's work, there is at no point any suggestion of a break or a radical shift in his mode of approach to national or general economic history. In each phase questions emerged which called for explorations in strange territories and it is difficult to escape the thrill of the chase one experiences in tracing through these adventurous excursions in the realm of ideas. "He was," . . . says Professor Brady, "in the grip of an exploratory spirit which would not let him be content with the traditional highways of economics."[9]

Turning back to the first phase of his explorations (1920-33), one name, from the beginning stands out in his readings—that of Veblen appears again and again throughout the 1920's, and his volumes were read and reread. This may account for one of the most revealing of Innis's publications, his **"A Bibliography of Thorstein Veblen."**[10] In it he sketches those influences which shaped Veblen's thought, putting heavy emphasis on his place on the frontier of the industrial revolution. "The constructive part of Veblen's work," he writes, "was essentially the elaboration of an extended argument showing the effects of the machine industry and the industrial revolution. Veblen's interest was in the state of the industrial arts which had got out of hand. . . ."[11] There is a reference to Veblen's search for laws of growth and decay and to his concern with the effects of industrialism on the preconceptions of economic science.

It is not without relevance here that Innis commented of Veblen: "It is much too early to appraise the validity of this work—certainly he attempted far too wide a field for one individual but it is the method of approach which must be stressed, and not the final conclusions."[12] And again: "His anxiety has always been to detect trends and to escape their effects."[13] "[His work] stands as a monument to the importance of an unbiased approach to economics. . . ."[14] Veblen, like Adam Smith, " . . . is an individualist and like most individualists in continental countries, . . . he is in revolt against mass education and standardization."[15] Such statements will recall Innis's use of George Jean Nathan's remark that "all biography is a form of unwitting self-betrayal." Like Veblen, Innis lived through the economic strains of a new country and sought to work out their more important characteristics through studies of the impact of industrialism on a continental background.

In his method of approach, in the selection of questions he regarded as most significant, and in his emphasis on the total environment of economic thought, Veblen's influence was great beyond question. But there was, none the less, one profound difference between the two men for, unlike Veblen, Innis brought a genuinely historical bent, an emphasis on empirical or dirt research, to his work. It was through his historical studies that he lived up to his expressed hope that Veblen's attempt at synthesis might be revised and steadily improved and it was his historical insights that were to carry him into areas beyond the reach of Veblen.

In this first phase, his reflections on economics centre on the state of the subject in Canada and the contributions of research in the economic history of new countries to an economic theory developed in older countries. In his note on **"The State of Economic Science in Canada"** he begins with the observation that "To the cynically inclined the above title may appear to parallel the title 'Snakes in Ireland'" but, quoting Dr. O. D. Skelton, "'an era of definite promise is beginning.'"[16] On more than one occasion there is expressed the view that the study of the development of new countries will have its uses in testing the validity of the principles of economic theory. "The conflict between the economics of a long and highly industrialized country such as England and the economics of the recently industrialized new and borrowing countries will become less severe as the study of cyclonics is worked out and incorporated in a general survey of the effects of the industrial revolution such as Veblen has begun and such as will be worked out and revised by later students."[17] In 1929, writing on **"The Teaching of Economic History in Canada,"** he comments: "A new country presents certain definite problems which appear to be more or less insoluble from the standpoint of the application of economic theory as worked out in the older highly industrialized countries. Economic history consequently becomes important as a tool by which the economic theory of the old countries can be amended."[18]

In the course of little more than a decade Innis had laid the foundations for a systematic treatment of industrialism in Canada. The dynamics of growth were to be found in changing technologies applied to abundant resources.[19] He had clearly demonstrated the possibilities of the "staples approach" as a method of attack on problems of new and developing countries. He had shown mastery of one element in Veblen's dichotomy, but the other, the pricing system and its historical implications, called for further study if he was to pass beyond what might be called technological history. His reflections on pricing factors in the next phase were to take him a long step in the direction of a more adequate formulation of the relation of economic history to economic theory.

II

He made a promising beginning in this direction in his article **"Economic Nationalism"** (1934). New techniques applied to such resources as hydroelectric power and petroleum, the appearance of new metals and new means of transportation are seen as productive of strains or tensions between areas of the old industrialism and the new. Early industrialism was marked by a free and expansive technology and an increasingly effective pricing system; the later or more modern stage by nationalism, regionalism, and the growth of new metropolitan areas as centres of control. The consequences were apparent in the increasingly important role of the state as an agency of adjustment and in the limitations of the pricing system in the face of disturbances resulting from new technologies which strengthened divisive tendencies. It was an exploratory essay which raised issues which were to concern him over this second phase of his researches. The distinction he drew between industrial techniques making for co-operation and industrial techniques making for division was similar to the distinction he drew later between communication devices which unite and communication devices which divide. In each area, industrialism and industrialization of communications, reflections on nationalism and the role of the state assume an increasingly important part in his thinking as he moves from early to late stages in their development.

In writing on **"Approaches to Canadian Economic History"**[20] he expresses the fear that economists' preoccupation with price statistics and their failure to take into account the unpredictable results of technological change and discoveries of new resources will rule out understanding of the historical role and functions of the pricing system and lead to neglect of the crucial role of pricing factors in economic change. Along with this growing interest in the pricing system in this phase there are signs of increasing awareness of the significance of communication techniques to modern society and to economics. His studies of modern industrialism and, in particular, of the pulp and paper industry led him to the conclusion that the newsprint industry possessed a dynamic of its own, that it exerted a pervasive influence on the climate of economic thought, and that to understand its place in economic and social change he must move beyond the well-tried staples approach. There appears in the late 1930's a shift of interest to the impact of industrialism on communications, and in this shift indications of a more adequate handling of technology and pricing. There is a faint sign of changes to come in his remark in 1936 to the Commerce students that "The increasing power of the state and its conquest of the press, the Church and the university, and of the tremendously improved system of communication . . . perhaps weighs more heavily against you than it did against us."[21]

Two years later, under the heading, **"The Passing of Political Economy,"** he writes: "The end of the nineteenth century and the twentieth century were marked by the extension of industrialism dependent on minerals, new sources of power, physics and chemistry and mathematics. These have led to the decline in freedom of trade and the hardening of political entities in the intensity of nationalism. With these has come the end of political economy, the emergence of specialization in the social sciences, and its subordination to nationalism."[22] And he continues: "It has been argued that the disappearance of political economy is an illusion and that it will emerge from behind the clouds. But the circumstances are not propitious for another great epoch of thought. The rise of literacy and improved communication promoted the rapid growth of groups, associations and nations and reduced social scientists to a position as defenders . . . of this and that particular cause. Under the influence of modern industrialism in the printing press and cheap paper, universities have become increasingly specialized, and increasing demands for space in the curriculum have enhanced the activity of administration and promoted the growth of vested interests."[23]

These reflections on modern industrialism and the state of communications were brought to a focus in **"The Penetrative Powers of the Price System."**[24] He had not yet embarked on intensive work on communications but his search for a more adequate formulation of the forces back of change, peaceful or disruptive, was moving him rapidly in this direction. There is apparent a growing awareness of the possibilities of communication studies for the treatment of change as a whole rather than change as looked at from one aspect or point of view only. There are few signs of this synthesis as yet; at some points the price system is treated almost as a thing apart, but the close relationship established between changes in the role of the price system, in techniques of communications, and in the power of such institutional elements as the state, underline the advance in his thinking which was to lead away from "the traditional highways of economics."

He writes: "The price system operated at a high state of efficiency in the occupation of the vacant spaces of the earth";[25] and he describes its part in the decline of feudal-

ism and mercantilism and in the rise of industrial capitalism. Its drive in turn evoked the new industrialism, increased strains between areas of early and late industrialism, and the resulting instability has led to increasing intervention by the state. Its limitations today are apparent in the appearance of monetary nationalism, changing concepts of the role of government, and the interest of economists in imperfections of competition. These developments, he continues, have "reduced the value of economic theory based on Adam Smith and increased the value of economic theory adapted to nationalism."[26] Study of the historical role of the price system, its possibilities and its limitations, is looked to for a more realistic approach to the economic problems of our time.

It was at this point that he moved to new ground. Back of the pricing system, its efficiency at one time, its distortion at another, have been developments in communications which at one time increased its penetrative powers over wide areas and which now in the twentieth century have limited these powers and produced the disease of economic nationalism. The key to economic change and much of its dynamic must be sought in changes in communications, for the penetrative power of the pricing system is but one aspect of the penetrative power of systems of communication. Innis's concern with the economic history of the price system had led him directly to the communication studies of the next phase of his work. This growing awareness of the strategic place of communications in change may explain the irritation he displayed in taking Schumpeter to task for his neglect of their importance to economics. Thus, " . . . Professor Schumpeter writes, 'we pass by paper,' 'we also pass by printing' . . . The reader will forgive the reviewer who has read 1050 pages if he insists on technological advance in these industries and the effects of the 'competing down' process on economic and other literature."[27]

III

Innis was now ready for the third stage of his researches—an intensive study of technology and pricing factors in communications—using these as he had used them in Canadian economic history as spearheads for investigations which went far beyond them alone. "Communication" is, unfortunately, as Melvin Knight has put it, " . . . an omnibus label for social relationships varying from simple, direct and merely practical transmissions between persons to the shifting continuity of institutions on a world scale and throughout human time."[28] The "practical transmissions" referred to ordinarily embrace transportation factors in addition to such developments as the telegraph and the cable, the press and radio, and are in the main related to the spatial aspect of communication, the ease or difficulty with which information is exchanged between individuals or groups. It may be said, with some minor qualifications, that in Innis's work in Canadian economic history problems of communication in this spatial sense occupied a central place long before he focussed attention on the role of communications in change.[29] But a more explicit treatment of this subject awaited further researches from which emerged questions that led him to concentrate on this area of study.

For the economic historian to venture into this field there is demanded an enormous extension in the scope of his inquiries, and it is worth noting that almost half Innis's reading, as indicated by his use of the resources of the University of Toronto and other libraries, was accomplished in the years following 1940. Apart from such demands on scholarly time and energy, studies in the economic history of communications raised a problem which was to occupy a central place in the last phase of his work. In his work in Canadian economic history he had viewed technology and pricing factors as an observer of events; now, in turning to communication studies he found himself inside or part of the universe he sought to explore, subject to influences productive of bias from which there could be no escape other than through knowledge of the forces which produce bias. Although he had not been unaware of the problem, witness his early reference to the need for ascertaining trends and escaping their effects, it now becomes so central in his thinking that it provides possibly the best clue to his research of the last decade.

The early years of the forties may be regarded as a period of preparation for study of what Knight referred to as "the shifting continuity of institutions." In embarking on intensive research in the economic history of communications, Innis turned from the position he had attained as a national economic historian of high standing to one which called for ventures into strange territories, many under the control of monopolies of knowledge, dominated by experts who viewed with suspicion and worse this intrusion by an economist, and therefore a barbarian, into the backyards they occupied. Nor were his brethren inclined to applaud this strange veering off into pioneer work in an area which seemed to have little to do with economics. This change of direction gives rise to the paradox that in this new concern with communication systems he faced for a time an almost complete breakdown in his communications with those who knew him best.

I have the impression that this shift to a new phase in his thinking was a vastly bigger step than he himself realized. There is apparent the intention to keep communication studies within the compass of more or less traditional economic history. He writes of his " . . . concern with the use of certain tools which have proved effective in the interpretation of the economic history of Canada and the British Empire."[30] Nor does his reading suggest at the beginning any marked shift of interest to the "big" problems of empires and civilizations, stability and progress, which so occupied his attention in the last years.

Beginning in July, 1940, his readings in Canadian history gave way almost completely to the reading of works on paper and printing, journalism and the press, literature and the book trade, censorship, advertising and propaganda, and memoirs, biographies, and autobiographies which throw light on these aspects of communication. Interest in the appearance and spread of machine techniques in printing took him to studies of the press in England and the Continent, and in the United States as the area of greatest freedom of technological change. There is the growing conviction that at the heart of industrial change lie these advances in communication technology, that early developments in printing and changes allied to them were back of the extension of markets and the spread of industrialism in the old world and the new.

His first important published work in this phase was **"The Newspaper in Economic Development"** (1942). It consists of a review of technological advances in printing and paper making, with the power press seen as the pioneer in the development of speed in communications and transportation, exerting pressure for more rapid transmission of news by cable, postal, and express systems and more efficient transportation services. The press provided the impetus to the spread of the price system over space and vertically in terms of income categories by its penetration to lower income groups. It appealed to a wide audience of all levels of literacy and strengthened the move to compulsory education and extension of the franchise.

As the pioneer in mass production and distribution, the press, in its emphasis on volume and rapid turnover, heralded the appearance of advertising and the giant department store. Increasing concentration of power in the newspaper field encouraged a corresponding concentration in business in areas making most effective use of new developments in communications. It is suggested that in the lumpiness of technological change in communications, and the instability resulting from the sensationalism of the press and its stress on the immediate, are present valuable clues for students of the business cycle and more broadly for those interested in the dynamics of change.

Innis's observations on economics in this third phase reflect these changes in his thinking. Following brief experiments with imperfect competition and liquidity preference, he turned with more profit to observations **"On the Economic Significance of Culture,"**[31] wherein he sought to bring technology and pricing together in a more coherent and unified approach. He writes: "The conflict between technology and the price system described by Veblen . . . can be resolved more easily with a broader perspective."[32] Schumpeter had tried to narrow the gap between pricing and technology but is seen as sacrificing much in both approaches and as neglecting the political factor. Silbering was more successful in his attempt "to coordinate the political, pecuniary and technological approaches," but weakened his effort by concentration on national boundaries.

Innis sought his broader perspective through studies in communications which passed beyond political boundaries and enabled consideration of the interrelations of politics, economics, and religion in historical change. Concerning the impact on religion of changes in communications he writes: "With the rise of a vast area of public opinion, which was essential to the rapid dissemination of information, and the growth in turn of marketing organizations, the expansion of credit, and the development of nationalism, the vast structure previously centering about religion declined."[33] Commerce succeeded religion as a force for stability, but new methods of communications have strengthened division, commerce is no longer the "great stabilizer" and the results are apparent in the radically altered role of the state.

New pressures are reflected in concern with the immediate and in the break-up of the classical tradition in economics. "At one time," he writes, "we are concerned with tariffs, at another with trusts, and still another with money. As newspapers seldom find it to their interest to pursue any subject for more than three or four days, so the economist becomes weary of particular interests or senses that the public is weary of them and changes accordingly."[34] As a corrective, Innis suggests that "Economic history may provide grappling irons with which to lay hold on the fringes of economics . . . and to rescue economics from the present-mindedness which pulverizes other subjects and makes a broad approach almost impossible."[35]

The sharp contrast between the synthesis he sought and modern tendencies in economics led to increasingly pointed comments on the unhealthy state of the subject. In his review of Ronald Walker's *From Economic Theory to Policy* he writes:

> Adam Smith was a distinguished representative of a century in which all knowledge was taken as a field: It was the supreme tragedy of his work that part of his contributions, namely the *Wealth of Nations,* developed around the principle of division of labour, and . . . that its application was made with devastating effects in the field of knowledge where he would have most abhorred it and where his writings stood most in contrast to it. The universe of Adam Smith was literally ground to atoms, or facts and figures, by the printing press and the calculating machine.[36]

In these years, Innis had moved from description of the state of economics to diagnosis of its condition.

The work of this phase led to an increasing interest on his part in the ability of machine-dominated cultures to survive. Growing instability and increasing reliance on force are productive of uncertainties which optimists of the nineteenth century could overlook. And since his studies of the media and techniques of communications had yielded new and valuable insight into problems centring on the character and course of historical change, it was perhaps inevitable that he should look to the state of modern communications for light on the survival powers of Western civilization. In so doing he raised anew a problem which was at the heart of communications itself,

namely the problem of understanding among peoples of different places and times.

In his article **"Industrialism and Cultural Values"** he speaks of " . . . the extraordinary, perhaps insuperable, difficulty of assessing the quality of a culture of which we are part or of assessing the quality of a culture of which we are not a part."[37] This "difficulty of assessment" is rooted in the bias of communications present in our own and other cultures. The clearest manifestations of this bias appear in attitudes toward time, and it was this search for clues as to the meaning of the time dimension in different cultures that led Innis to the fourth and final phase of his work. Interest in the spatial aspects of communications now gives way to concern with time concepts and the possibility of avoiding the fatal disease of bias by attainment of a balanced view of time and space as a condition of survival. The dichotomy of technology-price has given way to that of time-space and again he sought to resolve it by communication studies.

His interest at this time in the problem of understanding Russia may have been a factor in this new preoccupation with comparative history. In his **"Comments on Russia"** he wrote: "To be trained in political economy, a subject which has its roots in the West and which has suffered from the characteristic disease of specialization, and to realize suddenly that a vast powerful organisation built around the efforts of 180,000,000 people has arisen with little interest in this specialization is to find oneself compelled to search for possible contacts in the broader approach to its history."[38] And again: "Political economy as developed in the Western world will be compelled to broaden its range and to discuss the implications of competition between languages, religions and cultural phenomena largely neglected by it."[39]

IV

It is at this time (the mid-forties) that his readings take a new turn. The emphasis is now on the empires of the Mediterranean and, farther afield, of India and China, on law, religion, and the arts in classical and medieval cultures, on the character of communications as reflected in the alphabet and language and fashions in literature. There are increasing references to questions of power and stability, to nationalism, and to ancient and modern concepts of time. The first of his published works of this phase was the article **"Minerva's Owl"** of 1947, which like **"The Newspaper in Economic Development"** of 1942, provided the setting or outline for the following half decade. It represents a bird's-eye view of a larger work in process. *Empire and Communications* filled in some of the gaps and provided a more complete though still skeleton framework. The later sets of essays, *The Bias of Communications*[40] and *Changing Concepts of Time*[41] present the results of research arising out of problems encountered in these new explorations. In these years Innis worked back from the industrialization of communications to its antecedents and forward to its consequences for our time.

His studies of pre-industrial communications parallel in purpose and method his studies of early staples in Canadian economic history. The clay, papyrus, and parchment of the empires of the past, like the cod, beaver, and square timber of colonial North America, appear as the predecessors of industrialism and knowledge of their role and significance is looked to in both cases for light on the character and timing of the industrialism that was to emerge.

It is not difficult to discern the general pattern of change of this last phase of Innis's writings: the early stage of free and creative expansion eventually gives way before the rise of monopolies of knowledge which buttress hierarchies in state, religion, and economics; these monopolies in turn invite competition from marginal areas in which creative elements are strong; this competition is productive of disturbances as new forms of organization clash with established forms, and may be resolved only by the attainment of balance among competing forces. This solution by balance of opposing forces appears throughout his writings of this last phase wherein he juxtaposes time and space, Church and Empire, stability and change, written and oral traditions, Roman Law and Common Law, force and sanction.[42] Bias is lack of balance, it is the result of monopolies in communications representative of one point of view, and its explanation is to be found in the character of communication systems which shape attitudes and promote or destroy the possibility of understanding among peoples. The closed system rules out prospects for balance and no empire or civilization has escaped its effects.

Innis's approach "to the study of civilizations and of monopolies in relation to them" leads to conclusions which provide no optimism for the present. "Lack of interest in problems of duration in Western civilisation suggests that the bias of paper and printing has persisted in a concern with space."[43] States, divided by language, concern themselves with " . . . the enlargement of territories and the imposition of cultural uniformity . . . on [their] peoples."[44] This spatial bias of the present is productive of an emphasis on change, instability and progress, and presents " . . . graver threats to continuity than the tyranny of monopoly over time in the Middle Ages to the establishment of political organisation."[45]

These explorations of the last phase consist essentially of study of the devices by which control over space (how large an area did it cover) and time (how long did it last) has been attempted in other cultures and times—such devices as reliance on the power of the state or the sanctions of religion, architecture, and education. The problems of the present are rendered vastly more complex by the impact on cultural values of industrialism in communications, by the obstacles it presents to understanding of other cultures, and by its demands for specialization in technology and thought and its emphasis on the here and now. In the United States, as the area of sharpest impact and most dangerous manifestations, the affliction of bias appears in its most advanced stages. Canadians must search for balance elsewhere and this in the face of an increasingly heavy cultural bombardment from the south.

His reflections on Keynes[46] sum up his misgivings on the present state of economics. Keynes, under the spell of the immediate and of the Common Law tradition, is contrasted with the Adam Smith of Roman Law principles and a more balanced concern with time. It is less a critique of Keynes than a summing up of the forces that made Keynes run. More instructive is his unfinished paper, unhappily entitled **"The Decline in the Efficiency of Instruments Essential in Equilibrium."** In the main, this is concerned with the bias exerted by present-day communications on the state of mind of economists. It assumes close acquaintance with such writings as his *A Plea for Time,* **"The Bias of Communication,"**[47] and *Roman Law and the British Empire,*[48] wherein he has much to say about the nature of the obstacles in the way of any universal approach to economics or the appearance of "any central core of interest." The economic historian must take into account such obstacles and make others aware of their import.

He argues that the present state of communications rules out any effective contact between different cultural groups. Within Western civilization itself, the obstacles are almost as great, and by way of illustration he points to profound differences in outlook in the social sciences of Roman and Common Law countries.[49] Law, as an aspect of communications, leaves its impress on change and on economic thought, and the difference in points of view which results is as wide as that between Adam Smith and Keynes. Similarly, modern nationalism as a by-product of the new industrialization of communications presents new and dangerous obstacles to understanding, and press and radio steadily reinforce national differences in outlook. These differences are reflected in present-day preoccupation with national statistics; concentration on national problems subject to measurement, obsession with statistics determined by national boundaries, produce new obstacles to effective communication across such boundaries, the more so since statistics reflect the character of the state. Innis then turns to a familiar theme, the strategic position of communications in economic change, and in particular, to the role of the newspaper as the pioneer in mass production and distribution. And there the paper ends.

I do not think there is any doubt as to the direction in which he was proceeding. Modern developments in communications, with their emphasis on speed of change, their contributions to instability, and their concern with the moment, explain bias in economics as reflected in the disease of specialization and the prevailing obsession with the short run. The bias of economics is that of our culture and Innis saw little evidence of any concern with its perils and less of any attempts to correct it. I have the impression that he was saved from the role of historical pessimist by the sense of humour which pervades his writings as it did his conversation, and by his awareness of the importance of humour as an element in balance and a means of distinguishing between economics and insanity. And I cannot escape the feeling that leg-pulling was not entirely absent from his writings.

I have tried to set out some of the milestones on the road followed by Innis—those which mark out the increasing range and maturity of his thought and the course of his search for what he termed "an integration of basic approaches" as an offset to the fragmentation of knowledge which destroys prospects for understanding among peoples and nations. This understanding comes only through open lines of communications and he looked to social scientists to lead the way, even though the American Economic Association lag behind, providing as it did for Innis a case study in the sickness of liberal economics.

Toward the end there were signs of yet another phase, one suggested by Innis's growing interest in philosophy and more especially the philosophy of history. In his review of Cochrane's *Christianity and Classical Culture* he wrote: "A society dominated by Augustine will produce a fundamentally different type of historian, who approaches his problem from the standpoint of change and progress, from classicism with its emphasis on cyclical change and the tendency to equilibrium. . . . His [Cochrane's] contribution to the philosophy of history is shown in the development of general concepts at the basis of progress and the adjustment of order to meet the demands of change. . . ."[50] It is doubtful if any work exerted greater influence on the general outlook of the Innis of the last days than this volume. He, too, was searching for concepts useful in "the adjustment of order to meet the demands of change," a legitimate goal for an economic historian of cultures who sought to see things as a whole in the endeavour to throw light on the economic problems of his time.

NOTES

This paper was presented at the annual meeting of the Canadian Political Association in London, June 5, 1953.

[1] "The Decline in the Efficiency of Instruments Essential in Equilibrium," *American Economic Review,* May, 1953, 17-18.

[2] Toronto, 1933.

[3] *The Fur Trade in Canada: An Introduction to Canadian Economic History* (New Haven, 1930).

[4] This appeared in *Papers and Proceedings of the Canadian Political Science Association,* VI, 1934, 17-31 and in revised form in the Introduction to the volume *The Canadian Economy and Its Problems* edited by H. A. Innis and A. F. W. Plumptre (Toronto, 1934).

[5] *The Cod Fisheries: The History of an International Economy* (Toronto and New Haven, 1940).

[6] *Journal of Economic History,* vol. II, *Supplement,* Dec., 1942, 1-33.

[7] *Proceedings of the Royal Society of Canada,* 1947, Appendix A, Presidential Address, 83-108.

[8] Oxford, 1950.

[9] Alexander Brady, "Harold Adams Innis, 1894-1952," *Canadian Journal of Economics and Political Science,* XIX, no. 1, Feb., 1953, 92.

[10] *Southwestern Political and Social Science Quarterly,* X, no. 1, 1929, 56-68.

[11] *Ibid.,* 64.

[12] *Ibid.,* 65.

[13] *Ibid.,* 66.

[14] *Ibid.,* 67.

[15] *Ibid.,* 66.

[16] *Commerce Journal,* 1933, 5-8.

[17] "A Bibliography of Thorstein Veblen," 67-8.

[18] *Contributions to Canadian Economics,* in University of Toronto Studies, History and Economics, II, 1929, 52.

[19] A more complete survey would include reference to the influence of J. M. Clark. In the economics of overhead costs, Innis found much of the dynamic of change in both Canadian expansion westward and the spread of industrialized communications on a world scale. See H. A. Innis, "Unused Capacity as a Factor in Canadian Economic History," *Canadian Journal of Economics and Political Science,* II, no. 1, Feb., 1936, 1-15.

[20] *Commerce Journal,* 1936, 24-30.

[21] *Ibid.,* 1936, 30.

[22] *Ibid.,* 1938, 5.

[23] *Ibid.,* 1938, 6.

[24] *Canadian Journal of Economics and Political Science,* IV, no. 3, Aug., 1938, 299-319.

[25] *Ibid.,* 307.

[26] *Ibid.,* 318.

[27] *Canadian Journal of Economics and Political Science,* VI, no. 1, Feb., 1940, 95-6.

[28] *American Economic Review,* March, 1953, 180.

[29] See his "Transportation as a Factor in Canadian Economic History," *Papers and Proceedings of the Canadian Political Science Association,* III, 1931, 166-84,

also his "Significant Factors in Canadian Economic Development," *Canadian Historical Review,* XVIII, no. 4, Dec., 1937, 374-84.

[30] *Empire and Communications,* 5-6.

[31] *Journal of Economic History,* vol. IV, *Supplement,* Dec., 1944, 80-97.

[32] *Ibid.,* 83-4.

[33] *Ibid.,* 86-7.

[34] *Ibid.,* 92.

[35] *Ibid.,* 97.

[36] *Canadian Journal of Economics and Political Science,* X, no. 1, Feb., 1944, 107.

[37] *Papers and Proceedings of the American Economic Association,* in *American Economic Review,* XLI, May, 1951, 202.

[38] *International Journal,* I, no. 1, 31. See also his "The Problem of Mutual Understanding with Russia," *Queen's Quarterly,* LIII, no. 1, 1946, pp. 92-100.

[39] "Reflections on Russia" in *Political Economy in the Modern State* (Toronto, 1946), 262.

[40] Toronto, 1951.

[41] Toronto, 1952.

[42] There are strong suggestions of ideal type method in Innis's approach, e.g., his references to the oral tradition of Greece, the durable bureaucracy of the Byzantine Empire.

[43] *A Plea for Time.* Sesquicentennial Lectures, University of New Brunswick. (Fredericton, 1950), 8.

[45] "The Concept of Monopoly and Civilisation." A paper read at a meeting under the chairmanship of Professor Lucien Febvre, Paris, July 6, 1951.

[46] Review: John Maynard Keynes, *Two Memoirs—Dr. Melchior: A Defeated Enemy; and My Early Beliefs,* in *Canadian Journal of Economics and Political Science,* XVI, no. 2, Feb., 1950, 107-9. Also Review Article: "Sub Specie Temporis," *Canadian Journal of Economics and Political Science,* XVII, no. 4, Nov., 1951, 553-7.

[47] *Canadian Journal of Economics and Political Science,* XV, no. 4, Nov., 1949, 457-76.

[48] Sesquicentennial Lectures, University of New Brunswick. (Fredericton, 1950.)

[49] The Common Law with its flexibility and receptivity to change, its emphasis on facts and their interpretation favourable to the scientific tradition and to industrial development.

[50] "Charles Norris Cochrane, 1899-1945," *Canadian Journal of Economics and Political Science,* XII, no. 1, Feb., 1946, 97.

Robert F. Neill (essay date 1966)

SOURCE: "The Content and Context of the Work of H. A. Innis," in *The Journal of Economic History,* Vol. XXVI, No. 4, December, 1966, pp. 589-90.

[*In the following essay, Neill offers a short analysis of Innis's theories and the cultural environment in which he developed them.*]

The eccentric Innis was too complex a personality and too prolific and varied in his writings to be treated with justice in a short space. He ranks with James Mavor and Stephen Leacock as a great character in Canadian intellectual history. In the present sketch only the main lines of his contribution to economics can be drawn.

The context was an economy experiencing long-run growth with the aid of foreign investment. A period of severe short-run contraction had set in. Surpluses of fixed capital appeared, and structural stresses that had gone unnoticed during prosperity exposed themselves in the form of political demands for reorganization. In face of the problem Innis took his analytical lead from Thorstein Veblen. Neoclassical price economics had not concentrated on technical change or capital accumulation. These were the dominant characteristics of the Canadian case. A new economy required a new, more thoroughly "scientific" economics, and Veblen had pointed the way to it. Innis began the search by exploring the influence of geography and technology on the formation of institutions.

He treated institutions as means to ensure that prices reflect social values—particularly financial institutions as means to the expression of values when, in consequence of innovation, no market criteria exist. In a new country characterized by the uncertainty of pervasive technical change, new institutions had to be created by direct political action. For Innis, the Canadian state itself was essentially a financial institution tailored to a particular phase of technological development. In fact, in this view of things, every frontier area emerging in consequence of technical advance would necessarily be clothed with an appropriately advanced financial structure. From this Innis concluded that young economies don't grow up; they grow from the top down. Thus he offered a third answer to the questions raised by Frederick J. Turner and N. S. B. Gras. In the same way he provided an alternate rationalization for John Rae's opposition to Adam Smith: *laissez faire* in Britain would have been impossible without government intervention in areas on her economic frontier.

Canada's problems were a consequence of the failure of her institutions to cope with the demands of technique and accumulation. Accumulation itself had taken place, but at the expense of adjustments to relative scarcities. In Innis' reconstruction of the case, Canadian development had been predicated on the possibility of realizing a surplus by applying capital-intensive techniques to virgin resources. The capital had to be imported, raising the critical question of how the surplus, or a fair share of it, could be retained in Canada. The answer was to impose a tariff on imported capital goods, thus raising costs and reducing the profits of foreign investors. The tariff was in effect a tax on profits, the proceeds of which were used for the direct benefit of Canadians and to pay off the debt owed abroad. In large measure the scheme had succeeded, but there were weaknesses. The burden of the tariff had been shifted to exposed sectors of the economy, and initial success had led to uneconomic expansion with consequent excess capacity and unemployment. The whole development, as Innis told it, was an historical exercise in the Joan Robinson variety of capital theory.

The "revolutionary" monetary schemes of the 1930's appeared to Innis very much in the light, or the shadow, of his own insight into the past. They were simply the old device of governmentally supported finance operated by the more powerful machinery of the modern state. Under pressure from a disturbed democracy, the West was about to make the same mistake twice. A number of personal factors encouraged him in this view, not the least of which was his belief that monetary nationalism was just one aspect of a growing propensity to the use of force in international affairs. At the same time he was dismayed to see so many economists abandon "scientific objectivity" for the short-run preoccupations of the political arena. Innis thought of Keynes as a journalist rather than an economist.

The spectacle of the economist-turned-politician was profoundly disturbing to him. Following Veblen he had criticized price economics for its inability to handle values with scientific adequacy. As it became increasingly apparent to him that political bias was the foundation of economic doctrines and policies, he turned to the elaboration of a theory of value based on the determinants of public opinion. Financial institutions took shape in response to the physical characteristics of technique, and values were formed in response to the physical characteristics of the technique of communication. Technical constraints on talk created bias in its content. From this seminal notion he developed a new interpretation of the history of civilization.

During his last years he made an heroic attempt to trace the impact of changes in the media of communication on market commodity and time preferences. How were values related to techniques? How were they embodied in institutions? How had the physical characteristics of the means of communication reflected themselves in the spatial extension and duration of economic systems? He pursued these questions over a sufficient period to demonstrate the validity and usefulness of his insight, but no tidy answers were reached.

Taking Innis' work as a whole it can be summed up as an attempt to construct a new economic theory. The attempt led him through an exploration of the physical structure of capital to valuable insights into the role of institutions in economics and to a mature analysis of capital accumulation. It led him to develop a theory of value outside the concepts of price economics, but it did not lead him to a substitute for price economics itself.

James W. Carey (essay date 1967)

SOURCE: "Harold Adams Innis and Marshall McLuhan," in *The Antioch Review,* Vol. XXVII, No. 1, Spring, 1967, pp. 5-39.

[*In the following essay, Carey compares Innis's theories of communication with those of Marshall McLuhan.*]

Commenting on the abstruse and controversial scholarship of Harold Innis and Marshall McLuhan is a rather audacious and perhaps impertinent undertaking. It is also a thankless task. McLuhan has often argued that the attempt to analyze, classify, and criticize scholarship—the intent of my paper—is not only illegitimate; it also represents the dead hand of an obsolete tradition of scholarship. I am sensitive to treading forbidden waters in this paper. But I am content to let history or something else be the judge of what is the proper or only method of scholarship, as I at least am uncomfortable pronouncing on such weighty matters.

Despite the dangers in scrutinizing the work of Innis and McLuhan, I think students of the history of mass communication must assume the risks of analysis. Innis and McLuhan, alone among students of human society, make the history of the mass media central to the history of civilization at large. Both see the media not merely as technical appurtenances to society but as crucial determinants of the social fabric. For them, the history of the mass media is not just another avenue of historical research; rather it is another way of writing the history of Western civilization. Innis and McLuhan do not so much describe history as present a theory of history or, less grandiloquently, a theory of social change in the West. It is a theory which anchors social change in the transformations in the media of communication on which this civilization has been progressively dependent. Therefore, an assessment of the meaning and reasonableness of the positions they represent seems to me to be a principal task for students of the history of mass communication.

In this paper, I would like to suggest an interpretation of Innis and McLuhan and to compare the kinds of arguments they offer on the role of the mass media in social change. Second, I want to offer a critical commentary of their positions, principally directed at the relative merits of their arguments in organizing the historical material in question. Finally, I want to recommend a direction for future research on the role of the media in social change and to offer some reflections on the social meaning of the scholarship of Harold Innis and Marshall McLuhan.

Harold Adams Innis was a Canadian economist and historian who devoted most of his scholarly life to producing marvelously detailed studies of Canadian industries—the fur trading industry, the cod fisheries, the Canadian Pacific Railway, for example. During the last decade of his life (Innis died in 1952), he undertook an extensive analysis of all forms of human communication and produced two major works—*The Bias of Communication* and *Empire and Communications*—and two important collections of essays, *Changing Concepts of Time* and *Political Economy and the Modern State*. His interest in communications was not, however, independent of his concerns for economic history. Rather, the former grew out of the latter. In his studies of the economic history of Canada, Innis was confronted by two important questions: (1) What are the underlying causes of change in social organization, defined broadly to include both culture and social institutions? (2) What are the conditions which promote stability in any society? Stability here is defined as both the capacity to adapt to changing realities in politics and the economy and also as the capacity to preserve the integrity of culture, the continuity of attitude, sentiment, and morality upon which civilization is based. Further, Innis wanted to answer those questions in a manner that would capture not only the major currents of history in the West but also the eddies and tributaries, streams and backwaters of social change.[1]

Innis felt that the answer to his first question—the question of the source of social change—was to be found in technological innovation. He was, like McLuhan, a technological determinist, though unlike McLuhan a rather soft determinist. Innis and McLuhan agree that while there are various kinds of technology—military, industrial, administrative—these technologies were not equal in their impact on society or in their ontological status. For Innis, the technology of communication was central to all other technology. He does not make at all clear why this should be so. However, let me make this suggestion. There are presumably two reasons for the centrality of communications technology—one logical, one historical. Innis assumes that man stands in a unique, symbiotic relationship to his technology. In McLuhan's phrase, technology is literally an extension of man, as the ax is an extension of the hand, the wheel of the foot. Most instruments are attempts to extend man's physical capacity, a capacity shared with other animals. Communications technology, on the other hand, is an extension of thought, of consciousness, of man's unique perceptual capacities. Thus communication media, broadly used to include all modes of symbolic representation, are literally extensions of mind.

Innis also suggests that historically fundamental breakthroughs in technology are first applied to the process of communication. The age of mechanics was ushered in by the printing press, the age of electronics by the telegraph. The explanation for this historical fact Innis derived from a conception of society based upon a model of competition appropriated from economics and extended to all social institutions. And in this competitive model, competition for new means of communication was a principal axis of the competitive struggle. Innis argued that the available media of communication influence very strongly the forms of social organization that are possible. The media thus influence the kinds of human associations that can develop in any period. Because these patterns of association are not independent of the knowledge men have of themselves and others—indeed, consciousness is built on these associations—control of communications implies control of both consciousness and social organization. Thus, whenever a medium of communication and the groups which control the media have a hegemony in society, Innis assumes that a principal axis of competition will be the search for competing media of communication. New media are designed to undercut existing centers of power and to facilitate the creation of new patterns of association and the articulation of new forms of knowledge. I will return to this point later. Let me only note now that Innis assumed that disenfranchised groups in society would lead the search for new forms of technology in seeking to compete for some form of social power.

The bulk of Innis' work was devoted to analyzing the kinds of control inherent in communications media. He considered, as near as one can tell, all forms of communication from speech through printing, including what he took to be the four dominant pre-printing media—clay, papyrus, parchment, and paper. With each of these media he also considered the types of script employed and the kinds of writing instruments used. Innis argued that various stages of Western civilization could be characterized by the dominance of a particular medium of communication. The medium had a determinate influence on the form of social organization typical of the stage of society and on the character of the culture of that stage. Further, the succession of stages in Western civilization could be seen in terms of a competition between media of communication for dominance. The results of this competition among media progressively transformed the character of social institutions and the nature of culture.

I think it important to note Innis' emphasis on both culture and social organization. He was concerned not only with the ways in which culture and institutions were interrelated but also the sense in which they were *both* epiphenomena of communications technology. Usually the social history of the West takes either the route of August Comte, emphasizing the progressive transformation of culture from the theological to the metaphysical to the positivistic, or the route taken by Lewis Mumford, emphasizing the transformations in social organization from the tribe to the town to the city. Innis, however, attempts to marry these two traditions into a unified view of social change. Moreover, he attaches changes in both social organization and culture to changes in the technology of communication. The generality of Innis' argument is seldom recognized, I think, because of a failure to appreciate the meaning of the phrase "the bias of communication" and the dual sense in which he defines his two principal variables, space and time.

Innis argues that any given medium of communication is biased in terms of the control of time or space. Media which are durable and difficult to transport—parchment, clay, and stone—are time-binding or time-biased. Media which are light and less durable are space-binding or spatially biased. For example, paper and papyrus are space-binding, for they are light, easily transportable, can be moved across space with reasonable speed and great accuracy, and they thus favor administration over vast distance.

Any given medium will bias social organization, for it will favor the growth of certain kinds of interests and institutions at the expense of others and will also impose on these institutions a form of organization. Media which are space-binding facilitate and encourage the growth of empire, encourage a concern with expansion and with the present, and thus favor the hegemony of secular political authority. Space-binding media encourage the growth of the state, the military, and decentralized and expansionist institutions. Time-binding media foster concern with history and tradition, have little capacity for expansion of secular authority, and thus favor the growth of religion, of hierarchical organization, and of contractionist institutions. The hegemony of either religion or the state imposes a characteristic pattern on all secondary institutions, such as education, and also leads to a search for competing, alternative modes of communication to undercut this hegemony. Thus, the dynamic of social change resided in the search for alternative forms of communication alternately supporting the kingdom of God or man.

At the level of social structure, a time bias meant an emphasis upon religion, heirarchy, and contraction, whereas a space bias meant an emphasis upon the state, decentralization, and expansion. But the terms "time" and "space" also had a cultural meaning.

In cultural terms, time meant the sacred, the moral, the historical; space the present and the future, the technical and the secular. As media of communication favored the growth of certain kinds of institutions, it also assured the domination of the culture characteristic of those institutions. On the cultural level, his principal contrast was between the oral and written traditions. Let me try to develop the contrast.

Although speech is not the only means of communication in traditional societies, it certainly is the principal means. Traditional societies are organized in terms of, or are at least severely constrained by, certain features of speech. For example, spoken language can traverse only relatively short distances without being altered and distorted, giving rise to dialects. Speech not only moves over short distances but travels slowly compared with other means of communication. Speech also has a low capacity for storage; there is no way of preserving information except by storing it in the memories of individuals or by symbolizing it in some material form. Life in traditional societies must be collective, communal, and celebrative as the medium of communication requires it to be.

Innis argues that speech encourages the development of a society with a strong temporal bias, a society which focuses on the past and which emphasizes tradition, which attempts to conserve and preserve the existing stock of knowledge and values. Such societies are likely to have limited conceptions of space, conceptions restricted to the village or geographical area currently occupied by the tribe. Space beyond that is invested with magical qualities, frequently being the home of the gods; for example, cargo cults. While the mind of primitive man can traverse extraordinary reaches of time, it is radically limited in traversing space. The hegemony of speech is likely to also lead to magical beliefs in language. Words become icons, they do not represent things, they are themselves things. The care, nurture, and preservation of language is likely to occupy much collective energy of the society.

Oral cultures, then, are time-binding cultures. They have consequently a limited capacity for technical change. The imbalance toward time rooted in the available means of communication emphasizes the cohesion of people in the present by their "remembrances of things past." With media such as speech, Innis associated tradition, the sacred, and the institutionalization of magic and religion.

Speech as the dominant mode of communication gave rise to an oral tradition, a tradition that Innis not only described but admired. By an oral tradition Innis meant a "selection from the history of a people of a series of related events, culturally defined as significant, and their transmission from generation to generation." The recitation of artistic works within the oral tradition was a social ceremony which linked audiences to the past and celebrated their social cohesion in the present. While individual performers would modify an oral tradition to make it more servicable in present circumstances, they began with the tradition and thus became indissolubly linked to it.

Furthermore, the oral tradition was flexible and persistent. Linked as it was to the collective and communal life of a people, built into their linguistic habits and modes of symbolic expression, the oral tradition was difficult to destroy. Through endless repetition an oral tradition "created recognized standards and lasting moral and social institutions; it built up the soul of social organization and maintained their continuity. . . ."

Oral traditions and time-binding media led to the growth of a culture oriented toward a sacred tradition, which built consensus on the sharing of mutually affirmed and celebrated attitudes and values, and placed morals and metaphysics at the center of civilization.

Written traditions, in general, led to quite different cultures. They were usually space-binding and favored the growth of political authority and secular institutions and a culture appropriate to them. Let me warn you that Innis did not admire oral cultures and derogate written ones. Some of his language could easily lead one to that conclusion, but, as I hope to show, that was decidedly not the case.

Written traditions and their appropriate culture ground relations among men not on tradition but on attachment to secular authority. Rather than emphasizing the temporal relations among kinship, written tradition emphasizes spatial relations. Rather than emphasizing the past, it emphasizes the present and the future, particularly the future of empire. Rather than emphasizing knowledge grounded in moral order, it emphasizes the technical order and favors the growth of science and technical knowledge. Whereas the character of storage and reception of the oral tradition favor continuity over time, the written tradition favors discontinuity in time though continuity over space.

What Innis recognized was the hostility that seemed inevitably to develop between the written and the oral tradition. The innovation of writing would first lead to a recording of the oral tradition. It would thus freeze it and make it of interest to subsequent generations largely for antiquarian reasons. The written tradition, after its initial contact with the oral, would go its own way. It would favor change and innovation and progressive attenuation from the past as a residue of knowledge, values, and sentiment. The hostility between these traditions and between time-binding and space-binding media generally led to the creation of a monopoly of knowledge. He used the term monopoly in a straightforward economic sense. Very simply, Innis contended that the culture of the favored institution would infiltrate every aspect of social life and ultimately drive out, define as illegitimate, or radically transform competing traditions. Only knowledge that conformed to the concerns and cultural predispositions of the dominant medium would persist. In a written tradition, knowledge must be technical, secular, and future-oriented for it to be defined as legitimate or recognized as valid.

By now it should be obvious that Innis defined as the central problem of social science and social change the same problem which was the focus of Max Weber's work: the problem of authority. Innis wanted to know what, in general, determines the location of ultimate authority in a society and what will be recognizd as authoritative knowledge. His answer was this: That media of communication, depending on their bias, confer monopolies of authority and knowledge on the state, the technical order, and civil law or on religion, the sacred order, and moral law.[2]

Innis believed that an overemphasis or monopoly of either time or space, religion or the state, the moral or the technical, was the principal dynamic of the rise and fall of empire. Time and space were thus related as conjugant variables in which the progressive presence of one led to the progressive absence of the other. The bias toward time or space produced instability in society. A stable society was possible only with the development of mechanisms that preserved both temporal and spatial orientations, that preserved competition between religion and the state, and that preserved independence and tension between the moral and the technical. In *The Bias of Communication* Innis commented that

> in western civilization a stable society is dependent on an appreciation of a proper balance between the concepts of space and time. We are concerned with control over vast areas of space but also over vast stretches of time. We must appraise civilization in relation to its territory and in relation to its duration. The character of the medium of communication tends to create a bias in civilization favorable to an overemphasis on the time concept or on the space concept and only at rare intervals are the biases offset by the influence of another medium and stability achieved.

Classical Greece was such a rare interval. The relative isolation of Greece from the older civilizations of Egypt and the Near East enabled her to develop an oral tradition. The written tradition was slowly introduced into Greece from these neighboring cultures, but it did not destroy the oral tradition. The tradition was committed to writing, but the oral tradition continued to flourish. For example, the dialogue remained the principal instrument of Greek culture, and an oral literature constituted the common moral consciousness. The written tradition with its spatial emphasis encouraged the growth of political authority and allowed Greece to deal with problems of administration. Eventually, writing triumphed over the oral tradition in the latter part of the fifth centry B.C., and the spatial bias gave rise to a divisive individualism.

Generalizing from the experience of classical Greece, Innis argued that a healthy society requires competition not only in the marketplace but also in ideas, traditions, and institutions. Typically, media favor the development of cultural and institutional monopolies. Unless media favoring time and space exist as independent traditions offsetting and checking the biases of one another, the society will be dominated by a narrow monopoly. In such biased states, politics becomes sacralized or religion secularized; science destroys morality or morality emasculates science; tradition gives way to the notion of progress or chronic change obliterates tradition.

The history of the modern West, Innis argues, is the history of a bias of communication and a monopoly of knowledge founded on print. In one of his most quoted statements, Innis characterized modern Western history as beginning with temporal organization and ending with spatial organization. The introduction of printing attacked the temporal monopoly of the medieval church. Printing fostered the growth of nationalism and empire; it favored the extension of society in space. It encouraged the growth of bureaucracy and militarism, science and secular authority. Printing infiltrated all institutions, being the major force in creating what is currently celebrated as "the secular society." Not only did print destroy the oral tradition but it also drove underground the principal concerns of the oral tradition—morals, values, and metaphysics. While print did not destroy religion, it did, as Max Weber has argued, transform religion to meet the needs of the state and economy. Ultimately, the obsession with space, with the nation, with the moment, exposed the relativity of all values and led Western civilization, in Innis' eyes, to the brink of nihilism. The death of the oral tradition, the demise of concern with time, not only shifted the source of authority from the church to the state and of ultimate knowledge from religion to science; it also insisted on a transformation of religious concerns and language from the theological and sacred to the political and secular.

Innis viewed the rampaging nationalism of the twentieth century with anger and anguish, attitudes not untypical of contemporary intellectuals. But his emotion-charged writing should not obscure his central argument. The primary effect of changes in communication media is on the form of social organization that can be supported. Social organization produces a characteristic culture which constitutes the predispositions of individuals. The centrality of communication media to both culture and social structure implies that the principal axis of change, of the rise and fall of empire, will be alternations in the technologies of communcation upon which society is principally reliant.

There are many similarities between the thought of Innis and that of Marshall McLuhan. Although I do not intend to obscure those similarities, I would like to emphasize, at least in this paper, some significant points of difference. The question I am asking is this: What is absolutely central to Innis' argument and how does it compare with the central notion in McLuhan's work? Although McLuhan has occasionally characterized his work as an extension of Innis', I want to suggest that McLuhan has taken a relatively minor but recurring theme of Innis' work (perhaps only a suggestion) and made it central to his entire argument. Conversely, McLuhan has neglected or ignored the principal argument developed by Innis.

Both Innis and McLuhan agree that historically "the things on which words were written down count more than the words themselves"; that is, the medium is the message. Starting from this proposition, they engage in quite different kinds of intellectual book-keeping, however, and are seized by quite different kinds of implications.

Both McLuhan and Innis assume the centrality of communication technology; where they differ is in the principal kinds of effects they see deriving from this technology. Whereas Innis sees communication technology principally affecting social organization and culture, McLuhan sees its principal effect on sensory organization

and thought. McLuhan has much to say about perception and thought but little to say about institutions; Innis says much about institutions and little about perception and thought.

While McLuhan is intellectually linked to Innis, I think he can be more clearly and usefully tied to a line of speculation in socio-linguistics usually referred to as the Sapir-Whorf hypothesis.

The Sapir-Whorf hypothesis proposes that the language a speaker uses has a determining influence on the character of his thought. While it is a truism that men think with and through language, Edward Sapir and Benjamin Lee Whorf proposed that the very structure of reality—if I may use that grandiose and overworked phrase—is presented to individuals through language. When a person acquires a language he not only acquires a way of talking but also a way of seeing, a way of organizing experience, a way of discriminating the real world. Language, so the argument goes, has built into its grammar and lexicon the very structure of perception. Individuals discriminate objects and events in terms of the vocabulary provided by language. Further, individuals derive their sense of time, their patterns of classifications, their categories for persons, their perception of action, in terms of the tenses, the genders, the pronouns, the pluralizations that are possible in their language. This argument, then, largely reduces the structure of perception and thought to the structure of language.

McLuhan adopts the form of argument provided by the Sapir-Whorf hypothesis with two important modifications. First, he adopts a quite unorthodox characterization of the grammar of a language. Second, he extends the "grammatical analysis" to modes of communication such as print and television which are normally not treated as types of languages.

McLuhan does not view the grammar of a medium in terms of the formal properties of language, the parts of speech or morphemes, normally utilized in such an analysis. Instead, he argues that the grammar of a medium derives from the particular mixture of the senses that an individual characteristically uses in the utilization of the medium. For example, language—or better, speech—is the first of the mass media. It is a device for externalizing thought and for fixing and sharing perceptions. As a means of communication, speech elicits a particular orchestration of the sense. While speech is an oral phenomenon and gives rise to "ear-oriented cultures" (cultures in which people more easily believe what they hear than what they see), oral communication synthesizes or brings into play other sensual faculties. For example, in conversation men are aware not only of the sound of words but also of the visual properties of the speaker and the setting of the tactile qualities of various elements of the setting, and even certain olfactory properties of the person and the situation. These various faculties constitute parallel and simultaneous modes of communication, and thus McLuhan concludes that oral cultures synthesize these various modalities, elicit them all or bring them all into play in a situation utilizing all the sensory apparatus of the person. Oral cultures, then, involve the simultaneous interplay of sight, sound, touch, and smell and thus produce, in McLuhan's view, a depth of involvement in life as the principal communications medium—oral speech—simultaneously activates all the sensory faculties through which men acquire knowledge and share feeling.

However, speech is not the only mass medium, nor must it necessarily be the dominant mass medium. In technologically advanced societies, print, broadcasting, and film can replace speech as the dominant mode through which knowledge and feeling are communicated. In such societies speech does not disappear, but it assumes the characteristics of the dominant medium. For example, in literate communities oral traditions disappear and the content of spoken communication is the written tradition. Speech no longer follows its own laws. Rather it is governed by the laws of the written tradition. This means not only that the "content" of speech is what has previously been written but that the cadence and imagery of everyday speech is the cadence and imagery of writing. In literate communities, men have difficulty believing that the rich, muscular, graphic, almost multidimensional speech of Oscar Lewis' illiterate Mexican peasants was produced by such "culturally deprived" persons. But for McLuhan speech as an oral tradition, simultaneously utilizing many modes of communication, is almost exclusively the province of the illiterate.

McLuhan starts from the biological availability of parallel modes for the production and reception of messages. These modes—sight, touch, sound, and smell—do not exist independently but are interdependent with one another. Thus, to alter the capacity of one of the modes changes the total relations among the senses and thus alters the way in which individuals organize experience and fix perception. All this is clear enough. To remove one sense from a person leads frequently to the strengthening of the discriminatory powers of the other senses and thus to a rearrangement of not only the senses but of the kind of experience a person has. Blindness leads to an increasing reliance on and increasing power of smell and touch as well as hearing as modes of awareness. Loss of hearing particularly increases one's reliance on sight. But, McLuhan argues, the ratios between the senses and the power of the senses is affected by more than physical impairment or, to use his term, amputation. Media of communication also lead to the amputation of the senses. Media of communication also encourage the over-reliance on one sense faculty to the impairment or disuse of others. And thus, media of communication impart to persons a particular way of organizing experience and a particular way of knowing and understanding the world in which they travel.

Modes of communication, including speech, are, then, devices for fixing perception and organizing experience. Print, by its technological nature, has built into it a grammar for organizing experience, and its grammar is found in the particular ratio of sensory qualities it elicits in its users. All communications media are, therefore, extensions of man, or, better, are extensions of some mix of the sensory capacities of man. Speech is such an extension and thus the first mass medium. As an extension of man, it casts individuals in a unique, symbiotic relation to the dominant mode of communication in a culture. This symbiosis is not restricted to speech but extends to whatever medium of communication dominates a culture. This extension is by way of projecting certain sensory capacities of the individual. As I have mentioned, speech involves an extension and development of all the senses. Other media, however, are more partial in their appeal to the senses. The exploitation of a particular communications technology fixes particular sensory relations in members of society. By fixing such a relation, it determines a society's world view; that is, it stipulates a characteristic way of organizing experience. It thus determines the forms of knowledge, the structure of perception, and the sensory equipment attuned to absorb reality.

Media of communication, consequently, are vast social metaphors that not only transmit information but determine what is knowledge; that not only orient us to the world but tell us what kind of world exists; that not only excite and delight our sense but, by altering the ratio of sensory equipment that we use, actually change our character.

This is, I think, the core of McLuhan's argument. It can be most conveniently viewed as an attempt, albeit a creative and imaginative attempt, to extend the Sapir-Whorf hypothesis to include all forms of social communication.

Let me attempt to illustrate this abstruse argument with McLuhan's analysis of print. Print, the dominant means of communication in the West, depends on phonetic writing. Phonetic writing translated the oral into the visual; that is, it took sounds and translated them into visual symbols. Printing enormously extended and speeded up this process of translation, turning societies historically dependent upon the ear as the principal source of knowledge into societies dependent upon the eye. Print cultures are cultures in which seeing is believing, in which oral traditions are translated into written form, in which men have difficulty believing or remembering oral speech—names, stories, legends—unless they first see it written. In short, in print cultures knowledge is acquired and experience is confirmed by sight: as they say, by seeing it in writing. Men confirm their impressions of Saturday's football game by reading about it in Sunday morning's paper.

Besides making us dependent on the eye, printing imposes a particular logic on the organization of visual experience. Print organizes reality into discrete, uniform, harmonious, causal relations. The visual arrangement of the printed page becomes a perceptual model by which all reality is organized. The mental set of print—the desire to break things down into elementary units (words), the tendency to see reality in discrete units, to find causal relations and linear serial order (left to right arrangement of the page), to find orderly structure in nature (the orderly geometry of the printed page)—is transferred to all other social activities. Thus, science and government, art and architecture, work and education become organized in terms of the implicit assumption built into the dominant medium of communication.

Moreover, print encourages individualism and specialization. To live in an oral culture, one acquires knowledge only in contact with other people, in terms of communal activities. Printing, however, allows individuals to withdraw, to contemplate and meditate outside of communal activities. Print thus encourages privatization, the lonely scholar, and the development of private, individual points of view.

McLuhan thus concludes that printing detribalizes man. It removes him from the necessity of participating in a tightly knit oral culture. In a notion apparently taken from T. S. Eliot, McLuhan contends that print disassociates the senses, separating sight from sound; encourages a private and withdrawn existence; and supports the growth of specialization.

Above all, print leads to nationalism, for it allows for the visual apprehension of the mother tongue and through maps a visual apprehension of the nation. Printing allows the vernacular to be standardized and the mother tongue to be universalized through education.

While the book ushered in the age of print, developments such as newspapers and magazines have only intensified the implications of print: extreme visual nationalism, specialist technology and occupations, individualism and private points of view.

By such argument McLuhan insists that the meaning and effect of any communications innovation is to be found in the way it structures thought and perception. The excitement which currently surrounds McLuhan derives from his extension of this argument to the newer media of communication, particularly television, and the effect these newer media have on the venerated tradition of print and on the mental life of contemporary man.

For McLuhan, the civilization based on print is dead. A science based on its assumptions, which searches for causal relations, encourages orderly, non-contradictory argument, fosters the specialization and compartmentalization of knowledge, is obsolete. Education which relies on the book and the lecture—itself merely reading from written script—and the traditional modes of sciences is likewise obsolete.

Print culture was doomed, so McLuhan argues, by the innovation of telegraphy, the first of the electronic media. Radio further undercut the hegemony of print, but the triumph of electronic communication over print awaited the permeation of the entire society by television. We are now observing, McLuhan concludes, the first generation weaned on television for whom the book and printing are secondary, remote, and ephemeral kinds of media. It is not only that television, as Storm Jameson has recently argued, leads to a devaluation of the written word. Television is not only another means for transmitting information; it is also a radically new way of organizing experience. Unlike print, television is not merely an eye medium but utilizes a much broader range of sensory equipment. That television marries sight and sound is obvious; but McLuhan also argues that television is a tactile medium as well. Television, as a result of the scanning system on which it operates, is capable of conveying or eliciting a sense of touch. Thus, in the apprehension of television not only the eye but the ear and the hand are brought into play. Television re-orchestrates the senses; it engages, if you will, the whole man, the entire range of sensory qualities of the person.

Moreover, television is, in one of McLuhan's inimitable phrases, a cool medium. By this McLuhan means only that television, like the cartoon and line drawing, is low in information. You don't merely watch a television screen. You engage it; you are forced to add information to complete the message. The capacity of the screen to transmit information is determined by the number of lines in the scanning system. In American television the scanning system is particularly low, 525 lines, and thus the medium is low in information relative to say, movies. Thus the viewer must get involved; he must fill in auditory, visual, and tactile cues for the message on the screen to be completed. Because television appeals to all the senses, because it is a cool or active, participational medium in front of which a viewer cannot remain passive, a culture in which television is the dominant medium will produce a person characteristically different than will a culture based on print.

McLuhan observes we are now witnessing in maturity the first generation who were suckled on television, who acquired the conventions of television long before it acquired traditional print literacy. The generational gap we now observe by contrasting the withdrawn, private, specializing student of the fifties with the active, involved, generalist student of the sixties McLuhan rests at the door of television. For the characteristic differences in these generations are paralleled by the differences between print and television as devices of communication. The desire of students for involvement and participation, for talking rather than reading, for seminars rather than lectures, for action rather than reflection, in short for participation and involvement rather than withdrawal and observation he ascribes to the re-orchestration of the senses provoked by television.

The conflict between generations of which we are now so acutely aware is ultimately a conflict between a generation bred on the book and a generation bred on the tube and related forms of electronic communication. The generational gap involves much more than politics and education, of course. In every area of life McLuhan observes youth asserting forms of behavior, demanding kinds of experience, which engage the total self. Dance and dress, music and hair styles, must not only have a "look"; they must also have a "sound" and above all a "touch." They must appeal to all the senses simultaneously. It is not only that youth wants experience; it wants experience that unifies rather than dissociates the senses. Moreover, in the new styles of literature which destroy all the conventions of print, in the new argots which destroy all the conventions of traditional grammar, in the new styles of political action which demean the traditionally radical forms of ideology and organization, in the demands for change in education, in music, in art, in dance, in dress, McLuhan sees the re-tribalization of man restoring him to the integrated condition of the oral culture in which the sensual capacities of men are again made whole.

This re-tribalization presumably involves the extension in space of the entire nervous system. Sight, hearing, and tactility derive from a nervous system originally contained within the skin. Each of the media has in turn extended these mechanisms, these aspects of the nervous system, beyond the skin. They have externalized them. The book and camera extend the eye, radio and the listening device extend the ear, television extends not only the eye and the ear but also the hand. Electric circuitry in general represents an extension of the entire nervous system. Think, for example, of the imagery of the computer with its network of wires and nodes linked to a television system. This is the sense in which communications media are extensions of man—extending with the aid of the computer the entire sensory and neurological system of the person in space, heightening the capacity of the organism to receive and digest information, literally turning the person now extended by his technology into an information processing system.

It is through such an analysis that McLuhan arrives at or expresses his central point: every medium of communication possesses a logic or grammar which constitutes a set of devices for organizing experience. The logic or grammar of each medium which dominates an age impresses itself on the users of the medium, thus dictating what is defined as truth and knowledge. Communication media, then, determine not only what one thinks about but literally how one thinks.

In the exposition of this notion McLuhan, of course, treats more than print and television. These are merely the endpoints in an exposition that includes commentary on films, radio, cartoons, light bulbs, political candidates, and virtually every other technique and folly of man. But in each case he attempts to determine the grammar inherent in the technology of the medium. While McLuhan normally defines the grammar of a medium in terms of the sense ratios it elicits, he frequently resorts to the more simplified method of designating media as "hot" or "cold." A hot medium is one that presents a lot of information in one sense; it bombards the receiver with information or, in another favorite phrase, is in high definition. A cool medium, or one in low definition, is a medium that presents relatively little information; the re-

ceiver must complete the image, must add values to what is presented to him and is thus more involving or participational. The halftone photo in four colors is visually hot; the cartoon is visually cool. Print is a hot medium, television a cool medium. The quality of having temperature applies also to persons and cultures, dance and dress, autos and sports. Temperature, then, is another way of designating grammar. However, it is the least satisfactory of all McLuhan's concepts and arguments. This is unfortunate, because for most critics it is the terms "hot" and "cool" which are taken to be McLuhan's principal contribution to the study of media, and a lot of unanswerable critical fire can be heaped on McLuhan at this point. The terms "hot" and "cool" are applied in very haphazard ways. Media that are hot one minute seem to be cool another. It is impossible to tell if temperature is an absolute property of a medium or whether a medium is hot or cool relative only to some other medium. And the classification of media into these categories seems to be always quite arbitrary.

McLuhan's argument does not, however, stand or fall on the usage of the terms "hot" and "cool." One can simply agree that while media do possess an inherent grammar, the exact structure and logic of this grammar has not, as yet, been particularly well worked out. Some latitude should be allowed McLuhan at this point anyway. He obviously is doing a good deal of experimenting with the classification of media. There is little resemblance between the classification one finds in the "first edition" of *Understanding Media* (a report to the United States Office of Education, 1960) and that in the McGraw-Hill edition currently in circulation. His argument must, I think, be assessed in terms of its most general point: men stand in a symbiotic relation to all media, and consequently the dominant mode of communication dictates the character of perception and through perception the structure of mind.

At this point I would like to make some critical notes on the arguments that have been presented. My only reluctance in doing so is that Innis and McLuhan present rather convenient targets for criticism if only because their arguments are so unconventional. Also, criticism, let us be reminded, is easy. It is still harder to write novels than to write reviews. Further, not only the structure of McLuhan's argument but also his current popularity stand as an incautious invitation to criticism and thus most critical fire that I might muster would inevitably be aimed at McLuhan. Marshall McLuhan is, after all, not only a social analyst; he is also a prophet, a phenomenon, a happening, a social movement. His work has given rise to an ideology—*mcluhanisme*—and a mass movement producing seminars, clubs, art exhibits, and conferences in his name.

Besides, I'm convinced that a technical critique of McLuhan is a rather useless undertaking. If Robert Merton cannot dent his armor by pointing out inconsistencies in his argument and lacunae in his observations, I'm quite sure that my own lesser intellectual luminosity shall have little effect on McLuhan or his devotees. I am thinking here of such inconsistencies as the fact that while he is a serious critic of traditional logic and rationality, his argument is mechanistic, built upon linear causality, and illustrative of all the deficiencies of this type of analysis. His terminology is ill-defined and inconsistently used and maddeningly obtuse. More seriously, he has a view of mind, directly adopted from the *tabula rasa* of John Locke, that is not only simple-minded but contradicted by much of the work currently being done in linguistics, psychology, and psychotherapy. But I sense that such criticism is analogous to criticizing Christianity by pointing out contradictions in the Bible.

McLuhan is beyond criticism not only because he defines such activity as illegitimate but also because his work does not lend itself to critical commentary. It is a mixture of whimsy, pun, and innuendo. These things are all right in themselves, but unfortunately one cannot tell what he is serious about and what is mere whimsy. His sentences are not observations or assertions but, in his own language, "probes." Unfortunately, a probe is a neutral instrument about which one can say nothing but congratulate its inquisitiveness. One may resist his probes or yield to their delights, but to quarrel with them is rather beside the point.

Despite these disclaimers, a manageable enterprise remains. I would like to judge McLuhan's argument not in absolute or universal terms but only in relation to the work of Innis. If we can for the moment grant the central assumption on the role of communications technology in social change, who has presented us with the more powerful and useful argument? This is a question both manageable and germane to the paper. Less germane but at least of importance to me is the concluding question I would like to raise: what is it that makes McLuhan an acceptable prophet of our times? I think the answer to this question will also shed some important light on the argument of Innis.

I have suggested that Innis argued that the most visible and important effects of media technology were on social organization and through social organization on culture. Radio and television, I assume Innis would argue, are light media that quickly and easily transmit large amounts of information. Moreover, electronic signals, while highly perishable, are difficult to control. Unlike print, electronic media do not recognize national boundaries, as the Canadians have discovered. Thus, the effect of the electronic media is to extend the spatial bias of print, to make new forms of human association possible, and to foreshorten one's sense of time. As spatially biased media, radio and television, even when used by religious institutions, contribute to the growing hegemony of secular authority and to the extension of political influence in space. Further, they have contributed to the weakening of tradition and to the secularization of religion. Or so Innis might have it.

McLuhan treats quite a different effect of the media—the effect of the media not on social organization but on sensory organization. As I have previously mentioned, Innis and McLuhan do treat both kinds of effects. The effect of the media on sensory organization is a minor but persistent theme in Innis' writings.[3] McLuhan also treats the effects of media on social organization, as the previous discussion of nationalism, specialization, science, and education illustrated. However, the major direction and thus the implication of the two arguments is quite different. Moreover, McLuhan, deliberately or otherwise, confuses these two quite different effects of media technology. Much of his evidence is not directed at nor does it support his analysis of the sensory bias of media. Rather it supports Innis' claim for the institutional or organizational bias of media. For example, xerography, a process which very much interests McLuhan, is an important innovation in communication. While the innovation is based upon discoveries in electronic technology, its usual product nonetheless is the orderly, linear type of the printed page. The effect of xerography is not on sensory organization. However, by increasing the rate of speed at which information can be transmitted and reproduced, by allowing for the rapid recombination of printed materials, xerography does encourage the creation of novel vehicles of communication and novel groups of readers. That is, xerography encourages or at least permits certain structural reorganizations of social groups. Developments in offset printing have a similar effect.

My argument is simply that the most visible effects of communications technology are on social organization and not on sensory organization. Much of McLuhan's evidence can be more plausibly, directly, and productively used in support of the form of argument offered by Innis. I will subsequently return to this point. Here I much want to suggest that Innis provides a more plausible accounting of the principal phenomena in question and is of greater usefulness to students of the history of mass communication. My preferences for Innis are partly aesthetic; they stem partly from a simple aversion to much of what McLuhan represents. In addition I feel that Innis' argument will be ultimately productive of more significant scholarship. Finally, I feel that McLuhan's position awaits the same fate as the Sapir-Whorf hypothesis to which it is so closely tied. The Sapir-Whorf hypothesis, while it is a perfectly plausible notion, has never turned out to be productive of much insight or research or to have particularly advanced the study of language and perception.

The same fate awaits McLuhan, I fear, and stems from an argumentative similarity between the positions. For McLuhan states his case on very general grounds and defends it on very narrow grounds. Because he views the effect of the media as principally acting on the senses, his entire argument ultimately rests on the narrow grounds of the psychology of perception. This is, I think, a very weak foundation to support such a vast superstructure. This is not only because many of his comments on the psychology of perception are highly questionable, but also because given what we know about the complexity of behavior, it is hard to understand how such a vast range of social phenomena are to be so simply explained. When McLuhan is writing about the oral tradition and about print, areas where he is backed by the extensive scholarship of Innis, his work has a cogency and integration and is sensitive to the complexity of the problems at hand (for example, in large portions of *The Gutenberg Galaxy*). When he probes beyond these shores into the world of television and the computer, the water gets very muddy indeed, for here he attempts to explain every twitch in contemporary society on the basis of the sensory reorganization brought about by the media. I do not have the time, nor the knowledge, to examine McLuhan's theory of perception. However, a couple of problems should be pointed out.[4] The phenomenon of sensory closure upon which McLuhan's theory is built is a very primitive perceptual mechanism. It is found in all experiments on perception, though not always in predictable ways. Moreover, the gestalt movement in psychology was based upon the operation of this mechanism, though it was largely limited to the study of visual closure. An obvious strength of McLuhan's argument is his isolation of this primitive and important perceptual phenomenon and his generalization of the phenomenon beyond visual closure to include the relations among all the senses. However, the assumption that the pattern of sensory closure is dictated by the structure of the media seems to be an unnecessary and unwarranted oversimplification.

For example, McLuhan severely overestimates the inflexibility of media of communication. While any given medium confronts an artist with certain inherent constraints, media still allow wide latitude for innovation and artistic manipulation. McLuhan does not consider, for example, that any medium can be used, in any historical period, either discursively or presentationally. Speech and writing, while they have a bias toward discursive presentation, can also be used presentationally. It is difficult to imagine why McLuhan does not utilize the distinction between presentational and discursive forms, a distinction of some importance in modern aesthetic theory.[5] Elements in a presentational form have no individuated meaning but take on meaning only in relation to the whole. Elements in a discursive form have individuated meaning and the elements can be combined by formal rules. Ordinary language is highly discursive, but it can be used presentationally. And "this is the distinguishing mark of poetry. The significance of a poetic symbol can be appreciated only in the context of the entire poem."

The same can be said of other forms. A given medium of communication may favor discursive presentation or the presentation of perceptual gestalts, but they can be and are manipulated in either genre. These media are, of course, constaining forces: they limit and control to some degree the expressive capacities of men. But the history of these forms is the history of attempts to overcome the deficiencies seemingly inherent in media of communication, to make the media bend to thought and imagination rather than allowing thought and imagination to be imprisoned by them. Thus, metaphor and simile, incongruity and hyperbole, personification and irony, are all devices, imaginative and productive devices, for overcoming the formal constraints of speech and writing. Similarly, while print, radio and television, and movies have inherent technological constraints, artists within these media have constantly struggled to overcome the limitations of the form through invention of new modes of symbolic representation. Think only of the history of film editing.

While McLuhan frequently excludes artists from the laws of perceptual determinism, he does not exclude audiences. However, I want to suggest that devices such as metaphor, simile, and personification are used not only by artists but are part of the linguistic repertoire of every five-year-old child. They are devices through which all of us attempt to overcome the inherent constraints of speech. There is, I suspect, much more freedom in perception and invention in everyday communication than McLuhan is willing to admit. To propose the audience as an empty vessel, a black box, that has no significant autonomous existence but is, instead, filled or wired up by sources exclusively external to the self is not only to deny an enormous amount of everyday evidence but also to casually dismiss a significant amount of reasonably sound scientific evidence. The empty organism view of the self is, I think, not only pernicious but also unsupportable from the evidence at hand on perception.

But the most important criticism to make of McLuhan is that much of the argument he wants to make and most of the contemporary phenomena he wants to explain—particularly the conflict between generations—can be more effectively handled within the framework provided by Innis. Furthermore, the utilization of the perspective of Innis opens up, I think, a number of important and researchable questions and puts the argument once more in a historical context.

In this final section let me tentatively attempt to bring Innis' argument up to date; that is, to extend it from the early 1950's, where he left it, into the 1960's. You will remember that Innis argued that Western history began with temporal bias and was ending with spatial bias. I want to suggest that contemporary developments in the electronic media have intensified this spatial bias. Electronic media, particularly with the innovation of satellite broadcasting, increasingly transcend all national boundaries, thereby weakening nationalism or at least tending to undercut the parochial limitations of national identifications. Further, such media are a potent force in generating a more universal, world-wide culture which is urban, secular, and, in Innis' terms, unstable.

Let me put it this way. Among primitive societies and in earlier stages of Western history, relatively small discontinuities in space led to vast differences in culture and social organization. Tribal societies separated by a hundred miles could have entirely different forms of economic, political, and religious life and grossly dissimilar systems of expressive symbolism, myth, and ritual. However, within these societies there was a great continuity of culture and social structure over generations. Forms of life changed slowly, of course, and the attitudes, hopes, fears, and aspirations of a boy of fourteen and a man of sixty were remarkably similar. This does not mean there were no conflicts between age groups in such societies. Such conflicts are probably inevitable if only because of biological changes accompanying aging. However, the conflict occurred within a system of shared attitudes and values and within a system of mutual dependencies across age groups. Such societies were based on an oral tradition with a strong temporal bias. The continuity of culture was maintained by a shared, collective system of ritual and by the continuity of passage rites marking off the entrance of individuals into various stages of the life cycle. In such a world, then, there were vast differences between societies but relatively little variation between generations within a given society. In Innis' terms, temporal media produce vast continuity in time and great discontinuity in space.

The spatial bias of modern media, initiated by print but radically extended by film and the electronic media, has reversed the relations between time and space. Space in the modern world progressively disappears as a differentiating factor. As space becomes more continuous, regional variations in culture and social structure become ground down. Further, as I have already suggested and as other modern writers have persuasively argued, the rise of a world-wide urban civilization built upon the speed and extensiveness of travel and electronic media have progressively diminished—though they have come nowhere near eliminating—spatial, transnational variation in culture and social structure. It is this fact which has led Claude Levi-Strauss to re-echo the traditional keen of the anthropologist that primitive societies must be intensively studied now because they are rapidly disappearing.

If in fact the spatial bias of contemporary media does lead to a progressive reduction of regional variation within nations and trans-national variation between nations, one must not assume that differences between groups are being obliterated as some mass society theorists characterize the process of homogenization. As Levi-Strauss has argued, there may be a principle of diversity built into the species or, from our standpoint, built into the organization of man's communication. I am suggesting that the axis of diversity shifts from a spatial or structural dimension to a temporal or generational dimension. If in primitive societies time is continuous and space discontinuous, in modern societies as space becomes continuous time becomes discontinuous. In what seems like an ironic twist of language, spatially biased media obliterate space while temporally biased media obliterate time. The spatial bias of modern media, which have eliminated many spatial variations in culture and social structure, have simultaneously intensified the differences between generations within the same society. The differences in modern society between a boy of fourteen and a man of sixty—differences in language and values, symbols and meanings—are enormous. It is modern societies that face the problem of generations. It is

not only that conflict across age groups continues but there are gross discontinuities between generations in culture and symbols, perhaps best symbolized by the phrase, "Don't trust anyone over thirty."[6] This inversion in the relation of time and space in contemporary society seems to me a logical extension of Innis' argument. The inversion depends on the observation that spatially biased media obliterate space and lead men to live in a non-spatial world. Simultaneously, such media fragment time and make it progressively discontinuous. Temporal media, on the other hand, obliterate time, lead men to live in a non-temporal world, but fragment space.

I think it is important to remember that Innis argued that media possessed a bias or a predisposition toward time or space. He was not arguing for some simple mono-causality. Thus, if generations have become an increasingly important axis of diversity, in modern society, the causes include factors other than the media but to which the media are linked in a syndrome. I cannot, of course, attempt to trace out all such factors here, but a couple should be mentioned if only for their suggestive value. The importance of generations and the phenomena of generational discontinuity is linked most directly to the rate of technical change. In traditional societies, societies that change very slowly, the old are likely to be venerated as the repositories of the oral tradition and, consequently, as the storage banks of tribal wisdom. In societies such as ours, where knowledge and technique change very rapidly, the old are not likely to be so venerated. It is the young, the bearers of the new techniques and knowledge, that are likely to have both the power and the prestige. As the transmission of this knowledge is in the educational system, it is in this institution that generational discontinuities are likely to become most apparent. Also, because rapidly changing technical knowledge is difficult to acquire beyond school, the old are likely to be continually threatened by competition from the young, to be subject to fairly early obsolescence, and conflicts between generations bearing different knowledge and different values are likely to become a fact of life in all institutions.

This conflict is muted and disguised somewhat by the reorganization of the age composition of society. Some 40 per cent of the population is now under twenty, and within the year 50 per cent of the population will be under twenty-five. With the rapid expansion of the economy and institutions such as education, the young overwhelm older generations merely by numbers, and thus the intensity of the conflict is frequently masked by the ease of the political solutions. One thus must not discount the sheer fact of larger numbers in younger generations in heightening our awareness of generational discontinuity. The proportion of youth in the total population is also intensified by the progressive lengthening of adolescence; that is, one is young much longer today than in previous centuries.

Finally, the weakening of tradition caused not only by the media but also by the pace of technical change and progressive dominance of the educational system in the socialization process intensifies, I think, generational discontinuity. I am led to this argument by the belief that structural elements in the society are less able to provide useful and stable identity patterns to youth. Religious, ethnic, regional, and class identifications are weakening, and they are identifications which are *not* temporal in character. As religious and ethnic traditions weaken, generational identity becomes more important as a means of placing oneself and organizing one's own self-conception. This is true not only in the society at large but also in all subordinate institutions. The importance of generational identity is enhanced by the decline of ritual and passage rites which formerly served as devices for confirming and symbolizing structural identity. In addition, these structural identities simply come into conflict with one another, they counterpoint, and the young are frequently led to reject all past identities and seize upon membership in a generation as the key to understanding what is happening to them. This is a phenomenon Erik Erikson has usefully analyzed under the label the "totalism" of youth.

I am suggesting that generations are becoming more important sources of solidarity than other social groups in spite of Harold Rosenberg's observation that being a member of an age group is the lowest form of solidarity. The spread of a world-wide urban civilization built upon rapid and ephemeral means of communication ultimately means that individuals of the same age in Warsaw, Moscow, Tokyo, and New York sense a membership in a common age group and feel they have more in common with one another than with individuals older and younger within their own societies. This is a phenomenon which Innis did not anticipate. When Innis spoke of competition to establish a monopoly of knowledge, he normally was thinking of competition coming from institutions or structural groups: competition from the clergy, politicians, or the middle classes. Similarly, when other scholars have spoken of the role of groups in social change, they have normally thought of structural groups such as the burghers, the aristocracy, or the Jews. The implication of my suggestion is that the bearers of social change are increasingly age groups or generations rather than structural groups. Instead of groups representing individuals of all ages bound together by a common structural characteristic such as religion, race, or occupation, the most important groups of the future will be those of a common age who are structurally variegated. A generational group finds its solidarity in a common age even though some of its members are Catholic, some Jewish, some Protestant, some northerners, some southerners, some middle class, some working class. If this is correct, then political conflict, to choose just one example, which we have normally thought of in structural terms as conflict between regions, classes, and religions becomes focused instead around generations. If I correctly interpret the behavior of Robert Kennedy, he is aware of the phenomenon.

Now, unfortunately, things are neither as neat, as simple, or as true as I have painted them in these pages. There are still strong differences within generations. One must speak of generations of musicians and novelists, physicists and sociologists, northerners and southerners, Catholics and Jews. Obviously, one has to pay attention to the intersection of structural variables such as class and generational variables or the entire analysis quickly slides into a tautology. But I do think that in modern society generations become more important in all spheres of life. There is a competition to name generations, to symbolize them, to characterize the meaning of a generation. There is a competition within and between generations to choose the culture by which the generation shall be known. Further, there is competition to impose the culture of a generation on the entire society. And this, of course, is what Innis meant by a monopoly of knowledge. It was only a few years ago that David Riesman was suggesting that the media, particularly television, were devices for imposing the culture of the middle class on the entire society. Let me merely suggest that the media, particularly television, are devices by which the culture of youth is imposed on the entire society. In the competition to determine whose culture shall be the official culture and whose values the official norms, the axis of conflict is between generations.

These perhaps over-long notes on the sociology of generations illustrate, I hope, Innis' central point: the principal effect of media technology is on social organization. The capacity of Innis to deal with such phenomena in a reasonably direct and clear way leads me to prefer his characterization of media effects to that of McLuhan. However, this does not mean that Innis will ever have the social impact or perhaps even the intellectual impact of McLuhan, for McLuhan's appeal and his meaning reside not in the technical quality of his argument but in his capacity to be an acceptable prophet of our times. It is with an analysis of the basis of McLuhan's social appeal that I wish to close this paper.

Perhaps the most interesting thing about McLuhan is the degree of success he has enjoyed. Criticism of his position usually starts out, as does this paper, with the admission by the critic that he may represent an obsolete tradition, that McLuhan may be right in claiming that most scholars are merely "prisoners of print." Criticism, such as it is, usually gives away the game before the players are out of the dugout. No useful criticism can be made of McLuhan, I am now convinced, on technical grounds. There is no way of applying standards of verisimilitude and verification to his analysis. The only criticism of McLuhan that can hope to be effective is one that admits the possibility of a system of values and meanings preferable to those implicit in McLuhan's work.

It is unfortunate, I think, that some of the daring and exquisite insights McLuhan has into the communication process are largely vitiated by his style of presentation, his manner, and his method. The meaning of McLuhan is not in his message, his sentences, but in his *persona* as a social actor, in himself as a vessel of social meaning. The meaning of McLuhan is, I want to argue, mythical and utopian. Consequently, one cannot ask whether he is correct about the effects of communication technology, for this is a question irrelevant to his message. One can only determine how one feels about the attitudes toward life implicit in his utopian projections.

Unlike the traditional scholar, McLuhan deals with reality not by trying to understand it but by prescribing an attitude to take toward it. McLuhan is a poet of technology. His work represents a secular prayer to technology, a magical incantation of the gods, designed to quell one's fears that, after all, the machines may be taking over. Like any prayer, it is designed to sharpen up the pointless and to blunt the too sharply pointed.[7] It is designed to sharpen up the mindless and mundane world of popular culture which consumes so much of our lives and to blunt down the influence of modern technology on our personal existence. The social function of prayer is, I suppose, to numb us to certain gross realities of existence, realities too painful to contemplate, too complex to resolve. Ultimately, McLuhan himself is a medium and that is his message. As a medium, he tells us we need no longer ask the imperishable questions about existence or face the imperishable truths about the human condition. The fundamental problems of existence are to be solved automatically and irreversibly by the subliminal operation of the machines on our psychic life. McLuhan represents an apocalyptic vision, an eschatological prediction about the future that can quell our frequently ambivalent feelings about ourselves and our inventions. He represents in this guise the ultimate triumph of the technical over the moral, for he tells us that concerns for morals and values and meanings in the age of electric circuitry are unnecessary.

Harold Innis wanted to preserve the oral tradition and its characteristic concern for values and meaning in the face of a rampaging technology favoring the demands of space. The oral tradition and moral order were important *even if* contemporary media did not support such concerns. For McLuhan, on the other hand, modern technology obviates the necessity of raising moral problems and of struggling with moral dilemmas. When asked if one can make moral judgments about technology, McLuhan answers: "Does one ask a surgeon in the middle of an operation if surgery is ultimately good or bad?" I suppose not. But there are days on which the propriety of surgery must be questioned. If we had raised these questions some time ago we might have avoided a generation of frontal lobotomies.

Let me be clear on the utopian and mythical aspects of McLuhan. While McLuhan insists that he is not attacking print and he is not an enemy of books, his public meaning is unmistakably as follows: printing gave rise to the Age of Reason, to scientific logic, and to the liberal tradition. The liberal tradition argued that human freedom is solely the result of man's rationality. McLuhan contends, however, that the overemphasis on reason in the liberal tradition has resulted in man's alienation from himself, from other men, and from nature itself. This is an important

point, of course. It is a theme common to many critics of our civilization, is central to the argument of Innis, and is expressed much more cogently and persuasively in Norman O. Brown's *Life Against Death.*

McLuhan's relevance stems from the fact that he goes beyond this critique and argues that the reunification of man, the end of his alienation, the restoration of the "whole man" will result from autonomous developments in communications technology. All individuals have to do to be put back in touch with their essential nature is to detach themselves from tradition and submit to the sensory powers of the electronic media.

We are being saved again! This time, however, the salvation does not entail a determined act of will, the endurance of suffering, the selflessness of sacrifice, the torment of anxiety, but only the automatic operation of technology. I won't bore you by piling up quotations in which McLuhan argues that the effect of the media on sensory organization is automatic, without resistance, subliminal. Its operation is independent of the will and the wish of men. McLuhan thus represents a species of a secularized, religious determinism, a modern Calvinism which says, "Everything is gonna be all right, baby."

But is it? And should we take it seriously? The only thing of which we can all be sure is that even in the age of electric circuitry men are born alone and individually attached to nature and to society by an umbilical cord which all too quickly withers away. The fact of the terrible loneliness and isolation of existence is what has motivated much of the great art produced in any period of history. We should not need Eugene O'Neill to remind us in the face of McLuhan's onslaughts that "man is born broken; he lives by mending; the grace of God is glue."

Human communication, by language and every other technique, is the fragile means by which men attempt to overcome the isolation of existence and wed themselves to other men. Under the best of circumstances, communication is rarely successful, is always halting, is always tentative and tenuous. "Stammering *is* the native eloquence of we fog people." But the act of communication, as O'Neill and Camus among other modern artists remind us, is the only source of joy and tragedy humans have. One can all too easily forget that the word "communication" shares its root with "communion" and "community," and it is the attempt to establish this communion that theories of communication, vulgar as they are in present form, attempt to capture.

McLuhan's relevance and meaning resides in our attempts to deal with the dilemma of communion. In an age when men are more than ever divided from the basis of an authentic communion with one another, when men's relations with machines and technology seem more durable and important than their relation to one another, McLuhan finds man's salvation in the technology itself. For McLuhan (and I must admit for Innis also), the vision of the oral tradition and the tribal society is a substitute

Eden, a romantic but unsupportable vision of the past. What McLuhan is constructing, then, is a modern myth, and like all myths it attempts to adjust us to the uncomfortable realities of existence. The Iceman cometh again but this time in the cloak of the scientist. But even this shouldn't surprise one, for science is the only legitimate source of myths in the modern world. Science is, of course, the unquestioned source of authoritative knowledge in the modern world. Scientific myths enjoy the claim of being factually true even if they are in no way demonstrable, even if they must be taken on faith, even if they attempt to answer what are, after all, unanswerable questions. Scientific myths have the great advantage in this self-conscious society of not appearing as myths at all but as truths, verified by or capable of being verified by the inscrutable methods of the scientist.

McLuhan's parable on the restorative powers of the media in expanding the consciousness of man is one more myth, one more illusion by which men can organize their lives. Unlike most of the utopias of the modern world—*1984, Brave New World, The Rise of the Meritocracy,* and even B. F. Skinner's *Walden Two*—it celebrates not the evils of technology but its glories, not its inhumanity but its terrible humanity; it celebrates Eros and not Thanatos. In a world where electric technology is, like it or not, a reality of existence that shall not pass away, it attempts to offer a justification of optimism. McLuhan's vision quite closely parallels the specification of modern myths that Emerson offered in 1848. For modern myths to be effective they will have to be mechanical, scientific, democratic, and communal (socialistic).

What finally is one to think about this myth, this New Jerusalem the media are creating? One cannot help being overwhelmed by its awful vulgarity, by its disconnection from whatever sources of joy, happiness, and tragedy remain in this world. Scott Fitzgerald was right: Modern men would invent gods suitable only to seventeen-year-old Jay Gatsbys and then would be about their Father's business: "the service of a vast, vulgar, and meretricious beauty."

One need not be against myths. Men live by illusions; only gods and devils are without them, and it is our illusions ultimately that make us human. But it is the quality of moral imagination contained in McLuhan's myth that is disquieting; it is as if it were offered as a scientific footnote to Yeats' "The Second Coming."

Finally, let me note that McLuhan himself is the ultimate verification of the more prophetic aspects of Innis' work. For central to Harold Innis' vision was the certainty that the spatial bias of communication and the monopoly of knowledge forged in its name would lead to the triumph of the secular over the sacred. The divorce of the written from the oral tradition is now complete; the hegemony of science over religion, of technical authority over moral authority, has been accomplished. If McLuhan is the prophet of the collapse of all tradition, it is fitting, I suppose, that it should be evidenced by a concern with the media of communication. It is also ironic that it should come from a student of literature who views art as a vehicle of communication. For as Allen Tate has reminded us, the very concept of literature as communication represents an unexamined victory of modern secularism over the human spirit. "Our unexamined theory of literature as communication," he says in *The Forlorn Demon,* "could not have appeared in an age in which communion was still possible for any appreciable majority of persons. The world communication presupposes the victory of the secularized society, of means without ends."

McLuhan, then, is no more revolutionary than I am. The death of values he represents is not some twentieth-century revolution. It is the end point of a positivistic revolution against meaning and metaphysics. And thus it is no surprise that his utopianism should be based on the sanctity of science and the fact.

But let me remind you that it was precisely this revolution that Harold Innis tried to resist; it was precisely this revolution that he saw as ending the possibility of a stable civilization in the West. For Innis, the oral tradition representative of man's concern with history and metaphysics, morals and meanings had to be preserved if we were not to fall victim to a sacred politics and a sanctified science. It is an irony and an uncomfortable fact that the prophecy is borne out by one who has identified himself as a disciple. But such is the frequent result of discipleship.

NOTES

[1] The literary style adopted by Innis to convey the complexity of social change is a principal barrier to any adequate understanding of his work. He amasses on each page such an enormous body of fact, fact rarely summarized or generalized, that one becomes quickly lost in the thicket of data. Further, Innis disdains the conventions of written book scholarship; indeed, he attempts to break out of what he takes to be these limiting conventions by presenting an apparently disconnected kaleidoscope of fact and observation. He avoids arguing in a precise, serial order and instead, like the proprietor of a psychedelic delicatessen, flashes onto the page historic events widely separated in space and time. With such a method, he attempts to capture both the complexities of social existence and its multidimensional change. Nowhere does he present an orderly, systematic argument (except perhaps in the first and last chapters of *Empire and Communications*) depending rather on the reader to impose order, to capture not merely the fact of history but a vision of the dynamics of historic change.

[2] Innis was interested in all forms of monopolies of knowledge. In his teaching he was interested in the tendency of social science research to become focused around one man—a Keynes, Marx, or Freud—or one narrow attitude of speculation. He himself preferred an open and vigorous competition of viewpoints and felt

that the reliance of Western education on the book severely reduced the possibility of vigorous debate and discourse in education. See Donald Creighton, *Harold Adams Innis, Portrait of a Scholar* (Toronto: University of Toronto Press, 1957).

[3] Here are some examples culled at random from Innis' writings: "Scholars were concerned with letters rather than sounds and linguistic instruction emphasized eye philology rather than ear philology." (*Empire and Communications,* p. 159) "The discovery of printing in the middle of the 15th century implied the beginning of a return to a type of civilization dominated by the eye rather than the ear." (*The Bias of Communication,* p. 138) "Introduction of the alphabet meant a concern with sound rather than with sight or with the ear rather than the eye." (*The Bias of Communication,* pp. 40-41) "In oral intercourse the eye, ear and brain acted together in busy co-operation and rivalry each eliciting, stimulating and supplementing the other." (*The Bias of Communication,* p. 106) "The ear and the concern with time began to have its influence on the arts concerned with eye and space." (*The Bias of Communication,* p. 110)

[4] Here I am indebted to Sidney Robinovitch of the University of Illinois.

[5] Susanne K. Langer, *Philosophy in a New Key* (Harvard University Press, 1957).

[6] Of course, generational discontinuity is a universal of history. Normally, these discontinuities are explained by the periodic and random shocks to a system caused by relatively unsystematic variables such as wars, depressions, famines, etc. I am suggesting that generational discontinuity no longer depends on these random shocks to the system but that generational discontinuities are now endogenous factors, built into the normal operation of the system and very much "caused" by the bias of contemporary communication.

[7] Kenneth Burke, *A Grammar of Motives,* N.Y.: Prentice Hall, 1945, p. 393.

Leslie A. Pal (essay date 1977)

SOURCE: "Scholarship and the Later Innis," in *Journal of Canadian Studies/Revue d'études canadiennes,* Vol. 12, No. 5, Winter, 1977, pp. 32-44.

[*In the following essay, Pal explores Innis's later work within the context of his changing ideas.*]

The early Innis—the Innis of fish and fur—is fairly well known; the later Innis—the Innis of print and paper—less so. Part of the fault lies with Innis himself. His economic studies were never models of clarity but they seemed lucid next to the elliptical arguments, acrane terminology, and obscure conclusions of his communications works.

The list of his stylistic and substantive sins is a long one. But some of the fault also lies with the way that the later Innis has been analyzed and interpreted.

The later Innis, for example, has been almost universally interpreted as a communications theorist.[1] Marshall McLuhan, in search perhaps for the basis of his own theory of communications, probably reinforced this line of thinking. James Carey rightly complained that McLuhan had all but removed the political and economic elements of Innis's later work.[2] It is precisely this broader context and spectrum of relationships that we miss if we focus too narrowly on the simple biases of media and their presumed results. Communications is a protean term, the task of developing a general theory about it almost overwhelming. To ease this burden, Innis deliberately focused on communications within empires, or political entities. If we must think of the later Innis as a theorist therefore, it is perhaps best, as Christian argues, to think of him as a political theorist.[3] This restores the richness of Innis's vision without mistakenly winnowing away other important, if perhaps subsidiary, factors.

Another fundamental error habitually made by interpreters of the later Innis concerns the genesis of his communications work: they place it in the late 1930s or early 1940s when he was exploring pulp and paper as a staple industry.[4] In a trivial sense this is true: before Innis examined papyrus in Egypt, he studied paper in America. But in a more important sense, this is both false and misleading. W.T. Easterbrook has argued that the key article in the new phase of Innis's research was "The Newspaper in Economic Development,"[5] but if we mean by a new phase of research a period marked with a peculiar constellation of concerns, interests, and speculations, then Innis was laying the foundations for this new phase in the early 1930s, and not the early 1940s. There can be little doubt that his newsprint studies expanded his horizons and perhaps suggested new ideas, but Innis was already concerned about the effect of modern media on the state and public opinion by 1935. It was this concern, coupled with certain views on the duties and limits of scholarship, that led him to attempt a history of communications.

We lose much in our understanding of the later Innis if we ignore his preoccupations during the Depression. It is seldom noted, for example, that in this period Innis probably wrote and thought as much about universities and scholarship as he did about staples. ***The Bias of Communication*** and ***Empire and Communications*** represent the response to a problematic: the apparent decline of Western civilization. But if we wish to understand why Innis perceived the course of history as pessimistically as he did, or why he couched his analysis in certain terms and not others, or why he offered the particular solutions that he did, we must look to his early writings on social science, scholarship, and the role of the university. The major themes of his communications works, themes which unfortunately have been disregarded by analysts, such as the relationship between learning, public opinion, force and religion, or the requirements of liberty, are all adumbrated in these writings. His thoughts on social science were informed by a vigorous liberalism, and consequently by an epistemology of doubt, though this epistemology was probably tempered by the residues of an early religious training not completely erased by apostasy. A good measure of what has been called Innis's pessimism is attributable to these contrary tendencies: the conviction that certain factual and moral truths must exist, and the doubt that they can ever be found or established. It is reasonable, however, to examine Innis's thoughts on scholarship as the articulation of his liberalism. Such an examination will demonstrate that Innis's later works were, despite appearances, highly structured by methodological, as well as moral, principles.

I

In 1935, E.J. Urwick published a provocative article entitled, "The Role of Intelligence in the Social Process."[6] In it he argued that the paradigm of the natural sciences was inappropriate for the social sciences. The natural sciences had to remove the life from their subjects in order to study them; the social process, on the contrary, was a living, moving, changing pattern directed by value decisions made by free-willed beings. The life and vitality of the social process meant that "laws," analogous to the laws of natural science, were alien to it. The social process was essentially unpredictable because the human beings within in acted according to self-selected values. This argument undermined the subject matter of the social sciences but also endangered the social scientist. Urwick had made the familiar attack on "objectivity" by asserting that scientists inevitably infused their work with values: as human beings they had no choice.

While Innis shared some of Urwick's humanist sympathies, he was not prepared to give way entirely to them. He consequently tried to carve out some facets of the social process which could be handled with the tools of social science—not because he desired to keep social science alive for its own sake, but because he felt that these facets actually existed and were being ignored by Urwick's categorization. In his characteristic way, Innis tried to balance and combine his defence with Urwick's attacks.

The subject matter which Innis retained for social science was habit or (and he used the term here for the first time) bias. As he put it: "The 'sediment of experience' provides the basis for scientific investigation."[7] Innis was suggesting that while some human activity is consciously and spontaneously directed, much of it appears to be the result of unreflective and ingrained behaviour. Such behaviour is regular and, within limits, predictable. Innis acknowledged that these biases, habits, and unconscious forces shaped the behaviour of social scientists as well. But he postulated the existence of a cognitive ability which could perceive and transcend these biases; indeed the study and understanding of the biases in the social process might lead to self-awareness:

> The difficulty if not impossibility of predicting one's own course of action is decreased in predicting the course of action of others, as anyone knows who has been forced to live in close relations with one other person over a considerable period of time. . . . The habits or biases of individuals which permit prediction are reinforced in the cumulative bias of institutions and constitute the chief interest of the social scientist.[8]

There is a clear link between the definition of the subject matter of social science as habit and the importance of the concept of monopoly in Innis's communications works. One of the outstanding characteristics of monopolies for Innis was their rigidity in the face of change. Whatever the source of this rigidity, monopolies on this dimension are nothing more than habit, or institutionalized bias. Indeed, he was to see the "conservative character of institutions as a basic factor in method in the social sciences."[9]

Thus, out of the numerable difficulties surrounding the work of the social scientist Innis was able to discern an area for some sort of objectivity. It is notable that Innis was never completely clear about the likelihood of objectivity in the social sciences. While he had established a subject matter amenable to prediction, he retained Urwick's strictures against the possibility of escaping bias. In one place, for example, he said:

> We must all be aware of the extraordinary, perhaps insuperable, difficulty of assessing the quality of a culture of which we are a part or of assessing the quality of a culture of which we are not a part.[10]

Yet in another place he said of the social scientist: "It is impossible for him to avoid the bias of the period in which he writes."[11] While he was ambivalent about the possibility of totally transcending subjective factors, he did suggest a method which would at least hold out the goal of objectivity.

That method was simply the regular day-to-day research of the social scientist. The apparent banality of this solution disappears with the understanding that Innis considered, with Urwick, that the social scientist was part and parcel of what he studied, i.e., the social process. But Innis went further than Urwick with his assertion that the social scientist had the capacity to observe the regularities, habits, and determining relationships in this process. Thus, observation and discovery of bias in institutions or individuals was, because of the unity of the observer and observed, a method of introspection as well.

> The innumerable difficulties of the social scientist are paradoxically his only salvation. Since the social scientist cannot be 'scientific' or 'objective' because of the contradiction in terms, he can learn of his numerous limitations. . . . The never-ending shell of life suggested in the persistent character of bias provides possibilities of intense study of the limitations of life and its probable direction. 'Introspection' is a contradiction, but what is meant

by the word is the foremost limit of scientific investigation in a range extending back to geological time.[12]

An objective understanding of truth was still Innis's aim: social science could move towards this understanding by successive approximations. The bearings for these approximations were to be the biases in both the scientist and the subject matter. This conception of bias and scientific research clarifies a puzzling aspect of Innis's later work—its breadth. Much like Marx, Innis perceived of history as being in the living present. Past activities and patterns were not entombed in dusty books, neither were they once-and-forgotten affairs. History for Innis was the accumulated structure of bias which shaped contemporary activity. The most general receptacle for this accumulation was civilization, and this variable was of overwhelming importance in Innis's later work.

With objectivity as the goal, Innis examined the factors that could inhibit its attainment. It is an indication of Veblen's influence on Innis's thought that he paid special attention to the "corroding effects" of institutions on the objectivity of the social scientist. Veblen had highlighted the inhibiting effects of institutions on the purely economic functions of production and exchange; Innis highlighted the inhibiting force of institutions on the social scientist's attempts to escape bias. Institutions for Innis were always the embodiment of particular values or interests; they attempted to shape and mold their members accordingly. Institutions therefore (with the exception of the university) pursued interest, and it was purely fortuitous for interest and truth to coincide. The alliance of social science with self-interested institutions meant the demise of learning.

> But whether the social scientist succeeds in advancing the interests of any single enterprise or any group of enterprises by contributing to the solution of any problem, or whether he is employed by such an enterprise or group of enterprises for honorific purposes, his contribution is assumed by those who pay for it to have advanced their interests, probably at the expense of other interests and not necessarily to the advantage of the community as a whole—whatever that may mean. In any case, the social scientist is apt to develop strong vested interests in the prospects of an enterprise or of a group or of a society.[13]

Paradoxically, objectivity was being threatened as well by the belief in objectivity. Innis was deeply concerned with what he perceived as the pretentions of the social sciences to be free from bias. He saw political economy developing into a "new religion,"[14] and eventually came to feel that "it is the essence of the philosophy of the social sciences that concern should be given primarily to their limitations."[15] He wrote to A.H. Cole in 1944: "My only point is that we ought to put some thought on the limits or limitations of the social sciences."[16] In another letter he said: "We should keep raising our limitations."[17] Innis was suggesting that an emphasis on limits was not only important as an avenue to objectivity, but also that

unless the considerable problems of research were acknowledged, orthodoxies would spring up and stifle fresh ideas. Innis felt that social scientists were placing too much faith in their own generalizations: this heralded "the decline of skepticism."[18]

Innis tended to emphasize the complexity of human affairs (even though his work is marked with startling generalizations) and the multifaceted and total nature of truth. Objectivity for Innis was the frame of mind the social scientist needed to get at the truth; it was a precondition for, and not synonomous with, the truth. But any particular social science, by definition, emphasized one or a number of factors in favour of others. This necessary emphasis was what Innis meant by the limits of a social science. Such emphasis, if taken too far, implied the loss of Innisian objectivity—that is, objectivity as a complete openness to the whole truth. Objectivity was thus impossible within any one discipline, and particularly within any orthodoxy. But perhaps even more disheartening was the implication that truth was essentially ineffable: the whole cannot be expressed. Hence Innis's legendary distaste for "final answers."

> The task of the social scientist is to discover, not to persuade. There are fewer and fewer people who will admit that they do not know, or who have the courage to say that they have not solved the problem. And yet that is what the social scientist must continually keep saying if he hopes to maintain any hold on intellectual life.[19]

He was sceptical of the Rowell-Sirois Report, for example, because of "its pretence at final thoroughness and the danger of supporting the dogmatic fallacy."[20] He felt compelled to add that, "there is no last word in the writing of economic or of other history except in totalitarian states."[21] This sensitivity to the intricacy of the social process lent itself to an emphasis on questions rather than answers,[22] or as he put it elsewhere, the philosophical approach. He saw this type of approach as "vital"[23] because it shifted attention away from the preoccupation with dogmatisms and instead emphasized scepticism.

Innis's notions on the nature of truth and objectivity informed the methods he was to use when doing social science. He was to apply these methods throughout his later works. We have noted that Innis was quite unclear as to whether bias could be transcended, though he appears to have held out the possibility that it could. One of his own methods for circumventing the problem of bias was to deliberately consider the contradiction of whatever position he might be arguing, a method he later termed as "balance." This term occurs frequently in Innis's later writings but makes little sense unless related to his views on scholarship. Balance originally emerged as a remedy for the problem of complexity and bias. The balanced view on the one hand consciously seeks to take account of the contradictions surrounding a question or constituting a phenomenon and tries to reconcile them— if it cannot then at least it has not succumbed to the temptation of offering "final answers." On the other hand, a balanced view offers the possibility of transcending bias—a predilection to one side of a question or another—by pointing to the middle way. But it should be remembered that all institutions actively promote their interests—none, except the university, ever contemplates a balanced view because it serves them not one whit to do so. For Innis, not only did scholarship require balance as a duty, but as a refuge. The balanced view was not desired or possible anywhere outside the walls of the university.

The complexity problem meant a concern with limitations and a sense of humility but it also implied that one facet of society could not be studied in isolation from others. Innis saw the social in essentially organic terms, at least insofar as he was convinced that economics should be a branch of biology rather than physics and chemistry.[24] Thus, complexity should persuade the social sciences to act in unison or at very least to be aware of and grateful for contributions from other disciplines. That this did not happen was to Innis partially the function of a tendency to professionalization and specialization. Specialization was an evil he was to combat relentlessly after 1935 and his last works are a valiant attempt to cross the artificial boundaries of academe.

Innis saw specialization as detrimental to the development of a flexible social science and the cross-fertilization of ideas and approaches: "Specialization has contributed to the rigidity of the social sciences. . . . We are constantly reminded of the wonders of science and are always forgetting the eternal problems of society."[25] He felt that such specialization severely weakened an interest in scepticism[26] and once begun could only feed upon itself with the progressive splintering of subjects, all avidly competing on the basis of their own bias for university funds and research grants.[27] The problem affected him greatly in his last years, as a few excerpts from correspondence show:

> I have a feeling that the chief function of economic history is to protect against professionalization. It is difficult to make a case in a subject in which it is most important that we should emphasize the dangers of making cases. It seems to me that economic history should attempt to check the tendency toward intensive specialization in the social sciences, and that we cannot argue for an intense specialization of economic history.[28]

> It has seemed to me that one of the most crucial problems of the social sciences is to check the trend toward specialization in the humanities.[29]

> The great problem is that of checking this tendency to split up economic knowledge into little groups which develop vested interests of their own in publications and in meetings, joint or otherwise. The prospect of emphasizing a theoretical, universal, and all-inclusive approach is in consequence very difficult.[30]

It is not clear what Innis meant by an "all-inclusive approach" though it surely would have encompassed at least two elements. The first would have been the philosophical approach mentioned earlier. This would have implied a focus on "eternal question" which for Innis seemed to be the contradictions between individual creativity and organizational effectiveness and between freedom and order. These polarities intrigued Innis and he kept them in sight whenever analysing institutions. The second element would have been the recognition of complexity and interrelatedness mentioned above. For Innis it meant the incorporation of geography, economics, politics, biology, sociology and technology in any analysis of the social process.

Mathematics did not figure conspicuously in this method.[31] As a student, Innis had been trained to focus on the framework of the price system, on the values and interests that lay at the root of institutions. Innis was intrigued with the values that directed economic activity; his career in many respects was a search for the genesis of values. This emphasis on values and the consequent dynamic nature of the social process made Innis sceptical of the application of mathematics to society. On this point he seemed to move closer to Urwick's position.

In economics for example, Innis did not reject studies of the price system out of hand. What he did reject, and what alarmed him, was an excessive concentration on the price system because it could be easily studied with the aid of mathematics:

> The price system has presented material admirably adapted to the *penchant* for mathematics with the result that enormous numbers of studies in mathematical tabulations and small numbers of advanced mathematical arguments have been published: the possibilities of proliferation are endless.[32]

Innis felt this an abdication of scientific responsibilities in two senses: first, it indicated laxity and a desire to do what came easily; second, it suggested "a neglect of the limitations of precision."[33]

There is a certain petulance to Innis's attacks on mathematics.[34] Innis was a practitioner of a waning discipline: economic history was being rapidly eclipsed, in the United States at least, by the more mathematically inclined branches of economics. Innis's distaste for econometric analysis (and probably his unfamiliarity with it) was founded on a conviction that values were the important factors in shaping the social process, and that ultimately values were not susceptible to mathematical measurement or manipulation. Innis was suspicious of mathematics for two other reasons. The first had to do with the concept of bias discussed above. The tendency to apply mathematics to social phenomena, particularly in the concern for estimates, aggregates, and statistics, was peculiar to the bias of modern industrialism and the price system.[35] Innis argued that social scientists who adopted these methods unreflectively were only being swept along with the bias of their civilization. The effects of nationalism were not to be underestimated either.[36] The state has virtually always had an interest in effective taxation, and the modern state particularly had aided the growth of mathematics in its grasping efforts to subdue and control the citizenry. The connection between government and statistical methods in social science (which were only then coming into vogue) seemed fairly obvious to Innis: "This trend is in part a result of an interest in possible government support, or in a share of funds which have been made available on such large scale to the natural sciences."[37]

The second reason why Innis was suspicious of the logic of mathematics and the natural sciences refers back to his concept of balance. The radical elusiveness of a complete and unbiased picture of reality implied the need for tolerance and discretion. The dogmatist and simpleton alike cannot thrive when ideas, values, and culture are admitted to be impossibly complex and multi-faceted. A certain open texture in attitude and outlook is required. The premise of uncertainty is usually obscured with mathematics and the mathematical fallacy takes hold. Statistics, figures and numbers are only as exact as the tools of measurement will allow, and the problem becomes even more acute when so-called non-tangibles (love, friendship, affiliation) are subjected to measurement. In either case the mathematical fallacy is that the results of calculations made with measured values are exact *and therefore true* because the values are exact. A simple example would be the operationalization of an emotion as a difference in body temperature. Minute measurements would point without fail to exact differences in body temperature and consequently in emotion. The fallacy is based on the neglected possibility that the original measurement was faulty or indeed that the particular operationalization was inappropriate. Yet this specious exactitude banishes doubts. The intrusion of mathematics in law and politics was, to Innis, a harbinger of rigidities. Balance would become unnecessary, tolerance superfluous, and governments insensitive because of the assurance that calculations were correct. Innis's point was not that other non-mathematical approaches were not liable to foster this sense of certainty, but only that mathematics was more likely to.

Innis could only offer a solution to the problem through an emphasis on the humanities, particularly classical Greek contributions. He understood the Greek view of life as predicated on an ethic of balance, and hoped that a study of the humanities in general would focus attention on values and culture and perhaps broaden the scope of inquiry of social science:

> This is not to deny the importance of studies of pure phenomena or of statistics but to emphasize their limitations and inadequacies and their position as an introduction to social science. They are comparable in contributions to social science to studies of the palaeontologist or the archaeologist or the anthropologist or the geographer. Price phenomena are only a part of the 'sediment of experience' and throw light on its character similar to that of the study of architecture, literature, or

other evidences of cultural activity. Incidentally, the significance of a classical training to the social scientist should rest in the breadth of the approach and its emphasis on the range of human activity. . . .[38]

A pattern begins to emerge, and it is an important one. As early as 1935, Innis was already beginning to associate the university, scholarship, and social science with humanism, tolerance, culture, and civilization. Once he had made this connection, and it only becomes explicit around 1940, Innis could justly say that the destruction of the universities was the destruction of Western civilization.

There is a rigorous consistency in Innis's notions on social science, scholarship, and the university. As the preceding has suggested, his thinking on these matters took its departure from the problems of subject matter and objectivity in social science. Having articulated some assumptions about truth and objectivity, he proceeded to develop concepts and concerns crucial for his later work: bias, limits, balance, and specialization.

II

Social science is something one does; scholarship is more a way of life. Innis's conception of social science, or more concretely the problem of bias, implied certain strategies of circumvention. In one sense these strategies amounted to no more than vague "methods," but when seen as a total approach they suggested unremitting toil and effort. Faced with the complexity of the social process, the scholar must probe the limits and bias of his civilization, strive to attain a balanced view, and attempt to encompass—in a humanistic perspective—as many of the areas of human endeavour as possible. Little wonder that Innis argued that the scholar "must face the necessity of giving his life to the pursuit of truth and realize that he cannot hope to make contributions of significance with less than twenty to twenty-five years of his life and before he reaches an age of at least fifty."[39]

An effort of this magnitude requires suitable surroundings. Social scientists cannot hope to pursue truth disinterestedly while serving various institutions. As mentioned earlier, Innis saw institutions as organizations of raw interest: the everyday world was an arena of conflict over these interests and those who did battle were compelled to be committed or else perish because of their weakness. The scholar could not be thrust in such a milieu and still produce lasting contributions. As Innis wryly put it: "Peace is essential to effective discussion."[40] The university in Innis's eyes had to be an ivory tower to survive. The scholar must be protected from importunate institutions[41] so that he could pursue his task undisturbed. This separation from the world, a sort of new monasticism, was essential if scholars were to avoid bias and struggle to rise above specialization in the generation of a common view.[42] The everyday world was the world of commitment to interest—the scholarly world had to be one of commitment to truth. In the everyday world, commitment led to conviction; in the scholarly world, it would more likely lead to an enlightened doubt or suspension of belief. Indeed, Innis defined the university in his later years as the centre "where one has the right and duty not to make up one's mind."[43]

But if this was the function of the university in service to scholarship, Innis was convinced that universities also had a function for society:

> The place of the social sciences in Western civilization must be seen in relation to the role of universities. The university has played its greatest role in serving as a stabilizing factor. However inadequately it has played this role in various periods in the history of civilization, it has served as a repository of the reasoning of the ablest minds attracted to it. It has preferred reason to emotion, Voltaire to Rousseau, persuasion to power, ballots to bullets. . . . It must continue its vital function in checking the dangerous extremes to which all institutions with power are subject. The extreme tendencies of modern civilization shown in the rise of the modern state and in the tyranny of opinion compel universities to resist them.[44]

A year before this was written he quoted Rashdall to the effect that the function of the university lay in "providing stability and moderation in society."[45] Stability and moderation were, as we saw earlier, the results of balance and perspective, both elements of which Innis in 1944 identified with "the Greek tradition of the humanities."[46] That the university had a function for society suggests it was to be somewhat more than an ivory tower. It is difficult to clearly assess Innis's position, but it appears that he considered the major contribution of the university to be the young men and women that it produced—men and women with vision, culture, and the ability to take a balanced view.

In discussing Innis's notions of the role of the university we come to the very heart of his later work. On one level everything he valued was crystallized in the university tradition while everything he despised seemed to want to smash that tradition. But on another level he recommended the strengthening of the university because it seemed the best solution for the malaise of modern civilization. Any student of the later Innis will be familiar with the symptoms of this malaise: a bias towards space, the rise of the state, the lack of counter-balancing institutions, the rising tide of irrationality, nationalism, and force. In light of our previous discussion it is understandable that Innis's solutions were largely formalistic rather than substantial or specific. His abhorrence of "final answers" meant that any solutions he offered would favour a continuous, flexible frame of reference.

Innis's general solution was a call for balance. Bias in favour of either time or space in a civilization implied the inability to grapple with the total reality of human society, in that creativity, vision, and new needs were stifled.

In Innis's words, "in Western civilization a stable society is dependent on an appreciation of a proper balance between the concepts of space and time."[47] Modern civilization was biased towards space: "Under these circumstances the problem of duration or monopoly over time has been neglected, indeed obliterated. Time has been cut into pieces the length of a day's newspaper."[48] In the interest of balance therefore, Innis emphasized the need to develop a concern for time and duration, or as he put it, the "longer run."[49] The call for a broader time reference is a major motif in the later Innis. Indeed, he emphasized it in his own work by going back to 4241 B.C.

Innis urged, then, a need for balance; he was prescribing a concern for time because of the overwhelming and disastrous bias towards space in modern civilization. But what institution, what group, would be interested in balance and concerned with the long run? Religion was weakened, swallowed up by the state. Only the university and scholarship could play this crucial role.[50] Innis felt that the traditional perspective of the university had been long run: "The university is a very old institution and has been concerned throughout its history with long run problems. It is anxious to see its point of view recognized and to assist in any effort toward its achievement."[51] Innis assumed that the bias of modern culture led to a myopic focus on the immediate and had to be balanced by a longer view, but realized that few institutions were prepared or indeed interested in redressing the balance. This must be understood in light of Innis's conviction that the benchmark of scholarship is scepticism and the rejection of final answers. The complexity of the social process and the never-ending array of new problems to be faced precludes reliance on devices, institutional re-organization, or specialization. If the adversary is so elusive and chameleon-like, no special set of weapons will suffice. The best tactic, Innis saw, was to train capacity—to heighten general readiness for battle. To Innis an interest in time and the longer run was synonymous with a wider capacity to handle problems.

> It is to be expected that you will ask for cures and for some improvement from the state of chaos and strife in which we find ourselves in this century. There is no cure except the appeal to reason and an emphasis on long run considerations—on the future and on the past. By a determined effort to widen our perspective we may be able to stem the currents of the moment. And in all this such institutions as the university must be expected to play a major part in spite of the losses which it has sustained in Western Civilization during the present crisis. Throughout its history the university has always exercised a moderating influence.[52]

Innis was well aware of the many dangers that threatened the university tradition. Surrounded as it was by a multitude of institutions, and thoroughly enmeshed in the web of the state, the best that could be hoped for was a tenuous, struggling existence. But the survival of the university and its functions meant for Innis much more than merely the survival of one institution—with the death of the university Western culture would die as well. To resist the bias of the state and space was to encourage the existence of competing institutions: "It [the university] will always favour the existence of a number of centralized powers in the hope that no one of them will predominate and exert its will and that individual freedom will have a greater chance to survive."[53] Innis saw the task of the university, through its emphasis on time and balance, as the rejection of the dogmatisms of self-interested institutions; instead, scholarship was to pursue an unbiased truth, and in so doing, point out the limitations and fraudulent claims of competing organizations. By this very process it would prevent the domination of any one group and foster an appreciation of the necessity for limits to power.[54]

Innis felt that the universities were both the repositories and purveyors of Western culture.[55] He was horrified at the banality of the modern mind, its pulverization by the machine. In his history of communications, he had paid special attention to culture and argued that cultural growth was a "reflection of the tenacity of civilization."[56] Since the stability of civilizations seemed to depend on a balance of space and time, it appeared that culture was closely related to such a balance.[57] If the university was interested, as Innis argued, in balance, then it too imbibed the cathartic effect of culture. Innis felt quite strongly about the role of culture, indeed he felt it might "provide weapons for the human spirit,"[58] and check the power of church and state.[59] He pointed out that "States are destroyed by ignorance of the most important things in human life, by a profound lack of culture—which, following Plato, is the inability to secure a proper agreement between desire and intellect."[60] Thus culture appears here as the sort of capacity mentioned earlier, a balanced and sober view of things. Mass production and standardization threatened to crush the spirit of the West. Innis presumed that the modern wave had not yet completely washed over Europe, and consequently argued that "The future of the West depends on the cultural tenacity of Europe."[61]

But while culture meant in a vague sense a certain capacity, a balance of reason and passion, it also had a more specific reference to Greece and classical values. Innis was quite unequivocal about the Greek influence in the Western world: "The achievements of a rich oral tradition in Greek civilization became the basis of Western culture."[62] Though he acknowledged the influence of other cultures and civilizations, he tried to show that a pervasive Greek presence existed in the Mediterranean and Europe.[63] Greece had developed a culture which eventually formed the basis for the Roman Empire, and through it, Europe and eventually North America. The tradition of Hellas was impossible to escape, and indeed Innis relied heavily on what he perceived that tradition to be. His continual reiteration of the need for balance is evidence of this, for proportion and form are typically classical ideals.

Innis valued Greece as a civilization "concerned with balance and proportion," and he juxtaposed this with the civilization created by modern industrialism.[64] Greece had been able to strike a balance between religion and the state; it had, in other words, escaped the influence of priests and kings. It was because of the Greek influence that the West had had the opportunity to develop, in some rare instances, outside of the crushing weight of political hierarchies, absolutism, and bureaucracy.[65] This was because Greece, of all the early civilizations, had forged "the idea of individual responsibility for one's own fault which struck at the root of authority and pointed to the idea of the necessity for compromise and order."[66] Greece had focused on individual and personal development; it was fundamentally concerned with the training of character.[67] Innis found in Greece the concern for freedom,[68] personal capacity, reason, tolerance, and generally culture, which eventually motivated all of his work. Innis accepted the Platonic ideal and on the basis of this urged the study of classical works and an emphasis on the oral tradition. Indeed, he claimed that the glories of Greece were founded on the solid bedrock of an oral tradition: "Greek civilization was a reflection of the power of the spoken word."[69]

Innis's analysis of modernity and its problems called for a re-emphasis of the oral tradition. The spread of paper to Europe in 1275 as a medium favouring space over time and its combination with the printing press and the alphabet implied an emphasis on the vernacular. This emphasis reinforced a neglect of time and continuity. Mechanization, mass production, commercialism and the newspaper indicated to Innis that culture and civilization, legacies of the Greeks, were in danger. Innis felt that culture needed time,[70] not in the western Christian or Roman sense, but in the sense of continuity and stability implied in form. The savage violence of two World Wars had driven home that point.

The peculiarly pernicious and urgent problem in the modern age was that paper as a medium with a bias towards space had been dominant for so long that the habit of ignoring time was becoming too difficult to break. The radio, because it was an oral medium, was reintroducing a time element but solely to strengthen the interests of space, or the state. Another alarming point was the harnessing by media of the vernacular; consequently its bias was especially widespread, perhaps as never before. The media of Western civilization heavily emphasized space and thereby influenced knowledge and institutions along this dimension as well. University scholarship, traditionally concerned with culture, was in danger of submission to the immediate and the trendy. The passive act of reading (and today watching) emphasized the dependence on mechanized communication and implied a reliance on dead as opposed to living communication.[71] All of Western civilization was therefore in danger.

The need for balance was a need for a countervailing medium that would oppose the inherent tendencies of mechanization. The oral tradition in Innis's view was admirably suited to play this role: it emphasized time, fostered creativity, and fulfilled humanistic values. It was to be implemented, he hoped, in the university, the only institution left which held aloft the values of Western civilization—reason, moderation, balance, and the pursuit of truth and individual freedom. The interrelationship between these factors can be illustrated by Innis's arguments about the specific role of universities in a democracy.

We spoke earlier of Innis's conviction that there were no final solutions and that what must be done is to inculcate a sense of proportion or balanced view, a certain capacity for meeting problems. The connection with culture can now be made explicit: "Culture . . . is designed to train the individual to decide how much information he needs and how little he needs, to give him a sense of balance and proportion. . . . Culture is concerned with the capacity of the individual to appraise problems in terms of space and time and with enabling him to take the proper steps at the right time."[72] Culture in this sense was something that Innis felt the universities were best capable of conveying. It is here that the highly political character of his ideas about education and the state emerge once again.

> We have assumed that government in democratic countries is based on the will of the governed, that people can make up their minds, and that every encouragement should be given to enable them to do so. This implies that the state is concerned with strengthening intellectual capacity, and not with the weakening of that capacity by the expenditure of subsidies for the multiplication of facts. It also implies that adults have been so trained in the educational system that they can choose the facts and reach their own decisions. We should, then, be concerned like the Greeks with making men, not with overwhelming them by facts disseminated with paper and ink, film, radio and television. Education is the basis of the state and its ultimate aim and essence is the training of character.[73]

Innis realized that the character and vigour of any polity rests on the capacity of its people. The avoidance of monopoly and rigidity required the kind of training which emphasized balance and flexibility. Without this training and this capacity, modern civilization would collapse in a paroxysm of violence. But this kind of training was only possible within the walls of the university and it is in this sense that Innis quite seriously defended the maintenance of the university tradition on the grounds that without it Western civilization would collapse. The crisis in public opinion was a crisis for democracy[74] and the universities and scholarship were vital for the survival of democracy.[75]

III

As early as 1934, Innis was outlining the relationship between public opinion, politics, and the mechanization of words in newspaper and radio.

> Improved communication such as the press and the radio, improved transportation, and the

development of modern architecture (for example, the skyscraper) tend to stress similarities of language and ideas. Expansion of the pulp and paper industry has supported intensive advertising and revolutions in marketing essential to the demands of the city. It has coincided with the decline of editorials and of freedom of speech, and the emergence of headlines and the modern newspaper with its demands for excitement, including wars and peace, to appeal to a large range of lower mental types. The coincidences with the advent of radio of dictatorship in Russia, Germany, Italy, Great Britain, the United States, or Canada is not accidental. Mechanization, moreover, implies more effective utilization of physical force.[76]

It is clear from this that many of Innis's substantive ideas on communications were forming in the mid-1930s. Some of the analytical tools he was to use in his later works (e.g., the concept of centre periphery, cycles) were simply adapted from his earlier economic studies. But the third and perhaps most important ingredient of his later writings was a set of related notions on social science, scholarship and the role of the university. Had these notions remained isolated, Innis would perhaps merely have been one of many cantankerous scholars complaining about declining standards and eroding ideals. But for Innis the university embodied the best values of Western civilization: extinguishing that tradition could hence only further debase those values. Civilizations require culture and learning as healthy bodies require vitamins. Or so Innis believed.[77] Armed with this conviction, he quickly was led to speculate on the needs of learning, and indeed the kind of learning most desirable in the face of present circumstances. It is in this sense that his notions on scholarship form the scaffolding for his communications works.

Understanding the genesis of Innis's later works helps us understand them in other ways as well. The crucial concepts of balance, bias, and monopoly become clearer for example, as do their interrelationships. The paradox and pessimism in his later work is illuminated. Innis did not fear paradox or embrace consistency—it was quite the contrary. In many instances the inconsistency, the odd turn of phrase, or the obscure epigram were deliberate. In many others, however, they were not. There are real and apparently unresolvable tensions in Innis's thinking: between his individualism and his holism, between his elitism and his populism, and between his scepticism and his methodology (imputing biases towards time or space to media, and considering those biases as part of the nature or essence of those media). His pessimism, or at least one element of it, reflected his conviction that the values and traditions he thought noble and worthwhile were bound to succumb to the coarser tendencies in men and events. Good would not triumph; evil would prosper largely because it was so enticing.

In the accepted sense of the phrase, Innis was not a profound thinker. Yet when the verbiage and obscurities of his later works are washed away, there remains a simple structure of shining intensity. A few ideas, an awesome amount of research, and some daring generalizations shaped the structure; his sense of urgency provided the intensity. Scholars should however never be studied for their intensity alone. Some of his ideas were good—they were certainly all provocative. And they were provocative precisely in the way he would have hoped: not by providing answers but by raising important questions.

NOTES

[1] A notable exception is William Christian, "Harold Innis as a Political Theorist," *Canadian Journal of Political Science,* 10 (March, 1977), pp. 21-42. I am indebted to Professor Christian, and especially Professor Hugh Thorburn, for guidance and encouragement in writing the M.A. thesis upon which this paper is based. My gratitude extends as well to the Canada Council for providing the funds which enabled me to complete my M.A. work at Queen's University.

[2] James Carey, "Canadian Communication Theory: Extensions and Interpretations of Harold Innis," in *Studies in Canadian Communications,* ed. by G.J. Robinson and D.F. Theall (Montreal: McGill University, 1975), p. 27. (Page references are to a transcript held at the Thomas Fisher Rare Book Library. Innis's correspondence and unpublished material is held there as well.)

[3] Christian, *op. cit.*

[4] For an early and a recent example of this see John Nef, "Shapers of the Modern Outlook: Harold Adams Innis (1894-1952)," *Canadian Forum,* 32 (1953), p. 224, and Carl Berger, *The Writing of Canadian History: Aspects of English-Canadian Historical Writing 1900 to 1970* (Toronto: Oxford University Press, 1976), p. 188.

[5] W.T. Easterbrook, "Innis and Economics," *Canadian Journal of Economics and Political Science,* 19 (1953); p. 292.

[6] E.J. Urwick, "The Role of Intelligence in the Social Process," *Canadian Journal of Economics and Political Science,* 1 (1935), pp. 64-76.

[7] H.A. Innis, "The Role of Intelligence: Some Further Notes," *Canadian Journal of Economics and Political Science,* 1 (1935), p. 283.

[8] *Loc. cit;* also p. 284.

[9] H.A. Innis, "The Idea File" (unpublished manuscript, 1940-1952), p. 115.

[10] H.A. Innis, *The Bias of Communication* (Toronto: University of Toronto Press, 1971), p. 132.

[11] *Ibid.,* p. 62; also see Innis, "The Idea File," p. 147.

[12] Innis, "The Role of Intelligence," p. 283.

[13] *Ibid.,* p. 281.

[14] H.A. Innis, *Essays in Canadian Economic History,* ed. by Mary Q. Innis (Toronto: University of Toronto Press, 1956), pp. 292-3.

[15] H.A. Innis, *Political Economy in the Modern State* (Toronto: Ryerson Press, 1946), p. viii; also see Innis, "The Idea File," p. 119, 330c.

[16] Letter from Innis to A.H. Cole (April 11, 1944).

[17] Letter from Innis to A.H. Cole (no date).

[18] H.A. Innis, "Geography and Nationalism: A Discussion," *Geographical Review,* 35 (1945), p. 303.

[19] H.A. Innis, "Discussion in the Social Sciences," *Dalhousie Review,* 15 (1936), p. 408; also see Innis, *Essays in Canadian Economic History,* p. 79 and H.A. Innis, "Economics for Demos," *University of Toronto Quarterly,* 111 (1934), p. 393.

[20] H.A. Innis, "The Rowell-Sirois Report," *Canadian Journal of Economics and Political Science,* 6 (1940), p. 564.

[21] *Loc. cit.*

[22] H.A. Innis, *Empire and Communications* (Toronto: University of Toronto Press, 1972), p. 9.

[23] H.A. Innis, "Commentary on Father Gaudron" (unpublished address, no date), p. 2.

[24] Innis, *Essays in Canadian Economic History,* p. 272.

[25] Innis, "Geography and Nationalism," p. 304.

[26] *Ibid.,* p. 305.

[27] Innis, *The Bias of Communication,* p. 84; also Innis, *Political Economy in the Modern State,* p. viii.

[28] Letter from Innis to A.H. Cole (April 13, 1948).

[29] Letter from Innis to A.H. Cole (January 21, 1949).

[30] Letter from Innis to Joseph Willits (January 26, 1952).

[31] See Robin Neill, *A New Theory of Value: The Canadian Economics of H.A. Innis* (Toronto: University of Toronto Press, 1972), p. 87 and Gerald J. Graham, "Two Tributes to Harold Innis," *Saturday Night,* 67 (May 24, 1952), p. 13.

[32] Innis, "The Role of Intelligence," p. 284, emphasis in original; also see Innis, *Political Economy in the Modern State,* p. 84.

[33] H.A. Innis, *Changing Concepts of Time* (Toronto: University of Toronto Press, 1952), p. 107; also see Innis, "Geography and Nationalism," p. 303.

[34] I am indebted to Professor Scott Gordon for the following observation.

[35] Innis, "The Role of Intelligence," p. 284.

[36] H.A. Innis, "The Decline in the Efficiency of Instruments Essential in Equilibrium," *American Economic Review*, 43 (1953), p. 18.

[37] Letter from Innis to John Marshall (September 22, 1947).

[38] Innis, "The Role of Intelligence," p. 284; see also letter from Innis to A.H. Cole (April 13, 1948).

[39] H.A. Innis, "Social Sciences in the Post-War World," *Canadian Historical Review*, 22 (1941), p. 119.

[40] Innis, "The Rowell-Sirois Report," p. 571; also see Innis, "Discussion in the Social Sciences," p. 407.

[41] Innis, *Political Economy in the Modern State*, p. 69.

[42] Innis, "The Idea File," p. 380c.

[43] *Ibid.*, p. 332.

[44] Innis, *Political Economy in the Modern State*, p. 141.

[45] H.A. Innis, "The Problem of Graduate Work," *Third Annual Report of the Canadian Social Research Council: 1942-43* (Ottawa: The Canadian Social Research Council, 1944), p. 18.

[46] Innis, *Political Economy in the Modern State*, p. 65.

[47] Innis, *The Bias of Communication*, p. 64.

[48] H.A. Innis, "The Concept of Monopoly and Civilization," *Explorations*, 3 (1954), p. 94.

[49] Letter from Innis to A.H. Cole (December 15, 1943).

[50] Innis, "The Idea File," p. 330d.

[51] Innis, "Business and Government," *Commerce Journal* (1950), p. 39.

[52] Innis, "This Has Killed That," in this issue of the *Journal of Canadian Studies*, p. 5.

[53] *Ibid.*

[54] Innis, "The Idea File," p. 330f.

[55] *Ibid.*, p. 330d; also see Innis, *Political Economy in the Modern State*, p. 71.

[56] Innis, *Political Economy in the Modern State*, p. xvi.

[57] Innis, *The Bias of Communication*, p. 90.

[58] Innis, *Political Economy in the Modern State*, p. 269.

[59] Innis, "The Idea File," p. 27.

[60] Innis, *Political Economy in the Modern State*, p. x.

[61] Innis, *Essays in Canadian Economic History*, p. 412; also see Innis, *The Bias of Communication*, p. 169.

[62] Innis, *Empire and Communications*, p. 85; also see Innis, "Monopoly and Civilization," p. 93 and Innis, "The Idea File," p. 144, and Innis, *The Bias of Communication*, p. 10.

[63] Innis, *The Bias of Communication*, p. 137.

[64] *Ibid.*, pp. 140-89.

[65] Innis, *Political Economy in the Modern State*, p. 265; also see Innis, "The Problem of Mutual Understanding with Russia," *Queen's Quarterly*, LIII (1946), p. 95, and Innis, *Empire and Communications*, p. 166.

[66] Innis, *Empire and Communications*, p. 69.

[67] Innis, *Essays in Canadian Economic History*, p. 385; also see Innis, "The Problem of Mutual Understanding," p. 94.

[68] H.A. Innis, "A History of Communications," (unpublished manuscript, 1940-1948), p. 101.

[69] Innis, *Empire and Communications*, p. 56.

[70] Innis, *Changing Concepts of Time*, p. 15.

[71] Innis, *The Bias of Communication*, p. 191.

[72] *Ibid.*, p. 85.

[73] *Ibid.*, p. 203.

[74] Innis, "The Crisis in Public Opinion," (unpublished address, 1943), p. 17; also see Innis, "Geography and Nationalism," p. 303.

[75] Innis, "Geography and Nationalism," p. 305; also see H.A. Innis, "Social Sciences in the Post-War World," p. 120.

[76] Innis, *Essays in Canadian Economic History*, p. 127.

[77] Christian perceptively notes Innis's reliance on Charles Cochrane for this inspiration, *op. cit.*, p. 25.

William Christian (essay date 1977)

SOURCE: "The Inquisition of Nationalism," in *Journal of Canadian Studies/Revue d'études canadiennes*, Vol. 12, No. 5, Winter, 1977, pp. 62-71.

[*In the following essay, Christian investigates the question of Innis's nationalism.*]

Twenty-five years after his death Harold Innis's reputation is slowly regaining the heights that it held during his lifetime. It may be, as Marshall McLuhan suggests, that Innis is more admired than read; but nonetheless he is now generally esteemed as a great scholar, and perhaps held in even higher regard as an early and perceptive Canadian nationalist. Concerning his greatness as a scholar I take it that there is little controversy; later economic historians may challenge the details or the conclusions of his studies, but I doubt that there are many who would seriously deny that he was a commanding figure, not just in Canada, but throughout the English-speaking world.

Innis's supposed nationalism, however, is a quite different question. Shortly after Innis's death his friend J.B. Brebner wrote in a review of *Changing Concepts of Time* that: "It may be concluded that in spite of some anti-nationalistic comments . . . , Innis here exposed a nationalism that he had hitherto for the most part masked with irony and wit."[1] And in this *Journal* in 1969 Daniel Drache developed an interpretation of Innis along the lines that "To understand Harold Innis, there are two basic characteristics of him that should be stressed. He was a nationalist because of his liberalism. He was a liberal."[2] His biographer, Donald Creighton, also painted a picture of Innis's life compatible with the views advanced by Brebner and Drache. The reader of that work carries away the unmistakable impression of Innis as a determined, almost dedicated, nationalist, though the characterization is never made explicit.

Yet these readings of Innis sit strangely with some of the most sriking passages in his published work. In **"Industrialism and Cultural Values,"** for example, Innis shows himself sympathetic neither to the concept nor the phenomenon of nationalism. In one of his most brilliant passages, his rhetoric is obscure but the conclusion that nationalism is associated with great dangers is not.

> Von Eicken's thesis that the master key to history lies in the conclusion that human movements provoke violent reactions has much to support it. Roman imperialism created by intense nationalism ended by destroying the nationality of rulers and subjects. The nationalism of the Jews left them without a country. The Catholic church renounced the world and became the heir of the defunct Roman empire. Universal suffrage heralded the end of parliamentary government. The more successful a democracy in levelling population the less the resistance to despotism. The interest of the French Revolution in humanity kindled the fire of patriotism and nationalism in Spain, Germany, and Russia.[3]

If there are some who might think this passage enigmatic, they must come to terms with the note Innis made in his *Idea File* about 1946 or 1947[4]: "Warm fetid smell of

nationalism the breeding ground of the pestilences of the west, the worship of which kills its millions where the worship of the church in the inquisition killed its thousands."[5] There is, then, a paradox which it is important to resolve: how is it that Harold Innis, who wrote so vigorously against nationalism, has been widely understood to have been a nationalist? In an attempt to steer a way through this problem I shall first look at the factors which might have given rise to a belief in Innis's nationalism. That done, I shall examine Innis's own treatment of nationalism to see whether there is not an alternative reading of his ideas that points in another direction.

The case for a nationalistic Innis is, on the surface, a strong one. A number of facts about his intellectual and professional life lend credence to the interpretation of his career in such tones, as Donald Creighton has so skillfully shown. A nationalist spirit appears, in this version, to have been at work, guiding his intellectual destiny. When choosing a thesis topic at the University of Chicago Innis was, Creighton suggests, "moved by a strong inner compulsion, which the war had no doubt strengthened, to take up a theme in Canadian economic development."[6] Later, when his thesis was completed and published, and he had taken a permanent teaching position at the University of Toronto which he was not to relinquish until his death, he needed to determine the direction of his future researches. Although his request for a Canadian topic had been "perhaps made instinctively and without too much consideration," subsequently "he began to realize that this impulse had been prompted by some very potent influences. He was conscious of a great and compelling affection for Canada." As a consequence, Creighton assures us, Innis "felt obscurely that he must work for Canada. Canadians must explain their new nation to the outside world. Above all, Canadians must understand themselves. They must realize whence they had come and where they were probably going."[7] In choosing the fur trade in Canada as his topic of investigation the "great creative decision had been taken. He had settled upon his general plan of operations as a teacher-scholar for the future."[8]

Although Creighton presents no evidence for these strong inner compulsions, potent influences and obscure feelings, it is possible to find doctrines that are apparently their manifestations in the teachings of *The Fur Trade in Canada*. This work, in several ways Innis's masterpiece, has been the inspiration for many of the new wave of Canadian nationalists in the 1960s and 1970s, especially the new political economists and some of the believers in a distinctively Canadian school of political science. From it they have drawn intimations of Innis's own nationalism. Two considerations are central here. The first is methodological. Innis was genuinely dissatisfied with the results of the application of neo-classical economic analysis, drawn as he thought from the experience of more advanced industrial countries, when applied to the solution of contemporary Canadian economic difficulties, or to the explanation of the pattern of Canadian economic development. As he wrote in 1929:

... the textbooks of the United States and England pay little attention to the problems of conservation and of government ownership which are of foremost importance in a new country such as Canada. Canadians are obliged to teach the economic theory of old countries and to attempt to fit their analysis of new economic facts into an old background. The handicaps of this process are obvious, and there is evidence to show that the application of economic theories of old countries to the problems of new countries results in a new form of exploitation with dangerous consequences. The only escape can come from an intensive study of Canadian economic problems and from the development of a philosophy of economic history or an economic theory suited to Canadian needs.[9]

This escape Innis sought in a detailed historical analysis which paid particular attention to the institutions and practices associated with the exploitation of a staple product (beaver and other furs) for a European market. In this way he could draw attention to the changes in both pattern and structure which had occurred throughout the development of the fur trade and which the Newtonian timelessness of the neo-classical model both concealed and ignored. Although he drew on the writings of Thorstein Veblen and on the lectures of C. S. Duncan at Chicago[10] he was attempting to create a mode of understanding that was singularly appropriate to the Canadian case.

The second consideration that makes Innis's *Fur Trade* attractive to nationalist thinkers can be discovered in some of the conclusions he drew in the course of his narrative. For example, he made an eloquent case that it was "no mere accident that the present Dominion coincides roughly with the fur-trading areas of northern North America. The bases of supply for the fur trade in Quebec, in western Ontario, and in British Columbia represent the agricultural areas of the present Dominion. The Northwest Company was the forerunner of the present confederation."[11] In opposition to the continentalist school of which Goldwin Smith was a leading member, Innis held that the present Canadian state was not an eccentric abberation, put together by politicians for sentimental reasons, flying in the face of geographic reason and economic sense. Moreover, the Northwest Company had drawn its strength from roots which were sunk deeply into the very nature of the country, and had been all the more effective for that reason. It was "built on the work of the French *voyageur,* the contributions of the Indian, especially the canoe, Indian corn, and pemmican, and the organizing ability of Anglo-American merchants."[12] The general, but as we shall see precarious, conclusion that a casual reader can carry away from *The Fur Trade* is that Innis had shown the economic naturalness of the Canadian political community, and had provided a convincing account of the inherent conflict between the two states that had been created out of the great land mass of continental North America.

Those who had been persuaded that Innis's early career and writings bore witness to his nationalism could not help but be confirmed in this conclusion by considering his activities during the 1930s. During that decade he was not only active in establishing and promoting the learned societies which were to play such a vital role in creating a mature Canadian academic community, but he was also to be found fiercely insisting on the essential autonomy of Canadian scholarship in his terms for accepting an editorial role in *The Relations of Canada and the United States* series. Moreover, his second major work, **The Cod Fisheries,** published in 1940, was a further attack on the schools of history and economics which saw Canada decisively as a nation whose history and destiny were pre-eminently North American. The message that Creighton drew from that work was "that Canada in particular had been deeply dependent upon the markets, political power, and military assistance of Europe, precisely because Canada had been determined to maintain, as the real essence of its being, a separate and competitive position in North America."[13]

According to those who have mediated his thought to a later generation, the pace of this nationalism intensified during the Second World War, and especially after his visit to the Soviet Union in 1945. Already, before the end of the war, he had turned down a very generous offer from the University of Chicago, because, in his biographer's words: "He was a Canadian. He had struck deep roots in the Canadian scene. His previous research had lain chiefly in Canadian history. His friends, his interests, his influence, his authority, were all Canadian. Could he give them up?"[14] To the intense love of his own country, it has been suggested Innis added an equally powerful dislike of the United States.[15] This feature of his writings was thought to have become more and more important to the point where Brebner could write of the essays collected in his last published work: "All are polemical, partial, and provocative rather than balanced or hypothetical in intention, their common theme being almost absolute hostility to American influence on Canada and the world."[16]

There is, then, a case to be answered about Innis's alleged nationalism, and the testimony concerning it is all the more formidable since it comes from two men who were respected scholars as well as friends of Innis. It might be possible to prepare an appeal on the grounds that the charge is necessarily too vague to be answered, nationalism being such a procrustean doctrine; but I don't think that it is necessary to take this tack. I hope to show, by examining Innis's own treatment of nationalism, both in general and in a Canadian context, that he opposed that doctrine, and more especially, opposed the spirit which it incarnated, and that, moreover, such opposition was fundamental to his thought.

To begin, it is necessary to sketch, however briefly, the main lines of Innis's argument as he developed it in the 1940s, since this was the period during which he began to make explicit the thoughts and the principles that were embedded in the more limited studies in economic history that he had previously undertaken. It was then that he began to work toward a philosophy of history which might be summarized as follows.

Throughout history Innis had noted what appeared to be a powerful tendency for what he called monopolies of knowledge to develop in every society. These took on many shapes and forms, but they could be recognized in various establishments, hierarchies or authorized versions, and they were to be found in churches, empires, armies. The restrictiveness of such closed elite groups was the besetting weakness of the organization they maintained. Large organizations, such as empires, had to be constantly ready to make adjustments in relation to two factors. First they had to be constantly alive to their territorial space, expanding and contracting it according to changing circumstances. Equally they needed to be aware of the factors which contributed to preservation over time, particularly those factors which allowed the peaceful transition of power.

Most empires and civilizations eventually came to grief because the mental alertness and creative energy needed for adaptation had been allowed to atrophy. The ruling group, or groups, anxious to maintain its dominant position during times of stability, gradually built up increasingly complex barriers to entry into the inner circle. These monopolies of knowledge became closed, suspicious, intolerant and isolated. They discouraged creativity and they feared innovation. In short they sowed the seeds of their own destruction. Any number of factors—economic, political, religious, technological—could create a rift between the established methods of control and the society in which the organization was to be maintained. To compensate for this weakening of their control the ruling group was likely to resort to increasingly repressive measures, relying on armed force to substitute for the decay of its authority. In turn this would place progressively heavy burdens on the society that would bring it even closer to the brink. What was required to administer the coup de grace was a creative breakthrough—in commerce, in industry, in communication, in war—that would finally sweep away the encrusted old order. Given the ossification of the society in question, this thrust would most likely originate in some group that had been marginal to the society and had therefore escaped the full force of its stultification. A new dawn would then be born, but it would, alas, prefigure its own dusk.

This argument was not deterministic, only probabilistic. A creative breakthrough of sufficient power to sweep away the old oppressive order could not be generated at will, nor could it be relied upon. Moribund empires, staggering from crisis to crisis, could last an interminable time. But in the past the essential greatness of the human spirit, questing for freedom and self-realization, was the factor which, for Innis, had always been decisive.

This brief sketch of Innis's complex and subtle analysis[17] will, I think, be adequate to allow us to see his treatment of nationalism in perspective. The factors which ushered in, and gave their character to, the modern era were many. In one passage Innis mentions the increased use of paper, the growth of trade, the rise of cities, the prominence of monarchies, the rise of lawyers and the increased use of the vernacular.[18] Elsewhere he draws attention to changes in military technology, of which the use of gunpowder in war was perhaps the most important; to religious controversy, involving changing doctrine and forms of ecclesiastical organization; and to the development of new commercia and manufacturing practices. None of these factors was in itself decisive, but together they worked in co-operation to destroy the monopoly of knowledge that had developed in relation to the church in the Middle Ages. The process by which this change could be recognized—paper replacing parchment as the principal means of communication, and printers replacing copyists as the chief method of reproduction—were complex and are beyond the scope of this present analysis.

Nonetheless a decisive challenge to the church's authority had been mounted across a wide front. This confict turned out to be dialectical, rather than direct. The nature of the monopoly of knowledge that had developed in relation to the church had been predominantly concerned with control over time, and the concept of time that it had emphasized had been linear. Space, on the other hand, had been fragmentized, and it was the need to create more rational territorial units in economic, military and political terms that provided the impetus for the attack on the universal church.

The success of the rising nation states of Europe involved both gains and losses. For all its flaws mediaeval Christendom had been an international community and the interchange of ideas had been facilitated by the shared use of Latin as a language of learned discourse. Moreover the difficulties and expense of producing large numbers of copies of books using copyists and parchment had restricted the amount that could be published. The effect of this restriction was that there was a manageable amount of knowledge available in written form, and the dedicated scholar could aspire to master this corpus. As a corollary the mediaeval mind showed a tendency to synthesis as well as to the continual adaption of the material to new ideas and new circumstances. These appealing features of the Middle Ages were subsequently lost. "The printing press destroyed internationalism, and accentuated the importance of differences in language. . . ."[19]

The spread of paper from the Mohammedan areas in the late thirteenth and early fourteenth centuries, combined with the technical improvements in the quality of paper that the Europeans subsequently introduced, opened the way for the expression of new ideas and for the rise of new institutions. Innis noted these developments in his customary cryptic manner:

> A monopoly over time stimulated competitive elements in the organization of space. The introduction of paper from China to Baghdad and

to Cordova and to Italy and France contributed to the development of cursive writing and to the organization of space in relation to the vernaculars.[20]

Although paper had facilitated the escape of those men and organizations whose aim it was to foster the spread of ideas that weakened the control of the church, the religious character of the opponent had a contaminating effect on the subsequent character of printing.

> Greek scriptures following the translations of Erasmus and a concern with the possibility of translation into the vernaculars destroyed the monopoly of the church expressed in Latin. . . . Translations into the vernaculars gave them a sacred character and gave a powerful drive to nationalism. Milton was concerned with the production of an epic in English which would combine nationalism with Christianity.[21]

These two developments—the contribution of paper and printing to the organization of space, and the sacral aura that surrounded the printed page—were formidable both in destruction and creation. Forged together they found expression in nationalism. "The paper and printing industries supported the development of monopolies of space in nationalism and the state. Printing emphasized vernaculars, reduced the speed of movement of ideas, and divided the European mind."[22]

The speed with which the vernacular gained an ascendancy varied from country to country, but by "the end of the sixteenth century the flexibility of the alphabet and printing had contributed to the growth of diverse vernacular literatures and had produced a basis for divisive nationalism in Europe."[23] This process was exacerbated as the "application of power to communication industries hastened the consolidation of vernaculars, the rise of nationalism, revolution, and new outbreaks of savagery in the twentieth century."[24]

By the twentieth century the new means of communication, principally printing and photography, "had developed a monopoly which threatened to destroy Western civilization first in war and then in peace."[25] The resolution contained in the peace settlement after the First World War had been, Innis argued, in accord with "the impact of printing." However the monopoly which had arisen around printing gave rise to competition, this time in the form of appeals to the ear—the loud speaker and radio. In North America the new invention of radio was used to great effect by Franklin Roosevelt. But it proved much more disruptive in Europe, especially Germany. "Political boundaries related to the demands of the printing industry disappeared with the new instrument of communication. The spoken language provided a new base for the exploitation of nationalism and a far more effective device for appealing to large numbers. Illiteracy was no longer a serious barrier."[26] The appalling waste of the Second World War was further evidence, if such were needed, of the terrible costs involved in uncontrolled cultural change.

As well as inducing political leaders to try to redraw political boundaries along the lines of language, radio had one further corrupting effect. It lowered even further the possible level of political discussion. "The influence of mechanization on the printing industry had been evident in the increasing importance of the ephemeral. Superficiality became essential to meet the various demands of larger numbers of people and was developed as an art by those compelled to meet the demands. The radio accentuated the importance of the ephemeral and the superficial."[27] The power of the new journalism and of radio had been bought "at [the] expense of [a] universal approach."[28]

The printing press had fostered a nationalism which had fractured the unity of civilization. Now nationalism turned back and wrought havoc by means of the device that had given it birth. Not the least of its damage was to create economic disruptions, culminating in the Great Depression. As Innis speculated in his *Idea File:* "Extent to which depression result of nationalism built up on accentuated emphasis on vernacular and consequent growth of tariffs."[29] A "concern with monetary management" and the consequent "manipulation of currencies on a national basis"[30] were related phenomena. As well, nationalism had contributed to an exaggerated concern for the collection of statistics along national lines, "aggregates, estimates and averages" which have "accentuated a narrowing interest in mathematical abstractions and a neglect of the limitations of precision."[31]

These developments were serious enough. An even more dangerous consequence of the nationalism which had grown up in harness with printing was its tendency to place increasingly stringent restrictions on thought and speculation. In a long but unusually clear note in the *Idea File* Innis outlined this whole development.

> Significance of architecture—restriction of parchment emphasized need of expression especially with prosperity in buildings—these in turn favoured oral expression in cathedral schools and universities and rise of scholasticism—emphasis on large books—St. Thomas Aquinas *Summae*—cathedrals of thought— In this printing destroyed possibilities of architecture as expression except with wearing down of words by advertising and rise of skyscrapers to reinforce words. Use of language or vernacular as basis of force in development of state of absolute character of Hegel— But force transcends language and necessity of appeal to ideology cutting across language. Law still important as against history or romanticism. Printing means destruction of hierarchical values, reliance on force and mobilization of vernacular as force— Romanticism of 19th century—breakdown of rule of law—appeal to nationalism and history. Political myth revived when printing first developed—also compulsory education and rise of historicism and nationalism. Printing weakened initiative—opened way to totalitarian state.[32]

This rich and subtle note draws stark attention to the increasingly sinister alliance between nationalism and force. The dark hint of totalitarianism with which the passage ends is no mere rhetorical flourish, but follows naturally once the corrosive effects of nationalism had eroded the rule of law and replaced rational attachment to the political community by an irrationalist political myth, assiduously fostered by compulsory and universal education.

International sharing of learning and culture which might have served as a retardant or preventative were rendered impossible, and the sciences and social sciences, instead of serving as agents of enlightenment and toleration, were increasingly pressed into the service of the militarist and nationalist state. Under the influence of the state communication among scientists had become impossible because scientific discoveries often have implied military application.[33] This led to inefficiency and bigotry in science,[34] as well as to the general softening of science.[35] Nationalist science in turn ran a renewed danger of arrogance or immodesty because it is cut off from the healthy competition of ideas that breeds uncertainty or at least a salutary scepticism.[36]

The case of the social sciences was, if anything, worse. It was obvious to Innis that economics and political science had been pressed into the service of the state, during times of peace, and even more clearly when the state was imperilled by war. Innis contributed a particularly trenchant critique of geography to the *Geographical Review* in 1945 which was all the more telling since he thought geography to be in the strongest position of all the social sciences.[37] There he pointed out, with obvious scorn, that "even in peacetime, atlases have been published in Canada and the United States that show wind, rain, and temperature stopping at the 49th parallel. Scientific interest has been distorted to fit the mold of nationalism, and national boundaries have become cultural facts with the permanence of the features of geological phenomena."[38] The atmosphere of the war, combined with the increasing specialization of knowledge that Innis so dreaded, had fostered an aggressive and dogmatic cast of mind that was inimical to free inquiry. "Skepticism has been weakened by specialization, to the detriment of all concerned."[39] There was worse to come as nationalism drew strength from these developments. "Nationalism imposes tremendous burdens on democratic societies. Machine industry and, especially, inventions in transportation and communication have increased the possibilities of an international society, but they have also increased the defences of nationalism by enormously strengthening vested interests in language. The impact of propaganda has reached its most absurd limits in geopolitics—the social scientist and the natural scientist can take warning. It is the search for truth, not 'truth', that makes men free."[40]

Nationalism hammered the civilization from which it had grown. There was throughout the West a continual problem of the "adaptability of political machinery to shifting economic centres of production incidental to technological change especially in transportation—location of industry problem—significance of coal as a determinant—conflict with technological change in communications—

i.e. nationalism based on vernaculars—radio, etc. with little relation to results of industrial revolution."[41] In Europe the great disruptions and irrationalities in the aftermath of the Treaty of Versailles were manifestations of this phenomenon.

The English-speaking world had by no means escaped the baleful influences of nationalism. In the British Empire the centrifugal forces of language had begun to tear that organization apart.

> The British Empire, which gained from a fusion of Roman law traditions and common-law traditions, has been exposed to the effects of increasing nationalization based to an important extent on language under the influence of mechanization of the printed word and the spoken word as in the case of the French in Canada, the Dutch in South America, the languages of India and Pakistan, and the attempt to revive the Irish language in Eire.[42]

In the United States the situation was just as serious, perhaps even more so. There "with systems of mechanized communication and organized force" that country "has sponsored a new type of imperialism imposed on common law in which sovereignty is preserved *de jure* and used to expand imperialism *de facto.*"[43] Developments in the United States had become more dangerous because of the "disastrous effect of [the] common law in making politics part of law and emphasizing [the] position of [the] state. . . ."[44] With the complete destruction of the church's monopoly over time, mechanized communications and mechanized industry had filled the void and had created a sense of time preoccupied with the present and oblivious of the past and future. New and vicious substitutes had arisen to lend support to temporal continuity. "The disappearance of time monopolies facilitated the rapid extension of control by the state and the development of new religions evident in fascism, communism, and our way of life."[45]

Responding to these destructive pressures was by no means easy since the complete triumph of machine industry had carried with it a weakening of the powers of understanding its impact. It was supremely difficult to attempt a "universal approach in [the] face of nationalism, communication, etc. Machine industry emphasized regional civilization and [the] difficulties of [a] broad understanding. [The] Emphasis on [the] vernacular of [the] printing press accentuates [the] problem of [the] university in maintaining [a] bridge between world view and a shifting base of vernacular—Universities [have been] overwhelmed by [the] vernacular and common interest with little prospect of maintaining [an] interest in [the] problems of civilization."[46]

The problem which faced every civilization, and which was becoming a critical one for our own, was the one of creating cultured men. Culture is "designed to train the individual to decide how much information he needs and how little he needs, to give him a sense of balance and proportion, and to protect him from the fanatic who tells him that Canada will be lost to the Russians unless he knows more geography or more history or more economics or more science."[47] It was as part of this general deterioration of western civilization that Innis analyzed the Canadian predicament.

In spite of the apparent naturalness of the Canadian Confederation seen in the light of previous developments in the fur trade, Innis was ruthless in repudiating any suggestion that these political and economic coincidences were necessary relations. As he noted in his biography of Peter Pond, published in the same year as the *Fur Trade:*

> Like the other traders from the colonies . . . he felt no strong allegiance to any government but allegiance to Great Britain was a prerequisite to a supply of manufactured goods essential to the fur trade. . . . If lessons were to be drawn from his life, nothing would be more obvious than the fruitlessness of sentimental lamentations over the weakening ties of the British Empire. The Empire has grown and been maintained on stronger bonds than political bonds and it has grown in spite of its builders as well as because of them.[48]

Eighteen years later he made a similar observation in his introduction to the *Diary of Simion Perkins.* "In spite of strong family ties and business connections, Nova Scotia remained within the Empire. Because of these family ties and business connections the political bonds were of less importance."[49] Whatever Innis's fascination for the late George Ferguson's tittle-tattle and gossip about Canadian politics, it is fair to say that deep down there is some foundation for an observation that he was an unpolitical, or even an anti-political, man.

It is true that he deeply feared the influence of the United States which he thought had absorbed many of the worst and most dangerous features associated with mechanized industry and mechanized communications. He thought that Canadian cultural life was undergoing a constant battering from American commercialism, and that this had a dangerous impact in separating English and French-Canadian cultural life.[50] What was more Canada as an immature society was likely to prove unable to resist the influences of American imperialism.[51] Already there were grounds for fearing that Mackenzie King had "found Canada a nation and left it a colony in relation to [the] U.S.—particularly result of radio. . . ."[52] Towards the end of his life he drew particular and vigorous attention to the distorting effects of American industrialism and advertising on Canadian culture,[53] and advocated the need for an energetic programme to offset them.[54]

None of these fears or hopes led Innis to welcome nationalism as a contribution to the solution of Canada's problems, or to resolving the difficulties of Western civilization. Indeed, he dreaded it. As he wrote in 1946:

> States are destroyed by ignorance of the most important things in human life, by a profound lack of culture—which, following Plato, is the inability

to secure a proper agreement between desire and intellect. The state of the arts in Canada is threatened by a fanatical interest in nationalism reflecting our inability to grapple with the problems of Western Civilization. The drain of nationalism on our energies all but exhausts efforts to appreciate our position in the West.[55]

In practice Canadian nationalism had had a consistently debilitating effect. It has turned Canada into the Trojan horse of American penetration into the British Commonwealth,[56] and it had been systematically fostered by American branch plants who used nationalist appeals as an indirect means of weakening the central government and of encouraging regionalism. The consequence had been the accentuation of "back scratching small groups—Maritimes, Western Canada, Quebec. . . ."[58] In alliance, the "jackals of communications systems are constantly on the alert to destroy every vestige of sentiment towards Great Britain holding it no advantage if it threatens the omnipotence of American commercialism."[59]

Hangers-on were quick to take advantage wherever they could. "Nationalism in Canada [is] exploited by publishers"[60] though the ironic consequence of their attempts to promote their own interests had been that "except in French Canada nationalism prevents the growth of a large publishing industry."[61] The tourist trade and publicity departments exaggerated Canadian distinctiveness "through the necessity of appearing different from countries from which we hope to attract tourists."[62] University scholars themselves had been by no means slow to reap a personal harvest if they could. "On all sides the social scientist can be seen carrying fuel to Ottawa to make the flames of nationalism burn more brightly."[63]

Nationalism struck deep at the heart of the Canadian community, and it is, I think, fair to say that, for Innis, nationalism was precisely the spirit that had to be avoided if Canadians were to have any hope of overcoming their difficulties.

> Nationalism becomes more intense. The influence of the radio is canalized through the Canadian Broadcasting Corporation and interest in national culture is intensified. The intensification of nationalism increases the burden of tariffs and fixed charges, precipitates regionalism, and enhances the importance of the provinces. Particularism leads to the decline of national loyalties and to increase in imperial loyalties.[64]

It would have been surprising if Canadian politicians had been free from the attempt to take the advantage where it lay, and as Innis saw them, they were "quick to seize upon the possibility of capitalizing hostility to either the United States or Great Britain, and Canadian nationalism flourishes under these conditions, but it is nationalism in the interest of the short run rather than the long run."[65] Only in French Canada was nationalism a more wholesome endeavour, since there it stems from an interest in "culture, language and tradition" and represents a "reflection of the continual interest in time—i.e. influence of religion and church."[66] But even French-Canadian nationalism was harmful because it led them "to withdraw from interest in wider sphere."[67] In sum, the best that can be said of Canadian nationalism is that when it is not doing active harm, it is engaged in irrelevancies. "Emphasis on symbols of British sovereignty—use of Crown on highways—an indication of the penetration of American life—the greater the emphasis on form the greater the indication that the substance is inadequate—danger of intense interest in symbols—obscuring of basic factors."[68]

The United States was only the enemy in the sense that it represented the condition of crisis in the most acute form. "In the Anglo-Saxon world we have a new mobilization of force in the United States, with new perils, and all the resources of culture and language of the English-speaking peoples, *including those of the United States,* will be necessary to resist it."[69] It was rather mass production and standardization which were "the enemies of the West,"[70] and the "future of the West depends on the cultural tenacity of Europe. . . ."[71] And, as he had noted in his *Idea File* in 1948, the "Future of Europe [is] largely dependent on France with possible support from England—possibility of evading strangulation by Anglo-Saxon barbarism—especially North America—and by communism. Threat of mass production of North America to French culture and taste. . . ."[72] In this hope, Innis had returned to an old theme. After all, had he not begun his conclusion to **The Fur Trade in Canada** by noting: "Fundamentally the civilization of North America is the civilization of Europe and the interest of this volume is primarily in the effects of a vast new land area on European civilization."[73]

Was Harold Innis a nationalist? In the absence of any settled meaning for this term, it is obviously impossible to give an answer that will satisfy everyone. It is possible, for example, that for some a Canadian nationalist is someone who (1) loves his country; (2) dislikes or distrusts the United States; and (3) reveres some vague sort of British Imperial connection. In this case Innis might just qualify, though it is clear that he would never have described his own position as nationalist. This, however, is an unusually weak sense of nationalism, and its application to Innis, even if apt, is quite likely to generate a seriously misleading understanding of his overall position. The unmistakable conclusion that must be drawn from his writings is that in any sense stronger than the above usage, Innis was not a nationalist. It would be much fairer to say that he was opposed to nationalism as a programme or an ideology, and even more strongly opposed to the exclusivist and intolerant spirit which that doctrine usually incorporated. It is true that in his books and articles as in his life he revealed a deep dedication to his native land, but it drew that reaction from him because he saw in it the incarnation of a culture that represented much that was valuable in Western civilization from the age of Pericles on down the generations.

As for the future of his country and his civilization, Innis spoke only vaguely, and then in despairing tones. What was wrong was clearer than what ought to be done. A balanced perspective and a universal approach were clearly necessary. So was an awareness of the problems of time, or continuity, and of the dangers of an unreflective concern for the affairs of the moment. Reason had to be harmonized with the passions and a respect for individuality and creativity needed to be fostered. Such was the programme of a great and humane man who taught the "necessity of [a] university making available [the] standards of western civilization."[74]

As creative and original a thinker as Harold Innis was, he was not a Saint Augustine, and Innis's friend, Charles Cochrane, had shown in his *Christianity and Classical Culture* that it took a thinker of that power to resuscitate a dying civilization. But Innis could at least warn that fanaticism and intolerance were enemies and not friends. His beloved universities were becoming increasingly "small islands in [a] rising sea of barbarism"; and great care needed to be taken if the "inquisition of religion" were not to be "followed by [the] inquisition of nationalism."[75]

NOTES

[1] J.B. Brebner, "Review of *Changing Concepts of Time*" in *The Canadian Historical Review,* 34 (1953), p. 171. Carl Berger, whose chapters on Innis in *The Writing of Canadian History* (Toronto, 1976) I read only after this article was already in proof, echoes these sentiments. There he writes: "His was a passionate nationalism that had for long been masked by irony, humour, and cynical comments on the clichés of his day" (p. 111). I would also take strong exception to the emphasis Berger places on Innis's alleged determinism.

[2] Daniel Drache, "Harold Innis: A Canadian Nationalist," *Journal of Canadian Studies,* IV, No. 2 (1969), p. 7.

[3] Harold Innis, *The Bias of Communication* (Toronto, 1951, 1971), pp. 140-1.

[4] Sometime in the early 1940s Innis began to jot down his ideas, reading notes and the like on file cards. Subsequently he had these cards (now apparently lost) typed up to provide a typescript of 339 pages, now known as his *Idea File*. It was originally published on microfilm after his death. The edition was supervised by a committee consisting of Mrs. Innis, his son Donald, and some of his former colleagues; but it was published in an edition in which his ideas were reorganized according to alphabetical entries. The original version, that is, the one that was known to Innis, is in the University of Toronto Archives, and it is this version from which I have worked. It is, obviously, even more difficult to interpret these notes of about a decade than it is Innis's published work because of their (often) fragmentary nature. I have used the material from the *Idea File* with great care, and I trust that I have not produced an unrepresentative selection of en-

tries in this paper. For a longer discussion of the *Idea File,* see William Christian, "Harold Innis's *Idea File,*" *Queen's Quarterly,* forthcoming.

[5] Harold Innis, *Idea File* (unedited version, University of Toronto Archives), p. 213.

[6] Donald Creighton, *Harold Adams Innis: Portrait of a Scholar* (Toronto, 1957), p. 43.

[7] *Ibid.,* pp. 56-7.

[8] *Ibid.,* p. 60.

[9] Harold Innis, "The Teaching of Economic History in Canada," in *Essays in Canadian Economic History,* ed. M.Q. Innis (Toronto, 1958), p. 3.

[10] See Creighton, pp. 59-60.

[11] Harold Innis, *The Fur Trade in Canada,* revised edition (Toronto, 1962), p. 392.

[12] *Ibid.,* p. 262.

[13] Creighton, p. 105.

[14] *Ibid.,* p. 118.

[15] *Ibid.,* p. 125.

[16] Brebner, p. 171.

[17] For a fuller discussion see William Christian, "Harold Innis as Political Theorist," *Canadian Journal of Political Science,* X, No. 1 (March 1977), pp. 21-42.

[18] Innis, *Bias,* pp. 52-3.

[19] Harold Innis, "A Plea for the University Tradition," *Dalhousie Review,* vol. 24 (1944), p. 299.

[20] Innis, *Bias,* p. 124.

[21] *Ibid.,* p. 128.

[22] *Ibid.,* p. 129.

[23] *Ibid.,* p. 55.

[24] *Ibid.,* p. 29.

[25] *Ibid.,* p. 80.

[26] *Ibid.,* p. 81.

[27] *Ibid.,* p. 82.

[28] Innis, *Idea File,* p. 331.

[29] *Ibid.,* p. 223.

[30] *Ibid.,* p. 331.

[31] Harold Innis, *Changing Concepts of Time* (Toronto, 1952), p. 107.

[32] Innis, *Idea File,* p. 240.

[33] Innis, *Bias,* p. 193.

[34] Harold Innis, "Comments on Russia," *International Journal,* Vol. 1, no. 1 (1945), p. 35.

[35] Innis, *Idea File,* p. 230.

[36] *Ibid.,* p. 211.

[37] Harold Innis, "Geography and Nationalism: A Discussion," *Geographical Review,* vol. 35 (1945), p. 310.

[38] *Ibid.,* p. 302.

[39] *Ibid.,* p. 305.

[40] *Ibid.*

[41] Innis, *Idea File,* p. 326.

[42] Harold Innis, *Empire and Communications* (Toronto, 1950, 1972), p. 169.

[43] *Ibid.*

[44] Innis, *Idea File,* p. 142.

[45] Innis, *Bias,* p. 88.

[46] Innis, *Idea File,* p. 223.

[47] Innis, *Bias,* p. 85.

[48] Harold Innis, *Peter Pond: Fur Trader and Adventurer* (Toronto, 1930), pp. 141-2. Innis was a complex thinker, and his mind was often working on several problems at the same time. As well as pointing to the disjunction of economic and political trends mentioned in the text, it is quite possible that Innis was here also dealing with contemporary political controversy relating to the political and economic programmes of R.B. Bennett, who took office in 1930. It is also possible that he had in mind the earlier programme of the Imperial federationists. I owe this observation to Dr. Ian Drummond of the University of Toronto who was kind enough to give me his comments on the text as a whole.

[49] Simion Perkins, *The Diary of Simion Perkins, 1766-1780,* ed. H.A. Innis (Toronto, 1948), p. xxxiii.

[50] Innis, *Changing Concepts of Time,* p. 18.

[51] Harold Innis, "In the Tradition of Dissent," *University of Toronto Quarterly,* vol. 13 (1943), p. 131.

[52] Innis, *Idea File,* p. 139.

[53] Innis, *Changing Concepts of Time,* p. 14.

[54] *Ibid.,* p. 19.

[55] Harold Innis, *Political Economy in the Modern State* (Toronto, 1946), p. x.

[56] Innis, *Empire,* p. 169; see also, *Essays in Canadian Economic History,* p. 405.

[57] Innis, *Idea File,* p. 210.

[58] *Ibid.,* p. 213.

[59] Innis, *Changing Concepts of Time,* p. 19.

[60] Innis, *Idea File,* p. 150.

[61] Innis, *Political Economy,* p. xi.

[62] *Ibid.*

[63] *Ibid.,* p. xii.

[64] Innis, *Essays,* p. 236.

[65] *Ibid.,* p. 238.

[66] Innis, *Idea File,* p. 91.

[67] *Ibid.,* p. 88.

[68] *Ibid.,* p. 85.

[69] Innis, *Essays,* p. 412, my emphasis.

[70] Innis, *Empire,* p. 169.

[71] Innis, *Essays,* p. 412.

[72] Innis, *Idea File,* p. 141.

[73] Innis, *Fur Trade,* p. 383.

[74] Innis, *Idea File,* p. 213.

[75] *Ibid.,* p. 310.

Hugh J. G. Aitken (essay date 1977)

SOURCE: "Myth and Measurement: The Innis Tradition in Economic History," in *Journal of Canadian Studies/ Revue d'études canadiennes,* Vol. 12, No. 5, Winter, 1977, pp. 96-105.

[*In the following essay, Aitken offers his personal and professional insights on Innis's theories of economic history.*]

Most people past middle age would probably agree, if they look back on their early years, that there were a few individuals who, without ever intending to do so or being conscious of having done so, exercised a decisive influence on their later thoughts and attitudes. The effect of such people is, as it were, accidental; they transform without intent. Harold Innis played such a role in my life, as in the lives of many other scholars now in their fifties and sixties. I am sure that he never thought of me as in any sense "his" student. If, during my one year as a graduate student in economic history at Toronto, I was under the wing of any particular faculty member, it was Tom Easterbrook's, not Harold Innis's. Any suggestion to Innis that he was somehow responsible for the later trend of my thoughts and interests would have evoked from him no more than some characteristically acid-edged piece of ironic self-depreciation. Yet I am convinced that it was so. I suspect that Thorstein Veblen played a similar role—perhaps all great teachers do. North American scholarship is full of people who came under Veblen's influence, either personally or through his writings, and were irreversibly changed by the experience. But Veblen would not have taken kindly to any suggestion that he had been "influential" in a person-to-person sense. Influence of that kind carries with it an implication of responsibility. Veblen would have repudiated with scorn the suggestion that he was personally responsible for anyone's destiny other than his own; and I suspect that Innis's reaction would have been no different.

The comparison between Veblen and Innis is appropriate in another respect. In both cases one is conscious of tremendous intellectual power. This consciousness necessarily evokes respect, even when one disagrees with particular assertions. But this respect in both cases is time and again inter-mixed with what one must candidly call exasperation. In Veblen what exasperates is the deliberate search for paradox, the patent glee with which he turns convention on its head, the wilful contrariness of the man. With Innis it is the obscurity, the consistent refusal to write clearly and plainly, the shrouding of meaning in a fog of allusions and implications. At its worst this trait—in lectures and in writings—could be infuriating. One became infuriated because, in the last analysis, one was being asked to believe that, behind the ambiguity and imprecision there was profound meaning. What was required was, as Coleridge put it in another context, a willing suspension of disbelief. To be taught by Innis and to learn from Innis called for an act of faith. You had to believe that there was something really important there. Grains of doubt crept in from time to time—can anyone honestly deny it? Perhaps the Emperor had no new clothes after all.

It is very hard to find in Canadian scholarship today any serious criticism of Harold Innis. There has developed a kind of "cult of personality" rather like the mystique that now surrounds the *Annales* school of historians in Europe. There are interesting parallels between the two cases. Innis is known mostly for his work in the "staples theory" of Canadian history and for the later grand-scale extension of that theory to the "staple" of communications and the rise and fall of empires. The staples theory, it is now generally agreed, is not testable. It provides a framework for research, but no one can state what propositions one is required to accept or reject in order to qualify as a staples theorist. Melville Watkins, Gordon Bertram, and Kenneth Buckley have each in their own way gone as far as anyone can in the attempt to transform the staples theory into an operational model of development, but they would be the first to admit that their versions of the thesis—testable and quantifiable though they may be—fall far short of the rich suggestiveness of Innis's approach. Similarly with the *Annales* school. What is their method? What hypotheses are they testing? What assumptions are we asked to accept or reject? No one can say for sure. And so authority takes over where the logic of empiricism fails, and we have the cult of academic heroes. In the French case there is at least a line of succession: Febvre, Bloch, Braudel. In Canada no economic historian since Innis has come close to matching his reputation or his influence.

Such an outcome would have been anathema to Innis himself. No one could castigate monopolies of knowledge more vigorously than he. But we are discussing here his influence, not his intentions, and the fact of the matter is that, in Canadian economic history, Innis still dominates the field. In my personal judgment his influence has not been all to the good. Elsewhere, the last decade and a half in economic history has been one of the most exciting periods ever experienced in the history of the profession. Not so in Canada. There have been, it is true, a few echoes of the revolutionary experiments in methodology going on south of the border. John Dales and others have pointed out where the conventional wisdom is sadly in need of rethinking. And the statistical underpinning of the field is now in much better shape. But a reconstruction of the standard interpretation of Canadian economic history is still a long way off. That standard interpretation, enshrined in monographs and textbooks, is an interpretation on the Innis model. It is no compliment to Canadian scholarship that now, twenty-five years after his death, it still monopolizes the field.

The man's influence, it is clear, was powerful—perhaps more powerful than he knew, more powerful than he would have wished. Wherein did that power lie? Perhaps my own experience, as a professional economic historian who once passed through the field of influence of Harold Innis, can give some clues. When I came to Toronto in September, 1947, it was no part of my intention—nor of the intentions of my sponsor, the Hudson's Bay Company—that I should study economic history, far less specialize in it and make it my profession. Nevertheless, that is the way it turned out. And I have often tried to reconstruct the events and experiences that made it turn out

that way. It is not easy. There was certainly the assumption—unspoken but powerful—that only an idiot would be a graduate student in economics at Toronto and fail to take at least one course in economic history under Harold Innis. But this explains only one's initial introduction to the subject. It does not explain how at Toronto, and under Innis, the *idea* of economic history could reach out and take hold of a not-too-impressionable young man, and leave him convinced that, "Yes, certainly: this is what I want to do with my life."

The reason cannot have been that Harold Innis was, in any conventional sense of the word, an inspiring teacher. I can still recreate, in my imagination, the picture of that tall, stooped figure lecturing in the main auditorium of the old building on Bloor Street; just as clearly as I can hear the streetcars screeching down the tracks outside. And the truth is that, in his lecture courses, Harold Innis was often extraordinarily dull. And the same was true of his graduate seminar, in which indeed he spoke only infrequently, preferring to sit quietly in his chair in the corner, an inscrutable but somehow awe-inspiring figure.

No: it was not the teaching style of the man that inspired. It was the excitement of the ideas themselves. I had learned, as an undergraduate in Scotland, to conceive of economic history as a record of past economic activity—a record that it was the duty of scholars to make as comprehensive and accurate as possible, but nevertheless no more than a record. There was little there to inspire, little to elicit a commitment from students. What I got from Innis was something quite different. It was a sense of economic history as an enterprise, an exploration into the unknown. And in that enterprise a man's best aid came not from conscientious, careful diligence—though that was indispensable—but from the force of his ideas. The lectures indeed might seem dull and flat; the man himself clearly made no effort to entertain or amuse—to "relate to his students," as the cant phrase of today has it; but what was happening in Harold Innis's classes was that students were being introduced to the contest of ideas. And to those who had the native wit to sense what was going on, it was an exciting experience.

I have often been asked during my career, as all professors have, to make a judgment as to what is and what is not good teaching. Indeed, we have to make these judgments every day; because, although we may pride ourselves on our research and tell ourselves that research is the "really important" thing we do, nevertheless what we do most of the time is teach, and that is what we are mostly paid to do. I have been fortunate to have worked under some great teachers. Of these Harold Innis was the first. At Toronto I should also mention Tom Easterbrook. And later at Harvard there were men like Joseph Schumpeter and Leland Jenks. If I ask myself what these great teachers had in common, it was no particular quirk of personality, no gimmick of style or presentation. It was the power of their ideas—an almost uncanny ability, in lectures or in conversation, to throw out the ideas that, for their students, suddenly made everything they were learning make sense, so that all the particular things that were known suddenly fitted into a design. If this has ever happened to you, you will understand what I mean. It is not a matter of rhetoric; it is not something that a teacher can achieve by careful preparation and practice. It is an ability to make students *see* meaning in previously disjunct and disorganized data. The great teachers are those, I believe, who can give vision in this way.

I have spoken of the "power of their ideas" as one of the elements that made these men great teachers, and I mean by that not only explanatory power in the sense in which any scientific theory has explanatory power. I mean also the power to engage the imagination, the power to energize the often dull and tedious work of scholarly research and convert it into an exciting enterprise. It is no coincidence that each of the four master teachers I have mentioned was working out of a system of ideas which had this energizing power. For Innis it was originally his "staple thesis" of Canadian economic growth, broadening out at the time I first knew him into a comprehensive theory of the relationship between communications media and the rise and fall of empires. For Easterbrook it was his theme of enterprise and bureaucracy as the two basic organizational forms of economic life, each of them requiring a particular set of security conditions for its origin and survival. For Schumpeter it was his theory of the entrepreneur and his role in business cycles and economic development. And for Jenks it was Parsonian sociology, a conceptual apparatus of formidable complexity but also one of extreme comprehensiveness. Each of these men—and I think the same could be said of all good teachers—was teaching and thinking and writing out of a particular "idea-system." And it was the power of the idea-system that caught and held the attention of the student.

These "idea-systems" are what I have referred to, in the title of this article, as myths. And I think it will be clear that I am using the word in a particular, almost technical, sense. In popular usage, to refer to a system of beliefs as a myth is to sneer at it, to imply that it is somehow unworthy of the attention of the educated mind. This is not, I believe, a view that serious students of myths, be they anthropologists or theologians, are likely to accept, for they know very well that it is by their myths that men live; that men depend on myths to give meaning, significance, and purpose to their lives; and that cultures are formed as much by myths as by artifacts. Myths, in short, are important; they are functional; they have to be taken seriously. And if this is the view of the serious student of myth, it is also the view of those who create our myths: the poets and artists; the politicians; and, not least, some historians.

In the particular sense in which I am using the word, and with particular reference to economic history, I intend to distinguish between myths on the one hand and theories or hypotheses on the other. The basis for the distinction is simply that myths, as such, are not susceptible to disproof. They cannot, that is to say, be subjected to opera-

tional verification. And consequently they cannot be, in the positivistic sense, either true or false. To a logical positivist this would mean that myths have no meaning; they are made up of metaphysical statements. Within his system of definitions, this is undeniable. The position I wish to defend is simply that—whether or not they can be empirically tested, and perhaps even because there is no way in which they can be proved or disproved—myths are necessary for creative scholarship. Even more particularly, they are necessary for good teaching.

Let me illustrate my meaning by reference to a Canadian example: the so-called "staples approach" to Canadian economic history associated with the name of Harold Innis. Three points can be made:

1. There is no way in which the staples approach can be proved right or wrong. This is why one hesitates to refer to it as the staples theory or the staples hypothesis. These words seem too confining. We prefer the phrase "staples approach" precisely because it suggests not a series of testable propositions but a frame of reference, a point of view, a perspective, a way of *seeing* the data. One can, of course, reasonably discuss the usefulness of this point of view—and Canadian scholars have done so—suggesting that in certain phases of Canadian history the staples approach helps one to see what is really going on, while in other periods it obscures more than it illuminates. But, when we do this, we are discussing the instrumental value of the approach, not its empirical verifiability.

2. Nevertheless, even though not itself testable, it can be and in fact proved to be the source of a multitude of particular theories and hypotheses which could be and were tested. It provided, as it were, a frame of reference within which problems could be seen, and in terms of which hypotheses could be stated. Each of the individual theories or hypotheses is, so to speak, a translation of the myth into one possible testable form. But the particular hypothesis could fail without necessarily causing loss of faith in the myth itself.

3. The vitality of the myth, the power of the ideas that it contains, is shown precisely by its ability to call forth an outpouring of creative research activity. This is why the statement of a powerful myth is typically followed by a flowering of scholarship, a burst of creativity that sometimes makes one feel as if an obstacle to vision has been removed. And similarly, one evidence of the power of a myth is its ability to attract new talent into a field, as new possibilities become evident and new horizons opened up. As an example, we may recall the golden age of Canadian economic history that accompanied the statement and elaboration of the staples theme. Earlier, in the United States, much the same thing had happened after Frederick Jackson Turner's statement of the "frontier theory." And, on a much more modest scale, I was associated with something of the same kind at Harvard, in the pioneering days of research in entrepreneurial history.

Harold Innis was a great scholar and a great teacher because his myths had the power to energize, to inspire, to make one see meanings in history that one had not seen before. I make no distinction, in this respect, between the early and the late Innis. Whether he was writing about the fur trade or about the power of empires to control time and space, his technique was essentially the same. And this helps us to understand, also, the deliberate obscurity and difficulty of his writing. One does not expect the makers of myths to follow the canons of logical positivism. Indeed they cannot, for their myths are suggestive precisely to the extent that they lack identifiable operational meaning. The most precise language of all is mathematics; it can attain that level of precision because it is a purely formal language, devoid of content. One gains precision by losing the suggestibility, the ambiguity, the aura of associations and allusions that are characteristic of myth. Abandon these features of myth, and you may then hope to work comfortably with numbers, operational definitions, and precise measurement. But it is not possible to work in both modes simultaneously.

This is what I have referred to in the title of this article as the difference between myth and measurement. The terms are no more than convenient tags for different styles of historical writing, different techniques, if you will, of attaining historical plausibility. I do not mean to suggest that they are polar opposites. There are those, indeed, who would say that belief in measurement as a means of gaining understanding into the processes of history is the greatest myth of all. And Innis himself was never averse to using measurements to garnish his history, when measurements were available. But the difference is, nevertheless, real and important. It is a difference in the strategy of writing and teaching history, a difference between those who hold that truth can be found by counting and those who do not. Innis belonged to the latter way of thinking. And to be a historian in the Innisian mode is necessarily to lean toward myth rather than measurement.

If I am correct, developments in Canadian economic history over the last decade and a half—or rather, the relative lack of developments—become more readily understandable. For this has been a period in which the pendulum of style in the writing of economic history has swung decisively toward measurement. And the new modes of analysis, the new methods, have not proved easy to graft onto the main stem of the old myths. The puzzling question is why these myths have been so resistant to change in Canada, while in the United States most of them have proved vulnerable. The strength of the Innis tradition may be one explanation.

In the United States, the last fifteen or sixteen years in economic history have been a strange and somewhat paradoxical period. It has been a period of intense research activity, of very high productivity, of great excitement and change in the profession. And yet it has been a period in which the major thrust of work has been critical and revisionist—directed toward the destruction of old myths rather than the statement of new ones. In this period we have seen the birth of the new economic history, or what is now called cliometrics; and we have seen this movement transformed from a strange innovation into an accepted body of techniques and objectives. Its advocates, originally a small minority of scholars of the younger generation, are now the leaders of the profession, a new establishment if you will. And their view of the nature and purpose of economic history—what it should try to be, and how we should undertake to do it—has, in the United States at least, come to be the majority view of the active members of the profession. As all who have lived through it will agree, these years have been years of great excitement and interest. It may be an overstatement—indeed, I am sure it is—to refer to this period as constituting a revolution in the methods and philosophy of economic history. But is is unquestionably true that there have been very substantial changes concentrated in a relatively short span of time. Indeed, so substantial have been these changes that it has been a matter of surprise to some of us that the professional structure of economic history, and in particular its Association, has held together over this period, and that the formation of splinter groups and new forms of association has been held to a minimum. There has been more continuity in organization and in the spirit of the profession than one might have expected.

At this point it is necessary for me to give a brief sketch of the new economic history and to give some idea of what the advent of this new intellectual style in economic history has meant. Many readers may already be familiar with this information—from them I ask indulgence. But others may not be, and for them a few words of explanation are appropriate. I should make it clear, to begin with, that I do not consider myself to be one of the new economic historians, and I do not believe that anyone else considers me to be one of them. I am, however, in considerable sympathy with most of their objectives; and I am greatly impressed with the sense of new vigour and excitement that they have brought into a somewhat staid branch of scholarship. In particular, they have been responsible for an influx of talent into the field that is truly remarkable. But I cannot claim to be one of that number.

The best way to convey an idea of what the new economic history is may well be by the "way of negation"—that is, to describe what it is not. Let me begin, then, by stressing that it was not the creation of any one individual, or even of a small number. There have been leading figures, of course, and certain universities have from time to time enjoyed the reputation of being its spiritual home. But this was not a matter of a "school" forming under the influence and leadership of a great scholar. It was much more like a general movement within the profession, and specifically a movement of the younger members, almost a matter of generations. In some respects, indeed, it was a radical movement in economic history very characteristic of the climate of the 1960s; and just as disturbing to the morale and self-confidence of those of us of the older generation as were the radical movements in student politics to some conservative faculty members. Its earliest advocates were young doctoral candidates, instructors, and assistant professors, entering economic history from departments of economics in the late 1950s and early 1960s. What they brought with them into economic history was the desire to use, and the conviction that they could use, for purposes of historical analysis, the theoretical and computational skills that they had acquired during their graduate training as economists.

Now, this was a desire that others before them had had. The difference was not the desire to use theory in economic history but the confidence that it could be done and some advanced ideas as to how it could be done. The theory that they brought with them was, for the most part, modern neoclassical partial equilibrium theory. Supplementing this was usually a thorough training in statistics, econometrics, national income analysis, and in some cases skill in the handling of large masses of data by computer. If I had to specify the two most salient characteristics that all the early members of the new economic history had in common, I would say that they were all very good theorists, and none of them had any doubts about his ability to handle quantitative evidence on any scale that the historical record might provide.

The new economic history is sometimes referred to as quantitative economic history. It is true that its techniques are quantitative. It is not true that this is enough to define it. Quantitative research has always been characteristic of economic history; and even within the last fifteen years there has been much quantitative research done in economic history—for example, by Kuznets and his students—which is not part of the cliometric movement. No: it goes deeper than this. What is characteristic of the new economic history is the use of quantitative evidence to test hypotheses derived from theory and stated in terms of theoretical concepts. It is this blending of theory and measurement that is the defining characteristic. The theory has been neoclassical partial equilibrium theory, with some admixture of development theory; the techniques have been derived from statistics and econometrics.

This blending of theory and measurement has given the new economic history one of its characteristic techniques: the counterfactual hypothesis. A counterfactual hypothesis usually derives from the attempt to estimate the historical significance of an event by assuming the absence of that event—that is, something contrary to fact—or its change in some specified way, and asking what difference that would have made to the outcome. This is the kind of thing we do every day in a non-systematic way when we ask, "I wonder what would have happened if . . . ?" It is not a technique much approved by respectable historians. But it has become one of the hallmarks of the new economic history. Thus we find them asking, "What difference would it have made to 19th century economic development in the United States if the railroads had not been built? What difference

would it have made to the standard of living of American colonists if the Navigation Acts had been repealed? If Southern slaveowners had not invested their money in slaves, what would they have invested in, and would they have earned a higher or a lower rate of return? If slavery had been abolished in the United States in 1789, would the rate of economic development in the American South, or in the nation as a whole, have been higher or lower?" And so on. These are the kinds of questions the new economic historians ask. And not only ask, but also answer quantitatively, and in a way that, they believe, can convince the skeptic. It is the audacity with which such questions are asked, and the confident quantitative way in which they are answered, that have made the work of the new economic historians so controversial, and so intellectually stimulating.

Hypothetical history of this kind is not, as I have indicated, in much favour with respectable historians of the traditional school. What is it that makes the new economic historians believe they can execute it? It is precisely the marriage of economic theory and econometric technique to which I have just referred. Economic theory makes it possible to define the characteristics of a counter-factual situation—to define them so that "not everything is possible" once one departs from historical reality. Statistics and econometrics make it possible to estimate what difference such a counterfactual change would cause—if not one precise measure, at least an order of magnitude, an upper and lower bound. This is possible because economics has a developed body of theory with predictive power, so that it can be used by economic historians in a way that, so far, political or social theory cannot.

It is not measurement alone, then, that characterizes the new economic history, but measurement inspired by theory and guided by theory. The strengths of the new economic history, its impressive achievements, have been in those areas where economic theory has provided strong support. Its weaknesses and failures have been where the supporting theory has been weak, or where it has been called upon to serve purposes it is inadequate to serve. "The common thread running through the New Economic History is a commitment to the efficacy of theory in specifying useful counterfactuals, and to quantitative methods in implementing them." (Fishlow)

The adoption of this philosophy of research and of these techniques of enquiry has generated, over the last fifteen years, one of the most remarkable outbursts of productive activity in the history of our discipline. It is true that most of this activity has been critical in nature: a matter of questioning accepted myths and revising accepted interpretations rather than propounding new ones. And it is also true that, when one stands back and considers the end-result, many of the old interpretations have withstood the critical attack rather well. We now have to be more careful to say exactly what we mean; we have to be on guard against the dangerously dramatic phrase—the take-off, the revolution, the indispensability of this or that—

that says more than we are entitled to say. This is good for our souls, and the whole episode has had a pronounced cleansing and astringent effect on the discipline. It has also added very substantially to our factual knowledge of the past. And, perhaps most important, it has attracted into the discipline a cadre of highly intelligent and highly trained economists who, in all probability, would otherwise never have considered becoming economic historians.

All this is to the good. And yet the success has not been unqualified. And it seems now as if these qualifications are becoming apparent.

Neoclassical economic theory was a system of ideas designed to show the principles by which scarce resources are efficiently allocated among competing uses. As we all know, to elucidate these principles it considered the implications of incremental changes at the margin; and its typical device, particularly in its Marshallian form, was to consider only a single change at a time, all other factors in the situation being held constant. Consider for a moment what neoclassical economic theory was *not,* and what it was not intended to be. It was not a theory of long-run economic change. It was not a theory of non-market behaviour. It was not a theory of discontinuous change—"Nature makes no jumps," said Marshall. And it was not a theory of social institutions; in particular it had no theory of the state, and therefore was, strictly speaking, inapplicable to any problem in which the survival or growth of the state was a prime consideration.

In view of these rather obvious facts, it is remarkable that the new economic historians have been able to make such effective use of neoclassical economic theory. This may prove, as my friend John Dales has often said, that in economic history just a little theory will carry you a long way. Or it may be a tribute to the skill and ingenuity of the new economic historians in converting into a form with which neoclassical theory could come to grips, problems originally of a quite different nature: that is, converting general equilibrium problems into a partial equilibrium form; converting discontinuities into continuities; and conceiving of long-run development in terms of short-run shifts at the margin. The degree of success is still remarkable; for the problems the new economic historians have chosen to deal with—the influence of the railroads, the effects of slavery on long-run growth, large changes in government policy such as the dismantling of a mercantilist empire, and so on—are far distant indeed from any problems that neoclassical economic theory was designed to deal with.

It has been, I say, remarkable. And you will notice that I use the past tense. The reason for this is that there are clear signs of growing dissatisfaction with the limitations of the new economic history as it has been carried on so far. These limitations have been the limitations of the underlying theory; and they have been responsible for the often rather strained forcing of historical problems into a form with which an essentially ill-suited theory could

deal. This dissatisfaction is being voiced most strongly, not by outside critics, but by the leaders of the movement themselves. What they are calling for is not abandonment of the commitment to theory and measurement that has inspired their work for the last decade and a half. What they are calling for is the statement of theories that will be less restrictive. This is why I think we may be at some kind of a turning point in the history of economic history at this moment: a shift (in the terms I have been using in this paper) away from the phase of myth-destruction and myth-criticism that has occupied the last fifteen years, and towards a new phase of myth-statement and myth-creation.

It will be interesting to watch how this new phase develops. The characteristic techniques of the new economic history have involved an insistence on the explicit statement of theoretical models and on the quantitative testing of hypotheses. These techniques have been excellently adapted for the tasks of critical revision which have so far been the principal occupation of the movement. It remains to be seen how far they can be reconciled with the demands of myth-creation, which may involve a much looser use of concepts and the postulating of relationships that may be hard to test empirically.

Do I exaggerate the indications that a change of this kind is taking place? I think not. I turn to the pages of the *Journal of Economic History,* and I find a presidential address by William Parker of Yale entitled "From Old to New to Old in Economic History." In it he very appropriately commends the achievements of the new economic history (to which he has himself contributed in no small way), calling it "a gigantic test of the hypothesis of economic rationality," or alternatively, "A kind of hymn to what really happened . . . justifying the ways of the price system to man." But then he turns to what he calls the second great truth that modern economic history can teach us; and here the new myth enters. This second great truth turns out to be the Truth of the Recurring Opportunity, the truth of "the invisible hand which . . . within some societies . . . appears to have contrived their whole structure . . . in such a way as to create and refresh the stream of growth opportunities to which their economies can respond." And within a few pages we find him calling for a redirection of work, so that we may increase our understanding of "how social organizations are created through human action and how in turn they mold and channel human action."

Or alternatively we turn to the presidential address of Douglass North, long one of the most eloquent advocates of the new economic history, and we find him, in the March 1974 issue of the same journal, not listing its achievements but itemizing its limitations: its destructive thrust; its concentration on specific issues or institutions rather than long-run processes of change; its neglect of the role of government and of the "overwhelming percentage" of economic decisions that have always been made "outside the market"; and—this I find particularly significant—the fact that North finds the new economic history "curiously unteachable at the undergraduate level"—that it "leaves students frustrated" because of its failure to "provide any integrated explanation of man's economic past." This is clearly related to what Albert Fishlow of Berkeley has called the "dedramatizing" influence of the new economic history—what I would call its demythologizing influence—but North gives more emphasis to its failure to grapple with the dynamics of change. "If we have found slavery profitable," he writes, "railroads less than essential, and the burden of the Navigation Acts 'light,' we have not said what did make the system go." And, in pursuit of this goal of understanding "what did make the system go," North's own work has recently taken a decided turn toward the analysis of institutional change over the long run.

The clearest demonstration of my point, however, comes from the recent work of two scholars who are commonly regarded as among the leading exponents of the new economic history. I refer, of course, to Robert Fogel and Stanley Engerman and to their recent study of American slavery, *Time on the Cross*. I have no desire to add my quota to the intense controversy that the appearance of this book has aroused—controversy entirely typical of the forceful statement of a new myth. I ask you only to consider the authors' stated objectives. Chief among these objectives is "the recovery of black history": that is, its recovery from the racist interpretations promulgated by previous white historians, including particularly liberal white historians. Fogel and Engerman are concerned to present to the black man an image of his past in which he can take pride; and it is to the creation and elaboration of that image that all the quantitative calculations which fill the pages of *Time on the Cross* are directed. Their purpose is to destroy an unacceptable and, in their view, indefensible myth and replace it with one more acceptable and more defensible. Indeed, they are quite candid in stating this purpose. Here is the concluding paragraph of their text:

> Time on the cross did not come to an end for American blacks with the down-fall of the peculiar institution. For they were held on the cross not just by the chains of slavery but also by the spikes of racism. It is one of the bitterest ironies of history that the antislavery critics who worked so hard to break these chains probably did as much as any other group, perhaps more, to fasten the spikes that have kept blacks in the agony of racial discrimination during their century of freedom. The spikes are fashioned of myths that turned diligent and efficient workers into lazy loafers and bunglers, that turned love of family into a disregard for it, that turned those who struggled for self-improvement in the only way they could into "Uncle Toms." Three hundred and fifty years on the cross are enough. It's time to reveal not only to blacks but to whites as well, that part of American history which has been kept from them— the record of black achievement under adversity.

For the intellectual audacity that inspires these ventures—both those of Fogel and Engerman and the types

of work now projected by scholars like North and Parker—I have the highest respect. I do not wish to leave the impression that I regard them as in any way misguided. The only point I wish to make is that this kind of work is a far cry indeed from the explicitly specified models and quantified variables that were the standard fare of the new economic history in its earlier critical phase. And it is a fair question whether the techniques— and perhaps also the attitude of somewhat Puritanical self-righteousness—that characterized the earlier phase will also serve in the second. We are no longer tearing down myths that an older generation of economic historians created. We are creating myths of our own—ones that in time will no doubt be subjected to the same kind of radical criticism that has been the stock in trade of the new economic history in the past fifteen years.

Predicting the future course of fashion is no less hazardous in scholarship than in more commercial endeavors. As regards research and writing in U.S. economic history, however, the odds seem very high that the next fifteen years will prove at least as interesting and active as the last fifteen have been. The pendulum has begun its reverse swing; the urgent need for what I have called myths—for generalizations on a broader and more ambitious scale—is coming to be recognized; and the profession is now staffed by cadres of young scholars of exceptional technical competence. It will be an interesting period to watch.

But what of Canadian studies? The cliometric revolution south of the border has not been entirely without its "ripple effects" in Canada. There have been annual conferences, attended mostly by younger scholars who received their graduate training in the United States. One can cite a baker's dozen of Canadian cliometric contributions, each of them valuable but of limited scope. And there has been a healthy growth of dissatisfaction with economic history's conventional wisdom. None of this, however, has added up to the reconstruction of Canadian economic history that is now overdue by at least a quarter of a century. The traditional interpretations are still taught in classrooms across the country. A textbook written in the most conventional of "staples approach" modes still, wonder of wonders, retains its hold on the market. Only the most incurable of Pollyannas could discern symptoms of a creative stirring, far less of a new synthesis, in Canadian economic history at the moment. And this in Canada, which once under the leadership of Harold Innis, could make a fair claim to world eminence in the field.

Personally, I lean toward optimism. After all, why not? Any other attitude inhibits one's own work and stifles that of one's students. For economic history in general the omens look good. With the close of the initial phase of critical revisionism and myth-destruction, economic historians are once again starting to reach out toward those larger idea-systems that have the power to excite the imagination and elicit the kind of commitment to scholarship that Harold Innis could draw from his students. For economic history in Canada even more may be hoped, for here the reaction against the inherited truths has been muted and delayed, and the new synthesis, when it does come, may be more dramatic and more revolutionary than in the United States. The Innis tradition, after all, is a resource as well as a constraint, for no Canadian historian can afford to forget the courage, the audacity, the sheer power of Innis's ideas at their best. And there are broader issues at stake. If we can lift our eyes for a moment from purely academic concerns, we may remind ourselves that historical myths are important not only for the narrow fraternity of scholars but also for the larger community of which they are a part. What we teach in our lecture rooms and graduate seminars today is what will be taught in the high schools of the next generation—and what will be taken for granted as "what everyone knows" in the generation after that. It is the myths that are remembered by students long after the measurements are forgotten. And these myths are important because the way a people thinks of its past is important: important to the way it regards itself in the present and to what it thinks is possible in the future. The staples thesis, in the hands of Innis and his school, provided a rationale for the existence of the Canadian nation. It helped to make what had happened understandable and what existed acceptable. It placed Canada in historic time, so that you could see it whole and believe that you comprehended it. That myth has now lost its power, as all myths eventually must if they are not continually refreshed and reinterpreted. What takes its place is a matter of some importance, to Canadians and to all who wish them well.

W. J. Eccles (essay date 1979)

SOURCE: "A Belated Review of Harold Adams Innis, *The Fur Trade in Canada,*" in *Canadian Historical Review,* Vol. LX, No. 4, December, 1979, pp. 419-41.

[*In the following essay, Eccles compares the historic fur trade in Canada with Innis's scholarship on it.*]

A reappraisal of the Canadian fur trade is long overdue. For this to be done adequately there are two prerequisites: first, past misconceptions have to be cleared away; then the trade has to be placed in its historic and not just its economic context. This communication addresses itself primarily to the first of these presumptions.

Harold Adams Innis' major work, *The Fur Trade in Canada,* has long been regarded as the definitive work on the subject, an impeccable piece of scholarship, and a landmark in Canadian historiography. Robin W. Winks stated in his foreword to the 1962 edition, 'The book is of the greatest significance because of Innis' fundamental reinterpretation of North American history and because of the effect of that reinterpretation on subsequent scholarship.'[1] The statement is certainly true, but Professor Winks then went on to state that Innis 'never wrote an inadequately researched or thoughtless book.' A little

farther on, however, he qualified this encomium with the *caveat* 'his method of citation was somewhat quixotic,' as indeed it was.[2] The sweeping generalizations and conclusions of this work have been accepted uncritically by too many later historians. Unfortunately, neither his premises, both stated and unstated, his use of historical evidence, nor the conclusions drawn will stand up to close scrutiny and all too many erroneous interpretations of North American history have been made in consequence.

Innis saw clearly enough that in the early sixteenth century the trade in furs began as an adjunct of the cod fishery and that the coming into fashion of the beaver-felt hat had made the fur trade viable in its own right. His brief studies of the ecology of the beaver and of the manufacture and marketing of felt hats are certainly well done, albeit the latter study was derivative, being based on the work of French and British economic historians.[3] It was certainly the profits to be made in the garnering of furs from the Indians and their sale in France at a high profit that first enabled the French to establish permanent settlements in Acadia and the St Lawrence valley. Innis, however, took economic determinism to extremes and grossly exaggerated the role of the fur trade in the history of both North America and Europe. He stated, for example: 'The economic and institutional life of France undoubtedly suffered material disarrangement through the importation of furs on a large scale from New France.'[4] He produced no evidence in support of this claim and it is necessary only to examine the volume and value of the fur trade relative to the kingdom's total trade for it to be immediately apparent that the statement is, to say the least, a gross exaggeration.

Statistics are available for the years 1718–61 for furs imported at La Rochelle, the main port of entry for Canadian produce. These imports average out at roughly one million *livres* worth a year.[5] After 1739 some furs were shipped to Rouen by the Dugard *Compagnie du Canada,* which likely accounts for the decline in the La Rochelle import figures in the ensuing years.[6] The total amount entering Rouen could not have been very great, and thus the figure of about a million livres a year on average is as accurate as the work done to date will allow. A large amount of beaver was smuggled from Montreal to New York, but the participants in this clandestine trade were careful not to provide records. In any event these furs went to England; the Canadian economy benefitted thereby but that of France was not directly affected.

These statistics indicate clearly that the furs imported into France from Canada were a minuscule item in the country's trade balance. By 1741 the total value of French trade with the colonies was calculated to be worth 140 millions a year, and the total for all external trade was 300 million livres.[7] Compared to sugar, coffee, indigo, chocolate, and fish, fur was of minimal value.[8] Innis's assertion, therefore that the economy and institutions of France were thrown into disarray by the Canadian fur trade has to be regarded as a figment of his imagination.

Hard on the heels of the quest for furs as a motive for French colonization in Acadia and Canada came evangelism, the desire on the part of the French crown to carve out an empire in North America to rival that of Spain, and, also, the quest for precious metals and a water route through the unknown land mass to the Pacific. The charter of Richelieu's Company of One Hundred Associates states that its main purpose was to convert the Indians to Christianity.[9] The trade in furs was to be pursued to provide funds for this purpose. For the ensuing thirty years it was the French church that, directly or indirectly, provided the support that saved the colony from foundering. After the destruction of the Jesuit mission in Huronia by the Iroquois and the consequent opening of the western Great Lakes to French fur traders, the role of the church in the fur trade dwindled. Montreal, founded as a missionary centre, now became the main base for the exploitation of the western fur trade. Innis, however, failed to see the significance of these underlying factors. For him economics was all that counted.

When, in 1663, the crown took over responsibility for the colony from the moribund company, the monopoly on the marketing in France of all beaver pelts was purchased by a Quebec merchant, Aubert de la Chesnaye, then a year later it reverted to Colbert's newly established *Compagnie des Indes Occidentales*. In 1674 Colbert closed the books of that company and obliged a group of French tax farmers to take over the beaver marketing monopoly on a yearly lease of 350,000 *livres*. In his brief treatment of these complex arrangements Innis misunderstood what had actually transpired: that the fur trade did not loom as large on the French colonial balance sheet as he imagined.[10] What the new *Compagnie de la Ferme* of Jean Oudiette had wanted was control of the African slave trade and certain West Indies produce. That the beaver trade was not the company's main interest is demonstrated by the fact that it immediately subleased it to La Chesnaye for 119,000 *livres,* thereby taking a loss of 131,000 *livres* a year just to get it off its hands.[11] Similarly, Innis attributed the demise of the *Compagnie des Indes Occidentales* to heavy losses incurred in Canada when, in fact, the real reasons lay elsewhere.[12]

The pursuit of the fur trade for purely economic ends did not endure beyond the end of the seventeenth century. The amount of beaver exported to France had grown astronomically until, by the 1690s, it far exceeded what the market could absorb. By 1696 the French government had to face the fact that the beaver trade was bankrupt, although the trade in other furs continued to be profitable. The immediate reaction of the minister of marine was drastic. He ordered the suspension of the beaver trade and the abandonment of all but one of the trading posts in the west. At the one post to be held, St Louis des Illinois, no beaver was to be traded. It was to be retained solely for military purposes. England and France were then at war and for the past decade the Canadians had

been struggling desperately to repell the assaults of Britain's allies, the Iroquois confederacy. The minister's hasty decision had to be reversed the following year for political and military reasons. The senior officials in the colony were swift to point out to the minister that were France to withdraw from the west in such a fashion the English colonials would quickly take over the trade with the Indian nations. The commercial and military alliances with them would then be dissolved, they would be drawn into the English camp, and New France would quickly be overwhelmed. It is by no means certain that events would have fallen out at that point in time as these officials foretold, but they clearly saw a manifest danger that they believed had to be forfended. The French government thus found itself obliged to continue to support the fur trade even though its current mainstay, beaver, was then an economic liability.[13]

The accession of William of Orange to the English throne in 1689 and of Louis XIV's grandson to that of Spain in 1700 brought about a marked shift in the European balance of power and a prompt renewal of Anglo-French hostilities. From this point on the fur trade was mainly an economic weapon in Anglo-French imperial rivalry. What was now of primary importance to France was not the trade in furs *per se* but the military alliances it made possible with the Indian nations who were a far more important factor in this European power struggle than has yet been recognized. It was they, not the French or the English, who were sovereign in the west, despite the grandiose claims made by the rival powers. Indeed, their respective claims to sovereignty over the interior of the continent had about as much validity as the claims of the English crown to the throne of France, which were not relinquished until 1802. The French position was that, given their grossly inferior numbers, they had, at all costs, to keep the Indians from contact with the English. This meant they had to supply the Indians with the European goods they could no longer do without. Were the French not to supply them they would, of necessity, go over to the English. With the renewal of Anglo-French hostilities in 1702 fur trade posts became a chain of garrisoned military forts where furs had to be traded, at a loss if necessary, to retain the Indian nations in the French alliance and bar any attempted expansion of the English colonies west of the Alleghenies. If the fur trade at these posts showed a profit, so much the better. At least it was expected that the trade would help to defray the costs of this ambitious new imperial policy in North America.

This was a political factor that Innis failed completely to grasp. He viewed the events that occurred between 1696 and 1700 from the viewpoint merely of economics. He gives a confused account, including masses of dubious statistics culled from primary sources that are not subjected to critical scrutiny, but the overriding significance of the political decisions made during those years escaped him.[14] He mistakenly assumed that the French military effort in New France was intended solely to serve the economic ends of the fur trade.

In his preface to Murray G. Lawson, *Fur: A Study of English Mercantilism 1700-1775* (ix), Innis states: 'Military and naval efforts to check encroachment on the St. Lawrence from the Hudson route and Hudson Bay, and particularly the establishment of posts along the Great Lakes to check the Iroquois from the south and English competitors from the north, involved an enormous outlay of funds on the part of the government and sharp fluctuations in the supplies of varying grades of furs, depending in part on victories and defeats.' The French government's decision in 1696 to abandon the western posts and to curb the trade in beaver indicates clearly enough that the expenditures mentioned here were not made for the sake of the fur trade; neither was the subsequent decision of 1700 to establish a new base at Detroit and the colony of Louisiana to control the Mississippi valley. Innis also overlooked the fact that the British too had to make an enormous outlay of funds for military purposes in North America—for example, Forts Churchill, William Henry, Edward, and Oswego, not to mention Halifax. Nor will his statement that 'an increased burden of taxation to support militaristic ventures' placed the Canadians in a disadvantageous trading position bear scrutiny.[15] The only taxes paid by the Canadians were import and export duties on certain items and they were in no way affected by military expenditures. Those costs were borne by the French government and were certainly not a charge on the fur trade. Similarly, 'The increase in fixed capital which accompanied extension of military control . . .'[16] was not a drain on the fur trade; if anything it had the reverse effect. He also states: 'The vicious circle, in which cheaper English goods and more efficient English traders in the south necessitated greater expenditure on military measures to check competition, and the burden of increasing expenditures falling chiefly on the fur trade reduced the prices offered by the French to the Indians and encouraged competition . . .'[17] There is not a particle of evidence to support those claims but a great deal that refutes them, some of which, ironically, Innis cites himself in other contexts.[18]

A careful and extensive comparison of the prices of English and French trade goods has yet to be made, and so far as the French are concerned it is difficult to see how one could discover the prices they charged the Indians; whatever the market would bear, most likely. What evidence there is available indicates that some English goods were cheaper, some more expensive, but on the whole the difference between French and English prices was minimal. Too often comparisons that have been made are akin to those of apples and oranges and many of the comparisons made by the French in the seventeenth century, showing the prices of goods at Albany to be far lower than those at Montreal, are suspect since their compilers were pleading a case to have the *quart,* the 25 per cent export duty on beaver, removed to increase their profits.

English traders to the south were definitely not more efficient than the Canadians. Indeed, the reverse was the case. The fact that the merchants of New York obtained the bulk of their furs clandestinely from Montreal testifies to this.[19] *The American Gazetteer,* vol. II, published in London in 1762, in the entry on Montreal declared: 'the French have found some secret of conciliating the affections of the savages, which our traders seem stranger to, or at least take no care to put it in practice.'[20]

Military measures were neither required nor employed to check English competition in the fur trade; the burden of military expenditures most definitely did not fall on the trade, and there is no evidence to indicate that the French were obliged to reduce the prices they offered for furs for that reason. In fact, in 1754 when the French established Fort Duquesne at the forks of the Ohio the governor general ordered the commandant of the fort to regulate the prices charged the Indians for goods to put an end to their complaints of over-charging. This was done for political and military reasons. In short, military and political policy led to an increase in the prices offered by the French to the Indians, hence an improved competitive position; the reverse of what Innis claimed.[21] Again there is not a particle of evidence to support any of these claims, and that which Innis cites refutes them.[22]

A further figment of Innis's imagination is contained in his assertion: 'The military organization which had grown up because of the exigencies of the fur trade, though long effective, eventually collapsed.'[23] One would have thought that if there is one fact in Canadian history that is indisputable it is that New France was conquered, after five years of hostilities, by a British army and the Royal Navy, assisted by the fatal blunders committed by the French commander the Marquis de Montcalm at the battle of Quebec in 1759.[24] Innis, however, will not have it. He declares, 'The French power in New France collapsed of its own weight,'[25] but he subsequently advances a different reason for the British victory. 'The conquest of New France was largely the result of the efficiency of English manufactures combined with the control of shorter routes to the interior from New York and Hudson Bay.'[26] Wolfe, Murray, and Admiral Saunders would not likely have been in agreement. Moreover, Innis here blithely overlooked the fact that the Hudson's Bay Company men failed to establish themselves beyond the shores of the bay prior to the Conquest, and that the Anglo-American traders who eventually reached the Ohio valley were swiftly driven out.[27]

Two major points that Innis emphasized throughout his work were that the Canadian fur traders could not compete successfully with the Hudson's Bay Company owing to the latter's shorter trade route to the interior, hence lower costs, and the superiority and lower price of British trade goods.[28] He produced no viable evidence in support of these assertions; indeed, some of the evidence he cites contradicts them.[29] To deal first with the issue of the shorter trade route to the interior from Hudson Bay, this is, of course, true. Goods could be landed at the bay posts much more cheaply than at the main Canadian base at Michilimackinac, but once the goods arrived at the latter base they were only a short journey from the major fur trade areas. On the other hand, goods landed at the bay then had to be transported several hundred miles inland to the tribes that produced the furs.[30]

The Hudson's Bay Company lacked the two things required to transport goods to the interior—birch bark canoes and skilled canoemen. It was not until the York boat was developed in the nineteenth century that the Bay men were able to compete successfully with the Canadians. Prior to the Conquest the Bay Company had to rely on Cree middlemen to transport furs to the bay posts and the trade goods back to the fur producing tribes. This was a long hazardous journey through country where game was very scarce, hence supplies of food had to be carried both ways which reduced the amount of cargo that could be carried. The Cree canoemen undoubtedly expected to be recompensed for their labour, particularly when they could obtain the same goods from Canadian traders in their midst or nearby. Thus Innis's assertion that 'goods were obtained on a large scale, and with access by sea, at much more favourable rates' is, to say the least, dubious, and he produces no evidence to support it.[31]

Another important factor was that the Cree middlemen voyaging to the bay used small three-man canoes having a maximum capacity of 1000 pounds of goods,[32] whereas the Canadians used five- to eight-man *canots du maître* carrying loads of 4000 pounds.[33] At one point Innis gives as a reference evidence that contradicts his assertion.[34] The Canadians, in addition to larger canoes, had other advantages over the Bay traders. They had a much longer navigation season, April to October. For the Indians going to the bay it was a race to get there and back before freeze up.[35] The Canadians travelled through country where fish and game abounded in contrast to the hundreds of miles of 'starving country' west of Hudson Bay. Moreover, leached corn, the staple food of the fur brigades, could be obtained at Detroit and Michilimackinac.

When he came to deal with the rivalry between the Hudson's Bay Company and the North West Company, Innis again asserted that the former company had the advantage of a shorter route to the interior for the transport of heavier goods at lower cost, but in a footnote he cites the *Journals of Hearne and Turnor* who stated: 'The Canadians have greatly the advantage . . . in getting goods inland as five of their men with one canoe will carry as much goods as ten of the Honourable Company's servants can with 5 canoes.'[36] Exactly the same condition had obtained during the French régime, but Innis failed to draw the obvious inference from the evidence he cited.

The assertion Innis made that the Bay Company could transport heavier goods into the interior at lower cost than could the Canadians, failing to note that it was Indian middlemen and not company servants who performed the task, was accepted without question by some later historians of the fur trade. It has recently been stated that 'after 1714 the Hudson's Bay company managed to hold on to the major share of the trade of the subarctic Indians. The company was the primary supplier of bulky,

or heavy items such as kettles and guns that were difficult to transport overland in canoes in large quantities.'[37] The first statement is refuted by the tables produced by Murray Lawson which show a steady decline in Hudson's Bay Company fur receipts from 1713 to 1760 and also by the statistics given by Innis for fur receipts at the bay during the decades 1738-48.[38] The second statement, that the bay posts supplied the Indians with the bulk of the heavy goods is dubious in the extreme. The authors produced no evidence to support the assertion and it defies common sense. It would have been much easier for the Canadians to transport such goods in their eight-man *canots du maître* than it would have been for the Cree middlemen trading at the bay with their small three-man canoes. Thus the notion that 'a shorter route to the interior' gave the Hudson's Bay Company a marked competitive advantage over the Canadian traders, prior to the introduction of the York boat, has to be regarded as just another Innis myth that came to be accepted as conventional wisdom.

One point that Innis emphasized strongly was his *a priori* belief that the French were unable to compete successfully with the English in the fur trade owing to the superior quality and lower price of English goods.[39] A typical assertion of the claim occurs in the concluding chapter of the work in question: 'The importance of manufactures in the fur trade gave England, with her more efficient industrial development, a decided advantage. The competition of cheaper goods contributed in a definite fashion to the downfall of New France and enabled Great Britain to prevail in the face of its pronounced militaristic development.'[40] He made the same assertion in his preface to Lawson's *Fur: A study in English Mercantilism, 1700-1775*, even though the body of that work demonstrated the contrary. Innis, however, never allowed himself to be deterred by a want of evidence, or even conflicting evidence, in making his sweeping generalizations. He cited, for example, a lengthy statement dated 20 February 1765 which declared that the British traders in the west greatly feared the consequences were New Orleans to be ceded to Spain. The quoted writer stated: 'should that city pass into the hands of the Spaniards their allies the French will nevertheless supply them with suitable goods at a cheaper Rate than the English can do by reason of the high price of Labour among our Manufactures to wit, especially in Gunns, course cutlery etc . . .'[41] He also quoted from a letter written by a British trader at Michilimackinac to a gentleman in Quebec, published in the Quebec *Gazette* of 18 August 1768: 'All those who have wintered between this and the River Mississippi, complain of the French and Spaniards, of New Orleans, having undersold them considerably in every Article . . .'[42] That the French and Spaniards of Louisiana were then trading the same goods that the Canadians had used for decades Innis chose to ignore.

It is, of course, impossible to obtain first-hand evidence on the relative quality and price of French and British trade goods. The only available evidence is documentary, what interested parties wrote on the subject. This evidence has to be examined critically—all of it cannot be accepted at face value and the motives of the writers have to be taken into account. Moreover, one has to be reasonably sure, when price comparisons are made, that articles of the same quality are being compared.

Innis produced no evidence in support of his assumed 'growing supremacy of Great Britain in manufactures' in the first half of the eighteenth century. The assumption was, in fact, quite unfounded. Walter L. Dorn, in his *Competition for Empire,* published in 1940, wrote: 'There can be no question that before 1780 France was at least the manufacturing equal of England.'[43] This judgment was subsequently confirmed by more intensive research.[44] Nor should this come as any surprise since France, with a population three times that of England, was then the leading industrial power in Europe.

Had Innis consulted the letters written by the Hudson's Bay Company's traders he would have found a steady stream of complaints year after year, on the poor quality of the goods they received from England. Although the writers may have exaggerated somewhat to drive the point home, there is no reason to suspect that the burden of their complaints was not true. They had no discernible motive to make false statements. These Bay traders reported sadly and sometimes angrily that too much of their merchandise the Indians would not accept. It had to be shipped back and could not be replaced until the following year, meanwhile the Indians went to the nearby Canadian posts. As one disgruntled factor at York Fort commented, the Canadian traders inspected their goods very carefully at Montreal or Lachine before they were shipped west, whereas the Bay traders had to make do with whatever they received.[45]

English gun powder was notoriously inferior to that of the French and for the Indians this was a vital commodity since they depended on it for the hunting of the larger game that provided the bulk of their food supplies. Poor powder could mean starvation for an entire band. In 1734 the Bay traders at Moose River wrote to the company's governors: 'We cannot but take notice of the badness of the powder and the disservice it does us. It is so foul that in the winter time after firing three or four times it will freeze in the guns, thereby occasioning much danger, and in the summertime it will cause the foul, watery matter to run out both at bore and touch hole. But above all the Indians that sometimes trades with the French and know the difference between theirs and ours, utterly protest against our powder and tell us that they are not able to do any execution with it.'[46]

Samples of French goods were obtained from the Indians and sent to London with the urgent plea that quality be matched.[47] Surprisingly, serious complaints were made of the very items that Innis maintained the British produced of a quality far superior to the French products—cloth and metal goods.[48] Such comments as those of Joseph Isbister at Fort Albany in 1740 are typical: 'The Flannel last year proved but indifferent, and the duffles is alto-

gether useless, it being both thinner and narrower and not fit for either Indians or Englishmen.'[49] The cooking pots sent to the bay, a major trade item, appear to have been grossly inferior in quality to those supplied by the French. Many of those sent were much larger than was desired by the Indians, being too difficult to transport. There were frequent complaints that the handle lugs were weak and broke after short usage, or that the kettles themselves were as thin as paper, 'fit to be sold only for old brass.'[50] Knives, axes, and the bar iron sent to be made into axes and ice chisels were also often of inferior quality and shattered in sub-zero weather.[51] In 1716 the factor at Albany Fort requested that short-barrelled muskets such as the French supplied be sent in future 'for they are mighty taking with the Indians.'[52]

As for the rum that Innis claimed gave the Bay Company an advantage over the French,[53] The Indians preferred French brandy which was far too expensive at 7s. 6d. a gallon for the British traders. They went to great lengths to produce an 'English brandy' from cheap gin with rather alarming additives to make it look and taste something like the French product.[54] In any event, Canadian traders who were willing to defy the *ordonnances* of the Quebec officials could obtain all the rum they wanted at Oswego.[55]

The burden of the Bay traders' complaints of poor quality British goods was summed up by Thomas McCliesh at York Fort in 1728. After listing the large quantities of goods that he was sending back to England he declared:

> We have likewise sent home 18 barrels of powder that came over in 1726, for badness I never saw the like, for it will not kill fowl nor beast at thirty yards distance: and as for our kettles in general they are not fit to be put into an Indian's hand, being all of them thin, and eared with tender old brass that will not bear their weight when full of liquid, and soldered in several places. Never was any man so upbraided with our powder, kettles and hatchets, than we have been this summer by all the natives, especially by those that borders near the French. Our cloth likewise is almost torn from one end of the piece to the other . . . here came at least forty canoes of Indians this summer, most of them clothed in French clothing that they traded with the French last summer. They likewise brought several strong French kettles and some French powder in their horns, with which they upbraided us with, by comparing with ours, at same time told us that they would give us the same number of beaver as they gave the French, provided our kettles to be strong and clear of soldering.[56]

Evidence such as this makes a mockery of Innis's statement: 'Trade from York factory to the interior was rapidly developed after 1713, with no competition from the French in the interior.'[57]

Similar complaints of poor quality English woollens were voiced by a leading merchant in New York. In 1731 Cornelius Cuyler complained to his London supplier that the last shipment of strouds was 'almost good for nothing at all . . . I believe they are made of Dogs hair.' The following year he again complained 'the Strouds which you now Sent me are Course Refuse old musty Strouds good for nothing.'[58] Despite these complaints which referred to specific shipments and may have been the exception rather than the rule, the burden of the evidence appears to indicate that in this one item the British did indeed produce a superior product.[59] Governor General La Galissonière and intendant Bigot, however, claimed that the woollens of Montauban were just good as those of England but that the Montreal smugglers had convinced the fur traders that the product they brought in from Albany was preferred by the Indians. To have admitted that this was not, fact, the case would have put them out of business.[60] A particular piece of evidence is a *mémoire* of Governor General Vaudreuil written at the height of the Seven Years' War, wherein he declared that English *écarlatines* were essential to hold the Indians in their alliance with the French. The *Compagnie des Indes* obtained supplies from England by way of Holland, but losses at sea had been heavy; he therefore requested that future shipments be sent on the king's ships. He also reported that the intendant Bigot insisted that the cloth be sold pre-war prices despite higher costs and the company's demand for a per cent increase. This makes yet another example of the subordination of the fur trade to political and military ends.[61] In any event, the question as to whether or not English woollens were superior is academic one so far as the fur trade is concerned for the simple reason that the Canadian traders were well supplied by either the *Compagnie des Indes,* or the Albany merchants; thus the Hudson's Bay Company had no advantage. Moreover, woollens were only one item of trade goods; linen and cotton garments, hardware and spirits, made up a far larger proportion of the value of goods shipped to the west.[62]

The statistics that were available in Innis's day show quite conclusively that in the eighteenth century down to the Conquest the British share in the fur trade was in steady decline. Indeed, Innis himself gives figures for beaver traded at the bay during the decade 1738-48 showing a decline from 69,911 to 39,505 pounds.[63] The tables compiled by Lawson from the English customs entries show the value of furs for the years 1700-60, averaged out, amounted to the equivalent of approximately 400,000 *livres tournois* a year.[64] By comparison, French fur imports at La Rochelle for the years 1718-61 averaged over a million *livres* a year.[65] In addition, there were the furs imported at Rouen by Dugard and Company, and the beaver traded clandestinely at Albany, which likely accounted for some 20 per cent of the furs shipped to England.[66] In the mid-seventeenth century New York had exported 40,000 beaver pelts a year; by the end of the century the amount was reduced to 15,000 and almost all of it was obtained clandestinely from the Canadians.[67] These figures, unreliable though they undoubtedly are, still point to one inescapable conclusion— that Innis's claim, which he made over and over again, that the French were unable to compete successfully with

the British in the fur trade is quite erroneous. In fact, the reverse appears to be much closer to the truth. Had the Seven Years' War not intervened, the Hudson's Bay Company might well have been driven to the wall by the Canadians.[68]

As for the much vaunted price differential between Albany and Montreal, this too appears to have little basis in fact. Sir William Johnson cited prices for some staple trade goods in New York in 1746 and also immediately after the Seven Years' War.[69] Fortunately, in the second list he gave prices in both sterling and New York currency which indicates that the prices in the earlier list were in the latter currency. This is not an insignificant point since the exchange rate at both points in time was approximately £186 New York to £100 sterling.[70] When the price of such goods as blankets, shirts, knives, kettles, muskets, gun powder, mirrors, vermillion are compared, converting the *livre* at the current exchange rate of ten pence, the prices are virtually the same. For example, blankets in New York sold for 14 shillings and 7s. 7d.— quality being the most likely cause of the discrepancy— and in Montreal the price varied from 9 to 14 *livres*. A musket cost 17s. in New York, 20 *livres* or 16s. 6d. sterling in Montreal; knives were a shilling each in New York and 1s. 6d. to 11d., depending on size, in Montreal; kettles 2s. in New York, and in Montreal chaudières were 2s. 5d. sterling.[71] That the prices of such goods in both colonies were approximately the same should occasion no surprise. There is no discernible reason why they should not be. However, a much more intensive study of trade goods prices in both colonies is needed before definitive conclusions can be drawn. Had, however, goods at Albany been as cheap and of such superior quality as Innis claimed, compared to goods in Montreal, then it is impossible to see how the Canadians could have garnered the lion's share of the fur trade as the evidence clearly indicates they did.

On one significant aspect of the fur trade—monopolies— Innis appears confused and he has certainly spread confusion. He frequently alluded to the fur trade of New France as being monopolistic; sometimes, however, he qualified this by distinguishing between internal free trade and external monopoly,[72] but he failed to make it clear that after 1665 this external marketing monopoly applied only to beaver and moose hides. From 1700 on beaver represented less than half the total value of furs exported to France, thus this so-called monopoly applied to less than half of the furs traded. This confusion is heightened by Innis's continual failure to distinguish between furs and beaver, which he treats as synonymous.[73] He does, however, make it plain that he considers monopolies to be a bad thing in the case of New France and he attributes much to this. Thus he states: 'Through these organizations—the trading organization of the interior and the monopoly organization of external trade—there developed in the colony a highly centralized system of administration. This centralization was shown in agriculture, in industry, in the church, and in colonial government. The tendency towards centralization was responsible for the development of paternalistic government.'[74] What he implies here is that the fur trade was responsible for the framework and nature of all the colony's institutions, which is absurd. The other French colonies where the fur trade was of little importance, as in Louisiana, or non-existent as in the Antilles, had the same institutions. The fact that they were modelled on those of France he ignored. As for the one true monopoly in North America, the Hudson's Bay Company, this feature of that company is occasionally mentioned in passing, uncritically. It would appear that a British monopoly was without consequence, an imagined French one baneful.

Another, popular fallacy promulgated by Innis was that the fur trade had inhibited the proper economic development of New France. He declared that 'Dependence on the fur trade and a military organization was not compatible with agricultural and industrial development and large external trade'[75]; that 'The population of New France during the open season of navigation was increasingly engaged in carrying on the trade over longer distances to the neglect of agriculture and other phases of economic development';[76] and, finally, that 'A colony engaged in the fur trade was not in a position to develop industries to compete with manufactures of the mother country.'[77] The unstated premise here is that a colony should have a mixed economy with an agricultural, industrial, and commercial base that fostered a thriving foreign trade. In Innis's view the fur trade had prevented New France from developing its economy in that fashion.

It is true that in the last three decades of the seventeenth century the expansion of agriculture was hampered by a shortage of labour needed to clear virgin forest land and the crown officials complained vociferously of the large number of men who had left the settlements to engage illegally in the fur trade as *coureurs de bois*.[78] The lure of the fur trade was not alone responsible for this exodus of potential agricultural labourers; the imbalance in the sexes was also a major factor. There were fewer than half as many women of marriageable age as men,[79] and a wife was a necessity to establish a viable farm. Had the fur trade not existed most of the surplus men would, most likely, have returned to France. In any event, early in the eighteenth century the sexes came into balance, the number of men absorbed by the fur trade was limited, and the rapid expansion of the population, doubling every generation, allowed of their periodic absence in the west without other branches of the economy suffering unduly. Moreover, most of the voyageurs left the settlements after the spring plowing and returned in time for the harvest.

What really inhibited the economic development of New France were factors, some of them still operative today, that Innis failed to mention: namely, the harsh winter climate with its short growing season; the colony's inability to produce anything, except furs that could not be produced more cheaply in Europe or the English colonies; the great distance from available markets; and the prevailing economic policy of the mother country, usu-

ally referred to as 'mercantilism.' France would never allow any of its colonies to compete with it in the market place. In fact, there was a good deal more industry in New France than Innis realized, at the artisanal level. In Europe the only industries that employed large numbers of men were fishing, ship building, and iron foundries. In New France it was the same, except for fishing and the fur trade, and the Forges de St Maurice were first established out of the profits of the latter trade. Innis was, therefore, quite wrong in asserting that the economic development of New France was hindered by the fur trade.

In treating of the fur trade down to 1763 Innis had a simple, albeit erroneous, theme that gave the work some sort of cohesion—namely, the superiority of British industry, organization, trade goods, and routes to the interior, which not only made it impossible for the French to compete successfully but also made the conquest of New France inevitable.[80] In part three of the work, dealing with the fur trade from 1760 to 1821, the underlying theme is the rivalry between the Hudson's Bay Company and the North West Company. This presented problems since both were British, and used British goods. One was a monopoly, the other 'private enterprise,' and it was the former that won the struggle. What resulted was a scissors-and-paste narrative account with little analysis but a welter of poorly organized detail, the relevance of much of which is not easy to determine. Moreover, the mass of evidence cited does not appear to have been subjected to critical examination. It is all taken at face value. A great deal of useful information is provided, but in a barely coherent fashion.[81] Much of it could have been reduced to tables, or presented more succinctly by means of maps. Occasionally Innis failed to grasp the significance of the evidence he liberally presented. He mentioned in passing the introduction of the York boat but failed to see that this represented a revolution in northern communications and was an important factor in the eventual elimination of the Nor' Westers by the Hudson's Bay Company.[82] In his concluding chapter he made the baffling statement: 'Dependence on the York boat rather than the canoe was symbolic of the increasing importance of Capitalism.'[83] He noted that the amalgamation of the XY and North West Companies made possible a sizeable reduction in wages paid their employees.[84] He mentioned that there was some resentment of this expressed by the clerks, voyageurs, and interpreters, but there the matter was let drop; the economic and social consequences were not examined. The chapters end without any conclusions being drawn.

The ensuing section dealing with the Hudson's Bay Company's activities from 1821 to 1869 and the sale of Rupert's Land to the Dominion of Canada also consists mainly of details presented in an inchoate fashion. He manifestly had not digested the material. One sweeping generalization that had been introduced earlier is here discussed in greater depth—the basic conflict, as he saw it, of settlement and the fur trade. Here he took geographic determinism to absurd lengths. In his preface to

Lawson's book he stated that after 1713, 'With expansion of trade from New Orleans on the Mississippi, traders from the St. Lawrence were pushed to the Northwest, following La Vérendrye from Lake Superior to Lake Winnipeg and the Saskatchewan.'[85] This reveals that he had failed to discover how the fur trade was organized prior to the Conquest. The fur traders of Louisiana could not compete with the Montreal traders who controlled the trade of the Lake Michigan region and on the upper reaches of the Mississippi.[86] The Canadian traders were certainly not pushed north to the Saskatchewan by competition from New Orleans. The Canadian traders moved west on the Saskatchewan because the only other viable route, the Missouri, was blocked by the powerful and hostile Sioux nation. Moreover, the northern route gave access to tribes with greater supplies of the better grade furs. Innis stated further that 'Competition from the Hudson River drainage basin with the French and from Hudson Bay left only the territory northwest of Lake Superior.'[87] Here he ignored the richest fur region of all, that at La Baye (Green Bay), which included the headwaters of the Mississippi to the height of land, and the region south and east of Lake Michigan to the Wabash.

He also asserted that 'The present Dominion emerged not in spite of geography but because of it,'[88] and that the fur trade dictated the outcome of the American Revolution and the location of the Canadian-United States boundary.[89] He linked these events to his belief that the fur trade and settlement were incompatible and in continual conflict. In his concluding chapter he states: 'The history of the fur trade in North America has been shown as a retreat in the face of settlement.'[90] Yet two pages later he asserts that 'The area which was crucial to the development of the fur trade was the Pre-Cambrian shield.'[91] Since the Pre-Cambrian shield was eminently unsuitable for agriculture, hence for settlement, it is impossible to reconcile the two statements.[92] The only region where settlement came into conflict with the fur trade was the Selkirk settlement on the Red River, and here the conflict was not directly over furs but for control of the region where the fur brigades obtained the essential supplies of pemmican. Elsewhere he declares: 'To a very large extent the American Revolution and the fall of New France were phases of the struggle of settlement against furs.'[93] The causal connections of these great events to the fur trade he sees as the French occupation of the Ohio valley and the Proclamation of 1763. He failed to grasp the fact that the French did not occupy the Ohio valley for its furs. The Montreal traders had never shown any interest in the area. The French occupied the region, over the objections of the Canadians, for purely political and military reasons.[94] Similarly, the Proclamation of 1763 was a political document enunciating political decisions made to serve political ends. Any connection these decisions had with the fur trade was incidental.

The assertions that 'Canada emerged as a political entity with boundaries largely determined by the fur trade,'[95] that 'It is no mere accident that the present Dominion coincides roughly with the fur trading areas of Northern North America,'[96] that the North West Company was the forerunner of the present confederation,[97] and that the present boundaries were a result of the dominance of furs,[98] are all further examples of economic determinism carried to the extreme. Significantly, this assertion is the final conclusion of the book.

When the case is subjected to scrutiny it quickly collapses. The present border from the Atlantic to the western end of Lake Superior was in no way connected with the fur trade. In fact, if the fur trade were to have determined the border in the Great Lakes areas then it would presently run from the western end of Lake Erie south of Lake Michigan to the Mississippi. In 1783, despite the strong opposition of le comte de Vergennes, the French foreign minister, Britain ceded to the United States the territory south of the Great Lakes to the Mississippi for political reasons.[99] When, after the Louisiana Purchase, the border west of the Great Lakes had to be determined, it was only in the Columbia territory that the fur trade was a factor in the negotiations. Had the western boundary been determined by the fur trade it would today run along the Saskatchewan river to the Rocky Mountains, rather than the 49th parallel of latitude, for the fur trade country lay to the north of that river, and west of the Rockies it would follow the lower reaches of the Columbia River.

In a critique of a major work a detached, judicious balance has to be maintained in the rendering of judgment. It is, therefore, disturbing that virtually nothing can be found on the credit side of the ledger in this instance, except that Innis's *The Fur Trade in Canada* was a pioneering work which brought the Canadian fur trade to the attention of a wide audience. Unfortunately, it gave a distorted view of the trade and at the same time inhibited further investigation. The work contains a great mass of information, much of it presented in chapters that lack cohesion, and frequently the evidence presented contradicts the book's conclusions. The end result has been the establishment of myths as conventional wisdom.

The basic flaw in the work is that Innis manifestly approached the subject with certain *a priori* premises and conclusions already formed and he chose to disregard any evidence that pointed to different conclusions. Historians, if not economists, today begin—or at least they should—the study of any topic with a question, or series of questions, and study all the available evidence in search of answers. They may have some notion before they begin as to what the answers will be, but if the evidence subsequently indicates that they were wrong then they have to draw the conclusions that emerge from the evidence. Frequently it happens that the original questions are found to be of less significance than other questions that emerge from the evidence and have to be pursued. Innis, however, began with answers, not with questions, and thereby he went sadly astray. All too often his arguments defy both the evidence and logic, the latter sometimes being akin to asserting that wind is caused by the trees waving their branches.

For half a century this work has been regarded as definitive, and hence historians have, until very recently, shied away from a reexamination of the fur trade. This is most unfortunate since the trade played such an important role, not just in the economy of New France, but in the framing of its social structure, in military affairs, and in the execution of colonial policy that, in the final analysis, determined the fate of both the French and the British empires in North America. All of these aspects of the fur trade are long overdue for thorough investigation.

NOTES

[1] All references are to the 1962 reprint of the revised 1956 edition, it being the most readily available today. The book was first published in 1930.

[2] Harold Adams Innis, *The Fur Trade in Canada* (Toronto 1962), 83. The operative word in this statement is 'inadequately.' Professor Winks later noted (xiv), 'His only serious lack was failure to obtain access to the closed archives of the Hudson's Bay Company . . .' This implies that he attempted to gain access but was refused. It is difficult to see why this should have been since F. Merk was permitted to study documents in the archives of the company relevant to his work *Fur Trade and Empire,* published in 1931, and A.S. Morton made good use of those archives for his *History of the Canadian West to 1870-71,* published in 1939. Nor did Innis consult the great mass of fur-trade documents in the Archives judiciaires de Montréal. He did make use of some of the correspondence between the royal officials at Quebec and the Ministry of Marine, but only the transcripts of the documents at the Public Archives of Canada. Had he consulted the original documents in Paris he would have discovered that a considerable number of them were not transcribed for Ottawa. A list of those not to be transcribed, mostly dealing with economic affairs, was affixed to the inside of the cover of each volume. A considerable proportion of them dealt with the fur trade.

[3] Innis, *Fur Trade,* 76, notes 132, 133

[4] Ibid., 83

[5] La Rochelle, Archives de la Chambre de Commerce, Anciennes archives, carton 27, Récapitulation de . . . marchandises entrées dans . . . La Rochelle, 1718–1761. Cited in A. J. E. Lunn, 'Economic Development in New France, 1713–1760' (unpublished Ph. D. thesis, McGill University, 1942), 464-5. In 1715 Ruette d'Auteuil estimated the Canadian fur trade to be worth upwards of a million livres a year. See *Rapport de l'Archiviste de la Province de Québec, 1922-23,* 59-60. Fur and hide imports a La Rochelle, taken from the same source and for the same time span are cited in Emile Garnault, *Le Commerce rochelais! Le Rochelais et le Canada* (La Rochelle, 1893), 15-16. Emile Salone, *La colonisation de la Nouvelle-France* (Paris, 1905), 397-8, reproduces Garnault's figures with an amendment, the deduction of

the entry for hides, since these, he states, most likely came from the Antilles. Moose hides, deer, and seal skins, were, however, a not inconsiderable item in Canada's fur trade exports. There is a fairly consistent but puzzling discrepancy between Garnault's figures and those cited by Dr Lunn.

[6] Dale Miquelon, *Dugard of Rouen* (Montreal and London, 1978), 87

[7] Maurice Filion, *La pensée et l'action coloniale de Maurepas vis à vis du Canada 1723-1749* (Ottawa, 1972), 82. See also Fernand Braudel et Ernest Labrousse, éds., *Histoire économique et sociale de la France* (Paris, 1970), II, 499ff.

[8] The same was true in Britain where, in the eighteenth century, furs accounted for less than one half of one percent of the total value of imports. See Murray G. Lawson, *Fur: A Study in English Mercantilism 1700-1775* (Toronto, 1943), 70, 72. His concluding sentence says it all: 'In short, in the eighteenth century . . . it was acutally of no real importance either to the English or American economy.' Innis wrote a lengthy foreword to this work without noting that it contradicted much that he had written in his own study of the fur trade. That the cod exported from Louisbourg equalled or exceeded in value the furs exported from Canada is demonstrated by Christopher Moore, 'The Other Louisbourg: Trade and Merchant Enterprise in Ile Royale 1713-1758,' *Histoire sociale/Social History,* XII, May 1979, 84.

[9] *Edits, Ordonnances royaux, Déclarations et Arrêts du Conseil d'Etat du Roi concernat le Canada* (Québec 1854), 5-11.

[10] Innis, *Fur Trade,* 63-4

[11] Yves F. Zoltvany, 'Aubert de La Chesnaye, Charles,' *Dictionary of Canadian Biography,* II (Toronto 1969), 29

[12] See Stewart L. Mims, *Colbert's West India Policy* (New Haven 1912). Innis does not appear to have consulted this work.

[13] For a more detailed discussion of the beaver crisis of 1696 see W.J. Eccles, *Frontenac: The Courtier Governor* (Toronto 1959), 285-94.

[14] Here, as throughout his work, Innis failed to distinguish between beaver and other furs when citing the sources; to him they seemed synonymous. He also failed to distinguish between *livres* weight of fur and *livres* value which renders much of this statistical information meaningless or misleading.

[15] Innis, *Fur Trade,* 115

[16] Lawson, *Fur Trade,* ix

[17] Innis, *Fur Trade,* 110. See also page 391: 'The competition of cheaper goods contributed in a definite fashion to the downfall of New France and enabled Great Britain to prevail in the face of its pronounced militaristic development.'

[18] Ibid., 97, 106, 138, 167, 168-9, 175

[19] Thomas Elliot Norton, *The Fur Trade in Colonial New York 1686-1776* (Madison, Wisc. 1974), 56, 87, 124, 171-2

[20] The burden of the evidence indicates clearly enough that, all things being equal, the Indians preferred to trade with the French. They appear to have traded with the English mainly to preserve that option and thereby oblige the French to keep their prices competitive. James Knight at York Fort wrote on 19 September 1714: 'One of the Indians came to me when I hoisted the Union flag: he told me he did not love to see that, he loved to see the white one, so there is many of the Indians has great friendship for the French here.' Publications of the Hudson's Bay Record Society, xxv: K.G. Davies, ed., *Letters from Hudson Bay 1703-40* (London 1965), 37 [hereafter HBC Records]

[21] Fernand Grenier, éd., *Papiers Contrecœur et autres documents concernant le conflit anglo-français sur l'Ohio de 1745 à 1756* (Québec 1952), 264-5

[22] Innis, *Fur Trade,* 97, 106, 138, 167, 168-9, 175

[23] Ibid., 111

[24] See W.J. Eccles, 'The Battle of Quebec: A Reappraisal,' in The French Colonial Historical Society, *Proceedings of the Third Annual Meeting,* 1977.

[25] Innis, *Fur Trade,* 114

[26] Ibid., 166

[27] The Bay Company did establish Henley House in 1743 some 120 miles inland on the Albany River, but it proved almost impossible to maintain and in 1755 the staff was massacred by local Indians infuriated by the bad treatment they had received. Not until 1766 did the company succeed in re-establishing the post. See E.E. Rich, *The Fur Trade and the North West to 1857* (Toronto 1967), 105-8, 140.

[28] Innis, *Fur Trade,* 47, 52-3, 97, 109, 166

[29] Ibid., 138, 167

[30] Arthur J. Ray and Donald Freeman, *'Give us Good Measure': An Economic Analysis of Relations between the Indians and the Hudson's Bay Company before 1763* (Toronto 978), 41-51

[31] Innis, *Fur Trade,* 47

[32] HBC Records, 611; Ray and Freeman, *'Give us Good Measure,'* 161

[33] *Rapport de l'Archiviste de la Province de Québec 1923-24,* 44-5, Mémoire sur l'Etat de la Nouvelle-France 1757, Bougainville

[34] Innis, *Fur Trade,* 190. The reference is to J. Carver, *Travels Through the Interior Parts of North-America in the Years 1766, 1767, and 1768* (London 1778), 110-12. The relevant passage states, after mentioning Indian complaints of the shoddy quality of the goods they had obtained at the bay: 'The length of their journey to the Hudson's Bay factories, which they informed me took them up three months during the summer heats to go and return, and from the smallness of their canoes they could not carry more than a third of the beavers they killed. So that it is not to be wondered at, that these Indians should wish to have traders come to reside among them.'

[35] See the map in Ray and Freeman, *'Give us Good Measure,'* 46, which gives dates for the freeze up and the required dates of departure from York Factory for the Indians to return to their tribes before the rivers froze. Some of the dates given appear to be in error.

[36] Innis, *Fur Trade,* 164

[37] Ray and Freeman, *'Give us Good Measure,'* 33. Elsewhere they make statements that qualify or refute this assertion. See, for example, ' . . . the Indian's . . . per capita transport capacity remained fixed at a relatively low level' (129). See also 179, 197, 235, 239-40.

[38] Lawson, *Fur,* 87-92, 108, 136; Innis, *Fur Trade,* 138

[39] Innis, *Fur Trade,* 52-3, 78, 109, 110, 179

[40] Ibid., 391

[41] Ibid., 172, citing Public Archives of Canada, CO 42, II, 363-4

[42] Ibid., 172-3

[43] Walter L. Dorn, *Competition for Empire* (New York 1940), 254

[44] Braudel et Labrousse, éds., *Histoire,* 499-528

[45] HBC Records, 278-84. James Isham, York Fort, 20 July 1739. That the Canadian traders checked the goods shipped west carefully is confirmed by C. Nolan Lamarque, Livre de comptes, Archives nationales du Québec à Montréal.

[46] HBC Records, William Bevan and others, Moose River, 20 Aug. 1734, 196. See also Thomas White, York Fort, 9 Aug. 1734, 194-5.

[47] Ibid., Rowland Waggoner and others, Albany Fort, 15 Aug. 1739, 285; Richard Staunton and others, Moose Fort, 17 Aug. 1739, 306; Thomas McCliesh, Albany Fort, 16 July 1716, 44.

[48] Innis, *Fur Trade,* 85, 112

[49] HBC Records, 325; see also 43, 75, 232, 306.

[50] Ibid., Thomas McCliesh, Alban Fort, 16 July 1716, 43. See also 89, 99, 142, 149.

[51] Ibid., 44, 81, 99, 148, 150, 191, 232

[52] Ibid., Thomas McCliesh, Albany, 16 July 1716, 44

[53] Innis, *Fur Trade,* 85

[54] E.E. Rich, *The History of the Hudson's Bay Company 1670-1870,* I: *1670-1763* (London 1958), 547; HBC Records, 205

[55] Archives du Séminaire du Québec, Fonds Verreau, boîte 1, no 13, Duquesne à Contrecœur, Mtl., 30 avril 1753

[56] HBC Records, Thomas McCliesh, York Fort, 8 Aug. 1728, 136

[57] Innis, *Fur Trade,* 137

[58] Norton, *Fur Trade in Colonial New York,* 112

[59] Lunn, 'Economic Development,' 157-63. The Canadian traders, however, catered to Indian needs and preferences more astutely than did the British. Surcoats were made in Montreal and shipped to the west without sleeves attached; these last were shipped separately in three lengths so that the Indian customers could be sure of a good fit. Similarly, hatchets, axes, and 'casse têtes' were made with round eye holes, making it much easier to replace a broken handle in the bush. A factor at Fort Albany reported in 1727 that he was returning 170 hatchets 'all flat eyed which will not trade, they having lain upon account this ten years to my knowledge.' HBC Records, 125

[60] Paris, Archives Nationales, Colonies, C11A [hereafter AN C11A], vol. 91, ff 67-71, Galissonière et Bigot au ministre, Qué., 20 oct. 1748. They complained of some recent shipments of heavy and overly expensive cooking pots but stated that they were taking steps to prevent a recurrence. Their dispatch was written at the height the war, just after the loss of Louisbourg had resulted in a chronic shortage of trade goods. This had led to the defection of the western allies and attacks on the French posts. The governor general and intendant further declared that good quality trade goods at modest prices were essential, otherwise the trade would go to the English 'et les Mettra En Estat de tourner Contre nous Toutes les Nations dont l'alliance a Esté cy devant nôtre plus ferme apuy et le fleau des Colonies

angloises. C'Est princepalement dans cette Vue que nous insistons sur cet article.' This makes explicit that the fur trade was considered an economic means to a political and military end. Innis cited this document (85) as evidence of the superiority of British trade goods, failing to note the circumstances and ignoring the political context.

[61] AN C11A, vol. 103, ff 437-41, Mémoire

[62] See the itemized invoices of such shipments in the Livre de Comptes de C. Nolan Lamarque, Archives Nationales du Québec à Montréal.

[63] Innis, *Fur Trade,* 138

[64] Lawson, 108

[65] Lunn, 'Economic Development,' 455, 464-5

[66] Lawson, *Fur,* 34

[67] Norton, *Fur Trade in Colonial New York,* 100-3, 122, 124

[68] The same trend had developed in other commercial fields. France, by the 1740s, had succeeded in eliminating English goods from the Levant, her textiles from the Portuguese market, was making great inroads in the Spanish colonies, and took the lion's share of the fish on the Grand Banks. As French overseas trade increased by leaps and bounds that of England stagnated. See Roland Mousnier et Ernest Labrousse, *Histoire générale des civilisations,* v: *Le XVIIIe siècle* (Paris 1955), 213; Dorn, *Competition for Empire* 122-30. These economic factors were a main reason for England's seeking a spoiling war with France in 1744 and again a decade later. As Pares put it: 'These are the ambitions of the respectable tradesman who hopes to increase his custom by hiring the racketeer to destroy his neighbour's shop.' Richard Pares, *War and Trade in the West Indies, 1739-1763* (Oxford 1936), 181, also 61-4, 180. See also E.E. Rich and C.H. Wilson, *The Cambridge Economic History of Europe,* IV: *The Economy of Expanding Europe in the Sixteenth and Seventeenth Centuries* (Cambridge 1967), 536-7. Innis, however, without citing any evidence, stated: 'At the end of the period (1749) English products had made substantial inroads on the French market in Spain, Portugal, Italy and Germany' (*Fur Trade,* 101).

[69] *The Papers of Sir William Johnson* (Albany 1925), I, 72; IV, 559

[70] John J. McCusker, *Money and Exchange in Europe and America, 1600-1775: A Handbook* (Chapel Hill, NC 1978)

[71] New York prices are those given by Sir William Johnson, those at Montreal are from Le Livre de comptes de C. Nolan Lamarque. For clarity the Montreal prices

were converted into sterling at the current exchange rate of ten pence to the *livre tournois.*

[72] Innis, *Fur Trade,* 112-13

[73] Ibid., 102, 112, 386

[74] Ibid., 60 n1, 113. See also 115: 'The direct relation between the fur trade and the colonial administration as carried out from France, or in the colony, was unique. The paternalism of the French *regime* was characteristic of a colony dependent on the fur trade.' And again, 390 as well as xi, xiii of his preface to Lawson.

[75] Innis, *Fur Trade,* 115

[76] Ibid., 390

[77] Ibid., 391

[78] AN C11A, V, ff 297-8, Duchesneau à Seignelay, Qué., 13 nov. 1681; X, ff 65-7, Denonville à Seignelay, Qué., 10 août 1688

[79] Hubert Charbonneau et Yolande Lavoie, 'Introduction à la reconstitution de la population du Canada au XVIIe siècle: Etude critique des sources de la période 1665-1668,' *Revue d'histoire de l'Amérique française,* XXIV, 4, mars 1971, 485-511

[80] Innis, *Fur Trade,* 166

[81] See, for example, 190, 192-3, 195-8, 228-30, 237-42, 249ff, 258-9.

[82] Ibid., 154, 159-60, 289. For the significance of the York boat, and other factors that Innis ignored, see R. Glover, 'The Difficulties of the Hudson's Bay Company's Penetration of the West,' *Canadian Historical Review,* XXIX, Sept. 1948, 240-54.

[83] Innis, *Fur Trade,* 387

[84] Ibid., 241-2

[85] Lawson, *Fur,* X

[86] Guy Frégault, *Le Grand Marquis* (Montréal 1952), 317ff

[87] Lawson, *Fur,* X. See also Innis, *Fur Trade,* 110

[88] Ibid., 393

[89] Ibid., 67

[90] Ibid., 386

[91] Ibid., 388

[92] It is rather ironic that although there was no conflict in New France between settlement and the fur trade—Innis to the contrary—that conflict was quite pronounced in colonial New York. See Sung Bok Tim, *Landlord and Tenant in Colonial New York* (Chapel Hill, NC 1978), 75-6.

[93] Innis, *Fur Trade,* 178

[94] See Eccles, *Frontenac,* 334-6; *France in America* (New York 1972), 178-81; *Frégault, Le Grand Marquis,* 329ff.

[95] Innis, *Fur Trade,* 393

[96] Ibid., 392

[97] Ibid., 391

[98] Ibid., 401-2

[99] W.J. Eccles, 'The Role of the American Colonies in Eighteenth Century French Foreign Policy,' *Atti del I Congresso Internazionale di Storia Americana* (Genova 1976), 163-73

Donald Creighton (essay date 1981)

SOURCE: "Harold Adams Innis—An Appraisal," in *Culture, Communication, and Dependency: The Tradition of H. A. Innis,* William H. Melody, Liora Salter, Paul Heyer, eds., Ablex Publishing Corporation, 1981, pp. 13-25.

[*In the following essay, Creighton assesses Innis's education, career, and achievements.*]

Some little time ago, the head of one of the University of Toronto's new colleges put a sudden and very general question to me. What, he said in effect, is the importance of Harold Innis? I must admit that I was surprised and slightly annoyed by this abrupt inquiry and I made no serious attempt to answer it. I might have replied that Harold Innis had been the Head of the Department of Political Economy and the Dean of the Graduate School, that his published works in history and political economy numbered more than a dozen, that he had sat on several Royal Commissions and that his advice was almost invariably sought, during a large part of his career, on every important university issue and appointment in Canada. I might have made an answer along these lines, but I decided not to. I was repelled by the idea of summing up Harold Innis in what would have sounded like a short paragraph out of *Who's Who.* Besides, I could not help suspecting that my questioner was not likely to be much impressed by any brief answer I might make. His inquiry was not an honest request for information, but a disguised expression of disbelief. He probably knew little about Innis and his works, and he was not disposed to accept the Innis legend on trust. He rather brusquely invited me, a friend and a known admirer, to justify my faith in it.

It seems to me that this little incident makes a point, or raises a question of some importance. Has the time come for a reexamination, a reinterpretation, even a reappraisal of Innis and his work? The twenty-fifth anniversary of his death occurred in November 1977 and frequently this particular anniversary prompts a critical backward look at the work of a formerly popular author or prominent scholar. Harold Innis deserves such a retrospective review as much as any Canadian scholar and more than most; but the twenty-fifth anniversary came and went unmarked by any special effort at commemoration. The University of Toronto Press at first planned to publish a memorial volume of essays in his honor, but in the end this project fell through and only my own short biography, *Harold Adams Innis: Portrait of a Scholar,* was reissued in paperback. This absence of a special remembrance was perhaps unfortuante, but it by no means implies a decline in the high evaluation of Innis' work. The very existence of a symposium held early the next year, more than half a continent away from the city where he lived and wrote, is in itself a significant proof of the enduring vitality of his ideas. And in Toronto, the Innis Foundation, which for some years devoted itself to the task of converting the old Innis farm into a study and conference center, has now returned to its original and main purpose, which is encouragement and promotion of studies about Innis and his ideas.

It would be difficult to think of another Canadian scholar whose stature equals or approaches that of Harold Adams Innis. Banting won a Knighthood and the Nobel Prize. Wilder Penfield has been, so far, the only nonpolitical Canadian to become a member of that highly select body, the British Order of Merit. But these brilliantly creative scientists and medical men left behind them no great body of written work for the instruction and delight of their fellow Canadians. Harold Innis did, and the bulk, as well as the brilliance, of that work forces upon us the difficult but fascinating task of investigating the origins of the complex mind that conceived it.

The farm, in which he was born and grew to manhood, and the First World War, in which he almost lost his life, were the two most important early influences in his life. Both were to have important and permanent aftereffects; but the farm, the home, and the Baptist faith and morality, which pervaded it, were probably basic and primary. It was a complex varied influence and Innis' own attitude to it was extremely ambiguous. He hated its stultifying labor and was only too glad to escape from it forever, but he never forgot its seasonal rhythms or its complex daily operations. It taught him also, for his father's farm was a relatively poor one, the need and practice of hard work, and, throughout his entire academic career, he was repeatedly forced to increase his small income with student teaching. The farm gave him the directness and simplicity of his approach to people and things, his insatiable interest in significant detail, his capacity for hard sustained labor, and his enormous powers of endurance.

It also exercised, through the religious and cultural interests of the farm household, a direct and powerful influence on Innis' standards and values. The Innises were Baptists, "hard-shell" Baptists, their neighbors called them, who believed in adult baptism by total immersion and who lived a simple, narrow, and devout existence. Innis had not yet undergone the formidable rite of baptism when he left Otterville to join the Canadian army, but he was still a professed Christian, and he told his sister solemnly he did not believe he would have volunteered if it had not been for his Christian faith. How much of that faith survived the horrors of World War I is uncertain, but certainly there was none of it left in his later years. He had ceased to be a Baptist, but he clung tenaciously to certain convictions and values that have always been characteristic of his sect. He believed in the independence, dignity, and self-sufficiency of the individual, and he utterly rejected any compromise with his high standards in scholarship or teaching. Many people, when they are angered by an unjustified slight or an unmerited favor to others, go as far as to threaten resignation. Harold Innis did not threaten to resign; he just resigned. He resigned when a junior was appointed over his head in the Department of Political Economy at Toronto: He withdrew his resignation only when he was promoted to the same higher grade in the academic hierarchy. Years later, at the height of his career, he angrily resigned from the Royal Society of Canada on the ground that one of its awards had been bestowed on an unworthy fellow, and the academic world of Canada was confronted by the astonishing spectacle of one of its most distinguished members openly boycotting the proceedings of its most prestigious society!

There was still another important but negative influence of the Innis household: its undeniable cultural poverty, which, in my view, profoundly affected Innis' development. The *Family Herald* was the only periodical that arrived regularly at the farm; no metropolitan newspaper entered the home until Innis, who, like the rest of his family, was then a stout political Liberal, subscribed to the Toronto *Globe.* The family's speech was slovenly and ungrammatical, and Innis learnt his first big words from reading Borden's and Laurier's speeches on the Naval Bill in the House of Commons. There may have been a small library in the farmhouse, but, if so, its existence is not recorded. The young Innis no doubt gulped down a good many books, but they were books which, in the main, bore directly on the academic courses he was taking at Woodstock Collegiate Institute or McMaster University in Toronto. Even at McMaster, he never seems to have plunged into that fascinating debauch of extracurricular reading to which so many undergraduates succumb. At McMaster, he was known not as a bookworm, but as a debater, a powerful opponent in intercollegiate debates. And his success made him think of law as a career.

It was not until a good deal later, when Innis went to Chicago and fell in love with Mary Quayle, that he became dimly aware of this great, gaping hole in his general education. Mary Quayle was, as she later proved, a writer herself, and well versed in modern and contemporary English literature. During her engagement to Innis, she lent him a novel by Willa Cather, the leader of an early twentieth-century group of midwestern novelists in which she was interested. Innis later admitted that he had read the book, but had, if I remember correctly, nothing whatever to say about it; if the loan of Cather's *My Antonia* was intended to start him off on an extended course on the modern novel, it was a total failure! Years later, when Harold and Mary visited our Muskoka cottage, I tried to create a diversion from endless academic gossip, by reading some of the pieces from Stephen Leacock's *Nonsense Novels* or *Sunshine Sketches of a Little Town*. Innis was immensely amused and laughed uproariously, but it was obvious that this was the first time he had encountered Leacock! He had never even heard his name before!

Years later, in a series of lectures on prominent Canadian historians and economists, which was sponsored by the Department of Political Economy and the Department of History at Toronto, Innis gave a paper on Stephen Leacock. With laughable professional complacency, he attributed the vividness and accuracy of *Sunshine Sketches of a Little Town* to the fact that Leacock was an economist! In the entire history of English literary criticism there is probably no more hilarious absurdity than this inept remark. It was Leacock's inspired novelist's insight into the characters and circumstances of his little town—the gifts of a born storyteller—and not the laboriously acquired knowledge of an economist that gave his *Sunshine Sketches* their freshness and authenticity. What Harold Innis badly needed—and what he never took the trouble to acquire—was a thorough knowledge of the realistic and naturalistic novelists, French and English, of the nineteenth and early twentieth centuries. A thorough course of reading in Balzac, Flaubert, Zola, Trollope, Bennett, and Galsworthy would have shown him clearly how far novelists excel economists in depicting the social circumstances and class relationships of a given country and period.

There is one last formative influence on the development of the early Innis—World War I and its effects—that remains to be explored. When he left the Innis farm in South Norwich to join the Canadian artillery, he had felt himself to be a Christian soldier engaged in a holy crusade; when he came back, war had, for him, turned into a monstrous, sickening mixture of blood, filth, and stench. His experience left him with an enduring sense of sympathy and comradeship with the men who had actually risked the peril of front-line fighting; for everybody else supposedly engaged in the war, he had nothing but uncompromising contempt. As an economist, he might have been expected to realize that modern warfare was a vast, complicated enterprise in which thousands of non-combatants played essential parts, but, in fact, he was even more unwilling to apply Adam Smith's dictum about the necessary division of labor to World War II than he had been to World War I. In his view, noncombatants were simply bureaucrats who risked nothing and battened on the war's emoluments of money, prestige, and power. Bureaucracy meant regimentation and centralization and all the other evils of big government, which Innis instinctively hated. And World War II, directed and controlled by a triumvirate of War Lords, was an even more monstrous example of centralization. Innis simply endured it. He watched young university teachers go off to Ottawa, or London, or Washington, without interest and with barely concealed contempt. In his opinion, their real place was in their universities, guarding the threatened traditions of scholarship.

EARLY ACADEMIC CAREER

For Innis, World War I was a horrible but comparatively brief interlude in a life increasingly devoted to academic study. He had refused to take advantage of McMaster University's dubious offer of a free degree to fourth year students who enlisted before the end of the year and had stayed stubbornly on to write his examinations. In June, 1917, when he was stuck in the trenches at Vimy and there appeared not the remotest prospect of his release from fighting, he wrote to McMaster University asking for information about the requirements for the Master of Arts degree. A month later, a severe wound in his knee took him back to England and eventually to the Canadian General Hospital at Basingstoke. There he started in to read the formidable list of books Professor Duncan McGibbon had provided him and to write an M. A. thesis on his own chosen subject, "The Returned Soldier." He reached his home at Otterville at the end of March, 1918, and within only two days he was back again in Toronto, conferring with McGibbon. There was time for only a last fortnight of frantic study: On April 19, he wrote his examinations. Only a few days later he was honorably discharged from the army and on April 30, in Walmer Road Baptist Church, McMaster University's Annual Convocation awarded him the M. A. degree.

It was an astonishing record, carried out in an incredibly brief space of time. In only a little more than six months, a convalescent soldier, distressed by occasional periods of pain and weakness, had shown extraordinary powers of grim determination and compulsive speed. He had passed all the barriers now, academic and military; he richly deserved a holiday, but now, as always, he was in a hurry. There was the problem of his future career. In vain his mother renewed her old pleas that he become a Baptist clergyman. He himself had vaguely considered the law a profession; now he finally decided upon a legal career. His professional training at Osgoode Hall in Toronto was to begin in September, 1918, but before that happened, there were five empty months to be filled. Most young returned soldiers, if they had been academically as far advanced as Innis, would have welcomed a summer of comparative idleness, but Innis was not among their number. He discovered that the University of Chicago, to which McMaster was accustomed to send its most promising students for further study, had a graduate summer school. He decided to attend.

That summer at Chicago was decisive for Innis in a number of important ways. He made up his mind he would win his doctoral degree at Chicago and seek an academic career as a teacher of economics. He was launched on the study of Canadian economic history through the choice of his thesis subject, the Canadian Pacific Railway. Through an elementary course in economics, which he taught at this supervisor's request, he met, and soon fell in love with, one of his students, Mary Quayle. There was no doubt whatever about a job, for in both Canada and the United States the veterans were returning to their studies, and universities all over the continent were busily recruiting staff. A variety of academic openings were available, but Innis wanted to teach in Canada and preferred a senior and recognized university. Very quickly his hopes were realized, for Toronto offered him a position as lecturer in economics at a salary of $2,000 a year. In the autumn of 1920, he began to teach in the department of political economy and, in the spring of the following year, he married Mary Quayle.

Obviously, the first definite period in Innis' academic career begins with his appointment at Toronto in 1920, is neatly bisected by the publication of *The Fur Trade in Canada* in 1930, and ends with the appearance of *The Cod Fisheries: The History of an International Economy* in the early winter of 1940. For both Innis and his chosen subject, economics, it was a period of rapid advance and steady enlargement. In 1937, when he had been only seventeen years in the department, he was appointed its head. Those seventeen years witnessed an amazing increase in the range and depth of Canadian studies in economics. The revival of the Canadian Political Science Association in 1931 was followed four years later by the founding of the *Canadian Journal of Economics and Political Science*. The publication of the two volumes of Canadian Economic Documents, edited by Innis, and Innis and Arthur Lower, gave students for the first time an opportunity of getting at the roots of their subject. The launching of those two large scholarly enterprises, *Canadian Frontiers of Settlement* edited by W. A. Mackintosh, and *The Relations of Canada and the United States* edited by James T. Shotwell, gave senior scholars in economics, history, political science, and sociology more opportunities for publication than they had ever had before.

In contrast with the second period of Innis' career, which began in 1940, the first was essentially Canadian, North American in character. It was not, of course, that he carefully avoided contact with England and Europe. During the 1920s and early 1930s, he made perhaps half-a-dozen trips to England and the continent, chiefly in the guise of an economic geographer, which was the academic role he liked to assume at the time. He attended geographical conferences and made an investigation of German methods of teaching geography, but he never stayed long, never did any serious research in England or Europe and never attempted to learn a European language. By an odd coincidence, I encountered him myself on one of his brief European visits. In the summer of 1928, I was working at the Bibliothèque National on a subject in French Revolutionary history. At that time Innis and I knew each other slightly, but he showed a friendly interest in my researches and we went out together for a light luncheon, which probably consisted, as mine invariably did in that summer of abject poverty of "un sandwich au jambon." I remember that as we passed the guardian at the gate of the library, he muttered the one word "retourner." I never heard him speak a sentence or even a lengthy phrase in French. He may have come back again to the library, as he told the guardian he would, but I never saw him again that summer.

The brevity and infrequency of these European visits provide a striking contrast with the steady and unflagging zeal with which he explored Canada. The famous journey down the Mackenzie River in the summer of 1924 was only the most exciting and dangerous of his many travels. In those first ten crowded years at Toronto, he could be said to have realized the motto of the Canadian coat-of-arms: "He shall have Dominion from sea to sea, and from the river unto the ends of the earth." He became intimately acquainted with the land, its regions, resources, and industries. He got to know its universities, their principal scholars, and promising juniors. Through J. Bartlet Brebner, who had left Toronto for Columbia University, he became acquainted with James T. Shotwell, one of the directors of the Carnegie Endowment, and through him with Joseph Willits and Anne Bezanson of the Rockefeller Foundation, and Henry Allen Moe of the John Simon Guggenheim Foundation. These influential American associations were vital to Canadian scholarship in those days, for the establishment of the Canada Council was decades in the future. I had gone to Paris in 1928 on my own meager savings, but in 1940 I won a Guggenheim Fellowship, through, I am sure, the influence of Harold Innis.

The fact that Innis became a power in Canada and a potent influence in the United States was the result mainly of the two major works he produced during this period, *The Fur Trade in Canada* and *The Cod Fisheries: The History of an International Economy*. Both these books were applications of what came to be called the staples approach to Canadian economic history. Innis was not the sole inventor of this approach, but in the final chapter of *The Fur Trade in Canada,* which was one of the strongest chapters he ever wrote, he gave the classic exposition of the general theory upon which the staples approach was based. The migrant to a new country such as Canada, he assumed, was desperately dependent on the importation of manfactured goods from the homeland for the maintenance of the culture to which he or she was accustomed. For these, the migrant could pay only by the discovery of a native commodity or staple, which was available in fairly large quantities in the colony, was light enough to be carried for long distances in the little ships of the period, and was either unknown or scarce, and consequently desirable, in the Motherland. For Canada, the first two of these staples were fish and furs.

The *Fur Trade* and the *Cod Fisheries* are excellent examples of the way in which Innis carried out the application of this theory to Canadian economic history. His method of composition was unusual, highly distinctive and, at times, extremely exasperating. A large amount of the task of understanding his books was left to the reader. He insisted on including large chunks of original documents in an undigested and sometimes almost indigestible form. All too often his sentences were awkward collections of words, with a series of huge abstract nouns and a few rather feeble and frequently repeated passive verbs carrying the main action of the narrative or the chief burden of the argument. This dense, leaden exposition might go on for paragraphs, or even pages, when it could be suddenly interrupted by a brilliant generalization, a short paragraph that simply but superbly summed up pages of exposition, or a final chapter that suddenly seemed to open up vast horizons of understanding to the reader.

In those superb features of his work, the *Fur Trade* is surely the better of his first two books. Perhaps he tired in the end of the endless involutions of the story of the fisheries. Perhaps the sheer weight of his material overwhelmed him. At any rate, the vast untidy manuscript he finally sent down to New York was too much for James T. Shotwell, the general editor of the series on the *Relations of Canada and the United States*. He succeeded in persuading Innis that considerable revision was essential and Arthur W. MacFarlane, an old friend of Shotwell, came to Toronto and for more than a year worked with Innis over the revision. It was he who supplied the appendix to Chapter II, which explained the coins and money values of the period—a complicated subject Innis had majestically ignored.

Innis' uncompromising attitude to his readers had its origin in his conception of economics. He believed that it was a science, a difficult science certainly, with serious limitations, which invited study and exploration but definitely precluded any final, dogmatic conclusions. No word appeared more frequently in his work—it was part of the title of one of his collections of essays—than the word "bias." No man was ever more acutely aware of the fact that everybody, including the most supposedly detached economist, was a creature of his own generation and environment and deeply affected by its values, assumptions, and beliefs. Such arguments, carried to their logical extreme, could end only in complete relativism; they could mean only that an objective economic science was logically impossible. This absolute conclusion Innis refused to accept. Bias was the social scientist's greatest danger, but paradoxically it also was the best hope of salvation. Bias, he seemed to say, is an historical phenomenon that is always with us and can be studied and analyzed just like any other historical phenomenon. And through such study the economist could discover the cumulative force of biases, and their effect on institutions.

This was a modest defense of economics as a difficult science without dogmatic conclusions. It also provided a useful retort to the radical reformers of the 1930s, who suddenly appeared as a result of the world's worst depression and who were always demanding drastic economic or political changes and insisting economists should direct and aid the politicians in carrying them out. The League for Social Reconstruction—the very name was abhorrent to Innis—was founded early in the 1930s; the first Canadian Socialist Party—the Co-operative Commonwealth Federation, with a manifesto stuffed with huge economic and social generalizations—followed shortly after. Innis had nothing to do with either of these organizations. He dealt with them only when he was attacked by one of their members, or when the League for Social Reconstruction produced a book, *Social Planning for Canada,* which purported to be a serious intellectual exposition of its socialist principles. Innis gave this pretentious effort a highly critical review in the *University of Toronto Quarterly* a year later, at the first meeting of the revived Canadian Political Science Association, when F. H. Underhill denounced the Canadian economists as "the intellectual garage mechanics of the Canadian economy" and urged them to throw aside their timid academic scruples and join the holy crusade for a socialist Canada. Innis made such a devasting reply that thirty-five years later, George Ferguson, the editor of the Montreal *Star,* was still marveling over it!

For Innis all social planning on the grand scale was bad, but the social planning proposed by Canadian socialists was particularly bad because it assumed the federal government as the chief agent of social change. In sharp contrast with today, when a chorus of pious Canadians propose to save Confederation by pulling it to pieces or cutting it into shreds, the constitutional reformers of the 1930s were all strong federalists. It was their federalism almost as much as their socialism, which aroused Innis. He had nothing to do with the great federal Doomsday inquiry of the 1930s, the Royal Commission on Dominion-Provincial Relations. The only economic investigation of the 1930s in which he took part was Nova Scotia's Provincial Economic Inquiry of 1934 and even here he was careful to assert his own intellectual independence. The two other Commissioners signed the main report; Innis wrote a separate report, a complementary report he called it, that was mainly an economic history of Nova Scotia, with a few, relatively small specific recommendations tacked on.

LATER CAREER

The second and final period in Innis' career started with the real beginning of the World War II in the spring of 1940 and the commencement of his researches in the history of paper, printing, and the press, in the summer of the same year. This second period, which lasted only twelve years, differed markedly from the two decades that had preceded it. The range of Innis' work grew vastly larger and more ambitious. Before, his studies had been largely confined to North America; now, he seemed to appropriate the whole world and travel freely up and down the centuries of its history. He became much more deeply involved in the economic, political, and social issues of his time than he ever had been before and his criticism took on a much more pessimistic and intransigent tone. He had always dealt occasionally in generalizations and epigrams. Now the generalizations grew more frequent and sweeping, the paradoxes more daring, the conjunction of ideas and the association of events more unexpected and startling.

It seems to me that it is possible to explain the later Innis, the angry, gloomy, obscure, and overconfident Innis of the postwar period, and that the explanation is to be found partly in the radical change in his own researches and partly in the revolutionary transformation of the postwar world itself. It is difficult for historians and political scientists who now occupy the senior positions in Canadian universities to appreciate the profound impact this revolutionary transformation in world affairs had upon Innis. He lived through it all. He witnessed the British Empire's last desperate effort and the beginnings of its rapid decline. He saw the rise of the three great new Empires that were to dominate the postwar world—the United States, the Soviet Union, and the Republic of China. Canada, he realized, was passing inevitably from the light and easy obligations of an old empire to the uncompromising orders of a new one. During the war, this control took the form of an armed occupation of the Canadian North by American forces, virtually uncontrolled by the Canadian government. During the peace, it changed into a heavy diplomatic pressure that forced Canada to support American imperialistic policies in the Far East and eventually took us into the Korean War. The United Nations, under peremptory American direction, justified the Korean War and in those days Lester Pearson and the Canadian Department of External Affairs regarded the United Nations as a divine institution, created by God for the preservation of collective security and peace. Looking back now, after a lapse of nearly thirty years, we can realize how wonderfully correct they were in their confident expectations, can't we? In their eyes, the Korean War was a noble crusade for the collective system. Innis saw it for what it was, an American imperialist war decked out in a pious cloak of United Nations respectability!

These profound changes in world politics affected Innis deeply, but there was another important influence, the scope and nature of his new research, which also radically altered his outlook. Originally, pulp and paper had no doubt been conceived as another study of a Canadian staple industry, not unlike the fur trade and the fisheries; as time was to show fairly quickly it was, in fact, radically different. The fur trade and the fisheries had fairly definite limits in time and place, but once Innis had passed from pulp and paper to printing, the press and communications generally, he had entered an almost illimitable field. Communications was, in fact, an open-ended subject. It streched back into remote historical times and forward into the present and future. It was an enormous, monstrous subject and the fundamental difficulty Innis faced in tackling it was that he was almost as

ignorant of the immediate present as he was of the remote past. He was no great newspaper reader, found little interest in popular periodicals, rarely listened to the radio and, of course, never saw television. His ignorance of Latin and Greek was more abysmal than his unfamiliarity with French and it is probable that before the early 1940s he had barely heard of the Greek poets, dramatists and philosphers he quoted so freely in the fourth chapter of *Empire and Communications.*

Inevitably, the new, vast work he had undertaken forced him to adopt new methods that differed radically from the old. In the past, his work had always been based on a careful study of the available documentary evidence and on comprehensive knowledge of the geographical setting. Now, neither of these solid foundations could possibly be built. It was just as impossible for him to gain a detailed knowledge of the geography of Europe and the Middle East as it was for him to acquire an intimate acquaintance with the world's modern journalism. He had no time to turn himself into a Greek or Roman historian or an Egyptian archaeologist, and he could not spend his life reading daily newspapers. What he read, in fact, was *not* daily newspapers, or Greek philosphies and dramatists, or Latin historians, but books *about* them. Every night he arrived home with a bulging briefcase. He gulped down books like a man dying of hunger and thirst. He devoured what to other scholars would have been whole libraries.

As he worked, a theory rapidly developed. The *Fur Trade* and the *Cod Fisheries* had both produced a system of assumptions, which had come to be called the staples theory, but the staples theory applied only to colonial times and to limited areas. The new communications theory that Innis now rapidly elaborated was far more grandiose in conception: it was both global and eternal in its significance. The media of communications, he came to believe, were central to the history of organized society and changes in the character of the media meant alterations, often drastic, in institutions, social organizations, and cultural values. Two main classes of media had existed from the beginning of time, each with its different qualities and influences. A heavy, durable medium, such as stone, clay-baked tablets or parchment, emphasized stability, permanence, or time. A light, easily transported material like papyrus or paper meant rapid dissemination over distance or space. A medium of communication that favored time, he believed, emphasized local initiative, respect for antiquity, and religious observance. A space-based medium encouraged secular attitudes, centralized, bureaucratic government, imperialism, and technocracy. Like Oswald Spengler and Arnold Toynbee, Innis was attempting to explain the rise and fall of civilizations, the growth and collapse of empires; unlike Toynbee and Spengler, who found complex explanations laden with diversified historical evidence, Innis relied on a simple mechanical determinant, expressed in the twin categories of space and time. He did not openly predict the downfall of western civilization, as both Spengler and Toynbee had done, but from the angry despair with which he wrote of modern times, we can hardly doubt what he believed its inevitable end would be.

In June, 1946, Innis received a letter from the administrators of the Beit Fund at Oxford University, inviting him to give six lectures on any subject in the economic history of the British Empire. Innis had nothing new that he wanted to say about the economic history of the British Empire, but he was burning to deliver himself of the great new theory of communications that had been maturing rapidly in his mind for the last few years. The Beit lectures were given two years later, in the Trinity Term of 1948, but even before that Innis had crammed the substance of his great new theory into his presidential address to the Royal Society in the spring of 1947. In the next few years, he seemed to proclaim it everywhere. He lectured at the University of Nottingham and the University of London; he gave the Sesquicentennial lectures at the University of New Brunswick. In the last six years of his life, four books of his essays and lectures were published. It was as though he was driven by the desperate necessity of compulsion to deliver his last message to a sick and troubled world. And then, the cancer, which was to end all these efforts forever, began inexorably to destroy his life.

He was that rarest of all beings in Canadian history, a genius—not a flawless and immaculate genius, but a genius whose characteristic weaknesses and imperfections, the flaws of his upbringing and training, seem almost to heighten and intensify his special and unique brilliance.

James W. Carey (essay date 1981)

SOURCE: "Culture, Geography, and Communications: The Work of Harold Innis in an American Context," in *Culture, Communication, and Dependency: The Tradition of H. A. Innis,* William H. Melody, Liora Salter, Paul Heyer, eds., Ablex Publishing Corporation, 1981, pp. 73-91.

[*In the following essay, Carey evaluates Innis's contribution to the social sciences.*]

What is it about the ponderous and often unreadable texts of Harold Innis that makes them the subject of continuing interest, indeed, of a revival of interest some twenty-five years after his death? Despite their opacity, their maddening obscurity, their elliptical quality, I find myself drawn back to these texts precisely when seeking fresh departures in the study of communications. And the texts continue to yield because they combine an almost studied obscurity with a gift for pungent aphorism, producing, thereby, sudden flashes of juxtaposition and illumination. There was to Innis a natural depth, excess, and complexity, a sense of paradox and reversal that complicates his writing and provides permanent riddles rather than easy formulas. His books, in short, are not merely things to read but things to think with.

Beyond his intellectual qualities Innis had an indispensable moral gift; this was expressed throughout his life but perhaps most ardently in his opposition to the cold war and the absorption of Canada into it and in his defense of the university tradition against those who would use it as merely another expression of state or market power. His thought and conduct defied description by terms like radical or conservative, but represented nonetheless the best of western humanism. In an age when the social studies are tepid and antiseptic, and also more powerful, his example is a source of more than intellectual inspiration.

The very opaqueness and aphoristic quality of his writing, when combined with its critical moral stance, has left his work open to be assimilated to and contrasted with newer developments in scholarship that have occurred since his death. I am thinking, in particular, of developments in cultural geography, Marxism and critical theory, and in cultural anthropology and hermeneutics.

The significance that is my theme is of another kind. For me, the significance of his work is to be found in the light of our knowledge of, and literature about, human communication and, in particular, what we effortlessly but misleadingly call mass communication. I want to insert his work into that stream of understanding to highlight the significance of his scholarship for those of us in the United States whose own work, however pale by comparison, is derivative of it.

American research and scholarship on communication began as a cumulative tradition in the late 1880s when five people came together in Ann Arbor, Michigan. Two were young faculty—John Dewey and George Herbert Mead, two were students at the time—Robert Park and Charles Cooley. The final element of the pentad was an itinerant American journalist by the name of Franklin Ford, who shared with Dewey, indeed cultivated in him, the belief "A proper daily newspaper would be the only possible social science."[1]

Like most intellectuals of the period, this group was under the spell of Herbert Spencer's organic conception of society, through not enthralled by social Darwinism. The relationship between communication and transportation which organicism suggested—the nerves and arteries of society—had been realized in fact with the parallel growth of the telegraph and railroad: a thoroughly encephalated social nervous system with the control mechanism of communication divorced from the physical movement of people and things.

They saw in the developing technology of communications the capacity to transform, in Dewey's terms, the great society created by industry into a great community: a unified nation with one culture, a great public of common understanding and knowledge. This belief in communication as the cohesive force in society was, of course, part of the progressive creed. Communications technology was the key to improving the quality of politics and culture, the means for turning the United States into a continental village, a pulsating Greek democracy of discourse on a 3,000 mile scale. This was more than a bit of harmless romanticism; it was part of an unbroken tradition of thought on communications technology that continues to this day and that Leo Marx named and I appropriated as the "rhetoric of the technological sublime."[2]

Three other features of their work are worth noting. First, methodologically they were in a revolt against formalism, in Morton White's happy phrase: They attempted to return social studies to a branch of history and to emphasize the interdisciplinary nature of social knowledge.[3] Second, they were under the spell of the frontier hypothesis or at least a certain version thereof. The significance they found in the frontier was not that of the heroic individual breaking one's way into the wilderness, but rather they emphasized the process whereby strangers created the institutions of community life de novo in the small towns of the West. This process of community creation, of institution building, was, they argued, the formative process in the growth of American democracy. Again, although there is more than a little romance with the pastoral in all this, it also led to a positive achievement. In the absence of an inherited tradition, the active process of communication would have to serve as the source of social order and cohesion. Moreover, they conceived communication as something more than the imparting of information. Rather, they characterized communication as the entire process whereby a culture is brought into existence, maintained in time, and sedimented into institutions. Therefore, they saw communication in the envelope of art, architecture, custom and ritual, and, above all, politics. And this gave the third distinctive aspect to their thought: an intense concern with the nature of public life. As Alvin Gouldner has recently reemphasized, the idea of the public is a central notion in their thought and, although they agreed with Gabriel Tarde that the public is something brought into existence by the printing press, they went beyond him in trying to work through the conditions under which the public sphere gives rise to rational and critical discourse and action.[4] In the 1920s these concerns crested and yielded a continuous stream of literature on communications, a central feature of which was a concern with the "vanishing public" or the "eclipse of the public." Despite their youthful optimism, many of the Chicago School, as they were known, came to see that although the mass media brought the public into existence, it later threatened the possibility of public life and with it the possibility of rational discourse and enlightened public opinion.[5]

Harold Innis studied at the University of Chicago when Park and Mead were on the faculty and this tradition was in full flower. Moreover, these same intense concerns with communication were ripe within the city at large: in Jane Adams' Hull House, in Frank Lloyd Wright's architecture offices, in the writings of Louis Sullivan, and, above all, in the textures of the University of Chicago.[6] At a conference a few years back, I attempted to demonstrate some of the continuity of concerns of Innis and the Chicago School but also to dispute Marshall McLuhan's claim that Innis "should be considered as the most eminent member of the Chicago group headed by Robert Park."[7] Park had no direct influence on Innis and Innis was too singular a thinker to be described as a member of any school. Innis' transcript at the University of Chicago reveals he took a very narrow range of courses, strictly limited to traditional topics within political economy. His only outside work was one course in political science on municipal government offered by the greatest Chicago political scientist of the time, Charles Merriam.[8] My only claim is this: The significance of Innis for those of us working within United States' traditions is that he took the concerns of the Chicago School and, with the unvarnished eye of one peering across the Forty-ninth Parallel, corrected and completed these concerns, marvelously widened their range and precision and created a conception and historically grounded theory of communications that was purged of the inherited romanticism of the Chicago School and that led to a far more adequate view of the role of communications and communications technology in American life.

By the time Innis started to write about communications, Chicago sociology had pretty much run itself into the sand. During the 1930s it was transformed into symbolic interactionism, a social psychology of the self and others drawn from the work of Mead. However elegant this work might be, it was also safely tucked away from the questions of politics, rationality, power, and social change that Chicago sociologists had earlier engaged. American studies in communications then came under two influences. The first came from work on psychological behaviorism initiated by John B. Watson just prior to World War I. Watson, both a professor at Columbia and a vice-president of J. Walter Thompson advertising agency, drew upon an accumulating body of work, principally from E. L. Thorndike in animal psychology, and laid down a model of human action in which mind played no part in the arrangement of behavior. Transmitted into the study of communication, this provided the basis for a program of study in which communication became a branch of learning theory, in which learning was defined as the acquisition of behaviors and in which behaviors were governed in turn by conditioning and reinforcement. By removing mind from behavior, the possibility of rational action was removed also, but this was the precise and willing price to be paid for constructing a model of human social action on the postulates of physical science. Powerfully aided by the practical research demands of World War II, behaviorism gave rise to a power or domination model of communication in which study was narrowed into a focus on the means by which power and control is made effective through language, symbols, and media.

The second influence was more indirect but came initially, I think, from the powerful demonstration effect of the Hawthorn experiments. Conducted in a Western Electric plant in the Chicago suburbs, these studies gave rise to the often noted Hawthorn effect: that worker productivity rose over the cycle of the experiments because of the experiments themselves—Hawthorn gives us Heisenberg. What is less often noted is that the experiments were presumably a test of a model derived from Durkheim: that the factory should be viewed as an integrated social system to which the worker had to be adjusted. The findings of the experiments then gave rise to a new social role, a band of ambulatory counsellors whose task it was to resocialize the workers to their grievances. That is, the major lesson of the Hawthorn experiments was the discovery of the power of communication to serve as a means of therapy in the service of social control of the worker.

These movements in thought coalesced under Paul Lazarsfeld and his students and, impelled by the war effort and coordinate developments in cybernetics, communication studies in the immediate post war years was organized pretty strictly as a subdiscipline of social psychology. Moreover, the models that guided this research yielded two alternative formulations of communication: in one model, communication was seen as a mode of domination, in another as a form of therapy; in one model, men were motivated to pursue power, in the other to flee anxiety. I characterize such models in this way to emphasize one simple point: these models were not merely models of communication, representations of the communication process. They were also models for the enactment of the communication process, powerful models of an actual social practice.[9]

Finally, the growth of these models within the intellectual community and the marriage of this social science to imitations of the physical sciences signaled a shift in the nature of American social scientists in general and communications students in particular. I refer here to the transformation of social scientists from a prophetic to a priestly class. It signaled the ingestion of social science into the apparatus of rule and a surrendering of the critical function of independent intellectuals.

One final development should be noted. The transformation of communication studies into a branch of psychology not only ended the essentially interdisciplinary character of it in the United States but also separated it from historical studies. Conceived now as a natural science, communication studies could send historical studies elsewhere, implicitly into the humanities where they might retain curiosity value, but could not make claims as a form of knowledge of pertinence to the conduct of contemporary life. As a result, American historical studies in communications developed without a vital relationship to the social sciences. More unfortunately, they developed along a particular model which I, stealing a memorable phrase from Herbert Butterfield, have chosen to call a "Whig interpretation of communications history."[10] Butterfield used the notion of the Whig interpretation to describe the marriage of the doctrine of progress with the idea of history. The Whig interpretation of communications history, to put it all too briefly, views the history of the press as the slow steady expansion of freedom and knowledge from the political press to the commercial press, the setbacks into sensationalism and yellow journalism, the forward thrust into muckraking and social responsibility. History is seen as the rise and expansion of freedom and responsibility.[11] When communication technology is the subject for historical study, pretty much the same story emerges. The history of communications technology is the story of the expansion of the powers of human knowledge, the steady democratization of culture, the enlargement of freedom, and the erosion of monpolies of knowledge through more democratic sharing. From the onset of literacy through the latest in computational hardware, it is the story of the progressive liberation of the human spirit. More information is made available and is made to move further and faster, ignorance is ended, civil strife brought under control. In this version of the rhetoric of the technological sublime it is the machines that possess teleological insight.[12]

THE INNIS ACHIEVEMENT

This was the situation, admittedly reduced to a sketch, that pertained when Harold Innis died in the early 1950s. It is against this background that the achievement of Innis should be assessed, at least for those of us working in an American context. Let me briefly summarize that achievement: Innis produced a body of historical and theoretical speculation that sets out the major dimensions of communications history and the critical propositions and problems of communication theory, and he did so with maximal pertinance to the circumstances of North America. Much remains to be done with his work, both in moving outward to a more systematic cultural analysis, and in altering the entire framework to fit subsequent advances in the social sciences. However, while recognizing Innis' achievements, it is best to avoid excessive piety before it. Innis' books are not sacred texts to be exegetically struggled over. They are examples of what can be done and without his work we would lack a powerful place to begin.[13]

Let me briefly outline what it is that constitutes part of Innis' achievement when set against the background of the American scholarship I have mentioned.

First, and most obvious, Innis pursued communications in a genuinely interdisciplinary way. He was simultaneously geographer, historian, economist, and political scientist, and he located communications study at the point where these fields intersected. Like the Chicago School, he shared in the revolt against formalism and not only ransacked experience without regard to discipline but restored communications study to an historical foundation. For myself, what was most critical was that he rescued communications from a branch of social psychology and freed it from a reliance on natural science models. This seems to me to be the critical intervention. Innis recognized that all scholarship must be grounded in the analysis of the radical particularities of time and place, history and geography. However, scholars that adopted natural science models suggested they were expounding, like physical scientists, laws that were universal, that held without regard to time, place, and circumstance. He saw up close the consequence of adopting this view in his analysis of the applicability of Manchester economics to economies such as Canada's. To avoid intellectual colonization he felt Canada must, in scholarship as in other matters, turn to an analysis of the radical particularities of Canadian experience and reach out from them to the experience of others. As he said late in his life in an essay entitled, "Great Britain, the United States, and Canada," and here he was thinking of more than scholarship, "Whatever hope of continued autonomy Canada may have in the future must depend on her success in withstanding American influence and in assisting the development of a third bloc designed to withstand the pressure of the United States and Russia."[14]

He was committed to the notion of pluralistic centers of scholarship as essential to cultural stability. To this end he attempted to restore to economics and communications an historical model of analysis. The central terms that he brought to the study of communications—the limitations of technology, the spatial and temporal bias inherent in technology, the monopolies of knowledge toward which they tend and which they support, the analysis of social change, selective advantage, cultural stability and collapse, legitimacy, the dialetical method— were not the terms of a verification model. They were, instead, a made in the kitchen group of concepts with which to examine the actual historical record. As I suggested in a recent essay, rather too much time has been spent analyzing the dictionary meaning of these terms, as if they were designed to enter a deductive model or formal theory. What I tried to emphasize, and Ian Parker suggested that I did not emphasize it strongly enough, was that they were terms with which to examine the historical record, precisely to cut down and limit the legitimacy of formal and universal theories. And, if anything, in following out his work we have not been empirical enough, have not followed out the concrete historical investigations that would, utilizing many of his concepts, set this record straight.

In short, Innis provided in communication studies, at a moment when no one else in the United States was doing so, a model of scholarly investigation that was historical, empirical, interpretive, and critical. His work was historical, as I have said, in the precise sense that he wanted to test the limits of theoretical work, to show the actual variations in time and space that rendered transparent the dangerous claim of universal theory. The historical imagination checked off the bias of the theoretical one. It was empirical in that he attempted to exhume the actual historical record and not those ironclad laws of development with which we have been plagued from Hegel forward. His work was interpretive in that it sought the definitions, the varying definitions, people placed upon experience in relation to technology, law, religion, and politics.

Finally, his work was critical in the contemporary sense in that he was not proposing some natural value free study, but a standpoint from which to critique society and theories of it in light of humane and civilized values.

Second, Innis reformulated the idea of the Chicago School often in a quite explicit way and attacked, albeit indirectly, the notions of communications that had gained currency in American historical and scientific scholarship. In particular, from his earliest work, he argued against the major versions of the frontier hypothesis "so gratifyingly isolationist that the source of inspiration and action was not at the center but at the periphery of Western culture." Every frontier, in short, has a back tier. The "back tier" interest was determined by the extent to which the frontier products strengthened its economy, supplemented rather than competed with its products and enhanced its strategic position.[15] That first back tier was Europe and to that extent North American economic and communications development was part of the trajectory of European history. The development of this continent was decisively determined by the policies and struggles of European capitals. The consequences of those policies and struggles were outlined in his studies of staples: fur, fish, timber, etc. With the gradual decline of the influence of Europe, the back tier shifted to the North American metropolitan centers, both Canadian and American, but effective control shifted toward New York and Washington, relative to both the Canadian and American frontiers. The studies of paper and pulp brought that home and also led to the realization that in mechanized forms of communications new types of empire and back-tier/frontier relations were elaborated: "The United States, with systems of mechanized communication and organized force, has sponsored a new type of imperialism imposed on common law in which sovereignty is preserved de jure and used to expand imperialism de facto."[16]

In this observation, he founded the modern studies that now exist under the banner of media imperialism but his sense of the complexity of that relationship was considerably more subtle than that of most contemporary scholars. In particular, Innis knew something of the tensions, contradictions, and accommodations that existed between trading and communications partners. This allowed him, from the beginning, to pierce the organic metaphors that so often led the Chicago scholars astray and masked the facts of history, geography, and power in a veil of metaphysics. Even if society were like an organism, there would be some controlling element, some centralized brain in the body, some region and group that would collect the power necessary to direct the nerves of communication and the arteries of transportation. There would be no transformation of the great society into the great community by way of disinterested technology but only in terms of the ways in which knowledge and culture were monopolized by particular groups.

He saw in the growth of communication in the late eighteenth and nineteenth centuries a continual process of decentralization and recentralization that moved forward in a dialectical way as small hinterland communities attempted to outrun metropolitan influence, only later to be absorbed back into it. The prevailing pattern of communication prior to the American Revolution was a classically imperial one. Messages moved on an east-west axis between London and the Colonies. Communication between the Colonies moved slowly and erratically and in general the Colonies communicated with one another via London. Following the Revolution this same pattern prevailed for a time. News in early American newspapers was almost exclusively European in origin and communication was stronger between the port cities and England than between the cities and their own American hinterland. Internal communication was slow and problematic, good only on the Atlantic sea corridor and only then when not adversely affected by weather. American towns and cities were relatively isolated from one another and connected only by common port cities or European capitals.

Following the War of 1812, the country embarked on a vigorous campaign for what were benignly called "internal improvements," the object of which, again benignly expressed, was an attempt to bind the nation together or connect the east with the west. In fact, what developed was the same pattern of communication of the Colonial period but now with New York replacing London as the central element in the system. As Arthur Schlesinger, Sr., emphasized, what grew up over the first half of the eighteenth century was a pattern of city-state imperialism.[17] The major cities of the East vigorously competed with one another to replace London as the geographic center of trade and communications. By the early 1800s, New York was firmly established as the center of American communication and controlled the routes of trade and communication with the interior, a position it has never relinquished. It maintained first contacts with Europe through shipping and therefore information passed between American cities by being routed through New York. But every major city on the East coast made its bid for control of the interior. New York's hegemony was secured by the Hudson River, the Erie Canal, and the resultant access to the Great Lakes, and by Chicago allowing New York to service and drain the Mississippi Valley. Philadelphia also attempted to control the West through an elaborate series of canals whose failure brought Pennsylvania to the verge of bankruptcy. Baltimore attempted through the first national highway, from Cumberland, Maryland, to connect into the Ohio River and terminate in St. Louis at the headwaters of the Missouri. Baltimore later tried with the Baltimore and Ohio Railroad, the first national railroad, to build this connection surer and faster, and even Boston, although blocked from the West by New York, attempted to become a railroad center and create access independent of the Erie Canal. As Alan Pred's studies have documented most thoroughly, the effect of the hegemony of New York was to draw the hinterland cities within its information field and to isolate other East Coast cities. Even Columbus, Ohio, was being served by New York with both goods and information in the 1840s.[18] New York's hegemony was in turn strengthened by the construction of the Illinois Central Railroad from Chicago to New Orleans. At the time of its building it was popularly called the "great St. Louis cut-off" because it was designed to isolate St. Louis from its natural trading partner, Baltimore. When the first transcontinental railroad was placed along the northern route, this again strengthened the centrality of New York. When this was tied to the increasing access of New York and Washington along the Atlantic trade and information corridor, the basic pattern was complete. New York, and therefore its merchants, firms, and elites controlled an increasingly centralized system of information which tied the northern tier together and even acted as a source of supply from many Canadian Cities. It just as effectively isolated the South. By every measure of communication the South, with the exception of New Orleans, was isolated from the rest of the country. There were poor interconnections between southern cities, and southern cities dealt with one another and the rest of the North only by first channeling communication through New York.[19]

Although this pattern of information movement has been importantly altered since the 1840s, its persistence, at least in outline, is even more striking. The trade routes of culture laid down by the canal and railroad have been altered by the telegraph, wire services, magazines, films, telephone, broadcasting and jet aircraft to be sure. But the centrality of New York in the flow of communications and culture, the importance of the New York-Washington corridor, and the metropole-hinterland connections that flow east and west are still there to be observed. In other words, despite the enormous size of the United States, a particular pattern of geographic concentration developed that gave inordinate power to certain urban centers. This development undercut local and regional culture. Although it aided in forming a national culture, it disguised how local, even provincial, this national culture was: A national and even international culture was defined increasingly by how the world was seen from a couple of distinctively local places. The point is that since 1800 we have lived with essentially a dominant eastern corridor of American communication that has created an effective monopoly of knowledge in news and entertainment. This can be shown most graphically in the growth of the star system. Concretely, this means that today a few national figures and themes are pretty much exclusively focused on in politics and entertainment, that local issues are of interest only when they can be alchemized into national issues of concern in a few urban centers, and that the drama of news and entertainment must be made increasingly slick and abstract to appeal to national and, increasingly, international audiences.

That is only one-third of the story. Innis was also sensitive to the means by which the hinterland was in a continual struggle both to escape and accept metropolitan dominance. There was an important truth in the Chicago School's notion of the importance of local community building as a formative democratic experience. In his essay on **"Technology and Public Opinion in the United States"** Innis attempted to show how localities and regions resisted the spread of communication, how the issue was only decided by struggle over a protracted series of conflicts: the spread of standard time, of the mail order house, parcel post and rural free delivery, of the department store and regionalized corporation. Moreover, he was concerned to point out how the Western newspaper was an instrument for resisting metropolitan dominance, how the telegraph initially strengthened the local and regional press until that too was undercut by the power of the wire services and chain papers. That is, the spread of a spatially biased system of communication was not even and uniform but resulted in a complicated interplay of resistance and acceptance that we have yet to adequately lay out in detail.[20]

Moreover, the pattern of national spatial oraganization was reproduced in the organization of city after city and county after county. Seymour Mandelbaum's *Boss Tweed's New York* is a marvelous though complacent study of the reorganization of New York City essentially on a metropole-hinterland model.[21] My own studies suggest that same model of development holds true at the regional and county level.

The United States, then, at all levels of social structure pursued what I call high communications policy, one aimed solely at spreading messages further in space and reducing the cost of transmission. That is what Innis meant by exploiting the spatial bias of modern communication. Communication was seen, in other words, solely in the envelope of space and power. That communication might be seen as something else, as a container of human interaction that allows for the persistence and growth of culture, is a view that never entered United States policy. The distinction between power and container technology parallels Innis' distinction between space and time.[22] But what Innis saw more clearly than most was how modern institutions were thoroughly infected by the idea of space. The universities were not exempt. Economics, political science, urban planning, sociology, and the physical sciences charted the problems and challenges of society in space. Even time was converted to space as the social sciences, enamored by prediction, characterized the future as a frontier to be conquered. Even history had caught the bug for historical writing merely used time as a container to tell the narrative of progress: politics, power, empire, and rule.

In summary, as the United States pursued an almost exclusive policy of improving communication over long distance, as it saw communication as a form of power and transmission, the effective units of culture and social organization underwent major changes. There was a progressive shift from local and regional units to national and international ones, though not without considerable struggle and conflict. Individuals were linked into larger units of social organization without the necessity of appealing to them through local and proximate structures. Communication within these local units became less critical for the operation of society and less relevant to the solutions of personal problems. Finally, the growth of long distance communication cultivated new structures in which thought occurred—national classes and professions—new things thought about—speed, space, movement, mobility—and new things to think with—increasingly abstract, analytic, and manipulative symbols.

FREEDOM OF THE PRESS AND THE ORAL TRADITION

The third and final argument I want to make before concluding is that Innis also attacked the Whig interpretation of communications history. He did this by demonstrating at every point the paradoxical nature of changes in the technology of communication, and by disputing certain implicit notions concerning the nature of freedom and freedom of the press. I think this is the context of his long interest in Greek life and the nature of the oral tradition. That interest is to be understood, in other words, in terms of the relationship of democratic life to oral discourse and the public sphere.

As is well known, Innis argued that the first amendment to the United States Constitution did not so much grant freedom of speech and press as it gave constitutional protection to technology, and in this sense, restricted rather than expanded freedom:

> Freedom of the press has been given constitutional guarantees as in the United States [and] . . . has provided bulwarks for monopolies which have emphasized control over space. Under these conditions the problem of duration or monopoly over time has been neglected, indeed obliterated. Time has been cut into pieces the length of a day's newspaper.[23]

The free press clause served largely to consolidate the position of the newspaper's monopoly of knowledge and eventually, through the paper's dependence on advertising and news, was instrumental in telescoping time into a one-day world, in spreading the values of commercialism and industrialism and furthering the spatial bias of print. In granting freedom of the press, the constitution sacrificed, despite the qualifying clause, the right of people to speak to one another and to inform themselves. For such rights the Constitution substituted the more abstract right to be spoken to and to be informed by others, especially specialist, professional classes:

> The full impact of printing did not become possible until the adoption of the Bill of Rights in the United States with its guarantee of freedom of the press. A guarantee of freedom of the press in print was intended to further sanctify the printed word and to provide a rigid bulwark for the shelter of vested interests.[24]

He refused to yield to the modern notion that the level of democratic process correlates with the amount of capital invested in communication, capital that can do our knowing for us.

There certainly was something romantic in Innis' affection for the oral tradition but there was much more, a concern with the very possibility of public life. He identified the oral tradition with the Greeks and with Plato's attack on writing in the *Phaedrus:*

> If men learn this writing it will implant forgetfulness in their souls; they will cease to exercise memory because they rely on what is written, calling things to remembrance no longer from within themselves but by means of external marks; what you have discovered is a recipe not for memory but for reminder. And it is not true wisdom that you offer your disciples, but only its semblance. . . . [25]

The objections to writing here are twofold: It is inherently shallow in its effects, and essential principles of truth can only be arrived at dialectically. Writing is shallow in its effects because reading books may give a specious sense of knowledge, which in reality can only be attained by oral question and answer; and such knowledge in any case only goes deep when "it is written in the soul of the learner."[26]

We associate democracy with widespread literacy and a world of knowledge as transcending political units. Yet even though literacy can give rise to a form of democracy, it also makes impossible demands. Literacy produces instability and inconsistency because the written tradition is participated in so unevenly:

> Improvements in communication . . . make for increased difficulties of understanding. The cable compelled contraction of language and facilitated a rapid widening between the English and American languages. In the vast realm of fiction in the Anglo-Saxon world, the influence of the cinema and the radio has been evident in the best seller and the creation of special classes of readers with little prospect of communication between them. . . . The large-scale mechanization of knowledge is characterized by imperfect competition and the active creation of monopolies of language which prevent understanding. . . . [27]

That is, modern technology actually makes communication much more difficult. Rational agreement and democratic coherence become problematic when so little background is shared in common. As Bertha Phillpotts argued in 1931:

> Printing so obviously makes knowledge accessible to all that we are inclined to forget that it also makes knowledge easy to avoid. A shepherd in an Icelandic homestead . . . could not avoid spending his evenings listening to the kind of literature which interested the farmer. The result was a degree of really national culture, such as no nation of today has been able to achieve.[28]

Literate culture is much more easily avoided than an oral one and even when it is not avoided its actual effects may be relatively shallow. Lacking an oral culture one may

easily fall prey to experts in knowledge who do our knowing for us, who inform us but whose knowledge does not easily connect to our actual experience and to the basic transactions of life.

In short, Innis believed that the unstated presupposition of democratic life was the existence of a public sphere, of an oral tradition, or of a tradition of public discourse as a necessary counterweight to printing. In the more telegraphic prose of his notebooks Innis observed that:

> Commercialism tends to make for imperfect competition between levels of reading public and to fix various groups within level. Average man cut off from literature. Problem of making fiction a channel of communication between publics . . . reading public disintegrated by imperfect competition in publishing industry.[29]

The first amendment did not secure the permanence of public life; in fact, it acted against it because it finally placed the weight of education on the written tradition. Modern media of communication, largely for commercial purposes, created a system of communication that was essentially private. Private reading and the reading audience replaced the reading public and the public of discussion and argument. The system of communication that actually evolved was grounded, therefore, not merely in a spatial bias but in a privatized one as well. It was the privatization more than the Bill of Rights that led to the decline of censorship: "Decline in the practice of reading aloud led to a decline in the importance of censorship. The individual was taken over by the printing industry and his interest developed in material not suited to general conversation."[30] Under such conditions the public becomes a mere statistical artifact, public taste a measure of private opinion that has been both cultivated and objectified but not realized in discourse. With that, the public sphere goes into eclipse.

I think the breakdown in oral discourse is the key to Innis' thought and politics. The public he took to be grounded in the capacity through speech of rational discourse. He understood, of course, the difficulty of attaining these habits and realized the degree to which privatized existence inhibits the growth of such discourse. The strength of the oral tradition in his view was that it could not be easily monopolized. Once the habits of discourse were widespread, the public could take on an autonomous existence and not be subject to the easy control of the state or commerce. Therefore, the major intellectual project of Innis' later life, a project of importance to both politics and the university, was the restoration of the oral tradition—by which he meant a set of talents at memory, speech, and argument; and a sphere, a place of institutional home in which such a tradition might flourish. "Mass production and standardization are the enemies of the West. The limitations of the mechanization of the printed and the spoken word must be emphasized and determined efforts to recapture the vitality of the oral tradition must be made."[31] Here he agreed with John Dewey.[32] Speech is the agency of creative thought; printing of dissemination. It was precisely the imbalance between the processes of creativity and dissemination that Innis sought to correct. Mechanical communication transformed the reading and listening public into a reading and listening audience with disastrous consequences for democracy. Correcting the situation turned upon demonstrating that freedom of the press could ultimately stand as an enemy to freedom of expression.

Innis' attachment to the oral tradition finally, then, had a modern purpose: to demonstrate that the belief that the growth of mechanical communication necessarily expanded freedom and knowledge was both simplistic and misleading. For that to happen there would have to be a parallel and dialectical growth of public sphere, grounded in an oral tradition, where knowledge might be "written in the soul of the learner."

THE INVASION OF TIME

Let me emphasize, again, in conclusion, that the great challenge of Innis' work is not to attempt to figure out what he really meant. Rather, it is the attempt to apply and extend some of his major ideas by interpreting them within the context of concrete episodes. As one direction to take these interpretations, let me offer a closing observation on the relation of time, space, and communications.

The growth of communications in the nineteenth century had the practical effect of diminishing space as a differentiating criterion in human affairs. What Innis called the "penetrative powers of the price system"[33] was in effect the spread of a uniform price system throughout space so that for purposes of trade everyone was in the same place. In commerce this meant the decontextualization of markets such that local prices no longer depended on local factors of supply and demand but responded to national and international forces. The spread of the price system was part of the attempt to colonize space. The correlative to the penetration of the price system was what the late composer Igor Stravinsky called the "statisticalization of mind": the transformation of the entire mental world into quantity, and the distribution of quantities in space such that the relationship between things and people becomes solely one of numbers. Statistics widens and makes the market for everything more uniform and interdependent.

My interest is in that moment when the ecological niche of space was filled, so to speak, filled as an arena of commerce and control. Then, attention was shifted to filling time, now defined as an aspect of space, a continuation of space in another dimension. As the spatial frontier was filled, time became the new frontier. This is easiest to see in terms of trade. When the prices of commodities were equalized in space, largely as a result of the telegraph, speculation moved from a spatial to a temporal dimension. That is, the exhaustion of space as an arena of arbitrage gave rise to the futures market: a shifting of market activity from certain space to uncertain time. My

suspicion is that this was the first practical attempt to make time a new frontier, a newly defined zone of uncertainty, and to penetrate it by the price system.

There are two other dimensions of time I want to mention briefly. I think the second time to be penetrated once space was exhausted, was sacred time, in particular the sabbath. I believe that the greatest invention of the ancient Hebrews was the idea of the sabbath, though I am using this word in a fully secular sense: the invention of a region free from control of the state and commerce where another dimension of life could be experienced and where altered forms of social relationship could occur. As such, the sabbath has always been a major resistance to state and market power. For purposes of communication, the effective penetration of the sabbath came in the 1880s with the invention of the Sunday newspaper. It was Hearst with his New York Sunday *World* that popularized the idea of Sunday newspaper reading and created, in fact, a market where none had existed before— a sabbath market. Since then the penetration of the sabbath has been one of the "frontiers" of commercial activity. Finally, when the frontier in space was officially closed in 1893, the "new frontier" became the night, and since then there has been a continous spreading upward of commercial activity. In a recent and suggestive paper in the *American Sociological Review,* Murray Melbin of Boston University has attempted to characterize "night as a frontier."[34] In terms of communication, the steady expansion of commercial broadcasting into the night is one of the best examples. There were no twenty-four-hour radio stations in Boston, for example, from 1918 through 1954; now half of the stations in Boston operate all night. Television has slowly expanded into the night at one end and at the other initiated operations earlier and earlier. Now, indeed, there are twenty-four-hour television stations in major markets.[35]

The notion of night as frontier, a new frontier of time that opens once space is filled, is a metaphor but it is more than that. Melbin details some of the features common to the spatial and temporal frontiers: They both advance in stages, the population is more sparsely settled and homogenous, there is solitude, an absence of social constraints and less persecution, settlements are isolated, government is decentralized, law-lessness and violence as well as friendliness and helpfulness increase, new behavioral styles emerge.[36] That is, the same dialectic between centralization and decentralization occurs on the temporal frontier as on the spatial frontier. On the one hand, communication is even more privatized at night. On the other hand, people are less controlled by communication because of the absence of authority.

My point here is merely a suggestive one. The end of space led to the invasion of time by the forces of commerce and politics and with something of the same dialectic of decentralization and recentralization that was found in space. The way in which time was redefined as an ecological niche to be filled and the actual way it has been progressively filled since the closing of the spatial frontier in the nineteenth century is, I think, among the many practical research tasks that the work of Harold Innis left to us.

NOTES

[1] The phrase comes from notes taken by Charles Cooley on a Dewey lecture in Ann Arbor. Quoted in Fred H. Mathews, *Quest for an American Sociology: Robert E. Park and the Chicago School.* Montreal, McGill-Queen's University Press, 1977, p. 18.

[2] Marx, Leo. *The Machine in the Garden.* New York, Oxford University Press, 1964.

[3] White, Morton. *Social Thought in America: The Revolt Against Formalism.* Boston, Beacon Press, 1957.

[4] Gouldner, Alvin. *The Dialectic of Ideology and Technology.* New York, The Seabury Press, 1977, Chs. 4 and 5.

[5] See, in particular, John Dewey. *The Public and Its Problems.* New York, Henry Holt and Company, 1927.

[6] Quandt, Jean. *From the Small Town to the Great Community.* New Brunswick, New Jersey, Rutgers University Press, 1970.

[7] McLuhan, Marshall "Introduction," to *The Bias of Communication,* by Harold A. Innis. Toronto, University of Toronto Press, 1964, p. XVI.

[8] The Registrar of the University of Chicago was kind enough to send me a copy of Innis' transcript with grades appropriately and delicately blanked out.

[9] I have taken these matters up at greater length in "A Cultural Approach to Communication." In *Communication,* Vol. 2, No. 2, 1975, pp. 1-22.

[10] Butterfield, Herbert. *The Whig Interpretation of History* (1931). Harmondsworth, England, Penguin Books, 1973.

[11] Carey, James W. "The Problem of Journalism History." In *Journalism History,* Vol. 1, No. 1, Spring 1974, pp. 3-5, 27.

[12] For a more extended argument on these matters, particularly as they relate to Innis and McLuhan, see James W. Carey and John J. Quirk. "The Myths of the Electronic Revolution." In *American Scholar,* Vol. 39, Nos. 2 and 3, Spring, Summer 1970, pp. 219-241, 395-424.

[13] Carey, James W. "Canadian Communication Theory: Extensions and Interpretations of Harold Innis." In *Studies in Canadian Communications,* edited by Gertrude Joch Robinson and Donald F. Theall. Montreal, McGill Programme in Communications, 1975, pp. 27-59.

[14] Innis, H. A. *Essay in Canadian Economic History.* Toronto, University of Toronto Press, 1956, p. 411.

[15] Heaton, Herbert. *The Economics of Empire,* The James Ford Bell Lecture, No. 3, University of Minnesota, 1966.

[16] Innis H. A. *Empire and Communications.* Oxford, Oxford University Press, 1950, p. 215.

[17] Schlesinger, Sr., Arthur. *The Rise of the City 1878-1898.* New York, Macmillan, 1933, p. 86.

[18] This argument is based, specifically, on the work of Alan Pred. See: *Urban Growth and the Circulation of Information.* Cambridge, Harvard University Press, 1973. Pred, in turn, relies upon Innis' analysis.

[19] Again, the analysis relies on Pred's work but the outlines of the argument are presented in Innis' early work, particularly as it concerns the relations between the American South, the American North, and Canada. See: Innis, H. A. *The Fur Trade in Canada* (1930). Toronto, University of Toronto Press, 1956, particularly the concluding chapter.

[20] Innis, *Bias of Communication,* p. 156ff.

[21] Mandelbaum, Seymour J. *Boss Tweed's New York.* New York, John Wiley and Company, 1965.

[22] The distinction between power and container technology is taken from Lewis Mumford. *The Pentagon of Power.* New York, Harcourt, Brace, Javonovich, Inc., 1970, Ch. 6.

[23] Innis, H. A. "Concept of Monopoly and Civilization." In *Explorations,* No. 3, August 1954, pp. 89-95.

[24] Innis, *Bias of Communication,* p. 138.

[25] Hackworth, R. (Ed). *Plato's Phaedrus.* Cambridge, Cambridge University Press, 1972, p. 157.

[26] Hackworth, *Plato's Phaedrus,* p. 159.

[27] Innis, *Bias of Communication,* pp. 28-29.

[28] Quoted in Jack Good, (Ed). *Literacy in Traditional Societies.* Cambridge, Cambridge University Press, 1968, p. 60. This section borrows from and paraphrases Goody's work.

[29] Innis, H. A. *The Idea File.* In the collection of Thomas Fisher Library, University of Toronto, p. 30.

[30] Innis, H. A. *Changing Concepts of Time.* Toronto, University of Toronto Press, 1952, p. 10.

[31] Innis, *Empire and Communications,* p. 215.

[32] Dewey, John. *The Public and Its Problems,* Chicago, Swallow Press, 1927, Ch. 6.

[33] Innis, *Essays,* pp. 252-272.

[34] Melbin, Murray. "Night as Frontier." In *American Sociological Review,* Vol. 43, No. 1, February 1978, pp. 3-22.

[35] Melbin, "Night as Frontier," p. 4.

[36] Melbin, "Night as Frontier," pp. 6-18.

John Hutcheson (essay date 1982)

SOURCE: "Harold Innis and the Unity and Diversity of Confederation," in *Journal of Canadian Studies/Revue d'études canadiennes,* Vol. 17, No. 4, Winter, 1982-83, pp. 57-73.

[*In the following essay, Hutcheson examines Innis's views of Canadian economic development.*]

A prevalent view of the Canadian imagination, articulated by Northrop Frye, is that it has been dominated by a sense of dislocation occasioned by the enormity of the landscape and the sparseness of "civilization." Frye's view is that Canada has been seen as "a country of isolations and terror, and of the overwhelming of human values by an indifferent and wasteful nature." From this perspective Frye has claimed E. J. Pratt's "Brébeuf and His Brethren" as a statement of the central tragic theme of the Canadian imagination. The Iroquois are seen, in European fashion, as part of nature. Brébeuf represents an order which, through a hierarchical chain of command, extends outside of Canada to a civilization, and "head office," in Europe.

In Frye's view the central triumphant theme in the Canadian imagination also builds on the subject of "lines of communication," and "the theme of the epic act of communication in Canadian history, the linking of the east and west by a great railway, was thus also a logical one for Pratt to choose." In "Towards the Last Spike," Pratt portrays Macdonald's vision of the west:

> Seizing a telescope, he swept the skies
> The north-south drift, a self-illumined chart.
>
> . . . . .
>
> That stellar path looked too much like a road map
> Upon his wall—the roads all led to market—
> The north-south route. He lit a candle, held
> It to a second map full of blank spaces
> And arrows pointing west.

Macdonald's genius was to articulate an ideology of western expansion that would overcome all the obstacles, both natural and man made:

> The words
> British, the West instead of South, the Nation,
> the all-Canadian route—these terms were singing
> Fresher than ever. . . .

Van Horne, backed up by Shaughnessy and Stephen, overcomes the "reptile" shield, the "Laurentian monster," and then the "terror and beauty" of the mountain ranges to create a Canada *a mari usque ad mare.* It is a powerful theme and with only occasional dissent, such as F. R. Scott's "All the Spikes But the Last," has been renewed by writers as diverse as Gordon Lightfoot and Pierre Berton.

The vision owes much to Harold Innis. "Confederation," Innis declared, "has been to an important extent the creation of private enterprise represented by the Canadian Pacific Railway, supported by the federal government in a tariff and railway rate policy, and in the Canadian National Railways."[1] Innis also looked back beyond Confederation to see Canada as an extension of the St. Lawrence-Great Lakes water routes of the fur trade and even saw the North West Company as the "forerunner" of the Confederation that was consolidated by the CPR and the wheat economy.[2] But the celebration of Canada as the triumphant integration of a vast continental region by the heroic efforts of far-seeing merchants and politicians is a theme that belongs rather more to Donald Creighton than to Harold Innis. There are undoubtedly significant points of overlap between the work of Creighton and Innis. Both for example could see Canada and the United States as competing mercantilist empires. Creighton, however, writes from the political vantage point of the "imperial" centre, Montreal, Ottawa and ultimately London. Innis, in his concern to develop a theory of economic growth that encompassed the diverse regions of an economic empire had a keener eye for the ambiguities of empire.[3]

The line of analysis which flows directly from Innis' work situates the politics of Canadian nationalism and of federal-provincial strains in relation to the pattern of economic development in Canada. It thus evades a common pitfall in Canadian political history which is to trace Canadian politics, whether national or regional, in terms of the strength or weakness of European political ideas without linking the ideas to the nature of the European or Canadian social structures.[4]

Gerard Vano has recently examined regional tensions in Canada in the perspective of the "old Canadian ideology" which was "anti-Canadian" because based on an "internal distinction" of "feudal inspiration and derivation": "The *raison d'être* of the old order, the east-west trade in staples, has gone and with it went the unifying imperative and the will to sustain Confederation Canada."[5] Paradoxically, Vano suggests, the hope for the future lies in "popular Canadianism" of "liberal inspiration." Paradoxical because it has been created by multinational corporations and Americanization.

Vano's charge against Innis is that "Canada has not been, as Innis, Creighton and the staple theorists would claim, a product of Europe," because "the staples system was not capable of producing the social machinery to popularize liberal values."[6] But in Innis' sense Canada was a product of Europe. To say this did not imply a duplication in Canada of either European social structures or European ideas. Vano misses Innis' point about the differences between the centre and the margin.

Innis has been criticized recently by Professor Eccles for an "extreme" economic determinism[7] and there is no doubt that he did build a very substantial castle on the limited infrastructure of his study of the fur trade, though he later added supports with studies of other staples. He was given to dogmatic assertions, often of a paradoxical nature, which are at times, as Donald Creighton said,[8] "extremely exasperating" and it is not likely that any one reader can follow him in all of his conclusions. But his extreme assertions are often completed by significant qualifications which offset the central conclusions. As William Westfall has observed, Innis' work is "especially valuable in an area in which the new regionalism is quite weak—the historical relationship between the regions of Canada and the Canadian nation-state. The unity of Canada, Innis argued, was not tied to the physical features of the land, but to a way certain features of landscape could be used in relation to a specific type of economic enterprise. Other types of enterprise could lead to different "geographical" configurations. Boundaries—whether national or regional—were not "in the land" but rather tied to the character of staple production."[9]

The staple theory provided an explanation for the unity of Confederation. Canada "emerged not in spite of geography, but because of it."[10] But the staple theory also explains diversity and the strains that result from the experience of unequal development that is characteristic of empires.

Empires, as Innis' work leads us to see, create price systems which serve to define boundaries and which set up "centre-periphery" relationships within the boundaries. The "centre" or "core" country of the empire defines the price system by virtue of its ability to control the location of investment, international monetary policy and the rules of international trade. Its core status is maintained so long as it can wield the power to enforce those systems.[11]

The Canadian economy can be seen to have developed as the British price system encouraged the production of a series of staples in the various regions of Canada. Situated at the periphery of the system, Canada attempted to create its own "second-order" centre or "metropolis," which in turn led to the problem of regional balance within the new nation. The difficulties were enhanced by fluctuations in the success and failure of particular staples and indeed of the international system as a whole, and ultimately the emergence of the United States as a rival for Britain's role as "core" country induced a dangerous, and potentially fatal, complication.

This paper explores the theme of unity and diversity in Innis' theory of Canadian economic development. The first section is concerned with the way in which staples have created regional economies. The second section takes up the analysis of the role of government in economic development and the third examines Innis' view of the epochal economic changes that were occurring in his own lifetime.

THE LOCATION OF ECONOMIC ACTIVITY

At one level the staple theory is a theory of the location of economic activity. Innis was, throughout his life, concerned with working out a theory of the economic development of what were commonly called "new countries."[12] He had set himself this task by 1929 when he wrote that "perhaps the most serious obstacle to effective work in Canadian economics and economic history is the lack of a philosophy of economic history applicable to new countries."[13]

There were available several schools of thought that might have been considered to be relevant to the Canadian experience. One of these was the "frontier theory" which stressed the determining influence of the ever-moving margin of "civilization." Economically, the frontier theory stressed the self-sufficiency of an agrarian society, while politically it extolled the progressive and democratic aspects of the frontier. Innis rejected this approach for two reasons: firstly, because "Canada had no gradual development by which the frontier could exercise any continued and pervasive influence"[14]; secondly, and perhaps more importantly, because "the development of a new country means above all things continued relations, especially trade, with the old country."[15] Innis did not by any means neglect the impact of the Canadian environment and geography, but he recognized the equally important point that the "frontier" was only the end of a long chain of commercial links that bound farmers and miners to merchants and bankers. The links extended through the Canadian cities and outside the country to the imperial centres. Canada was "fundamentally a product of Europe."[16]

To see trade as important was not a sufficient rejoinder to the frontier school. The view of Canada as a "product" of Europe emphasizes the point that trade was *imperial* trade and that the starting point of economic activity was not the "margin" but the "centre" of the empire. "Throughout the economic history of Canada, the dominance of water transportation in the Maritime Provinces and the St. Lawrence has accentuated dependence on Europe for manufactured products and for markets of staple raw materials . . . European markets and European capital dominated Canadian economic development through the background of water transportation."[17] Innis, in 1930, was the first economist to use the centre-periphery framework.

This perception of empire differentiates Innis from W. A. Mackintosh. In 1922 Mackintosh had indicated the significance of staple exports in his lecture, "Economic Factors in Canadian History."[18] He acknowledged the work of the American historian G. S. Callendar on colonial economic development and the role of staple products which had enabled pioneer communities to "come into close contact with the commercial world and leave behind the disabilities of a pioneer existence."[19] The perspective is that of the colonial society seeking out a suitable staple product and then developing the necessary transportation routes to send the product to market. Mackintosh stressed the fact that transportation became a problem as the North American colonies moved inland from the Atlantic coast. In Canada the Laurentian Shield posed a formidable barrier until the CPR made possible the opening of the west. "Canadian nationality was assured" with the world staple of western wheat and thus Canada was created "in defiance of geography."[20]

The Laurentian Shield was, however, only a barrier to the "opening" of the west from the perspective of a Canadian "empire" in the west. Innis' study of the fur trade showed that the Shield did not prevent Montreal from dominating an area "which approximated the present boundaries of the Dominion,"[21] but it also showed that not only had Montreal had to compete with New York for continental dominance, it had also had to compete with Hudson Bay. In 1821 the North West Company was defeated by the Hudson's Bay Company which had linked "the west" with Britain by means of a trade along the Saskatchewan and Nelson rivers.[22]

Thus Confederation should not be seen as the result of the "maturation" of a colonial society that had spread out from the Atlantic seaboard. Confederation was a political unification of established economic units which had undergone some common experiences but which were separated by their individual histories and by different types of economic links with Britain. The units that were amalgamated by Confederation were the Maritimes, the Canadas, and the West. Each was undergoing its own form of development in relation to Britain and the economic effect of Confederation was to redefine the links of the three regions with Britain and, through the National Policy, to reorient the Maritimes and the West to Central Canada.

As far as eastern Canada is concerned the shared experiences of the colonies were largely a result of the relationship with Britain. "The success of industrialism in England evident in the advent of freedom of trade compelled the colonies to rely on their own devices, which included tariffs, railways and canals, debts, and Confederation. Tariffs became a source of the revenue needed for the construction of transportation systems and a source of protection against the competition of an increasingly efficient area under free trade."[23] Innis' studies of two major staples, cod and fur, showed the different patterns of development that characterized the Atlantic provinces and the central provinces.

The economy of the Atlantic provinces was developed in response to the requirements of a single staple—fish and, in particular, cod. The fishing industry gave rise to a pattern of expansion along the coastline which entailed numerous ports and thus economic decentralization. "The scattered character of the fishing grounds, importance of individual initiative, short seasons and dependence on a foreign market all led to a strong sense of local importance in scattered communities."[24]

Somewhat paradoxically, Innis thought that the Maritime provinces had been integrated into the British Empire because they had been successful, but not too successful. The French hold on the western Atlantic had been precarious because "the French Empire had failed to link up the fur trade on the St. Lawrence, the fishing industry of the Maritimes, and the sugar plantations of the West Indies."[25] On the other hand, the first British Empire had failed to contain the "aggressive commercialism" of New England within a mercantile system that required that the colonies be primarily staple producing regions. Nova Scotia, which had ceased to be an outpost of New England because of the "requirement that for the greatest efficiency the fishery be conducted from the land nearest the fishing grounds," attempted to establish a place in the second British Empire comparable to that of New England in the first. The high price St. Lawrence region was "inadequate as a continental base to support Nova Scotia in relation to the West Indies and Newfoundland," but through a relatively successful combination of the fishery, shipping and trade, Nova Scotia was able to strengthen her autonomy within the British Empire, and even to influence the development of the continent.[26]

The economic similarities, and thus antagonism, between Nova Scotia and New England played a part in checking the expansion of the United States: "Commercial organization based on the fishing industry contributed to the expansion and influential character of New England and Nova Scotia in the development of the continent. . . . New England and Nova Scotia reinforced and strengthened the division of North America dictated by the St. Lawrence. The separatist character of the economic life of the Maritimes has been written into the federal constitutions of the continent and has been fundamental in the position of Massachusetts and Nova Scotia."[27] In fact, as Innis went on to argue, it was as a result of continued competition from New England that Nova Scotia "turned toward the St. Lawrence" and ultimately Confederation.[28] The price to the Maritimes of Confederation was "acceptance of the high price system of the St. Lawrence."[29] But simultaneously, Nova Scotia lost the battle with its maritime rival as labour moved southward, while capital equipment and financial control moved north from New England.[30]

The retreat from world markets resulted in the "revolution from an economy facing the sea with a large number of ports to an economy dependent on a central port and railways to the interior. . . . The disappearance of an active commercial region as a result of the impact of machine industry has been a major calamity to the fishing regions of France, New England, Nova Scotia, and Newfoundland. . . . The transition from dependence on a maritime economy to dependence on a continental economy has been slow, painful, and disastrous."[31] The decentralized economy of the Maritimes had been pushed into a unification with a centralized economy.

In continental Canada, centralization had its origins in the fur trade and it was Innis' study of the fur trade that led him to the far-ranging generalizations about the nature of staple development.[32] The fur trade was a battleground in the clash of empires: "The shift from Paris to London of the fur trade was significant of the industrial growth of France and England—just as possession of Canada after the American Revolution was significant of the industrial limitations of the United States."[33] As a consequence of its position in the British Empire, Canada's energy was directed towards the exploitation of staple products. Geography—in the character of water routes, for example—and technology—available from industrial centres, especially the United States—combined with the demands of industrial centres for staple imports to develop Canada as a peripheral economy: "The result was that the Canadian economic structure had the peculiar characteristics of areas dependent on staples—especially weakness in other lines of development, dependence on highly industrialized areas for markets and for supplies of manufactured goods, and the dangers of fluctuations in the staple commodity."[34]

The economic history of central Canada[35] showed clear signs of its development by means of a succession of staple industries. When fur gave way to lumber and timber, immigration was stimulated and the trade created a demand for labour and for agricultural products. This in turn led to a demand for improved transportation systems—canals and then railways. The significant point is that industrialization occurred in relation to the success of the staple export. This remained true in the second half of the nineteenth century as the transportation system, ports, towns, capital equipment, the iron and steel industry were all built up in response to the demands of the western wheat economy, and furthermore it remained true in the twentieth century as Ontario and Quebec developed their waterpower resources and their pulp and paper and mining staples. The "industrialized area is powerfully influenced by fluctuation in the basic industries as shown in wheat, pulp and paper, and mining," Innis observed in 1933.[36]

Confederation and the wheat economy had returned to Canada dominance over an area which it had lost in 1821 when the Hudson's Bay Company assumed control of the fur trade. Despite the hiatus of fifty years, the western "empire" of the St. Lawrence was quickly re-established and "the superposition of machine industry on an institutional background characteristic of the fur trade was effected with remarkably little disturbance."[37] Immediate growth was facilitated by the combination of authority and independence which was the legacy of the fur trade and which was institutionalized in such "peculiar tendencies" in Canadian development as an economically active central government, branch banking and transcontinental railway systems: "The relationship which existed with the opening of western Canada, in which important officials of the Hudson's Bay Company were prominent in the activities of the Bank of Montreal, of the Canadian Pacific Railway Company, and of the Dominion government, was not accidental."[38]

While the prairie west was passing from a fur economy, in which the southern plains were integrated with the Shield and Hudson Bay,[39] to a wheat economy linked to central Canada, the Pacific coast region was undergoing its own development. But once again the development was characterized by a succession of staple products. The fur trade, which had been controlled by the separate Western Department of the Hudson's Bay Company, retreated before the rapid increase of population and improved transportation which followed the series of gold rushes. Mining, smelting, and lumbering were developed as capital and labour moved to resources that were in demand in world markets. Innis observed that it was not just the wheat economy which linked the regions of the new Canada: "The development of mining provided a new industry for the Precambrian and Cordilleran regions which facilitated and hastened a restoration of the unity of Canada in the construction of a transcontinental railway."[40] Mining promoted a "highly integrated advanced type of industrial community" which "rounded out" metropolitan growth across the country. In fact, Innis suggested, the linkages produced by mining softened the effects of dependence on wheat and worked "in the main to reduce the evils of dependence on a staple economy."[41]

Innis' analysis of the development of each region stressed the fact that Canada had been at the "margin" of western civilization, rather than at the centre, and thus Canada's role had been to provide a succession of staple products, or raw materials, for the manufacturing industries of the centre countries. Canada has been linked to imperial centres through cod and fur exports, then through forest products, beginning with square timber and progressing to pulp and paper, as well as through agriculture and mining. The importance of the staple approach lies in its suggestion that staple exports have been more than just significant sectors of the economy. The staple industries have not been merely "leading sectors"—they have dominated the whole of Canadian society through their economic, social, and political ramifications and they have imposed upon Canada a particular pattern of settlement.

The Act of Union and responsible government were brought about by the need for capital investment on a large scale as Montreal competed with New York for the trade of the interior of the continent.[42] The agricultural produce of Upper Canada could move to the Erie Canal as easily as to the St. Lawrence, and to some extent the emergence of a rivalry between Toronto and Montreal was a continuation of the New York-Montreal rivalry. Innis' analysis stressed the centralization inherent in the Canadian economy and thus the predominance of

Montreal as the metropolis, but he recognized the emergence of Toronto, later in the century, as a "relatively independent financial centre" as a result of the efforts of Senator McMaster and the Canadian Bank of Commerce in competition with the Bank of Montreal.[43]

The concept of a metropolis as the locus of a mature financial system has to be modified in the case of a staple economy since the Canadian metropolis, whether Montreal or Toronto, is itself located by reference to an outside "metropolis" and it is by no means clear that the local metropolis can establish a self-propelling form of economic development. Montreal owed its position to the success of a "national policy" which in Fowke's words had as its objective "the creation of a new frontier of investment opportunities for the commercial and financial interests of the St. Lawrence area."[44] Those investment opportunities were tied to staple exports and Toronto's growth may result from a similar form of dependency. Jacob Spelt has shown that Toronto was "started on the road towards metropolitan predominance not by its economic strength but by the deliberate actions of a self-interested governmental clique" and that up to the 1880s Toronto remained mainly a service centre. Spelt claims that by the late nineteenth century a "self-propelling" manufacturing industry became the major factor in the city's growth.[45] The latter claim, however, ignores the significance, clearly seen by Innis, of the development of Northern Ontario's staples and also the significance of branch plant location in the Toronto economic region. In fact it seems possible that the Canadian economy has been able to support only one metropolitan centre—a position held by Montreal as long as the National Policy survived, but taken up by Toronto as the Canadian economy was re-oriented toward the American market.[46]

THE POLITICS OF STAPLE DEVELOPMENT

Staple development determined the nature of Canadian economic growth as capital and technology from "older centres" exploited Canadian resources. Not only the pace of economic growth but also the location of economic activity in Canada were to a very considerable extent made subject to the requirements of the industrial centre countries. Innis' work is thus an explicit rejection of any model of economic development which suggests that development occurs as the result of the shift of resources from a self-sufficient agriculture into trade and then into manufacturing. Innis makes not only the point that an economy may be, from the first, exploited as a capitalist venture and brought into an existing "world" economy through its export staple, but also the point that such an economy may remain linked to the "world" economy as a staple producer. Thus exogenous demands will remain a significant factor in the determination of the location of economic activity. Trading centres will be encouraged, and some "residentiary" industry may develop to supply local markets, but there is no certainty that a staple economy will progress into an industrial economy.[47]

The staple approach rejects any assumption of "stages" of development theory, and in so doing it also rejects the view that economic development will of necessity give rise to the proliferation of metropolitan areas within the staple-producing country. This means that regional imbalances may persist in staple-producing countries, and such imbalances may in fact be caused by the nature of staple development.[48] In saying this, however, one should guard against the suggestion that geographical and technological factors are the sole cause of such imbalances. Innis' work shows very clearly the way in which political decisions interacted with the geographical and technological: "The structure of the Canadian economy was an extension of the European or British economy, with a consequent increase in efficiency guaranteed by cheap water transport, imperial preferences, and the opening of new resources. It was handicapped by the extent of government intervention, the rigidity of government indebtedness, railway rates and tariffs, and dependence on a commodity subject to wide fluctuations in yield and price."[49] The analysis of regional imbalances is bound up with the analysis of the role of governments in a staple economy.

Transportation played a key role in the creation of a staple economy: "Cheap water transportation in the St. Lawrence economy accentuated dependence on export of staples to Europe, the specialization of technique in relation to those commodities, and support from government intervention."[50] Control from Great Britain, Innis observed, meant "a rigidity of finances without benefit of bankruptcy" and ultimately the need for tax revenue to finance the development of the transportation network required a measure of responsible government, in addition to a continued dependence on British capital. What was needed was not simply a strong government to provide assurance for the capital required to overcome the natural obstacles to water transportation by the building of canals and railways. Private capital had to be supplemented by government sponsorship to promote a strategy of economic development which would check competition from the United States.

The National Policy accompanied a political extension of the economy of the St. Lawrence: "The fixed charges involved, . . . especially in canals and the improvement of water transportation and in railways, led to a demand for new markets in the East and in the West. Expansion eastward and westward involved Confederation."[51] Confederation was thus seen by Innis to be a consequence of a progressive extension of a staple producing economy. "Federation was a device to secure ample supplies of capital for the construction of railways from the Atlantic to the Pacific in a region handicapped by concentration on staples such as fur, timber, and agricultural products and without an iron and steel industry."[52]

Innis' writings show an awareness of the fact that Confederation was a two-sided arrangement. On the one hand, a federation implied the continuation of regional powers within the new nation: "Cultural areas with their special interests of language, religion, and political and economic organization were given assurance of permanence by the federation. The position of the provinces under the British North America Act is a recognition of the differences in cultural characteristics: of Nova Scotia based on the fishing industry, of New Brunswick on the timber trade, of Quebec on the fur trade and later on agriculture and the timber trade, and of Ontario on the timber trade and agriculture."[53] In fact the powers of the provinces were enhanced by the "new industrialism" of hydro-electric power, mining and pulp and paper. Innis went so far as to suggest that provincial control of resources, particularly forests, had given rise to a "feudalistic structure" which contrasted with the centralization of the wheat economy: "The problem of Canadian federalism is linked to the disparity between economies stamped with the influence of the lumber industries and economies dependent on wheat, and the provincialism of the one has accentuated the federalism of the other."[54]

On the other hand, there was no doubt that Confederation had established a new centre of power. A national policy which extended the staple producing economy of the St. Lawrence region and attempted to check an expansive American imperialism led Canada to develop what Innis saw as "her own type of imperialism."[55] The St. Lawrence economy took on characteristics reminiscent of dependent development elsewhere: it became a metropolitan area which controlled a vast hinterland but was itself a hinterland in a larger "international" empire.

The National Policy was characteristic of the two-sided nature of Canadian development. Innis saw the history of the second half of the nineteenth century as indicative of the decline of the old British mercantile system, or "commercial system" as Adam Smith had called it: "Into the moulds of the commercial period, set by successive heavier and cheaper commodities, and determined by geographic factors, such as the St. Lawrence River and the Precambrian formation; by cultural considerations, such as the English and French languages, by technology, such as the canoe and the raft; by business organization such as the Northwest Company and Liverpool timber firms; and by political institutions peculiar to France and England, were poured the rivers of iron and steel in the form of steamships and railways which hardened into modern capitalism."[56] The decline of the old colonial system was marked by the change to free trade which, in the middle of the century, was extended throughout North America by means of the Reciprocity Treaty, and the change was reflected in the achievement of responsible government in Canada. In this use of the terms "commercialism" and "modern capitalism" Innis clearly was referring to the displacement of an economic system based on short-term credit by a system requiring long-term credit, and in particular the growing importance of capital equipment for transportation as industrial Britain became dependent on staple areas for its supply of foodstuffs. For Canada this meant that "the commercial class, supported by the mother country in the French and British empires and with their chief interests in the fur trade and the

timber trade, tended now to be displaced by the capitalist class. The earlier appeals on the part of commercial groups for continuations of the preference were replaced by the appeals of Hincks and Galt for capital support from the houses of Baring and others. The autonomous capitalist state replaced commercial capitalism."[57]

Autonomy, however, was only relative: "Political control from Great Britain declined in importance, but its decline was essential to the expansion of economic control." Britain remained the "metropolitan centre of the world."[58] The "rivers of iron and steel" required new forms of economic organization but they were there to move the staples from the hinterland to the metropolis and the National Policy was not simply the Canadian version of the transition from mercantilism to industrial society.

Notwithstanding Adam Smith's view of the "commercial system" as an interference with the extension of the market which was necessary to economic development, there has been a long tradition in the analysis of economic history, going back at least to William Cunningham's *The Growth of English Industry and Commerce,* which sees mercantilism as a necessary step in preparation for industrialization. Charles Wilson entitles his economic history of England in the seventeenth and eighteenth centuries *England's Apprenticeship.* In *Economic Backwardness in Historical Perspective,* Alexander Gerschenkron built on this perspective by arguing that "follower" nations in the early stages of industrialization might have to substitute government economic activities for market institutions and thus in effect carry over some mercantilist elements into the stage of industrialization. Applied to Canada this model could explain features of the National Policy as a substitution for market activity made necessary by Canada's relative backwardness and, in addition, by such peculiarities of Canadian geography as the Laurentian Shield.

This line of approach, however, ignores the problem of dependency. Britain and the United States were able to move from mercantilism to an industrial society because their mercantilism was imperialist, as Christopher Hill and W. A. Williams have shown for the respective countries.[59] The opposite side of the coin is that mercantilism does not necessarily lead in such a direction for countries that have become dependent. Furthermore, in such dependent countries, the policies of the government, rather than providing substitutes for the market in order to bring about industrialization, may in fact perpetuate dependency on resource exploitation. Innis' work strongly suggests that in Canada the government has in fact played this latter role and much recent work in Canadian political economy has been devoted to the subject.[60]

The National Policy resulted in industrial development in central Canada, but it did so precisely because of the success of the policy in promoting Canada's development as a staple economy. The consequences of the policy were continued dependency and regional imbalances. Central Canada established itself as a "metropolis," but it was a "second order" metropolis and if its relative dominance created discontent in the west and in the Maritimes, it was also true, as Acheson has pointed out, that many Maritime industries failed because central Canada could not absorb the output of the new regional industries.[61]

Innis saw the problem of regional inequalities in terms not only of the rigidities of the staple economy but also of the inequality of political power. Staple exports resulted in a fluctuating economy as a result of the varying returns as prices and yields changed in relation to rigid costs characteristic of high transportation charges and a protected system.[62] The tariff in conjunction with the transportation network was a major feature of the National Policy, but as Innis observed it was an increasingly unreliable force: "The problem of protection is . . . that of increasing the traffic of manufactured goods and thereby increasing earnings, with the result that railroad costs may be decreased to the producers of raw materials to an amount equal to or more than the rise in the price of manufactured goods as a result of protection. Dependence on the application of mature technique, especially in transport, to virgin natural resources must steadily recede in importance as a basis for the tariff. It will become increasingly difficult to wield the tariff as the crude but effective weapon by which we have been able to obtain a share of our natural resources."[63] The rigidities of the Canadian economy had, however, been shared unequally: "The elasticity of the economy of Ontario has been based on a wealth of developed natural resources and has been obtained in part through inelastic developments which bear with undue weight on less favoured areas of the Dominion. The strength of Ontario may emphasize the weakness of the federation. An empire has its obligations as well as its opportunities."[64] The "development of government in the interests of capital expansion through canals and railways" produced a strong central government and by the late 1930s Innis was clearly disturbed by what he saw as excessive centralization. He worried about the disappearance of "the lack of unity which has preserved Canadian unity."[65]

THE DECLINE OF THE "PRICE SYSTEM"

The difficulties created by unequal regional development were compounded by new circumstances which resulted from a combination of economic and political changes. In the short run, the problem was produced by ten years of depression. In the long run the emergence of what Innis called "national capitalism" had profound implications for Canada's political economy.

The coincidence of depression and a relative decline of natural resources, Innis observed, had had disastrous results. The analysis of the new situation was hampered by the paucity of "valid economic thinking" which Innis believed to be a consequence of the "abysmal ignorance of the economic structure in Canada."[66] Innis did believe, however, that the depression had given rise to one "outstanding contribution" to the economic literature and that

was *The Report of the Royal Commission on Price Spreads.* The *Report,* heavily influenced by H. H. Stevens, mounted a stinging attack on the corporate organization of economic power. "Unregulated competition," it argued, "no longer guarantees efficiency and maximum production at fair prices. Competition degenerates sometimes into economic warfare where victory may go to the strong, rather than to the efficient."[67] Innis felt that the Commission had touched on a vulnerable spot in Canadian politics: "The low cultural level of Canadian business, conspicuous in speeches, architecture, the standard of living, and in an inconceivable narrowness of outlook, together with the relative inability of the large corporate organization characteristic of transcontinental development, to meet problems of adjustment during periods of depression—these have not been things pleasant to contemplate."[68] Despite his admiration for R. B. Bennett, Innis saw that the tradition of "evangelical bourgeois meliorism" was inadequate to the times.

The Price Spreads *Report* had noted that the social inequities which had resulted from corporate concentration also had a regional aspect: "Agricultural exporters, open to all the strains and stresses of world conditions, are defenceless in the face of a drastic decline in prices, but the more powerful domestic manufactures and traders have in many cases been able to offer an effective resistance to that decline."[69] The regional impact of the depression had given rise to a second major document. But Innis was not nearly so favourably impressed by *The Report of the Royal Commission on Dominion-Provincial Relations.* The Rowell-Sirois Commission recommended a national minimum standard of social services as well as the use of the fiscal and monetary powers of the central government to enhance growth and counter the downward effects of the business cycle. The consequence was nothing less than the redefinition of the National Policy. A succession of Liberal governments introduced a wide range of social welfare policies which were to be administered uniformly across the country by a combination of federal and provincial government bureaucracies.

The Commission had originated in a concern with the inadequacy of government finances and Innis shared the concern. He saw the federal government as "a credit instrument" and thus "the problem of debt is the problem of Canadian federalism."[70] But by the mid-1930s Innis was concerned with the "break-up of Confederation" as a result of rigidities made evident by the depression[71] and he did not think that the Rowell-Sirois Commission had been sufficiently concerned with the conflict between the federal and provincial governments which was inherent in the Canadian political economy. The old National Policy reflected a disequilibrium between eastern and western Canada and "accentuated it through land, tariff and railway policies and bonuses indirectly and directly to the steel and coal industries of Nova Scotia." But the Commission did not direct itself to the problems of economic growth, transportation costs, tariffs and the staple economy. Later Innis would add the criticism that the new "national policy" of emphasis on central monetary and fiscal policy was destroying the basis of federalism.[72]

Federal-provincial relations were being changed by major upheavals in the price system. Innis perceived the price system as the creator of an international economy. The price system, he observed in his 1938 article, "The Penetrative Powers of the Price System," "had eaten out the rotting timbers of European colonial structures" and "as it had destroyed the feudalism so it destroyed the defences of commercialism." In the long process of the decline of commercialism, or mercantilism, "Great Britain emerged as a dominant metropolitan unit."[73] Canada has developed on the margin of this metropolis. In this analysis of the price system, however, Innis clearly was identifying the price system as a *market-price* system.[74] But, as Innis himself saw, capitalism could "run in the direction of commercialism" or even, as in Canada, towards the "highly centralized state" where the "state became capital equipment."[75] These developments could modify the prevailing price system.

Mercantilist policies and the creation of a highly centralized state can be seen as attempts to change existing centre-margin relations by the creation of a new metropolitan unit. Inevitably, however, the attempt to create a new Canadian centre further peripheralized the "regions" of the Canadian economy, and in a federal polity raised the question of which state should decide on the modifications.

The situation was complicated by the fact that the central provinces were also involved in the success of the new "provincial" staples but, as Chester Martin noted, the acquisition of the Hudson's Bay land had transformed Canada from a "Confederation of equal provinces into a miniature Empire, with a vast domain of subordinate colonial territory under its control."[76] The powers of the federal government were designed, as J. R. Mallory has shown, for "rapid capital accumulation" and for the development of the West as "Canada's empire." Federal disallowance power has been "an imperial device for holding other provinces under the sway of the predominant economic interest of the central provinces."[77] Thus while the commercial and financial interests of central Canada remained committed to the success of the staple industries in Ontario and Quebec and thus to a continuing dependency of the Canadian economy, they exercised their dominance over the western hinterland and increasingly over the Maritime region as the National Policy created a pattern of unequal levels of development.[78]

The rigidities of central policy and the opportunities afforded by new staples ultimately pushed the provinces into their own "neo-mercantilism." Just as nations had reacted to the old international price system by neo-mercantilist policies which were in effect attempts to create new price systems with new metropolitan centres, so did provincial governments attempt to promote their own metropolitan centres by means of neo-mercantilist policies. Economically the provinces were aided in the con-

flict with the old, centrally dominated east-west price system by the interests of the American economy. Politically, however, the provinces were hindered through the limitation of their powers with regard to tariffs and monetary policy.

Ultimately, the attempt to establish new metropolitan centres has been defeated by more powerful price systems. For that reason federal-provincial conflicts have the character of wars between ghosts. The centre, object of so much provincial resentment, is itself a spectral presence. The status of Montreal as Canada's metropolis vanished with the National Policy. Toronto was the immediate beneficiary of the influx of American branch plants but, as we can see now, Toronto is, like Montreal before it, merely a second order metropolis. As Garth Stevenson has remarked: "The health of the Ontario economy depends less on decisions made in Ottawa about freight rates and tariffs than on decisions made in Washington about defence contracts and the automotive industry. . . . From being the metropolitan region of Canada and the principal beneficiary of Confederation, Ontario has moved towards the position of being in effect, a province like any other."[79]

As Donald Smiley has noted, Innis did not think that the Rowell-Sirois Commission had dealt with the "disequilibrium" produced by the National Policy.[80] But not only had the Report failed to do justice to the analysis of regional inequalities, it had paid insufficient attention to economic developments in the United States and Great Britain in recent years. Innis' analysis suggested that inequalities between groups and regions in Canada were exacerbated by the "conflict between a price structure dominated by Great Britain and a price structure increasingly dominated by the continent."[81]

As a result of long-run changes, the conflict between regionalism and centralization was being given a new dimension as the "second unity" of Canada began to "drift in the direction of the first." Added to the effect of depression was the fact that the Canadian federal structure was being "wrenched between the influence of British policies and their effect on wheat, and of American policies and their effect on minerals and newsprint and on the rigidity of such important costs of wheat production as railway rates and interest charges.[82] Innis' analysis of the federal-provincial conflicts of the 1930s derives from his perception that "international industrialism" was giving way to "national industrialism."

Canadian politicians had two standard responses to depression: tariffs and public works. In the past these policies had been successful because each wave of capital imports had tapped fresh natural resources and the capital expenditures had reduced transportation costs. Each round of expansion had left a legacy of heavy fixed charges and government debt which could only be financed while natural resource markets remained buoyant, but a powerful central government, the legacy of New France, had "enabled Canadians through governmental activity to develop their natural resources by construction of canals, railways, hydro-electric power facilities and other undertakings."[83] Expansion within the framework of the National Policy had also assumed the orientation of the Canadian economy towards the St. Lawrence and thus to Great Britain in opposition to the pressures for a continental integration with the United States: "Periods of depression accompanied by migration to the United States have been accompanied by a hardening of the central structure and appeal to imperialist sentiment, and this in turn has increased the importance of governmental intervention during periods of prosperity. Government ownership in Canada is based on a hard core of defence against the United States."[84]

Innis did not, however, think that Canada could escape from the depression of the 1930s by means of the habitual remedies. Other countries were experiencing serious difficulties of readjustment, but Canada's depression was peculiarly the result of the rigidities imposed by staple development with large overhead costs and no simple importation of fiscal or monetary prescriptions would cure the malady. New trade weapons had taken the place of war. Exchange controls, quotas, empire agreements, economic autarchy—all imposed a particular burden on a Canadian economy dependent on staple exports: "Canada with inadequate, badly coordinated, machinery stands on the one hand in danger of being burned at the stake of natural resources and on the other hand in danger of being boiled in the oil of unrestricted competition."[85] The low price of raw materials required market controls and also relief measures to ease the suffering of regions which were particularly hard hit by the closing of foreign markets.

Canada had emerged from the "intense baptism of fire of the 1914-18 war" with a determination to control its own destiny, but the problem, as Innis saw it, was that the National Policy had operated in the context of an international economy which by the 1930s no longer existed. The entire Canadian economy was concerned with the demands of an international market and each region of Canada had its "conditions of equilibrium" with regard to powerful external economies such as Britain and the United States. The shocks of the 1930s were profound and in Innis' view they had "exposed the limitations of finance capitalism." From the late 1930s until the end of his life Innis grappled with the analysis of an international economy which was characterized by the "spread of national capitalism" and thus the declining efficacy of a price system which had unified the international economy. The new national capitalism was also marked by a change, particularly fateful for Canada, as the United States displaced Britain in the international hierarchy of power.[86]

Innis found that the analysis of the decline of the price system and the rise of national capitalism was hampered by the limitations of economic thought. Economic thought itself had been bound up with the framework of the price system. It was even possible to note a "bias" of

economics "which makes the best economists come from powerful countries." What was needed was a "sociology or a philosophy of the social sciences and particularly of economics" which would make clear the limitations of scientific thought and Innis embarked upon an intellectual voyage that eventually led him a long way from orthodox economic theory. It was not an easy undertaking for Innis because, while he increasingly feared the "outbreak of irrationality which is the tragedy of our time" and perhaps looked back with some fondness to a phase of capitalism when commerce had acted as a "stabilizer of power," his own analysis suggested that the new world of national capitalism was in fact a result of the very success of the price system which brought the formation of monopolies and ultimately the weakening of even the profit motive by its "emphasis on management." Innis was in the uncomfortable position of a nineteenth-century liberal who was perspicacious enough to recognize that the foundations of his belief were being undermined by historical developments.[87] The results of Innis' search for a philosophy of social science were fragmentary, but Innis continued to produce penetrating insights into the workings of the Canadian economy.

World War I had marked the final end of the free-trade capitalism of the nineteenth century. The old capitalism had been replaced by a system which Innis called variously "the new industrialism," "neotechnic industrialism," or "national capitalism." Industrialism had moved beyond the "metropolitan" area of the Atlantic basin with its coal and iron and year-round water transportation to new centres which relied on hydro-electric power and oil. Accompanying this change was a nationalism which Innis identified with "neo-mercantilist economics." Competition for markets for manufactured goods was leading to protective tariffs and other forms of regulation. More countries were discovering the advantages of "national self-sufficiency" to the extent of protecting their home markets while continuing to invade foreign markets. The result was a situation not very favourable to "specialization."[88] Yet the old system, "palaeotechnic industrialism," had developed Canada as a large-scale producer of basic commodities.

In fact the old "international" economy had not worked to the equal advantage of all. The central role of the London money market enabled Britain to solve payments imbalances by making bank rate changes rather than price adjustments, thus shifting the burden to capital receiving, and commodity exporting, countries.[89] The National Policy had managed to integrate Canada into this system with some success, but the rise of the "neotechnic industrialism" meant a concern with base metals, hydro-electric power, and pulp and newsprint rather than wheat, and it was accompanied by the re-orientation of the Canadian economy towards the capital markets of the United States and this required a new policy.

Kari Levitt has argued that the primary feature of the "new mercantilism" is the multinational corporation: "The subsidiaries and branch plants of large American-based multinational corporations have replaced the operations of the earlier European-based mercantile venture companies in extracting the staple and organizing the supply of manufactured goods."[90] As Abraham Rotstein has suggested, it is possible to see a further similarity between multinational corporations and the old mercantilist empires in that multinationals, as much as possible, operate a trading system in which prices are administered rather than accepting the international market price system which Innis believed had been characteristic of nineteenth-century capitalism.[91]

Innis, curiously, did not pay much attention to the multinational corporation as a new form of economic organization. He did, of course, observe the increasing "penetration of American capital and control in the basic industries during the speculative boom of the twenties . . . followed by further migration to Canada of branch plants during the depression under the shelter of the high tariff of 1930 and the extension of imperial markets," and he noted the paradox that Canadian nationalism and even imperialist sentiment had worked to the advantage of American branch plants. In a similar way even the rejection of reciprocity in 1911 had favoured the United States. Thus, Innis concluded, the result of the far-reaching, cumulative influence of the United States was to "twist" both Canadian financial structures and the Canadian federal structure which were oriented to a western expansion of the St. Lawrence economy. The consequences were profound for Canadian nationalism and regionalism.[92]

Canada had moved "from colony to nation to colony." This perception of Canada's situation produced an ambivalence in Innis' attitude to nationalism. Nationalism in the sense of neo-mercantilism and the "monetary nationalism" of Keynesian policies had destroyed the international economy in which Canada had developed as a nation and trade barriers and monopolies were "deadly enemies" of "free-enterprise" capitalism. Yet given that this international system had been destroyed, it was necessary for Canada to protect itself: "The stupidity of nationalism is tempered by the chaos of internationalism." Canada's difficulties were enhanced by neo-mercantilism in the United States and, as "American imperialism . . . replaced and exploited British imperialism," Canada's very national existence was called into question. "We are indeed fighting for our lives," Innis concluded, and "the pride taken in improving our status in the British Commonwealth of Nations has made it difficult for us to realize that our status on the North American continent is on the verge of disappearing. Continentalism assisted in the achievement of autonomy and has consequently become more dangerous. We can only survive by taking persistent action at strategic points against American imperialism in all its attractive guises."[93]

The complexities of nationalism were increased by the divisiveness of regionalism which was promoted as a result of the decline of the St. Lawrence as the centre of the Dominion. The activities of the provinces assumed a new importance with the American demand for resources which were controlled by provincial governments. "The pull to the north and south," as Innis put it, "has tended to become stronger in contrast with the pull east and west." The pulp and paper and mining industries were indicative of a new economic system which contrasted with the economy that underlay the British North America Act. The influence of the United States, combined with the centralizing tendencies of the Liberal governments under Mackenzie King were sharpening the differences between federal and provincial governments.[94]

The price system of the nineteenth century, controlled effectively from London, had brought railways and industrial capitalism to Canada. The second half of the nineteenth century had, nonetheless, been one long period of depression and, ironically, prosperity came to Canada in the early years of the twentieth century as the National Policy was being undermined by new sources of power and the emergence of new centres of capital accumulation. In fact, as Innis knew, the international price system had had mixed results in staple producing areas of the world and Confederation and the National Policy were merely a mercantilist modification of the price system which shifted some power to a second-order metropolis. But if Canada needed protection from the full working of the nineteenth-century economy with its international division of labour, the blasts of the twentieth century were even more chilling. In a world of "national capitalism" and American empire the old international order offered an attractive ideal. Yet, as Innis saw, the situation had changed and it was not possible to avoid the conclusion that "nationalism provides the only sure basis for internationalism."[95]

Innis' contribution to our understanding was the consequence of the tragic vision of nineteenth-century Canadian liberalism faced with the disappearance of the conditions which gave it its meaning. The causes of Canada's deformation did not reside merely in the replacement of Imperial politics by continentalist politics as Creighton has argued. The causes were embedded in the political economy of staple development. It was a short step from Innis' despair to George Grant's *Lament for a Nation.*

NOTES

[1] H. A. Innis, *Essays in Canadian Economic History,* ed. Mary Q. Innis (Toronto: University of Toronto Press, 1954), p. 368.

[2] Innis, *The Fur Trade in Canada, An Introduction to Canadian Economic History* (Toronto: University of Toronto Press, 1962), p. 392.

[3] William Westfall has recently remarked that Careless' "metropolitanism," which is an offshoot of Creighton's "Laurentianism," also focuses on the "centre" rather than

the "edge." See W. Westfall, "The Ambivalent Verdict: Harold Innis and Canadian History," in William H. Melody, Liora Salter and Paul Heyer, eds., *Culture, Communication and Dependency* (New Jersey, 1981), p. 37.

[4] See my *Dominance and Dependency: Liberalism and National Policies in the North Atlantic Triangle* (Toronto, 1978), Chapter 1.

[5] Gerard S. Vano, *Neo-Feudalism: The Canadian Dilemma* (Toronto, 1981), pp. 126, 128.

[6] *Ibid.*, pp. 137 and 27. This is not a problem for Innis' analysis, though, as I have suggested (in *Dominance and Dependency*, ch. 1), Innis' work does need to be extended into an enquiry into the social relationships produced in a staple economy. Vano's problem, however, begins with his ideological definition of liberalism as "universal" and "progressive."

[7] See W. J. Eccles, "A Belated Review of Harold Adams Innis, *The Fur Trade in Canada*," *Canadian Historical Review* LX (1979), pp. 419-41; Hugh M. Grant, "One Step Forward, Two Steps Back: Innis, Eccles and the Canadian Fur Trade," *Canadian Historical Review* LXII (1981), pp. 304-22; Eccles, "A Response to Hugh M. Grant on Innis," *Canadian Historical Review* LXII (1981), pp. 323-29.

Eccles questions the reputation of *The Fur Trade in Canada* on what I see as seven points: 1) Innis wrongly asserted that "the economy and institutions of France were thrown into disarray by the Canadian fur trade"; 2) Innis "failed completely to grasp" the political factor (and the religious factor) in the policies of New France and missed the military factor in its defeat; 3) the Hudson Bay route was superior to the Montreal route only after the introduction of the York boat in the nineteenth century, and prior to that there is no evidence for British superiority in the fur trade; 4) centralization in New France was not simply a consequence of the fur trade but was typical of French administration everywhere; 5) the fur trade was not itself a problem in limiting the economic development of New France; 6) Innis failed to produce a coherent account of the triumph of the monopolistic Hudson's Bay Company over the North West Company; 7) the "extreme" economic determinist view that "Canada emerged with a political entity with boundaries largely determined by the fur trade" is an example of Innis' "*a priori* premises and conclusions."

Eccles does, I think, sustain the claim that Innis overemphasized the significance of the fur trade in the North American theatre of the clash between Britain and France. As he says in his riposte to Grant: "In my view one of the main weaknesses of Innis' work on the fur trade was his failure to elucidate the real purpose of French western policy" (p. 327).

It is also true that Innis did push his conclusions to extremities, and Grant's reply does not do much to refute

Eccles' specific points. Yet in the end Eccles' article does not really confront the main issues of the staple approach that Innis delineated. His criticism on this issue is peripheral.

[8] Donald Creighton, "Harold Adams Innis—An Appraisal," in W. Melody *et al.*, eds., *Culture, Communication and Dependency*, p. 20.

[9] Westfall, "Ambivalent Verdict," p. 48.

[10] *Fur Trade*, p. 393.

[11] For an analysis of core economies which pays tribute to Harold Innis, see Robert Gilpin, *U.S. Power and the Multinational Corporation* (New York, 1975), Chapter II.

[12] This is not the place to discuss the appropriateness of this term. Suffice it to say that in general it was applied to countries of European settlement in which the precolonial population had evolved a hunting and pastoral economy rather than a peasant agriculture.

[13] *Essays*, p. 10.

[14] *Ibid.*, p. 11.

[15] *Ibid.*

[16] *Fur Trade*, p. 401.

[17] *Essays*, p. 208.

[18] See W. A. Mackintosh, "Economic Factors in Canadian History," reprinted in W. T. Easterbrook and M. H. Watkins, eds., *Approaches to Canadian Economic History* (Toronto, 1967). On the influence as well of C. R. Fay on the "staple approach," see R. Neill, *A New Theory of Value: The Canadian Economics of H. A. Innis* (Toronto, 1972), p. 39.

[19] Mackintosh, "Economic Factors," p. 4.

[20] *Ibid.*, p. 15.

[21] *Essays*, p. 156.

[22] The technological factors contributing to this development are discussed by Innis in terms of the competition between canoes and York boats (see *Essays*, p. 65). Innis also pointed out that "dependence on the York boat rather than the canoe was symbolic of the increasing importance of capitalism" (*Fur Trade*, p. 387). The political implications were that accessibility to the continent through the St. Lawrence and Hudson Bay reinforced British control. The interior of the United States was less accessible.

[23] Innis, *The Cod Fisheries: The History of an International Economy* (Toronto: University of Toronto Press, 1954), p. 505.

[24] *Essays,* pp. 38-39. See also the Conclusion to *Cod Fisheries* where Innis suggests that this coastal decentralization offset the centralization of the commercial group in Halifax. I have not included Innis' specific comments on Newfoundland in this paper, but *The Cod Fisheries* and several essays contain an analysis of the economic factors peculiar to the history of that province. As will be apparent, this discussion of the "Maritimes" is primarily related to Nova Scotia.

[25] *Cod Fisheries,* p. 504.

[26] See *Essays,* pp. 204, 365, 367. Innis observed that control from the Atlantic was based largely on the relative success of the integration of the trade and industry of the European empires. The second British Empire was "more flexible" than the first and was more efficient at "coordinating the interests of staple-producing regions" which depended on Britain for a market and for capital. Cod from Newfoundland, beaver from Canada, sugar from the West Indies, all "depended on commercial and industrial England." See *Essays,* pp. 100, 106.

[27] *Cod Fisheries,* p. 499. See also *Essays,* p. 234: "Separatist Nova Scotia and New England accentuated differences between the northern and southern parts of the continent."

[28] *Cod Fisheries,* p. 504.

[29] *Essays,* p. 367.

[30] *Cod Fisheries,* p. 492.

[31] *Ibid.,* pp. 507-8. Innis (p. 485) referred to the "disastrous results" of recent industrialism (mining, pulp and paper), although his pessimism about Nova Scotia could be said to be modified by his analysis of Newfoundland: "An industry which flourished with commercialism and an international economy was crushed by the demands of capitalism and nationalism. The impact was less striking in Nova Scotia because of her more divergent resources and also because of influences inherent in Confederation" (p. 497).

[32] See *Essays,* pp. 28, 39.

[33] *Fur Trade,* p. 386. Innis adds that "the northern half of North America remained British because of the importance of fur as a staple product" (p. 391).

[34] *Essays,* p. 66.

[35] With the exception of a few comments, Innis did not distinguish between Quebec and Ontario in his analysis of the economy of the St. Lawrence. He noted that the displacement of the government and trading organizations of New France had left the Church as "the shield and sword of a race and language exposed to foreign domination" (*Essays,* p. 177). Innis also suggested that Quebec was less vulnerable to American influence in that

a combination of "French tradition and more direct accessibility to European markets provided a less suitable environment for American technique" (*Essays,* p. 166). See also his comment that "Imperialism which is not imperialistic has been particularly effective in Canada with its difficulty in dealing precisely and directly with foreign problems because of a division between French and English" (*Essays,* p. 407).

[36] *Essays,* p. 95.

[37] *Fur Trade,* pp. 397-98.

[38] *Ibid.,* p. 397. See also *Essays,* p. 15.

[39] See W. L. Morton, *Manitoba: A History* (Toronto, 1957), for a discussion of the complex society which occupied what Pratt saw as the "blank spaces" of Macdonald's map.

[40] Innis, *Settlement and the Mining Frontier,* Canadian Frontiers of Settlement, vol. IX (Toronto, 1936), p. 397.

[41] *Ibid.,* p. 403.

[42] See *Essays,* p. 117. Innis suggested that the struggle between New York and Montreal was a continuation of the Iroquois-Huron conflict (p. 110).

[43] *Essays,* p. 118. See also Innis, "The Rise and Decline of Toronto," *Canadian Forum,* XIII (1933), p. 251. Innis thought that transportation and finance continued to favour Montreal in the 1930s. D. C. Masters' *The Rise of Toronto* (Toronto, 1947), is based on N. S. B. Gras' concept of a metropolis as the centre of a mature financial system.

[44] V. C. Fowke, "The National Policy—Old and New," reprinted in Easterbrook and Watkins, *Approaches,* p. 243.

[45] J. Spelt, *The Urban Development in South-Central Ontario* (Toronto, 1972), pp. 49, 137, 224.

[46] On branch plant location see William Alonso, *Industrial Location and Regional Policy in Economic Development,* Centre for Planning and Development Research, University of California, Berkeley, Working Paper no. 74. W. T. Easterbrook ("Long Period Comparative Study: Some Historical Cases," *Journal of Economic History,* 17 [1957], pp. 571-95), makes the point that Canada differed from the U.S. where a number of expansion points emerged with inter-urban rivalries for control of hinterlands.

[47] See *Essays,* pp. 289-90. A stages of growth theory is outlined by D. C. North, "Location Theory and Regional Economic Growth," *Journal of Political Economy,* 63 (1955), pp. 243-58. North modifies the "traditional" development and location theory but he still concludes that "regionalism will tend to disappear" (p. 256) as accumu-

lated capital overflows into other activities. On the subject of "linkages" between staples and other industries, see M. H. Watkins, "A Staple Theory of Economic Growth," reprinted in Easterbrook and Watkins, *Approaches*, pp. 49-73.

[48] See, for example, W. Alonso, "Urban and Regional Imbalances in Economic Development," *Economic Development and Cultural Change*, 17 (1968), pp. 1-14.

[49] *Essays*, p. 234. See also Innis' comment that geography has been effective in "determining the grooves of economic life through its effects on transportation and communication" (*Essays*, p. 88).

[50] *Ibid.*, p. 228. Paradoxically, according to Innis, control from Great Britain was strengthened by the import of American technique: "The acceleration of development in Canada through contributions from the United States accentuated dependence on British capital and the increase of public debt" (p. 230).

[51] *Ibid.*, p. 71. See also p. 76.

[52] *Ibid.*, p. 313.

[53] *Ibid.*, p. 207. See also p. 251.

[54] *Ibid.*, p. 368. See also Innis, *Political Economy in the Modern State* (Toronto, 1946): "In Canada feudalism continued in the ownership of natural resources by the provinces and produced the dual mixture of a capitalistic federal government and feudalistic provincial governments" (p. 88).

[55] Innis, *Changing Concepts of Time* (Toronto, 1952), p. 69.

[56] *Essays*, p. 258.

[57] *Ibid.*, p. 206.

[58] *Ibid.*, pp. 353-56.

[59] See C. Hill, *Reformation to Industrial Revolution* (Harmondsworth, 1969) and W. A. Williams, *The Contours of American History* (Chicago, 1966).

[60] See Mel Watkins, "The Staple Theory Revisited," *Journal of Canadian Studies* 12:5 (Winter 1977), pp. 83-95.

[61] T. W. Acheson, "The Maritimes and 'Empire Canada,'" in D.J. Bercuson, ed., *Canada and the Burden of Unity* (Toronto, 1977), p. 95.

[62] *Essays*, p. 288.

[63] *Ibid.*, p. 77.

[64] *Ibid.*, p. 122.

[65] *Political Economy in the Modern State;* the quotations are from pp. 132-33.

[66] Innis, "For the People," *University of Toronto Quarterly*, 5 (1935-36), p. 284.

[67] *Report of the Royal Commission on Price Spreads* (Ottawa, 1937), p. 12. The Report added (p. 13) that the corporate form "facilitates the evasion of moral responsibility for inequitable and uneconomic practices." It is instructive to compare this document with the recent report of the Royal Commission on Corporate Concentration.

[68] Innis, "For the People," p. 286. Innis noted elsewhere that "Adam Smith might have said of capitalists as he said of merchants: 'The government of an exclusive company of merchants is perhaps the worst of all governments for any country whatever'" (*Essays*, p. 163).

[69] *Report of the Royal Commission on Price Spreads*, p. 11.

[70] *Essays*, p. 265.

[71] *Ibid.*, p. 267.

[72] Innis, "The Rowell-Sirois Report," *Canadian Journal of Economics and Political Science*, 6 (1940), p. 570; *Changing Concepts of Time*, p. 74. Innis recognized the problem of the Commission in facing "the Charybdis of increasing provincial powers and the Scylla of railway amalgamation masquerading as national unity" (*Essays*, p. 210).

[73] *Essays*, p. 257.

[74] On market and non-market price systems, see Abraham Rotstein, "Innis: The Alchemy of Fur and Wheat," *Journal of Canadian Studies*, 12:5 (Winter 1977).

[75] *Essays*, p. 260.

[76] Quoted in Carl Berger, *The Writing of Canadian History* (Toronto, 1976), p. 38.

[77] J. R. Mallory, *Social Credit and the Federal Power in Canada* (Toronto, 1976), pp. 6, 169, 177. Mallory makes the point that "at least as far as disallowance is concerned, provincial legislation on the subject of property and civil rights has very definite limits . . . although the Padlock Act failed signally to arouse the Department of Justice to the pitch of indignation it might have reached if the property padlocked had been a branch of a chartered bank" (pp. 176-77).

[78] See T. W. Acheson, "The National Policy and the Industrialization of the Maritimes, 1880-1910," *Acadiensis* 1 (1972), pp. 3-28; Acheson, "The Maritimes and 'Empire Canada,'" pp. 87-114; and, also in the Bercuson volume, Ernest R. Forbes, "Misguided Symmetry: The

Destruction of Regional Transportation Policy for the Maritimes" and T. D. Regehr, "Western Canada and the Burden of National Transportation Policies."

[79] Garth Stevenson, "Continental Integration and Canadian Unity," in W. A. Axline *et al., Continental Community? Independence and Integration in North America* (Toronto, 1974), p. 209.

[80] Donald V. Smiley, "Canada and the Quest for a National Policy," *Canadian Journal of Political Science,* vol. 8 (1975), pp. 46-47. Creighton ("Harold Adams Innis—An Appraisal," p. 22) refers to Innis' "anti-federalist perspective."

[81] *Essays,* p. 198.

[82] *Ibid.,* pp. 74, 279. See also pp. 368-69.

[83] *Ibid.,* p. 384. See also pp. 80-81.

[84] *Ibid.,* p. 195.

[85] *Ibid.,* pp. 130, 140. See also p. 155.

[86] *Ibid.,* pp. 291, 371. Innis noted that "commercial capitalism" had given way to the free trade of "finance capitalism" as a result of the conflicts produced by mercantilism. The American War of Independence had been one of the conflicts but "it was precisely the contributions of the United States to the solution of the problems of commercial capitalism which made it impossible for her to solve the problems of finance capitalism." Innis here uses the term "finance capitalism" to refer to what he had earlier called "modern capitalism," i.e., a system requiring long-term credit as opposed to the short-term credit of commercial capitalism.

[87] *Changing Concepts of Time,* p. 104 and also pp. 105-07; *Essays,* pp. 83, 97-100, 269. See *Essays,* pp. 123-140, for examples of Innis' despair at the collapse of the old order: "Democracy, nationalism and regionalism are involved in vicious circles which imply lowering of the standard of living . . ." (p. 131).

[88] See "The Canadian Economy and the Depression," *Essays,* pp. 123-35. (This essay incorporates an earlier one entitled "Economic Nationalism.") See also *Essays,* pp. 252-72, and "Preface" to *Political Economy in the Modern State.*

[89] See, for example, Joan Robinson, *The New Mercantilism* (Cambridge, 1966), pp. 5-6.

[90] K. Levitt, *Silent Surrender* (Toronto, 1970), p. 23.

[91] Rotstein, "The Alchemy of Fur and Wheat." Innis did note, however, that "the rapidity of development accentuated by the position of overhead costs incidental to fixed capital equipment such as transcontinental railways weakens the effect of price as an organizing factor"

(*Settlement and the Mining Frontier,* p. 404). On the significance of multinational corporations, see my *Dominance and Dependency,* pp. 56-63 and 136-43.

[92] *Essays,* pp. 156-75. See also p. 174, and "Preface" to *Political Economy in the Modern State.*

[93] *Essays,* pp. 405, 395, 410, 271; *Changing Concepts of Time,* pp. 19-20. Innis noted that sentiment towards Great Britain had been "at the heart of our cultural life in Canada" but that by the 1940s a transition to the U.S. empire was linked with opposition to "socialistic trends" in Britain (*Essays,* p. 405).

[94] *Essays,* p. 209; *Changing Concepts of Time,* p. 74.

[95] *Essays,* p. 83.

Ronald Keast (essay date 1985)

SOURCE: "It Is Written—But I Say Unto You: Innis on Religion," in *Journal of Canadian Studies/Revue d'études canadiennes,* Vol. 20, No. 4, Winter, 1985-86, pp. 12-25.

[*In the following essay, Keast outlines Innis's ideas on the influence of religion.*]

INTRODUCTION

When Harold Innis died in 1952 he had achieved an international scholarly reputation and was recognized as Canada's foremost historian. That reputation had been established by his early published works, those dealing with the Canadian Pacific Railway, the fur trade in Canada, and the cod fisheries. In these Innis showed how technique (the method or means) and technology (the hardware), especially of transportation, affected the development of economic and political monopolies. Canadian history was viewed in terms of the evolution of spatial monopolies of commerce and national politics, and the struggle for commercial and political freedom. His reputation grew during the last decade of his life as his interest in monopolies extended from Canada to the whole of western civilization and from transportation to communication. During this later period he showed how technique and technology, especially of communication, have affected the development of monopolies in the long history of the West. He viewed history in terms of the evolution of monopolies of knowledge and the struggle for individual spiritual freedom.

Innis's breadth and depth are greater in his later works than in his earlier ones, but as his approach was similar there is a continuity throughout. His early works reflect the thesis, elucidated so well in the works of Thorstein Veblen, that habits of thought are the outcome of habits of life, especially habits of work. His later works focus on habits of mind as he develops the thesis that habits of work and habits of mind are in large measure effects of communication and that all human thought reflects the technique and technology of communication. If the way man communicates influences what he communicates as well as his perception and understanding of what is communicated, then man's perception and understanding of truths and values, at least in part, are effects of communication. Since it is truths and values which we think of when we use the word "religion," this article proposes that, based on the later works of Harold Innis, religion in the West may be considered as an effect of communication.

Innis used the term religion, and certainly considered the concept of religion, in a much broader sense than is usual. It was for him the basis of empire, whether ecclesiastical or political. It provided the truths or myths which allow for the control of time or space. He referred to large-scale truths or systems of truths as monopolies of knowledge. Whether a civilization tends to be influenced by truths of time or of space is a reflection of its dominant medium of communication. Media that are light and easily transportable favour space; those that are durable and not so easily transportable favour time. However, he also identified a fundamental religious experience outside any organizational or institutional setting, free of bias, which is an effect of oral communication. This is a spiritual creativity which implies individual freedom and the pursuit of truth.

Innis placed great stress on the importance of personal interaction, of mind with mind and emotion with emotion, for the evolution of new ideas, for spiritual breakthrough, for individual freedom from the monopoly of truths characteristic of large-scale organization, and for the free pursuit of truth. He believed that because oral communication involves all the senses "in busy interplay," and because it involves both intellect and emotion, it is singularly reflective of the whole man. It is, therefore, singularly spiritual.

Innis emphasized the value of questioning all "religious" truths. Since they are the basis of large-scale control, all must be continually questioned in order for man to be truly religious. An agnostic state of mind is indispensable for individual freedom and spiritual creativity. This is an effect of oral communication and Innis's works suggest that it is of the essence of religion.

No means of mechanized communication adequately or fully communicates the oral tradition. Each technique and technology imposes a message of its own. This suggests that the message of the Christian gospels, for example, which came out of an oral milieu, will be changed when communicated in mechanized forms. It will be different from, and less than, the original. An understanding of the effects of communication is important, therefore, for an understanding of the gospel message. Innis helped to provide such an understanding.

Man's thinking is biased by the way he communicates. Therefore, he may never know in any absolute sense what truth is. He may, however, have faith that truth exists. This brings an important perspective to the understanding of religion.

THE HISTORY OF COMMUNICATIONS

In his two major published works, **Empire and Communications** and **The Bias of Communication,** as well as numerous other works including a huge unpublished document entitled *"A History of Communications,"* Innis provided an historical analysis of the effects of communication in the West from the pre-alphabet civilizations of Egypt and Babylonia to the age of radio in Europe and North America. A brief review of this enormous body of work is necessary in order to appreciate his thesis.

The sections on Egypt and Babylonia provide an understanding of the limitations of such early forms of mechanized communication as pictographic writing on stone and papyrus and cuneiform patterns of triangles and massed parallel lines pressed into clay. These complicated styles necessitated long training and the development of a class of priest-scribes. Because of the resulting monopolies of writing exercised by the priests, succeeding political empires were limited in their ability to control space. As a result, societies on the fringes of these empires, with their own religious truths, such as the Jews in Palestine, were able to develop their oral traditions in relative freedom.

It was in such societies, marginal to the great empires, that a more simple system of writing began to emerge. Semitic peoples adapted elements of Egyptian writing to their own strong oral tradition and developed the phonetic alphabet over a long period of time. This more flexible means of mechanized communication, utilizing papyrus and parchment, efficiently captured the oral traditions and allowed for a far more efficient organization and communication of truths relating both to time and space.

The oral tradition was the creative fount from which flowed both religion and philosophy. With the alphabet the creative and evolving religious truths, inherent in oral societies, became fossilized and a monopoly of knowledge could be built up. "The writing of books necessitates presenting a case as the final argument. As a result books contribute powerfully to the closing of minds, particularly of writers, as they have strong vested interests in positions which they have elaborated."[1] Innis understood writing to be, essentially, a product of pure intelligence. It encourages intellectual freedom but restricts emotional freedom. It thus tends to retard the development and expression of the creative spiritual component in man. Truths are defended; the free pursuit of truth retarded. Writing by means of the phonetic alphabet emphasizes reason, individualism, and equality. Truths become those things that appeal to man's reason. Thus, the invention and use of the alphabet changed man's very concept of truth. Rational truths became the basis of control over space and time. A linear, rational method of thinking was imposed. "Dogmatism followed the conclusion that power governing the universe was rational."[2]

The alphabet was developed among the Hebrews as an aid to memory. Writing was given religious sanction by saying that Moses introduced it at the command of God to prevent the possible disappearance of the oral tradition. "For the Hebrews the word is the word of Wisdom. Word, Wisdom, and God were almost identical theological concepts." Gradually, however, "the written letter replaced the graven image as an object of worship."[3] The prohibition of images, following the experience in Egypt, and the concentration on the abstract in writing which was an effect of the alphabet allowed the Hebrews to advance from relationships based on blood—that is, kinship relationships—to universal ethical standards that were grounded in monotheism. It also helped to strengthen the influence of the prophets in opposition to the absolute power of the king. The alphabet was flexible enough to allow for the powerful oral tradition, communicated by the prophets, to be collected and preserved. As a result, the power and creative energy of the oral tradition, at least partially preserved in the scriptures, has influenced religious development to this day. Gradually, however, mechanized communication exerted its inevitable effect on the dynamic oral tradition. It killed much though not all, of the spirit of oral communication and set up a body of unchangeable truths by which the priests were able to monopolize time. The written word took on the power of the ancient spoken word and became the principle of authority. The interpreters of this sacred writing were the priests. "The written bible assumed monotheism, doctrine, and priesthood. No book, no doctrine, no doctrine, no book."[4] In general, the alphabet brought greater efficiency in the control of both time and space. It facilitated a more efficient control of time in monotheism by the Hebrews; more efficient trade and commerce by the Phoenicians and Aramaeans; more efficient control of space by the Assyrians, the Persians, and later empires.

Innis believed that Greek culture was particularly creative because it was able to escape the stupifying tendencies of writing until a comparatively late date. When its oral tradition was finally committed to writing, the flexible alphabet allowed its creative power to be more accurately reflected than would have been possible earlier. The oral tradition in the Greek, as in the Hebrew, civilization implied an emphasis on time, tradition, continuity, and religion. But "the Greeks had no bible with a sacred literature attempting to give reasons and coherence to the scheme of things, making dogmatic assertions and strangling science in infancy."[5] The relative absence of dogma allowed for the evolution of truths. The effects of writing and the phonetic alphabet could be seen clearly in Greece by the second half of the fifth century. Written laws were considered universally valid. Compromise became more difficult. In Athens the old communal bond was broken. In the fourth century Plato recognized the dangers inherent in writing and attempted to save the remnants of Greek culture by reflecting the oral tradition in the style of the Socratic dialogues. Socrates knew that "the letter is designed to kill much (though not all) of the life that the spirit has given."[6]

Similar to the Greek experience was the evolution of Roman society from one based on a strong oral tradition to one based on writing. At first laws were oral, passed down by memory, and applied to all disputes. The oral tradition gave continuity to early Roman society. It was flexible and allowed for compromise and change to take place gradually and without violent conflict. An interest in the codification of laws developed with the spread of writing. Gradually the letter of the law became supreme. Truths became fixed and unchangeable.

The great creative periods of Hebrew religion, Greek philosophy, and Roman law all were seen by Innis as effects of a strong oral tradition. In each case the flexibility of the phonetic alphabet allowed these great traditions to be preserved, to the enormous benefit of western civilization. However, it changed them in the very act of preservation. The other great tradition which grew out of the same oral creativity and suffered a similar fate was Christianity.

Christianity arose out of a ferment within Judaism, partially as a protest against theocratic rigidity, itself a response to the gap that had developed between Hebrew as a sacred written "dead" language and the oral vernacular language of the area which was Aramaic. The Pharisaic concern with the law (written truths) was repudiated: "The strength of sin is in the law."[7] The early Christians developed their own oral tradition which they traced back to the apostles. In these early stages, copies of short written works were probably made on papyrus, as well as parchment. Gradually, the oral tradition was committed to writing on parchment. A growing demand for authoritative scriptures led to the development of the canon of the New Testament and the production of complete Bibles. The primacy of the Roman Church within Christianity was established by the end of the first century and a Catholic confederation emerged about A.D. 180. In 313, Christianity became a licensed cult. With the Edict of Milan, the empire of Constantine recognized the Christian Church as a corporation by giving it permission to hold property. Paganism was dethroned as a state religion. Libraries were recopied on parchment and the wholesale destruction of pagan writings on papyrus took place. Christianity, now based on a book as the carrier of everlasting and unchangeable truths, absorbed or drove out other religions and moved to a position of close cooperation with the state. In summarizing this period, Innis explained that "the bureaucratic development of the Roman Empire and success in solving problems of administration over vast areas were dependent on supplies of papyrus. The bias of this medium became apparent in the monopoly of bureaucracy and its inability to find a satisfactory solution to the problem of time. The problem of the Roman Empire in relation to time was solved by the support of religion in the Christian Church."[8]

The Roman Empire was successful in the East, with its capital at Constantinople, at least in part because it was based on competing media. "A [political] bureaucracy built up in relation to papyrus and the alphabet was supplemented by a [religious] hierarchy built up in relation to parchment. The consequent stability was evident in the continuity of the Byzantine Empire to 1453."[9] A balance was maintained between the truths of time and space. While politics was supreme it was tempered by religion. Justinian contributed much to the strengthening of the eastern part of the empire with his code of written civil law, with its spatial bias. This code of Roman law has influenced European life more than any written work except the Bible. In addition, the great manuscripts of Christian literature, with their time bias, were produced in the first part of the fourth century. For Innis, this was the ideal arrangement for the survival of political empire. The time and spatial biases co-existed. One kind of truth did not gain a monopoly.

The situation in the western part of the empire was different. As a result of barbarian encroachment, the political position of the empire was weakened and the hierarchy of the empire became to a large extent the hierarchy of the Roman Church. There was a growth of ecclesiastical empire with its monopoly of knowledge of time. Monarchy in the western papacy closely paralleled monarchy in the eastern empire. The difference was that while religious divisions occurred in the East, the empire remained firm. In the West there was relative religious stability but constant political instability.

Parchment gave a powerful impetus to monasticism. The truths of the Church could be copied and maintained in decentralized monastic locations. Each monastery had a library. There was little check on the growth of monasticism in the West and this accentuated the influence of celibacy, Latin, and a monopoly of knowledge of time. The "ecclesiastical empire" resisted all spatial pressures until the time bias of parchment was undermined by a new medium, paper, with its spatial bias.

The monopoly of knowledge of time achieved by the Church in the West invited competition from areas marginal to the effects of the ecclesiastical empire. The demands and needs of lower levels of society were first expressed within the oral tradition. The emphasis on Latin by the Church, an attempt to protect its monopoly, widened the gap with the oral and the growing vernacular, written traditions. The courts were important centres of literary activity in the vernacular and supported the poetry of the troubadours as well as the literature of writers such as Dante, Petrarch, Boccaccio, and Chaucer. The influx of Greek scholars from the East, following the destruction of Constantinople, contributed to the growing interest in classical civilization with its rich oral tradition. "The vitality of the classics of Greece which reflected the power of civilization based on an oral tradition gradually weakened the monopoly of knowledge held by the Church."[10]

Innis believed that a centralizing trend, manifest particularly in national politics but also in the development of commerce and industry, began with paper as a medium of communication. Because linen rags were the main raw material and because the large cities provided the chief market, the production and use of paper promoted centralizing tendencies which were opposite to the tendencies of parchment. The manufacture and increasing use of paper in urban centres began to undermine the monopoly over writing held by the monasteries. During this period of increasing use of paper there was a steady development in secular, and vernacular, education. This was occasioned by and helped to further the development of trade and commerce and the increasing centralization manifest in the growing importance of cities. To protect its monopoly, the Church reacted against this secular education and closed the monastery schools to secular students. This favoured the growth of cathedral schools, the development of the oral tradition in the universities, and finally the breaking forth of the oral tradition in the Reformation. "Decline of the monopoly of knowledge based on parchment in which an ecclesiastical organization emphasized control over time followed the competition of paper which supported the growth of trade and of cities, the rise of vernaculars, and the increasing importance of lawyers, and emphasized the concept of space in nationalism."[11]

The full impact of this development came with the invention of the printing press. Printing in the vernacular offered a tremendous impetus to the spatial bias inherent in writing and paper. It communicated these effects to large numbers of people. The vernacular languages offered a wider market for new authors and readers. Its effects were revolutionary. It became the instrument of the Reformation. The many vernacular translations of the Bible, as well as the Greek translations, destroyed the monopoly of time as expressed in Latin. "Publication of the scriptures in the vernacular was followed by new interpretations and by the intensive controversies conducted in pamphlets and sheets which ended in the establishment of Protestantism." "The prolific source of Protestant sectarianism was the notion that the scriptures speak unmistakably."[12]

The new spatial truths, relating to nationalism and commerce, grew and developed parallel with Protestantism, all as effects of printing and paper. The new "religious" truths, relating to control of geographical area, were supported by vernacular translations of the Bible. Nationalism was based on the mass communication of vernacular languages. As vernacular translations of the Bible gave these languages sacred appeal, so the concept of nationalism and the nation itself gained sacred appeal. "After the introduction of paper and the printing press, religious monopoly was followed by monopolies of vernaculars in modern states. A monopoly of time was followed by a monopoly of space."[13]

Innis believed that only in England were the "religious" truths relating to the control of space somewhat undermined by a strong oral tradition. It is not that Britain did not reflect a spatial bias; in fact, it reflected the bias of both nationalism and commercialism. But the effects of its strong oral tradition meant more flexibility and compromise in the political organization than had been possible in any other nation in the West. In England, as in early Greece and Rome, common law evolved from customs which had developed over a long period of time and which were carried in the minds of men. "The law was not made, it was only proved."[14] The importance of the strong oral tradition meant that, in law, truths and dogma reflecting the power of writing and printing did not easily monopolize the mind of man. This made possible the development of the jury system and parliament. The oral tradition and the early restrictions on printing in England accentuated an interest in the drama. Shakespeare was able to exploit and to expand the capacities of the vernacular language which had not been conventionalized or repressed by print. Tragedy flourished in Athens in the years before writing became firmly established, whereas in England it flourished before printing was able to exercise its full power.

But with the publication of the King James version of the Bible in 1611, prose achieved a position of predominance over poetry and drama. It influenced the development of a common written vernacular language, a spatial bias, individualism, and a more rational mode of thinking. As in the case of Greece, the increase in the reading and writing of prose accentuated the development of individualism, of pure reason, and of science. This was particularly true in England among Protestants who had a much more intense interest in the Bible and Bible reading. The spirit of individualism, which was expounded by Hobbes and which became the basis of the concept of *laissez-faire* as explained by Adam Smith, was, at least in part, an effect of printing. Also, as a result of printing, specifically the printing of the Bible, the Puritans developed the concept of a fundamental common or natural law in politics which was an embodiment of reason and which was above all the sovereign powers of the state. In the Instrument of Government which set up the Protectorate in England in 1653, the Puritans attempted to limit the power of parliament by a written constitution. This was the first and last attempt in England to do so. However, the impact of Puritanism and of a linear, rational mode of thinking persisted in the colonies where written constitutions, as the products of reason, persisted.

The effects of the written tradition on the Puritan mind meant the imposition of written truths in the political sphere. This undermined the flexibility inherent in the oral tradition. It meant a growing slavery to the truths of space. With their strong Puritan tradition, the colonies recognized the written law (truths) of God in the Bible as the only absolute law for man. However, they also imposed an absolute law on man through their written constitution. The written constitution of the United States, in reaction to the absolute power of the English parliament, restricted the absolute power of government. But the fact that it was written left the United States with a relatively inflexible constitution which tended to be seen as an embodiment of truths, not unlike the absolute truths of the Puritan Bible. "The full impact of printing did not become possible until the adoption of the Bill of Rights in the United States with its guarantee of freedom of the press. A guarantee of freedom of the press in print was intended to further sanctify the printed word and to provide a rigid bulwark for the shelter of vested interests."[15] The prominent role of the newspaper in the American Revolution was recognized in the first article of the Bill of Rights.

The written constitution and the impetus it gave to printing, especially to newspapers, and to the effects of printing and paper, meant that the United States, from the very beginning of its political history, was firmly gripped by "religious" truths relating to the control of space. The press, through its sanctification in the written constitution, became the guardian and expositor of the truths on which the nation was founded. These truths reflect, almost completely, national politics and commerce.

Innis saw a similar pattern in the development of commonwealth countries, notably Canada. He did not believe that culture could survive in such a monopolized environment; knowledge is not possible. In Canada there was, in his mind, a real question as to whether or not Confederation could survive. With a written constitution there is less and less room for compromise in federal and provincial negotiations. The divine truths of federalism struggle against the divine truths of provincialism. Innis believed that resistance to this spatial monopoly of knowledge is possible only by adherence to the oral common law tradition of Britain and to the cultural heritage of Europe, notably France. In other words, he advocated a return to the roots of Canadian society in order to escape the dominance of the new secular religion emanating principally from the United States.

Innis's later works provide a vast amount of detail regarding the development and the effects of mass communications in the western world. Such detail furthered his thesis that spatial truths, the secular "religious" truths of national politics and capitalism, have been imposed on the mind of western man in a manner and to an extent never before possible. He described modern states, even democratic ones, as totalitarian. It was this powerful monopoly of knowledge and the possibility of violent conflicts resulting from the clash of spatial truths which he feared. Much of his later work consists of an effort to expose these modern truths as in no way absolute, but rather as effects of communication, and to emphasize the importance of oral communication in undermining all truths in the pursuit of truth. "States are destroyed by ignorance of the most important thing in human life, by a profound lack of culture—which, following Plato, is the inability to secure a proper agreement between desire and intellect."[16] Culture is an effect of oral communication.

Innis valued the oral tradition, as manifest particularly in Greek culture, because it tends to undermine monopolies of knowledge; to introduce a balanced view of life; to allow for flexibility and for compromise in thinking and in acting; and to permit change and the evolution of truths. Modern spatial truths of national politics and commerce are simply too dangerous not to be constantly questioned. He believed that the university can offer an important bastion of resistance to the spatial monopoly of knowledge which is threatening mankind's survival in the West, because the oral tradition is of the very essence of university education. The university has a critically important role in maintaining and strengthening this tradition. It must emphasize the pursuit of truth rather than the defence of truths. It must emphasize balance and perspective, that is, culture. By denying all claims to truth, philosophy and religion may grow and blossom and democracy will be protected, for in a practical as well as a spiritual sense, "it is the search for truth, not truth, that makes men free."[17]

CHRISTIANITY AND COMMUNICATIONS

Innis's works on communication are studies of the struggle between freedom and slavery, both of society and the individual. In religious terms this may be described as a struggle between law and prophecy, between written truths and oral communication: "It is written . . . but, I say unto you."[18] When Innis used the passage from Holy Writ—"without vision the people perish"[19]—the vision referred to is an effect of oral communication. It is a spiritual effect, basic both to philosophy and religion, to wisdom and to faith.

Innis pointed out that in the Bible "Word, Wisdom, and God were almost identical theological concepts."[20] Innis himself seems to have seen them as identical also. Certainly, oral communication has a very special spiritual effect, analogous at least to the Christian concept of the working of the Word in the world: that is, the working of the Holy Spirit in the individual and within society. This interpretation suggests that oral communication is essential to Christian faith, that it results in the continuous pursuit of truth in the faith that truth exists. The pursuit gives freedom in the knowledge that there are no truths to monopolize the mind. Only faith remains, or nihilism.

The concept that faith (faith that truth exists) precedes understanding (the wisdom that it may never be comprehended intellectually), and that this understanding leads to faith, is a powerful, though implicit, message in Innis's later works. This concept was clearly elucidated by Charles Norris Cochrane in his book, *Christianity and Classical Culture*. There is every probability that Cochrane had considerable influence on Innis's mature thinking, as perhaps Innis had on Cochrane's.

Innis's works stress that the way man communicates affects what he communicates. The very way man thinks, and certainly what he thinks of as true, tend to be biased by his mechanized means of communication. Therefore, man cannot know in any absolute sense what truth is. Cochrane's work presents a similar thesis. According to Augustine, man cannot know what truth is because his thinking is biased by the very fact that he is man. However, this understanding that man cannot know what truth is helps to provide the basis for Christian faith. The Church fathers emphasized that Christ *was* the truth, not merely that he *had* the truth. The total person of Christ was the one avenue to truth. The Christian's duty was to apprehend rather than to investigate. Such an attitude, however, constituted an essential breach between science and faith. The emphasis placed by the Church fathers on apprehension rather than scientific investigation appears to be similar to the emphasis placed on oral communication by Innis. Both rejected the belief that truths may be discovered by reason. The Church fathers considered the belief that this can be done to be a reflection of man's inherent pride, his faith in his own reason. Innis saw it as reflecting a similar faith, but as an effect of writing and printing utilizing the phonetic alphabet. The truths of reason, for Innis and Cochrane, as for Augustine, were projections of man's own mind, illusions which he worships and which control him. Their rejection may be seen as a rejection of idolatry, pride, and sin. "Secular pride, i.e. the original sin, became the key to the weakness of classical civilization and the doctrine of original sin became the fatal weapon against the pretentions of emperors."[21] Man must question all truths; he must be agnostic, in order to be Christian.

For neither Cochrane nor Innis did the scepticism of the truths of reason mean reliance of some kind of instinctive or mystical apprehension of truth. Cochrane explained that for Augustine this revolt from faith in reason "points the way to an attitude from which, if faith precedes understanding, understanding in turn becomes the reward of faith."[22] For Innis, understanding is possible only when one realizes that one is biased, that one cannot know what truth is. As bias is an effect of mechanized communication, so understanding is an effect of oral communication. This is an understanding of one's own idolatry, of one's own sin. It is an understanding that one knows nothing. When this is considered in the light of Cochrane's elucidation of Augustine, one sees how it can lead to Christian faith, to the faith that truth exists without the knowledge of what truth is. In this sense faith becomes the reward of understanding. Also, if the concept of oral communication is interpreted in the Christian sense of the Word at work in the world, then faith and understanding become the product of the working of the Holy Spirit, or of grace. Thus, understanding becomes the reward of faith. Augustine said, "believe in order that you may understand."[23] Implicit in Innis's later works is a message similar to this. Oral communication allows one to escape the domination of "religious" truths. It brings one to an understanding that, since we cannot know *what* truth is, we have freedom to believe *that* truth is. This faith gives freedom from bondage to truths.

Innis's works clearly indicate that oral communication effects a spiritual creativity and freedom. Cochrane's work indicates that this spiritual creativity is of the essence of Christianity—the Holy Spirit, the Word, at work in the world. It is therefore possible to understand the

Word as being, in a literal sense, oral communication. Christianity may thus be seen as an effect of oral communication, the person of Jesus Christ being the Incarnation of the spirituality of oral communication, the perfect example of this process at work in the world. With this understanding one may better appreciate the statement in Matthew (18:19), "For where two or three have met together in my name, I am there among them."

According to Cochrane, Augustine was aware that written works operate just as effectively to embalm as to enshrine truth. Both he and Innis invoked the authority of St. Paul in their rejection of literalism: "the letter killeth." Augustine believed that the full understanding of words came only in the light of the Spirit. Innis elucidated the process by which the Spirit operates. Therefore, while the Bible may be considered as a written record of the apprehension of truth, and authoritative because of this, the record cannot be considered as truth nor used as a basis for a rational analysis and understanding of what truth is.

Innis's works help explain why the Bible has tended to be misunderstood as a record of what truth is, of truths open to rational analysis. The effect of the written and printed linear display is to impose a rational, logical method of thinking and a faith in the results of this method. The fact that it is written tends to impose on it the mantle of unchanging truth. Both the technique and the technology of mechanized communication impose their own truths. The Bible has not escaped these effects. The written record of the Word may be valuable if it is understood as a record of a spiritual process which in itself it does not fully contain or reflect. It is the record of an oral tradition. It may be useful if it is appreciated as a means to the means. If it is not, then it will hinder the pursuit of truth. The Bible is the record of the communication of values. It is open to faith, not to reason. Printing imposes a faith in reason itself which tends to neglect value for fact.

The works of both Innis and Cochrane suggest, clearly, that God is manifest in human interaction. It is through human interaction that God may be apprehended and pursued, and that freedom may be effected. This human interaction, oral communication, is of the essence of Christianity. While both Innis and Cochrane may be seen as part of a well-recognized liberal tradition in the West in their rejection of truths and emphasis on the pursuit of truth and on individual freedom, they must also be seen to stand outside this tradition, to be part of the Christian tradition dating from Augustine. The freedom sought by Innis is more than the freedom of the classical or the liberal traditions. It is freedom from all truths, especially the truths of reason. He moved beyond a tradition which he saw as a reflection of mechanized communication, a tradition that reflected a faith in man's ability to discover truth, to a position where truth can be pursued in freedom. Innis, like Cochrane, and like Augustine, combined a questioning of all truths with faith in truth. He was both agnostic and Christian. In fact, on

the basis of his and Cochrane's works, it can be concluded that one must be agnostic in order to be Christian.

CONCLUSION

Innis's later works have profound significance for the study of religion, as they have for the study of western thought and social organization in general. He believed that we must be prepared to question every truth, every value, every thought; that we must question our very questions. He showed particular interest in stressing the need to question our faith in scientific objectivity and the truths of reason. However, he did not mean to imply that objectivity is not to be desired or that one should not strive for a scientific point of view. Indeed, he attempted to view society from just this perspective. He believed that bias itself may be studied. But he stressed that the social scientist in particular must be aware that he is continually under the influence of the bias of his culture, even while he is attempting to study it. He cannot escape this influence. A wise man, a truly educated man, is one who is aware that he is biased, that objectivity in any absolute sense is impossible. He is therefore humble in his assessment of his own infallibility. Only by reaching this plateau of knowledge may a man consider himself to be either wise or free. Freedom is not possible without knowledge, the knowledge that one knows nothing, the knowledge that there are no truths.

In his later works Innis was clearly proselytizing. He took a firm stand against the degeneration of the secular, spatially biased society he saw around him. A central theme is the need for a spiritual renewal in order to escape the mechanical petrification of modern western society. Mechanical petrification is an effect of mechanical communication. Spiritual awakening requires spiritual communication.

Besides the suggestion that mechanized communication works to destroy human spirituality and freedom, Innis was clear in his understanding that it never fully communicates the oral tradition. This is significant for an understanding of religion, especially Christianity. It implies that the gospel message, which was originally communicated within an oral environment, will be changed when it is communicated in written, printed, or electronic forms. Each different technique and technology imposes its own message. All will be different from, and less than, the original oral message. The essence of the Christian religion is represented by the phrase "I say unto you." This is the Word at work.

Innis believed that the apprehension of truth which the Bible records, as well as the record of the pursuit of truth contained in the Platonic dialogues, are better recorded than not recorded. When the bias of communication is understood, these records of a dynamic oral tradition may act as a leaven for our mechanized civilization. Nevertheless, an understanding of the effects of communication is essential before either the gospels or the dialogues can be fully appreciated, before the spirit of the oral tradition which they contain can cut through the darkness imposed by mechanized technique and technology. Innis, like Plato, St. Paul, and St. Augustine believed that mechanized communication kills much, though not all, of the spirit of oral communication.

Innis's works on the effects of communication point to the vacuity of modern secular pride which tells us that truth is that which appeals to our reason. Yet his works, while cutting the ground from under our faith that we have the truth or that we can discover what truth is, leaves freedom for the faith that truth exists, that God exists. They may be viewed as an attempt to free man from "religious" truths in order that he may be truly religious.

NOTES

1 Harold Innis Collection, University of Toronto Archives, Box 10A, *Idea File*, p. 157.

2 Harold Innis, *Empire and Communications* (Oxford: Clarendon Press, 1950), p. 115.

3 *Ibid.*, p. 53.

4 Harold Innis, *The Bias of Communication* (Toronto: University of Toronto Press, 1951), p. 13.

5 Innis, *Empire and Communications*, p. 80.

6 *Ibid.*, p. 68.

7 Innis, *Bias of Communication*, p. 115.

8 *Ibid.*, p. 47.

9 *Ibid.*, p. 117.

10 *Ibid.*, p. 22.

11 *Ibid.*, p. 53.

12 Innis, *Empire and Communications*, p. 184; *Bias of Communication*, p. 64.

13 Innis, *Bias of Communication*, p. 64.

14 Innis, *Empire and Communications*, p. 164.

15 Innis, *Bias of Communication*, p. 138.

16 Harold Innis, *Political Economy in the Modern State* (Toronto: Ryerson Press, 1946), p. x.

17 Harold Innis and Jan O.M. Brock, "Geography and Nationalism: a discussion," *Geographical Review,* vol. XXXV (1945), 303.

18 Innis, *Bias of Communication*, p. 14.

19 *Ibid.*, p. 91.

20 Innis, *Empire and Communications,* p. 53.

21 Harold Innis, "Charles Norris Cochrane, 1889-1945," *Canadian Journal of Economics and Political Science,* vol. XII (1946), 95-97.

22 Charles Norris Cochrane, *Christianity and Classical Culture* (New York: Oxford University Press, 1957), p. 400.

23 *Ibid.*, p. 402.

Robin Neill (essay date 1987)

SOURCE: "Rationality and the Informational Environment: A Reassessment of the Work of Harold Adams Innis," in *Journal of Canadian Studies/Revue d'études canadiennes,* Vol. 22, No. 4, Winter, 1987-88, pp. 78-92.

[*In the following essay, Neill examines the significance of Innis's writings on communications and economics.*]

A NEW PERSPECTIVE

Harold Innis's message was not well communicated, because, in part, those who received it did not occupy a perceptual vantage point from which it could be understood. The consequence has been a multiplication of interpretations of Innis, many cited in R.F. Neill's intellectual biography,[1] others appearing since 1972 in the continuing flow of commentaries. None has captured Innis's fundamental insight into the nature and consequences of the informational environment of decision-making.

Over the past fifteen years, with no reference to Innis—perhaps because they have misunderstood him, perhaps because they have never heard of him—a number of economists have taken a new approach in which Innis's work makes consistent sense. In the consequent perspective, his general research program may appear to be clearly separated from the sequence of subjects to which it applies and with which it deals. Indeed, in this light, the underlying unity of his economic analysis, his Canadian history, and his essays on communication becomes increasingly evident. The methodological issues at the root of his studies, his general scientific contribution, and his innovative interpretation of the Canadian economy all come to the fore.

The new approach in economics was undertaken by the proponents of New Classical Economics in their attempt to single out and negate the principal tenets of Keynesian theory. The broad Keynesian judgement—that there is something wrong with the market system that has to be corrected by government—had to be effectively challenged by a neoconservative assertion that just the opposite is the case, that is, that there is something wrong with government intervention that has to be corrected by increased reliance on the market system. In generating this challenge, the new conservatives replaced the theory of irrational expectations that was the foundation of the Keynesian interpretation with a theory of rational expectations. This, in turn, triggered a renewed awareness that a theory of the informational environment—that is, a theory of the decision-making process—is central to all economic analysis.

A few years before Innis's death in 1952, empirical development of the theory of decision-making accelerated under the influence of Herbert Simon and his associates.[2] Like Innis's theorizing, Simon's work has not been accepted within the mainstream of economics. Nonetheless, it has had a regenerating influence on the discipline because of its more analytic approach to consumer and producer choice. It is a basic and inductive, rather than an applied, approach. It focuses more narrowly on the process of deciding and its consequences than on the expectant outcomes of the decision-makers. A listing of Simon's conclusions helps to put Innis's contribution into an appropriate perspective. According to Simon there are specifiable limits or "bounds" to the use of reason in decision-making. These are: (1) the limits of computational ability, set by the limits of short-term and long-term memory; (2) the limits of perception, set by the path of information search; (3) the limits set by the availability and certitude of information; (4) the limits set by the presence of multiple goals; and (5) the limits set by preoriented attention. Innis was particularly concerned with the historical effects of the bounding of rationality by limited perception and attention.

An important conclusion drawn by Simon is that the rational, maximizing economic man as assumed in neoclassical economics has no empirical validity. Agents are, as he puts it, "satisficing" rather than maximizing. Innis, who was innocent of empirical psychology, never used the term "satisficing," but he agreed with the substance of this proposition,[3] and he sought with a different kind of empiricism to specify its consequences in economic behaviour. He prefaced his essays on the bias of communication with the comment, "They emphasize the importance of communication in determining 'the things to which we attend' . . . ,"[4] that is, in determining the extent to which decisions deviate from substantive (objective) rationality.

We need not agree that positive, neoclassical economics is effectively dismissed either by Simon's empiricism or Innis's historicism. The troublesome relationship between theory, history and empiricism in economics can be resolved in the context of decision theory, but not so easily or so destructively as both Simon and Innis seem to have thought; but that is another subject.

Keynes was a theorist, and the New Classical economists and Herbert Simon are theorists, though all are associated with methodologically distinct empiricisms. Innis used theory in historical analysis, thereby subjecting theory to history. New Classical, rational expectations theory presumes that decisions are based on unlimited reasoning power and unlimited, though costly, access to information. Accordingly, decisions are effectively maximizing. They are what Simon calls "substantively rational." Rational expectations theory admits to a degree of uncertainty in the information environment, but, by endowing agents with the ability to reduce uncertainties to true, objective probabilities, and by asserting that these probabilities are described by the statistical laws of random events, it can assert that any deviations from substantive rationality are minor and of short duration. Keynes, on the contrary, asserted that decisions are affected by habit, custom, historical factors, and psychological factors such as "herd instincts," that is, that decisions are substantively irrational. Irrational expectations determine actual outcomes.[5] On this matter Keynes and the New Classical economists, obviously, do not agree. Both would agree, however, that the subject over which disagreement occurs is the degree of objective rationality in decisions or, in other words, the characteristics of the informational environment. Simon carried out psychological tests to specify the extent and the characteristics of the limits to rationality in decision-making. Innis's contribution was the description of historically specific limits to rationality. He described particular informational environments and he formulated the effects of specifiable conditions in those environments.

Over the past thirty years, Herbert Simon and his associates have provided the empirical foundation in psychology for Innis's reconstruction of the effects of information systems on the structure and evolution of institutions. Over the past fifteen years, debate between Keynesians and New Classical economists has re-emphasized the importance of the informational environment in the analysis of market and non-market behaviour. From the vantage point provided by these related research programs, it is possible to see Innis's work as a largely successful attempt both to present the evidence of history concerning the importance of informational environments and to formulate and corroborate hypotheses concerning the character of substantive non-rationality, that is, of the "bias" of decision-making behaviour.

INNIS IN THE NEW PERSPECTIVE

The multiplicity of commentaries since Neill's comprehensive study has revealed new details of Innis's position in the Canadian social science community. These details do not, however, constitute the basis for a re-interpretation. Rather, they help to fill out the picture which itself takes on meaning only when seen in the new perspective of theories of decision-making and of the informational environment.

In company with Adam Shortt, Oscar Skelton, W.A. Mackintosh, and a number of non-Canadian-born scholars, such as James Mavor and C.R. Fay, Innis brought Canadians to an understanding of the key economic factors in the development of their country.[6] He did so at a time when the academic disciplines of history and social science were being indigenized in Canada. Innis, especially, exploited the economic interpretation of history to make the point that a unique economy, built on a particular geographical and technological base, had given Canada a unique identity. There have been suggestions that Innis, insisting that foreign-trained scholars did not know the country, consciously exploited this view to improve the position of native Canadians in the academic community.[7] Perhaps he himself rode the tide of Canadianization to what, it is alleged, he most wanted to have, advancement in the University of Toronto. Seen in this suggested perspective, however, Innis's behaviour follows logically from his conviction that the substance of Simon's conclusions was correct. He wanted immigrant economists to undergo a reorientation program lest they teach courses and prescribe policies based on inappropriate perceptions and preconceptions.[8]

Despite the wealth of new detail provided in recent years, commentators have continued to find difficulty in specifying a theory or view that can confidently be called Innis's scientific contribution, that is, some empirically tested or testable hypothesis or hypotheses of his upon which others might build. They have instead referred to his "concerns" or to an "Innis tradition."[9] Despite his voluminous scholarly output, his own generation thought his work to be unfinished. There was talk, at first, that his son, Donald, or Marshall McLuhan might finish it. No one, except perhaps McLuhan, identified anything that could be called "Innis Law" or "the Innis Theorem," or even an "Innis Effect." W.T. Easterbrook's explicit pursuit of Innisian "concerns" in his elaboration of the historical effects of changes in the "macroeconomic uncertainty environment of decisions"[10] was innocent of the more recent theories of decision-making, in the light of which, as I contend, Innis's contribution appears complete and his work finished.

It is now uncontroversial to attribute the Staple Theory of Canadian economic development to W.A. Mackintosh[11] rather than to Innis. The theory is too consonant with normative neoclassical analysis to be the product of a devoted disciple of Thorstein Veblen or of someone whose work can be identified with Simonean decision theory.[12] In fact, the idea that the Canadian economy had acquired a special character and set of policies from its reliance on a narrow, primary products export base was being applied by Adam Shortt[13] long before either Innis or Mackintosh received his first degree. That the neoclassical version of the Staple Theory is now questioned even in the standard texts cannot, then, be taken as a direct criticism of Innis. In the 1970s a western Marxian version of the Staple Theory was developed with much reference to Innis, but the most capable exponent of the resulting "Theory of the Staple Trap" has clearly indicated that it cannot be drawn directly from Innis.[14] Thus, Innis's contribution, in this regard, was not to establish Canada's reliance on staple exports; rather, it was to establish that this reliance was a less than efficient consequence of a distinctive, national informational environment.

It came as no surprise to Innis's contemporaries that a leftist theory, like the Theory of the Staple Trap, could not be drawn from his interpretation of Canadian history. Founding members of the League for Social Reconstruction, a sort of "brains trust" for Canada's socialist party, recall Innis as a pre-converted Paul acting on behalf of the "conservative establishment."[15] There was no subsequent conversion in his case. Indeed, the picture that has been presented is not altogether appealing.[16] While praising his political skill and his energy, Innis's contemporaries note how self-serving his purpose was as he rode the fashions of materialism, nationalism, and conservatism to the top of his profession. They recall that his disorganized and confusing presentations were somehow a success because they were at once methodologically fashionable and comforting to established interests. They accuse him of lacking a liberal education, of being intellectually naive, of being a perennial sophomore, forever half discovering everything. These personal reminiscences have special interest because Innis rejected the Keynesian paradigm that most of his contemporaries accepted.[17] When put in perspective, they are enlightening with respect to Innis's contribution because he was as judgemental about the older, neoclassical paradigm as he was about its contemporary critics. It may be, as commentators seem to suggest, that Innis arrogated to himself the role of spokesman for scientific purity when, in fact, he was no purer than the others. What is of scientific interest, however, is the possibility of locating some objective meaning that informed his behaviour.

Innis received his intellectual formation during the early decades of the twentieth century when attention turned from moral to materialistic determinants of social behaviour.[18] This new emphasis characterized the writing of Canadian history in the years of Innis's maturity. William Wallace, Frank Underhill, and Donald Creighton all drew extensively from economic interpretations of American history to tell Canada's story. Like Innis,[19] they were not philosophically committed materialists, but they did let their attention dwell on the materialistic factors in historical development. A.R.M. Lower approached the problem of Canadian nationalism through the timber trade. Creighton approached Canadian imperialism through the commercial possibilities of a river basin.[20] Innis approached the rise and decline of empires about the North Atlantic through the fur trade, the fish trade, and the mining frontier. Collectively, they produced the idea that fur and the canoe had first united the northern half of North America, that wheat and the railway had reunited it, and that the federal government had been the political instrument of that reunification. Perhaps Innis was most responsible for this vision, but something very much like it had appeared in the writings of Edward Porritt and Gustavus Myers, as well as in certain regional complaints against the bias of federal power.[21] The difference was that these voices sought to expose the inequities and inefficiencies of Canadian development. After Innis had turned his attention away from Canadian history, other, explicitly neoclassical scholars approached Canadian development as an optimal response to well-understood opportunities.[22] Innis's position was, then, distinguished because it seemed acceptable in part to both views. Canadian development had been a limited success.[23] The result was not substantively optimal. Still, Innis concluded, the country was viable. We might say it was a typical piece of Simonean "satisficing."

Although their careers overlapped in time, there is no evidence that Harold Innis and H.A. Simon were in any way aware of one another. The similarities in their research programs was a consequence of their common intellectual roots in American Institutionalism. Innis turned to history, Simon to empirical testing. Their research programs, however, complement and support one another, each putting the other in a different perspective.[24] When Innis's work is seen in the perspective of decision-making theory, subsequent rejection of the normative, neoclassical Staple Theory of Canadian development[25] appears as a justification of his emphasis on the role of the information environment in producing substantively non-optimal decisions. In the light of Simon's critique of methodologies that combine quantitative analysis with normative neoclassical theory, the apparent contradiction between, on the one hand, Innis's repeated downgrading of studies that he considered "non-scientific," and, on the other, his rejection of "statistics" and of positivism disappears.[26] Innis rejected contemporary methods of positivism. He rejected the abuse of statistics in normative studies. He was not opposed to empirical science, to quantification, or, indeed, to the goals of positivism itself.

INNIS'S CONTRIBUTION IN PERSPECTIVE

In the second and third chapters of *Reason in Human Affairs,* Herbert Simon speculates about the evolution of institutions. His discussion is based entirely on empirical tests of his "behavioral model of rationality." Nowhere does he use the history of institutions to illustrate or corroborate his model; neither does he use the model to explain long-run historical phenomena, though that suggests itself as a natural extension of his inquiry. Innis, whose interests ran in another direction, undertook that extension. Innis's focus was narrow, returning persistently to the effects of the physical characteristics of information systems on attention, perception, and the consequent organization of decisions. He made frequent comments on such things as the efficiency of techniques of warfare, the effects of mathematics on computational capacity, the roles of emotion, of multiple goals, and of ignorance and uncertainty in the rise and decline of institutional arrangements; but he always returned to stress the physical characteristics of information systems, that is, to what he called the bias of communications. His distinctive contribution was to suggest testable hypotheses with respect to this influence on the long-run evolution of decision-making organizations.

Innis described the historical path of less than substantively rational decisions. He described the forces that he thought important in controlling deviations from objective rationality and in shaping the consequent organization of social behaviour. In normative, neoclassical

theory, equilibrium is a fixed, conclusive termination of a substantively rational process, and that is all. Whether equilibrium occurs in particular historical conditions is a secondary concern, as is specification of the historical conditions under which the processes by which equilibrium is reached terminate. Innis recorded conditions that had caused deviations from substantive rationality and had frustrated the termination process. He called it the study of "economic pathology."[27] This research project was the common root connecting what has been called "the early" and the "later" Innis.[28] During the period when neo-Keynesian doctrines were the stuff of normal science in economics, when some basic elements in Keynes's analysis were pushed out of sight, Innis's preoccupation with these matters left him out of the mainstream of his discipline. However, with the advent of Rational Expectations theory and its insights into the conditions of objectively rational decisions, Innis's interest in the bias generating imperfections of the informational environment has regained relevance.

Commentators who have pointed to a relationship between the views of Innis and of the philosopher, George Grant,[29] have caught a glimpse of the Innisian project, but not of its definitive core elements. Innis did not share Grant's judgement that liberalism was morally vacuous. He was not a "Red Tory." He was an individualist, and a liberal in that sense, first, last, and always.[30] What Innis and Grant have in common is a perception of an informational environment in which it is possible for decisions to deviate from what is appropriate for institutional survival, that is, in which things can go wrong. Innis was not a philosopher. Paul Feyerabend subsequently developed a philosophy of science with which Innis would have been perfectly comfortable.[31] Like Simon and Innis, Feyerabend focuses on the limitations of reason in human affairs. Feyerabend's "methodological anarchy" has the same relation to Innis's work as Simon's empirical decision theory. It is a research program with a set of conclusions that complements and supports Innis's historical analysis.

The Feyerabendian perspective on Innis (or the Innisian perspective on Feyerabend) may need clarification. Consider Feyerabend's repeated assertion that there are no objective facts, that all facts are theory-laden. Consider also his argument that we cannot separate the subject of science from its observational instruments,[32] and immediately becomes evident that he was dealing with the bias of the media of communication, or the imperfections of the informational environment, however one wants to phrase it. Innis's reconstruction of the history of institutional arrangements turns on two factors. One, materialistic and Veblenesque, was the technical limits of the information media. In explaining the structure of decision-making in terms of available information and information-handling techniques, Innis reveals this Simonean element in his analysis.[33] The other was a moral or philosophical factor that Innis drew from his contemporaries in the Department of Classics at the University of Toronto, the interplay of reason and passion, of virtue and fate, in the informational environment.[34] While there are elements of this other awareness in Simon's work,[35] it is Feyerabend's understanding of the mere instrumentality of reason and its false pretentions to intellectual sovereignty that most closely suggests Innis's insight in this regard.[36]

INNIS'S SCIENTIFIC CONTRIBUTION

Innis's contribution was the formulation and preliminary historical corroboration of several "operationally viable" hypotheses about the role of the informational environment in the structure of decisions.[37] Despite his often turgid exposition and his lack of a normal scientific presentation, his repetitiveness and his tendency to build up masses of examples make it relatively easy to extract four of the more important of these hypotheses. They should not be characterized as "laws." There may be no "laws" in the science of the artificial. They are better viewed as "effects." That is, they can all be characterized by a shared formula: given certain definable characteristics in the informational environment, certain definable behaviour patterns (i.e., institutional arrangements or structures of decisions) have been and will be a consequence. These effects may be called the Accelerating Disequilibrium Effect, the Initial Disorientation Effect, the Reorientation Conflict Effect, and the Minerva's Owl Effect.

The Accelerating Disequilibrium Effect is a generalization drawn from Canadian historical development. It may be stated as follows: when there is a social pre-commitment in uncertainty to large expenditures on physical and institutional capital, the resulting structure of alternative, subsequent decisions does not include an objectively rational decision to liquidate. That is, some decisions include a structuring of the informational environment that precludes reversibility. There are decisions from which there is no going back.

Innis owed the Accelerating Disequilibrium Effect to J.M. Clark. Like Innis, Clark attempted to extend Veblen's "Non Euclidian Economics." In the spirit of Simon's concept of bounded rationality, both Clark and Innis set out to make economics scientific by including in its considerations the constraints of engineering technique.[38] Clark's work was the foundation of the modern "Accelerator Theory" of business cycles, the idea that, when any other sector experiences growth, the capital goods sector accelerates the pace of growth by responding at an even faster rate. Clark originally developed the idea to explain alternating booms and slumps in frontier towns. Seeing the effect as a recurring phenomenon in Canadian history, Innis took it a step further by using it to explain the frontier's apparent inability to accept a strategic, organized reversal of expansion.

Innis turned the accelerator phenomenon into a general account of the effects of "overhead costs" in shaping the Canadian economy.[39] Development in a modern industrial economy required relatively large, up-front investments.

Arrangements for the placement of the moneys and provision for the long period between investment and ultimate pay-off required considerable overhead in the form of social organization. The consequence was possible heavy losses, especially for the decision-making elite that would have to authorize rational liquidation in case of failure. In narrowly based frontier economies, because region-specific and industry-specific capital could not be reallocated, the prospects for associated labour were only slightly better. Faced with their own possible bankruptcy, the decision-making elite chose a less than objectively rational alternative: they reinforced the original decision to expand. Innis did not assert, like Simon, that unit monetary losses are more heavily weighted in preference functions than are unit monetary gains; he did not question the scientific basis of subjective, expected utility analysis. Innis as historian simply noted that "the economics of losses is not less significant than the economics of profits."[40]

In normative neoclassical economics it is assumed that market forces, in the long run, eliminate inefficient enterprise. Innis's point was that in certain circumstances, clearly documentable in the Canadian experience, something less than substantive efficiency is viable. Where there are industry- and region-specific activities involving significant private and social capital, and especially where there is a region-specific government with sufficient power,[41] the information environment will generate recurring decisions to repeat strategies that reinforce inefficiency. He did not think the Canadian case was unique. The Accelerating Disequilibrium Effect seemed to him to be evident in the experiences of the United States and most European countries in the late nineteenth and early twentieth centuries.[42] It is not difficult for anyone familiar with Canadian experience over the past ten years to think of evidence that would further corroborate the Effect. The histories of Dome Petroleum and the east coast fish processors are telling examples.

The Initial Disorientation and Reorientation Conflict Effects occur when the information environment undergoes fundamental restructuring as a result of a change in perception. According to Simon, who has established the empirical validity of the phenomenon,[43] the perceived identity of an object is dependent on the search procedures used in the recognition process. Search procedures, in turn, are dictated by the preconceptions of the searcher and by the sequence in which information is presented to him. Innis's point was that different media for presenting information are associated with different sequences of presentation and, consequently, different perceptions of objective reality. Preconceptions can be explained, at least in part, by the limitations of the various media used in earlier search exercises. These are the simple, basic elements of Innis's concept of the bias of an information environment. When fully elaborated, the concept is a very general notion, relating to certain specific media in much the way that Thomas Kuhn's notion of a scientific paradigm relates to the specific theory at its centre, by including the totality of the organization of the scientific community around the theory.[44]

Initially, however, Innis considered only the technical characteristics of the media in question. A change in media characteristics constitutes an external, unexpected disruption of the informational environment. Rational expectations become impossible as the informational basis of expectations suddenly reforms itself through a radical change in perception. The consequence is uncertainty, disorientation, confusion, and paralysis in decision-making processes. This is the Initial Disorientation Effect. In time, a new informational environment is built into new structures of decision-making in which a new priority of values obtains. Conflict then occurs between new organizations developing under the influence of the new media, and older, established institutions.

References to the Initial Disorientation Effect are scattered through a number of Innis's essays. Consider, for example, the three following observations:

> Instability of public opinion . . . follows the introduction of new inventions in communication.
>
> . . .
>
> Profound disturbances in Egyptian civilization . . . coincided with a shift in emphasis on stone as a medium of communication . . . to an emphasis on papyrus.
>
> The consequent maladjustments were evident in the boom of the Twenties and the depression, and were to an important extent a result of expansion of the press and of a new instrument of communication—the radio. Public opinion became less stable and instability became a prime weakness, serving as a forced draft in the expansion of the twenties, and exposed to collapse in the depression.[45]

It is best, however, not to multiply citations from Innis to show that there are testable hypotheses to be drawn from his work. His own presentation did not follow the canons and style of positive science, and his massing of overlapping examples tends often to confuse, rather than to focus, attention. For example, passages that describe the perceptual disorientation and instability caused by the advent of a new media of communication tend to run over into passages describing subsequent interest group conflict. Note, for example, Innis's statement that "The spread of writing contributed to the downfall of the Republic (of Rome) and the emergence of Empire."[46]

Following an initial change in communication technique, institutions, according to Innis, organize around the consequent new perception of reality to exploit its possibilities. This is an "operationally viable," or positivist, hypothesis for which he provides ample historical support. The development of mathematics in Babylonia led to the reorganization of business enterprise. The development of a non-pictoral alphabet in Ancient Greece led to the reorganization of city states into the Hellenic empire.

Organization of decision-making and the ranking of priorities varied with the use of papyrus, parchment, and the printing press.[47] In every case, except those in which perception and organization were dominated by primitive oral communication, some form of inter-group rivalry was a factor in the result. Innis was convinced by his reading of history that organizations retaining the imprint of oral communication had a superior ability to absorb new values without conflict. In the absence of an oral tradition, technological progress in communication had been and would continue to be accompanied by wasteful conflict in which the more efficient alternatives might not be the winners.[48]

In the context of empirical decision theory, the Reorientation Conflict Effect suggests experimentation with individual and group problem solving using different and changing means of communication. Innis did not take that approach, and no one else has tested his hypotheses. What Innis repeatedly did call for was some kind of balanced approach to the resolution of conflict between extremist views. He sought a greater degree of objectivity and adaptability in facing the perceptual consequences of changes in communication techniques, but he said nothing of what specific steps could be taken to meet this need.

Herbert Simon projected a "science of design,"[49] the subject of which would be the effects of changes in the bounds of reason on the organization of decisions. This was a first step in the direction suggested by Innis. Although he did not attempt it, Simon considered extending this "science of the artificial" to nations and multinational entities, that is, to the macroeconomic informational environment. By documenting a number of historical effects, Innis provided a beginning for the pursuit of Simon's project. The pieces fit. Simon's contribution led to a neoclassical elaboration of the economics of uncertainty and information,[50] the subject matter of Innis's work, though in a different paradigm.

Consideration of Innis's Minerva's Owl Effect[51] leads in the same direction. The Effect suggests that the elements of an organization may survive a change in communication technique, but also that they may not, and that those most necessary to the conservation and advancement of the organization may not be the survivors. More specifically, the Minerva's Owl Effect suggests the petrification of a creative contribution to the ends of an organization as the contribution passes from one medium of communication to another. What was vital and growing in one informational environment, rigidifies in another, monopolizing thought and preventing further growth along the same lines. What had been common and useful, rather than sacred and revered, flowers into classic form and ceases to develop. It becomes a dead thing, disfunctional from the point of view of its earlier existence. As Innis noted in this regard, "Freedom of the press as guaranteed by the Bill of Rights in the United States has become the great bulwark of monopolies of time."[52]

The Minerva's Owl Effect was, for Innis, the most personally disturbing of his hypotheses. In its light, he could see that the values and institutions that constituted the survival equipment of western civilization had appeared in different forms in technically different circumstances. These values and institutions had survived, but only under constant threat. As successive informational environments replaced one another, different elements in the basic values of western civilization blossomed in new forms and spread over the areas influenced by the relevant means of communication. Whether western civilization or, indeed, any civilization could survive these increasingly frequent jolts of technological change remained uncertain. Witnessing the disturbances of the Great Depression of the 1930s and of the subsequent total world war immediately after, it is not surprising that Innis was deeply pessimistic.

The Minerva's Owl Effect is related to the Reorientation Conflict Effect and, as such, could be readily tested in and refined in the context of empirical decision theory. A small group instructed in some written form to perform a co-operative task could be compared, with respect to its organizational behaviour, with another small group instructed by tape recorder to perform the same task. Alternatively, the same group could be instructed through different media to perform the same or a different task, with internal conflict being the object of observation. In this light, it is now difficult to understand why the media buffs surrounding McLuhan did not undertake such simple, positivist procedures.

THE REASSESSMENT

Innis's insights into the nature and importance of macro informational environments constitute a major contribution. He specified a set of testable, informational environment effects. His attempt to validate these hypotheses by historical reconstruction was a success. Of course, he made mistakes in detail. He tended to overgeneralize. He occasionally thought his generalizations to be validated in very dubious cases. However, quite apart from his position as a "conservative" at the beginning of a "liberal" era, and without reference to his position in the social science community in Canada, he made a recognizable scientific contribution on which others may build. Indeed, practitioners of the science of administrative design and, to some extent, those developing the economics of information, are proceeding toward the end product designated by him. Aspects of the "New Institutional Economics" in the Coase-Williamson tradition that are closely related to Herbert Simon's work[53] are also related to elements of Innis's thought. Still, no one has taken up the specific task toward which Innis directed attention, that of designing organizational procedures that would routinize adaptation to changes in media of communication.

On another level, in the new perspective in which Innis now appears, two additional tasks have become evident. First, with respect to social science in general, there is the need to work out a methodology for the science of design that can include history, empirical decision theory, and neoclassical economic analysis in mutually supporting roles, thus reducing the conflict that grows out of different disciplinary perceptions. Secondly, with respect to Canadian economic history, the elaboration of Canadian development as a series of satisficing decisions under the influence of biased informational environments, a study begun by Innis, has yet to be completed.

NOTES

[1] R.F. Neill, *A New Theory of Value: The Canadian Economics of H.A. Innis* (Toronto: University of Toronto Press, 1972).

[2] The work of H.A. Simon is well known. Nonetheless, I make special reference to his work on the significance of paths of information search (see *Models of Thought* [New Haven: Yale University Press, 1975], pp. 355-62) and of preoriented attention ("Rationality in Psychology and Business," *Journal of Business* 59 [1986], pp. 209-24).

[3] Neill, *A New Theory,* p. 40.

[4] H.A. Innis, *The Bias of Communication* (Toronto: University of Toronto Press, 1951), p. vii.

[5] J.M. Keynes, *The General Theory of Employment Interest and Money* (London: Macmillan, 1936), Chapter 5, pp. 95-97, 148, 156, 203, 238.

[6] Neill, *A New Theory,* pp. 35-40; C. Berger, *The Writing of Canadian History* (Toronto: Oxford, 1976), p. 84; C.D.W. Goodwin, *Canadian Economic Thought* (Durham: Duke University Press, 1961), pp. 176-95.

[7] D. Creighton, "Harold Innis—An Appraisal," in W.H. Melody, L. Salter and P. Heyer, eds., *Culture, Communication and Dependency* (Norwood: ABLEX Publishing, 1981), pp. 13-25; E. Havelock, "Harold Innis: A Man of His Times, The Philosophic Historian," *E.T.C.* 38 (1981), pp. 141-68.

[8] Neill, *A New Theory,* pp. 37, 65.

[9] W.T. Easterbrook, "Innis and Economics," *Canadian Journal of Economics and Political Science* 19 (1953), pp. 291-303; M. Watkins, "The Innis Tradition in Canadian Political Economy," *Canadian Journal of Political and Social Theory* 6 (1982), pp. 12-33.

[10] W.T. Easterbrook, "The North American Pattern of Growth and Development—The Continental Context," ed. Ian Parker (unpublished, 1984).

[11] M. Watkins, "The Staple Theory Revisited," *Journal of Canadian Studies* 12, 5 (1977), pp. 83-95; W.A. Mackintosh, "Economic Factors in Canadian History," *Canadian Historical Review* 4 (1923), pp. 12-23.

[12] Neill, *A New Theory*, p. 37; H.A. Simon, *Reason In Human Affairs* (Stanford: California University Press, 1983), pp. 12-17.

[13] A. Shortt, "The History of Canadian Currency, Banking and Exchange: Lord Sydenham's Measures," *Journal of the Canadian Bankers' Association* 10 (1902), pp. 21-40.

[14] D. Drache, "Harold Innis and Canadian Capitalist Development," *Canadian Journal of Social and Political Theory* 6 (1982), pp. 35-39; Watkins, "Staple Theory Revisited."

[15] Havelock, "Harold Innis."

[16] Berger, pp. 85-111; S.D. Clark, "The Contribution of H.A. Innis to Canadian Scholarship," in Melody *et al.* pp. 27-35; Creighton, "Harold Innis"; G.S. Dunbar, "Harold Innis and Canadian Geography," *Canadian Geography* 29 (1985), pp. 159-64; Havelock, "Harold Innis"; and A.R.M. Lower, "Harold Innis as I Remember Him," *Journal of Canadian Studies* 20, 4 (1985-86), pp. 3-11.

[17] H.A. Innis, "Sub-Specie Temporis," *Canadian Journal of Economics and Political Science* 17 (1951), pp. 553-57.

[18] S.E.D. Shortt, *Search for an Ideal* (Toronto: University of Toronto Press, 1976); Berger, p. 100.

[19] Berger, pp. 55, 211; Neill, *A New Theory*, pp. 101, 17, 87.

[20] Berger, pp. 113-36; 236.

[21] A. Rotstein, "The Alchemy of Fur and Wheat," *Journal of Canadian Studies* 12, 5 (1977), pp. 6-31; G. Myers, *The History of Canadian Wealth* (Chicago: Charles H. Kerr, 1914); E. Porritt, *Sixty Years of Protection in Canada* (London: Macmillan, 1908); C. Martin, *The Natural Resources Question: The Historical Basis of Provincial Claims* (Winnipeg: King's Printer, 1920); E.R. Forbes, *The Maritime Rights Movement 1919-1927* (Montreal: McGill-Queen's University Press, 1977).

[22] A.W. Currie, *Canadian Economic Development* (Toronto: Nelson, 1943); D.C. North, "Location Theory and Regional Economic Growth," *Journal of Political Economy* 63 (1955), pp. 243-58; R.E. Caves, "Vent for Surplus Models of Trade and Growth," in J.D. Theberge, ed., *The Economics of Trade and Development* (New York: Wiley, 1968), pp. 211-29.

[23] Neill, *A New Theory*, pp. 66-67.

[24] *Ibid.*, pp. 24-34, 40; H.A. Simon, "Rational Decision Making in Business Organizations," *American Economic Review* 69 (1979), pp. 493-513, 499.

[25] K.J. Buckley, "The Role of Staples Industries in Canadian Economic Development," *Journal of Economic History* 19 (1985), pp. 439-52; P. George, "Rates of Return for Railway Investment and the Implications for Subsidization of the C.P.R.," *Canadian Journal of Economics* 1 (1968), pp. 740-62; E.J. Chambers and G.W. Bertram, "Urbanization and Manufacturing in Canada 1870-1890," *Canadian Political Science Association Conference on Statistics* (1964), pp. 225-58. Also, E.J. Chambers and D.J. Gordon, "Primary Products and Economic Growth: An Empirical Measurement," *Journal of Political Economy* 74 (1966), pp. 315-52; R.E. Caves, "Export-Led Growth and the New Economic History," in J.N. Bhagwati, ed., *Trade, Balance of Payments and Growth* (Amsterdam: North Holland, 1971), pp. 403-42.

[26] H.A. Simon, *Models of Bounded Rationality* (Cambridge: Yale University Press, 1982), pp. 503-06; Neill, *A New Theory*, p. 41; W. Westfall, "The Ambivalent Verdict: Harold Innis and Canadian History," in Melody *et al.*, pp. 37-51.

[27] Neill, *A New Theory*, pp. 64, 148.

[28] G. Patterson, "Harold Innis and the Writing of History," *Canadian Literature* 83 (1979), pp. 118-30; H.A. Innis, *Changing Concepts of Time* (Toronto: University of Toronto Press, 1952), p. iii.

[29] A. Kroker, *Technology and the Canadian Mind: Innis, Grant and McLuhan* (New York: St. Martin's Press, 1984); John Hutcheson, "Harold Innis and the Unity and Diversity of Canadian Federation," *Journal of Canadian Studies* 17, 4 (1982-83), pp. 57-73.

[30] Neill, *A New Theory*, p. 10.

[31] R.F. Neill, "Rethinking Canadian Political Economy," *Studies in Political Economy* 9 (1982), pp. 147-54.

[32] P.K. Feyerabend, *Against Method: Outline of an Anarchistic Theory of Knowledge* (London: N.L.B., 1975).

[33] Neill, "Rethinking," p. 97; Simon, *Models of Bounded Rationality*, pp. 56-57.

[34] W. Christian, "Harold Innis as Economist and Moralist," *Occasional Papers #2*, University of Guelph, 1981; R. Keast, "It Is Written—But I Say Unto You': Innis on Religion," *Journal of Canadian Studies* 20, 4 (1985-86), pp. 12-25; A.J. Watson, "Harold Innis and Classical Scholarship," *Journal of Canadian Studies* 12, 5 (1977), pp. 45-61.

[35] Simon, "Rational Decision Making," pp. 29-38.

[36] P.K. Feyerabend, "Science, the Myth and its Role in Society," *Inquiry* 18 (1975), pp. 167-81; H.A. Innis, "Economic Nationalism," *Papers and Proceedings of the Canadian Political Science Association for 1934* (1934), pp. 17-31; Innis, "Economics for Demos," *University of Toronto Quarterly* 3 (1934), pp. 389-95; Innis, "The Role of Intelligence: Some Further Notes," *Canadian*

Journal of Economics and Political Science 1 (1935), pp. 280-87.

[37] P. Samuelson, *Foundations of Economic Analysis* (Cambridge: Harvard University Press, 1975).

[38] Neill, *A New Theory,* pp. 32-33.

[39] I.M. Spry, "Overhead Costs, Rigidities of Production Capacity and the Price System," in Melody *et al.,* pp. 155-66; H.A. Innis, *Essays in Canadian Economic History* (Toronto: University of Toronto Press, 1956), pp. 141-65.

[40] Simon, *Reason in Human Affairs,* pp. 12-17; Simon, "Rational Decision Making," pp. 493-513, 506; Innis, *Essays in Canadian Economic History,* p. 272.

[41] Neill, *A New Theory,* pp. 66-70, 146-49; H.A. Innis, "Government Ownership in Canada," *Schriften des Vereins fur Sozial-politick* 176 (1931), pp. 241-79.

[42] H.A. Innis, "The Decline in the Efficiency of Instruments Essential in Equilibrium," *American Economic Review* 42 (1953), pp. 16-22; Innis, *Essays in Canadian Economic History,* p. 78.

[43] Simon, *Models of Thought,* pp. 292-305, 353-62.

[44] T.S. Kuhn, *The Structure of Scientific Revolutions* (Chicago: University of Chicago Press, 1970).

[45] H.A. Innis, *Empire and Communications* (Clarendon: Oxford University Press, 1950), pp. iv, 17; Innis, *Changing Concepts,* pp. 102-03.

[46] Innis, *Empire and Communications,* p. 121.

[47] *Ibid.,* pp. 40, 98-99, 140ff, 173ff.

[48] *Ibid.,* p. 41; Innis, *Bias of Communication,* pp. 92-93.

[49] H.A. Simon, *The Science of the Artificial* (Cambridge: M.I.T. Press, 1969).

[50] K. Arrow, *The Economics of Information. Vol. 3: Collected Papers of Kenneth Arrow* (Cambridge: Belknap Press of Harvard University Press, 1984).

[51] Innis, *Bias of Communication,* pp. 3-52.

[52] Innis, *Changing Concepts,* p. 108.

[53] Simon, *Models of Bounded Rationality,* pp. 480, 487.

FURTHER READING

Biography

Creighton, Donald. *Harold Adams Innis: Portrait of a Scholar.* Toronto: University of Toronto Press, 1957, 146 p.
> The definitive Innis biography, written by an associate who conducted extensive interviews with Mary Quayle Innis and others close to Innis himself.

Havelock, Eric A. "Harold Innis: A Man of His Times." *Et cetera* 38, No. 3 (Fall 1981): 242-54.
> A personal reminiscence of Innis by a colleague, with emphasis on the controversial Underhill affair.

Innis, Harold Adams. *The Idea File of Harold Adams Innis,* introduced and edited by William Christian. Toronto: University of Toronto Press, 1980, 287 p.
> A wide-ranging collection of Innis's notes, observations, and annotations which offers a key to his thought processes and to the breadth of his interests.

Lower, Arthur. "Harold Innis As I Remember Him." *Journal of Canadian Studies* 20, No. 4 (Winter 1985/86): 3-11.
> Recollections of Innis by a friend and colleague, along with an assessment of his stature as a scholar and an analysis "of what made Innis 'tick'."

Criticism

Comor, Edward. "Harold Innis's Dialectical Triad." *Journal of Canadian Studies* 29, No. 2 (Summer 1994): 111-27.
> An examination of Innis's seldom-understood dialectic of "wealth-knowledge-force," and an application of this to a study of late twentieth-century systems, including the "information economy."

Marvin, Carolyn. "Innis, McLuhan and Marx." *Visible Language* 20, No. 3 (Summer 1986): 355-59.
> A comparison of Innis's, McLuhan's, and Marx's views on the relation of media and political power which takes issue with aspects of Innis's work, particularly his inability to incorporate permutations of oral-gestural modes within his categories of spatial and temporal bias.

Neil, Robin. *A New Theory of Value: The Canadian Economics of Harold Adams Innis.* Toronto: University of Toronto Press, 1972, 159 p.
> A study of Innis's economic thought which its author offers as a companion piece to the biographical material in D.G. Creighton's *Harold Adams Innis: Portrait of a Scholar.*

Parkman, F. Review of *Select Documents in Canadian Economic History, 1497-1783,* edited by H.A. Innis. *The New England Quarterly* III, No. IV (October 1930): 775.
> A mixed review which praises the volume's first half

for its insights on the history of French and English fisheries over three centuries, but faults the latter half for straying far from its ostensible subject, the fur trade.

Stevenson, Garth. Review of *The Idea File of Harold Adams Innis,* edited by William Christian. *Canadian Historical Review* LXI, No. 4 (December 1980): 549-50.
    A positive review which nonetheless pronounces *The Idea File* of interest chiefly to Innis scholars and not to students of Canadian history as a whole.

The following source published by Gale Research contains further information on Innis's life and works: *Dictionary of Literary Biography,* Vol. 88

Twentieth-Century
Literary Criticism

Cumulative Indexes
Volumes 1-77

How to Use This Index

See also CA 57-60; CANR 13, 44; DLB 171

Angelou, Maya 1928-**CLC 12, 35, 64, 77; BLC; DA; DAB; DAC; DAM MST, MULT, POET, POP; WLCS**
See also AAYA 7, 20; BW 2; CA 65-68; CANR 19, 42; DLB 38; MTCW; SATA 49

Anna Comnena 1083-1153 .... **CMLC 25**

Annensky, Innokenty (Fyodorovich) 1856-1909 **TCLC 14**
See also CA 110; 155

Annunzio, Gabriele d'
See D'Annunzio, Gabriele

Anodos
See Coleridge, Mary E(lizabeth)

Anon, Charles Robert
See Pessoa, Fernando (Antonio Nogueira)

Anouilh, Jean (Marie Lucien Pierre) 1910-1987 **CLC 1, 3, 8, 13, 40, 50; DAM DRAM; DC 8**
See also CA 17-20R; 123; CANR 32; MTCW

Anthony, Florence
See Ai

Anthony, John
See Ciardi, John (Anthony)

Anthony, Peter
See Shaffer, Anthony (Joshua); Shaffer, Peter (Levin)

Anthony, Piers 1934- .... **CLC 35; DAM POP**
See also AAYA 11; CA 21-24R; CANR 28, 56; DLB 8; MTCW; SAAS 22; SATA 84

Antoine, Marc
See Proust, (Valentin-Louis-George-Eugene-) Marcel

Antoninus, Brother
See Everson, William (Oliver)

Antonioni, Michelangelo 1912- .... **CLC 20**
See also CA 73-76; CANR 45

Antschel, Paul 1920-1970
See Celan, Paul
See also CA 85-88; CANR 33, 61; MTCW

Anwar, Chairil 1922-1949 .... **TCLC 22**
See also CA 121

Apollinaire, Guillaume 1880-1918**TCLC 3, 8, 51; DAM POET; PC 7**
See also Kostrowitzki, Wilhelm Apollinaris de
See also CA 152

Appelfeld, Aharon 1932- .... **CLC 23, 47**
See also CA 112; 133

Apple, Max (Isaac) 1941- .... **CLC 9, 33**
See also CA 81-84; CANR 19, 54; DLB 130

Appleman, Philip (Dean) 1926- .... **CLC 51**
See also CA 13-16R; CAAS 18; CANR 6, 29, 56

Appleton, Lawrence
See Lovecraft, H(oward) P(hillips)

Apteryx
See Eliot, T(homas) S(tearns)

Apuleius, (Lucius Madaurensis) 125(?)-175(?) **CMLC 1**

Aquin, Hubert 1929-1977 .... **CLC 15**
See also CA 105; DLB 53

Aragon, Louis 1897-1982 .. **CLC 3, 22; DAM NOV, POET**
See also CA 69-72; 108; CANR 28; DLB 72; MTCW

Arany, Janos 1817-1882 .... **NCLC 34**

Arbuthnot, John 1667-1735 .... **LC 1**
See also DLB 101

Archer, Herbert Winslow
See Mencken, H(enry) L(ouis)

Archer, Jeffrey (Howard) 1940- ..... **CLC 28; DAM POP**
See also AAYA 16; BEST 89:3; CA 77-80;

CANR 22, 52; INT CANR-22

Archer, Jules 1915- .... **CLC 12**
See also CA 9-12R; CANR 6; SAAS 5; SATA 4, 85

Archer, Lee
See Ellison, Harlan (Jay)

Arden, John 1930-**CLC 6, 13, 15; DAM DRAM**
See also CA 13-16R; CAAS 4; CANR 31; DLB 13; MTCW

Arenas, Reinaldo 1943-1990 . **CLC 41; DAM MULT; HLC**
See also CA 124; 128; 133; DLB 145; HW

Arendt, Hannah 1906-1975 .... **CLC 66, 98**
See also CA 17-20R; 61-64; CANR 26, 60; MTCW

Aretino, Pietro 1492-1556 .... **LC 12**

Arghezi, Tudor .... **CLC 80**
See also Theodorescu, Ion N.

Arguedas, Jose Maria 1911-1969 **CLC 10, 18**
See also CA 89-92; DLB 113; HW

Argueta, Manlio 1936- .... **CLC 31**
See also CA 131; DLB 145; HW

Ariosto, Ludovico 1474-1533 .... **LC 6**

Aristides
See Epstein, Joseph

Aristophanes 450B.C.-385B.C.**CMLC 4; DA; DAB; DAC; DAM DRAM, MST; DC 2; WLCS**
See also DLB 176

Arlt, Roberto (Godofredo Christophersen) 1900-1942**TCLC 29; DAM MULT; HLC**
See also CA 123; 131; HW

Armah, Ayi Kwei 1939-**CLC 5, 33; BLC; DAM MULT, POET**
See also BW 1; CA 61-64; CANR 21, 64; DLB 117; MTCW

Armatrading, Joan 1950- .... **CLC 17**
See also CA 114

Arnette, Robert
See Silverberg, Robert

Arnim, Achim von (Ludwig Joachim von Arnim) 1781-1831 ...... **NCLC 5; SSC 29**
See also DLB 90

Arnim, Bettina von 1785-1859 .... **NCLC 38**
See also DLB 90

Arnold, Matthew 1822-1888**NCLC 6, 29; DA; DAB; DAC; DAM MST, POET; PC 5; WLC**
See also CDBLB 1832-1890; DLB 32, 57

Arnold, Thomas 1795-1842 .... **NCLC 18**
See also DLB 55

Arnow, Harriette (Louisa) Simpson 1908-1986 **CLC 2, 7, 18**
See also CA 9-12R; 118; CANR 14; DLB 6; MTCW; SATA 42; SATA-Obit 47

Arp, Hans
See Arp, Jean

Arp, Jean 1887-1966 .... **CLC 5**
See also CA 81-84; 25-28R; CANR 42

Arrabal
See Arrabal, Fernando

Arrabal, Fernando 1932- .... **CLC 2, 9, 18, 58**
See also CA 9-12R; CANR 15

Arrick, Fran .... **CLC 30**
See also Gaberman, Judie Angell

Artaud, Antonin (Marie Joseph) 1896-1948 **TCLC 3, 36; DAM DRAM**
See also CA 104; 149

Arthur, Ruth M(abel) 1905-1979 ...... **CLC 12**
See also CA 9-12R; 85-88; CANR 4; SATA 7, 26

Artsybashev, Mikhail (Petrovich) 1878-1927 **TCLC 31**

Arundel, Honor (Morfydd) 1919-1973**CLC 17**
See also CA 21-22; 41-44R; CAP 2; CLR 35; SATA 4; SATA-Obit 24

Arzner, Dorothy 1897-1979 .... **CLC 98**

Asch, Sholem 1880-1957 .... **TCLC 3**
See also CA 105

Ash, Shalom
See Asch, Sholem

Ashbery, John (Lawrence) 1927-**CLC 2, 3, 4, 6, 9, 13, 15, 25, 41, 77; DAM POET**
See also CA 5-8R; CANR 9, 37; DLB 5, 165; DLBY 81; INT CANR-9; MTCW

Ashdown, Clifford
See Freeman, R(ichard) Austin

Ashe, Gordon
See Creasey, John

Ashton-Warner, Sylvia (Constance) 1908-1984 **CLC 19**
See also CA 69-72; 112; CANR 29; MTCW

Asimov, Isaac 1920-1992 **CLC 1, 3, 9, 19, 26, 76, 92; DAM POP**
See also AAYA 13; BEST 90:2; CA 1-4R; 137; CANR 2, 19, 36, 60; CLR 12; DLB 8; DLBY 92; INT CANR-19; JRDA; MAICYA; MTCW; SATA 1, 26, 74

Assis, Joaquim Maria Machado de
See Machado de Assis, Joaquim Maria

Astley, Thea (Beatrice May) 1925- ... **CLC 41**
See also CA 65-68; CANR 11, 43

Aston, James
See White, T(erence) H(anbury)

Asturias, Miguel Angel 1899-1974 **CLC 3, 8, 13; DAM MULT, NOV; HLC**
See also CA 25-28; 49-52; CANR 32; CAP 2; DLB 113; HW; MTCW

Atares, Carlos Saura
See Saura (Atares), Carlos

Atheling, William
See Pound, Ezra (Weston Loomis)

Atheling, William, Jr.
See Blish, James (Benjamin)

Atherton, Gertrude (Franklin Horn) 1857-1948 **TCLC 2**
See also CA 104; 155; DLB 9, 78, 186

Atherton, Lucius
See Masters, Edgar Lee

Atkins, Jack
See Harris, Mark

Atkinson, Kate .... **CLC 99**

Attaway, William (Alexander) 1911-1986 **CLC 92; BLC; DAM MULT**
See also BW 2; CA 143; DLB 76

Atticus
See Fleming, Ian (Lancaster)

Atwood, Margaret (Eleanor) 1939-**CLC 2, 3, 4, 8, 13, 15, 25, 44, 84; DA; DAB; DAC; DAM MST, NOV, POET; PC 8; SSC 2; WLC**
See also AAYA 12; BEST 89:2; CA 49-52; CANR 3, 24, 33, 59; DLB 53; INT CANR-24; MTCW; SATA 50

Aubigny, Pierre d'
See Mencken, H(enry) L(ouis)

Aubin, Penelope 1685-1731(?) .... **LC 9**
See also DLB 39

Auchincloss, Louis (Stanton) 1917-**CLC 4, 6, 9, 18, 45; DAM NOV; SSC 22**
See also CA 1-4R; CANR 6, 29, 55; DLB 2; DLBY 80; INT CANR-29; MTCW

Auden, W(ystan) H(ugh) 1907-1973**CLC 1, 2, 3, 4, 6, 9, 11, 14, 43; DA; DAB; DAC; DAM DRAM, MST, POET; PC 1; WLC**
See also AAYA 18; CA 9-12R; 45-48; CANR

5, 61; CDBLB 1914-1945; DLB 10, 20;
MTCW
Audiberti, Jacques 1900-1965 **CLC 38; DAM
DRAM**
See also CA 25-28R
Audubon, John James 1785-1851 .. **NCLC 47**
Auel, Jean M(arie) 1936- **CLC 31, 107; DAM
POP**
See also AAYA 7; BEST 90:4; CA 103; CANR
21, 64; INT CANR-21; SATA 91
Auerbach, Erich 1892-1957 .... **TCLC 43**
See also CA 118; 155
Augier, Emile 1820-1889 .... **NCLC 31**
August, John
See De Voto, Bernard (Augustine)
Augustine, St. 354-430 .... **CMLC 6; DAB**
Aurelius
See Bourne, Randolph S(illiman)
Aurobindo, Sri 1872-1950 .... **TCLC 63**
Austen, Jane 1775-1817 **NCLC 1, 13, 19, 33,
51; DA; DAB; DAC; DAM MST, NOV;
WLC**
See also AAYA 19; CDBLB 1789-1832; DLB
116
Auster, Paul 1947- .... **CLC 47**
See also CA 69-72; CANR 23, 52
Austin, Frank
See Faust, Frederick (Schiller)
Austin, Mary (Hunter) 1868-1934 . **TCLC 25**
See also CA 109; DLB 9, 78
Autran Dourado, Waldomiro
See Dourado, (Waldomiro Freitas) Autran
Averroes 1126-1198 .... **CMLC 7**
See also DLB 115
Avicenna 980-1037 .... **CMLC 16**
See also DLB 115
Avison, Margaret 1918- **CLC 2, 4, 97; DAC;
DAM POET**
See also CA 17-20R; DLB 53; MTCW
Axton, David
See Koontz, Dean R(ay)
Ayckbourn, Alan 1939- **CLC 5, 8, 18, 33, 74;
DAB; DAM DRAM**
See also CA 21-24R; CANR 31, 59; DLB 13;
MTCW
Aydy, Catherine
See Tennant, Emma (Christina)
Ayme, Marcel (Andre) 1902-1967 .... **CLC 11**
See also CA 89-92; CLR 25; DLB 72; SATA 91
Ayrton, Michael 1921-1975 .... **CLC 7**
See also CA 5-8R; 61-64; CANR 9, 21
Azorin .... **CLC 11**
See also Martinez Ruiz, Jose
Azuela, Mariano 1873-1952 . **TCLC 3; DAM
MULT; HLC**
See also CA 104; 131; HW; MTCW
Baastad, Babbis Friis
See Friis-Baastad, Babbis Ellinor
Bab
See Gilbert, W(illiam) S(chwenck)
Babbis, Eleanor
See Friis-Baastad, Babbis Ellinor
Babel, Isaac
See Babel, Isaak (Emmanuilovich)
Babel, Isaak (Emmanuilovich) 1894-1941(?)
TCLC 2, 13; SSC 16
See also CA 104; 155
Babits, Mihaly 1883-1941 .... **TCLC 14**
See also CA 114
Babur 1483-1530 .... **LC 18**
Bacchelli, Riccardo 1891-1985 .... **CLC 19**
See also CA 29-32R; 117
Bach, Richard (David) 1936- **CLC 14; DAM**

NOV, POP
See also AITN 1; BEST 89:2; CA 9-12R; CANR
18; MTCW; SATA 13
Bachman, Richard
See King, Stephen (Edwin)
Bachmann, Ingeborg 1926-1973 .... **CLC 69**
See also CA 93-96; 45-48; DLB 85
Bacon, Francis 1561-1626 .... **LC 18, 32**
See also CDBLB Before 1660; DLB 151
Bacon, Roger 1214(?)-1292 .... **CMLC 14**
See also DLB 115
Bacovia, George .... **TCLC 24**
See also Vasiliu, Gheorghe
Badanes, Jerome 1937- .... **CLC 59**
Bagehot, Walter 1826-1877 .... **NCLC 10**
See also DLB 55
Bagnold, Enid 1889-1981 .... **CLC 25; DAM
DRAM**
See also CA 5-8R; 103; CANR 5, 40; DLB 13,
160; MAICYA; SATA 1, 25
Bagritsky, Eduard 1895-1934 .... **TCLC 60**
Bagrjana, Elisaveta
See Belcheva, Elisaveta
Bagryana, Elisaveta .... **CLC 10**
See also Belcheva, Elisaveta
See also DLB 147
Bailey, Paul 1937- .... **CLC 45**
See also CA 21-24R; CANR 16, 62; DLB 14
Baillie, Joanna 1762-1851 .... **NCLC 2**
See also DLB 93
Bainbridge, Beryl (Margaret) 1933- **CLC 4, 5,
8, 10, 14, 18, 22, 62; DAM NOV**
See also CA 21-24R; CANR 24, 55; DLB 14;
MTCW
Baker, Elliott 1922- .... **CLC 8**
See also CA 45-48; CANR 2, 63
Baker, Jean H. .... **TCLC 3, 10**
See also Russell, George William
Baker, Nicholson 1957- **CLC 61; DAM POP**
See also CA 135; CANR 63
Baker, Ray Stannard 1870-1946 .... **TCLC 47**
See also CA 118
Baker, Russell (Wayne) 1925- .... **CLC 31**
See also BEST 89:4; CA 57-60; CANR 11, 41,
59; MTCW
Bakhtin, M.
See Bakhtin, Mikhail Mikhailovich
Bakhtin, M. M.
See Bakhtin, Mikhail Mikhailovich
Bakhtin, Mikhail
See Bakhtin, Mikhail Mikhailovich
Bakhtin, Mikhail Mikhailovich 1895-1975
CLC 83
See also CA 128; 113
Bakshi, Ralph 1938(?)- .... **CLC 26**
See also CA 112; 138
Bakunin, Mikhail (Alexandrovich) 1814-1876
NCLC 25, 58
Baldwin, James (Arthur) 1924-1987 **CLC 1, 2,
3, 4, 5, 8, 13, 15, 17, 42, 50, 67, 90; BLC;
DA; DAB; DAC; DAM MST, MULT, NOV,
POP; DC 1; SSC 10; WLC**
See also AAYA 4; BW 1; CA 1-4R; 124; CABS
1; CANR 3, 24; CDALB 1941-1968; DLB
2, 7, 33; DLBY 87; MTCW; SATA 9; SATA-
Obit 54
Ballard, J(ames) G(raham) 1930- **CLC 3, 6, 14,
36; DAM NOV, POP; SSC 1**
See also AAYA 3; CA 5-8R; CANR 15, 39; DLB
14; MTCW; SATA 93
Balmont, Konstantin (Dmitriyevich) 1867-1943
TCLC 11
See also CA 109; 155

Balzac, Honore de 1799-1850 **NCLC 5, 35, 53;
DA; DAB; DAC; DAM MST, NOV; SSC
5; WLC**
See also DLB 119
Bambara, Toni Cade 1939-1995 **CLC 19, 88;
BLC; DA; DAC; DAM MST, MULT;
WLCS**
See also AAYA 5; BW 2; CA 29-32R; 150;
CANR 24, 49; DLB 38; MTCW
Bamdad, A.
See Shamlu, Ahmad
Banat, D. R.
See Bradbury, Ray (Douglas)
Bancroft, Laura
See Baum, L(yman) Frank
Banim, John 1798-1842 .... **NCLC 13**
See also DLB 116, 158, 159
Banim, Michael 1796-1874 .... **NCLC 13**
See also DLB 158, 159
Banjo, The
See Paterson, A(ndrew) B(arton)
Banks, Iain
See Banks, Iain M(enzies)
Banks, Iain M(enzies) 1954- .... **CLC 34**
See also CA 123; 128; CANR 61; INT 128
Banks, Lynne Reid .... **CLC 23**
See also Reid Banks, Lynne
See also AAYA 6
Banks, Russell 1940- .... **CLC 37, 72**
See also CA 65-68; CAAS 15; CANR 19, 52;
DLB 130
Banville, John 1945- .... **CLC 46**
See also CA 117; 128; DLB 14; INT 128
Banville, Theodore (Faullain) de 1832-1891
NCLC 9
Baraka, Amiri 1934- **CLC 1, 2, 3, 5, 10, 14, 33;
BLC; DA; DAC; DAM MST, MULT,
POET, POP; DC 6; PC 4; WLCS**
See also Jones, LeRoi
See also BW 2; CA 21-24R; CABS 3; CANR
27, 38, 61; CDALB 1941-1968; DLB 5, 7,
16, 38; DLBD 8; MTCW
Barbauld, Anna Laetitia 1743-1825 **NCLC 50**
See also DLB 107, 109, 142, 158
Barbellion, W. N. P. .... **TCLC 24**
See also Cummings, Bruce F(rederick)
Barbera, Jack (Vincent) 1945- .... **CLC 44**
See also CA 110; CANR 45
Barbey d'Aurevilly, Jules Amedee 1808-1889
NCLC 1; SSC 17
See also DLB 119
Barbusse, Henri 1873-1935 .... **TCLC 5**
See also CA 105; 154; DLB 65
Barclay, Bill
See Moorcock, Michael (John)
Barclay, William Ewert
See Moorcock, Michael (John)
Barea, Arturo 1897-1957 .... **TCLC 14**
See also CA 111
Barfoot, Joan 1946- .... **CLC 18**
See also CA 105
Baring, Maurice 1874-1945 .... **TCLC 8**
See also CA 105; DLB 34
Barker, Clive 1952- .... **CLC 52; DAM POP**
See also AAYA 10; BEST 90:3; CA 121; 129;
INT 129; MTCW
Barker, George Granville 1913-1991 **CLC 8,
48; DAM POET**
See also CA 9-12R; 135; CANR 7, 38; DLB
20; MTCW
Barker, Harley Granville
See Granville-Barker, Harley
See also DLB 10

Barker, Howard 1946- .... **CLC 37**
See also CA 102; DLB 13
Barker, Pat(ricia) 1943- .... **CLC 32, 94**
See also CA 117; 122; CANR 50; INT 122
Barlow, Joel 1754-1812 .... **NCLC 23**
See also DLB 37
Barnard, Mary (Ethel) 1909- .... **CLC 48**
See also CA 21-22; CAP 2
Barnes, Djuna 1892-1982**CLC 3, 4, 8, 11, 29; SSC 3**
See also CA 9-12R; 107; CANR 16, 55; DLB 4, 9, 45; MTCW
Barnes, Julian (Patrick) 1946-**CLC 42; DAB**
See also CA 102; CANR 19, 54; DLBY 93
Barnes, Peter 1931- .... **CLC 5, 56**
See also CA 65-68; CAAS 12; CANR 33, 34, 64; DLB 13; MTCW
Baroja (y Nessi), Pio 1872-1956**TCLC 8; HLC**
See also CA 104
Baron, David
See Pinter, Harold
Baron Corvo
See Rolfe, Frederick (William Serafino Austin Lewis Mary)
Barondess, Sue K(aufman) 1926-1977 **CLC 8**
See also Kaufman, Sue
See also CA 1-4R; 69-72; CANR 1
Baron de Teive
See Pessoa, Fernando (Antonio Nogueira)
Barres, Maurice 1862-1923 .... **TCLC 47**
See also DLB 123
Barreto, Afonso Henrique de Lima
See Lima Barreto, Afonso Henrique de
Barrett, (Roger) Syd 1946- .... **CLC 35**
Barrett, William (Christopher) 1913-1992 **CLC 27**
See also CA 13-16R; 139; CANR 11; INT CANR-11
Barrie, J(ames) M(atthew) 1860-1937 **T C L C 2; DAB; DAM DRAM**
See also CA 104; 136; CDBLB 1890-1914; CLR 16; DLB 10, 141, 156; MAICYA; YABC 1
Barrington, Michael
See Moorcock, Michael (John)
Barrol, Grady
See Bograd, Larry
Barry, Mike
See Malzberg, Barry N(athaniel)
Barry, Philip 1896-1949 .... **TCLC 11**
See also CA 109; DLB 7
Bart, Andre Schwarz
See Schwarz-Bart, Andre
Barth, John (Simmons) 1930-**CLC 1, 2, 3, 5, 7, 9, 10, 14, 27, 51, 89; DAM NOV; SSC 10**
See also AITN 1, 2; CA 1-4R; CABS 1; CANR 5, 23, 49, 64; DLB 2; MTCW
Barthelme, Donald 1931-1989**CLC 1, 2, 3, 5, 6, 8, 13, 23, 46, 59; DAM NOV; SSC 2**
See also CA 21-24R; 129; CANR 20, 58; DLB 2; DLBY 80, 89; MTCW; SATA 7; SATA-Obit 62
Barthelme, Frederick 1943- .... **CLC 36**
See also CA 114; 122; DLBY 85; INT 122
Barthes, Roland (Gerard) 1915-1980**CLC 24, 83**
See also CA 130; 97-100; MTCW
Barzun, Jacques (Martin) 1907- .... **CLC 51**
See also CA 61-64; CANR 22
Bashevis, Isaac
See Singer, Isaac Bashevis
Bashkirtseff, Marie 1859-1884 ...... **NCLC 27**
Basho

See Matsuo Basho
Bass, Kingsley B., Jr.
See Bullins, Ed
Bass, Rick 1958- .... **CLC 79**
See also CA 126; CANR 53
Bassani, Giorgio 1916- .... **CLC 9**
See also CA 65-68; CANR 33; DLB 128, 177; MTCW
Bastos, Augusto (Antonio) Roa
See Roa Bastos, Augusto (Antonio)
Bataille, Georges 1897-1962 .... **CLC 29**
See also CA 101; 89-92
Bates, H(erbert) E(rnest) 1905-1974**CLC 46; DAB; DAM POP; SSC 10**
See also CA 93-96; 45-48; CANR 34; DLB 162; MTCW
Bauchart
See Camus, Albert
Baudelaire, Charles 1821-1867 .**NCLC 6, 29, 55; DA; DAB; DAC; DAM MST, POET; PC 1; SSC 18; WLC**
Baudrillard, Jean 1929- .... **CLC 60**
Baum, L(yman) Frank 1856-1919 ... **TCLC 7**
See also CA 108; 133; CLR 15; DLB 22; JRDA; MAICYA; MTCW; SATA 18
Baum, Louis F.
See Baum, L(yman) Frank
Baumbach, Jonathan 1933- .... **CLC 6, 23**
See also CA 13-16R; CAAS 5; CANR 12; DLBY 80; INT CANR-12; MTCW
Bausch, Richard (Carl) 1945- .... **CLC 51**
See also CA 101; CAAS 14; CANR 43, 61; DLB 130
Baxter, Charles (Morley) 1947- **CLC 45, 78; DAM POP**
See also CA 57-60; CANR 40, 64; DLB 130
Baxter, George Owen
See Faust, Frederick (Schiller)
Baxter, James K(eir) 1926-1972 .... **CLC 14**
See also CA 77-80
Baxter, John
See Hunt, E(verette) Howard, (Jr.)
Bayer, Sylvia
See Glassco, John
Baynton, Barbara 1857-1929 .... **TCLC 57**
Beagle, Peter S(oyer) 1939- .... **CLC 7, 104**
See also CA 9-12R; CANR 4, 51; DLBY 80; INT CANR-4; SATA 60
Bean, Normal
See Burroughs, Edgar Rice
Beard, Charles A(ustin) 1874-1948 **TCLC 15**
See also CA 115; DLB 17; SATA 18
Beardsley, Aubrey 1872-1898 .... **NCLC 6**
Beattie, Ann 1947-**CLC 8, 13, 18, 40, 63; DAM NOV, POP; SSC 11**
See also BEST 90:2; CA 81-84; CANR 53; DLBY 82; MTCW
Beattie, James 1735-1803 .... **NCLC 25**
See also DLB 109
Beauchamp, Kathleen Mansfield 1888-1923
See Mansfield, Katherine
See also CA 104; 134; DA; DAC; DAM MST
Beaumarchais, Pierre-Augustin Caron de 1732-1799 .... **DC 4**
See also DAM DRAM
Beaumont, Francis 1584(?)-1616**LC 33; DC 6**
See also CDBLB Before 1660; DLB 58, 121
Beauvoir, Simone (Lucie Ernestine Marie Bertrand) de 1908-1986**CLC 1, 2, 4, 8, 14, 31, 44, 50, 71; DA; DAB; DAC; DAM MST, NOV; WLC**
See also CA 9-12R; 118; CANR 28, 61; DLB 72; DLBY 86; MTCW

Becker, Carl (Lotus) 1873-1945 ..... **TCLC 63**
See also CA 157; DLB 17
Becker, Jurek 1937-1997 .... **CLC 7, 19**
See also CA 85-88; 157; CANR 60; DLB 75
Becker, Walter 1950- .... **CLC 26**
Beckett, Samuel (Barclay) 1906-1989 **CLC 1, 2, 3, 4, 6, 9, 10, 11, 14, 18, 29, 57, 59, 83; DA; DAB; DAC; DAM DRAM, MST, NOV; SSC 16; WLC**
See also CA 5-8R; 130; CANR 33, 61; CDBLB 1945-1960; DLB 13, 15; DLBY 90; MTCW
Beckford, William 1760-1844 .... **NCLC 16**
See also DLB 39
Beckman, Gunnel 1910- .... **CLC 26**
See also CA 33-36R; CANR 15; CLR 25; MAICYA; SAAS 9; SATA 6
Becque, Henri 1837-1899 .... **NCLC 3**
Beddoes, Thomas Lovell 1803-1849 **NCLC 3**
See also DLB 96
Bede c. 673-735 .... **CMLC 20**
See also DLB 146
Bedford, Donald F.
See Fearing, Kenneth (Flexner)
Beecher, Catharine Esther 1800-1878 **N C L C 30**
See also DLB 1
Beecher, John 1904-1980 .... **CLC 6**
See also AITN 1; CA 5-8R; 105; CANR 8
Beer, Johann 1655-1700 .... **LC 5**
See also DLB 168
Beer, Patricia 1924- .... **CLC 58**
See also CA 61-64; CANR 13, 46; DLB 40
Beerbohm, Max
See Beerbohm, (Henry) Max(imilian)
Beerbohm, (Henry) Max(imilian) 1872-1956 **TCLC 1, 24**
See also CA 104; 154; DLB 34, 100
Beer-Hofmann, Richard 1866-1945**TCLC 60**
See also CA 160; DLB 81
Begiebing, Robert J(ohn) 1946- .... **CLC 70**
See also CA 122; CANR 40
Behan, Brendan 1923-1964 **CLC 1, 8, 11, 15, 79; DAM DRAM**
See also CA 73-76; CANR 33; CDBLB 1945-1960; DLB 13; MTCW
Behn, Aphra 1640(?)-1689**LC 1, 30; DA; DAB; DAC; DAM DRAM, MST, NOV, POET; DC 4; PC 13; WLC**
See also DLB 39, 80, 131
Behrman, S(amuel) N(athaniel) 1893-1973 **CLC 40**
See also CA 13-16; 45-48; CAP 1; DLB 7, 44
Belasco, David 1853-1931 .... **TCLC 3**
See also CA 104; DLB 7
Belcheva, Elisaveta 1893- .... **CLC 10**
See also Bagryana, Elisaveta
Beldone, Phil "Cheech"
See Ellison, Harlan (Jay)
Beleno
See Azuela, Mariano
Belinski, Vissarion Grigoryevich 1811-1848 **NCLC 5**
Belitt, Ben 1911- .... **CLC 22**
See also CA 13-16R; CAAS 4; CANR 7; DLB 5
Bell, Gertrude 1868-1926 .... **TCLC 67**
See also DLB 174
Bell, James Madison 1826-1902 ...**TCLC 43; BLC; DAM MULT**
See also BW 1; CA 122; 124; DLB 50
Bell, Madison Smartt 1957- ...... **CLC 41, 102**
See also CA 111; CANR 28, 54
Bell, Marvin (Hartley) 1937-**CLC 8, 31; DAM**

POET
See also CA 21-24R; CAAS 14; CANR 59; DLB 5; MTCW
Bell, W. L. D.
See Mencken, H(enry) L(ouis)
Bellamy, Atwood C.
See Mencken, H(enry) L(ouis)
Bellamy, Edward 1850-1898 .... **NCLC 4**
See also DLB 12
Bellin, Edward J.
See Kuttner, Henry
Belloc, (Joseph) Hilaire (Pierre Sebastien Rene Swanton) 1870-1953 **TCLC 7, 18; DAM POET**
See also CA 106; 152; DLB 19, 100, 141, 174; YABC 1
Belloc, Joseph Peter Rene Hilaire
See Belloc, (Joseph) Hilaire (Pierre Sebastien Rene Swanton)
Belloc, Joseph Pierre Hilaire
See Belloc, (Joseph) Hilaire (Pierre Sebastien Rene Swanton)
Belloc, M. A.
See Lowndes, Marie Adelaide (Belloc)
Bellow, Saul 1915-**CLC 1, 2, 3, 6, 8, 10, 13, 15, 25, 33, 34, 63, 79; DA; DAB; DAC; DAM MST, NOV, POP; SSC 14; WLC**
See also AITN 2; BEST 89:3; CA 5-8R; CABS 1; CANR 29, 53; CDALB 1941-1968; DLB 2, 28; DLBD 3; DLBY 82; MTCW
Belser, Reimond Karel Maria de 1929-
See Ruyslinck, Ward
See also CA 152
Bely, Andrey .... **TCLC 7; PC 11**
See also Bugayev, Boris Nikolayevich
Benary, Margot
See Benary-Isbert, Margot
Benary-Isbert, Margot 1889-1979 .... **CLC 12**
See also CA 5-8R; 89-92; CANR 4; CLR 12; MAICYA; SATA 2; SATA-Obit 21
Benavente (y Martinez), Jacinto 1866-1954 **TCLC 3; DAM DRAM, MULT**
See also CA 106; 131; HW; MTCW
Benchley, Peter (Bradford) 1940- **CLC 4, 8; DAM NOV, POP**
See also AAYA 14; AITN 2; CA 17-20R; CANR 12, 35; MTCW; SATA 3, 89
Benchley, Robert (Charles) 1889-1945**T C L C 1, 55**
See also CA 105; 153; DLB 11
Benda, Julien 1867-1956 .... **TCLC 60**
See also CA 120; 154
Benedict, Ruth (Fulton) 1887-1948 **TCLC 60**
See also CA 158
Benedikt, Michael 1935- .... **CLC 4, 14**
See also CA 13-16R; CANR 7; DLB 5
Benet, Juan 1927- .... **CLC 28**
See also CA 143
Benet, Stephen Vincent 1898-1943 . **TCLC 7; DAM POET; SSC 10**
See also CA 104; 152; DLB 4, 48, 102; YABC 1
Benet, William Rose 1886-1950 .... **TCLC 28; DAM POET**
See also CA 118; 152; DLB 45
Benford, Gregory (Albert) 1941- ...... **CLC 52**
See also CA 69-72; CAAS 27; CANR 12, 24, 49; DLBY 82
Bengtsson, Frans (Gunnar) 1894-1954**T C L C 48**
Benjamin, David
See Slavitt, David R(ytman)
Benjamin, Lois

See Gould, Lois
Benjamin, Walter 1892-1940 .... **TCLC 39**
Benn, Gottfried 1886-1956 .... **TCLC 3**
See also CA 106; 153; DLB 56
Bennett, Alan 1934-**CLC 45, 77; DAB; DAM MST**
See also CA 103; CANR 35, 55; MTCW
Bennett, (Enoch) Arnold 1867-1931**TCLC 5, 20**
See also CA 106; 155; CDBLB 1890-1914; DLB 10, 34, 98, 135
Bennett, Elizabeth
See Mitchell, Margaret (Munnerlyn)
Bennett, George Harold 1930-
See Bennett, Hal
See also BW 1; CA 97-100
Bennett, Hal .... **CLC 5**
See also Bennett, George Harold
See also DLB 33
Bennett, Jay 1912- .... **CLC 35**
See also AAYA 10; CA 69-72; CANR 11, 42; JRDA; SAAS 4; SATA 41, 87; SATA-Brief 27
Bennett, Louise (Simone) 1919-**CLC 28; BLC; DAM MULT**
See also BW 2; CA 151; DLB 117
Benson, E(dward) F(rederic) 1867-1940 **TCLC 27**
See also CA 114; 157; DLB 135, 153
Benson, Jackson J. 1930- .... **CLC 34**
See also CA 25-28R; DLB 111
Benson, Sally 1900-1972 .... **CLC 17**
See also CA 19-20; 37-40R; CAP 1; SATA 1, 35; SATA-Obit 27
Benson, Stella 1892-1933 .... **TCLC 17**
See also CA 117; 155; DLB 36, 162
Bentham, Jeremy 1748-1832 .... **NCLC 38**
See also DLB 107, 158
Bentley, E(dmund) C(lerihew) 1875-1956 **TCLC 12**
See also CA 108; DLB 70
Bentley, Eric (Russell) 1916- .... **CLC 24**
See also CA 5-8R; CANR 6; INT CANR-6
Beranger, Pierre Jean de 1780-1857**NCLC 34**
Berdyaev, Nicolas
See Berdyaev, Nikolai (Aleksandrovich)
Berdyaev, Nikolai (Aleksandrovich) 1874-1948 **TCLC 67**
See also CA 120; 157
Berdyayev, Nikolai (Aleksandrovich)
See Berdyaev, Nikolai (Aleksandrovich)
Berendt, John (Lawrence) 1939- ...... **CLC 86**
See also CA 146
Berger, Colonel
See Malraux, (Georges-)Andre
Berger, John (Peter) 1926- .... **CLC 2, 19**
See also CA 81-84; CANR 51; DLB 14
Berger, Melvin H. 1927- .... **CLC 12**
See also CA 5-8R; CANR 4; CLR 32; SAAS 2; SATA 5, 88
Berger, Thomas (Louis) 1924-**CLC 3, 5, 8, 11, 18, 38; DAM NOV**
See also CA 1-4R; CANR 5, 28, 51; DLB 2; DLBY 80; INT CANR-28; MTCW
Bergman, (Ernst) Ingmar 1918- **CLC 16, 72**
See also CA 81-84; CANR 33
Bergson, Henri 1859-1941 .... **TCLC 32**
Bergstein, Eleanor 1938- .... **CLC 4**
See also CA 53-56; CANR 5
Berkoff, Steven 1937- .... **CLC 56**
See also CA 104
Bermant, Chaim (Icyk) 1929- .... **CLC 40**
See also CA 57-60; CANR 6, 31, 57

Bern, Victoria
See Fisher, M(ary) F(rances) K(ennedy)
Bernanos, (Paul Louis) Georges 1888-1948 **TCLC 3**
See also CA 104; 130; DLB 72
Bernard, April 1956- .... **CLC 59**
See also CA 131
Berne, Victoria
See Fisher, M(ary) F(rances) K(ennedy)
Bernhard, Thomas 1931-1989 **CLC 3, 32, 61**
See also CA 85-88; 127; CANR 32, 57; DLB 85, 124; MTCW
Bernhardt, Sarah (Henriette Rosine) 1844-1923 **TCLC 75**
See also CA 157
Berriault, Gina 1926- .... **CLC 54**
See also CA 116; 129; DLB 130
Berrigan, Daniel 1921- .... **CLC 4**
See also CA 33-36R; CAAS 1; CANR 11, 43; DLB 5
Berrigan, Edmund Joseph Michael, Jr. 1934-1983
See Berrigan, Ted
See also CA 61-64; 110; CANR 14
Berrigan, Ted .... **CLC 37**
See also Berrigan, Edmund Joseph Michael, Jr.
See also DLB 5, 169
Berry, Charles Edward Anderson 1931-
See Berry, Chuck
See also CA 115
Berry, Chuck .... **CLC 17**
See also Berry, Charles Edward Anderson
Berry, Jonas
See Ashbery, John (Lawrence)
Berry, Wendell (Erdman) 1934- **CLC 4, 6, 8, 27, 46; DAM POET**
See also AITN 1; CA 73-76; CANR 50; DLB 5, 6
Berryman, John 1914-1972**CLC 1, 2, 3, 4, 6, 8, 10, 13, 25, 62; DAM POET**
See also CA 13-16; 33-36R; CABS 2; CANR 35; CAP 1; CDALB 1941-1968; DLB 48; MTCW
Bertolucci, Bernardo 1940- .... **CLC 16**
See also CA 106
Berton, Pierre (Francis De Marigny) 1920- **CLC 104**
See also CA 1-4R; CANR 2, 56; DLB 68
Bertrand, Aloysius 1807-1841 .... **NCLC 31**
Bertran de Born c. 1140-1215 .... **CMLC 5**
Besant, Annie (Wood) 1847-1933 .... **TCLC 9**
See also CA 105
Bessie, Alvah 1904-1985 .... **CLC 23**
See also CA 5-8R; 116; CANR 2; DLB 26
Bethlen, T. D.
See Silverberg, Robert
Beti, Mongo ...... **CLC 27; BLC; DAM MULT**
See also Biyidi, Alexandre
Betjeman, John 1906-1984 **CLC 2, 6, 10, 34, 43; DAB; DAM MST, POET**
See also CA 9-12R; 112; CANR 33, 56; CDBLB 1945-1960; DLB 20; DLBY 84; MTCW
Bettelheim, Bruno 1903-1990 .... **CLC 79**
See also CA 81-84; 131; CANR 23, 61; MTCW
Betti, Ugo 1892-1953 .... **TCLC 5**
See also CA 104; 155
Betts, Doris (Waugh) 1932- ...... **CLC 3, 6, 28**
See also CA 13-16R; CANR 9; DLBY 82; INT CANR-9
Bevan, Alistair
See Roberts, Keith (John Kingston)
Bialik, Chaim Nachman 1873-1934 **TCLC 25**
Bickerstaff, Isaac

See Swift, Jonathan
Bidart, Frank 1939- .... **CLC 33**
 See also CA 140
Bienek, Horst 1930- .... **CLC 7, 11**
 See also CA 73-76; DLB 75
Bierce, Ambrose (Gwinett) 1842-1914(?)
 **TCLC 1, 7, 44; DA; DAC; DAM MST; SSC
 9; WLC**
 See also CA 104; 139; CDALB 1865-1917;
 DLB 11, 12, 23, 71, 74, 186
Biggers, Earl Derr 1884-1933 .... **TCLC 65**
 See also CA 108; 153
Billings, Josh
 See Shaw, Henry Wheeler
Billington, (Lady) Rachel (Mary) 1942- **C L C
 43**
 See also AITN 2; CA 33-36R; CANR 44
Binyon, T(imothy) J(ohn) 1936- .... **CLC 34**
 See also CA 111; CANR 28
Bioy Casares, Adolfo 1914-1984**CLC 4, 8, 13,
 88; DAM MULT; HLC; SSC 17**
 See also CA 29-32R; CANR 19, 43; DLB 113;
 HW; MTCW
Bird, Cordwainer
 See Ellison, Harlan (Jay)
Bird, Robert Montgomery 1806-1854**NCLC 1**
Birney, (Alfred) Earle 1904-1995**CLC 1, 4, 6,
 11; DAC; DAM MST, POET**
 See also CA 1-4R; CANR 5, 20; DLB 88;
 MTCW
Bishop, Elizabeth 1911-1979 **CLC 1, 4, 9, 13,
 15, 32; DA; DAC; DAM MST, POET; PC
 3**
 See also CA 5-8R; 89-92; CABS 2; CANR 26,
 61; CDALB 1968-1988; DLB 5, 169;
 MTCW; SATA-Obit 24
Bishop, John 1935- .... **CLC 10**
 See also CA 105
Bissett, Bill 1939- .... **CLC 18; PC 14**
 See also CA 69-72; CAAS 19; CANR 15; DLB
 53; MTCW
Bitov, Andrei (Georgievich) 1937- ... **CLC 57**
 See also CA 142
Biyidi, Alexandre 1932-
 See Beti, Mongo
 See also BW 1; CA 114; 124; MTCW
Bjarme, Brynjolf
 See Ibsen, Henrik (Johan)
Bjornson, Bjornstjerne (Martinius) 1832-1910
 TCLC 7, 37
 See also CA 104
Black, Robert
 See Holdstock, Robert P.
Blackburn, Paul 1926-1971 .... **CLC 9, 43**
 See also CA 81-84; 33-36R; CANR 34; DLB
 16; DLBY 81
Black Elk 1863-1950**TCLC 33; DAM MULT**
 See also CA 144; NNAL
Black Hobart
 See Sanders, (James) Ed(ward)
Blacklin, Malcolm
 See Chambers, Aidan
Blackmore, R(ichard) D(oddridge) 1825-1900
 TCLC 27
 See also CA 120; DLB 18
Blackmur, R(ichard) P(almer) 1904-1965
 CLC 2, 24
 See also CA 11-12; 25-28R; CAP 1; DLB 63
Black Tarantula
 See Acker, Kathy
Blackwood, Algernon (Henry) 1869-1951
 TCLC 5
 See also CA 105; 150; DLB 153, 156, 178

Blackwood, Caroline 1931-1996**CLC 6, 9, 100**
 See also CA 85-88; 151; CANR 32, 61; DLB
 14; MTCW
Blade, Alexander
 See Hamilton, Edmond; Silverberg, Robert
Blaga, Lucian 1895-1961 .... **CLC 75**
Blair, Eric (Arthur) 1903-1950
 See Orwell, George
 See also CA 104; 132; DA; DAB; DAC; DAM
 MST, NOV; MTCW; SATA 29
Blais, Marie-Claire 1939-**CLC 2, 4, 6, 13, 22;
 DAC; DAM MST**
 See also CA 21-24R; CAAS 4; CANR 38; DLB
 53; MTCW
Blaise, Clark 1940- .... **CLC 29**
 See also AITN 2; CA 53-56; CAAS 3; CANR
 5; DLB 53
Blake, Fairley
 See De Voto, Bernard (Augustine)
Blake, Nicholas
 See Day Lewis, C(ecil)
 See also DLB 77
Blake, William 1757-1827 . **NCLC 13, 37, 57;
 DA; DAB; DAC; DAM MST, POET; PC
 12; WLC**
 See also CDBLB 1789-1832; DLB 93, 163;
 MAICYA; SATA 30
Blasco Ibanez, Vicente 1867-1928 **TCLC 12;
 DAM NOV**
 See also CA 110; 131; HW; MTCW
Blatty, William Peter 1928-**CLC 2; DAM POP**
 See also CA 5-8R; CANR 9
Bleeck, Oliver
 See Thomas, Ross (Elmore)
Blessing, Lee 1949- .... **CLC 54**
Blish, James (Benjamin) 1921-1975 . **CLC 14**
 See also CA 1-4R; 57-60; CANR 3; DLB 8;
 MTCW; SATA 66
Bliss, Reginald
 See Wells, H(erbert) G(eorge)
Blixen, Karen (Christentze Dinesen) 1885-1962
 See Dinesen, Isak
 See also CA 25-28; CANR 22, 50; CAP 2;
 MTCW; SATA 44
Bloch, Robert (Albert) 1917-1994 .... **CLC 33**
 See also CA 5-8R; 146; CAAS 20; CANR 5;
 DLB 44; INT CANR-5; SATA 12; SATA-Obit
 82
Blok, Alexander (Alexandrovich) 1880-1921
 TCLC 5; PC 21
 See also CA 104
Blom, Jan
 See Breytenbach, Breyten
Bloom, Harold 1930- .... **CLC 24, 103**
 See also CA 13-16R; CANR 39; DLB 67
Bloomfield, Aurelius
 See Bourne, Randolph S(illiman)
Blount, Roy (Alton), Jr. 1941- .... **CLC 38**
 See also CA 53-56; CANR 10, 28, 61; INT
 CANR-28; MTCW
Bloy, Leon 1846-1917 .... **TCLC 22**
 See also CA 121; DLB 123
Blume, Judy (Sussman) 1938- ... **CLC 12, 30;
 DAM NOV, POP**
 See also AAYA 3; CA 29-32R; CANR 13, 37;
 CLR 2, 15; DLB 52; JRDA; MAICYA;
 MTCW; SATA 2, 31, 79
Blunden, Edmund (Charles) 1896-1974 **C L C
 2, 56**
 See also CA 17-18; 45-48; CANR 54; CAP 2;
 DLB 20, 100, 155; MTCW
Bly, Robert (Elwood) 1926-**CLC 1, 2, 5, 10, 15,
 38; DAM POET**

 See also CA 5-8R; CANR 41; DLB 5; MTCW
Boas, Franz 1858-1942 .... **TCLC 56**
 See also CA 115
Bobette
 See Simenon, Georges (Jacques Christian)
Boccaccio, Giovanni 1313-1375 ... **CMLC 13;
 SSC 10**
Bochco, Steven 1943- .... **CLC 35**
 See also AAYA 11; CA 124; 138
Bodenheim, Maxwell 1892-1954 .... **TCLC 44**
 See also CA 110; DLB 9, 45
Bodker, Cecil 1927- .... **CLC 21**
 See also CA 73-76; CANR 13, 44; CLR 23;
 MAICYA; SATA 14
Boell, Heinrich (Theodor) 1917-1985 **CLC 2,
 3, 6, 9, 11, 15, 27, 32, 72; DA; DAB; DAC;
 DAM MST, NOV; SSC 23; WLC**
 See also CA 21-24R; 116; CANR 24; DLB 69;
 DLBY 85; MTCW
Boerne, Alfred
 See Doeblin, Alfred
Boethius 480(?)-524(?) .... **CMLC 15**
 See also DLB 115
Bogan, Louise 1897-1970 . **CLC 4, 39, 46, 93;
 DAM POET; PC 12**
 See also CA 73-76; 25-28R; CANR 33; DLB
 45, 169; MTCW
Bogarde, Dirk .... **CLC 19**
 See also Van Den Bogarde, Derek Jules Gaspard
 Ulric Niven
 See also DLB 14
Bogosian, Eric 1953- .... **CLC 45**
 See also CA 138
Bograd, Larry 1953- .... **CLC 35**
 See also CA 93-96; CANR 57; SAAS 21; SATA
 33, 89
Boiardo, Matteo Maria 1441-1494 .... **LC 6**
Boileau-Despreaux, Nicolas 1636-1711 . **LC 3**
Bojer, Johan 1872-1959 .... **TCLC 64**
Boland, Eavan (Aisling) 1944- .. **CLC 40, 67;
 DAM POET**
 See also CA 143; CANR 61; DLB 40
Bolt, Lee
 See Faust, Frederick (Schiller)
Bolt, Robert (Oxton) 1924-1995 ..... **CLC 14;
 DAM DRAM**
 See also CA 17-20R; 147; CANR 35; DLB 13;
 MTCW
Bombet, Louis-Alexandre-Cesar
 See Stendhal
Bomkauf
 See Kaufman, Bob (Garnell)
Bonaventura .... **NCLC 35**
 See also DLB 90
Bond, Edward 1934- **CLC 4, 6, 13, 23; DAM
 DRAM**
 See also CA 25-28R; CANR 38; DLB 13;
 MTCW
Bonham, Frank 1914-1989 .... **CLC 12**
 See also AAYA 1; CA 9-12R; CANR 4, 36;
 JRDA; MAICYA; SAAS 3; SATA 1, 49;
 SATA-Obit 62
Bonnefoy, Yves 1923-... **CLC 9, 15, 58; DAM
 MST, POET**
 See also CA 85-88; CANR 33; MTCW
Bontemps, Arna(ud Wendell) 1902-1973**C L C
 1, 18; BLC; DAM MULT, NOV, POET**
 See also BW 1; CA 1-4R; 41-44R; CANR 4,
 35; CLR 6; DLB 48, 51; JRDA; MAICYA;
 MTCW; SATA 2, 44; SATA-Obit 24
Booth, Martin 1944- .... **CLC 13**
 See also CA 93-96; CAAS 2
Booth, Philip 1925- .... **CLC 23**

See also CA 5-8R; CANR 5; DLBY 82

Booth, Wayne C(layson) 1921- .... **CLC 24**
See also CA 1-4R; CAAS 5; CANR 3, 43; DLB 67

Borchert, Wolfgang 1921-1947 .... **TCLC 5**
See also CA 104; DLB 69, 124

Borel, Petrus 1809-1859 .... **NCLC 41**

Borges, Jorge Luis 1899-1986 CLC 1, 2, 3, 4, 6, 8, 9, 10, 13, 19, 44, 48, 83; DA; DAB; DAC; DAM MST, MULT; HLC; SSC 4; WLC
See also AAYA 19; CA 21-24R; CANR 19, 33; DLB 113; DLBY 86; HW; MTCW

Borowski, Tadeusz 1922-1951 .... **TCLC 9**
See also CA 106; 154

Borrow, George (Henry) 1803-1881 NCLC 9
See also DLB 21, 55, 166

Bosman, Herman Charles 1905-1951 **T C L C 49**
See also Malan, Herman
See also CA 160

Bosschere, Jean de 1878(?)-1953 ... **TCLC 19**
See also CA 115

Boswell, James 1740-1795 . **LC 4; DA; DAB; DAC; DAM MST; WLC**
See also CDBLB 1660-1789; DLB 104, 142

Bottoms, David 1949- .... **CLC 53**
See also CA 105; CANR 22; DLB 120; DLBY 83

Boucicault, Dion 1820-1890 .... **NCLC 41**

Boucolon, Maryse 1937(?)-
See Conde, Maryse
See also CA 110; CANR 30, 53

Bourget, Paul (Charles Joseph) 1852-1935 **TCLC 12**
See also CA 107; DLB 123

Bourjaily, Vance (Nye) 1922- .... **CLC 8, 62**
See also CA 1-4R; CAAS 1; CANR 2; DLB 2, 143

Bourne, Randolph S(illiman) 1886-1918 **TCLC 16**
See also CA 117; 155; DLB 63

Bova, Ben(jamin William) 1932- ...... **CLC 45**
See also AAYA 16; CA 5-8R; CAAS 18; CANR 11, 56; CLR 3; DLBY 81; INT CANR-11; MAICYA; MTCW; SATA 6, 68

Bowen, Elizabeth (Dorothea Cole) 1899-1973 **CLC 1, 3, 6, 11, 15, 22; DAM NOV; SSC 3, 28**
See also CA 17-18; 41-44R; CANR 35; CAP 2; CDBLB 1945-1960; DLB 15, 162; MTCW

Bowering, George 1935- .... **CLC 15, 47**
See also CA 21-24R; CAAS 16; CANR 10; DLB 53

Bowering, Marilyn R(uthe) 1949- .... **CLC 32**
See also CA 101; CANR 49

Bowers, Edgar 1924- .... **CLC 9**
See also CA 5-8R; CANR 24; DLB 5

Bowie, David .... **CLC 17**
See also Jones, David Robert

Bowles, Jane (Sydney) 1917-1973 **CLC 3, 68**
See also CA 19-20; 41-44R; CAP 2

Bowles, Paul (Frederick) 1910-1986 CLC 1, 2, 19, 53; SSC 3
See also CA 1-4R; CAAS 1; CANR 1, 19, 50; DLB 5, 6; MTCW

Box, Edgar
See Vidal, Gore

Boyd, Nancy
See Millay, Edna St. Vincent

Boyd, William 1952- .... **CLC 28, 53, 70**
See also CA 114; 120; CANR 51

Boyle, Kay 1902-1992 CLC 1, 5, 19, 58; SSC 5
See also CA 13-16R; 140; CAAS 1; CANR 29,

61; DLB 4, 9, 48, 86; DLBY 93; MTCW

Boyle, Mark
See Kienzle, William X(avier)

Boyle, Patrick 1905-1982 .... **CLC 19**
See also CA 127

Boyle, T. C. 1948-
See Boyle, T(homas) Coraghessan

Boyle, T(homas) Coraghessan 1948- CLC 36, 55, 90; DAM POP; SSC 16
See also BEST 90:4; CA 120; CANR 44; DLBY 86

Boz
See Dickens, Charles (John Huffam)

Brackenridge, Hugh Henry 1748-1816 N C L C 7
See also DLB 11, 37

Bradbury, Edward P.
See Moorcock, Michael (John)

Bradbury, Malcolm (Stanley) 1932- CLC 32, 61; DAM NOV
See also CA 1-4R; CANR 1, 33; DLB 14; MTCW

Bradbury, Ray (Douglas) 1920- CLC 1, 3, 10, 15, 42, 98; DA; DAB; DAC; DAM MST, NOV, POP; SSC 29; WLC
See also AAYA 15; AITN 1, 2; CA 1-4R; CANR 2, 30; CDALB 1968-1988; DLB 2, 8; MTCW; SATA 11, 64

Bradford, Gamaliel 1863-1932 ...... **TCLC 36**
See also CA 160; DLB 17

Bradley, David (Henry, Jr.) 1950- .. **CLC 23; BLC; DAM MULT**
See also BW 1; CA 104; CANR 26; DLB 33

Bradley, John Ed(mund, Jr.) 1958- .. **CLC 55**
See also CA 139

Bradley, Marion Zimmer 1930- CLC 30; DAM POP
See also AAYA 9; CA 57-60; CAAS 10; CANR 7, 31, 51; DLB 8; MTCW; SATA 90

Bradstreet, Anne 1612(?)-1672 LC 4, 30; DA; DAC; DAM MST, POET; PC 10
See also CDALB 1640-1865; DLB 24

Brady, Joan 1939- .... **CLC 86**
See also CA 141

Bragg, Melvyn 1939- .... **CLC 10**
See also BEST 89:3; CA 57-60; CANR 10, 48; DLB 14

Braine, John (Gerard) 1922-1986 CLC 1, 3, 41
See also CA 1-4R; 120; CANR 1, 33; CDBLB 1945-1960; DLB 15; DLBY 86; MTCW

Bramah, Ernest 1868-1942 .... **TCLC 72**
See also CA 156; DLB 70

Brammer, William 1930(?)-1978 .... **CLC 31**
See also CA 77-80

Brancati, Vitaliano 1907-1954 .... **TCLC 12**
See also CA 109

Brancato, Robin F(idler) 1936- .... **CLC 35**
See also AAYA 9; CA 69-72; CANR 11, 45; CLR 32; JRDA; SAAS 9; SATA 23

Brand, Max
See Faust, Frederick (Schiller)

Brand, Millen 1906-1980 .... **CLC 7**
See also CA 21-24R; 97-100

Branden, Barbara .... **CLC 44**
See also CA 148

Brandes, Georg (Morris Cohen) 1842-1927 **TCLC 10**
See also CA 105

Brandys, Kazimierz 1916- .... **CLC 62**

Branley, Franklyn M(ansfield) 1915- CLC 21
See also CA 33-36R; CANR 14, 39; CLR 13; MAICYA; SAAS 16; SATA 4, 68

Brathwaite, Edward Kamau 1930- . **CLC 11;**

DAM POET
See also BW 2; CA 25-28R; CANR 11, 26, 47; DLB 125

Brautigan, Richard (Gary) 1935-1984 CLC 1, 3, 5, 9, 12, 34, 42; DAM NOV
See also CA 53-56; 113; CANR 34; DLB 2, 5; DLBY 80, 84; MTCW; SATA 56

Brave Bird, Mary 1953-
See Crow Dog, Mary (Ellen)
See also NNAL

Braverman, Kate 1950- .... **CLC 67**
See also CA 89-92

Brecht, (Eugen) Bertolt (Friedrich) 1898-1956 **TCLC 1, 6, 13, 35; DA; DAB; DAC; DAM DRAM, MST; DC 3; WLC**
See also CA 104; 133; CANR 62; DLB 56, 124; MTCW

Brecht, Eugen Berthold Friedrich
See Brecht, (Eugen) Bertolt (Friedrich)

Bremer, Fredrika 1801-1865 .... **NCLC 11**

Brennan, Christopher John 1870-1932 T C L C 17
See also CA 117

Brennan, Maeve 1917- .... **CLC 5**
See also CA 81-84

Brent, Linda
See Jacobs, Harriet

Brentano, Clemens (Maria) 1778-1842 N C L C 1
See also DLB 90

Brent of Bin Bin
See Franklin, (Stella Maraia Sarah) Miles

Brenton, Howard 1942- .... **CLC 31**
See also CA 69-72; CANR 33; DLB 13; MTCW

Breslin, James 1930-1996
See Breslin, Jimmy
See also CA 73-76; CANR 31; DAM NOV; MTCW

Breslin, Jimmy .... **CLC 4, 43**
See also Breslin, James
See also AITN 1

Bresson, Robert 1901- .... **CLC 16**
See also CA 110; CANR 49

Breton, Andre 1896-1966 CLC 2, 9, 15, 54; PC 15
See also CA 19-20; 25-28R; CANR 40, 60; CAP 2; DLB 65; MTCW

Breytenbach, Breyten 1939(?)- . **CLC 23, 37; DAM POET**
See also CA 113; 129; CANR 61

Bridgers, Sue Ellen 1942- .... **CLC 26**
See also AAYA 8; CA 65-68; CANR 11, 36; CLR 18; DLB 52; JRDA; MAICYA; SAAS 1; SATA 22, 90

Bridges, Robert (Seymour) 1844-1930 T C L C 1; DAM POET
See also CA 104; 152; CDBLB 1890-1914; DLB 19, 98

Bridie, James .... **TCLC 3**
See also Mavor, Osborne Henry
See also DLB 10

Brin, David 1950- .... **CLC 34**
See also AAYA 21; CA 102; CANR 24; INT CANR-24; SATA 65

Brink, Andre (Philippus) 1935- **CLC 18, 36, 106**
See also CA 104; CANR 39, 62; INT 103; MTCW

Brinsmead, H(esba) F(ay) 1922- .... **CLC 21**
See also CA 21-24R; CANR 10; CLR 47; MAICYA; SAAS 5; SATA 18, 78

Brittain, Vera (Mary) 1893(?)-1970 . **CLC 23**
See also CA 13-16; 25-28R; CANR 58; CAP 1;

MTCW

Broch, Hermann 1886-1951 .... **TCLC 20**
　See also CA 117; DLB 85, 124
Brock, Rose
　See Hansen, Joseph
Brodkey, Harold (Roy) 1930-1996 .... **CLC 56**
　See also CA 111; 151; DLB 130
Brodsky, Iosif Alexandrovich 1940-1996
　See Brodsky, Joseph
　See also AITN 1; CA 41-44R; 151; CANR 37;
　　DAM POET; MTCW
Brodsky, Joseph 1940-1996 **CLC 4, 6, 13, 36,
　100; PC 9**
　See also Brodsky, Iosif Alexandrovich
Brodsky, Michael (Mark) 1948- .... **CLC 19**
　See also CA 102; CANR 18, 41, 58
Bromell, Henry 1947- .... **CLC 5**
　See also CA 53-56; CANR 9
Bromfield, Louis (Brucker) 1896-1956 **T C L C
　11**
　See also CA 107; 155; DLB 4, 9, 86
Broner, E(sther) M(asserman) 1930- **CLC 19**
　See also CA 17-20R; CANR 8, 25; DLB 28
Bronk, William 1918- .... **CLC 10**
　See also CA 89-92; CANR 23; DLB 165
Bronstein, Lev Davidovich
　See Trotsky, Leon
Bronte, Anne 1820-1849 .... **NCLC 4**
　See also DLB 21
Bronte, Charlotte 1816-1855 **NCLC 3, 8, 33,
　58; DA; DAB; DAC; DAM MST, NOV;
　WLC**
　See also AAYA 17; CDBLB 1832-1890; DLB
　　21, 159
Bronte, Emily (Jane) 1818-1848 **NCLC 16, 35;
　DA; DAB; DAC; DAM MST, NOV, POET;
　PC 8; WLC**
　See also AAYA 17; CDBLB 1832-1890; DLB
　　21, 32
Brooke, Frances 1724-1789 .... **LC 6**
　See also DLB 39, 99
Brooke, Henry 1703(?)-1783 .... **LC 1**
　See also DLB 39
Brooke, Rupert (Chawner) 1887-1915 **T C L C
　2, 7; DA; DAB; DAC; DAM MST, POET;
　WLC**
　See also CA 104; 132; CANR 61; CDBLB
　　1914-1945; DLB 19; MTCW
Brooke-Haven, P.
　See Wodehouse, P(elham) G(renville)
Brooke-Rose, Christine 1926(?)- .... **CLC 40**
　See also CA 13-16R; CANR 58; DLB 14
Brookner, Anita 1928- **CLC 32, 34, 51; DAB;
　DAM POP**
　See also CA 114; 120; CANR 37, 56; DLBY
　　87; MTCW
Brooks, Cleanth 1906-1994 .... **CLC 24, 86**
　See also CA 17-20R; 145; CANR 33, 35; DLB
　　63; DLBY 94; INT CANR-35; MTCW
Brooks, George
　See Baum, L(yman) Frank
Brooks, Gwendolyn 1917- **CLC 1, 2, 4, 5, 15,
　49; BLC; DA; DAC; DAM MST, MULT,
　POET; PC 7; WLC**
　See also AAYA 20; AITN 1; BW 2; CA 1-4R;
　　CANR 1, 27, 52; CDALB 1941-1968; CLR
　　27; DLB 5, 76, 165; MTCW; SATA 6
Brooks, Mel .... **CLC 12**
　See also Kaminsky, Melvin
　See also AAYA 13; DLB 26
Brooks, Peter 1938- .... **CLC 34**
　See also CA 45-48; CANR 1
Brooks, Van Wyck 1886-1963 .... **CLC 29**

See also CA 1-4R; CANR 6; DLB 45, 63, 103
Brophy, Brigid (Antonia) 1929-1995 **CLC 6,
　11, 29, 105**
　See also CA 5-8R; 149; CAAS 4; CANR 25,
　　53; DLB 14; MTCW
Brosman, Catharine Savage 1934- ..... **CLC 9**
　See also CA 61-64; CANR 21, 46
Brother Antoninus
　See Everson, William (Oliver)
The Brothers Quay
　See Quay, Stephen; Quay, Timothy
Broughton, T(homas) Alan 1936- ..... **CLC 19**
　See also CA 45-48; CANR 2, 23, 48
Broumas, Olga 1949- .... **CLC 10, 73**
　See also CA 85-88; CANR 20
Brown, Alan 1951- .... **CLC 99**
Brown, Charles Brockden 1771-1810 **N C L C
　22**
　See also CDALB 1640-1865; DLB 37, 59, 73
Brown, Christy 1932-1981 .... **CLC 63**
　See also CA 105; 104; DLB 14
Brown, Claude 1937- ... **CLC 30; BLC; DAM
　MULT**
　See also AAYA 7; BW 1; CA 73-76
Brown, Dee (Alexander) 1908- .. **CLC 18, 47;
　DAM POP**
　See also CA 13-16R; CAAS 6; CANR 11, 45,
　　60; DLBY 80; MTCW; SATA 5
Brown, George
　See Wertmueller, Lina
Brown, George Douglas 1869-1902 **TCLC 28**
Brown, George Mackay 1921-1996 **CLC 5, 48,
　100**
　See also CA 21-24R; 151; CAAS 6; CANR 12,
　　37, 62; DLB 14, 27, 139; MTCW; SATA 35
Brown, (William) Larry 1951- .... **CLC 73**
　See also CA 130; 134; INT 133
Brown, Moses
　See Barrett, William (Christopher)
Brown, Rita Mae 1944- **CLC 18, 43, 79; DAM
　NOV, POP**
　See also CA 45-48; CANR 2, 11, 35, 62; INT
　　CANR-11; MTCW
Brown, Roderick (Langmere) Haig-
　See Haig-Brown, Roderick (Langmere)
Brown, Rosellen 1939- .... **CLC 32**
　See also CA 77-80; CAAS 10; CANR 14, 44
Brown, Sterling Allen 1901-1989 **CLC 1, 23,
　59; BLC; DAM MULT, POET**
　See also BW 1; CA 85-88; 127; CANR 26; DLB
　　48, 51, 63; MTCW
Brown, Will
　See Ainsworth, William Harrison
Brown, William Wells 1813-1884 ... **NCLC 2;
　BLC; DAM MULT; DC 1**
　See also DLB 3, 50
Browne, (Clyde) Jackson 1948(?)- .... **CLC 21**
　See also CA 120
Browning, Elizabeth Barrett 1806-1861
　**NCLC 1, 16, 61, 66; DA; DAB; DAC; DAM
　MST, POET; PC 6; WLC**
　See also CDBLB 1832-1890; DLB 32
Browning, Robert 1812-1889 **NCLC 19; DA;
　DAB; DAC; DAM MST, POET; PC 2;
　WLCS**
　See also CDBLB 1832-1890; DLB 32, 163;
　　YABC 1
Browning, Tod 1882-1962 .... **CLC 16**
　See also CA 141; 117
Brownson, Orestes (Augustus) 1803-1876
　NCLC 50
Bruccoli, Matthew J(oseph) 1931- ... **CLC 34**
　See also CA 9-12R; CANR 7; DLB 103

Bruce, Lenny .... **CLC 21**
　See also Schneider, Leonard Alfred
Bruin, John
　See Brutus, Dennis
Brulard, Henri
　See Stendhal
Brulls, Christian
　See Simenon, Georges (Jacques Christian)
Brunner, John (Kilian Houston) 1934-1995
　CLC 8, 10; DAM POP
　See also CA 1-4R; 149; CAAS 8; CANR 2, 37;
　　MTCW
Bruno, Giordano 1548-1600 .... **LC 27**
Brutus, Dennis 1924- ... **CLC 43; BLC; DAM
　MULT, POET**
　See also BW 2; CA 49-52; CAAS 14; CANR 2,
　　27, 42; DLB 117
Bryan, C(ourtlandt) D(ixon) B(arnes) 1936-
　CLC 29
　See also CA 73-76; CANR 13; INT CANR-13
Bryan, Michael
　See Moore, Brian
Bryant, William Cullen 1794-1878 . **NCLC 6,
　46; DA; DAB; DAC; DAM MST, POET;
　PC 20**
　See also CDALB 1640-1865; DLB 3, 43, 59
Bryusov, Valery Yakovlevich 1873-1924
　TCLC 10
　See also CA 107; 155
Buchan, John 1875-1940 ..... **TCLC 41; DAB;
　DAM POP**
　See also CA 108; 145; DLB 34, 70, 156; YABC
　　2
Buchanan, George 1506-1582 .... **LC 4**
Buchheim, Lothar-Guenther 1918- .... **CLC 6**
　See also CA 85-88
Buchner, (Karl) Georg 1813-1837 . **NCLC 26**
Buchwald, Art(hur) 1925- .... **CLC 33**
　See also AITN 1; CA 5-8R; CANR 21; MTCW;
　　SATA 10
Buck, Pearl S(ydenstricker) 1892-1973 **CLC 7,
　11, 18; DA; DAB; DAC; DAM MST, NOV**
　See also AITN 1; CA 1-4R; 41-44R; CANR 1,
　　34; DLB 9, 102; MTCW; SATA 1, 25
Buckler, Ernest 1908-1984 .... **CLC 13; DAC;
　DAM MST**
　See also CA 11-12; 114; CAP 1; DLB 68; SATA
　　47
Buckley, Vincent (Thomas) 1925-1988 **CLC 57**
　See also CA 101
Buckley, William F(rank), Jr. 1925- **CLC 7, 18,
　37; DAM POP**
　See also AITN 1; CA 1-4R; CANR 1, 24, 53;
　　DLB 137; DLBY 80; INT CANR-24; MTCW
Buechner, (Carl) Frederick 1926- **CLC 2, 4, 6,
　9; DAM NOV**
　See also CA 13-16R; CANR 11, 39, 64; DLBY
　　80; INT CANR-11; MTCW
Buell, John (Edward) 1927- .... **CLC 10**
　See also CA 1-4R; DLB 53
Buero Vallejo, Antonio 1916- ..... **CLC 15, 46**
　See also CA 106; CANR 24, 49; HW; MTCW
Bufalino, Gesualdo 1920(?)- .... **CLC 74**
Bugayev, Boris Nikolayevich 1880-1934
　See Bely, Andrey
　See also CA 104
Bukowski, Charles 1920-1994 **CLC 2, 5, 9, 41,
　82, 108; DAM NOV, POET; PC 18**
　See also CA 17-20R; 144; CANR 40, 62; DLB
　　5, 130, 169; MTCW
Bulgakov, Mikhail (Afanas'evich) 1891-1940
　TCLC 2, 16; DAM DRAM, NOV; SSC 18
　See also CA 105; 152

Bulgya, Alexander Alexandrovich 1901-1956
TCLC 53
See also Fadeyev, Alexander
See also CA 117

Bullins, Ed 1935-... CLC 1, 5, 7; BLC; DAM
DRAM, MULT; DC 6
See also BW 2; CA 49-52; CAAS 16; CANR
24, 46; DLB 7, 38; MTCW

Bulwer-Lytton, Edward (George Earle Lytton)
1803-1873 .... NCLC 1, 45
See also DLB 21

Bunin, Ivan Alexeyevich 1870-1953 TCLC 6;
SSC 5
See also CA 104

Bunting, Basil 1900-1985 ..... CLC 10, 39, 47;
DAM POET
See also CA 53-56; 115; CANR 7; DLB 20

Bunuel, Luis 1900-1983 .. CLC 16, 80; DAM
MULT; HLC
See also CA 101; 110; CANR 32; HW

Bunyan, John 1628-1688 ... LC 4; DA; DAB;
DAC; DAM MST; WLC
See also CDBLB 1660-1789; DLB 39

Burckhardt, Jacob (Christoph) 1818-1897
NCLC 49

Burford, Eleanor
See Hibbert, Eleanor Alice Burford

Burgess, AnthonyCLC 1, 2, 4, 5, 8, 10, 13, 15,
22, 40, 62, 81, 94; DAB
See also Wilson, John (Anthony) Burgess
See also AITN 1; CDBLB 1960 to Present; DLB
14

Burke, Edmund 1729(?)-1797 LC 7, 36; DA;
DAB; DAC; DAM MST; WLC
See also DLB 104

Burke, Kenneth (Duva) 1897-1993 CLC 2, 24
See also CA 5-8R; 143; CANR 39; DLB 45,
63; MTCW

Burke, Leda
See Garnett, David

Burke, Ralph
See Silverberg, Robert

Burke, Thomas 1886-1945 .... TCLC 63
See also CA 113; 155

Burney, Fanny 1752-1840 .... NCLC 12, 54
See also DLB 39

Burns, Robert 1759-1796 .... PC 6
See also CDBLB 1789-1832; DA; DAB; DAC;
DAM MST, POET; DLB 109; WLC

Burns, Tex
See L'Amour, Louis (Dearborn)

Burnshaw, Stanley 1906- .... CLC 3, 13, 44
See also CA 9-12R; DLB 48

Burr, Anne 1937- .... CLC 6
See also CA 25-28R

Burroughs, Edgar Rice 1875-1950 . TCLC 2,
32; DAM NOV
See also AAYA 11; CA 104; 132; DLB 8;
MTCW; SATA 41

Burroughs, William S(eward) 1914-1997 CLC
1, 2, 5, 15, 22, 42, 75; DA; DAB; DAC;
DAM MST, NOV, POP; WLC
See also AITN 2; CA 9-12R; 160; CANR 20,
52; DLB 2, 8, 16, 152; DLBY 81; MTCW

Burton, Richard F. 1821-1890 .... NCLC 42
See also DLB 55, 184

Busch, Frederick 1941- ..... CLC 7, 10, 18, 47
See also CA 33-36R; CAAS 1; CANR 45; DLB
6

Bush, Ronald 1946- .... CLC 34
See also CA 136

Bustos, F(rancisco)
See Borges, Jorge Luis

Bustos Domecq, H(onorio)
See Bioy Casares, Adolfo; Borges, Jorge Luis

Butler, Octavia E(stelle) 1947- CLC 38; DAM
MULT, POP
See also AAYA 18; BW 2; CA 73-76; CANR
12, 24, 38; DLB 33; MTCW; SATA 84

Butler, Robert Olen (Jr.) 1945- CLC 81; DAM
POP
See also CA 112; DLB 173; INT 112

Butler, Samuel 1612-1680 .... LC 16
See also DLB 101, 126

Butler, Samuel 1835-1902 . TCLC 1, 33; DA;
DAB; DAC; DAM MST, NOV; WLC
See also CA 143; CDBLB 1890-1914; DLB 18,
57, 174

Butler, Walter C.
See Faust, Frederick (Schiller)

Butor, Michel (Marie Francois) 1926- CLC 1,
3, 8, 11, 15
See also CA 9-12R; CANR 33; DLB 83; MTCW

Butts, Mary 1892(?)-1937 .... TCLC 77
See also CA 148

Buzo, Alexander (John) 1944- .... CLC 61
See also CA 97-100; CANR 17, 39

Buzzati, Dino 1906-1972 .... CLC 36
See also CA 160; 33-36R; DLB 177

Byars, Betsy (Cromer) 1928- .... CLC 35
See also AAYA 19; CA 33-36R; CANR 18, 36,
57; CLR 1, 16; DLB 52; INT CANR-18;
JRDA; MAICYA; MTCW; SAAS 1; SATA
4, 46, 80

Byatt, A(ntonia) S(usan Drabble) 1936- C L C
19, 65; DAM NOV, POP
See also CA 13-16R; CANR 13, 33, 50; DLB
14; MTCW

Byrne, David 1952- .... CLC 26
See also CA 127

Byrne, John Keyes 1926-
See Leonard, Hugh
See also CA 102; INT 102

Byron, George Gordon (Noel) 1788-1824
NCLC 2, 12; DA; DAB; DAC; DAM MST,
POET; PC 16; WLC
See also CDBLB 1789-1832; DLB 96, 110

Byron, Robert 1905-1941 .... TCLC 67
See also CA 160

C. 3. 3.
See Wilde, Oscar (Fingal O'Flahertie Wills)

Caballero, Fernan 1796-1877 .... NCLC 10

Cabell, Branch
See Cabell, James Branch

Cabell, James Branch 1879-1958 .... TCLC 6
See also CA 105; 152; DLB 9, 78

Cable, George Washington 1844-1925 T C L C
4; SSC 4
See also CA 104; 155; DLB 12, 74; DLBD 13

Cabral de Melo Neto, Joao 1920- ... CLC 76;
DAM MULT
See also CA 151

Cabrera Infante, G(uillermo) 1929- CLC 5, 25,
45; DAM MULT; HLC
See also CA 85-88; CANR 29; DLB 113; HW;
MTCW

Cade, Toni
See Bambara, Toni Cade

Cadmus and Harmonia
See Buchan, John

Caedmon fl. 658-680 .... CMLC 7
See also DLB 146

Caeiro, Alberto
See Pessoa, Fernando (Antonio Nogueira)

Cage, John (Milton, Jr.) 1912- .... CLC 41
See also CA 13-16R; CANR 9; INT CANR-9

Cahan, Abraham 1860-1951 .... TCLC 71
See also CA 108; 154; DLB 9, 25, 28

Cain, G.
See Cabrera Infante, G(uillermo)

Cain, Guillermo
See Cabrera Infante, G(uillermo)

Cain, James M(allahan) 1892-1977 CLC 3, 11,
28
See also AITN 1; CA 17-20R; 73-76; CANR 8,
34, 61; MTCW

Caine, Mark
See Raphael, Frederic (Michael)

Calasso, Roberto 1941- .... CLC 81
See also CA 143

Calderon de la Barca, Pedro 1600-1681 .. L C
23; DC 3

Caldwell, Erskine (Preston) 1903-1987 CLC 1,
8, 14, 50, 60; DAM NOV; SSC 19
See also AITN 1; CA 1-4R; 121; CAAS 1;
CANR 2, 33; DLB 9, 86; MTCW

Caldwell, (Janet Miriam) Taylor (Holland)
1900-1985 CLC 2, 28, 39; DAM NOV, POP
See also CA 5-8R; 116; CANR 5

Calhoun, John Caldwell 1782-1850 NCLC 15
See also DLB 3

Calisher, Hortense 1911- CLC 2, 4, 8, 38; DAM
NOV; SSC 15
See also CA 1-4R; CANR 1, 22; DLB 2; INT
CANR-22; MTCW

Callaghan, Morley Edward 1903-1990 CLC 3,
14, 41, 65; DAC; DAM MST
See also CA 9-12R; 132; CANR 33; DLB 68;
MTCW

Callimachus c. 305B.C.-c. 240B.C. CMLC 18
See also DLB 176

Calvin, John 1509-1564 .... LC 37

Calvino, Italo 1923-1985 CLC 5, 8, 11, 22, 33,
39, 73; DAM NOV; SSC 3
See also CA 85-88; 116; CANR 23, 61; MTCW

Cameron, Carey 1952- .... CLC 59
See also CA 135

Cameron, Peter 1959- .... CLC 44
See also CA 125; CANR 50

Campana, Dino 1885-1932 .... TCLC 20
See also CA 117; DLB 114

Campanella, Tommaso 1568-1639 .... LC 32

Campbell, John W(ood, Jr.) 1910-1971 C L C
32
See also CA 21-22; 29-32R; CANR 34; CAP 2;
DLB 8; MTCW

Campbell, Joseph 1904-1987 .... CLC 69
See also AAYA 3; BEST 89:2; CA 1-4R; 124;
CANR 3, 28, 61; MTCW

Campbell, Maria 1940- .... CLC 85; DAC
See also CA 102; CANR 54; NNAL

Campbell, (John) Ramsey 1946- CLC 42; SSC
19
See also CA 57-60; CANR 7; INT CANR-7

Campbell, (Ignatius) Roy (Dunnachie) 1901-
1957 .... TCLC 5
See also CA 104; 155; DLB 20

Campbell, Thomas 1777-1844 .... NCLC 19
See also DLB 93; 144

Campbell, Wilfred .... TCLC 9
See also Campbell, William

Campbell, William 1858(?)-1918
See Campbell, Wilfred
See also CA 106; DLB 92

Campion, Jane .... CLC 95
See also CA 138

Campos, Alvaro de
See Pessoa, Fernando (Antonio Nogueira)

Camus, Albert 1913-1960 CLC 1, 2, 4, 9, 11, 14,

32, 63, 69; DA; DAB; DAC; DAM DRAM, MST, NOV; DC 2; SSC 9; WLC
See also CA 89-92; DLB 72; MTCW

Canby, Vincent 1924- .... **CLC 13**
See also CA 81-84

Cancale
See Desnos, Robert

Canetti, Elias 1905-1994 **CLC 3, 14, 25, 75, 86**
See also CA 21-24R; 146; CANR 23, 61; DLB 85, 124; MTCW

Canin, Ethan 1960- .... **CLC 55**
See also CA 131; 135

Cannon, Curt
See Hunter, Evan

Cape, Judith
See Page, P(atricia) K(athleen)

Capek, Karel 1890-1938 ... **TCLC 6, 37; DA; DAB; DAC; DAM DRAM, MST, NOV; DC 1; WLC**
See also CA 104; 140

Capote, Truman 1924-1984 **CLC 1, 3, 8, 13, 19, 34, 38, 58; DA; DAB; DAC; DAM MST, NOV, POP; SSC 2; WLC**
See also CA 5-8R; 113; CANR 18, 62; CDALB 1941-1968; DLB 2; DLBY 80, 84; MTCW; SATA 91

Capra, Frank 1897-1991 .... **CLC 16**
See also CA 61-64; 135

Caputo, Philip 1941- .... **CLC 32**
See also CA 73-76; CANR 40

Caragiale, Ion Luca 1852-1912 ..... **TCLC 76**
See also CA 157

Card, Orson Scott 1951- **CLC 44, 47, 50; DAM POP**
See also AAYA 11; CA 102; CANR 27, 47; INT CANR-27; MTCW; SATA 83

Cardenal, Ernesto 1925- .... **CLC 31; DAM MULT, POET; HLC**
See also CA 49-52; CANR 2, 32; HW; MTCW

Cardozo, Benjamin N(athan) 1870-1938
TCLC 65
See also CA 117

Carducci, Giosue (Alessandro Giuseppe) 1835-1907 .... **TCLC 32**

Carew, Thomas 1595(?)-1640 .... **LC 13**
See also DLB 126

Carey, Ernestine Gilbreth 1908- .... **CLC 17**
See also CA 5-8R; SATA 2

Carey, Peter 1943- .... **CLC 40, 55, 96**
See also CA 123; 127; CANR 53; INT 127; MTCW; SATA 94

Carleton, William 1794-1869 .... **NCLC 3**
See also DLB 159

Carlisle, Henry (Coffin) 1926- .... **CLC 33**
See also CA 13-16R; CANR 15

Carlsen, Chris
See Holdstock, Robert P.

Carlson, Ron(ald F.) 1947- .... **CLC 54**
See also CA 105; CANR 27

Carlyle, Thomas 1795-1881 . **NCLC 22; DA; DAB; DAC; DAM MST**
See also CDBLB 1789-1832; DLB 55; 144

Carman, (William) Bliss 1861-1929 **TCLC 7; DAC**
See also CA 104; 152; DLB 92

Carnegie, Dale 1888-1955 .... **TCLC 53**

Carossa, Hans 1878-1956 .... **TCLC 48**
See also DLB 66

Carpenter, Don(ald Richard) 1931-1995 **C L C 41**
See also CA 45-48; 149; CANR 1

Carpentier (y Valmont), Alejo 1904-1980 **CLC 8, 11, 38; DAM MULT; HLC**

See also CA 65-68; 97-100; CANR 11; DLB 113; HW

Carr, Caleb 1955(?)- .... **CLC 86**
See also CA 147

Carr, Emily 1871-1945 .... **TCLC 32**
See also CA 159; DLB 68

Carr, John Dickson 1906-1977 .... **CLC 3**
See also Fairbairn, Roger
See also CA 49-52; 69-72; CANR 3, 33, 60; MTCW

Carr, Philippa
See Hibbert, Eleanor Alice Burford

Carr, Virginia Spencer 1929- .... **CLC 34**
See also CA 61-64; DLB 111

Carrere, Emmanuel 1957- .... **CLC 89**

Carrier, Roch 1937- **CLC 13, 78; DAC; DAM MST**
See also CA 130; CANR 61; DLB 53

Carroll, James P. 1943(?)- .... **CLC 38**
See also CA 81-84

Carroll, Jim 1951- .... **CLC 35**
See also AAYA 17; CA 45-48; CANR 42

Carroll, Lewis ..... **NCLC 2, 53; PC 18; WLC**
See also Dodgson, Charles Lutwidge
See also CDBLB 1832-1890; CLR 2, 18; DLB 18, 163, 178; JRDA

Carroll, Paul Vincent 1900-1968 ...... **CLC 10**
See also CA 9-12R; 25-28R; DLB 10

Carruth, Hayden 1921- **CLC 4, 7, 10, 18, 84; PC 10**
See also CA 9-12R; CANR 4, 38, 59; DLB 5, 165; INT CANR-4; MTCW; SATA 47

Carson, Rachel Louise 1907-1964 .. **CLC 71; DAM POP**
See also CA 77-80; CANR 35; MTCW; SATA 23

Carter, Angela (Olive) 1940-1992 **CLC 5, 41, 76; SSC 13**
See also CA 53-56; 136; CANR 12, 36, 61; DLB 14; MTCW; SATA 66; SATA-Obit 70

Carter, Nick
See Smith, Martin Cruz

Carver, Raymond 1938-1988 **CLC 22, 36, 53, 55; DAM NOV; SSC 8**
See also CA 33-36R; 126; CANR 17, 34, 61; DLB 130; DLBY 84, 88; MTCW

Cary, Elizabeth, Lady Falkland 1585-1639 **LC 30**

Cary, (Arthur) Joyce (Lunel) 1888-1957 **TCLC 1, 29**
See also CA 104; CDBLB 1914-1945; DLB 15, 100

Casanova de Seingalt, Giovanni Jacopo 1725-1798 .... **LC 13**

Casares, Adolfo Bioy
See Bioy Casares, Adolfo

Casely-Hayford, J(oseph) E(phraim) 1866-1930 **TCLC 24; BLC; DAM MULT**
See also BW 2; CA 123; 152

Casey, John (Dudley) 1939- .... **CLC 59**
See also BEST 90:2; CA 69-72; CANR 23

Casey, Michael 1947- .... **CLC 2**
See also CA 65-68; DLB 5

Casey, Patrick
See Thurman, Wallace (Henry)

Casey, Warren (Peter) 1935-1988 ..... **CLC 12**
See also CA 101; 127; INT 101

Casona, Alejandro .... **CLC 49**
See also Alvarez, Alejandro Rodriguez

Cassavetes, John 1929-1989 .... **CLC 20**
See also CA 85-88; 127

Cassian, Nina 1924- .... **PC 17**

Cassill, R(onald) V(erlin) 1919- .... **CLC 4, 23**

See also CA 9-12R; CAAS 1; CANR 7, 45; DLB 6

Cassirer, Ernst 1874-1945 .... **TCLC 61**
See also CA 157

Cassity, (Allen) Turner 1929- .... **CLC 6, 42**
See also CA 17-20R; CAAS 8; CANR 11; DLB 105

Castaneda, Carlos 1931(?)- .... **CLC 12**
See also CA 25-28R; CANR 32; HW; MTCW

Castedo, Elena 1937- .... **CLC 65**
See also CA 132

Castedo-Ellerman, Elena
See Castedo, Elena

Castellanos, Rosario 1925-1974 **CLC 66; DAM MULT; HLC**
See also CA 131; 53-56; CANR 58; DLB 113; HW

Castelvetro, Lodovico 1505-1571 .... **LC 12**

Castiglione, Baldassare 1478-1529 ...... **LC 12**

Castle, Robert
See Hamilton, Edmond

Castro, Guillen de 1569-1631 .... **LC 19**

Castro, Rosalia de 1837-1885 **NCLC 3; DAM MULT**

Cather, Willa
See Cather, Willa Sibert

Cather, Willa Sibert 1873-1947 **TCLC 1, 11, 31; DA; DAB; DAC; DAM MST, NOV; SSC 2; WLC**
See also CA 104; 128; CDALB 1865-1917; DLB 9, 54, 78; DLBD 1; MTCW; SATA 30

Cato, Marcus Porcius 234B.C.-149B.C.
CMLC 21

Catton, (Charles) Bruce 1899-1978 .. **CLC 35**
See also AITN 1; CA 5-8R; 81-84; CANR 7; DLB 17; SATA 2; SATA-Obit 24

Catullus c. 84B.C.-c. 54B.C. .... **CMLC 18**

Cauldwell, Frank
See King, Francis (Henry)

Caunitz, William J. 1933-1996 .... **CLC 34**
See also BEST 89:3; CA 125; 130; 152; INT 130

Causley, Charles (Stanley) 1917- .... **CLC 7**
See also CA 9-12R; CANR 5, 35; CLR 30; DLB 27; MTCW; SATA 3, 66

Caute, (John) David 1936- ..... **CLC 29; DAM NOV**
See also CA 1-4R; CAAS 4; CANR 1, 33, 64; DLB 14

Cavafy, C(onstantine) P(eter) 1863-1933 **TCLC 2, 7; DAM POET**
See also Kavafis, Konstantinos Petrou
See also CA 148

Cavallo, Evelyn
See Spark, Muriel (Sarah)

Cavanna, Betty .... **CLC 12**
See also Harrison, Elizabeth Cavanna
See also JRDA; MAICYA; SAAS 4; SATA 1, 30

Cavendish, Margaret Lucas 1623-1673 **LC 30**
See also DLB 131

Caxton, William 1421(?)-1491(?) .... **LC 17**
See also DLB 170

Cayrol, Jean 1911- .... **CLC 11**
See also CA 89-92; DLB 83

Cela, Camilo Jose 1916- **CLC 4, 13, 59; DAM MULT; HLC**
See also BEST 90:2; CA 21-24R; CAAS 10; CANR 21, 32; DLBY 89; HW; MTCW

Celan, Paul .... **CLC 10, 19, 53, 82; PC 10**
See also Antschel, Paul
See also DLB 69

Celine, Louis-Ferdinand **CLC 1, 3, 4, 7, 9, 15,**

47
See also Destouches, Louis-Ferdinand
See also DLB 72
Cellini, Benvenuto 1500-1571 .... **LC 7**
Cendrars, Blaise 1887-1961 ..... **CLC 18, 106**
See also Sauser-Hall, Frederic
Cernuda (y Bidon), Luis 1902-1963 **CLC 54; DAM POET**
See also CA 131; 89-92; DLB 134; HW
Cervantes (Saavedra), Miguel de 1547-1616
LC 6, 23; DA; DAB; DAC; DAM MST, NOV; SSC 12; WLC
Cesaire, Aime (Fernand) 1913- . **CLC 19, 32; BLC; DAM MULT, POET**
See also BW 2; CA 65-68; CANR 24, 43; MTCW
Chabon, Michael 1963- .... **CLC 55**
See also CA 139; CANR 57
Chabrol, Claude 1930- .... **CLC 16**
See also CA 110
Challans, Mary 1905-1983
See Renault, Mary
See also CA 81-84; 111; SATA 23; SATA-Obit 36
Challis, George
See Faust, Frederick (Schiller)
Chambers, Aidan 1934- .... **CLC 35**
See also CA 25-28R; CANR 12, 31, 58; JRDA; MAICYA; SAAS 12; SATA 1, 69
Chambers, James 1948-
See Cliff, Jimmy
See also CA 124
Chambers, Jessie
See Lawrence, D(avid) H(erbert Richards)
Chambers, Robert W. 1865-1933 ... **TCLC 41**
Chandler, Raymond (Thornton) 1888-1959
TCLC 1, 7; SSC 23
See also CA 104; 129; CANR 60; CDALB 1929-1941; DLBD 6; MTCW
Chang, Eileen 1921- .... **SSC 28**
Chang, Jung 1952- .... **CLC 71**
See also CA 142
Channing, William Ellery 1780-1842 **NCLC 17**
See also DLB 1, 59
Chaplin, Charles Spencer 1889-1977 **CLC 16**
See also Chaplin, Charlie
See also CA 81-84; 73-76
Chaplin, Charlie
See Chaplin, Charles Spencer
See also DLB 44
Chapman, George 1559(?)-1634 **LC 22; DAM DRAM**
See also DLB 62, 121
Chapman, Graham 1941-1989 .... **CLC 21**
See also Monty Python
See also CA 116; 129; CANR 35
Chapman, John Jay 1862-1933 .... **TCLC 7**
See also CA 104
Chapman, Lee
See Bradley, Marion Zimmer
Chapman, Walker
See Silverberg, Robert
Chappell, Fred (Davis) 1936- ..... **CLC 40, 78**
See also CA 5-8R; CAAS 4; CANR 8, 33; DLB 6, 105
Char, Rene(-Emile) 1907-1988 **CLC 9, 11, 14, 55; DAM POET**
See also CA 13-16R; 124; CANR 32; MTCW
Charby, Jay
See Ellison, Harlan (Jay)
Chardin, Pierre Teilhard de
See Teilhard de Chardin, (Marie Joseph) Pierre

Charles I 1600-1649 .... **LC 13**
Charriere, Isabelle de 1740-1805 .. **NCLC 66**
Charyn, Jerome 1937- .... **CLC 5, 8, 18**
See also CA 5-8R; CAAS 1; CANR 7, 61; DLBY 83; MTCW
Chase, Mary (Coyle) 1907-1981 .... **DC 1**
See also CA 77-80; 105; SATA 17; SATA-Obit 29
Chase, Mary Ellen 1887-1973 .... **CLC 2**
See also CA 13-16; 41-44R; CAP 1; SATA 10
Chase, Nicholas
See Hyde, Anthony
Chateaubriand, Francois Rene de 1768-1848 **NCLC 3**
See also DLB 119
Chatterje, Sarat Chandra 1876-1936(?)
See Chatterji, Saratchandra
See also CA 109
Chatterji, Bankim Chandra 1838-1894 **NCLC 19**
Chatterji, Saratchandra .... **TCLC 13**
See also Chatterje, Sarat Chandra
Chatterton, Thomas 1752-1770 . **LC 3; DAM POET**
See also DLB 109
Chatwin, (Charles) Bruce 1940-1989 **CLC 28, 57, 59; DAM POP**
See also AAYA 4; BEST 90:1; CA 85-88; 127
Chaucer, Daniel
See Ford, Ford Madox
Chaucer, Geoffrey 1340(?)-1400 **LC 17; DA; DAB; DAC; DAM MST, POET; PC 19; WLCS**
See also CDBLB Before 1660; DLB 146
Chaviaras, Strates 1935-
See Haviaras, Stratis
See also CA 105
Chayefsky, Paddy .... **CLC 23**
See also Chayefsky, Sidney
See also DLB 7, 44; DLBY 81
Chayefsky, Sidney 1923-1981
See Chayefsky, Paddy
See also CA 9-12R; 104; CANR 18; DAM DRAM
Chedid, Andree 1920- .... **CLC 47**
See also CA 145
Cheever, John 1912-1982 **CLC 3, 7, 8, 11, 15, 25, 64; DA; DAB; DAC; DAM MST, NOV, POP; SSC 1; WLC**
See also CA 5-8R; 106; CABS 1; CANR 5, 27; CDALB 1941-1968; DLB 2, 102; DLBY 80, 82; INT CANR-5; MTCW
Cheever, Susan 1943- .... **CLC 18, 48**
See also CA 103; CANR 27, 51; DLBY 82; INT CANR-27
Chekhonte, Antosha
See Chekhov, Anton (Pavlovich)
Chekhov, Anton (Pavlovich) 1860-1904 **TCLC 3, 10, 31, 55; DA; DAB; DAC; DAM DRAM, MST; SSC 2, 28; WLC**
See also CA 104; 124; SATA 90
Chernyshevsky, Nikolay Gavrilovich 1828-1889 **NCLC 1**
Cherry, Carolyn Janice 1942-
See Cherryh, C. J.
See also CA 65-68; CANR 10
Cherryh, C. J. .... **CLC 35**
See also Cherry, Carolyn Janice
See also DLBY 80; SATA 93
Chesnutt, Charles W(addell) 1858-1932
TCLC 5, 39; BLC; DAM MULT; SSC 7
See also BW 1; CA 106; 125; DLB 12, 50, 78; MTCW

Chester, Alfred 1929(?)-1971 .... **CLC 49**
See also CA 33-36R; DLB 130
Chesterton, G(ilbert) K(eith) 1874-1936
TCLC 1, 6, 64; DAM NOV, POET; SSC 1
See also CA 104; 132; CDBLB 1914-1945; DLB 10, 19, 34, 70, 98, 149, 178; MTCW; SATA 27
Chiang Pin-chin 1904-1986
See Ding Ling
See also CA 118
Ch'ien Chung-shu 1910- .... **CLC 22**
See also CA 130; MTCW
Child, L. Maria
See Child, Lydia Maria
Child, Lydia Maria 1802-1880 .... **NCLC 6**
See also DLB 1, 74; SATA 67
Child, Mrs.
See Child, Lydia Maria
Child, Philip 1898-1978 .... **CLC 19, 68**
See also CA 13-14; CAP 1; SATA 47
Childers, (Robert) Erskine 1870-1922 **TCLC 65**
See also CA 113; 153; DLB 70
Childress, Alice 1920-1994 **CLC 12, 15, 86, 96; BLC; DAM DRAM, MULT, NOV; DC 4**
See also AAYA 8; BW 2; CA 45-48; 146; CANR 3, 27, 50; CLR 14; DLB 7, 38; JRDA; MAICYA; MTCW; SATA 7, 48, 81
Chin, Frank (Chew, Jr.) 1940- .... **DC 7**
See also CA 33-36R; DAM MULT
Chislett, (Margaret) Anne 1943- ...... **CLC 34**
See also CA 151
Chitty, Thomas Willes 1926- .... **CLC 11**
See also Hinde, Thomas
See also CA 5-8R
Chivers, Thomas Holley 1809-1858 **NCLC 49**
See also DLB 3
Chomette, Rene Lucien 1898-1981
See Clair, Rene
See also CA 103
Chopin, Kate **TCLC 5, 14; DA; DAB; SSC 8; WLCS**
See also Chopin, Katherine
See also CDALB 1865-1917; DLB 12, 78
Chopin, Katherine 1851-1904
See Chopin, Kate
See also CA 104; 122; DAC; DAM MST, NOV
Chretien de Troyes c. 12th cent. - .. **CMLC 10**
Christie
See Ichikawa, Kon
Christie, Agatha (Mary Clarissa) 1890-1976
CLC 1, 6, 8, 12, 39, 48; DAB; DAC; DAM NOV
See also AAYA 9; AITN 1, 2; CA 17-20R; 61-64; CANR 10, 37; CDBLB 1914-1945; DLB 13, 77; MTCW; SATA 36
Christie, (Ann) Philippa
See Pearce, Philippa
See also CA 5-8R; CANR 4
Christine de Pizan 1365(?)-1431(?) .... **LC 9**
Chubb, Elmer
See Masters, Edgar Lee
Chulkov, Mikhail Dmitrievich 1743-1792 **LC 2**
See also DLB 150
Churchill, Caryl 1938- ..... **CLC 31, 55; DC 5**
See also CA 102; CANR 22, 46; DLB 13; MTCW
Churchill, Charles 1731-1764 .... **LC 3**
See also DLB 109
Chute, Carolyn 1947- .... **CLC 39**
See also CA 123
Ciardi, John (Anthony) 1916-1986 . **CLC 10, 40, 44; DAM POET**

See also CA 5-8R; 118; CAAS 2; CANR 5, 33;
CLR 19; DLB 5; DLBY 86; INT CANR-5;
MAICYA; MTCW; SATA 1, 65; SATA-Obit
46

Cicero, Marcus Tullius 106B.C.-43B.C.
CMLC 3

Cimino, Michael 1943- .... **CLC 16**
See also CA 105

Cioran, E(mil) M. 1911-1995 .... **CLC 64**
See also CA 25-28R; 149

Cisneros, Sandra 1954-**CLC 69; DAM MULT;
HLC**
See also AAYA 9; CA 131; CANR 64; DLB 122,
152; HW

Cixous, Helene 1937- .... **CLC 92**
See also CA 126; CANR 55; DLB 83; MTCW

Clair, Rene .... **CLC 20**
See also Chomette, Rene Lucien

Clampitt, Amy 1920-1994 ..... **CLC 32; PC 19**
See also CA 110; 146; CANR 29; DLB 105

Clancy, Thomas L., Jr. 1947-
See Clancy, Tom
See also CA 125; 131; CANR 62; INT 131;
MTCW

Clancy, Tom .... **CLC 45; DAM NOV, POP**
See also Clancy, Thomas L., Jr.
See also AAYA 9; BEST 89:1, 90:1

Clare, John 1793-1864 **NCLC 9; DAB; DAM
POET**
See also DLB 55, 96

Clarin
See Alas (y Urena), Leopoldo (Enrique Garcia)

Clark, Al C.
See Goines, Donald

Clark, (Robert) Brian 1932- .... **CLC 29**
See also CA 41-44R

Clark, Curt
See Westlake, Donald E(dwin)

Clark, Eleanor 1913-1996 ....**CLC 5, 19**
See also CA 9-12R; 151; CANR 41; DLB 6

Clark, J. P.
See Clark, John Pepper
See also DLB 117

Clark, John Pepper 1935-......**CLC 38; BLC;
DAM DRAM, MULT; DC 5**
See also Clark, J. P.
See also BW 1; CA 65-68; CANR 16

Clark, M. R.
See Clark, Mavis Thorpe

Clark, Mavis Thorpe 1909- .... **CLC 12**
See also CA 57-60; CANR 8, 37; CLR 30;
MAICYA; SAAS 5; SATA 8, 74

Clark, Walter Van Tilburg 1909-1971**CLC 28**
See also CA 9-12R; 33-36R; CANR 63; DLB
9; SATA 8

Clarke, Arthur C(harles) 1917-**CLC 1, 4, 13,
18, 35; DAM POP; SSC 3**
See also AAYA 4; CA 1-4R; CANR 2, 28, 55;
JRDA; MAICYA; MTCW; SATA 13, 70

Clarke, Austin 1896-1974 .... **CLC 6, 9; DAM
POET**
See also CA 29-32; 49-52; CAP 2; DLB 10, 20

Clarke, Austin C(hesterfield) 1934-**CLC 8, 53;
BLC; DAC; DAM MULT**
See also BW 1; CA 25-28R; CAAS 16; CANR
14, 32; DLB 53, 125

Clarke, Gillian 1937- .... **CLC 61**
See also CA 106; DLB 40

Clarke, Marcus (Andrew Hislop) 1846-1881
NCLC 19

Clarke, Shirley 1925- .... **CLC 16**

Clash, The
See Headon, (Nicky) Topper; Jones, Mick;

Simonon, Paul; Strummer, Joe

Claudel, Paul (Louis Charles Marie) 1868-1955
TCLC 2, 10
See also CA 104

Clavell, James (duMaresq) 1925-1994**CLC 6,
25, 87; DAM NOV, POP**
See also CA 25-28R; 146; CANR 26, 48;
MTCW

Cleaver, (Leroy) Eldridge 1935- ..... **CLC 30;
BLC; DAM MULT**
See also BW 1; CA 21-24R; CANR 16

Cleese, John (Marwood) 1939- .... **CLC 21**
· See also Monty Python
See also CA 112; 116; CANR 35; MTCW

Cleishbotham, Jebediah
See Scott, Walter

Cleland, John 1710-1789 .... **LC 2**
See also DLB 39

Clemens, Samuel Langhorne 1835-1910
See Twain, Mark
See also CA 104; 135; CDALB 1865-1917; DA;
DAB; DAC; DAM MST, NOV; DLB 11, 12,
23, 64, 74, 186; JRDA; MAICYA; YABC 2

Cleophil
See Congreve, William

Clerihew, E.
See Bentley, E(dmund) C(lerihew)

Clerk, N. W.
See Lewis, C(live) S(taples)

Cliff, Jimmy .... **CLC 21**
See also Chambers, James

Clifton, (Thelma) Lucille 1936- **CLC 19, 66;
BLC; DAM MULT, POET; PC 17**
See also BW 2; CA 49-52; CANR 2, 24, 42;
CLR 5; DLB 5, 41; MAICYA; MTCW; SATA
20, 69

Clinton, Dirk
See Silverberg, Robert

Clough, Arthur Hugh 1819-1861 ... **NCLC 27**
See also DLB 32

Clutha, Janet Paterson Frame 1924-
See Frame, Janet
See also CA 1-4R; CANR 2, 36; MTCW

Clyne, Terence
See Blatty, William Peter

Cobalt, Martin
See Mayne, William (James Carter)

Cobb, Irvin S. 1876-1944 .... **TCLC 77**
See also DLB 11, 25, 86

Cobbett, William 1763-1835........... **NCLC 49**
See also DLB 43, 107, 158

Coburn, D(onald) L(ee) 1938- .... **CLC 10**
See also CA 89-92

Cocteau, Jean (Maurice Eugene Clement) 1889-
1963**CLC 1, 8, 15, 16, 43; DA; DAB; DAC;
DAM DRAM, MST, NOV; WLC**
See also CA 25-28; CANR 40; CAP 2; DLB
65; MTCW

Codrescu, Andrei 1946-**CLC 46; DAM POET**
See also CA 33-36R; CAAS 19; CANR 13, 34,
53

Coe, Max
See Bourne, Randolph S(illiman)

Coe, Tucker
See Westlake, Donald E(dwin)

Coen, Ethan 1958- ....**CLC 108**
See also CA 126

Coen, Joel 1955-...............................**CLC 108**
See also CA 126

Coetzee, J(ohn) M(ichael) 1940- **CLC 23, 33,
66; DAM NOV**
See also CA 77-80; CANR 41, 54; MTCW

Coffey, Brian

See Koontz, Dean R(ay)

Cohan, George M(ichael) 1878-1942**TCLC 60**
See also CA 157

Cohen, Arthur A(llen) 1928-1986 . **CLC 7, 31**
See also CA 1-4R; 120; CANR 1, 17, 42; DLB
28

Cohen, Leonard (Norman) 1934- **CLC 3, 38;
DAC; DAM MST**
See also CA 21-24R; CANR 14; DLB 53;
MTCW

Cohen, Matt 1942- .... **CLC 19; DAC**
See also CA 61-64; CAAS 18; CANR 40; DLB
53

Cohen-Solal, Annie 19(?)- .... **CLC 50**

Colegate, Isabel 1931- .... **CLC 36**
See also CA 17-20R; CANR 8, 22; DLB 14;
INT CANR-22; MTCW

Coleman, Emmett
See Reed, Ishmael

Coleridge, M. E.
See Coleridge, Mary E(lizabeth)

Coleridge, Mary E(lizabeth) 1861-1907**TCLC
73**
See also CA 116; DLB 19, 98

Coleridge, Samuel Taylor 1772-1834**NCLC 9,
54; DA; DAB; DAC; DAM MST, POET;
PC 11; WLC**
See also CDBLB 1789-1832; DLB 93, 107

Coleridge, Sara 1802-1852 .... **NCLC 31**

Coles, Don 1928- .... **CLC 46**
See also CA 115; CANR 38

Coles, Robert (Martin) 1929- .... **CLC 108**
See also CA 45-48; CANR 3, 32; INT CANR-
32; SATA 23

Colette, (Sidonie-Gabrielle) 1873-1954**T C L C
1, 5, 16; DAM NOV; SSC 10**
See also CA 104; 131; DLB 65; MTCW

Collett, (Jacobine) Camilla (Wergeland) 1813-
1895 .... **NCLC 22**

Collier, Christopher 1930- .... **CLC 30**
See also AAYA 13; CA 33-36R; CANR 13, 33;
JRDA; MAICYA; SATA 16, 70

Collier, James L(incoln) 1928-**CLC 30; DAM
POP**
See also AAYA 13; CA 9-12R; CANR 4, 33,
60; CLR 3; JRDA; MAICYA; SAAS 21;
SATA 8, 70

Collier, Jeremy 1650-1726 .... **LC 6**

Collier, John 1901-1980 .... **SSC 19**
See also CA 65-68; 97-100; CANR 10; DLB
77

Collingwood, R(obin) G(eorge) 1889(?)-1943
TCLC 67
See also CA 117; 155

Collins, Hunt
See Hunter, Evan

Collins, Linda 1931- .... **CLC 44** ·
See also CA 125

Collins, (William) Wilkie 1824-1889**NCLC 1,
18**
See also CDBLB 1832-1890; DLB 18, 70, 159

Collins, William 1721-1759 . **LC 4, 40; DAM
POET**
See also DLB 109

Collodi, Carlo 1826-1890 .... **NCLC 54**
See also Lorenzini, Carlo
See also CLR 5

Colman, George
See Glassco, John

Colt, Winchester Remington
See Hubbard, L(afayette) Ron(ald)

Colter, Cyrus 1910- .... **CLC 58**
See also BW 1; CA 65-68; CANR 10; DLB 33

Crane, (Harold) Hart 1899-1932 **TCLC 2, 5; DA; DAB; DAC; DAM MST, POET; PC 3; WLC**
See also CA 104; 127; CDALB 1917-1929; DLB 4, 48; MTCW

Crane, R(onald) S(almon) 1886-1967**CLC 27**
See also CA 85-88; DLB 63

Crane, Stephen (Townley) 1871-1900 **TCLC 11, 17, 32; DA; DAB; DAC; DAM MST, NOV, POET; SSC 7; WLC**
See also AAYA 21; CA 109; 140; CDALB 1865-1917; DLB 12, 54, 78; YABC 2

Crase, Douglas 1944- .... **CLC 58**
See also CA 106

Crashaw, Richard 1612(?)-1649 .... **LC 24**
See also DLB 126

Craven, Margaret 1901-1980 . **CLC 17; DAC**
See also CA 103

Crawford, F(rancis) Marion 1854-1909**TCLC 10**
See also CA 107; DLB 71

Crawford, Isabella Valancy 1850-1887**NCLC 12**
See also DLB 92

Crayon, Geoffrey
See Irving, Washington

Creasey, John 1908-1973 .... **CLC 11**
See also CA 5-8R; 41-44R; CANR 8, 59; DLB 77; MTCW

Crebillon, Claude Prosper Jolyot de (fils) 1707-1777 .... **LC 28**

Credo
See Creasey, John

Credo, Alvaro J. de
See Prado (Calvo), Pedro

Creeley, Robert (White) 1926-**CLC 1, 2, 4, 8, 11, 15, 36, 78; DAM POET**
See also CA 1-4R; CAAS 10; CANR 23, 43; DLB 5, 16, 169; MTCW

Crews, Harry (Eugene) 1935- **CLC 6, 23, 49**
See also AITN 1; CA 25-28R; CANR 20, 57; DLB 6, 143; MTCW

Crichton, (John) Michael 1942-**CLC 2, 6, 54, 90; DAM NOV, POP**
See also AAYA 10; AITN 2; CA 25-28R; CANR 13, 40, 54; DLBY 81; INT CANR-13; JRDA; MTCW; SATA 9, 88

Crispin, Edmund .... **CLC 22**
See also Montgomery, (Robert) Bruce
See also DLB 87

Cristofer, Michael 1945(?)- .... **CLC 28; DAM DRAM**
See also CA 110; 152; DLB 7

Croce, Benedetto 1866-1952 .... **TCLC 37**
See also CA 120; 155

Crockett, David 1786-1836 .... **NCLC 8**
See also DLB 3, 11

Crockett, Davy
See Crockett, David

Crofts, Freeman Wills 1879-1957 .. **TCLC 55**
See also CA 115; DLB 77

Croker, John Wilson 1780-1857 .... **NCLC 10**
See also DLB 110

Crommelynck, Fernand 1885-1970 .. **CLC 75**
See also CA 89-92

Cronin, A(rchibald) J(oseph) 1896-1981**CLC 32**
See also CA 1-4R; 102; CANR 5; SATA 47; SATA-Obit 25

Cross, Amanda
See Heilbrun, Carolyn G(old)

Crothers, Rachel 1878(?)-1958 ...... **TCLC 19**
See also CA 113; DLB 7

Croves, Hal
See Traven, B.

Crow Dog, Mary (Ellen) (?)- .... **CLC 93**
See also Brave Bird, Mary
See also CA 154

Crowfield, Christopher
See Stowe, Harriet (Elizabeth) Beecher

Crowley, Aleister .... **TCLC 7**
See also Crowley, Edward Alexander

Crowley, Edward Alexander 1875-1947
See Crowley, Aleister
See also CA 104

Crowley, John 1942- .... **CLC 57**
See also CA 61-64; CANR 43; DLBY 82; SATA 65

Crud
See Crumb, R(obert)

Crumarums
See Crumb, R(obert)

Crumb, R(obert) 1943- .... **CLC 17**
See also CA 106

Crumbum
See Crumb, R(obert)

Crumski
See Crumb, R(obert)

Crum the Bum
See Crumb, R(obert)

Crunk
See Crumb, R(obert)

Crustt
See Crumb, R(obert)

Cryer, Gretchen (Kiger) 1935- .... **CLC 21**
See also CA 114; 123

Csath, Geza 1887-1919 .... **TCLC 13**
See also CA 111

Cudlip, David 1933- .... **CLC 34**

Cullen, Countee 1903-1946**TCLC 4, 37; BLC; DA; DAC; DAM MST, MULT, POET; PC 20; WLCS**
See also BW 1; CA 108; 124; CDALB 1917-1929; DLB 4, 48, 51; MTCW; SATA 18

Cum, R.
See Crumb, R(obert)

Cummings, Bruce F(rederick) 1889-1919
See Barbellion, W. N. P.
See also CA 123

Cummings, E(dward) E(stlin) 1894-1962**CLC 1, 3, 8, 12, 15, 68; DA; DAB; DAC; DAM MST, POET; PC 5; WLC 2**
See also CA 73-76; CANR 31; CDALB 1929-1941; DLB 4, 48; MTCW

Cunha, Euclides (Rodrigues Pimenta) da 1866-1909 .... **TCLC 24**
See also CA 123

Cunningham, E. V.
See Fast, Howard (Melvin)

Cunningham, J(ames) V(incent) 1911-1985 **CLC 3, 31**
See also CA 1-4R; 115; CANR 1; DLB 5

Cunningham, Julia (Woolfolk) 1916-**CLC 12**
See also CA 9-12R; CANR 4, 19, 36; JRDA; MAICYA; SAAS 2; SATA 1, 26

Cunningham, Michael 1952- .... **CLC 34**
See also CA 136

Cunninghame Graham, R(obert) B(ontine) 1852-1936 .... **TCLC 19**
See also Graham, R(obert) B(ontine) Cunninghame
See also CA 119; DLB 98

Currie, Ellen 19(?)- .... **CLC 44**

Curtin, Philip
See Lowndes, Marie Adelaide (Belloc)

Curtis, Price

See Ellison, Harlan (Jay)

Cutrate, Joe
See Spiegelman, Art

Cynewulf c. 770-c. 840 .... **CMLC 23**

Czaczkes, Shmuel Yosef
See Agnon, S(hmuel) Y(osef Halevi)

Dabrowska, Maria (Szumska) 1889-1965**CLC 15**
See also CA 106

Dabydeen, David 1955- .... **CLC 34**
See also BW 1; CA 125; CANR 56

Dacey, Philip 1939- .... **CLC 51**
See also CA 37-40R; CAAS 17; CANR 14, 32, 64; DLB 105

Dagerman, Stig (Halvard) 1923-1954 **TCLC 17**
See also CA 117; 155

Dahl, Roald 1916-1990**CLC 1, 6, 18, 79; DAB; DAC; DAM MST, NOV, POP**
See also AAYA 15; CA 1-4R; 133; CANR 6, 32, 37, 62; CLR 1, 7, 41; DLB 139; JRDA; MAICYA; MTCW; SATA 1, 26, 73; SATA-Obit 65

Dahlberg, Edward 1900-1977 .. **CLC 1, 7, 14**
See also CA 9-12R; 69-72; CANR 31, 62; DLB 48; MTCW

Daitch, Susan 1954- .... **CLC 103**
See also CA 161

Dale, Colin .... **TCLC 18**
See also Lawrence, T(homas) E(dward)

Dale, George E.
See Asimov, Isaac

Daly, Elizabeth 1878-1967 .... **CLC 52**
See also CA 23-24; 25-28R; CANR 60; CAP 2

Daly, Maureen 1921- .... **CLC 17**
See also AAYA 5; CANR 37; JRDA; MAICYA; SAAS 1; SATA 2

Damas, Leon-Gontran 1912-1978 .... **CLC 84**
See also BW 1; CA 125; 73-76

Dana, Richard Henry Sr. 1787-1879**NCLC 53**

Daniel, Samuel 1562(?)-1619 .... **LC 24**
See also DLB 62

Daniels, Brett
See Adler, Renata

Dannay, Frederic 1905-1982 . **CLC 11; DAM POP**
See also Queen, Ellery
See also CA 1-4R; 107; CANR 1, 39; DLB 137; MTCW

D'Annunzio, Gabriele 1863-1938**TCLC 6, 40**
See also CA 104; 155

Danois, N. le
See Gourmont, Remy (-Marie-Charles) de

Dante 1265-1321 .... **CMLC 3, 18; DA; DAB; DAC; DAM MST, POET; PC 21; WLCS**

d'Antibes, Germain
See Simenon, Georges (Jacques Christian)

Danticat, Edwidge 1969- .... **CLC 94**
See also CA 152

Danvers, Dennis 1947- .... **CLC 70**

Danziger, Paula 1944- .... **CLC 21**
See also AAYA 4; CA 112; 115; CANR 37; CLR 20; JRDA; MAICYA; SATA 36, 63; SATA-Brief 30

Da Ponte, Lorenzo 1749-1838 .... **NCLC 50**

Dario, Ruben 1867-1916 .... **TCLC 4; DAM MULT; HLC; PC 15**
See also CA 131; HW; MTCW

Darley, George 1795-1846 .... **NCLC 2**
See also DLB 96

Darwin, Charles 1809-1882 .... **NCLC 57**
See also DLB 57, 166

Daryush, Elizabeth 1887-1977 ...... **CLC 6, 19**

See also CA 49-52; CANR 3; DLB 20

Dashwood, Edmee Elizabeth Monica de la Pasture 1890-1943
See Delafield, E. M.
See also CA 119; 154

Daudet, (Louis Marie) Alphonse 1840-1897
NCLC 1
See also DLB 123

Daumal, Rene 1908-1944 .... **TCLC 14**
See also CA 114

Davenport, Guy (Mattison, Jr.) 1927-**CLC 6, 14, 38; SSC 16**
See also CA 33-36R; CANR 23; DLB 130

Davidson, Avram 1923-
See Queen, Ellery
See also CA 101; CANR 26; DLB 8

Davidson, Donald (Grady) 1893-1968**CLC 2, 13, 19**
See also CA 5-8R; 25-28R; CANR 4; DLB 45

Davidson, Hugh
See Hamilton, Edmond

Davidson, John 1857-1909 .... **TCLC 24**
See also CA 118; DLB 19

Davidson, Sara 1943- .... **CLC 9**
See also CA 81-84; CANR 44

Davie, Donald (Alfred) 1922-1995 . **CLC 5, 8, 10, 31**
See also CA 1-4R; 149; CAAS 3; CANR 1, 44; DLB 27; MTCW

Davies, Ray(mond Douglas) 1944- ... **CLC 21**
See also CA 116; 146

Davies, Rhys 1903-1978 .... **CLC 23**
See also CA 9-12R; 81-84; CANR 4; DLB 139

Davies, (William) Robertson 1913-1995 **C L C 2, 7, 13, 25, 42, 75, 91; DA; DAB; DAC; DAM MST, NOV, POP; WLC**
See also BEST 89:2; CA 33-36R; 150; CANR 17, 42; DLB 68; INT CANR-17; MTCW

Davies, W(illiam) H(enry) 1871-1940**TCLC 5**
See also CA 104; DLB 19, 174

Davies, Walter C.
See Kornbluth, C(yril) M.

Davis, Angela (Yvonne) 1944- **CLC 77; DAM MULT**
See also BW 2; CA 57-60; CANR 10

Davis, B. Lynch
See Bioy Casares, Adolfo; Borges, Jorge Luis

Davis, Gordon
See Hunt, E(verette) Howard, (Jr.)

Davis, Harold Lenoir 1896-1960 ...... **CLC 49**
See also CA 89-92; DLB 9

Davis, Rebecca (Blaine) Harding 1831-1910
TCLC 6
See also CA 104; DLB 74

Davis, Richard Harding 1864-1916**TCLC 24**
See also CA 114; DLB 12, 23, 78, 79; DLBD 13

Davison, Frank Dalby 1893-1970 ..... **CLC 15**
See also CA 116

Davison, Lawrence H.
See Lawrence, D(avid) H(erbert Richards)

Davison, Peter (Hubert) 1928- .... **CLC 28**
See also CA 9-12R; CAAS 4; CANR 3, 43; DLB 5

Davys, Mary 1674-1732 .... **LC 1**
See also DLB 39

Dawson, Fielding 1930-....................... **CLC 6**
See also CA 85-88; DLB 130

Dawson, Peter
See Faust, Frederick (Schiller)

Day, Clarence (Shepard, Jr.) 1874-1935
TCLC 25
See also CA 108; DLB 11

Day, Thomas 1748-1789 .... **LC 1**
See also DLB 39; YABC 1

Day Lewis, C(ecil) 1904-1972 . **CLC 1, 6, 10; DAM POET; PC 11**
See also Blake, Nicholas
See also CA 13-16; 33-36R; CANR 34; CAP 1; DLB 15, 20; MTCW

Dazai, Osamu .... **TCLC 11**
See also Tsushima, Shuji
See also DLB 182

de Andrade, Carlos Drummond
See Drummond de Andrade, Carlos

Deane, Norman
See Creasey, John

de Beauvoir, Simone (Lucie Ernestine Marie Bertrand)
See Beauvoir, Simone (Lucie Ernestine Marie Bertrand) de

de Beer, P.
See Bosman, Herman Charles

de Brissac, Malcolm
See Dickinson, Peter (Malcolm)

de Chardin, Pierre Teilhard
See Teilhard de Chardin, (Marie Joseph) Pierre

Dee, John 1527-1608 .... **LC 20**

Deer, Sandra 1940- .... **CLC 45**

De Ferrari, Gabriella 1941- .... **CLC 65**
See also CA 146

Defoe, Daniel 1660(?)-1731 **LC 1; DA; DAB; DAC; DAM MST, NOV; WLC**
See also CDBLB 1660-1789; DLB 39, 95, 101; JRDA; MAICYA; SATA 22

de Gourmont, Remy(-Marie-Charles)
See Gourmont, Remy (-Marie-Charles) de

de Hartog, Jan 1914- .... **CLC 19**
See also CA 1-4R; CANR 1

de Hostos, E. M.
See Hostos (y Bonilla), Eugenio Maria de

de Hostos, Eugenio M.
See Hostos (y Bonilla), Eugenio Maria de

Deighton, Len .... **CLC 4, 7, 22, 46**
See also Deighton, Leonard Cyril
See also AAYA 6; BEST 89:2; CDBLB 1960 to Present; DLB 87

Deighton, Leonard Cyril 1929-
See Deighton, Len
See also CA 9-12R; CANR 19, 33; DAM NOV, POP; MTCW

Dekker, Thomas 1572(?)-1632 .. **LC 22; DAM DRAM**
See also CDBLB Before 1660; DLB 62, 172

Delafield, E. M. 1890-1943 .... **TCLC 61**
See also Dashwood, Edmee Elizabeth Monica de la Pasture
See also DLB 34

de la Mare, Walter (John) 1873-1956**TCLC 4, 53; DAB; DAC; DAM MST, POET; SSC 14; WLC**
See also CDBLB 1914-1945; CLR 23; DLB 162; SATA 16

Delaney, Franey
See O'Hara, John (Henry)

Delaney, Shelagh 1939-**CLC 29; DAM DRAM**
See also CA 17-20R; CANR 30; CDBLB 1960 to Present; DLB 13; MTCW

Delany, Mary (Granville Pendarves) 1700-1788
LC 12

Delany, Samuel R(ay, Jr.) 1942-**CLC 8, 14, 38; BLC; DAM MULT**
See also BW 2; CA 81-84; CANR 27, 43; DLB 8, 33; MTCW

De La Ramee, (Marie) Louise 1839-1908
See Ouida

See also SATA 20

de la Roche, Mazo 1879-1961 .... **CLC 14**
See also CA 85-88; CANR 30; DLB 68; SATA 64

De La Salle, Innocent
See Hartmann, Sadakichi

Delbanco, Nicholas (Franklin) 1942- **CLC 6, 13**
See also CA 17-20R; CAAS 2; CANR 29, 55; DLB 6

del Castillo, Michel 1933- .... **CLC 38**
See also CA 109

Deledda, Grazia (Cosima) 1875(?)-1936
TCLC 23
See also CA 123

Delibes, Miguel .... **CLC 8, 18**
See also Delibes Setien, Miguel

Delibes Setien, Miguel 1920-
See Delibes, Miguel
See also CA 45-48; CANR 1, 32; HW; MTCW

DeLillo, Don 1936- **CLC 8, 10, 13, 27, 39, 54, 76; DAM NOV, POP**
See also BEST 89:1; CA 81-84; CANR 21; DLB 6, 173; MTCW

de Lisser, H. G.
See De Lisser, H(erbert) G(eorge)
See also DLB 117

De Lisser, H(erbert) G(eorge) 1878-1944
TCLC 12
See also de Lisser, H. G.
See also BW 2; CA 109; 152

Deloney, Thomas 1560-1600 .... **LC 41**

Deloria, Vine (Victor), Jr. 1933- ..... **CLC 21; DAM MULT**
See also CA 53-56; CANR 5, 20, 48; DLB 175; MTCW; NNAL; SATA 21

Del Vecchio, John M(ichael) 1947- ... **CLC 29**
See also CA 110; DLBD 9

de Man, Paul (Adolph Michel) 1919-1983
CLC 55
See also CA 128; 111; CANR 61; DLB 67; MTCW

De Marinis, Rick 1934- .... **CLC 54**
See also CA 57-60; CAAS 24; CANR 9, 25, 50

Dembry, R. Emmet
See Murfree, Mary Noailles

Demby, William 1922- . **CLC 53; BLC; DAM MULT**
See also BW 1; CA 81-84; DLB 33

de Menton, Francisco
See Chin, Frank (Chew, Jr.)

Demijohn, Thom
See Disch, Thomas M(ichael)

de Montherlant, Henry (Milon)
See Montherlant, Henry (Milon) de

Demosthenes 384B.C.-322B.C. ...... **CMLC 13**
See also DLB 176

de Natale, Francine
See Malzberg, Barry N(athaniel)

Denby, Edwin (Orr) 1903-1983 .... **CLC 48**
See also CA 138; 110

Denis, Julio
See Cortazar, Julio

Denmark, Harrison
See Zelazny, Roger (Joseph)

Dennis, John 1658-1734 .... **LC 11**
See also DLB 101

Dennis, Nigel (Forbes) 1912-1989 .... **CLC 8**
See also CA 25-28R; 129; DLB 13, 15; MTCW

Dent, Lester 1904(?)-1959 .... **TCLC 72**
See also CA 112; 161

De Palma, Brian (Russell) 1940- .... **CLC 20**
See also CA 109

See also CA 134

Durkheim, Emile 1858-1917 .... **TCLC 55**

Durrell, Lawrence (George) 1912-1990 **C L C 1, 4, 6, 8, 13, 27, 41; DAM NOV**
See also CA 9-12R; 132; CANR 40; CDBLB 1945-1960; DLB 15, 27; DLBY 90; MTCW

Durrenmatt, Friedrich
See Duerrenmatt, Friedrich

Dutt, Toru 1856-1877 .... **NCLC 29**

Dwight, Timothy 1752-1817 .... **NCLC 13**
See also DLB 37

Dworkin, Andrea 1946- .... **CLC 43**
See also CA 77-80; CAAS 21; CANR 16, 39; INT CANR-16; MTCW

Dwyer, Deanna
See Koontz, Dean R(ay)

Dwyer, K. R.
See Koontz, Dean R(ay)

Dye, Richard
See De Voto, Bernard (Augustine)

Dylan, Bob 1941- .... **CLC 3, 4, 6, 12, 77**
See also CA 41-44R; DLB 16

Eagleton, Terence (Francis) 1943-
See Eagleton, Terry
See also CA 57-60; CANR 7, 23; MTCW

Eagleton, Terry .... **CLC 63**
See also Eagleton, Terence (Francis)

Early, Jack
See Scoppettone, Sandra

East, Michael
See West, Morris L(anglo)

Eastaway, Edward
See Thomas, (Philip) Edward

Eastlake, William (Derry) 1917-1997 **CLC 8**
See also CA 5-8R; 158; CAAS 1; CANR 5, 63; DLB 6; INT CANR-5

Eastman, Charles A(lexander) 1858-1939 **TCLC 55; DAM MULT**
See also DLB 175; NNAL; YABC 1

Eberhart, Richard (Ghormley) 1904- **CLC 3, 11, 19, 56; DAM POET**
See also CA 1-4R; CANR 2; CDALB 1941-1968; DLB 48; MTCW

Eberstadt, Fernanda 1960- .... **CLC 39**
See also CA 136

Echegaray (y Eizaguirre), Jose (Maria Waldo) 1832-1916 .... **TCLC 4**
See also CA 104; CANR 32; HW; MTCW

Echeverria, (Jose) Esteban (Antonino) 1805-1851 .... **NCLC 18**

Echo
See Proust, (Valentin-Louis-George-Eugene-) Marcel

Eckert, Allan W. 1931- .... **CLC 17**
See also AAYA 18; CA 13-16R; CANR 14, 45; INT CANR-14; SAAS 21; SATA 29, 91; SATA-Brief 27

Eckhart, Meister 1260(?)-1328(?) ... **CMLC 9**
See also DLB 115

Eckmar, F. R.
See de Hartog, Jan

Eco, Umberto 1932- **CLC 28, 60; DAM NOV, POP**
See also BEST 90:1; CA 77-80; CANR 12, 33, 55; MTCW

Eddison, E(ric) R(ucker) 1882-1945 **TCLC 15**
See also CA 109; 156

Eddy, Mary (Morse) Baker 1821-1910 **T C L C 71**
See also CA 113

Edel, (Joseph) Leon 1907-1997 .. **CLC 29, 34**
See also CA 1-4R; 161; CANR 1, 22; DLB 103; INT CANR-22

Eden, Emily 1797-1869 .... **NCLC 10**

Edgar, David 1948- ... **CLC 42; DAM DRAM**
See also CA 57-60; CANR 12, 61; DLB 13; MTCW

Edgerton, Clyde (Carlyle) 1944- ...... **CLC 39**
See also AAYA 17; CA 118; 134; CANR 64; INT 134

Edgeworth, Maria 1768-1849 .... **NCLC 1, 51**
See also DLB 116, 159, 163; SATA 21

Edmonds, Paul
See Kuttner, Henry

Edmonds, Walter D(umaux) 1903- ... **CLC 35**
See also CA 5-8R; CANR 2; DLB 9; MAICYA; SAAS 4; SATA 1, 27

Edmondson, Wallace
See Ellison, Harlan (Jay)

Edson, Russell .... **CLC 13**
See also CA 33-36R

Edwards, Bronwen Elizabeth
See Rose, Wendy

Edwards, G(erald) B(asil) 1899-1976 **CLC 25**
See also CA 110

Edwards, Gus 1939- .... **CLC 43**
See also CA 108; INT 108

Edwards, Jonathan 1703-1758 .... **LC 7; DA; DAC; DAM MST**
See also DLB 24

Efron, Marina Ivanovna Tsvetaeva
See Tsvetaeva (Efron), Marina (Ivanovna)

Ehle, John (Marsden, Jr.) 1925- .... **CLC 27**
See also CA 9-12R

Ehrenbourg, Ilya (Grigoryevich)
See Ehrenburg, Ilya (Grigoryevich)

Ehrenburg, Ilya (Grigoryevich) 1891-1967 **CLC 18, 34, 62**
See also CA 102; 25-28R

Ehrenburg, Ilyo (Grigoryevich)
See Ehrenburg, Ilya (Grigoryevich)

Eich, Guenter 1907-1972 .... **CLC 15**
See also CA 111; 93-96; DLB 69, 124

Eichendorff, Joseph Freiherr von 1788-1857 **NCLC 8**
See also DLB 90

Eigner, Larry .... **CLC 9**
See also Eigner, Laurence (Joel)
See also CAAS 23; DLB 5

Eigner, Laurence (Joel) 1927-1996
See Eigner, Larry
See also CA 9-12R; 151; CANR 6

Einstein, Albert 1879-1955 .... **TCLC 65**
See also CA 121; 133; MTCW

Eiseley, Loren Corey 1907-1977 .... **CLC 7**
See also AAYA 5; CA 1-4R; 73-76; CANR 6

Eisenstadt, Jill 1963- .... **CLC 50**
See also CA 140

Eisenstein, Sergei (Mikhailovich) 1898-1948 **TCLC 57**
See also CA 114; 149

Eisner, Simon
See Kornbluth, C(yril) M.

Ekeloef, (Bengt) Gunnar 1907-1968 **CLC 27; DAM POET**
See also CA 123; 25-28R

Ekelof, (Bengt) Gunnar
See Ekeloef, (Bengt) Gunnar

Ekelund, Vilhelm 1880-1949 .... **TCLC 75**

Ekwensi, C. O. D.
See Ekwensi, Cyprian (Odiatu Duaka)

Ekwensi, Cyprian (Odiatu Duaka) 1921- **C L C 4; BLC; DAM MULT**
See also BW 2; CA 29-32R; CANR 18, 42; DLB 117; MTCW; SATA 66

Elaine .... **TCLC 18**

See also Leverson, Ada

El Crummo
See Crumb, R(obert)

Elder, Lonne III 1931-1996 .... **DC 8**
See also BLC; BW 1; CA 81-84; 152; CANR 25; DAM MULT; DLB 7, 38, 44

Elia
See Lamb, Charles

Eliade, Mircea 1907-1986 .... **CLC 19**
See also CA 65-68; 119; CANR 30, 62; MTCW

Eliot, A. D.
See Jewett, (Theodora) Sarah Orne

Eliot, Alice
See Jewett, (Theodora) Sarah Orne

Eliot, Dan
See Silverberg, Robert

Eliot, George 1819-1880 **NCLC 4, 13, 23, 41, 49; DA; DAB; DAC; DAM MST, NOV; PC 20; WLC**
See also CDBLB 1832-1890; DLB 21, 35, 55

Eliot, John 1604-1690 .... **LC 5**
See also DLB 24

Eliot, T(homas) S(tearns) 1888-1965 **CLC 1, 2, 3, 6, 9, 10, 13, 15, 24, 34, 41, 55, 57; DA; DAB; DAC; DAM DRAM, MST, POET; PC 5; WLC 2**
See also CA 5-8R; 25-28R; CANR 41; CDALB 1929-1941; DLB 7, 10, 45, 63; DLBY 88; MTCW

Elizabeth 1866-1941 .... **TCLC 41**

Elkin, Stanley L(awrence) 1930-1995 **CLC 4, 6, 9, 14, 27, 51, 91; DAM NOV, POP; SSC 12**
See also CA 9-12R; 148; CANR 8, 46; DLB 2, 28; DLBY 80; INT CANR-8; MTCW

Elledge, Scott .... **CLC 34**

Elliot, Don
See Silverberg, Robert

Elliott, Don
See Silverberg, Robert

Elliott, George P(aul) 1918-1980 .... **CLC 2**
See also CA 1-4R; 97-100; CANR 2

Elliott, Janice 1931- .... **CLC 47**
See also CA 13-16R; CANR 8, 29; DLB 14

Elliott, Sumner Locke 1917-1991 ..... **CLC 38**
See also CA 5-8R; 134; CANR 2, 21

Elliott, William
See Bradbury, Ray (Douglas)

Ellis, A. E. .... **CLC 7**

Ellis, Alice Thomas .... **CLC 40**
See also Haycraft, Anna

Ellis, Bret Easton 1964- .. **CLC 39, 71; DAM POP**
See also AAYA 2; CA 118; 123; CANR 51; INT 123

Ellis, (Henry) Havelock 1859-1939 **TCLC 14**
See also CA 109

Ellis, Landon
See Ellison, Harlan (Jay)

Ellis, Trey 1962- .... **CLC 55**
See also CA 146

Ellison, Harlan (Jay) 1934- ... **CLC 1, 13, 42; DAM POP; SSC 14**
See also CA 5-8R; CANR 5, 46; DLB 8; INT CANR-5; MTCW

Ellison, Ralph (Waldo) 1914-1994 . **CLC 1, 3, 11, 54, 86; BLC; DA; DAB; DAC; DAM MST, MULT, NOV; SSC 26; WLC**
See also AAYA 19; BW 1; CA 9-12R; 145; CANR 24, 53; CDALB 1941-1968; DLB 2, 76; DLBY 94; MTCW

Ellmann, Lucy (Elizabeth) 1956- ...... **CLC 61**
See also CA 128

See also AAYA 17; CA 13-14; 25-28R; CAP 1;
　CLR 27; DLB 22; JRDA; MAICYA; SATA 2
Forche, Carolyn (Louise) 1950- **CLC 25, 83,**
　86; DAM POET; PC 10
　See also CA 109; 117; CANR 50; DLB 5; INT
　117
Ford, Elbur
　See Hibbert, Eleanor Alice Burford
Ford, Ford Madox 1873-1939 **TCLC 1, 15, 39,**
　57; DAM NOV
　See also CA 104; 132; CDBLB 1914-1945;
　DLB 162; MTCW
Ford, Henry 1863-1947 .... **TCLC 73**
　See also CA 115; 148
Ford, John 1586-(?) .... **DC 8**
　See also CDBLB Before 1660; DAM DRAM;
　DLB 58
Ford, John 1895-1973 .... **CLC 16**
　See also CA 45-48
Ford, Richard .... **CLC 99**
Ford, Richard 1944- .... **CLC 46**
　See also CA 69-72; CANR 11, 47
Ford, Webster
　See Masters, Edgar Lee
Foreman, Richard 1937- .... **CLC 50**
　See also CA 65-68; CANR 32, 63
Forester, C(ecil) S(cott) 1899-1966 ... **CLC 35**
　See also CA 73-76; 25-28R; SATA 13
Forez
　See Mauriac, Francois (Charles)
Forman, James Douglas 1932- .... **CLC 21**
　See also AAYA 17; CA 9-12R; CANR 4, 19,
　42; JRDA; MAICYA; SATA 8, 70
Fornes, Maria Irene 1930- .... **CLC 39, 61**
　See also CA 25-28R; CANR 28; DLB 7; HW;
　INT CANR-28; MTCW
Forrest, Leon 1937- .... **CLC 4**
　See also BW 2; CA 89-92; CAAS 7; CANR 25,
　52; DLB 33
Forster, E(dward) M(organ) 1879-1970 **C L C**
　1, 2, 3, 4, 9, 10, 13, 15, 22, 45, 77; DA; DAB;
　DAC; DAM MST, NOV; SSC 27; WLC
　See also AAYA 2; CA 13-14; 25-28R; CANR
　45; CAP 1; CDBLB 1914-1945; DLB 34, 98,
　162, 178; DLBD 10; MTCW; SATA 57
Forster, John 1812-1876 .... **NCLC 11**
　See also DLB 144, 184
Forsyth, Frederick 1938- **CLC 2, 5, 36; DAM**
　NOV, POP
　See also BEST 89:4; CA 85-88; CANR 38, 62;
　DLB 87; MTCW
Forten, Charlotte L. .... **TCLC 16; BLC**
　See also Grimke, Charlotte L(ottie) Forten
　See also DLB 50
Foscolo, Ugo 1778-1827 .... **NCLC 8**
Fosse, Bob .... **CLC 20**
　See also Fosse, Robert Louis
Fosse, Robert Louis 1927-1987
　See Fosse, Bob
　See also CA 110; 123
Foster, Stephen Collins 1826 1864 **NCLC 26**
Foucault, Michel 1926-1984 . **CLC 31, 34, 69**
　See also CA 105; 113; CANR 34; MTCW
Fouque, Friedrich (Heinrich Karl) de la Motte
　1777-1843 .... **NCLC 2**
　See also DLB 90
Fourier, Charles 1772-1837 .... **NCLC 51**
Fournier, Henri Alban 1886-1914
　See Alain-Fournier
　See also CA 104
Fournier, Pierre 1916- .... **CLC 11**
　See also Gascar, Pierre
　See also CA 89-92; CANR 16, 40

Fowles, John 1926- **CLC 1, 2, 3, 4, 6, 9, 10, 15,**
　33, 87; DAB; DAC; DAM MST
　See also CA 5-8R; CANR 25; CDBLB 1960 to
　Present; DLB 14, 139; MTCW; SATA 22
Fox, Paula 1923- .... **CLC 2, 8**
　See also AAYA 3; CA 73-76; CANR 20, 36,
　62; CLR 1, 44; DLB 52; JRDA; MAICYA;
　MTCW; SATA 17, 60
Fox, William Price (Jr.) 1926- .... **CLC 22**
　See also CA 17-20R; CAAS 19; CANR 11; DLB
　2; DLBY 81
Foxe, John 1516(?)-1587 .... **LC 14**
Frame, Janet 1924- **CLC 2, 3, 6, 22, 66, 96; SSC**
　29
　See also Clutha, Janet Paterson Frame
France, Anatole .... **TCLC 9**
　See also Thibault, Jacques Anatole Francois
　See also DLB 123
Francis, Claude 19(?)- .... **CLC 50**
Francis, Dick 1920- **CLC 2, 22, 42, 102; DAM**
　POP
　See also AAYA 5, 21; BEST 89:3; CA 5-8R;
　CANR 9, 42; CDBLB 1960 to Present; DLB
　87; INT CANR-9; MTCW
Francis, Robert (Churchill) 1901-1987 **C L C**
　15
　See also CA 1-4R; 123; CANR 1
Frank, Anne(lies Marie) 1929-1945 **TCLC 17;**
　DA; DAB; DAC; DAM MST; WLC
　See also AAYA 12; CA 113; 133; MTCW; SATA
　87; SATA-Brief 42
Frank, Elizabeth 1945- .... **CLC 39**
　See also CA 121; 126; INT 126
Frankl, Viktor E(mil) 1905-1997 ...... **CLC 93**
　See also CA 65-68; 161
Franklin, Benjamin
　See Hasek, Jaroslav (Matej Frantisek)
Franklin, Benjamin 1706-1790 .. **LC 25; DA;**
　DAB; DAC; DAM MST; WLCS
　See also CDALB 1640-1865; DLB 24, 43, 73
Franklin, (Stella Maraia Sarah) Miles 1879-
　1954 .... **TCLC 7**
　See also CA 104
Fraser, (Lady) Antonia (Pakenham) 1932-
　CLC 32, 107
　See also CA 85-88; CANR 44; MTCW; SATA-
　Brief 32
Fraser, George MacDonald 1925- ...... **CLC 7**
　See also CA 45-48; CANR 2, 48
Fraser, Sylvia 1935- .... **CLC 64**
　See also CA 45-48; CANR 1, 16, 60
Frayn, Michael 1933- **CLC 3, 7, 31, 47; DAM**
　DRAM, NOV
　See also CA 5-8R; CANR 30; DLB 13, 14;
　MTCW
Fraze, Candida (Merrill) 1945- .... **CLC 50**
　See also CA 126
Frazer, J(ames) G(eorge) 1854-1941 **TCLC 32**
　See also CA 118
Frazer, Robert Caine
　See Creasey, John
Frazer, Sir James George
　See Frazer, J(ames) G(eorge)
Frazier, Ian 1951- .... **CLC 46**
　See also CA 130; CANR 54
Frederic, Harold 1856-1898 .... **NCLC 10**
　See also DLB 12, 23; DLBD 13
Frederick, John
　See Faust, Frederick (Schiller)
Frederick the Great 1712-1786 .... **LC 14**
Fredro, Aleksander 1793-1876 .... **NCLC 8**
Freeling, Nicolas 1927- .... **CLC 38**
　See also CA 49-52; CAAS 12; CANR 1, 17,

50; DLB 87
Freeman, Douglas Southall 1886-1953 **T C L C**
　11
　See also CA 109; DLB 17
Freeman, Judith 1946- .... **CLC 55**
　See also CA 148
Freeman, Mary Eleanor Wilkins 1852-1930
　TCLC 9; SSC 1
　See also CA 106; DLB 12, 78
Freeman, R(ichard) Austin 1862-1943 **T C L C**
　21
　See also CA 113; DLB 70
French, Albert 1943- .... **CLC 86**
French, Marilyn 1929- **CLC 10, 18, 60; DAM**
　DRAM, NOV, POP
　See also CA 69-72; CANR 3, 31; INT CANR-
　31; MTCW
French, Paul
　See Asimov, Isaac
Freneau, Philip Morin 1752-1832 ... **NCLC 1**
　See also DLB 37, 43
Freud, Sigmund 1856-1939 .... **TCLC 52**
　See also CA 115; 133; MTCW
Friedan, Betty (Naomi) 1921- .... **CLC 74**
　See also CA 65-68; CANR 18, 45; MTCW
Friedlander, Saul 1932- .... **CLC 90**
　See also CA 117; 130
Friedman, B(ernard) H(arper) 1926- **CLC 7**
　See also CA 1-4R; CANR 3, 48
Friedman, Bruce Jay 1930- ...... **CLC 3, 5, 56**
　See also CA 9-12R; CANR 25, 52; DLB 2, 28;
　INT CANR-25
Friel, Brian 1929- .... **CLC 5, 42, 59; DC 8**
　See also CA 21-24R; CANR 33; DLB 13;
　MTCW
Friis-Baastad, Babbis Ellinor 1921-1970 **CLC**
　12
　See also CA 17-20R; 134; SATA 7
Frisch, Max (Rudolf) 1911-1991 **CLC 3, 9, 14,**
　18, 32, 44; DAM DRAM, NOV
　See also CA 85-88; 134; CANR 32; DLB 69,
　124; MTCW
Fromentin, Eugene (Samuel Auguste) 1820-
　1876 .... **NCLC 10**
　See also DLB 123
Frost, Frederick
　See Faust, Frederick (Schiller)
Frost, Robert (Lee) 1874-1963 **CLC 1, 3, 4, 9,**
　10, 13, 15, 26, 34, 44; DA; DAB; DAC;
　DAM MST, POET; PC 1; WLC
　See also AAYA 21; CA 89-92; CANR 33;
　CDALB 1917-1929; DLB 54; DLBD 7;
　MTCW; SATA 14
Froude, James Anthony 1818-1894 **NCLC 43**
　See also DLB 18, 57, 144
Froy, Herald
　See Waterhouse, Keith (Spencer)
Fry, Christopher 1907- **CLC 2, 10, 14; DAM**
　DRAM
　See also CA 17-20R; CAAS 23; CANR 9, 30;
　DLB 13; MTCW; SATA 66
Frye, (Herman) Northrop 1912-1991 **CLC 24,**
　70
　See also CA 5-8R; 133; CANR 8, 37; DLB 67,
　68; MTCW
Fuchs, Daniel 1909-1993 .... **CLC 8, 22**
　See also CA 81-84; 142; CAAS 5; CANR 40;
　DLB 9, 26, 28; DLBY 93
Fuchs, Daniel 1934- .... **CLC 34**
　See also CA 37-40R; CANR 14, 48
Fuentes, Carlos 1928- **CLC 3, 8, 10, 13, 22, 41,**
　60; DA; DAB; DAC; DAM MST, MULT,
　NOV; HLC; SSC 24; WLC

See also AAYA 4; AITN 2; CA 69-72; CANR 10, 32; DLB 113; HW; MTCW

Fuentes, Gregorio Lopez y
See Lopez y Fuentes, Gregorio

Fugard, (Harold) Athol 1932-**CLC 5, 9, 14, 25, 40, 80; DAM DRAM; DC 3**
See also AAYA 17; CA 85-88; CANR 32, 54; MTCW

Fugard, Sheila 1932- .... **CLC 48**
See also CA 125

Fuller, Charles (H., Jr.) 1939- **CLC 25; BLC; DAM DRAM, MULT; DC 1**
See also BW 2; CA 108; 112; DLB 38; INT 112; MTCW

Fuller, John (Leopold) 1937- .... **CLC 62**
See also CA 21-24R; CANR 9, 44; DLB 40

Fuller, Margaret .... **NCLC 5, 50**
See also Ossoli, Sarah Margaret (Fuller marchesa d')

Fuller, Roy (Broadbent) 1912-1991**CLC 4, 28**
See also CA 5-8R; 135; CAAS 10; CANR 53; DLB 15, 20; SATA 87

Fulton, Alice 1952- .... **CLC 52**
See also CA 116; CANR 57

Furphy, Joseph 1843-1912 .... **TCLC 25**

Fussell, Paul 1924- .... **CLC 74**
See also BEST 90:1; CA 17-20R; CANR 8, 21, 35; INT CANR-21; MTCW

Futabatei, Shimei 1864-1909 .... **TCLC 44**
See also DLB 180

Futrelle, Jacques 1875-1912 .... **TCLC 19**
See also CA 113; 155

Gaboriau, Emile 1835-1873 .... **NCLC 14**

Gadda, Carlo Emilio 1893-1973 .... **CLC 11**
See also CA 89-92; DLB 177

Gaddis, William 1922- **CLC 1, 3, 6, 8, 10, 19, 43, 86**
See also CA 17-20R; CANR 21, 48; DLB 2; MTCW

Gage, Walter
See Inge, William (Motter)

Gaines, Ernest J(ames) 1933- **CLC 3, 11, 18, 86; BLC; DAM MULT**
See also AAYA 18; AITN 1; BW 2; CA 9-12R; CANR 6, 24, 42; CDALB 1968-1988; DLB 2, 33, 152; DLBY 80; MTCW; SATA 86

Gaitskill, Mary 1954- .... **CLC 69**
See also CA 128; CANR 61

Galdos, Benito Perez
See Perez Galdos, Benito

Gale, Zona 1874-1938**TCLC 7; DAM DRAM**
See also CA 105; 153; DLB 9, 78

Galeano, Eduardo (Hughes) 1940- ... **CLC 72**
See also CA 29-32R; CANR 13, 32; HW

Galiano, Juan Valera y Alcala
See Valera y Alcala-Galiano, Juan

Gallagher, Tess 1943- ...... **CLC 18, 63; DAM POET; PC 9**
See also CA 106; DLB 120

Gallant, Mavis 1922- ... **CLC 7, 18, 38; DAC; DAM MST; SSC 5**
See also CA 69-72; CANR 29; DLB 53; MTCW

Gallant, Roy A(rthur) 1924- .... **CLC 17**
See also CA 5-8R; CANR 4, 29, 54; CLR 30; MAICYA; SATA 4, 68

Gallico, Paul (William) 1897-1976 ..... **CLC 2**
See also AITN 1; CA 5-8R; 69-72; CANR 23; DLB 9, 171; MAICYA; SATA 13

Gallo, Max Louis 1932- .... **CLC 95**
See also CA 85-88

Gallois, Lucien
See Desnos, Robert

Gallup, Ralph

See Whitemore, Hugh (John)

Galsworthy, John 1867-1933**TCLC 1, 45; DA; DAB; DAC; DAM DRAM, MST, NOV; SSC 22; WLC 2**
See also CA 104; 141; CDBLB 1890-1914; DLB 10, 34, 98, 162; DLBD 16

Galt, John 1779-1839 .... **NCLC 1**
See also DLB 99, 116, 159

Galvin, James 1951- .... **CLC 38**
See also CA 108; CANR 26

Gamboa, Federico 1864-1939 .... **TCLC 36**

Gandhi, M. K.
See Gandhi, Mohandas Karamchand

Gandhi, Mahatma
See Gandhi, Mohandas Karamchand

Gandhi, Mohandas Karamchand 1869-1948 **TCLC 59; DAM MULT**
See also CA 121; 132; MTCW

Gann, Ernest Kellogg 1910-1991 ...... **CLC 23**
See also AITN 1; CA 1-4R; 136; CANR 1

Garcia, Cristina 1958- .... **CLC 76**
See also CA 141

Garcia Lorca, Federico 1898-1936**TCLC 1, 7, 49; DA; DAB; DAC; DAM DRAM, MST, MULT, POET; DC 2; HLC; PC 3; WLC**
See also CA 104; 131; DLB 108; HW; MTCW

Garcia Marquez, Gabriel (Jose) 1928-**CLC 2, 3, 8, 10, 15, 27, 47, 55, 68; DA; DAB; DAC; DAM MST, MULT, NOV, POP; HLC; SSC 8; WLC**
See also AAYA 3; BEST 89:1, 90:4; CA 33-36R; CANR 10, 28, 50; DLB 113; HW; MTCW

Gard, Janice
See Latham, Jean Lee

Gard, Roger Martin du
See Martin du Gard, Roger

Gardam, Jane 1928- .... **CLC 43**
See also CA 49-52; CANR 2, 18, 33, 54; CLR 12; DLB 14, 161; MAICYA; MTCW; SAAS 9; SATA 39, 76; SATA-Brief 28

Gardner, Herb(ert) 1934- .... **CLC 44**
See also CA 149

Gardner, John (Champlin), Jr. 1933-1982 **CLC 2, 3, 5, 7, 8, 10, 18, 28, 34; DAM NOV, POP; SSC 7**
See also AITN 1; CA 65-68; 107; CANR 33; DLB 2; DLBY 82; MTCW; SATA 40; SATA-Obit 31

Gardner, John (Edmund) 1926-**CLC 30; DAM POP**
See also CA 103; CANR 15; MTCW

Gardner, Miriam
See Bradley, Marion Zimmer

Gardner, Noel
See Kuttner, Henry

Gardons, S. S.
See Snodgrass, W(illiam) D(e Witt)

Garfield, Leon 1921-1996 .... **CLC 12**
See also AAYA 8; CA 17-20R; 152; CANR 38, 41; CLR 21; DLB 161; JRDA; MAICYA; SATA 1, 32, 76; SATA-Obit 90

Garland, (Hannibal) Hamlin 1860-1940 **TCLC 3; SSC 18**
See also CA 104; DLB 12, 71, 78

Garneau, (Hector de) Saint-Denys 1912-1943 **TCLC 13**
See also CA 111; DLB 88

Garner, Alan 1934-**CLC 17; DAB; DAM POP**
See also AAYA 18; CA 73-76; CANR 15, 64; CLR 20; DLB 161; MAICYA; MTCW; SATA 18, 69

Garner, Hugh 1913-1979 .... **CLC 13**

See also CA 69-72; CANR 31; DLB 68

Garnett, David 1892-1981 .... **CLC 3**
See also CA 5-8R; 103; CANR 17; DLB 34

Garos, Stephanie
See Katz, Steve

Garrett, George (Palmer) 1929-**CLC 3, 11, 51**
See also CA 1-4R; CAAS 5; CANR 1, 42; DLB 2, 5, 130, 152; DLBY 83

Garrick, David 1717-1779 ....**LC 15; DAM DRAM**
See also DLB 84

Garrigue, Jean 1914-1972 .... **CLC 2, 8**
See also CA 5-8R; 37-40R; CANR 20

Garrison, Frederick
See Sinclair, Upton (Beall)

Garth, Will
See Hamilton, Edmond; Kuttner, Henry

Garvey, Marcus (Moziah, Jr.) 1887-1940 **TCLC 41; BLC; DAM MULT**
See also BW 1; CA 120; 124

Gary, Romain .... **CLC 25**
See also Kacew, Romain
See also DLB 83

Gascar, Pierre .... **CLC 11**
See also Fournier, Pierre

Gascoyne, David (Emery) 1916- .... **CLC 45**
See also CA 65-68; CANR 10, 28, 54; DLB 20; MTCW

Gaskell, Elizabeth Cleghorn 1810-1865**NCLC 5; DAB; DAM MST; SSC 25**
See also CDBLB 1832-1890; DLB 21, 144, 159

Gass, William H(oward) 1924-**CLC 1, 2, 8, 11, 15, 39; SSC 12**
See also CA 17-20R; CANR 30; DLB 2; MTCW

Gasset, Jose Ortega y
See Ortega y Gasset, Jose

Gates, Henry Louis, Jr. 1950- **CLC 65; DAM MULT**
See also BW 2; CA 109; CANR 25, 53; DLB 67

Gautier, Theophile 1811-1872 .. **NCLC 1, 59; DAM POET; PC 18; SSC 20**
See also DLB 119

Gawsworth, John
See Bates, H(erbert) E(rnest)

Gay, Oliver
See Gogarty, Oliver St. John

Gaye, Marvin (Penze) 1939-1984 ..... **CLC 26**
See also CA 112

Gebler, Carlo (Ernest) 1954- .... **CLC 39**
See also CA 119; 133

Gee, Maggie (Mary) 1948- .... **CLC 57**
See also CA 130

Gee, Maurice (Gough) 1931- .... **CLC 29**
See also CA 97-100; SATA 46

Gelbart, Larry (Simon) 1923- .... **CLC 21, 61**
See also CA 73-76; CANR 45

Gelber, Jack 1932- .... **CLC 1, 6, 14, 79**
See also CA 1-4R; CANR 2; DLB 7

Gellhorn, Martha (Ellis) 1908- .. **CLC 14, 60**
See also CA 77-80; CANR 44; DLBY 82

Genet, Jean 1910-1986**CLC 1, 2, 5, 10, 14, 44, 46; DAM DRAM**
See also CA 13-16R; CANR 18; DLB 72; DLBY 86; MTCW

Gent, Peter 1942- .... **CLC 29**
See also AITN 1; CA 89-92; DLBY 82

Gentlewoman in New England, A
See Bradstreet, Anne

Gentlewoman in Those Parts, A
See Bradstreet, Anne

George, Jean Craighead 1919- .... **CLC 35**
See also AAYA 8; CA 5-8R; CANR 25; CLR 1;

DLB 52; JRDA; MAICYA; SATA 2, 68

George, Stefan (Anton) 1868-1933TCLC **2, 14**
See also CA 104

Georges, Georges Martin
See Simenon, Georges (Jacques Christian)

Gerhardi, William Alexander
See Gerhardie, William Alexander

Gerhardie, William Alexander 1895-1977
CLC **5**
See also CA 25-28R; 73-76; CANR 18; DLB
36

Gerstler, Amy 1956- .... CLC **70**
See also CA 146

Gertler, T. .... CLC **34**
See also CA 116; 121; INT 121

Ghalib .... NCLC **39**
See also Ghalib, Hsadullah Khan

Ghalib, Hsadullah Khan 1797-1869
See Ghalib
See also DAM POET

Ghelderode, Michel de 1898-1962CLC **6, 11;**
DAM DRAM
See also CA 85-88; CANR 40

Ghiselin, Brewster 1903- .... CLC **23**
See also CA 13-16R; CAAS 10; CANR 13

Ghose, Zulfikar 1935- .... CLC **42**
See also CA 65-68

Ghosh, Amitav 1956- .... CLC **44**
See also CA 147

Giacosa, Giuseppe 1847-1906 .... TCLC **7**
See also CA 104

Gibb, Lee
See Waterhouse, Keith (Spencer)

Gibbon, Lewis Grassic .... TCLC **4**
See also Mitchell, James Leslie

Gibbons, Kaye 1960-CLC **50, 88; DAM POP**
See also CA 151

Gibran, Kahlil 1883-1931 . TCLC **1, 9; DAM**
POET, POP; PC **9**
See also CA 104; 150

Gibran, Khalil
See Gibran, Kahlil

Gibson, William 1914- .. CLC **23; DA; DAB;**
DAC; DAM DRAM, MST
See also CA 9-12R; CANR 9, 42; DLB 7; SATA
66

Gibson, William (Ford) 1948- ... CLC **39, 63;**
DAM POP
See also AAYA 12; CA 126; 133; CANR 52

Gide, Andre (Paul Guillaume) 1869-1951
TCLC **5, 12, 36; DA; DAB; DAC; DAM**
MST, NOV; SSC **13; WLC**
See also CA 104; 124; DLB 65; MTCW

Gifford, Barry (Colby) 1946- .... CLC **34**
See also CA 65-68; CANR 9, 30, 40

Gilbert, Frank
See De Voto, Bernard (Augustine)

Gilbert, W(illiam) S(chwenck) 1836-1911
TCLC **3; DAM DRAM, POET**
See also CA 104; SATA 36

Gilbreth, Frank B., Jr. 1911- .... CLC **17**
See also CA 9-12R; SATA 2

Gilchrist, Ellen 1935-CLC **34, 48; DAM POP;**
SSC **14**
See also CA 113; 116; CANR 41, 61; DLB 130;
MTCW

Giles, Molly 1942- .... CLC **39**
See also CA 126

Gill, Patrick
See Creasey, John

Gilliam, Terry (Vance) 1940- .... CLC **21**
See also Monty Python
See also AAYA 19; CA 108; 113; CANR 35;

INT 113

Gillian, Jerry
See Gilliam, Terry (Vance)

Gilliatt, Penelope (Ann Douglass) 1932-1993
CLC **2, 10, 13, 53**
See also AITN 2; CA 13-16R; 141; CANR 49;
DLB 14

Gilman, Charlotte (Anna) Perkins (Stetson)
1860-1935 .... TCLC **9, 37; SSC 13**
See also CA 106; 150

Gilmour, David 1949- .... CLC **35**
See also CA 138, 147

Gilpin, William 1724-1804 .... NCLC **30**

Gilray, J. D.
See Mencken, H(enry) L(ouis)

Gilroy, Frank D(aniel) 1925- .... CLC **2**
See also CA 81-84; CANR 32, 64; DLB 7

Gilstrap, John 1957(?)- .... CLC **99**
See also CA 160

Ginsberg, Allen 1926-1997CLC **1, 2, 3, 4, 6, 13,**
36, 69; DA; DAB; DAC; DAM MST,
POET; PC **4; WLC 3**
See also AITN 1; CA 1-4R; 157; CANR 2, 41,
63; CDALB 1941-1968; DLB 5, 16, 169;
MTCW

Ginzburg, Natalia 1916-1991CLC **5, 11, 54, 70**
See also CA 85-88; 135; CANR 33; DLB 177;
MTCW

Giono, Jean 1895-1970 .... CLC **4, 11**
See also CA 45-48; 29-32R; CANR 2, 35; DLB
72; MTCW

Giovanni, Nikki 1943-CLC **2, 4, 19, 64; BLC;**
DA; DAB; DAC; DAM MST, MULT,
POET; PC **19; WLCS**
See also AAYA 22; AITN 1; BW 2; CA 29-32R;
CAAS 6; CANR 18, 41, 60; CLR 6; DLB 5,
41; INT CANR-18; MAICYA; MTCW; SATA
24

Giovene, Andrea 1904- .... CLC **7**
See also CA 85-88

Gippius, Zinaida (Nikolayevna) 1869-1945
See Hippius, Zinaida
See also CA 106

Giraudoux, (Hippolyte) Jean 1882-1944
TCLC **2, 7; DAM DRAM**
See also CA 104; DLB 65

Gironella, Jose Maria 1917- .... CLC **11**
See also CA 101

Gissing, George (Robert) 1857-1903TCLC **3,**
24, 47
See also CA 105; DLB 18, 135, 184

Giurlani, Aldo
See Palazzeschi, Aldo

Gladkov, Fyodor (Vasilyevich) 1883-1958
TCLC **27**

Glanville, Brian (Lester) 1931- .... CLC **6**
See also CA 5-8R; CAAS 9; CANR 3; DLB 15,
139; SATA 42

Glasgow, Ellen (Anderson Gholson) 1873(?)-
1945 .... TCLC **2, 7**
See also CA 104; DLB 9, 12

Glaspell, Susan 1882(?)-1948 .... TCLC **55**
See also CA 110; 154; DLB 7, 9, 78; YABC 2

Glassco, John 1909-1981 .... CLC **9**
See also CA 13-16R; 102; CANR 15; DLB 68

Glasscock, Amnesia
See Steinbeck, John (Ernst)

Glasser, Ronald J. 1940(?)- .... CLC **37**

Glassman, Joyce
See Johnson, Joyce

Glendinning, Victoria 1937- .... CLC **50**
See also CA 120; 127; CANR 59; DLB 155

Glissant, Edouard 1928- . CLC **10, 68; DAM**

MULT
See also CA 153

Gloag, Julian 1930- .... CLC **40**
See also AITN 1; CA 65-68; CANR 10

Glowacki, Aleksander
See Prus, Boleslaw

Gluck, Louise (Elisabeth) 1943-CLC **7, 22, 44,**
81; DAM POET; PC **16**
See also CA 33-36R; CANR 40; DLB 5

Glyn, Elinor 1864-1943 .... TCLC **72**
See also DLB 153

Gobineau, Joseph Arthur (Comte) de 1816-
1882 .... NCLC **17**
See also DLB 123

Godard, Jean-Luc 1930- .... CLC **20**
See also CA 93-96

Godden, (Margaret) Rumer 1907- ... CLC **53**
See also AAYA 6; CA 5-8R; CANR 4, 27, 36,
55; CLR 20; DLB 161; MAICYA; SAAS 12;
SATA 3, 36

Godoy Alcayaga, Lucila 1889-1957
See Mistral, Gabriela
See also BW 2; CA 104; 131; DAM MULT;
HW; MTCW

Godwin, Gail (Kathleen) 1937- CLC **5, 8, 22,**
31, 69; DAM POP
See also CA 29-32R; CANR 15, 43; DLB 6;
INT CANR-15; MTCW

Godwin, William 1756-1836 .... NCLC **14**
See also CDBLB 1789-1832; DLB 39, 104, 142,
158, 163

Goebbels, Josef
See Goebbels, (Paul) Joseph

Goebbels, (Paul) Joseph 1897-1945TCLC **68**
See also CA 115; 148

Goebbels, Joseph Paul
See Goebbels, (Paul) Joseph

Goethe, Johann Wolfgang von 1749-1832
NCLC **4, 22, 34; DA; DAB; DAC; DAM**
DRAM, MST, POET; PC **5; WLC 3**
See also DLB 94

Gogarty, Oliver St. John 1878-1957TCLC **15**
See also CA 109; 150; DLB 15, 19

Gogol, Nikolai (Vasilyevich) 1809-1852NCLC
5, 15, 31; DA; DAB; DAC; DAM DRAM,
MST; DC **1; SSC 4, 29; WLC**

Goines, Donald 1937(?)-1974 CLC **80; BLC;**
DAM MULT, POP
See also AITN 1; BW 1; CA 124; 114; DLB 33

Gold, Herbert 1924- .... CLC **4, 7, 14, 42**
See also CA 9-12R; CANR 17, 45; DLB 2;
DLBY 81

Goldbarth, Albert 1948- .... CLC **5, 38**
See also CA 53-56; CANR 6, 40; DLB 120

Goldberg, Anatol 1910-1982 .... CLC **34**
See also CA 131; 117

Goldemberg, Isaac 1945- .... CLC **52**
See also CA 69-72; CAAS 12; CANR 11, 32;
HW

Golding, William (Gerald) 1911-1993CLC **1,**
2, 3, 8, 10, 17, 27, 58, 81; DA; DAB; DAC;
DAM MST, NOV; WLC
See also AAYA 5; CA 5-8R; 141; CANR 13,
33, 54; CDBLB 1945-1960; DLB 15, 100;
MTCW

Goldman, Emma 1869-1940 .... TCLC **13**
See also CA 110; 150

Goldman, Francisco 1955- .... CLC **76**

Goldman, William (W.) 1931- .... CLC **1, 48**
See also CA 9-12R; CANR 29; DLB 44

Goldmann, Lucien 1913-1970 .... CLC **24**
See also CA 25-28; CAP 2

Goldoni, Carlo 1707-1793LC **4; DAM DRAM**

Goldsberry, Steven 1949- .... **CLC 34**
See also CA 131

Goldsmith, Oliver 1728-1774**LC 2; DA; DAB; DAC; DAM DRAM, MST, NOV, POET; DC 8; WLC**
See also CDBLB 1660-1789; DLB 39, 89, 104, 109, 142; SATA 26

Goldsmith, Peter
See Priestley, J(ohn) B(oynton)

Gombrowicz, Witold 1904-1969**CLC 4, 7, 11, 49; DAM DRAM**
See also CA 19-20; 25-28R; CAP 2

Gomez de la Serna, Ramon 1888-1963**CLC 9**
See also CA 153; 116; HW

Goncharov, Ivan Alexandrovich 1812-1891
NCLC 1, 63

Goncourt, Edmond (Louis Antoine Huot) de 1822-1896 .... **NCLC 7**
See also DLB 123

Goncourt, Jules (Alfred Huot) de 1830-1870
NCLC 7
See also DLB 123

Gontier, Fernande 19(?)- .... **CLC 50**

Gonzalez Martinez, Enrique 1871-1952
TCLC 72
See also HW

Goodman, Paul 1911-1972 ...... **CLC 1, 2, 4, 7**
See also CA 19-20; 37-40R; CANR 34; CAP 2; DLB 130; MTCW

Gordimer, Nadine 1923-**CLC 3, 5, 7, 10, 18, 33, 51, 70; DA; DAB; DAC; DAM MST, NOV; SSC 17; WLCS**
See also CA 5-8R; CANR 3, 28, 56; INT CANR-28; MTCW

Gordon, Adam Lindsay 1833-1870 **NCLC 21**

Gordon, Caroline 1895-1981**CLC 6, 13, 29, 83; SSC 15**
See also CA 11-12; 103; CANR 36; CAP 1; DLB 4, 9, 102; DLBY 81; MTCW

Gordon, Charles William 1860-1937
See Connor, Ralph
See also CA 109

Gordon, Mary (Catherine) 1949- **CLC 13, 22**
See also CA 102; CANR 44; DLB 6; DLBY 81; INT 102; MTCW

Gordon, N. J.
See Bosman, Herman Charles

Gordon, Sol 1923- .... **CLC 26**
See also CA 53-56; CANR 4; SATA 11

Gordone, Charles 1925-1995**CLC 1, 4; DAM DRAM; DC 8**
See also BW 1; CA 93-96; 150; CANR 55; DLB 7; INT 93-96; MTCW

Gore, Catherine 1800-1861 .... **NCLC 65**
See also DLB 116

Gorenko, Anna Andreevna
See Akhmatova, Anna

Gorky, Maxim 1868-1936**TCLC 8; DAB; SSC 28; WLC**
See also Peshkov, Alexei Maximovich

Goryan, Sirak
See Saroyan, William

Gosse, Edmund (William) 1849-1928**TCLC 28**
See also CA 117; DLB 57, 144, 184

Gotlieb, Phyllis Fay (Bloom) 1926- .. **CLC 18**
See also CA 13-16R; CANR 7; DLB 88

Gottesman, S. D.
See Kornbluth, C(yril) M.; Pohl, Frederik

Gottfried von Strassburg fl. c. 1210- **CMLC 10**
See also DLB 138

Gould, Lois .... **CLC 4, 10**
See also CA 77-80; CANR 29; MTCW

Gourmont, Remy (-Marie-Charles) de 1858-1915 .... **TCLC 17**
See also CA 109; 150

Govier, Katherine 1948- .... **CLC 51**
See also CA 101; CANR 18, 40

Goyen, (Charles) William 1915-1983**CLC 5, 8, 14, 40**
See also AITN 2; CA 5-8R; 110; CANR 6; DLB 2; DLBY 83; INT CANR-6

Goytisolo, Juan 1931- . **CLC 5, 10, 23; DAM MULT; HLC**
See also CA 85-88; CANR 32, 61; HW; MTCW

Gozzano, Guido 1883-1916 .... **PC 10**
See also CA 154; DLB 114

Gozzi, (Conte) Carlo 1720-1806 .... **NCLC 23**

Grabbe, Christian Dietrich 1801-1836**NCLC 2**
See also DLB 133

Grace, Patricia 1937- .... **CLC 56**

Gracian y Morales, Baltasar 1601-1658**LC 15**

Gracq, Julien .... **CLC 11, 48**
See also Poirier, Louis
See also DLB 83

Grade, Chaim 1910-1982 .... **CLC 10**
See also CA 93-96; 107

Graduate of Oxford, A
See Ruskin, John

Grafton, Garth
See Duncan, Sara Jeannette

Graham, John
See Phillips, David Graham

Graham, Jorie 1951- .... **CLC 48**
See also CA 111; CANR 63; DLB 120

Graham, R(obert) B(ontine) Cunninghame
See Cunninghame Graham, R(obert) B(ontine)
See also DLB 98, 135, 174

Graham, Robert
See Haldeman, Joe (William)

Graham, Tom
See Lewis, (Harry) Sinclair

Graham, W(illiam) S(ydney) 1918-1986**CLC 29**
See also CA 73-76; 118; DLB 20

Graham, Winston (Mawdsley) 1910- **CLC 23**
See also CA 49-52; CANR 2, 22, 45; DLB 77

Grahame, Kenneth 1859-1932**TCLC 64; DAB**
See also CA 108; 136; CLR 5; DLB 34, 141, 178; MAICYA; YABC 1

Grant, Skeeter
See Spiegelman, Art

Granville-Barker, Harley 1877-1946**TCLC 2; DAM DRAM**
See also Barker, Harley Granville
See also CA 104

Grass, Guenter (Wilhelm) 1927-**CLC 1, 2, 4, 6, 11, 15, 22, 32, 49, 88; DA; DAB; DAC; DAM MST, NOV; WLC**
See also CA 13-16R; CANR 20; DLB 75, 124; MTCW

Gratton, Thomas
See Hulme, T(homas) E(rnest)

Grau, Shirley Ann 1929- .. **CLC 4, 9; SSC 15**
See also CA 89-92; CANR 22; DLB 2; INT CANR-22; MTCW

Gravel, Fern
See Hall, James Norman

Graver, Elizabeth 1964- .... **CLC 70**
See also CA 135

Graves, Richard Perceval 1945- .... **CLC 44**
See also CA 65-68; CANR 9, 26, 51

Graves, Robert (von Ranke) 1895-1985 **CLC 1, 2, 6, 11, 39, 44, 45; DAB; DAC; DAM MST, POET; PC 6**

See also CA 5-8R; 117; CANR 5, 36; CDBLB 1914-1945; DLB 20, 100; DLBY 85; MTCW; SATA 45

Graves, Valerie
See Bradley, Marion Zimmer

Gray, Alasdair (James) 1934- .... **CLC 41**
See also CA 126; CANR 47; INT 126; MTCW

Gray, Amlin 1946- .... **CLC 29**
See also CA 138

Gray, Francine du Plessix 1930- ..... **CLC 22; DAM NOV**
See also BEST 90:3; CA 61-64; CAAS 2; CANR 11, 33; INT CANR-11; MTCW

Gray, John (Henry) 1866-1934 ...... **TCLC 19**
See also CA 119

Gray, Simon (James Holliday) 1936- **CLC 9, 14, 36**
See also AITN 1; CA 21-24R; CAAS 3; CANR 32; DLB 13; MTCW

Gray, Spalding 1941-**CLC 49; DAM POP; DC 7**
See also CA 128

Gray, Thomas 1716-1771**LC 4, 40; DA; DAB; DAC; DAM MST; PC 2; WLC**
See also CDBLB 1660-1789; DLB 109

Grayson, David
See Baker, Ray Stannard

Grayson, Richard (A.) 1951- .... **CLC 38**
See also CA 85-88; CANR 14, 31, 57

Greeley, Andrew M(oran) 1928- ..... **CLC 28; DAM POP**
See also CA 5-8R; CAAS 7; CANR 7, 43; MTCW

Green, Anna Katharine 1846-1935 **TCLC 63**
See also CA 112; 159

Green, Brian
See Card, Orson Scott

Green, Hannah
See Greenberg, Joanne (Goldenberg)

Green, Hannah 1927(?)-1996 .... **CLC 3**
See also CA 73-76; CANR 59

Green, Henry 1905-1973 .... **CLC 2, 13, 97**
See also Yorke, Henry Vincent
See also DLB 15

Green, Julian (Hartridge) 1900-
See Green, Julien
See also CA 21-24R; CANR 33; DLB 4, 72; MTCW

Green, Julien .... **CLC 3, 11, 77**
See also Green, Julian (Hartridge)

Green, Paul (Eliot) 1894-1981**CLC 25; DAM DRAM**
See also AITN 1; CA 5-8R; 103; CANR 3; DLB 7, 9; DLBY 81

Greenberg, Ivan 1908-1973
See Rahv, Philip
See also CA 85-88

Greenberg, Joanne (Goldenberg) 1932- **CLC 7, 30**
See also AAYA 12; CA 5-8R; CANR 14, 32; SATA 25

Greenberg, Richard 1959(?)- .... **CLC 57**
See also CA 138

Greene, Bette 1934- .... **CLC 30**
See also AAYA 7; CA 53-56; CANR 4; CLR 2; JRDA; MAICYA; SAAS 16; SATA 8

Greene, Gael .... **CLC 8**
See also CA 13-16R; CANR 10

Greene, Graham (Henry) 1904-1991**CLC 1, 3, 6, 9, 14, 18, 27, 37, 70, 72; DA; DAB; DAC; DAM MST, NOV; SSC 29; WLC**
See also AITN 2; CA 13-16R; 133; CANR 35, 61; CDBLB 1945-1960; DLB 13, 15, 77,

100, 162; DLBY 91; MTCW; SATA 20

Greene, Robert 1558-1592 .... LC 41

Greer, Richard
See Silverberg, Robert

Gregor, Arthur 1923- .... CLC 9
See also CA 25-28R; CAAS 10; CANR 11;
SATA 36

Gregor, Lee
See Pohl, Frederik

Gregory, Isabella Augusta (Persse) 1852-1932
TCLC 1
See also CA 104; DLB 10

Gregory, J. Dennis
See Williams, John A(lfred)

Grendon, Stephen
See Derleth, August (William)

Grenville, Kate 1950- .... CLC 61
See also CA 118; CANR 53

Grenville, Pelham
See Wodehouse, P(elham) G(renville)

Greve, Felix Paul (Berthold Friedrich) 1879-
1948
See Grove, Frederick Philip
See also CA 104; 141; DAC; DAM MST

Grey, Zane 1872-1939 .. TCLC 6; DAM POP
See also CA 104; 132; DLB 9; MTCW

Grieg, (Johan) Nordahl (Brun) 1902-1943
TCLC 10
See also CA 107

Grieve, C(hristopher) M(urray) 1892-1978
CLC 11, 19; DAM POET
See also MacDiarmid, Hugh; Pteleon
See also CA 5-8R; 85-88; CANR 33; MTCW

Griffin, Gerald 1803-1840 .... NCLC 7
See also DLB 159

Griffin, John Howard 1920-1980 ..... CLC 68
See also AITN 1; CA 1-4R; 101; CANR 2

Griffin, Peter 1942- .... CLC 39
See also CA 136

Griffith, D(avid Lewelyn) W(ark) 1875(?)-1948
TCLC 68
See also CA 119; 150

Griffith, Lawrence
See Griffith, D(avid Lewelyn) W(ark)

Griffiths, Trevor 1935- .... CLC 13, 52
See also CA 97-100; CANR 45; DLB 13

Griggs, Sutton Elbert 1872-1930(?)TCLC 77
See also CA 123; DLB 50

Grigson, Geoffrey (Edward Harvey) 1905-1985
CLC 7, 39
See also CA 25-28R; 118; CANR 20, 33; DLB
27; MTCW

Grillparzer, Franz 1791-1872 .... NCLC 1
See also DLB 133

Grimble, Reverend Charles James
See Eliot, T(homas) S(tearns)

Grimke, Charlotte L(ottie) Forten 1837(?)-1914
See Forten, Charlotte L.
See also BW 1; CA 117; 124; DAM MULT,
POET

Grimm, Jacob Ludwig Karl 1785-1863NCLC
3
See also DLB 90; MAICYA; SATA 22

Grimm, Wilhelm Karl 1786-1859 .... NCLC 3
See also DLB 90; MAICYA; SATA 22

Grimmelshausen, Johann Jakob Christoffel von
1621-1676 .... LC 6
See also DLB 168

Grindel, Eugene 1895-1952
See Eluard, Paul
See also CA 104

Grisham, John 1955- .... CLC 84; DAM POP
See also AAYA 14; CA 138; CANR 47

Grossman, David 1954- .... CLC 67
See also CA 138

Grossman, Vasily (Semenovich) 1905-1964
CLC 41
See also CA 124; 130; MTCW

Grove, Frederick Philip .... TCLC 4
See also Greve, Felix Paul (Berthold Friedrich)
See also DLB 92

Grubb
See Crumb, R(obert)

Grumbach, Doris (Isaac) 1918-CLC 13, 22, 64
See also CA 5-8R; CAAS 2; CANR 9, 42; INT
CANR-9

Grundtvig, Nicolai Frederik Severin 1783-1872
NCLC 1

Grunge
See Crumb, R(obert)

Grunwald, Lisa 1959- .... CLC 44
See also CA 120

Guare, John 1938- . CLC 8, 14, 29, 67; DAM
DRAM
See also CA 73-76; CANR 21; DLB 7; MTCW

Gudjonsson, Halldor Kiljan 1902-
See Laxness, Halldor
See also CA 103

Guenter, Erich
See Eich, Guenter

Guest, Barbara 1920- .... CLC 34
See also CA 25-28R; CANR 11, 44; DLB 5

Guest, Judith (Ann) 1936- CLC 8, 30; DAM
NOV, POP
See also AAYA 7; CA 77-80; CANR 15; INT
CANR-15; MTCW

Guevara, Che .... CLC 87; HLC
See also Guevara (Serna), Ernesto

Guevara (Serna), Ernesto 1928-1967
See Guevara, Che
See also CA 127; 111; CANR 56; DAM MULT;
HW

Guild, Nicholas M. 1944- .... CLC 33
See also CA 93-96

Guillemin, Jacques
See Sartre, Jean-Paul

Guillen, Jorge 1893-1984 .... CLC 11; DAM
MULT, POET
See also CA 89-92; 112; DLB 108; HW

Guillen, Nicolas (Cristobal) 1902-1989 C L C
48, 79; BLC; DAM MST, MULT, POET;
HLC
See also BW 2; CA 116; 125; 129; HW

Guillevic, (Eugene) 1907- .... CLC 33
See also CA 93-96

Guillois
See Desnos, Robert

Guillois, Valentin
See Desnos, Robert

Guiney, Louise Imogen 1861-1920 TCLC 41
See also CA 160; DLB 54

Guiraldes, Ricardo (Guillermo) 1886-1927
TCLC 39
See also CA 131; HW; MTCW

Gumilev, Nikolai Stephanovich 1886-1921
TCLC 60

Gunesekera, Romesh 1954- .... CLC 91
See also CA 159

Gunn, Bill .... CLC 5
See also Gunn, William Harrison
See also DLB 38

Gunn, Thom(son William) 1929-CLC 3, 6, 18,
32, 81; DAM POET
See also CA 17-20R; CANR 9, 33; CDBLB
1960 to Present; DLB 27; INT CANR-33;
MTCW

Gunn, William Harrison 1934(?)-1989
See Gunn, Bill
See also AITN 1; BW 1; CA 13-16R; 128;
CANR 12, 25

Gunnars, Kristjana 1948- .... CLC 69
See also CA 113; DLB 60

Gurdjieff, G(eorgei) I(vanovich) 1877(?)-1949
TCLC 71
See also CA 157

Gurganus, Allan 1947- . CLC 70; DAM POP
See also BEST 90:1; CA 135

Gurney, A(lbert) R(amsdell), Jr. 1930- . C L C
32, 50, 54; DAM DRAM
See also CA 77-80; CANR 32, 64

Gurney, Ivor (Bertie) 1890-1937 ... TCLC 33

Gurney, Peter
See Gurney, A(lbert) R(amsdell), Jr.

Guro, Elena 1877-1913 .... TCLC 56

Gustafson, James M(oody) 1925- ... CLC 100
See also CA 25-28R; CANR 37

Gustafson, Ralph (Barker) 1909- ..... CLC 36
See also CA 21-24R; CANR 8, 45; DLB 88

Gut, Gom
See Simenon, Georges (Jacques Christian)

Guterson, David 1956- .... CLC 91
See also CA 132

Guthrie, A(lfred) B(ertram), Jr. 1901-1991
CLC 23
See also CA 57-60; 134; CANR 24; DLB 6;
SATA 62; SATA-Obit 67

Guthrie, Isobel
See Grieve, C(hristopher) M(urray)

Guthrie, Woodrow Wilson 1912-1967
See Guthrie, Woody
See also CA 113; 93-96

Guthrie, Woody .... CLC 35
See also Guthrie, Woodrow Wilson

Guy, Rosa (Cuthbert) 1928- .... CLC 26
See also AAYA 4; BW 2; CA 17-20R; CANR
14, 34; CLR 13; DLB 33; JRDA; MAICYA;
SATA 14, 62

Gwendolyn
See Bennett, (Enoch) Arnold

H. D. .... CLC 3, 8, 14, 31, 34, 73; PC 5
See also Doolittle, Hilda

H. de V.
See Buchan, John

Haavikko, Paavo Juhani 1931- .. CLC 18, 34
See also CA 106

Habbema, Koos
See Heijermans, Herman

Habermas, Juergen 1929- .... CLC 104
See also CA 109

Habermas, Jurgen
See Habermas, Juergen

Hacker, Marilyn 1942- CLC 5, 9, 23, 72, 91;
DAM POET
See also CA 77-80; DLB 120

Haggard, H(enry) Rider 1856-1925TCLC 11
See also CA 108; 148; DLB 70, 156, 174, 178;
SATA 16

Hagiosy, L.
See Larbaud, Valery (Nicolas)

Hagiwara Sakutaro 1886-1942TCLC 60; PC
18

Haig, Fenil
See Ford, Ford Madox

Haig-Brown, Roderick (Langmere) 1908-1976
CLC 21
See also CA 5-8R; 69-72; CANR 4, 38; CLR
31; DLB 88; MAICYA; SATA 12

Hailey, Arthur 1920-CLC 5; DAM NOV, POP
See also AITN 2; BEST 90:3; CA 1-4R; CANR

2, 36; DLB 88; DLBY 82; MTCW

Hailey, Elizabeth Forsythe 1938- ..... **CLC 40**
See also CA 93-96; CAAS 1; CANR 15, 48; INT CANR-15

Haines, John (Meade) 1924- .... **CLC 58**
See also CA 17-20R; CANR 13, 34; DLB 5

Hakluyt, Richard 1552-1616 .... **LC 31**

Haldeman, Joe (William) 1943- .... **CLC 61**
See also CA 53-56; CAAS 25; CANR 6; DLB 8; INT CANR-6

Haley, Alex(ander Murray Palmer) 1921-1992 **CLC 8, 12, 76; BLC; DA; DAB; DAC; DAM MST, MULT, POP**
See also BW 2; CA 77-80; 136; CANR 61; DLB 38; MTCW

Haliburton, Thomas Chandler 1796-1865 **NCLC 15**
See also DLB 11, 99

Hall, Donald (Andrew, Jr.) 1928- **CLC 1, 13, 37, 59; DAM POET**
See also CA 5-8R; CAAS 7; CANR 2, 44, 64; DLB 5; SATA 23

Hall, Frederic Sauser
See Sauser-Hall, Frederic

Hall, James
See Kuttner, Henry

Hall, James Norman 1887-1951 ..... **TCLC 23**
See also CA 123; SATA 21

Hall, (Marguerite) Radclyffe 1886-1943 **TCLC 12**
See also CA 110; 150

Hall, Rodney 1935- .... **CLC 51**
See also CA 109

Halleck, Fitz-Greene 1790-1867 .... **NCLC 47**
See also DLB 3

Halliday, Michael
See Creasey, John

Halpern, Daniel 1945- .... **CLC 14**
See also CA 33-36R

Hamburger, Michael (Peter Leopold) 1924- **CLC 5, 14**
See also CA 5-8R; CAAS 4; CANR 2, 47; DLB 27

Hamill, Pete 1935- .... **CLC 10**
See also CA 25-28R; CANR 18

Hamilton, Alexander 1755(?)-1804 **NCLC 49**
See also DLB 37

Hamilton, Clive
See Lewis, C(live) S(taples)

Hamilton, Edmond 1904-1977 .... **CLC 1**
See also CA 1-4R; CANR 3; DLB 8

Hamilton, Eugene (Jacob) Lee
See Lee-Hamilton, Eugene (Jacob)

Hamilton, Franklin
See Silverberg, Robert

Hamilton, Gail
See Corcoran, Barbara

Hamilton, Mollie
See Kaye, M(ary) M(argaret)

Hamilton, (Anthony Walter) Patrick 1904-1962 **CLC 51**
See also CA 113; DLB 10

Hamilton, Virginia 1936- .... **CLC 26; DAM MULT**
See also AAYA 2, 21; BW 2; CA 25-28R; CANR 20, 37; CLR 1, 11, 40; DLB 33, 52; INT CANR-20; JRDA; MAICYA; MTCW; SATA 4, 56, 79

Hammett, (Samuel) Dashiell 1894-1961 **C L C 3, 5, 10, 19, 47; SSC 17**
See also AITN 1; CA 81-84; CANR 42; CDALB 1929-1941; DLBD 6; DLBY 96; MTCW

Hammon, Jupiter 1711(?)-1800(?) ..**NCLC 5;**

BLC; DAM MULT, POET; PC 16
See also DLB 31, 50

Hammond, Keith
See Kuttner, Henry

Hamner, Earl (Henry), Jr. 1923- ...... **CLC 12**
See also AITN 2; CA 73-76; DLB 6

Hampton, Christopher (James) 1946- **CLC 4**
See also CA 25-28R; DLB 13; MTCW

Hamsun, Knut .... **TCLC 2, 14, 49**
See also Pedersen, Knut

Handke, Peter 1942-**CLC 5, 8, 10, 15, 38; DAM DRAM, NOV**
See also CA 77-80; CANR 33; DLB 85, 124; MTCW

Hanley, James 1901-1985 ..... **CLC 3, 5, 8, 13**
See also CA 73-76; 117; CANR 36; MTCW

Hannah, Barry 1942- .... **CLC 23, 38, 90**
See also CA 108; 110; CANR 43; DLB 6; INT 110; MTCW

Hannon, Ezra
See Hunter, Evan

Hansberry, Lorraine (Vivian) 1930-1965**CLC 17, 62; BLC; DA; DAB; DAC; DAM DRAM, MST, MULT; DC 2**
See also BW 1; CA 109; 25-28R; CABS 3; CANR 58; CDALB 1941-1968; DLB 7, 38; MTCW

Hansen, Joseph 1923- .... **CLC 38**
See also CA 29-32R; CAAS 17; CANR 16, 44; INT CANR-16

Hansen, Martin A. 1909-1955 .... **TCLC 32**

Hanson, Kenneth O(stlin) 1922- .... **CLC 13**
See also CA 53-56; CANR 7

Hardwick, Elizabeth 1916- .... **CLC 13; DAM NOV**
See also CA 5-8R; CANR 3, 32; DLB 6; MTCW

Hardy, Thomas 1840-1928**TCLC 4, 10, 18, 32, 48, 53, 72; DA; DAB; DAC; DAM MST, NOV, POET; PC 8; SSC 2; WLC**
See also CA 104; 123; CDBLB 1890-1914; DLB 18, 19, 135; MTCW

Hare, David 1947- .... **CLC 29, 58**
See also CA 97-100; CANR 39; DLB 13; MTCW

Harewood, John
See Van Druten, John (William)

Harford, Henry
See Hudson, W(illiam) H(enry)

Hargrave, Leonie
See Disch, Thomas M(ichael)

Harjo, Joy 1951- .... **CLC 83; DAM MULT**
See also CA 114; CANR 35; DLB 120, 175; NNAL

Harlan, Louis R(udolph) 1922- .... **CLC 34**
See also CA 21-24R; CANR 25, 55

Harling, Robert 1951(?)- .... **CLC 53**
See also CA 147

Harmon, William (Ruth) 1938- .... **CLC 38**
See also CA 33-36R; CANR 14, 32, 35; SATA 65

Harper, F. E. W.
See Harper, Frances Ellen Watkins

Harper, Frances E. W.
See Harper, Frances Ellen Watkins

Harper, Frances E. Watkins
See Harper, Frances Ellen Watkins

Harper, Frances Ellen
See Harper, Frances Ellen Watkins

Harper, Frances Ellen Watkins 1825-1911 **TCLC 14; BLC; DAM MULT, POET; PC 21**
See also BW 1; CA 111; 125; DLB 50

Harper, Michael S(teven) 1938- .... **CLC 7, 22**

See also BW 1; CA 33-36R; CANR 24; DLB 41

Harper, Mrs. F. E. W.
See Harper, Frances Ellen Watkins

Harris, Christie (Lucy) Irwin 1907- **CLC 12**
See also CA 5-8R; CANR 6; CLR 47; DLB 88; JRDA; MAICYA; SAAS 10; SATA 6, 74

Harris, Frank 1856-1931 .... **TCLC 24**
See also CA 109; 150; DLB 156

Harris, George Washington 1814-1869**NCLC 23**
See also DLB 3, 11

Harris, Joel Chandler 1848-1908 ... **TCLC 2; SSC 19**
See also CA 104; 137; DLB 11, 23, 42, 78, 91; MAICYA; YABC 1

Harris, John (Wyndham Parkes Lucas) Beynon 1903-1969
See Wyndham, John
See also CA 102; 89-92

Harris, MacDonald .... **CLC 9**
See also Heiney, Donald (William)

Harris, Mark 1922- .... **CLC 19**
See also CA 5-8R; CAAS 3; CANR 2, 55; DLB 2; DLBY 80

Harris, (Theodore) Wilson 1921- ..... **CLC 25**
See also BW 2; CA 65-68; CAAS 16; CANR 11, 27; DLB 117; MTCW

Harrison, Elizabeth Cavanna 1909-
See Cavanna, Betty
See also CA 9-12R; CANR 6, 27

Harrison, Harry (Max) 1925- .... **CLC 42**
See also CA 1-4R; CANR 5, 21; DLB 8; SATA 4

Harrison, James (Thomas) 1937- **CLC 6, 14, 33, 66; SSC 19**
See also CA 13-16R; CANR 8, 51; DLBY 82; INT CANR-8

Harrison, Jim
See Harrison, James (Thomas)

Harrison, Kathryn 1961- .... **CLC 70**
See also CA 144

Harrison, Tony 1937- .... **CLC 43**
See also CA 65-68; CANR 44; DLB 40; MTCW

Harriss, Will(ard Irvin) 1922- .... **CLC 34**
See also CA 111

Harson, Sley
See Ellison, Harlan (Jay)

Hart, Ellis
See Ellison, Harlan (Jay)

Hart, Josephine 1942(?)-**CLC 70; DAM POP**
See also CA 138

Hart, Moss 1904-1961**CLC 66; DAM DRAM**
See also CA 109; 89-92; DLB 7

Harte, (Francis) Bret(t) 1836(?)-1902**TCLC 1, 25; DA; DAC; DAM MST; SSC 8; WLC**
See also CA 104; 140; CDALB 1865-1917; DLB 12, 64, 74, 79; SATA 26

Hartley, L(eslie) P(oles) 1895-1972**CLC 2, 22**
See also CA 45-48; 37-40R; CANR 33; DLB 15, 139; MTCW

Hartman, Geoffrey H. 1929- .... **CLC 27**
See also CA 117; 125; DLB 67

Hartmann, Sadakichi 1867-1944 ... **TCLC 73**
See also CA 157; DLB 54

Hartmann von Aue c. 1160-c. 1205**CMLC 15**
See also DLB 138

Hartmann von Aue 1170-1210 ...... **CMLC 15**

Haruf, Kent 1943- .... **CLC 34**
See also CA 149

Harwood, Ronald 1934- .... **CLC 32; DAM DRAM, MST**
See also CA 1-4R; CANR 4, 55; DLB 13

Hasek, Jaroslav (Matej Frantisek) 1883-1923
TCLC **4**
See also CA 104; 129; MTCW

Hass, Robert 1941- ... CLC **18, 39, 99; PC 16**
See also CA 111; CANR 30, 50; DLB 105;
SATA 94

Hastings, Hudson
See Kuttner, Henry

Hastings, Selina .... CLC **44**

Hathorne, John 1641-1717 .... LC **38**

Hatteras, Amelia
See Mencken, H(enry) L(ouis)

Hatteras, Owen .... TCLC **18**
See also Mencken, H(enry) L(ouis); Nathan,
George Jean

Hauptmann, Gerhart (Johann Robert) 1862-
1946 .... TCLC **4; DAM DRAM**
See also CA 104; 153; DLB 66, 118

Havel, Vaclav 1936- ... CLC **25, 58, 65; DAM
DRAM; DC 6**
See also CA 104; CANR 36, 63; MTCW

Haviaras, Stratis .... CLC **33**
See also Chaviaras, Strates

Hawes, Stephen 1475(?)-1523(?) .... LC **17**

Hawkes, John (Clendennin Burne, Jr.) 1925-
CLC **1, 2, 3, 4, 7, 9, 14, 15, 27, 49**
See also CA 1-4R; CANR 2, 47, 64; DLB 2, 7;
DLBY 80; MTCW

Hawking, S. W.
See Hawking, Stephen W(illiam)

Hawking, Stephen W(illiam) 1942- . CLC **63,
105**
See also AAYA 13; BEST 89:1; CA 126; 129;
CANR 48

Hawthorne, Julian 1846-1934 .... TCLC **25**

Hawthorne, Nathaniel 1804-1864 NCLC **39;
DA; DAB; DAC; DAM MST, NOV; SSC
3, 29; WLC**
See also AAYA 18; CDALB 1640-1865; DLB
1, 74; YABC 2

Haxton, Josephine Ayres 1921-
See Douglas, Ellen
See also CA 115; CANR 41

Hayaseca y Eizaguirre, Jorge
See Echegaray (y Eizaguirre), Jose (Maria
Waldo)

Hayashi Fumiko 1904-1951 .... TCLC **27**
See also CA 161; DLB 180

Haycraft, Anna
See Ellis, Alice Thomas
See also CA 122

Hayden, Robert E(arl) 1913-1980 . CLC **5, 9,
14, 37; BLC; DA; DAC; DAM MST,
MULT, POET; PC 6**
See also BW 1; CA 69-72; 97-100; CABS 2;
CANR 24; CDALB 1941-1968; DLB 5, 76;
MTCW; SATA 19; SATA-Obit 26

Hayford, J(oseph) E(phraim) Casely
See Casely-Hayford, J(oseph) E(phraim)

Hayman, Ronald 1932- .... CLC **44**
See also CA 25-28R; CANR 18, 50; DLB 155

Haywood, Eliza (Fowler) 1693(?)-1756 LC **1**

Hazlitt, William 1778-1830 .... NCLC **29**
See also DLB 110, 158

Hazzard, Shirley 1931- .... CLC **18**
See also CA 9-12R; CANR 4; DLBY 82;
MTCW

Head, Bessie 1937-1986 ... CLC **25, 67; BLC;
DAM MULT**
See also BW 2; CA 29-32R; 119; CANR 25;
DLB 117; MTCW

Headon, (Nicky) Topper 1956(?)- ..... CLC **30**

Heaney, Seamus (Justin) 1939- CLC **5, 7, 14,
25, 37, 74, 91; DAB; DAM POET; PC 18;
WLCS**
See also CA 85-88; CANR 25, 48; CDBLB
1960 to Present; DLB 40; DLBY 95; MTCW

Hearn, (Patricio) Lafcadio (Tessima Carlos)
1850-1904 .... TCLC **9**
See also CA 105; DLB 12, 78

Hearne, Vicki 1946- .... CLC **56**
See also CA 139

Hearon, Shelby 1931- .... CLC **63**
See also AITN 2; CA 25-28R; CANR 18, 48

Heat-Moon, William Least .... CLC **29**
See also Trogdon, William (Lewis)
See also AAYA 9

Hebbel, Friedrich 1813-1863 NCLC **43; DAM
DRAM**
See also DLB 129

Hebert, Anne 1916- CLC **4, 13, 29; DAC; DAM
MST, POET**
See also CA 85-88; DLB 68; MTCW

Hecht, Anthony (Evan) 1923- CLC **8, 13, 19;
DAM POET**
See also CA 9-12R; CANR 6; DLB 5, 169

Hecht, Ben 1894-1964 .... CLC **8**
See also CA 85-88; DLB 7, 9, 25, 26, 28, 86

Hedayat, Sadeq 1903-1951 .... TCLC **21**
See also CA 120

Hegel, Georg Wilhelm Friedrich 1770-1831
NCLC **46**
See also DLB 90

Heidegger, Martin 1889-1976 .... CLC **24**
See also CA 81-84; 65-68; CANR 34; MTCW

Heidenstam, (Carl Gustaf) Verner von 1859-
1940 .... TCLC **5**
See also CA 104

Heifner, Jack 1946- .... CLC **11**
See also CA 105; CANR 47

Heijermans, Herman 1864-1924 .... TCLC **24**
See also CA 123

Heilbrun, Carolyn G(old) 1926- .... CLC **25**
See also CA 45-48; CANR 1, 28, 58

Heine, Heinrich 1797-1856 .... NCLC **4, 54**
See also DLB 90

Heinemann, Larry (Curtiss) 1944- ... CLC **50**
See also CA 110; CAAS 21; CANR 31; DLBD
9; INT CANR-31

Heiney, Donald (William) 1921-1993
See Harris, MacDonald
See also CA 1-4R; 142; CANR 3, 58

Heinlein, Robert A(nson) 1907-1988 CLC **1, 3,
8, 14, 26, 55; DAM POP**
See also AAYA 17; CA 1-4R; 125; CANR 1,
20, 53; DLB 8; JRDA; MAICYA; MTCW;
SATA 9, 69; SATA-Obit 56

Helforth, John
See Doolittle, Hilda

Hellenhofferu, Vojtech Kapristian z
See Hasek, Jaroslav (Matej Frantisek)

Heller, Joseph 1923- CLC **1, 3, 5, 8, 11, 36, 63;
DA; DAB; DAC; DAM MST, NOV, POP;
WLC**
See also AITN 1; CA 5-8R; CABS 1; CANR 8,
42; DLB 2, 28; DLBY 80; INT CANR-8;
MTCW

Hellman, Lillian (Florence) 1906-1984 CLC **2,
4, 8, 14, 18, 34, 44, 52; DAM DRAM; DC 1**
See also AITN 1, 2; CA 13-16R; 112; CANR
33; DLB 7; DLBY 84; MTCW

Helprin, Mark 1947- CLC **7, 10, 22, 32; DAM
NOV, POP**
See also CA 81-84; CANR 47, 64; DLBY 85;
MTCW

Helvetius, Claude-Adrien 1715-1771 .. LC **26**

Helyar, Jane Penelope Josephine 1933-
See Poole, Josephine
See also CA 21-24R; CANR 10, 26; SATA 82

Hemans, Felicia 1793-1835 .... NCLC **29**
See also DLB 96

Hemingway, Ernest (Miller) 1899-1961 C L C
**1, 3, 6, 8, 10, 13, 19, 30, 34, 39, 41, 44, 50,
61, 80; DA; DAB; DAC; DAM MST, NOV;
SSC 25; WLC**
See also AAYA 19; CA 77-80; CANR 34;
CDALB 1917-1929; DLB 4, 9, 102; DLBD
1, 15, 16; DLBY 81, 87, 96; MTCW

Hempel, Amy 1951- .... CLC **39**
See also CA 118; 137

Henderson, F. C.
See Mencken, H(enry) L(ouis)

Henderson, Sylvia
See Ashton-Warner, Sylvia (Constance)

Henderson, Zenna (Chlarson) 1917-1983 S S C
29
See also CA 1-4R; 133; CANR 1; DLB 8; SATA
5

Henley, Beth .... CLC **23; DC 6**
See also Henley, Elizabeth Becker
See also CABS 3; DLBY 86

Henley, Elizabeth Becker 1952-
See Henley, Beth
See also CA 107; CANR 32; DAM DRAM,
MST; MTCW

Henley, William Ernest 1849-1903 .. TCLC **8**
See also CA 105; DLB 19

Hennissart, Martha
See Lathen, Emma
See also CA 85-88; CANR 64

Henry, O. .... TCLC **1, 19; SSC 5; WLC**
See also Porter, William Sydney

Henry, Patrick 1736-1799 .... LC **25**

Henryson, Robert 1430(?)-1506(?) ...... LC **20**
See also DLB 146

Henry VIII 1491-1547 .... LC **10**

Henschke, Alfred
See Klabund

Hentoff, Nat(han Irving) 1925- .... CLC **26**
See also AAYA 4; CA 1-4R; CAAS 6; CANR
5, 25; CLR 1; INT CANR-25; JRDA;
MAICYA; SATA 42, 69; SATA-Brief 27

Heppenstall, (John) Rayner 1911-1981 C L C
10
See also CA 1-4R; 103; CANR 29

Heraclitus c. 540B.C.-c. 450B.C. .. CMLC **22**
See also DLB 176

Herbert, Frank (Patrick) 1920-1986 CLC **12,
23, 35, 44, 85; DAM POP**
See also AAYA 21; CA 53-56; 118; CANR 5,
43; DLB 8; INT CANR-5; MTCW; SATA 9,
37; SATA-Obit 47

Herbert, George 1593-1633 ..... LC **24; DAB;
DAM POET; PC 4**
See also CDBLB Before 1660; DLB 126

Herbert, Zbigniew 1924- .. CLC **9, 43; DAM
POET**
See also CA 89-92; CANR 36; MTCW

Herbst, Josephine (Frey) 1897-1969 CLC **34**
See also CA 5-8R; 25-28R; DLB 9

Hergesheimer, Joseph 1880-1954 .. TCLC **11**
See also CA 109; DLB 102, 9

Herlihy, James Leo 1927-1993 .... CLC **6**
See also CA 1-4R; 143; CANR 2

Hermogenes fl. c. 175- .... CMLC **6**

Hernandez, Jose 1834-1886 .... NCLC **17**

Herodotus c. 484B.C.-429B.C. ...... CMLC **17**
See also DLB 176

Herrick, Robert 1591-1674 LC **13; DA; DAB;**

DAC; DAM MST, POP; PC 9
See also DLB 126

Herring, Guilles
See Somerville, Edith

Herriot, James 1916-1995 CLC 12; DAM POP
See also Wight, James Alfred
See also AAYA 1; CA 148; CANR 40; SATA 86

Herrmann, Dorothy 1941- .... CLC 44
See also CA 107

Herrmann, Taffy
See Herrmann, Dorothy

Hersey, John (Richard) 1914-1993 CLC 1, 2, 7, 9, 40, 81, 97; DAM POP
See also CA 17-20R; 140; CANR 33; DLB 6; MTCW; SATA 25; SATA-Obit 76

Herzen, Aleksandr Ivanovich 1812-1870 NCLC 10, 61

Herzl, Theodor 1860-1904 .... TCLC 36

Herzog, Werner 1942- .... CLC 16
See also CA 89-92

Hesiod c. 8th cent. B.C.- .... CMLC 5
See also DLB 176

Hesse, Hermann 1877-1962 CLC 1, 2, 3, 6, 11, 17, 25, 69; DA; DAB; DAC; DAM MST, NOV; SSC 9; WLC
See also CA 17-18; CAP 2; DLB 66; MTCW; SATA 50

Hewes, Cady
See De Voto, Bernard (Augustine)

Heyen, William 1940- .... CLC 13, 18
See also CA 33-36R; CAAS 9; DLB 5

Heyerdahl, Thor 1914- .... CLC 26
See also CA 5-8R; CANR 5, 22; MTCW; SATA 2, 52

Heym, Georg (Theodor Franz Arthur) 1887-1912 .... TCLC 9
See also CA 106

Heym, Stefan 1913- .... CLC 41
See also CA 9-12R; CANR 4; DLB 69

Heyse, Paul (Johann Ludwig von) 1830-1914 TCLC 8
See also CA 104; DLB 129

Heyward, (Edwin) DuBose 1885-1940 T C L C 59
See also CA 108; 157; DLB 7, 9, 45; SATA 21

Hibbert, Eleanor Alice Burford 1906-1993 CLC 7; DAM POP
See also BEST 90:4; CA 17-20R; 140; CANR 9, 28, 59; SATA 2; SATA-Obit 74

Hichens, Robert (Smythe) 1864-1950 T C L C 64
See also CA 162; DLB 153

Higgins, George V(incent) 1939-CLC 4, 7, 10, 18
See also CA 77-80; CAAS 5; CANR 17, 51; DLB 2; DLBY 81; INT CANR-17; MTCW

Higginson, Thomas Wentworth 1823-1911 TCLC 36
See also DLB 1, 64

Highet, Helen
See MacInnes, Helen (Clark)

Highsmith, (Mary) Patricia 1921-1995 CLC 2, 4, 14, 42, 102; DAM NOV, POP
See also CA 1-4R; 147; CANR 1, 20, 48, 62; MTCW

Highwater, Jamake (Mamake) 1942(?)- C L C 12
See also AAYA 7; CA 65-68; CAAS 7; CANR 10, 34; CLR 17; DLB 52; DLBY 85; JRDA; MAICYA; SATA 32, 69; SATA-Brief 30

Highway, Tomson 1951-CLC 92; DAC; DAM MULT

See also CA 151; NNAL

Higuchi, Ichiyo 1872-1896 .... NCLC 49

Hijuelos, Oscar 1951- CLC 65; DAM MULT, POP; HLC
See also BEST 90:1; CA 123; CANR 50; DLB 145; HW

Hikmet, Nazim 1902(?)-1963 .... CLC 40
See also CA 141; 93-96

Hildegard von Bingen 1098-1179 . CMLC 20
See also DLB 148

Hildesheimer, Wolfgang 1916-1991 .. CLC 49
See also CA 101; 135; DLB 69, 124

Hill, Geoffrey (William) 1932- CLC 5, 8, 18, 45; DAM POET
See also CA 81-84; CANR 21; CDBLB 1960 to Present; DLB 40; MTCW

Hill, George Roy 1921- .... CLC 26
See also CA 110; 122

Hill, John
See Koontz, Dean R(ay)

Hill, Susan (Elizabeth) 1942- . CLC 4; DAB; DAM MST, NOV
See also CA 33-36R; CANR 29; DLB 14, 139; MTCW

Hillerman, Tony 1925- . CLC 62; DAM POP
See also AAYA 6; BEST 89:1; CA 29-32R; CANR 21, 42; SATA 6

Hillesum, Etty 1914-1943 .... TCLC 49
See also CA 137

Hilliard, Noel (Harvey) 1929- .... CLC 15
See also CA 9-12R; CANR 7

Hillis, Rick 1956- .... CLC 66
See also CA 134

Hilton, James 1900-1954 .... TCLC 21
See also CA 108; DLB 34, 77; SATA 34

Himes, Chester (Bomar) 1909-1984 CLC 2, 4, 7, 18, 58, 108; BLC; DAM MULT
See also BW 2; CA 25-28R; 114; CANR 22; DLB 2, 76, 143; MTCW

Hinde, Thomas .... CLC 6, 11
See also Chitty, Thomas Willes

Hindin, Nathan
See Bloch, Robert (Albert)

Hine, (William) Daryl 1936- .... CLC 15
See also CA 1-4R; CAAS 15; CANR 1, 20; DLB 60

Hinkson, Katharine Tynan
See Tynan, Katharine

Hinton, S(usan) E(loise) 1950- CLC 30; DA; DAB; DAC; DAM MST, NOV
See also AAYA 2; CA 81-84; CANR 32, 62; CLR 3, 23; JRDA; MAICYA; MTCW; SATA 19, 58

Hippius, Zinaida .... TCLC 9
See also Gippius, Zinaida (Nikolayevna)

Hiraoka, Kimitake 1925-1970
See Mishima, Yukio
See also CA 97-100; 29-32R; DAM DRAM; MTCW

Hirsch, E(ric) D(onald), Jr. 1928- .... CLC 79
See also CA 25-28R; CANR 27, 51; DLB 67; INT CANR-27; MTCW

Hirsch, Edward 1950- .... CLC 31, 50
See also CA 104; CANR 20, 42; DLB 120

Hitchcock, Alfred (Joseph) 1899-1980 CLC 16
See also AAYA 22; CA 159; 97-100; SATA 27; SATA-Obit 24

Hitler, Adolf 1889-1945 .... TCLC 53
See also CA 117; 147

Hoagland, Edward 1932- .... CLC 28
See also CA 1-4R; CANR 2, 31, 57; DLB 6; SATA 51

Hoban, Russell (Conwell) 1925- . CLC 7, 25;

DAM NOV
See also CA 5-8R; CANR 23, 37; CLR 3; DLB 52; MAICYA; MTCW; SATA 1, 40, 78

Hobbes, Thomas 1588-1679 .... LC 36
See also DLB 151

Hobbs, Perry
See Blackmur, R(ichard) P(almer)

Hobson, Laura Z(ametkin) 1900-1986 CLC 7, 25
See also CA 17-20R; 118; CANR 55; DLB 28; SATA 52

Hochhuth, Rolf 1931- .. CLC 4, 11, 18; DAM DRAM
See also CA 5-8R; CANR 33; DLB 124; MTCW

Hochman, Sandra 1936- .... CLC 3, 8
See also CA 5-8R; DLB 5

Hochwaelder, Fritz 1911-1986 CLC 36; DAM DRAM
See also CA 29-32R; 120; CANR 42; MTCW

Hochwalder, Fritz
See Hochwaelder, Fritz

Hocking, Mary (Eunice) 1921- .... CLC 13
See also CA 101; CANR 18, 40

Hodgins, Jack 1938- .... CLC 23
See also CA 93-96; DLB 60

Hodgson, William Hope 1877(?)-1918 T C L C 13
See also CA 111; DLB 70, 153, 156, 178

Hoeg, Peter 1957- .... CLC 95
See also CA 151

Hoffman, Alice 1952- ...CLC 51; DAM NOV
See also CA 77-80; CANR 34; MTCW

Hoffman, Daniel (Gerard) 1923-CLC 6, 13, 23
See also CA 1-4R; CANR 4; DLB 5

Hoffman, Stanley 1944- .... CLC 5
See also CA 77-80

Hoffman, William M(oses) 1939- ...... CLC 40
See also CA 57-60; CANR 11

Hoffmann, E(rnst) T(heodor) A(madeus) 1776-1822 .... NCLC 2; SSC 13
See also DLB 90; SATA 27

Hofmann, Gert 1931- .... CLC 54
See also CA 128

Hofmannsthal, Hugo von 1874-1929 TCLC 11; DAM DRAM; DC 4
See also CA 106; 153; DLB 81, 118

Hogan, Linda 1947- ... CLC 73; DAM MULT
See also CA 120; CANR 45; DLB 175; NNAL

Hogarth, Charles
See Creasey, John

Hogarth, Emmett
See Polonsky, Abraham (Lincoln)

Hogg, James 1770-1835 .... NCLC 4
See also DLB 93, 116, 159

Holbach, Paul Henri Thiry Baron 1723-1789 LC 14

Holberg, Ludvig 1684-1754 .... LC 6

Holden, Ursula 1921- .... CLC 18
See also CA 101; CAAS 8; CANR 22

Holderlin, (Johann Christian) Friedrich 1770-1843 .... NCLC 16; PC 4

Holdstock, Robert
See Holdstock, Robert P.

Holdstock, Robert P. 1948- .... CLC 39
See also CA 131

Holland, Isabelle 1920- .... CLC 21
See also AAYA 11; CA 21-24R; CANR 10, 25, 47; JRDA; MAICYA; SATA 8, 70

Holland, Marcus
See Caldwell, (Janet Miriam) Taylor (Holland)

Hollander, John 1929- .... CLC 2, 5, 8, 14
See also CA 1-4R; CANR 1, 52; DLB 5; SATA 13

See also CA 5-8R; CANR 3, 24; DLB 15
Humphreys, Josephine 1945- ..... **CLC 34, 57**
See also CA 121; 127; INT 127
Huneker, James Gibbons 1857-1921**TCLC 65**
See also DLB 71
Hungerford, Pixie
See Brinsmead, H(esba) F(ay)
Hunt, E(verette) Howard, (Jr.) 1918-. **CLC 3**
See also AITN 1; CA 45-48; CANR 2, 47
Hunt, Kyle
See Creasey, John
Hunt, (James Henry) Leigh 1784-1859**N C L C
1; DAM POET**
Hunt, Marsha 1946- .... **CLC 70**
See also BW 2; CA 143
Hunt, Violet 1866-1942 .... **TCLC 53**
See also DLB 162
Hunter, E. Waldo
See Sturgeon, Theodore (Hamilton)
Hunter, Evan 1926-. **CLC 11, 31; DAM POP**
See also CA 5-8R; CANR 5, 38, 62; DLBY 82;
INT CANR-5; MTCW; SATA 25
Hunter, Kristin (Eggleston) 1931- .... **CLC 35**
See also AITN 1; BW 1; CA 13-16R; CANR
13; CLR 3; DLB 33; INT CANR-13;
MAICYA; SAAS 10; SATA 12
Hunter, Mollie 1922- .... **CLC 21**
See also McIlwraith, Maureen Mollie Hunter
See also AAYA 13; CANR 37; CLR 25; DLB
161; JRDA; MAICYA; SAAS 7; SATA 54
Hunter, Robert (?)-1734 .... **LC 7**
Hurston, Zora Neale 1903-1960**CLC 7, 30, 61;
BLC; DA; DAC; DAM MST, MULT, NOV;
SSC 4; WLCS**
See also AAYA 15; BW 1; CA 85-88; CANR
61; DLB 51, 86; MTCW
Huston, John (Marcellus) 1906-1987 **CLC 20**
See also CA 73-76; 123; CANR 34; DLB 26
Hustvedt, Siri 1955- .... **CLC 76**
See also CA 137
Hutten, Ulrich von 1488-1523 .... **LC 16**
See also DLB 179
Huxley, Aldous (Leonard) 1894-1963 **CLC 1,
3, 4, 5, 8, 11, 18, 35, 79; DA; DAB; DAC;
DAM MST, NOV; WLC**
See also AAYA 11; CA 85-88; CANR 44;
CDBLB 1914-1945; DLB 36, 100, 162;
MTCW; SATA 63
Huxley, T. H. 1825-1895 .... **NCLC 67**
See also DLB 57
Huysmans, Charles Marie Georges 1848-1907
See Huysmans, Joris-Karl
See also CA 104
Huysmans, Joris-Karl .... **TCLC 7, 69**
See also Huysmans, Charles Marie Georges
See also DLB 123
Hwang, David Henry 1957- ... **CLC 55; DAM
DRAM; DC 4**
See also CA 127; 132; INT 132
Hyde, Anthony 1946- .... **CLC 42**
See also CA 136
Hyde, Margaret O(ldroyd) 1917- ..... **CLC 21**
See also CA 1-4R; CANR 1, 36; CLR 23; JRDA;
MAICYA; SAAS 8; SATA 1, 42, 76
Hynes, James 1956(?)- .... **CLC 65**
Ian, Janis 1951- .... **CLC 21**
See also CA 105
Ibanez, Vicente Blasco
See Blasco Ibanez, Vicente
Ibarguengoitia, Jorge 1928-1983 ..... **CLC 37**
See also CA 124; 113; HW
Ibsen, Henrik (Johan) 1828-1906 **TCLC 2, 8,
16, 37, 52; DA; DAB; DAC; DAM DRAM,**

MST; DC 2; WLC
See also CA 104; 141
Ibuse Masuji 1898-1993 .... **CLC 22**
See also CA 127; 141; DLB 180
Ichikawa, Kon 1915- .... **CLC 20**
See also CA 121
Idle, Eric 1943-................................. **CLC 21**
See also Monty Python
See also CA 116; CANR 35
Ignatow, David 1914- .... **CLC 4, 7, 14, 40**
See also CA 9-12R; CAAS 3; CANR 31, 57;
DLB 5
Ihimaera, Witi 1944- .... **CLC 46**
See also CA 77-80
Ilf, Ilya .... **TCLC 21**
See also Fainzilberg, Ilya Arnoldovich
Illyes, Gyula 1902-1983 .... **PC 16**
See also CA 114; 109
Immermann, Karl (Lebrecht) 1796-1840
NCLC 4, 49
See also DLB 133
Inchbald, Elizabeth 1753-1821 ...... **NCLC 62**
See also DLB 39, 89
Inclan, Ramon (Maria) del Valle
See Valle-Inclan, Ramon (Maria) del
Infante, G(uillermo) Cabrera
See Cabrera Infante, G(uillermo)
Ingalls, Rachel (Holmes) 1940- .... **CLC 42**
See also CA 123; 127
Ingamells, Rex 1913-1955 .... **TCLC 35**
Inge, William (Motter) 1913-1973 . **CLC 1, 8,
19; DAM DRAM**
See also CA 9-12R; CDALB 1941-1968; DLB
7; MTCW
Ingelow, Jean 1820-1897 .... **NCLC 39**
See also DLB 35, 163; SATA 33
Ingram, Willis J.
See Harris, Mark
Innaurato, Albert (F.) 1948(?)- .. **CLC 21, 60**
See also CA 115; 122; INT 122
Innes, Michael
See Stewart, J(ohn) I(nnes) M(ackintosh)
Innis, Harold Adams 1894-1952 .... **TCLC 77**
See also DLB 88
Ionesco, Eugene 1909-1994**CLC 1, 4, 6, 9, 11,
15, 41, 86; DA; DAB; DAC; DAM DRAM,
MST; WLC**
See also CA 9-12R; 144; CANR 55; MTCW;
SATA 7; SATA-Obit 79
Iqbal, Muhammad 1873-1938 .... **TCLC 28**
Ireland, Patrick
See O'Doherty, Brian
Iron, Ralph
See Schreiner, Olive (Emilie Albertina)
Irving, John (Winslow) 1942-**CLC 13, 23, 38;
DAM NOV, POP**
See also AAYA 8; BEST 89:3; CA 25-28R;
CANR 28; DLB 6; DLBY 82; MTCW
Irving, Washington 1783-1859 . **NCLC 2, 19;
DA; DAB; DAM MST; SSC 2; WLC**
See also CDALB 1640-1865; DLB 3, 11, 30,
59, 73, 74; YABC 2
Irwin, P. K.
See Page, P(atricia) K(athleen)
Isaacs, Susan 1943- .... **CLC 32; DAM POP**
See also BEST 89:1; CA 89-92; CANR 20, 41;
INT CANR-20; MTCW
Isherwood, Christopher (William Bradshaw)
1904-1986 .... **CLC 1, 9, 11, 14, 44; DAM
DRAM, NOV**
See also CA 13-16R; 117; CANR 35; DLB 15;
DLBY 86; MTCW
Ishiguro, Kazuo 1954- **CLC 27, 56, 59; DAM**

NOV
See also BEST 90:2; CA 120; CANR 49;
MTCW
Ishikawa, Hakuhin
See Ishikawa, Takuboku
Ishikawa, Takuboku 1886(?)-1912 **TCLC 15;
DAM POET; PC 10**
See also CA 113; 153
Iskander, Fazil 1929- .... **CLC 47**
See also CA 102
Isler, Alan (David) 1934- .... **CLC 91**
See also CA 156
Ivan IV 1530-1584 .... **LC 17**
Ivanov, Vyacheslav Ivanovich 1866-1949
TCLC 33
See also CA 122
Ivask, Ivar Vidrik 1927-1992 .... **CLC 14**
See also CA 37-40R; 139; CANR 24
Ives, Morgan
See Bradley, Marion Zimmer
J. R. S.
See Gogarty, Oliver St. John
Jabran, Kahlil
See Gibran, Kahlil
Jabran, Khalil
See Gibran, Kahlil
Jackson, Daniel
See Wingrove, David (John)
Jackson, Jesse 1908-1983 .... **CLC 12**
See also BW 1; CA 25-28R; 109; CANR 27;
CLR 28; MAICYA; SATA 2, 29; SATA-Obit
48
Jackson, Laura (Riding) 1901-1991
See Riding, Laura
See also CA 65-68; 135; CANR 28; DLB 48
Jackson, Sam
See Trumbo, Dalton
Jackson, Sara
See Wingrove, David (John)
Jackson, Shirley 1919-1965 . **CLC 11, 60, 87;
DA; DAC; DAM MST; SSC 9; WLC**
See also AAYA 9; CA 1-4R; 25-28R; CANR 4,
52; CDALB 1941-1968; DLB 6; SATA 2
Jacob, (Cyprien-)Max 1876-1944 .... **TCLC 6**
See also CA 104
Jacobs, Harriet 1813(?)-1897 .... **NCLC 67**
Jacobs, Jim 1942-............................... **CLC 12**
See also CA 97-100; INT 97-100
Jacobs, W(illiam) W(ymark) 1863-1943
TCLC 22
See also CA 121; DLB 135
Jacobsen, Jens Peter 1847-1885 .... **NCLC 34**
Jacobsen, Josephine 1908-........ **CLC 48, 102**
See also CA 33-36R; CAAS 18; CANR 23, 48
Jacobson, Dan 1929- .... **CLC 4, 14**
See also CA 1-4R; CANR 2, 25; DLB 14;
MTCW
Jacqueline
See Carpentier (y Valmont), Alejo
Jagger, Mick 1944- .... **CLC 17**
Jahiz, Al- c. 776-869 .... **CMLC 25**
Jakes, John (William) 1932- .. **CLC 29; DAM
NOV, POP**
See also BEST 89:4; CA 57-60; CANR 10, 43;
DLBY 83; INT CANR-10; MTCW; SATA 62
James, Andrew
See Kirkup, James
James, C(yril) L(ionel) R(obert) 1901-1989
CLC 33
See also BW 2; CA 117; 125; 128; CANR 62;
DLB 125; MTCW
James, Daniel (Lewis) 1911-1988
See Santiago, Danny

See Disch, Thomas M(ichael)

Koch, C(hristopher) J(ohn) 1932- .... **CLC 42**
　See also CA 127

Koch, Christopher
　See Koch, C(hristopher) J(ohn)

Koch, Kenneth 1925- ..... **CLC 5, 8, 44; DAM POET**
　See also CA 1-4R; CANR 6, 36, 57; DLB 5; INT CANR-36; SATA 65

Kochanowski, Jan 1530-1584 .... **LC 10**

Kock, Charles Paul de 1794-1871 . **NCLC 16**

Koda Shigeyuki 1867-1947
　See Rohan, Koda
　See also CA 121

Koestler, Arthur 1905-1983 **CLC 1, 3, 6, 8, 15, 33**
　See also CA 1-4R; 109; CANR 1, 33; CDBLB 1945-1960; DLBY 83; MTCW

Kogawa, Joy Nozomi 1935- .. **CLC 78; DAC; DAM MST, MULT**
　See also CA 101; CANR 19, 62

Kohout, Pavel 1928- .... **CLC 13**
　See also CA 45-48; CANR 3

Koizumi, Yakumo
　See Hearn, (Patricio) Lafcadio (Tessima Carlos)

Kolmar, Gertrud 1894-1943 .... **TCLC 40**

Komunyakaa, Yusef 1947- .... **CLC 86, 94**
　See also CA 147; DLB 120

Konrad, George
　See Konrad, Gyoergy

Konrad, Gyoergy 1933- .... **CLC 4, 10, 73**
　See also CA 85-88

Konwicki, Tadeusz 1926- .... **CLC 8, 28, 54**
　See also CA 101; CAAS 9; CANR 39, 59; MTCW

Koontz, Dean R(ay) 1945- ..... **CLC 78; DAM NOV, POP**
　See also AAYA 9; BEST 89:3, 90:2; CA 108; CANR 19, 36, 52; MTCW; SATA 92

Kopit, Arthur (Lee) 1937- **CLC 1, 18, 33; DAM DRAM**
　See also AITN 1; CA 81-84; CABS 3; DLB 7; MTCW

Kops, Bernard 1926- .... **CLC 4**
　See also CA 5-8R; DLB 13

Kornbluth, C(yril) M. 1923-1958 .... **TCLC 8**
　See also CA 105; 160; DLB 8

Korolenko, V. G.
　See Korolenko, Vladimir Galaktionovich

Korolenko, Vladimir
　See Korolenko, Vladimir Galaktionovich

Korolenko, Vladimir G.
　See Korolenko, Vladimir Galaktionovich

Korolenko, Vladimir Galaktionovich 1853-1921 .... **TCLC 22**
　See also CA 121

Korzybski, Alfred (Habdank Skarbek) 1879-1950 .... **TCLC 61**
　See also CA 123; 160

Kosinski, Jerzy (Nikodem) 1933-1991 **CLC 1, 2, 3, 6, 10, 15, 53, 70; DAM NOV**
　See also CA 17-20R; 134; CANR 9, 46; DLB 2; DLBY 82; MTCW

Kostelanetz, Richard (Cory) 1940- .. **CLC 28**
　See also CA 13-16R; CAAS 8; CANR 38

Kostrowitzki, Wilhelm Apollinaris de 1880-1918
　See Apollinaire, Guillaume
　See also CA 104

Kotlowitz, Robert 1924- .... **CLC 4**
　See also CA 33-36R; CANR 36

Kotzebue, August (Friedrich Ferdinand) von 1761-1819 .... **NCLC 25**

See also DLB 94

Kotzwinkle, William 1938- ..... **CLC 5, 14, 35**
　See also CA 45-48; CANR 3, 44; CLR 6; DLB 173; MAICYA; SATA 24, 70

Kowna, Stancy
　See Szymborska, Wislawa

Kozol, Jonathan 1936- .... **CLC 17**
　See also CA 61-64; CANR 16, 45

Kozoll, Michael 1940(?)- .... **CLC 35**

Kramer, Kathryn 19(?)- .... **CLC 34**

Kramer, Larry 1935- **CLC 42; DAM POP; DC 8**
　See also CA 124; 126; CANR 60

Krasicki, Ignacy 1735-1801 .... **NCLC 8**

Krasinski, Zygmunt 1812-1859 .... **NCLC 4**

Kraus, Karl 1874-1936 .... **TCLC 5**
　See also CA 104; DLB 118

Kreve (Mickevicius), Vincas 1882-1954 **TCLC 27**

Kristeva, Julia 1941- .... **CLC 77**
　See also CA 154

Kristofferson, Kris 1936- .... **CLC 26**
　See also CA 104

Krizanc, John 1956- .... **CLC 57**

Krleza, Miroslav 1893-1981 .... **CLC 8**
　See also CA 97-100; 105; CANR 50; DLB 147

Kroetsch, Robert 1927- **CLC 5, 23, 57; DAC; DAM POET**
　See also CA 17-20R; CANR 8, 38; DLB 53; MTCW

Kroetz, Franz
　See Kroetz, Franz Xaver

Kroetz, Franz Xaver 1946- .... **CLC 41**
　See also CA 130

Kroker, Arthur (W.) 1945- .... **CLC 77**
　See also CA 161

Kropotkin, Peter (Aleksieevich) 1842-1921 **TCLC 36**
　See also CA 119

Krotkov, Yuri 1917- .... **CLC 19**
　See also CA 102

Krumb
　See Crumb, R(obert)

Krumgold, Joseph (Quincy) 1908-1980 **C L C 12**
　See also CA 9-12R; 101; CANR 7; MAICYA; SATA 1, 48; SATA-Obit 23

Krumwitz
　See Crumb, R(obert)

Krutch, Joseph Wood 1893-1970 ...... **CLC 24**
　See also CA 1-4R; 25-28R; CANR 4; DLB 63

Krutzch, Gus
　See Eliot, T(homas) S(tearns)

Krylov, Ivan Andreevich 1768(?)-1844 **N C L C 1**
　See also DLB 150

Kubin, Alfred (Leopold Isidor) 1877-1959 **TCLC 23**
　See also CA 112; 149; DLB 81

Kubrick, Stanley 1928- .... **CLC 16**
　See also CA 81-84; CANR 33; DLB 26

Kumin, Maxine (Winokur) 1925- **CLC 5, 13, 28; DAM POET; PC 15**
　See also AITN 2; CA 1-4R; CAAS 8; CANR 1, 21; DLB 5; MTCW; SATA 12

Kundera, Milan 1929- . **CLC 4, 9, 19, 32, 68; DAM NOV; SSC 24**
　See also AAYA 2; CA 85-88; CANR 19, 52; MTCW

Kunene, Mazisi (Raymond) 1930- .... **CLC 85**
　See also BW 1; CA 125; DLB 117

Kunitz, Stanley (Jasspon) 1905- **CLC 6, 11, 14; PC 19**

See also CA 41-44R; CANR 26, 57; DLB 48; INT CANR-26; MTCW

Kunze, Reiner 1933- .... **CLC 10**
　See also CA 93-96; DLB 75

Kuprin, Aleksandr Ivanovich 1870-1938 **TCLC 5**
　See also CA 104

Kureishi, Hanif 1954(?)- .... **CLC 64**
　See also CA 139

Kurosawa, Akira 1910- **CLC 16; DAM MULT**
　See also AAYA 11; CA 101; CANR 46

Kushner, Tony 1957(?)- **CLC 81; DAM DRAM**
　See also CA 144

Kuttner, Henry 1915-1958 .... **TCLC 10**
　See also Vance, Jack
　See also CA 107; 157; DLB 8

Kuzma, Greg 1944- .... **CLC 7**
　See also CA 33-36R

Kuzmin, Mikhail 1872(?)-1936 ...... **TCLC 40**

Kyd, Thomas 1558-1594 **LC 22; DAM DRAM; DC 3**
　See also DLB 62

Kyprianos, Iossif
　See Samarakis, Antonis

La Bruyere, Jean de 1645-1696 .... **LC 17**

Lacan, Jacques (Marie Emile) 1901-1981 **CLC 75**
　See also CA 121; 104

Laclos, Pierre Ambroise Francois Choderlos de 1741-1803 .... **NCLC 4**

La Colere, Francois
　See Aragon, Louis

Lacolere, Francois
　See Aragon, Louis

La Deshabilleuse
　See Simenon, Georges (Jacques Christian)

Lady Gregory
　See Gregory, Isabella Augusta (Persse)

Lady of Quality, A
　See Bagnold, Enid

La Fayette, Marie (Madelaine Pioche de la Vergne Comtes 1634-1693 .... **LC 2**

Lafayette, Rene
　See Hubbard, L(afayette) Ron(ald)

Laforgue, Jules 1860-1887 **NCLC 5, 53; PC 14; SSC 20**

Lagerkvist, Paer (Fabian) 1891-1974 **CLC 7, 10, 13, 54; DAM DRAM, NOV**
　See also Lagerkvist, Par
　See also CA 85-88; 49-52; MTCW

Lagerkvist, Par .... **SSC 12**
　See also Lagerkvist, Paer (Fabian)

Lagerloef, Selma (Ottiliana Lovisa) 1858-1940 **TCLC 4, 36**
　See also Lagerlof, Selma (Ottiliana Lovisa)
　See also CA 108; SATA 15

Lagerlof, Selma (Ottiliana Lovisa)
　See Lagerloef, Selma (Ottiliana Lovisa)
　See also CLR 7; SATA 15

La Guma, (Justin) Alex(ander) 1925-1985 **CLC 19; DAM NOV**
　See also BW 1; CA 49-52; 118; CANR 25; DLB 117; MTCW

Laidlaw, A. K.
　See Grieve, C(hristopher) M(urray)

Lainez, Manuel Mujica
　See Mujica Lainez, Manuel
　See also HW

Laing, R(onald) D(avid) 1927-1989 .. **CLC 95**
　See also CA 107; 129; CANR 34; MTCW

Lamartine, Alphonse (Marie Louis Prat) de 1790-1869 **NCLC 11; DAM POET; PC 16**

Lamb, Charles 1775-1834 ..... **NCLC 10; DA;**

DAB; DAC; DAM MST; WLC
See also CDBLB 1789-1832; DLB 93, 107, 163;
SATA 17

Lamb, Lady Caroline 1785-1828 ... **NCLC 38**
See also DLB 116

Lamming, George (William) 1927- **CLC 2, 4, 66; BLC; DAM MULT**
See also BW 2; CA 85-88; CANR 26; DLB 125;
MTCW

L'Amour, Louis (Dearborn) 1908-1988 **C L C 25, 55; DAM NOV, POP**
See also AAYA 16; AITN 2; BEST 89:2; CA 1-
4R; 125; CANR 3, 25, 40; DLBY 80; MTCW

Lampedusa, Giuseppe (Tomasi) di 1896-1957
TCLC 13
See also Tomasi di Lampedusa, Giuseppe
See also DLB 177

Lampman, Archibald 1861-1899 ... **NCLC 25**
See also DLB 92

Lancaster, Bruce 1896-1963 .... **CLC 36**
See also CA 9-10; CAP 1; SATA 9

Lanchester, John .... **CLC 99**

Landau, Mark Alexandrovich
See Aldanov, Mark (Alexandrovich)

Landau-Aldanov, Mark Alexandrovich
See Aldanov, Mark (Alexandrovich)

Landis, Jerry
See Simon, Paul (Frederick)

Landis, John 1950- .... **CLC 26**
See also CA 112; 122

Landolfi, Tommaso 1908-1979 .... **CLC 11, 49**
See also CA 127; 117; DLB 177

Landon, Letitia Elizabeth 1802-1838 **N C L C 15**
See also DLB 96

Landor, Walter Savage 1775-1864 **NCLC 14**
See also DLB 93, 107

Landwirth, Heinz 1927-
See Lind, Jakov
See also CA 9-12R; CANR 7

Lane, Patrick 1939- ... **CLC 25; DAM POET**
See also CA 97-100; CANR 54; DLB 53; INT
97-100

Lang, Andrew 1844-1912 .... **TCLC 16**
See also CA 114; 137; DLB 98, 141, 184;
MAICYA; SATA 16

Lang, Fritz 1890-1976 .... **CLC 20, 103**
See also CA 77-80; 69-72; CANR 30

Lange, John
See Crichton, (John) Michael

Langer, Elinor 1939- .... **CLC 34**
See also CA 121

Langland, William 1330(?)-1400(?) ... **LC 19; DA; DAB; DAC; DAM MST, POET**
See also DLB 146

Langstaff, Launcelot
See Irving, Washington

Lanier, Sidney 1842-1881 ..... **NCLC 6; DAM POET**
See also DLB 64; DLBD 13; MAICYA; SATA
18

Lanyer, Aemilia 1569-1645 .... **LC 10, 30**
See also DLB 121

Lao Tzu .... **CMLC 7**

Lapine, James (Elliot) 1949- .... **CLC 39**
See also CA 123; 130; CANR 54; INT 130

Larbaud, Valery (Nicolas) 1881-1957**TCLC 9**
See also CA 106; 152

Lardner, Ring
See Lardner, Ring(gold) W(ilmer)

Lardner, Ring W., Jr.
See Lardner, Ring(gold) W(ilmer)

Lardner, Ring(gold) W(ilmer) 1885-1933

TCLC 2, 14
See also CA 104; 131; CDALB 1917-1929;
DLB 11, 25, 86; DLBD 16; MTCW

Laredo, Betty
See Codrescu, Andrei

Larkin, Maia
See Wojciechowska, Maia (Teresa)

Larkin, Philip (Arthur) 1922-1985**CLC 3, 5, 8, 9, 13, 18, 33, 39, 64; DAB; DAM MST, POET; PC 21**
See also CA 5-8R; 117; CANR 24, 62; CDBLB
1960 to Present; DLB 27; MTCW

Larra (y Sanchez de Castro), Mariano Jose de
1809-1837 .... **NCLC 17**

Larsen, Eric 1941- .... **CLC 55**
See also CA 132

Larsen, Nella 1891-1964**CLC 37; BLC; DAM MULT**
See also BW 1; CA 125; DLB 51

Larson, Charles R(aymond) 1938- ... **CLC 31**
See also CA 53-56; CANR 4

Larson, Jonathan 1961-1996 .... **CLC 99**
See also CA 156

Las Casas, Bartolome de 1474-1566 ... **LC 31**

Lasch, Christopher 1932-1994 .... **CLC 102**
See also CA 73-76; 144; CANR 25; MTCW

Lasker-Schueler, Else 1869-1945 ... **TCLC 57**
See also DLB 66, 124

Laski, Harold 1893-1950 .... **TCLC 79**

Latham, Jean Lee 1902- .... **CLC 12**
See also AITN 1; CA 5-8R; CANR 7; MAICYA;
SATA 2, 68

Latham, Mavis
See Clark, Mavis Thorpe

Lathen, Emma .... **CLC 2**
See also Hennissart, Martha; Latsis, Mary J(ane)

Lathrop, Francis
See Leiber, Fritz (Reuter, Jr.)

Latsis, Mary J(ane)
See Lathen, Emma
See also CA 85-88

Lattimore, Richmond (Alexander) 1906-1984
CLC 3
See also CA 1-4R; 112; CANR 1

Laughlin, James 1914- .... **CLC 49**
See also CA 21-24R; CAAS 22; CANR 9, 47;
DLB 48; DLBY 96

Laurence, (Jean) Margaret (Wemyss) 1926-
1987 .. **CLC 3, 6, 13, 50, 62; DAC; DAM MST; SSC 7**
See also CA 5-8R; 121; CANR 33; DLB 53;
MTCW; SATA-Obit 50

Laurent, Antoine 1952- .... **CLC 50**

Lauscher, Hermann
See Hesse, Hermann

Lautreamont, Comte de 1846-1870**NCLC 12; SSC 14**

Laverty, Donald
See Blish, James (Benjamin)

Lavin, Mary 1912-1996**CLC 4, 18, 99; SSC 4**
See also CA 9-12R; 151; CANR 33; DLB 15;
MTCW

Lavond, Paul Dennis
See Kornbluth, C(yril) M.; Pohl, Frederik

Lawler, Raymond Evenor 1922- .... **CLC 58**
See also CA 103

Lawrence, D(avid) H(erbert Richards) 1885-
1930**TCLC 2, 9, 16, 33, 48, 61; DA; DAB; DAC; DAM MST, NOV, POET; SSC 4, 19; WLC**
See also CA 104; 121; CDBLB 1914-1945;
DLB 10, 19, 36, 98, 162; MTCW

Lawrence, T(homas) E(dward) 1888-1935

TCLC 18
See also Dale, Colin
See also CA 115

Lawrence of Arabia
See Lawrence, T(homas) E(dward)

Lawson, Henry (Archibald Hertzberg) 1867-
1922 .... **TCLC 27; SSC 18**
See also CA 120

Lawton, Dennis
See Faust, Frederick (Schiller)

Laxness, Halldor .... **CLC 25**
See also Gudjonsson, Halldor Kiljan

Layamon fl. c. 1200- .... **CMLC 10**
See also DLB 146

Laye, Camara 1928-1980 .. **CLC 4, 38; BLC; DAM MULT**
See also BW 1; CA 85-88; 97-100; CANR 25;
MTCW

Layton, Irving (Peter) 1912-**CLC 2, 15; DAC; DAM MST, POET**
See also CA 1-4R; CANR 2, 33, 43; DLB 88;
MTCW

Lazarus, Emma 1849-1887 .... **NCLC 8**

Lazarus, Felix
See Cable, George Washington

Lazarus, Henry
See Slavitt, David R(ytman)

Lea, Joan
See Neufeld, John (Arthur)

Leacock, Stephen (Butler) 1869-1944**TCLC 2; DAC; DAM MST**
See also CA 104; 141; DLB 92

Lear, Edward 1812-1888 .... **NCLC 3**
See also CLR 1; DLB 32, 163, 166; MAICYA;
SATA 18

Lear, Norman (Milton) 1922- .... **CLC 12**
See also CA 73-76

Leavis, F(rank) R(aymond) 1895-1978**CLC 24**
See also CA 21-24R; 77-80; CANR 44; MTCW

Leavitt, David 1961- ..... **CLC 34; DAM POP**
See also CA 116; 122; CANR 50, 62; DLB 130;
INT 122

Leblanc, Maurice (Marie Emile) 1864-1941
TCLC 49
See also CA 110

Lebowitz, Fran(ces Ann) 1951(?)-**CLC 11, 36**
See also CA 81-84; CANR 14, 60; INT CANR-
14; MTCW

Lebrecht, Peter
See Tieck, (Johann) Ludwig

le Carre, John .... **CLC 3, 5, 9, 15, 28**
See also Cornwell, David (John Moore)
See also BEST 89:4; CDBLB 1960 to Present;
DLB 87

Le Clezio, J(ean) M(arie) G(ustave) 1940-
CLC 31
See also CA 116; 128; DLB 83

Leconte de Lisle, Charles-Marie-Rene 1818-
1894 .... **NCLC 29**

Le Coq, Monsieur
See Simenon, Georges (Jacques Christian)

Leduc, Violette 1907-1972 .... **CLC 22**
See also CA 13-14; 33-36R; CAP 1

Ledwidge, Francis 1887(?)-1917 .... **TCLC 23**
See also CA 123; DLB 20

Lee, Andrea 1953-**CLC 36; BLC; DAM MULT**
See also BW 1; CA 125

Lee, Andrew
See Auchincloss, Louis (Stanton)

Lee, Chang-rae 1965- .... **CLC 91**
See also CA 148

Lee, Don L. .... **CLC 2**
See also Madhubuti, Haki R.

POET; PC 13
  See also CA 104; 151; DLB 54, 140
Lowell, James Russell 1819-1891 .... **NCLC 2**
  See also CDALB 1640-1865; DLB 1, 11, 64, 79
Lowell, Robert (Traill Spence, Jr.) 1917-1977 **CLC 1, 2, 3, 4, 5, 8, 9, 11, 15, 37; DA; DAB; DAC; DAM MST, NOV; PC 3; WLC**
  See also CA 9-12R; 73-76; CABS 2; CANR 26, 60; DLB 5, 169; MTCW
Lowndes, Marie Adelaide (Belloc) 1868-1947 **TCLC 12**
  See also CA 107; DLB 70
Lowry, (Clarence) Malcolm 1909-1957 **TCLC 6, 40**
  See also CA 105; 131; CANR 62; CDBLB 1945-1960; DLB 15; MTCW
Lowry, Mina Gertrude 1882-1966
  See Loy, Mina
  See also CA 113
Loxsmith, John
  See Brunner, John (Kilian Houston)
Loy, Mina .... **CLC 28; DAM POET; PC 16**
  See also Lowry, Mina Gertrude
  See also DLB 4, 54
Loyson-Bridet
  See Schwob, (Mayer Andre) Marcel
Lucas, Craig 1951- .... **CLC 64**
  See also CA 137
Lucas, E(dward) V(errall) 1868-1938 **TCLC 73**
  See also DLB 98, 149, 153; SATA 20
Lucas, George 1944- .... **CLC 16**
  See also AAYA 1; CA 77-80; CANR 30; SATA 56
Lucas, Hans
  See Godard, Jean-Luc
Lucas, Victoria
  See Plath, Sylvia
Ludlam, Charles 1943-1987 .... **CLC 46, 50**
  See also CA 85-88; 122
Ludlum, Robert 1927- **CLC 22, 43; DAM NOV, POP**
  See also AAYA 10; BEST 89:1, 90:3; CA 33-36R; CANR 25, 41; DLBY 82; MTCW
Ludwig, Ken .... **CLC 60**
Ludwig, Otto 1813-1865 .... **NCLC 4**
  See also DLB 129
Lugones, Leopoldo 1874-1938 .... **TCLC 15**
  See also CA 116; 131; HW
Lu Hsun 1881-1936 .... **TCLC 3; SSC 20**
  See also Shu-Jen, Chou
Lukacs, George .... **CLC 24**
  See also Lukacs, Gyorgy (Szegeny von)
Lukacs, Gyorgy (Szegeny von) 1885-1971
  See Lukacs, George
  See also CA 101; 29-32R; CANR 62
Luke, Peter (Ambrose Cyprian) 1919-1995 **CLC 38**
  See also CA 81-84; 147; DLB 13
Lunar, Dennis
  See Mungo, Raymond
Lurie, Alison 1926- .... **CLC 4, 5, 18, 39**
  See also CA 1-4R; CANR 2, 17, 50; DLB 2; MTCW; SATA 46
Lustig, Arnost 1926- .... **CLC 56**
  See also AAYA 3; CA 69-72; CANR 47; SATA 56
Luther, Martin 1483-1546 .... **LC 9, 37**
  See also DLB 179
Luxemburg, Rosa 1870(?)-1919 ..... **TCLC 63**
  See also CA 118
Luzi, Mario 1914- .... **CLC 13**

See also CA 61-64; CANR 9; DLB 128
Lyly, John 1554(?)-1606 **LC 41; DAM DRAM; DC 7**
  See also DLB 62, 167
L'Ymagier
  See Gourmont, Remy (-Marie-Charles) de
Lynch, B. Suarez
  See Bioy Casares, Adolfo; Borges, Jorge Luis
Lynch, David (K.) 1946- .... **CLC 66**
  See also CA 124; 129
Lynch, James
  See Andreyev, Leonid (Nikolaevich)
Lynch Davis, B.
  See Bioy Casares, Adolfo; Borges, Jorge Luis
Lyndsay, Sir David 1490-1555 .... **LC 20**
Lynn, Kenneth S(chuyler) 1923- .... **CLC 50**
  See also CA 1-4R; CANR 3, 27
Lynx
  See West, Rebecca
Lyons, Marcus
  See Blish, James (Benjamin)
Lyre, Pinchbeck
  See Sassoon, Siegfried (Lorraine)
Lytle, Andrew (Nelson) 1902-1995 ... **CLC 22**
  See also CA 9-12R; 150; DLB 6; DLBY 95
Lyttelton, George 1709-1773 .... **LC 10**
Maas, Peter 1929- .... **CLC 29**
  See also CA 93-96; INT 93-96
Macaulay, Rose 1881-1958 .... **TCLC 7, 44**
  See also CA 104; DLB 36
Macaulay, Thomas Babington 1800-1859 **NCLC 42**
  See also CDBLB 1832-1890; DLB 32, 55
MacBeth, George (Mann) 1932-1992 **CLC 2, 5, 9**
  See also CA 25-28R; 136; CANR 61; DLB 40; MTCW; SATA 4; SATA-Obit 70
MacCaig, Norman (Alexander) 1910- **CLC 36; DAB; DAM POET**
  See also CA 9-12R; CANR 3, 34; DLB 27
MacCarthy, (Sir Charles Otto) Desmond 1877-1952 .... **TCLC 36**
MacDiarmid, Hugh **CLC 2, 4, 11, 19, 63; PC 9**
  See also Grieve, C(hristopher) M(urray)
  See also CDBLB 1945-1960; DLB 20
MacDonald, Anson
  See Heinlein, Robert A(nson)
Macdonald, Cynthia 1928- .... **CLC 13, 19**
  See also CA 49-52; CANR 4, 44; DLB 105
MacDonald, George 1824-1905 .... **TCLC 9**
  See also CA 106; 137; DLB 18, 163, 178; MAICYA; SATA 33
Macdonald, John
  See Millar, Kenneth
MacDonald, John D(ann) 1916-1986 **CLC 3, 27, 44; DAM NOV, POP**
  See also CA 1-4R; 121; CANR 1, 19, 60; DLB 8; DLBY 86; MTCW
Macdonald, John Ross
  See Millar, Kenneth
Macdonald, Ross .... **CLC 1, 2, 3, 14, 34, 41**
  See also Millar, Kenneth
  See also DLBD 6
MacDougal, John
  See Blish, James (Benjamin)
MacEwen, Gwendolyn (Margaret) 1941-1987 **CLC 13, 55**
  See also CA 9-12R; 124; CANR 7, 22; DLB 53; SATA 50; SATA-Obit 55
Macha, Karel Hynek 1810-1846 .... **NCLC 46**
Machado (y Ruiz), Antonio 1875-1939 **TCLC 3**
  See also CA 104; DLB 108

Machado de Assis, Joaquim Maria 1839-1908 **TCLC 10; BLC; SSC 24**
  See also CA 107; 153
Machen, Arthur .... **TCLC 4; SSC 20**
  See also Jones, Arthur Llewellyn
  See also DLB 36, 156, 178
Machiavelli, Niccolo 1469-1527 **LC 8, 36; DA; DAB; DAC; DAM MST; WLCS**
MacInnes, Colin 1914-1976 .... **CLC 4, 23**
  See also CA 69-72; 65-68; CANR 21; DLB 14; MTCW
MacInnes, Helen (Clark) 1907-1985 **CLC 27, 39; DAM POP**
  See also CA 1-4R; 117; CANR 1, 28, 58; DLB 87; MTCW; SATA 22; SATA-Obit 44
Mackay, Mary 1855-1924
  See Corelli, Marie
  See also CA 118
Mackenzie, Compton (Edward Montague) 1883-1972 .... **CLC 18**
  See also CA 21-22; 37-40R; CAP 2; DLB 34, 100
Mackenzie, Henry 1745-1831 .... **NCLC 41**
  See also DLB 39
Mackintosh, Elizabeth 1896(?)-1952
  See Tey, Josephine
  See also CA 110
MacLaren, James
  See Grieve, C(hristopher) M(urray)
Mac Laverty, Bernard 1942- .... **CLC 31**
  See also CA 116; 118; CANR 43; INT 118
MacLean, Alistair (Stuart) 1922(?)-1987 **CLC 3, 13, 50, 63; DAM POP**
  See also CA 57-60; 121; CANR 28, 61; MTCW; SATA 23; SATA-Obit 50
Maclean, Norman (Fitzroy) 1902-1990 **CLC 78; DAM POP; SSC 13**
  See also CA 102; 132; CANR 49
MacLeish, Archibald 1892-1982 **CLC 3, 8, 14, 68; DAM POET**
  See also CA 9-12R; 106; CANR 33, 63; DLB 4, 7, 45; DLBY 82; MTCW
MacLennan, (John) Hugh 1907-1990 **CLC 2, 14, 92; DAC; DAM MST**
  See also CA 5-8R; 142; CANR 33; DLB 68; MTCW
MacLeod, Alistair 1936- **CLC 56; DAC; DAM MST**
  See also CA 123; DLB 60
Macleod, Fiona
  See Sharp, William
MacNeice, (Frederick) Louis 1907-1963 **CLC 1, 4, 10, 53; DAB; DAM POET**
  See also CA 85-88; CANR 61; DLB 10, 20; MTCW
MacNeill, Dand
  See Fraser, George MacDonald
Macpherson, James 1736-1796 .... **LC 29**
  See also DLB 109
Macpherson, (Jean) Jay 1931- .... **CLC 14**
  See also CA 5-8R; DLB 53
MacShane, Frank 1927- .... **CLC 39**
  See also CA 9-12R; CANR 3, 33; DLB 111
Macumber, Mari
  See Sandoz, Mari(e Susette)
Madach, Imre 1823-1864 .... **NCLC 19**
Madden, (Jerry) David 1933- .... **CLC 5, 15**
  See also CA 1-4R; CAAS 3; CANR 4, 45; DLB 6; MTCW
Maddern, Al(an)
  See Ellison, Harlan (Jay)
Madhubuti, Haki R. 1942- **CLC 6, 73; BLC; DAM MULT, POET; PC 5**

Marsh, (Edith) Ngaio 1899-1982 **CLC 7, 53; DAM POP**
See also CA 9-12R; CANR 6, 58; DLB 77; MTCW

Marshall, Garry 1934- .... **CLC 17**
See also AAYA 3; CA 111; SATA 60

Marshall, Paule 1929-**CLC 27, 72; BLC; DAM MULT; SSC 3**
See also BW 2; CA 77-80; CANR 25; DLB 157; MTCW

Marsten, Richard
See Hunter, Evan

Marston, John 1576-1634**LC 33; DAM DRAM**
See also DLB 58, 172

Martha, Henry
See Harris, Mark

Marti, Jose 1853-1895**NCLC 63; DAM MULT; HLC**

Martial c. 40-c. 104 .... **PC 10**

Martin, Ken
See Hubbard, L(afayette) Ron(ald)

Martin, Richard
See Creasey, John

Martin, Steve 1945- .... **CLC 30**
See also CA 97-100; CANR 30; MTCW

Martin, Valerie 1948- .... **CLC 89**
See also BEST 90:2; CA 85-88; CANR 49

Martin, Violet Florence 1862-1915 **TCLC 51**

Martin, Webber
See Silverberg, Robert

Martindale, Patrick Victor
See White, Patrick (Victor Martindale)

Martin du Gard, Roger 1881-1958 **TCLC 24**
See also CA 118; DLB 65

Martineau, Harriet 1802-1876 .... **NCLC 26**
See also DLB 21, 55, 159, 163, 166; YABC 2

Martines, Julia
See O'Faolain, Julia

Martinez, Enrique Gonzalez
See Gonzalez Martinez, Enrique

Martinez, Jacinto Benavente y
See Benavente (y Martinez), Jacinto

Martinez Ruiz, Jose 1873-1967
See Azorin; Ruiz, Jose Martinez
See also CA 93-96; HW

Martinez Sierra, Gregorio 1881-1947**TCLC 6**
See also CA 115

Martinez Sierra, Maria (de la O'LeJarraga) 1874-1974 .... **TCLC 6**
See also CA 115

Martinsen, Martin
See Follett, Ken(neth Martin)

Martinson, Harry (Edmund) 1904-1978**C L C 14**
See also CA 77-80; CANR 34

Marut, Ret
See Traven, B.

Marut, Robert
See Traven, B.

Marvell, Andrew 1621-1678**LC 4; DA; DAB; DAC; DAM MST, POET; PC 10; WLC**
See also CDBLB 1660-1789; DLB 131

Marx, Karl (Heinrich) 1818-1883 . **NCLC 17**
See also DLB 129

Masaoka Shiki .... **TCLC 18**
See also Masaoka Tsunenori

Masaoka Tsunenori 1867-1902
See Masaoka Shiki
See also CA 117

Masefield, John (Edward) 1878-1967**CLC 11, 47; DAM POET**
See also CA 19-20; 25-28R; CANR 33; CAP 2; CDBLB 1890-1914; DLB 10, 19, 153, 160;

MTCW; SATA 19

Maso, Carole 19(?)- .... **CLC 44**

Mason, Bobbie Ann 1940-**CLC 28, 43, 82; SSC 4**
See also AAYA 5; CA 53-56; CANR 11, 31, 58; DLB 173; DLBY 87; INT CANR-31; MTCW

Mason, Ernst
See Pohl, Frederik

Mason, Lee W.
See Malzberg, Barry N(athaniel)

Mason, Nick 1945- .... **CLC 35**

Mason, Tally
See Derleth, August (William)

Mass, William
See Gibson, William

Masters, Edgar Lee 1868-1950 **TCLC 2, 25; DA; DAC; DAM MST, POET; PC 1; WLCS**
See also CA 104; 133; CDALB 1865-1917; DLB 54; MTCW

Masters, Hilary 1928- .... **CLC 48**
See also CA 25-28R; CANR 13, 47

Mastrosimone, William 19(?)- .... **CLC 36**

Mathe, Albert
See Camus, Albert

Mather, Cotton 1663-1728 .... **LC 38**
See also CDALB 1640-1865; DLB 24, 30, 140

Mather, Increase 1639-1723 .... **LC 38**
See also DLB 24

Matheson, Richard Burton 1926- ..... **CLC 37**
See also CA 97-100; DLB 8, 44; INT 97-100

Mathews, Harry 1930- .... **CLC 6, 52**
See also CA 21-24R; CAAS 6; CANR 18, 40

Mathews, John Joseph 1894-1979 .. **CLC 84; DAM MULT**
See also CA 19-20; 142; CANR 45; CAP 2; DLB 175; NNAL

Mathias, Roland (Glyn) 1915- .... **CLC 45**
See also CA 97-100; CANR 19, 41; DLB 27

Matsuo Basho 1644-1694 .... **PC 3**
See also DAM POET

Mattheson, Rodney
See Creasey, John

Matthews, Greg 1949- .... **CLC 45**
See also CA 135

Matthews, William 1942- .... **CLC 40**
See also CA 29-32R; CAAS 18; CANR 12, 57; DLB 5

Matthias, John (Edward) 1941- .... **CLC 9**
See also CA 33-36R; CANR 56

Matthiessen, Peter 1927-**CLC 5, 7, 11, 32, 64; DAM NOV**
See also AAYA 6; BEST 90:4; CA 9-12R; CANR 21, 50; DLB 6, 173; MTCW; SATA 27

Maturin, Charles Robert 1780(?)-1824**N C L C 6**
See also DLB 178

Matute (Ausejo), Ana Maria 1925- .. **CLC 11**
See also CA 89-92; MTCW

Maugham, W. S.
See Maugham, W(illiam) Somerset

Maugham, W(illiam) Somerset 1874-1965 **CLC 1, 11, 15, 67, 93; DA; DAB; DAC; DAM DRAM, MST, NOV; SSC 8; WLC**
See also CA 5-8R; 25-28R; CANR 40; CDBLB 1914-1945; DLB 10, 36, 77, 100, 162; MTCW; SATA 54

Maugham, William Somerset
See Maugham, W(illiam) Somerset

Maupassant, (Henri Rene Albert) Guy de 1850-1893**NCLC 1, 42; DA; DAB; DAC; DAM**

MST; SSC 1; WLC
Scc also DLB 123

Maupin, Armistead 1944-**CLC 95; DAM POP**
See also CA 125; 130; CANR 58; INT 130

Maurhut, Richard
See Traven, B.

Mauriac, Claude 1914-1996 .... **CLC 9**
See also CA 89-92; 152; DLB 83

Mauriac, Francois (Charles) 1885-1970 **C L C 4, 9, 56; SSC 24**
See also CA 25-28; CAP 2; DLB 65; MTCW

Mavor, Osborne Henry 1888-1951
See Bridie, James
See also CA 104

Maxwell, William (Keepers, Jr.) 1908-**CLC 19**
See also CA 93-96; CANR 54; DLBY 80; INT 93-96

May, Elaine 1932- .... **CLC 16**
See also CA 124; 142; DLB 44

Mayakovski, Vladimir (Vladimirovich) 1893-1930 .... **TCLC 4, 18**
See also CA 104; 158

Mayhew, Henry 1812-1887 .... **NCLC 31**
See also DLB 18, 55

Mayle, Peter 1939(?)- .... **CLC 89**
See also CA 139; CANR 64

Maynard, Joyce 1953- .... **CLC 23**
See also CA 111; 129; CANR 64

Mayne, William (James Carter) 1928-**CLC 12**
See also AAYA 20; CA 9-12R; CANR 37; CLR 25; JRDA; MAICYA; SAAS 11; SATA 6, 68

Mayo, Jim
See L'Amour, Louis (Dearborn)

Maysles, Albert 1926- .... **CLC 16**
See also CA 29-32R

Maysles, David 1932- .... **CLC 16**

Mazer, Norma Fox 1931- .... **CLC 26**
See also AAYA 5; CA 69-72; CANR 12, 32; CLR 23; JRDA; MAICYA; SAAS 1; SATA 24, 67

Mazzini, Guiseppe 1805-1872 .... **NCLC 34**

McAuley, James Phillip 1917-1976 .. **CLC 45**
See also CA 97-100

McBain, Ed
See Hunter, Evan

McBrien, William Augustine 1930-.. **CLC 44**
See also CA 107

McCaffrey, Anne (Inez) 1926-**CLC 17; DAM NOV, POP**
See also AAYA 6; AITN 2; BEST 89:2; CA 25-28R; CANR 15, 35, 55; DLB 8; JRDA; MAICYA; MTCW; SAAS 11; SATA 8, 70

McCall, Nathan 1955(?)- .... **CLC 86**
See also CA 146

McCann, Arthur
See Campbell, John W(ood, Jr.)

McCann, Edson
See Pohl, Frederik

McCarthy, Charles, Jr. 1933-
See McCarthy, Cormac
See also CANR 42; DAM POP

McCarthy, Cormac 1933- **CLC 4, 57, 59, 101**
See also McCarthy, Charles, Jr.
See also DLB 6, 143

McCarthy, Mary (Therese) 1912-1989**CLC 1, 3, 5, 14, 24, 39, 59; SSC 24**
See also CA 5-8R; 129; CANR 16, 50, 64; DLB 2; DLBY 81; INT CANR-16; MTCW

McCartney, (James) Paul 1942- **CLC 12, 35**
See also CA 146

McCauley, Stephen (D.) 1955- .... **CLC 50**
See also CA 141

McClure, Michael (Thomas) 1932-**CLC 6, 10**

NOV
See also CA 13-16R; CANR 8, 43; CDBLB 1960 to Present; DLB 14; INT CANR-8; MTCW

Murfree, Mary Noailles 1850-1922 ... **SSC 22**
See also CA 122; DLB 12, 74

Murnau, Friedrich Wilhelm
See Plumpe, Friedrich Wilhelm

Murphy, Richard 1927- .... **CLC 41**
See also CA 29-32R; DLB 40

Murphy, Sylvia 1937- .... **CLC 34**
See also CA 121

Murphy, Thomas (Bernard) 1935- ... **CLC 51**
See also CA 101

Murray, Albert L. 1916- .... **CLC 73**
See also BW 2; CA 49-52; CANR 26, 52; DLB 38

Murray, Judith Sargent 1751-1820 **NCLC 63**
See also DLB 37

Murray, Les(lie) A(llan) 1938- **CLC 40; DAM POET**
See also CA 21-24R; CANR 11, 27, 56

Murry, J. Middleton
See Murry, John Middleton

Murry, John Middleton 1889-1957 **TCLC 16**
See also CA 118; DLB 149

Musgrave, Susan 1951- .... **CLC 13, 54**
See also CA 69-72; CANR 45

Musil, Robert (Edler von) 1880-1942 **TCLC 12, 68; SSC 18**
See also CA 109; CANR 55; DLB 81, 124

Muske, Carol 1945- .... **CLC 90**
See also Muske-Dukes, Carol (Anne)

Muske-Dukes, Carol (Anne) 1945-
See Muske, Carol
See also CA 65-68; CANR 32

Musset, (Louis Charles) Alfred de 1810-1857 **NCLC 7**

My Brother's Brother
See Chekhov, Anton (Pavlovich)

Myers, L(eopold) H(amilton) 1881-1944 **TCLC 59**
See also CA 157; DLB 15

Myers, Walter Dean 1937- ..... **CLC 35; BLC; DAM MULT, NOV**
See also AAYA 4; BW 2; CA 33-36R; CANR 20, 42; CLR 4, 16, 35; DLB 33; INT CANR-20; JRDA; MAICYA; SAAS 2; SATA 41, 71; SATA-Brief 27

Myers, Walter M.
See Myers, Walter Dean

Myles, Symon
See Follett, Ken(neth Martin)

Nabokov, Vladimir (Vladimirovich) 1899-1977 **CLC 1, 2, 3, 6, 8, 11, 15, 23, 44, 46, 64; DA; DAB; DAC; DAM MST, NOV; SSC 11; WLC**
See also CA 5-8R; 69-72; CANR 20; CDALB 1941-1968; DLB 2; DLBD 3; DLBY 80, 91; MTCW

Nagai Kafu 1879-1959 .... **TCLC 51**
See also Nagai Sokichi
See also DLB 180

Nagai Sokichi 1879-1959
See Nagai Kafu
See also CA 117

Nagy, Laszlo 1925-1978 .... **CLC 7**
See also CA 129; 112

Naipaul, Shiva(dhar Srinivasa) 1945-1985 **CLC 32, 39; DAM NOV**
See also CA 110; 112; 116; CANR 33; DLB 157; DLBY 85; MTCW

Naipaul, V(idiadhar) S(urajprasad) 1932-

CLC 4, 7, 9, 13, 18, 37, 105; DAB; DAC; DAM MST, NOV
See also CA 1-4R; CANR 1, 33, 51; CDBLB 1960 to Present; DLB 125; DLBY 85; MTCW

Nakos, Lilika 1899(?)- .... **CLC 29**

Narayan, R(asipuram) K(rishnaswami) 1906- **CLC 7, 28, 47; DAM NOV; SSC 25**
See also CA 81-84; CANR 33, 61; MTCW; SATA 62

Nash, (Frediric) Ogden 1902-1971 . **CLC 23; DAM POET; PC 21**
See also CA 13-14; 29-32R; CANR 34, 61; CAP 1; DLB 11; MAICYA; MTCW; SATA 2, 46

Nashe, Thomas 1567-1601 .... **LC 41**

Nathan, Daniel
See Dannay, Frederic

Nathan, George Jean 1882-1958.... **TCLC 18**
See also Hatteras, Owen
See also CA 114; DLB 137

Natsume, Kinnosuke 1867-1916
See Natsume, Soseki
See also CA 104

Natsume, Soseki 1867-1916 .... **TCLC 2, 10**
See also Natsume, Kinnosuke
See also DLB 180

Natti, (Mary) Lee 1919-
See Kingman, Lee
See also CA 5-8R; CANR 2

Naylor, Gloria 1950- **CLC 28, 52; BLC; DA; DAC; DAM MST, MULT, NOV, POP; WLCS**
See also AAYA 6; BW 2; CA 107; CANR 27, 51; DLB 173; MTCW

Neihardt, John Gneisenau 1881-1973 **CLC 32**
See also CA 13-14; CAP 1; DLB 9, 54

Nekrasov, Nikolai Alekseevich 1821-1878 **NCLC 11**

Nelligan, Emile 1879-1941 .... **TCLC 14**
See also CA 114; DLB 92

Nelson, Willie 1933- .... **CLC 17**
See also CA 107

Nemerov, Howard (Stanley) 1920-1991 **CLC 2, 6, 9, 36; DAM POET**
See also CA 1-4R; 134; CABS 2; CANR 1, 27, 53; DLB 5, 6; DLBY 83; INT CANR-27; MTCW

Neruda, Pablo 1904-1973 **CLC 1, 2, 5, 7, 9, 28, 62; DA; DAB; DAC; DAM MST, MULT, POET; HLC; PC 4; WLC**
See also CA 19-20; 45-48; CAP 2; HW; MTCW

Nerval, Gerard de 1808-1855 **NCLC 1, 67; PC 13; SSC 18**

Nervo, (Jose) Amado (Ruiz de) 1870-1919 **TCLC 11**
See also CA 109; 131; HW

Nessi, Pio Baroja y
See Baroja (y Nessi), Pio

Nestroy, Johann 1801-1862 .... **NCLC 42**
See also DLB 133

Netterville, Luke
See O'Grady, Standish (James)

Neufeld, John (Arthur) 1938- .... **CLC 17**
See also AAYA 11; CA 25-28R; CANR 11, 37, 56; MAICYA; SAAS 3; SATA 6, 81

Neville, Emily Cheney 1919- .... **CLC 12**
See also CA 5-8R; CANR 3, 37; JRDA; MAICYA; SAAS 2; SATA 1

Newbound, Bernard Slade 1930-
See Slade, Bernard
See also CA 81-84; CANR 49; DAM DRAM

Newby, P(ercy) H(oward) 1918-1997 **CLC 2, 13; DAM NOV**

See also CA 5-8R; 161; CANR 32; DLB 15; MTCW

Newlove, Donald 1928- .... **CLC 6**
See also CA 29-32R; CANR 25

Newlove, John (Herbert) 1938- .... **CLC 14**
See also CA 21-24R; CANR 9, 25

Newman, Charles 1938- .... **CLC 2, 8**
See also CA 21-24R

Newman, Edwin (Harold) 1919- .... **CLC 14**
See also AITN 1; CA 69-72; CANR 5

Newman, John Henry 1801-1890 .. **NCLC 38**
See also DLB 18, 32, 55

Newton, Suzanne 1936- .... **CLC 35**
See also CA 41-44R; CANR 14; JRDA; SATA 5, 77

Nexo, Martin Andersen 1869-1954 **TCLC 43**

Nezval, Vitezslav 1900-1958 .... **TCLC 44**
See also CA 123

Ng, Fae Myenne 1957(?)- .... **CLC 81**
See also CA 146

Ngema, Mbongeni 1955- .... **CLC 57**
See also BW 2; CA 143

Ngugi, James T(hiong'o) .... **CLC 3, 7, 13**
See also Ngugi wa Thiong'o

Ngugi wa Thiong'o 1938- **CLC 36; BLC; DAM MULT, NOV**
See also Ngugi, James T(hiong'o)
See also BW 2; CA 81-84; CANR 27, 58; DLB 125; MTCW

Nichol, B(arrie) P(hillip) 1944-1988 **CLC 18**
See also CA 53-56; DLB 53; SATA 66

Nichols, John (Treadwell) 1940- .... **CLC 38**
See also CA 9-12R; CAAS 2; CANR 6; DLBY 82

Nichols, Leigh
See Koontz, Dean R(ay)

Nichols, Peter (Richard) 1927- **CLC 5, 36, 65**
See also CA 104; CANR 33; DLB 13; MTCW

Nicolas, F. R. E.
See Freeling, Nicolas

Niedecker, Lorine 1903-1970 .... **CLC 10, 42; DAM POET**
See also CA 25-28; CAP 2; DLB 48

Nietzsche, Friedrich (Wilhelm) 1844-1900 **TCLC 10, 18, 55**
See also CA 107; 121; DLB 129

Nievo, Ippolito 1831-1861 .... **NCLC 22**

Nightingale, Anne Redmon 1943-
See Redmon, Anne
See also CA 103

Nik. T. O.
See Annensky, Innokenty (Fyodorovich)

Nin, Anais 1903-1977 **CLC 1, 4, 8, 11, 14, 60; DAM NOV, POP; SSC 10**
See also AITN 2; CA 13-16R; 69-72; CANR 22, 53; DLB 2, 4, 152; MTCW

Nishiwaki, Junzaburo 1894-1982 .... **PC 15**
See also CA 107

Nissenson, Hugh 1933- .... **CLC 4, 9**
See also CA 17-20R; CANR 27; DLB 28

Niven, Larry .... **CLC 8**
See also Niven, Laurence Van Cott
See also DLB 8

Niven, Laurence Van Cott 1938-
See Niven, Larry
See also CA 21-24R; CAAS 12; CANR 14, 44; DAM POP; MTCW; SATA 95

Nixon, Agnes Eckhardt 1927- .... **CLC 21**
See also CA 110

Nizan, Paul 1905-1940 .... **TCLC 40**
See also CA 161; DLB 72

Nkosi, Lewis 1936- .... **CLC 45; BLC; DAM MULT**

See also Oneal, Elizabeth
See also AAYA 5; CLR 13; JRDA
O'Neill, Eugene (Gladstone) 1888-1953 **TCLC 1, 6, 27, 49; DA; DAB; DAC; DAM DRAM, MST; WLC**
See also AITN 1; CA 110; 132; CDALB 1929-1941; DLB 7; MTCW
Onetti, Juan Carlos 1909-1994 ... **CLC 7, 10; DAM MULT, NOV; SSC 23**
See also CA 85-88; 145; CANR 32, 63; DLB 113; HW; MTCW
O Nuallain, Brian 1911-1966
See O'Brien, Flann
See also CA 21-22; 25-28R; CAP 2
Ophuls, Max 1902-1957 .... **TCLC 79**
See also CA 113
Opie, Amelia 1769-1853 .... **NCLC 65**
See also DLB 116, 159
Oppen, George 1908-1984 ...... **CLC 7, 13, 34**
See also CA 13-16R; 113; CANR 8; DLB 5, 165
Oppenheim, E(dward) Phillips 1866-1946 **TCLC 45**
See also CA 111; DLB 70
Opuls, Max
See Ophuls, Max
Origen c. 185-c. 254 .... **CMLC 19**
Orlovitz, Gil 1918-1973 .... **CLC 22**
See also CA 77-80; 45-48; DLB 2, 5
Orris
See Ingelow, Jean
Ortega y Gasset, Jose 1883-1955 .... **TCLC 9; DAM MULT; HLC**
See also CA 106; 130; HW; MTCW
Ortese, Anna Maria 1914- .... **CLC 89**
See also DLB 177
Ortiz, Simon J(oseph) 1941-.. **CLC 45; DAM MULT, POET; PC 17**
See also CA 134; DLB 120, 175; NNAL
Orton, Joe .... **CLC 4, 13, 43; DC 3**
See also Orton, John Kingsley
See also CDBLB 1960 to Present; DLB 13
Orton, John Kingsley 1933-1967
See Orton, Joe
See also CA 85-88; CANR 35; DAM DRAM; MTCW
Orwell, George . **TCLC 2, 6, 15, 31, 51; DAB; WLC**
See also Blair, Eric (Arthur)
See also CDBLB 1945-1960; DLB 15, 98
Osborne, David
See Silverberg, Robert
Osborne, George
See Silverberg, Robert
Osborne, John (James) 1929-1994 **CLC 1, 2, 5, 11, 45; DA; DAB; DAC; DAM DRAM, MST; WLC**
See also CA 13-16R; 147; CANR 21, 56; CDBLB 1945-1960; DLB 13; MTCW
Osborne, Lawrence 1958- .... **CLC 50**
Oshima, Nagisa 1932- .... **CLC 20**
See also CA 116; 121
Oskison, John Milton 1874-1947 .. **TCLC 35; DAM MULT**
See also CA 144; DLB 175; NNAL
Ossoli, Sarah Margaret (Fuller marchesa d') 1810-1850
See Fuller, Margaret
See also SATA 25
Ostrovsky, Alexander 1823-1886 **NCLC 30, 57**
Otero, Blas de 1916-1979 .... **CLC 11**
See also CA 89-92; DLB 134
Otto, Whitney 1955- .... **CLC 70**

See also CA 140
Ouida .... **TCLC 43**
See also De La Ramee, (Marie) Louise
See also DLB 18, 156
Ousmane, Sembene 1923- .... **CLC 66; BLC**
See also BW 1; CA 117; 125; MTCW
Ovid 43B.C.-18(?) **CMLC 7; DAM POET; PC 2**
Owen, Hugh
See Faust, Frederick (Schiller)
Owen, Wilfred (Edward Salter) 1893-1918 **TCLC 5, 27; DA; DAB; DAC; DAM MST, POET; PC 19; WLC**
See also CA 104; 141; CDBLB 1914-1945; DLB 20
Owens, Rochelle 1936- .... **CLC 8**
See also CA 17-20R; CAAS 2; CANR 39
Oz, Amos 1939- **CLC 5, 8, 11, 27, 33, 54; DAM NOV**
See also CA 53-56; CANR 27, 47; MTCW
Ozick, Cynthia 1928- **CLC 3, 7, 28, 62; DAM NOV, POP; SSC 15**
See also BEST 90:1; CA 17-20R; CANR 23, 58; DLB 28, 152; DLBY 82; INT CANR-23; MTCW
Ozu, Yasujiro 1903-1963 .... **CLC 16**
See also CA 112
Pacheco, C.
See Pessoa, Fernando (Antonio Nogueira)
Pa Chin .... **CLC 18**
See also Li Fei-kan
Pack, Robert 1929- .... **CLC 13**
See also CA 1-4R; CANR 3, 44; DLB 5
Padgett, Lewis
See Kuttner, Henry
Padilla (Lorenzo), Heberto 1932-..... **CLC 38**
See also AITN 1; CA 123; 131; HW
Page, Jimmy 1944- .... **CLC 12**
Page, Louise 1955- .... **CLC 40**
See also CA 140
Page, P(atricia) K(athleen) 1916- **CLC 7, 18; DAC; DAM MST; PC 12**
See also CA 53-56; CANR 4, 22; DLB 68; MTCW
Page, Thomas Nelson 1853-1922 .... **SSC 23**
See also CA 118; DLB 12, 78; DLBD 13
Pagels, Elaine Hiesey 1943- .... **CLC 104**
See also CA 45-48; CANR 2, 24, 51
Paget, Violet 1856-1935
See Lee, Vernon
See also CA 104
Paget-Lowe, Henry
See Lovecraft, H(oward) P(hillips)
Paglia, Camille (Anna) 1947- .... **CLC 68**
See also CA 140
Paige, Richard
See Koontz, Dean R(ay)
Paine, Thomas 1737-1809 .... **NCLC 62**
See also CDALB 1640-1865; DLB 31, 43, 73, 158
Pakenham, Antonia
See Fraser, (Lady) Antonia (Pakenham)
Palamas, Kostes 1859-1943 .... **TCLC 5**
See also CA 105
Palazzeschi, Aldo 1885-1974 .... **CLC 11**
See also CA 89-92; 53-56; DLB 114
Paley, Grace 1922- **CLC 4, 6, 37; DAM POP; SSC 8**
See also CA 25-28R; CANR 13, 46; DLB 28; INT CANR-13; MTCW
Palin, Michael (Edward) 1943- .... **CLC 21**
See also Monty Python
See also CA 107; CANR 35; SATA 67

Palliser, Charles 1947- .... **CLC 65**
See also CA 136
Palma, Ricardo 1833-1919 .... **TCLC 29**
Pancake, Breece Dexter 1952-1979
See Pancake, Breece D'J
See also CA 123; 109
Pancake, Breece D'J .... **CLC 29**
See also Pancake, Breece Dexter
See also DLB 130
Panko, Rudy
See Gogol, Nikolai (Vasilyevich)
Papadiamantis, Alexandros 1851-1911 **TCLC 29**
Papadiamantopoulos, Johannes 1856-1910
See Moreas, Jean
See also CA 117
Papini, Giovanni 1881-1956 .... **TCLC 22**
See also CA 121
Paracelsus 1493-1541 .... **LC 14**
See also DLB 179
Parasol, Peter
See Stevens, Wallace
Pareto, Vilfredo 1848-1923 .... **TCLC 69**
Parfenie, Maria
See Codrescu, Andrei
Parini, Jay (Lee) 1948- .... **CLC 54**
See also CA 97-100; CAAS 16; CANR 32
Park, Jordan
See Kornbluth, C(yril) M.; Pohl, Frederik
Park, Robert E(zra) 1864-1944 ...... **TCLC 73**
See also CA 122
Parker, Bert
See Ellison, Harlan (Jay)
Parker, Dorothy (Rothschild) 1893-1967 **CLC 15, 68; DAM POET; SSC 2**
See also CA 19-20; 25-28R; CAP 2; DLB 11, 45, 86; MTCW
Parker, Robert B(rown) 1932- **CLC 27; DAM NOV, POP**
See also BEST 89:4; CA 49-52; CANR 1, 26, 52; INT CANR-26; MTCW
Parkin, Frank 1940- .... **CLC 43**
See also CA 147
Parkman, Francis, Jr. 1823-1893 .. **NCLC 12**
See also DLB 1, 30
Parks, Gordon (Alexander Buchanan) 1912- **CLC 1, 16; BLC; DAM MULT**
See also AITN 2; BW 2; CA 41-44R; CANR 26; DLB 33; SATA 8
Parmenides c. 515B.C.-c. 450B.C. **CMLC 22**
See also DLB 176
Parnell, Thomas 1679-1718 .... **LC 3**
See also DLB 94
Parra, Nicanor 1914- ...... **CLC 2, 102; DAM MULT; HLC**
See also CA 85-88; CANR 32; HW; MTCW
Parrish, Mary Frances
See Fisher, M(ary) F(rances) K(ennedy)
Parson
See Coleridge, Samuel Taylor
Parson Lot
See Kingsley, Charles
Partridge, Anthony
See Oppenheim, E(dward) Phillips
Pascal, Blaise 1623-1662 .... **LC 35**
Pascoli, Giovanni 1855-1912 .... **TCLC 45**
Pasolini, Pier Paolo 1922-1975 . **CLC 20, 37, 106; PC 17**
See also CA 93-96; 61-64; CANR 63; DLB 128, 177; MTCW
Pasquini
See Silone, Ignazio
Pastan, Linda (Olenik) 1932- **CLC 27; DAM**

POET
See also CA 61-64; CANR 18, 40, 61; DLB 5
Pasternak, Boris (Leonidovich) 1890-1960
    **CLC 7, 10, 18, 63; DA; DAB; DAC; DAM
    MST, NOV, POET; PC 6; WLC**
See also CA 127; 116; MTCW
Patchen, Kenneth 1911-1972 ... **CLC 1, 2, 18;
    DAM POET**
See also CA 1-4R; 33-36R; CANR 3, 35; DLB
    16, 48; MTCW
Pater, Walter (Horatio) 1839-1894 .. **NCLC 7**
See also CDBLB 1832-1890; DLB 57, 156
Paterson, A(ndrew) B(arton) 1864-1941
    TCLC 32
See also CA 155
Paterson, Katherine (Womeldorf) 1932-**C L C
    12, 30**
See also AAYA 1; CA 21-24R; CANR 28, 59;
    CLR 7; DLB 52; JRDA; MAICYA; MTCW;
    SATA 13, 53, 92
Patmore, Coventry Kersey Dighton 1823-1896
    NCLC 9
See also DLB 35, 98
Paton, Alan (Stewart) 1903-1988 **CLC 4, 10,
    25, 55, 106; DA; DAB; DAC; DAM MST,
    NOV; WLC**
See also CA 13-16; 125; CANR 22; CAP 1;
    MTCW; SATA 11; SATA-Obit 56
Paton Walsh, Gillian 1937-
See Walsh, Jill Paton
See also CANR 38; JRDA; MAICYA; SAAS 3;
    SATA 4, 72
Patton, George S. 1885-1945 .... **TCLC 79**
Paulding, James Kirke 1778-1860 ... **NCLC 2**
See also DLB 3, 59, 74
Paulin, Thomas Neilson 1949-
See Paulin, Tom
See also CA 123; 128
Paulin, Tom .... **CLC 37**
See also Paulin, Thomas Neilson
See also DLB 40
Paustovsky, Konstantin (Georgievich) 1892-
    1968 .... **CLC 40**
See also CA 93-96; 25-28R
Pavese, Cesare 1908-1950 ... **TCLC 3; PC 13;
    SSC 19**
See also CA 104; DLB 128, 177
Pavic, Milorad 1929- .... **CLC 60**
See also CA 136; DLB 181
Payne, Alan
See Jakes, John (William)
Paz, Gil
See Lugones, Leopoldo
Paz, Octavio 1914-**CLC 3, 4, 6, 10, 19, 51, 65;
    DA; DAB; DAC; DAM MST, MULT,
    POET; HLC; PC 1; WLC**
See also CA 73-76; CANR 32; DLBY 90; HW;
    MTCW
p'Bitek, Okot 1931-1982**CLC 96; BLC; DAM
    MULT**
See also BW 2; CA 124; 107; DLB 125; MTCW
Peacock, Molly 1947- .... **CLC 60**
See also CA 103; CAAS 21; CANR 52; DLB
    120
Peacock, Thomas Love 1785-1866 . **NCLC 22**
See also DLB 96, 116
Peake, Mervyn 1911-1968 .... **CLC 7, 54**
See also CA 5-8R; 25-28R; CANR 3; DLB 15,
    160; MTCW; SATA 23
Pearce, Philippa .... **CLC 21**
See also Christie, (Ann) Philippa
See also CLR 9; DLB 161; MAICYA; SATA 1,
    67

Pearl, Eric
See Elman, Richard
Pearson, T(homas) R(eid) 1956- .... **CLC 39**
See also CA 120; 130; INT 130
Peck, Dale 1967- .... **CLC 81**
See also CA 146
Peck, John 1941- .... **CLC 3**
See also CA 49-52; CANR 3
Peck, Richard (Wayne) 1934- .... **CLC 21**
See also AAYA 1; CA 85-88; CANR 19, 38;
    CLR 15; INT CANR-19; JRDA; MAICYA;
    SAAS 2; SATA 18, 55
Peck, Robert Newton 1928- ..... **CLC 17; DA;
    DAC; DAM MST**
See also AAYA 3; CA 81-84; CANR 31, 63;
    CLR 45; JRDA; MAICYA; SAAS 1; SATA
    21, 62
Peckinpah, (David) Sam(uel) 1925-1984**C L C
    20**
See also CA 109; 114
Pedersen, Knut 1859-1952
See Hamsun, Knut
See also CA 104; 119; CANR 63; MTCW
Peeslake, Gaffer
See Durrell, Lawrence (George)
Peguy, Charles Pierre 1873-1914 .. **TCLC 10**
See also CA 107
Pena, Ramon del Valle y
See Valle-Inclan, Ramon (Maria) del
Pendennis, Arthur Esquir
See Thackeray, William Makepeace
Penn, William 1644-1718 .... **LC 25**
See also DLB 24
PEPECE
See Prado (Calvo), Pedro
Pepys, Samuel 1633-1703 **LC 11; DA; DAB;
    DAC; DAM MST; WLC**
See also CDBLB 1660-1789; DLB 101
Percy, Walker 1916-1990**CLC 2, 3, 6, 8, 14, 18,
    47, 65; DAM NOV, POP**
See also CA 1-4R; 131; CANR 1, 23, 64; DLB
    2; DLBY 80, 90; MTCW
Perec, Georges 1936-1982 .... **CLC 56**
See also CA 141; DLB 83
Pereda (y Sanchez de Porrua), Jose Maria de
    1833-1906 .... **TCLC 16**
See also CA 117
Pereda y Porrua, Jose Maria de
See Pereda (y Sanchez de Porrua), Jose Maria
    de
Peregoy, George Weems
See Mencken, H(enry) L(ouis)
Perelman, S(idney) J(oseph) 1904-1979 **C L C
    3, 5, 9, 15, 23, 44, 49; DAM DRAM**
See also AITN 1, 2; CA 73-76; 89-92, CANR
    18; DLB 11, 44; MTCW
Peret, Benjamin 1899-1959 .... **TCLC 20**
See also CA 117
Peretz, Isaac Loeb 1851(?)-1915 ... **TCLC 16;
    SSC 26**
See also CA 109
Peretz, Yitzkhok Leibush
See Peretz, Isaac Loeb
Perez Galdos, Benito 1843-1920 .... **TCLC 27**
See also CA 125; 153; HW
Perrault, Charles 1628-1703 .... **LC 2**
See also MAICYA; SATA 25
Perry, Brighton
See Sherwood, Robert E(mmet)
Perse, St.-John .... **CLC 4, 11, 46**
See also Leger, (Marie-Rene Auguste) Alexis
    Saint-Leger
Perutz, Leo 1882-1957 .... **TCLC 60**

See also DLB 81
Peseenz, Tulio F.
See Lopez y Fuentes, Gregorio
Pesetsky, Bette 1932- .... **CLC 28**
See also CA 133; DLB 130
Peshkov, Alexei Maximovich 1868-1936
See Gorky, Maxim
See also CA 105; 141; DA; DAC; DAM DRAM,
    MST, NOV
Pessoa, Fernando (Antonio Nogueira) 1888-
    1935 .... **TCLC 27; HLC; PC 20**
See also CA 125
Peterkin, Julia Mood 1880-1961 .... **CLC 31**
See also CA 102; DLB 9
Peters, Joan K(aren) 1945- .... **CLC 39**
See also CA 158
Peters, Robert L(ouis) 1924- .... **CLC 7**
See also CA 13-16R; CAAS 8; DLB 105
Petofi, Sandor 1823-1849 .... **NCLC 21**
Petrakis, Harry Mark 1923- .... **CLC 3**
See also CA 9-12R; CANR 4, 30
Petrarch 1304-1374 **CMLC 20; DAM POET;
    PC 8**
Petrov, Evgeny .... **TCLC 21**
See also Kataev, Evgeny Petrovich
Petry, Ann (Lane) 1908-1997 ... **CLC 1, 7, 18**
See also BW 1; CA 5-8R; 157; CAAS 6; CANR
    4, 46; CLR 12; DLB 76; JRDA; MAICYA;
    MTCW; SATA 5; SATA-Obit 94
Petursson, Halligrimur 1614-1674 .... **LC 8**
Phaedrus 18(?)B.C.-55(?) .... **CMLC 25**
Philips, Katherine 1632-1664 .... **LC 30**
See also DLB 131
Philipson, Morris H. 1926- .... **CLC 53**
See also CA 1-4R; CANR 4
Phillips, Caryl 1958- .. **CLC 96; DAM MULT**
See also BW 2; CA 141; CANR 63; DLB 157
Phillips, David Graham 1867-1911 **TCLC 44**
See also CA 108; DLB 9, 12
Phillips, Jack
See Sandburg, Carl (August)
Phillips, Jayne Anne 1952-**CLC 15, 33; SSC 16**
See also CA 101; CANR 24, 50; DLBY 80; INT
    CANR-24; MTCW
Phillips, Richard
See Dick, Philip K(indred)
Phillips, Robert (Schaeffer) 1938- .... **CLC 28**
See also CA 17-20R; CAAS 13; CANR 8; DLB
    105
Phillips, Ward
See Lovecraft, H(oward) P(hillips)
Piccolo, Lucio 1901-1969 .... **CLC 13**
See also CA 97-100; DLB 114
Pickthall, Marjorie L(owry) C(hristie) 1883-
    1922 .... **TCLC 21**
See also CA 107; DLB 92
Pico della Mirandola, Giovanni 1463-1494**LC
    15**
Piercy, Marge 1936- **CLC 3, 6, 14, 18, 27, 62**
See also CA 21-24R; CAAS 1; CANR 13, 43;
    DLB 120; MTCW
Piers, Robert
See Anthony, Piers
Pieyre de Mandiargues, Andre 1909-1991
See Mandiargues, Andre Pieyre de
See also CA 103; 136; CANR 22
Pilnyak, Boris .... **TCLC 23**
See also Vogau, Boris Andreyevich
Pincherle, Alberto 1907-1990 ... **CLC 11, 18;
    DAM NOV**
See also Moravia, Alberto
See also CA 25-28R; 132; CANR 33, 63;
    MTCW

Pinckney, Darryl 1953- .... **CLC 76**
See also BW 2; CA 143
Pindar 518B.C.-446B.C. .... **CMLC 12; PC 19**
See also DLB 176
Pineda, Cecile 1942- .... **CLC 39**
See also CA 118
Pinero, Arthur Wing 1855-1934 ... **TCLC 32;
DAM DRAM**
See also CA 110; 153; DLB 10
Pinero, Miguel (Antonio Gomez) 1946-1988
CLC 4, 55
See also CA 61-64; 125; CANR 29; HW
Pinget, Robert 1919-1997 .... **CLC 7, 13, 37**
See also CA 85-88; 160; DLB 83
Pink Floyd
See Barrett, (Roger) Syd; Gilmour, David; Mason, Nick; Waters, Roger; Wright, Rick
Pinkney, Edward 1802-1828 .... **NCLC 31**
Pinkwater, Daniel Manus 1941- .... **CLC 35**
See also Pinkwater, Manus
See also AAYA 1; CA 29-32R; CANR 12, 38;
CLR 4; JRDA; MAICYA; SAAS 3; SATA 46,
76
Pinkwater, Manus
See Pinkwater, Daniel Manus
See also SATA 8
Pinsky, Robert 1940-**CLC 9, 19, 38, 94; DAM
POET**
See also CA 29-32R; CAAS 4; CANR 58;
DLBY 82
Pinta, Harold
See Pinter, Harold
Pinter, Harold 1930-**CLC 1, 3, 6, 9, 11, 15, 27,
58, 73; DA; DAB; DAC; DAM DRAM,
MST; WLC**
See also CA 5-8R; CANR 33; CDBLB 1960 to
Present; DLB 13; MTCW
Piozzi, Hester Lynch (Thrale) 1741-1821
NCLC 57
See also DLB 104, 142
Pirandello, Luigi 1867-1936**TCLC 4, 29; DA;
DAB; DAC; DAM DRAM, MST; DC 5;
SSC 22; WLC**
See also CA 104; 153
Pirsig, Robert M(aynard) 1928-**CLC 4, 6, 73;
DAM POP**
See also CA 53-56; CANR 42; MTCW; SATA
39
Pisarev, Dmitry Ivanovich 1840-1868 **NCLC
25**
Pix, Mary (Griffith) 1666-1709 .... **LC 8**
See also DLB 80
Pixerecourt, Guilbert de 1773-1844**NCLC 39**
Plaatje, Sol(omon) T(shekisho) 1876-1932
TCLC 73
See also BW 2; CA 141
Plaidy, Jean
See Hibbert, Eleanor Alice Burford
Planche, James Robinson 1796-1880**NCLC 42**
Plant, Robert 1948- .... **CLC 12**
Plante, David (Robert) 1940- **CLC 7, 23, 38;
DAM NOV**
See also CA 37-40R; CANR 12, 36, 58; DLBY
83; INT CANR-12; MTCW
Plath, Sylvia 1932-1963 **CLC 1, 2, 3, 5, 9, 11,
14, 17, 50, 51, 62; DA; DAB; DAC; DAM
MST, POET; PC 1; WLC**
See also AAYA 13; CA 19-20; CANR 34; CAP
2; CDALB 1941-1968; DLB 5, 6, 152;
MTCW; SATA 96
Plato 428(?)B.C.-348(?)B.C. .... **CMLC 8; DA;
DAB; DAC; DAM MST; WLCS**
See also DLB 176

Platonov, Andrei .... **TCLC 14**
See also Klimentov, Andrei Platonovich
Platt, Kin 1911- .... **CLC 26**
See also AAYA 11; CA 17-20R; CANR 11;
JRDA; SAAS 17; SATA 21, 86
Plautus c. 251B.C.-184B.C. .... **DC 6**
Plick et Plock
See Simenon, Georges (Jacques Christian)
Plimpton, George (Ames) 1927- .... **CLC 36**
See also AITN 1; CA 21-24R; CANR 32;
MTCW; SATA 10
Pliny the Elder c. 23-79 .... **CMLC 23**
Plomer, William Charles Franklin 1903-1973
CLC 4, 8
See also CA 21-22; CANR 34; CAP 2; DLB
20, 162; MTCW; SATA 24
Plowman, Piers
See Kavanagh, Patrick (Joseph)
Plum, J.
See Wodehouse, P(elham) G(renville)
Plumly, Stanley (Ross) 1939- .... **CLC 33**
See also CA 108; 110; DLB 5; INT 110
Plumpe, Friedrich Wilhelm 1888-1931**T C L C
53**
See also CA 112
Po Chu-i 772-846 .... **CMLC 24**
Poe, Edgar Allan 1809-1849**NCLC 1, 16, 55;
DA; DAB; DAC; DAM MST, POET; PC
1; SSC 1, 22; WLC**
See also AAYA 14; CDALB 1640-1865; DLB
3, 59, 73, 74; SATA 23
Poet of Titchfield Street, The
See Pound, Ezra (Weston Loomis)
Pohl, Frederik 1919- .... **CLC 18; SSC 25**
See also CA 61-64; CAAS 1; CANR 11, 37;
DLB 8; INT CANR-11; MTCW; SATA 24
Poirier, Louis 1910-
See Gracq, Julien
See also CA 122; 126
Poitier, Sidney 1927- .... **CLC 26**
See also BW 1; CA 117
Polanski, Roman 1933- .... **CLC 16**
See also CA 77-80
Poliakoff, Stephen 1952- .... **CLC 38**
See also CA 106; DLB 13
Police, The
See Copeland, Stewart (Armstrong); Summers,
Andrew James; Sumner, Gordon Matthew
Polidori, John William 1795-1821.**NCLC 51**
See also DLB 116
Pollitt, Katha 1949- .... **CLC 28**
See also CA 120; 122; MTCW
Pollock, (Mary) Sharon 1936-**CLC 50; DAC;
DAM DRAM, MST**
See also CA 141; DLB 60
Polo, Marco 1254-1324 .... **CMLC 15**
Polonsky, Abraham (Lincoln) 1910- **CLC 92**
See also CA 104; DLB 26; INT 104
Polybius c. 200B.C.-c. 118B.C. ...... **CMLC 17**
See also DLB 176
Pomerance, Bernard 1940- .... **CLC 13; DAM
DRAM**
See also CA 101; CANR 49
Ponge, Francis (Jean Gaston Alfred) 1899-1988
CLC 6, 18; DAM POET
See also CA 85-88; 126; CANR 40
Pontoppidan, Henrik 1857-1943 .... **TCLC 29**
Poole, Josephine .... **CLC 17**
See also Helyar, Jane Penelope Josephine
See also SAAS 2; SATA 5
Popa, Vasko 1922-1991 .... **CLC 19**
See also CA 112; 148; DLB 181
Pope, Alexander 1688-1744 **LC 3; DA; DAB;**

DAC; DAM MST, POET; WLC
See also CDBLB 1660-1789; DLB 95, 101
Porter, Connie (Rose) 1959(?)- .... **CLC 70**
See also BW 2; CA 142; SATA 81
Porter, Gene(va Grace) Stratton 1863(?)-1924
TCLC 21
See also CA 112
Porter, Katherine Anne 1890-1980**CLC 1, 3, 7,
10, 13, 15, 27, 101; DA; DAB; DAC; DAM
MST, NOV; SSC 4**
See also AITN 2; CA 1-4R; 101; CANR 1; DLB
4, 9, 102; DLBD 12; DLBY 80; MTCW;
SATA 39; SATA-Obit 23
Porter, Peter (Neville Frederick) 1929-**CLC 5,
13, 33**
See also CA 85-88; DLB 40
Porter, William Sydney 1862-1910
See Henry, O.
See also CA 104; 131; CDALB 1865-1917; DA;
DAB; DAC; DAM MST; DLB 12, 78, 79;
MTCW; YABC 2
Portillo (y Pacheco), Jose Lopez
See Lopez Portillo (y Pacheco), Jose
Post, Melville Davisson 1869-1930 **TCLC 39**
See also CA 110
Potok, Chaim 1929- . **CLC 2, 7, 14, 26; DAM
NOV**
See also AAYA 15; AITN 1, 2; CA 17-20R;
CANR 19, 35, 64; DLB 28, 152; INT CANR-
19; MTCW; SATA 33
Potter, (Helen) Beatrix 1866-1943
See Webb, (Martha) Beatrice (Potter)
See also MAICYA
Potter, Dennis (Christopher George) 1935-1994
CLC 58, 86
See also CA 107; 145; CANR 33, 61; MTCW
Pound, Ezra (Weston Loomis) 1885-1972
**CLC 1, 2, 3, 4, 5, 7, 10, 13, 18, 34, 48, 50;
DA; DAB; DAC; DAM MST, POET; PC
4; WLC**
See also CA 5-8R; 37-40R; CANR 40; CDALB
1917-1929; DLB 4, 45, 63; DLBD 15;
MTCW
Povod, Reinaldo 1959-1994 .... **CLC 44**
See also CA 136; 146
Powell, Adam Clayton, Jr. 1908-1972**CLC 89;
BLC; DAM MULT**
See also BW 1; CA 102; 33-36R
Powell, Anthony (Dymoke) 1905-**CLC 1, 3, 7,
9, 10, 31**
See also CA 1-4R; CANR 1, 32, 62; CDBLB
1945-1960; DLB 15; MTCW
Powell, Dawn 1897-1965 .... **CLC 66**
See also CA 5-8R
Powell, Padgett 1952- .... **CLC 34**
See also CA 126; CANR 63
Power, Susan 1961- .... **CLC 91**
Powers, J(ames) F(arl) 1917-**CLC 1, 4, 8, 57;
SSC 4**
See also CA 1-4R; CANR 2, 61; DLB 130;
MTCW
Powers, John J(ames) 1945-
See Powers, John R.
See also CA 69-72
Powers, John R. .... **CLC 66**
See also Powers, John J(ames)
Powers, Richard (S.) 1957- .... **CLC 93**
See also CA 148
Pownall, David 1938- .... **CLC 10**
See also CA 89-92; CAAS 18; CANR 49; DLB
14
Powys, John Cowper 1872-1963**CLC 7, 9, 15,
46**

See also CA 85-88; DLB 15; MTCW
Powys, T(heodore) F(rancis) 1875-1953
TCLC 9
See also CA 106; DLB 36, 162
Prado (Calvo), Pedro 1886-1952 ... **TCLC 75**
See also CA 131; HW
Prager, Emily 1952- .... **CLC 56**
Pratt, E(dwin) J(ohn) 1883(?)-1964 **CLC 19;**
DAC; DAM POET
See also CA 141; 93-96; DLB 92
Premchand .... **TCLC 21**
See also Srivastava, Dhanpat Rai
Preussler, Otfried 1923- .... **CLC 17**
See also CA 77-80; SATA 24
Prevert, Jacques (Henri Marie) 1900-1977
CLC 15
See also CA 77-80; 69-72; CANR 29, 61;
MTCW; SATA-Obit 30
Prevost, Abbe (Antoine Francois) 1697-1763
LC 1
Price, (Edward) Reynolds 1933-**CLC 3, 6, 13,**
43, 50, 63; DAM NOV; SSC 22
See also CA 1-4R; CANR 1, 37, 57; DLB 2;
INT CANR-37
Price, Richard 1949- .... **CLC 6, 12**
See also CA 49-52; CANR 3; DLBY 81
Prichard, Katharine Susannah 1883-1969
CLC 46
See also CA 11-12; CANR 33; CAP 1; MTCW;
SATA 66
Priestley, J(ohn) B(oynton) 1894-1984**CLC 2,**
5, 9, 34; DAM DRAM, NOV
See also CA 9-12R; 113; CANR 33; CDBLB
1914-1945; DLB 10, 34, 77, 100, 139; DLBY
84; MTCW
Prince 1958(?)- .... **CLC 35**
Prince, F(rank) T(empleton) 1912- .. **CLC 22**
See also CA 101; CANR 43; DLB 20
Prince Kropotkin
See Kropotkin, Peter (Aleksieevich)
Prior, Matthew 1664-1721 .... **LC 4**
See also DLB 95
Prishvin, Mikhail 1873-1954 .... **TCLC 75**
Pritchard, William H(arrison) 1932-**CLC 34**
See also CA 65-68; CANR 23; DLB 111
Pritchett, V(ictor) S(awdon) 1900-1997 **C L C**
5, 13, 15, 41; DAM NOV; SSC 14
See also CA 61-64; 157; CANR 31, 63; DLB
15, 139; MTCW
Private 19022
See Manning, Frederic
Probst, Mark 1925- .... **CLC 59**
See also CA 130
Prokosch, Frederic 1908-1989 ...... **CLC 4, 48**
See also CA 73-76; 128; DLB 48
Prophet, The
See Dreiser, Theodore (Herman Albert)
Prose, Francine 1947- .... **CLC 45**
See also CA 109; 112; CANR 46
Proudhon
See Cunha, Euclides (Rodrigues Pimenta) da
Proulx, E. Annie 1935- .... **CLC 81**
Proust, (Valentin-Louis-George-Eugene-)
Marcel 1871-1922 **TCLC 7, 13, 33; DA;**
DAB; DAC; DAM MST, NOV; WLC
See also CA 104; 120; DLB 65; MTCW
Prowler, Harley
See Masters, Edgar Lee
Prus, Boleslaw 1845-1912 .... **TCLC 48**
Pryor, Richard (Franklin Lenox Thomas) 1940-
CLC 26
See also CA 122
Przybyszewski, Stanislaw 1868-1927**TCLC 36**

See also CA 160; DLB 66
Pteleon
See Grieve, C(hristopher) M(urray)
See also DAM POET
Puckett, Lute
See Masters, Edgar Lee
Puig, Manuel 1932-1990**CLC 3, 5, 10, 28, 65;**
DAM MULT; HLC
See also CA 45-48; CANR 2, 32, 63; DLB 113;
HW; MTCW
Pulitzer, Joseph 1847-1911 .... **TCLC 76**
See also CA 114; DLB 23
Purdy, Al(fred Wellington) 1918-**CLC 3, 6, 14,**
50; DAC; DAM MST, POET
See also CA 81-84; CAAS 17; CANR 42; DLB
88
Purdy, James (Amos) 1923-**CLC 2, 4, 10, 28,**
52
See also CA 33-36R; CAAS 1; CANR 19, 51;
DLB 2; INT CANR-19; MTCW
Pure, Simon
See Swinnerton, Frank Arthur
Pushkin, Alexander (Sergeyevich) 1799-1837
NCLC 3, 27; DA; DAB; DAC; DAM
DRAM, MST, POET; PC 10; SSC 27;
WLC
See also SATA 61
P'u Sung-ling 1640-1715 .... **LC 3**
Putnam, Arthur Lee
See Alger, Horatio, Jr.
Puzo, Mario 1920-**CLC 1, 2, 6, 36, 107; DAM**
NOV, POP
See also CA 65-68; CANR 4, 42; DLB 6;
MTCW
Pygge, Edward
See Barnes, Julian (Patrick)
Pyle, Ernest Taylor 1900-1945
See Pyle, Ernie
See also CA 115; 160
Pyle, Ernie 1900-1945 .... **TCLC 75**
See also Pyle, Ernest Taylor
See also DLB 29
Pym, Barbara (Mary Crampton) 1913-1980
CLC 13, 19, 37
See also CA 13-14; 97-100; CANR 13, 34; CAP
1; DLB 14; DLBY 87; MTCW
Pynchon, Thomas (Ruggles, Jr.) 1937-**CLC 2,**
3, 6, 9, 11, 18, 33, 62, 72; DA; DAB; DAC;
DAM MST, NOV, POP; SSC 14; WLC
See also BEST 90:2; CA 17-20R; CANR 22,
46; DLB 2, 173; MTCW
Pythagoras c. 570B.C.-c. 500B.C. . **CMLC 22**
See also DLB 176
Qian Zhongshu
See Ch'ien Chung-shu
Qroll
See Dagerman, Stig (Halvard)
Quarrington, Paul (Lewis) 1953- ..... **CLC 65**
See also CA 129; CANR 62
Quasimodo, Salvatore 1901-1968 ..... **CLC 10**
See also CA 13-16; 25-28R; CAP 1; DLB 114;
MTCW
Quay, Stephen 1947- .... **CLC 95**
Quay, Timothy 1947- .... **CLC 95**
Queen, Ellery .... **CLC 3, 11**
See also Dannay, Frederic; Davidson, Avram;
Lee, Manfred B(ennington); Marlowe,
Stephen; Sturgeon, Theodore (Hamilton);
Vance, John Holbrook
Queen, Ellery, Jr.
See Dannay, Frederic; Lee, Manfred
B(ennington)
Queneau, Raymond 1903-1976 **CLC 2, 5, 10,**

42
See also CA 77-80; 69-72; CANR 32; DLB 72;
MTCW
Quevedo, Francisco de 1580-1645 .... **LC 23**
Quiller-Couch, Arthur Thomas 1863-1944
TCLC 53
See also CA 118; DLB 135, 153
Quin, Ann (Marie) 1936-1973 .... **CLC 6**
See also CA 9-12R; 45-48; DLB 14
Quinn, Martin
See Smith, Martin Cruz
Quinn, Peter 1947- .... **CLC 91**
Quinn, Simon
See Smith, Martin Cruz
Quiroga, Horacio (Sylvestre) 1878-1937
TCLC 20; DAM MULT; HLC
See also CA 117; 131; HW; MTCW
Quoirez, Francoise 1935- .... **CLC 9**
See also Sagan, Francoise
See also CA 49-52; CANR 6, 39; MTCW
Raabe, Wilhelm 1831-1910 .... **TCLC 45**
See also DLB 129
Rabe, David (William) 1940-... **CLC 4, 8, 33;**
DAM DRAM
See also CA 85-88; CABS 3; CANR 59; DLB 7
Rabelais, Francois 1483-1553**LC 5; DA; DAB;**
DAC; DAM MST; WLC
Rabinovitch, Sholem 1859-1916
See Aleichem, Sholom
See also CA 104
Rachilde 1860-1953 .... **TCLC 67**
See also DLB 123
Racine, Jean 1639-1699 . **LC 28; DAB; DAM**
MST
Radcliffe, Ann (Ward) 1764-1823**NCLC 6, 55**
See also DLB 39, 178
Radiguet, Raymond 1903-1923 ...... **TCLC 29**
See also DLB 65
Radnoti, Miklos 1909-1944 .... **TCLC 16**
See also CA 118
Rado, James 1939- .... **CLC 17**
See also CA 105
Radvanyi, Netty 1900-1983
See Seghers, Anna
See also CA 85-88; 110
Rae, Ben
See Griffiths, Trevor
Raeburn, John (Hay) 1941- .... **CLC 34**
See also CA 57-60
Ragni, Gerome 1942-1991 .... **CLC 17**
See also CA 105; 134
Rahv, Philip 1908-1973 .... **CLC 24**
See also Greenberg, Ivan
See also DLB 137
Raine, Craig 1944- .... **CLC 32, 103**
See also CA 108; CANR 29, 51; DLB 40
Raine, Kathleen (Jessie) 1908- ...... **CLC 7, 45**
See also CA 85-88; CANR 46; DLB 20; MTCW
Rainis, Janis 1865-1929 .... **TCLC 29**
Rakosi, Carl .... **CLC 47**
See also Rawley, Callman
See also CAAS 5
Raleigh, Richard
See Lovecraft, H(oward) P(hillips)
Raleigh, Sir Walter 1554(?)-1618 . **LC 31, 39**
See also CDBLB Before 1660; DLB 172
Rallentando, H. P.
See Sayers, Dorothy L(eigh)
Ramal, Walter
See de la Mare, Walter (John)
Ramon, Juan
See Jimenez (Mantecon), Juan Ramon
Ramos, Graciliano 1892-1953 .... **TCLC 32**

17; DLB 53; MAICYA; MTCW; SATA 44;
SATA-Brief 27

Richter, Conrad (Michael) 1890-1968**CLC 30**
See also AAYA 21; CA 5-8R; 25-28R; CANR
23; DLB 9; MTCW; SATA 3

Ricostranza, Tom
See Ellis, Trey

Riddell, J. H. 1832-1906 .... **TCLC 40**

Riding, Laura .... **CLC 3, 7**
See also Jackson, Laura (Riding)

Riefenstahl, Berta Helene Amalia 1902-
See Riefenstahl, Leni
See also CA 108

Riefenstahl, Leni .... **CLC 16**
See also Riefenstahl, Berta Helene Amalia

Riffe, Ernest
See Bergman, (Ernst) Ingmar

Riggs, (Rolla) Lynn 1899-1954 ..... **TCLC 56;
DAM MULT**
See also CA 144; DLB 175; NNAL

Riley, James Whitcomb 1849-1916**TCLC 51;
DAM POET**
See also CA 118; 137; MAICYA; SATA 17

Riley, Tex
See Creasey, John

Rilke, Rainer Maria 1875-1926**TCLC 1, 6, 19;
DAM POET; PC 2**
See also CA 104; 132; CANR 62; DLB 81;
MTCW

Rimbaud, (Jean Nicolas) Arthur 1854-1891
**NCLC 4, 35; DA; DAB; DAC; DAM MST,
POET; PC 3; WLC**

Rinehart, Mary Roberts 1876-1958**TCLC 52**
See also CA 108

Ringmaster, The
See Mencken, H(enry) L(ouis)

Ringwood, Gwen(dolyn Margaret) Pharis
1910-1984 .... **CLC 48**
See also CA 148; 112; DLB 88

Rio, Michel 19(?)- .... **CLC 43**

Ritsos, Giannes
See Ritsos, Yannis

Ritsos, Yannis 1909-1990 .... **CLC 6, 13, 31**
See also CA 77-80; 133; CANR 39, 61; MTCW

Ritter, Erika 1948(?)- .... **CLC 52**

Rivera, Jose Eustasio 1889-1928 ... **TCLC 35**
See also HW

Rivers, Conrad Kent 1933-1968 .... **CLC 1**
See also BW 1; CA 85-88; DLB 41

Rivers, Elfrida
See Bradley, Marion Zimmer

Riverside, John
See Heinlein, Robert A(nson)

Rizal, Jose 1861-1896 .... **NCLC 27**

Roa Bastos, Augusto (Antonio) 1917-**CLC 45;
DAM MULT; HLC**
See also CA 131; DLB 113; HW

Robbe-Grillet, Alain 1922- **CLC 1, 2, 4, 6, 8,
10, 14, 43**
See also CA 9-12R; CANR 33; DLB 83; MTCW

Robbins, Harold 1916-1997 ..... **CLC 5; DAM
NOV**
See also CA 73-76; CANR 26, 54; MTCW

Robbins, Thomas Eugene 1936-
See Robbins, Tom
See also CA 81-84; CANR 29, 59; DAM NOV,
POP; MTCW

Robbins, Tom .... **CLC 9, 32, 64**
See also Robbins, Thomas Eugene
See also BEST 90:3; DLBY 80

Robbins, Trina 1938- .... **CLC 21**
See also CA 128

Roberts, Charles G(eorge) D(ouglas) 1860-1943

TCLC 8
See also CA 105; CLR 33; DLB 92; SATA 88;
SATA-Brief 29

Roberts, Elizabeth Madox 1886-1941 **T C L C
68**
See also CA 111; DLB 9, 54, 102; SATA 33;
SATA-Brief 27

Roberts, Kate 1891-1985 .... **CLC 15**
See also CA 107; 116

Roberts, Keith (John Kingston) 1935-**CLC 14**
See also CA 25-28R; CANR 46

Roberts, Kenneth (Lewis) 1885-1957**TCLC 23**
See also CA 109; DLB 9

Roberts, Michele (B.) 1949- .... **CLC 48**
See also CA 115; CANR 58

Robertson, Ellis
See Ellison, Harlan (Jay); Silverberg, Robert

Robertson, Thomas William 1829-1871**NCLC
35; DAM DRAM**

Robeson, Kenneth
See Dent, Lester

Robinson, Edwin Arlington 1869-1935**T C L C
5; DA; DAC; DAM MST, POET; PC 1**
See also CA 104; 133; CDALB 1865-1917;
DLB 54; MTCW

Robinson, Henry Crabb 1775-1867**NCLC 15**
See also DLB 107

Robinson, Jill 1936- .... **CLC 10**
See also CA 102; INT 102

Robinson, Kim Stanley 1952- .... **CLC 34**
See also CA 126

Robinson, Lloyd
See Silverberg, Robert

Robinson, Marilynne 1944- .... **CLC 25**
See also CA 116

Robinson, Smokey .... **CLC 21**
See also Robinson, William, Jr.

Robinson, William, Jr. 1940-
See Robinson, Smokey
See also CA 116

Robison, Mary 1949- .... **CLC 42, 98**
See also CA 113; 116; DLB 130; INT 116

Rod, Edouard 1857-1910 .... **TCLC 52**

Roddenberry, Eugene Wesley 1921-1991
See Roddenberry, Gene
See also CA 110; 135; CANR 37; SATA 45;
SATA-Obit 69

Roddenberry, Gene .... **CLC 17**
See also Roddenberry, Eugene Wesley
See also AAYA 5; SATA-Obit 69

Rodgers, Mary 1931- .... **CLC 12**
See also CA 49-52; CANR 8, 55; CLR 20; INT
CANR-8; JRDA; MAICYA; SATA 8

Rodgers, W(illiam) R(obert) 1909-1969**CLC 7**
See also CA 85-88; DLB 20

Rodman, Eric
See Silverberg, Robert

Rodman, Howard 1920(?)-1985 .... **CLC 65**
See also CA 118

Rodman, Maia
See Wojciechowska, Maia (Teresa)

Rodriguez, Claudio 1934- .... **CLC 10**
See also DLB 134

Roelvaag, O(le) E(dvart) 1876-1931**TCLC 17**
See also CA 117; DLB 9

Roethke, Theodore (Huebner) 1908-1963**CLC
1, 3, 8, 11, 19, 46, 101; DAM POET; PC 15**
See also CA 81-84; CABS 2; CDALB 1941-
1968; DLB 5; MTCW

Rogers, Thomas Hunton 1927- .... **CLC 57**
See also CA 89-92; INT 89-92

Rogers, Will(iam Penn Adair) 1879-1935
TCLC 8, 71; DAM MULT

See also CA 105; 144; DLB 11; NNAL

Rogin, Gilbert 1929- .... **CLC 18**
See also CA 65-68; CANR 15

Rohan, Koda .... **TCLC 22**
See also Koda Shigeyuki

Rohlfs, Anna Katharine Green
See Green, Anna Katharine

Rohmer, Eric .... **CLC 16**
See also Scherer, Jean-Marie Maurice

Rohmer, Sax .... **TCLC 28**
See also Ward, Arthur Henry Sarsfield
See also DLB 70

Roiphe, Anne (Richardson) 1935- .. **CLC 3, 9**
See also CA 89-92; CANR 45; DLBY 80; INT
89-92

Rojas, Fernando de 1465-1541 .... **LC 23**

**Rolfe, Frederick (William Serafino Austin
Lewis Mary)** 1860-1913 .... **TCLC 12**
See also CA 107; DLB 34, 156

Rolland, Romain 1866-1944 .... **TCLC 23**
See also CA 118; DLB 65

Rolle, Richard c. 1300-c. 1349 ...... **CMLC 21**
See also DLB 146

Rolvaag, O(le) E(dvart)
See Roelvaag, O(le) E(dvart)

Romain Arnaud, Saint
See Aragon, Louis

Romains, Jules 1885-1972 .... **CLC 7**
See also CA 85-88; CANR 34; DLB 65; MTCW

Romero, Jose Ruben 1890-1952 .... **TCLC 14**
See also CA 114; 131; HW

Ronsard, Pierre de 1524-1585 ... **LC 6; PC 11**

Rooke, Leon 1934- .. **CLC 25, 34; DAM POP**
See also CA 25-28R; CANR 23, 53

Roosevelt, Theodore 1858-1919 ..... **TCLC 69**
See also CA 115; DLB 47

Roper, William 1498-1578 .... **LC 10**

Rosa, Joao Guimaraes 1908-1967 .... **CLC 23**
See also CA 89-92; DLB 113

Rose, Wendy 1948-**CLC 85; DAM MULT; PC
13**
See also CA 53-56; CANR 5, 51; DLB 175;
NNAL; SATA 12

Rosen, R. D.
See Rosen, Richard (Dean)

Rosen, Richard (Dean) 1949- .... **CLC 39**
See also CA 77-80; CANR 62; INT CANR-30

Rosenberg, Isaac 1890-1918 .... **TCLC 12**
See also CA 107; DLB 20

Rosenblatt, Joe .... **CLC 15**
See also Rosenblatt, Joseph

Rosenblatt, Joseph 1933-
See Rosenblatt, Joe
See also CA 89-92; INT 89-92

Rosenfeld, Samuel
See Tzara, Tristan

Rosenstock, Sami
See Tzara, Tristan

Rosenstock, Samuel
See Tzara, Tristan

Rosenthal, M(acha) L(ouis) 1917-1996 . **C L C
28**
See also CA 1-4R; 152; CAAS 6; CANR 4, 51;
DLB 5; SATA 59

Ross, Barnaby
See Dannay, Frederic

Ross, Bernard L.
See Follett, Ken(neth Martin)

Ross, J. H.
See Lawrence, T(homas) E(dward)

Ross, Martin

See Ozu, Yasujiro

Schwartz, John Burnham 1965- .... **CLC 59**
See also CA 132

Schwartz, Lynne Sharon 1939- .... **CLC 31**
See also CA 103; CANR 44

Schwartz, Muriel A.
See Eliot, T(homas) S(tearns)

Schwarz-Bart, Andre 1928- .... **CLC 2, 4**
See also CA 89-92

Schwarz-Bart, Simone 1938-............... **CLC 7**
See also BW 2; CA 97-100

Schwob, (Mayer Andre) Marcel 1867-1905
TCLC 20
See also CA 117; DLB 123

Sciascia, Leonardo 1921-1989 . **CLC 8, 9, 41**
See also CA 85-88; 130; CANR 35; DLB 177;
MTCW

Scoppettone, Sandra 1936- .... **CLC 26**
See also AAYA 11; CA 5-8R; CANR 41; SATA
9, 92

Scorsese, Martin 1942- .... **CLC 20, 89**
See also CA 110; 114; CANR 46

Scotland, Jay
See Jakes, John (William)

Scott, Duncan Campbell 1862-1947 **TCLC 6;**
DAC
See also CA 104; 153; DLB 92

Scott, Evelyn 1893-1963 .... **CLC 43**
See also CA 104; 112; CANR 64; DLB 9, 48

Scott, F(rancis) R(eginald) 1899-1985 **CLC 22**
See also CA 101; 114; DLB 88; INT 101

Scott, Frank
See Scott, F(rancis) R(eginald)

Scott, Joanna 1960- .... **CLC 50**
See also CA 126; CANR 53

Scott, Paul (Mark) 1920-1978 .... **CLC 9, 60**
See also CA 81-84; 77-80; CANR 33; DLB 14;
MTCW

Scott, Walter 1771-1832 **NCLC 15; DA; DAB;**
DAC; DAM MST, NOV, POET; PC 13;
WLC
See also AAYA 22; CDBLB 1789-1832; DLB
93, 107, 116, 144, 159; YABC 2

Scribe, (Augustin) Eugene 1791-1861 **N C L C**
16; DAM DRAM; DC 5

Scrum, R.
See Crumb, R(obert)

Scudery, Madeleine de 1607-1701 .... **LC 2**

Scum
See Crumb, R(obert)

Scumbag, Little Bobby
See Crumb, R(obert)

Seabrook, John
See Hubbard, L(afayette) Ron(ald)

Sealy, I. Allan 1951- .... **CLC 55**

Search, Alexander
See Pessoa, Fernando (Antonio Nogueira)

Sebastian, Lee
See Silverberg, Robert

Sebastian Owl
See Thompson, Hunter S(tockton)

Sebestyen, Ouida 1924- .... **CLC 30**
See also AAYA 8; CA 107; CANR 40; CLR 17;
JRDA; MAICYA; SAAS 10; SATA 39

Secundus, H. Scriblerus
See Fielding, Henry

Sedges, John
See Buck, Pearl S(ydenstricker)

Sedgwick, Catharine Maria 1789-1867 **NCLC**
19
See also DLB 1, 74

Seelye, John 1931- .... **CLC 7**

Seferiades, Giorgos Stylianou 1900-1971

See Seferis, George
See also CA 5-8R; 33-36R; CANR 5, 36;
MTCW

Seferis, George .... **CLC 5, 11**
See also Seferiades, Giorgos Stylianou

Segal, Erich (Wolf) 1937- . **CLC 3, 10; DAM**
POP
See also BEST 89:1; CA 25-28R; CANR 20,
36; DLBY 86; INT CANR-20; MTCW

Seger, Bob 1945- .... **CLC 35**

Seghers, Anna .... **CLC 7**
See also Radvanyi, Netty
See also DLB 69

Seidel, Frederick (Lewis) 1936- .... **CLC 18**
See also CA 13-16R; CANR 8; DLBY 84

Seifert, Jaroslav 1901-1986 .. **CLC 34, 44, 93**
See also CA 127; MTCW

Sei Shonagon c. 966-1017(?) .... **CMLC 6**

Selby, Hubert, Jr. 1928- **CLC 1, 2, 4, 8; SSC 20**
See also CA 13-16R; CANR 33; DLB 2

Selzer, Richard 1928- .... **CLC 74**
See also CA 65-68; CANR 14

Sembene, Ousmane
See Ousmane, Sembene

Senancour, Etienne Pivert de 1770-1846
NCLC 16
See also DLB 119

Sender, Ramon (Jose) 1902-1982 **CLC 8; DAM**
MULT; HLC
See also CA 5-8R; 105; CANR 8; HW; MTCW

Seneca, Lucius Annaeus 4B.C.-65 . **CMLC 6;**
DAM DRAM; DC 5

Senghor, Leopold Sedar 1906- **CLC 54; BLC;**
DAM MULT, POET
See also BW 2; CA 116; 125; CANR 47; MTCW

Serling, (Edward) Rod(man) 1924-1975 **C L C**
30
See also AAYA 14; AITN 1; CA 65-68; 57-60;
DLB 26

Serna, Ramon Gomez de la
See Gomez de la Serna, Ramon

Serpieres
See Guillevic, (Eugene)

Service, Robert
See Service, Robert W(illiam)
See also DAB; DLB 92

Service, Robert W(illiam) 1874(?)-1958 **TCLC**
15; DA; DAC; DAM MST, POET; WLC
See also Service, Robert
See also CA 115; 140; SATA 20

Seth, Vikram 1952- **CLC 43, 90; DAM MULT**
See also CA 121; 127; CANR 50; DLB 120;
INT 127

Seton, Cynthia Propper 1926-1982 .. **CLC 27**
See also CA 5-8R; 108; CANR 7

Seton, Ernest (Evan) Thompson 1860-1946
TCLC 31
See also CA 109; DLB 92; DLBD 13; JRDA;
SATA 18

Seton-Thompson, Ernest
See Seton, Ernest (Evan) Thompson

Settle, Mary Lee 1918- .... **CLC 19, 61**
See also CA 89-92; CAAS 1; CANR 44; DLB
6; INT 89-92

Seuphor, Michel
See Arp, Jean

Sevigne, Marie (de Rabutin-Chantal) Marquise
de 1626-1696 .... **LC 11**

Sewall, Samuel 1652-1730 .... **LC 38**
See also DLB 24

Sexton, Anne (Harvey) 1928-1974 **CLC 2, 4, 6,**
8, 10, 15, 53; DA; DAB; DAC; DAM MST,
POET; PC 2; WLC

See also CA 1-4R; 53-56; CABS 2; CANR 3,
36; CDALB 1941-1968; DLB 5, 169;
MTCW; SATA 10

Shaara, Michael (Joseph, Jr.) 1929-1988 **C L C**
15; DAM POP
See also AITN 1; CA 102; 125; CANR 52;
DLBY 83

Shackleton, C. C.
See Aldiss, Brian W(ilson)

Shacochis, Bob .... **CLC 39**
See also Shacochis, Robert G.

Shacochis, Robert G. 1951-
See Shacochis, Bob
See also CA 119; 124; INT 124

Shaffer, Anthony (Joshua) 1926- .... **CLC 19;**
DAM DRAM
See also CA 110; 116; DLB 13

Shaffer, Peter (Levin) 1926- **CLC 5, 14, 18, 37,**
60; DAB; DAM DRAM, MST; DC 7
See also CA 25-28R; CANR 25, 47; CDBLB
1960 to Present; DLB 13; MTCW

Shakey, Bernard
See Young, Neil

Shalamov, Varlam (Tikhonovich) 1907(?)-1982
CLC 18
See also CA 129; 105

Shamlu, Ahmad 1925- .... **CLC 10**

Shammas, Anton 1951- .... **CLC 55**

Shange, Ntozake 1948- **CLC 8, 25, 38, 74; BLC;**
DAM DRAM, MULT; DC 3
See also AAYA 9; BW 2; CA 85-88; CABS 3;
CANR 27, 48; DLB 38; MTCW

Shanley, John Patrick 1950- .... **CLC 75**
See also CA 128; 133

Shapcott, Thomas W(illiam) 1935- ... **CLC 38**
See also CA 69-72; CANR 49

Shapiro, Jane .... **CLC 76**

Shapiro, Karl (Jay) 1913- ... **CLC 4, 8, 15, 53**
See also CA 1-4R; CAAS 6; CANR 1, 36; DLB
48; MTCW

Sharp, William 1855-1905 .... **TCLC 39**
See also CA 160; DLB 156

Sharpe, Thomas Ridley 1928-
See Sharpe, Tom
See also CA 114; 122; INT 122

Sharpe, Tom .... **CLC 36**
See also Sharpe, Thomas Ridley
See also DLB 14

Shaw, Bernard .... **TCLC 45**
See also Shaw, George Bernard
See also BW 1

Shaw, G. Bernard
See Shaw, George Bernard

Shaw, George Bernard 1856-1950 **TCLC 3, 9,**
21; DA; DAB; DAC; DAM DRAM, MST;
WLC
See also Shaw, Bernard
See also CA 104; 128; CDBLB 1914-1945;
DLB 10, 57; MTCW

Shaw, Henry Wheeler 1818-1885 .. **NCLC 15**
See also DLB 11

Shaw, Irwin 1913-1984 **CLC 7, 23, 34; DAM**
DRAM, POP
See also AITN 1; CA 13-16R; 112; CANR 21;
CDALB 1941-1968; DLB 6, 102; DLBY 84;
MTCW

Shaw, Robert 1927-1978 .... **CLC 5**
See also AITN 1; CA 1-4R; 81-84; CANR 4;
DLB 13, 14

Shaw, T. E.
See Lawrence, T(homas) E(dward)

Shawn, Wallace 1943- .... **CLC 41**
See also CA 112

Southworth, Emma Dorothy Eliza Nevitte
  1819-1899 .... NCLC 26
Souza, Ernest
  See Scott, Evelyn
Soyinka, Wole 1934-CLC 3, 5, 14, 36, 44; BLC;
  DA; DAB; DAC; DAM DRAM, MST,
  MULT; DC 2; WLC
  See also BW 2; CA 13-16R; CANR 27, 39; DLB
  125; MTCW
Spackman, W(illiam) M(ode) 1905-1990 C L C
  46
  See also CA 81-84; 132
Spacks, Barry (Bernard) 1931-......... CLC 14
  See also CA 154; CANR 33; DLB 105
Spanidou, Irini 1946- .... CLC 44
Spark, Muriel (Sarah) 1918-CLC 2, 3, 5, 8, 13,
  18, 40, 94; DAB; DAC; DAM MST, NOV;
  SSC 10
  See also CA 5-8R; CANR 12, 36; CDBLB 1945-
  1960; DLB 15, 139; INT CANR-12; MTCW
Spaulding, Douglas
  See Bradbury, Ray (Douglas)
Spaulding, Leonard
  See Bradbury, Ray (Douglas)
Spence, J. A. D.
  See Eliot, T(homas) S(tearns)
Spencer, Elizabeth 1921- .... CLC 22
  See also CA 13-16R; CANR 32; DLB 6;
  MTCW; SATA 14
Spencer, Leonard G.
  See Silverberg, Robert
Spencer, Scott 1945- .... CLC 30
  See also CA 113; CANR 51; DLBY 86
Spender, Stephen (Harold) 1909-1995CLC 1,
  2, 5, 10, 41, 91; DAM POET
  See also CA 9-12R; 149; CANR 31, 54; CDBLB
  1945-1960; DLB 20; MTCW
Spengler, Oswald (Arnold Gottfried) 1880-1936
  TCLC 25
  See also CA 118
Spenser, Edmund 1552(?)-1599LC 5, 39; DA;
  DAB; DAC; DAM MST, POET; PC 8;
  WLC
  See also CDBLB Before 1660; DLB 167
Spicer, Jack 1925-1965 CLC 8, 18, 72; DAM
  POET
  See also CA 85-88; DLB 5, 16
Spiegelman, Art 1948-......................... CLC 76
  See also AAYA 10; CA 125; CANR 41, 55
Spielberg, Peter 1929-.......................... CLC 6
  See also CA 5-8R; CANR 4, 48; DLBY 81
Spielberg, Steven 1947- .... CLC 20
  See also AAYA 8; CA 77-80; CANR 32; SATA
  32
Spillane, Frank Morrison 1918-
  See Spillane, Mickey
  See also CA 25-28R; CANR 28, 63; MTCW;
  SATA 66
Spillane, Mickey .... CLC 3, 13
  See also Spillane, Frank Morrison
Spinoza, Benedictus de 1632-1677 .... LC 9
Spinrad, Norman (Richard) 1940- ..... CLC 46
  See also CA 37-40R; CAAS 19; CANR 20; DLB
  8; INT CANR-20
Spitteler, Carl (Friedrich Georg) 1845-1924
  TCLC 12
  See also CA 109; DLB 129
Spivack, Kathleen (Romola Drucker) 1938-
  CLC 6
  See also CA 49-52
Spoto, Donald 1941- .... CLC 39
  See also CA 65-68; CANR 11, 57
Springsteen, Bruce (F.) 1949-............ CLC 17

See also CA 111
Spurling, Hilary 1940- .... CLC 34
  See also CA 104; CANR 25, 52
Spyker, John Howland
  See Elman, Richard
Squires, (James) Radcliffe 1917-1993CLC 51
  See also CA 1-4R; 140; CANR 6, 21
Srivastava, Dhanpat Rai 1880(?)-1936
  See Premchand
  See also CA 118
Stacy, Donald
  See Pohl, Frederik
Stael, Germaine de
  See Stael-Holstein, Anne Louise Germaine
  Necker Baronn
  See also DLB 119
Stael-Holstein, Anne Louise Germaine Necker
  Baronn 1766-1817 .... NCLC 3
  See also Stael, Germaine de
Stafford, Jean 1915-1979CLC 4, 7, 19, 68; SSC
  26
  See also CA 1-4R; 85-88; CANR 3; DLB 2, 173;
  MTCW; SATA-Obit 22
Stafford, William (Edgar) 1914-1993 CLC 4,
  7, 29; DAM POET
  See also CA 5-8R; 142; CAAS 3; CANR 5, 22;
  DLB 5; INT CANR-22
Stagnelius, Eric Johan 1793-1823 . NCLC 61
Staines, Trevor
  See Brunner, John (Kilian Houston)
Stairs, Gordon
  See Austin, Mary (Hunter)
Stannard, Martin 1947- .... CLC 44
  See also CA 142; DLB 155
Stanton, Elizabeth Cady 1815-1902TCLC 73
  See also DLB 79
Stanton, Maura 1946- .... CLC 9
  See also CA 89-92; CANR 15; DLB 120
Stanton, Schuyler
  See Baum, L(yman) Frank
Stapledon, (William) Olaf 1886-1950 T C L C
  22
  See also CA 111; DLB 15
Starbuck, George (Edwin) 1931-1996CLC 53;
  DAM POET
  See also CA 21-24R; 153; CANR 23
Stark, Richard
  See Westlake, Donald E(dwin)
Staunton, Schuyler
  See Baum, L(yman) Frank
Stead, Christina (Ellen) 1902-1983 CLC 2, 5,
  8, 32, 80
  See also CA 13-16R; 109; CANR 33, 40;
  MTCW
Stead, William Thomas 1849-1912 TCLC 48
Steele, Richard 1672-1729 .... LC 18
  See also CDBLB 1660-1789; DLB 84, 101
Steele, Timothy (Reid) 1948- .... CLC 45
  See also CA 93-96; CANR 16, 50; DLB 120
Steffens, (Joseph) Lincoln 1866-1936 T C L C
  20
  See also CA 117
Stegner, Wallace (Earle) 1909-1993CLC 9, 49,
  81; DAM NOV; SSC 27
  See also AITN 1; BEST 90:3; CA 1-4R; 141;
  CAAS 9; CANR 1, 21, 46; DLB 9; DLBY
  93; MTCW
Stein, Gertrude 1874-1946TCLC 1, 6, 28, 48;
  DA; DAB; DAC; DAM MST, NOV, POET;
  PC 18; WLC
  See also CA 104; 132; CDALB 1917-1929;
  DLB 4, 54, 86; DLBD 15; MTCW
Steinbeck, John (Ernst) 1902-1968CLC 1, 5, 9,

13, 21, 34, 45, 75; DA; DAB; DAC; DAM
  DRAM, MST, NOV; SSC 11; WLC
  See also AAYA 12; CA 1-4R; 25-28R; CANR
  1, 35; CDALB 1929-1941; DLB 7, 9; DLBD
  2; MTCW; SATA 9
Steinem, Gloria 1934- .... CLC 63
  See also CA 53-56; CANR 28, 51; MTCW
Steiner, George 1929- ... CLC 24; DAM NOV
  See also CA 73-76; CANR 31; DLB 67; MTCW;
  SATA 62
Steiner, K. Leslie
  See Delany, Samuel R(ay, Jr.)
Steiner, Rudolf 1861-1925 .... TCLC 13
  See also CA 107
Stendhal 1783-1842NCLC 23, 46; DA; DAB;
  DAC; DAM MST, NOV; SSC 27; WLC
  See also DLB 119
Stephen, Adeline Virginia
  See Woolf, (Adeline) Virginia
Stephen, Leslie 1832-1904 .... TCLC 23
  See also CA 123; DLB 57, 144
Stephen, Sir Leslie
  See Stephen, Leslie
Stephen, Virginia
  See Woolf, (Adeline) Virginia
Stephens, James 1882(?)-1950 .... TCLC 4
  See also CA 104; DLB 19, 153, 162
Stephens, Reed
  See Donaldson, Stephen R.
Steptoe, Lydia
  See Barnes, Djuna
Sterchi, Beat 1949- .... CLC 65
Sterling, Brett
  See Bradbury, Ray (Douglas); Hamilton,
  Edmond
Sterling, Bruce 1954- .... CLC 72
  See also CA 119; CANR 44
Sterling, George 1869-1926 .... TCLC 20
  See also CA 117; DLB 54
Stern, Gerald 1925- .... CLC 40, 100
  See also CA 81-84; CANR 28; DLB 105
Stern, Richard (Gustave) 1928- .... CLC 4, 39
  See also CA 1-4R; CANR 1, 25, 52; DLBY 87;
  INT CANR-25
Sternberg, Josef von 1894-1969 .... CLC 20
  See also CA 81-84
Sterne, Laurence 1713-1768LC 2; DA; DAB;
  DAC; DAM MST, NOV; WLC
  See also CDBLB 1660-1789; DLB 39
Sternheim, (William Adolf) Carl 1878-1942
  TCLC 8
  See also CA 105; DLB 56, 118
Stevens, Mark 1951- .... CLC 34
  See also CA 122
Stevens, Wallace 1879-1955 TCLC 3, 12, 45;
  DA; DAB; DAC; DAM MST, POET; PC
  6; WLC
  See also CA 104; 124; CDALB 1929-1941;
  DLB 54; MTCW
Stevenson, Anne (Katharine) 1933-CLC 7, 33
  See also CA 17-20R; CAAS 9; CANR 9, 33;
  DLB 40; MTCW
Stevenson, Robert Louis (Balfour) 1850-1894
  NCLC 5, 14, 63; DA; DAB; DAC; DAM
  MST, NOV; SSC 11; WLC
  See also CDBLB 1890-1914; CLR 10, 11; DLB
  18, 57, 141, 156, 174; DLBD 13; JRDA;
  MAICYA; YABC 2
Stewart, J(ohn) I(nnes) M(ackintosh) 1906-
  1994 .... CLC 7, 14, 32
  See also CA 85-88; 147; CAAS 3; CANR 47;
  MTCW
Stewart, Mary (Florence Elinor) 1916-CLC 7,

See Ashton-Warner, Sylvia (Constance)

Symmes, Robert Edward
See Duncan, Robert (Edward)

Symonds, John Addington 1840-1893 **N C L C 34**
See also DLB 57, 144

Symons, Arthur 1865-1945 .... **TCLC 11**
See also CA 107; DLB 19, 57, 149

Symons, Julian (Gustave) 1912-1994 **CLC 2, 14, 32**
See also CA 49-52; 147; CAAS 3; CANR 3, 33, 59; DLB 87, 155; DLBY 92; MTCW

Synge, (Edmund) J(ohn) M(illington) 1871-1909 ... **TCLC 6, 37; DAM DRAM; DC 2**
See also CA 104; 141; CDBLB 1890-1914; DLB 10, 19

Syruc, J.
See Milosz, Czeslaw

Szirtes, George 1948- .... **CLC 46**
See also CA 109; CANR 27, 61

Szymborska, Wislawa 1923-.............. **CLC 99**
See also CA 154; DLBY 96

T. O., Nik
See Annensky, Innokenty (Fyodorovich)

Tabori, George 1914- .... **CLC 19**
See also CA 49-52; CANR 4

Tagore, Rabindranath 1861-1941 **TCLC 3, 53; DAM DRAM, POET; PC 8**
See also CA 104; 120; MTCW

Taine, Hippolyte Adolphe 1828-1893 . **N C L C 15**

Talese, Gay 1932-................................ **CLC 37**
See also AITN 1; CA 1-4R; CANR 9, 58; INT CANR-9; MTCW

Tallent, Elizabeth (Ann) 1954- .... **CLC 45**
See also CA 117; DLB 130

Tally, Ted 1952-................................... **CLC 42**
See also CA 120; 124; INT 124

Tamayo y Baus, Manuel 1829-1898 **NCLC 1**

Tammsaare, A(nton) H(ansen) 1878-1940 **TCLC 27**

Tam'si, Tchicaya U
See Tchicaya, Gerald Felix

Tan, Amy (Ruth) 1952-**CLC 59; DAM MULT, NOV, POP**
See also AAYA 9; BEST 89:3; CA 136; CANR 54; DLB 173; SATA 75

Tandem, Felix
See Spitteler, Carl (Friedrich Georg)

Tanizaki, Jun'ichiro 1886-1965**CLC 8, 14, 28; SSC 21**
See also CA 93-96; 25-28R; DLB 180

Tanner, William
See Amis, Kingsley (William)

Tao Lao
See Storni, Alfonsina

Tarassoff, Lev
See Troyat, Henri

Tarbell, Ida M(inerva) 1857-1944 . **TCLC 40**
See also CA 122; DLB 47

Tarkington, (Newton) Booth 1869-1946**TCLC 9**
See also CA 110; 143; DLB 9, 102; SATA 17

Tarkovsky, Andrei (Arsenyevich) 1932-1986 **CLC 75**
See also CA 127

Tartt, Donna 1964(?)- .... **CLC 76**
See also CA 142

Tasso, Torquato 1544-1595 .... **LC 5**

Tate, (John Orley) Allen 1899-1979**CLC 2, 4, 6, 9, 11, 14, 24**
See also CA 5-8R; 85-88; CANR 32; DLB 4, 45, 63; MTCW

Tate, Ellalice
See Hibbert, Eleanor Alice Burford

Tate, James (Vincent) 1943- ..... **CLC 2, 6, 25**
See also CA 21-24R; CANR 29, 57; DLB 5, 169

Tavel, Ronald 1940-............................ **CLC 6**
See also CA 21-24R; CANR 33

Taylor, C(ecil) P(hilip) 1929-1981 .... **CLC 27**
See also CA 25-28R; 105; CANR 47

Taylor, Edward 1642(?)-1729 ..... **LC 11; DA; DAB; DAC; DAM MST, POET**
See also DLB 24

Taylor, Eleanor Ross 1920- .... **CLC 5**
See also CA 81-84

Taylor, Elizabeth 1912-1975 ..... **CLC 2, 4, 29**
See also CA 13-16R; CANR 9; DLB 139; MTCW; SATA 13

Taylor, Frederick Winslow 1856-1915 **T C L C 76**

Taylor, Henry (Splawn) 1942- .... **CLC 44**
See also CA 33-36R; CAAS 7; CANR 31; DLB 5

Taylor, Kamala (Purnaiya) 1924-
See Markandaya, Kamala
See also CA 77-80

Taylor, Mildred D. .... **CLC 21**
See also AAYA 10; BW 1; CA 85-88; CANR 25; CLR 9; DLB 52; JRDA; MAICYA; SAAS 5; SATA 15, 70

Taylor, Peter (Hillsman) 1917-1994**CLC 1, 4, 18, 37, 44, 50, 71; SSC 10**
See also CA 13-16R; 147; CANR 9, 50; DLBY 81, 94; INT CANR-9; MTCW

Taylor, Robert Lewis 1912- .... **CLC 14**
See also CA 1-4R; CANR 3, 64; SATA 10

Tchekhov, Anton
See Chekhov, Anton (Pavlovich)

Tchicaya, Gerald Felix 1931-1988 .. **CLC 101**
See also CA 129; 125

Tchicaya U Tam'si
See Tchicaya, Gerald Felix

Teasdale, Sara 1884-1933 .... **TCLC 4**
See also CA 104; DLB 45; SATA 32

Tegner, Esaias 1782-1846 .... **NCLC 2**

Teilhard de Chardin, (Marie Joseph) Pierre 1881-1955 .... **TCLC 9**
See also CA 105

Temple, Ann
See Mortimer, Penelope (Ruth)

Tennant, Emma (Christina) 1937-**CLC 13, 52**
See also CA 65-68; CAAS 9; CANR 10, 38, 59; DLB 14

Tenneshaw, S. M.
See Silverberg, Robert

Tennyson, Alfred 1809-1892 ... **NCLC 30, 65; DA; DAB; DAC; DAM MST, POET; PC 6; WLC**
See also CDBLB 1832-1890; DLB 32

Teran, Lisa St. Aubin de .... **CLC 36**
See also St. Aubin de Teran, Lisa

Terence 195(?)B.C.-159B.C. **CMLC 14; DC 7**

Teresa de Jesus, St. 1515-1582 .... **LC 18**

Terkel, Louis 1912-
See Terkel, Studs
See also CA 57-60; CANR 18, 45; MTCW

Terkel, Studs .... **CLC 38**
See also Terkel, Louis
See also AITN 1

Terry, C. V.
See Slaughter, Frank G(ill)

Terry, Megan 1932- .... **CLC 19**
See also CA 77-80; CABS 3; CANR 43; DLB 7

Tertz, Abram

See Sinyavsky, Andrei (Donatevich)

Tesich, Steve 1943(?)-1996 .... **CLC 40, 69**
See also CA 105; 152; DLBY 83

Teternikov, Fyodor Kuzmich 1863-1927
See Sologub, Fyodor
See also CA 104

Tevis, Walter 1928-1984 .... **CLC 42**
See also CA 113

Tey, Josephine .... **TCLC 14**
See also Mackintosh, Elizabeth
See also DLB 77

Thackeray, William Makepeace 1811-1863 **NCLC 5, 14, 22, 43; DA; DAB; DAC; DAM MST, NOV; WLC**
See also CDBLB 1832-1890; DLB 21, 55, 159, 163; SATA 23

Thakura, Ravindranatha
See Tagore, Rabindranath

Tharoor, Shashi 1956- .... **CLC 70**
See also CA 141

Thelwell, Michael Miles 1939- .... **CLC 22**
See also BW 2; CA 101

Theobald, Lewis, Jr.
See Lovecraft, H(oward) P(hillips)

Theodorescu, Ion N. 1880-1967
See Arghezi, Tudor
See also CA 116

Theriault, Yves 1915-1983 .... **CLC 79; DAC; DAM MST**
See also CA 102; DLB 88

Theroux, Alexander (Louis) 1939-**CLC 2, 25**
See also CA 85-88; CANR 20, 63

Theroux, Paul (Edward) 1941- **CLC 5, 8, 11, 15, 28, 46; DAM POP**
See also BEST 89:4; CA 33-36R; CANR 20, 45; DLB 2; MTCW; SATA 44

Thesen, Sharon 1946- .... **CLC 56**

Thevenin, Denis
See Duhamel, Georges

Thibault, Jacques Anatole Francois 1844-1924
See France, Anatole
See also CA 106; 127; DAM NOV; MTCW

Thiele, Colin (Milton) 1920- .... **CLC 17**
See also CA 29-32R; CANR 12, 28, 53; CLR 27; MAICYA; SAAS 2; SATA 14, 72

Thomas, Audrey (Callahan) 1935-**CLC 7, 13, 37, 107; SSC 20**
See also AITN 2; CA 21-24R; CAAS 19; CANR 36, 58; DLB 60; MTCW

Thomas, D(onald) M(ichael) 1935- . **CLC 13, 22, 31**
See also CA 61-64; CAAS 11; CANR 17, 45; CDBLB 1960 to Present; DLB 40; INT CANR-17; MTCW

Thomas, Dylan (Marlais) 1914-1953**TCLC 1, 8, 45; DA; DAB; DAC; DAM DRAM, MST, POET; PC 2; SSC 3; WLC**
See also CA 104; 120; CDBLB 1945-1960; DLB 13, 20, 139; MTCW; SATA 60

Thomas, (Philip) Edward 1878-1917 . **T C L C 10; DAM POET**
See also CA 106; 153; DLB 19

Thomas, Joyce Carol 1938- .... **CLC 35**
See also AAYA 12; BW 2; CA 113; 116; CANR 48; CLR 19; DLB 33; INT 116; JRDA; MAICYA; MTCW; SAAS 7; SATA 40, 78

Thomas, Lewis 1913-1993 .... **CLC 35**
See also CA 85-88; 143; CANR 38, 60; MTCW

Thomas, Paul
See Mann, (Paul) Thomas

Thomas, Piri 1928- .... **CLC 17**
See also CA 73-76; HW

Thomas, R(onald) S(tuart) 1913- **CLC 6, 13,**

See also CA 123
Vassa, Gustavus
See Equiano, Olaudah
Vassilikos, Vassilis 1933- .... **CLC 4, 8**
See also CA 81-84
Vaughan, Henry 1621-1695 .... **LC 27**
See also DLB 131
Vaughn, Stephanie .... **CLC 62**
Vazov, Ivan (Minchov) 1850-1921 . **TCLC 25**
See also CA 121; DLB 147
Veblen, Thorstein (Bunde) 1857-1929 **T C L C 31**
See also CA 115
Vega, Lope de 1562-1635 .... **LC 23**
Venison, Alfred
See Pound, Ezra (Weston Loomis)
Verdi, Marie de
See Mencken, H(enry) L(ouis)
Verdu, Matilde
See Cela, Camilo Jose
Verga, Giovanni (Carmelo) 1840-1922 **T C L C 3; SSC 21**
See also CA 104; 123
Vergil 70B.C.-19B.C. ... **CMLC 9; DA; DAB; DAC; DAM MST, POET; PC 12; WLCS**
Verhaeren, Emile (Adolphe Gustave) 1855-1916 **TCLC 12**
See also CA 109
Verlaine, Paul (Marie) 1844-1896 **NCLC 2, 51; DAM POET; PC 2**
Verne, Jules (Gabriel) 1828-1905 **TCLC 6, 52**
See also AAYA 16; CA 110; 131; DLB 123; JRDA; MAICYA; SATA 21
Very, Jones 1813-1880 .... **NCLC 9**
See also DLB 1
Vesaas, Tarjei 1897-1970 .... **CLC 48**
See also CA 29-32R
Vialis, Gaston
See Simenon, Georges (Jacques Christian)
Vian, Boris 1920-1959 .... **TCLC 9**
See also CA 106; DLB 72
Viaud, (Louis Marie) Julien 1850-1923
See Loti, Pierre
See also CA 107
Vicar, Henry
See Felsen, Henry Gregor
Vicker, Angus
See Felsen, Henry Gregor
Vidal, Gore 1925- **CLC 2, 4, 6, 8, 10, 22, 33, 72; DAM NOV, POP**
See also AITN 1; BEST 90:2; CA 5-8R; CANR 13, 45; DLB 6, 152; INT CANR-13; MTCW
Viereck, Peter (Robert Edwin) 1916- . **CLC 4**
See also CA 1-4R; CANR 1, 47; DLB 5
Vigny, Alfred (Victor) de 1797-1863 **NCLC 7; DAM POET**
See also DLB 119
Vilakazi, Benedict Wallet 1906-1947 **TCLC 37**
Villiers de l'Isle Adam, Jean Marie Mathias Philippe Auguste Comte 1838-1889 **NCLC 3; SSC 14**
See also DLB 123
Villon, Francois 1431-1463(?) .... **PC 13**
Vinci, Leonardo da 1452-1519 .... **LC 12**
Vine, Barbara .... **CLC 50**
See also Rendell, Ruth (Barbara)
See also BEST 90:4
Vinge, Joan D(ennison) 1948- **CLC 30; SSC 24**
See also CA 93-96; SATA 36
Violis, G.
See Simenon, Georges (Jacques Christian)
Visconti, Luchino 1906-1976 .... **CLC 16**
See also CA 81-84; 65-68; CANR 39

Vittorini, Elio 1908-1966 .... **CLC 6, 9, 14**
See also CA 133; 25-28R
Vizenor, Gerald Robert 1934- **CLC 103; DAM MULT**
See also CA 13-16R; CAAS 22; CANR 5, 21, 44; DLB 175; NNAL
Vizinczey, Stephen 1933- .... **CLC 40**
See also CA 128; INT 128
Vliet, R(ussell) G(ordon) 1929-1984 **CLC 22**
See also CA 37-40R; 112; CANR 18
Vogau, Boris Andreyevich 1894-1937(?)
See Pilnyak, Boris
See also CA 123
Vogel, Paula A(nne) 1951- .... **CLC 76**
See also CA 108
Voight, Ellen Bryant 1943- .... **CLC 54**
See also CA 69-72; CANR 11, 29, 55; DLB 120
Voigt, Cynthia 1942- .... **CLC 30**
See also AAYA 3; CA 106; CANR 18, 37, 40; CLR 13,48; INT CANR-18; JRDA; MAICYA; SATA 48, 79; SATA-Brief 33
Voinovich, Vladimir (Nikolaevich) 1932- **CLC 10, 49**
See also CA 81-84; CAAS 12; CANR 33; MTCW
Vollmann, William T. 1959- ... **CLC 89; DAM NOV, POP**
See also CA 134
Voloshinov, V. N.
See Bakhtin, Mikhail Mikhailovich
Voltaire 1694-1778 . **LC 14; DA; DAB; DAC; DAM DRAM, MST; SSC 12; WLC**
von Daeniken, Erich 1935- .... **CLC 30**
See also AITN 1; CA 37-40R; CANR 17, 44
von Daniken, Erich
See von Daeniken, Erich
von Heidenstam, (Carl Gustaf) Verner
See Heidenstam, (Carl Gustaf) Verner von
von Heyse, Paul (Johann Ludwig)
See Heyse, Paul (Johann Ludwig von)
von Hofmannsthal, Hugo
See Hofmannsthal, Hugo von
von Horvath, Odon
See Horvath, Oedoen von
von Horvath, Oedoen
See Horvath, Oedoen von
von Liliencron, (Friedrich Adolf Axel) Detlev
See Liliencron, (Friedrich Adolf Axel) Detlev von
Vonnegut, Kurt, Jr. 1922- **CLC 1, 2, 3, 4, 5, 8, 12, 22, 40, 60; DA; DAB; DAC; DAM MST, NOV, POP; SSC 8; WLC**
See also AAYA 6; AITN 1; BEST 90:4; CA 1-4R; CANR 1, 25, 49; CDALB 1968-1988; DLB 2, 8, 152; DLBD 3; DLBY 80; MTCW
Von Rachen, Kurt
See Hubbard, L(afayette) Ron(ald)
von Rezzori (d'Arezzo), Gregor
See Rezzori (d'Arezzo), Gregor von
von Sternberg, Josef
See Sternberg, Josef von
Vorster, Gordon 1924- .... **CLC 34**
See also CA 133
Vosce, Trudie
See Ozick, Cynthia
Voznesensky, Andrei (Andreievich) 1933- **CLC 1, 15, 57; DAM POET**
See also CA 89-92; CANR 37; MTCW
Waddington, Miriam 1917- .... **CLC 28**
See also CA 21-24R; CANR 12, 30; DLB 68
Wagman, Fredrica 1937- .... **CLC 7**
See also CA 97-100; INT 97-100
Wagner, Linda W.

See Wagner-Martin, Linda (C.)
Wagner, Linda Welshimer
See Wagner-Martin, Linda (C.)
Wagner, Richard 1813-1883 .... **NCLC 9**
See also DLB 129
Wagner-Martin, Linda (C.) 1936- .... **CLC 50**
See also CA 159
Wagoner, David (Russell) 1926- **CLC 3, 5, 15**
See also CA 1-4R; CAAS 3; CANR 2; DLB 5; SATA 14
Wah, Fred(erick James) 1939- .... **CLC 44**
See also CA 107; 141; DLB 60
Wahloo, Per 1926-1975 .... **CLC 7**
See also CA 61-64
Wahloo, Peter
See Wahloo, Per
Wain, John (Barrington) 1925-1994 . **CLC 2, 11, 15, 46**
See also CA 5-8R; 145; CAAS 4; CANR 23, 54; CDBLB 1960 to Present; DLB 15, 27, 139, 155; MTCW
Wajda, Andrzej 1926- .... **CLC 16**
See also CA 102
Wakefield, Dan 1932- .... **CLC 7**
See also CA 21-24R; CAAS 7
Wakoski, Diane 1937- **CLC 2, 4, 7, 9, 11, 40; DAM POET; PC 15**
See also CA 13-16R; CAAS 1; CANR 9, 60; DLB 5; INT CANR-9
Wakoski-Sherbell, Diane
See Wakoski, Diane
Walcott, Derek (Alton) 1930- **CLC 2, 4, 9, 14, 25, 42, 67, 76; BLC; DAB; DAC; DAM MST, MULT, POET; DC 7**
See also BW 2; CA 89-92; CANR 26, 47; DLB 117; DLBY 81; MTCW
Waldman, Anne 1945- .... **CLC 7**
See also CA 37-40R; CAAS 17; CANR 34; DLB 16
Waldo, E. Hunter
See Sturgeon, Theodore (Hamilton)
Waldo, Edward Hamilton
See Sturgeon, Theodore (Hamilton)
Walker, Alice (Malsenior) 1944- **CLC 5, 6, 9, 19, 27, 46, 58, 103; BLC; DA; DAB; DAC; DAM MST, MULT, NOV, POET, POP; SSC 5; WLCS**
See also AAYA 3; BEST 89:4; BW 2; CA 37-40R; CANR 9, 27, 49; CDALB 1968-1988; DLB 6, 33, 143; INT CANR-27; MTCW; SATA 31
Walker, David Harry 1911-1992 .... **CLC 14**
See also CA 1-4R; 137; CANR 1; SATA 8; SATA-Obit 71
Walker, Edward Joseph 1934-
See Walker, Ted
See also CA 21-24R; CANR 12, 28, 53
Walker, George F. 1947- . **CLC 44, 61; DAB; DAC; DAM MST**
See also CA 103; CANR 21, 43, 59; DLB 60
Walker, Joseph A. 1935- .... **CLC 19; DAM DRAM, MST**
See also BW 1; CA 89-92; CANR 26; DLB 38
Walker, Margaret (Abigail) 1915- **CLC 1, 6; BLC; DAM MULT; PC 20**
See also BW 2; CA 73-76; CANR 26, 54; DLB 76, 152; MTCW
Walker, Ted .... **CLC 13**
See also Walker, Edward Joseph
See also DLB 40
Wallace, David Foster 1962- .... **CLC 50**
See also CA 132; CANR 59
Wallace, Dexter

BLC; DAM MULT
See also BW 2; CA 53-56; CAAS 3; CANR 6, 26, 51; DLB 2, 33; INT CANR-6

Williams, Jonathan (Chamberlain) 1929-
CLC 13
See also CA 9-12R; CAAS 12; CANR 8; DLB 5

Williams, Joy 1944- .... CLC 31
See also CA 41-44R; CANR 22, 48

Williams, Norman 1952- .... CLC 39
See also CA 118

Williams, Sherley Anne 1944-CLC 89; BLC; DAM MULT, POET
See also BW 2; CA 73-76; CANR 25; DLB 41; INT CANR-25; SATA 78

Williams, Shirley
See Williams, Sherley Anne

Williams, Tennessee 1911-1983CLC 1, 2, 5, 7, 8, 11, 15, 19, 30, 39, 45, 71; DA; DAB; DAC; DAM DRAM, MST; DC 4; WLC
See also AITN 1, 2; CA 5-8R; 108; CABS 3; CANR 31; CDALB 1941-1968; DLB 7; DLBD 4; DLBY 83; MTCW

Williams, Thomas (Alonzo) 1926-1990CLC 14
See also CA 1-4R; 132; CANR 2

Williams, William C.
See Williams, William Carlos

Williams, William Carlos 1883-1963CLC 1, 2, 5, 9, 13, 22, 42, 67; DA; DAB; DAC; DAM MST, POET; PC 7
See also CA 89-92; CANR 34; CDALB 1917-1929; DLB 4, 16, 54, 86; MTCW

Williamson, David (Keith) 1942- ...... CLC 56
See also CA 103; CANR 41

Williamson, Ellen Douglas 1905-1984
See Douglas, Ellen
See also CA 17-20R; 114; CANR 39

Williamson, Jack .... CLC 29
See also Williamson, John Stewart
See also CAAS 8; DLB 8

Williamson, John Stewart 1908-
See Williamson, Jack
See also CA 17-20R; CANR 23

Willie, Frederick
See Lovecraft, H(oward) P(hillips)

Willingham, Calder (Baynard, Jr.) 1922-1995
CLC 5, 51
See also CA 5-8R; 147; CANR 3; DLB 2, 44; MTCW

Willis, Charles
See Clarke, Arthur C(harles)

Willy
See Colette, (Sidonie-Gabrielle)

Willy, Colette
See Colette, (Sidonie-Gabrielle)

Wilson, A(ndrew) N(orman) 1950- ... CLC 33
See also CA 112; 122; DLB 14, 155

Wilson, Angus (Frank Johnstone) 1913-1991
CLC 2, 3, 5, 25, 34; SSC 21
See also CA 5-8R; 134; CANR 21; DLB 15, 139, 155; MTCW

Wilson, August 1945- CLC 39, 50, 63; BLC; DA; DAB; DAC; DAM DRAM, MST, MULT; DC 2; WLCS
See also AAYA 16; BW 2; CA 115; 122; CANR 42, 54; MTCW

Wilson, Brian 1942- .... CLC 12

Wilson, Colin 1931- .... CLC 3, 14
See also CA 1-4R; CAAS 5; CANR 1, 22, 33; DLB 14; MTCW

Wilson, Dirk
See Pohl, Frederik

Wilson, Edmund 1895-1972CLC 1, 2, 3, 8, 24

See also CA 1-4R; 37-40R; CANR 1, 46; DLB 63; MTCW

Wilson, Ethel Davis (Bryant) 1888(?)-1980
CLC 13; DAC; DAM POET
See also CA 102; DLB 68; MTCW

Wilson, John 1785-1854 .... NCLC 5

Wilson, John (Anthony) Burgess 1917-1993
See Burgess, Anthony
See also CA 1-4R; 143; CANR 2, 46; DAC; DAM NOV; MTCW

Wilson, Lanford 1937- CLC 7, 14, 36; DAM DRAM
See also CA 17-20R; CABS 3; CANR 45; DLB 7

Wilson, Robert M. 1944- .... CLC 7, 9
See also CA 49-52; CANR 2, 41; MTCW

Wilson, Robert McLiam 1964- .... CLC 59
See also CA 132

Wilson, Sloan 1920- .... CLC 32
See also CA 1-4R; CANR 1, 44

Wilson, Snoo 1948- .... CLC 33
See also CA 69-72

Wilson, William S(mith) 1932- .... CLC 49
See also CA 81-84

Wilson, Woodrow 1856-1924 .... TCLC 73
See also DLB 47

Winchilsea, Anne (Kingsmill) Finch Counte 1661-1720
See Finch, Anne

Windham, Basil
See Wodehouse, P(elham) G(renville)

Wingrove, David (John) 1954- .... CLC 68
See also CA 133

Wintergreen, Jane
See Duncan, Sara Jeannette

Winters, Janet Lewis .... CLC 41
See Lewis, Janet
See also DLBY 87

Winters, (Arthur) Yvor 1900-1968 CLC 4, 8, 32
See also CA 11-12; 25-28R; CAP 1; DLB 48; MTCW

Winterson, Jeanette 1959-CLC 64; DAM POP
See also CA 136; CANR 58

Winthrop, John 1588-1649 .... LC 31
See also DLB 24, 30

Wiseman, Frederick 1930- .... CLC 20
See also CA 159

Wister, Owen 1860-1938 .... TCLC 21
See also CA 108; DLB 9, 78; SATA 62

Witkacy
See Witkiewicz, Stanislaw Ignacy

Witkiewicz, Stanislaw Ignacy 1885-1939
TCLC 8
See also CA 105

Wittgenstein, Ludwig (Josef Johann) 1889-1951
TCLC 59
See also CA 113

Wittig, Monique 1935(?)- .... CLC 22
See also CA 116; 135; DLB 83

Wittlin, Jozef 1896-1976 .... CLC 25
See also CA 49-52; 65-68; CANR 3

Wodehouse, P(elham) G(renville) 1881-1975
CLC 1, 2, 5, 10, 22; DAB; DAC; DAM NOV; SSC 2
See also AITN 2; CA 45-48; 57-60; CANR 3, 33; CDBLB 1914-1945; DLB 34, 162; MTCW; SATA 22

Woiwode, L.
See Woiwode, Larry (Alfred)

Woiwode, Larry (Alfred) 1941- ....CLC 6, 10
See also CA 73-76; CANR 16; DLB 6; INT CANR-16

Wojciechowska, Maia (Teresa) 1927-CLC 26
See also AAYA 8; CA 9-12R; CANR 4, 41; CLR 1; JRDA; MAICYA; SAAS 1; SATA 1, 28, 83

Wolf, Christa 1929- .... CLC 14, 29, 58
See also CA 85-88; CANR 45; DLB 75; MTCW

Wolfe, Gene (Rodman) 1931- CLC 25; DAM POP
See also CA 57-60; CAAS 9; CANR 6, 32, 60; DLB 8

Wolfe, George C. 1954- .... CLC 49
See also CA 149

Wolfe, Thomas (Clayton) 1900-1938TCLC 4, 13, 29, 61; DA; DAB; DAC; DAM MST, NOV; WLC
See also CA 104; 132; CDALB 1929-1941; DLB 9, 102; DLBD 2, 16; DLBY 85; MTCW

Wolfe, Thomas Kennerly, Jr. 1931-
See Wolfe, Tom
See also CA 13-16R; CANR 9, 33; DAM POP; INT CANR-9; MTCW

Wolfe, Tom .... CLC 1, 2, 9, 15, 35, 51
See also Wolfe, Thomas Kennerly, Jr.
See also AAYA 8; AITN 2; BEST 89:1; DLB 152

Wolff, Geoffrey (Ansell) 1937- .... CLC 41
See also CA 29-32R; CANR 29, 43

Wolff, Sonia
See Levitin, Sonia (Wolff)

Wolff, Tobias (Jonathan Ansell) 1945- . C L C 39, 64
See also AAYA 16; BEST 90:2; CA 114; 117; CAAS 22; CANR 54; DLB 130; INT 117

Wolfram von Eschenbach c. 1170-c. 1220
CMLC 5
See also DLB 138

Wolitzer, Hilma 1930- .... CLC 17
See also CA 65-68; CANR 18, 40; INT CANR-18; SATA 31

Wollstonecraft, Mary 1759-1797 .... LC 5
See also CDBLB 1789-1832; DLB 39, 104, 158

Wonder, Stevie .... CLC 12
See also Morris, Steveland Judkins

Wong, Jade Snow 1922- .... CLC 17
See also CA 109

Woodberry, George Edward 1855-1930
TCLC 73
See also DLB 71, 103

Woodcott, Keith
See Brunner, John (Kilian Houston)

Woodruff, Robert W.
See Mencken, H(enry) L(ouis)

Woolf, (Adeline) Virginia 1882-1941TCLC 1, 5, 20, 43, 56; DA; DAB; DAC; DAM MST, NOV; SSC 7; WLC
See also CA 104; 130; CANR 64; CDBLB 1914-1945; DLB 36, 100, 162; DLBD 10; MTCW

Woolf, Virginia Adeline
See Woolf, (Adeline) Virginia

Woollcott, Alexander (Humphreys) 1887-1943
TCLC 5
See also CA 105; 161; DLB 29

Woolrich, Cornell 1903-1968 .... CLC 77
See also Hopley-Woolrich, Cornell George

Wordsworth, Dorothy 1771-1855 .. NCLC 25
See also DLB 107

Wordsworth, William 1770-1850..NCLC 12, 38; DA; DAB; DAC; DAM MST, POET; PC 4; WLC
See also CDBLB 1789-1832; DLB 93, 107

Wouk, Herman 1915-CLC 1, 9, 38; DAM NOV, POP

Literary Criticism Series
Cumulative Topic Index

This index lists all topic entries in Gale's *Classical and Medieval Literature Criticism, Contemporary Literary Criticism, Literature Criticism from 1400 to 1800, Nineteenth-Century Literature Criticism,* and *Twentieth-Century Literary Criticism.*

Topic Index

Topic Index

Twentieth-Century Literary Criticism
Cumulative Nationality Index

Nationality Index

Brown, George Douglas **28**
Buchan, John **41**
Cunninghame Graham, R(obert) B(ontine) **19**
Davidson, John **24**
Frazer, J(ames) G(eorge) **32**
Gibbon, Lewis Grassic **4**
Lang, Andrew **16**
MacDonald, George **9**
Muir, Edwin **2**
Sharp, William **39**
Tey, Josephine **14**

SOUTH AFRICAN
Bosman, Herman Charles **49**
Campbell, (Ignatius) Roy (Dunnachie) **5**
Mqhayi, S(amuel) E(dward) K(rune Loliwe) **25**
Plaatje, Sol(omon) T(shekisho) **73**
Schreiner, Olive (Emilie Albertina) **9**
Smith, Pauline (Urmson) **25**
Vilakazi, Benedict Wallet **37**

SPANISH
Alas (y Urena), Leopoldo (Enrique Garcia) **29**
Barea, Arturo **14**
Baroja (y Nessi), Pio **8**
Benavente (y Martinez), Jacinto **3**
Blasco Ibanez, Vicente **12**
Echegaray (y Eizaguirre), Jose (Maria Waldo) **4**
Garcia Lorca, Federico **1, 7, 49**
Jimenez (Mantecon), Juan Ramon **4**
Machado (y Ruiz), Antonio **3**
Martinez Sierra, Gregorio **6**
Martinez Sierra, Maria (de la O'LeJarraga) **6**
Miro (Ferrer), Gabriel (Francisco Victor) **5**
Ortega y Gasset, Jose **9**
Pereda (y Sanchez de Porrua), Jose Maria de **16**
Perez Galdos, Benito **27**
Salinas (y Serrano), Pedro **17**
Unamuno (y Jugo), Miguel de **2, 9**
Valera y Alcala-Galiano, Juan **10**
Valle-Inclan, Ramon (Maria) del **5**

SWEDISH
Bengtsson, Frans (Gunnar) **48**
Dagerman, Stig (Halvard) **17**
Ekelund, Vilhelm **75**
Heidenstam, (Carl Gustaf) Verner von **5**
Key, Ellen **65**
Lagerloef, Selma (Ottiliana Lovisa) **4, 36**
Soderberg, Hjalmar **39**
Strindberg, (Johan) August **1, 8, 21, 47**

SWISS
Ramuz, Charles-Ferdinand **33**
Rod, Edouard **52**
Saussure, Ferdinand de **49**
Spitteler, Carl (Friedrich Georg) **12**
Walser, Robert **18**

SYRIAN
Gibran, Kahlil **1, 9**

TURKISH
Sait Faik **23**

UKRAINIAN
Aleichem, Sholom **1, 35**
Bialik, Chaim Nachman **25**

URUGUAYAN
Quiroga, Horacio (Sylvestre) **20**

Sanchez, Florencio **37**

WELSH
Davies, W(illiam) H(enry) **5**
Lewis, Alun **3**
Machen, Arthur **4**
Thomas, Dylan (Marlais) **1, 8, 45**

Nationality Index

TCLC-77 Title Index

ISBN 0-7876-2023-8

90000

9 780787 620233